Teacher's Edition

PRENTICE HALL

SCIENCE EXPLORER

Grade 6

VIRGINIA

The Natural Bridge

Needham, Massachusetts
Upper Saddle River, New Jersey
Glenview, Illinois

Grade 6 Science Teacher's Edition
Virginia Science Explorer

Print Components
Student Edition
Teacher's Edition
Unit Resources Books
Color Transparencies
Chapter and Unit Tests
Performance Assessment
SOL Assessment Test Preparation Book
Laboratory Manual
Laboratory Manual, Teacher's Edition
Computer Microscope Lab Manual
Inquiry Skills Activity Book
Southeast Student-Centered Science Activity Books
Guided Reading and Study Workbook
Reading in the Content Area with Literature Connections
How to Manage Instruction in the Block
How to Assess Student Work
Teacher's Ell Handbook: Strategies for English Language Learners
Navigation Guide and Lesson Plans

Media/Technology
iText, the interactive text online and on CD-ROM
ExamView®, Computer Test Bank Book with CD-ROM
Resource Pro® CD-ROM
Presentation Pro CD-ROM
Probeware Lab Manual with CD-ROM
Order Assistant Plus CD-ROM
Student Edition on Audio CD
Lab Activity Videotape Library
Concept Videotape Library
Companion Web site at PHSchool.com

ISBN: 0-13-190231-8

1 2 3 4 5 6 7 8 9 10 07 06 05 04 03

TEACHER'S EDITION

Virginia Standards of Learning for Grade 6 Science

Prentice Hall Virginia Science Explorer

Now more than ever, every Virginia middle school student needs a solid science education, and *Prentice Hall Virginia Science Explorer* helps you provide just that. The skills and content in *Science Explorer* will fully prepare Virginia students for success on the Grade 8 SOL Test. This three-book series contains a wealth of resources to help Virginia students access and better understand the core science concepts developed through the middle grades, and assessed on the Grade 8 SOL Test.

Take a look at pages TVA5–TVA13 and explore for yourself the depth and breadth of science content found in every page of *Prentice Hall Virginia Science Explorer.*

Don't stop there. Continue exploring all of the activities... breathtaking visuals... reading support... multiple opportunities for ongoing, integrated assessment... and incredible supplementary resources that accompany this brand-new program.

What will you see? Solid science content developed specifically to help Virginia students understand the skills and content that will lead to success on the Grade 8 SOL Test.

A comprehensive Virginia science exploration is designed around the Virginia Standards of Learning (SOL).

Unmatched depth of content and hands-on activities give students the solid science they need to succeed on the Grade 8 SOL test.

Virginia Navigation Guide and Lesson Plans correlates selected resources with the Organizing topics and Standards of Learning (SOL) for Virginia's Science Curriculum. Available for Grade 6, Life Science, and Physical Science.

Built-in reading support enhances student comprehension.

GUIDE FOR READING

- How do stress forces affect rock?
- Why do faults form and where do they occur?
- How does movement along faults change Earth's surface?

Vivid graphics and dynamic photos bring science concepts to life.

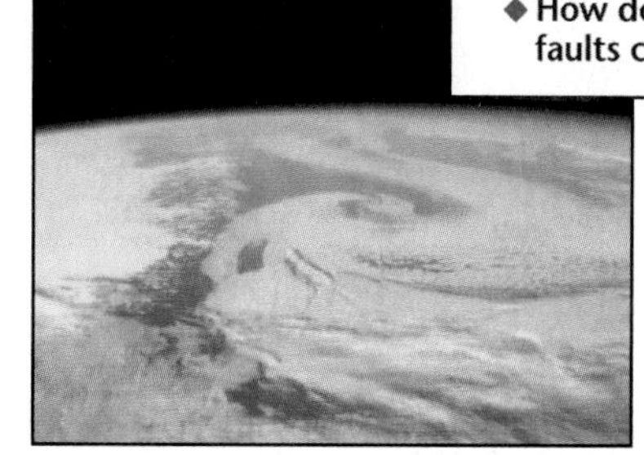

Flexible, self-contained sections give you more options for meeting your curriculum needs.

Wealth of assessment resources—both traditional and performance-based—make regular progress checks easy.

for today's students.

Grade 6

Table of Contents

Unit 4 Weather and Climate

Chapter 11 The Atmosphere

1. The Air Around You
2. Integrating Environmental Science: Air Pollution
3. Air Pressure
4. Layers of the Atmosphere

Chapter 12 Weather Factors

1. Energy in the Atmosphere
2. Integrating Physics: Heat Transfer
3. Winds
4. Water in the Atmosphere
5. Precipitation

Chapter 13 Weather Patterns

1. Air Masses and Fronts
2. Storms
3. Integrating Health: Floods
4. Predicting the Weather

Chapter 14 Climate and Climate Change

1. What Causes Climate?
2. Climate Regions
3. Long-Term Changes in Climate
4. Integrating Environmental Science: Global Changes in the Atmosphere

Unit 5 Energy and the Environment

Chapter 15 Energy and Power

1. The Nature of Energy
2. Energy Conversion and Conservation
3. Photosynthesis and Fossil Fuels
4. Integrating Mathematics: Power

Chapter 16 Energy Resources

1. Fossil Fuels
2. Renewable Sources of Energy
3. Integrating Chemistry: Nuclear Energy
4. Energy Conservation

Chapter 17 Environmental Issues

2. Recognizing Environmental Issues
2. Forests and Fisheries
3. Biodiversity
4. Integrating Health: The Search for New Medicines

Unit 6 Introduction to Astronomy

Chapter 18 Earth, Moon, and Sun

1. Earth in Space
2. Phases, Eclipses, and Tides
3. Integrating Technology: Rockets and Satellites
4. Earth's Moon

Chapter 19 The Solar System

1. Observing the Solar System
2. The Sun
3. The Inner Planets
4. The Outer Planets
5. Comets, Asteroids, and Meteors
6. Integrating Life Science: Is There Life Beyond Earth?

Interdisciplinary Exploration: The Solar System

Virginia students utilize a rich asssortment of activities to promote inquiry learning.

Prentice Hall Virginia Science Explorer gives you more activities—and more types of activities—than any other middle school program available. This rich, flexible assortment of activities reinforces content, meets a variety of learning and teaching styles, and allows Virginia students to investigate and understand concepts covered on the Virginia SOL (8th grade) science assessment.

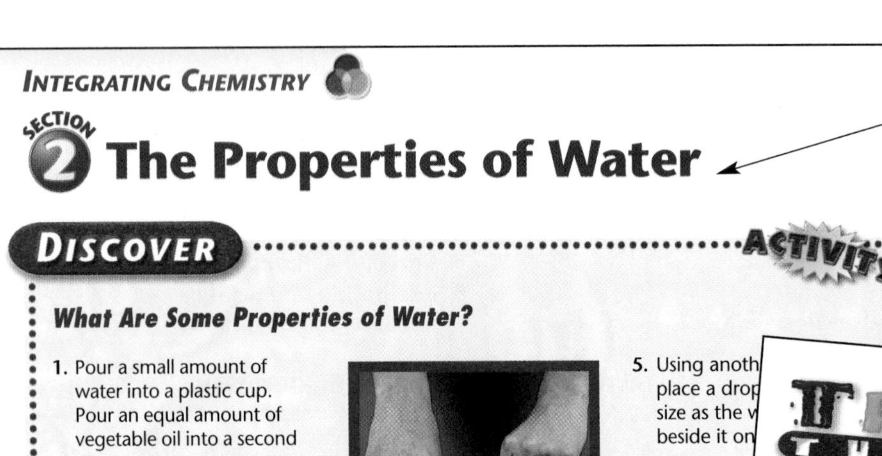

INTEGRATING CHEMISTRY

SECTION 2 The Properties of Water

DISCOVER ACTIVITY

What Are Some Properties of Water?

1. Pour a small amount of water into a plastic cup. Pour an equal amount of vegetable oil into a second cup.
2. Cut two strips of paper towel. Hold the strips so that the bottom of one strip is in the water and the other is in the oil.
3. After one minute, measure how high each substance climbed up the pape...
5. Using anoth... place a drop... size as the w... beside it on...
6. Observe th... two drops...
7. Follow you... instruction... the oil wh... after this...

TRY THIS

How Do Your Algae Grow? ACTIVITY

In this activity you will observe how fertilizers affect the growth of algae in pond water.

1. Label two jars A and B. Pour tap water into each jar until it is half full.
2. Add water from a pond or aquarium to each jar until it is three-quarters full.

3. Add 5 mL of liquid fertilizer to jar A only.
4. Cover both jars tightly and place them on a windowsill in the sunlight. Wash your hands with soap.
5. Observe the jars every day for a week.

Drawing Conclusions How did the fertilizer affect the growth of the algae in jar A? What was the purpose of jar B in this experiment?

Real-World Lab

You, the Consumer

Testing the Waters

How does the bottled water sold in supermarkets differ from the water that comes out of your kitchen faucet? In this lab, you will discover some differences among various types of water.

Problem

How do distilled water, spring water, and mineral water differ from tap water?

Skills Focus

observing, inferring, drawing conclusions

Materials

hot plate
ruler
tap water, 200 mL
spring water, 200 mL
4 200-mL beakers
4 pieces of pH paper
25-mL graduated cylinder
4 paper cups per person
liquid soap
wax pencil
distilled water, 200 mL
mineral water, 200 mL
4 test tubes and stoppers
pH indicator chart

Procedure

... your notebook.

2. Label the beakers A, B, ... 100 mL of tap water in... 100 mL of the other w... correct beaker (refer...
3. Heat each water sample ... about 20 mL remains. Do not allow the ... to boil completely away. **CAUTION:** *Do not touch the hot plate or beakers.*
4. After the water samples have cooled, look for solids that make the water cloudy. Rank the samples from 1 to 4, where 1 has the fewest visible solids and 4 has the most visible solids. Record your rankings in the data table.
5. Label the test tubes A, B, C, and D. Pour 10 mL of each water sample from the source bottle in... correct test tube.
6. Dip a pi... measure its acidity. ... paper to a number on the pH indicator chart. Record the pH (1–14) in your data table.

- **Discover Activities** provide quick exploration and inquiry before learning, at start of every lesson.
- **Chapter Projects** are long-term inquiry opportunities, one per chapter.
- **Try This Activities** gives quick reinforcement of key concepts, two per chapter.
- **Sharpen Your Skills Activities** provide quick practice of a specific inquiry skill, two per chapter.
- **Skills Labs** give in-depth practice of an inquiry skill, one per chapter.
- **Real-World Labs** are everyday applications of science concepts, one per chapter.

Solid science content

Ongoing assessment, right in the Virginia Student Edition, keeps students on track.

Prentice Hall Virginia Science Explorer features a remarkable range of strategies for checking student progress—including both traditional and performance assessment. With this variety of assessment approaches, students are better prepared to succeed on the SOL Test.

- **Comprehensive Chapter Reviews** include a broad range of question types that students will encounter on state and local standardized tests: multiple choice, enhanced true/false, concept mastery, visual thinking, skill application, and critical thinking.
- **Chapter Projects** with two-part Wrap Ups (Present Your Project and Reflect and Record) and Getting Involved ideas present ample performance assessment opportunities in every Chapter Review.
- **Caption Questions** maximize the usefulness of the visuals, and help keep students on track by assessing critical thinking skills.
- **Checkpoint Questions** give students an immediate content check as new concepts are presented.
- **Section Reviews** provide "Check Your Progress" opportunities for the Chapter Project, Science at Home, and review questions for the section.

Monocots

Seed

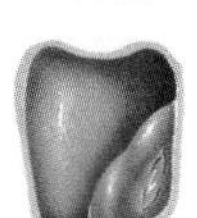

One cotyledon

Leaf

Parallel veins

Stem

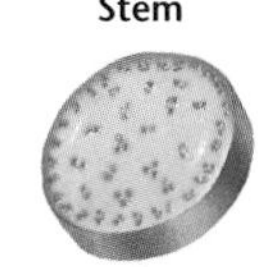

Scattered bundles of vascular tissue

Flower

Flower parts in threes

Dicots

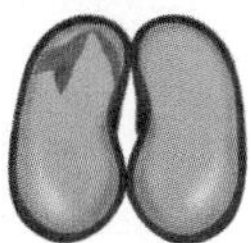

Two cotyledons

Branching veins

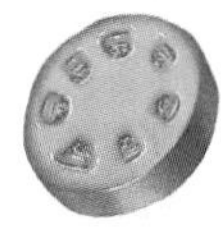

Circle of vascular tissue

Flower parts in four or fives

Figure 16 Monocots and dicots are the two groups of angiosperms. The groups differ in the number of cotyledons, the arrangement of veins and vascular tissue, and the number of petals. *Classifying Would a plant whose flowers have 20 petals be a monocot or a dicot?*

Types of Angiosperms

Angiosperms are divided into two major groups: monocots and dicots. "Cot" is short for *cotyledon.* Recall from Section 1 that the cotyledon, or seed leaf, provides food for the embryo. *Mono* means "one" and *di* means "two". **Monocots** are angiosperms that have only one seed leaf. **Dicots,** on the other hand, produce seeds with two seed leaves. Look at Figure 16 to compare the characteristics of monocots and dicots.

Monocots Grasses, including corn, wheat, and rice, and plants such as lilies and tulips are monocots. The flowers of a monocot usually have either three petals or a multiple of three petals. Monocots usually have long, slender leaves with veins that run parallel to one another like train rails. The bundles of vascular tissue in monocot stems are usually scattered randomly throughout the stem.

Dicots Dicots include plants such as roses and violets, as well as dandelions. Both oak and maple trees are dicots, as are food plants such as beans and apples. The flowers of dicots often have either four or five petals or multiples of these numbers. The leaves are usually wide, with veins that branch off from one another. Dicot stems usually have bundles of vascular tissue arranged in a circle.

✓ *Checkpoint How do the petals of monocots and dicots differ in number?*

Section 3 Review

1. What two characteristics do all angiosperms share? Explain the importance of those characteristics.
2. Give a brief description of how reproduction occurs in angiosperms.
3. List the parts of a typical flower. What is the function of each part?
4. **Thinking Critically Inferring** A certain plant has small, dull-colored flowers with no scent. Do you think the plant is pollinated by animals or by the wind? Explain.

CHAPTER PROJECT

Check Your Progress

Your plants should now have, or will soon have, flowers. Make a diagram of the flower's structure. When the flowers open, you'll have to pollinate them. This work is usually done by insects or birds. After pollination, watch how the flower changes. (*Hint:* Discuss with your teacher and classmates how to pollinate the flowers.)

Innovative resources: SOL-specific materials to teach the skills and content in Virginia

- **Virginia Student Editions—**content-rich, vivid, and accessible. Solid science built around the SOLs.
- **Virginia Teacher's Editions—**comprehensive teacher support puts you in charge. Suggested answers, easy-to-manage lesson plans, and multiple assessment opportunities are located exactly where you need them. Plus, ideas for meeting the needs of diverse learners are also included.
- **Laboratory Manuals (Student Consumable)—**classroom-proven inquiry opportunities bring the excitement of hands-on science to your students.
- **Guided Reading and Study Workbooks—**promote active reading and enhance students' study skills using innovative questioning strategies and exercises—linked to the student text.

Teaching Resources and SOL Support

All the day-to-day resources you need to manage instruction effectively.

- **Virginia Navigation Guide and Lesson Plans—**correlates selected resources with the Organizing topics and Standards of Learning (SOL) for Virginia's Science Curriculum, and targets resources that may be used to enhance and strengthen coverage of each essential understanding, knowledge, and skills outlined from the Virginia Scope and Sequence.
- **Unit Resource Books—**organized by chapter, include Chapter Projects, Lesson Plans, Section Summaries, Review & Reinforce Worksheets, Enrich Worksheets, Skills Labs and Real-World Labs, complete with Answer Keys.
- **Laboratory Manual, Teacher's Edition—**in-depth labs with complete teaching support.
- **Color Transparencies—**vibrant color transparencies bring difficult-to-understand concepts to life.
- **Resource Pro® CD-ROM—**the ultimate lesson planning and scheduling tool, with electronic access to worksheets. Lets you plan by the day, week, month, or year!
- **How to Manage Instruction in the Block—**comprehensive collection of block scheduling resources—from managing classroom routines to checklists for monitoring and assessing small-group learning.
- **Correlation to National Science Education Standards**

Assessment Resources for the SOLs

Comprehensive assessment tools—all in one place!

- **Virginia SOL Assessments Test Preparation Book—** provides students with hints, tips, strategies, and practice to help them prepare for the Grade 8 SOL Test.
- **Chapter and Unit Tests—** provides students with practice in writing responses to essay questions and in answering questions that require interpretation of graphs, data tables, diagrams, and maps.
- **Performance Assessment—** assess student problem-solving and process skills using easy-to-score rubrics.
- **ExamView® Computer Test Bank Book with CD-ROM—** contains chapter tests featuring a variety of question types. Powerful Computer Test Bank software makes it easy to create customized tests, correlated to the Virginia SOLs.
- **How to Assess Student Work—** contains articles and activities on integrating assessments, using rubrics, and establishing a portfolio.

Student Performance Resources

Components to improve science comprehension and enhance process skills.

- **Section Summaries on Audio CD—** offers students summaries of important concepts from each section of every chapter.
- **Guided Reading and Study Workbook, Teacher's Edition—** contains blackline master worksheets for assessing, understanding, and developing study skills.
- **Reading in the Content Area with Literature Connections—** contains reading strategies to improve student comprehension.
- **Inquiry Skills Activity Book—** has additional activities that introduce basic and advanced inquiry skills.

Additional Program-wide Resources

- **Order Assistant Plus CD-ROM—** generates a Master Materials List based on the activities you choose to teach.
- **Southeast Student-Centered Science Activity Book**
- **Teacher's ELL Handbook—** provides multiple strategies for reaching language learners. Select appropriate activities to meet the needs of individual students.

See next page for technology resources

for today's students.

Prentice Hall Virginia Science Explorer connects your classroom to the power of interactivity.

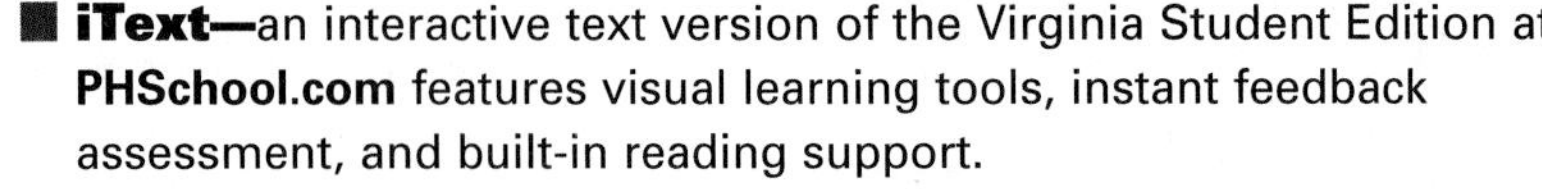

■ **iText—**an interactive text version of the Virginia Student Edition at **PHSchool.com** features visual learning tools, instant feedback assessment, and built-in reading support.

■ **ExamView® Computer Test Bank Book with CD-ROM—** contains chapter tests featuring a variety of question types. Powerful Computer Test Bank software makes it easy to create customized tests, correlated to the Virginia SOLs.

■ **Lab Activity Videotape Library—**provides step-by-step instruction with students performing activities from every chapter.

■ **Student Edition on Audio CD—**includes the complete text read to students section-by-section, providing support for English Language Learners and reluctant readers.

■ **Concept Videotape Library—**explores and visualizes concepts through spectacular short documentaries and computer animations.

■ **Presentation Pro® CD-ROM—**provides electronic access to all teaching transparencies, allowing you to create custom presentations with the click of a mouse.

■ **Probeware Lab Manual with CD-ROM—**provides detailed instruction for using Probeware to perform selected labs. Contains blackline masters of labs. Includes CD-ROM, workbook, and blackline masters.

■ **Resource Pro® CD-ROM—**the ultimate lesson planning and scheduling tool, with electronic access to worksheets and lessons.

Online activities and teaching resources for every chapter of the text.

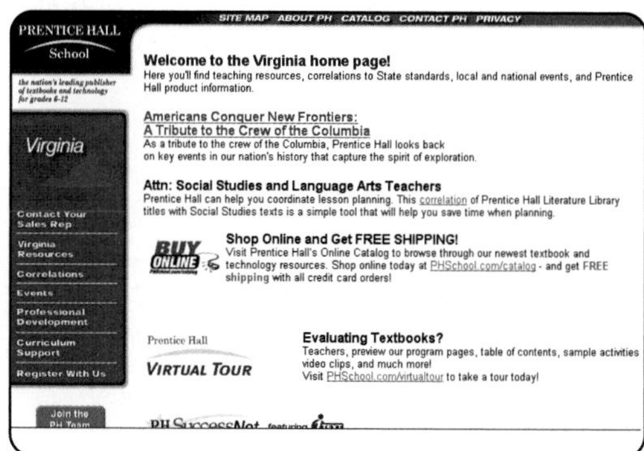

For Teachers

- **What's New—**Create enthusiasm with our dynamic Internet activities—at least one per chapter.
- **Further Exploration—**Links enhance and reinforce Internet activity concepts.
- **Teaching Links—**Web sites relate to chapter content.

SCIENCE NEWS

- **Science News®—**A weekly electronic and print newsletter provides the latest information on science news in earth science, biology, technology, and more.

For Students

- **Hot Links to Web Sites—**Access additional material that extends chapter content.
- **Internet Activities—**Enhance concepts with interactive, hands-on/minds-on activities.
- **Self-Tests—**Help students to check how they are doing, and obtain scores instantly.

Plus! PlanetDiary

- **PlanetDiary—**Get weekly reports on environmental news and natural phenomena, directly correlated to the *Virginia Science Explorer* series.

for today's students.

Virginia Standards of Learning Grade 6 Science Year-at-a-Glance

VIRGINIA STANDARDS OF LEARNING	PRENTICE HALL GRADE 6 SCIENCE CHAPTERS																			
	Int	1	2	3	4	5	6	7	8	9	10	11	12	13	14	15	16	17	18	19
Scientific Investigation, Reasoning, and Logic																				
6.1 The student will plan and conduct investigations in which																				
a) observations are made involving fine discrimination between similar objects and organisms;	◆	◆	◆	◆	◆	◆	◆	◆	◆	◆	◆	◆	◆	◆	◆	◆	◆	◆	◆	◆
b) a classification system is developed based on multiple attributes;		◆		◆																
c) precise and approximate measures are recorded;	◆	◆		◆	◆	◆	◆	◆	◆	◆		◆	◆	◆	◆	◆	◆	◆	◆	◆
d) scale models are used to estimate distance, volume, and quantity;	◆	◆				◆	◆	◆			◆		◆			◆			◆	◆
e) hypotheses are stated in ways that identify the independent (manipulated) and dependent (responding) variables;	◆	◆			◆	◆	◆	◆			◆	◆	◆		◆		◆		◆	◆
f) a method is devised to test the validity of predictions and inferences;	◆	◆			◆	◆	◆							◆	◆	◆	◆	◆		◆
g) one variable is manipulated over time with many repeated trials;		◆				◆		◆		◆					◆		◆		◆	◆
h) data are collected, recorded, analyzed, and reported using appropriate metric measurement;		◆		◆	◆	◆	◆	◆	◆	◆	◆	◆	◆	◆	◆	◆	◆	◆	◆	◆
i) data are organized and communicated through graphical representation (graphs, charts, and diagrams);	◆		◆			◆	◆	◆	◆	◆	◆	◆	◆	◆	◆	◆		◆	◆	◆
j) models are designed to explain a sequence; and	◆	◆	◆	◆	◆	◆	◆	◆	◆	◆	◆		◆	◆		◆		◆	◆	◆
k) an understanding of the nature of science is developed and reinforced.	◆	◆		◆		◆	◆	◆	◆		◆		◆	◆	◆		◆			◆
Force, Motion, and Energy																				
6.2 The student will investigate and understand basic sources of energy, their origins, transformations, and uses. Key concepts include																				
a) potential and kinetic energy;									◆	◆						◆				
b) the role of the sun in the formation of most energy sources on Earth;										◆			◆		◆	◆	◆			
c) nonrenewable energy sources (fossil fuels, including petroleum, natural gas, and coal);																◆	◆			
d) renewable energy sources (wood, wind, hydro, geothermal, tidal, and solar); and									◆	◆							◆			
e) energy transformations (heat/light to mechanical, chemical, and electrical energy).		◆		◆		◆			◆							◆	◆			

VIRGINIA STANDARDS OF LEARNING	PRENTICE HALL GRADE 6 SCIENCE CHAPTERS																			
	Int	1	2	3	4	5	6	7	8	9	10	11	12	13	14	15	16	17	18	19
Force, Motion, and Energy (continued)																				
6.3 The student will investigate and understand the role of solar energy in driving most natural processes within the atmosphere, the hydrosphere, and on the Earth's surface. Key concepts include																				
a) the Earth's energy budget;													◆							
b) the role of radiation and convection in the distribution of energy;													◆	◆	◆					
c) the motion of the atmosphere and the oceans;						◆				◆			◆		◆					
d) cloud formation; and													◆							
e) the role of heat energy in weather-related phenomena including thunderstorms and hurricanes.													◆							
Matter																				
6.4 The student will investigate and understand that all matter is made up of atoms. Key concepts include																				
a) atoms are made up of electrons, protons, and neutrons;		◆																		
b) atoms of any element are alike but are different from atoms of other elements;		◆																		
c) elements may be represented by chemical symbols;				◆																
d) two or more atoms may be chemically combined;		◆	◆	◆								◆								
e) compounds may be represented by chemical formulas;		◆	◆	◆												◆				
f) chemical equations can be used to model chemical changes; and		◆		◆												◆				
g) a limited number of elements comprise the largest portion of the solid Earth, living matter, the oceans, and the atmosphere.		◆								◆		◆			◆					
6.5 The student will investigate and understand the unique properties and characteristics of water and its roles in the natural and human-made environment. Key concepts include																				
a) water as the universal solvent;			◆																	
b) the properties of water in all three states;			◆																	
c) the action of water in physical and chemical weathering;					◆	◆				◆										
d) the ability of large bodies of water to store heat and moderate climate;										◆					◆					
e) the origin and occurrence of water on Earth;								◆		◆	◆									
f) the importance of water for agriculture, power generation, and public health; and									◆				◆							
g) the importance of protecting and maintaining water resources.									◆				◆							
6.6 The student will investigate and understand the properties of air and the structure and dynamics of the Earth's atmosphere. Key concepts include																				
a) air as a mixture of gaseous elements and compounds;												◆	◆							
b) air pressure, temperature, and humidity;												◆	◆	◆						
c) how the atmosphere changes with altitude;												◆								
d) natural and human-caused changes to the atmosphere;													◆		◆					

VIRGINIA STANDARDS OF LEARNING	PRENTICE HALL GRADE 6 SCIENCE CHAPTERS																				
	Int	1	2	3	4	5	6	7	8	9	10	11	12	13	14	15	16	17	18	19
Matter (continued)																				
e) the relationship of atmospheric measures and weather conditions;													◆	◆	◆					
f) basic information from weather maps including fronts, systems, and basic measurements; and													◆	◆						
g) the importance of protecting and maintaining air quality.															◆					
Living Systems																				
6.7 The student will investigate and understand the natural processes and human interactions that affect watershed systems. Key concepts include																				
a) the health of ecosystems and the abiotic factors of a watershed;								◆			◆									
b) the location and structure of Virginia's regional watershed systems;								◆			◆									
c) divides, tributaries, river systems, and river and stream processes;					◆	◆		◆												
d) wetlands;								◆												
e) estuaries;											◆									
f) major conservation, health, and safety issues associated with watersheds; and								◆			◆									
g) water monitoring and analysis using field equipment including hand-held technology.															◆					
Interrelationships in Earth/Space Systems																				
6.8 The student will investigate and understand the organization of the solar system and the relationships among the various bodies that comprise it. Key concepts include																				
a) the, sun, moon, Earth, other planets and their moons, meteors, asteroids, and comets;	◆						◆												◆	◆
b) relative size of and distance between planets;																				◆
c) the role of gravity;																			◆	◆
d) revolution and rotation;																			◆	◆
e) the mechanics of day and night and phases of the moon;																			◆	
f) the unique properties of Earth as a planet;							◆												◆	
g) the relationship of the Earth's tilt and seasons;																			◆	
h) the cause of tides; and																			◆	
i) the history and technology of space exploration.	◆																		◆	◆
Resources																				
6.9 The student will investigate and understand public policy decisions relating to the environment. Key concepts include																				
a) management of renewable resources (water, air, soil, plant life, animal life);					◆			◆	◆		◆	◆			◆			◆		
b) management of nonrenewable resources (coal, oil, natural gas, nuclear power, mineral resources);		◆									◆						◆			
c) the mitigation of land-use and environmental hazards through preventive measures; and					◆			◆	◆					◆				◆		
d) cost/benefit tradeoffs in conservation policies.					◆			◆	◆		◆							◆		

Virginia Standards of Learning Scope and Sequence for Science

The scope and sequence of content is organized around the major stands and specific objectives in the Virginia Standards of Learning, which are an important part of Virginia's implementation of the No Child Left Behind Act. This chart will help you prepare students for the Grade 8 SOL Test

VIRGINIA STANDARDS OF LEARNING	GRADE 6	LIFE SCIENCE	PHYSICAL SCIENCE
GRADE 6			
Scientific Investigation, Reasoning, and Logic			
6.1 The student will plan and conduct investigations in which			
a) observations are made involving fine discrimination between similar objects and organisms;	◆	◆	◆
b) a classification system is developed based on multiple attributes;	◆	◆	◆
c) precise and approximate measures are recorded;	◆	◆	◆
d) scale models are used to estimate distance, volume, and quantity;	◆	◆	◆
e) hypotheses are stated in ways that identify the independent (manipulated) and dependent (responding) variables;	◆	◆	
f) a method is devised to test the validity of predictions and inferences;	◆	◆	◆
g) one variable is manipulated over time with many repeated trials;	◆	◆	◆
h) data are collected, recorded, analyzed, and reported using appropriate metric measurement;	◆	◆	◆
i) data are organized and communicated through graphical representation (graphs, charts, and diagrams);	◆	◆	◆
j) models are designed to explain a sequence;	◆	◆	
k) an understanding of the nature of science is develop reinforced.	◆	◆	◆
Force, Motion, and Energy			
6.2 The student will investigate and understand basic sources of energy, their origins, transformations, and uses. Key concepts include			
a) potential and kinetic energy;	◆		◆
b) the role of the sun in the formation of most energy sources on Earth;	◆	◆	◆
c) nonrenewable energy sources (fossil fuels, including petroleum, natural gas, and coal);	◆	◆	◆
d) renewable energy sources (wood, wind, hydro, geothermal, tidal, and solar);	◆		◆
e) energy transformations (heat/light to mechanical, chemical, and electrical energy).	◆	◆	◆
6.3 The student will investigate and understand the role of solar energy in driving most natural processes within the atmosphere, the hydrosphere, and on the Earth's surface. Key concepts include			
a) the Earth's energy budget;	◆		
b) the role of radiation and convection in the distribution of energy;	◆		
c) the motion of the atmosphere and the oceans;	◆		
d) cloud formation;	◆		
e) the role of heat energy in weather-related phenomena including thunderstorms and hurricanes.	◆		
Matter			
6.4 The student will investigate and understand that all matter is made up of atoms. Key concepts include			
a) atoms are made up of electrons, protons, and neutrons;	◆		◆
b) atoms of any element are alike but are different from atoms of other elements;	◆		◆
c) elements may be represented by chemical symbols;	◆		◆
d) two or more atoms may be chemically combined;	◆		◆
e) compounds may be represented by chemical formulas;	◆		◆
f) chemical equations can be used to model chemical changes;	◆		◆
g) a limited number of elements comprise the largest portion of the solid Earth, living matter, the oceans, and the atmosphere.	◆	◆	◆

VIRGINIA STANDARDS OF LEARNING	GRADE 6	LIFE SCIENCE	PHYSICAL SCIENCE
GRADE 6			
Matter (continued)			
6.5 The student will investigate and understand the unique properties and characteristics of water and its roles in the natural and human-made environment. Key concepts include			
a) water as the universal solvent;	◆		◆
b) the properties of water in all three states;	◆		◆
c) the action of water in physical and chemical weathering;	◆		
d) the ability of large bodies of water to store heat and moderate climate;	◆		
e) the origin and occurrence of water on Earth;	◆		
f) the importance of water for agriculture, power generation, and public health;	◆		
g) the importance of protecting and maintaining water resources.	◆		
6.6 The student will investigate and understand the properties of air and the structure and dynamics of the Earth's atmosphere. Key concepts include			
a) air as a mixture of gaseous elements and compounds;	◆		
b) air pressure, temperature, and humidity;	◆		
c) how the atmosphere changes with altitude;	◆		◆
d) natural and human-caused changes to the atmosphere;	◆		
e) the relationship of atmospheric measures and weather conditions;	◆		
f) basic information from weather maps including fronts, systems, and basic measurements;	◆		
g) the importance of protecting and maintaining air quality.	◆		
Living Systems			
6.7 The student will investigate and understand the natural processes and human interactions that affect watershed systems. Key concepts include			
a) the health of ecosystems and the abiotic factors of a watershed;	◆	◆	
b) the location and structure of Virginia's regional watershed systems;	◆		
c) divides, tributaries, river systems, and river and stream processes;	◆		
d) wetlands;	◆	◆	
e) estuaries;	◆	◆	
f) major conservation, health, and safety issues associated with watersheds;	◆		
g) water monitoring and analysis using field equipment including hand-held technology.	◆		
Interrelationships in Earth/Space Systems			
6.8 The student will investigate and understand the organization of the solar system and the relationships among the various bodies that comprise it. Key concepts include			
a) the, sun, moon, Earth, other planets and their moons, meteors, asteroids, and comets;	◆		
b) relative size of and distance between planets;	◆		
c) the role of gravity;	◆		
d) revolution and rotation;	◆		
e) the mechanics of day and night and phases of the moon;	◆		
f) the unique properties of Earth as a planet;	◆		
g) the relationship of the Earth's tilt and seasons;	◆		
h) the cause of tides;	◆		
i) the history and technology of space exploration.	◆		
Resources			
6.9 The student will investigate and understand public policy decisions relating to the environment. Key concepts include			
a) management of renewable resources (water, air, soil, plant life, animal life);	◆	◆	
b) management of nonrenewable resources (coal, oil, natural gas, nuclear power, mineral resources);	◆	◆	
c) the mitigation of land-use and environmental hazards through preventive measures;	◆	◆	
d) cost/benefit tradeoffs in conservation policies.	◆	◆	

VIRGINIA STANDARDS OF LEARNING	GRADE 6	LIFE SCIENCE	PHYSICAL SCIENCE
LIFE SCIENCE			
LS.1 The student will plan and conduct investigations in which			
a) data are organized into tables showing repeated trials and means;	◆	◆	◆
b) variables are defined;	◆	◆	◆
c) metric units (SI – International System of Units) are used;	◆	◆	◆
d) models are constructed to illustrate and explain phenomena;	◆	◆	
e) sources of experimental error are identified;		◆	
f) dependent variables, independent variables, and constants are identified;		◆	
g) variables are controlled to test hypotheses and trials are repeated;	◆	◆	◆
h) continuous line graphs are constructed, interpreted, and used to make predictions;	◆	◆	
i) interpretations from the same set of data are evaluated and defended;	◆	◆	◆
j) an understanding of the nature of science is developed and reinforced.	◆	◆	◆
LS.2 The student will investigate and understand that all living things are composed of cells. Key concepts include			
a) cell structure and organelles (cell membrane, cell wall, cytoplasm, vacuole, mitochondrion, endoplasmic reticulum, nucleus and chloroplast);		◆	
b) similarities and differences between plant and animal cells;		◆	
c) development of cell theory;		◆	
d) cell division (mitosis and meiosis).		◆	
LS.3 The student will investigate and understand that living things show patterns of cellular organization. Key concepts include			
a) cells, tissues, organs, and systems;		◆	
b) life functions and processes of cells, tissues, organs, and systems (respiration, removal of wastes, growth, reproduction, digestion, and cellular transport).		◆	
LS.4 The student will investigate and understand that the basic needs of organisms must be met in order to carry out life processes. Key concepts include			
a) plant needs (light and energy sources, water, gases, nutrients);	◆	◆	
b) animal needs (food, water, gases, shelter, space); and factors that influence life processes.	◆	◆	
LS.5 The student will investigate and understand how organisms can be classified. Key concepts include			
a) distinguishing characteristics among kingdoms of organisms;		◆	
b) distinguishing characteristics of major animal and plant phyla;		◆	
c) the characteristics of the species.		◆	
LS.6 The student will investigate and understand the basic physical and chemical processes of photosynthesis and its importance to plant and animal life. Key concepts include			
a) energy transfer between sunlight and chlorophyll;	◆	◆	
b) transformation of water and carbon dioxide into sugar and oxygen;	◆	◆	
c) photosynthesis as the foundation of virtually all food webs.	◆	◆	◆
LS.7 The student will investigate and understand that organisms within an ecosystem are dependent on one another and on nonliving components of the environment. Key concepts include			
a) the carbon, water, and nitrogen cycles;	◆	◆	
b) interactions resulting in a flow of energy and matter throughout the system;	◆	◆	
c) complex relationships within terrestrial, freshwater, and marine ecosystems;	◆	◆	
d) energy flow in food webs and energy pyramids.		◆	
LS.8 The student will investigate and understand that interactions exist among members of a population. Key concepts include			
a) competition, cooperation, social hierarchy, territorial imperative;		◆	
b) influence of behavior on a population.		◆	
LS.9 The student will investigate and understand interactions among populations in a biological community. Key concepts include			
a) the relationship among producers, consumers, and decomposers in food webs;	◆	◆	
b) the relationship of predators and prey;	◆	◆	
c) competition and cooperation;		◆	

VIRGINIA STANDARDS OF LEARNING	GRADE 6	LIFE SCIENCE	PHYSICAL SCIENCE
LIFE SCIENCE			
d) symbiotic relationships;		◆	
e) niches.		◆	
LS.10 The student will investigate and understand how organisms adapt to biotic and abiotic factors in an ecosystem. Key concepts include			
a) differences between ecosystems and biomes;		◆	
b) characteristics of land, marine, and freshwater ecosystems;	◆	◆	
c) adaptations that enable organisms to survive within a specific ecosystem.	◆	◆	
LS.11 The student will investigate and understand that ecosystems, communities, populations, and organisms are dynamic and change over time (daily, seasonal, and long term). Key concepts include			
a) phototropism, hibernation, and dormancy;		◆	
b) factors that increase or decrease population size;		◆	
c) eutrophication, climate change, and catastrophic disturbances.	◆	◆	
LS.12 The student will investigate and understand the relationships between ecosystem dynamics and human activity. Key concepts include			
a) food production and harvest;	◆	◆	
b) change in habitat size, quality, and structure;	◆	◆	
c) change in species competition;		◆	
d) population disturbances and factors that threaten and enhance species survival;	◆	◆	
e) environmental issues (water supply, air quality, energy production, and waste management).	◆	◆	
LS.13 The student will investigate and understand that organisms reproduce and transmit genetic information to new generations. Key concepts include			
a) the role of DNA;		◆	
b) the function of genes and chromosomes;		◆	
c) genotypes and phenotypes;		◆	
d) factors affecting the expression of traits;		◆	
e) characteristics that can and cannot be inherited;		◆	
f) genetic engineering and its applications;		◆	
g) historical contributions and significance of discoveries related to genetics.		◆	
LS.14 The student will investigate and understand that organisms change over time. Key concepts include			
a) the relationships of mutation, adaptation, natural selection, and extinction;		◆	
b) evidence of evolution of different species in the fossil record;		◆	
c) how environmental influences, as well as genetic variation, can lead to diversity of organisms.		◆	
PHYSICAL SCIENCE			
PS.1 The student will plan and conduct investigations in which			
a) chemicals and equipment are used safely;	◆	◆	◆
b) length, mass, volume, density, temperature, weight, and force are accurately measured and reported using the International System of Units (SI – metric);	◆	◆	◆
c) conversions are made among metric units applying appropriate prefixes;		◆	◆
d) triple beam and electronic balances, thermometers, metric rulers, graduated cylinders, and spring scales are used to gather data;	◆	◆	◆
e) numbers are expressed in scientific notation where appropriate;			◆
f) research skills are utilized using a variety of resources;	◆	◆	◆
g) independent and dependent variables, constants, controls, and repeated trials are identified;		◆	◆
h) data tables showing the independent and dependent variables, derived quantities, and the number of trials are constructed and interpreted;		◆	◆
i) data tables for descriptive statistics showing specific measures of central tendency, the range of the data set, and the number of repeated trials are constructed and interpreted;		◆	◆
j) frequency distributions, scattergrams, line plots, and histograms are constructed and interpreted;		◆	◆
k) valid conclusions are made after analyzing data;	◆	◆	◆
l) research methods are used to investigate practical problems and questions;	◆	◆	◆
m) experimental results are presented in appropriate written form;	◆	◆	◆
n) an understanding of the nature of science is developed and reinforced.	◆	◆	◆

VIRGINIA STANDARDS OF LEARNING	GRADE 6	LIFE SCIENCE	PHYSICAL SCIENCE
PHYSICAL SCIENCE			
PS.2 The student will investigate and understand the basic nature of matter. Key concepts include			
a) the particle theory of matter;	◆	◆	◆
b) elements, compounds, mixtures, acids, bases, and salts;	◆	◆	◆
c) solids, liquids, and gases;	◆	◆	◆
d) characteristics of types of matter based on physical and chemical properties;	◆		◆
e) physical properties (shape, density, solubility, odor, melting point, boiling point, color);	◆		◆
f) chemical properties (acidity, basicity, combustibility, reactivity).	◆		◆
PS.3 The student will investigate and understand the modern and historical models of atomic structure. Key concepts include			
a) the contributions of Dalton, Thomson, Rutherford, and Bohr in understanding the atom;	◆		◆
b) the modern model of atomic structure.			◆
PS.4 The student will investigate and understand the organization and use of the periodic table of elements to obtain information. Key concepts include			
a) symbols, atomic number, atomic mass, chemical families (groups), and periods;	◆	◆	◆
b) classification of elements as metals, metalloids, and nonmetals;			◆
c) simple compounds (formulas and nature of bonding).	◆	◆	◆
PS.5 The student will investigate and understand changes in matter and the relationship of these changes to the Law of Conservation of Matter and Energy. Key concepts include			
a) physical changes;	◆		◆
b) nuclear reactions (products of fusion and fission and their effects on human beings and the environment);	◆		◆
c) chemical changes (types of reactions, reactants and products, and balanced equations).	◆	◆	◆
PS.6 The student will investigate and understand states and forms of energy and how energy is transferred and transformed. Key concepts include			
a) potential and kinetic energy;	◆		◆
b) mechanical, chemical, and electrical energy;	◆	◆	◆
c) heat, light, and sound.	◆	◆	◆
PS.7 The student will investigate and understand temperature scales, heat, and heat transfer. Key concepts include			
a) Celsius and Kelvin temperature scales and absolute zero;			◆
b) phase change, freezing point, melting point, boiling point, vaporization, and condensation;	◆		◆
c) conduction, convection, radiation,			◆
d) applications of heat transfer (heat engines, thermostats, refrigeration, and heat pumps).	◆		◆
PS.8 The student will investigate and understand characteristics of sound and technological applications of sound waves. Key concepts include			
a) wavelength, frequency, speed, and amplitude;			◆
b) resonance;			◆
c) the nature of mechanical waves;			◆
d) technological applications of sound.			◆
PS.9 The student will investigate and understand the nature and technological applications of light. Key concepts include			
a) the wave behavior of light (reflection, refraction, diffraction, and interference);			◆
b) images formed by lenses and mirrors;			◆
c) the electromagnetic spectrum.			◆
PS.10 The student will investigate and understand scientific principles and technological applications of work, force, and motion. Key concepts include			
a) speed, velocity, and acceleration;			◆
b) Newton's laws of motion;			◆
c) work, force, mechanical advantage, efficiency, and power;	◆		◆
d) applications (simple machines, compound machines, powered vehicles, rockets, and restraining devices).	◆		◆
PS.11 The student will investigate and understand basic principles of electricity and magnetism. Key concepts include			
a) static, current, circuits;			◆
b) magnetic fields and electromagnets;			◆
c) motors and generators.			◆

Virginia Standards of Learning Grade 6 Science Lesson-by-Lesson Correlation and Pacing Guide

CHAPTER/SECTION	VIRGINIA STANDARDS OF LEARNING	PACING GUIDE DAYS	BLOCKS
Introduction to Science			
What is Science?	**6.1a, c, d, e, i, j, k; 6.8a, i**	**4**	**2**
Skills Lab: Cool Crystals	6.1c, e, f, h, k	lab time included above	
Chapter 1 Introduction to Matter			
Chapter Project	**6.1a, c, e, f g, h, k**	**Ongoing: 2 weeks**	
1 Describing Matter and Energy	6.2e; 6.4 a b, d, g	3-4	1 1/2 - 2
2 Measuring Matter	6.1d	2-3	1- 1 1/2
Skills Lab: Making Sense of Density	6.1a, c, e, f, g, h, k	lab time included above	
3 Particles of Matter	6.4a, b, e	2	1
4 Integrating Earth Science: Elements From Earth	6.9b	2	1
Real-World Lab: Isolating Copper	6.1a, b, f, k; 6.4f		
Chapter 2 Water and Solutions			
Chapter Project	**6.1a, i, j**	**Ongoing: 1 week**	
1 The Properties of Water	6.1a; 6.4d, e; 6.5a, b	2	1
Skills Lab: Speeding Up Evaporation	6.1a, e, f, i, k	lab time included above	
2 Understanding Solutions	6.1a; 6.5a	2	1
Chapter 3 Chemical Interactions			
Chapter Project	**6.1a b, h, k**	**Ongoing: 1 week**	
1 Observing Chemical Reactions	6.2e; 6.4f	2-3	1-1 1/2
Skills Lab: Where's the Evidence?	6.1a, k	lab time included above	
2 Writing Chemical Equations	6.1a, c, j; 6.4c, d, e, f	2	1
Chapter 4 Weathering and Soil Formation			
Chapter Project	**6.1a, c, e, f h**	**Ongoing: 2 weeks**	
1 Rocks and Weathering	6.1a, c; 6.5c	3	1 1/2
Skills Lab: Rock Shake	6.1a, f, h, j	lab time included above	
2 Soil Formation and Composition	6.1a; 6.7c	2	1
3 Conserving Land and Soil	6.9a, c	1	1/2
4 Integrating Environmental Science: Waste Disposal and Recycling	6.9c, d,	2	1
Chapter 5 Erosion and Deposition			
Chapter Project	**6.1f, i**	**Ongoing: 2 weeks**	
1 Earth's Changing Surface	6.1e, f; 6.5c	2	1
Skills Lab: Sand Hills	6.1c, d, e, f, g, h, j, k, i	lab time included above	
2 Water Erosion	6.1a, d, j; 6.5c	2	1

CHAPTER/SECTION	VIRGINIA STANDARDS OF LEARNING	PACING GUIDE DAYS	BLOCKS
Chapter 5 Erosion and Deposition (continued)			
Real-World Lab: Streams in Action	6.1a, c, d, f, g, h, i, j, k	lab time included above	
3 Integrating Physics: The Force of Moving Water	6.1f; 6.2e; 6.7c	1	1/2
4 Glaciers	6.1a, d, j; 6.5c	1	1/2
5 Waves	6.1a; 6.3c	1	1/2
6 Wind	6.1a; 6.3c	1	1/2
Chapter 6 Earth's Land Resources			
Chapter Project	**6.1a, c, h, i**	**Ongoing: 2 weeks**	
1 Exploring Earth's Surface	6.1a, c, h, i; 6.8a, f	1	1/2
2 Topographic Maps	6.1a, c, j; 6.8a, f	1	1/2
3 Integrating Life Science: Earth's Land Biomes	6.1a, c, e, f; 6.8a, f	2-3	1-1 1/2
Skills Lab: Save That Soil	6.1a, c, d, e, f, j, k	lab time included above	
Chapter 7 Fresh Water			
Chapter Project	**6.1a, c, h, i, k**	**Ongoing: 2 weeks**	
1 The Water Cycle	6.1a, j; 6.5e	1	1/2
2 Water on the Surface	6.1a, b, i; 6.5e; 6.7c; 6.9c, d	3	1 1/2
3 Water Underground	6.1a; 6.5e; 6.9a, c, d	3	1 1/2
Real-World Lab: Soil Testing	6.1a, c, d, e, g, j, k	lab time included above	
4 Integrating Life Science: Wetland Environments	6.1a, j; 6.5e; 6.7a, b, c, d, f; 6.9a	2	1
Chapter 8 Freshwater Resources			
Chapter Project	**6.1a, j, k**	**Ongoing: 2 weeks**	
1 Water to Drink	6.5f, g; 6.7f; 6.9a	2-3	1-1 1/2
Real-World Lab: Testing the Waters	6.1a, c, h, i, k; 6.7g	lab time included above	
2 Balancing Water Needs	6.5f; 6.9a, c, d	2	1
Skills Lab: Getting the Salt Out	6.1a, j	lab time included above	
3 Freshwater Pollution	6.1 a, j; 6.9a, c, d	1	1/2
4 Integrating Physics: Water as an Energy Resource	6.1a; 6.2a, d, e; 6.5f	1	1/2
Chapter 9 Ocean Motions			
Chapter Project	**6.1a, j**	**Ongoing: 1 week**	
1 Wave Action	6.1a; 6.3c; 6.5c	1	1/2
2 Integrating Space Science: Tides	6.1c, h; 6.2a, b, d; 6.3c	1	1/2
3 Ocean Water Chemistry	6.1a; 6.4g; 6.5d, e	1-2	1/2-1
Skills Lab: Investigating Changes in Density	6.1a, c, g, h, i, j	lab time included above	
4 Currents and Climate	6.3c; 6.5d	1-2	1/2-1
Real-World Lab: Modeling Ocean Currents	6.1a, c, i, j	lab time included above	
Chapter 10 Ocean Zones			
Chapter Project	**6.1a, d, j**	**Ongoing: 2 weeks**	
1 Exploring the Ocean	6.5e	2	1
Skills Lab: The Shape of the Ocean Floor	6.1a, e, h, i, k	lab time included above	
2 Integrating Life Science: Life at the Ocean's Edge	6.7a, e, f	2	1
3 Integrating Life Science: The Neritic Zone and Open Ocean	6.7a; 6.9a	1	1/2

CHAPTER/SECTION	VIRGINIA STANDARDS OF LEARNING	PACING GUIDE DAYS	PACING GUIDE BLOCKS
Chapter 10 Ocean Zones (continued)			
4 Resources From the Ocean	6.9a, b, d	2-3	1-1 1/2
Real-World Lab: Cleaning Up an Oil Spill	6.1a; 6.9c, d	lab time included above	
Interdisciplinary Exploration: Chesapeake Bay	**6.7b; 6.9a**	**2**	**1**
Chapter 11 The Atmosphere			
Chapter Project	**6.1a, c, h**	**Ongoing: 1 1/2 weeks**	
1 The Air Around You	6.1a, h; 6.4d, g; 6.6a	2	1
Real-World Lab: How Clean Is the Air?	6.1a, c, e, h, i	lab time included above	
2 Integrating Environmental Science: Air Pollution	6.6d, g; 6.9a	2	1
3 Air Pressure	6.6b, c	2	1
4 Layers of the Atmosphere	6.6c	1-2	1/2-1
Chapter 12 Weather Factors			
Chapter Project	**6.1a, c, h, i**	**Ongoing: 2 weeks**	
1 Energy in the Atmosphere	6.1a, c, h; 6.2b; 6.3a	2-3	1-1 1/2
Skills Lab: Heating Earth's Surface	6.1a, c, e, h, i, k	lab time included above	
2 Integrating Physics: Heat Transfer	6.1a; 6.2b; 6.3b	1	1/2
3 Winds	6.1a, j; 6.3c, e; 6.6a, d, e	2	1
Real-World Lab: Where's the Wind?	6.1a, c, d, h, i	lab time included above	
4 Water in the Atmosphere	6.1a, j; 6.3d; 6.6b	1-2	1/2-1
5 Precipitation	6.1a, j; 6.5f, g; 6.6e, f	1-2	1/2-1
Chapter 13 Weather Patterns			
Chapter Project	**6.1a, c, h, i, j, k; 6.6f**	**Ongoing: 2 weeks**	
1 Air Masses and Fronts	6.1a; 6.3b, e; 6.6f	1-2	1/2-1
2 Storms	6.1a; 6.3e; 6.6e; 6.9c	2-3	1-1 1/2
Real-World Lab: Tracking a Hurricane	6.1a, c, f, h, i	lab time included above	
3 Integrating Health: Floods	6.1a; 6.7g	1	1/2
4 Predicting Weather	6.1a; 6.6b, f	3	1 1/2
Skills Lab: Reading a Weather Map	6.1a, h	lab time included above	
Chapter 14 Climate and Climate Change			
Chapter Project	**6.1a, c, e, g, h, i**	**Ongoing: 2 weeks**	
1 What Causes Climate?	6.1a; 6.3c; 6.5d; 6.6e	3	1 1/2
Skills Lab: Sunny Rays and Angles	6.1a, c, e, f, h, i, k	lab time included above	
2 Climate Regions	6.3c; 6.5d	3	1 1/2
Real-World Lab: Cool Climate Graphs	6.1h, i	lab time included above	
3 Long-Term Changes in Climate	6.1a; 6.2b; 6.4g	1	1/2
4 Integrating Environmental Science: Global Changes in the Atmosphere	6.2b; 6.3b; 6.6d, g; 6.9a	2	1
Chapter 15 Energy and Power			
Chapter Project	**6.1c, d, h, i, j**	**Ongoing: 1 week**	
1 The Nature of Energy	6.1a, c, f; 6.2a	2	1
Skills Lab: Soaring Straws	6.1a, c, g, h, i	lab time included above	

CHAPTER/SECTION	VIRGINIA STANDARDS OF LEARNING	PACING GUIDE DAYS	PACING GUIDE BLOCKS
Chapter 15 Energy and Power (continued)			
2 Energy Conversion and Conservation	6.1a, f; 6.2e	1	1/2
3 Photosynthesis and Fossil Fuels	6.1a, c; 6.2a, b, c, e; 6.4e, f	1	1/2
4 Integrating Mathematics: Power	6.1a; 6.2e	1	1/2
Real-World Lab: Can You Feel the Power?	6.1a, c, f, h	lab time included above	
Chapter 16 Energy Resources			
Chapter Project	**6.1a, c**	**Ongoing: 1 1/2 weeks**	
1 Fossil Fuels	6.1a; 6.2c, e; 6.9b	2	1
2 Renewable Sources of Energy	6.1a, c, e; 6.2b, d	2	1
3 Integrating Chemistry: Nuclear Energy	6.1a, j; 6.2d, e	1	1/2
Skills Lab: Keeping Comfortable	6.1a, c, e, f, g, h, k	lab time included above	
4 Energy Conservation	6.1a, c, f; 6.2c, d, e; 6.9b	2	1
Chapter 17 Environmental Issues			
Chapter Project	**6.1a, c, h, i**	**Ongoing: 1 1/2 weeks**	
1 Recognizing Environmental Issues	6.9a, c, d	2	1
Real-World Lab: Is Paper a Renewable Resource?	6.1a, f	lab time included above	
2 Forests and Fisheries	6.9a, c, d	2	1
Skills Lab: Tree Cookie Tales	6.1a, c, f, j	lab time included above	
3 Biodiversity	6.7a, f; 6.9a, c, d	1	1/2
4 Integrating Health: The Search for New Medicines	6.1a, j; 6.9c, d	1	1/2
Chapter 18 Earth, Moon, and Sun			
Chapter Project	**6.1a, c, h, i**	**Ongoing: 2 weeks**	
1 Earth in Space	6.1a, j; 6.8a, d, f, g	2	1
Skills Lab: Reasons for the Seasons	6.1a, c, j	lab time included above	
2 Phases, Eclipses, and Tides	6.1a, j; 6.8c, e, h	3	1 1/2
Skills Lab: A Moonth of Phases	6.1a, j	lab time included above	
3 Integrating Technology: Rockets and Satellites	6.1a, j; 6.8i	2	1
4 Earth's Moon	6.1a, c, d, e, g; 6.8a, d	2	1
Chapter 19 The Solar System			
Chapter Project	**6.1a, c, d, j, i**	**Ongoing: 2 weeks**	
1 Observing the Solar System	6.1a, f; 6.8c, i	1	1/2
2 The Sun	6.1a; 6.8a	1-2	1/2-1
Real-World Lab: Stormy Sunspots	6.1a, c, e, h, i, k	lab time included above	
3 The Inner Planets	6.1a, c, j; 6.8a, b, d	2	1
4 The Outer Planets	6.1a, c, h; 6.8a, b, d	3	1 1/2
Skills Lab: Speeding Around the Sun	6.1a, c, e, f, g, h, j, k	lab time included above	
5 Comets, Asteroids, and Meteors	6.1a, j; 6.8a	2	1
6 Integrating Life Science: Is There Life Beyond Earth?	6.1a; 6.8i	1	1/2
Interdisciplinary Exploration: The Solar System	**6.8a, i**	**2**	**1**

National Science Education Standards and *Benchmarks*

Project 2061 was established by the American Association for the Advancement of Science (AAAS) as a long-term project to improve science education nationwide. A primary goal of Project 2061 is to define a "common core of learning"—the knowledge and skills we want all students to achieve. Project 2061 published *Science for All Americans* in 1989 and followed this with *Benchmarks for Science Literacy* in 1993. *Benchmarks* recommends what students should know and be able to do by the end of grades 2, 5, 8, and 12. Project 2061 clearly states that *Benchmarks* is not a curriculum, but a tool for designing successful curricula.

The National Research Council (NRC) utilized *Science for All Americans* and *Benchmarks* to develop the National Science Education Standards (NSES), which were published in 1996. The NSES are organized into six categories (Content, Teaching, Assessment, Professional Development, Program, and System) to help schools establish the conditions necessary to achieve scientific literacy for all students.

Michael Padilla, the lead author of *Science Explorer*, guided one of six teams of teachers whose work led to the publication of *Benchmarks*. He also was a contributing writer of the National Science Education Standards. Under his guidance, *Science Explorer* has implemented these standards through its inquiry approach, a focus on student learning of important concepts and skills, and teacher support aligned with the NSES teaching standards.

Neither *Benchmarks* nor the NSES requires a single, uniform national curriculum, and in fact there is a great diversity nationwide in science curricula. The correlations that follow are designed to help you utilize the *Science Explorer* program to meet your particular curriculum needs.

National Science Education Standards Correlation

National Science Education Standards	*Grade 6 Science* Sections	*Life Science* Sections	*Physical Science* Sections
CONTENT STANDARD A: SCIENCE AS INQUIRY			
A-1 Identify Questions that Can Be Answered Through Scientific Investigations.	Chapter Projects: 11, 18	1.1, 7.2, 7.3, 10.2, 10.4, 15.1, 15.3, 15.4, 16.1, 16.2, 17.1, 17.3, 18.1; Chapter Projects: 1, 10, 11, 14, 20	19.1; Chapter Projects: 1, 3, 7, 8, 14, 16, 18
A-2 Design and Conduct a Scientific Investigation.	Intro, 4.1, 6.3, 9.3, 11.1, 14.1; Chapter Projects: 4, 7–10, 14, 17	Intro, 2.4, 7.2, 8.1, 10.4, 12.2, 13.3,20.1; Chapter Projects: 1, 7, 9, 10, 11, 14, 20, 22–24	Intro, 6.2, 9.2, 13.4, 15.2–15.3, 16.1, 16.3, 18.2; Chapter Projects: 1, 3, 6, 8, 11, 12, 19, 20
A-3 Use Appropriate Tools and Techniques to Gather, Analyze, and Interpret Data.	6.3, 8.1, 10.1, 12.3, 13.2, 13.4, 14.2, 15.4, 16.2, 16.4; Chapter Projects: 11–14, 16	Intro, 1.3, 2.1, 2.5, 3.1, 6.3, 22.2; Chapter Projects: 1, 3, 6, 8, 10, 15, 16, 22, 23	Intro, 8.1, 9.1, 14.1, 14.2; Chapter Projects: 1, 3, 5–9, 17, 21
A-4 Develop Descriptions, Explanations, Predictions, and Models Using Evidence.	Intro, 1.2, 1.4, 2.1, 4.2, 5.1, 5.2, 9.4, 10.4, 17.1, 17.2, 19.4; Chapter Projects: 5, 6, 10, 18, 19	3.1, 4.1, 5.1, 5.3, 19.2, 22.1, 23.4, 23.5, 24.1, 24.2; Chapter Projects: 1–5, 10–15, 17–20	1.2, 1.4, 3.1, 3.3, 3.4, 4.1–4.3, 11.1; Chapter Projects: 2, 4, 8, 15, 22
A-5 Think Critically and Logically to Make the Relationships between Evidence and Explanations.	1.47.1, 7.3, 8.2	Intro, 4.1, 9.4, 14.2, 20.4; Chapter Projects: 1–4, 11, 15, 20	Intro, 1.4, 21.4; Chapter Projects: 6, 13, 14, 19, 21
A-6 Recognize and Analyze Alternative Explanations and Predictions.	Chapter Projects: 12, 13	Chapter Projects: 13, 16	21.3
A-7 Communicate Scientific Procedures and Explanations.	3.2; Chapter Projects: 1-19	Intro, 4.1, 12.2; Chapter Projects: 1, 3–9, 13–19, 21–24	Intro, 5.1, 11.3, 19.3; Chapter Projects: 1–7, 9–22
A-8 Use Mathematics in All Aspects of Scientific Inquiry.	15.1, 15.4, Chapter Projects: 14	3.1, 3.2, 6.4, 7.2, 7.3, 19.3, 21.3; Chapter Projects: 3, 5, 6, 12, 13, 16	2.2, 2.3, 9.1–9.3, 11.1,11.3, 13.1, 13.4, 22.1, 22.3, Chapter Projects: 9, 17, 21

National Science Education Standards Correlation			
National Science Education Standards	***Grade 6 Science* Sections**	***Life Science* Sections**	***Physical Science* Sections**
CONTENT STANDARD B: PHYSICAL SCIENCE			
B-1 Properties and Changes of Properties in Matter	1.1, 1.2, 2.1, 2.2, 3.1, 3.2, 9.3, 11.1–11.3	2.2, 5.2, 5.3, 10.4, 11.1, 15.1, 16.1, 16.2, 17.2, 18.1, 19.2, 21.1, 23.2	1.1–1.4, 2.1–2.4, 3.1–3.5, 4.1–4.3, 5.1–5.4, 6.1–6.5, 7.1–7.3, 8.1–8.4, 9.1, 11.3, 13.1, 13.2, 14.1, 14.3, 17.3, 19.1, 19.3, 20.1, 21.4, 22.1
B-2 Motions and Forces		1.2, 11.1, 13.2, 17.1, 17.2, 18.1	2.1, 3.1, 4.1, 4.2, 9.1–9.3, 10.1–10.5, 11.1–11.4, 15.1–15.4, 16.2, 17.1, 17.2, 19.1, 19.3, 19.4, 20.1, 20.2, 21.1–21.4
B-3 Transfer of Energy	3.1, 5.3, 5.5, 7.1, 7.2, 9.1–9.3, 12.1–12.3, 15.1–15.3, 16.1, 16.4, 19.2; Chapter Project: 15	13.1, 16.1, 19.4, 20.3, 23.1, 23.2	2.4, 3.5, 4.1, 5.1, 5.3, 5.4, 6.4, 7.3 8.3, 12.1–12.3, 13.1–13.4, 14.1–14.4, 15.1, 15.2, 15.4, 16.2, 17.1–17.4, 18.1–18.4, 19.3, 19.4, 20.1–20.3, 21.1–21.4, 22.1, 22.2
CONTENT STANDARD C: LIFE SCIENCE			
C-1 Structure and Function in Living Systems		1.1–1.4, 2.1–2.5, 3.1, 3.3, 3.4, 6.1–6.4, 7.1–7.3, 8.1–8.4, 9.1–9.4, 10.1–10.4, 11.1, 11.2, 12.1–12.4, 13.1–13.4, 15.1–15.4, 16.2, 16.3, 17.1–17.4, 18.1–18.3, 19.1–19.4, 20.1–20.4, 21.1–21.3	5.1, 6.5, 7.2, 7.3, 8.1, 11.1, 11.4, 12.4, 14.2, 16.4, 18.4, 20.4
C-2 Reproduction and Heredity		1.1, 3.1–3.4, 4.1–4.3, 6.3, 6.4, 7.3, 8.1–8.3, 9.1–9.3, 10.1, 10.3, 10.4, 11.2,11.3, 11.5, 12.2–12.4, 21.2, 21.3	
C-3 Regulation and Behavior		1.1, 1.4, 2.2, 6.3, 6.4, 7.1–7.3, 8.1–8.3, 9.1–9.4, 11.4, 14.1, 14.2, 15.1, 15.3, 20.1–20.4, 21.1–21.3, 22.1–22.3, 23.1	16.5
C-4 Populations and Ecosystems	4.2, 5.3, 7.2, 7.4, 10.2, 10.3, 14.2; Chapter Project: 10	2.3, 2.4, 5.1, 6.3, 7.2, 10.3, 11.3, 12.3, 13.1, 14.1, 14.2, 22.1–22.3, 23.1–23.5	
C-5 Diversity and Adaptations of Organisms	17.3, 17.4; Chapter Project: 17	5.1–5.3, 6.1, 6.3, 6.4, 7.1–7.3, 8.1–8.3, 10.1–10.4, 11.1–11.5, 12.1–12.4, 13.1–13.4, 14.1, 14.2, 22.3, 23.4, 24.3	7.2, 7.3, 10.4, 11.2
CONTENT STANDARD D: EARTH AND SPACE SCIENCE			
D-1 Structure of the Earth System	4.1–4.3, 5.1, 5.2, 6.1, 7.1–7.4, 10.1–10.3, 11.1, 11.4, 12.1–12.5, 13.1–13.3, 19.3; Chapter Projects: 4, 5	11.1, 23.2, 23.5	1.4, 2.1, 2.4, 3.3, 3.4, 4.3, 5.2, 6.3, 7.1, 9.2, 14.2, 15.4, 19.2, 20.1

National Science Education Standards Correlation			
National Science Education Standards	***Grade 6 Science* Sections**	***Life Science* Sections**	***Physical Science* Sections**
CONTENT STANDARD D: EARTH AND SPACE SCIENCE *(continued)*			
D-2 Earth's History	14.3, 18.4	1.4, 5.1, 5.2, 12.1	8.4, 9.2, 13.3, 19.2
D-3 Earth in the Solar System	9.2, 12.1, 12.3, 12.4, 14.1, 18.1, 18.2, 18.4, 19.3	22.3	3.5, 10.3, 10.5, 17.2, 18.5, 19.2
CONTENT STANDARD E: SCIENCE AND TECHNOLOGY			
E-1 Abilities of Technological Design	1.4, 11.2, 15.1, 18.3; Chapter Projects: 6, 8, 9, 15		1.3, 1.4, 3.3, 5.4, 6.4, 7.3, 8.1, 8.2, 10.3, 11.2, 11.3, 11.4, 12.1–12.3, 13.1, 13.2, 14.4, 17.3, 17.4, 19.1, 19.3, 19.4, 20.1–20.4, 21.1–21.4, 22.1–22.4; Chapter Projects: 6, 7, 10–14, 16, 18–20, 22
E-2 Understandings about Science and Technology	Intro, 8.2, 8.4, 10.1, 10.4, 15.4, 16.1–16.4	1.2, 4.2, 4.3, 5.3, 12.3, 14.1, 15.3, 17.1, 19.4, 24.1, 24.2	Intro, 3.3, 4.2, 5.4, 6.3, 7.1, 7.2, 8.1–8.4, 10.3, 10.5, 12.1, 13.2, 13.4, 14.2, 15.4, 16.5, 17.3, 17.4, 19.2, 21.3, 22.3, 22.4
CONTENT STANDARD F: SCIENCE IN PERSONAL AND SOCIAL PERSPECTIVES			
F-1 Personal Health	8.1, 8.3, 13.2, 13.2	1.2, 2.4, 3.4, 4.2, 4.3, 6.4, 15.1–15.4, 16.1, 17.4, 18.2, 18.3, 19.1–19.4, 20.2–20.4, 21.3	5.4, 6.5, 7.3, 8.4, 9.2, 14.2, 16.4, 16.5, 17.2, 18.5, 20.4
F-2 Populations, Resources, and Environments	8.2, 10.4, 17.3	2.3, 8.4, 10.3, 22.2, 24.1–24.3	3.3, 5.2, 6.4, 8.4, 13.3, 21.2, 21.4
F-3 Natural Hazards	7.2, 7.3, 8.2, 11.2, 13.2	12.3, 15.4, 19.4	7.2, 8.1, 15.4, 20.1, 20.4
F-4 Risks and Benefits	5.2, 7.2, 7.3, 13.2, 19.6	8.4, 12.3, 17.4, 20.2, 20.3, 20.4, 24.1, 24.3	5.4, 7.3, 8.4, 16.4, 17.2, 21.2, 22.4
F-5 Science and Technology in Society	4.3, 4.4, 7.1, 7.3, 8.2, 8.3, 13.4, 14.4, 16.2, 17.1; Chapter Projects: 2, 6, 7	4.3, 8.4, 22.2, 24.1, 24.2	1.3, 5.4, 8.4, 9.1, 12.3, 16.3, 16.5, 17.2–17.4, 18.2, 18.5, 22.1–22.4
CONTENT STANDARD G: HISTORY AND NATURE OF SCIENCE			
G-1 Science as a Human Endeavor	Intro, 4.3, 18.4	Intro, 1.2, 3.3, 5.1, 14.1, 16.2, 17.3, 17.4, 19.1, 19.3, 24.1, 24.3	Intro, 3.1, 3.2, 16.3, 17.4, 18.5
G-2 Nature of Science	Intro	Intro, 1.2, 16.2, 19.1	Intro, 3.1
G-3 History of Science	Intro, 6.1, 11.4, 17.1, 19.1, 18.4, 20.1, 20.3–20.5	1.1, 1.2, 1.4, 3.1, 3.2, 5.1, 6.1, 13.1, 14.1, 16.2, 17.3, 17.4, 19.1, 19.3, 24.1	1.2, 1.3, 2.2, 3.1, 3.2, 8.1–8.3, 10.1–10.5, 11.2–11.4, 13.2, 13.4 16.2, 17.4, 18.5, 19.1–19.3, 20.2, 20.4, 21.3, 22.3, 22.4

National Science Education Standards and *Benchmarks* (continued)

***Benchmarks* Correlation**

Benchmarks for Science Literacy	*Grade 6 Science* Chapters	*Life Science* Chapters	*Physical Science* Chapters
1 THE NATURE OF SCIENCE			
1A The Scientific World View	Intro; Chapter Project: 3	8, 16, 19	5, 17, 18, 21
1B Scientific Inquiry	Intro, 1, 4–17; 1, 2, 4, 5, 11–14	Intro, 1–8, 10, 11, 14, 17, 22, 23, 24	Intro, –3, 6–8, 13, 15, 20
1C The Scientific Enterprise	Intro, 17	Intro, 1, 3, 5, 19, 20, 24	Intro, 11, 19, 22
2 THE NATURE OF MATHEMATICS			
2A Patterns and Relationships	19	10, 22	3, 4, 15
2B Mathematics, Science, and Technology	8, 9	22	12, 21
2C Mathematical Inquiry	19	6, 17, 21	16, 20
3 THE NATURE OF TECHNOLOGY			
3A Technology and Science	Intro, 6, 8, 10, 11, 13, 16–18	1, 4, 11, 24	Intro, 5, 8, 9, 18, 22
3B Design and Systems	8, 15, 16, 18		8, 10, 11, 13, 14, 20–22
3C Issues in Technology	1, 4, 6–8, 10, 11, 14, 16, 17	4, 6–8, 13, 15, 17, 24	1, 8, 12, 14, 16, 17, 21, 22
4 THE PHYSICAL SETTING			
4A The Universe	19		
4B The Earth	4–9, 11–15, 17–19	23, 24	13
4C Processes that Shape the Earth	4, 5, 9, 14, 18	5, 23	15
4D Structure of Matter	1, 2, 3, 9, 11	18	1–8, 11, 14, 21
4E Energy Transformations	3, 5, 9, 11, 12, 15, 19		2–5, 12–14, 17, 20–22
4F Motion	12, 18	11	9, 10, 15, 16, 18
4G Forces of Nature	19		3, 19
5 THE LIVING ENVIRONMENT			
5A Diversity of Life	10, 17	1, 5–13, 23, 24	
5B Heredity		3, 4	
5C Cells		1, 2, 3, 8, 9, 15, 20	18
5D Interdependence of Life	4, 10, 14	2, 6, 7, 10–12, 22, 23	
5E Flow of Matter and Energy	15	1, 2, 8, 16, 18, 23	6, 7, 13
5F Evolution of Life		1, 5, 12, 13, 14	
6 THE HUMAN ORGANISM			
6A Human Identity		14, 15	12, 16, 18
6B Human Development		15, 21	
6C Basic Functions		13, 15–18, 20	6, 7, 16
6D Learning		20	22
6E Physical Health	13	15–20	7
6F Mental Health		15	
7 HUMAN SOCIETY			
7A Cultural Effects on Behavior		18	22
7B Group Behavior	16	15	
7C Social Change	13, 16	24	
7D Social Trade-Offs	5, 10, 13	22, 24	8

***Benchmarks* Correlation**			
Benchmarks for Science Literacy	***Grade 6 Science* Chapters**	***Life Science* Chapters**	***Physical Science* Chapters**
7 HUMAN SOCIETY *(continued)*			
7E Political and Economic Systems	11		
7F Social Conflict	8, 10		
7G Global Interdependence	7, 14, 16	24	
8 THE DESIGNED WORLD			
8A Agriculture	4, 7, 8	8, 9	
8B Materials and Manufacturing		24	3, 8
8C Energy Sources and Use	8, 9, 11, 15, 16		8, 12–14, 19–21
8D Communication	18		17, 18, 22
8E Information Processing			22
8F Health Technology		4, 15, 17–19, 24	8
9 THE MATHEMATICAL WORLD			
9A Numbers		3	9
9B Symbolic Relationships	10, 14, 15		2, 9, 12, 13, 15
9C Shapes	1	10	4, 7
9D Uncertainty		3	9
9E Reasoning		6, 14	3, 7, 10
10 HISTORICAL PERSPECTIVES			
10A Displacing the Earth from the Center of the Universe	18, 19		9
10B Uniting the Heavens and Earth	19		10
10C Relating Matter & Energy and Time & Space			
10D Extending Time		5	
10E Moving the Continents			
10F Understanding Fire			1, 4
10G Splitting the Atom			8
10H Explaining the Diversity of Life		3, 5	
10I Discovering Germs	15	1, 19	
10J Harnessing Power			13, 14
11 COMMON THEMES			
11A Systems		17	12, 16, 20
11B Models	1, 2, 7, 9, 10, 19	12	1, 4, 11
11C Constancy and Change	3, 18	9, 10, 15, 18	5, 6, 15
11D Scale		7	4
12 HABITS OF MIND			
12A Values and Attitudes	Chapter Projects: (all)	10; Chapter Projects (all)	6, 21; Chapter Projects (all)
12B Computation and Estimation	11		2, 9
12C Manipulation and Observation	12		8, 10
12D Communication Skills	7, 11, 14; Chapter Projects: 1, 2	Intro, 1, 4, 6, 11–13, 15, 16, 19	Intro, 1, 7, 10
12E Critical-Response Skills	8	6, 13, 20, 24	6, 7, 8, 10, 17

Inquiry Skills Chart

The Prentice Hall ***Science Explorer*** program provides comprehensive teaching, practice, and assessment of science skills, with an emphasis on the process skills necessary for inquiry. The chart lists the skills covered in the program and cites the page numbers where each skill is covered.

Basic Process SKILLS			
	Student Text: Projects and Labs	**Student Text: Activities**	**Student Text: Caption and Review Questions**
Observing	9, 42–43, 76–77, 91, 108, 142–143, 165, 199, 214–215, 225, 228–229, 259, 282–283, 329, 248–349, 529, 536, 559, 568–569	50, 59, 70, 109, 129, 158, 181, 210, 232, 243, 251, 260, 262, 271, 314, 373, 403, 419, 432, 468, 479, 484, 500, 552, 579, 581, 600, 606	79, 137, 170, 188, 339, 389, 409, 450, 472, 615, 618, 625
Inferring	42–43, 108, 199, 228–229, 282–283, 348–349, 440–441	18, 25, 35, 56, 62, 71, 92, 145, 149, 183, 192, 278, 290, 298, 308, 313, 330, 347, 368, 387, 415, 435, 447, 454, 459, 490, 515, 521, 537, 543, 570, 601, 612, 617, 624	21, 46, 71, 78, 97, 120, 162, 188, 213, 223, 227, 235, 249, 257, 275, 296, 315, 321, 368, 437, 471, 497, 508, 547, 554, 586, 588, 591, 621, 629
Predicting	125, 142–143, 361, 395, 412–413, 513	96, 103, 132, 236, 239, 266, 351, 594, 597	58, 64, 66, 88, 97, 122, 129, 133, 146, 151, 157, 160, 168, 223, 233, 257, 287, 320, 343, 350, 358, 384, 386, 418, 425, 458, 462, 478, 512, 524, 556, 578, 591, 627
Classifying	69	20, 118, 200, 245, 311, 401, 449, 614	15, 39, 60, 73, 75, 89, 109, 122, 222, 286, 320, 358, 386, 392, 393, 402, 428, 451, 486, 519, 526, 527
Making Models	125, 142–143, 191, 225, 241, 259, 282–283, 289, 318, 361, 467, 568–569, 576–577, 593	78, 81, 173, 194, 202, 212, 372, 429, 516, 560, 574, 617	67, 635
Communicating	17, 49, 91, 125, 165, 191, 225, 259, 289, 329, 361, 395, 431, 467, 499, 529, 559, 593	416, 535, 629	122, 162, 188, 232, 256, 286, 320, 358, 392, 428, 464, 496, 497, 526, 556, 590, 634
Measuring	34, 130–131, 214–215, 334–335, 339, 348–349, 366–367, 374–375, 474–475, 492–493, 542	362	389, 465
Calculating	34, 49, 199, 297, 492–493	82, 174, 193, 226, 230, 273, 389, 404, 517, 531, 540, 561, 587	47, 155, 163, 359, 393, 527
Creating Data Tables	49, 69, 329, 361, 366–367, 431, 440–441, 474–475, 499, 520, 529, 559		
Graphing	49, 276–277, 297, 361, 431, 440–441, 452–453, 605	117, 268, 487, 502, 609	287, 359, 393, 557

Inquiry Skills Chart

Advanced Process SKILLS

	Student Text: Projects and Labs	Student Text: Activities	Student Text: Caption and Review Questions
Posing Questions	17, 69, 108	154	11, 123, 321, 429, 590
Developing Hypotheses	9, 56–57, 130–131, 186, 366–367, 431, 622–623	126, 147, 178, 252, 332, 381, 396, 507, 583	123, 156, 163, 257, 439, 557
Designing Experiments	17, 98–99, 130–131, 142–143, 186, 241, 276–277, 440–441, 474–475, 513, 520, 536, 622–623	40, 63	123, 257
Controlling Variables	9, 56-57, 98–99, 186, 276–277, 440–441, 467, 520		
Forming Operational Definitions	69, 318, 513	101, 166, 442, 476, 482, 530, 628	376
Interpreting Data	17, 34, 49, 91, 130–131, 297, 334–335, 374–375, 412–413, 452–453, 492–493, 542, 605	115, 175, 296, 370, 383, 422, 426, 602	47, 67, 89, 230, 331, 429, 465, 527, 557, 635
Drawing Conclusions	9, 17, 56–57, 214–215, 228–229, 366–367, 374–375, 452–453	28, 53, 106, 134, 248, 280, 345, 426, 461	47, 67. 223, 287, 356, 393, 497, 527, 635

Critical Thinking SKILLS

	Student Text: Projects and Labs	Student Text: Activities	Student Text: Caption and Review Questions
Comparing and Contrasting	91, 395	266, 273	4, 46, 54, 66, 120, 141, 159, 162, 172, 182, 185, 188, 217, 222, 256, 267, 284, 286, 301, 392, 428, 446, 448, 464, 494, 526, 535, 541, 582, 604, 634
Applying Concepts	108, 142–143, 199, 214–215, 228–229, 282–283, 318, 334–335, 366–367, 374–375, 412–413, 452–453, 513, 536, 605		27, 42–43, 36, 47, 51, 58, 66, 84, 88, 122, 162, 188, 203, 209, 240, 261, 270, 286, 316, 333, 342, 352, 358, 365, 371, 378, 380, 290, 397, 404, 411, 417, 434, 451, 460, 469, 481, 482, 485, 489, 490, 506, 518, 524, 534, 544, 561, 590, 591, 599, 630, 631, 634
Interpreting Diagrams, Graphs, Photographs, and Maps	395		7, 8, 24, 26, 39, 80, 102, 107, 111, 123, 135, 140, 167, 177, 211, 213, 219, 223, 253, 257, 263, 264, 269, 272, 279, 291, 305, 307, 309, 312, 321, 337, 341, 359, 363, 377, 400, 402, 408, 424, 429, 433, 458, 465, 470, 504, 517, 538, 543, 547, 564, 567, 573, 575, 578, 595, 598, 607, 635

Critical Thinking SKILLS (continued)

	Student Text: Projects and Labs	Student Text: Activities	Student Text: Caption and Review Questions
Relating Cause and Effect			15, 64, 66, 107, 122, 127, 128, 129, 148, 155, 162, 163, 184, 198, 209, 222, 237, 244, 247, 265, 281, 286, 310, 320, 358, 392, 428, 443, 464, 496, 506, 526, 556, 567, 590, 604, 613, 634
Making Generalizations			32, 180, 222, 270, 302, 320, 510, 551, 556, 634
Making Judgments			15, 44, 162, 220, 240, 250, 256, 303, 316, 428, 464, 526, 556
Problem Solving			15, 33, 46, 81, 88, 114, 162, 254, 256, 392, 473, 494, 496

Basic Process SKILLS

	Student Text: Projects and Labs	Student Text: Activities	Student Text: Caption and Review Questions
Concept Maps			45, 87, 187, 255, 357, 391, 463, 495, 555, 589
Compare/ Contrast Tables			121, 319, 427, 525, 633
Venn Diagrams			
Flowcharts			65, 161, 285
Cycle Diagrams			221

Master Materials List

The Master Materials list cross-references items to activities and defines the quantities needed for a class of 30 students working in 5 groups of 6.

CONSUMABLE ITEMS

Description	Qty per class	Textbook Section(s)
Adhesive Materials	5	10-2 (DIS)
Agar, Block	10	10-4 (TT)
Alka Seltzer Tablets, Pkg/24	1	1-1 (SYS), 4-1 (DIS), 18-3 (TT)
Aluminum Foil, Roll ,12" x 25'	1	3-1 (Lab), 8-2 (Lab), 16-2 (Lab)
Bag, Plastic Zip Lip, 6" x 8"	20	1-1 (SYS), 11-4 (DIS), 16-2 (DIS)
Bag, Plastic Zip Lip 9" x 12"	5	12-1 (DIS)
Bags, Plastic Small, Box/80, w/Ties	1	7-1 (Lab), 14-4 (TT)
Bags, Trash, Heavy Plastic	15	8-1 (DIS), 8-4 (DIS)
Baking Powder, 200 g	1	1-1 (TT)
Baking Soda, 454 g	1	2-1 (TT), 3-1 (DIS), 19-4 (TT)
Ball, Styrofoam, 2"	5	8-4 (TT)
Ball, Styrofoam, 3"	5	19-4 (TT)
Balloons, Round, 15", Pkg/5	2	11-3 (DIS), 11-3 (Lab)
Balloons, Round 9", Pkg/35	1	18-3 (DIS)
Battery, 6 V, Lantern	5	1-4 (Lab)
Battery, Size D	10	2-2 (TT), 14-1 (DIS), 18-1 (Lab)
Bromothymol Blue, 500 mL	1	1-1 (SYS)
Bulb, Fluorescent, 15 Watt	5	16-4 (DIS)
Bulb, Incandescent, 100 Watt	6	2-1 (Lab), 7-1 (TT), 14-1 (Lab), 16-4 (DIS), 18-1 (DIS), 18-2 (Lab)
Bulb, Incandescent, 60 Watt	5	16-4 (DIS)
Bulb, 150 Watt	5	12-1 (Lab)
Candle, Warming	5	(INT), 11-1 (DIS), 12-2 (DIS)
Candles, Birthday, Pkg/36	1	3-1 (Lab)
Cardboard, Corrugated	55	6-2 (DIS), 12-3 (Lab), 13-1 (DIS), 19-1 (TT)
Cardboard, Piece	10	11-3 (Lab), 19-2 (DIS), 19-2 (TT)
Cards, Index, 3" x 5", Pkg/100	1	1-4 (Lab), 2-1 (Lab), 15-2 (DIS)
Chalk, White, Pkg/12	1	9-4 (Lab)
Cheesecloth, 2 sq yds	1	7-3 (Lab)
Clay, Modeling (water-resistant) 1 lb	10	1-2 (Lab), 3-1 (Lab), 4-3 (DIS), 7-3 (TT), 9-4 (Lab), 11-1 (DIS), 11-3 (TT) 11-3 (Lab), 19-5 (DIS)
Clay, Powder, 454 g	1	7-3 (Lab)
Cornmeal, 454 g	1	5-6 (DIS)
Cornstarch, 500 g	1	1-1 (TT)
Cotton Balls, Pkg/300	1	10-4 (Lab)
Crayon	5	1-2 (Lab)
Cup, Plastic 270 mL, Squat, Pkg/50	2	1-1 (TT), 1-2 (DIS), 1-2 (TT), 2-1 (DIS), 2-1 (TT), 2-2 (DIS), 3-1 (DIS), 3-1 (TT), 3-1 (Lab), 5-4 (DIS), 11-2 (TT), 17-3 (DIS)
Cup, Styrofoam, 180 mL., pkg/25	1	5-2 (Lab), 16-4 (Lab)
Cupric Chloride Crystals, 100 g	1	1-4 (Lab)
Cupric Sulfate, 500 g	1	3-1 (Lab)
Cups, Paper 100 mL, pkg/25	1	4-2 (DIS), 18-3 (TT)
Cups, Paper 200 mL, pkg/100	2	6-3 (Lab), 7-4 (DIS), 8-1 (Lab), 10-4 (Lab), 16-4 (Lab)
Cups, Plastic Clear 300 mL, pkg/50	1	2-1 (TT), 7-1 (SYS), 9-4 (DIS), 11-1 (TT), 13-3 (DIS), 16-4 (Lab), 17-4 (DIS)
Detergent, Household	1	5-2 (Lab), 8-1 (Lab), 13-2 (DIS)

KEY: **DIS**: Discover; **SYS**: Sharpen Your Skills; **TT**: Try This; **Lab**: Lab; **INT**: Introduction Lab

CONSUMABLE ITEMS (continued)		
Description	**Qty per class**	**Textbook Section(s)**
Egg, Uncooked	10	9-3 (DIS)
Feather, White	5	10-4 (Lab)
Fertilizer, Granular	1	8-3 (TT)
Filter Paper, 15 cm Diam, Pkg/100	1	17-4 (DIS)
Filters, Coffee Box/100	1	8-3 (DIS), 11-1 (Lab)
Flour 2 lb	1	10-3 (DIS)
Food Coloring, Blue, 30 mL	1	2-1 (TT), 5-2 (Lab), 13-1 (DIS)
Food Coloring, Red, 30 mL	1	8-3 (DIS), 9-4 (DIS), 13-1 (DIS)
Gelatin, Box	1	2-2 (TT)
Glue	1	11-3 (Lab), 16-2 (Lab)
Graph Paper, Metric Coordinates, Pkg/100	1	4-2 (Lab), 4-4 (DIS), 9-2 (SYS), 10-1 (Lab), 12-1 (Lab), 12-2 (TT), 14-1 (Lab), 14-2 (Lab), 17-2 (DIS), 19-2 (Lab), 19-3 (SYS)
Guava Juice or other Fruit Juice	5	10-4 (TT)
Hydrochloric Acid, 1 L, 1.0 M	1	3-1 (Lab)
Ice Cubes, Bucket	7	(INT), 7-1 (DIS), 8-2 (Lab), 9-3 (Lab), 9-4 (DIS), 12-4 (DIS), 12-5 (DIS)
Lemon Juice, 500 mL	1	11-2 (TT)
Lid for 200-mL Paper Cup	25	16-4 (Lab)
Lid for Styrofoam Cup	25	16-4 (Lab)
Lid for 300-mL Cup	50	16-4 (Lab)
Lid, Plastic	5	10-3 (DIS)
Limewater Solution, 1L	1	3-1 (TT), 11-1 (TT)
Live Cacti, Set/5	1	6-3 (TT)
Live Pond Culture, 240 mL	1	7-2 (DIS)
Marker, Black, Permanent	5	4-1 (Lab), 8-3 (DIS), 9-4 (Lab), 10-3 (DIS), 10-4 (Lab) , 15-1 (Lab)
Marker, Black, Water Soluble	5	17-4 (DIS)
Marshmallows, Bag	1	16-2 (Lab)
Masking Tape, Roll	5	1-2 (TT), 4-1 (Lab), 5-1 (Lab), 6-3 (DIS), 10-3 (DIS), 11-3 (Lab), 12-2 (DIS), 12-3 (DIS), 12-3 (TT), 12-3 (Lab), 14-1 (DIS), 14-1 (Lab), 15-1 (Lab), 16-2 (Lab), 17-4 (DIS), 18-3 (TT), 19-2 (DIS) 19-3 (TT)
Matches, Wood Safety, Box/30	5	3-1 (Lab), 11-1 (DIS), 12-2 (DIS), 15-3 (DIS)
Newspaper	5	5-2 (TT), 6-3 (Lab), 7-3 (TT), 9-4 (Lab), 17-1 (Lab)
Oil, Vegetable, 16 oz	1	2-1 (DIS), 2-1 (TT), 10-4 (Lab)
Overhead Transparency	5	19-4 (TT)
Pan, Aluminum Foil 22.5 cm	10	8-4 (TT), 12-2 (DIS)
Paper Towel Roll	2	1-2 (Lab), 1-4 (DIS), 2-1 (DIS), 2-1 (Lab), 4-1 (Lab), 4-2 (DIS), 5-4 (DIS), 7-2 (TT), 10-4 (Lab)
Paper, Construction, Black Pkg/50	1	12-3 (TT), 14-1 (Lab), 14-4 (DIS)
Paper, Construction, Blue Pkg/50	1	9-4 (Lab)
Paper, Construction, Red Pkg/50	1	9-4 (Lab)
Paper, Oaktag, Sheet	15	16-2 (Lab)
Paper, Tracing, 9" x 12", Pad/50	1	13-2 (Lab)
Pebbles, Gravel, 2.5 kg	2	4-3 (DIS), 5-3 (DIS), 7-1 (TT), 7-1 (Lab), 7-3 (DIS), 7-3 (Lab), 9-1 (DIS)
Pencils, Colored, Pkg/12	5	13-2 (Lab), 14-2 (Lab), 17-2 (Lab)
Pepper, 60 g	1	2-2 (DIS)
Peppercorns, Black, 30 g	1	19-4 (TT)
Perfume	1	11-2 (DIS)
pH Test Paper, Wide Range, 100/Vial	5	8-1 (Lab), 11-2 (TT)
Phenyl Salicylate Crystals, Salol, 100 g	1	(INT)

KEY: **DIS**: Discover; **SYS**: Sharpen Your Skills; **TT**: Try This; **Lab**: Lab; **INT**: Introduction Lab

Master Materials List

CONSUMABLE ITEMS (continued)		
Description	Qty per class	Textbook Section(s)
Plastic Wrap Roll, 50 sq ft	1	7-1 (TT), 14-2 (TT), 14-4 (DIS), 17-1 (Lab)
Plates, Paper, 9", Pkg/50	1	8-3 (DIS), 17-3 (DIS)
Rheoscopic Fluid, Kalliroscope 32 oz	2	9-4 (Lab)
Rock, Limestone Chips, 4 oz	2	4-1 (Lab)
Rubber Bands, Assorted 4 oz	1	7-1 (TT), 7-3 (Lab), 11-1 (Lab), 11-3 (Lab), 11-4 (DIS), 14-2 (TT), 15-1 (Lab), 15-2 (DIS)
Salt, Non-Iodized, 737 g	2	1-1 (TT), 2-1 (TT), 2-2 (DIS), 2-2 (TT), 2-2 (SYS), 8-2 (Lab), 9-3 (DIS), 9-3 (Lab), 12-5 (DIS), 13-1 (DIS)
Sand Collected from a Beach, Sample	2	5-5 (DIS)
Sand, Fine, 2.5 kg	5	1-4 (DIS), 5-1 (Lab), 5-3 (DIS), 5-4 (DIS), 7-3 (DIS), 7-3 (TT), 7-3 (Lab), 9-1 (DIS), 12-1 (Lab), 18-4 (DIS)
Sand, Quartz, Coarse, 1 lb	1	5-3 (DIS)
Soap, Ivory, Bar	10	5-2 (DIS), 5-4 (DIS)
Sod	5	6-3 (Lab)
Sodium Carbonate Anhydrous, 500 g	1	3-1 (Lab)
Soil, Clay, 2.5 kg	1	5-2 (TT), 5-3 (DIS)
Soil, Diatomaceous Earth, 1 lb	4	5-2 (Lab)
Soil, Loam, 2.5 kg	2	4-2 (DIS), 4-2 (Lab), 4-3 (DIS), 5-3 (DIS), 6-3 (Lab)
Splints, Wooden, Pkg/25	1	12-3 (Lab), 15-3 (DIS)
Spoons, Plastic, Pkg/24	2	(INT), 1-1 (TT), 1-1 (SYS), 2-1 (TT), 2-2 (DIS), 3-1 (DIS), 3-1 (Lab), 4-2 (Lab), 5-1 (Lab), 5-2 (Lab), 5-5 (DIS), 7-2 (TT), 8-2 (DIS), 8-2 (Lab), 9-3 (DIS), 9-3 (Lab), 19-6 (DIS)
Steel Wool Pads, Pkg/6	1	4-1 (TT)
Sticks, Craft, Pkg/50	2	1-2 (Lab), 4-2 (TT), 4-3 (DIS), 10-4 (Lab)
Stirrer Sticks, Pkg/50	1	5-2 (Lab)
Straw, Flexible Plastic, Pkg/50	1	9-4 (Lab)
Straws, Plastic, Pkg/200	1	1-2 (TT), 5-6 (DIS), 7-3 (TT), 10-1 (DIS), 11-1 (TT), 11-3 (TT), 11-3 (Lab), 12-3 (TT), 15-1 (Lab)
String, Cotton, 200 ft	2	2-1 (TT), 4-2 (TT), 9-1 (TT), 10-3 (DIS), 12-1 (Lab), 15-2 (TT), 19-1 (TT), 19-4 (Lab), 19-5 (DIS)
Sugar, Granulated, 454 g	2	2-2 (SYS), 3-1 (Lab), 10-4 (TT), 19-6 (DIS)
Sugar, Powdered, 454 g	1	1-1 (TT)
Sunprint Paper, 12 Sheets	2	14-4 (TT)
Sunscreen	2	14-4 (TT)
Tape, Adding Machine Roll	1	6-3 (DIS), 14-1 (DIS)
Tape, Transparent Dispenser Roll	1	19-4 (TT)
Thread, White	1	12-2 (DIS)
Tongue Depressor	5	9-1 (DIS)
Toothpicks, Round, Pkg/250	1	4-2 (DIS), 4-2 (Lab), 8-4 (TT), 12-3 (Lab), 18-1 (Lab), 19-4 (TT)
Trash, Bag with Household Wastes	5	4-4 (DIS)
Tube, Cardboard 13 cm x 5.5 cm OD	5	15-1 (Lab)
Vinegar, 500 mL	5	1-1 (TT), 1-1 (SYS), 3-1 (DIS), 4-1 (Lab)
Water, Carbonated, 5 mL	5	3-1 (TT)
Water, Distilled, 4 Liters	1	8-1 (Lab)
Water, Mineral	1	8-1 (Lab)
Water, Pond or Aquarium	5	8-3 (TT)
Water, Spring	1	8-1 (Lab)
Wax Paper, 75 sq ft	1	2-1 (DIS)
Wax Pencil, Black	5	2-1 (TT), 8-1 (Lab), 12-3 (DIS)
Yeast, Dry Baking, 7 g	5	19-6 (DIS)

KEY: **DIS**: Discover; **SYS**: Sharpen Your Skills; **TT**: Try This; **Lab**: Lab; **INT**: Introduction Lab

NONCONSUMABLE ITEMS

Description	Qty per class	Textbook Section(s)
Ball, Inflatable (Beach Ball)	5	12-3 (DIS)
Ball, Styrene, 3"	5	18-1 (Lab)
Ball, Styrofoam, 4"	5	18-2 (Lab)
Ball, Ping Pong, Pkg/6	1	8-4 (DIS), 10-2 (DIS)
Ball, Tennis	5	15-1 (DIS)
Beaker, 100 mL	15	2-2 (TT), 7-3 (Lab)
Beaker, 250 mL	20	1-4 (Lab), 2-2 (SYS), 4-1 (DIS), 7-3 (Lab), 8-1 (Lab), 8-2 (Lab), 9-3 (DIS), 9-3 (Lab)
Beaker, 400 mL	10	12-1 (Lab), 12-5 (DIS), 16-4 (Lab)
Board, 2.5 cm x 30 cm x 120 cm	5	15-4 (Lab)
Bolt, Small	25	3-2 (TT)
Book	50	9-1 (DIS), 14-1 (Lab), 15-4 (Lab), 17-1 (Lab), 18-1 (Lab)
Bottle, Plastic, 1 L	5	7-1 (SYS)
Bottle, Plastic, 2 L	5	11-3 (TT), 12-4 (DIS)
Bowl, Plastic, 2 L	10	1-2 (TT), 1-4 (DIS), 3-1 (DIS), 7-1 (SYS), 7-1 (TT), 8-1 (TT), 8-2 (DIS), 17-1 (Lab), 18-4 (DIS)
Bowl, Plastic, Small	10	8-2 (DIS), 14-2 (TT), 19-6 (DIS)
Box	15	1-3 (DIS), 10-1 (DIS), 14-4 (DIS)
Bucket	5	5-2 (Lab), 10-3 (DIS)
Calculator	5	14-2 (Lab), 15-4 (Lab), 17-2 (Lab)
Can, Aluminum	5	1-2 (DIS)
Checkers, Pkg/24	1	1-1 (DIS)
Clock or Watch	1	5-2 (Lab), 16-2 (Lab), 16-4 (Lab)
Cloth, Cotton, White, 18" x 22"	1	4-1 (Lab)
Coins, Assorted	120	3-2 (DIS)
Compass with Pencil	5	19-3 (DIS), 19-4 (TT)
Compass, Magnetic, Pkg/6	1	6-1 (DIS)
Container and Lid, Glass	5	16-4 (Lab)
Container and Lid, Metal	5	16-4 (Lab)
Container, Clear Plastic, 3 L	5	9-4 (DIS), 13-1 (DIS), 13-3 (DIS)
Cork	25	8-4 (DIS), 9-1 (TT)
Dominoes, Box of 28	3	16-3 (DIS)
Dowel, Wood	15	16-2 (Lab)
Droppers, Plastic, pkg/6	1	1-1 (SYS), 2-1 (DIS), 2-1 (Lab), 4-2 (Lab), 5-2 (TT), 7-1 (SYS), 8-2 (DIS), 9-4 (DIS), 10-4 (Lab)
Dropping Bottle, 30 mL	5	3-1 (Lab)
Egg Beater	5	17-1 (Lab)
Fan	1	19-5 (DIS)
Film Canister	5	18-3 (TT)
Flashlight, Plastic	5	2-2 (TT), 14-1 (DIS), 18-1 (Lab)
Flask, Erlenmeyer, 500 mL	5	8-2 (Lab), 15-3 (DIS)
Funnel, Plastic	15	7-3 (TT), 7-3 (Lab), 12-5 (SYS), 13-3 (DIS)
Glass	5	7-1 (DIS)
Graduated Cylinder, Plastic, 10 mL	5	3-1 (TT), 3-1 (Lab)
Graduated Cylinder, Plastic, 25 mL	5	8-1 (Lab), 8-3 (TT)
Graduated Cylinder, Plastic, 100 mL	5	1-2 (Lab), 4-1 (DIS), 7-1 (SYS), 9-3 (Lab), 10-4 (Lab)
Graduated Cylinder, Plastic, 250 mL	5	4-1 (Lab), 9-3 (Lab), 16-2 (DIS)
Grid, Acetate	5	18-1 (Lab)

KEY: **DIS**: Discover; **SYS**: Sharpen Your Skills; **TT**: Try This; **Lab**: Lab; **INT**: Introduction Lab

Master Materials List

NONCONSUMABLE ITEMS (continued)

Description	Qty per class	Textbook Section(s)
Hairdryer	5	15-4 (DIS)
Hole Punch	5	9-4 (Lab)
Jar, Clear Plastic, 850 mL	15	7-3 (DIS), 7-3 (Lab), 8-3 (TT), 8-4 (DIS)
Jar, Plastic, 16 oz	20	4-1 (TT), 4-1 (Lab), 5-3 (DIS)
Jar, Plastic, Tall, 12 oz	5	12-5 (SYS), 13-2 (DIS)
Jar, Glass, 4 oz	5	7-1 (TT), 11-1 (DIS)
Jar, Glass, 16 oz	5	11-1 (DIS), 11-3 (Lab), 11-4 (DIS)
Labels from Household Products	5	10-4 (DIS)
Lid, Metal for 850-mL Jar	15	8-3 (TT)
Lid, Metal for 12 oz. Jar	5	13-2 (DIS)
Lid, Metal for 16 oz Jar	20	4-1 (TT), 4-1 (Lab), 5-3 (DIS)
Light Socket, Clamp-on w/Shade	5	2-1 (Lab), 7-1 (TT), 12-1 (Lab), 14-1 (Lab), 16-4 (DIS)
Light Socket, Porcelain	1	18-1 (DIS), 18-2 (Lab)
Magnifying Glasses, Pkg/6	1	(INT), 1-1 (TT), 4-2 (DIS), 4-2 (TT), 5-2 (Lab), 5-5 (DIS), 6-3 (TT), 7-2 (DIS), 7-3 (Lab), 16-1 (DIS), 17-2 (Lab)
Map, U. S. with City Names and Latitude Lines	5	14-2 (Lab)
Marble, Large, 1"	5	18-4 (DIS)
Marbles, 5/8", Pkg/20	3	1-1 (DIS), 5-1 (DIS), 8-4 (DIS), 13-2 (DIS), 16-3 (TT), 18-4 (DIS)
Marbles, 9/16", Pkg/6	1	18-4 (DIS)
Measuring Cup, Plastic, 500 mL	5	2-1 (TT), 4-3 (DIS), 5-2 (Lab), 5-3 (DIS), 8-2 (DIS), 8-2 (SYS)
Meter Stick	5	5-2 (TT), 6-3 (DIS), 10-3 (DIS), 12-2 (TT), 12-3 (Lab), 15-1 (DIS), 15-1 (Lab), 15-2 (TT), 15-4 (Lab), 18-4 (DIS), 19-4 (Lab)
Microscope Slide, Pkg/72	1	(INT), 7-2 (DIS), 17-1 (Lab)
Nut, Small	25	1-4 (DIS), 3-2 (TT)
Objects, Assorted	5	1-3 (DIS)
Pan, Aluminum, Small	5	15-3 (DIS)
Pan, Aluminum Foil, 11 cm x 21 cm x 6 cm	5	7-3 (TT)
Pan, Aluminum Foil, 13" x 10" x 2"	10	5-1 (Lab), 5-2 (Lab), 6-3 (Lab), 7-4 (DIS), 9-1 (DIS), 9-4 (Lab), 10-2 (DIS), 10-4 (Lab)
Pan, Aluminum Foil, Round, 22.5 cm	5	(INT), 1-4 (DIS), 4-3 (DIS), 5-6 (DIS), 8-2 (Lab), 11-1 (DIS)
Pan, Aluminum Foil, 8" x 8" x 1-1/4"	5	17-1 (Lab)
Paper Clips, Box/100	1	4-3 (DIS), 10-3 (DIS)
Paper Clips, Jumbo Box/100	1	1-1 (DIS), 1-4 (Lab)
Paper Clips, Plastic Pkg/100	1	1-1 (DIS)
Penny	5	18-2 (DIS)
Petri Dishes, Plastic, Pkg/6	2	2-1 (Lab), 4-2 (Lab), 5-2 (TT), 7-2 (DIS)
Pins, Straight, Pkg/150	1	12-3 (TT)
Pinwheel	5	15-4 (DIS)
Pitcher, 2 qt w/Lid	5	8-1 (DIS)
Plastic Products, Assortment	5	4-4 (TT)
Protractor	5	14-1 (Lab), 18-1 (Lab)
Pushpins, Pkg/100	1	19-1 (TT)
Quarter	5	18-2 (DIS), 19-4 (DIS)

KEY: **DIS**: Discover; **SYS**: Sharpen Your Skills; **TT**: Try This; **Lab**: Lab; **INT**: Introduction Lab

NONCONSUMABLE ITEMS (continued)

Description	Qty per class	Textbook Section(s)
Rock, Coal, Bituminous, Pkg/6	1	16-1 (DIS)
Rocks	25	1-2 (DIS), 10-2 (DIS), 19-1 (DIS)
Ruler	5	2-1 (DIS), 4-2 (TT), 4-4 (DIS), 5-1 (Lab), 8-1 (Lab), 9-3 (Lab), 9-4 (Lab), 11-3 (Lab), 12-1 (Lab), 13-2 (Lab), 14-1 (Lab), 14-2 (Lab), 15-1 (Lab), 15-2 (DIS), 17-2 (Lab), 18-2 (SYS), 19-1 (TT), 19-2 (Lab), 19-3 (DIS), 19-4 (DIS), 19-5 (DIS)
Sandpaper, Sheet	5	5-1 (DIS)
Saucepan, Cooking	5	10-4 (TT)
Scissors	5	5-2 (Lab), 6-2 (DIS), 6-3 (TT), 8-4 (TT), 10-3 (DIS), 11-3 (Lab), 12-3 (TT), 14-1 (Lab), 14-4 (DIS), 15-1 (Lab), 15-2 (DIS), 16-2 (Lab), 18-3 (TT), 19-2 (DIS), 19-2 (TT), 19-4 (TT), 19-5 (DIS)
Screen, Window	5	17-1 (Lab)
Screw, Small	15	1-4 (DIS)
Seeds, 15 Bean Mix, 454 g	1	17-3 (DIS)
Seeds, Bean, Kidney, 1 lb	1	17-3 (DIS)
Seeds, Black Bean, 1 lb	1	17-3 (DIS)
Seeds, White Bean, 4 oz	1	17-3 (DIS)
Shallow Pan, Cooking	5	10-4 (TT)
Skewer, Wood	5	5-1 (Lab)
Slide, Elodea Leaf wm	5	15-3 (TT)
Slide, Lily Leaf	5	15-3 (TT)
Slide, Lilac Leaf	5	15-3 (TT)
Sponge	10	7-4 (DIS), 8-3 (DIS)
Spool	5	8-4 (DIS)
Spray Bottle	5	5-2 (Lab), 8-4 (DIS)
Stirring Rod, Plastic	5	4-1 (DIS), 8-2 (Lab)

Description	Qty per class	Textbook Section(s)
Stopper, Rubber Size 3, 1-Hole	5	19-4 (Lab)
Stopper, Rubber Size 7, 1-Hole	5	8-2 (Lab)
Stopper, Rubber, Size 1, Solid	20	8-1 (Lab)
Stopwatch	5	2-1 (Lab), 4-1 (DIS), 7-3 (Lab), 8-2 (DIS), 11-1 (DIS), 12-1 (Lab), 14-1 (Lab), 15-4 (Lab), 19-4 (Lab)
Test Tube Support	5	8-1 (Lab)
Test Tube, 18 mm x 150 mm	20	8-1 (Lab), 12-5 (DIS)
Thermometer	15	2-2 (SYS), 9-3 (Lab), 11-1 (Lab), 12-1 (DIS), 12-1 (Lab), 12-2 (TT), 14-1 (Lab), 14-4 (DIS), 15-3 (DIS), 16-2 (DIS), 16-2 (Lab), 16-4 (DIS), 16-4 (Lab)
Thumbtacks, Pkg/100	1	9-3 (Lab)
Tongs, Flask and Test Tube	5	(INT), 3-1 (Lab)
Trash Barrel, Large	10	8-1 (DIS)
Tree Cross-Section	5	17-2 (Lab)
Trowel	5	4-2 (TT)
Truck, Toy Dump	5	19-1 (DIS)
Tube, Cardboard for Flashlight	5	14-1 (DIS)
Tube, Cardboard	5	5-1 (Lab)
Tube, Clear Plastic	5	19-4 (Lab)
Tubing, Rigid Plastic, 6"	5	8-2 (Lab)
Tubing, Vinyl Plastic, Ft	10	8-1 (TT), 8-2 (Lab)
Vacuum Cleaner with Intake Hose	1	11-1 (Lab)
Washer, Metal, 3/4"	75	9-1 (TT), 15-2 (TT)
Washers, Metal, 1-1/2", Pkg/6	3	19-4 (Lab)
Watering Can	5	7-3 (DIS)
Wire Lead w/Alligator Clips	10	1-4 (Lab)
Wire, Bare Copper, 20 Gauge, 4 oz.	1	5-2 (Lab)
Wood, Block, 1" Cube	5	5-1 (DIS)
Wood, Board, 1" x 4" x 8"	10	5-1 (DIS), 5-2 (Lab), 6-3 (Lab)

KEY: **DIS**: Discover; **SYS**: Sharpen Your Skills; **TT**: Try This; **Lab**: Lab; **INT**: Introduction Lab

Master Materials List

EQUIPMENT/SAFETY ITEMS					
Description	**Qty per class**	**Textbook Section(s)**	**Description**	**Qty per class**	**Textbook Section(s)**
Apron, Lab	30	several activities	Globe	5	14-1 (DIS), 18-1 (DIS)
Aquarium	5	9-1 (TT)	Gloves, Latex, Box/100	1	4-4 (DIS)
Balance, Triple Beam	5	1-2 (DIS), 1-2 (Lab), 2-2 (SYS), 3-2 (TT), 4-1 (Lab), 7-1 (Lab), 9-3 (Lab), 11-3 (DIS), 15-1 (Lab)	Goggles, Chemical Splash - Class Set	1	several activities
Binoculars	5	19-2 (DIS), 19-2 (TT)	Hot Plate	5	2-2 (SYS), 8-1 (Lab), 8-2 (Lab), 9-3 (Lab), 16-4 (Lab)
Buret Clamp, Round Jaws	10	12-1 (Lab), 15-2 (TT), 15-3 (DIS)	Microscope	5	7-2 (DIS), 11-1 (Lab), 15-3 (TT), 17-1 (Lab)
Clamp, Three-Pronged with Coated Jaws	5	19-2 (DIS), 19-2 (TT)	Oven Mitt	5	8-1 (Lab), 8-2 (Lab), 9-3 (Lab), 11-1 (DIS)
Computer w/Graphing Program (optional)	1	1-2 (Lab), 15-1 (Lab)	Ring Stand	5	12-1 (Lab), 15-2 (TT), 15-3 (DIS), 19-2 (DIS), 19-2 (TT)
			Stereomicroscope	5	4-2 (Lab)

KEY: **DIS**: Discover; **SYS**: Sharpen Your Skills; **TT**: Try This; **Lab**: Lab; **INT**: Introduction Lab

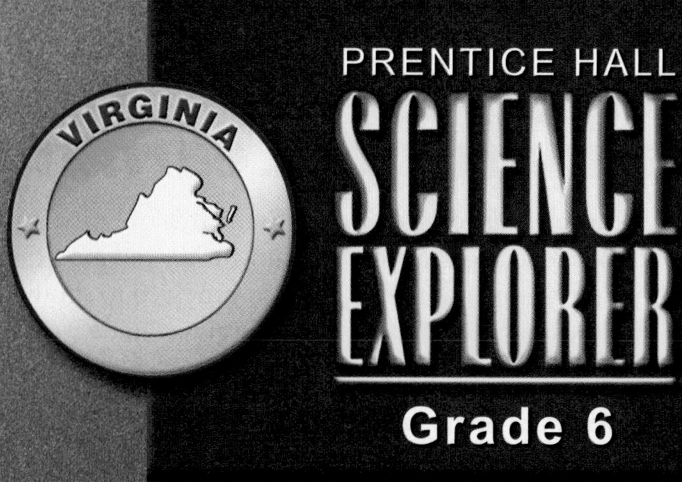

Virginia Standards of Learning Handbook

ISBN 0-13-190228-8
1 2 3 4 5 6 7 8 9 10 07 06 05 04 03

Grade 6 Science Standards of Learning

Here is a complete list of the Virginia Standards of Learning (SOL) for Grade 6 Science, so that you can know what you are expected to learn this year. Sample test items are also provided to show you how these standards might be tested on the Virginia Grade 8 (SOL) Test.

Scientific Investigation, Reasoning, and Logic

6.1 plan and conduct investigations in which

a) observations are made involving fine discrimination between similar objects and organisms;
b) a classification system is developed based on multiple attributes;
c) precise and approximate measures are recorded;
d) scale models are used to estimate distance, volume, and quantity;
e) hypotheses are stated in ways that identify the independent (manipulated) and dependent (responding) variables;
f) a method is devised to test the validity of predictions and inferences;
g) one variable is manipulated over time with many repeated trials;
h) data are collected, recorded, analyzed, and reported using appropriate metric measurement;
i) data are organized and communicated through graphical representation (graphs, charts, and diagrams);
j) models are designed to explain a sequence; and
k) an understanding of the nature of science is developed and reinforced.

What It Means to You

All of Standard 6.1 will be tested on the Grade 8 Science Test. There will be a total of 11 items on the test from this category.

Where You Will Learn This

This material is covered in the **Introduction to Science and in the labs** you will do throughout this course. Controlling variables, collecting data, and organizing data are important skills to acquire.

EXAMPLE A student wanted to find out how the amount of salt added to water affects the density of the solution. First, the student prepared several solutions with different amounts of salt in the same volume of water. Then the student tested the density of each solution. What was the manipulated variable in this experiment?

A The amount of water
* B The amount of salt
C The temperature of the water
D The density of the water

TVA42

Force, Motion, and Energy

6.2 investigate and understand basic sources of energy, their origins, transformations, and uses.

Key concepts include

a) potential and kinetic energy;
b) the role of the sun in the formation of most energy sources on Earth;
c) nonrenewable energy sources (fossil fuels, including petroleum, natural gas, and coal);
d) renewable energy sources (wood, wind, hydro, geothermal, tidal, and solar); and
e) energy transformations (heat/light to mechanical, chemical, and electrical energy).

What It Means to You

Standards 6.2.a through d will be tested on the Grade 8 Science Test. There will be a total of 18 items from the category of Force, Motion, Energy, and Matter, which includes **Standards 6.2 through 6.7.**

Where You Will Learn This

This material is covered in **Chapters 1, 3, 5, 8, 9, 12, and 14 through 16.**

EXAMPLES

1 When gasoline is burned in a car's engine, the chemical energy in the fuel is converted to the car's —

A potential energy
B gravitational energy
★ C mechanical energy
D solar energy

2 An archer pulls back on the string of the bow. Just before the archer releases it, the string of the bow has —

★ F elastic potential energy
G gravitational potential energy
H power
J kinetic energy

Force, Motion, and Energy (continued)

6.3 investigate and understand the role of solar energy in driving most natural processes within the atmosphere, the hydrosphere, and on the Earth's surface.

Key concepts include

a) the Earth's energy budget;
b) the role of radiation and convection in the distribution of energy;
c) the motion of the atmosphere and the oceans;
d) cloud formation; and
e) the role of heat energy in weather-related phenomena including thunderstorms and hurricanes.

What It Means to You

All of Standard 6.3 will be tested on the Grade 8 Science Test. There will be a total of 18 items from the category of Force, Motion, Energy, and Matter, which includes **Standards 6.2 through 6.7.**

Where You Will Learn This

This material is covered in **Chapters 5, 9, and 12 through 14.**

EXAMPLES

1 Uneven heating of the air near Earth's surface causes —

* **A** wind
B rain
C cloud formation
D ice storms

2 Earth's rotation causes currents in the ocean to curve. This is known as —

F a surface current
G a deep current
* **H** the Coriolis effect
J an upwelling

Matter

6.4 investigate and understand that all matter is made up of atoms.

Key concepts include

a) atoms are made up of electrons, protons, and neutrons;
b) atoms of any element are alike but are different from atoms of other elements;
c) elements may be represented by chemical symbols;
d) two or more atoms may be chemically combined;
e) compounds may be represented by chemical formulas;
f) chemical equations can be used to model chemical changes; and
g) a limited number of elements comprise the largest portion of the solid Earth, living matter, the oceans, and the atmosphere.

What It Means to You

Standards 6.4.a through e will be tested on the Grade 8 Science Test. There will be a total of 18 items from the category of Force, Motion, Energy, and Matter, which includes **Standards 6.2 through 6.7.**

Where You Will Learn This

This material is covered in **Chapters 1 through 3, 9, 11, 14, and 15.**

EXAMPLE

Chemical Formulas

Compound	Formula
Water	H_2O
Hydrogen Peroxide	H_2O_2
Ammonia	NH_3
Baking Soda	$NaHCO_3$

Which of the compounds shown in the chart contains three atoms?

* **A** Water
B Hydrogen Peroxide
C Ammonia
D Baking Soda

TVA45

Matter (continued)

6.5 investigate and understand the unique properties and characteristics of water and its roles in the natural and human-made environment.

Key concepts include

a) water as the universal solvent;
b) the properties of water in all three states;
c) the action of water in physical and chemical weathering;
d) the ability of large bodies of water to store heat and moderate climate;
e) the origin and occurrence of water on Earth;
f) the importance of water for agriculture, power generation, and public health; and
g) the importance of protecting and maintaining water resources.

What It Means to You

All of Standard 6.5 will be tested on the Grade 8 Science Test. There will be a total of 18 items from the category of Force, Motion, Energy, and Matter, which includes **Standards 6.2 through 6.7.**

Where You Will Learn This

This material is covered in **Chapters 2, 4, 5, 7 through 10, 12, and 14.**

EXAMPLES

1 Where is most of Earth's water located?

A Oceans
B Lakes and rivers
C Groundwater
*D Ice

2 A river slows when it reaches the ocean and deposits sediment in a formation called —

F an alluvial fan
*G a delta
H a meander
J an oxbow

TVA46

Matter (continued)

6.6 investigate and understand the properties of air and the structure and dynamics of the Earth's atmosphere.

Key concepts include

a) air as a mixture of gaseous elements and compounds;

b) air pressure, temperature, and humidity;

c) how the atmosphere changes with altitude;

d) natural and human-caused changes to the atmosphere;

e) the relationship of atmospheric measures and weather conditions;

f) basic information from weather maps including fronts, systems, and basic measurements; and

g) the importance of protecting and maintaining air quality.

What It Means to You

All of Standard 6.6 will be tested on the Grade 8 Science Test. There will be a total of 18 items from the category of Force, Motion, Energy, and Matter, which includes **Standards 6.2 through 6.7.**

Where You Will Learn This

This material is covered in **Chapters 11 through 14.**

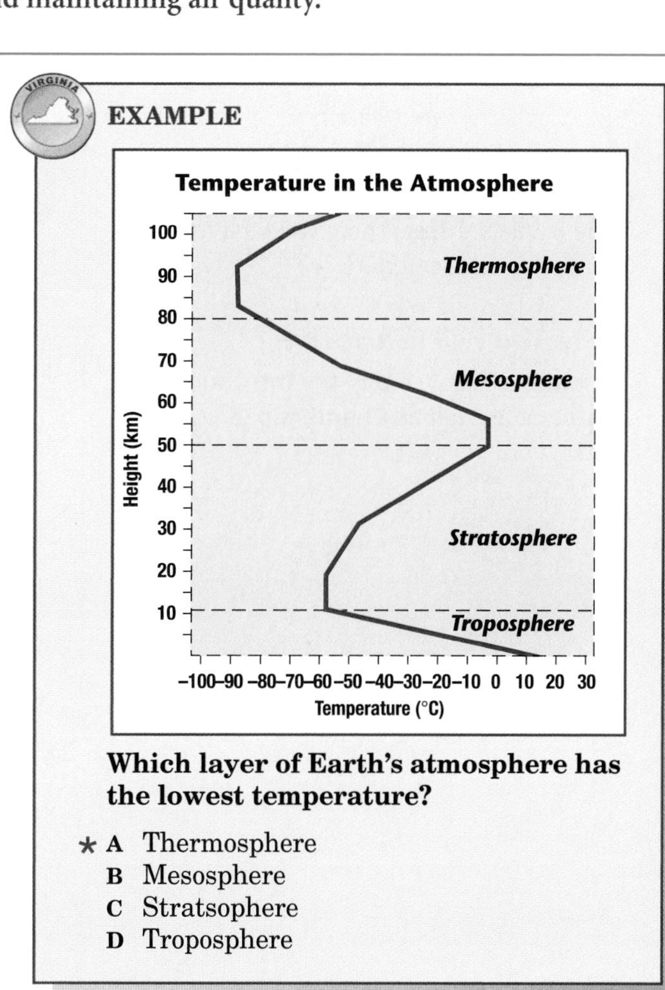

Which layer of Earth's atmosphere has the lowest temperature?

★ **A** Thermosphere
B Mesosphere
C Stratsophere
D Troposphere

TVA47

Living Systems

6.7 investigate and understand the natural processes and human interactions that affect watershed systems.

Key concepts include

a) the health of ecosystems and the abiotic factors of a watershed;
b) the location and structure of Virginia's regional watershed systems;
c) divides, tributaries, river systems, and river and stream processes;
d) wetlands;
e) estuaries;
f) major conservation, health, and safety issues associated with watersheds; and
g) water monitoring and analysis using field equipment including hand-held technology.

What It Means to You

All of Standard 6.7 will be tested on the Grade 8 Science Test. There will be a total of 7 items from this category.

Where You Will Learn This

This material is covered in the **Introduction to Science as well as Chapters 4, 5, 7, 8, 10, and 13.**

EXAMPLES

1 One watershed is separated from another by a ridge of land called —

A a tributary
B an estuary
* **C** a divide
D a river system

2 Which watershed covers the largest area in Virginia?

F Potomac River Watershed
G Yadkin River Watershed
H York River Watershed
* **J** James River Watershed

Interrelationships in Earth/Space Systems

6.8 investigate and understand the organization of the solar system and the relationships among the various bodies that comprise it.

Key concepts include

a) the sun, moon, Earth, other planets and their moons, meteors, asteroids, and comets;
b) relative size of and distance between planets;
c) the role of gravity;
d) revolution and rotation;
e) the mechanics of day and night and phases of the moon;
f) the unique properties of Earth as a planet;
g) the relationship of the Earth's tilt and seasons;
h) the cause of tides; and
i) the history and technology of space exploration.

What It Means to You

Standards 6.8a through h will be tested on the Grade 8 Science Test. There will be a total of 6 items from this category.

Where You Will Learn This

This material is covered in the **Introduction to Science as well as Chapters 6, 18, and 19.**

EXAMPLE

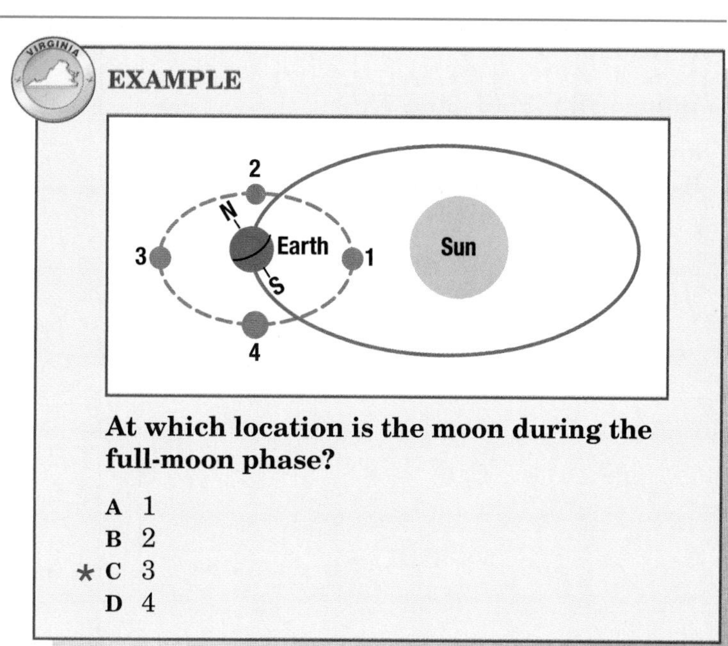

At which location is the moon during the full-moon phase?

A 1
B 2
* C 3
D 4

TVA49

Resources

6.9 investigate and understand public policy decisions relating to the environment.

Key concepts include

a) management of renewable resources (water, air, soil, plant life, animal life);

b) management of nonrenewable resources (coal, oil, natural gas, nuclear power, mineral resources);

c) the mitigation of land-use and environmental hazards through preventive measures; and

d) cost/benefit tradeoffs in conservation policies.

What It Means to You

All of Standard 6.9 will be tested on the Grade 8 Science Test. There will be a total of 7 items from this category.

Where You Will Learn This

This material is covered in **Chapters 1, 4, 7, 8, 10, 11, 13, 14, 16, and 17.**

EXAMPLES

1 One problem with air quality in some cities is a thick brownish haze that forms when certain gases in the air react with sunlight, causing —

A acid rain
B temperature inversions
* C smog
D greenhouse gases

2 Where land is not flat, farmers reduce soil erosion by not plowing and planting in straight rows. Instead, the farmers follow the curves of the land, a practice called —

F conservation plowing
* G contour plowing
H crop rotation
J land reclamation

Test-Taking Strategies

Charts

Charts display information in a visual form. The information is organized into columns and rows. Charts often display numerical data, but they can also be used to present other information, such as descriptions or observations. Here are some strategies to help you answer questions about charts.

1. Read the title of the chart to learn what it is about. The title of the chart gives the main idea of the chart. Reading the title first will help to focus your thinking. In the chart shown here, the title is "The Speed of Sound."

2. Read the passage, if there is one, to get an idea of what the passage is about. Then, read the question. Be sure that you understand what the question is asking. Think about how the chart can help you answer the question.

3. Examine the labels for each column that are found at the top of a chart. They indicate the categories of information included in the columns below them. Looking at these labels will help you understand the relationships among the columns of information. For example, the labels in the chart shown here are "Air Temperature" and "Speed". This information tells you that there may be a relationship between the air temperature and how fast sound travels through it.

4. Study the data in the first column. In the chart shown here, notice that the air temperature increases by 10°C as you read down the column.

5. Study the data in the second column. In the chart shown here, notice that the speed of sound increases as you read down the column.

6. Read the question again. When you are sure of what you are being asked, refer to the chart to find the data you need. To answer the question shown here, look at the first column to find the two rows that give the two temperatures, –10°C and 20°C, mentioned in the question. Then, look across each row to find its speed of sound (324 m/s and 342 m/s). Now find the difference in the speed of sound between the two temperatures (18 m/s).

The Speed of Sound

Air Temperature (°C)	Speed (m/s)
–20	318
–10	324
0	330
10	336
20	342
30	348

How much does the speed of sound in air change as air is heated from –10°C to 20°C?

A 6 m/s
★B 18 m/s
C 30 m/s
D 342 m/s

TVA51

Test-Taking Strategies

Graphs

Graphs display numerical data in a visual form. There are several kinds of graphs, including line graphs, bar graphs, and circle graphs. Line graphs are used to show patterns or trends. Bar graphs are used to display quantities. Circle graphs are used to show parts of a whole. Circle graphs often are labeled in percents, and the percents of the sections of the graph add up to 100 percent.

1. Read the title of the graph to learn what it is about. The title of the graph gives the main idea of the graph. Reading the title first will help to focus your thinking. The title of the graph shown here is "Masses and Lifetimes of Stars."
2. Read the passage, if there is one. Then read the question. Be sure that you understand what the question is asking. Think about how the graph can help you answer the question.
3. Study the structure of the graph. If it is a line graph or bar graph, read the labels on the axes of the graph. Like the headings at the tops of columns in a chart, the axes of a graph will help you understand the relationship or information presented in the graph. The horizontal axis of the graph shown here is labeled "Mass of Star" and the vertical axis is labeled "Lifetime of Star." Note that there are no axes on a circle graph. For a circle graph, you should begin by skimming the labels of the sections of the circle.
4. Look at the data in the graph. If it is a line graph, think about the direction of the line. Is the line straight, or does it curve? If it is a bar graph, look at the shortest and tallest bars. If it is a circle graph, look at the largest and smallest sections of the circle.
5. Read the question again. When you are sure of what you are being asked, refer to the graph to find the data you need. To answer the question shown, first find the point on the line for the sun. Then look down to the horizontal axis to see what the sun's mass is. Look to the right to find twice that value, and then find the point on the line above this value. Look at the vertical axis to see what the lifetime would be for that mass. Compare this lifetime to the lifetime of the sun, and you can see that a star with twice the mass of the sun would have less than half the lifetime of the sun.

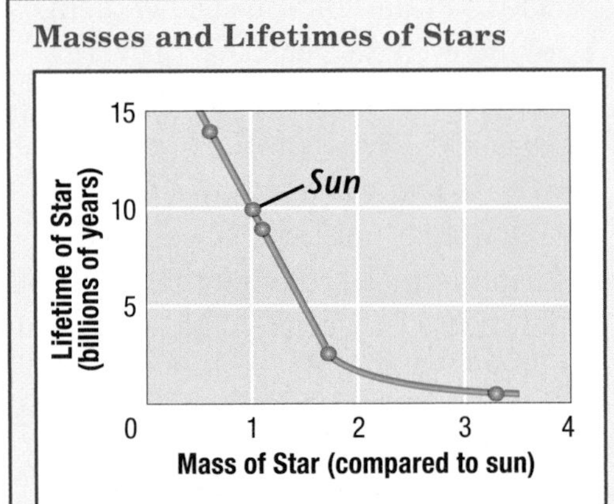

Compared to the lifetime of the sun, what would be the lifetime of a star with twice as much mass as the sun?

★**A** Less than half as long
B Half as long
C Twice as long
D More than twice as long

TVA52

Test-Taking Strategies

Diagrams

Diagrams display information in a visual form. Diagrams are pictures that present information that is not numerical. A diagram can show the structure of an object, such as a cell or the sun. It can also show a process, such as photosynthesis.

1. Read the title of the diagram to learn what it is about. The title of a diagram tells the main idea of the diagram. Reading this first will help focus your thinking. The title of the diagram shown here is "Profile of the Ocean Floor."
2. Read the passage, if there is one. Then read the question. Be sure that you understand what the question is asking. Think about how the diagram can help you answer the question.
3. Study the structure of the diagram. If the diagram has labels, read them and look to see what each label identifies. If the diagram shows a process, look for arrows that show the flow of the process. Follow the arrows and identify the steps that are shown. You may find it helpful to use your finger to trace the arrows as you study the diagram.
4. Read the question again. Find the points on the diagram that relate to the question. To answer the question shown here, find points A and C, then look at the part of the ocean floor between these points. Read the four descriptions and choose the description that best fits the slope of the ocean floor. Note that the diagram has other labels that are not mentioned in the question. Do not let these labels distract you. Just look at points A and C, and you will be able to tell that the ocean floor slopes downward slightly, then slopes upward.

Profile of the Ocean Floor

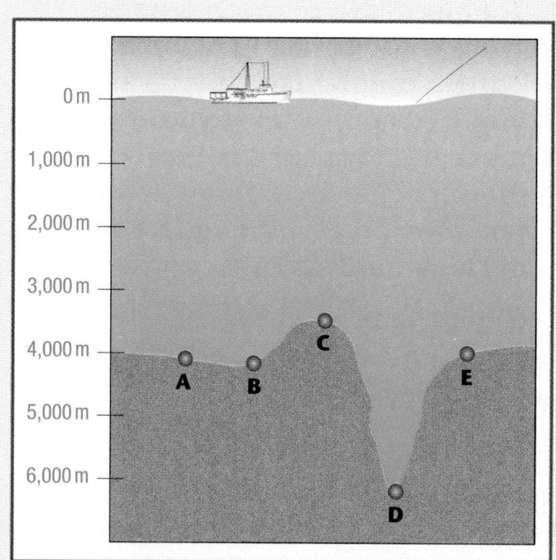

How does the slope of the ocean floor change from point A to point C?

A It slopes upward steadily.
B It slopes upward slightly, then more steeply.
*★**C** It slopes downward slightly, then slopes upward.
D It rises slowly, then slopes downward steeply.

TVA53

Preparing for the Test

By the time you have completed your study of science in Grade 8 you should be able to answer these questions and questions like them.

DIRECTIONS

Read each question carefully and choose the best answer.

1 Temperature decreases as you climb a mountain. The biomes you pass through also change as you climb a mountain. If you were in a boreal forest at the base of a mountain, which biome would you most likely find at the top of the mountain?

A Rain forest
B Desert
* C Tundra
D Deciduous forest

2 Parallel and Series Circuits

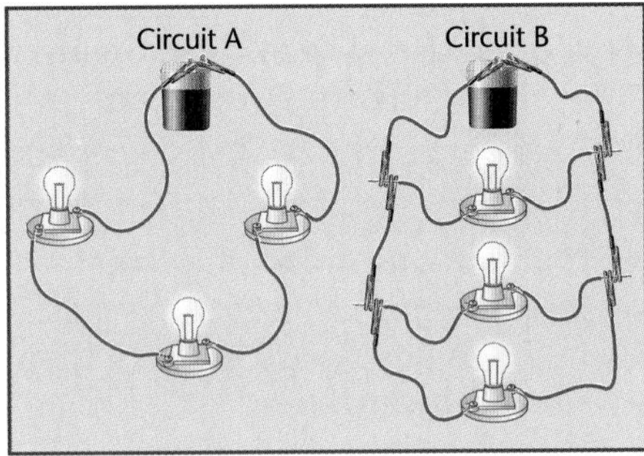

What will happen to the bulbs in Circuit B if one of the bulbs is removed?

F They will go out.
* G They will continue to light with the same brightness.
H They will continue to light, but be brighter.
J They will continue to light, but be dimmer.

3 An atom has a neutral charge if —

* A the number of electrons equals the number of protons
B the number of electrons equals the number of neutrons
C the number of protons equals the number of neutrons
D the number of protons equals the number of neutrons plus electrons

4 Clouds form when water vapor in the air —

F becomes heated
* G condenses
H evaporates
J precipitates

5 Which of the following is a difference between plant cells and animals cells?

* A Plant cells have cell walls and animal cells do not.
B Plant cells have vacuoles and animal cells do not.
C Animal cells have mitochondria and plant cells do not.
D Animal cells have cell membranes and plant cells do not.

6 Earth's rotation causes Earth to have —

F equinoxes
G solstices
H tides
* J day and night

TVA54

7

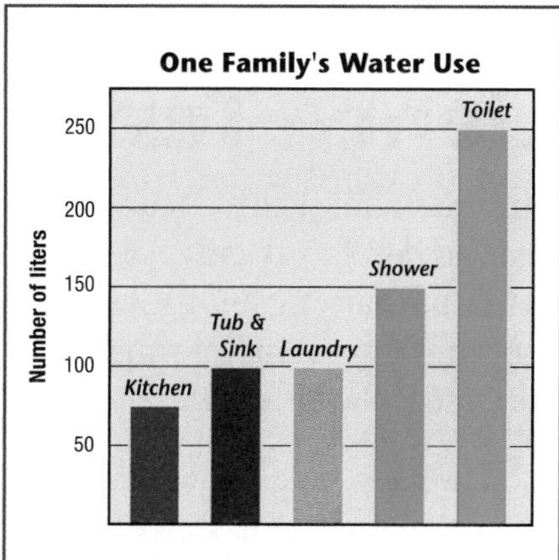

A family conducted a survey of their water use. The graph shows their typical water use for one day. If everyone in the family agreed to take 5-minute showers instead of the 10-minute showers they usually take, about how many liters of water would they save each day?

A 5

B 25

* C 75

D 150

8 A student added 50 g of ice at 0°C to a beaker that contained 100 g of water at 20°C. The student then added 50 g of water at 0°C to a second beaker that contained 100 g of water at 20°C. The student measured the temperature of the mixtures every minute. After five minutes, the water to which ice had been added had a lower temperature than the water to which cold water had been added. What was the responding variable in this experiment?

F The temperature of the ice

G The temperature of the 100 g of water

H The time over which the temperatures were measured

* J The temperatures of the mixtures

9 What causes an echo?

* A Reflection of sound waves

B Refraction of sound waves

C Diffraction of sound waves

D Interference of sound waves

10 Energy from the sun is transferred to chemical energy in cells through the process of —

F respiration

* G photosynthesis

H fermentation

J nitrogen fixation

11 The appropriate unit to express the distance a school bus travels on its morning route is the —

A meter

B millimeter

C centimeter

* D kilometer

12 Flow and Sediment in a River

Month	Volume of Flow (cubic meters/s)	Sediment Load (metric tons/day)
January	1.5	200
February	1.7	320
March	2.6	725
April	4.0	1600
May	3.2	1100
June	2.8	900

What may have occurred in the river's watershed in April to cause the changes in volume of flow and sediment load?

* F Rains and melting snow increased the amount of runoff.

G A late spring frost covered most of the watershed.

H The river had been frozen all winter, and it thawed suddenly.

J The watershed was affected by a long drought.

TVA55

Important Facts: Grade 8 Science Test

The Commonwealth of Virginia has published a document explaining how your Grade 8 Science Test was developed and organized. This document is called the Standards of Learning (SOL) Test Blueprint. The Blueprint also contains specific, important information that can assist you in preparing for the Grade 8 Science Test.

Blueprint Highlights

- ✔ *The test will be untimed, so you should take your time choosing your answers. Be sure to double check all of your answers.*
- ✔ *You will be scored on the number of correct answers, so try to answer all questions.*
- ✔ *You are permitted to use scratch paper, a 4-function calculator, a standard ruler (inches) and a metric ruler (centimeters) during the test. If possible, bring these materials with you.*
- ✔ *Measurements are given in SI (metric) or English units where appropriate. Be sure that you are familiar with both types of measurement units.*
- ✔ *Each test item is a multiple-choice item containing four choices. Eliminating just one of the four possible choices greatly increases your chance of selecting the correct answer. Choices such as "None of the above," "All of the above," and "Not here" are not used.*
- ✔ *Information is presented through written text or through visual materials such as graphs, tables, models, or other illustrations. Before the test, become comfortable with interpreting these types of materials.*
- ✔ *Answer choices are given in words, as numerical expressions including appropriate units, graphics, or other appropriate expressions. Read all choices carefully before selecting your answer.*
- ✔ *Because of the large number of SOL in science, every SOL will not be assessed on every test. Instead, each test will sample the SOL from a category. So it is important to study all the SOL.*

Program Authors

Michael J. Padilla, Ph.D.
Professor
Department of Science Education
University of Georgia
Athens, Georgia

Michael Padilla is a leader in middle school science education. He has served as an editor and elected officer for the National Science Teachers Association. He has been principal investigator of several National Science Foundation and Eisenhower grants and served as a writer of the National Science Education Standards.

As lead author of *Science Explorer,* Mike has inspired the team in developing a program that meets the needs of middle grades students, promotes science inquiry, and is aligned with the National Science Education Standards.

Ioannis Miaoulis, Ph.D.
Dean of Engineering
College of Engineering
Tufts University
Medford, Massachusetts

Martha Cyr, Ph.D.
Director, Engineering Educational Outreach
College of Engineering
Tufts University
Medford, Massachusetts

Science Explorer was created in collaboration with the College of Engineering at Tufts University. Tufts has an extensive engineering outreach program that uses engineering design and construction to excite and motivate students and teachers in science and technology education.

Faculty from Tufts University participated in the development of *Science Explorer* chapter projects, reviewed the student books for content accuracy, and helped coordinate field testing.

CHAPTER PROJECT

Series Authors

Elizabeth Coolidge-Stolz, M.D.
Medical Writer
North Reading, Massachusetts

Linda Cronin-Jones, Ph.D.
Professor, College of Education
University of Florida
Gainesville, Florida

Donald Cronkite, Ph.D.
Professor of Biology
Hope College
Holland Michigan

Joseph D. Exline, M.A., Ed.D.
President
Exline Consulting Services, Inc.
Beaverdam, Virginia

David V, Frank, Ph.D.
Head, Department of Physical Sciences
Ferris State Unversity
Big Rapids, Michigan

Dawn Graff-Haight, Ph.D., CHES
Associate Professor, Health Education
Linfield College
McMinnville, Oregon

Fred Holtzclaw
Science Instructor
Oak Ridge High School
Oak Ridge, Tennessee

Jan Jenner, Ph.D.
Science Writer
Talladega, Alabama

John G. Little
Science Teacher
St. Mary's High School
Stockton, California

Steve Miller
Science Writer
State College, Pennsylvania

Barbara Brooks Simons
Science Writer
Boston Massachusetts

Carole Garbuny Vogel, M.A.T.
Science Writer
Lexington, Massachusetts

Camille L. Wainwright, Ph.D.
Professor of Science Education
Pacific University
Forest Grove, Oregon

Thomas R. Wellnitz
Science Teacher
The Paideia School
Atlanta, Georgia

Contributing Writers

W. Russell Blake, Ph.D.
Planetarium Director
Plymouth Community Intermediate School
Plymouth, Massachusetts

Alfred B. Bortz, Ph.D.
School of Education
Duquesne University
Pittsburgh, Pennsylvania

Rose-Marie Botting
Science Teacher
Broward County School District
Fort Lauderdale, Florida

Jeffrey C. Callister
Science Teacher
Newburgh Free Academy
Newburgh, New York

Colleen Campos
Science Teacher
Laredo Middle School
Aurora, Colorado

Holly Estes
Science Teacher
Hale Middle School
Stow, Massachusetts

Edward Evans
Former Science Teacher
Hilton Central School
Hilton, New York

Greg Hutton
Science and Health Curriculum Coordinator
School Board of Sarasota County
Sarasota, Florida

Lauren Magruder
Science Teacher
St. Michael's Country Day School
Newport, Rhode Island

Emery Pineo
Science Instructor
Barrington Middle School
Barrington, Rhode Island

Karen Riley Sievers
Science Teacher
Callanan Middle School
Des Moines, Iowa

Sharon M. Stroud
Science Teacher
Widefield High School
Colorado Springs, Colorado

Reading Consultant

Bonnie B. Armbruster, Ph.D.
Department of Curriculum and Instruction
University of Illinois
Champaign, Illinois

Interdisciplinary Consultant

Heidi Hayes Jacobs, Ed.D.
Teachers College
Columbia University
New York, New York

Safety Consultants

W. H. Breazeale, Ph.D.
Department of Chemistry
College of Charleston
Charleston, South Carolina

Ruth Hathaway, Ph.D.
Hathaway Consulting
Cape Girardeau, Missouri

Content Reviewers

Jack W. Beal, Ph.D.
Department of Physics
Fairfield University
Fairfield, Connecticut

W. Russell Blake, Ph.D.
Planetarium Director
Plymouth Community Intermediate School
Plymouth, Massachusetts

Howard E. Buhse, Jr., Ph.D.
Department of Biological Sciences
University of Illinois
Chicago, Illinois

Dawn Smith Burgess, Ph.D.
Department of Geophysics
Stanford University
Palo Alto, California

A. Malcolm Campbell, Ph.D.
Assistant Professor
Davidson College
Davidson, North Carolina

Elizabeth A. De Stasio, Ph.D.
Associate Professor of Biology
Lawrence University
Appleton, Wisconsin

John M. Fowler, Ph.D.
Former Director of Special Projects
National Science Teachers Association
Arlington, Virginia

Jonathan Gitlin, M.D.
School of Medicine
Washington University
St. Louis, Missouri

Deborah L. Gumucio, Ph.D.
Associate Professor
Department of Anatomy and Cell Biology
University of Michigan
Ann Arbor, Michigan

William S. Harwood, Ph.D.
Dean of University Division and Associate Professor of Education
Indiana University
Bloomington, Indiana

Cyndy Henzel, Ph.D.
Department of Geography and Regional Development
University of Arizona
Tucson, Arizona

Greg Hutton
Science and Health Curriculum Coordinator
School Board of Sarasota County
Sarasota, Florida

Susan K. Jacobson, Ph.D.
Department of Wildlife Ecology and Conservation
University of Florida
Gainesville, Florida

Judy Jernstedt, Ph.D.
Department of Agronomy and Range Science
University of California, Davis
Davis, California

John L. Kermond, Ph.D.
Office of Global Programs
National Oceanographic and Atmospheric Administration
Silver Spring, Maryland

David E. LaHart, Ph.D.
Institute of Science and Public Affairs
Florida State University
Tallahassee, Florida

Joe Leverich, Ph.D.
Department of Biology
St. Louis University
St. Louis, Missouri

Dennis K. Lieu, Ph.D.
Department of Mechanical Engineering
University of California
Berkeley, California

Cynthia J. Moore, Ph.D.
Science Outreach Coordinator
Washington University
St. Louis, Missouri

Joseph M. Moran, Ph.D.
Department of Earth Science
University of Wisconsin–Green Bay
Green Bay, Wisconsin

Joseph Stukey, Ph.D.
Department of Biology
Hope College
Holland, Michigan

Seetha Subramanian
Lexington Community College
University of Kentucky
Lexington, Kentucky

Carl L. Thurman, Ph.D.
Department of Biology
University of Northern Iowa
Cedar Falls, Iowa

Edward D. Walton, Ph.D.
Department of Chemistry
California State Polytechnic University
Pomona, California

Robert S. Young, Ph.D.
Department of Geosciences and Natural Resource Management
Western Carolina University
Cullowhee, North Carolina

Edward J. Zalisko, Ph.D.
Department of Biology
Blackburn College
Carlinville, Illinois

iii

Tufts University Program Reviewers

Behrouz Abedian, Ph.D.
Department of Mechanical Engineering

Wayne Chudyk, Ph.D.
Department of Civil and Environmental Engineering

Eliana De Bernardez-Clark, Ph.D.
Department of Chemical Engineering

Anne Marie Desmarais, Ph.D.
Department of Civil and Environmental Engineering

David L. Kaplan, Ph.D.
Department of Chemical Engineering

Paul Kelley, Ph.D.
Department of Electro-Optics

George S. Mumford, Ph.D.
Professor of Astronomy, Emeritus

Jan A. Pechenik, Ph.D.
Department of Biology

Livia Racz, Ph.D.
Department of Mechanical Engineering

Robert Rifkin, M.D.
School of Medicine

Jack Ridge, Ph.D.
Department of Geology

Chris Swan, Ph.D.
Department of Civil and Environmental Engineering

Peter Y. Wong, Ph.D.
Department of Mechanical Engineering

Teacher Reviewers

Stephanie Anderson
Sierra Vista Junior High School
Canyon Country, California

John W. Anson
Mesa Intermediate School
Palmdale, California

Pamela Arline
Lake Taylor Middle School
Norfolk, Virginia

Lynn Beason
College Station Jr. High School
College Station, Texas

Richard Bothmer
Hollis School District
Hollis, New Hampshire

Jeffrey C. Callister
Newburgh Free Academy
Newburgh, New York

Judy D'Albert
Harvard Day School
Corona Del Mar, California

Betty Scott Dean
Guilford County Schools
McLeansville, North Carolina

Sarah C. Duff
Baltimore City Public Schools
Baltimore, Maryland

Melody Law Ewey
Holmes Junior High School
Davis, California

Sherry L. Fisher
Lake Zurich Middle School North
Lake Zurich, Illinois

Melissa Gibbons
Fort Worth ISD
Fort Worth, Texas

Debra J. Goodding
Kraemer Middle School
Placentia, California

Jack Grande
Weber Middle School
Port Washington, New York

Steve Hills
Riverside Middle School
Grand Rapids, Michigan

Sandra M. Justin
Swift Junior High School
Oakville, Connecticut

Carol Ann Lionello
Kraemer Middle School
Placentia, California

Jaime A. Morales
Henry T. Gage Middle School
Huntington Park, California

Patsy Partin
Cameron Middle School
Nashville, Tennessee

Deedra H. Robinson
Newport News Public Schools
Newport News, Virginia

Bonnie Scott
Clack Middle School
Abilene, Texas

Charles M. Sears
Belzer Middle School
Indianapolis, Indiana

Barbara M. Strange
Ferndale Middle School
High Point, North Carolina

Jackie Louise Ulfig
Ford Middle School
Allen, Texas

Kathy Usina
Belzer Middle School
Indianapolis, Indiana

Heidi M. von Oetinger
L'Anse Creuse Public School
Harrison Township, Michigan

Pam Watson
Hill Country Middle School
Austin, Texas

Activity Field Testers

Nicki Bibbo
Russell Street School
Littleton, Massachusetts

Connie Boone
Fletcher Middle School
Jacksonville Beach, Florida

Rose-Marie Botting
Broward County School District
Fort Lauderdale, Florida

Colleen Campos
Laredo Middle School
Aurora, Colorado

Elizabeth Chait
W. L. Chenery Middle School
Belmont, Massachusetts

Holly Estes
Hale Middle School
Stow, Massachusetts

Laura Hapgood
Plymouth Community Intermediate School
Plymouth, Massachusetts

Sandra M. Harris
Winman Junior High School
Warwick, Rhode Island

Jason Ho
Walter Reed Middle School
Los Angeles, California

Joanne Jackson
Winman Junior High School
Warwick, Rhode Island

Mary F. Lavin
Plymouth Community Intermediate School
Plymouth, Massachusetts

James MacNeil, Ph.D.
Concord Public Schools
Concord, Massachusetts

Lauren Magruder
St. Michael's Country Day School
Newport, Rhode Island

Jeanne Maurand
Glen Urquhart School
Beverly Farms, Massachusetts

Warren Phillips
Plymouth Community Intermediate School
Plymouth, Massachusetts

Carol Pirtle
Hale Middle School
Stow, Massachusetts

Kathleen M. Poe
Kirby-Smith Middle School
Jacksonville, Florida

Cynthia B. Pope
Ruffner Middle School
Norfolk, Virginia

Anne Scammell
Geneva Middle School
Geneva, New York

Karen Riley Sievers
Callanan Middle School
Des Moines, Iowa

David M. Smith
Howard A. Eyer Middle School
Macungie, Pennsylvania

Derek Strohschneider
Plymouth Community Intermediate School
Plymouth, Massachusetts

Sallie Teames
Rosemont Middle School
Fort Worth, Texas

Gene Vitale
Parkland Middle School
McHenry, Illinois

Zenovia Young
Meyer Levin Junior High School (IS 285)
Brooklyn, New York

v

Contents

Grade 6 Science

Unit 2 Earth's Changing Surface

vii

Unit 3 Earth's Waters

Unit 4 Weather and Climate

Unit 5 Energy and the Environment

x

Unit 6 Introduction to Astronomy

xi

Reference Section

xii

Activities

Inquiry Activities

CHAPTER PROJECT

Opportunities for long-term inquiry

DISCOVER

Exploration and inquiry before reading

xiii

DISCOVER

continued

xiv

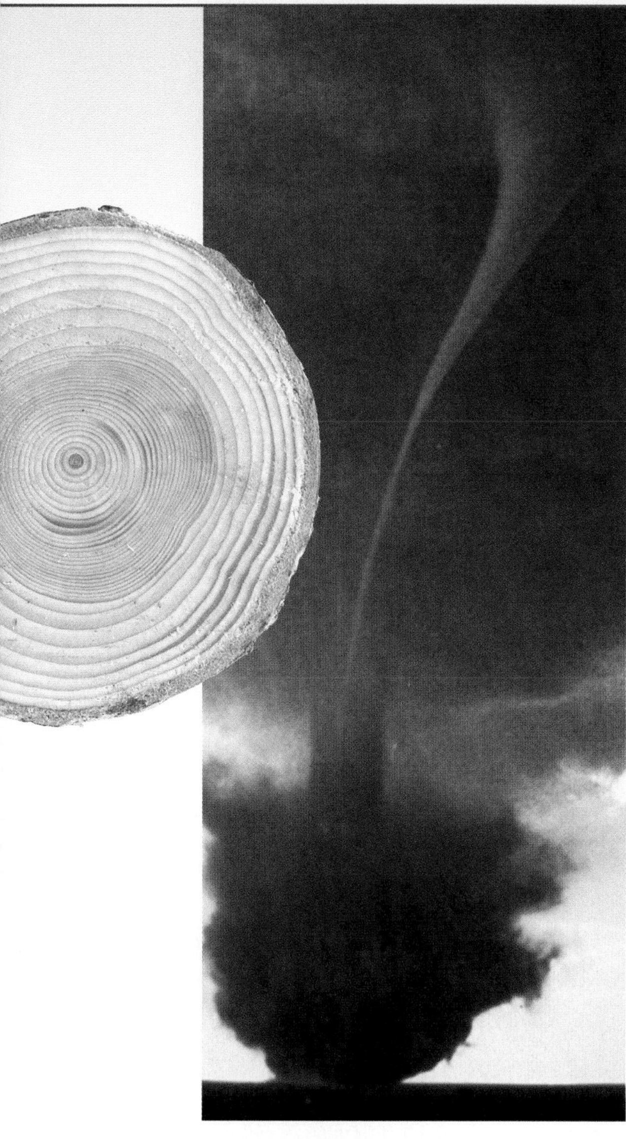

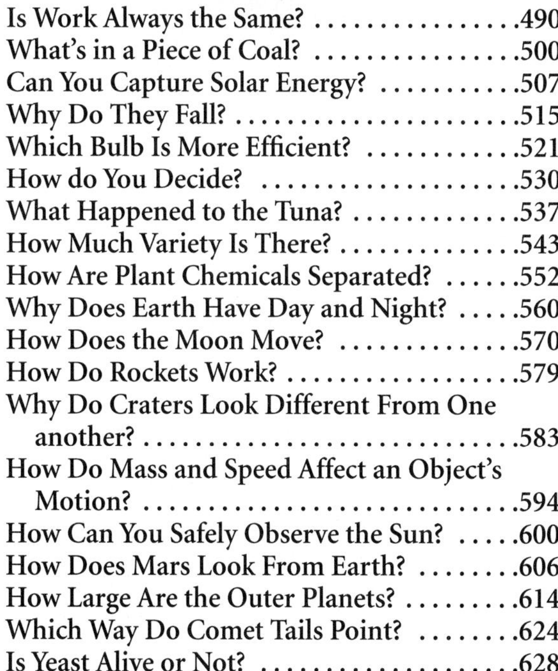

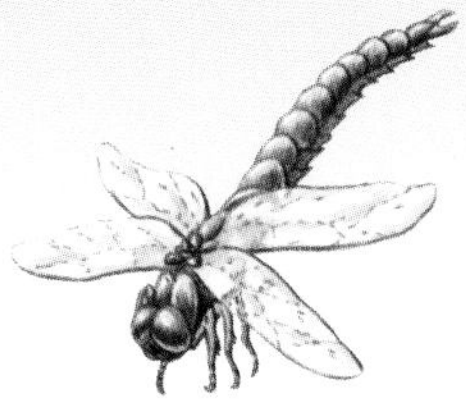

Sharpen your Skills

Practice of specific science inquiry skills

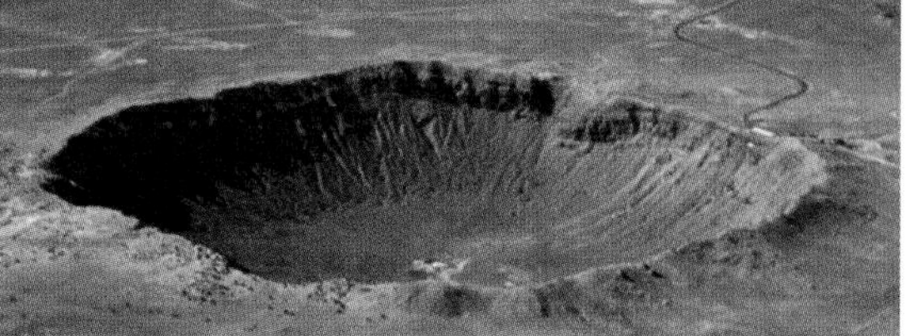

Try This

Reinforcement of key concepts

Skills Lab

In-depth practice of inquiry skills

xvi

Real-World Lab

Everyday application of science concepts

Science at Home

Family involvement in science exploration

Science at Home

continued

EXPLORING

Visual exploration of concepts

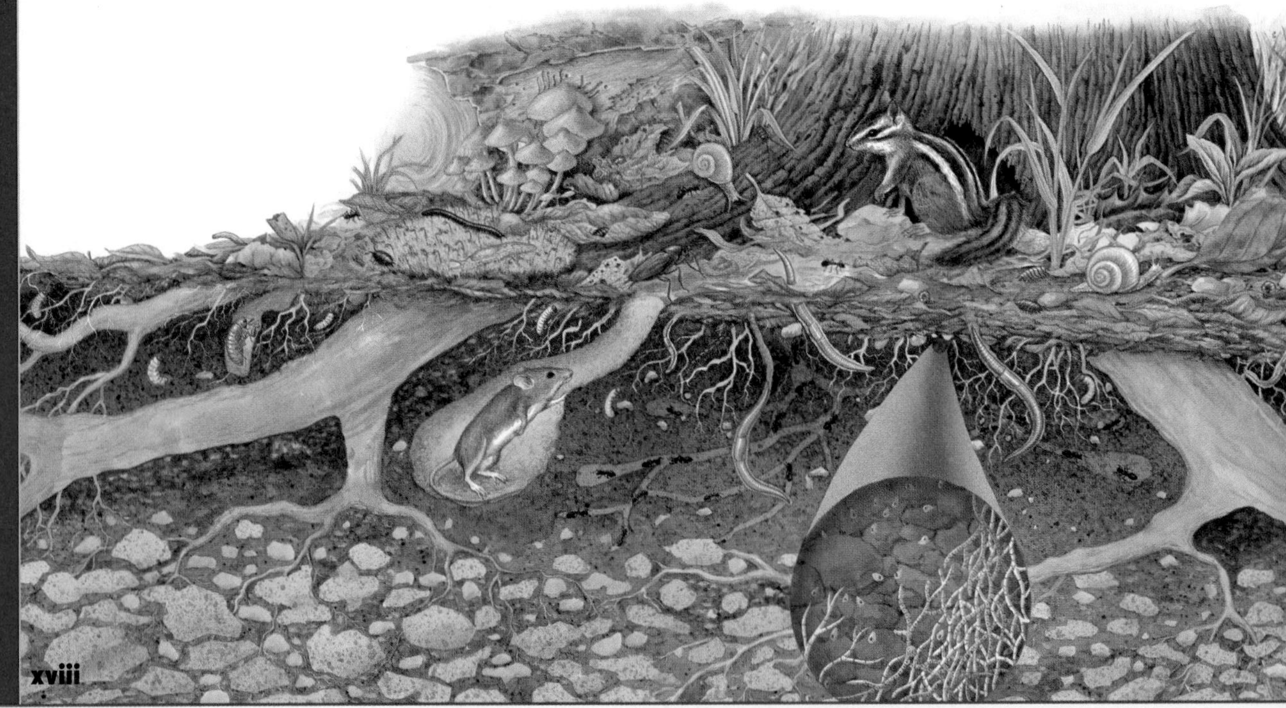

Interdisciplinary Activities

xix

Introduction to Science

Objectives	Time	Student Edition Activities	Other Activities
◆ Explain how scientists, using scientific inquiry, seek to understand the natural world. ◆ Explain observation and inference. ◆ Describe scientific methods, including the process of developing a hypothesis and testing the hypothesis through a controlled experiment. ◆ Explain what a scientific theory is.	4 periods/ 2 blocks	**Skills Lab: Developing Hypotheses** Cool Crystals, p. 9	**TE** Addressing Naive Conceptions, p. 5 **TE** Building Inquiry Skills: Hypothesizing, p. 6 **TE** Including All Students, p. 13 **LM** Introduction, "How to Use a Balance"

For Standard or Block Schedule The Resource Pro® CD-ROM gives you maximum flexibility for planning your instruction for any type of schedule. Resource Pro® contains Planning Express®, an advanced scheduling program, as well as the entire contents of the Teaching Resources and the Computer Test Bank.

Meeting the National Science Education Standards and AAAS Benchmarks

National Science Education Standards	Benchmarks for Science Literacy	Unifying Themes
Science As Inquiry (Content Standard A) ◆ **Design and conduct a scientific investigation** Students conduct an experiment about how cooling rate affects crystal size. *(Skills Lab)* ◆ **Develop descriptions, explanations, and models using evidence** Students develop hypotheses and collect evidence about how cooling rate affects crystal size. *(Skills Lab)* **Science and Technology** (Content Standard E) ◆ **Understandings about science and technology** Scientists use computers and satellites to gather information. **History and Nature of Science** (Content Standard G) ◆ **Science as a human endeavor** Many different kinds of people are involved in science and its related fields. ◆ **Nature of science** Scientists use observation, experimentation, and theoretical and mathematical models to explain nature. ◆ **History of science** Over the years many scientists have contributed to today's scientific knowledge.	**1A The Scientific World View** New information can lead to new scientific theories and alterations of existing theories. **1B Scientific Inquiry** Students investigate the scientific process. **1C The Scientific Enterprise** Many different kinds of people have advanced scientific thought over a long time. **3A Technology and Science** Scientists use computers, robots, satellites, and space probes to gather information.	◆ **Modeling** Scientists use models to study phenomena in the natural world.

PLANNING GUIDE

Program Resources	Assessment Strategies	Media and Technology
UR Introduction Lesson Plan **UR** Introduction Section Summary **UR** Introduction Review and Reinforce **UR** Introduction Enrich **UR** Introduction Skills Lab blackline master	**TE** Ongoing Assessment, p. 7 **TE** Performance Assessment, p. 11 **SE** Study Guide/Assessment, pp. 14–15 **PA** Introduction Performance Assessment **CUT** Introduction Test **CTB** Introduction Test	Science Explorer Internet Site at www.phschool.com Student Edition on Audio CD, Introduction Computer Test Bank, Introduction Test

Key: **SE** Student Edition
CTB Computer Test Bank
ISAB Inquiry Skills Activity Book
GRSW Guided Reading and Study Workbook
TE Teacher's Edition
PTA Product Testing Activities by *Consumer Reports*
RCA Reading in the Content Area
PA Performance Assessment
UR Unit Resources
LM Laboratory Manual
IES Interdisciplinary Explorations Series
CUT Chapter and Unit Tests

Student Edition Activities Planner

ACTIVITY	Time (minutes)	Materials *Quantities for one work group*	Skills
Skills Lab, p. 9	30	**Consumable** salol, candle, matches, ice cubes **Nonconsumable** plastic spoon, 2 microscope slides, tongs, hand lens	**Developing Hypotheses, Controlling Variables, Drawing Conclusions**

A list of all materials required for the Student Edition activities can be found on pages TVA34–TVA40. You can obtain information about ordering materials by calling 1-800-848-9500 or by accessing the Science Explorer Internet site at: **www.phschool.com**

Take It to the Net

Interactive text at www.phschool.com

Science Explorer comes alive with iText.

- **Complete student text** is accessible from any computer with Internet access or a CD-ROM drive.
- **Animations, simulations, and videos** enhance student understanding and retention of concepts.
- **Self-tests and online study tools** assess student understanding.

STAY CURRENT with **SCIENCE NEWS®**

Find out the latest research and information about The Nature of Science at: **www.phschool.com**

Go to **www.phschool.com** and click on the Science icon.Then click on Science Explorer: Life, Earth, and Physical Science under PH@school.

Searching for the Home of Comets

Focus on Astronomy

This four-page feature introduces the process of scientific inquiry by involving students in a high-interest, magazine-like feature about a working scientist, astronomer Jane Luu. Using Dr. Luu's investigation of the source of comets, the feature focuses on persistence, patience, and reasoning as key elements of scientific inquiry.

Comets are presented in Chapter 19 of this book. However, students need not have any previous knowledge of that chapter's content to understand and appreciate this feature.

Scientific Inquiry

- Before students read the feature let them read the title, examine the pictures, and read the captions on their own. Then ask: **What questions came into your mind as you looked at these pictures?** *(Students might suggest questions such as "Do comets come from a single place?" "What is astronomy?" "Why are there observatories in Hawaii?" and "What does it mean for Pluto to be on a different plane?")* Point out to students that just as they had questions about what they were seeing, scientists too have questions about what they observe.

Searching for the home of COMETS

It's a long way from astronomer Jane Luu's office in the Netherlands to the mountaintop in Hawaii where she searches the night sky. But astronomers need dark skies, far from city lights. They also need clean, clear air to see deep into the solar system. That's why Jane Luu travels all the way to the high mountain observatory in Hawaii. Jane Luu has traveled long distances before. Born in Vietnam, she came to the United States at the age of 12.

"As a kid in Vietnam," she says, "I didn't have a single class in science. But after studying physics in college, I got a job at the Jet Propulsion Laboratory, the place where they track all the unmanned space missions. It was a summer job, pretty unimportant stuff. But when I saw the pictures taken by *Voyager I* and *Voyager II* in the mid-1980s, I thought they were spectacular. Those pictures of the planets were what made me go to graduate school in planetary astronomy."

Dr. Jane Luu arrived in the United States from Vietnam as a young girl. Dr. Luu studied physics at Stanford University in California and astronomy at the Massachusetts Institute of Technology. She now works at Leiden University in the Netherlands.

Background

Astronomy is the study of all natural objects in space. These bodies range from comets and meteors, to planets and moons, to stars, galaxies and interstellar matter.

Within astronomy, scientists specialize in areas such as astrometry (the study of the positions and motions of objects such as stars and planets), celestial mechanics (the mathematical study of the motions of objects in space), and cosmology (the study of the development of the universe as a whole).

TALKING WITH DR. JANE LUU

What Jane Luu looks at now lies just beyond the farthest planets in our solar system. It's a ring made of millions of pieces of ice-rock that circle the sun. Luu and her co-worker David Jewitt first discovered these objects in 1992. The rocky planet Pluto is the biggest object in this ring, which is called the Kuiper (KY pur) Belt. Pluto travels through space along with thousands of other objects that Luu and Jewitt have named "Plutinos" (little Plutos). Objects in the Kuiper Belt sometimes escape from the belt and approach the sun. The sun's heat then makes them light up and they become comets.

These color-enhanced images of Jupiter (above), Saturn (right), and Neptune (below) were taken from a *Voyager* spacecraft.

Q *Why did you start searching for the Kuiper Belt?*

A There were two reasons. We wanted to know if there was anything beyond Neptune besides Pluto. Why should that space be empty when there were so many planets and smaller objects nearer the sun? Scientists had predicted there would be a group of comets not too far beyond Neptune, but no one had seen these objects. There were other people trying to find the same thing, so it was a bit of a race. We're glad we won it.

Q *Where did you start looking?*

A Most things in the solar system are in a plane, a basically flat disk where the planets and the sun are. So you start looking there. Then, you want to look opposite the sun. Also, you look at a time of the year when the Milky Way, our home galaxy, isn't in the part of the sky you're searching. That's so the light of all those stars doesn't make it hard to see.

Q *Once you knew where to look, what did you do?*

A We took pictures. We started in 1987 and saw the first object in 1992, five years later. In the beginning we didn't have a computer at the telescope that was fast enough to analyze the pictures. So we'd make three pictures and then take them home to analyze. We'd take images, say a half-hour apart, of the same piece of sky. Then we'd look to see if any point of light had moved

- Explain that astronomers are scientists who study objects in the universe such as stars, planets, comets, asteroids, and galaxies.
- Encourage students to tell what they already know about comets. Ask students who have seen a comet to describe how it appeared. Ask students what they know about Halley's Comet or other famous comets.
- If a student knows the difference between meteors and comets, ask the student to explain the difference to the class.
- If students have access to the Internet, they can find images of comets at: **www.nasa.gov**
- Ask: **Why is an observatory at the top of a mountain in Hawaii?** *(The sky is dark and the air is clean and clear.)* **Why is the sky dark?** *(There are no city lights nearby.)* Challenge interested students to find out the remote locations of some other observatories.
- If students seem particularly interested in the Kuiper Belt, share the information in Background below. Also suggest that they consult library books to learn more about comets. (See Further Reading, page 3.)

Background

Drs. Luu and Jewitt found the first Kuiper Belt object in August 1992, and the second in March 1993. By May 1996, 32 objects had been found by Luu, Jewitt, and other scientists. These objects are all outside Neptune's orbit. They travel in a similar plane. They have diameters ranging from 100 kilometers to 400 kilometers.

About half the objects that scientists have found so far revolve around the sun in the same amount of time that Pluto takes to revolve around the sun. Luu and Jewitt estimate that there are several thousand such objects in the Kuiper Belt.

Nature of Science

- Using volunteers, demonstrate what it means for Pluto to be on a different plane from the other planets. Clear a large space in the classroom or take the students to a hall or field. Have one student hold a basketball or other large ball at waist-height to represent the sun. Have other students walk around this student holding tennis balls or other small balls at waist-height. Arrange students so they are in concentric circles of different radii around the "sun." Explain that the smaller balls represent planets. Point out that the sun and the planets are on one plane. Now take a different ball and walk around the "sun" while moving the ball above and below the plane of the other balls. Lead students to recognize that the plane of Pluto lies on an angle to the plane of the other planets.
- Ask: **What are the objects that Dr. Luu found in the Kuiper Belt?** *(pieces of ice-rock)*
- **What do you think it means for telescope time to be valuable?** *(Students' answers will vary. Sample: Many astronomers want to use the telescope for different projects so each astronomer is given a limited amount of time.)*
- Ask students if they have ever lived at or visited high altitudes. Invite a volunteer to explain what happens to your body when you visit a high altitude and why Dr. Luu would need an extra night to adjust to the altitude. Ask: **What does it mean for the air to be thin?** *(The air is less dense and therefore there is less oxygen to breathe.)*
- Challenge interested students to find out more about comets and the people who discovered them. Invite students to share their findings with the class.

These observatories are located on top of Mauna Kea, an inactive volcano in Hawaii.

between the three pictures. If it moves, we know it's near us in the solar system, and not a distant star. Since our first discovery in 1992, scientists have found many more objects in the Kuiper Belt. David and I have found about two thirds of those.

Q *Do you stay up all night?*

A Yes, we have to. Telescope time is valuable so you don't want to waste a single minute. We observe for a week or so, staying up for 5 or 6 nights in a row. It's hard work, switching from a daytime to a nighttime schedule. In Hawaii, we observe on top of Mauna Kea volcano at 14,000 feet. So we have to add an extra night at the beginning to get used to the altitude and thin air.

The Kuiper Belt lies beyond the part of the solar system where the planets revolve around the sun. Objects in the Kuiper Belt revolve far from Earth and the sun. Pluto's orbit is on a different plane from the other planets.

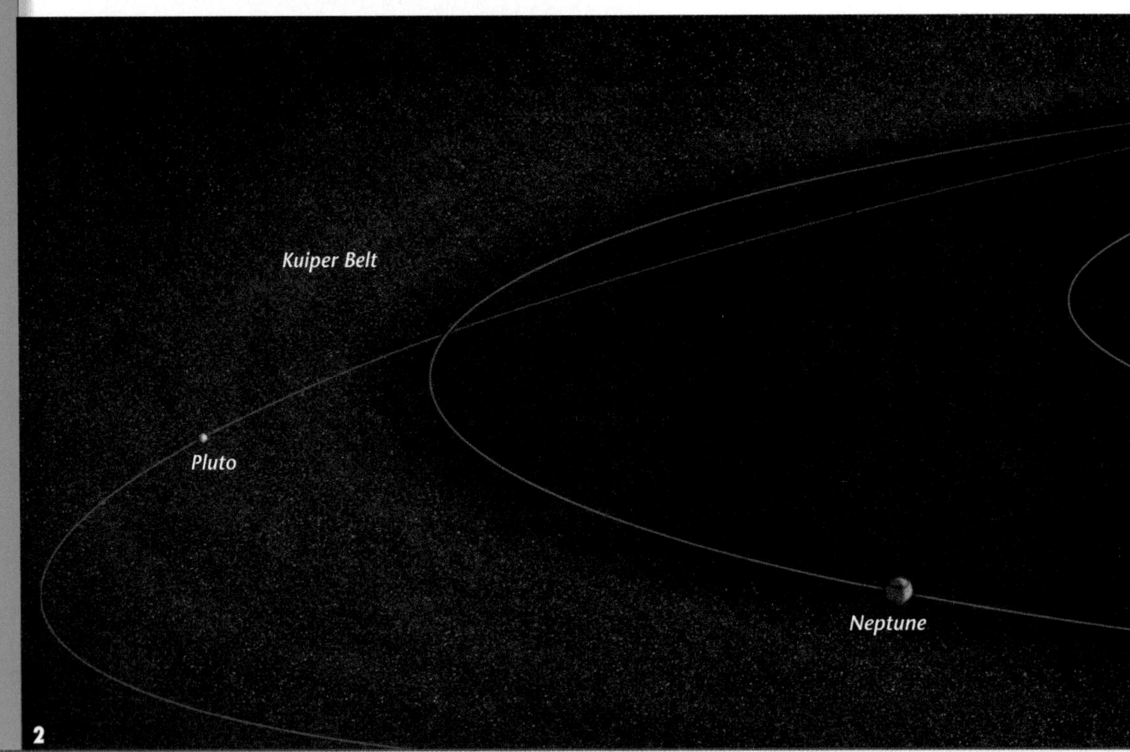

Background

In 1951, an astronomer named Gerard Kuiper theorized that the solar system contained numerous small objects revolving around the sun at or beyond Pluto's orbit. Kuiper believed that these objects would be made of material similar to comets, frozen water mixed with other frozen gases.

For years, many scientists did not take Kuiper's theory seriously. They instead believed that comets entered the solar system from interstellar space. In 1988, however, scientists used computer simulations to show that it was unlikely that comets originated from far beyond our solar system.

Even before the results of the computer simulation were published, Drs. Luu and Jewitt decided to explore whether there were objects in the solar system beyond Pluto and Neptune. Their discoveries supported Kuiper's theory.

Q ***Five years is a long time to wait for a discovery. Didn't you get discouraged?***

A We told ourselves that after we'd covered a certain part of the sky without finding anything, we would stop. We were pretty near that limit. But the newer cameras could take bigger pictures of the sky. They helped us do in a month what at first had taken two years. We could see something and know right away where to look the next night.

Because I've been lucky, I've participated in discoveries. There's such a satisfaction you get when you solve a puzzle, when you find out something that nobody has known before. And it's really fun after a lot of hard work, when you've finally found what you wanted to find.

In Your Journal

Jane Luu describes working night after night for five years, observing and recording data for one part of the night sky. "It was so time-consuming, and we didn't know if anything was going to come from it." Fortunately, in the end, she was rewarded. How did Jane Luu's persistence, as well as her skill, energy, and step-by-step reasoning, lead to her success?

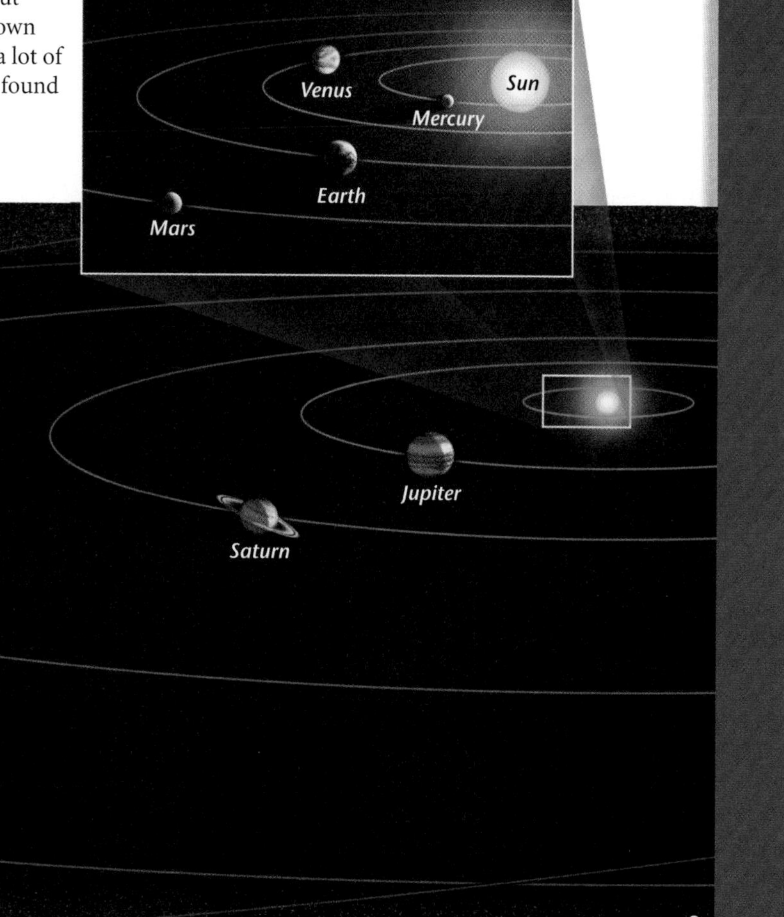

3

In Your Journal To help students appreciate Dr. Luu's persistence, have students recall where they were five years ago. Have students imagine that they began working on a project five years ago and worked on it every night since. Ask: **What would motivate you to keep working on your project night after night for so long?** *(Student answers will vary. Sample: the satisfaction of being the first to discover something)* Extend the discussion by asking: **What kind of person do you think would make a good astronomer?** *(Student answers will vary. Samples: patient, determined, persistent, detail-oriented)*

READING STRATEGIES

Further Reading

- Marsh, Carole and Arthur R. Upgren. *Asteroids, Comets, and Meteors.* Twenty First Century Books, 1996.
- Sagan, Carl and Ann Druyan. *Comet.* Ballantine Books, 1997.

What is Science?

Objectives

After completing this introduction, students will be able to
- explain how scientists, using scientific inquiry, seek to understand the natural world;
- explain observation and inference;
- describe scientific methods, including the process of developing a hypothesis and testing the hypothesis through a controlled experiment;
- explain what a scientific theory is.

Key Terms science, scientific inquiry, observation, inference, hypothesis, controlled experiment, variable, manipulated variable, responding variable, data, scientific theory, chemist, geologist, oceanographer, meteorologist, astronomer, environmental scientist

1 Engage/Explore

Activating Prior Knowledge

Ask students what they think scientists do. Students will likely say that scientists work in a laboratory and carry out experiments. Have students preview pages 12–13. Then discuss that scientists work in many kinds of places.

What is SCIENCE?

GUIDE FOR READING

- What is science?
- What methods do scientists use?

Reading Tip **Before you begin reading, make a list of boldfaced terms. As you read, write the definition for each term.**

Astronomer Jane Luu's search for the home of comets began with curiosity. Her curiosity led her to ask many questions: Where do comets come from? What is at the outer edge of the solar system? In asking these questions, Dr. Luu was acting like a scientist, a person who studies the natural world.

Science is a way of learning about the natural world and the knowledge gained through that process. The word *science* comes from a Latin word that means "knowing." The natural world includes not just Earth, but everything in the universe.

As they study the natural world, scientists use scientific inquiry. **Scientific inquiry** is the diverse ways in which scientists explore problems and seek to answer questions about the natural world. Scientific inquiry involves how scientists think as well as the techniques they use.

About 500 years ago, the astronomer Copernicus developed this model of the solar system. *Comparing and Contrasting* *How does this model compare with the modern one on pages 2–3?* ▶

Reading Strategies

Reading Tip Have students write a question for each of the terms they list. They may combine terms in a compare-and-contrast statement. Sample answer: How does a manipulated variable differ from a responding variable?

Program Resources

- **Unit 1 Resources** Introduction Lesson Plan; Introduction Section Summary
- **Guided Reading and Study Workbook** Introduction

Media and Technology

Student Edition on Audio CD Introduction

Using a telescope designed for the purpose, this student can safely observe a solar eclipse.

Thinking Like a Scientist

As you study science, you will need to think like a scientist. In fact, you probably have used some kinds of scientific thinking already. For example, as you get ready for school in the morning, you may observe that the sky is cloudy. Then you infer, or make an inference, that rain is likely. Observation and inference are just two of the skills that scientists use.

Observation involves using sight, hearing, smell, and sometimes taste to gather information. An **inference** is an interpretation based on your observation and prior knowledge. See the Skills Handbook on pages 642–654 to learn more about observing, inferring, and other skills that will help you think like a scientist.

To find answers to her questions Jane Luu used observation and inference. She also used other kinds of scientific thinking, including predicting and making models.

Years before Jane Luu made her discovery, a scientist named Gerard Kuiper predicted that there might be comets at the outer edge of the solar system. Kuiper based his prediction on the idea that some material may have been left over after the solar system formed. Kuiper thought that this left-over material would be found in the form of icy comets beyond the orbit of Neptune. Jane Luu wanted to find out if Kuiper's prediction was correct.

Before Dr. Luu's discovery of the Kuiper belt, scientists' model of the solar system showed empty space between Neptune and Pluto. After Dr. Luu's discovery, scientists changed their model of the solar system to include the Kuiper belt. Scientists named the Kuiper belt in honor of Gerard Kuiper, who had predicted its existence.

☑ *Checkpoint* *What is the difference between an observation and an inference?*

2 Facilitate

Thinking Like a Scientist

Addressing Naive Conceptions

Materials *beaker, water, hot plate*

Help students distinguish between making observations and inferences. Heat a beaker of water on a hot plate until the water boils. When the water has reached the boiling point, ask students to describe what they see. Students will likely say that the water is boiling. Ask them to describe what they see without using the word *boiling*. Students should describe observing bubbles forming inside the water, rising, and breaking at the surface. Students may also be able to observe a fog-like layer above the surface of the water. Point out that these are observations, and the statement that the water is boiling is an inference based on observing the hot, bubbling water and using what they know about boiling. **learning modality: visual**

Background

For students, the most important task is learning to distinguish *observations* (evidence gathered through the senses) from *inferences* (logical thinking about those observations). Students often mistake one for the other. By making the distinction, they take a major step in modeling the way scientists think. Use the Addressing Naive Conceptions activity on this page to help students practice making the distinction.

Answers to Self-Assessment

Caption Question

Both show the sun at the center and the orbiting planets. The models differ in the number and position of planets.

☑ *Checkpoint*

An observation is information that is gathered by the senses. An inference is an interpretation of an observation and involves a person's prior knowledge.

Building Inquiry Skills: Hypothesizing

Materials *beaker, water, hot plate, ice cube, tongs*

Heat water in a beaker on a hot plate. When the water is boiling, ask students: **What does boiling water feel like?** *(Very hot)* Show students an ice cube. Ask: **What does an ice cube feel like?** *(Very cold)* On the board write, "If an ice cube is placed into boiling water..." and invite students to suggest endings for the sentence. List the endings on the board. Tell students that these statements are hypotheses. Discuss how the hypotheses can be tested. Then use the tongs to place the ice cube into the boiling water so that students can see if their hypotheses are supported. **learning modality: visual**

Including All Students

At the time that the first humans landed on the moon, several areas of the United States had heavy rains. Some people said that the rain was caused by the moon landing. Ask students if this is a valid hypothesis. *(No, because it is based on a coincidence, and even if the observation were repeated, this would not support the hypothesis. Also, this is not a testable hypothesis because all the relevant variables could never be controlled in a way that would establish a causal relationship between moon landings and rain.)* **learning modality: logical/ mathematical**

Building Inquiry Skills: Communicating

Divide students into two groups. Have one group take the part of the Swiss scientists who believed that glaciers did not move. Have the other group take the part of the Swiss scientists who believed that glaciers did move. Have each group list observations that led to its point of view. **learning modality: verbal**

Using the Visual

Have students identify the glacier and the dark bands in the photograph. Ask how the glacier differs from the mountains around it. **learning modality: visual**

Scientific Methods

Scientists use many methods as they search for answers to questions about the natural world. **Scientific methods generally include posing questions, developing and testing hypotheses, and drawing conclusions. Scientists often test hypotheses by conducting controlled experiments.**

In the 1800s, scientists applied scientific methods to the study of glaciers. Glaciers are usually found on and around high mountains, such as the Alps in Switzerland. Two hundred years ago, scientists knew very little about glaciers. Some scientists thought that glaciers could move. But others claimed that it was impossible for such huge masses of ice to move. To settle this dispute, some scientists in Switzerland decided to investigate.

Posing Questions Scientists begin with a question about something that is unexplained. The Swiss scientists studying glaciers asked, "Do glaciers move?"

Developing Hypotheses After posing a question, scientists often gather information or make observations. They then use this information to form a hypothesis. A **hypothesis** is a possible explanation for observations that relate to a scientific question. A hypothesis can be tested by observation or experiment. Scientists do not accept a hypothesis after just one test. Repeated tests must provide evidence that supports the hypothesis.

People in the Alps had long observed boulders in the valleys below glaciers. Did that mean that moving ice had carried the boulders? Such observations led scientists to the hypothesis that glaciers move slowly over the land.

☑ *Checkpoint* *What is a hypothesis?*

Designing a Controlled Experiment The controlled experiment is a method that scientists use to test hypotheses and predictions. A **controlled experiment** is a test of a hypothesis under conditions established by the scientist. In a controlled

The Gorner glacier winds down from high peaks in the Swiss Alps. The dark bands in the glacier are pieces of rock broken off and picked up by the moving ice.

6

Background

The term *hypothesis* refers to a proposed explanation that can be tested. In science, many hypotheses are developed as inferences, that is, through logical thinking. But some hypotheses have resulted from imagination, creative leaps, chance events, and even dreams. The key characteristic of a hypothesis is that it is testable. Use the Building Inquiry Skills activity on this page to help students practice identifying a valid hypothesis.

experiment, a scientist determines how one variable affects the outcome of the experiment. A **variable** is one of the factors that can change in an experiment.

The variable that a scientist changes is called the **manipulated variable.** The manipulated variable is also called the independent variable. The variable that changes because of the manipulated variable is the **responding variable,** or dependent variable.

In a controlled experiment, scientists control, or keep constant, all other variables. Controlling variables enables the scientist to eliminate the effects of the other variables as factors in the results of the experiment. Over time, variables can be manipulated and tested with many repeated trials. You will design and conduct controlled experiments at many points in this textbook. You can learn more about controlled experiments in the Skills Handbook on pages 646–647.

Testing Hypotheses In the real world, conducting a controlled experiment can be difficult or impossible. Scientists may have to study objects that are very large or very small, or processes that take millions of years. Scientists can test hypotheses through observation and measurement, as did the Swiss scientists who studied glaciers. The figure above shows how these scientists measured the movement of a glacier.

Collecting and Interpreting Data The facts, figures, and other evidence gained through observation are called **data.** Observation often involves measurements to obtain data that can be expressed as numbers. Scientists then interpret the data to determine whether or not the data support their hypothesis.

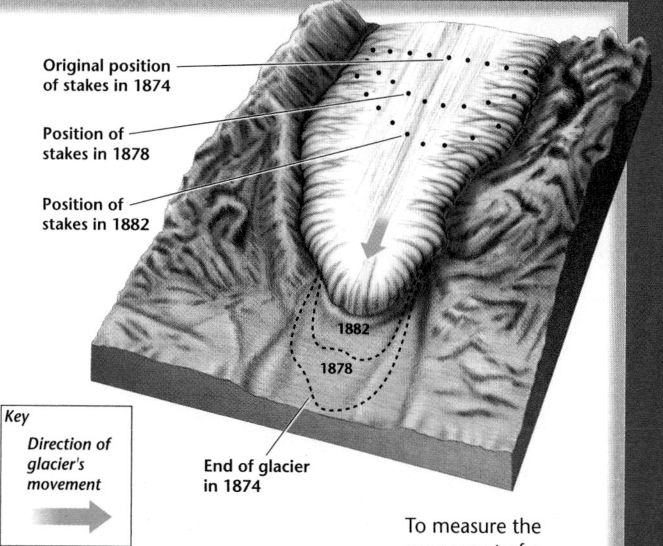

To measure the movement of a glacier, scientists drove a row of stakes into the glacier. They then measured how much the stakes moved in relation to the rocky sides of the valley. *Interpreting Diagrams Which part of the glacier appears to be moving the fastest? How can you tell?*

Measuring Measurement enables scientists to record what they observe in a way that others can understand easily. That's because units of measurement used by scientists are the same worldwide. This system of measurement is the International System of Units, also called SI units. For more about measurement and SI units, see pages 644–645 of the Skills Handbook.

Drawing Conclusions Once scientists have reviewed their data, they are ready to draw a conclusion. The data may support the hypothesis or show that the hypothesis was incorrect. Sometimes, no conclusion can be reached, and more data are needed.

The Swiss scientists studying glaciers concluded that their data supported their hypothesis. Glaciers do indeed move slowly. But the scientists' data also revealed a surprise. As the glacier was moving downhill, it was also melting back at its lower end. A surprising finding like this one can lead scientists to form new hypotheses.

You can practice developing hypotheses in the Skills Lab on page 9. Review Appendix A before you begin.

Using the Visual

Ask students: **How did the edge of the glacier change from 1874 to 1882?** *(The glacier's edge appeared to move back.)* **Suggest hypotheses that could explain this observation.** *(Possible hypotheses: the glacier is moving backward; the glacier is melting at its edge.)* Then direct students to look at the stakes in the glacier. Ask: **How have the positions of the stakes in the glacier changed?** *(They moved downhill.)* **How does this observation affect hypotheses about the change at the edge of the glacier?** *(If the stakes moved downhill, the hypothesis that the glacier moved uphill is unlikely.)* **learning modality: visual**

Background

The words *inference* and *conclusion* have the same meaning in everyday language, and one term is often used to define the other. In science, however, *inference* is often used as the broader term, while *conclusion* is used for the culminating, formal inference of an experiment. In keeping with this distinction, *drawing a conclusion* refers here to making a statement that summarizes how experimental data relates to the hypothesis tested.

Answers to Self-Assessment

Caption Question

The right-hand side of the glacier appears to be moving faster because the stakes moved farther on this side.

☑ Checkpoint

A hypothesis is a possible explanation for a set of observations.

Ongoing Assessment

Skills Check Have students draw flowcharts that show how scientists test a hypothesis. *(Sample flowchart: design a controlled experiment → collect data → interpret data → draw conclusions)*

Scientific Methods, continued

Including all Students

Ask students to list objects that are too large to study in the classroom. *(Answers will vary, but may include skyscrapers, airplanes, ships, the moon, or planets.)* Than ask what kinds of models might help students to study these objects? *(Three-dimensional models, drawings, maps, blueprints of buildings, ships, or planes.)* **learning modality: verbal**

Addressing Naive Conceptions

Some students may think that a theory that has been tested and supported is now a law. Point out that a theory is an explanation, and is always subject to change. A law describes a pattern that occurs in nature. **learning modality: logical/mathematical**

Skills Lab

Developing Hypotheses

Cool Crystals

Preparing for Inquiry

Key Concept In general, crystal size decreases as the rate of cooling increases.

Skills Objectives Students will be able to:

- develop hypotheses about how the rate of cooling affects crystal formation;
- identify variables;
- draw conclusions about the relationship beween hypotheses and experiments.

Time 30 minutes

Advance Planning Obtain salol (phenylsalicylate) from a drugstore or a chemical supply house.

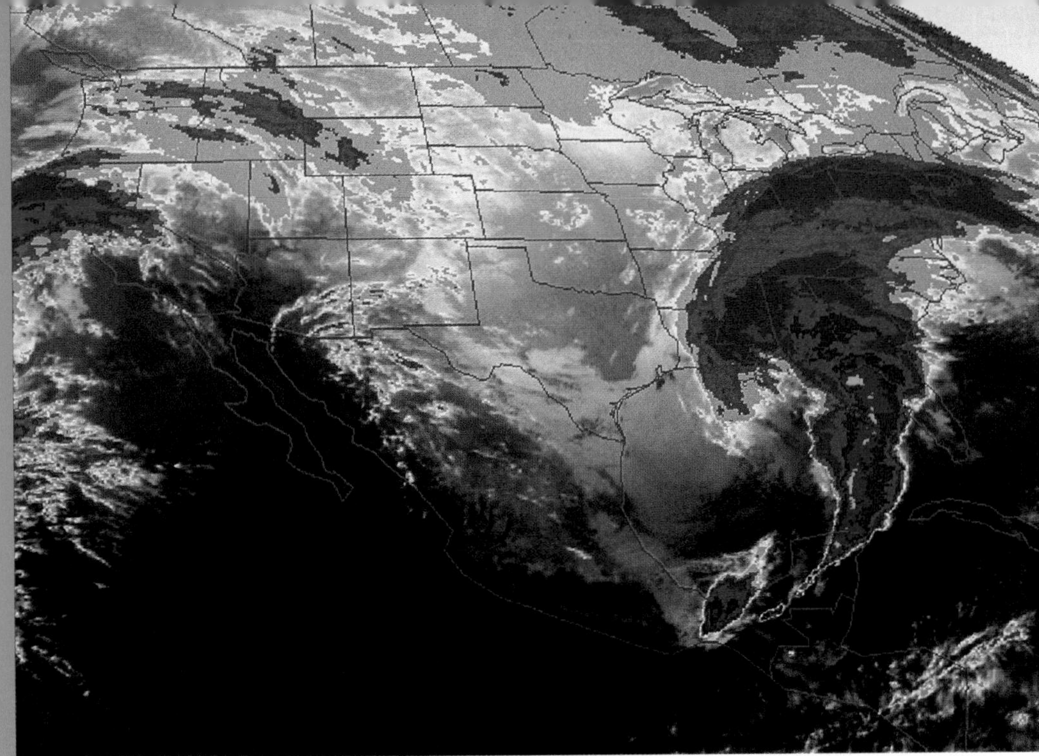

A weather map is a model of changing conditions in Earth's atmosphere. This map, based on satellite data, shows a storm over the eastern United States. Models can also be used to show a sequence of events or to help explain a process. *Interpreting Maps Which color on the map do you think represents areas of heavy rain? Explain your answer.*

Models and Simulations To test a hypothesis, scientists may also create models or simulations. A simulation is a model that imitates something in the real world. Scientists compare the results obtained from a simulation with known facts. This helps them decide whether this evidence supports the hypothesis.

Today, scientists know much more than they did during the 1800s about how glaciers move. For example, scientists working in laboratories have used simulations to model how glaciers move. The scientists studied samples of hot metal to see how the metal changed shape when under great pressure. The metal served as a model of the slowly flowing ice in a glacier. Studying such models helps scientists develop new hypotheses and ways of testing them. Above, you can see another type of model: a weather map.

Scientific Theories

Since the 1800s, scientists studying glaciers have made repeated observations of glacial movement. These observations confirmed the Swiss scientists' work. For a hypothesis to be widely accepted, other scientists must be able to repeat an experiment and obtain the same results.

As scientists study the natural world, they do more than just collect facts. Their goal is to develop concepts that explain their observations. These concepts are called scientific theories. A **scientific theory** is a well-tested scientific concept that explains a wide range of observations. An accepted theory has withstood repeated tests. But if tests fail to support a theory, scientists change the theory or abandon it.

☑ *Checkpoint* *What is a scientific theory?*

Answers to Self-Assessment

Caption Question

Answers may vary. Some students may suggest that shades of purple, blue, and magenta on the map represent the heaviest rain because they occupy the inner areas of the storm.

☑ *Checkpoint*

A scientific theory is a scientific concept that has been well tested and that explains a wide range of observations.

Developing Hypotheses

Cool Crystals

In this lab, you will develop and test a hypothesis about crystal formation.

Problem

How does the rate of cooling affect crystals?

Materials

goggles
plastic spoon
salol
2 microscope slides
tongs
candle
matches
ice cube
hand lens

Procedure

1. Read the whole procedure. Write a hypothesis describing how the rate of cooling will affect the formation of crystals.
2. Put on your goggles. Use a plastic spoon to place a small amount of salol near one end of each of two microscope slides. You need just enough to form a spot 0.5 to 1.0 cm in diameter.
3. Carefully hold one slide with tongs. Warm it gently over a lit candle until the salol is almost completely melted. **CAUTION:** *Move the slide in and out of the flame to avoid cracking the glass.*

4. Set the slide aside to cool slowly.
5. While the first slide is cooling, hold the second slide with tongs and heat it as in Step 3. Cool the slide quickly by placing it on an ice cube. Carefully blow out the candle.
6. Observe the slides under a hand lens. Make a sketch of the crystals that you observe.
7. Compare the appearance of the crystals that form on the two slides.
8. Wash your hands when you are finished.

Analyze and Conclude

1. What was the manipulated variable in this experiment?
2. What was the responding variable?
3. How did the appearance of the crystals on the two slides compare?
4. Describe how your data did or did not support your hypothesis.
5. **Predicting** Inside Earth, some minerals form crystals as melted rock cools slowly. If a mineral forms by slow cooling, would you expect the crystals to be large or small?
6. **Think About It** How did this experiment enable you to test your hypothesis?

Design an Experiment

Design an experiment to test how the rate of evaporation affects the formation of salt crystals from a water and salt mixture. Obtain your teacher's approval before carrying out your experiment.

Program Resources

◆ **Unit 1 Resources** Introduction Skills Lab blackline masters

Safety

Caution students to be careful when heating the slide. Review the safety guidelines in Appendix A.

Guiding Inquiry

Invitation Invitation Ask students: **Why do you think crystals vary in appearance?** *(Accept all reasonable responses at this time.)* Have students contrast manipulated and responding variables. *(A manipulated variable is one that changes in an experiment and a responding variable is one that changes because of the manipulated variable.)*

Introducing the Procedure

◆ Have students read through the complete procedure before beginning. As a class, discuss any questions they might have.

Troubleshooting the Experiment

◆ Students should wear goggles to make sure they do not get salol in their eyes.
◆ Caution students not to overheat the slide, especially the one placed on ice because it might break. Moving the slide from side to side over the flame will prevent overheating.
◆ Keep the slides on which the salol has hardened for remelting by other classes.

Expected Outcome

The crystals that form on the two slides will be of different sizes. On the first slide, the crystals should be smaller, because of the more rapid cooling.

Analyze and Conclude

1. The manipulated variable is the rate of cooling of the salol.
2. The responding variable is the crystal size.
3. The crystals on the first slide are larger than those on the second slide.
4. Answers will vary. Some students may have foreseen the results correctly and confirmed their hypothesis through the experiment.
5. Predicting The crystals formed by slow cooling will be large.
6. Think About It Answers will vary, but should mention the relationship between the hypothesis and the variable involved.

Design an Experiment

A typical design might suggest mixing a solution of water and salt, pouring equal amounts into two identical pans, and then exposing one pan to heat to increase its evaporation rate.

Laboratory Safety

Including all Students

Remind students that electrical devices should not be used near water unless they are specifically designed for such purposes. When using both electricity and water, be sure to keep the two far apart. Also, be sure that all electrical equipment has GFI switches. **learning modality: verbal**

Technology and the Internet in Science

Integrating Technology

Access the Science Explorer website at: **www.phschool.com** Here you will find additional information on topics for every chapter in this book. **learning modality: logical/mathematical**

Laboratory Safety

As you use this textbook, you will conduct many science experiments and other activities. In experiments and activities, it is very important to think about safety. Always follow your teacher's instructions on safety in the laboratory. Before conducting any experiments, review with your teacher the Science Safety Rules in Appendix A on pages 656–657. Also watch for the safety symbols that appear at the beginning of a lab or activity. The symbols alert you to needed precautions, such as wearing goggles to protect your eyes. Learn to recognize the safety symbols and know what precautions they require you to take. The safety symbols are listed in Appendix A on page 655.

Technology and the Internet in Science

Today, many scientists use the latest technology to explore Earth's surface and outer space. Computers, robots, satellites, and space probes are just some of the tools used by scientists. For example, many different satellites constantly scan Earth's surface, collecting data for scientists.

Technology helps scientists collect data. But technology also helps scientists communicate their discoveries to other scientists and to the public. You can find large amounts of information about current research and discoveries in science on the Internet. Web sites maintained by several United States government agencies such as NASA, the U.S. Geological Survey (USGS), and the National Oceanic and Atmospheric Administration (NOAA) are often excellent sources of information. The Web sites of private research institutes and scientific associations also can be very helpful. These Web sites provide data about everything from earthquakes and volcanoes to hurricanes.

Some Branches of Science

Throughout history, people have observed the Earth around them and the skies above them. Over thousands of years, scientists have built a body of knowledge based on these observations.

Chemistry In Unit 1, you will study matter and its properties, key topics in chemistry. **Chemists** are scientists who investigate the particles that make up everything around you and how those particles interact.

Geology Unit 2 of this book deals mainly with geology. Geology is the study of the solid Earth. **Geologists** study the forces that have shaped Earth throughout its long history. Geologists study the material that

These science students are using the Internet to find information on oceanography.

Chandra X-ray Observatory is a satellite placed in orbit in 1999 to detect X-rays given off by distant stars and galaxies.
Posing Questions *What do you think are some questions that astronomers would like to answer with data from* Chandra's *observations?*

forms Earth's surface and interior. Geologists describe landforms, the features sculptured in rock and soil by water, wind, and waves.

Oceanography In Unit 3, you will learn about the water that covers about 75 percent of Earth's surface. Oceanography is the study of Earth's oceans. **Oceanographers** study everything from the chemistry of ocean water to the shape of the ocean floor to living things in the ocean's depths. Scientists in related fields study Earth's fresh water in lakes, rivers, and glaciers and beneath the surface.

Meteorology Unit 4 presents meteorology. Meteorology is the study of Earth's atmosphere. Meteorologists do much more than just forecast tomorrow's weather. **Meteorologists** are scientists who gather information about conditions in the atmosphere from around the world. Scientists in related fields study the forces that slowly change Earth's climate.

Environmental Science Some scientists, called **environmental scientists,** study Earth's environment and resources, which you will learn about in Unit 5. Environmental scientists work together to determine the effects of human activities on Earth's land, air, water, and living things. They try to solve problems, such as pollution, that result from the use of resources. Throughout this textbook, you will find examples of how environmental science relates to the other sciences.

Astronomy Astronomy, the study of the universe beyond Earth, is the subject of Unit 6. Some **astronomers,** like Jane Luu, focus on the solar system. Other astronomers observe stars and galaxies in an effort to understand the universe and its history.

As you can see in *Exploring Careers in Science*, scientists do many different things.

☑ *Checkpoint* *What is astronomy?*

Branches of Science

Real-Life Learning

Ask students: **How often do you check the weather forecast on television?** *(Answers will vary, but students will likely say they check the weather when they have an outdoor activity planned.)* **How do you think the weather report is prepared?** If students do not know the answer, tell them that the weather forecast is prepared by scientists called meteorologists, although on some television stations the person who reports the weather is a reporter, not a scientist. **learning modality: verbal**

Answers to Self-Assessment

Caption Question

Answers will vary, but may include "What are stars made of? What happens when a star explodes? How do stars and galaxies form?"

☑ *Checkpoint*

Astronomy is the study of the universe beyond Earth.

Performance Assessment

Skills Check Have students make concept maps to show the branches of science and what is included in each branch.

EXPLORING

Careers in Science

Have students look at the photographs of the scientists. Point out that most of the scientists are working outdoors. Divide students into five groups and assign each group one of the careers highlighted on the page. Encourage each group to list what they know about the work "their scientist" does and what they would like to learn. Have groups share their knowledge and questions with the whole class. Some questions might be: What kind of education is needed by each scientist? Where might each scientist work? What is the pay scale for jobs in this type of science?

Have each group prepare a notebook with information about this scientist's career. **learning modality: verbal**

Addressing Naive Conceptions

The names of the careers may mislead some students. Emphasize that an oceanographer may study fresh water and climate while an astronomer may study meteors; and environmental scientists may study many of the same things that other scientists do, but from a viewpoint of conserving resources.

Ask students to make a Venn diagram that shows each type of scientist and what they study. Have them show how environmental science might intersect with the other sciences. **learning modality: visual**

EXPLORING Careers in Science

If you worked as a scientist, you might release a weather balloon into the atmosphere. Or you might pilot a submersible deep beneath the ocean or chip samples of rock from a mountain top.

Oceanographers

These oceanographers have donned scuba gear to observe the interactions of living things with the environment on a measured square of ocean floor.

Geologists

The work of geologists often takes them outdoors—from caves beneath the surface (above) to mountainsides (below).

Background

Astronomers usually have at least a college degree and many hold doctoral degrees. There are, however, jobs as assistants available to interested people without as much formal training. Most astronomers do research. Some specialize in studying the motions of planets and other bodies in space. Other astronomers study the makeup of planets or stars.

Geologists usually hold at least a bachelor's degree with a master's degree or a Ph.D. Again, support jobs are available to interested people without as much training. The field of geology offers many choices. Geologists may specialize in the study of Earth's structure and how it relates to earthquakes. Other geologists study types of soil and what can be done to prevent the loss of soil through erosion.

Astronomers

Astronomers use radio telescopes like this one in New Mexico to detect radio waves from distant stars and galaxies.

Meteorologists

Meteorologists use data from weather satellites to monitor storms such as hurricanes. Computers are important in processing and displaying weather data.

Environmental Scientists

These environmental scientists are gathering data by testing water samples to find evidence of environmental change or pollution.

13

Including all Students

Materials *One index card per student*
Time *10 minutes*

Have each student choose one of the five scientific careers shown and draw a picture of one or more things that scientists might study. Group cards by field of science chosen and use them for student presentations about each field. **learning modality: visual, verbal**

Real-Life Learning

Ask students: **If you decided to work as a scientist, which branch would you choose? List your choice and reasons.** After students have completed this book, have them revisit their choices and see if they still feel the same way. **learning modality: verbal**

Cultural Diversity

Ask students why studying one or more languages other than English might be useful to scientists. *(Possible answers: To communicate with scientists from other places in the world, to study work done by scientists in other languages, to facilitate field work or research in another country)*

3 Assess

Ongoing Assessment

Writing Have students list five types of scientists and under each type one thing each might study.

ASSESSMENT

Reviewing Content

True or False

1. inference **2.** true **3.** true
4. Astronomers **5.** true

Multiple Choice

6. b **7.** d **8.** a **9.** d **10.** b

Checking Concepts

11. Science is a way of knowing about the natural world based on observations and logical reasoning.
12. Answers should explain how the evidence gained from the observation led to the student's inference.
13. Scientists cannot always use controlled experiments because many of the things that they study take a very long time, are very large, happened millions of years ago, or are located in space.
14. A hypothesis is a possible explanation for an observation or answer to a scientific question. A hypothesis can be tested by observation or experiment. A scientific theory is a concept that explains a wide range of observations. If scientists test a hypothesis repeatedly and find that the evidence supports the hypothesis, that hypothesis may be accepted as a scientific theory.
15. Scientists interpret the data collected during an experiment to determine whether the data support their hypothesis. Scientists can then draw a conclusion about the hypothesis.
16. Following safety rules ensures that nobody involved in the experiment will be injured. It also protects equipment from damage.
17. A geologist

Thinking Critically

18. Answers may vary. Students may say that you would need to observe the color of sunsets over time and then record what kinds of weather occurred on each following day. If fair weather consistently followed a colorful sunset, then you could conclude that the evidence supported the hypothesis.
19. By controlling all variables but one, scientists can draw a valid conclusion. If more than one variable is changing, scientists cannot tell which variable is the cause of the results that are observed.
20. Other scientists should not accept the hypothesis. For a hypothesis to be accepted, other scientists must be able to repeat the experiment many times and obtain the same results.
21. Astronomy would investigate the temperature of a star; oceanography would investigate the temperature at the bottom of the sea, and meteorology would investigate air temperature on a mountaintop.

ASSESSMENT

Study Guide

Key Ideas

- Science is a way of learning about the natural world and the knowledge gained from that process.
- Scientific methods generally include posing questions, developing and testing hypotheses, and drawing conclusions. Scientists often test hypotheses by conducting controlled experiments.
- A scientific theory is a well-tested scientific concept that explains a wide range of observations.
- The System of International Units (SI) is the standard system of measurement in science.
- In experiments and activities, it is very important to think about safety. Always follow your teacher's instructions on safety in the laboratory.
- Science has several branches, including geology, the study of the solid Earth, and oceanography, the study of the oceans. Meteorology is the science concerned with Earth's atmosphere and the processes that cause the weather. Astronomy is the exploration of the origin and structure of planets, moons, stars, and galaxies.

Key Terms

science	responding variable
scientific inquiry	data
observation	scientific theory
inference	chemists
hypothesis	geologists
controlled experiment	oceanographers
variable	meteorologists
manipulated variable	astronomers
	environmental scientists

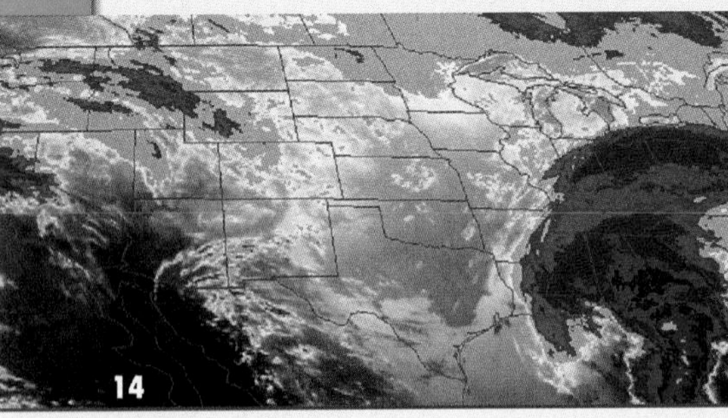

Reviewing Content

True or False

If the statement is true, write true. If it is false, change the underlined word or words to make the statement true.

1. A variable is an interpretation of an observation.
2. The information that a scientist obtains through observation is called data.
3. If an experiment fails to support a scientific theory, scientists will change the theory or abandon it.
4. Meteorologists are scientists who study stars, planets, and other bodies in space.
5. Environmental scientists study the effects of human activities on Earth's land, air, water, and living things.

Multiple Choice

Choose the answer that best completes the sentence.

6. Scientists seek to answer questions about the natural world in a process of
a. modeling. **b.** scientific inquiry.
c. predicting. **d.** developing hypotheses.

7. An explanation that can be tested by observation or experiment is called a(n)
a. experiment. **b.** scientific theory.
c. scientific fact. **d.** hypothesis.

8. One of the factors that can change in an experiment is called a(n)
a. variable. **b.** theory.
c. hypothesis. **d.** observation.

9. One way in which scientists test a hypothesis is by
a. asking questions.
b. drawing conclusions.
c. interpreting data.
d. conducting a controlled experiment.

10. A scientist who studies the features sculptured in rock and soil by water, wind, and waves is a(n)
a. oceanographer.
b. geologist.
c. meteorologist.
d. environmental scientist.

Checking Concepts

11. In your own words, explain briefly what science is.

12. Give an example of an observation of the natural world that you have made. Then give an example of an inference that you made based on that observation. Explain.

13 Why is it often difficult to use controlled experiments to test hypotheses in science? Explain.

14. What is the difference between a hypothesis and a scientific theory?

15 Explain how a scientist would use the data gathered through a controlled experiment.

16. Explain the importance of following safety rules in laboratory experiments.

17. Which kind of scientist would you consult to find out how a feature on Earth's surface like a beach is formed?

Thinking Critically

18. Problem Solving You may have heard the saying, "Red sky at night/Sailor's delight." This expression is a hypothesis: A colorful red sunset means there will be fair weather the next day. Describe a scientific method of testing this hypothesis.

19. Relating Cause and Effect In a controlled experiment, why do scientists try to control all of the variables except one?

20. Making Judgments As a result of just one experiment, a scientist finds evidence that supports a hypothesis. Should other scientists around the world accept this hypothesis? Explain your answer.

21. Classifying Which science would investigate the surface temperature of a star? Water temperature at the bottom of the sea? Air temperature at the top of a mountain?

Test Preparation

Use these questions to prepare for standardized tests.

Read the passage. Then answer Questions 22–25.

It may surprise you to learn that the climate in a large city can be different from the climate just outside the city. Climate is the average, year-to-year, weather conditions in a region. Meteorologists have collected data on these climate differences. The data show that the climate in a city is often warmer and wetter than the climate in the nearby countryside. Cities are also less sunny and windy than the country around them.

Why are cities warmer? One reason is that buildings and paved surfaces absorb and store more of the sun's energy than do grass, crops, and trees. Another reason is that cars, factories, heating, and air conditioning in cities all give off heat.

Scientists think several factors cause increased rainfall in cities. One hypothesis is that the built-up areas of a city form an obstacle to passing storms. As a result, the storms take longer to move over the city, allowing more rain to fall.

22. The best title for this reading selection is
a. Sunny Weather Ahead
b. Meteorologists at Work
c. The Climates of Cities
d. What Causes Storms?

23. Meteorologists found that the climate in a city differs from the climate in the country by
a. asking city residents.
b. collecting data.
c. observing clouds.
d. performing controlled experiments.

24. How would you predict a city could lower its outdoor temperature in the summer?
a. by building more factories
b. by having more parks with grass and trees
c. by putting more cars on the road
d. by adding more air conditioners

25. The idea that a city's buildings can increase rainfall by slowing down a passing storm is an example of a(n)
a. variable. **b.** scientific theory.
c. determining factor. **d.** hypothesis.

Test Preparation

22. c **23.** b **24.** b **25.** d

Program Resources

- **Unit 1 Resources** Introduction Review and Reinforce; Introduction Enrich
- **Performance Assessment** Introduction
- **Chapter and Unit Tests** Introduction Test

Media and Technology

Computer Test Bank
Introduction Test

CHAPTER 1

Introduction to Matter

Sections	Time	Student Edition Activities	ACTIVITY Other Activities
CHAPTER PROJECT **Product Testing** p. 17	Ongoing (2 weeks)	Check Your Progress, pp. 37, 39, 44 Present Your Project, p. 47	
1 Describing Matter and Energy pp. 18–27 ◆ Define matter and energy. ◆ Explain that substances can be identified or classified by their physical and chemical properties. ◆ Explain the differences among elements, compounds, and mixtures. ◆ Distinguish between physical and chemical changes. ◆ Identify different forms of energy, and give examples of energy transformations that affect matter.	3–4 periods/ $1\frac{1}{2}$–2 blocks	**Discover** What is a Mixture?, p. 18 **Try This** Alike or Different?, p. 20 **Sharpen Your Skills** Inferring, p. 25	**TE** Real-Life Learning, pp. 21, 26 **TE** Building Inquiry Skills: Inferring, p. 22 **TE** Demonstration, p. 24 **TE** Including All Students, pp. 24, 25
2 Measuring Matter pp. 28–34 ◆ Explain the difference between weight and mass. ◆ Calculate the density of substances using SI units for mass and volume.	2–3 periods/ 1–$1\frac{1}{2}$ blocks	**Discover** Which Has More Mass?, p. 28 **Try This** Bubble Time, p. 29 **Science at Home,** p. 33 **Skills Lab: Interpreting Data** Making Sense of Density, p. 34	**TE** Building Inquiry Skills: Applying Concepts, p. 29; Making Measurements, p. 32 **TE** Integrating Mathematics, p. 30 **TE** Including All Students, p. 31 **LM** 1, "Determining the Density of Liquids"
3 Particles of Matter pp. 35–39 ◆ Identify atoms as the smallest particles of an element. ◆ Describe Dalton's theory of atoms. ◆ Identify chemical bonds as the force holding atoms together in molecules.	2 periods/ 1 block	**Discover** What's in the Box?, p. 35	**TE** Demonstration, p. 37
4 INTEGRATING EARTH SCIENCE **Elements From Earth** pp. 40–44 ◆ Describe how the density of gold allows it to be panned. ◆ Explain that a chemical reaction is needed to obtain an element from one of its compounds.	2 periods/ 1 block	**Discover** How Can You Separate Bolts From Sand?, p. 40 **Real-World Lab: How It Works** Isolating Copper, pp. 42–43	**TE** Demonstration, p. 44
Study Guide/Chapter Assessment pp. 45–47	1 period/ $\frac{1}{2}$ block	**PLM** Provides blackline masters for Probeware labs	**ISAB** Provides teaching and review of all inquiry skills

For Standard or Block Schedule The Resource Pro® CD-ROM gives you maximum flexibility for planning your instruction for any type of schedule. Resource Pro® contains Planning Express®, an advanced scheduling program, as well as the entire contents of the Teaching Resources and the Computer Test Bank.

CHAPTER PLANNING GUIDE

Program Resources	Assessment Strategies	Media and Technology
UR Chapter 1 Project Teacher Notes **UR** Chapter 1 Project Overview and Worksheets	**SE** Performance Assessment: Present Your Project, p. 47 **TE** Check Your Progress, pp. 37, 39, 44 **UR** Chapter 1 Project Scoring Rubric	Science Explorer Internet Site at www.phschool.com Student Edition on Audio CD, Chapter 1
UR 1-1 Section Lesson Plan **UR** 1-1 Section Summary **UR** 1-1 Review and Reinforce **UR** 1-1 Enrich	**SE** Section 1 Review, p. 27 **TE** Ongoing Assessment, pp. 19, 21, 23, 25 **TE** Performance Assessment, p. 27	
UR 1-2 Section Lesson Plan **UR** 1-2 Section Summary **UR** 1-2 Review and Reinforce **UR** 1-2 Enrich **UR** Skills Lab blackline masters	**SE** Section 2 Review, p. 33 **TE** Ongoing Assessment, pp. 29, 31 **TE** Performance Assessment, p. 33	Concept Videotape Library, Grade 6, Tape 1, "Density"; "The Metric System"; "What's a Cubit?" Lab Activity Videotapes, Grade 6 Tape 1
UR 1-3 Section Lesson Plan **UR** 1-3 Section Summary **UR** 1-3 Review and Reinforce **UR** 1-3 Enrich	**SE** Section 3 Review, p. 39 **TE** Ongoing Assessment, p. 37 **TE** Performance Assessment, p. 39	Concept Videotape Library, Grade 6, Tape 1, "Rutherford's Experiment" Transparency 1, "Models of Molecules"
UR 1-4 Section Lesson Plan **UR** 1-4 Section Summary **UR** 1-4 Review and Reinforce **UR** 1-4 Enrich **UR** Real-World Lab blackline masters	**SE** Section 4 Review, p. 44 **TE** Ongoing Assessment, p. 41 **TE** Performance Assessment, p. 44	Lab Activity Videotapes, Grade 6 Tape 1
RCA Provides strategies to improve science reading skills **GRSW** Provides worksheets to promote student comprehension of content	**SE** Chapter 1 Study Guide/Assessment, pp. 47–47 **PA** Chapter 1 Performance Assessment **CUT** Chapter 1 Test **CTB** Chapter 1 Test	Computer Test Bank, Chapter 1 Test

Key: **SE** Student Edition
CTB Computer Test Bank
ISAB Inquiry Skills Activity Book
GRSW Guided Reading and Study Workbook
TE Teacher's Edition
PTA Product Testing Activities by *Consumer Reports*
RCA Reading in the Content Area
PA Performance Assessment
UR Unit Resources
LM Laboratory Manual
IES Interdisciplinary Explorations Series
CUT Chapter and Unit Tests

Meeting the National Science Education Standards and AAAS Benchmarks

National Science Education Standards	Benchmarks for Science Literacy	Unifying Themes
Science as Inquiry (Content Standard A) ◆ **Develop descriptions, explanations, predictions, and models using evidence** Students investigate density and conclude that the density of a homogeneous substance does not depend on the size of the sample. Students infer chemical characteristics based on evidence. *(Skills Lab, Real-World Lab)* ◆ **Think critically and logically to make the relationships between evidence and explanations** Students construct an apparatus for electrolysis of copper chloride and infer that copper chloride is a compound. *(Real-World Lab)* **Physical Science** (Content Standard B) ◆ **Properties and changes of properties in matter** Each specific substance has its own combination of properties. When matter changes state, physical properties change, but chemical properties do not change. *(Sections 1, 2; Skills Lab)* **Science and Technology** (Content Standard E) ◆ **Abilities of technological design** The physical and chemical properties of elements such as iron, gold, and copper allow them to be commercially exploited. *(Section 4, Real-World Lab)*	**1B Scientific Inquiry** Students investigate the nature of density and investigate how electrolysis can be used to separate an element from a compound. Students design an experiment to compare properties of a consumer product. *(Skills Lab, Real-World Lab, Chapter Project)* **3C Issues in Technology** Mining of gold and other dense metals is made possible by taking advantage of density to separate the metal mechanically. *(Section 4)* **4D Structure of Matter** Matter has both physical and chemical properties. Physical properties can change when the state of matter changes, but chemical properties do not change during changes of state. *(Section 1; Skills Lab)* **11B Models** Students use models to investigate a property of matter, density. *(Skills Lab)* **12D Communication Skills** Students investigate properties of a consumer product and compile and present information to the class. *(Chapter Project)*	◆ **Patterns of Change** When matter changes state, physical properties change, but chemical properties do not change. *(Section 1)* ◆ **Scale and Structure** The physical properties of a substance depend on the arrangement of particles that make up the substance. Mass and volume depend on the amount of substance present, but their ratio, density, is a characteristic property of a substance. *(Section 2; Real-World Lab)* ◆ **Unity and Diversity** The general properties of matter are physical properties. All matter is made of particles. Elements are composed of particles that are all identical. Compounds contain different kinds of particles in fixed ratios. *(Section 1; Real-World Lab)* ◆ **Systems and Interactions** In physical changes, the substances remain unchanged. During chemical changes, new substances with different properties are formed. *(Section 1)* ◆ **Stability** When a substance undergoes a change of state, its physical properties change but it remains the same substance. *(Section 1)*

Take It to the Net

Interactive text at www.phschool.com

Science Explorer comes alive with iText.

- **Complete student text** is accessible from any computer with Internet access or a CD-ROM drive.
- **Animations, simulations, and videos** enhance student understanding and retention of concepts.
- **Self-tests and online study tools** assess student understanding.

STAY CURRENT with **SCIENCE NEWS®**

Find out the latest research and information about Properties of Matter at: **www.phschool.com**

Go to **www.phschool.com** and click on the Science icon.Then click on Science Explorer: Life, Earth, and Physical Science under PH@school.

Student Edition Activities Planner

ACTIVITY	Time (minutes)	Materials *Quantities for one work group*	Skills
Section 1			
Discover, p. 18	15	**Nonconsumable** small objects such as checkers, marbles, and paper clips of different colors and sizes	Inferring
Try This, p. 20	20	**Consumable** powdered sugar, salt, cornstarch, baking powder, water, vinegar **Nonconsumable** hand lens, plastic cup or test tube	Classifying
Sharpen your Skills, p. 25	15	**Consumable** vinegar, bromthymol blue indicator, antacid tablet, resealable plastic bag **Nonconsumable** plastic spoon	Inferring
Section 2			
Discover, p. 28	15	**Nonconsumable** triple-beam balance; objects of different weights such as rocks, plastic drinking cups, aluminum cans, pencils	Drawing Conclusions
Try This, p. 29	10	**Consumable** water, tape, flexible drinking straw **Nonconsumable** large container, clear plastic cup	Inferring
Science at Home, p. 33	home	**Consumable** water, salt, food coloring, clear plastic straw **Nonconsumable** two cups with flat bottoms	Communicating
Skills Lab, p. 34	30	**Consumable** water, paper towels **Nonconsumable** balance; wooden stick, approximately 6 cm long; ball of modeling clay, approximately 5 cm wide; crayon with paper covering removed; graduated cylinder, 100 mL, computer and spreadsheet program (optional)	Interpreting Data, Measuring, Calculating
Section 3			
Discover, p. 35	10	**Nonconsumable** shoe box containing one or more objects such as a candle, pencil, empty soda can, sock, marble, sponge	Inferring
Section 4			
Discover, p. 40	15	**Consumable** water, paper towels **Nonconsumable** dry sand, metal bolts, plastic tray or pie pan, bowl	Designing an Experiment
Real-World Lab, pp. 42–43	30	**Consumable** two paper clips; copper chloride solution (0.6 M), 50–100 mL; index card **Nonconsumable** glass jar, about 250 mL; wires with alligator clips or battery holder with wires; 6-volt battery	Observing, Inferring

A list of all materials required for the Student Edition activities can be found on pages TVA34–TVA40. You can obtain information about ordering materials by calling 1-800-848-9500 or by accessing the Science Explorer Internet site at **www.phschool.com**.

CHAPTER 1 PROJECT

Product Testing

Many students consider chemistry and chemicals as divorced from everyday matter. They can see in this project how properties of matter can be investigated by comparing household products.

Purpose In this project, students design experiments to test a chosen property of three similar brands of a consumer product. The emphasis is on designing experiments that are easily duplicated and have reproducible results. The project should help students recognize the physical properties of everyday consumer products.

Skills Focus After completing the Chapter 1 Project, students will be able to

- pose questions about the properties of matter;
- design experiments in which they control variables, interpret data, and draw conclusions;
- compare results from having two people follow the same procedure;
- communicate their findings about their product to their classmates.

Project Time Line This project will take approximately two weeks to complete. During the first week, students brainstorm a list of products they might select to study, then design experiments and develop procedures to study a physical property of their products. Students should consult with a first partner to get advice about their experimental designs. During the beginning of the second week, students conduct their experiments, collect data, and draw conclusions. At this time, assign students new partners with whom they can exchange procedures and materials. Students then conduct their partners' experiments. At the end of the second week, students complete their projects, compare their results with those of their second partner, and present their work to the class.

Before beginning the project, see the Chapter 1 Project Teacher Notes in Unit 1 Resources for more details on carrying out the project. Distribute to students the Chapter 1 Project Overview, Worksheets, and Scoring Rubric in Unit 1 Resources.

Possible Materials Possible materials include paper towels, batteries, tomato sauces, adhesive tapes, and laundry detergents. Encourage students to suggest and use other materials, but make sure they consider the cost of the products when they design their experiments. Students should also obtain enough materials so they and their partners can conduct experiments with repeated trials.

Launching the Project To introduce the project, bring two brands of a product into the classroom, for example, two brands of paper towels. Ask: **How could you determine which product works better?** *(Sample: Conduct an experiment that measures a physical property, such as the absorbency of the paper towels.)*

Allow time for students to read the description of the project in their text and the Chapter Project Overview in Unit 1 Resources. Then discuss the physical properties of matter and materials that could be used. Distribute copies of the Chapter 1 Project Worksheets in Unit 1 Resources for students to review.

Review experimental design with the class, as outlined in the Skills Handbook. Make sure students understand their results should be measurable. They should record their data in a data table, and may present the data in a graph at the end of the project. Students should be able to interpret their data and draw conclusions they can discuss in their class presentation.

CHAPTER 1 PROJECT

Product Testing

Antiques at a Virginia country store

Blue glass bottles, wooden chairs, a doll and her dress, a metal pitcher, and a straw hat are for sale at a country store. These items and others in the photo are just some examples of the materials that make up our world. The scientific name for these materials is matter. Every object in this photograph—actually, every object in the world—is an example of matter. Also, materials have different properties, such as color, shape, and hardness. It's the properties of a particular material that determine whether it is useful for a specific purpose.

Your Goal Compare a property of matter in three different brands of a consumer product.

To complete the project you will

- design a comparison test of a consumer-product property
- conduct the comparison test designed by a partner
- analyze the data you and a partner obtained
- follow the safety guidelines in Appendix A

Get Started As a class, brainstorm a list of different products to compare. For each product, write down several properties that could be compared, including those related to promotional claims of manufacturers. For example, paper towels may absorb different amounts of water. Review Designing an Experiment in the Skills Handbook.

Check Your Progress You'll be working on this project as you study this chapter. To keep your project on track, look for Check Your Progress boxes at the following points.

Section 1 Review, page 27: Design an experiment.
Section 3 Review, page 39: Perform the procedure.
Section 4 Review, page 44: Trade procedures with your partner.

Present Your Project At the end of the chapter (page 47), you and your second partner will present the data collected.

Integrating Earth Science

SECTION 4 **Elements From Earth**

Discover **How Can You Separate Bolts From Sand?**
Real-World Lab **Isolating Copper**

17

Performance Assessment

The Chapter 1 Project Scoring Rubric in Unit 1 Resources will help you evaluate how well students complete the Chapter 1 Project.

Students are assessed on

- how well their procedures test the properties chosen to study and allow for conclusive tests in the time allowed;
- whether their experimental procedures are clearly written, easy to follow, and allow for repeated trials and quantifiable results;
- whether their presentations and data comparisons are thorough and well organized;
- how well they work with other students in exchanging procedures.

By sharing the Chapter 1 Project Scoring Rubric with students at the beginning of the project, you will make it clear to them what they are expected to do.

Program Resources

- **Unit 1 Resources** Chapter 1 Project Teacher Notes; Chapter 1 Project Overview and Worksheets; Chapter 1 Project Scoring Rubric

Media and Technology

Student Edition on Audio CD
Chapter 1

www.phschool.com

You will find an Internet activity, chapter self-tests for students, and links to other chapter topics at this site.

SECTION 1 Describing Matter and Energy

Objectives

After completing the lesson, students will be able to

- ◆ define matter and energy;
- ◆ explain that substances can be identified or classified by their physical and chemical properties;
- ◆ explain the differences among elements, compounds, and mixtures;
- ◆ distinguish between physical and chemical changes;
- ◆ identify different forms of energy, and give examples of energy transformations that affect matter.

Key Terms matter, energy, chemistry, substance, physical property, chemical property, element, compound, mixture, physical change, state, chemical change

1 Engage/Explore

Activating Prior Knowledge

Ask students to describe how they identify unfamiliar objects. Challenge them to make a list of qualities they observe, such as size, color, shape, texture, smell, and weight. Then ask a volunteer to describe a common object to the class using descriptions from each category on the list. The other students should listen to the description and identify the object.

DISCOVER ACTIVITY

Skills Focus inferring
Materials *small objects such as checkers, marbles, and paper clips of different colors and sizes*
Time 15 minutes
Tips Encourage students to think about the properties of objects as they sort the objects.
Think It Over Students will likely group objects of the same type together, for example checkers in one group, paper clips in another group. Students may infer that a substance has one set of properties, while a mixture may be made of parts that have different properties.

SECTION 1 Describing Matter and Energy

DISCOVER ACTIVITY

What Is a Mixture?

1. Your teacher will give you a handful of objects, such as checkers, marbles, and paper clips of different sizes and colors.
2. Examine the objects. Then sort them into at least three groups. Each item should be grouped with other similar items.
3. Describe the differences between the unsorted handful and the sorted groups of objects. Then make a list of the characteristics of each sorted group.

Think It Over

Inferring The handful of objects represents a mixture. Your sorted groups represent substances. Using your observations, infer what the terms *mixture* and *substance* mean.

GUIDE FOR READING

- ◆ Why is it useful to know the physical and chemical properties of matter?
- ◆ What happens when elements combine?
- ◆ How do physical and chemical changes differ?
- ◆ How are energy and changes in matter related?

Reading Tip Before you read, use the headings to outline the section. As you read, add information to your outline.

You're watching a soccer game on an autumn afternoon. There's the whistle. The player kicks the ball, and it moves straight down the field into the net! You've just seen a goal. You've also just seen an example of the interaction of matter and energy. People use the words *matter* and *energy* in different ways. How often have you heard someone say, "As a matter of fact, . . ." or "Hey, what's the matter?" Maybe you've heard, "That team plays with a lot of energy!" Are these phrases familiar? What do the words mean in science?

Defining Matter and Energy

Scientists define **matter** as anything that has mass and takes up space. Mass is how much of something you have. As you learn more about matter and mass in this chapter, these terms will become more meaningful to you. Thinking about examples of matter is an easy way to get an idea of what matter is.

Examples of matter ▶

READING STRATEGIES

Reading Tip Help students preview the section and locate the blue-green main headings and purple sub-headings. Remind students to leave space below headings so that they can add information as they read. Students' outlines might begin like this:

I. Describing Matter and Energy
  A. Defining Matter and Energy
  B. Classifying Matter
    1. Physical Properties
    2. Chemical Properties
  C. Kinds of Matter
    1. Elements
    2. Compounds
    3. Mixtures

Figure 1 Fuel burning in the engines of this boat provides energy that turns the paddle wheel.

Matter is the "stuff" that makes up everything in the universe. Fruit, softballs, tools, animals, rain, flowers—all these are examples of matter. Even air is matter. It may be invisible, but you know it is there when you feel a cool breeze on your face or watch bubbles rise in a fish tank.

Energy is the ability to do work or cause change. Change can sometimes mean motion, that is, moving matter from one place to another. When you pound a nail, energy moves the hammer that drives the nail into a board. Energy even moves your hand. Change can also mean a change in form. A kettle of water that goes from room temperature to boiling on the stove tells you something about energy. Energy is always involved when changes in matter occur. The study of the properties of matter and how matter changes is called **chemistry.**

Classifying Matter by Its Physical and Chemical Properties

In addition to having mass and taking up space, matter has a variety of characteristics, or properties, that can differ. For example, matter can be solid, liquid, or gas. In turn, solid matter can be hard or soft, rough or smooth, square or round. Some kinds of matter catch fire easily. Others don't. The properties of matter usually fall into two groups—physical properties and chemical properties. **Physical and chemical properties are used to identify, describe, and classify matter.** A single kind of matter that has distinct physical and chemical properties is called a **substance.**

Program Resources

- **Unit 1 Resources** 1-1 Lesson Plan; 1-1 Section Summary
- **Guided Reading and Study Workbook** Section 1-1

2 Facilitate

Defining Matter and Energy

Inquiry Challenge

ACTIVITY

Students can learn more about matter and energy by using the five senses of smell, sight, taste, hearing, and touch. Have students list the five senses and then describe examples of matter and energy that they might detect using each sense. For example, if students hear a thunderstorm, they are detecting electrical energy and the matter that makes up clouds and rain. **learning modality: logical/mathematical**

Language Arts Connection

Have students use dictionaries to compare the meanings of the terms *matter, material, mass,* and *substance.* Have students share the various definitions they found. Help them distinguish between scientific and everyday meanings of the terms. **learning modality: verbal**

Classifying Matter by Its Physical and Chemical Properties

Including All Students

Point out that both matter and energy have properties, or characteristics, and that these can be used to classify matter and energy into different types. Have students describe three types of matter; for example, solids, liquids, and gases. Then ask for three types of energy. Students may mention heat, light, motion, and nuclear. Explain that, as students learn more about matter and energy, they will be able to create more comprehensive classification systems. **learning modality: logical/mathematical**

Ongoing Assessment

Writing Ask students to briefly define matter and energy in their own words.

Classifying Matter by Its Physical and Chemical Properties, continued

Addressing Naive Conceptions

List common substances such as wood, plastic, or metals on the board, and have student describe properties of each. Write the properties next to the items. Ask: **Which of these properties do you think could be used to identify a substance?** *(Sample answer: color, size, shape, odor)* Help students understand that properties such as size or weight refer to an individual object and not to the substance of which it is made. **learning modality: logical/ mathematical**

TRY THIS — ACTIVITY

Skills Focus classifying

Materials *powdered sugar, salt, cornstarch, baking powder, hand lens, plastic cup or test tube, water, vinegar*

Time 20 minutes

Tips Have students make five-column data tables to record and compare their observations. The column titles can be: Substance, Appearance, Texture, With Water, and With Vinegar.

Expected Outcome In Steps 1 and 2, students are looking for physical properties such as color and texture. The sugar and salt will look like crystals when examined with the hand lens; the cornstarch and baking powder will appear dusty. In Steps 3 and 4 students observe another physical property—how easily each substance dissolves in water or vinegar. In addition, the baking powder will fizz, or create bubbles. This is evidence of a chemical property because a new substance—the gas—has been produced. *(The gas is carbon dioxide.)*

Extend Have students choose several other common kitchen substances such as corn syrup, lemon juice, and cooking oil. Students can look for physical and chemical properties of these substances and add them to their data tables. **learning modality: tactile/ kinesthetic**

Alike or Different? — ACTIVITY

1. Examine samples of powdered sugar, salt, cornstarch, and baking powder.
2. With a hand lens, look closely at each substance. Then rub a little of one substance between your fingers. Repeat with each of the other substances. Record your observations. Wash your hands.
3. Place one spoonful of each substance in a different plastic cup or test tube. Add two spoonfuls of water to each substance. Record any changes.
4. Repeat Step 3, using vinegar instead of water. Record any changes.

Classifying Make a list of properties for each of the substances. Based on your observations, can you group any of the substances together? Explain.

Physical Properties Have you ever smelled a bottle of vinegar? Whew! You can't miss its sharp odor. You wouldn't mistake its taste for the sweet taste of sugar, either. Odor and taste are physical properties. A **physical property** is a characteristic of a substance that can be observed without changing the substance into something else.

Other physical properties include hardness, texture, color, and the temperature at which a solid melts or a liquid boils. Every diamond, for example, is hard enough to scratch glass. Every sample of pure water boils at 100°C. Even when you describe a substance as a solid, a liquid, or a gas, you are stating one of its physical properties. Some types of matter can be easily classified based on their physical properties. Iron, copper, and aluminum may be different substances, but you know by looking at them that they are all metals.

Chemical Properties Some properties can't be determined just by looking at or touching a substance. Instead, you must change the substance to find out about such properties. A **chemical property** is a characteristic that is observed when a substance interacts with another substance. Like physical properties, chemical properties are used to classify substances. If you hold a toothpick and an iron rod in a candle flame, the toothpick will burn, but the rod will not. Burning, or flammability, is a chemical property of the substances in wood but is not a property of iron. Another chemical property involves rusting. Suppose you place an iron rod and a toothpick on a paper towel moistened with salt water. In a few days, the toothpick will remain unchanged, but the iron will react with water to form rust. Still other chemical properties determine whether a substance will explode like fireworks or tarnish like a piece of silverware.

☑ ***Checkpoint*** *What is an example of a physical property of a candle? What is an example of a chemical property of a candle?*

Figure 2 These medals are made of different substances but share many physical properties that classify them as metals.

20

Background

Integrating Science In chemistry, water is discussed as a pure compound, H_2O. In nature, water is found not as a pure compound, but as a mixture. Sea water contains a mixture of salts, mostly sodium chloride. The water in lakes and rivers contains varying amounts of dissolved minerals. After a heavy rain, river water also contains particles of silt in suspension. Drinking water is not pure H_2O. Water from a well contains dissolved minerals. Water from a city water distribution system often contains dissolved minerals and also small amounts of chlorine or other chemicals added to reduce the amount of bacteria.

For laboratory use, chemists often need pure water. Water can be purified for lab use by distillation. Tap water is boiled and the water vapor that is given off is condensed. The condensed water is pure H_2O.

Figure 3 A geodesic dome, a bridge, and a skyscraper are all made from steel, but their uses are very different. *Inferring Based on the uses shown in these photos, what properties of steel make it useful for a variety of construction projects?*

Kinds of Matter

Take an imaginary walk through your city or town and notice all the buildings. Their shapes, sizes, and uses are very different, but they are all constructed of a few kinds of materials. Bricks, wood, glass, stone, concrete, and steel are some of the most common forms of matter used in building. Using these forms of matter, people have built many different structures.

Elements Just as many different buildings are made from a few kinds of materials, all the different kinds of matter in the universe are made from a few more than 100 different substances, called elements. An **element** is a substance that cannot be broken down into any other substances by chemical or physical means. Each element can be identified by its specific physical and chemical properties. Elements and the letter symbols used to represent them are shown on the Periodic Table in Appendix C.

You have experience with some elements in the world around you. Examples include aluminum foil and copper coatings on pennies. Oxygen and nitrogen gases are two elements in the air you breathe.

Answers to Self-Assessment

Caption Question

Figure 3 Steel is strong and it resists rusting.

☑ Checkpoint

Examples of physical properties of a candle may be: solid, smooth texture; soft enough to cut with a knife. Flammability is an example of a chemical property.

Kinds of Matter

Real-Life Learning

ACTIVITY

Have students collect samples of items around their homes that are made of common elements. Encourage students to look for items made of iron, copper, aluminum, and carbon. Make a display of the items students find. You may wish to have students use periodic tables of elements to check that their choices are elements rather than compounds or mixtures. **learning modality: tactile/ kinesthetic**

Addressing Naive Conceptions

Students may think that familiar substances such as glass, wood, and steel must be elements because they are so common. Emphasize the definition—that an element is not made of other substances. Point out that students may not be able to identify whether a substance is an element by looking at it. They may need to check books or other reference sources to find out what a substance is made of. For example, steel is an alloy of iron and carbon. **learning modality: verbal**

Building Inquiry Skills: Classifying

Materials *worksheets with simplified periodic table of element*
Time 20 minutes

Introduce the periodic table of the elements to students. Explain that it is a way of organizing all the known elements. Point out that each element has a chemical symbol—usually one or two letters that stand for the element. Have students find familiar elements such as iron, gold, silver, and oxygen. Have each student choose three familiar elements, name one or two properties of each, and state whether each element ordinarily exists as a solid, a liquid, or a gas. **learning modality: visual**

Ongoing Assessment

Oral Presentation Ask students to give examples of properties that would help them identify water.

Math TOOLBOX

Encourage students to use ratios to compare items in the classroom. Ask them to find the ratio of boys to girls, brown eyes to blue eyes, and so on. Point out that in each case they may write the ratio, 1 to 4, or use symbols, 1:4. Have students use the information they gather to compose sentences. For example, "In this class, the ratio of boys to girls is 12 to 13." **learning modality: logical/mathematical**

Building Inquiry Skills: Inferring

ACTIVITY

Organize the class into three groups. Give each group an index card on which you have written one of the following terms: *mixture, compound,* or *element.* Groups can take turns asking other groups indirect questions that can be answered yes or no, with the goal of finding out which card each group holds. Students may not ask, for example, "Is it an element?" or "Is it a mixture?" Encourage students to ask questions that will give the most information in the least number of turns. For instance, "Is it made of elements?" will yield a yes answer regardless of which card is chosen. In contrast, "Can it be broken down into parts?" separates mixtures and compounds *(yes)* from elements *(no)* in a single turn. **cooperative learning**

Math TOOLBOX

Ratios

A ratio compares two numbers. It tells you how much you have of one item in comparison to how much you have of another. For example, a recipe for cookies calls for 2 cups of flour for every 1 cup of sugar. You can write the ratio of flour to sugar as:

2 to 1 or 2 : 1

The elements in a compound are present in a specific ratio. If two compounds contain the same elements in different ratios, such as CO and CO_2, they are different compounds.

Compounds Most elements are found in nature combined with other elements. A **compound** is a substance made of two or more elements chemically combined in a set ratio, or proportion. For example, the carbon dioxide gas you breathe out is a compound made of carbon and oxygen. Any sample of carbon dioxide will always be made of one part carbon to two parts oxygen (CO_2). Table salt (sodium chloride) is made of one part sodium to one part chlorine (NaCl).

You use many compounds every day. The fruit sugar that makes juice taste sweet, the water that you drink when you are thirsty, and the cavity-fighting ingredient in your toothpaste are all compounds made from different combinations of elements. Each compound has its own specific properties. Water at room temperature, for example, is a clear, colorless liquid.

When elements are combined to make a compound, the new substance has properties different from those of the original elements. Consider table sugar, for example. It is a compound made from three elements—carbon, oxygen, and hydrogen. The sugar crystals do not resemble the carbon you see in charcoal or the colorless gases oxygen and hydrogen.

Mixtures Most matter that you find in the environment occurs as mixtures. A **mixture** is made from two or more substances—elements, compounds, or both—that are in the same place but are not chemically combined. Mixtures differ from compounds in two ways. First, the substances in a mixture keep their individual properties. Second, the parts of a mixture are not necessarily present in set ratios.

Consider a handful of moist soil. If you look at the soil through a hand lens, you will find particles of sand, tiny bits of clay, maybe even pieces of decaying plants. If you squeeze the soil, you might force out a few drops of water. Another sample of soil won't necessarily contain the same amount of water or any other material. Soil from a flowerpot in your home may be very different from the soil in a nearby park.

☑ *Checkpoint* *Why is soil a mixture and not a compound?*

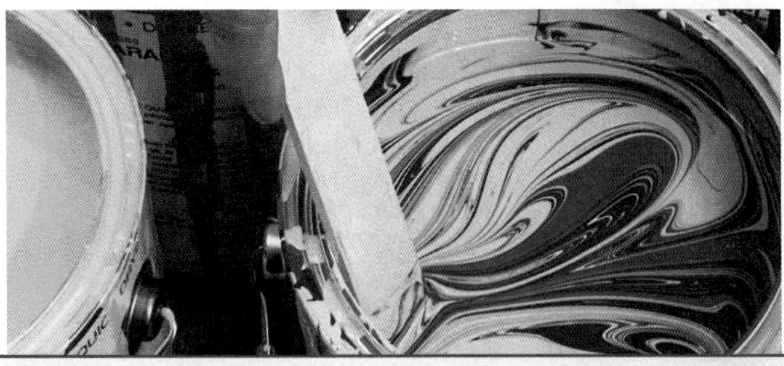

Figure 4 The element silver (above) is sometimes found in a wiry, tree-shaped form. The paints (right) are mixtures of several compounds. The compounds that give paints their colors are called pigments.

22

Background

Integrating Earth Science About one eighth of Earth's crust is made up of silica minerals. Quartz, which is made of silicon dioxide (SiO_2), is the most common of these minerals. It is a valuable natural resource; industries consume millions of tons of quartz yearly. Sand, a primary ingredient of concrete and mortar, is largely quartz. Many common building stones are also quartz. Its hardness has made it indispensable in sandpaper and for polishing and cutting glass, stone, and metal. Carbonate minerals make up approximately one seventh of Earth's sediments and sedimentary rocks and about one fiftieth of its crust. Calcite, one type of carbonate known for beautiful crystals, is widely distributed. It is the main ingredient in limestones and marbles. A particular form of calcite, Iceland spar, is used in optical instruments.

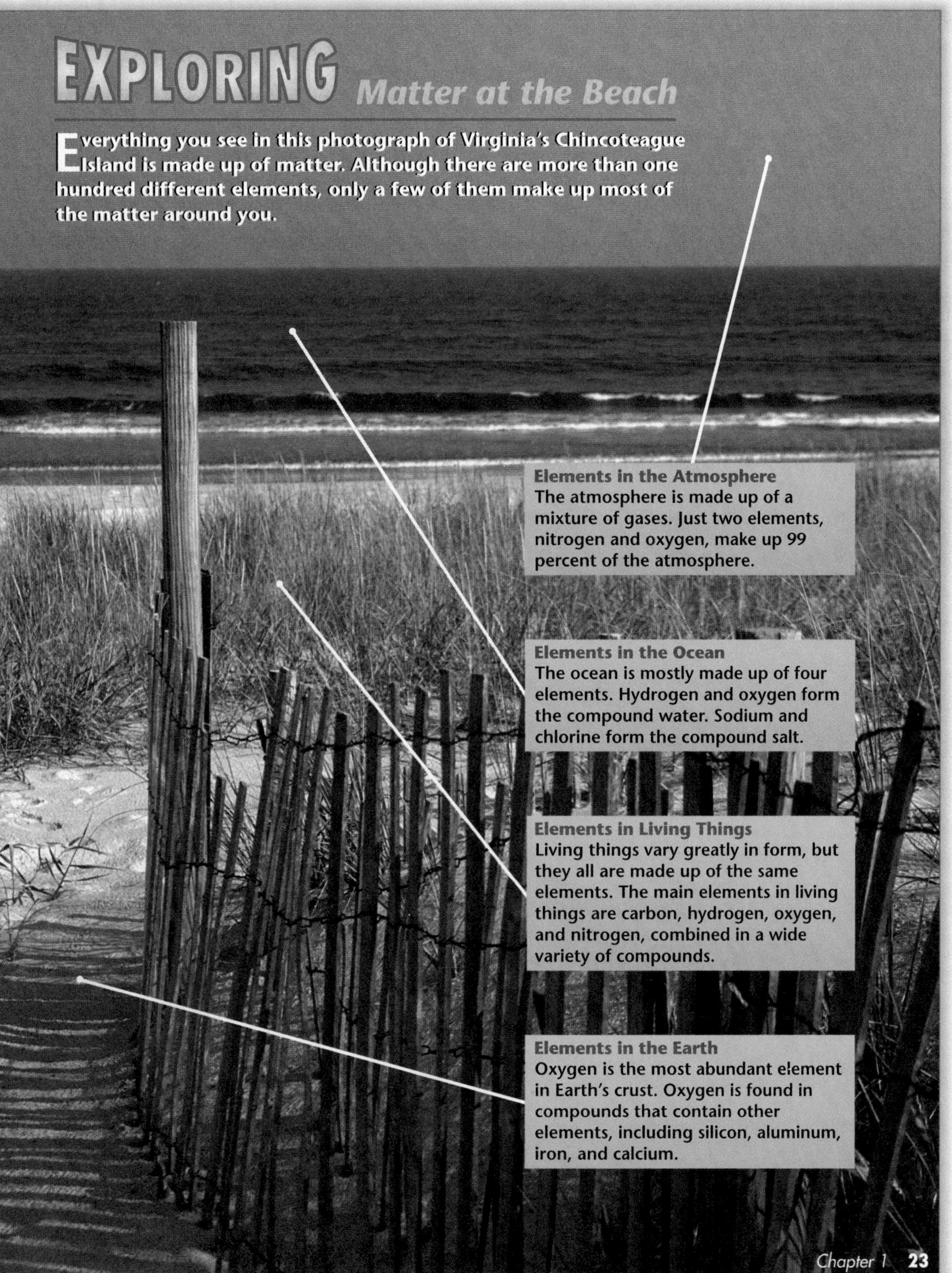

Answers to Self-Assessment

Checkpoint

The substances that make up soil are not chemically combined, and they may not be present in the same ratio in two different samples of soil.

EXPLORING

Matter at the Beach

Direct student's attention to the description of matter in Earth. Explain that the crust is Earth's outermost layer. Some students may find it strange that oxygen is so abundant in the solid crust. Inform students that the crust contains many compounds, called minerals, that contain oxygen. For example, some beach sand is a mixture of a mineral called quartz and tiny fragments of shells. Quartz is actually silicon dioxide, SiO_2, a compound containing silicon and oxygen. Ask: **How is the compound silicon dioxide different from its element, oxygen?** *(Oxygen is a gas, whereas silicon dioxide is a solid.)* Then, have students identify the living things in the photograph. Explain that organisms like these contain compounds called carbohydrates and fats, which are all made of the elements carbon, hydrogen, and oxygen. Other compounds in living things include proteins, which in addition to carbon, hydrogen, and oxygen contain nitrogen and sometimes other elements such as sulfur and phosphorus.

Extend Obtain several different samples of sand and allow students to examine the samples with a hand lens. Ask students how the mixtures are similar and how they are different. **learning modality: visual**

Building Inquiry Skills: Classifying

Encourage students to think about the objects around them, at home, and at places they may have visited. Suggest they classify some of the materials around them first as mixtures, elements, or compounds. Encourage them to find at least two examples of each type. Have the class share their classifications and come to an agreement on each object, then compose a master list. **learning modality: verbal**

Ongoing Assessment

Oral Presentation Ask students to give examples of mixtures and compounds.

Changes in Matter

Demonstration

Materials *tin can, matches, paper*
Time 10 minutes

Tear some of the paper into small pieces, dropping them into the can. Ask: **Is this a physical or chemical change? Why?** *(Physical; the appearance changed but the original substances are still present.)* Next, carefully burn a piece of paper in the can. Again, ask students to identify the change as chemical or physical and to give a reason. *(Chemical; a new substance—ash—is now in the can and the paper is gone.)* **limited English proficiency**

Including All Students

Materials *small paper cups, ice cubes*
Time 10 minutes

To give extra help to students who have difficulty understanding how matter can change properties, distribute ice cubes in small paper cups to each student. Ask them to describe the ice cube using terms in the text, such as *smooth, hard, soft, colorless, cold,* or other appropriate terms. As the ice cube melts, have students use new terms to describe the new properties of water. Ask them which properties changed and which stayed the same as the ice cube melted. **learning modality: tactile/kinesthetic**

Changes in Matter

Try to think of a world where nothing ever changes. Pretty boring, isn't it? Actually, you couldn't even survive in such a world because changes must occur inside your body if you are to remain alive. A sandwich that you eat for lunch must be changed by your body into muscle, blood, and other things you need. Chemists study both physical and chemical changes.

Physical Change Think of going to a costume party and seeing someone dressed as a clown. Could it be someone you know? How can you tell? Putting on a costume can make someone look quite different, but the person hasn't changed. So it is with some changes in matter. A change that alters the form or appearance of a material but does not make the material into another substance is called a **physical change.** Examples of physical changes include chopping wood, bending copper wire into new shapes, or molding clay.

Matter has three principal **states,** or forms—solid, liquid, and gas. A change in state is another example of physical change. Matter can change from one state to another when the temperature changes. For example, ice cubes are made of solid (frozen) water. They will melt in a tray left on your kitchen table, forming liquid water. If you return the tray to the freezer, the water will become ice again. But if you leave the tray on the table overnight, some of the water will escape into the air as a gas. Water remains the same substance whether it's in the form of a solid, a liquid, or a gas. It is still made of two parts hydrogen and one part oxygen (H_2O).

Checkpoint *Why is a change in state considered to be a physical change?*

Figure 5 Wood can be chopped into different shapes (above). The bubble below is a thin film of liquid that changes shape around a body of air.
Interpreting Photographs *How can you tell that these changes are physical changes?*

24

Background

Facts and Figures Four physical states of matter are solid, liquid, gas, and plasma. While the first three are familiar, the fourth is quite rare on Earth. The sun and other stars consist of plasma, gas-like matter made of bare atomic nuclei and free electrons.

Five changes in the physical state of matter are melting, freezing, vaporization, condensation, and sublimation. (In sublimation, a substance goes directly from a solid to a gas without passing through the liquid state.) Energy changes are always involved when a change of state occurs. Energy is lost by a substance when it changes from a gas to a liquid or from a liquid to a solid. A change from a solid to a liquid or from a liquid to a gas requires the addition of energy.

Figure 6 Unlike a physical change, a chemical change alters the identity of a substance. In a forest fire, wood is changed into gases and other substances, and energy is released.

Chemical Change A change in matter that produces new substances is called a **chemical change,** or a chemical reaction. In a chemical change, elements may combine to form compounds, or compounds may be broken down into elements, or compounds may change into other compounds. **Unlike a physical change, a chemical change produces new substances with properties different from the original substances.**

Some familiar examples of chemical changes include the souring of milk and the burning of wood. When wood burns, the compounds of the wood combine with oxygen in the air to make new substances. These new substances include carbon dioxide, water, and other compounds. The element carbon is left in the ashes. Each of these new substances can be identified by its properties, which are different from those of the original wood.

Energy and Matter

As you learned earlier, energy and changes in matter go hand-in-hand. Recall that energy may be defined as the ability to do work or cause change. Energy can have different forms, and it can be transformed from one form to another. The idea of energy becomes easier to understand if you remember that what you often observe is the *effects* of energy on matter. Soup boiling on a stove and the sound of clapping hands both result from energy affecting matter. You can detect the effects of energy when matter is moved, when it reacts, or when energy is transformed from one form to another. **Energy is always involved when physical and chemical changes occur in matter.** The following pages describe some forms of energy and its interactions with matter.

Sharpen your Skills

Inferring

1. Put a large spoonful of vinegar into a large resealable plastic bag. As instructed by your teacher, carefully smell the contents.
2. Add a drop of bromthymol blue indicator to the bag. (Bromthymol blue has a different color in different types of some water mixtures.)
3. Add an antacid tablet and seal the bag. Note any changes to the matter in the bag.
4. Based on the changes you observed, do you think there was a physical change to the matter in the bag? Explain.

Answers to Self-Assessment

Caption Question

Figure 5 The changes are physical because the materials are changing in shape. No new substances are produced.

Checkpoint

A change in state alters the form and appearance of a substance but does not transform it into a new substance.

Sharpen your Skills

Inferring

Materials *vinegar, resealable plastic bag, plastic spoon, bromthymol blue indicator, antacid tablet*

ACTIVITY

Time 15 minutes

Tips Show students how to smell the contents of the bag by waving one hand over the bag to move some of the fumes toward the nose.

Expected Outcome The bromthymol blue will change color from yellow to blue, showing that the liquid has become less acidic. Students can infer that the antacid tablet changed the vinegar into one or more other substances. Thus, the change was chemical. Students may also observe bubbles or fizzing, evidence for a chemical change.

Extend Have students repeat the experiment using liquid antacid. Students may observe that the chemical change occurs more quickly. **learning modality: logical/mathematical**

Energy and Matter

Including All Students

Materials *sponge, balloon, tuning fork, wood block*

ACTIVITY

Time 10 minutes

Have small groups of students perform these activities and identify the energy source and the object that gains energy.

- blow up a balloon *(energy source—diaphragm and chest muscles; object—the stretched balloon)*
- strike a tuning fork on a table *(energy source—hand or arm; object—the vibrating tuning fork)*
- compress a large soft sponge with a brick *(energy source—weight of the brick; object—compressed sponge)*

learning modality: tactile/kinesthetic

Ongoing Assessment

Skills Check Have students describe examples of a physical change and a chemical change in a metal. *(Sample: Melting is physical; rusting is chemical.)*

Energy and Matter, continued

Addressing Naive Conceptions

Some students may think that energy cannot change form. Show students a flashlight with the batteries next to it. Ask them to identify the form of energy stored in the batteries. *(chemical)* Then place the batteries in the flashlight and turn it on. Ask: **What form of energy do you see?** *(electromagnetic)* Allow students to place their hands near the bulb of the flashlight. Ask: **What form of energy do you feel?** *(thermal)* **learning modality: visual**

Building Inquiry Skills: Applying Concepts

Encourage students to describe each type of energy in their own words. Challenge students to think of one or two examples of each type of energy. **limited English proficiency**

Real Life Learning

Materials *wintergreen candies, small mirrors*
Time 15 minutes

Not all wintergreen candies work. Test different brands to see which do work.

CAUTION: *Since small pieces of candy can stick in the throat, give students access to a water fountain. Some students may find the wintergreen flavor unpleasant.* Pass out candies to each student. Darken the room. (Note: The room must be very dark and time must be allowed for eyes to adjust.) Have students chew the candies with their lips open as they watch themselves in the mirrors. As each piece of candy is crushed, they will see tiny flashes of white or bluish-white light. Ask: **What kind of energy did the mints have?** *(chemical)* **What kind of energy did your teeth add?** *(mechanical)* **What kind of energy did you see?** *(electromagnetic)* Explain that this is an example of triboluminescence, luminescence induced by friction. **learning modality: visual**

Figure 7 A tornado strikes buildings in Pampa, Texas. *Interpreting Diagrams Will the houses in the path of this tornado undergo a physical or a chemical change? Explain your answer.*

Mechanical Energy Mechanical energy is related to the motion or position of matter. When you shoot a basketball, energy is transferred from your hands to the ball. If you transfer just the right amount of mechanical energy in just the right way, the ball flies into the basket. A skateboard rolling down a hill is another example of mechanical energy.

Thermal Energy One of the most familiar forms of energy is thermal energy, which you sense as heat. All matter is made of small particles that are constantly in motion. If thermal energy is added to matter, the particles move faster, and the matter feels warmer than it did before the energy was added. If thermal energy is lost, the particles move more slowly, and the matter feels cooler than before. Remember the ice cube tray mentioned earlier? To make ice, you would put liquid water into the tray and leave it in the freezer. Thermal energy is lost from the water to the surroundings, and the water freezes. On a hot day, thermal energy in your surroundings will quickly melt the ice if you take the tray out and forget to put it back.

Electromagnetic Energy A familiar form of electromagnetic energy is light. X-rays, microwaves, radio and TV signals, and ultraviolet rays are also forms of electromagnetic energy. When electromagnetic energy interacts with matter, it can produce physical or chemical changes. For example, a microwave oven can change a frozen block of spaghetti and tomato sauce into a piping hot meal—a physical change. This change occurs with the transformation of electromagnetic energy to thermal energy. A similar kind of transformation can produce chemical changes, too. Without sunblock, people at a beach who are exposed to electromagnetic energy from the sun can experience painful chemical changes to the matter that makes up their skin. You know this effect as sunburn.

Electrical Energy A moving electric charge produces electricity. The energy of these moving charges is electrical energy. Electrical energy becomes useful when it is transformed into other forms of energy. In factories, for example, electrical energy is transformed into mechanical energy that turns the large motors

26

Background

Integrating Science As the sun warms Earth's land and water, water evaporates and thermal energy is stored in the air containing the evaporated water. When this stored thermal energy is released, it can cause violent storms. The thermal energy is released when warm air cools and condenses, forming liquid water. An average thunderstorm releases about 36 terajoules of energy. Severe storms can release up to 100 times more energy.

The thermal energy stored in warm air also forms tornadoes and hurricanes. A tornado may have wind speeds that exceed 800 km per hour. Hurricanes, which are much larger than tornadoes, release even more energy. They form over warm ocean waters where evaporation takes place. Winds near the eye may be as high as 300 kilometers per hour, and a hurricane may be over 2,000 km in diameter.

of manufacturing equipment. In a light bulb, electrical energy is transformed as it interacts with the metal wire in the bulb. With the flick of a switch, electrical energy is transformed into thermal energy and light.

Chemical Energy Matter itself contains energy known as chemical energy. Chemical energy is transformed to other forms of energy during a chemical reaction. When a candle burns, the chemical energy in candle wax becomes thermal and electromagnetic energy. You detect the change as heat and light.

INTEGRATING LIFE SCIENCE One of the most important energy transformations on Earth involves chemical energy. Plants transform electromagnetic energy from the sun into chemical energy. These plants, and animals and other living things that eat plants, then transform this chemical energy once again. It becomes the mechanical, electrical, and thermal energy needed to carry out life activities. The potato you have for dinner might supply the energy you need to go for a walk or read this book!

Figure 8 Light can result from more than one kind of energy transformation. In glowsticks, chemical energy is changed to light by the reaction of two liquids. Electrical energy lights the bulbs on this ship's rigging.

Section 1 Review

1. Name several properties used to classify matter. Tell whether each is a physical property or a chemical property.
2. How are compounds formed?
3. Explain the difference between a physical change and a chemical change.
4. In what way are energy and matter related?
5. Describe a change in matter that you observed today. Tell what kind of energy change you think was involved.
6. **Thinking Critically Applying Concepts** You see a solid that looks like an ice cube, but it does not melt at room temperature. Can the solid be frozen water? Explain.

CHAPTER PROJECT

Check Your Progress

Choose which product and property you will test. Design a procedure to test the property you have selected. Decide which variables you will keep constant. Describe how you will measure and organize the data you collect. Discuss ideas for your procedure with a partner. Answer your partner's questions about the procedure, listen to any comments offered, and incorporate appropriate comments into your plan.

Program Resources

◆ **Unit 1 Resources** 1-1 Review and Reinforce; 1-1 Enrich

Answers to Self-Assessment

Caption Question

Figure 7 The houses will undergo physical changes. Their appearance will change but no new substances will be produced unless a fire starts or an explosion occurs.

Integrating Life Science

Invite students to brainstorm a list of energy transformations in animals. Motion (mechanical energy) and body heat (thermal energy) are likely responses. Prompt students to think of other kinds of energy, such as light (firefly) or electricity (electric eel)

3 Assess

Section 1 Review Answers

1. Sample: Physical properties—taste, odor, hardness, texture, color, melting temperature, and boiling temperature. Chemical properties—how easily a substance burns, reacts with water to form rust, explodes, or tarnishes.
2. A compound forms when two or more elements are chemically combined.
3. Physical change: matter may change form or appearance, but no new substances are formed. Chemical change: one or more new substances are produced.
4. Energy is involved when matter undergoes a physical or a chemical change.
5. Accept all answers in which students correctly identify changes as physical or chemical.
6. No. If the solid was frozen water, it would melt at room temperature because the melting temperature of ice is 0°C.

CHAPTER PROJECT

Check Your Progress

Students can work with their first partner to design their procedures. The written procedures should tell how to test the chosen property of the consumer products. The procedure should indicate that students have made predictions about results they will obtain. You may want to require students to include a summary of their partner's comments with their plans. Check students' procedures for safety.

Performance Assessment

Writing Have students use the major headings in the section to write brief summaries. Students' summaries should include examples.

Measuring Matter

Objectives

After completing the lesson, students will be able to

- explain the difference between weight and mass;
- calculate the density of substances using SI units for mass and volume.

Key Terms weight, mass, International System of Units, volume, density

1 Engage/Explore

Activating Prior Knowledge

Obtain two bars of hand soap, one that floats (such as Ivory) and one that does not. Remove the packaging. Show students the two bars, and ask: **What will happen when I place the two bars in a pan of water about 10 cm deep?** *(One will float and one will sink.)* Put the bars in the water. Let students observe the results and try to explain them.

Discover Activity

Skills Focus drawing conclusions
Materials *triple-beam balance, objects of different weights such as rocks, plastic drinking cups, aluminum cans, pencils*
Time 15 minutes
Tips Choose objects that are small but heavy (lead weights, small rocks, bolts, or paperweights), and objects that are larger but lightweight (plastic drinking cups, pieces of plastic foam, empty aluminum cans).
Think It Over Students may predict that the larger objects are heavier, but should conclude that small objects can be heavier than large objects, depending on density (although they may not know the term yet).

Section 2 Measuring Matter

Discover Activity

Which Has More Mass?

1. Your teacher will provide you with some small objects, such as a rock, a plastic cup, an aluminum can, and a pencil. Look at the objects, but do not touch them.
2. Predict which object is lightest, which is second lightest, and so on. Record your predictions.

3. Use a triple-beam balance to find the mass of each object.
4. Based on your results, list the objects from lightest to heaviest.

Think It Over

Drawing Conclusions How did your predictions compare to your results? Are bigger objects always heavier than smaller objects? Why or why not?

Guide for Reading

- What is the difference between weight and mass?
- How is density calculated?

Reading Tip Before you read, define *mass, volume,* and *density* in your own words. Then revise your definitions as you read.

Here's a riddle for you: Which weighs more, a pound of feathers or a pound of bricks? If you answered "the pound of bricks," think again. Both weigh exactly the same—one pound!

There are all sorts of ways of measuring matter, and you use these measurements every day. Scientists rely on measurements as well. In fact, scientists work hard to make sure that their measurements are as accurate as possible.

Mass

A veterinarian wants an updated weight for a dog at its annual checkup. To find the weight, the owner steps on a spring scale, holding the dog. Their combined body weight presses down on springs inside the scale. The more the girl and her dog weigh, the more the springs compress, and the higher the reading. When the owner's weight is subtracted from the total, the vet has an answer.

A spring scale would not give the same result on the moon. If the girl and her dog were to step on a spring scale on the moon, the springs inside wouldn't compress as much as on Earth. The vet would record a lower weight.

Figure 9 A spring scale measures the weight of an object.

Reading Strategies

Reading Tip Have students write their definitions in their notebooks, leaving space for additions or corrections. Before reading the section, students may define *density* as "how heavy something is." After students have read the section and revised their definitions, call on volunteers to read their revised definitions. Make sure that all incorrect preliminary definitions are revised accurately.

Background

Facts and Figures Weight is a measure of the force of gravity on an object, and is measured using a scale. Mass is a measure of the amount of matter in an object, and is measured using a balance.

Weight and Mass Your **weight** is a measure of the force of gravity on you. On Earth, all objects are attracted downward by Earth's gravity. On other planets, the force of gravity may be more or less. On the moon, the force of gravity is much weaker than on Earth. You would weigh less on the moon.

In everyday life, weight is a useful measurement of how much matter you have. But scientists rely on a property that is constant wherever the object may be. The **mass** of an object is the measurement of how much matter it contains. **Unlike weight, an object's mass will not change if the force of gravity on it changes. For this reason, mass is a useful physical property for describing and measuring matter.**

Units of Mass To measure the properties of matter, scientists use a system of units called the **International System of Units.** The system is abbreviated "SI," after its French name, Système International. For mass, the SI unit is the kilogram (kg). If you weigh 90 pounds on Earth, then your mass is approximately 40 kilograms.

Although you sometimes will see kilograms used in this textbook, usually you will see a smaller unit—the gram (g). There are exactly 1,000 grams in a kilogram. A nickel has a mass of about 5 grams, the mass of a baseball is about 150 grams, and the water in a medium-sized glass has a mass of about 200 grams.

☑ *Checkpoint* *What is the SI unit for mass?*

Volume

The amount of space that matter occupies is called its **volume.** It's easy to see the volume that solid and liquid objects take up. But gases have volume, too. Watch a balloon as you blow into it. You're actually increasing its volume with your breath.

Bubble Time

Do gases have volume?

1. Fill a large container with water. Completely submerge a clear plastic cup, right-side up, in the container.
2. Mark the water level with a piece of tape on the outside of the container.
3. Turn the cup upside-down under water, without letting any air bubbles enter the cup.
4. Insert the short end of the straw into the water and up into the cup. Then blow into the straw.

Inferring Did blowing air into the cup change the water level in the container? Explain your observations.

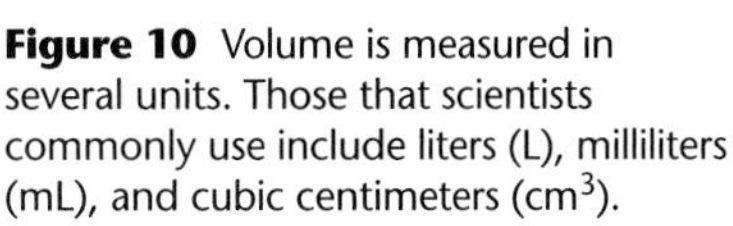

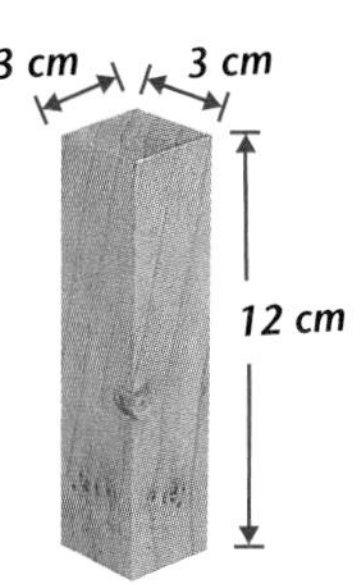

Figure 10 Volume is measured in several units. Those that scientists commonly use include liters (L), milliliters (mL), and cubic centimeters (cm^3).

2 Facilitate

Mass

Building Inquiry Skills: Applying Concepts

Materials *spring scale, objects from Discover activity, string*
Time 20 minutes

Have students weigh the objects on the spring scale. Be sure students zero the spring scales. Challenge students to infer how a spring scale measures the weight of an object. *(It measures the force required to resist gravity.)* Have students list the items in order of weight. Compare this list with the list from the Discover. Ask: **How are mass and weight related?** *(Objects with greater mass have greater weight.)* **What would happen if you weighed the objects using the same spring scale on the moon?** *(The objects would weigh less.)* **learning modality: logical/mathematical**

Volume

TRY THIS

Skills Focus inferring
Materials *water, large container, clear plastic cup, tape, flexible drinking straw*
Time 10 minutes

Tips Use a container large enough for students to invert the cup without lifting it out of the water.
Expected Outcome The water level in the container will rise because the air blown into the cup will push water out of the cup and into the container.
Extend Have students develop a method to determine whether the increase in the water's volume is equal to the volume of gas in the cup. *(Students can use graduated containers to measure the volumes.)* **learning modality: tactile/kinesthetic**

Ongoing Assessment

Writing Ask students to give brief definitions of weight and mass.

Program Resources

- **Unit 1 Resources** 1-2 Lesson Plan; 1-2 Section Summary
- **Guided Reading and Study Workbook** Section 1-2

Answers to Self-Assessment

☑ *Checkpoint*

Kilogram

Integrating Mathematics

ACTIVITY

Students often have difficulty recognizing how to convert units of area or volume. Have students calculate how many cubic centimeters are in a cubic meter. Remind students that 1 m = 100 cm.

$1\ m^3 = 100\ cm \times 100\ cm \times 100\ cm$

$1\ m^3 = 1{,}000{,}000\ cm^3$

SCIENCE & History

Time 20 minutes

Tips To determine whether students are reading the time line correctly, ask: **How many years are represented by this time line?** *(3,500)* Ask: **Were the early systems of measurement as accurate as those we use today? Why?** *(No, because they depended on things that are not the same for all people at all times, such as the length of a person's arm or how much land oxen can plow in two days)* Then ask students to infer why people still use units of measurement that are not part of the SI system. *(Sample: Because they are familiar with them; because the units are traditionally used in some fields)*

Extend Have students list SI units they use in their everyday lives. Refer to the **ELL Handbook** for additional teaching strategies.

In Your Journal Encourage students to define and explain the units they choose. For example, a *carat,* a unit of weight for precious gems, is equal to 200 milligrams. Horses are measured in *hands,* a unit of height equal to about 10 centimeters. In sailing, a *fathom* (about 2 meters) is used to measure the depth of water. **learning modality: verbal**

INTEGRATING MATHEMATICS For rectangular objects such as a block of wood, the volume is found by multiplying the measurements of length, width, and height.

$$\text{Volume} = \text{Length} \times \text{Width} \times \text{Height}$$

When you multiply the three measurements, you must multiply the units as well as the numbers. So, just as $2 \times 2 \times 2 = 2^3$, $cm \times cm \times cm = cm^3$. If a block of wood has a length of 3 centimeters, a width of 3 centimeters, and a height of 12 centimeters, then the volume would equal the product of those values.

$$\text{Volume} = 3\ cm \times 3\ cm \times 12\ cm = 108\ cm^3$$

Measurement Systems

Like so much else in science, systems of measurement developed gradually over time in different parts of the world.

1400 B.C.

Egypt

The ancient Egyptians developed the first known weighing instrument, a simple balance with a pointer. Earlier, they had been the first to standardize a measure of length. The length, called a cubit, was originally defined as the distance between the elbow and the tip of the middle finger.

1500 B.C. | **1000 B.C.** | **500 B.C.** | **A.D. 1**

640 B.C.

Lydia

Merchants in the Middle East and Mediterranean used units of weight to be sure that they received the correct amount of gold and silver in trade and to check the purity of the metal. A *talent* was about 25 kilograms and a *mina* about 500 grams. The Lydians minted the first true coins to have standard weight and value.

200 B.C.

China

Shih Huang Ti, the first emperor of China, set standards for weight, length, and volume. Even earlier, the Chinese were the first to use decimal notation, the number system based on 10 digits. This is the system most people use today.

30

Background

Facts and Figures Students may be interested in hearing more about units of measurement.

- A *furlong,* a distance now used only in horse racing, is approximately equal to 200 meters. It comes from an old English unit of length that was based on the length of an average furrow in a plowed field.
- The *knot,* a measure of speed at sea, is approximately equal to 1.15 miles per hour, or 1.85 km per hour. The term probably originated because of knots made in a length of rope which were used to measure the speed of a ship through water.
- A *fathom* is a measure of depth of water. A fathom is 6 feet, or 1.83 meters. Originally, a fathom was the distance between the tips of the middle fingers of a large man holding his arms fully outstretched.

The abbreviation "cm^3" is read as *cubic centimeter(s),* which is a common unit of volume. Other units of volume include the liter (L) and the milliliter (mL), both of which are often used to measure liquids. A milliliter is exactly 1 cubic centimeter. There are 1,000 milliliters in one liter.

How can you measure the volume of an object with an irregular shape, such as a piece of fruit or a rock? One way is to put the object in a graduated cylinder containing water and measure the change in the volume of the water.

Checkpoint *How can you calculate the volume of a rectangular object like a shoe box?*

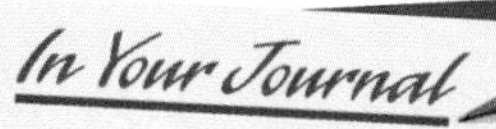

In Your Journal

Although scientists rely on SI units, people use other measurement units for many different purposes. Research the units used in diamond cutting, horse breeding, sailing, or other activities that interest you. Write a brief essay describing your findings.

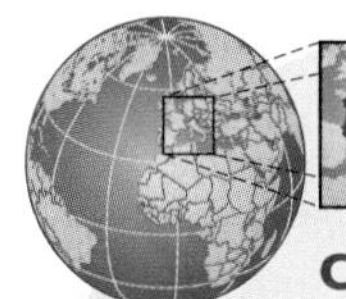

A.D. 789
Central Europe

The foot of Charlemagne, emperor of most of central Europe, was set as the standard unit of length. The standard unit of weight was the *Karlspfund,* translated as "Charlemagne's pound."

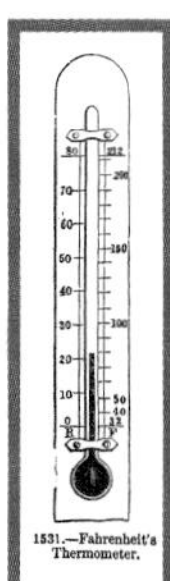

A.D. 1714
Germany

Gabriel Fahrenheit invented the thermometer, a temperature-measuring device that relies on the expansion of mercury with heat. His name later came to be used as the name for a temperature scale.

A.D. 500 **A.D. 1000** **A.D. 1500** **A.D. 2000**

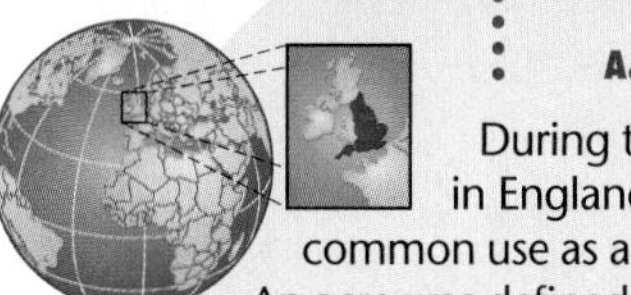

A.D. 700 **England**

During the reign of Ethelbert II in England, the term *acre* was in common use as a measurement of area. An acre was defined as the amount of land two oxen could plow in one day.

A.D. 1983
France

The International Bureau of Weights and Measures defines a single set of units that is the same everywhere. Scientists throughout the world use these units in their work.

Including All Students

Materials *unit cubes (manipulatives used in math class)*
Time 10 minutes

Students who need extra challenges may enjoy visualizing how a small increase in the dimensions of an object can cause a large change in the volume of the object. Ask: **If you make a cube that is 1 cm longer, 1 cm wider, and 1 cm taller than another cube, how much more volume does the bigger cube have?** *(Some students may say the cube will be 1 cm larger.)* Suggest students use unit cubes to model three cubes, the first with one unit cube, the second with dimensions of $2 \times 2 \times 2$, and the third with dimensions of $3 \times 3 \times 3$. Ask students to compare the volume (in unit cubes) of the $2 \times 2 \times 2$ cube *(8)* and the $3 \times 3 \times 3$ cube *(27)*. Have students calculate the volume in unit cubes of a cube that is 4 units tall, 4 units wide, and 4 units long. *(64)* **learning modality: logical/mathematical**

Media and Technology

Concept Videotape Library
Grade 6, Tape 1 "Density"

Program Resources

- **Laboratory Manual** 1, "Determining the Density of Liquids"

Answers to Self-Assessment

Checkpoint

Multiply the length of the shoe box by its width and by its height.

Ongoing Assessment

Skills Check Have students calculate the volumes of several rectangular items such as a textbook, a shoe box, and the classroom. For each item, students should draw diagrams that explain how they arrived at their answers.

Density—A Physical Property of Matter

Building Inquiry Skills: Making Measurements

ACTIVITY

Materials *assorted small irregularly shaped objects, 1,000-mL graduated cylinder, water, balance, string*
Time 15 minutes

To show students how to find the density of irregular objects, first have them find the masses of the objects. They can then use the graduated cylinder, filled with water to the 50-mL line, to find their volumes. (If they are available, you can use an overflow can or a 1,000-mL graduated cylinder to measure the density of larger objects.) To do this, students can tie the string around each object, then slowly lower the object into the cylinder. Each object will displace a certain volume of water, and students can measure how much the water level rises by noting the graduations on the cylinder. Ask: **How can you use the new water level to find the volume of the object?** *(New level − 50 mL = volume of solid)* Finally, have students calculate the density of each object. **learning modality: tactile/kinesthetic**

Sample Problem

Reproduce the sample problem on the board, and work through the steps with students. Point out that density is a ratio of two quantities, mass and volume. Show students how to check their answers by checking the units. The units of density are always expressed in mass per unit volume (so the answer is read as "grams per cubic centimeter"). If students find other units, they are not doing the problem correctly. **learning modality: logical/mathematical**

Practice Problems

1. 24 g ÷ 16 mL = 1.5 g/mL
2. 43.5 g ÷ 15 cm^3 = 2.9 g/cm^3

Figure 11 This table lists commonly used units of mass, volume, and distance. *Making Generalizations Which units show the amount of space an object occupies? Which units show the amount of matter in an object?*

Common Units and Conversions

Quantity	SI/Metric Units	Other Units	Conversions
Mass	Kilogram (kg) Gram (g)		1 kilogram = 1,000 grams
Volume	Cubic meter (m^3) Liter (L) Milliliter (mL) Cubic centimeter (cm^3)	Quart Gallon	1 liter = 1,000 milliliters 1 milliliter = 1 cm^3
Distance	Meter (m) Kilometer (km) Centimeter (cm)	Foot Mile Inch	1 kilometer = 1,000 meters 1 centimeter = 0.01 meter

Density—A Physical Property of Matter

Different substances may have the same mass, but they don't necessarily fill the same volume. Remember the riddle about the bricks and the feathers? A kilogram of bricks takes up a much smaller volume than the same mass of feathers. This is because bricks and feathers have different densities—a very important property of matter. **Density** is a physical property that relates the mass and volume of an object or material. **To calculate the density of a sample, divide its mass by its volume.**

$$Density = \frac{Mass}{Volume}$$

A unit of density is always a unit of mass, such as grams, divided by a unit of volume, such as cubic centimeters. One typical unit of density is written as "g/cm^3," which is read as "grams per cubic centimeter." The word *per* means "for each," which in mathematics is the same as "divided by." For liquids, density is often stated in grams per milliliter, or g/mL. The density of water is 1.0 g/mL, which is the same as 1.0 g/cm^3.

Figure 12 An object sinks or floats in water depending, in part, on its density. This stone statue remains on the sea floor where it was placed. A statue of solid wood, with a density less than that of water, would float.

Sometimes you can compare the densities of substances just by observing them. For example, suppose you have a solid block of wood and a solid block of gold. When you drop each block into a tub of water, the wood floats and the gold sinks. You know the density of water is 1.0 g/cm^3. You can conclude that the density of wood is less than 1.0 g/cm^3. In contrast, the density of the gold is greater than 1.0 g/cm^3. In the same way, you can conclude that the density of the solid stone statue in Figure 12 is greater than the density of the water around it.

32

Background

History of Science A popular legend about the Greek scientist Archimedes offers a useful application of density. King Hieron II of Syracuse suspected a goldsmith of using a mix of metals rather than pure gold to make his crown. Archimedes reasoned that the density of a lump of pure gold and a crown of pure gold would be the same. He then reasoned that a lump of pure gold with the same mass as the crown should have the same volume. To test the trustworthiness of the goldsmith, he placed that lump of pure gold and then the crown in water. The crown displaced more water than the lump of gold with the same mass, indicating that it had a greater volume. Therefore, Archimedes could say with certainty that the crown was not made of pure gold because its density was less than the density of pure gold.

Sample Problem

A small block of wood floats on water. It has a volume of 25 cubic centimeters and a mass of 20 grams. What is the density of the wood?

Analyze. You know the mass and the volume. You want to find the density.

Write the formula. $Density = \frac{Mass}{Volume}$

Substitute and solve. $Density = \frac{20\ g}{25\ cm^3}$

$Density = 0.8\ g/cm^3$

Think about it. The answer shows mass per unit volume.

Practice Problems

1. A sample of liquid has a mass of 24 grams and a volume of 16 milliliters. What is the density of the liquid?
2. A metal sample has a mass of 43.5 grams and a volume of 15 cubic centimeters. What is its density?

Watch a bottle of oil-and-vinegar salad dressing after it's been shaken. You will see oil droplets rise toward the top of the bottle. Eventually, the oil forms a separate layer above the other ingredients. What can you conclude? You're right if you said that the oil is less dense than the rest of the liquid dressing.

Density is a physical property of a substance. As a result, density can be used to help identify a substance. For example, all samples of pure gold at a certain temperature have a density of 19.3 g/cm^3. Finding the density of a shiny yellow material is one way to test whether or not that material is gold.

Section 2 Review

1. Why is mass more useful than weight for measuring matter?
2. What two quantities do you need to know in order to calculate density?
3. Describe how you could measure the volume of an object with an irregular shape.
4. **Thinking Critically Problem Solving** The density of aluminum is 2.7 g/cm^3. A metal sample has a mass of 52.0 grams and a volume of 17.1 cubic centimeters. Could the sample be aluminum? Explain your answer.

Science at Home

Density Demonstration Label two cups A and B and place a cup of water in each. Stir 3 small spoonfuls of salt and several drops of food coloring into Cup B. Dip a clear straw into Cup A to a depth of about 2 cm. Place your finger on the end of the straw and transfer the straw into Cup B to a depth of about 4 cm. Remove your finger from the straw and then replace it. Remove the straw from the cup. Explain to your family what density has to do with the results.

3 Assess

Section 2 Review Answers

1. Unlike weight, mass does not change if the force of gravity changes.
2. Mass and volume
3. Fill a container with enough water to submerge the object. Measure the volume of the water. Place the object in the water and find the increase in volume. The increase in volume is equal to the volume of the object.
4. The density of the metal sample is 52.0 g ÷ 17.1 cm^3 = 3.04 g/cm^3. This density is greater than the density of aluminum, so the sample is not aluminum.

Science at Home

ACTIVITY

Materials *two cups with flat bottoms, water, salt, food coloring, clear plastic straw*

Have students predict what will happen before they try this activity. When students have dipped the straw into both cups, the water in the straw will be in two bands. Water from cup A will be at the top, and water from cup B will be at the bottom. Students should explain that the water from cup A is less dense, so it floats on the water from cup B without mixing. This activity can also be performed with three solutions of different densities.

Program Resources

- **Unit 1 Resources** 1-2 Review and Reinforce; 1-2 Enrich

Media and Technology

Concept Videotape Library Grade 6, Tape 1 "The Metric System"; "What's a Cubit?"

Answers to Self-Assessment

Caption Question

Figure 11 Amount of space—liters, milliliters, cubic meters, and cubic centimeters, as well as quarts and gallons; amount of matter—kilograms and grams

Performance Assessment

Skills Check Have students prepare presentations that explain how to find the density of a small, irregularly shaped solid. Students can use illustrations to explain one or all of the steps.

Students can include their illustrations in their portfolios.

Skills Lab

Interpreting Data

Making Sense of Density

Preparing for Inquiry

Key Concept The density of a substance is a property that can be used to identify that substance.

Skills Objectives Students will be able to
- measure mass using a balance;
- measure volume using the method of water displacement;
- calculate density.

Time 30 minutes

Advance Planning
- Make sure the objects to be tested can be broken easily and will fit into graduated cylinders.
- Make sure students know the proper procedure for using the balance.
- *Computer use is optional.*

Guiding Inquiry

Introducing the Procedure
Review the procedure briefly. Students should record each object's initial and new volume in Steps 2 and 3 in case they need to check their calculations.

Troubleshooting the Experiment
Have students develop a method for submerging objects that might float, such as some wood and crayons, in order to measure their volumes. Encourage students to examine what effect this will have on the accuracy of their results.

Expected Outcome
Density values for all samples of each object should be approximately equal.

Skills Lab

Interpreting Data

MAKING SENSE OF DENSITY

In this lab you will find out if an object's density changes when its size changes.

Problem

Does the density of a substance change if it is broken into pieces?

Materials 

balance
water
paper towels
wooden stick, approximately 6 cm long
ball of modeling clay, approximately 5 cm wide
crayon with paper covering removed
graduated cylinder, 100 mL
computer and spreadsheet program (optional)

Procedure

1. Use a balance to find the mass of the wooden stick. Record the mass in a data table like the one at the right or in a computer spreadsheet.
2. Add enough water to a graduated cylinder so that the stick can be completely submerged. Measure the initial volume of the water.
3. Place the stick in the graduated cylinder. Measure the new volume of the water.
4. The volume of the stick is the difference between the water levels in Steps 2 and 3. Calculate this volume and record it.
5. The density of the stick equals its mass divided by its volume. Calculate and record its density.
6. Thoroughly dry the stick with a paper towel. Then carefully break the stick into two pieces. Repeat Steps 1 through 5 to calculate the density of each of the two pieces.
7. Repeat Steps 1 through 6 using the clay rolled into a rope.
8. Repeat Steps 1–6 again using the crayon.

Analyze and Conclude

1. For each of the three objects you tested, compare the density of the whole object with the densities of the pieces of the object.
2. Use your results to explain how density can be used to identify a substance.
3. Why did you dry the objects in Step 6?
4. **Think About It** Predict the results of this experiment if you had used a pencil with an eraser on one end instead of a wooden stick. Explain your prediction.

More to Explore

Wrap the modeling clay around the wooden stick and predict the density of the object you created. Then measure mass and volume and calculate the density to see if your prediction was correct.

DATA TABLE

Object	Mass (g)	Volume Change (cm^3)	Density (g/cm^3)
Wooden Stick			
Whole			
Piece 1			
Piece 2			
Modeling Clay			
Whole			
Piece 1			
Piece 2			
Crayon			
Whole			
Piece 1			
Piece 2			

34

Analyze and Conclude
1. The density of the whole object should equal the density of each piece.
2. Because every sample of a substance has the same density, density can be used to identify that substance.
3. If the object were wet, then the mass measurements would include water, introducing a source of error into the calculations.
4. The density of the eraser would most likely differ from the density of the rest of the pencil. Thus, the density of pencil pieces would differ from the density of the whole pencil.

Extending the Inquiry

More to Explore Students should discover that the density of a mixture falls in between the highest and lowest densities of the substances in the mixture.

Program Resources
- **Unit 1 Resources** Chapter 1 Skills Lab blackline masters
- **Inquiry Skills Activity Book** Provides teaching and review of all inquiry skills

Media and Technology
 **Lab Activity Videotapes**
Grade 6, Tape 1

Particles of Matter

DISCOVER ACTIVITY

What's in the Box?

1. Your teacher will give you a sealed box that contains one or more objects. Without opening the box, try to find out as much as you can about the contents. Try tilting, turning, shaking, or tapping the box.
2. Ask yourself questions such as these: Are the objects inside round or flat? Do they slide or roll? How many objects are there?
3. Make a list of your observations about the objects in the box.
4. Trade boxes with another group of students and repeat the activity.

Think It Over

Inferring Try to imagine what familiar objects would fit your observations. Make a sketch showing what you think the contents look like. How is it possible to make an inference from indirect evidence?

Glance at the painting below and you see people enjoying an afternoon in the park. Look again and notice that some people are in the sunlight and others are in the shade. How did the artist make your eyes see bright light, dark shadows, and shades in between? You can find the answer by looking closely at the circled detail of the painting. The artist used thousands of small spots of color.

Are you surprised that such a rich painting can be created from lots of small spots? Matter is like that too. The properties you can observe are produced by tiny objects and events that you cannot observe.

GUIDE FOR READING

- What did Dalton conclude about atoms?
- What are molecules made of?

Reading Tip As you read, take notes on the main points under each heading.

"Sunday Afternoon on the Island of La Grande Jatte," by Georges Seurat, at the Art Institute of Chicago

READING STRATEGIES

Reading Tip Suggest that before they read the section, students write the headings in their notebooks, leaving space between the headings. For example, under "Early Ideas About Atoms," a student could write: In 440 B.C., Democritus thought matter was made up of tiny unbreakable pieces called atoms.

Program Resources

- **Unit 1 Resources** 1-3 Lesson Plan; 1-3 Section Summary
- **Guided Reading and Study Workbook** Section 1-3

Section 3 Particles of Matter

Objectives

After completing the lesson, students will be able to

- identify atoms as the smallest particles of an element;
- describe Dalton's theory of atoms;
- identify chemical bonds as the force holding atoms together in molecules.

Key Terms atom, nucleus, proton, neutron, electron, chemical bond, molecule

1 Engage/Explore

Activating Prior Knowledge

Distribute hand lenses and sections from the Sunday comics. Have students examine the comics with the hand lenses and describe what they see. Ask students to describe how a whole picture can be made up of many tiny parts.

DISCOVER

Skills Focus inferring

Materials *shoe box containing one or more objects such as a candle, pencil, empty soda can, sock, marble, sponge*

Time 10 minutes

Tips Have students work in pairs or groups of 3. Make certain each shoe box is opaque and taped firmly closed. When students exchange shoe boxes, encourage them to evaluate each other's observations and inferences.

Think It Over Students' answers should be appropriate to their observations. Emphasize to students that they may not have enough information to draw precise conclusions. Students should realize that they can make inferences from indirect evidence by making repeated observations and revising their inferences to fit the observations.

2 Facilitate

Early Ideas About Atoms

Including All Students

Many students have difficulty when scientific concepts deal with things that cannot be directly observed. Divide the class into small groups, and have students consider the way a crime is solved when there is no direct evidence, such as an eyewitness. Crime solvers make careful measurements and collect as much indirect evidence as possible. Eventually, the evidence can be enough to convince a jury. Have a reporter from each group share the group's finding with the class. Then explain that scientists also collect indirect evidence until they are convinced a particular theory is correct. **cooperative learning**

Using the Visuals: Figure 13

While mercury is a liquid at room temperature, small amounts of mercury vaporize, so mercury vapor is always present. Mercury vapor can be inhaled and can then accumulate in body tissues until concentrations are high enough to cause serious health problems, even brain damage and death. Ask students if they think the smallest droplets of mercury pictured contain just a few atoms of mercury or many atoms. *(many)* Tell students that the smallest droplets pictured, which might have a mass of 0.01 g, still contain around 3 billion billion atoms (3.0×10^{18}). **learning modality: visual**

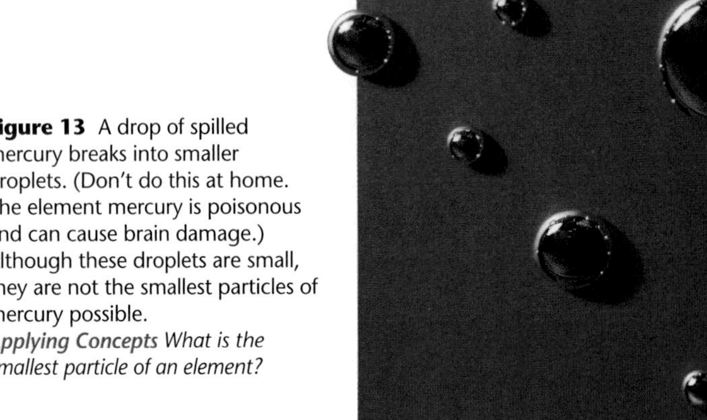

Figure 13 A drop of spilled mercury breaks into smaller droplets. (Don't do this at home. The element mercury is poisonous and can cause brain damage.) Although these droplets are small, they are not the smallest particles of mercury possible.
Applying Concepts *What is the smallest particle of an element?*

Early Ideas About Atoms

What's the smallest possible piece of an element? Think of tearing a sheet of aluminum foil in half, and then tearing the halves into quarters, and the quarters into eighths. Could you keep tearing forever, producing smaller and smaller pieces? Or would you eventually reach the smallest possible piece of aluminum? And if matter is made of such tiny pieces, what are those pieces like? How can they explain the properties of matter that you observe? Philosophers and scientists have asked these kind of questions for more than 2,000 years.

One of the first people known to have thought that matter is formed of small pieces was Democritus, a Greek philosopher who lived about 440 B.C. He thought that you could cut matter into ever smaller pieces until you got to its smallest piece, which couldn't be divided any further. Democritus called this smallest piece *atomos*, which is Greek for "uncuttable." Does that word look familiar? Of course! It's where the word *atom* comes from. An **atom** is the smallest particle of an element.

Dalton's Ideas About Atoms

A major step in understanding atoms occurred in 1802 when a British school teacher, John Dalton, proposed an atomic theory. No one knows how much Dalton was influenced by the ideas of Democritus. Unlike Democritus and the ancient Greeks, Dalton used experiments to test his ideas.

Background

History of Science John Dalton (1766–1844) began teaching in a Quaker school at the age of 12. At 21, Dalton began his first scientific work, a diary recording the meteorological changes of the district in which he lived. Ultimately, the diary contained 200,000 entries. In 1793, Dalton published his *Meteorological Observations and Essays.*

Dalton preferred to make his own observations and draw his conclusions from them. He also built his own instruments.

Dalton investigated the behavior of gases and discovered that for a mixture of gases, the total pressure equals the sum of the pressures of the individual gases. He also studied color blindness, a condition that he had. Although his theory was later discarded, his work was so influential that color blindness was referred to as *Daltonism.*

Based on evidence from experiments, Dalton inferred that atoms had certain characteristics. Here are his main conclusions.

- *Atoms can't be broken into smaller pieces.* **Dalton thought of atoms as similar to tiny marbles, or rigid spheres that are impossible to break.**
- *In any element, all the atoms are exactly alike.* This idea explains why an element always has the same properties.
- *Atoms of different elements are different.* This idea explains why different elements have their own set of properties.
- *Atoms of two or more elements can combine to form compounds.* Compounds can be broken down into elements, so Dalton concluded that compounds had to be made of atoms as well.
- *Atoms of each element have a unique mass.* Dalton and other scientists of his day were not actually able to measure the mass of individual atoms, however.
- *The masses of the elements in a compound are always in a constant ratio.* Water is made up of hydrogen atoms and oxygen atoms. In any two samples of pure water, the ratio of the mass of hydrogen to the mass of oxygen is always the same.

Today, scientists have identified some important exceptions to Dalton's statements. Even so, Dalton's ideas form the basis of our understanding of atoms.

☑ **Checkpoint** *What were two of Dalton's ideas about atoms?*

Math TOOLBOX

Constant Ratios

When two pairs of numbers produce the same ratio, the ratio is said to be constant. Suppose you wanted to increase the recipe in the Math Toolbox on page 22. To double the recipe, you would need 4 cups of flour and 2 cups of sugar. The ratio 4:2 reduces to 2:1 by dividing each number by 2.

$$\frac{4}{2} = \frac{2}{1}$$

To triple the recipe you would need 6 cups of flour and 3 cups of sugar. The ratio 6:3 reduces to 2:1 by dividing each number by 3.

$$\frac{6}{3} = \frac{2}{1}$$

The two ratios are constant because they both reduce to 2:1.

Similarly, for any quantity of a compound, the ratio of the masses of the elements in the compound is constant.

Figure 14 The compound calcium oxide is part of mortar, the "glue" that holds bricks together. In this compound, the ratio of the mass of calcium to the mass of oxygen is always 5 to 2.

Dalton's Ideas About Atoms

Demonstration

ACTIVITY

Materials *two glasses of water, a few drops of milk, bright flashlight with a narrow beam*
Time 10 minutes

Out of sight of the students, place a few drops of milk into one glass of water and stir thoroughly. Be careful not to use too much. The two glasses of water should appear to be the same under room lights. Now darken the room lights, and from the side shine a powerful flashlight beam into each glass. Have students write down their observations. Return the room lights to normal and tell the students that you placed a few drops of milk in one glass. Can they tell which? Have students describe the observations that allowed them to distinguish. *(The beam from the flashlight was clearly visible in the glass with the milk droplets but was invisible in the other.)* Explain that this process shows one way to detect tiny particles that cannot be seen under normal conditions. Point out that what students saw were not individual atoms, but were particles from the milk mixed into the water. **learning modality: visual**

Math TOOLBOX

Review the concepts of writing ratios as fractions and the steps for reducing fractions to their smallest whole-number values. Point out that in the first example, both the numerator and denominator are divisible by 2. Ask: **In the second example, what was done to reduce the fraction $\frac{6}{3}$ to its smallest whole-number values?** *(The numerator and denominator were divided by 3.)* Stress the importance of performing the same operation on both numerator and denominator if ratios are to be kept constant. **learning modality: logical/ mathematical**

Media and Technology

Concept Videotape Library
Grade 6, Tape 1 "Rutherford's Experiment"

Answers to Self-Assessment

Caption Question
Figure 13 An atom

☑ **Checkpoint**
Any two: Atoms of one element are exactly alike; atoms are indivisible; atoms of each element have a unique mass; atoms of two or more elements can combine to form compounds; the masses of the elements in a compound always have the same ratio.

Ongoing Assessment

Writing Ask students to briefly describe atoms in their own words.

Ideas About Atoms Today

Language Arts CONNECTION

Encourage students to think of other stories or movies about people becoming very small. Point out that a person who is the size of a cell in the human body would be visible only under a microscope. Remind students that atoms are much smaller than cells.

In Your Journal If students have trouble writing their stories, encourage them to imagine that they are the size of an atom in or on a specific object, such as a flower or tennis ball. Encourage students to be creative and to remember how small atoms are as they write. **learning modality: verbal**

Atoms and Molecules

Using the Visuals: Figure 16

It is very difficult to accurately represent molecules. Scientists and teachers have traditionally used two approaches, known as the "ball-and-stick" model and the "space-filling" model. Figure 16 shows space-filling models of water, oxygen, acetic acid, and part of a DNA molecule. The ball-and-stick model can better show angles and distances between atomic centers, while the space-filling model is better at showing sizes of atoms and shapes of molecules. Direct student's attention to the water molecule and ask them which is hydrogen and which is oxygen. *(Small spheres are hydrogen.)* **How do the sizes of the atoms compare?** *(Oxygen is much larger.)* Point out that the DNA molecule and water molecule are not shown to the same scale. **learning modality: visual**

Figure 15 An atom's tiny nucleus contains protons and neutrons. The electrons move in the space around the nucleus.

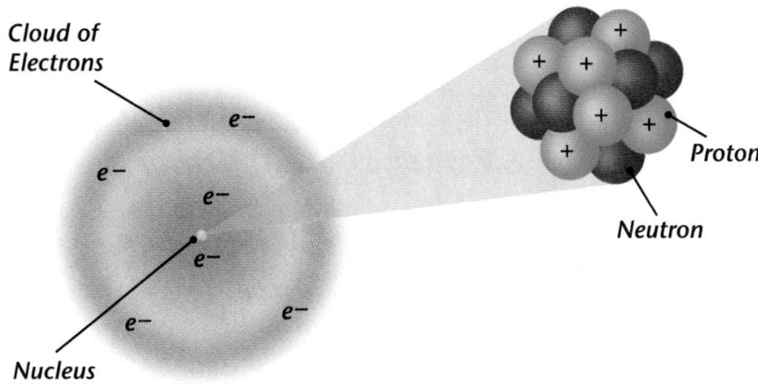

Ideas About Atoms Today

Atoms are so small that one grain of sand on a typical beach contains more atoms than there are grains of sand on the entire beach. Although they are extremely small, atoms are made of even smaller parts. An atom's **nucleus** (NOO clee us) (plural *nuclei*) is the tiny, central core of an atom. Nuclei contain particles called protons and neutrons. **Protons** have a positive electric charge (indicated by a plus symbol, +). **Neutrons** have no charge. They are neutral. (Could you guess that from their name?) A third type of particle moves in the space around the nucleus. These are very energetic particles, called **electrons,** which move rapidly in all directions. Electrons carry a negative charge (indicated by a negative symbol, –). Figure 15 shows the structure of an atom of carbon.

All atoms of a particular element have the same number of protons. For example, all atoms of carbon have 6 protons. Because the number of protons is unique to each element, this number is called the element's atomic number.

Language Arts CONNECTION

In Isaac Asimov's science fiction story *Fantastic Voyage,* people are shrunk down to the size of a single cell. Their experiences inside the body of a full-sized person are "fantastic" reading. Imagine what it would be like to shrink down to the size of a single atom!

In Your Journal

Write a one-page story about what you would see and experience as you shrink down to the size of an atom. Explore your new world, describing the other atoms and molecules around you. What happens as you grow back to normal size?

Atoms and Molecules

An atom can frequently be linked with one or more other atoms. The force that holds two atoms together is a **chemical bond.** Often, two or more atoms that are bonded together form a particle called a **molecule.** Some molecules are made of atoms that are alike, as in the oxygen gas (O_2) that you breathe. **Most molecules are made of two or more different types of atoms bonded together.** Water molecules have 2 hydrogen atoms combined with 1 oxygen atom (H_2O). Acetic acid, the compound that gives vinegar its sharp odor and sour taste, has 2 carbon atoms, 4 hydrogen atoms, and 2 oxygen atoms ($C_2H_4O_2$). Molecules can be huge. Some molecules in your body contain millions of atoms.

Background

Facts and Figures The scanning tunneling microscope can actually capture images of atoms. It was first developed in 1981 by Gerd Binnig and Heinrich Rohrer in Zurich, Switzerland. Its operation is based on the phenomenon known as tunneling, which occurs when electrons "jump" out of a surface to a conductor that is very close to the surface. The sharp tip of a tungsten needle is positioned about one billionth of a meter above the surface and slowly moved across the surface in a regular pattern. The tunneling current is read at each position, and a computer is used to build up a three-dimensional image of the surface. When the image is displayed on a television monitor, precisely arranged layers of atoms and even individual atoms can clearly be seen. For their discovery, Binnig and Rohrer were awarded the Nobel Prize in physics in 1986.

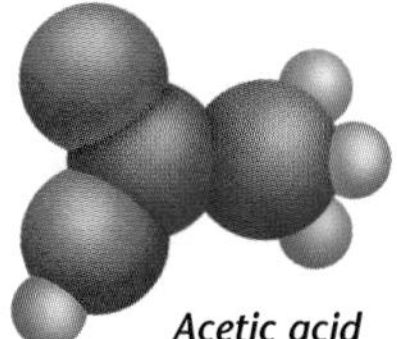

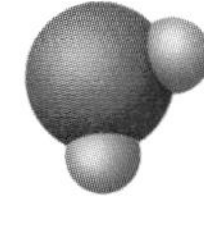

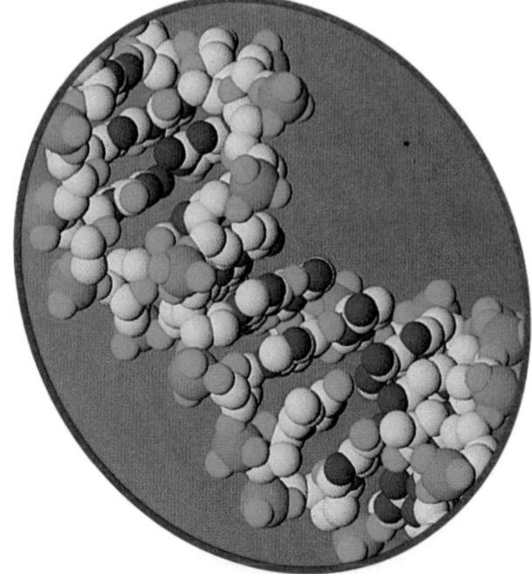

Figure 16 Each diagram on the left is a model of a molecule made of atoms bonded together. The molecule on the right shows a small part of the DNA in living cells. (This computer image of DNA was made using a color code for atoms different from the code used in this book.) *Classifying Which one of these models shows a molecule of an element? How do you know?*

The Atom as a Model

If you looked at a water drop through a high-powered microscope, you couldn't really see what atoms look like or how they might work. Like a person trying to imagine what's in a box by shaking it, scientists studying atoms must make inferences about them based on observations.

In this way, atoms act as models. In science, a model may be a diagram, a mental picture, a mathematical statement, or an object that helps explain ideas about the natural world. Scientists use models to make and test predictions. In chemistry, models of atoms and molecules are often used to explain how matter behaves. Dalton's description of atoms was one of the first atomic models. Ideas about atoms have changed greatly since Dalton's time, but models continue to be valuable tools in science. You will see models many times in this book. In the next chapter, for example, simple models of atoms and molecules will be used to help explain the nature of water.

Section 3 Review

1. What images did Dalton use to help describe atoms?
2. How are atoms and molecules related?
3. An ice cube consists of molecules of water (H_2O). Could you continue, forever, to break an ice cube into smaller and smaller pieces of ice? Explain your answer.
4. **Thinking Critically Interpreting Diagrams** Examine the model of acetic acid ($C_2H_4O_2$) in Figure 16. Which elements are represented by each of the three colors? How do you know? What does the model tell you about the way the different atoms are arranged?

CHAPTER PROJECT

Check Your Progress

Get your teacher's approval of your procedure for testing your product. Then obtain the materials you need and perform the test. If you alter the procedure, change the instructions to reflect your alterations. (*Hint:* A good experimental procedure should be reliable—repeatable. Test more than one sample to see if your results are repeated.)

The Atom as a Model

Including All Students

Review with students the use of a model to represent something that can't be easily viewed. Models can be used to study atoms, which are too tiny to see, or the solar system, which is to huge to view all at once. **learning modality: logical/mathematical**

3 Assess

Section 3 Review Answers

1. Tiny marbles or spheres that are impossible to break.
2. A molecule is made of two or more atoms joined together with a chemical bond.
3. No, the smallest possible piece of ice is one molecule of H_2O.
4. Blue—hydrogen, red—oxygen, black—carbon; the four blue spheres must represent the four hydrogen atoms; if oxygen is red, as in the two other models, the black spheres are carbon. The model shows which atoms are connected to other atoms.

CHAPTER PROJECT

Check Your Progress

After students obtain their materials and begin to conduct their experiments, ask whether they have had to modify their procedures. If so, make sure their instructions reflect these changes. Also, make sure students are conducting multiple trials with the same product. Encourage students to average the results of their trials.

Program Resources

◆ **Unit 1 Resources** 1-3 Review and Reinforce; 1-3 Enrich

Media and Technology

Transparencies "Models of Molecules," Transparency 1

Answers to Self-Assessment

Caption Question

Figure 16 Oxygen, because it is the only molecule made from one kind of atom.

Performance Assessment

Skills Check Have students model atoms with small clay balls, then use their models to illustrate one of Dalton's ideas. *(Sample: Several identical clay balls together— all atoms of a given element are identical.)*

Integrating Earth Science

Section 4 Elements From Earth

Objectives

After completing the lesson, students will be able to

- describe how the density of gold allows it to be panned;
- explain that a chemical reaction is needed to obtain an element from one of its compounds.

Key Terms electrolysis, electrode

1 Engage/Explore

Activating Prior Knowledge

Supply students with samples of rocks that contain metals or metal compounds, such as iron pyrite or galena. Samples can probably be borrowed from the earth science teacher. Ask students to speculate how engineers could identify what kind of metal is in the rock and how they could extract it.

Discover

Skills Focus designing an experiment

Materials *wet sand, metal bolts and screws, plastic tray or pie pan, water, bowl, paper towels*

Time 15 minutes

Tips One way to separate the mixture is to use a stream of water to wash the sand off the bolts. The sand can be collected in a bowl, then dried on paper towels.

Think It Over Procedures and their successes will vary. The suggested procedure separates the bolts from the sand by taking advantage of the difference in their masses. The lightweight sand particles are carried away by the stream of water, while the heavier bolts sink.

Integrating Earth Science

Section 4 Elements From Earth

Discover Activity

How Can You Separate Bolts From Sand?

1. Mix wet sand with a few small metal bolts and screws. Place the mixture in a tray or pie pan.
2. Think of a way to separate the sand from the bolts. You may not use a magnet, but you may use water, a bowl, paper towels, and other supplies available in your classroom.
3. With your teacher's permission, try your procedure.

Think It Over

Designing an Experiment What properties of matter did you use to separate the sand and the bolts? How successful was your procedure?

Guide for Reading

- What physical property of gold allows it to be panned?
- What must be done to obtain an element from one of its compounds?

Reading Tip As you read, list the ways that people obtain elements from the forms in which they are found in nature.

Gold! In 1848, several gold nuggets were found in the American River in northern California near a mill owned by John Sutter. Thousands of people rushed to California with pans, pickaxes, and shovels. They searched the riverbanks and stream beds hoping to find more nuggets or even gold flakes.

Some people got rich, but many went home empty-handed. Perhaps the most disappointed of all were those who found pyrite, a substance that looks like gold. Pyrite is actually a compound of iron and sulfur. Can you tell why pyrite is also called "fool's gold"?

A miner pans for gold in northern California ▶

Reading Strategies

Reading Tip Before students begin reading, have them preview the photographs and captions in the section. Then challenge students to describe or speculate about ways that people take matter out of the earth. List students' responses on the board. Then have students read the section and follow directions for the Reading Tip. Students should list panning, electrolysis, and heating. Revise or add to the items on the board after students have read the section.

Gold and Density

Figure 17 Gold nuggets contain the element gold.

During the California gold rush, miners needed a way to remove the precious metal from a mixture that also contained dirt and sand. **Gold can be separated from other materials in a mixture because of its density.** As you read in Section 2, gold has a density of 19.3 g/cm^3. This density is much higher than that of most other materials, including fool's gold, which has a density of only 5.0 g/cm^3.

The miners used a technique called panning. They put the mixture of gold, dirt, and sand into a shallow pan and covered it with water. They then swirled the contents around and carefully poured off the water. The water carried the less dense dirt and sand with it. The more dense gold sank and was left behind. The miners repeated this process until only gold remained in the pan.

Today, gold mining is done on a much larger scale using machines called dredges. But the basic process of separating gold by its density is the same. The dredge scrapes up large amounts of dirt and sand, washes the mixture, and separates the gold in a way that's similar to panning.

☑ *Checkpoint* *What could you do to tell the difference between real gold and fool's gold?*

Copper and Electrolysis

In nature, finding an element that's not part of a compound is unusual. Most elements, including those that people use for industrial purposes in great amounts, are usually found as compounds. For example, copper compounds are most often found in a certain kind of ore. An ore is any rock that contains a metal or other economically useful material.

The process of obtaining copper from one of its compounds is more complicated than panning for gold. **To obtain an element from its compound, it is necessary to cause a chemical reaction to take place.** In that chemical change, the copper atoms must be separated from the other atoms in the compound.

Figure 18 Ores contain useful elements that are combined with other substances. **A.** Malachite contains copper. **B.** Iron pyrite contains iron.
Applying Concepts Why do ores have different properties from the elements that they contain?

2 Facilitate

Gold and Density

Real-Life Learning

Materials *bunch of fresh spinach, large bowl of water*
Time 5 minutes

Tell students that many cooks rely on the same principle used to pan for gold to clean spinach. Because spinach grows in sandy soil, the leaves are often full of sand and can be difficult to clean. Place a bunch of spinach in the water so it is completely submerged and swirl it around. Ask students to predict what will happen. After a few minutes, lift the spinach out of the water and allow students to observe the water in the bowl. The bottom of the bowl should be covered with the sand that was in the spinach. Ask students to explain what happened. *(The sand is more dense than the water, and so it sank to the bottom, allowing you to lift out the clean spinach.)* **learning modality: visual**

Copper and Electrolysis

Addressing Naive Conceptions

Some students may think that the process of electrolysis separates copper from the *rock* that contains it. The copper compounds are separated from the rock first. Then electrolysis separates copper from other *elements* in the copper compound by breaking the chemical bonds between them. **learning modality: verbal**

Program Resources

- **Unit 1 Resources** 1-4 Lesson Plan; 1-4 Section Summary
- **Guided Reading and Study Workbook** Section 1-4

Answers to Self-Assessment

Caption Question

Figure 18 Ores are mixtures of many substances, often including the useful element in the form of a compound.

☑ *Checkpoint*

Find the density of the sample. Real gold has a density of 19.3 g/cm^3 and fool's gold has a density of 5.0 g/cm^3.

Ongoing Assessment

Oral Presentation Ask students to describe ways metals are found in nature. *(Some metals, such as gold, are found as elements. Other metals, such as copper, are found in compounds)*

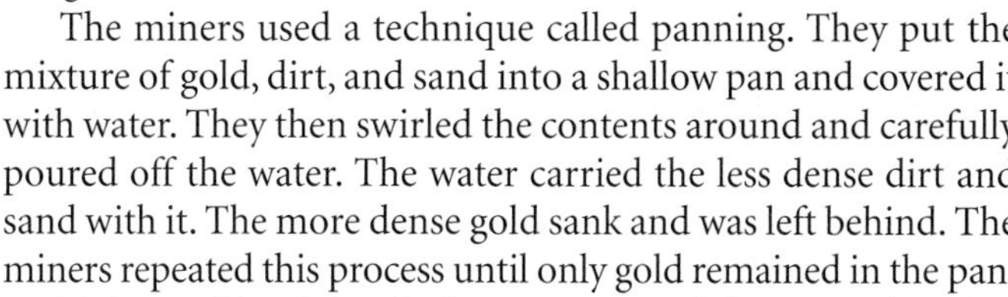

Real-World Lab

How It Works

Isolating Copper

Preparing for Inquiry

Key Concept Elements can be isolated from some compounds by passing an electric current through a solution containing the compound.

Skills Objectives Students will be able to
- observe the outcome of electrolysis;
- infer the changes occurring in a copper chloride solution during electrolysis.

Time 30 minutes

Advance Planning
- To make the 0.6 M copper (II) chloride (cupric chloride) solution, add 9.5 g of copper (II) chloride dihydrate, $CuCl_2 \cdot 2H_2O$, to 100 mL of distilled water. For 12 pairs of students, you will need about 600–1,200 mL of the solution.
- The electrodes can be used repeatedly, but the tips must be cleaned with #0000 steel wool between uses to remove plated copper.
- To make wire connections, any small leads with alligator clips on both ends will work for this lab. A length of at least 8 cm is easier for students to handle.

Alternative Materials

You may also use a copper sulfate solution.

Guiding Inquiry

Invitation

Show students a bright new penny. Ask students how the copper in the penny was found. *(Many will say the copper was in the ground in the pure elemental state).* Point out that most elements are not found in their elemental states, and they have to be processed to extract the pure element.

Introducing the Procedure
- Set up a sample apparatus for students to look at as they set up their own.
- Point out the positive and negative poles on the 9-volt battery. Remind students that they will be asked which electrode (+ or −) collected the copper.

Many steps are involved in obtaining copper from its ores. The last step in the process is called **electrolysis.** This term literally means "electric cutting." In one kind of electrolysis, a copper compound is dissolved in water, forming a mixture called a solution. Two metal strips called **electrodes** are placed in the copper compound solution. Each electrode is attached to a wire, and the wires are connected to a source of electric current such as a battery.

Real-World Lab

How It Works

Isolating Copper

In nature, copper is usually found in compounds with other elements. In this investigation, you will perform an electrolysis procedure to isolate copper from a compound called copper chloride.

Problem

How can copper be isolated from a compound by electrolysis?

Skills Focus

observing, inferring

Materials

glass jar, about 250 mL
6-volt battery
two paper clips
index card
wires with alligator clips or battery holder with wires
copper chloride solution (0.6 *M*), 100 mL

Procedure   

1. Unbend a paper clip and make a hook shape. Push the long end through an index card until the hooked part touches the card.
2. Repeat Step 1 with another paper clip so that the clips are about 2–3 cm apart. The paper clips serve as your electrodes.
3. Pour enough copper chloride solution into a jar to cover at least half the length of the paper clips when the index card is set on top of the jar. **CAUTION:** *Copper chloride solution can be irritating to the skin and eyes. Do not touch it with your hands or get it in your mouth. The solution can stain your skin and clothes.*
4. Place the index card on top of the jar. If the straightened ends of the paper clips are not at least half-covered by the copper chloride solution, add more solution.

42

Troubleshooting the Experiment
- Caution students to avoid breaking the electrodes.
- Some students may have difficulty detecting chlorine gas in Step 7. There may not be enough produced to be noticeable, or students may be unfamiliar with the odor.

Expected Outcome
- The pale yellow-gold or pinkish color on the tip of the negative electrode shows that copper has been deposited there.
- The faint odor of chlorine tells students that another substance was also produced by this reaction. They may see small bubbles being produced at the positive electrode. They may or may not be able to identify this substance.

Analyze and Conclude

1. Check students' diagrams. Make sure labels are correct.
2. Copper forms on the negative electrode, and chlorine gas bubbles at the positive electrode.

When the electric current is turned on, one electrode in the solution becomes coated with copper metal. At the same time, other materials form on the second electrode. In a laboratory, electrolysis produces only small amounts of copper metal. In industry, the isolation of copper from its ores happens on a huge scale and involves several complex steps. Because many copper compounds do not dissolve in water, the method of electrolysis used in the last step can vary.

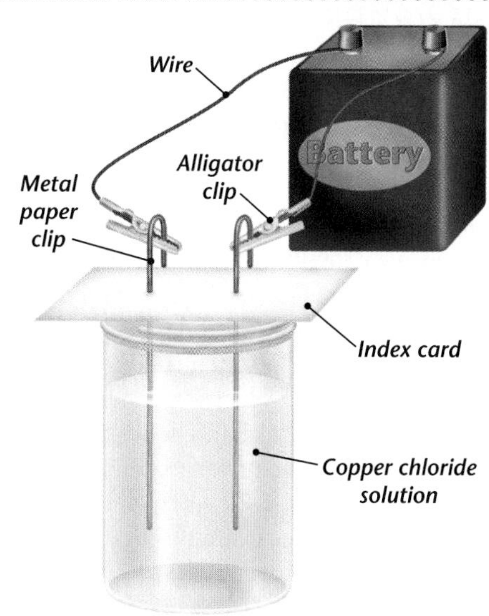

5. Attach a wire to each pole of a battery. Attach the other ends of the wires to a separate paper clip. (See the drawing.) Prevent the paper clips from touching each other.
6. Predict what you think will happen if you allow the current to run for 2–3 minutes. (*Hint:* What elements are present in the copper chloride solution?)
7. Let the setup run for 2–3 minutes or until you see a deposit forming on one of the electrodes. Also look for bubbles.
8. Disconnect the wires. Remove the index card. Bring your face close to the jar and gently wave your hand toward your nose. Note any odor.
9. Note whether the color of the solution has changed since you began the procedure.
10. Note the color of the tips of the electrodes.
11. Discard the solution as directed by your teacher, and wash your hands.

Analyze and Conclude

1. Make a labeled diagram of your experimental setup. Indicate which electrode is connected to the positive side of the battery and which is connected to the negative side.
2. On which electrode was the copper produced? On which electrode was the chlorine produced?
3. If the color of the solution changed, how can you explain the change?
4. Compare the properties of copper, chlorine, and copper chloride solution.
5. Describe the changes in matter that you observed. Classify them as physical changes or chemical changes.
6. **Apply** Using your observations during this lab as evidence, explain why you think copper chloride is a compound, not a mixture.

More to Explore

Suppose you were to reconnect the wires with the positive and negative sides reversed. Predict how your results would differ under these conditions. With your teacher's permission, carry out the electrolysis with the connections reversed. Was your prediction correct?

3. The color changed because the copper compound producing the color was changed during a chemical reaction.
4. Copper is a shiny, gold-colored metal. Chlorine is a dense, green, irritating gas. Copper chloride solution is a clear green liquid.
5. The dissolved copper chloride underwent a chemical change to form new substances, copper and chlorine. As the chemical change took place, the copper became a solid and the chlorine became a gas through physical changes.
6. Copper chloride must be a compound because the electrolysis caused a chemical change by breaking its chemical bonds, and two elements—copper and chlorine—were produced.

Extending the Inquiry

More to Explore Students may predict that the copper and chlorine will form on the opposite electrodes when the polarity is reversed.

Safety

Dispose of the copper chloride according to state or local regulation. Chlorine gas, a toxic substance, is produced in small quantities in this lab. Ensure good ventilation in the room during the lab. Review the safety guidelines in Appendix A.

Program Resources

◆ **Unit 1 Resources** Chapter 1 Real-World Lab blackline masters

Media and Technology

 **Lab Activity Videotapes** Grade 6, Tape 1

Iron and the Blast Furnace

Demonstration

Use gumdrops and toothpicks to show students how iron oxide is changed in a blast furnace. Connect one "iron atom" with two "oxygen atoms". Show students a single "carbon atom". Move the "oxygen atoms" to the "carbon atom". Ask students if the carbon atom is an element or a compound. *(element)*

3 Assess

Section 4 Review Answers

1. Gold is more dense than sand and dirt. When the mixture is swirled with water, the gold sinks. When the water is poured off, it carries away the sand and dirt.
2. A chemical change (chemical bonds must be broken)
3. The carbon in coke reacts with the oxygen that is bonded with the iron and leaves pure iron behind.
4. Recycling programs will probably become more important because more metals will be needed by Earth's growing population.

CHAPTER PROJECT

Check Your Progress

Assign students a new partner and have them exchange procedures and materials. After students conduct each other's experiments, set aside class time for them to discuss their results and to share ways they could make their procedures easier to follow.

Performance Assessment

Writing Have students create two flowcharts for the processes of removing metal from its ore by using heating and electrolysis.

Figure 19 Industry uses large-scale chemical reactions to produce useful materials. This blast furnace is used to make carbon react with iron ore to produce iron metal. The source of the carbon is coke, a substance produced from coal.

Iron and the Blast Furnace

Industry uses huge amounts of the element iron. Like copper, iron is usually found in an ore in the form of a compound. And also like copper, the element iron must be separated from its compounds by a chemical reaction.

Iron ores usually contain compounds formed of iron and oxygen. In order to release the iron, chunks of iron ore are placed in a hot fire along with coke, a source of carbon. In the intense heat of a blast furnace like the one in Figure 19, the carbon reacts with the oxygen. The element iron is left behind.

After leaving the blast furnace, iron is often used with other materials to produce mixtures having specific properties. For example, iron may be mixed with carbon and other metals to produce steel, which is stronger than iron alone. Adding chromium and nickel makes stainless steel, which resists rusting. Iron, copper, and gold are just three examples of useful elements that are extracted from Earth's surface.

Section 4 Review

1. Describe how panning for gold takes advantage of a specific property of gold.
2. What kind of change must take place to remove an element from its compound? Explain.
3. What happens to the elements in iron ore when the ore is mixed with carbon and heated?
4. **Thinking Critically Making Judgments** Planet Earth contains a limited supply of all metals. Predict whether programs to recycle aluminum, iron, and other metals will become more important in the future.

CHAPTER PROJECT

Check Your Progress

Trade your written procedure and product samples with a new partner. Repeat this partner's procedure, following the directions as exactly as you can. Share your results with your new partner. Think of ways to improve both your procedure and your partner's procedure to make them clearer to follow.

Program Resources

- **Unit 1 Resources** 1-4 Review and Reinforce; 1-4 Enrich

CHAPTER 1 STUDY GUIDE

Section 1 Describing Matter and Energy

Key Ideas

- Each specific substance has its own physical and chemical properties. These properties can be used to identify the substance.
- Matter is made up of elements. Elements can be chemically combined in compounds.
- Physical changes alter the form of a substance, but not its identity. Chemical changes result in one or more new substances.
- Energy is needed for both physical and chemical changes. There are different types of energy, which interact with matter in different ways.

Key Terms

matter, energy, chemistry, substance, physical property, chemical property, element, compound, mixture, physical change, state, chemical change

Section 2 Measuring Matter

Key Ideas

- Mass is a measurement of how much matter an object contains. If you move an object away from Earth, its weight changes, but its mass stays the same.
- The density of an object equals its mass divided by its volume. A unit of density is always a mass unit divided by a volume unit, such as grams per cubic centimeter (g/cm^3).

Key Terms

weight, mass, International System of Units (SI), volume, density

Section 3 Particles of Matter

Key Ideas

- Atoms are the smallest particles of an element.
- Dalton stated that atoms are unbreakable, rigid spheres. He also said that atoms of different elements are different from one another.
- Atoms can be combined into molecules, which are held together by chemical bonds.

Key Terms

atom, nucleus, proton, neutron, electron, molecule, chemical bond

Section 4 Elements From Earth

Integrating Earth Science

Key Ideas

- Gold, which is usually found in nature as an element, can be separated from other materials because of its density.
- Earth contains deposits of many elements in the form of compounds. A chemical reaction is needed to remove an element from its compound.

Key Terms

electrolysis, electrode

Organizing Information

Concept Map Copy the concept map about classifying matter onto a separate sheet of paper. Then complete the map and add a title. (For more on concept maps, see the Skills Handbook.)

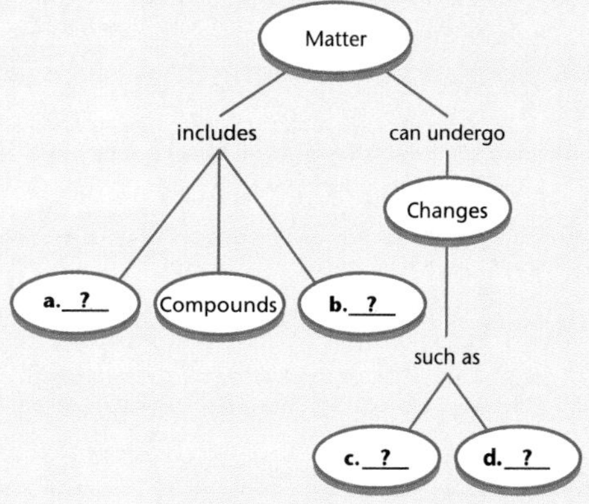

Program Resources

- **Unit 1 Resources** Chapter 1 Project Scoring Rubric
- **Performance Assessment** Chapter 1
- **Chapter and Unit Tests** Chapter 1 Test

Media and Technology

Computer Test Bank Chapter 1 Test

Organizing Information

Concept Map Sample title: Classifying Matter; **a.** Elements **b.** Mixtures **c.** Physical changes **d.** Chemical changes

Reviewing Content

Multiple Choice

1. a **2.** b **3.** d **4.** a **5.** a

True or False

6. Elements **7.** true **8.** mass
9. density **10.** true

Checking Concepts

11. When a piece of paper is torn into two pieces, its parts have the same kinds of properties as the original piece of paper. Thus, the paper has undergone a physical change.
12. Place a small amount of water in the graduated cylinder. Record the volume. Submerge the rock and record the new volume. The difference between the new and old volumes is the volume of the rock.
13. Its density is less than that of water (1.0 g/cm^3).
14. The water releases energy as it changes from a liquid to a solid.
15. Encourage students to think creatively about observing properties of matter and writing about them. Challenge students to describe each object so that others can identify it from the description.

Thinking Critically

16. Salt is a solid, water is a liquid, but salt water is a solution, or mixture. Students may suggest boiling the solution to produce water vapor and solid salt.
17. Atoms and molecules are both extremely small particles of matter. Molecules are made up of two or more atoms bonded together. For example, a carbon atom alone is the smallest piece of the element carbon. In the molecule CO_2, a carbon atom is bonded to two oxygen atoms.
18. Dalton reasoned that since every atom of an element is identical and unique to that element, every sample of a substance has the same properties.
19. Since the density of the gold decreases but the mass stays the same, the volume must increase.

CHAPTER 1 ASSESSMENT

Reviewing Content

Multiple Choice

Choose the letter of the answer that best completes the statement or answers the question.

1. Matter made of two or more substances is a(n)
   a. mixture. **b.** element.
   c. compound. **d.** property.
2. One form of electromagnetic energy is
   a. motion. **b.** light.
   c. electricity. **d.** energy in matter.
3. The density of an object equals
   a. the product of its length, width, and height.
   b. its volume divided by its mass.
   c. the product of the mass and volume.
   d. its mass divided by its volume.
4. Dalton imagined atoms to be
   a. rigid, unbreakable spheres.
   b. all exactly alike.
   c. always joined together in compounds.
   d. of equal mass.
5. A method used to release iron metal from its ore involves
   a. heating the ore and carbon together.
   b. cooling the ore in an ice bath.
   c. breaking the ore into small pieces.
   d. panning.

True or False

If the statement is true, write true. If it is false, change the underlined word to make it true.

6. Compounds are substances that cannot be broken down into other substances by any chemical means.
7. Energy is always involved when changes in matter occur.
8. If you move an object from place to place in the universe, the weight of the object will stay the same.
9. Grams per milliliter (g/mL) is an example of a unit of volume.
10. One of Dalton's principles is that each element is made of its own kind of atom.

Checking Concepts

11. When a piece of paper is torn into two pieces, has it undergone a chemical change or a physical change? Explain.
12. How could you find the volume of a small rock, using only a graduated cylinder and water?
13. What can you infer about the density of a substance if a block of that substance floats in water?
14. In terms of energy, describe what happens to water in a freezer.
15. **Writing to Learn** In a novel or short story, the author describes the properties of objects he or she is writing about. These details add interest to the story. Select at least six different kinds of objects. You might include objects from nature as well as objects made by people. List the properties of each object. Now use that list to write the first paragraph of a story.

Thinking Critically

16. **Problem Solving** How can you show that salt water is a mixture and not a compound? First compare the properties of the solution to the properties of the individual components. Then come up with a plan to separate the solution into its components.
17. **Comparing and Contrasting** Compare and contrast atoms and molecules. What do the two kinds of particles have in common? How are they related? Give an example that shows this relationship.
18. **Applying Concepts** How can you use Dalton's atomic theory to explain why every sample of a particular substance has the same properties?
19. **Inferring** Solid gold has a greater density than liquid gold. What must happen to the volume of a given mass of solid gold when it becomes a liquid? Explain.

Applying Skills

20. A: 7.6 g/cm^3; B: 8.0 g/cm^3; C: 7.2 g/cm^3; D: 8.4 g/cm^3; E: 8.9 g/cm^3; F: 7.5 g/cm^3
21. Coin D
22. The density of Coin E (8.9 g/cm^3) is very close to 8.92 g/cm^3, so Coin E very likely could be pure copper. The density of Coin C (7.2 g/cm^3) is close enough to 7.14 (g/cm^3) that there is a good chance Coin C could be pure zinc.

Applying Skills

Use the table below to answer Questions 20–22. The table lists the mass and volume of six coins.

Coin	Mass (g)	Volume (cm^3)
A	3.1	0.41
B	4.0	0.50
C	8.6	1.2
D	8.0	0.95
E	9.8	1.1
F	5.0	0.67

20. Calculating Based on the data in the table, calculate the density of Coins A–F.

21. Interpreting Data In Altrusia, all coins are made of a mixture of copper and zinc that has a density of 8.42 g/cm^3. Which coins could be from Altrusia?

22. Drawing Conclusions The density of copper is 8.92 g/cm^3 and the density of zinc is 7.14 g/cm^3. If you assume that only copper and zinc were used to make the coins, can any of the coins be pure copper? Can any be pure zinc? Explain.

Performance Assessment

Present Your Project Work with your second partner to show the data each of you collected. Present your data so that other students can see whether the procedure produced similar results each time. Briefly describe why or why not you think your data is reliable.

Reflect and Record In your journal, record the results of your experiment and describe why you think your conclusions are valid. Describe how your data compares with the advertising message promoted by the product's manufacturer.

Test Preparation

Use these questions to prepare for standardized tests.

Use the diagram to answer Questions 23–26.

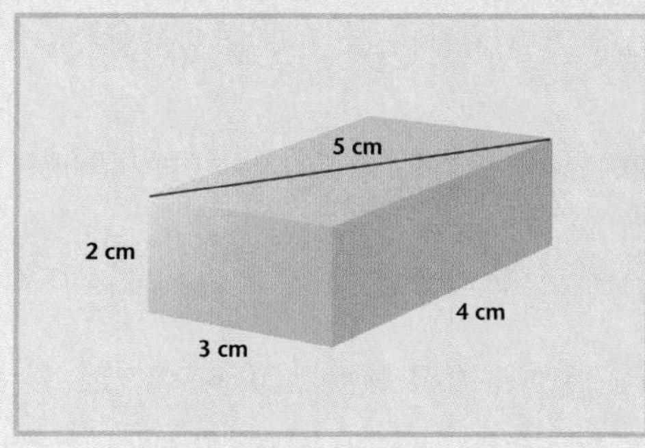

Alexander found a solid block of an unknown material. He used a metric ruler to measure the size of the block. The measurements he recorded are shown in the diagram.

23. What is the volume of the block?
a. 9 cm **b.** 24 cm^2
c. 24 cm^3 **d.** 60 cm^3

24. Which measurement shown in the diagram was not needed to find the volume of the box?
a. length (4 cm) **b.** height (2 cm)
c. width (3 cm) **d.** diagonal (5 cm)

25. Alexander knows that the density of the material from which the block is made is 2 g/cm^3. Knowing this, what is the mass of the block?
a. 4.8 g **b.** 48 g
c. 480 g **d.** 4,800 g

26. If the block could be molded into a flatter and longer shape, then the
a. mass, volume, and density all would change.
b. volume would change, but the mass and density would remain the same.
c. mass and volume would change, but the density would remain the same.
d. mass, volume, and density all would remain the same.

Performance Assessment (Chapter Project)

Present Your Project Allow students time in class to meet with their partners so that they can prepare the data for each of their procedures. Both partners should plot their data on the same graph. If the students graph their own trials, the scales of the graphs may not be the same and comparing data sets will be difficult. Have students question their classmates about why they chose particular properties to measure and how their experimental designs test these properties.

Reflect and Record Students should include questions they have after performing their experiments and describe how they think they could answer them.

Test Preparation

23. c 24. d 25. b 26. d

Program Resources

- **Inquiry Skills Activity Book** Provides teaching and review of all inquiry skills

CHAPTER 2 Water and Solutions

Sections	Time	Student Edition Activities	Other Activities
CHAPTER PROJECT **Every Drop Counts** p. 49	Ongoing (2 weeks)	Check Your Progress, pp. 58, 64 Present Your Project, p. 67	
1 *INTEGRATING CHEMISTRY* **The Properties of Water** pp. 50–58 ◆ Describe the physical and chemical properties of water. ◆ Explain how water dissolves other polar substances. ◆ Identify the three states in which water exists on Earth.	2 periods/ 1 block	**Discover** What Are Some Properties of Water?, p. 50 **Try This** Follow That String, p. 52 **Try This** Comparing Solvents, p. 53 **Skills Lab: Developing Hypotheses** Speeding Up Evaporation, pp. 56–57	**TE** Inquiry Challenge, p. 51 **TE** Addressing Naive Conceptions, p. 52 **TE** Building Inquiry Skills: Designing an Experiment, p. 53 **TE** Demonstration, p. 54 **TE** Language Arts Connection, p. 55 **LM** 2, "Properties of Water"
2 **Understanding Solutions** pp. 59–64 ◆ Define and compare solutions, suspensions, and colloids. ◆ Explain what happens to particles of a solute when a solution forms. ◆ Describe how solutes affect the freezing and boiling points of solvents.	2 periods/ 1 block	**Discover** What Makes a Mixture a Solution?, p. 59 **Try This** Scattered Light, p. 62 **Sharpen Your Skills** Designing Experiments, p. 63	**TE** Inquiry Challenge, p. 60 **TE** Integrating Life Science, p. 60 **TE** Real-Life Learning, p. 61 **TE** Building Inquiry Skills: Inferring, p. 63 **TE** "Soap From Concept to Consumer," pp. 27–30
Study Guide/Assessment pp. 65–67	1 period/ $\frac{1}{2}$ block		**ISAB** Provides teaching and review of all inquiry skills

For Standard or Block Schedule The Resource Pro® CD-ROM gives you maximum flexibility for planning your instruction for any type of schedule. Resource Pro® contains Planning Express®, an advanced scheduling program, as well as the entire contents of the Teaching Resources and the Computer Test Bank.

CHAPTER PLANNING GUIDE

Program Resources	Assessment Strategies	Media and Technology
UR Chapter 2 Project Teacher Notes **UR** Chapter 2 Project Overview and Worksheets	**TE** Check Your Progress, pp. 58, 64 **TE** Performance Assessment: Chapter 2 Present Your Project, p. 67 **UR** Chapter 2 Project Scoring Rubric	Science Explorer Internet Site at www.phschool.com Student Edition on Audio CD, Chapter 2
UR 1-1 Lesson Plan **UR** 1-1 Section Summary **UR** 1-1 Review and Reinforce **UR** 1-1 Enrich **UR** Skills Lab blackline masters	**SE** Section 1 Review, p. 58 **SE** Analyze and Conclude, p. 57 **TE** Ongoing Assessment, pp. 51, 53, 55 **TE** Performance Assessment, p. 58	Lab Activity Videotapes, Grade 6 Tape 1 Concept Videotape Library, Grade 6, Tape 1, "Opposites Atrract" Concept Videotape Library, Grade 6, Tape 1, "The Disappearing Ice Cube" Transparency 2, "Structure of Water Molecules" Transparency 3, "Three States of Water"
UR 2-2 Lesson Plan **UR** 2-2 Section Summary **UR** 2-2 Review and Reinforce **UR** 2-2 Enrich	**SE** Section 2 Review, p. 64 **TE** Ongoing Assessment, pp. 61, 63 **TE** Performance Assessment, p. 64	Transparencies 4, "Solution of An Ionic Solid"; 5 "Effect of Solutes on Freezing and Boiling" Concept Videotape Library, Grade 6, Tape 1, "Opposites Attract"
RCA Provides strategies to improve science reading skills **GRSW** Provides worksheets to promote student comprehension of content	**SE** Chapter 2 Study Guide/Assessment, pp. 65–67 **PA** Chapter 2 Performance Assessment **CUT** Chapter 2 Test **CTB** Chapter 2 Test	Computer Test Bank, Chapter 2 Test

Key: **SE** Student Edition
CTB Computer Test Bank
ISAB Inquiry Skills Activity Book
GRSW Guided Reading and Study Workbook
TE Teacher's Edition
PTA Product Testing Activities by *Consumer Reports*
RCA Reading in the Content Area
PA Performance Assessment
UR Unit Resources
LM Laboratory Manual
IES Interdisciplinary Explorations Series
CUT Chapter and Unit Tests

Meeting the National Science Education Standards and AAAS Benchmarks

National Science Education Standards	Benchmarks for Science Literacy	Unifying Themes
Science as Inquiry (Content Standard A) ◆ **Develop descriptions, explanations, predictions, and models using evidence** Students investigate factors that affect evaporation. *(Skills Lab)* **Physical Science** (Content Standard B) ◆ **Properties and changes of properties of matter** Water has a unique chemical structure that gives it unusual properties. Substances that dissolve in a solvent are called solutes. *(Sections 1, 2)* **Science in Personal and Social Perspectives** (Content Standard F) ◆ **Science and technology in society** People use water for many purposes. *(Chapter Project)*	**1B Scientific Inquiry** Students investigate what factors increase the rate at which water evaporates. *(Skills Lab)* **4D Structure of Matter** Water has a unique chemical structure that gives it unusual properties. *(Section 1)* **11B Models** Students use models to investigate evaporation. *(Skills Lab)* **12D Communication Skills** Students monitor water use in their homes and community and share their findings. *(Chapter Project)*	◆ **Scale and Structure** Water has a unique structure that gives it unusual properties. *(Section 1)* ◆ **Energy** Water molecules gain or lose energy when water changes state. Compared to other substances, water has a high specific heat. The sun is the source of energy that drives the water cycle. *(Section 1; Skills Lab)* ◆ **Systems and Interactions** Solutions are made up of solutes and solvents. The particles of a solute separate into ions or molecules as they are surrounded by solvent particles in a solution. *(Section 2)* ◆ **Unity and Diversity** All solutions are made up of solutes and solvents. *(Section 2)*

Take It to the Net

Interactive text at www.phschool.com

Science Explorer comes alive with iText.

- **Complete student text** is accessible from any computer with Internet access or a CD-ROM drive.
- **Animations, simulations, and videos** enhance student understanding and retention of concepts.
- **Self-tests and online study tools** assess student understanding.

STAY CURRENT with

Find out the latest research and information about Earth's Waters at: **www.phschool.com**

Go to **www.phschool.com** and click on the Science icon.Then click on Science Explorer: Life, Earth, and Physical Science under PH@school.

Student Edition Activities Planner

ACTIVITY	Time (minutes)	Materials *Quantities for one work group*	Skills
Section 1			
Discover, p. 50	15	**Consumable** water, vegetable oil, paper towels, wax paper **Nonconsumable** 2 plastic cups, scissors, meter stick, 2 plastic droppers	Observing
Try This, p. 52	20	**Consumable** string, water, tape **Nonconsumable** scissors, pitcher, plastic cup	Inferring
Try This, p. 53	20	**Consumable** water, vegetable oil, salt, baking soda, food coloring **Nonconsumable** 6 plastic cups, permanent marker, 6 plastic spoons, plastic dropper	Drawing Conclusions
Skills Lab, pp. 56–57	40	**Consumable** water, 3 index cards, paper towels **Nonconsumable** 2 plastic petri dishes, 1 petri dish cover, plastic dropper, lamp, stopwatch	Developing Hypotheses, Controlling Variables, Drawing Conclusions
Section 2			
Discover, p. 59	80	**Consumable** 2 plastic cups, water, pepper, salt **Nonconsumable** plastic spoon	Observing
Try This, p. 62	15	**Consumable** liquid gelatin, salt water **Nonconsumable** small glass beakers or jars, small flashlight (such as a penlight)	Inferring
Sharpen Your Skills, p. 63	10	No special materials are required.	Designing Experiments

A list of all materials required for the Student Edition activities can be found on pages TVA34–TVA40. You can obtain information about ordering materials by calling 1-800-848-9500 or by accessing the Science Explorer Internet site at: **www.phschool.com**

CHAPTER 2 PROJECT

Every Drop Counts

Opening a faucet is so routine that many students are unaware of how often they run water in the home. Equally as significant, they are probably unaware of the total amount of water used, as most of it swirls down the drain.

Purpose In this project, students will measure how much water they themselves use during a week, how much water is used in their homes during the same week, and how much water is used in another type of building in a week. Gathering this information should give students a greater understanding of the importance of water and water resources.

Skills Focus After completing the Chapter 2 Project, students will be able to

- ◆ interpret data collected from a home water meter and from another building in their community;
- ◆ create data tables about home water use;
- ◆ calculate how much water is used in their home and in another building during a one-week period;
- ◆ graph the data collected about household water use;
- ◆ communicate the results of the project in a presentation to the class.

Project Timeline The entire project will require at least two weeks. See Chapter 2 Project Teacher Notes in Unit 1 Resources for hints and detailed directions. Also distribute to students Chapter 2 Project Overview and Worksheets and Scoring Rubric in Unit 1 Resources.

Early in the project, allow class time for students to discuss how to make their data tables. Although students will be making their measurements at home through the week, they will need some class time for you to check their progress.

You may want students to begin immediately looking for an appropriate nonresidential building to study. Tell students they should ask parents and other adults for suggestions. Often parents will know someone who could help students gain access to a building manager or building records. Allow the second week of the project for the gathering of this information, as well as for the preparation of student presentations.

SECTION 1 The Properties of Water

Discover What Are Some Properties of Water?
Try This Follow That String
Try This Comparing Solvents
Skills Lab Speeding Up Evaporation

SECTION 2 Understanding Solutions

Discover What Makes a Mixture a Solution?
Try This Scattered Light
Sharpen Your Skills Designing Experiments

48

Suggested Shortcuts If the project seems too long or involved for your students, you could have them do only the home study for one or two weeks, eliminating the monitoring of a second building. As an alternative, you could ask for a small group of student volunteers to monitor a nonresidential building and report to the class.

A further shortcut would be to simply have students monitor their own water use over several days. This would eliminate the cooperation of family members but would still fulfill the purpose of the project.

Possible Materials Students need nothing more than paper and pencil to collect the data for the project. In presenting their results at the end of the project, some students may want to use poster board to mount their graphs or other visual aids.

CHAPTER 2 PROJECT

Every Drop Counts

With an almost deafening roar, water rushes over this waterfall and plunges into the rocky pool below. Every day, hundreds of thousands of liters of water flow over the falls. How do you think this amount compares with the amount of water that flows out of your faucets at home each day?

In this chapter, you will explore the many ways that living things depend on Earth's water. To learn how water is used in your own home and community, you will design a method for tracking water use over a one-week period.

Your Goal To monitor water use in your home and in another building in your community for one week.

To complete the project you will

- ◆ track your personal water use at home
- ◆ determine the total amount of water used in your home
- ◆ find out how much water is used by a business, school, hospital, or other building in your community

Get Started Begin now by brainstorming the ways you use water at home. Use this list to create a data table in which you will record each time you perform these activities during the week.

Check Your Progress You'll be working on this project as you study this chapter. To keep your project on track, look for Check Your Progress boxes at the following points.

Section 1 Review, page 58: Calculate your total water use.

Section 2 Review, page 64: Investigate water use at another building in your community.

Present Your Project At the end of the chapter (page 67), you will graph your household water-use data and share the information with your classmates.

Hikers in California's Yosemite National Park are awed by its thundering waterfalls.

49

Launching the Project To introduce this project to students, ask: **What are some of the ways you and your family use water daily in and around the home?** *(Flushing toilets, taking baths and showers, brushing teeth, cleaning dishes, washing clothes, watering the lawn, washing the car, and so on)* Write students' suggestions on the board. Then challenge students to estimate how many liters of water each of them uses in a day. After students have shared their estimates, tell them that in this country residential water use averages about 300 L per person per day. Encourage students to compare this average with their own water use to estimate if they use more or less than the average.

Finally, have students read the description of the project in their text and in the Chapter 2 Project Overview in Unit 1 Resources. Encourage students to come up with their own ideas of how they could accomplish the tasks involved.

Performance Assessment

The Chapter 2 Project Scoring Rubric in Unit 1 Resources will help you evaluate how well students complete the Chapter 2 Project. Students will be assessed on

- ◆ how completely and accurately they collect data from their homes and a second building,
- ◆ how thorough and interesting their class presentations are,
- ◆ their participation in their groups.

By sharing the Chapter 2 Project Scoring Rubric with students at the beginning of the project, you will make it clear to them what they are expected to do.

Program Resources

- ◆ **Unit 1 Resources** Chapter 2 Project Teacher Notes; Chapter 2 Project Student Materials; Chapter 2 Project Scoring Rubric

Media and Technology

Student Edition on Audio CD Chapter 2

You will find an Internet activity, chapter self-tests for students, and links to other chapter topics at this site.

Integrating Chemistry 

The Properties of Water

Objectives

After completing the lesson, students will be able to

- describe the physical and chemical properties of water;
- explain how water dissolves other polar substances;
- identify the three states in which water exists on Earth.

Key Terms polar molecule, surface tension, capillary action, solution, solvent, state, evaporation, condensation, specific heat

1 Engage/Explore

Activating Prior Knowledge

Hold a clear glass full of water in your hand and, as students watch, place two large ice cubes in the water. Ask: **How is the ice in the glass related to the liquid?** *(Ice is the solid state of liquid water.)* **Why do you think the ice floats?** *(Some students may know that ice is less dense than liquid water.)* Challenge students to describe other properties of water. Note their misconceptions. Tell them that they will learn about the properties of water in this section.

Discover

Skills Focus observing
Materials *water, 2 plastic cups, vegetable oil, paper towel, scissors, meter stick, 2 pieces of wax paper, 2 plastic droppers*
Time 15 minutes
Tips Students need only a small amount of water and oil in the cups. You may want to cut the strips of paper towel yourself, before class begins.
Think It Over The water climbs up the paper towel faster than the oil, and the water forms a taller, rounder drop on the wax paper than the oil.

Section 1 The Properties of Water

Discover Activity

What Are Some Properties of Water?

1. Pour a small amount of water into a plastic cup. Pour an equal amount of vegetable oil into a second cup.
2. Cut two strips of paper towel. Hold the strips so that the bottom of one strip is in the water and the other is in the oil.
3. After one minute, measure how high each substance climbed up the paper towel.
4. Using a plastic dropper, place a big drop of water onto a piece of wax paper.

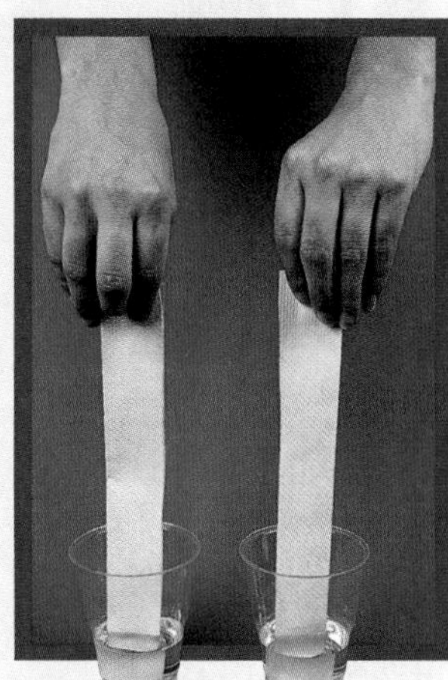

5. Using another dropper, place a drop of oil the same size as the water drop beside it on the wax paper.
6. Observe the shape of the two drops from the side.
7. Follow your teacher's instructions for disposing of the oil when you clean up after this activity.

Think It Over
Observing What differences do you notice between the water and the oil in each experiment?

Guide for Reading

- How does the chemical structure of water molecules cause them to stick together?
- How does water dissolve other polar substances?
- What are the three states in which water exists on Earth?

Reading Tip As you read, make a list of water's properties. Write a sentence describing each property.

How would you describe water to someone who had never seen it before? You might say that pure water has no color, no taste, and no odor. You might even say that water is a rather plain, ordinary substance. But if you asked a chemist to describe water, the response would be different. The chemist would say that water is very unusual. Its properties differ from those of most other familiar substances.

Are you and the chemist talking about the same substance? To understand the chemist's description of water, you need to know something about the chemical structure of water.

Water's Unique Structure

Like all matter, water is made up of atoms. Just as the 26 letters of the alphabet combine in different ways to form all the words in the English language, about 100 types of atoms combine in different ways to form all types of matter. Atoms bond to form molecules. Recall from Chapter 1 that two hydrogen atoms bonded to an oxygen atom form a water molecule. A short way of writing this is to use the chemical formula for water, H_2O.

Reading Strategies

Reading Tip Remind students that a property of a substance is a characteristic of it. Help students with limited English proficiency to distinguish this meaning from the meaning of property as real estate or other possessions by pointing out that water cannot have possessions, but it does have unique characteristics. Then ask students to identify some properties of water. Student lists should include the following: surface tension, capillary action, high specific heat, dissolves many substances, and is less dense in the solid state than the liquid state. Have students share their sentences describing each property with the class.

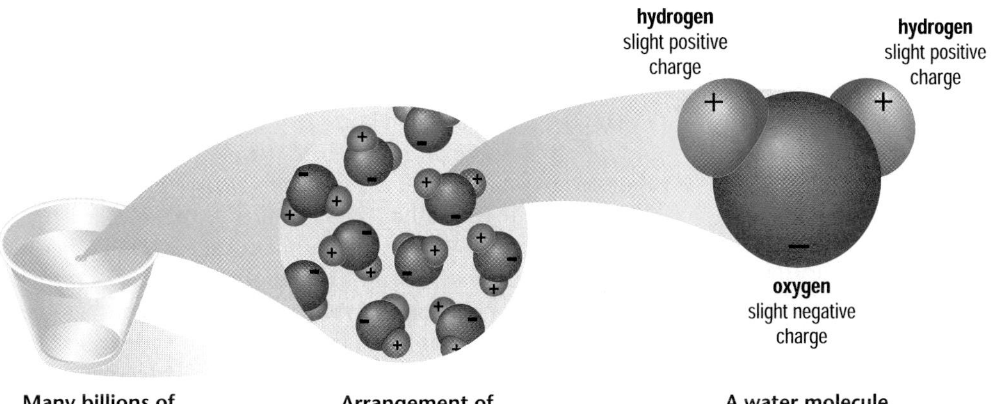

Figure 1 A glass of water contains many billions of water molecules. Notice how the water molecules are arranged in the center image. The positive ends of one molecule are attracted to the negative end of another molecule.

Figure 1 shows how the hydrogen and oxygen atoms are arranged in a water molecule. Each end of the molecule has a slight electric charge. The oxygen end has a slight negative charge. The hydrogen ends have a slight positive charge. A molecule that has electrically charged areas is called a **polar molecule.** Because water consists of polar molecules, it is called a polar substance.

Have you ever played with bar magnets? If so, you know that the opposite poles of two magnets attract each other. The same is true with polar molecules, except that an electric force rather than a magnetic force causes the attraction. **The positive hydrogen ends of one water molecule attract the negative oxygen ends of nearby water molecules. As a result, the water molecules tend to stick together.** Many of water's unusual properties occur because of this attraction among the polar water molecules.

☑ *Checkpoint Describe the arrangement of the atoms in a water molecule. What makes it a polar molecule?*

Surface Tension

Have you ever watched a water strider like the one at the left? These insects can skate across the surface of a pond without sinking. They are supported by the surface tension of the water. **Surface tension** is the tightness across the surface of water that is caused by the polar molecules pulling on each other. The molecules at the surface are being pulled by the molecules next to them and below them. The pulling forces the surface of the water into a curved shape. Surface tension also causes raindrops to form round beads when they fall onto a car windshield.

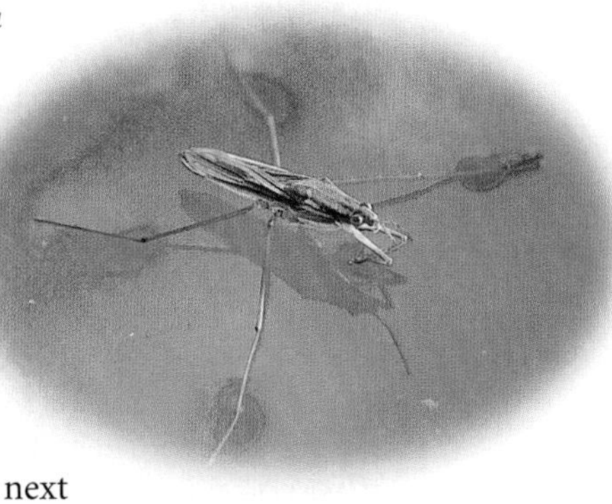

Figure 2 A water strider skips lightly across the surface of a pond. *Applying Concepts How do water's polar molecules keep the insect from falling into the water?*

2 Facilitate

Water's Unique Structure

Using the Visuals: Figure 1

First, point out that there is a scale difference between each part of this figure. Then call students' attention to the middle illustration in the figure. Ask: **What accounts for the attraction between water molecules?** *(The positive charges of the hydrogen atoms are attracted to the negative charges of the oxygen atoms on different molecules.)* **Why do you think beads of water stick to other substances?** *(The charged ends of water molecules are attracted to the charged parts of molecules of the other substances.)* **learning modality: visual**

Surface Tension

Inquiry Challenge

Materials *water, bowl, pepper, liquid detergent*
Time 20 minutes
Pose this question to students: **What effect does detergent have on the surface tension of water?** Provide each group with the materials, and challenge them to investigate this question. Students should find that the pepper easily floats on the surface of the water until they add the detergent. Then some of the pepper will sink and much of it will move to the side of the bowl, away from the detergent, where surface tension remains strong. Students should conclude that detergent lowers water's surface tension. This characteristic of detergents helps water to penetrate soiled materials more completely. **learning modality: kinesthetic**

Program Resources

- **Unit 1 Resources** 2-1 Lesson Plan; 2-1 Section Summary
- **Guided Reading and Study Workbook** Section 2-1

Answers to Self-Assessment

Caption Question

Figure 2 Water's molecules pull on each other, which causes surface tension. This surface tension supports the water strider.

☑ *Checkpoint*

Two hydrogen atoms bonded to an oxygen atom form a water molecule. A water molecule is polar because it has electrically charged areas.

Ongoing Assessment

Drawing Challenge students to draw and cut out three water molecules and use them to show how the charged ends of one molecule attract the ends of other water molecules.

Capillary Action

Skills Focus inferring
Materials *string, scissors, water, pitcher, plastic cup, tape*
Time 20 minutes
Tips Make sure students keep tension on the string and pour the water from the pitcher slowly. Do this activity outside or over a big sink.
Expected Outcome As the student slowly moves the cup away from the pitcher, the water should flow down the string into the cup. Students may infer that water molecules on the wet string cling to the string and the water molecules flowing from the pitcher are attracted to the water molecules on the string.
Extend Students can explore whether the pitcher height affects how the water flows down the string. **learning modality: kinesthetic**

Water, the Universal Solvent

Addressing Naive Conceptions

Materials *sugar, water, spoon, plastic cup, plastic saucer*
Time 5 minutes × 2 days
Many students assume that when a solute "disappears" into a solvent, the original components can never be separated, as in a chemical reaction. Invite students to stir several spoonfuls of sugar into a cup of water. Students will observe that the sugar is "gone" and that the water remains clear. Then have students pour some of the solution into a small saucer and place the saucer in a warm spot. After the water evaporates, students can observe the residue of sugar that remains. **learning modality: visual**

Follow That String

You can use a string to pour water sideways! Try this activity over a sink or outdoors.

1. Cut a piece of string as long as your arm. Wet the string.
2. Fill a pitcher with water. Tie the string to the handle.
3. Drape the string across the spout and let the other end dangle into a plastic cup. Tape the end of the string to the inside of the cup.

4. Hold the cup below the pitcher so that the string is pulled tight. As your partner gently pours the water into the cup, slowly move the cup to the right of the spout, keeping the string tight.

Inferring How do water's polar molecules cause it to follow the string?

Capillary Action

The next time you have a drink with a straw in it, look closely at the level of the liquid outside and inside the straw. You will see that the liquid rises higher inside the straw. Similarly, water will climb up into the pores of a brick or piece of wood. How does water move up against the force of gravity? Just as water molecules stick to each other, they also stick to the sides of a tube. As water molecules are attracted to the tube, they pull other water molecules up with them. The combined force of attraction among water molecules and with the molecules of surrounding materials is called **capillary action.** Capillary action allows water to move through materials with pores or narrow spaces inside.

Capillary action causes water molecules to cling to the fibers of materials like paper and cloth. You may have seen outdoor or athletic clothing that claims to "wick moisture away from the skin." The capillary action that occurs along the cloth's fibers pulls water away from your skin. By pulling the water away from your skin, the fibers keep you dry.

Water, the Universal Solvent

What happens when you make lemonade from a powdered mix? As you stir the powder into a pitcher of water, the powder seems to disappear. When you make lemonade, you are making a solution. A **solution** is a mixture that forms when one substance dissolves another. The substance that does the dissolving is called the **solvent.** In this example, the water is the solvent.

One reason that water is able to dissolve many substances is that it is polar. The charged ends of the water molecule attract the molecules of other polar substances. Sugar is a familiar polar substance. When you add a sugar cube to a cup of hot tea, the polar water molecules in the tea pull on the polar sugar molecules on the surfaces of the cube. As those sugar molecules

Figure 3 Water's ability to dissolve limestone created the spiky stalactites and stalagmites in this cave in Arkansas' Ozark Mountains. As the water evaporated, the rock formations were left behind.

52

Background

Facts and Figures A hydrogen atom consists of a proton and an electron. In a water molecule, the electrons of the two hydrogen atoms are usually found close to the oxygen atom. The result is that each hydrogen atom tends to behave like a free proton, with a positive charge. This positive charge, in turn, causes a strong attraction to the negative oxygen atoms of nearby water molecules.

Capillary action is a form of adhesion, the attracting force that acts between the particles of different substances. The term *capillary* is derived from the Latin word for hair. Capillary action occurs in fine tubes, like hairs, such as the fibers of a paper towel or blotting paper or the tiny tubular cells in plants.

dissolve, other sugar molecules are exposed to the water. Eventually the sugar cube dissolves into many individual molecules too small to see. The result is a solution of sweetened tea.

Water dissolves so many substances that it is often called the "universal solvent." It can dissolve solids, such as salt and soap, and liquids, such as bleach and rubbing alcohol. Water also dissolves many gases, including oxygen and carbon dioxide. These dissolved gases are important for organisms that live in the water.

However, some substances, such as oils and wax, do not dissolve in water. You have observed this if you have ever seen the oil separate from the vinegar and water in salad dressing. The molecules of oil are nonpolar molecules — they have no charged regions. Nonpolar molecules do not dissolve well in water.

☑ *Checkpoint* *List a solid, a liquid, and a gas that dissolve in water.*

Changing State

It's a hot, humid summer day. To cool down, you put some ice cubes in a glass and add cold water. Is there anything unusual about this scene? Surprisingly, yes! You are interacting with water in three different states, or forms: solid, liquid, and gas. **The ice is a solid, the water is a liquid, and the water vapor in the air is a gas.** In terms of chemistry, this is a remarkable situation. Water is the only substance on Earth that commonly exists in all of its different states.

As you know if you have ever boiled water or made ice cubes, water can change from one state to another. Most other substances require extremes of hot or cold to change state. A steel car door doesn't melt in a July heat wave. In fact, steel would remain a solid even inside your kitchen oven. The air you breathe remains a gas whether the weather is hot or cold. Water, however, can change states within the range of Earth's normal temperatures.

Melting To understand how temperature is related to change of state, start by thinking about an ice cube. The ice is a solid. It has a regular shape because its molecules are arranged in a rigid structure. Suppose that the temperature of the ice is −10°C. What does the temperature tell you? Temperature is a measurement of the average speed of the molecules. Although you can't see them, all the molecules in a substance are constantly moving. At −10°C, the molecules in the ice cube are vibrating back and forth, but they are not moving fast enough to break free of their structure.

Now suppose that you put the ice cube in a pan on the stove. As heat energy is added, the molecules in the ice start moving faster. The temperature rises. When the temperature reaches 0°C, the solid ice melts and becomes liquid water.

Comparing Solvents

ACTIVITY

In this activity you will compare how well water and oil dissolve several substances.

1. Label six small plastic cups A, B, C, D, E, and F.
2. Add water to cups A, B, and C until they are half full. Add the same amount of vegetable oil to cups D, E, and F.
3. Make a table like the one shown below to help organize your observations.

Cup	Contents	Result
A	Water Salt	

4. Now stir a spoonful of salt into cups A and D. Record your observations.
5. Stir a spoonful of baking soda into cups B and E. Record your observations.
6. Add two drops of food coloring to cups C and F. Do not stir. Record your observations.

Drawing Conclusions In which solvent did each substance dissolve better? Propose an explanation for your results. (*Hint:* Think about the difference between polar and nonpolar molecules.)

ACTIVITY

Skills Focus drawing conclusions
Materials *6 small plastic cups, permanent marker, water, vegetable oil,*
6 plastic spoons, salt, baking soda, food coloring, plastic dropper
Time 20 minutes
Tips Students should use a clean spoon to add the substance to each cup.
Expected Outcome Each of the three substances dissolves better in water than in oil. The substances must have had charged particles that were attracted to water's polar molecules, but not to the nonpolar oil molecules.
Extend Have students test whether a variety of other substances will dissolve in water. **learning modality: kinesthetic**

Changing State

Building Inquiry Skills: Designing an Experiment

ACTIVITY

After students have learned about melting and freezing, ask: **Are the melting point and the freezing point of water the same temperature?** Have students meet in groups to design an experiment to investigate this question. Explain that their designs should use materials that could be found in a school or home. Ask that they write a hypothesis, a list of materials, and a step-by-step procedure. *(A typical experiment might use a thermometer to measure the temperature at which ice cubes melt in a glass of water and the temperature at which water freezes in a freezer.)* **cooperative learning**

Media and Technology

Transparencies "Structure of Water Molecules," Transparency 2

Concept Videotape Library Grade 6, Tape 1 "Opposites Attract"

Answers to Self-Assessment

☑ *Checkpoint*

Answers may vary. Sample answer: Sugar is a solid that dissolves in water, bleach is a liquid that dissolves in water, and carbon dioxide is a gas that dissolves in water.

Ongoing Assessment

Skills Check Have students define *state.* Then challenge them to identify the state of three familiar substances.

Changing State, continued

Using the Visuals: Figure 4

Use the illustrations of molecules in the figure to emphasize the differences at the molecular level among the three states. Ask: **Why can't a solid flow like a gas or a liquid?** *(A solid's molecules are rigidly held in place, unlike the molecules of a liquid or a gas.)* **How is the arrangement of molecules of liquid water different from the arrangement of molecules of water vapor?** *(The molecules of liquid water are arranged much closer together than the molecules of water vapor).* **learning modality: visual**

Demonstration

Materials *goggles, lab apron, water, beaker, hot plate*
Time 15 minutes

Wear goggles and a lab apron. Add a little water to a beaker and place the beaker on a hot plate. Shortly, the water will begin to boil. Ask: **What caused the water to boil?** *(The heat from the hot plate added energy to the water molecules.)* **What happened to the water molecules after they boiled?** *(They changed from liquid water to water vapor.)* **Why didn't the glass in the beaker change state as well?** *(It requires a higher temperature to change state.)* **learning modality: visual**

Including All Students

To help students understand differences among the three states of water, display pictures of (1) a military formation, (2) a milling crowd of people, and (3) soccer players dispersed on a field. Ask students to make analogies between each picture and a state of matter. *(The pictures represent the molecular arrangements of a solid, a liquid, and a gas, respectively.)* **learning modality: visual**

Boiling and Evaporation As you know, liquid water looks very different from solid ice. The liquid flows and takes the shape of the pan. This is true because the molecules in liquid water have more energy than the molecules in ice. The molecules move more freely, bouncing off each other.

What happens if you continue to heat the water on the stove? As more energy is added to the liquid water, the speed of the molecules increases and the temperature rises. At 100°C, the water boils and another change of state occurs. The molecules have enough energy to escape the liquid and become invisible water vapor. The molecules in a gas move even more freely than those in a liquid. They spread out to fill their container — in this example, your whole kitchen!

Another way that liquid water can become a gas is through evaporation. **Evaporation** is the process by which molecules at the surface of a liquid absorb enough energy to change to the gaseous state. If you let your hair air-dry after going swimming, you are taking advantage of evaporation.

Condensation As water vapor cools down, it releases some of its energy to its surroundings. The molecules slow down and the temperature decreases. As the temperature of the gas reaches the boiling point, the water vapor begins to change back to the liquid state. The process by which a gas changes to a liquid is called **condensation.** When you fog up a window by breathing on it, you are seeing the effects of condensation. The invisible water vapor in your breath is cooled by the window and forms visible drops of liquid water.

Figure 4 Water exists on Earth in all three states: solid, liquid, and gas. **A.** The molecules in solid ice are close together and form a rigid structure. **B.** In liquid water, the molecules move more freely and the water takes the shape of its container. **C.** The molecules in gaseous water vapor move very freely and spread out to fill a space. *Comparing and Contrasting In which state do the molecules move the slowest? The fastest?*

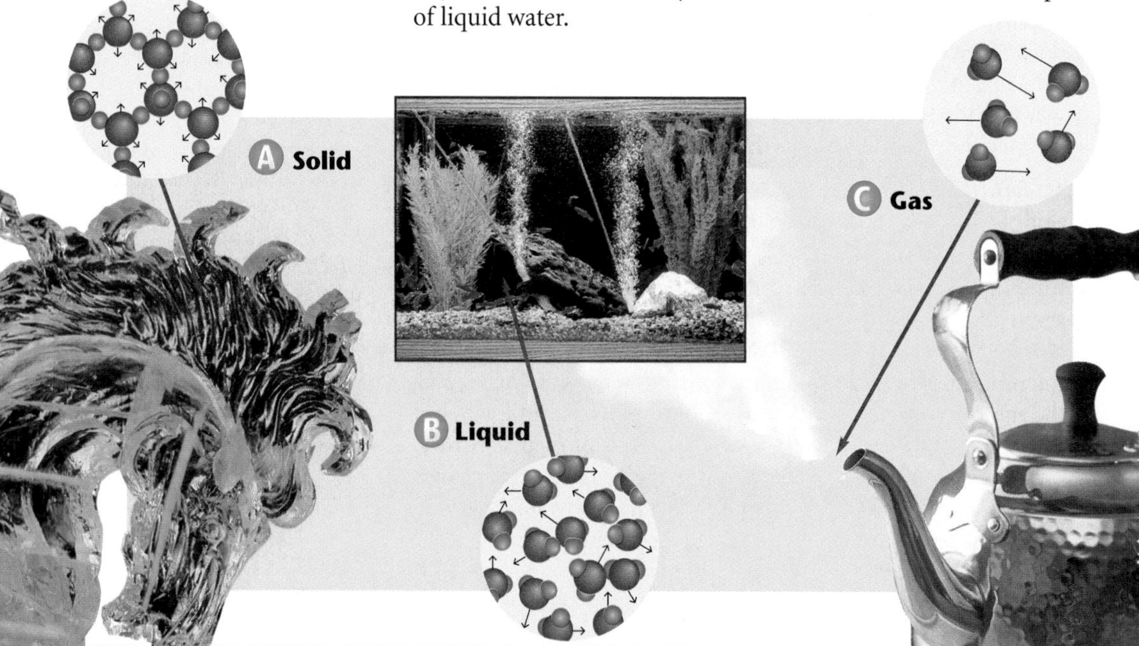

Background

Facts and Figures In liquid water, the water molecules are constantly moving at a variety of speeds and in all directions. Thus, some molecules are moving upward. The fastest of these can escape the attraction of the other water molecules. These fast-moving molecules escape into the air through the surface of the liquid—that is, they evaporate. Evaporation occurs at all temperatures. If enough heat is added to raise the temperature of liquid water to 100°C, the water boils. Now even molecules moving at an average speed can escape the attraction of other water molecules, and a change of state occurs throughout the liquid. Thus, boiling is different from evaporation in two ways: (1) boiling occurs only at the boiling point, while evaporation occurs at all temperatures; and (2) boiling occurs throughout the liquid, while evaporation occurs only at the surface.

Freezing If the liquid water continues to be cooled, the molecules continue to lose energy. They move more and more slowly. At 0°C, the liquid water freezes, changing back into solid ice. If you have ever observed an icicle forming from water dripping off a roof, you have seen this change of state in progress.

***Checkpoint* In which state do water molecules have the most energy?**

Why Ice Floats

You know from experience that ice cubes in a glass float at the top of the water. If you combine the solid and liquid forms of most other substances, the solid sinks to the bottom. You have observed this if you have ever melted wax to make candles. The solid wax pieces sink to the bottom of the hot liquid wax.

As most liquids cool, their molecules slow down and move closer together until they reach their compact solid form. But surprisingly, something different happens to water. When water cools below about 4°C, the molecules begin to line up in a gridlike crystal structure. The molecules take up more space in this crystal structure than as a liquid. Frozen water in an ice cube tray contains the same amount of matter as when it was a liquid. However, the water takes up more space as ice than it did as a liquid. This means that ice is less dense than liquid water. Less dense substances, like the ice, float on more dense substances, like the liquid water.

INTEGRATING LIFE SCIENCE The fact that ice floats has important consequences for fish and other organisms that live in water. When lakes and ponds freeze in the winter, the ice stays at the top. The ice layer shelters the water below from the coldest winds and air. The fish are able to live in the water below the ice and find food on the bottom of the lake. If water acted as most substances do when they freeze, the ice would sink to the bottom of the lake as it formed.

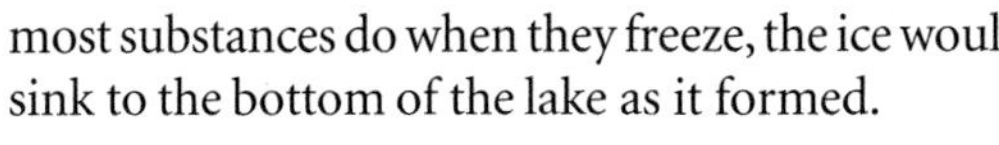

Language Arts CONNECTION

Imagine that you work at an advertising agency. Your agency has just been hired to design an advertising campaign for water. You know that water has many properties that make it unique. Your plan is to highlight one or more of these properties in an ad to show people what an unusual substance water is.

In Your Journal

Before you begin to write, decide which properties you will highlight in your ad. Write down some facts about each property that you think will interest people. Now you are ready to create the ad. Use humor, pictures, and everyday examples to make your point in an appealing way. Will your ad convince people that water is a unique substance?

Figure 5 One of water's unusual properties helped this ice fisherman catch a pike. Because solid ice is less dense than liquid water, the ice floats on top of the lake. Fish can live all winter in the water below.

Media and Technology

Transparencies "Three States of Water," Transparency 3

Concept Videotape Library Grade 6, Tape 1 "The Disappearing Ice Cube"

Answers to Self-Assessment

Caption Question

Figure 4 Slowest in the solid state; fastest in the gas state

Checkpoint

In the gas state

Why Ice Floats

Integrating Life Science

Encourage students to imagine a frozen-over lake in winter. Ask: **Is there anything living in this lake during wintertime?** *(A variety of living things, including fish, turtles, and many different protists.)* **What would happen to these organisms if ice were more dense than liquid water?** *(The ice would sink as it formed instead of forming a protective shield for the organisms in the water below.)* **learning modality: verbal**

Language Arts CONNECTION

ACTIVITY

Show students several examples of magazine ads. Ask: **What are some characteristics that all these ads have in common?** *(Students might mention large type for key words, attractive pictures, and persuasive language.)* **What strategies did the ad writers use to capture the reader's attention?** *(Students might suggest that writers tried to appeal to a need of the consumer.)* Encourage students to use these techniques in their ads. **learning modality: verbal**

Ongoing Assessment

Skills Check Have students make a compare/contrast table of the three states of water. They should include information about movement of particles and temperatures.

Skills Lab

Developing Hypotheses

Speeding Up Evaporation

Preparing for Inquiry

Key Concept Various factors influence the rate at which water evaporates, including exposure to a heat source, the use of a cover, and the presence of wind.

Skills Objectives Students will be able to

- develop hypotheses about factors affecting the evaporation of water;
- control variables to determine the effect of different factors;
- draw conclusions about how various factors affect evaporation.

Time 40 minutes

Advance Planning Have locations picked out for each group's dishes for all three parts. The locations for the dishes in Part 1 are especially important because of the need for an electrical outlet.

Alternative Materials In Part 1, you may want to shorten the time of evaporation by having students place the dish in direct sunlight on a dark surface. You could also have students use a heat source in Part 2, as long as both dishes are exposed to the same amount of heat. In Part 3, you could shorten the time by having students use small fans set on low.

Guiding Inquiry

Invitation To help students think of prior experiences with evaporation, ask: **Do you think evaporation occurs faster in a desert or a forest?** *(in a desert)* **Does it occur faster on a windy day or a calm day?** *(on a windy day)* Then challenge students to explain why evaporation would be faster in each situation.

Introducing the Procedure

- Call on students to describe the process of evaporation at the molecular level. If students have difficulty, have them read again the explanation of evaporation on page 55.
- Have students read through the complete procedure. Then ask: **What variable is being tested in each part?** *(In Part 1, exposure to a heat source; in Part 2, the use of a cover; in Part 3, the presence of wind)*

Skills Lab

Developing Hypotheses

Speeding Up Evaporation

You have just learned that water changes from a liquid to a gas through evaporation. In this lab, you will develop hypotheses as you investigate this process.

Problem

What factors increase the rate at which water evaporates?

Materials

water
plastic dropper
2 plastic petri dishes
1 petri dish cover
3 index cards
paper towels
stopwatch
lamp

Procedure

Part 1 Effect of Heat

1. Copy the data table into your notebook.
2. How do you think heating a water sample will affect how fast it evaporates? Record your hypothesis in the data table.
3. Place each petri dish on an index card.
4. Add a single drop of water to each of the petri dishes. Try to make the two drops the same size.
5. Position the lamp over one of the dishes as a heat source. Turn on the light. Make sure the light does not shine on the other dish. **CAUTION:** *The light bulb will become very hot. Avoid touching the bulb or getting water on it.*
6. Observe the dishes every 3 minutes to see which sample evaporates faster. Record your result in the data table.

DATA TABLE	
Part 1 Effect of Heat	
Hypothesis	
Result	
Part 2 Effect of a Cover	
Hypothesis	
Result	
Part 3 Effect of Wind	
Hypothesis	
Result	

Part 2 Effect of a Cover

7. How do you think placing a cover over the water sample will affect how fast it evaporates? Record your hypothesis in the data table.
8. Dry both petri dishes and place them side by side over the index cards. Add a drop of water to each dish as you did in Step 4.
9. Place a cover over one dish. Leave the other dish uncovered.
10. Observe the dishes after 10 minutes to see which sample evaporates faster. Record your result in the data table.

Part 3 Effect of Wind

11. How do you think fanning the water sample will affect how fast it evaporates? Record your hypothesis in the data table.
12. Dry both petri dishes and place them over the index cards. Add a drop of water to each dish as you did in Step 4.

Troubleshooting the Experiment

- Emphasize that in each part, both dishes should contain the same amount of water. Thus, the single drops of water must be the same size. You may want to demonstrate the use of the plastic dropper, modeling how to make two small drops the same size.
- You may want to have students set up Part 1 and Part 2 and then proceed to Part 3 without waiting for results of the first two parts. Part 3 requires students to fan the water sample continuously until it evaporates. Once results in that part are obtained, students can turn their attention back to the first two parts.

Expected Outcome

In Part 1, the water exposed to a lamp's heat will evaporate faster. In Part 2, the water in the uncovered dish will evaporate faster. In Part 3, the water fanned by the index card will evaporate faster.

13. Use an index card to fan one of the dishes for 5 minutes. Be careful not to fan the other dish as well.
14. Observe the dishes to see which sample evaporates faster. Record your result in the data table.

Analyze and Conclude

1. In which cases were your hypotheses correct? In which cases were they incorrect?
2. For each part of the experiment, explain why the water evaporated faster in one dish than the other. (*Hint:* Think about what happened to the water molecules in each dish.)
3. Make a general statement about factors that increase the rate at which water evaporates.
4. Based on this experiment, predict what would happen in each of the following situations.
   a. Would a wet swimsuit dry faster in a plastic bag or out in the open? Explain.
   b. Would wet clothes on a clothesline dry faster on a windy day or on a calm day? Explain.
   c. Would wet clothes dry faster if they were hung on a clothesline located on the sunny side of a house or on the shady side? Explain.
5. **Think About It** What knowledge or everyday experiences helped you make your hypotheses at the beginning of the experiment? Explain how hypotheses differ from guesses.

More to Explore

How do you think increasing the surface area of a water sample will affect how fast it evaporates? Write your hypothesis and then design an experiment to test it. Be sure to check your plan with your teacher before carrying out your experiment.

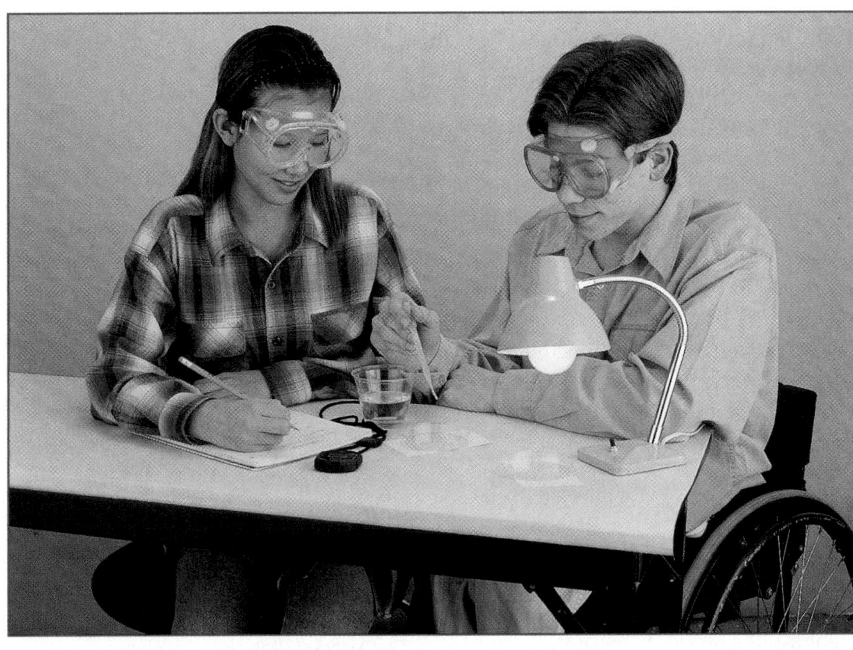

Sample Data Table

	Hypothesis	*Result*
Effect of Heat	*Water exposed to heat will evaporate faster.*	*The water in the dish under the light evaporated faster.*
Effect of a Cover	*Water in an uncovered container will evaporate faster than water in a covered container.*	*The water in the uncovered dish evaporated faster.*
Effect of Wind	*Water exposed to wind will evaporate faster than water not exposed to wind.*	*The water that was fanned evaporated faster.*

Program Resources

◆ **Unit 1 Resources** Skills Lab blackline masters

Media and Technology

Lab Activity Videotapes
Grade 6, Tape 1

Analyze and Conclude

1. Answers will vary. Some students may have foreseen the results correctly in each case and confirmed their hypotheses through the experiment.
2. In Part 1, the water in the dish exposed to the heat source evaporated faster because the heat energy caused the water molecules in that dish to move faster. In Part 2, the water in the uncovered dish evaporated faster because a cover limits the movement of the water vapor. In Part 3, the water exposed to the wind evaporated faster because the wind increases the energy of the molecules at the surface.
3. Factors that increase the rate of evaporation of water include exposure to a heat source, the absence of a cover over a container, and exposure to wind.
4 a. A swimsuit would dry faster out in the open because the movement of water vapor is not limited as it would be in a plastic bag.
b. Clothes would dry faster on a windy day because water molecules would absorb energy from the wind.
c. Clothes would dry faster on the sunny side because the water molecules could absorb energy from sunlight.
5. A typical response might mention how quickly wet clothes or a car or puddle dries when in the sun or exposed to wind and how covers usually keep foods from drying out. Hypotheses are based on information gathered through study or experience, whereas guesses are based only on feelings or intuition.

Extending the Inquiry

More to Explore A typical hypothesis might suggest that increasing the surface area of a water sample will increase the rate of evaporation. A typical design might suggest pouring equal amounts of water into a deep bowl and a shallow pan and then exposing both to the same amount of heat or wind. As you review students' hypotheses and plans, challenge them to explain why they think increasing the surface area would increase the rate of evaporation.

Safety

Caution students to be careful when handling the lamp, because the bulb gets hot and can explode if splashed with water. Review the safety guidelines in Appendix A.

Specific Heat

Including All Students

On a map, point out Bismarck, North Dakota, and Juneau, Alaska. Ask: **Why is Bismarck colder than Juneau when Juneau is farther north?** *(Juneau is on the coast while Bismarck is not near any large body of water. Because of water's high specific heat, the air over water is warmer than the air over land in the winter, and this helps to moderate Juneau's winter temperatures.)* **learning modality: logical/mathematical**

3 Assess

Section 1 Review Answers

1. The positive hydrogen ends of one water molecule attract the negative oxygen ends of nearby water molecules.
2. Sugar dissolves well in water because sugar is a polar substance. The charged ends of the water molecule attract the molecules of other polar substances.
3. As ice melts, the water molecules absorb energy and move faster and faster.
4. Ice floats in liquid water because ice is less dense than liquid water.
5. The sand will heat up faster than the water because of water's high specific heat. The temperature of water does not increase as quickly as the temperature of sand that is heated the same amount.

CHAPTER PROJECT

Check Your Progress

To calculate the total amount of water used in the home over the week, most students should have recorded readings of a water meter. Students without access to a water meter should have made estimates based on their daily records. At this stage, encourage students to identify another type of building to monitor.

Performance Assessment

Drawing Have students make a series of drawings showing why land near a large body of water has less dramatic temperature changes than areas far inland.

Specific Heat

Imagine a steamy July day. The air is hot, the sidewalk is hot, and the sandy beach is hot. You jump into a pool or the ocean, and the water is surprisingly cool! But if you go for an evening swim, the water is warm compared to the cool air.

You feel this difference in temperature because of water's unusually high specific heat. **Specific heat** is the amount of heat needed to increase the temperature of a certain mass of a substance by 1°C. Compared to other substances, water re-quires a lot of heat to increase its temperature.

Water's high specific heat is due to the many attractions among water molecules. Other substances, such as air and rocks, have fewer attractions between their molecules. Their temperature increases more quickly as they are heated than water that is heated the same amount.

One effect of water's high specific heat is that land areas located near large bodies of water experience less dramatic temperature changes than areas far inland. In the summer, the sun's heat warms the land more quickly than the water. The warm land heats the air above it to a higher temperature than the air over the ocean. As a result, the air is warmer inland than on the coast. Just the opposite effect occurs in the winter. The land loses heat to the air more quickly than the water. The water remains warm and keeps the air above it warmer than the air over the cold land.

Figure 6 What could be more refreshing than a swim on a hot summer day? This swimmer is taking advantage of water's high specific heat. *Applying Concepts How does this property of water help the swimmer cool off?*

Section 1 Review

1. What causes water molecules to be attracted to each other?
2. Why does sugar dissolve well in water?
3. Describe what is happening to the water molecules as ice melts.
4. What unusual fact about ice causes it to float in liquid water?
5. **Thinking Critically Predicting** If you place a cup of sand and a cup of water in the sun, which one will heat up faster? Explain your prediction in terms of a property of water.

CHAPTER PROJECT

Check Your Progress

Complete your water-use data table by calculating the total amount of water you used during the week. Use the chart on page 198 to estimate the water used for some common activities. Then determine how much water your family used during the week. You can do this by reading your water meter, estimating based on your personal water use, or having your family members record their usage. (*Hint:* Convert all amounts to liters.)

Program Resources

- **Unit 1 Resources** 2-1 Review and Reinforce; 2-1 Enrich
- **Laboratory Manual** 2, "Properties of Water"

Answers to Self-Assessment

Caption Question

Figure 6 Because of water's high specific heat, it does not heat up as fast as the air and land around it. Therefore, on a hot summer day, the water is cooler than the surrounding air and land.

Section 2 Understanding Solutions

DISCOVER

What Makes a Mixture a Solution?

1. Put about 50 or 60 milliliters of water into a plastic cup. Add a spoonful of pepper and stir well.
2. To a similar amount of water in a second cup, add a spoonful of table salt. Stir well.
3. Compare the appearance of the two mixtures.

Think It Over

Observing What is the difference between the two mixtures? What other mixtures have you seen that are similar to pepper and water? That are similar to table salt and water?

GUIDE FOR READING

- How does a solution differ from other mixtures?
- What happens to the particles of a solute when a solution forms?
- How do solutes affect the freezing point and boiling point of a solvent?

Reading Tip As you read, list the properties of solutions, suspensions and colloids.

Imagine a hot summer day. You've been outdoors and now you're really thirsty. A tall, cool glass of just plain water would taste great. Or would it? Have you ever tasted distilled water? It tastes flat. Distilled water is "plain water." To make it, you boil tap water until it becomes water vapor. Then you cool the vapor and recollect it as a liquid. This process separates the water from dissolved materials that give it flavor.

Tap water is a mixture of pure water (H_2O) and a variety of other substances, such as chloride, fluoride, and metallic ions. Gases, such as oxygen and carbon dioxide, are also dissolved in water. As with all mixtures, the composition of tap water can vary. The water coming out of the tap can differ from one home to the next, across a town, or from state to state. Tap water is an example of a kind of mixture called a solution.

Solutions and Suspensions

What happens if you make a mixture of water and pepper? Not much. No matter how much you stir pepper and water, the two never really seem to "mix." When you stop stirring, you can still see pepper flakes floating on the water's surface and collecting at the bottom of the cup. You could scoop them out if you wanted to. Pepper and water make a suspension. A **suspension** (suh SPEN shun) is a mixture in which particles can be seen and easily separated by settling or filtration. If you tasted the pepper suspension, you might find that one mouthful of it tastes more peppery than another mouthful. Such a mixture is not evenly mixed.

READING STRATEGIES

Reading Tip Suggest that, before they read the section, students list in their notebooks the terms *solution, suspension,* and *colloid.* Remind students to leave space beneath each term. As they read, students can fill in the properties of each type of mixture. Sample answer: Suspension—particles can be seen; particles can be separated by filtration

Program Resources

- **Unit 1 Resources** 2-2 Lesson Plan; 2-2 Section Summary
- **Guided Reading and Study Workbook** Section 2-2

Section 2 Understanding Solutions

Objectives

After completing the lesson, students will be able to

- define and compare solutions, suspensions, and colloids;
- explain what happens to particles of a solute when a solution forms;
- describe how solutes affect the freezing and boiling points of solvents.

Key Terms suspension, solute, colloid, freezing point, boiling point

1 Engage/Explore

Activating Prior Knowledge

Show students containers of water, water and sugar solution, and salt water. Ask students to compare the three containers and tell you if they can detect the difference just by looking. Have students discuss how they could distinguish between the solutions.

DISCOVER

Skills Focus observing
Materials *2 paper cups, water, plastic spoon, pepper, table salt*
Time 10 minutes
Tips Remind students to wash the spoon before making their second mixture.
Expected Outcome The pepper will not dissolve in the water, but the table salt will.
Think It Over First mixture: the pepper is visible; second mixture: the table salt dissolves and forms a clear mixture. Students may recall that sugar and water resemble salt and water and that sand and water resemble pepper and water. Accept other answers that demonstrate the same concepts.

2 Facilitate

Solutions and Suspensions

Inquiry Challenge

Materials *2 coffee filters, 500 mL water, 50 g sugar crystals, 50 g sand, 2 stirrer sticks, four 500-mL beakers*

ACTIVITY

Have students predict how they can separate mixtures of sand and water and sugar and water. If possible use turbinado sugar, which looks like sand. After approving students' plans, have them carry out their experiments. *(Sample experiment: Prepare two identical sugar and water solutions and two identical mixtures of sand and water; filter one sand mixture and one sugar mixture, then allow the other two to sit for a day or so. Sand will remain in the filter and quickly settle out from the mixture. Dissolved sugar will pass through the filter but will form small crystals as the water evaporates.)* **learning modality: kinesthetic**

Solvents and Solutes

Integrating Life Science

Materials *slice of fresh onion skin, slice of dried onion skin, hand lens*

Time 15 minutes

Allow students to compare slices of cells of the two onion skins, and note how water affects the appearance of living cells. **learning modality: visual**

Figure 7 Glitter mixes with the water when you shake the paperweight, but settles out later. *Classifying Are the glitter particles in solution or in suspension?*

On the other hand, if you stir table salt into water, the salt disappears. Water and salt form a solution—a well-mixed mixture. If you taste a salt solution, any sip tastes just as salty as the next. **Unlike a suspension, a solution has the same properties throughout. Solutions and suspensions also differ in the size of their particles and the way the parts of the mixtures can be separated.** Dissolved particles are much smaller than suspended particles. They do not settle out of solution, and they pass through a filter. However, salt can be separated from water by boiling. Letting the water evaporate also works.

Solvents and Solutes

All solutions have at least two parts: the solvent and one or more solutes. Recall that the solvent is the substance that does the dissolving. It is the part of a solution present in the largest amount. A substance that is present in a solution in a smaller amount and dissolved by the solvent is a **solute.** In a solution of table salt and water, the solvent is water and the solute is salt.

In many common solutions, the solvent is water. Sugar in water, for example, is the starting solution for flavored soft drinks. Adding food coloring gives the drink color. Dissolving carbon dioxide gas in the mixture produces a soda.

INTEGRATING LIFE SCIENCE Life depends on water solutions. Nutrients used by plants are dissolved in water in the soil. Sap is a solution that carries sugar to tree cells. Water is the solvent in blood, saliva, and tears. Reactions in cells take place in solution. To keep cells working, you must replace the water you lose in sweat and urine—two other water solutions.

Figure 8 When air bubbles are blown through a fish tank, oxygen gas dissolves in the water. Fish take in this oxygen through their gills. Without oxygen, the fish would die.

Background

Facts and Figures Almost everything you eat or drink is a mixture. Drinks like iced tea are uniform, or homogeneous, mixtures called solutions. Foods like fruit salad are nonuniform, or heterogeneous, mixtures.

Some foods, such as whipped cream, gelatin, mayonnaise, uncooked egg white, milk, and butter are colloids. Colloids differ from solutions and suspensions in the size of their dispersed particles. Whereas particles in true solutions are ions or relatively small molecules too tiny to scatter light, and particles in suspensions are visible to the eye, colloids contain particles or clumps of particles that range in size from about 1 to 1000 nanometers and have very high molecular masses. The scattering of light by a colloid (or a suspension) is called the Tyndall Effect. An example of this phenomenon can be seen when the beam of a car headlight is scattered by fog.

Particles in a Solution

Why do solutes seem to disappear when you mix them with water? If you had a microscope powerful enough to look at the particles in the mixture, what would you see? **Whenever a solution forms, particles of the solute leave each other and become surrounded by particles of the solvent.**

Ionic Solids in Water When they dissolve, some solids break into particles with a positive or negative charge. These charged particles are called ions, and such solids are called ionic solids. Figure 9 shows what happens when an ionic solid mixes with water. A crystal of table salt, sodium chloride, is added to water. The positive sodium ions and negative chloride ions are attracted to polar water molecules, and bonds within the crystal are broken. Water molecules surround each ion as it leaves the surface of the crystal. As each layer of the solid is exposed, more ions can dissolve.

Molecular Solids in Water Not every substance breaks into ions when it dissolves in water. A molecular solid, such as sugar, breaks up into individual neutral molecules. The polar water molecules attract the slightly polar sugar molecules. This causes the sugar molecules to move away from each other. But bonds within the molecules are not broken. Like ions, the sugar molecules become surrounded by water.

Saturated Solutions As you can see in Figure 9, when the salt has completely dissolved, its particles have become spread throughout the water. What would happen if you added more and more salt to the solution? There is a limit to the amount of solute that a solvent can dissolve. When a solution contains the maximum amout of solute, it is a saturated solution. Any extra solute settles to the bottom.

Figure 9 Water molecules surround and separate positive and negative ions as an ionic solid dissolves. Notice that sodium ions attract the oxygen ends of the water molecules.

1 Water Cl^- Na^+

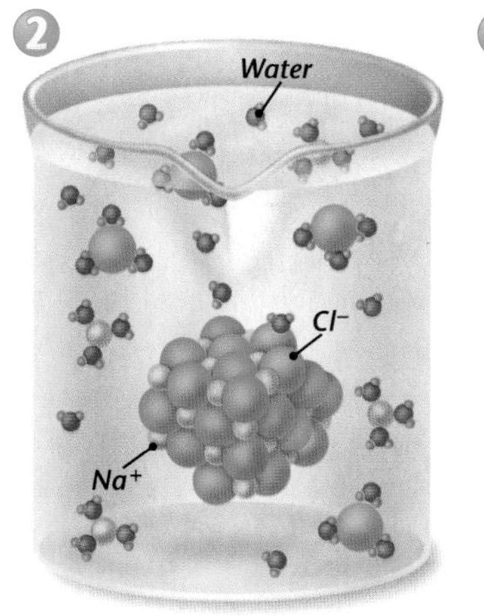

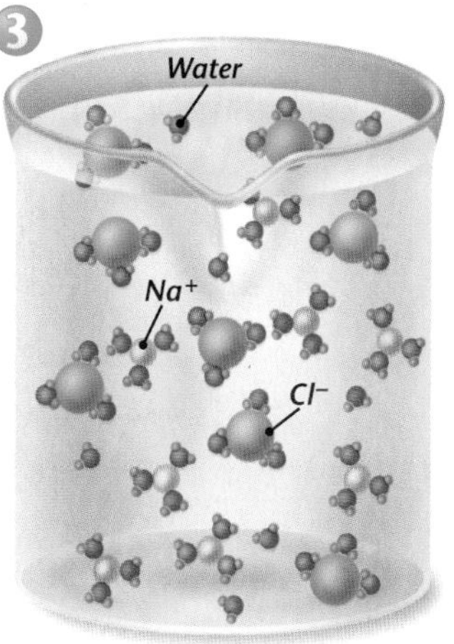

Real-Life Learning

ACTIVITY

Materials *labels from items such as soup, juice, salad dressing, ketchup, mustard, soft drinks, shampoo*
Time 15 minutes

Ask each student to examine the ingredients on one label. Challenge students to determine if the product is a solution or a suspension and then identify the solvent and solutes. Ask: **How can you tell which ingredient is a solvent?** *(It is present in the largest quantity, so it is listed first on the product label.)* **learning modality: verbal**

Particles in a Solution

Using the Visuals: Figure 9

Have students identify the sodium ions and the chloride ions in the first diagram. Ask students to describe what situation the diagram could represent. *(Sample: A visible piece of table salt is placed in a container of water.)* Then have students use their own words to describe what is happening in the second diagram. *(Sample: The salt is dissolving as water molecules surround the positive and negative ions.)* Ask students to describe what is happening in the third diagram. *(All the ions in the salt have been surrounded by water molecules and the salt is completely dissolved.)* **learning modality: visual**

Answers to Self-Assessment

Caption Question

Figure 7 The glitter particles are in suspension because the particles can be seen and easily separated, and they settle out.

Ongoing Assessment

Oral Presentation Ask students to name some common water solutions and identify the solvent and the solute in each. *(Sample: Soft drinks are water solutions. Water is the solvent; sugar, food coloring, and carbon dioxide gas are the solutes.)*

Colloids

TRY THIS

Skills Focus inferring
Materials *gelatin and water mixture, salt water, small glass beakers or jars, small flashlights (such as penlights)*
Time 15 minutes
Tips Use any brand of flavored or unflavored gelatin, mixed according to directions and left as a liquid. Mix a dilute saltwater solution ahead of time. If the solution is cloudy, add more water until it becomes clear.
Inferring The beam of light is visible through the gelatin, but not in the salt water. The gelatin is a colloid because the particles scatter light, but they are not visible and they do not settle.
Extend Have students investigate what happens when the liquid gelatin is filtered. **learning modality: visual**

Scattered Light

ACTIVITY

Find out how a beam of light is affected by a colloid.

1. Pour about 50 mL of a gelatin and water mixture into a small, clean glass beaker or jar.
2. Similarly, pour the same amount of a saltwater solution into another clean beaker or jar that is about the same size.
3. Compare the appearance of the two liquids.
4. In a darkened room, shine a small flashlight through the side of the container of gelatin. Repeat with the saltwater solution.
5. Compare the appearance of the light in each case.

Inferring What evidence tells you gelatin is a colloid?

Solutions and Electricity You have a water solution, but you don't know if the solute is salt or sugar. How could you find out? (Remember, never taste chemicals!) Electric current flows through a solution of ionic solids in water, but may not flow through a solution of molecular solids in water. You could test the solution to see if current flows through it. If no ions were present (as in a sugar solution), current would not flow.

Checkpoint *How do ionic and molecular solids differ from each other in solution?*

Colloids

Have you ever made a gelatin dessert? To do so, you stir powdered gelatin in hot water until the two substances are uniformly mixed. The liquid looks like a solution, but it's not. It isn't a suspension either. Gelatin is a colloid. A **colloid** (KAHL oyd) is a mixture with small undissolved particles that do not settle out. A colloid has properties that differ from both solutions and suspensions.

Solutions and colloids differ in the size of their particles and how they affect the path of light. The particles in a colloid are larger than the particles in a solution, but not as large as the particles in a suspension. The particles in a colloid are large enough to affect the way light passes through a colloid. Fog is a colloid. You may have noticed that you can see the beams of light from a car's headlights on a foggy night. You can see this because the fog scatters the beam of light. Other colloids include mayonnaise, shaving cream, and whipped cream.

Effects of Solutes on Solutions

Have you ever made ice cream? First you mix cream, sugar, and other ingredients. Then you freeze the mixture by placing it in an outer container full of ice and water. But ice water by itself is not

Figure 10 Milk bought in most grocery stores is a colloid. It has been processed to make the particles of water, proteins, and fats small enough to remain uniformly mixed.

Background

History of Science The discovery that water solutions freeze at lower temperatures than pure water led to advances in food preparation and storage. Pure water freezes at 0°C, but foods must be colder because they are composed of different solutes dissolved in water.

People have been eating frozen ices for at least 2,000 years, but they were difficult to make until people learned to use salt to lower the temperature of ice. Soon people were able to make ice cream at home. A Baltimore company produced the first commercially made ice cream in 1851.

Solutions of salt and water were also used to freeze fish and chicken. In the 1920s, Clarence Birdseye received a patent for a method of freezing fish between two metal plates cooled by a solution of calcium chloride. This allowed fish to cool to –40°C.

cold enough to do the job. Cream freezes at a temperature lower than the temperature at which water freezes (0°C). Adding rock salt to the ice water in the outer container creates a mixture that is several degrees cooler. This salt-ice-water mixture is cold enough to freeze the cream mixture. Mmm!

Salt can affect boiling, too. When cooking spaghetti, people often add table salt to the water. As a result, the water boils at a temperature higher than 100°C, the temperature at which pure water boils. One small spoonful of salt in a liter of water will raise the temperature at which it boils about 0.25°C. A few large spoonfuls of salt in a liter of water could increase the boiling temperature by about 0.5 degrees. This change will cause the spaghetti to cook slightly faster.

It isn't just salt that can make cold water colder when it freezes and hot water hotter when it boils. Any solute can affect freezing or boiling. How? The answer to this question depends on solute particles.

Lower Freezing Points The **freezing point** is the temperature at which a substance freezes, or changes from a liquid to a solid. **Solutes lower the freezing point of a solvent.** When liquid water freezes, the movement of molecules slows considerably. Instead, they form crystals of solid ice. Look at Figure 11 to compare the particles in pure water with those in a saltwater solution. Notice that pure water is made only of water molecules. In the salt solution, solute particles are present, too. In fact, they're in the way. The solute particles make it harder for the water molecules to form crystals. The temperature must drop lower than 0°C for a solid to form.

Designing Experiments

ACTIVITY

How does the mass of a solute affect the boiling temperature of water? Design an experiment using a solute, water, a balance, a hot plate, and a thermometer.

What variables should remain constant in your experiment? What is the manipulated variable? What will be the responding variable?

With approval from your teacher, do the experiment. Report on your results.

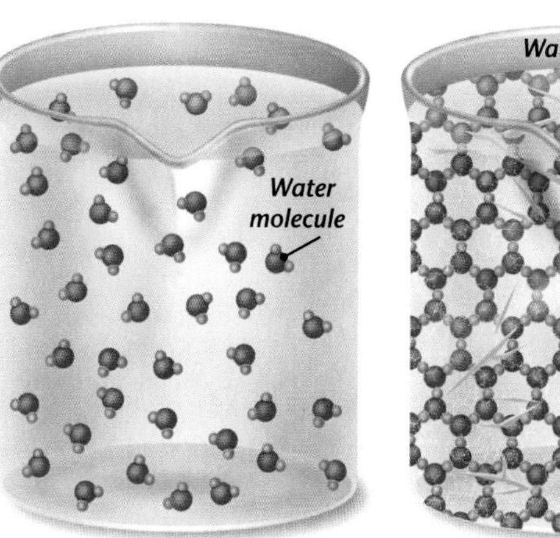

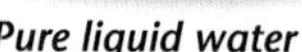

Figure 11 The freezing point and boiling point of water are affected by solute particles, which interfere with changes in state.

Effects of Solutes on Solutions

Building Inquiry Skills: Inferring

ACTIVITY

Materials *very cold distilled, tap, and salt water; stainless steel bowls; small paper cups; ice; salt; marker*
Time 15 minutes for set up, 1 hour for observation

Prepare the solutions. Also make several cold saltwater baths by placing ice, water, and salt in the bowls. Have students work in small groups to add a small amount of each solution into each of three paper cups. Ask students: **Which solution will freeze first?** To test their predictions, students can float the cups in the saltwater baths, then check the cups every 10 minutes. Ask: **What do your observations tell you about distilled water?** *(Its freezing point is higher, so it must contain fewer or no solutes.)* **cooperative learning**

Sharpen your Skills

Designing Experiments

ACTIVITY

Time 10 minutes
Tips Constant variables—quantity of water, type of solute; manipulated variable—mass of the solute; responding variable—temperature at which water boils.
Expected Outcome Increasing the mass of the solute raises the boiling temperature of water.
Extend Challenge students to determine whether different solutes cause water to boil at different temperatures.

Media and Technology

Transparencies "Solution of an Ionic Solid," Transparency 4

Answers to Self-Assessment

☑ *Checkpoint*

In solution, ionic solids conduct electricity because they form ions in the water. Molecular solids do not form ions; they dissolve into separate molecules.

Ongoing Assessment

Drawing Have students make diagrams that show how a molecular solute dissolves.

Students can save their diagrams in their portfolios.

Effects of Solutes on Solutions, continued

Integrating Technology

Challenge students to infer whether a car would be better protected by pure antifreeze or a mixture of half antifreeze and half water. Ask students to explain their inferences. *(Half antifreeze and half water, because the mixture has a lower freezing point and a higher boiling point than either water or antifreeze.)*
learning modality: verbal

3 Assess

Section 2 Review Answers

1. The particles of a solution will not settle out, are not visible to the eye and will pass through a filter. The particles of a suspension will settle out, are visible to the eye, and will not pass through a filter.
2. The molecules of sugar separate from each other and become surrounded by water molecules, but the molecules do not separate into ions or atoms. When an ionic compound dissolves, it breaks up into ions, which are surrounded by water molecules.
3. The salt is a solute, which lowers the freezing point of the water as the two substances begin to mix.
4. Ocean water is a solution of salt and water. The salt lowers the freezing point of water below that of fresh water.

CHAPTER PROJECT

Check Your Progress

Review student's choices of buildings. Help students decide whom might be best to contact to get the needed information. Lead a roleplay interview or phone call with students so they can practice.

Performance Assessment

Oral Presentation Call on students to describe the characteristics of solutions, suspensions, and colloids.

Figure 12 The coolant in a car radiator is a solution.
Predicting On a very cold day, what might happen to a car that had only water in the radiator?

Higher Boiling Points The **boiling point** is the temperature at which a substance boils, or changes from a liquid to a gas. **Solutes raise the boiling point of a solvent.** To see why this happens, think about what you learned Section 1 about evaporation. As a liquid evaporates, molecules from its surface leave the liquid and enter the air above. If the temperature goes up, more evaporation takes place. When the temperature is high enough, bubbles of gas actually form within the liquid. That is, you see the liquid boil. Now, suppose you add solute particles to the liquid. The more solute particles added, the fewer solvent molecules there are exposed to the surface. So fewer escape to the air. As a result, the temperature must go higher for the solution to boil. In the case of water, that would be higher than 100°C.

INTEGRATING TECHNOLOGY Car manufacturers make use of the effects of solutes to protect engines from heat and cold. The coolant in a car radiator is a solution of water and another liquid called antifreeze. Often the antifreeze is ethylene glycol, which freezes at –13°C and boils at 197°C. The mixture of the two liquids has a lower freezing point and higher boiling point than water alone. This solution can absorb more of the heat given off by the running engine. Risk of damage to the car from overheating is greatly reduced. So is the risk of damage from freezing in very cold weather.

Section 2 Review

1. List three ways to tell the difference between a solution and a suspension.
2. Describe what happens to the molecules of a solid, such as a sugar cube, when it dissolves in water. How does the process differ for an ionic compound, such as table salt?
3. Why does salt sprinkled on icy roads cause the ice to melt?
4. **Thinking Critically Relating Cause and Effect** Why is the temperature needed to freeze ocean water lower than the temperature needed to freeze the surface of a freshwater lake?

CHAPTER PROJECT

Check Your Progress

By now you should have chosen a building in your community to monitor. How will you determine the amount and type of water usage there? Be sure to check with your teacher before contacting anyone at the site. (*Hint:* A building manager or facilities manager often has information about water use. You may find it helpful to write down your questions before you interview the person.)

Program Resources

- **Unit 1 Resources** 2-2 Review and Reinforce; 2-2 Enrich

Media and Technology

 **Transparencies** "Effect of Solutes on Freezing and Boiling," Transparency 5

Answers to Self-Assessment

Caption Question

Figure 12 The car's engine might be damaged because the water inside the radiator could freeze on a very cold day.

The Properties of Water

Key Ideas

- A water molecule consists of two hydrogen atoms bonded to an oxygen atom. The hydrogen ends of the molecule have a slight positive charge. The oxygen end of the molecule has a slight negative charge.
- The charged ends of water's polar molecules attract the charged ends of other water molecules. Water molecules are also attracted to other charged particles.
- Some properties caused by the attractions among water molecules are surface tension, capillary action, and high specific heat.
- Water dissolves so many substances that it is sometimes called the "universal solvent."
- Water on Earth exists in three states: liquid water; ice, a solid; and water vapor, a gas.
- Energy must be added or released for water molecules to change state.
- Unlike most other substances, the solid form of water is less dense than the liquid form.

Key Terms

polar molecule
surface tension
capillary action
solution
solvent
evaporation
condensation
specific heat

Understanding Solutions

Key Ideas

- A solution is a well-mixed mixture, having smaller particles than a suspension or a colloid.
- When a solution forms, particles of solute are surrounded by particles of solvent.
- Solutes lower the freezing point and raise the boiling point of a solvent.

Key Terms

suspension
solute
colloid
freezing point
boiling point

Organizing Information

Flowchart The flowchart below shows how ice melts. Copy the flowchart onto a piece of paper. Then complete it and add a title. (For more on Flowcharts, see the Skills Handbook.)

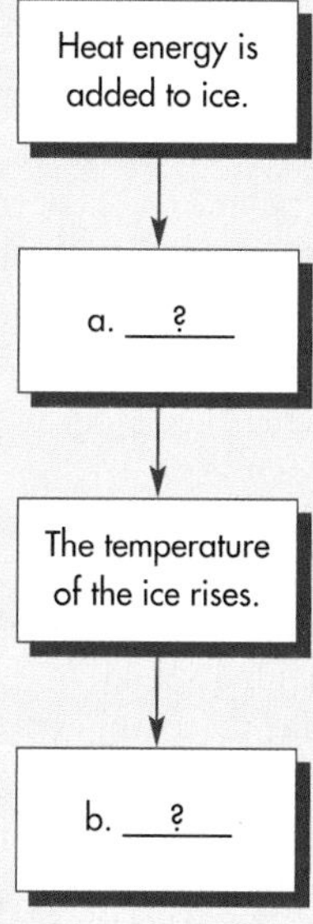

Program Resources

- **Unit 1 Resources** Chapter 2 Project Scoring Rubric
- **Performance Assessment** Chapter 2
- **Chapter and Unit Tests** Chapter 2 Test

Media and Technology

Computer Test Bank Chapter 2 Test

Organizing Information

Flow Chart **a.** Molecules in the ice start moving faster. **b.** Solid ice melts and becomes liquid water. Sample title: The Melting of Ice

Reviewing Content

Multiple Choice

1. b 2. a 3. c 4. b 5. d

True or False

6. true 7. freezing point 8. condensation 9. solute 10. true

Checking Concepts

11. The presence of a solute in a solution lowers the temperature at which the solvent freezes.
12. Water is called the "universal solvent" because it dissolves many substance.
13. A light beam will scatter when shined through a colloid, but will not scatter when shined through a solution.
14. Students' diagrams should be similar to the illustration of a water molecule in Figure 1 on page 51, with labels for one oxygen atom and two hydrogen atoms. The hydrogen atoms should be labeled as having a positive charge; the oxygen atom should be labeled as having a negative charge.
15. Answers may vary. Properties that depend on water's polarity include surface tension, capillary action, the ability to dissolve many substances, water's unusually high specific heat, and the fact that solid ice is less dense than liquid water.
16. Water occurs on Earth as a solid in the form of ice, as liquid water, and as a gas in the form of water vapor. Water is unique in that it is the only substance on Earth that exists in all three states.

Thinking Critically

17. Water molecules in the solid state move slowly and are arranged in a rigid structure. Water molecules in the liquid state move more rapidly and spread out to take the shape of their container. Water molecules in the gas state are moving fastest of all, and they spread out to fill an enclosed space.
18. Water is a polar substance. The charged ends of water molecules attract the molecules of other polar substances, allowing those substances to dissolve in water. Oil is a nonpolar substance, so its molecules are not attracted to the water molecules. Therefore the oil does not dissolve in water.

CHAPTER 2 ASSESSMENT

Reviewing Content

Multiple Choice

Choose the letter of the best answer.

1. Sugar water is an example of a
a. suspension. **b.** solution.
c. solute. **d.** colloid.

2. When salt is added to an ice and water mixture at 0°C,
a. the temperature of the mixture drops.
b. more of the water freezes.
c. more of the water evaporates.
d. there is no noticeable change.

3. A molecule with electrically charged areas is a
a. nonpolar molecule.
b. solution.
c. polar molecule.
d. gas.

4. When you stir salt into water, the water acts as a
a. solution. **b.** solvent.
c. solute. **d.** molecule.

5. The amount of heat needed to increase the temperature of a certain mass of a substance by 1°C is called the
a. boiling point. **b.** freezing point.
c. capillary action. **d.** specific heat.

True or False

If the statement is true, write true. If it is false, change the underlined word or words to make the statement true.

6. The property of surface tension allows insects to walk on water.
7. At the boiling point, a substance changes from a liquid to a solid.
8. Through the process of evaporation, a gas changes to a liquid.
9. In a solution, the substance that gets dissolved is the solvent.
10. Electric current will flow through a water solution of ionic solids.

Checking Concepts

11. How does a solute affects the temperature at which a solvent freezes?
12. Explain why water is called the "universal solvent."
13. Explain how you could tell the difference between a solution and a clear colloid.
14. Draw a diagram of a water molecule that shows how it is polar. Be sure to include labels in your diagram.
15. Give examples of two properties of water that are caused by the attractions between water molecules.
16. **Writing to Learn** As the information officer aboard a starship, you are assigned to write a handbook describing Earth's waters to visitors from other galaxies. Write a description of the states in which water occurs on Earth and explain why these states make water unique.

Thinking Critically

17. **Comparing and Contrasting** Compare the three states of water in terms of the speed and arrangement of their molecules.
18. **Applying Concepts** You may have heard the saying, "Oil and water don't mix." Explain this statement in terms of the chemistry of water.
19. **Predicting** The city of Charleston, South Carolina, is located on the Atlantic coast. The city of Macon, Georgia, is located about 340 kilometers inland to the west. Predict which city is likely to be cooler in the summer. Explain your answer.
20. **Relating Cause and Effect** A molecule of water is likely to evaporate more quickly from the Caribbean Sea near the equator than from the Arctic Ocean. Explain why this statement is true.

66

19. Charleston is likely to be cooler in summer because it is nearer to a large body of water than Macon. Because of water's high specific heat, land heats up more quickly than water. The warmer land warms the air above it, while the air above water remains cool. Breezes from the ocean, then, should keep Charleston cooler in summer.
20. The sun's heat provides the energy to evaporate water, and the sun's heat is more intense near the equator than at the Arctic Ocean.

Applying Skills

21. Bonds within the molecules of the unknown substance are broken so that their atoms are separated into ions.
22. Students' diagrams should show water molecules surrounding and separating ions of the unknown substance as it dissolves.
23. The dissolved particles would be neutral molecules rather than individual atoms.

Applying Skills

The diagram below shows the particles of an unknown substance in a water solution. Use the diagram to answer Questions 21–23.

21. **Interpreting Data** How can you tell from the diagram that the unknown substance is an ionic solid rather than a molecular solid??
22. **Making Models** Make a diagram to show the role water molecules play in dissolving the unknown substance.
23. **Drawing Conclusions** How would the diagram differ if the unknown substance were a molecular solid?

Performance CHAPTER PROJECT Assessment

Present Your Project Now you are ready to share the data you have collected. Make a graph of your household water-use data. As a class, discuss any surprising results. How do your findings compare to those of your classmates?

Reflect and Record In your project notebook, reflect on the data collection process. What part of the project was the most difficult? How might you approach this task differently? Write a paragraph summarizing what your class discovered about how water is used in your community. Do you notice any similarities among buildings where a lot of water is used, or among those where little water is used?

Test Preparation

Use these questions to prepare for standardized tests.

Study the table showing common solutions. Then answer Questions 24–27.

Examples of Common Solutions

Solute	Solvent	Solution
Gas	Gas	Air (oxygen and other gases in nitrogen)
Gas	Liquid	Soda water (carbon dioxide in water)
Liquid	Liquid	Antifreeze (ethylene glycol in water)
Solid	Liquid	Dental filling (silver in mercury)
Solid	Liquid	Ocean water (sodium chloride and other compounds in water)
Solid	Solid	Brass (zinc in copper)

24. Mixing carbon dioxide and water produces which solution?
    a. antifreeze **b.** dental filling
    c. soda water **d.** brass
25. In which solution are both the solute and the solvent a solid?
    a. antifreeze **b.** dental filling
    c. soda water **d.** brass
26. The solvent in dental filling is
    a. a solid. **b.** a gas.
    c. mercury. **d.** silver.
27. The boiling point of ocean water is most likely
    a. higher than that of pure water.
    b. lower than that of pure water.
    c. the same as that of pure water.
    d. the same as that of sodium chloride.

Program Resources

- **Inquiry Skills Activity Book** Provides teaching and review of all inquiry skills

Performance CHAPTER PROJECT Assessment

Present Your Project To maximize sharing of information and to give students an opportunity to compare their models, try to schedule all the presentations in no more than two class periods or one block, allocating a specific maximum amount of time for each model. If possible, arrange the room with the students forming a large circle so everyone can see each model as it is presented.

Prompt students to identify the specific features in the model by name, explain how the features are formed in nature, and describe the role they play in the river system. Encourage the other students to ask questions about each model as it is presented. Make sure you provide all students with positive feedback about their model. Suggest that students save their models for presentation on Parents' Night or at a science fair.

Reflect and Record Encourage students to use the Chapter 2 Project Scoring Rubric to help assess their models. Suggest that they review their sketches to make sure their models accomplished what they planned. Students might also evaluate the materials they used to make the models for their effectiveness to the application.

Test Preparation

24. a **25.** d **26.** c **27.** a

CHAPTER 3

Chemical Interactions

Sections	Time	Student Edition Activities	Other Activities
CHAPTER PROJECT **Keep a Chemical Change Log** p. 69	Ongoing (2 weeks)	Check Your Progress, pp. 75, 86 Project Wrap Up, p. 89	
1 Observing Chemical Reactions pp. 70–77 ◆ Define and compare elements, compounds, mixtures, atoms, and molecules. ◆ Compare chemical changes to physical changes. ◆ Explain how chemical bonds are changed during chemical reactions. ◆ Identify evidence of chemical reactions.	2–3 periods/ 1–1$\frac{1}{2}$ blocks	**Discover** What Happens When Chemicals React?, p. 70 **Try This** Mostly Cloudy, p. 71 **Skills Lab: Making Observations** Where's the Evidence?, pp. 76–77	**TE** Demonstration, p. 73
2 Writing Chemical Equations pp. 78–86 ◆ Describe the information conveyed in a chemical equation. ◆ Apply the principle of conservation of mass to chemical reactions. ◆ Identify and describe the three categories of chemical reactions.	2 periods/ 1 block	**Discover** Do You Lose Anything?, p. 78 **Try This** Still There, p. 81 **Sharpen Your Skills** Calculating, p. 82	**TE** Inquiry Challenge, p. 80 **TE** Including All Students, p. 82 **TE** Demonstration, p. 84 **LM** 3, "The Law of Definite Proportions" **IES** "The Glory of Ancient Rome," pp. 24–25
Study Guide/Assessment pp. 87–89	1 period/ $\frac{1}{2}$ block		**ISAB** Provides teaching and review of all inquiry skills

For Standard or Block Schedule The Resource Pro® CD-ROM gives you maximum flexibility for planning your instruction for any type of schedule. Resource Pro® contains Planning Express®, an advanced scheduling program, as well as the entire contents of the Teaching Resources and the Computer Test Bank.

CHAPTER PLANNING GUIDE

Program Resources	Assessment Strategies	Media and Technology
UR Chapter 3 Project Teacher Notes **UR** Chapter 3 Project Overview and Worksheets	**SE** Performance Assessment: Present Your Project, p. 89 **TE** Check Your Progress, pp. 75, 86 **UR** Chapter 3 Project Scoring Rubric	Science Explorer Internet Site at www.phschool.com Student Edition on Audio CD, Chapter 3
UR 3-1 Lesson Plan **UR** 3-1 Section Summary **UR** 3-1 Review and Reinforce **UR** 3-1 Enrich **UR** Chapter 3 Skills Lab blackline masters	**SE** Section 1 Review, p. 75 **TE** Ongoing Assessment, pp. 71, 73 **TE** Performance Assessment, p. 75	Concept Videotape Library, Grade 6, Tape 1, "Designing Fireworks" Lab Activity Videotapes, Grade 6 Tape 1
UR 3-2 Lesson Plan **UR** 3-2 Section Summary **UR** 3-2 Review and Reinforce **UR** 3-2 Enrich	**SE** Section 2 Review, p. 86 **TE** Ongoing Assessment, pp. 79, 81, 83 **TE** Performance Assessment, pp. 85, 86	Transparency 6, "Balancing an Equation"
RCA Provides strategies to improve science reading skills **GRSW** Provides worksheets to promote student comprehension of content	**SE** Chapter 3 Study Guide/Assessment, pp. 87–89 **PA** Chapter 3 Performance Assessment **CUT** Chapter 3 Test **CTB** Chapter 3 Test	Computer Test Bank, Chapter 3 Test

Key: **SE** Student Edition
CTB Computer Test Bank
ISAB Inquiry Skills Activity Book
GRSW Guided Reading and Study Workbook
TE Teacher's Edition
PTA Product Testing Activities by *Consumer Reports*
RCA Reading in the Content Area
PA Performance Assessment
UR Unit Resources
LM Laboratory Manual
IES Interdisciplinary Explorations Series
CUT Chapter and Unit Tests

Meeting the National Science Education Standards and AAAS Benchmarks

National Science Education Standards	Benchmarks for Science Literacy	Unifying Themes
Science as Inquiry (Content Standard A) ◆ **Communicate scientific procedures and explanations** Students report on how successfully they were able to observe chemical reactions in the world around them. *(Skills Lab)* **Physical Science** (Content Standard B) ◆ **Properties and changes of properties in matter** A chemical reaction changes the original reactants into new substances with different properties. *(Sections 1, 2)* ◆ **Transfer of energy** Chemical reactions always involve transfer of energy between reactants and changes in the energy level of products. *(Section 1)*	**1A The Scientific World View** Chemistry and chemical processes are all around us and are essential for understanding the world. *(Chapter Project)* **4D The Structure of Matter** Matter is composed of a few simple building blocks called elements. Elements can form compounds with properties different from the elements. *(Sections 1, 2)* **4E Energy Transformations** Chemical reactions always involve energy changes. *(Section 1)* **11C Constancy and Change** Mass is always conserved in chemical reactions. *(Section 2)*	◆ **Energy** The energy of the reactants changes during a chemical reaction. A chemical reaction can give off energy or absorb energy. *(Section 1)* ◆ **Patterns of Change** A chemical reaction changes the original reactants into new substances with different properties. *(Sections 1, 2)* ◆ **Scale and Structure** The types of atoms and how they are joined determine the properties of a substance. Elements combine to form compounds. Molecules are made of atoms bonded together. *(Sections 1, 2)* ◆ **Unity and Diversity** All chemical reactions share certain characteristics. Different kinds of chemical reactions can be classified. *(Section 1, 2; Skills Lab)* ◆ **Stability** Mass is always conserved in chemical reactions. *(Section 2)*

Take It to the Net

Interactive text at www.phschool.com

Science Explorer comes alive with iText.

- **Complete student text** is accessible from any computer with Internet access or a CD-ROM drive.
- **Animations, simulations, and videos** enhance student understanding and retention of concepts.
- **Self-tests and online study tools** assess student understanding.

STAY CURRENT with **SCIENCE NEWS®**

Find out the latest research and information about Chemical Reactions at: **www.phschool.com**

Go to **www.phschool.com** and click on the Science icon.Then click on Science Explorer: Life, Earth, and Physical Science under PH@school.

Student Edition Activities Planner

ACTIVITY	Time *(minutes)*	Materials *Quantities for one work group*	Skills
Section 1			
Discover, p. 70	10	**Consumable** baking soda, white vinegar, clear plastic cups **Nonconsumable** large bowl or sink, sfety goggles	Observing
Try This, p. 71	10	**Consumable** carbonated water, limewater, tap water, plastic cups **Nonconsumable** graduated cylinder, safety goggles, lab apron	Inferring
Skills Lab, pp. 76–77	40	**Consumable** 4 small plastic cups; 2 plastic spoons; matches; sodium carbonate (powder); aluminum foil, about 10-cm square; dilute hydrochloric acid in a dropper bottle; copper sulfate solution; sodium carbonate solution; sugar **Nonconsumable** tongs; graduated cylinder, 10 mL; birthday candles; clay	Observing
Section 2			
Discover, p. 78	10	**Nonconsumable** about 24 coins of various denominations	Making Models
Try This, p. 81	15	**Nonconsumable** hex nuts and short bolts, balance	Making Models
Sharpen Your Skills, p. 82	10	No special materials are required.	Calculating

A list of all materials required for the Student Edition activities can be found on pages TVA34–TVA40. You can obtain information about ordering materials by calling 1-800-848-9500 or by accessing the Science Explorer Internet site at: **www.phschool.com**

CHAPTER 3 PROJECT

Keep a Chemical Change Log

Many students think of "chemistry" as something that happens only in the school lab. They may think that chemistry has nothing to do with them. As students learn about the concepts of chemical reactions, they will discover the large number of chemical changes that occur around them and how these reactions are an important part of their daily lives.

Purpose In this project, students will keep a log of chemical changes that they observe in their daily lives. They will use the signs of chemical change mentioned in Section 1 to distinguish between physical and chemical changes and will further classify these changes. They will also design their own record-keeping format for recording their observations.

Skills Focus Students will be able to

- form operational definitions about physical and chemical changes;
- pose questions and make inferences based on observations of chemical reactions;
- create tables to record observations;
- classify chemical reactions as synthesis, decomposition, or replacement reactions.

Project Time Line The project requires almost two weeks. On the first day, have students survey the chapter to learn what is meant by a chemical change. Use the Chapter 3 Project Worksheet 1 to help students start thinking about differences between physical and chemical changes. On the second or third day, have students list the signs of a chemical reaction and discuss their lists in pairs. On the next day, students should prepare data tables. Students should then spend a week making their observations and completing the tables.

Before beginning the project, see Chapter 3 Project Teacher Notes in Unit 1 Resources for more details on carrying out the project. Also distribute to students the Chapter 3 Project Overview, Worksheets, and Scoring Rubric in Unit 1 Resources.

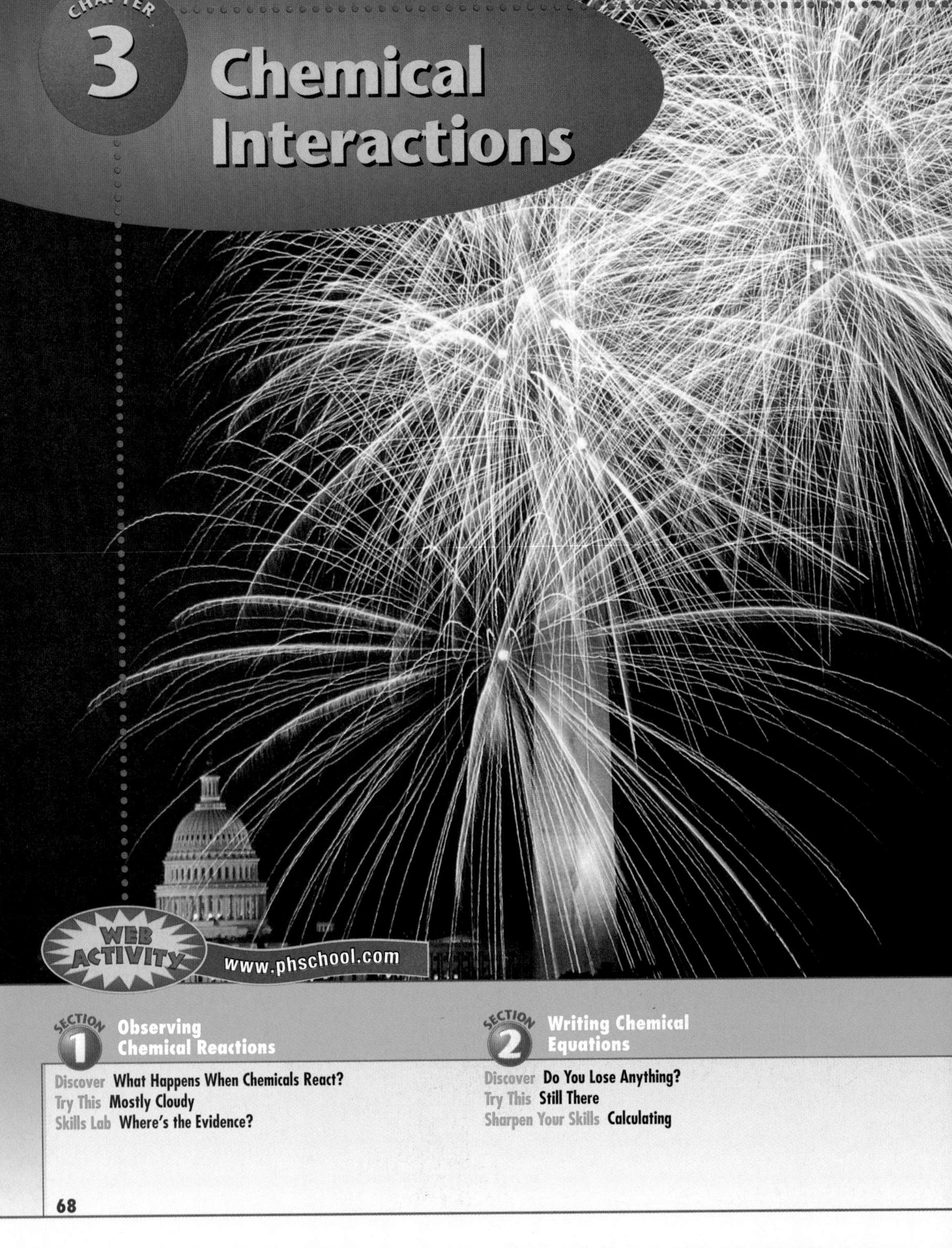

SECTION 1 Observing Chemical Reactions

Discover What Happens When Chemicals React?
Try This Mostly Cloudy
Skills Lab Where's the Evidence?

SECTION 2 Writing Chemical Equations

Discover Do You Lose Anything?
Try This Still There
Sharpen Your Skills Calculating

68

Suggested Shortcuts To save time, students can observe and record the chemical reactions they observe during a 24 hour period.

Possible Materials Students need only paper and pencil to record data for the project. Students should design their own record-keeping sheets, using Chapter 3 Project Worksheet 2 as an example.

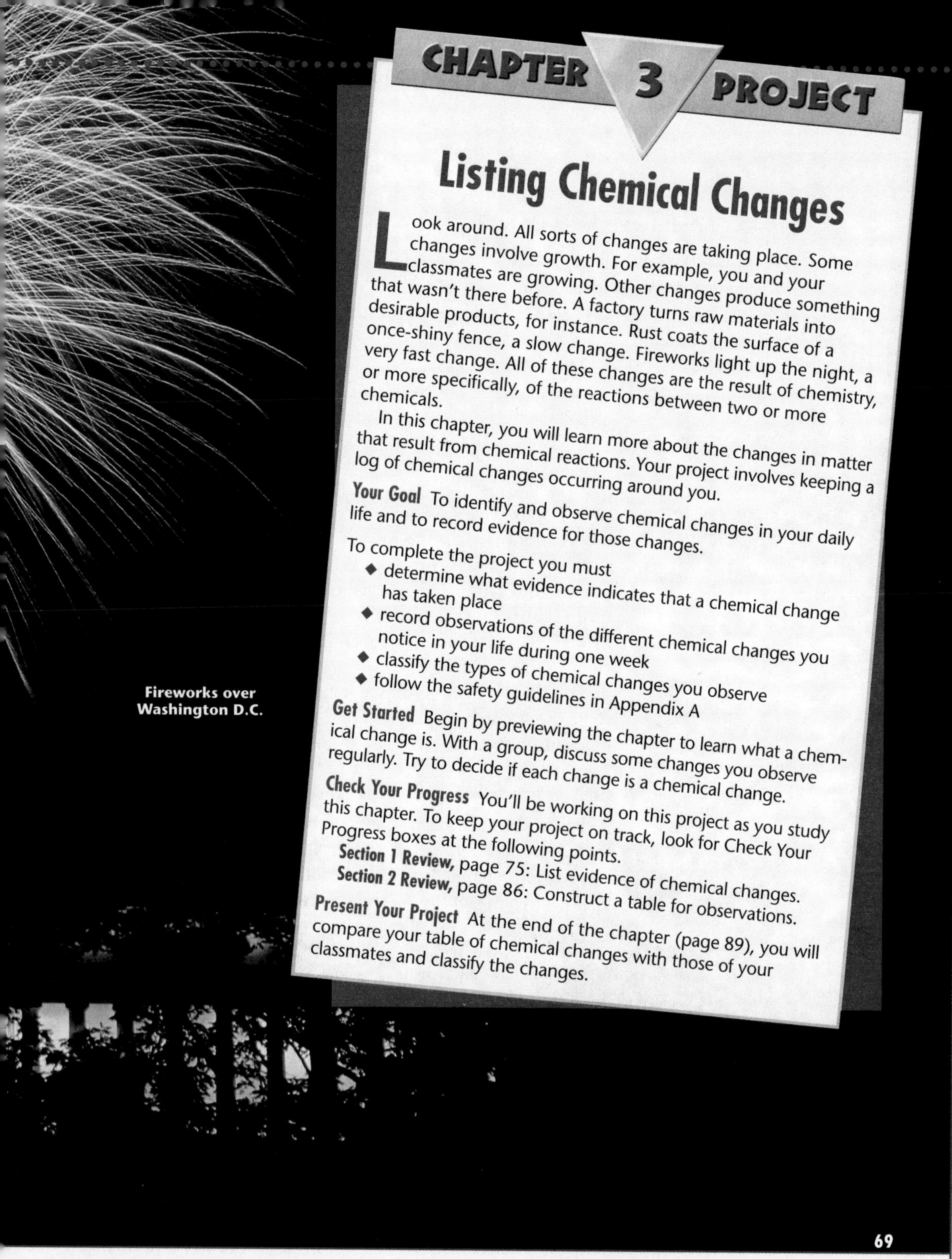

CHAPTER 3 PROJECT

Listing Chemical Changes

Look around. All sorts of changes are taking place. Some changes involve growth. For example, you and your classmates are growing. Other changes produce something that wasn't there before. A factory turns raw materials into desirable products, for instance. Rust coats the surface of a once-shiny fence, a slow change. Fireworks light up the night, a very fast change. All of these changes are the result of chemistry, or more specifically, of the reactions between two or more chemicals.

In this chapter, you will learn more about the changes in matter that result from chemical reactions. Your project involves keeping a log of chemical changes occurring around you.

Your Goal To identify and observe chemical changes in your daily life and to record evidence for those changes.

To complete the project you must

- determine what evidence indicates that a chemical change has taken place
- record observations of the different chemical changes you notice in your life during one week
- classify the types of chemical changes you observe
- follow the safety guidelines in Appendix A

Get Started Begin by previewing the chapter to learn what a chemical change is. With a group, discuss some changes you observe regularly. Try to decide if each change is a chemical change.

Check Your Progress You'll be working on this project as you study this chapter. To keep your project on track, look for Check Your Progress boxes at the following points.

Section 1 Review, page 75: List evidence of chemical changes.

Section 2 Review, page 86: Construct a table for observations.

Present Your Project At the end of the chapter (page 89), you will compare your table of chemical changes with those of your classmates and classify the changes.

Fireworks over Washington D.C.

Launching the Project To illustrate physical change, cut a piece of paper into smaller parts and point out that the small pieces are still paper. Then burn a piece of paper and show students the ash. Explain that this is a chemical change. Point out that the key difference between chemical and physical changes is that a chemical change produces substance(s) that were not there before the reaction. Explain that sometimes it is difficult to tell if a new substance is produced. Hold up a battery. Tell students that a chemical change occurs inside the battery as it operates, but it is not visible or obvious.

Distribute copies of the Chapter 3 Project Worksheet 1 in Unit 1 Resources and have small groups of students discuss the project. To ensure that every student participates in discussions, limit group size to three students.

Allow time for students to read the description of the project in their text and the Chapter Project Overview in Unit 1 Resources.

Program Resources

- **Unit 1 Resources** Chapter 3 Project Teacher Notes; Chapter 3 Overview and Worksheets; Chapter 3 Project Scoring Rubric

Media and Technology

Student Edition on Audio CD Chapter 3

www.phschool.com

You will find an Internet activity, chapter self-tests for students, and links to other chapter topics at this site.

Performance Assessment

The Chapter 3 Project Scoring Rubric in Unit 1 Resources will help you evaluate how well students complete the Chapter 3 Project. You may wish to share the scoring rubric with your students so they are clear about what will be expected of them.

Students will be assessed on

- their understanding of and ability to identify chemical change;
- the number of different observations dealing with chemical change that they are able to accumulate during one week;
- the accuracy of their classifications of the types of chemical changes observed;
- their participation in classroom discussions.

Section 1 Observing Chemical Reactions

Objectives

After completing the lesson, students will be able to

- explain that the production of new substances having different properties shows that a chemical reaction has occurred;
- compare endothermic and exothermic reactions;
- explain how chemical bonds are changed during chemical reactions.

Key Terms precipitate, endothermic reaction, exothermic reaction

1 Engage/Explore

Activating Prior Knowledge

Invite volunteers to name some changes to matter that they are familiar with. Prompt students by suggesting rusting bicycle chains, growing plants, burning candles, melting ice, and so on. Record students' responses on the board and refer to them as students work through the section.

Discover Activity

Skills Focus observing
Materials *safety goggles, baking soda, white vinegar, clear plastic cups, large bowl or sink*
Time 10 minutes
Tips Demonstrate the wafting technique (see Appendix A, Science Safety Rules). Remind students not to taste the mixture.
Expected Outcome The mixture will fizz, the contents of the cup will become cooler, and the vinegar smell will disappear.
Think It Over Students may say they could hear the products fizzing, feel the cup become cool, and smell that the mixture no longer smelled like vinegar.

Section 1 Observing Chemical Reactions

Discover Activity

What Happens When Chemicals React?

1. Put on your safety goggles.
2. Put 2 small spoonfuls of baking soda into a clear plastic cup.
3. Holding the cup over a large bowl or sink, add about 125 mL of vinegar. Swirl the cup gently.
4. Observe any changes to the material in the cup. Feel the outside of the cup. What do you notice about the temperature?
5. Carefully fan some air over the liquid toward you. What does the mixture smell like?

Think It Over

Observing Looking at an experiment is not the only way to get information. Your other senses can be equally useful in making observations. What changes did you detect using your senses of smell and touch?

Guide for Reading

- What are the observable characteristics of a chemical reaction?
- What two kinds of energy changes can occur during a chemical reaction?
- How might chemical bonds change during a chemical reaction?

Reading Tip As you read, write one or two sentences to summarize the main ideas under each heading.

Suppose you are a sculptor choosing the material for a new outdoor statue. You don't want your work destroyed by chemical reactions with substances in the air. What material would you use? The artist who created the statue below chose bronze, a brownish yellow alloy of copper, tin, and other metals. Bronze is harder than iron and more resistant to chemical changes. However, its outer surface does react with oxygen, producing the dark color you see here. The new surface helps preserve the statue by acting as a protective layer for the unreacted metal atoms beneath it.

Evidence for Chemical Reactions

Picture yourself toasting marshmallows over a campfire. You use your senses to detect chemical changes. You see the burning logs change from a hard solid to a soft pile of ash. You hear popping and hissing sounds as gases produced by the reaction cause the wood to expand. You smell smoke. You feel the heat. You can even taste the results. The brown surface of the toasted marshmallow is a big change from the soft white marshmallow just out of its bag. Like the toasting of marshmallows, other chemical reactions involve two main kinds of observable changes.

◀ Bronze statue with its surface darkened by chemical reactions

Reading Strategies

Reading Tip Before students read the section, help them preview it to locate the main headings. Students can copy the headings into their notebooks, leaving space to write their summary sentences.
Sample summary:
Evidence for Chemical Reactions
One kind of evidence is the production of new substances with new properties. Another kind of evidence is an energy change.

Study and Comprehension After students read the section, have them use the summary sentences they created to generate questions about matter and its changes. Have partners quiz each other using the questions. Suggest that students save their questions to use as study guides for the section.

Figure 1 Brilliant, bombastic fireworks add excitement to many holidays. ***Inferring*** *What evidence tells you that fireworks involve chemical reactions?*

Changes in Properties One way to detect chemical reactions is to observe changes in the properties of the materials involved. Those changes result when new substances form. But what specific kinds of changes should you look for? First, a gas might be produced. If the reaction occurs in a liquid, you may see the gas as bubbles. Second, a color change may signal that a new substance has formed. Third, a solid may appear when two solutions are mixed. A solid that forms from solution during a chemical reaction is called a **precipitate** (pree SIP uh tayt). Finally, other kinds of observable changes in properties can also signal a chemical reaction. For example, hard marble forms a crumbly solid when it reacts with acid rain.

A single property change such as the formation of a gas may indicate that a chemical reaction has taken place, but it's not a guarantee. Sometimes physical changes give similar results. The sign of a chemical change is that one or more new substances are produced. When water changes physically, the resulting water vapor, ice, or liquid is made of the same particles as the starting substance. For example, when water boils, the gas bubbles you see are made of molecules of H_2O, just as the original liquid was. When water changes chemically, however, the H_2O molecules undergo a change. For example, when an electric current is passed through water during electrolysis, two gases are produced, hydrogen gas (H_2) and oxygen gas (O_2). **One observable characteristic of a chemical reaction is the production of new materials with properties that are different from those of the starting materials.**

Mostly Cloudy 

How can you tell if a chemical reaction is taking place?

1. Put on your safety goggles and apron.
2. Pour about 5 mL of limewater into a plastic cup.
3. Pour an equal amount of plain water into another plastic cup.
4. Add about 5 mL of carbonated water to each of the cups.

Inferring In which cup do you think a chemical reaction occurred? What evidence supports your inference?

2 Facilitate

Evidence for Chemical Reactions

TRY THIS

Skills Focus inferring

Materials *carbonated water, limewater, tap water, plastic cups, graduated cylinder, safety goggles, lab apron*

Time 10 minutes

Tips To make limewater, dissolve solid lime (calcium hydroxide, available at garden centers) in water until no more solid will dissolve. CAUTION: *Wear safety goggles.* Filter the solution.

Expected Outcome The reaction in the limewater cup will produce a white precipitate (calcium carbonate). As it settles, it will form a layer on the bottom of the cup. There will be no reaction in the plain water cup.

Inferring There was a chemical reaction in the limewater cup. The evidence for this is the white precipitate.

Extend Ask students: **How can you be sure there was no chemical reaction in the other cup?** *(Sample: None of the indicators of a chemical reaction were observed.)*

Program Resources

- **Unit 1 Resources** 3-1 Lesson Plan; 3-1 Section Summary
- **Guided Reading and Study Workbook** Section 3-1

Answers to Self-Assessment

Caption Questions

Figure 1 Examples of evidence of chemical reactions include: changes in colors, noise from explosions, burning, and smoke.

Ongoing Assessment

Oral Presentation Call on students to describe changes in properties that can result from a chemical reaction.

EXPLORING

Evidence for Chemical Reactions

Draw students' attention to the photograph showing a precipitate forming in solution. Ask: **Why is a precipitate forming in a solution an evidence of a chemical change?** (*The precipitate is a new material formed by a chemical reaction of the original materials.*) Have students explain how they know a chemical reaction is occurring in each photo. Make sure students understand that the water is undergoing a physical change as it boils, but the natural gas is producing heat as a result of a chemical reaction. The color changes in autumn leaves are due, in part, to the *cessation* of a chemical reaction. The plants stop making chlorophyll while existing chlorophyll is broken down. **learning modality: verbal**

Extend Have students work in pairs to prepare a storyboard or poster about a chemical-reaction detective. The poster should illustrate, with examples other than those shown in the text, five clues the detective can use to tell if a chemical reaction has taken place.

EXPLORING Evidence for Chemical Reactions

Chemical reactions produce new substances. The signs of a reaction vary, but many reactions include one or more of the following types of evidence.

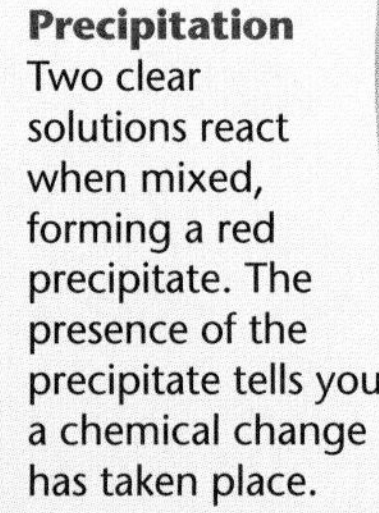

Precipitation Two clear solutions react when mixed, forming a red precipitate. The presence of the precipitate tells you a chemical change has taken place.

Color Change A color change often is a sign that a chemical reaction has occurred. The brilliant colors of fall foliage result when green chlorophyll in leaves breaks down. Then colors of other substances in the leaves become visible.

Changes in Temperature The burning of natural gas (a chemical reaction) supplies heat to boil water (a physical change). A temperature change can result from the changes in energy during a chemical reaction.

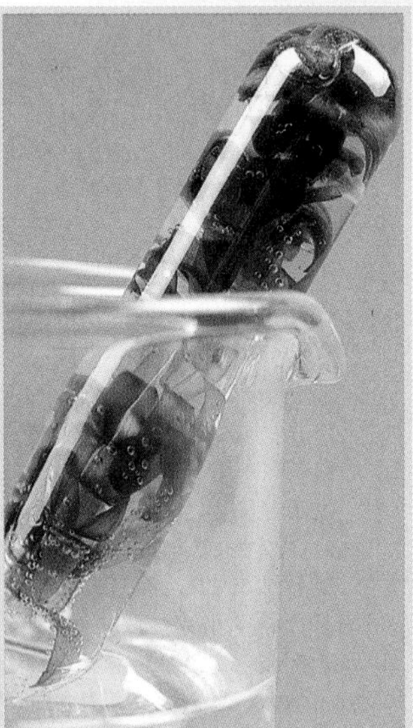

Gas Production Oxygen bubbles formed during photosynthesis collect on the leaves of this underwater plant. Oxygen is a product of the reaction between carbon dioxide and water inside the cells of the plant.

Changes in Properties Baking turns flour, water, and other ingredients into light, flaky bread. The loaf of bread with its crunchy crust has very different properties from the soft dough that went into the oven.

Background

Facts and Figures The release of heat is familiar evidence of a chemical reaction. Light can also be evidence of a chemical reaction. Often light is given off with heat, as in a combustion reaction. But in some reactions, light is released without being accompanied by a large amount of heat. For example, the blinking light of a firefly is the result of a chemical reaction in specialized cells in the insect's abdomen.

"Light sticks" use a chemical reaction that gives off light but not heat. To make a "light stick" glow, one must bend the stick to break a small tube inside the larger one. When the small tube breaks, it releases chemicals into the larger tube. The chemicals in the smaller tube mix with the chemicals in the larger tube, and the reaction that takes place releases light.

Changes in Energy From your everyday experience, you know about various types of energy, such as light and electricity. As matter changes, it can either absorb or release energy. **The second observable characteristic of a chemical reaction is a change in energy. Some reactions absorb energy, while others release energy.** One common indication that energy has been absorbed or released is a change in temperature.

If you did the Discover activity on page 70, you observed that the mixture became colder. When baking soda (sodium bicarbonate) reacts with vinegar, the reaction takes heat from the solution, making it feel cooler. This kind of reaction, which absorbs energy, is called an **endothermic reaction** (en doh THUR mik). The reaction that occurs in the cold pack in Figure 2 is another example of an endothermic reaction.

In contrast, the reaction between fuel and oxygen in an airplane engine releases the energy that lifts the plane off the ground and keeps it in the air. Some energy is also given off as heat. A reaction that releases energy in the form of heat is called an **exothermic reaction** (eks oh THUR mik).

☑ *Checkpoint* *How are endothermic reactions different from exothermic reactions?*

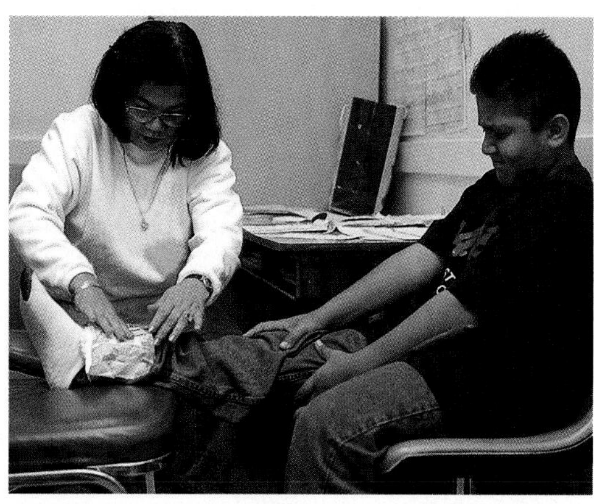

Figure 2 When this cold pack was squeezed, a reaction between water and another compound occurred and the temperature of the pack decreased. The resulting cooling effect reduces pain in the injured ankle and speeds up the healing process. *Classifying Is this reaction exothermic or endothermic? Explain.*

Figure 3 Burning airplane fuel releases a huge amount of energy. This exothermic reaction keeps a plane moving fast enough to remain in the air.

Including All Students

Some students may need extra help to remember the difference between the terms *exothermic* and *endothermic.* Suggest students say to themselves "Exo—go out; endo—go in" to help them remember that during an exothermic reaction, energy moves outward, and during an endothermic reaction, energy is absorbed. **limited English proficiency**

Demonstration

ACTIVITY

Obtain an instant cold pack and/or hot pack. Cold packs are often found in first-aid kits. Hot packs are usually available in stores that sell camping and hiking equipment. Allow students to feel the pack before you activate the chemical reaction in the pack. After you squeeze or bend the pack to mix the contents and start the reaction, allow students to feel the pack again, and classify the reaction inside the pack as endothermic or exothermic. Ask students: **Do you think the pack will continue to give off or absorb heat for a long time?** *(No)* **What will happen?** *(Eventually, the chemicals in the pack will react completely. Once the reaction stops, the energy change will also stop.)* If time permits, allow students to feel the pack again after a half-hour or more has passed, to see if the temperature of the pack has changed. **learning modality: kinesthetic**

Answers to Self-Assessment

Caption Questions

Figure 2 Endothermic; the reaction absorbed energy, resulting in a drop in temperature.

☑ *Checkpoint*

Endothermic reactions absorb energy; exothermic reactions release energy.

Ongoing Assessment

Skills Check Have students create a table or concept map to compare endothermic and exothermic reactions.

Chemical Reactions on a Small Scale

Addressing Naive Conceptions

Because complex chemical processes can be stated in an overall reaction, students may think that such chemical processes take place in one simple step. In a previous science class, students may have learned about photosynthesis. Ask a volunteer to state a word equation for photosynthesis. *(Water plus carbon dioxide in sunlight produce oxygen and sugar.)* Tell students that this process is much more complex than this summary. Photosynthesis is a series of reactions. Each reaction produces the materials required by the next step.

Chemical Bonds and Chemical Reactions

Using the Visuals: Figure 5

Use Figure 5 to help students visualize molecular models. Draw students' attention to the art representing the oxygen molecule. Ask: **How many oxygen atoms bond together to form a single molecule of oxygen?** *(two)* **Are the oxygen ions present in magnesium oxide in pairs ?** *(No. They are distributed evenly throughout the ionic compound.)* Ask students to infer what happens to the oxygen molecules when oxygen reacts with magnesium to form magnesium oxide. *(The oxygen molecule is broken apart, and the individual atoms bond with the magnesium atoms in a one-to-one ratio.)* **learning modality: visual**

Including All Students

If students have trouble visualizing the combination of magnesium and oxygen atoms, suggest that they draw electron dot diagrams of these elements. Invite a volunteer to draw electron dot diagrams of magnesium and oxygen on the board. Ask students: **How many valence electrons does magnesium have?** *(Two)* **How many valence electrons does oxygen have?** *(Six)* Use the electron dot diagrams to show students how the ionic bond between magnesium and oxygen forms. **learning modality: visual**

Chemical Reactions on a Small Scale

If you walk along a beach, you leave footprints in the sand. Over time, the incoming tide erases them. A beach is constantly changing as each wave carries new sand in from the ocean and takes some of the shore sand back with it. Sometimes a violent storm can change the outline of a shore in just a few hours, but mostly the beach is changed by wind and water moving sand a little at a time.

Chemical reactions also occur one small step at a time. When you use your senses to observe evidence of a chemical change, you are detecting the combined effect of countless small, invisible changes. These changes involve the rearrangement of atoms. Recall that the force that holds atoms together is called a chemical bond. **Chemical reactions occur when chemical bonds break or when new bonds form.** In order for new bonds to form, all of the reacting atoms must come into contact with one another.

Chemical Bonds and Chemical Reactions

In any substance, the types of atoms that are present and the types of chemical bonds they form determine the properties of the substance. For example, before the reaction in Figure 5, only magnesium atoms were present in the solid gray ribbon. When they burn, magnesium atoms (Mg) give up negatively charged electrons to oxygen atoms (O). Magnesium and oxygen react together rapidly. The product of the reaction, magnesium oxide (MgO), is an ionic solid with properties that are different from

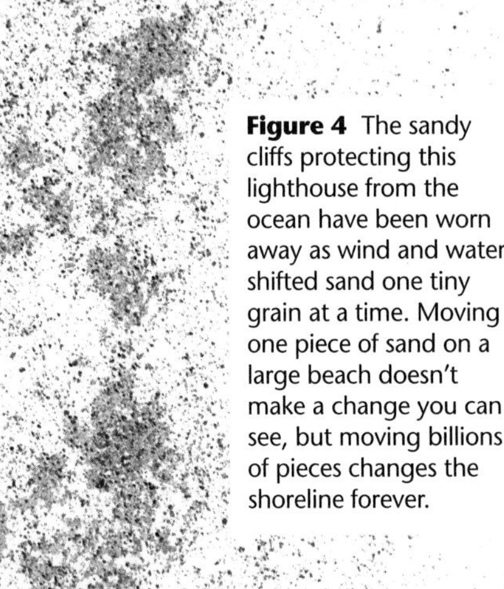

Figure 4 The sandy cliffs protecting this lighthouse from the ocean have been worn away as wind and water shifted sand one tiny grain at a time. Moving one piece of sand on a large beach doesn't make a change you can see, but moving billions of pieces changes the shoreline forever.

Background

Facts and Figures One very obvious chemical reaction is the oxidation that occurs when photochromatic eyeglasses get dark when exposed to sunlight, and lighten when the light is reduced.

Some photochromatic lenses contain tiny crystals of silver chloride (AgCl) and copper chloride (CuCl) which are added during manufacture. The crystals become uniformly embedded in the glass.

When light hits the silver chloride, the chloride ions lose an electron to become chlorine atoms. The silver ions grab the free electrons and become ordinary silver. The presence of silver in the glass makes it darker. Normally, the chlorine gas would escape and the lenses would be permanently darkened, but the copper ions convert the chlorine back to chloride ions.

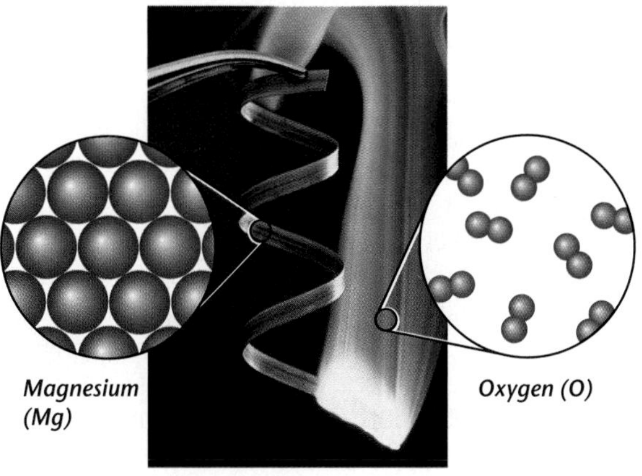

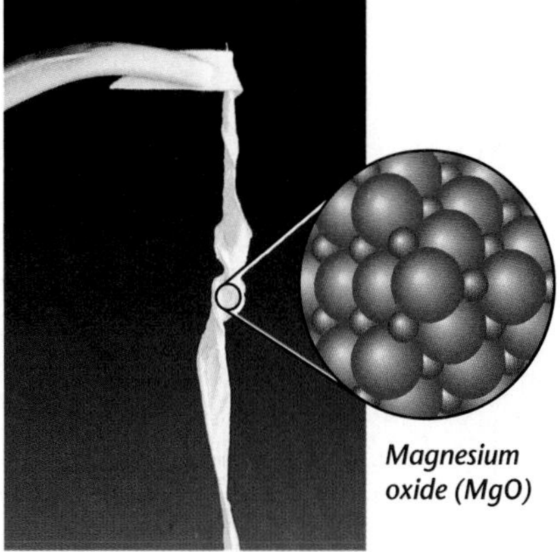

Figure 5 When magnesium burns (left), its atoms give up electrons to oxygen atoms, forming magnesium oxide (right). Notice that the resulting ions are different in size compared to the original atoms.

those of magnesium and oxygen. For example, while magnesium melts at about 650°C, temperatures of more than 2,800°C are required to melt magnesium oxide.

Chemical bonds also determine whether or not a chemical reaction will occur in a specific set of circumstances. Some bonds, such as those in glass, are strong and hard to change. Windows in buildings hundreds of years old show no damage from weather, while wood frames around the glass have rotted away. The wood is made of compounds that react easily with other substances in the environment. It can be softened by water and rotted by fungi.

Section 1 Review

1. What are some examples of evidence for a chemical reaction?
2. What two kinds of energy changes can take place during a chemical reaction?
3. What happens to the chemical bonds in a substance during a chemical reaction?
4. When a solid forms as two solutions are mixed together, what is that solid called?
5. **Thinking Critically Classifying** Classify the following as an endothermic or exothermic reaction: The temperature of two separate solutions is found to be 20°C. When the solutions are mixed, a precipitate forms and the temperature changes to 18°C. Explain your reasoning.

CHAPTER PROJECT

Check Your Progress

Use the information from the section to make a list of signs or evidence that a chemical reaction is taking place. Discuss your list with another classmate. (*Hint:* Look outside your home, think about reactions inside your body, and look for reactions that may occur either very slowly or very quickly.) Consider changes you might observe that shouldn't be classified as chemical reactions.

Program Resources

- **Unit 1 Resources** 3-1 Review and Reinforce; 3-1 Enrich

3 Assess

Section 1 Review Answers

1. The production of a gas or a precipitate, a change in color, or a change in temperature
2. Energy may be absorbed in an endothermic reaction, or energy may be released in an exothermic reaction.
3. Bonds are broken, and new bonds may form.
4. A precipitate
5. Endothermic; the temperature dropped, indicating that energy was absorbed.

CHAPTER PROJECT

Check Your Progress

Have students work together to make their lists and check each others' work. Students should develop rules for classifying situations in which evidence of a chemical change may actually signal a physical change. If students have difficulty thinking of places to look for chemical changes, suggest they list rooms in their homes, places they visit during a day, and products they use.

Performance Assessment

Skills Check Ask students to state several kinds of evidence for a chemical reaction.

Skills Lab

Making Observations

Where's the Evidence?

Preparing for Inquiry

Key Concept There is often visible evidence that a chemical change is taking place or has taken place. Production of gas bubbles, color change, or production of a precipitate are all indications of chemical reactions.

Skills Objectives Students will be able to
- make predictions of results of reactions;
- observe evidence of chemical reactions;
- infer that a chemical reaction has occurred.

Time 40 minutes

Advance Planning Prepare copper  sulfate solution by dissolving 25 g of $CuSO_4 \cdot 5H_2O$, in 1 liter of water. Prepare sodium carbonate solution by dissolving 13 g of $Na_2CO_3 \cdot H_2O$, in 1 liter of water. Prepare 1.0 M HCl solution by carefully adding 83 mL of concentrated HCl into enough water to make 1,000 mL of solution. CAUTION: *Always add acid to water, never the other way around.* Pour the dilute HCl into individual dropper bottles for student use.

Guiding Inquiry

Invitation

Review the difference between a physical change and a chemical change. Ask students to describe the difference between making careful observations and reaching a conclusion by inference. *(Observations describe only what is taking place. Reaching a conclusion by inference means interpreting the meaning of those observations.)*

Skills Lab

Observing

Where's the Evidence?

Chemical reactions occur all around you. In this lab you will observe different types of evidence of chemical reactions.

Problem

What are some signs that a chemical reaction has taken place?

Materials

4 small plastic cups
2 plastic spoons
tongs
matches
sodium carbonate (powdered solid)
graduated cylinder, 10 mL
aluminum foil, about 10-cm square
dilute hydrochloric acid in a dropper bottle
copper sulfate solution
sodium carbonate solution
birthday candles
sugar
clay

Procedure

Preview the steps for each reaction and copy the data table into your notebook.

Part 1

1. Put a pea-sized pile of sodium carbonate into a clean plastic cup. Record in the data table the appearance of the sodium carbonate.
2. Observe a dropper containing hydrochloric acid. Record the appearance of the acid. **CAUTION:** *Hydrochloric acid can burn you or anything else it touches. Wash spills immediately with water.*
3. Make a prediction about how you think the acid and the sodium carbonate will react when mixed. Record your prediction.
4. Add about 10 drops of hydrochloric acid to the sodium carbonate. Swirl to mix the contents of the cup. Record your observations.

Part 2

5. Fold up the sides of the aluminum foil square to make a small tray.
6. Use a plastic spoon to place a pea-sized pile of sugar into the tray.
7. Carefully describe the appearance of the sugar in your data table.

DATA TABLE

Reaction	Observations Before Reaction	Predictions	Observations During Reaction	Observations After Reaction
1. Sodium carbonate (powder) + hydrochloric acid				
2. Sugar + heat				
3. Copper sulfate + sodium carbonate solutions				

76

Introducing the Procedure
- Have students read through the procedure before class, and ask them to predict some of the observations they will make during each reaction. Remind students that important information is often missed just because no one was looking for it.

Troubleshooting the Experiment
- Part 1: Students will call the bubbles air bubbles. Remind them that not all gases are air and they should not jump to conclusions about the gas's identify.

Program Resources
- **Unit 1 Resources** Skills Lab blackline masters

Safety

Caution students not to mix or burn any materials except as directed in the procedure. Fire safety should be reviewed before students perform Part 2. Instruct students how to safely light the candle. Review the safety guidelines in Appendix A.

8. Secure a small candle on your desktop in a lump of clay. Carefully light the candle with a match only after being instructed to do so by your teacher. **CAUTION:** *Tie back long hair and loose clothing.*
9. Predict what you think will happen if you heat the sugar. Record your prediction.
10. Use tongs to hold the aluminum tray. Heat the sugar slowly by moving the tray gently back and forth over the flame. Make observations while the sugar is heating.
11. When you think there is no longer a chemical reaction occurring, blow out the candle.
12. Allow the tray to cool for a few seconds and set it down on your desk. Record your observations of the material left in the tray.

Part 3

13. Put about 2 mL of copper sulfate solution in one cup. **CAUTION:** *Copper sulfate is poisonous and can stain your skin and clothes. Do not touch it or get it in your mouth.* Put an equal amount of sodium carbonate solution in another cup. Record the appearance of both liquids.
14. Predict what you think will happen when the two solutions are mixed. Record your prediction.
15. Combine the two solutions and record your observations. **CAUTION:** *Dispose of the solutions as directed by your teacher.*
16. Wash your hands when you have finished working.

Analyze and Conclude

1. How do the results of each reaction compare with your predictions for that reaction?
2. How did you know when Reaction 1 was over?
3. Was the product of the reaction in Part 1 a solid, a liquid, or a gas? How do you know?
4. How are the properties of the material remaining after the reaction in Part 2 different from those of the sugar?
5. Was the product of the reaction in Part 3 a solid, a liquid, or a gas? How do you know?
6. How do you know if new substances were formed in each reaction?
7. **Think About It** What senses did you use to make observations during this lab? How might you use scientific instruments to extend your senses in order to make more observations?

More to Explore

Use your observation skills to find evidence of chemical reactions involving foods in your kitchen. Look for production of gases, color changes, and formation of precipitates. Share your findings with your classmates.

Sample Data Table

Reaction	Observations Before Reaction	Predictions	Observations During Reaction	Observations After Reaction
1. Sodium carbonate (powder) + hydrochloric acid	white powder and colorless liquid	accept all answers	bubbles and foaming	colorless liquid, maybe some white solid
2. Sugar+ heat	white, granular crystals	accept all answers	bubbles, smoke, turning black	black solid
3.Copper sulfate + sodium carbonate solutions	blue liquid and colorless liquid	accept all answers	reaction too fast	green precipitate

- Part 2: Students must pay attention so they don't miss the melting of the sugar before the chemical reaction begins. They will probably say that "smoke" is produced. It is actually water vapor produced by the decomposition of the sugar. The solid product is pure carbon.
- Part 3: The green color of the copper carbonate precipitate may be difficult to see in the blue copper sulfate solution.

Expected Outcome

- Part 1: Sodium carbonate and hydrochloric acid react to produce carbon dioxide gas as one of the products.
- Part 2: Sugar melts and then decomposes into pure carbon and water vapor. Students will see vapor and a black crusty product. They will smell a cotton candy smell.
- Part 3: The solutions of copper sulfate and sodium carbonate react to produce copper carbonate (a green precipitate) as well as sodium sulfate solution in a double replacement reaction.

Analyze and Conclude

1. Accept all well-explained, logical answers relating predictions to observations.
2. Students may suggest that there was no more bubbling or vapor.
3. The product is a gas. It made gas bubbles in the liquid.
4. The product is black and crusty.
5. Solid. A precipitate was produced.
6. The properties (color, physical state, solubility) changed for the substances in the reactions. This is evidence that there are new substances present.
7. Answers may include sight, sound, smell, or touch. Thermometers could be used to measure changes in temperature. Balances could be used to measure the masses of reactants and products. Microscopes could be used to observe the formation of the precipitate.

Extending the Inquiry

More to Explore Possible answers include: an egg white changing color and texture as an egg is fried; meat changing color when it is cooked; the rising of a cake as a gas (CO_2) is released inside the cake.

Section 2 Writing Chemical Equations

Objectives

After completing the lesson, students will be able to

- ◆ describe the information conveyed in a chemical equation;
- ◆ apply the principle of conservation of mass to chemical reactions;
- ◆ identify and describe the three classes of chemical reactions.

Key Terms chemical equation, subscript, reactant, product, conservation of mass, coefficient, synthesis, decomposition, replacement

1 Engage/Explore

Activating Prior Knowledge

As a class, brainstorm a list of symbols that the students are familiar with. Ask: **What symbols did you observe on your way to school today?** *(Samples: bus stop sign, stop sign, crosswalk, school bell)* Ask students to use examples to illustrate how symbols are helpful.

Discover Activity

Skills Focus making models
Materials *about 24 coins of various denominations*
Time 10 minutes
Tips Suggest that students use data tables to record their counts for each trial.
Think It Over The total value and types of coins did not change. Rearranging the coins did not change any individual coins. Students should infer that, like the total value and kinds of coins in the activity, the total number of atoms and the kinds of atoms do not change during chemical reactions.

Section 2 Writing Chemical Equations

Discover Activity

Do You Lose Anything?

1. Place about two dozen coins on a table. Sort them into stacks of pennies, nickels, dimes, and quarters.
2. Count and record the number of coins in each stack. Calculate and record the value of each stack and the total of all stacks combined.
3. Mix all the coins together and then divide them randomly into four unsorted stacks.
4. Again calculate the value of each stack and the total amount of money. Count the total number of each type of coin.
5. Repeat Steps 3 and 4.

Think It Over

Making Models What happened to the total value and types of coins in this activity? Did rearranging the coins change any individual coin? If you think of the coins as representing different types of atoms, what does this model tell you about chemical reactions?

Guide for Reading

- ◆ What does a chemical equation tell you?
- ◆ How does mass change during a chemical reaction?
- ◆ What are three categories of chemical reactions?

Reading Tip As you read, describe how each boldfaced vocabulary word relates to a chemical reaction.

Suppose you were to take a walk in a foreign country where the language is unfamiliar to you. Think of the signs you might see—two doors with drawings of a man and a woman, the receiver of a telephone, a drawing of a bicycle, and a picture of a trash can with something dropping into it. You would have no trouble figuring out what these signs mean.

Symbols express a concept in a shorter form. "Hydrogen molecules react with oxygen molecules to form water molecules," is a sentence that describes the reaction between hydrogen and oxygen. But writing it is slow and awkward. A **chemical equation** is a shorter, easier way to show chemical reactions, using symbols instead of words.

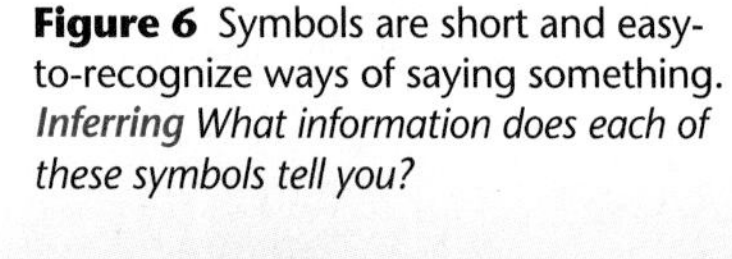

Figure 6 Symbols are short and easy-to-recognize ways of saying something. *Inferring What information does each of these symbols tell you?*

78

Reading Strategies

Reading Tip Before students begin reading, have them preview the chapter to look for boldfaced vocabulary words. Direct students to write these words on a sheet of notebook paper, leaving at least two lines of space to write a description of each term. Sample description: A chemical equation is a way to write what happens in a chemical reaction.

Study and Comprehension After students finish reading, have them review each section and jot down the main points and important details. Then have students use these notes to write summaries of the information in the section. Students may also want to use the descriptions they wrote for the Reading Tip to summarize the section. Remind students that in a summary, they should briefly state the main points and key details in their own words.

Formulas of Some Familiar Compounds			
Compound	**Formula**	**Compound**	**Formula**
Water	H_2O	Fool's gold (pyrite)	FeS_2
Hydrogen peroxide	H_2O_2	Propane	C_3H_8
Ammonia	NH_3	Rubbing alcohol	C_3H_8O
Aspirin	$C_9H_8O_4$	Rust	Fe_2O_3
Baking soda	$NaHCO_3$	Sodium chloride	NaCl
Bleach	NaClO	Sugar (sucrose)	$C_{12}H_{22}O_{11}$
Carbon dioxide	CO_2	Sulfur dioxide	SO_2
Carbon monoxide	CO	Washing soda	Na_2CO_3
Hemoglobin	$C_{3032}H_{4816}O_{780}N_{780}S_8Fe_4$		

Figure 7 Formulas for compounds tell you what elements as well as how many atoms of each element are present. ***Observing*** *How many oxygen atoms are present in water, carbon dioxide, and sugar?*

Understanding Chemical Equations

You may be surprised to learn that although chemical equations are shorter than sentences, they contain more information. That's partly because equations use chemical formulas and other symbols instead of the words. Also, equations follow a common structure that all chemists understand.

Writing Chemical Formulas You have already seen chemical formulas, such as H_2O and H_2O_2 and letter symbols that stand for specific elements. (You can review those symbols in the periodic table in Appendix C.) If you think of these symbols as being like the letters of the alphabet, a formula is like a "word" that represents a compound. Figure 7 shows you the formulas for some common compounds.

In addition to identifying the elements in a compound, a formula shows the ratio of the atoms that make up that substance. In the case of molecular compounds, the formula shows the number and kind of atoms in a molecule. You can see at a glance which atoms make up a molecule of table sugar, $C_{12}H_{22}O_{11}$. For ionic compounds, the formula shows the ratio of the different ions that are present. In aluminum chloride, $AlCl_3$, there are 3 chloride ions for every 1 aluminum ion.

Notice that there are numbers in a formula that are written smaller and lower than the letter symbols. These numbers are subscripts. **Subscripts** show the number of atoms of an element in a molecule or the ratio of elements in a compound. If a letter symbol in a chemical formula doesn't have a subscript, the number 1 is understood. For example, a carbon dioxide molecule, CO_2, has one carbon atom and two oxygen atoms. How many atoms in total does the molecule H_2O have? Since the absence of a subscript means that there is one oxygen atom, there are three atoms altogether.

Math TOOLBOX

Ratios and Subscripts

A ratio compares two numbers. In a chemical formula, subscripts show the ratio of one kind of atom to another. $CaBr_2$ for instance, shows that there are 2 bromide atoms for every 1 calcium atom. Write a formula for a compound that has atoms in the following ratios:

- Twice as many silver atoms as carbon atoms
- Three times as many oxygen atoms as carbon atoms

In this formula, show the elements in this order: silver (Ag), carbon (C), and oxygen (O).

2 Facilitate

Understanding Chemical Equations

Using the Visuals: Figure 7

Make sure students understand that ionic compounds do not occur as individual molecules (except in the gaseous state). The subscripts in ionic compound represent ratios of atoms in the compound, not atoms in a molecule. After students study the table of formulas in Figure 7, ask: **How many elements make up rubbing alcohol?** *(three)* **How many atoms are in each sugar molecule?** *(12 + 22 + 11 = 45)* Invite students to work in small groups to develop a three-question quiz based on data found in the table. Prompt students' creativity by asking: **Which molecule has 2 elements and 11 atoms?** *(propane)* **Which compounds have the same number of sodium (Na) atoms in their formulas?** *(salt, baking soda)* Allow groups to exchange and answer their quizzes. **cooperative learning**

Math TOOLBOX

(Ag_2CO_3) Remind students that a formula does not count how many atoms of each element are present in a sample of a compound, but rather the proportion of atoms present. Have students identify the ratios of atoms in each formula listed in Figure 7. Ask volunteers to say the answers so the class can become accustomed to how a ratio is expressed in words, as in "1 nitrogen atom for every 3 hydrogen atoms," or "three times as many hydrogen atoms as nitrogen atoms." **learning modality: logical/mathematical**

Program Resources

- **Unit 1 Resources** 3-2 Lesson Plan; 3-2 Section Summary
- **Guided Reading and Study Workbook** Section 3-2

Answers to Self-Assessment

Caption Questions

Figure 6 Bicycle path; rest rooms; traffic signal; waste basket; telephone; No U-turn

Figure 7 1 oxygen atom in water, 2 oxygen atoms in carbon dioxide, 11 oxygen atoms in sugar

Ongoing Assessment

Skills Check Have each student choose three compounds from Figure 7 besides water, carbon dioxide, or sugar, then list the elements that are present in the compounds and how many atoms of each are in the formulas.

Understanding Chemical Equations, continued

Building Inquiry Skills: Making Generalizations

Ask students to compare the general chemical equation and the two equations for specific reactions shown on this page. Ask: **Are there any elements on the left side of the equations that are not also on the right side?** *(No)* Have students rewrite each equation as a sentence. *(Calcium carbonate yields calcium oxide and carbon dioxide; iron plus sulfur yields iron sulfide.)* **learning modality: logical/mathematical**

Inquiry Challenge: Making Measurements

ACTIVITY

Materials *self-sealing plastic bag, baking soda, 10 mL vinegar, small spoon, plastic cup, balance, safety goggles*
Time 20 minutes
Tips CAUTION: *Vinegar is a mild acid. Wash spills with water. Make sure students wear goggles.* To begin the activity, have students put a small spoonful of baking soda in the corner of a dry plastic bag and use the balance to find the mass of the baking soda and the bag. Then have students find the mass of an empty plastic cup, add about 10 mL of vinegar, and find the combined mass. Then subtract to find the mass of the vinegar. Ask: **What will the mass of the product and the plastic bag be after the baking soda and vinegar react?** *(It will be equal to the mass of the baking soda, vinegar, and bag before the reaction.)* Then instruct students to carefully pour the vinegar into the bag containing the baking soda and quickly seal the bag. After the contents of the bag mix, students can find the total mass and compare it to their predictions. **learning modality: kinesthetic**

Structure of an Equation A chemical equation summarizes a reaction. It tells you the substances you start with and the substances you get at the end. The materials you have at the beginning are called the **reactants.** When the reaction is complete, you have different materials, called the **products** of the reaction. **A chemical equation uses symbols and formulas to show the reactants and the products of a chemical reaction.**

Chemical equations have a definite structure. The formulas for the reactants are written on the left, followed by an arrow. You read the arrow as "yields." The products are written on the right. When there are two or more reactants—or two or more products—they are separated from each other by plus signs.

$$\text{Reactant} + \text{Reactant} \rightarrow \text{Product} + \text{Product}$$

The number of reactants and products can vary. Some reactions have only one reactant or product. Other reactions have two, three, or more reactants or products. Find the number of products that result when limestone ($CaCO_3$) is heated.

$$\underset{\text{Reactant}}{CaCO_3} \rightarrow \underset{\text{Product}}{CaO} + \underset{\text{Product}}{CO_2}$$

Conservation of Mass No matter how many reactants and products are involved, all the atoms present at the start of a reaction are present at the end. Think about what happens when classes change at your school. A class is made up of a group of students and a teacher together in a room. When the bell rings, people from each class move from room to room, ending up in new and different classes. The number of students and teachers in the school has not changed. But their arrangement is different and the new groups interact differently.

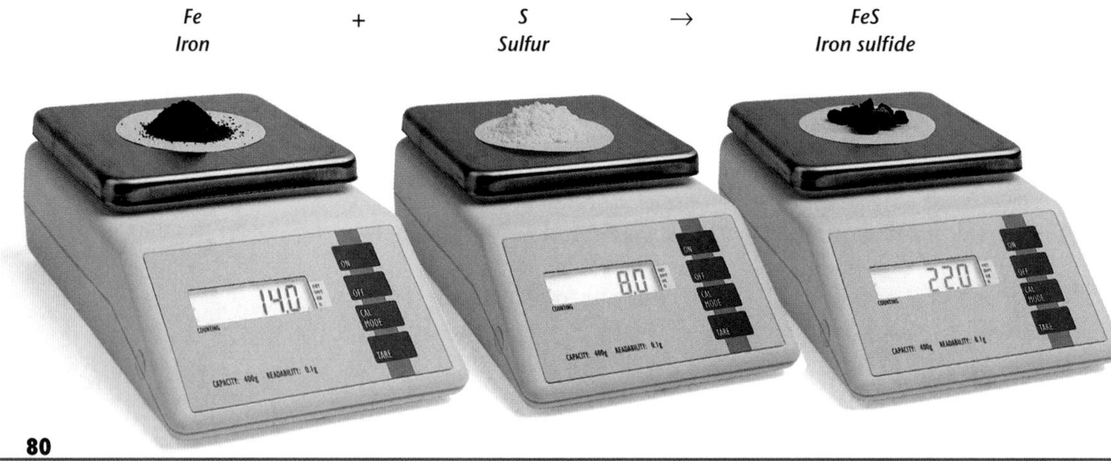

Figure 8 When iron filings and sulfur are mixed and heated, the product is the compound iron sulfide. *Interpreting Diagrams How do you know that mass has been conserved in the reaction?*

Background

History of Science The principle of conservation of mass was first expressed by Antoine Lavoisier (1743–1794). Lavoisier is often called "The Father of Modern Chemistry." He was a meticulous experimenter and was one of the first to apply quantitative analysis to chemical experiments. He experimented with burning sulfur and phosphorus, carefully measuring the mass of the reactants and the products. He also duplicated Joseph Priestly's investigations into the combustion of mercury oxide. In these investigations, Lavoisier precisely measured the reactants and products. He concluded that the mass of the reactants in a chemical equation was the same as the mass of the products of that same reaction—nothing is created or destroyed. Lavoisier published his findings in 1789.

Figure 9 Burnt wood and gray ash are all that remain from a roaring fire.
Problem Solving When wood burns, it reacts with oxygen in the air. What masses would you need to measure before and after the fire to show conservation of mass?

Now imagine that all the students and teachers are atoms, and each class is a molecule. At the end of a reaction (similar to a class change), the same atoms are present, but they are grouped together in different molecules. **The amount of matter involved in a chemical reaction does not change. The total mass of the reactants must equal the total mass of the products.** This principle, called the **conservation of mass,** means that during a chemical reaction, matter is not created or destroyed.

At first glance, some reactions seem to violate the principle of conservation of mass. If you measured the cooled ash left from a wood fire, for example, it wouldn't have the same mass as the wood that had been burned. What happened to the missing mass? It has escaped into the air as carbon dioxide gas and water vapor. If you could trap and measure these gases, you'd be able to prove that the mass didn't change.

Checkpoint *How do the masses of the atoms in the reactants of a chemical reaction compare with the atoms in the products?*

Balancing Chemical Equations

How does the principle of conservation of mass relate to a chemical equation? It indicates that the same number of atoms exist in the products as were present in the reactants. So to describe a reaction accurately, a chemical equation must show the same number of each type of atom on both sides of the equation. When that happens, chemists say the equation is balanced. To balance an equation, begin by looking at the formulas.

$$H_2 + O_2 \rightarrow H_2O$$

How many atoms does the hydrogen molecule have? How about oxygen? How many of each kind of atom are present in one water molecule?

Still There ACTIVITY

Use nuts and bolts to model the principle of conservation of mass.

1. Measure the mass of a collection of bolts, each with a nut attached to it.
2. Remove all the nuts from the bolts. Measure the total mass of the nuts. Then do the same with the bolts. Add these values.
3. Rearrange your collection, putting two or three nuts on one bolt, one nut on another bolt, and so on. You can even leave a few pieces unattached.
4. Measure the total mass again. Compare this figure with the totals from Steps 1 and 2.

Making Models How are the nuts and bolts similar to atoms and molecules in a chemical reaction? How do your observations model conservation of mass?

TRY THIS

Skills Focus making models
Materials *hex nuts and short bolts, balance*
Time 15 minutes
Tips Encourage students to think of the original group of bolts and nuts as reactants and the final group of nuts and bolts as products.
Expected Outcome The total mass of the nuts and bolts will be the same.
Making Models The nuts and bolts are similar to the atoms in a chemical reaction because even though they are rearranged during the activity, no nuts or bolts are created or destroyed.
Extend Have students use the nuts and bolts to model a reaction. Let the bolts represent iron atoms and the hex nuts represent sulfur atoms. Then model the reaction: $Fe + S \rightarrow FeS$. **learning modality: kinesthetic**

Balancing Chemical Equations

Building Inquiry Skills: Inferring

On the board, write "Carbon reacts with oxygen to form carbon dioxide." Ask a volunteer to write the appropriate chemical equation below this statement. Ask: **How can we tell this is a balanced equation?** *(It has the same number of carbon and oxygen atoms in the product as in the reactants.)* Explain that when carbon burns in a limited supply of oxygen, carbon monoxide (CO) is formed instead of carbon dioxide. Ask: **How would the balanced equation for this new reaction be different from the one we just completed?** *($2C + O_2 \rightarrow 2CO$)* **learning modality: logical/mathematical**

Media and Technology

Transparencies "Balancing an Equation," Transparency 6

Answers to Self-Assessment

Caption Questions

Figure 10 The mass of the reactants (14 grams + 8 grams) equals the mass of the product (22 grams).
Figure 11 Measure the masses of the oxygen and wood before the fire, and the ashes and escaped gases afterward.

Checkpoint

The numbers of atoms remain equal and their total mass is unchanged.

Ongoing Assessment

Writing Have students explain conservation of mass in chemical reactions in terms of atoms.

Including All Students

Materials *two colors of modeling clay, 2 paper plates, marker*
Time 20 minutes

Some students may need extra help to understand how to balance chemical equations. Write these statements on the board:

- One molecule of oxygen has two oxygen atoms.
- One molecule of hydrogen has two hydrogen atoms.
- One molecule of water has two hydrogen atoms and one oxygen atom.

Direct students to use the clay to model an oxygen molecule, a hydrogen molecule, and a water molecule. Have students label one paper plate *Reactants* and the other *Products,* then place their model molecules on the appropriate plates. Ask: **What do you need to do to make the product balance the reactants?** *(Add one hydrogen molecule to the reactants and one water molecule to the product.)* Allow students who are still mastering English to demonstrate their answers with their models. **limited English proficiency**

Sharpen your Skills

Calculating

ACTIVITY

Time 10 minutes
Tips Have volunteers show their calculations on the board. Students should multiply the subscript by the coefficient to find the number of atoms of a substance. If there is no coefficient, the subscript is the number of atoms.
Expected Outcome 3 H_2O: 6 H atoms, 3 O atoms; 2 H_2SO_4: 4 H atoms, 2 S atoms, 8 O atoms; 4 Fe_2O_3: 8 Fe atoms, 12 O atoms; 6 NaCl: 6 Na atoms, 6 Cl atoms; NO_2: 1 N atom, 2 O atoms
Extend Have students compute the number of atoms of each element for other chemical formulas that have coefficients written before them. **learning modality: logical/mathematical**

Calculating ACTIVITY

Each chemical formula below is written just as it might be in a balanced chemical equation. For each formula, calculate the number of each kind of atom.

3 H_2O
2 H_2SO_4
4 Fe_2O_3
6 NaCl
NO_2

When a coefficient is in front of a formula, how do you find the total number of atoms of one kind? What do you do if there is no coefficient?

Look at the chemical equation and models for the reaction:

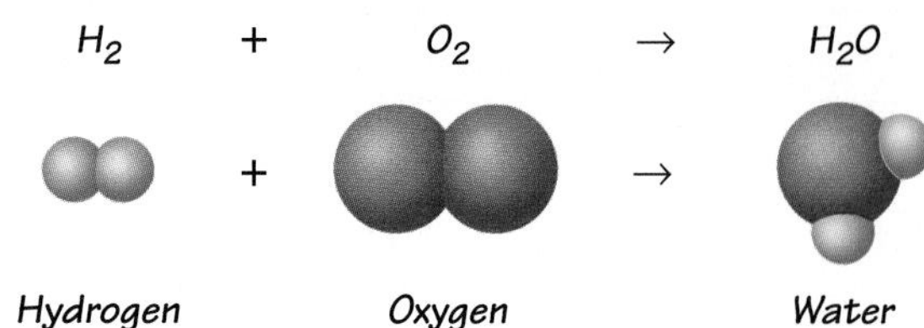

Count the number of atoms of each element on each side of the equation. You find 2 atoms of oxygen in the reactants but only 1 atom of oxygen in the products.

How can you get the number of oxygen molecules on both sides to be the same? You might be tempted to balance the oxygen by changing the formula for water to H_2O_2. Don't even think about it! Remember that H_2O_2 is the formula for hydrogen peroxide, a completely different compound.

To balance the equation, use a coefficient. A **coefficient** (koh uh FISH unt) is a number placed *in front of* a chemical formula in an equation. It tells you how many atoms or molecules of each reactant and product take part in the reaction. If the coefficient is 1, you don't need to write it. Balance the number of oxygen atoms by writing the coefficient 2 for water. That's like saying "2 × H_2O." Now there are 2 oxygen atoms in the product.

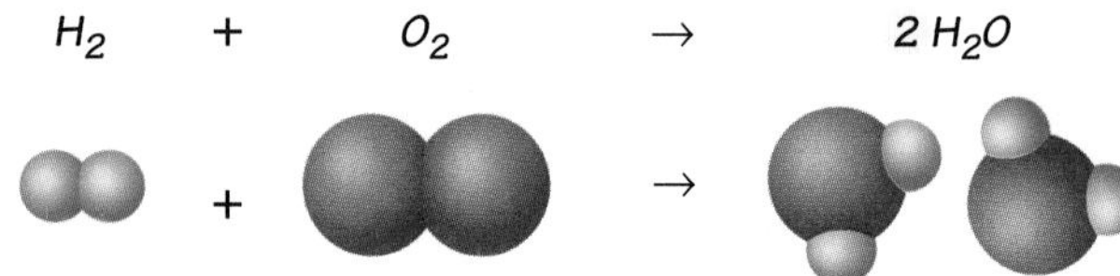

Okay, you've balanced the oxygen atoms. But now there are 2 hydrogen atoms in the reactants and 4 in the product. How can you balance the hydrogen? Try doubling the number of hydrogen atoms on the left side of the equation by changing the coefficient for hydrogen to 2. That's it!

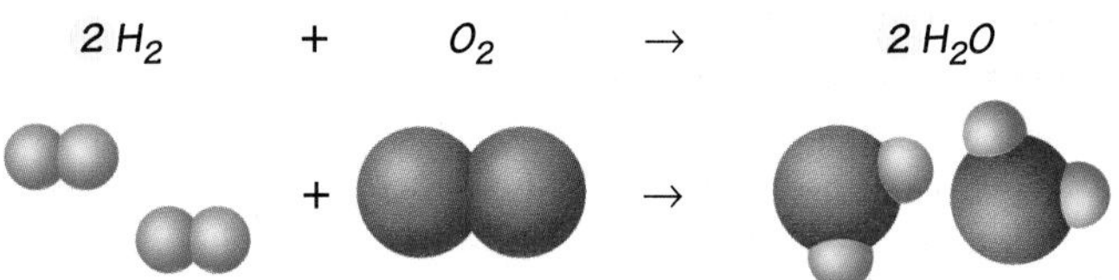

Now there are 4 hydrogen atoms and 2 oxygen atoms on each side. The equation is balanced. It tells you that 2 molecules of hydrogen react with 1 molecule of oxygen to yield 2 molecules of water. Count the atoms in the final diagram. Prove to yourself that the balanced equation is correct.

Background

Integrating Science Students may suggest that photosynthesis and cell respiration are, respectively, examples of synthesis and decomposition reactions. From a chemist's perspective, however, these reactions do not fit the strict definitions of the terms. A decomposition yields two or more simple products from one complex reactant. A synthesis does just the opposite—forming one product from two or more simpler reactants. Photosynthesis yields two products (sugar and oxygen), while cell respiration, an oxidation reaction, uses two reactants (glucose and oxygen).

The classification of chemical reactions is useful for understanding basic mechanisms, but only to a point. Many reactions involve more than one kind of change and/or several steps, and cannot be cleanly categorized as synthesis, decomposition, or replacement.

Sample Problem

When magnesium metal, Mg, reacts with oxygen, O_2, the product of the reaction is magnesium oxide, MgO. Write a balanced equation for this reaction.

Write the word equation.	*Magnesium + Oxygen → Magnesium oxide*
Write the chemical equation.	$Mg + O_2 \rightarrow MgO$
Count the number of atoms of each element on each side of the equation.	*Mg* one; *O* two; *Mg* one, *O* one
Choose coefficients to balance the equation.	$2\,Mg + O_2 \rightarrow 2\,MgO$
Think about it.	The answer shows 2 magnesium atoms and 2 oxygen atoms on each side, so the equation is balanced.

Practice Problems

1. Balance the equation: $C + Cl_2 \rightarrow CCl_4$
2. Balance the equation: $Al_2O_3 \rightarrow Al + O_2$

Classifying Chemical Reactions

Chemical reactions can be classified by what happens to the reactants and products. Substances may add together to make a more complex substance. They may break apart to make simpler substances. Or substances may even exchange parts. In each case, new materials form. **Many chemical reactions can be classified in one of three categories: synthesis, decomposition, or replacement.** As you read about each of these kinds of reactions, look at the examples. Compare the reactants and the products to see how they change.

Synthesis Have you ever listened to music from a synthesizer? You can hear many different notes and types of musical sounds. The synthesizer combines these sounds to make a complicated piece of music. When two or more substances (elements or compounds) combine to make a more complex substance, the process is called **synthesis** (SIN thuh sis). To synthesize is to put things together. Look back at the reaction of hydrogen and oxygen to make water. You should see now that this is a synthesis reaction—two elements come together, making a compound.

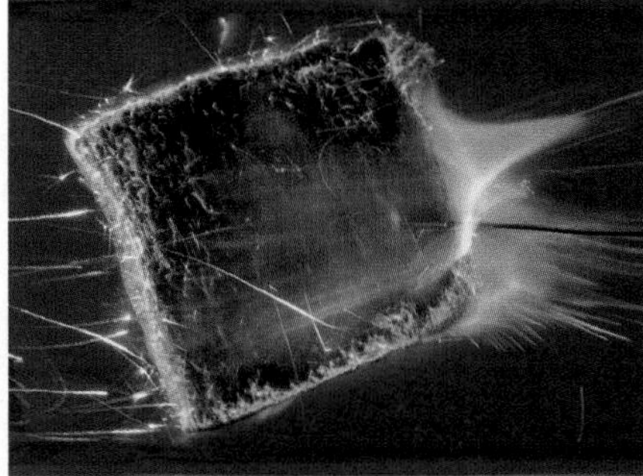

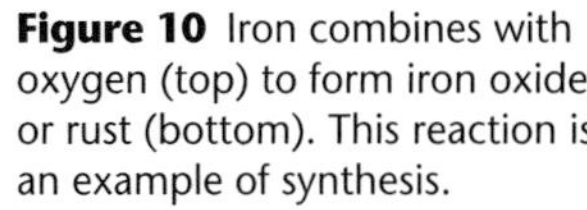

Figure 10 Iron combines with oxygen (top) to form iron oxide, or rust (bottom). This reaction is an example of synthesis.

Sample Problem

Have a volunteer demonstrate how to count the number of atoms of each element on each side of the equation. Invite a second volunteer to explain how to choose coefficients that will balance the equation.

Practice Problems

1. $C + 2\,Cl_2 \rightarrow CCl_4$
2. $2\,Al_2O_3 \rightarrow 4\,Al + 3\,O_2$

Classifying Chemical Reactions

Building Inquiry Skills: Applying Concepts

To help students understand the classifications for chemical reactions, write these statements on the board:

- hand + kerchief → handkerchief
- schoolbook → school + book
- television screen + door knob → television knob + screen door

Tell students the words and word pairs represent reactants or products. Inform them that the first statement represents *synthesis* (two words combine to make a more complex word), the second statement represents *decomposition* (a word broken apart to make simpler words), and the third represents *replacement* (two word pairs exchange parts to form two new word pairs) Challenge students to come up with new statements for each type of reaction. **learning modality: verbal**

Program Resources

- **Laboratory Manual** 3, "The Law of Definite Proportions"
- **Interdisciplinary Explorations Series** "The Glory of Ancient Rome," pp. 24–25

Ongoing Assessment

Writing Have students prepare step-by-step directions explaining how to write a balanced equation for tarnished silver. The reactants are silver (Ag) and hydrogen sulfide (H_2S). The products are Ag_2S and H_2. *($2\,Ag + H_2S \rightarrow Ag_2S + H_2$)*

Classifying Chemical Reactions, continued

Integrating Environmental Science

Open the discussion by asking what students know about acid rain. Then have them visit the Environmental Protection Agency's Web site at **www.epa.gov** and follow the links to the information on acid rain. Or you may have students do research in the library. When they have finished, students can prepare reports about the problem and suggest ways the amount of acid rain might be reduced. **learning modality: verbal**

Demonstration

Materials *safety goggles, lab aprons, granulated sugar, concentrated sulfuric acid, 50-mL heat-resistant beaker, 100-mL graduated cylinder*

ACTIVITY

Time 15 minutes

Tips CAUTION: *Sulfuric acid will burn skin and clothing. Avoid direct contact. You and your students should wear safety goggles and lab aprons, and you should wear protective gloves. Wash spills and splashes with plenty of water.* Remind students that the formula for sugar is $C_{12}H_{22}O_{11}$. Ask them to predict what will happen when sulfuric acid is added to sugar. Then pour in ordinary table sugar to the 20-mL mark on the beaker. CAUTION: *You may wish to use a slightly larger beaker because the volume of the product will be significantly greater than the volume of the sugar, and it will overflow the beaker if it is too small.* Next, slowly add 7–10 mL of the acid to the sugar. The reaction takes 60–90 seconds to finish, and the beaker will be VERY hot. Explain that the black column formed is primarily carbon. They may notice the water vapor that is given off. Ask students: **Is this reaction synthesis, decomposition, or replacement? Why?** *(Decomposition, because the sugar was broken down into the simpler products.)* The simplest way of explaining this reaction is to tell students that sulfuric acid attracts water so strongly that it will pull hydrogen and oxygen right out of the sugar, forming water and leaving the carbon behind. **learning modality: visual**

INTEGRATING ENVIRONMENTAL SCIENCE Acid rain is a product of synthesis reactions. In one case, sulfur dioxide, oxygen, and water combine to make sulfuric acid. Look at the equation for the reaction. Can you find the 8 oxygen atoms on each side of the equation?

$$2\,SO_2 + O_2 + 2\,H_2O \rightarrow 2\,H_2SO_4$$

Sulfur dioxide — Oxygen — Water — Sulfuric acid

Sulfur dioxide comes from car engines or from power plants that burn coal. Oxygen and water vapor are in the air. Together they produce sulfuric acid, which causes rainwater to become corrosive. This acid water then eats away at stone and metal, and can damage living organisms.

Decomposition While a synthesis reaction builds compounds from simpler reactants, a process called **decomposition** breaks down compounds into simpler products. Many people keep a bottle of hydrogen peroxide to clean cuts. If you keep such a bottle for a very long time, you'll have water instead. The hydrogen peroxide decomposes into water and oxygen gas.

$$2\,H_2O_2 \rightarrow 2\,H_2O + O_2$$

The oxygen that is produced escapes into the air.

Checkpoint *How do synthesis and decomposition differ?*

Figure 11 Safety airbags in cars inflate as a result of a decomposition reaction. On impact, a detonator cap inside the air bag explodes. The explosion causes a compound made of sodium and nitrogen to decompose. One product is a large quantity of nitrogen gas.
Applying Concepts Why would quick inflation of airbags be important?

Background

Facts and Figures Sulfuric acid, also called oil of vitriol, or hydrogen sulfate, is a dense, colorless, oily, corrosive liquid. The acid, sometimes referred to as the "king of chemicals" is produced worldwide in enormous quantities. Annual production in the United States, the world's leading producer, is well over 39 billion kilograms. Nearly half the manufactured acid is used to produce phosphates and other fertilizers. Other uses for sulfuric acid include the manufacture of high-octane gasoline, explosives, rayon, the processing of uranium, and the pickling of steel. The acid also is used in the manufacture of pigments, dyes, drugs, and detergents. In its most familiar application, sulfuric acid is the electrolyte in lead-acid storage batteries.

Smelting Iron Ore

Iron usually occurs as the ores hematite or magnetite. Iron ores must be smelted, a process that involves replacement reactions, to separate the iron from the oxygen and other substances in the ores. Then the iron is refined and processed into steel.

1. Iron ore is crushed and then mixed with crushed limestone and coke (baked coal), which is rich in carbon.

2. The coke and iron ore are placed in a blast furnace. Hot air is blown through, making the coke burn easily.

3. As the coke burns, chemical changes occur in the mixture. Carbon reacts with iron oxide to produce carbon dioxide gas and molten iron in a replacement reaction.

4. The iron sinks to the bottom of the furnace. Impurities left in the ore combine with the limestone to create slag.

5. The slag and molten iron are poured off through taps in the blast furnace.

EXPLORING

Smelting Iron Ore

On the board, write the formulas for magnetite (Fe_3O_4) and hematite (Fe_2O_3). Both are a compound of iron and oxygen. Then ask volunteers to read the annotations for each step in the smelting process. Ask: **What is the purpose of smelting?** *(To separate the iron from the oxygen in iron ore)* **What is added to the ore to accomplish this purpose?** *(coke and limestone)* The product of smelting can be made into either cast-iron objects or used to make steel. **learning modality: verbal**

Program Resources

- **Unit 1 Resources** 13-2 Review and Reinforce; 3-2 Enrich

Answers to Self-Assessment

Caption Question

Figure 11 In a car crash, the airbags must inflate in time to stop the passengers from hitting the dashboard or windshield.

Checkpoint

Synthesis reactions build compounds from simpler reactants; decomposition reactions break down compounds into simpler substances.

Performance Assessment

Skills Check Have students make a flowchart showing the steps involved in smelting iron ore.

3 Assess

Section 2 Review Answers

1. The reactants, the products, and their chemical formulas
2. In a chemical reaction, the total mass of the reactants is equal to the total mass of the products.
3. In a synthesis reaction, substances combine to form a new substance. In a decomposition reaction, compounds break apart into simpler substances. In a replacement reaction, one element replaces another in a compound.
4. a. already balanced; **b.** $2\ Fe_2O_3 + 3\ C \rightarrow 4\ Fe + 3\ CO_2$; **c.** $2\ SO_2 + O_2 \rightarrow 2\ SO_3$
5. a. decomposition; **b.** replacement; **c.** synthesis

Check Your Progress

Make sure students generate clearly organized tables with sufficient space to record descriptions of and evidence for observed changes. Check that the evidence listed is consistent with students' observations. Discuss with the class how to record examples of chemical changes for which they cannot directly observe evidence, such as photosynthesis in a leaf or reactions in a dry cell battery. Invite students to think about the materials that are present before and after the reaction. Have students form small discussion groups to help each other classify reactions by type.

Performance Assessment

Drawing Direct students to compose posters explaining how to classify a chemical reaction. Posters should describe the differences and similarities between the types of reactions.

Students can save their posters in their portfolios.

Figure 12 Copper metal can be smelted from copper ore. Copper oxide (in the ore) reacts with carbon in a replacement reaction.

Replacement When one element replaces another in a compound, or when two elements in different compounds trade places, the process is called **replacement.** *Exploring Smelting Iron Ore* on page 85 shows a process in which replacement reactions are used to obtain pure iron from iron ore. Similarly, copper metal can be obtained by heating rock containing copper oxide in the presence of charcoal. The carbon of the charcoal takes the place of copper in the copper oxide.

$$2\ CuO + C \rightarrow 2\ Cu + CO_2$$

Medications for an upset stomach may contain calcium carbonate. Notice how this replacement reduces the amount of stomach acid (HCl).

$$CaCO_3 + 2\ HCl \rightarrow CaCl_2 + H_2CO_3$$

Not all reactions can be classified as synthesis, decomposition, or replacement, however.

Section 2 Review

1. What information do you need in order to write a chemical equation?
2. What is the principle of conservation of mass?
3. List and define three categories of chemical reactions.
4. **Thinking Critically Applying Concepts** Balance the following chemical equations by adding coefficients:
   a. $HCl + NaOH \rightarrow H_2O + NaCl$
   b. $Fe_2O_3 + C \rightarrow Fe + CO_2$
   c. $SO_2 + O_2 \rightarrow SO_3$
5. **Thinking Critically Classifying** Classify each of the following reactions as synthesis, decomposition, or replacement:
   a. $2\ NH_4NO_3 \rightarrow 2\ N_2 + O_2 + 4\ H_2O$
   b. $2\ Al + Fe_2O_3 \rightarrow Al_2O_3 + 2\ Fe$
   c. $P_4O_{10} + 6\ H_2O \rightarrow 4\ H_3PO_4$

Check Your Progress

CHAPTER PROJECT

Prepare a table to keep track of the chemical changes you observe. Have your teacher check your table to be sure it contains the proper headings. Record the different chemical changes you observe for a week. Make sure you can describe the evidence for each chemical change. If possible, classify each reaction as a synthesis, decomposition, or replacement reaction. Also classify it as occurring in a living or nonliving setting.

CHAPTER 3 STUDY GUIDE

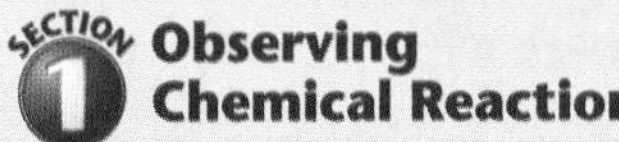

Observing Chemical Reactions

Key Ideas

- A chemical reaction produces materials that have different properties than the starting materials had. Each reaction either absorbs or releases energy.
- Color change, production of a gas or a precipitate, a change in temperature, or a change in the properties of a substance are all clues that a chemical reaction has taken place.
- Chemical reactions occur when chemical bonds are formed or broken.

Key Terms

precipitate
endothermic reaction
exothermic reaction

Writing Chemical Equations

Key Ideas

- A chemical equation uses symbols to show the reactants and products of a chemical reaction.
- Matter is neither created nor destroyed during a chemical reaction.
- Chemical reactions may be classified by the types of changes in reactants and products.

Key Terms

chemical equation
subscript
reactants
products
conservation of mass
coefficient
synthesis
decomposition
replacement reaction

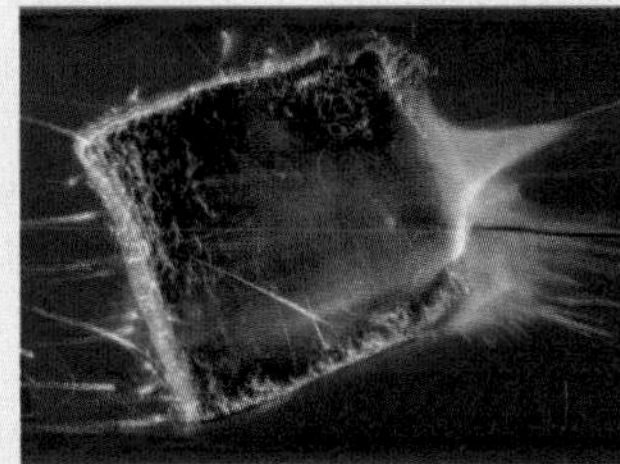

Organizing Information

Concept Map Copy the chemical reactions concept map onto a separate sheet of paper. Then complete it and add a title. (For more on concept maps, see the Skills Handbook.)

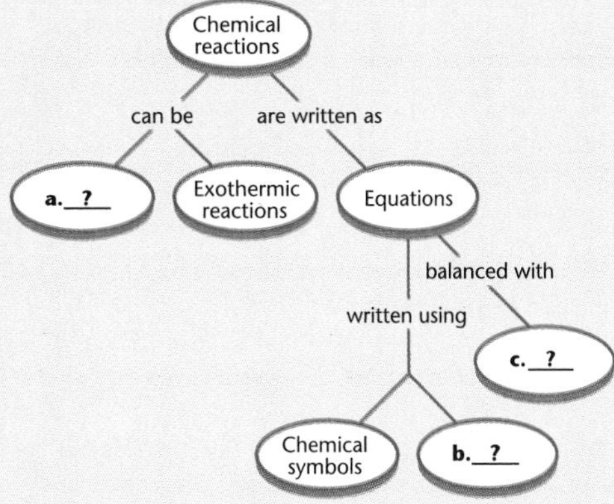

Program Resources

- **Unit 1 Resources** Chapter 3 Project Scoring Rubric
- **Performance Assessment** Chapter 3
- **Chapter and Unit Tests** Chapter 3 Test; Unit 1 Test

Media and Technology

 **Computer Test Bank** Chapter 3 Test

Organizing Information

Concept Map Sample title: *Chemical Reactions*
a. Endothermic reactions **b.** Chemical formulas **c.** Coefficients

Reviewing Content

Multiple Choice

1. c **2.** a **3.** b **4.** a **5.** d

True or False

6. true **7.** releases **8.** true **9.** true
10. products

Checking Concepts

11. Changing the subscripts in a compound's formula changes it to the formula for a different compound.
12. No. The extra mass in rust (iron oxide) is from oxygen, which was not accounted for in the original measurement because it was in the air.
13. Carbon dioxide gas bubbles are produced by the reaction of the baking soda with the food.
14. Answers will vary, but should reflect the steps, processes, and equipment shown in the *Explore* on page 85.

Thinking Critically

15. a. $Fe + 2\,HCl \rightarrow FeCl_2 + H_2$; replacement **b.** $2\,N_2 + 5\,O_2 \rightarrow 2\,N_2O_5$; synthesis **c.** balanced; decomposition **d.** balanced; replacement
16. Sample: Paint the metal on the ship so that the salt water is prevented from coming into contact with the metal.
17. The two masses will be equal. According to the principle of conservation of mass, matter is not created or destroyed during a chemical reaction.
18. The equation is balanced. There are the same number and kinds of atoms on each side of the equation. The reaction is classified as combustion because a fuel reacts with oxygen.

CHAPTER 3 ASSESSMENT

Reviewing Content

Multiple Choice

Choose the letter of the best answer.

1. Which one of the following does NOT indicate a chemical change?
a. formation of a precipitate
b. change of color
c. change in surface area
d. production of a gas

2. You can balance a chemical equation by changing the
a. coefficients. **b.** products.
c. reactants. **d.** formulas.

3. The reaction between sulfur trioxide and water ($SO_3 + H_2O \rightarrow H_2SO_4$) is called
a. replacement.
b. synthesis.
c. decomposition.
d. conservation.

4. When one element replaces another in a compound during a chemical reaction, the process is called
a. replacement.
b. synthesis.
c. decomposition.
d. conservation.

5. Chemical reactions occur when
a. chemical bonds break.
b. solids lose mass.
c. chemical bonds form.
d. both a and c.

True or False

If the statement is true, write true. If it is false, change the underlined word or words to make the statement true.

6. A solid that falls out of solution during a chemical reaction is called a precipitate.
7. An exothermic reaction absorbs energy.
8. In a chemical formula, symbols identify which elements are present.
9. In a chemical reaction, the properties of the products are different from the properties of the starting materials.
10. The materials you have when a reaction is complete are the reactants.

Checking Concepts

11. Why can't you balance a chemical equation by changing the subscripts?
12. You find the mass of a piece of iron metal, let it rust, and measure the mass again. The mass has increased. Does this violate the law of conservation of mass? Explain.
13. A fire starts in a frying pan in your kitchen. You throw baking soda into the pan. Bubbling and foaming occur, and the fire goes out. What is the evidence that a chemical reaction has occurred?
14. Writing to Learn Imagine that you are writing to your pen pal in another state. In a letter, describe what you saw during a recent tour of a smelting plant.

Thinking Critically

15. Applying Concepts Balance the following equations and tell whether they are synthesis, decomposition, or replacement reactions.
a. $Fe + HCl \rightarrow FeCl_2 + H_2$
b. $N_2 + O_2 \rightarrow N_2O_5$
c. $H_2CO_3 \rightarrow H_2O + CO_2$
d. $CuO + H_2SO_4 \rightarrow CuSO_4 + H_2O$

16. Problem Solving Steel that is exposed to water and salt rusts quickly. If you were a shipbuilder, how would you protect a new ship? Explain why your idea works.

17. Predicting Equal amounts of sodium iodide (NaI) solution and lead nitrate [$Pb(NO_3)_2$] solution are poured into separate compartments of a container. The container is sealed and its mass is determined. The container is then shaken and a yellow solid, lead iodide (PbI_2), forms. If the container's mass is determined again, how will the two masses compare? Explain.

18. Applying Concepts Gasohol is a fuel made up of gasoline and alcohol. When gasohol burns, it releases fewer pollutants than pure gasoline. The chemical reaction is:
$C_2H_5OH + 3O_2 \rightarrow 2CO_2 + 3H_2O$
Is this equation balanced correctly? How do you know?

Applying Skills

19. It decreases.
20. endothermic
21. Answers will vary. Sample answer: the reaction of baking soda with vinegar

Applying Skills

Use the data table to answer Questions 19–21.

Temperature Changes in a Chemical Reaction

Time (min)	Temperature (°C)
0	20
1	18
2	17
3	16
4	16

19. **Interpreting Data** How does the temperature change as the reaction takes place?
20. **Classifying** Tell whether this reaction is exothermic or endothermic. Explain.
21. **Predicting** Give an example of a reaction that could be represented by these data.

Performance Assessment (Chapter Project)

Present Your Project Compare the reactions in your chemical change log with those of your classmates. How many of the same processes did you observe? Defend your opinions as to whether or not your observations were chemical changes. Together make a list of the types of evidence you observed, and classify the reactions as endothermic or exothermic.

Reflect and Record In your journal, answer these questions. What evidence of chemical change is easiest to detect? What types of chemical reactions did you observe most frequently? Give an example of a chemical reaction you suspect was taking place, but for which you could not find direct evidence.

Test Preparation

Use these questions to prepare for standardized tests.

Read the information below. Then answer Questions 22–26.

A laboratory assistant was experimenting with chemical reactions when she combined a small amount of zinc (Zn) with hydrochloric acid (HCl). She discovered that zinc chloride ($ZnCl_2$) and hydrogen (H_2) were produced.

22. Which of the following substances are the reactants?
    - **a.** $Zn + HCl$
    - **b.** $ZnCl_2 + H_2$
    - **c.** $Zn + H_2$
    - **d.** $ZnCl_2 + HCl$
23. Which of the following substances are the products?
    - **a.** $Zn + HCl$
    - **b.** $ZnCl_2 + H_2$
    - **c.** $Zn + H_2$
    - **d.** $ZnCl_2 + HCl$
24. Which equation correctly describes this reaction?
    - **a.** $Zn + HCl \rightarrow ZnCl_2 + H_2$
    - **b.** $ZnCl_2 + H_2 \rightarrow Zn + 2\,HCl$
    - **c.** $Zn + 2HCl \rightarrow ZnCl_2 + H_2$
    - **d.** $2\,Zn + 2\,HCl \rightarrow 2\,(ZnCl_2 + H_2)$
25. How should the assistant classify this reaction?
    - **a.** synthesis
    - **b.** decomposition
    - **c.** replacement
    - **d.** combustion
26. The 2 in H_2 is a
    - **a.** subscript.
    - **b.** coefficient.
    - **c.** symbol for hydrogen.
    - **d.** symbol for zinc.

Performance Assessment (Chapter Project)

Present Your Project As students compare their observations and compile a list, have them identify common observations and make sure they classified them the same way. It may help to have volunteers make a poster or a large data table on the board for students to fill in. Have students work together to classify the reactions as endothermic or exothermic.

Reflect and Record Students should identify changes that were easy to observe and classify, as well as those that were difficult. Students should give an example of a reaction they had trouble analyzing.

Test Preparation

22. a **23.** b **24.** c **25.** c **26.** a

Program Resources

- **Inquiry Skills Activity Book** Provides teaching and review of all inquiry skills

Weathering and Soil Formation

Sections	Time	Student Edition Activities	Other Activities
CHAPTER PROJECT **Soils for Seeds** p. 91	Ongoing (2 weeks)	Check Your Progress, p. 107, 114 Present Your Project, p. 123	
1 Rocks and Weathering pp. 92–100 ◆ Identify what causes mechanical weathering. ◆ Identify what causes chemical weathering. ◆ Describe the factors that determine how fast weathering occurs.	3 periods/ $1\frac{1}{2}$ blocks	**Discover** How Fast Can It Fizz, p. 92 **Try This** Rusting Away, p. 96 **Science at Home,** p. 97 **Skills Lab: Controlling Variables** Rock Shake, pp. 98–99	TE Demonstration, pp. 93, 95 TE Integrating Physics, p. 94 TE Building Inquiry Skills: Designing Experiments, p. 94 TE Real-Life Learning, p. 95 TE Inquiry Challenge, p. 97 LM 4, "Investigating Soils and Drainage"
2 Soil Formation and Composition pp. 101–108 ◆ Describe the composition of soil. ◆ Explain how soil is formed and how soil horizons develop. ◆ Identify the roles of plants and animals in soil formation.	2 periods/ 1 block	**Discover** What is Soil?, p. 101 **Sharpen Your Skills** Predicting, p. 103 **Try This** A Square Meter of Soil, p. 106 **Real-World Lab: Careers in Science** Getting to Know the Soil, p. 108	TE Building Inquiry Skills: Comparing and Contrasting, p. 103; Calculating, p. 105 TE Integrating Life Science, p. 104 TE Including All Students, p. 104 TE Inquiry Challenge, p. 105
3 Conserving Land and Soil pp. 109–114 ◆ Describe some major forms of land use. ◆ Explain why soil is a valuable resource. ◆ List ways that soil can be lost or destroyed. ◆ Identify some ways that soil can be conserved.	1 period/ $\frac{1}{2}$ block	**Discover** How Can You Keep Soil From Washing Away?, p. 109	TE Inquiry Challenge, p. 111 TE Real-Life Learning, p. 113 TE Building Inquiry Skills: Comparing, p. 113
4 *Integrating Environmental Science* **Waste Disposal and Recycling** pp. 115–120 ◆ Describe methods for managing solid waste. ◆ List the four major types of recyclable waste. ◆ Identify methods for managing hazardous wastes.	2 periods/ 1 block	**Discover** What's in the Trash?, p. 115 **Sharpen Your Skills** Graphing, p. 117 **Try This** It's in the Numbers, p. 118 **Science at Home** p. 120	TE Building Inquiry Skills: Making Models, p. 116; Calculating, p. 117; Communicating, p. 118; Classifying, p. 119 PTA "Testing Orange Juice"; "Testing Toilet Paper," pp. 1–8 TE Real-Life Learning p. 119
Study Guide/Chapter Assessment pp. 121–123	1 period/ $\frac{1}{2}$ block		ISAB Provides teaching and review of all inquiry skills

For Standard or Block Schedule The Resource Pro® CD-ROM gives you maximum flexibility for planning your instruction for any type of schedule. Resource Pro® contains Planning Express®, an advanced scheduling program, as well as the entire contents of the Teaching Resources and the Computer Test Bank.

CHAPTER PLANNING GUIDE

Program Resources	Assessment Strategies	Media and Technology
UR Chapter 4 Project Teacher Notes **UR** Chapter 4 Project Overview and Worksheets	**SE** Performance Assessment: Present Your Project, p. 123 **TE** Check Your Progress, pp. 107, 114 **UR** Chapter 4 Project Scoring Rubric	Science Explorer Internet Site at www.phschool.com Student Edition on Audio CD, Chapter 4
UR 4-1 Lesson Plan **UR** 4-1 Section Summary **UR** 4-1 Review and Reinforce **UR** 4-1 Enrich **UR** Chapter 4 Skills Lab	**SE** Section 1 Review, p. 97 **TE** Ongoing Assessment, pp. 93, 95 **TE** Performance Assessment, p. 97	Transparency 7, "Forces of Mechanical Weathering" Lab Activity Videotapes, Grade 6 Tape 1
UR 4-2 Lesson Plan **UR** 4-2 Section Summary **UR** 4-2 Review and Reinforc **UR** 4-2 Enrich **UR** Chapter 4 Real-World Lab	**SE** Section 2 Review, p. 107 **TE** Ongoing Assessment, pp. 103, 105 **TE** Performance Assessment, p. 107	Transparencies 8, "Soil Composition and Soil Horizons"; 9, "Exploring Living Organisms in Soil"; 10, "Soils of North America" Concept Videotape Library, Grade 6, Tape 1, "Ancient Farmers"; "Cycles in Nature"
UR 4-3 Lesson Plan **UR** 4-3 Section Summary **UR** 4-3 Review and Reinforce **UR** 4-3 Enrich	**SE** Section 3 Review, p. 114 **TE** Ongoing Assessment, pp. 111, 113 **TE** Performance Assessment, p. 114	Concept Videotape Library, Grade 6, Tape 1, "Is Our Soil Endangered?"
UR 4-4 Lesson Plan **UR** 4-4 Section Summary **UR** 4-4 Review and Reinforce **UR** 4-4 Enrich	**SE** Section 4 Review, p. 120 **TE** Ongoing Assessment, pp. 117, 119 **TE** Performance Assessment, p. 120	Concept Videotape Library, Grade 6, Tape 1, "Where Does Your Garbage Go?"; "It Really Isn't Garbage" Transparency 11, "Exploring a Landfill" Lab Activity Videotapes, Grade 6 Tape 1
RCA Provides strategies to improve science reading skills **GRSW** Provides worksheets to promote student comprehension of content	**SE** Chapter 4 Study Guide/Assessment, pp. 121–123 **PA** Chapter 4 Performance Assessment **CUT** Chapter 4 Test **CTB** Chapter 4 Test	Computer Test Bank, Chapter 4 Test

Key: **SE** Student Edition
CTB Computer Test Bank
ISAB Inquiry Skills Activity Book
GRSW Guided Reading and Study Workbook
TE Teacher's Edition
PTA Product Testing Activities by *Consumer Reports*
RCA Reading in the Content Area
PA Performance Assessment
UR Unit Resources
LM Laboratory Manual
IES Interdisciplinary Explorations Series
CUT Chapter and Unit Tests

Meeting the National Science Education Standards and AAAS Benchmarks

National Science Education Standards	Benchmarks for Science Literacy	Unifying Themes
Science As Inquiry (Content Standard A) ◆ **Design and conduct a scientific investigation** Students investigate how soil composition affects plant growth. Students compare the rates of weathering that take place under different conditions. *(Chapter Project; Skills Lab)* ◆ **Develop descriptions, explanations, predictions, and models using evidence** Students observe a sample of soil to determine its characteristics. *(Real-World Lab)* **Life Science** (Content Standard C) ◆ **Populations and ecosystems** Some soil organisms mix the soil and make spaces in it for air and water; others make humus. *(Section 2)* **Earth and Space Science** (Content Standard D) ◆ **Structure of the Earth system** Weathering is the process that breaks down rock and other materials at Earth's surface. Soil forms as rock is broken down by weathering and mixes with other materials. Soil is one of Earth's most valuable resources. *(Sections 1, 2, 3; Chapter Project; Skills Lab; Real-World Lab)* **Science in Personal and Social Perspectives** (Content Standard F) ◆ **Science and technology in society** Students examine the issue of preserving stone monuments. Soil conservation is the management of soil to prevent its destruction. The problem of disposing of solid waste is handled by burying it, burning it, or recycling it. *(Science and Society; Sections 3, 4)*	**1B Scientific Inquiry** Students investigate how soil composition affects plant growth. Students compare the rates of weathering that take place under different conditions. Students observe a sample of soil to determine its characteristics. *(Chapter Project; Skills Lab; Real-World Lab)* **3C Issues in Technology** Students examine the issue of preserving stone monuments. Soil conservation is the management of soil to prevent its destruction. The problem of disposing of solid waste is handled by burying it, burning it, or recycling it. *(Science and Society; Sections 3, 4)* **4B The Earth** Soil is one of Earth's most valuable resources. A wide range of materials can be recycled. *(Sections 3, 4)* **4C Processes That Shape the Earth** Weathering is the process that breaks down rock and other materials at Earth's surface. Soil forms as rock is broken down by weathering and mixes with other materials. Plowing removed the grass from the Great Plains and exposed the soil, which led to the Dust Bowl. *(Sections 1, 2, 3; Skills Lab; Real-World Lab)* **5D Interdependence of Life** Some soil organisms mix the soil and make spaces in it for air and water; others make humus. *(Section 2)*	◆ **Energy** The forces of weathering break rocks. Many burrowing animals break up compacted soil and mix humus through it. Wind blew away the soil in the Dust Bowl. The burning of solid waste is called incineration. Recycling saves energy. *(Sections 1, 2, 3, 4; Skills Lab)* ◆ **Evolution** Over time, weathering breaks down even the biggest, hardest rocks. Soil formation continues over a long period of time, and gradually soil horizons develop. *(Sections 1, 2)* ◆ **Patterns of Change** Once rocks become exposed at Earth's surface, they begin to undergo weathering. Soil forms as rock is broken down and mixes with other materials. *(Sections 1, 2; Science and Society)* ◆ **Scale and Structure** Soil is a mixture of rock particles, minerals, decayed organic material, air, and water. *(Section 2; Real-World Lab)* ◆ **Systems and Interactions** Soil composition can affect how plants grow. Weathering breaks rock down into particles of soil. Some soil organisms mix the soil and make spaces in it for air and water. Two ways that soil can be conserved include contour plowing and conservation plowing. *(Chapter Project; Sections 1, 2, 3)* ◆ **Unity and Diversity** The two kinds of weathering are mechanical weathering and chemical weathering. Soil is classified into three horizons. *(Sections 1, 2; Skills Lab)* ◆ **Stability** Weathering and erosion work together continuously to wear down and carry away the rocks at Earth's surface. *(Section 1)*

Take It to the Net

Interactive text at www.phschool.com

Science Explorer comes alive with iText.

- **Complete student text** is accessible from any computer with Internet access or a CD-ROM drive.
- **Animations, simulations, and videos** enhance student understanding and retention of concepts.
- **Self-tests and online study tools** assess student understanding.

STAY CURRENT with **SCIENCE NEWS®**

Find out the latest research and information about Earth's Surface: Weathering, Erosion, and Deposition at: **www.phschool.com**

Go to **www.phschool.com** and click on the Science icon.Then click on Science Explorer: Life, Earth, and Physical Science under PH@school.

ACTIVITY	Time (minutes)	Materials Quantities for one work group	Skills
Section 1			
Discover, p. 92	10	**Consumable** 2 fizzing antacid tablets, warm water **Nonconsumable** 2 beakers, plastic stirring rod, plastic bowl, stopwatch	Inferring
Try This, p. 96	5; 5	**Consumable** 2 pads of steel wool, water **Nonconsumable** jar with lid	Predicting
Science at Home, p. 97	home	**Consumable** plastic drinking straw, modeling clay, water **Nonconsumable** freezer	Drawing Conclusions
Skills Lab, pp. 98–99	30; 30	**Consumable** 300 mL of water, paper towels, masking tape, 2 pieces of thin cloth, 300 mL of vinegar, 80 small pieces of limestone **Nonconsumable** balance, marking pen or pencil, 250-mL plastic graduated cylinder, 4 500-mL watertight plastic containers with screw-on caps	Measuring, Predicting, Controlling Variables, Creating Data Tables, Drawing Conclusions
Section 2			
Discover, p. 101	15	**Consumable** soil sample, paper cup, paper towel, toothpick **Nonconsumable** hand lens	Forming Operational Definitions
Sharpen Your Skills, p. 103	5	No special materials are required.	Predicting
Try This, p. 106	30	**Consumable** string **Nonconsumable** metric ruler, stakes, trowel, hand lens	Drawing Conclusions
Real-World Lab, p. 108	40	**Consumable** 20–30 grams of soil, toothpick, water, graph paper ruled with 1- or 2-mm spacing **Nonconsumable** plastic spoon, plastic dropper, stereomicroscope, plastic petri dish or jar lid	Observing, Inferring, Posing Questions
Section 3			
Discover, p. 109	15	**Consumable** soil, water, craft sticks, paper clips, pebbles, modeling clay, paper **Nonconsumable** pie plate, container	Observing
Section 4			
Discover, p. 115	15	**Consumable** trash bag, 10–15 items commonly found in household waste, plastic gloves, graph paper **Nonconsumable** ruler	Interpreting Data
Sharpen Your Skills, p. 117	5	**Nonconsumable** protractor, drawing compass	Graphing
Try This, p. 118	30	**Nonconsumable** pieces of plastic products with recycling codes	Classifying
Science at Home, p. 120	home	**Consumable** household trash collected for one week **Nonconsumable** scale, calculator (optional)	Calculating

A list of all materials required for the Student Edition activities can be found on pages TVA34–TVA40. You can obtain information about ordering materials by calling 1-800-848-9500 or by accessing the Science Explorer Internet site at: **www.phschool.com**

CHAPTER 4 PROJECT

Soils for Seeds

Many students may think that all soil is a substance that varies little from place to place, especially if they have always lived in the same general area. Students may not realize how important the composition of soil is to the growth and health of plants.

Purpose In the Chapter 4 Project, students will work in small groups to examine soils, plant bean seeds in different kinds of soils, collect and record data about the growth of the bean plants, compare how the plants fared in different soils, and draw conclusions about how much effect a soil has on the plants it holds. By doing this project, students will gain a better understanding of soil composition and fertility.

Skills Focus Students will be able to:

- design an experiment that investigates different soils and their effects on plant growth;
- control variables in setting up an experiment that isolates soil as the only variable among different plants;
- make measurements of plant growth over the course of the project;
- create a data table to record observations about the growth and health of the plants;
- draw conclusions about how soil composition affects plant growth.

Project Time Line The entire project will require about two to three weeks. Depending on how much class time students can spend working on the project, planning and setup should take only one or two days. Observing plant growth requires a minimum of two weeks. The presentations can be done in a day. The project will require groups to carry out the following phases.

- Meet to decide on which soils to use and how to set up the experiment.
- Examine the different soils and note their characteristics.
- Plant the seeds and set up the experiment.
- Create a data table to record growth data.
- Observe and record the growth and health of the plants in different soils.
- Draw conclusions about the effect soil had on the data collected.
- Present the results and conclusions to the class.

For more detailed information on planning and supervising the Chapter 4 Project, see Chapter 4 Project Teacher Notes in Unit 2 Resources.

Suggested Shortcuts

- You can make this project shorter and less involved by explaining the experiment to students and having them observe the growth of plants in sand, gravel, vermiculite, potting soil, and local topsoil over a two-week period. Each student can make individual observations and create a data table to record those observations.
- You can make this project shorter by planting bean seeds about a week in advance. You can give each student group three or four pots to observe, each pot containing plants in a different type of soil.

Possible Materials Sand, gravel, vermiculite, and potting soil can be purchased from any

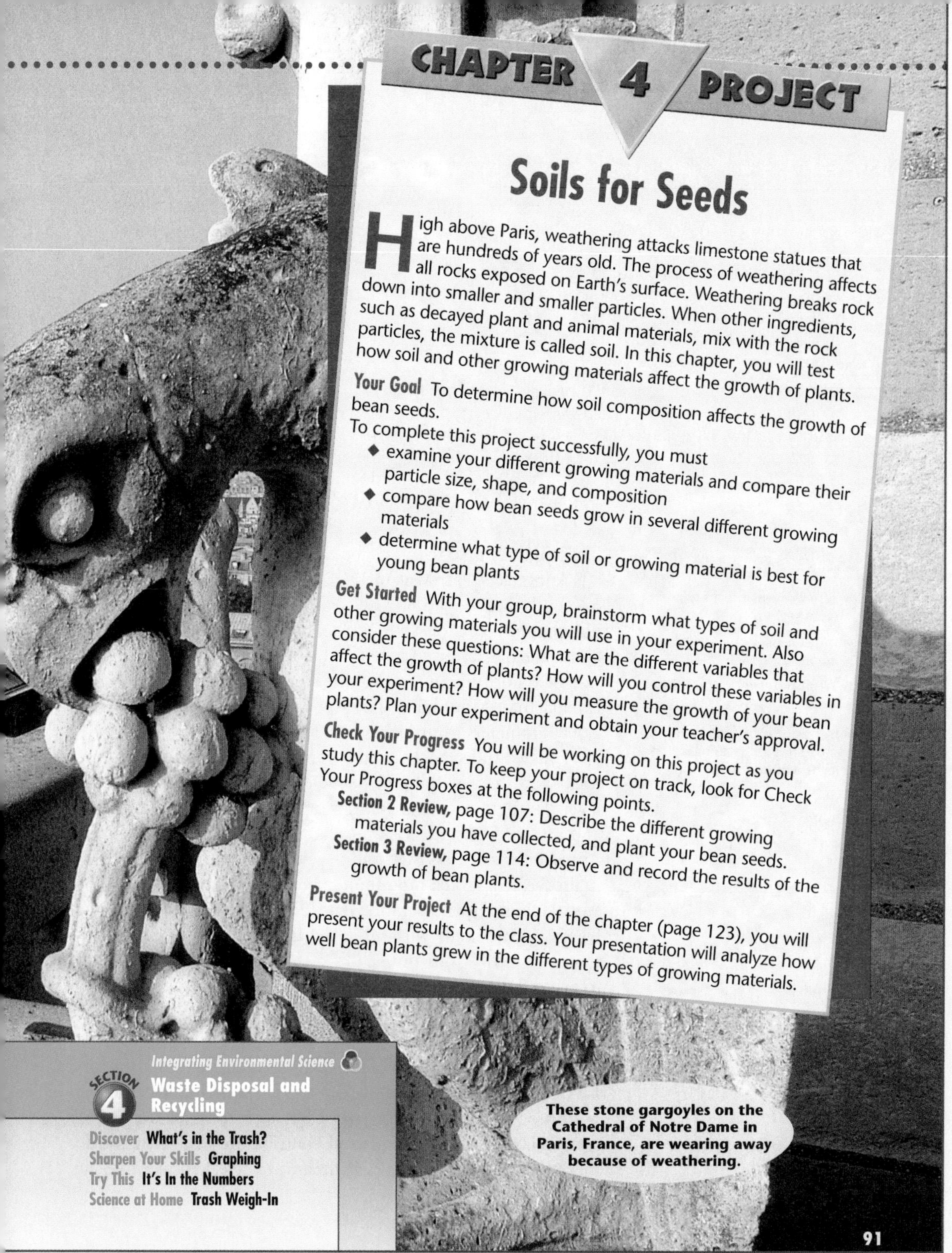

CHAPTER 4 PROJECT

Soils for Seeds

High above Paris, weathering attacks limestone statues that are hundreds of years old. The process of weathering affects all rocks exposed on Earth's surface. Weathering breaks rock down into smaller and smaller particles. When other ingredients, such as decayed plant and animal materials, mix with the rock particles, the mixture is called soil. In this chapter, you will test how soil and other growing materials affect the growth of plants.

Your Goal To determine how soil composition affects the growth of bean seeds.

To complete this project successfully, you must

- examine your different growing materials and compare their particle size, shape, and composition
- compare how bean seeds grow in several different growing materials
- determine what type of soil or growing material is best for young bean plants

Get Started With your group, brainstorm what types of soil and other growing materials you will use in your experiment. Also consider these questions: What are the different variables that affect the growth of plants? How will you control these variables in your experiment? How will you measure the growth of your bean plants? Plan your experiment and obtain your teacher's approval.

Check Your Progress You will be working on this project as you study this chapter. To keep your project on track, look for Check Your Progress boxes at the following points.

Section 2 Review, page 107: Describe the different growing materials you have collected, and plant your bean seeds.

Section 3 Review, page 114: Observe and record the results of the growth of bean plants.

Present Your Project At the end of the chapter (page 123), you will present your results to the class. Your presentation will analyze how well bean plants grew in the different types of growing materials.

Integrating Environmental Science

SECTION 4 **Waste Disposal and Recycling**

These stone gargoyles on the Cathedral of Notre Dame in Paris, France, are wearing away because of weathering.

Program Resources

- **Unit 2 Resources** Chapter 4 Project Teacher Notes; Chapter 4 Project Overview and Worksheets; Chapter 4 Project Scoring Rubric

Media and Technology

Student Edition on Audio CD
Chapter 4

www.phschool.com

You will find an Internet activity, chapter self-tests for students, and links to other chapter topics at this site.

local garden or large hardware store. Students can collect local topsoil; they will need a trowel and a bucket. Each group will also need 12 to 15 pinto bean seeds and three or four small pots in which to plant their beans. (Plastic foam cups with a small hole punched in the bottom can be used for pots.) To make measurements of plant growth, students should use metric rulers.

Launching the Project Introduce the Chapter 4 Project by displaying a healthy potted plant. Ask: **If you wanted to grow a healthy plant like this, how could you meet the plant's requirements?** *(Answers will vary. Most students will mention the right amount of sunlight and water. Some may mention good soil.)* Point out that each one of these factors could be investigated to find out what effect it has on plant growth. In this project, students will investigate only one factor—how soil affects plants. Thus, type of soil will be the variable in the experiment they will design. They will have to control other factors so that only soil makes a difference in how plants grow. To help students get started, pass out Chapter 4 Project Overview and Worksheets in Unit 2 Resources. You may also wish to pass out the Chapter 4 Project Scoring Rubric at this time.

Performance Assessment

Use the Chapter 4 Project Scoring Rubric to assess students' work. Students will be assessed on

- how well they examine various soils and set up the experiment;
- how well they observe and record the growth of their plants in a data table;
- how effectively they present their results and conclusions to the class;
- how much they contribute to their group's effort.

Rocks and Weathering

Objectives

After completing the lesson, students will be able to

- ◆ identify what causes mechanical weathering;
- ◆ identify what causes chemical weathering;
- ◆ describe the factors that determine how fast weathering occurs.

Key Terms weathering, erosion, mechanical weathering, abrasion, ice wedging, chemical weathering, permeable

1 Engage/Explore

Activating Prior Knowledge

Many students have probably seen old headstones in cemeteries. Ask: **How would you describe the difference between a new headstone and one that is a hundred years old?** *(A typical answer might describe the old headstone as rounded and crumbling with a faded inscription.)* Invite students to speculate about what processes change a headstone through the years.

DISCOVER ACTIVITY

Skills Focus inferring
Materials *2 fizzing antacid tablets, 2 beakers, warm water, plastic stirring rod, plastic bowl, stopwatch*
Time 10 minutes
Tips Demonstrate how to grind up a tablet by using the stirring rod in a plastic bowl. Have students use warm water from the tap. If stopwatches are unavailable, students can observe a second hand on a watch or wall clock.
Expected Outcome Typical dissolving times are 30 seconds for the whole tablet, 10 seconds for the ground-up tablet.
Think It Over The ground-up tablet dissolved faster than the whole tablet. Inferences may vary. Some students might correctly suggest that the ground-up tablet had more surface area exposed to the water than the whole tablet, and therefore dissolved faster.

Section 1 Rocks and Weathering

DISCOVER ACTIVITY

How Fast Can It Fizz?

1. Place a fizzing antacid tablet in a small beaker. Then grind up a second tablet and place it in another beaker. The whole tablet is a model of solid rock. The ground-up tablet is a model of rock fragments.
2. Add 100 mL of warm water to the beaker containing the whole tablet. Then stir with a stirring rod until the tablet dissolves completely. Use a stopwatch to time how long it takes.
3. Add 100 mL of warm water to the beaker containing the ground-up tablet. Then stir until all of the ground-up tablet dissolves. Time how long it takes.

Think It Over

Inferring Which dissolved faster, the whole antacid tablet or the ground-up tablet? What difference between the two affected how long it took them to dissolve?

GUIDE FOR READING

- ◆ What causes mechanical weathering?
- ◆ What causes chemical weathering?
- ◆ What determines how fast weathering occurs?

Reading Tip As you read, use the headings to make an outline about weathering.

Imagine a hike that lasts for months and covers hundreds of kilometers. Each year, many hikers go on such treks. They hike trails that run the length of America's great mountain ranges. For example, the John Muir Trail follows the Sierra Nevada mountains. The Sierras extend about 640 kilometers along the eastern side of California. In the east, the Appalachian Trail follows the Appalachian Mountains. The Appalachians stretch more than 2,000 kilometers from Alabama to Maine.

The two trails cross very different landscapes. The Sierras are rocky and steep, with many peaks rising 3,000 meters above sea level. The Appalachians are more rounded and gently sloping, and are covered with soil and plants. The highest peaks in the Appalachians are less than half the elevation of the highest peaks in the Sierras. Which mountain range do you think is older? The Appalachians formed more than 250 million years ago. The Sierras formed only within the last 10 million years. The forces that wear down rock on Earth's surface have had much longer to grind down the Appalachians.

The Effects of Weathering

The process of mountain building thrusts rock up to the Earth's surface. There, the rock becomes exposed to weathering. **Weathering** is the process that breaks down rock and other substances at Earth's surface. Heat, cold, water, and ice all contribute to weathering. So do the oxygen and carbon dioxide in the atmosphere. Repeated freezing

READING STRATEGIES

Reading Tip You may wish to have students prepare the main heads of the outline by previewing the headings in the section before they read. Remind students to leave space below each heading so that they can add information as they read. Students' outlines might begin as follows:
I. The Effect of Weathering
II. Mechanical Weathering
III. Chemical Weathering

Vocabulary Help clarify the difference between the terms *mechanical weathering* and *chemical weathering* by referring to physical change and chemical change. Physical changes include changes in size, shape, phase, and so on. Such changes don't alter the basic substance. Chemical changes, by contrast, refer to changes from chemical reactions, in which substances change into other substances.

and thawing, for example, can crack rock apart into smaller pieces. Rainwater can dissolve minerals that bind rock together. You don't need to go to the mountains to see examples of weathering. The forces that wear down mountains also cause bicycles to rust, paint to peel, sidewalks to crack, and potholes to form.

The forces of weathering break rocks into smaller and smaller pieces. Then the forces of erosion carry the pieces away. **Erosion** (ee ROH zhun) is the movement of rock particles by wind, water, ice, or gravity. Weathering and erosion work together continuously to wear down and carry away the rocks at Earth's surface.

There are two kinds of weathering: mechanical weathering and chemical weathering. Both types of weathering act slowly, but over time they break down even the biggest, hardest rocks.

☑ *Checkpoint* *What is the difference between weathering and erosion?*

Figure 1 The jagged, rocky peaks of the Sierra Nevadas (left) show that the mountains are young. The more gently sloping Appalachians (right) have been exposed to weathering for 250 million years.

Mechanical Weathering

If you hit a rock hard enough with a hammer, the rock will break into pieces. Some forces of weathering can also break rock into pieces. The type of weathering in which rock is physically broken into smaller pieces is called **mechanical weathering.** These smaller pieces of rock have the same composition as the rock they came from. If you have seen rocks that are cracked or peeling in layers, then you have seen rocks that are undergoing mechanical weathering.

Mechanical weathering breaks rock into pieces by freezing and thawing, release of pressure, growth of plants, actions of animals, and abrasion. The term **abrasion** (uh BRAY zhun) refers to the grinding away of rock by rock particles carried by water, ice, wind, or gravity. Mechanical weathering works slowly. But over very long periods of time, it does more than wear down rocks. Mechanical weathering eventually wears away whole mountains.

2 Facilitate

The Effects of Weathering

Using the Visuals: Figure 1

Explain that the Sierra Nevada mountains formed less than 10 million years ago. Ask: **How much longer has weathering acted on the Appalachians?** *(250 million years)* **Do you think in another 250 million years the Sierra will look like the Appalachians?** *(Answers may vary. Many students will think they will.)* Advise students to keep this question in mind when they read about the causes of weathering and differences in the rate of weathering later in the section. **learning modality: logical/mathematical**

Mechanical Weathering

Demonstration

Materials *2 pieces of sandstone, newspaper*
Time 5 minutes

As students watch, have a volunteer rub two pieces of sandstone together over a spread-out newspaper. Students will observe particles fall onto the paper. Ask: **What kind of mechanical weathering does this model?** *(abrasion)* Ask: **How could such abrasion occur in nature?** *(Water or wind could carry sand particles into rock, grinding part of it away.)* **learning modality: visual**

Program Resources

- **Unit 2 Resources** 4-1 Lesson Plan; 4-1 Section Summary
- **Guided Reading and Study Workbook** Section 4-1
- **Laboratory Manual** 4, "Investigating Soils and Drainage"

Answers to Self-Assessment

☑ *Checkpoint*

Weathering is the process that breaks down rock and other materials at Earth's surface, while erosion is the movement of rock particles by wind, water, ice, or gravity.

Ongoing Assessment

Oral Presentation Call on students at random to classify examples as either weathering or erosion. Each time you call on a student, give a brief, general description of an agent of weathering or an instance of erosion, without using any technical terms.

Mechanical Weathering, continued

Integrating Physics

ACTIVITY

Materials *small steel mixing bowl, plastic saucer, 4–5 kg weight, water, freezer*
Time 5 minutes for setup; 5 minutes the next day for observation

As students observe, fill the bowl to the top with water. Place the saucer over the top of the bowl. On top of the saucer place a small weight. Then place this apparatus in a freezer overnight. The next day, students will see that the expansion of water as it turned to ice pushed the weight up. **learning modality: visual**

EXPLORING the Forces of Mechanical Weathering

Ask students to describe any evidence they have seen of mechanical weathering, then ask: **With which of the five forces is the composition of rock different after mechanical weathering occurs?** *(None. In each case, the composition of the rock remains the same.)* **How are rocks changed after mechanical weathering?** *(Rocks are either cracked or broken into smaller pieces.)* **learning modality: verbal**

Building Inquiry Skills: Designing Experiments

ACTIVITY

Materials *charcoal briquettes, plastic sandwich bags, water, marking pen, freezer*
Time 20 minutes for design and setup; 5 minutes the next day

Challenge small groups to use the materials given to design an experiment that shows how freezing and thawing water affects rock. A typical experiment might include soaking one briquette with water while keeping the other dry, and then placing each in a plastic bag and freezing both overnight. The next day, the water-saturated briquette would be cracked or in pieces, while the other would not. Review each group's design before permitting them to proceed. **learning modality: kinesthetic**

INTEGRATING PHYSICS In cool climates, the most important force of mechanical weathering is freezing and thawing of water. Water seeps into cracks in rocks and then freezes when the temperature drops. Water expands when it freezes. Ice therefore acts like a wedge, a simple machine that forces things apart. Wedges of ice in rocks widen and deepen cracks. This process is called **ice wedging.** When the ice melts, the water seeps deeper into the cracks. With repeated freezing and thawing, the cracks slowly expand until pieces of rock break off. *Exploring the Forces of Mechanical Weathering* shows how this process weathers rock.

☑ *Checkpoint* *How does ice wedging weather rock?*

EXPLORING the Forces of Mechanical Weathering

Mechanical weathering affects all the rock on Earth's surface. Given enough time, mechanical weathering can break down a massive mountain into tiny particles of sand.

Release of Pressure
As erosion removes material from the surface of a mass of rock, pressure on the rock below is reduced. This release of pressure causes the outside of the rock to crack and flake off like the layers of an onion.

Freezing and Thawing
When water freezes in a crack in a rock, it expands and makes the crack bigger. The process of ice wedging also widens cracks in sidewalks and causes potholes in streets.

Background

Facts and Figures Ice wedging, or frost wedging, is a powerful force of mechanical weathering. When water freezes, it expands about 9 percent larger than it was as a liquid. When water freezes within a crack in rock, it exerts a pressure of about 110 kg/cm^2. Such pressure is roughly equal to the force of a 98-kg object dropped from a height of 3 m. Freezing and thawing over and over eventually breaks rock apart. It also causes significant destruction to the roadways of the northern United States, particularly during the early spring when freezing and thawing are common. At this time, pavement can become buckled and scarred with potholes.

Chemical Weathering

In addition to mechanical weathering, another type of weathering attacks rock. **Chemical weathering** is the process that breaks down rock through chemical changes. **The agents of chemical weathering include water, oxygen, carbon dioxide, living organisms, and acid rain.**

Chemical weathering produces rock particles that have a different mineral makeup from the rock they came from. Each rock is made up of one or more minerals. For example, granite is made up of several minerals, including feldspar, quartz, and mica. But chemical weathering of granite eventually changes the feldspar minerals to clay minerals.

Plant Growth
Roots of trees and other plants enter cracks in rocks. As the roots grow, they force the cracks farther apart. Over time, the roots of even small plants can pry apart cracked rocks.

Abrasion
Sand and other rock particles that are carried by wind, water, or ice can wear away exposed rock surfaces like sandpaper on wood. Wind-driven sand helped shape the rocks shown here.

Animal Actions
Animals that burrow in the ground—including moles, gophers, prairie dogs, and some insects—loosen and break apart rocks in the soil.

Media and Technology

Transparencies "Forces of Mechanical Weathering," Transparency 7

Answers to Self-Assessment

Checkpoint

Water seeps into cracks in rock and then freezes. Because water expands when it freezes, the ice acts as a wedge, widening and deepening the cracks.

Real-Life Learning

Time *15 minutes* ACTIVITY

Have students look for examples of mechanical weathering caused by plant growth on or around the school grounds. Students can do this during lunch or after school. They should be able to find examples of plants growing up through cracks in the sidewalk or blacktop or plant roots displacing stones or concrete. Encourage students to sketch what they see and then tell the class about it. **learning modality: visual**

Chemical Weathering

Addressing Naive Conceptions

Many students may believe that weathering, especially chemical weathering, occurs as large and dramatic events. Ask: **Have any of you ever seen rock weather?** *(No one will probably have seen rock weather.)* Emphasize that weathering usually occurs slowly over great spans of time. A person's lifetime is not long enough to observe any dramatic changes caused by weathering, such as mountains being worn down. **learning modality: verbal**

Demonstration

Materials *samples of limestone and granite, 2 plates, dilute hydrochloric acid or vinegar, plastic dropper, gloves* ACTIVITY
Time 5 minutes

Display two plates, with a limestone sample on one and a granite sample on the other. Then, as students observe, use the dropper to apply the acid to each rock. The limestone will dramatically fizz and deteriorate, while the granite will remain unchanged. Ask: **What does this demonstration model?** *(The way that carbonic acid weathers limestone)* **learning modality: visual**

Ongoing Assessment

Writing Have students explain in their own words the difference between mechanical weathering and chemical weathering.

Students can save their paragraphs in their portfolios.

Chemical Weathering, continued

Using the Visuals: Figure 2

To help students understand that more surface area means more weathering, propose that the faces of the unbroken cube in the figure are each 10 × 10 m and the rock is sitting on Earth's surface. Ask: **How many square meters of rock are exposed to the forces of chemical weathering?** *(600 m^2, 6×10^2, are exposed to weathering.)* **If the rock fractures into eight pieces as shown, how much surface area is exposed?** *(Now each face is 25 m^2. Thus, there would be 1,200 m^2 exposed to chemical weathering: 8 pieces × 6 sides each = 48; 48 × 25 m^2 = 1200 m^2.)* **learning modality: logical/mathematical**

TRY THIS

Skills Focus predicting
Materials *2 pads of steel wool, water, jar with lid*
Time 5 minutes for setup; 5 minutes a few days later
Tips Don't use steel-wool pads that contain soap. To cut down on the cost of materials, cut each pad in half.
Expected Outcome The moistened steel wool left in the jar will rust. When squeezed, it will crumble and stay compacted, while the new piece will spring back to the original shape. Like the oxidation of rock, the steel wool becomes crumbly and turns reddish.
Extend Encourage interested students to set up a long-term experiment by placing half a steel-wool pad somewhere outside where it will not be disturbed and keeping the other half inside as a control. After a month, compare the two to observe the effects of weathering.
learning modality: kinesthetic

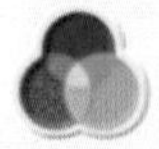

Integrating Environmental Science

Ask students: **What do you and your family do to contribute to the problem of acid rain?** *(Students should mention driving and electricity use.)* **How could you reduce your contribution to this problem?** *(Students might mention using more efficient vehicles and electric appliances or using them less often.)* **learning modality: verbal**

Figure 2 As weathering breaks apart rock, the surface area exposed to further weathering increases.

Chemical weathering creates holes or soft spots in rock, so the rock breaks apart more easily. Chemical and mechanical weathering often work together. As mechanical weathering breaks rock into pieces, more surface area becomes exposed to chemical weathering. The Discover activity in this section shows how increasing the surface area increases the rate of a chemical reaction.

Water Water is the most important agent of chemical weathering. Water weathers rock by dissolving it. When a rock or other substance dissolves in water, it mixes uniformly throughout the water to make a solution. Over time, many rocks will dissolve in water.

Oxygen The oxygen gas in air is an important cause of chemical weathering. If you have ever left a bicycle or metal tool outside in the rain, then you have seen how oxygen can weather iron. Iron combines with oxygen in the presence of water in a process called oxidation. The product of oxidation is rust. Rock that contains iron also oxidizes, or rusts. Rust makes rock soft and crumbly and gives it a red or brown color.

Carbon Dioxide Another gas found in air, carbon dioxide, also causes chemical weathering. Carbon dioxide becomes dissolved in rainwater and in water that sinks through air pockets in the soil. The result is a weak acid called carbonic acid. Carbonic acid easily weathers marble and limestone.

Living Organisms Imagine a seed landing on a rock face. As it sprouts, its roots push into cracks in the rock. As the plant's roots grow, they produce weak acids that slowly dissolve rock around the roots. Lichens—plantlike organisms that grow on rocks—also produce weak acids that chemically weather rock.

Acid Rain Over the past 150 years, people have been burning large amounts of coal, oil, and gas for energy. Burning these fuels can pollute the air with sulfur, carbon, and nitrogen compounds. Such compounds react chemically with the water vapor in clouds, forming acids. These acids mix with raindrops and fall as acid rain. Acid rain causes very rapid chemical weathering.

INTEGRATING ENVIRONMENTAL SCIENCE

TRY THIS

Rusting Away

Here's how you can observe weathering.

1. Moisten some steel wool and place it in a closed container so it will not dry out.
2. Observe the steel wool after a few days. What has happened to the steel wool?
3. Take a new piece of steel wool and squeeze it between your fingers. Remove the steel wool from the container and squeeze it between your fingers. What happens? Wash your hands when you have finished.

Predicting If you kept the steel wool moist for a longer time, what would eventually happen to it? How is the weathering of steel wool like the weathering of a rock?

96

Background

Facts and Figures Chemical weathering cannot take place without water. Some moisture is available for chemical weathering even in deserts, but the processes of chemical weathering are much more significant in wetter climates. Solution, oxidation, formation of carbonic acid, and acid rain all require water.

Chemical weathering works to prepare rock for erosion. First, such weathering often results in softer and smaller rocks that erode more easily. Second, chemical weathering often involves dissolving minerals in solution. Such dissolved minerals are easily transported by the flow of water, a process called chemical erosion.

Rate of Weathering

Visitors to New England's historic cemeteries may notice a surprising fact. Slate tombstones from the 1700s are less weathered and easier to read than marble gravestones from the 1800s. Why is this so? **The most important factors that determine the rate at which weathering occurs are type of rock and climate.**

Type of Rock Some kinds of rocks weather more rapidly than others. The minerals that make up the rock determine how fast it weathers. Rock made of minerals that do not dissolve easily in water weathers slowly. Rock made of minerals that dissolve easily in water weathers faster.

Some rock weathers easily because it is permeable. **Permeable** (PUR mee uh bul) means that a material is full of tiny, connected air spaces that allow water to seep through it. Permeable rock weathers chemically at a fast rate. Why? As water seeps through the spaces in the rock, it removes dissolved material formed by weathering.

Climate Climate refers to the average weather conditions in an area. Both chemical and mechanical weathering occur faster in wet climates. Rainfall provides the water needed for chemical changes as well as for freezing and thawing.

Chemical reactions occur faster at higher temperatures. That is why chemical weathering occurs more quickly where the climate is both hot and wet. Granite, for example, is a very hard rock that forms when molten material cools inside Earth. Granite weathers so slowly in cool climates that it is often used as a building stone. But in hot and wet climates, granite weathers faster and eventually crumbles apart.

Figure 3 The rate of weathering of these tombstones depends on the type of rock. Slate (top) resists weathering better than marble (bottom). *Inferring What type of weathering probably wore away the letters on the marble tombstone?*

Section 1 Review

1. What factors cause mechanical weathering?
2. Describe three causes of chemical weathering.
3. What factors affect the rate of weathering?
4. Explain why chemical weathering occurs faster in hot, wet climates than in cool, dry climates.
5. **Thinking Critically Predicting** Suppose you see a large boulder with several cracks in it. What would you expect to see if you could observe the boulder again in several hundred years? Explain.

Science at Home

Ice in a Straw Here's how to demonstrate one type of weathering for your family. Plug one end of a drinking straw with a small piece of clay. Fill the straw with water. Now plug the top of the straw with clay. Make sure that the clay plugs do not leak. Lay the straw flat in the freezer overnight. Remove the straw the next day. What happened to the clay plugs? What process produced this result? Be sure to dispose of the straw so that no one will use it for drinking.

Program Resources

- **Unit 2 Resources** 4-1 Review and Reinforce; 4-1 Enrich

Answers to Self-Assessment

Caption Question

Figure 3 A typical answer might correctly suggest that chemical weathering probably wore away the letters.

Rate of Weathering

Inquiry Challenge

ACTIVITY

Divide students into small groups and challenge each group to develop a hypothesis about which factor plays the greater role in rate of weathering, type of rock or climate. Then have students design an experiment that could test their hypothesis. Finally, have a member of each group describe the experiment to the class. **cooperative learning**

3 Assess

Section 1 Review Answers

1. Freezing and thawing, heating and cooling, growth of plants, actions of animals, and abrasion
2. Answers may vary. Students should describe any three of the following: the presence of water to dissolve rocks, the presence of oxygen to cause oxidation, the presence of carbon dioxide dissolved in rainwater, the presence of living organisms, and the presence of acid rain.
3. The most important factors are type of rock and climate.
4. In hot, wet climates, rainfall provides the water needed for chemical changes and higher temperatures cause chemical reactions to occur faster.
5. Answers may vary. Students might suggest that they would see a crumbled rock, a rock with much larger cracks, or a rock with plants growing in the cracks.

Science at Home

ACTIVITY

Encourage students to try this model of ice wedging at home. Use a plastic straw. After freezing the straw overnight, students should observe that the ice has forced one or both of the clay plugs out of the straw because water expands when it freezes.

Performance Assessment

Skills Check Have students make a compare/contrast table that includes every agent of mechanical and chemical weathering.

Skills Lab

Controlling Variables

Rock Shake

Preparing for Inquiry

Key Concept Both mechanical weathering and chemical weathering break down rocks into smaller pieces.

Skills Objectives Students will be able to:

- measure the amount of water and acid poured into each container;
- make predictions about whether an acid or water will weather limestone pieces more;
- control variables by setting up four different variations of weathering;
- create a data table by recording data related to change in mass and percent change in mass;
- draw conclusions about weathering from their data.

Time 30 minutes on Day 1; 30 minutes on Day 2

Advance Planning Collect and prepare the pieces of limestone at least a day in advance. Each student will need 80 pieces. Small limestone gravel is the best material to use. Use a hammer to break up any large pieces. Soak the limestone pieces in water 24 hours in advance.

The cloth students use should be about 10 × 10 centimeters; cheesecloth will work the best. The vinegar should be a vinegar-water solution. Make this in advance by using 75 percent white vinegar and 25 percent distilled water. The water used in containers A and B should be distilled water, because tap water is slightly acidic.

Since there are many varieties of limestone, you should perform the activity in advance at least once to determine likely changes in mass for the pieces in each container.

Designate a space for students to place their containers overnight. Have students write their initials on the masking tape label of each container to avoid confusion about which containers belong to whom.

Alternative Materials If standard plastic containers are unavailable, use small plastic soft-drink bottles.

Skills Lab

Controlling Variables

ROCK SHAKE

Which do you think would weather faster, a rock attacked by plant acids or a rock in the rushing waters of a stream? Many factors affect the rate at which rock weathers. In this lab, you will compare the rates of weathering that take place under different conditions.

Problem

How will shaking and acid conditions affect the rate at which limestone weathers?

Materials

300 mL of water
balance
paper towels
masking tape
2 pieces of thin cloth
marking pen or pencil
300 mL of vinegar, an acid
plastic graduated cylinder, 250 mL
80 small pieces of water-soaked limestone
4 watertight plastic containers with screw-on caps, 500-mL

Procedure 

Part 1—Day 1

1. Using masking tape, label the four 500-mL containers A, B, C, and D.
2. Separate the 80 pieces of limestone into four sets of 20.
3. Copy the data table in your notebook. Then place the first 20 pieces of limestone on the balance and record their mass in the data table. Place the rocks in Container A.
4. Repeat Step 3 for the other sets of rocks and place them in containers B, C, and D.
5. Pour 150 mL of water into container A and container B. Put caps on both containers.
6. Pour 150 mL of vinegar into container C and also into container D. Put caps on both containers.
7. Predict the effect of weathering on the mass of the limestone pieces. Which will weather more: the limestone in water or the limestone in vinegar? (*Hint:* Vinegar is an acid.) Also predict the effect of shaking on the limestone in containers B and D. Record your predictions in your notebook.
8. Allow the pieces to soak overnight.

Container	Total Mass Start	Total Mass Next Day	Change in Mass	Percent Change in Mass
A (water, no shaking)				
B (water, shaking)				
C (vinegar, no shaking)				
D (vinegar, shaking)				

98

Guiding Inquiry

Introducing the Procedure

- After students have read the procedure, ask: **What variables are you testing in this experiment?** *(The effect of acid and the effect of shaking on limestone)*
- **What is the purpose of container A?** *(Since container A contains no acid and the pieces are not shaken, it is the control.)*

Troubleshooting the Experiment

- On Day 1, make sure students write their predictions in their journals.
- On Day 2, students should be able to see a clock so they can time how long they shake containers B and D. Students can work in pairs, with each student shaking one container. If students get tired, they can rest, as long as each container is shaken the same total amount of time.
- Demonstrate how to pour the water through the cloth. Advise students to pick out the 20 largest pieces, ignoring any tiny sediment in the containers.
- Help students determine percent change by doing an example problem on the board.

Part 2—Day 2

9. Screw the caps tightly on containers B and D. Shake both containers for 10 to 15 minutes. Make sure that each container is shaken for exactly the same amount of time and at the same intensity. After shaking, set the containers aside. Do not shake containers A and C.
10. Open the top of container A. Place one piece of thin cloth over the opening of the container. Carefully pour all of the water out through the cloth into a waste container. Be careful not to let any of the pieces flow out with the water. Dry these pieces carefully and record their mass in your data table.
11. Next, determine how much limestone was lost through weathering in container A. (*Hint:* Subtract the mass of the limestone pieces remaining on Day 2 from the mass of the pieces on Day 1.)
12. Repeat Steps 10 and 11 for containers B, C, and D.

Analyze and Conclude

1. Calculate the percent change in mass of the 20 pieces for each container.

$$\% \text{ change} = \frac{\text{Change in mass} \times 100}{\text{Total mass start}}$$

Record the results in the data table.

2. Do your data show a change in mass of the 20 pieces in each of the four containers?
3. Is there a greater change in total mass for the pieces in one container than for the pieces in the other? Explain.
4. How correct were your predictions of how shaking and acid would affect the weathering of limestone? Explain.
5. If your data showed a greater change in the mass of the pieces in one of the containers, how might this change be explained?
6. **Think About It** Based on your data, which variable do you think was more responsible for breaking down the limestone: the vinegar or the shaking? Explain.

Design an Experiment

Would your results for this experiment change if you changed the variables? For example, you could soak or shake the pieces for a longer time, or test rocks other than limestone. You could also test whether adding more limestone pieces (30 rather than 20 in each set) would make a difference in the outcome. Design an experiment on the rate of weathering to test the effects of changing one of these variables. Have your teacher approve your experiment before you begin.

Expected Outcome
The pieces in container D will show the greatest change in mass, because those pieces were subjected to both chemical and mechanical weathering (acid and shaking). The pieces in container A will show little or no change in mass, because they were subjected to neither chemical nor mechanical weathering. The pieces in container C will probably show a greater change in mass than the pieces in container B, depending on the type of limestone students use.

Analyze and Conclude

1. The percent change in mass of the 20 pieces in each container will vary significantly, depending on the variety of limestone used, the original mass of the pieces, the strength of the acid, and the amount of shaking. The exact figures are unimportant. How the figures compare with one another will be telling.
2. Answers will vary. Students should see a change in mass of the pieces in containers B, C, and D. There should be little or no change in mass of the pieces in container A.
3. The pieces in container D should show the greatest change in total mass, because they were subjected to both the acid and the shaking. The pieces in container A should show little change in total mass, because they were not subject to acid or shaking.
4. Answers will vary according to predictions. Most students will probably have correctly predicted that the acid and shaking will cause the mass of the limestone pieces to change more than the mass of the pieces not exposed to these forms of "weathering."
5. The mass of the pieces in container D showed the greatest change because those pieces of limestone were both soaked overnight in acid and shaken the next day, while none of the pieces in the other containers were subjected to both types of weathering.
6. Answers will vary. Most students will suggest that the acid was more responsible for breaking down the limestone, because the change in mass of the pieces in container C was greater than the change in mass of the pieces in container B.

Extending the Inquiry

Design an Experiment Encourage students to continue testing limestone or other types of rock. Granite, for example, is more resistant to both acid and shaking. Different students can test different kinds of rocks, and then collaborate in a compare/contrast table.

Media and Technology

Lab Activity Videotapes
Grade 6, Tape 1

Program Resources

◆ **Unit 2 Resources** Chapter 4 Skills Lab

Safety

Caution students to wear their goggles when pouring the vinegar and shaking the containers. Have them make sure the caps are screwed on tightly. Review the safety guidelines in Appendix A.

Science and Society

Preserving Stone Monuments

Purpose Students will become more familiar with the pros and cons of preserving stone monuments.

Role Play

Time 40 minutes

After students have read the feature, divide the class into small groups and have them meet for 10 minutes to prepare for a panel discussion. Assign each group a position to support. One group could advocate restoring stone monuments whatever the cost. Another group could focus on instituting regulations to diminish air pollution around the world. Another group could advance the notion that there are much better ways to spend money, such as for famine relief. A fourth group could advocate covering important monuments until techniques can be developed to save them. Then invite all groups to participate in a UN-sponsored assembly where these matters can be discussed. Have a student volunteer moderate the discussion, and encourage groups to strongly express their positions though avoid any personal attacks.

Extend Encourage interested students to contact a local historical society to find out what stone structures in their area are threatened by weathering and pollution. Students could make a list of these structures, complete with locations, descriptions of the problems, and possible solutions. Consider having student volunteers meet and develop this list before the panel discussion.

You Decide

After the panel discussion has concluded, encourage students to reflect on what they've said and heard as they identify the problem and analyze the options. Then encourage each student to take a position by writing an advocacy letter to a public official. Assess these letters on the soundness of their argument, not on the position a student takes on the issue.

Science and Society

Preserving Stone Monuments

A statue with a human head and a lion's body crouches in the desert beside the pyramids of Egypt. This is the great Sphinx. It was carved out of limestone about 4,500 years ago. Thousands of years of weathering by water, wind, and sand have worn away much of the Sphinx's face. In the 1800s, sand that had protected the Sphinx's body was cleared away. Weathering attacked the newly exposed parts of the Sphinx. Flakes and even chunks of stone fell from the statue. Workers tried to repair the Sphinx with cement. But the repairs weakened the statue and changed its shape.

The Issues

Should Structures Be Restored?
Weathering threatens many ancient stone monuments throughout the world. Pollutants in air and rain make stone weather faster. But there are ways to slow the weathering of a monument without changing or damaging it. In 1998, workers in Egypt completed a new restoration of the Sphinx. They removed the added cement. They replaced the damaged stones with new, hand-cut limestone blocks of the same size and weight. The new stone will help protect what remains of the monument. Visitors to the Sphinx will now see only the original statue and repairs made with original materials. The new repairs preserve the statue's original shape.

Most people want the Sphinx and other monuments to be restored. But restoration is time-consuming and very expensive. And in some cases, repair work can damage or change the original structure.

Can New Technology Slow Weathering?
Advances in technology may provide some solutions. At the Sphinx, scientists measure wind direction, wind speed, and moisture in the air. This information helps scientists follow the weathering process and provides data that will help prevent more damage. Similar instruments are used at other monuments.

Other scientists are working on a way of coating stone with a chemical compound to strengthen and repair the surface. So far, they have found a compound that sticks well to sandstone, but not to marble or limestone.

What Else Can People Do? Repair and restoration are not the only options. Some say that ancient monuments should be buried again after being uncovered by archaeologists. Some people suggest that the Sphinx itself should be reburied in the sand that protected it for so many centuries. But scholars, archaeologists, and tourists disagree. Meanwhile, as people seek solutions, rain, wind, sun, and polluted air continue to take their toll.

You Decide

1. Identify the Problem
In your own words, explain the difficulties involved in preserving ancient monuments.

2. Analyze the Options
List methods for preserving ancient buildings and monuments. Note the advantages and disadvantages of repair work, technology, and other approaches.

3. Find a Solution
Make a plan to preserve a monument in your city. Write your recommendations in the form of a letter to a city mayor or town council.

Background

Facts and Figures The deterioration of the Sphinx is not all modern. The nose has been missing since the fourteenth century, and the first repairs of the structure date from ancient times. In the 1990s, the Egyptian government undertook to repair the structure as best it could, keeping in mind that it will remain an ancient ruin.

The Sphinx is far from the only concern for those wanting to save ancient monuments. The Acropolis in Athens, Greece, is deteriorating at an alarming rate, in no small part because of the polluted Athens air. The acid precipitation in large cities takes a toll on all monuments.

Section 2 Soil Formation and Composition

DISCOVER ACTIVITY

What Is Soil?

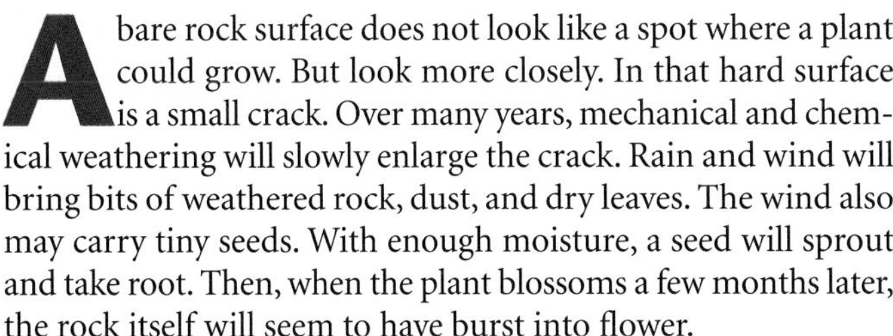

1. Use a toothpick to separate a sample of soil into individual particles. With a hand lens, try to identify the different types of particles in the sample. Wash your hands when you are finished.
2. Write a "recipe" for the sample of soil, naming each of the "ingredients" that you think the soil contains. Include what percentage of each ingredient would be needed to create the soil.
3. Compare your recipe with those of your classmates.

Think It Over

Forming Operational Definitions Based on your observations, how would you define *soil*?

A bare rock surface does not look like a spot where a plant could grow. But look more closely. In that hard surface is a small crack. Over many years, mechanical and chemical weathering will slowly enlarge the crack. Rain and wind will bring bits of weathered rock, dust, and dry leaves. The wind also may carry tiny seeds. With enough moisture, a seed will sprout and take root. Then, when the plant blossoms a few months later, the rock itself will seem to have burst into flower.

GUIDE FOR READING

- How does soil form?
- What is soil made of?
- What is the role of plants and animals in soil formation?

Reading Tip Before you read, rewrite the headings as *how, what, where,* and *why* questions. Then look for answers as you read.

Soil Formation

The crack in the rock seems to have little in common with a flower garden containing thick, rich soil. But soil is what the weathered rock and other materials in the crack have started to become. **Soil** is the loose, weathered material on Earth's surface in which plants can grow. **Soil forms as rock is broken down by weathering and mixes with other materials on the surface.**

Soil is constantly being formed wherever bedrock is exposed. **Bedrock** is the solid layer of rock beneath the soil. Once exposed at the surface, bedrock gradually weathers into smaller and smaller particles that are the basic material of soil.

Figure 4 A crack between rocks holds just enough soil for this plant.

READING STRATEGIES

Reading Tip Possible questions might include, "How does soil form? What is the composition of soil? What determines soil texture?" After students read the section, suggest they trade questions with a classmate and test their reading comprehension by answering each other's questions.

Program Resources

- **Unit 2 Resources** 4-2 Lesson Plan; 4-2 Section Summary
- **Guided Reading and Study Workbook** Section 4-2

Section 2 Soil Formation and Composition

Objectives

After completing the lesson, students will be able to

- describe the composition of soil;
- explain how soil is formed and how soil horizons develop;
- identify the roles of plants and animals in soil formation.

Key Terms soil, bedrock, humus, loam, soil horizon, topsoil, subsoil, litter, decomposer

1 Engage/Explore

Activating Prior Knowledge

Ask students: **How would you describe the soil of this area in terms of color, feel, and makeup?** *(Answers will vary, depending on the local soil type. Students should mention whether the local soil is black, brown, or red; sandy or clayey; and so on.)* Then let students examine and feel a commercial potting soil. Challenge students to explain why that soil is different from the local soil.

DISCOVER

Skills Focus forming operational definitions

Materials *soil sample, paper cup, paper towel, toothpick, hand lens*

Time 15 minutes

Tips Provide each student with about 50 mL of soil in a paper cup. You can collect this soil from your local area or buy commercial topsoil. Advise students to pour the sample onto a paper towel for examination.

Expected Outcome Students should observe a variety of different substances in the soil, including rock particles and organic matter. Their recipes should reflect these observations.

Think It Over Answers may vary. A typical answer might suggest that soil is a mixture of different substances, including sand, clay, rock particles, and material derived from living things.

2 Facilitate

Soil Formation

Using the Visuals: Figure 4

To emphasize the connection between weathering and soil formation, have students make a flowchart that shows how bedrock changes to become soil embedded in the crack of a rock. **learning modality: verbal**

Soil Composition

Using the Visuals: Figure 5

After students have examined the circle graph, ask: **How is the large percentage of air and water related to the amount of humus in loam?** *(Humus helps create spaces for air and water.)* **If the percentage of clay greatly increased, say to 35 percent, how would that probably change the percentages of other materials? How would that affect the soil's quality for growth of plants?** *(Increasing the clay percentage would likely increase the water percentage, because clay soils hold water. The percentages of sand, silt, and air would probably, therefore, decrease. More water and less air would make the soil's quality for plant growth poorer.)* **learning modality: logical/mathematical**

Sharpen your Skills

Predicting

Time 5 minutes
Expected Outcome
Answers may vary. A typical answer might suggest that adding compost would change the composition of the soil, increasing its percentage of organic matter and decreasing its percentage of other materials. The addition of compost will help the sandy soil hold more water and air and will make it more fertile.
Extend Ask: **Which soil horizon is the soil most like before the compost is added, and which is it like after compost is added?** *(It is like the B horizon before and the A horizon after.)* **learning modality: logical/mathematical**

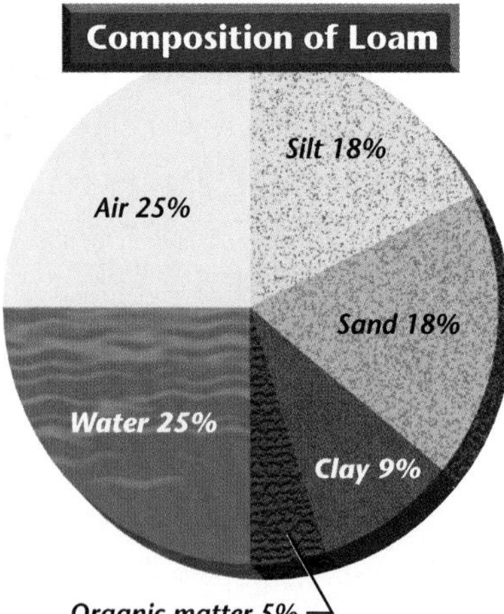

Figure 5 Loam, a type of soil, is made up of air, water, and organic matter as well as materials from weathered rock. The circle graph shows the composition of loam by volume. *Interpreting Graphs What two materials make up the major portion of this soil?*

Soil Composition

Soil is more than just particles of weathered bedrock. **Soil is a mixture of rock particles, minerals, decayed organic material, air, and water.**

The type of rock particles and minerals in any given soil depends on two factors: the bedrock that was weathered to form the soil and the type of weathering. Together, sand, silt, and clay make up the portion of soil that comes from weathered rock.

The decayed organic material in soil is humus. **Humus** (HYOO mus) is a dark-colored substance that forms as plant and animal remains decay. Humus helps create spaces in soil for the air and water that plants must have. Humus is also rich in the nitrogen, sulfur, phosphorus, and potassium that plants need to grow.

Soil Texture

Sand feels coarse and grainy, but clay feels smooth and silky. These differences are differences in texture. Soil texture depends on the size of individual soil particles.

The particles of rock in soil are classified by size. As you can see in Figure 6, the largest soil particles are gravel. Small pebbles and even large boulders are considered gravel. Next in size are particles of sand, followed by silt particles, which are smaller than sand. The smallest soil particles are clay. Clay particles are smaller than the period at the end of this sentence.

Soil texture is important for plant growth. Soil that is mostly clay has a dense, heavy texture. Some clay soils hold a lot of water, so plants grown in them may "drown" for lack of air. In contrast, sandy soil has a coarse texture. Water quickly drains through it, so plants may die for lack of water.

Soil that is made up of about equal parts of clay, sand, and silt is called **loam.** It has a crumbly texture that holds both air and water. Loam is best for growing most types of plants.

Figure 6 Soil particles range in size from gravel to clay particles too small to be seen by the unaided eye. The sand, silt, and clay shown here have been enlarged.

Background

Facts and Figures The air in soil is important not only for plants but also for the microorganisms and animals in the soil. Without the air, the plants and other living things would not have the oxygen and carbon dioxide they need to carry out their life processes. The problem with too much water in soil is not the water itself but the resulting lack of air for the soil organisms.

Soil color is another characteristic scientists use to classify soils. A black or brown color usually indicates a high level of humus. A red or yellow color usually indicates the presence of iron compounds. A light gray or white color means different things depending on the climate. In wetter climates, it means the soil is low in iron; in drier areas, it means the soil is high in salts.

Soil Horizons

Soil formation continues over a long period of time. Gradually, soil develops layers called horizons. A **soil horizon** is a layer of soil that differs in color and texture from the layers above or below it.

If you dug a hole in the ground about half a meter deep, you would see the different soil horizons. Figure 7 shows how soil scientists classify the soil into three horizons. The A horizon is made up of **topsoil,** a crumbly, dark brown soil that is a mixture of humus, clay, and other minerals. The B horizon, often called **subsoil,** usually consists of clay and other particles washed down from the A horizon, but little humus. The C horizon contains only partly weathered rock.

☑ *Checkpoint* *What are soil horizons?*

The Rate of Soil Formation

The rate at which soil forms depends on the climate and type of rock. Remember that weathering occurs most rapidly in areas with a warm, rainy climate. As a result, soil develops more quickly in these areas. In contrast, weathering and soil formation take place slowly in areas where the climate is cold and dry.

Some types of rock weather and form soil faster than others. For example, limestone weathers faster than granite. Thus, soil forms more quickly from limestone than from granite.

Sharpen your Skills

Predicting ACTIVITY

Gardeners often improve soil by adding materials to it. These added materials change the soil's composition. They make the soil more fertile or improve its ability to hold water. For example, a gardener might add compost (partly decayed leaves) to sandy soil. How would the compost change the sandy soil?

Figure 7 Soil horizons form in three steps.

1. The C horizon forms as bedrock weathers and rock breaks up into soil particles.

C horizon

Bedrock

2. The A horizon develops from the C horizon when plant roots weather the rock mechanically and chemically. Plants also add organic material to the soil.

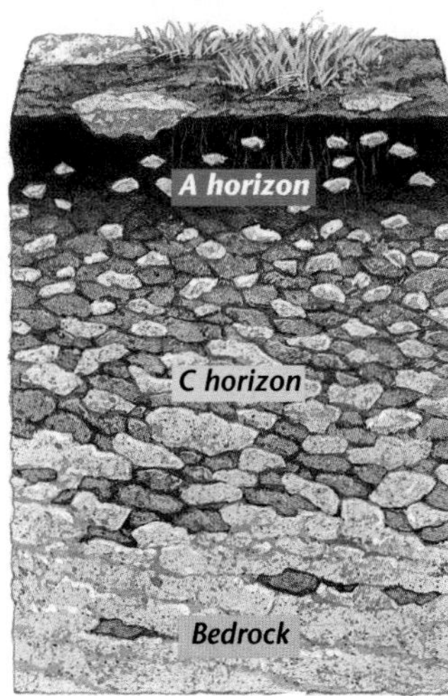

3. The B horizon develops as rainwater washes clay and minerals from the A horizon to the B horizon.

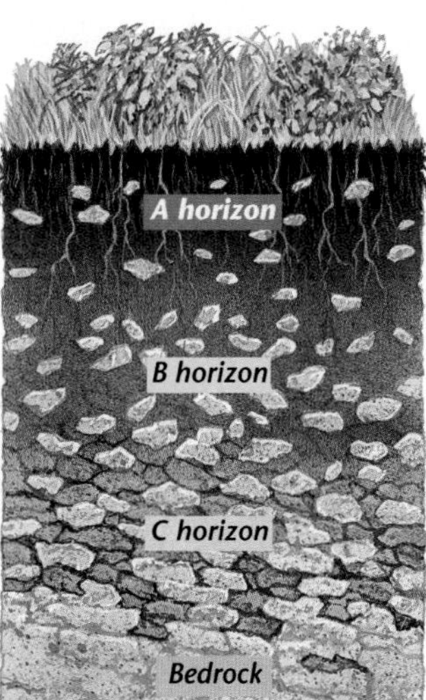

Media and Technology

Transparencies "Soil Composition and Soil Horizons," Transparency 8

Answers to Self-Assessment

Caption Question

Figure 5 Air and water make up the major portion of loam.

☑ *Checkpoint*

A soil horizon is a layer of soil that differs in color and texture from the layers above or below it.

Soil Texture

Building Inquiry Skills: Comparing and Contrasting

ACTIVITY

Materials *hand lens, toothpick, white paper, samples of soil with different textures, including loam, sandy soil, clay soil, silty soil*

Time 15 minutes

Obtain commercially classified soil samples. Then have pairs of students examine a sample of each. Encourage students to separate the gravel, sand, silt, clay, and humus in each sample and estimate the proportions. **learning modality: kinesthetic**

Soil Horizons

Using the Visuals: Figure 7

ACTIVITY

Materials *soil samples from different levels of a roadcut, white paper, toothpick, hand lens*

Time 15 minutes

Collect soil samples from different levels of a local roadcut or similar vertical exposure of soil horizons. Then have small groups of students compare and contrast samples from each level, identifying the sample that most likely is from the A horizon, B horizon, and C horizon. **learning modality: visual**

The Rate of Soil Formation

Including All Students

To support students who need more help in making a connection between weathering and soil formation, ask: **What factors determine the rate of weathering?** *(Type of rock and climate)* **What factors determine the rate of soil formation?** *(Type of rock and climate)* Emphasize that weathering and soil formation are essentially parts of the same process, determined by the same factors. **learning modality: verbal**

Ongoing Assessment

Drawing Have students make a drawing of the A, B, and C horizons, writing a brief description of each.

EXPLORING

Living Organisms in Soil

Give students a few minutes to examine the feature. Then elicit their experiences in observing these organisms. Ask: **What do decomposers make in soil as they break down plant and animal remains?** *(humus)* Emphasize that without humus in soil, most plants could not grow. **learning modality: verbal**

Integrating Life Science

ACTIVITY

Materials *plastic bag, soil sample, petri dish with agar and cover, incubator*
Time 5 minutes for setup; 5 minutes the next day for observation

To demonstrate the presence of bacteria in soil, place a soil sample in a plastic bag. Then, as students watch, sprinkle a tiny amount of the soil on nutrient agar in a petri dish. Cover the dish and incubate for 24 hours. Have students observe the results. They should see colonies of bacteria growing on the surface of the nutrient. (Follow the guidelines for disposing of bacteria cultures in Appendix A, Teacher's Edition. Make sure you follow all local and state guidelines for disposing of such cultures.) **learning modality: visual**

Including All Students

ACTIVITY

Materials *earthworms, large plastic container, plastic trash bag, shredded newspapers, fallen leaves*
Time 30 minutes

Encourage students who need additional challenges to find out how to build a worm compost bin in which plant materials can be added to make fertile soil for gardens. A typical bin is simply a large container with drainage holes in the bottom. To prepare the bin for worms, fill it halfway with strips of newspaper and fallen leaves. Then add worms and cover the container with plastic. The worms will digest most food scraps except meat and dairy products. **learning modality: kinesthetic**

Life in Soil

INTEGRATING LIFE SCIENCE

Soil is more than just bits of rock. If you look closely at some soil, you can see that it is teeming with living things. **Some soil organisms mix the soil and make spaces in it for air and water. Other soil organisms make humus, the material that makes soil fertile.** Fertile soil is rich in nutrients that plants need, such as nitrogen and phosphorus.

Plants contribute most of the organic remains that form humus. As plants shed leaves, they form a loose layer called **litter.**

EXPLORING Living Organisms in Soil

In every cubic meter of soil live billions of organisms. All organisms that live in soil enrich humus with their remains or wastes. Animals and plant roots break up the soil, opening spaces for air and water.

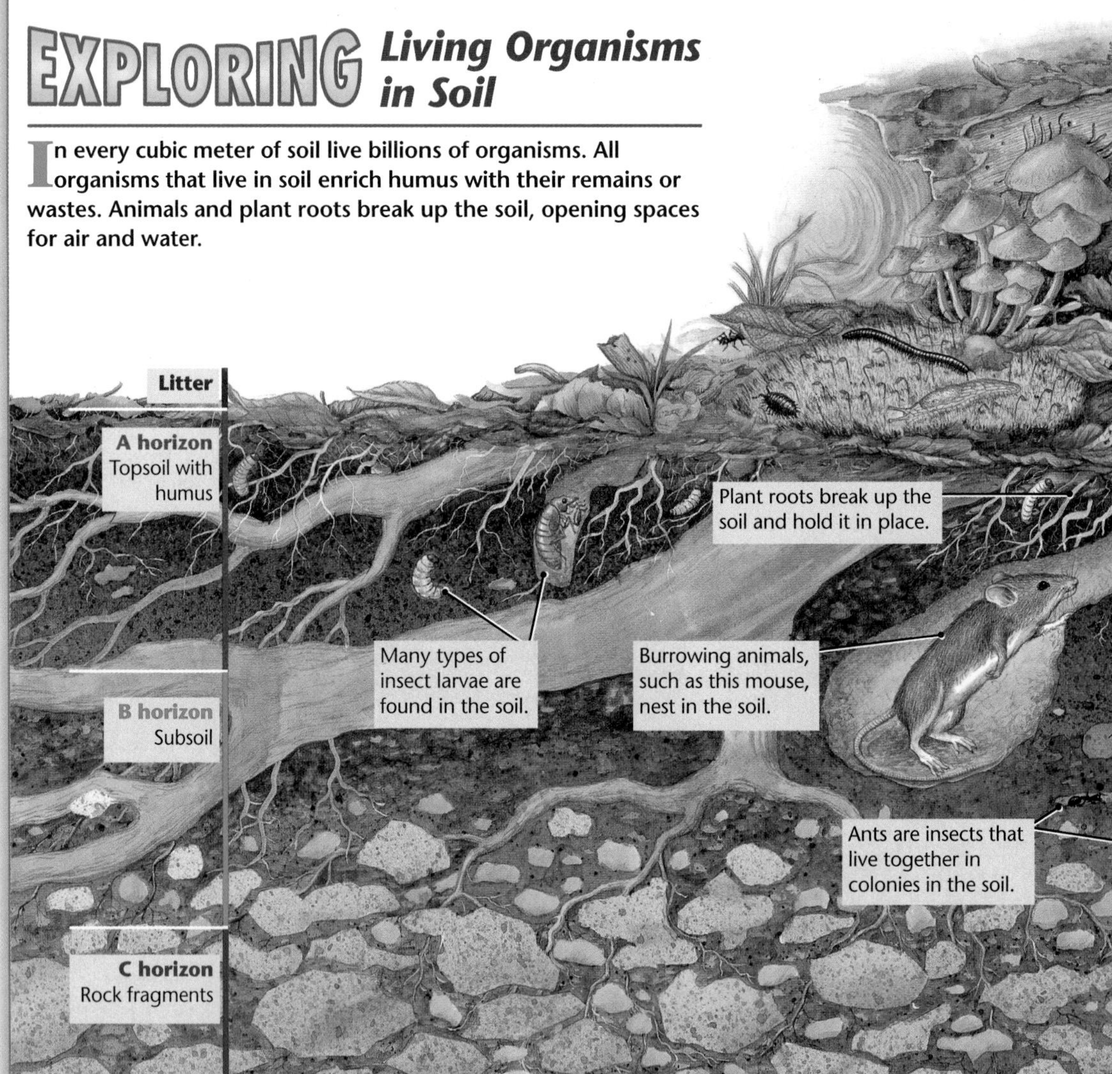

Background

History of Science In the 1940s at Rutgers University, microbiologist Selman Waksman began searching for soil organisms that produced chemicals that killed bacteria. He discovered a moldlike type of bacteria in the genus *Streptomyces* that was very effective. From that bacteria, the medicine streptomycin was made. It was Waksman who coined the term *antibiotic.* Further research discovered other soil microorganisms from which antibiotics were derived, including the tetracyclines.

Integrating Science Fresh soil owes its distinctive smell in part to chemicals produced by *Streptomyces* bacteria. Commercial potting soil does not have this smell because it has been sterilized. Once plants are added to the soil, the "fresh" smell becomes evident because bacteria arrives on plant roots.

When plants die, their remains fall to the ground and become part of the litter. Plant roots also die and begin to decay underground. Although plant remains are full of stored nutrients, they are not yet humus.

Humus forms in a process called decomposition. As decomposition occurs, organisms that live in soil turn dead organic material into humus. These organisms are called decomposers. **Decomposers** are the organisms that break the remains of dead organisms into smaller pieces and digest them with chemicals.

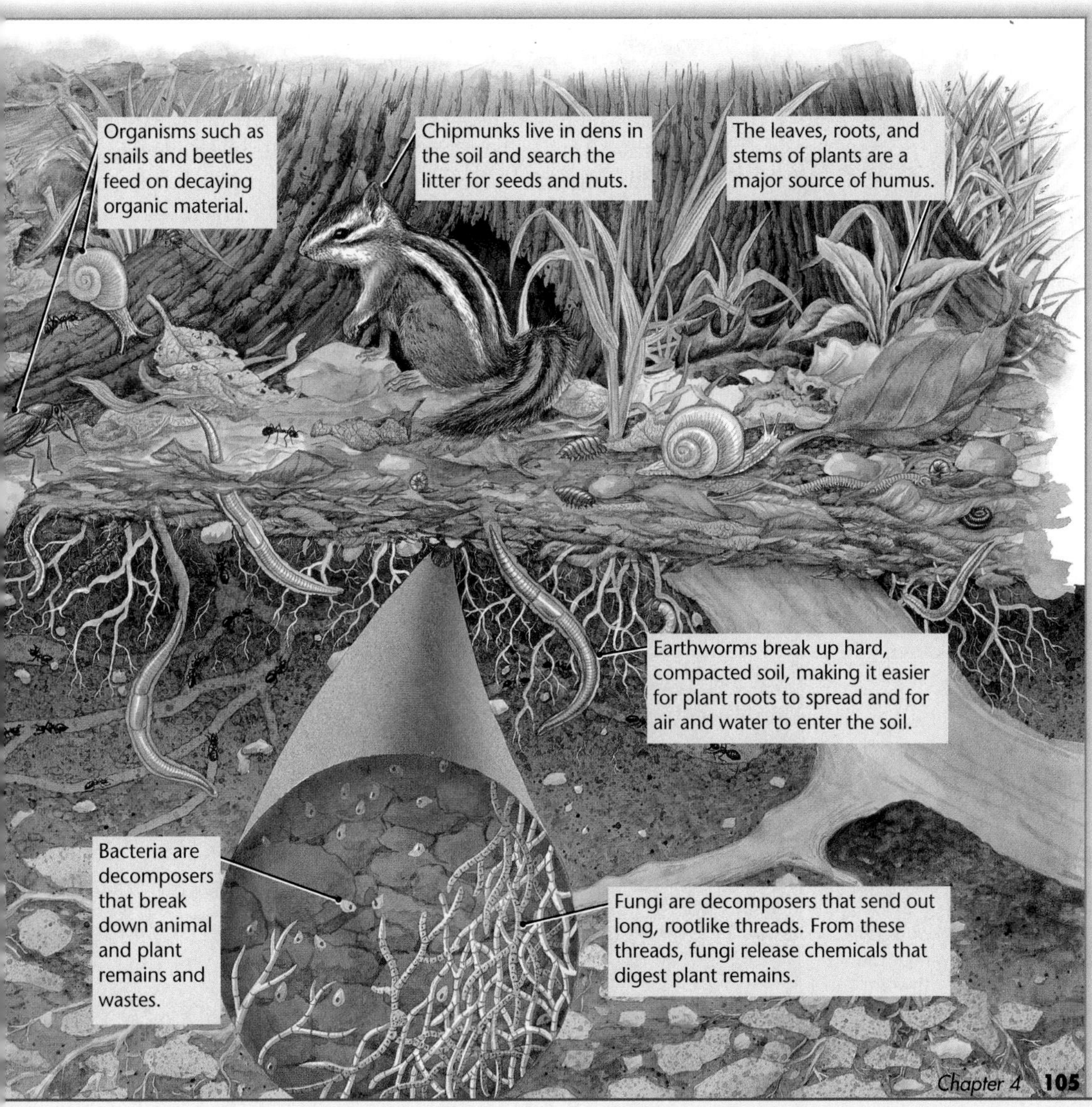

Organisms such as snails and beetles feed on decaying organic material.

Chipmunks live in dens in the soil and search the litter for seeds and nuts.

The leaves, roots, and stems of plants are a major source of humus.

Earthworms break up hard, compacted soil, making it easier for plant roots to spread and for air and water to enter the soil.

Bacteria are decomposers that break down animal and plant remains and wastes.

Fungi are decomposers that send out long, rootlike threads. From these threads, fungi release chemicals that digest plant remains.

Media and Technology

Transparencies "Exploring Living Organisms in Soil," Transparency 9

Concept Videotape Library Grade 6, Tape 1 "Ancient Farmers"; "Cycles in Nature"

Building Inquiry Skills: Calculating

Materials *soil sample, 2 measuring cups, trowel, water*
Time 15 minutes

Point out that many of the living things in soil need oxygen from air to carry out their life processes. Then challenge small groups of students to determine the amount of air in a soil sample by adding a measured volume of soil to a measuring cup and then pouring an equal volume of water into the cup. The water will fill the air spaces in the soil, and as a result, the amount of soil and water in the cup will be less than the two volumes added together. Students can find the volume of air in the original volume of soil by subtracting the final volume in the cup from the sum of the original volumes of soil and water. **learning modality: logical/mathematical**

Inquiry Challenge

ACTIVITY

Divide the class into small groups, and have each group develop a hypothesis about how well plants will grow in soil that contains no living organisms. After groups have written a hypothesis, challenge them to design an experiment that can test their hypothesis. A typical experiment might involve eliminating living things from a soil sample by removing worms and other animals and using a microwave oven to kill fungi and bacteria. (You might need to suggest this part of the procedure to students.) Then seeds can be planted in the sterile soil. Growth of these plants can be compared with a control—plants growing in normal soil. Have students discuss their groups' designs, modify them as needed, and then carry out their revised designs. **cooperative learning**

Ongoing Assessment

Oral Presentation Call on students at random to explain how each different kind of soil organism contributes to soil formation.

Skills Focus drawing conclusions

Materials *metric ruler, string, stakes, trowel, hand lens*

Time 30 minutes

Tips Students can carry out this investigation on the school grounds or on a private, vacant lot. For either option, permission should be obtained in advance. Choose areas that are not completely sod-covered, and advise students not to remove plants from their sites. Encourage students to keep notes of their observations as they go along. To help students observe the materials in the soil, give each student a piece of white table paper on which they can spread out their diggings. The light background will make it easier for students to observe the makeup of the soil.

Expected Outcome Students should find a variety of materials in their square area, including rocks, sand, silt, clay, insects, worms, plants, and even human-made objects. Students can draw conclusions about the soil's fertility based on its composition, particularly the amount of humus in it, and on the kinds of plants growing in the area.

Extend Encourage interested students to examine a second plot of ground in a very different location. For example, if the first was in a field, the second might be in a forest or along a stream. Students can compare and contrast what they observe in the two different places. **learning modality: kinesthetic**

Soil Types in the United States

Real-Life Learning

Obtain a soil profile of the local soil. Your public library may have soil profiles of your county. If not, contact either a federal farm agency or an office of the state department of natural resources or agriculture in your area. Give small groups copies of the profile, and challenge them to interpret its information. Then review their findings in a whole-class discussion. **learning modality: verbal**

A Square Meter of Soil

1. Outdoors, measure an area of one square meter. Mark your square with string.
2. Observe the color and texture of the surface soil. Is it dry or moist? Does it contain sand, clay, or gravel? Are there plants, animals, or humus?
3. Use a trowel to dig down several centimeters into the soil. What is the soil's color and texture there?
4. When you finish, leave the soil as you found it. Wash your hands.

Drawing Conclusions What can you conclude about the soil's fertility? What evidence supports your conclusions?

Fungi, protists, bacteria, and worms are the main soil decomposers. Fungi are organisms such as molds and mushrooms. Fungi grow on, and digest, plant remains. Bacteria are microscopic decomposers that cause decay. Bacteria attack dead organisms and their wastes in soil. Other very small animals, such as mites and worms, also decompose dead organic material and mix it with the soil.

Earthworms do most of the work of mixing humus with other materials in soil. As earthworms eat their way through soil, they carry humus down to the subsoil and subsoil up to the surface. Earthworms also pass out the soil they eat as waste. The waste soil is enriched with substances that plants need to grow, such as nitrogen.

Many burrowing mammals such as mice, moles, prairie dogs, and gophers break up hard, compacted soil and mix humus through it. These animals also add nitrogen to the soil when they excrete waste. They add organic material when they die and decay.

Earthworms and burrowing animals also help to aerate, or mix air into, the soil. Plant roots need the oxygen that this process adds to the soil.

✓ ***Checkpoint*** *How do decomposers contribute to the formation of soil?*

Soil Types in the United States

If you were traveling across the hills of north-central Georgia, you would see soils that seem to be made of red clay. In other parts of the country, soils can be black, brown, yellow, or gray. In the United States alone, differences in climate and local bedrock have led to the formation of thousands of different types of soil.

Figure 8 Earthworms break up the soil, allowing in air and water. An earthworm eats its own weight in soil every day.

Background

Integrating Science The amount of living organic matter in soil varies greatly. In typical topsoil found in the eastern United States, living organisms make up about 0.2 percent of the top 15 cm of soil. In 1 hectare (which is over twice the size of an acre), there are about 2,000 kg of living roots, about 700 kg of animals (mostly worms), about 500 kg of bacteria, and about 400 kg of fungi.

Facts and Figures In classifying soils, scientists consider the physical and chemical properties of the soil, much as geologists consider similar properties in classifying rocks. Climate is also a major factor in classification because it is so important in soil formation. Among other things, climate determines temperature, precipitation, vegetation, and kind and amount of soil organisms.

Soils of North America

Tundra soils	Form where it is cold year-round; thin soil with little humus.
Northern forest soils	Form in cool, wet climates; range from thick and fertile to thin with little humus.
Prairie soils	Form in cool, dry climates of grasslands; topsoil thick and rich in humus.
Mountain soils	Topsoil often thin because cold temperatures slow chemical weathering and erosion causes soil loss.
Southern forest soils	Form in warm, wet climates; may be low in humus.
Desert soils	Form in dry areas with few plants and little chemical weathering; often sandy, thin soil that is low in humus.
Tropical soils	Form in wet, tropical climates; often low in humus and minerals.

Figure 9 An area's climate and plant life help to determine what type of soil forms from bedrock. ***Interpreting Maps*** *Recall that soil forms more rapidly in warm, wet areas than in cold, dry areas. Which types of soil on the map would you expect to form most slowly?*

Scientists classify the different types of soil into groups. These groups are based partly on the climate in a region. The most common plants found in a region are also used to help classify the soil. In addition, scientists classify soil by its composition—whether it is rocky, sandy, or rich in clay. Major soil types found in North America include forest, prairie, desert, mountain, tundra, and tropical soils. Look at Figure 9 to see where each of the major soil types is found. Which soil type is found in your part of the country?

Section 2 Review

1. What role does weathering play in the formation of soil?
2. What are the different materials that make up soil?
3. How do plants and animals affect the formation and composition of soil?
4. How do forest soils differ from prairie soils?
5. **Thinking Critically Relating Cause and Effect** Earthworms breathe by absorbing air in the soil through their skin. Why do you think earthworms crawl to the surface when it rains? Explain.

CHAPTER PROJECT

Check Your Progress

Obtain samples of the soil and growing materials you will use to grow your bean seeds. Choices include sand, vermiculite, gravel, potting soil, and local topsoil. **CAUTION:** *Avoid collecting soil near animal droppings. Wash your hands after handling the soil.* Make notes describing each sample. Predict which soil or mixture will be best for the growth of bean seeds. Design a method for recording the growth of your bean plants. Plant the bean seeds in the growing materials.

Program Resources

- **Unit 2 Resources** 4-2 Review and Reinforce; 4-2 Enrich

Media and Technology

Transparencies "Soils of North America," Transparency 10

Answers to Self-Assessment

Caption Question

Figure 9 Tundra soils and desert soils would probably form most slowly.

Checkpoint

Decomposers turn dead organic material into humus.

Using the Visuals: Figure 9

Ask students: **What are the two main variables that determine a region's climate?** *(Average temperature and average rainfall)* Then guide students to understand that those variables also determine the common plants as well as the kind and rate of weathering of the bedrock of the region. Since soil is a mixture of rock and organic materials, climate greatly determines soil type. **learning modality: verbal**

3 Assess

Section 2 Review Answers

1. Soil forms as rock is broken down by weathering and mixes with other materials on the surface.
2. Rock particles, minerals, decayed organic material, air, and water
3. Some soil organisms mix the soil and make spaces in it for air and water. Other soil organisms make humus, the material that makes soil fertile.
4. Prairie soils have topsoil that is thick and rich in humus, while northern and southern forest soils may be low in humus.
5. When the soil becomes full of water, there are no spaces for air in the soil. Worms must crawl to the surface to find air.

CHAPTER PROJECT

Check Your Progress

Make sure groups have chosen the soils they will use and planted the bean seeds. Each student should write a description of each soil and make a prediction about which soil will prove best for plant growth. Demonstrate how to plant the seeds in soil. Provide places for groups to place their growing plants.

Performance Assessment

Writing Challenge students to design and write a two-page pamphlet, such as a local park might hand out, that explains the formation and composition of the local soil. This pamphlet should be complete with drawings of soil horizons and any other relevant visual aids.

Real-World Lab

Careers in Science

Getting to Know the Soil

Preparing for Inquiry

Key Concept Scientists classify soil by its composition.

Skills Objectives Students will be able to:
- observe a soil sample to determine its composition;
- infer the type of environment from which the soil came;
- pose questions to help determine the soil's fertility.

Time 40 minutes

Advance Planning Collect soil at least a day in advance, and make sure the soil is relatively dry. Use a balance to prepare individual samples of 20–30 grams each.

Guiding Inquiry

Introducing the Procedure

Ask students: **What materials do you expect to find in a soil sample?** *(Rock fragments, sand, silt, clay, organic material)* **How do you predict that each of these materials will be affected by water?** *(The rocks and sand will look wet; the silt and clay will cloud the water; organic material will probably float.)*

Troubleshooting the Experiment

- Students can observe both the wet and dry soil under the stereomicroscope. Advise students to leave the wet soil in the petri dish.

Expected Outcome

Specific outcomes will depend on the composition of the soil samples used. All students should be able to observe various characteristics of their sample.

Real-World Lab

Careers in Science

Getting to Know the Soil

Soil scientists observe soil to determine its composition and how well it holds water. Farmers use this information in growing their crops.

Problem

What are the characteristics of a sample of soil?

Skills Focus

observing, inferring, posing questions

Materials

20–30 grams of soil
plastic spoon
plastic dropper
toothpick
water
stereomicroscope
graph paper ruled with 1- or 2-mm spacing
plastic petri dish or jar lid

Procedure 

1. Your teacher will give you a dry sample of soil. As you observe the sample, record your observations in your lab notebook.
2. Spread half of the sample on the graph paper. Spread the soil thinly so that you can see the lines on the paper through the soil. Using graph paper as a background, estimate the sizes of the particles that make up the soil.
3. Place the rest of the sample in the palm of your hand, rub it between your fingers, and squeeze it. Is it soft or gritty? Does it clump together or crumble when you squeeze it?
4. Place about half the sample in a plastic petri dish. Using the dropper, add water one drop at a time. Watch how the sample changes. Does any material in the sample float? As the sample gets wet, do you notice any odor?
5. Look at some of the soil under the stereomicroscope. (*Hint:* Use the toothpick to examine the particles in the soil.) Sketch what you see. Label the particles, such as gravel, organic matter, or strangely shaped grains.
6. Clean up and dispose of your soil sample as directed by your teacher. **CAUTION:** *Wash your hands when you finish handling the soil.*

Analyze and Conclude

1. What did you notice about the appearance of the soil sample when you first obtained it?
2. What can you infer about the composition of the soil from the different sizes of its particles? From your observations of its texture? From how the sample changed when water was added? What surprised you the most about the composition of your sample?
3. Based on the composition of your soil sample, can you determine the type of environment from which it was taken?
4. **Apply** List several questions that a soil scientist would need to answer to determine whether a soil sample was good for growing flowers or vegetables. Did your observations answer these questions for your soil sample?

More to Explore

Repeat the procedure using a soil sample from a different location. How does it compare with the first soil sample you tested?

108

Analyze and Conclude

1. Students should notice various characteristics, including color and texture.
2. From observations of particle size, texture, and how water changed the sample, students should be able to estimate what proportions of the sample are sand, clay, silt, and organic material. Students may be most surprised by the kinds of organic material in the sample.
3. Answers will vary. Students should support their inferences with evidence from their observations.
4. Questions will vary. *Sample questions:* What percentage of the soil is composed of humus? What is the texture of the soil?

Extending the Inquiry

More to Explore Have soil samples from different locations available. They should find that samples from different locations have different characteristics.

Program Resources

- **Unit 2 Resources** Chapter 4 Real-World Lab

Safety

Caution students to wear their goggles when handling the soil sample and to wash their hands thoroughly when finished. Review the safety guidelines in Appendix A.

Conserving Land and Soil

DISCOVER ACTIVITY

How Can You Keep Soil From Washing Away?

1. Pour about 500 mL of soil into a pie plate, forming a pile.
2. Devise a way to keep the soil from washing away when water is poured over it. To protect the pile of soil, you may use craft sticks, paper clips, pebbles, modeling clay, strips of paper, or other materials approved by your teacher.
3. After arranging your materials to protect the soil, hold a container containing 200 mL of water about 20 cm above the center of the soil. Slowly pour the water in a stream onto the pile of soil.
4. Compare your pan of soil with those of your classmates.

Think It Over

Observing Based on your observations, what do you think is the best way to prevent soil on a slope from washing away?

GUIDE FOR READING

- How do people use land?
- Why is soil one of Earth's most valuable resources?
- What are some ways that soil can be conserved?

Reading Tip As you read, make a list of activities that can harm the soil and a list of activities that can help save the soil.

Less than a quarter of Earth's surface is dry land. Except for the small amount added when volcanoes erupt, new land cannot be created. All the people on Earth must share this limited amount of land to produce their food, build shelter, and obtain other resources. Land is a precious resource. As the American author Mark Twain once said about land, "They don't make it anymore."

Types of Land Use

People use land in many ways. **Three uses that change the land are agriculture, development, and mining.** There are many other types of land use. Figure 10 shows what percentage of land in the United States is devoted to several major land uses.

Agriculture Since land is the source of most food, agriculture is an important land use. Crops such as wheat require large areas of fertile land. New farmland must be created by clearing forests, draining wetlands, and irrigating deserts. Other land serves as pasture or rangeland for grazing animals.

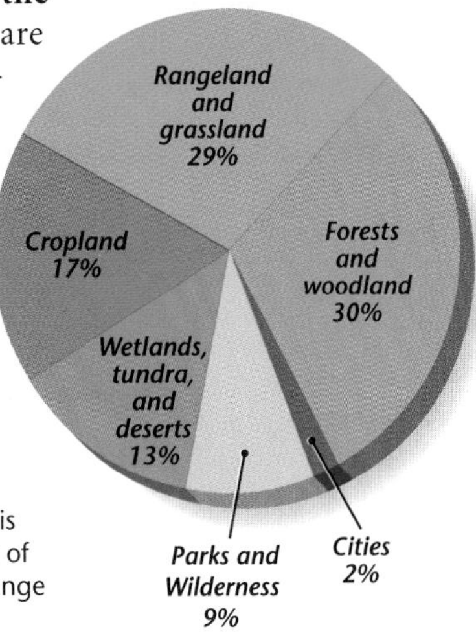

Figure 10 Land in the United States is used in many ways. *Classifying* Which of these land uses cause the greatest change in the land's natural appearance?

READING STRATEGIES

Reading Tip Harmful activities mentioned in the section include exhausting the soil and poor farming practices, including overgrazing. Beneficial activities include contour plowing and conservation plowing. Encourage students to add to their lists any practices that arise during class discussions or as a result of activities and research they do about soil conservation.

Program Resources

- **Unit 2 Resources** 4-3 Lesson Plan; 4-3 Section Summary

Answers to Self-Assessment

Caption Question

Figure 10 The development of cities causes the greatest change in the land's natural appearance.

Section 3 Conserving Land and Soil

Objectives

After completing the lesson, students will be able to

- describe some major forms of land use;
- explain why soil is a valuable resource;
- list ways that soil can be lost or destroyed;
- identify some ways that soil can be conserved.

Key Terms development, desertification, sod, Dust Bowl, soil conservation, contour plowing, fallow, crop rotation, land reclamation

1 Engage/Explore

Activating Prior Knowledge

Recall for students a place in town that is a wide area of dirt, such as a construction site or a vacant lot used for parking. Ask: **What happens when it rains?** *(The area becomes a sea of mud.)* **What is the water like that runs off the area?** *(It is dirty, full of mud.)* **Is there anything that could be done to prevent this erosion of soil?** *(Answers will vary. Some students might suggest barriers. Others might suggest planting grass or some other ground cover.)*

DISCOVER ACTIVITY

Focus observing

Materials *soil, pie plate, water, container, craft sticks, paper clips, pebbles, modeling clay, paper*

Time 15 minutes

Tips Provide students with soil in measured amounts, or prepare each pie plate with 500 mL of soil before class. Encourage students to be creative in their arrangements.

Expected Outcome Students should discover a variety of ways to prevent the soil from washing away.

Think It Over Answers may vary. A typical answer might suggest that a barrier of clay or clay mixed with other materials best prevents soil from washing away.

2 Facilitate

Types of Land Use

Using the Visuals: Figures 10 and 11

After students have examined the photographs in Figure 11, have them identify the type of land use shown in each photograph. *(from left to right: agriculture, development, and mining)* Ask: **Which of the land uses pictured is not represented in the circle graph in Figure 10?** *(mining)* **Why do you think it is not represented?** *(The percentage of land in the United States used for mining is likely less than 1 percent, too small to be represented on the circle graph.)* **Of the other two land uses pictured in the photographs, which accounts for a greater percentage of land in the United States? Explain your answer.** *(Agriculture accounts for a greater percentage than development. Agriculture, which is represented as cropland and rangeland in the graph, accounts for 17 percent and 29 percent of land use. Development, which is represented as cities, accounts for only 2 percent.)* Ask students to hypothesize about why agriculture uses a significantly greater percentage of land than development does. **learning modality: logical/mathematical**

Social Studies CONNECTION

Display a large map of your town or region. Have students locate areas of dense economic development and major landmarks in the area such as airports, railroads, highways, and ports. Have students examine the location of this development relative to local topographical features such as mountains, plains, and large bodies of water and hypothesize why this development occurred where it did.

In Your Journal Provide physical or topographic maps, atlases, historical descriptions, or Web links for students to use as starting points for their research. Also consider having students research and present their ideas about a current local development issue.

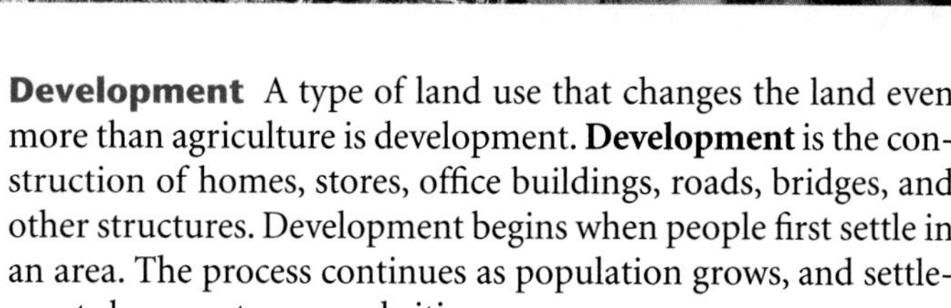

Figure 11 Agriculture, mining, and development are land uses that affect the soil.

Social Studies CONNECTION

The economic development of an area is influenced by many factors, including the topography, climate, and natural and human resources of that area. For example, historically many cities grew because of their proximity to ocean harbors or rivers. In the mid to late 1800s, the discovery of gold and other precious metals caused many towns to be built almost overnight, only to become "ghost towns" almost as quickly when the local mines were tapped out.

In Your Journal

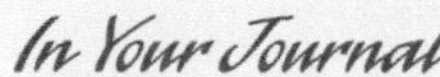

Use library or Internet resources to find out which factors have played an important role in the economic development of a city near where you live. Then write a journal entry explaining how these factors influenced local development and whether they are still as important now as they were in the past.

Development A type of land use that changes the land even more than agriculture is development. **Development** is the construction of homes, stores, office buildings, roads, bridges, and other structures. Development begins when people first settle in an area. The process continues as population grows, and settlements become towns and cities.

In the United States, about a million hectares of farmland (an area half the size of New Jersey) are developed each year. Development not only reduces the amount of farmland, but can also destroy wildlife habitats.

Mining Mining changes the land as mineral resources such as iron, copper, and coal are removed. There are three main kinds of mining: strip mining, underground mining, and open-pit mining. Once land has been mined, it is often difficult to use the land for another purpose.

Checkpoint What are three main kinds of land use?

The Value of Soil

Soil is one of Earth's most valuable resources because everything that lives on land depends directly or indirectly on soil. Plants depend directly on the soil to live and grow. Animals depend on plants—or on other animals that depend on plants—for food. Soil is a renewable resource that can be found wherever weathering occurs. But soil formation takes a long time. It can take hundreds of years for just a few centimeters of soil to form. The thick, fertile soil may take thousands of years to develop.

Fertile soil is valuable because there is a limited supply. Less than one eighth of the land on Earth has soils that are well suited for farming. In many areas, farming is difficult and little food is produced. The reasons for this include low soil fertility, lack of water, steep slopes, or a short growing season.

Background

History of Science George Washington Carver was born a slave in Missouri at the end of the Civil War, shortly before slavery was abolished. An orphan, Carver was raised by a family that provided for his education. He ultimately received degrees from Iowa State Agricultural College, along with many awards and honors for his work.

Carver spent most of his adult life as director of the Department of Agricultural Research at the Tuskegee Institute in Tuskegee, Alabama. He helped the South enormously by showing farmers how to enrich soil that was infertile due to growing only cotton and tobacco. To accomplish this, Carver used muck from swamps and composted organic matter. He also advised the planting of peanuts and sweet potatoes, crops that enrich the soil.

Soil Damage and Loss

Soil is one of Earth's most important resources. But soil can be lost or damaged. For example, soil can become exhausted, or lose its fertility. This occurred in large parts of the South in the late 1800s. Soils in which only cotton had been grown were exhausted. Many farmers abandoned their farms. Early in the 1900s in Alabama, a scientist named George Washington Carver developed new crops and farming methods that helped to restore soil fertility in the South. Peanuts were one crop that helped make the soil fertile again.

Soil may be polluted by human activities such as mining or chemical spills. It can be lost to erosion by water and wind. Water erosion can also occur wherever soil is not protected by plant cover. Plants break the force of falling rain, and plant roots hold the soil together. Wind erosion is another cause of soil loss.

In parts of the world that receive little rain, desertification is an important cause of soil loss. **Desertification** is the advance of desertlike conditions into areas that previously were fertile. In the past 50 years, desertification has occurred on about five billion hectares of land. Figure 13 shows regions where desertification is a threat.

One cause of desertification is climate. During periods of drought, crops fail. Without plant cover, the exposed soil easily blows away. The overgrazing of grasslands by cattle and sheep or the cutting down of trees for firewood can also cause desertification.

Desertification is a very serious problem. People cannot grow crops and graze livestock where desertification has occurred. Parts of the United States were severely affected by desertification during the 1930s. Wind erosion and farming methods not suited to dry conditions created a "Dust Bowl" on the Great Plains.

Figure 12 George Washington Carver (1864–1943) taught new methods of soil conservation to farmers in the South.

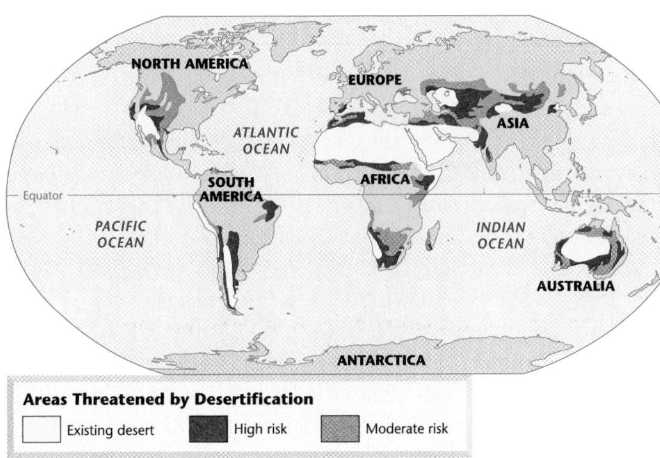

Figure 13 Large areas of the world are at risk of desertification. One cause is overgrazing. Without grass to hold the soil in place, the Senegal plain is becoming a barren desert. *Interpreting Maps Which continents are most threatened by desertification?*

The Value of Soil

Real-Life Learning

Have student volunteers call several local garden stores and greenhouses to find out how much it would cost to have a truckload of topsoil delivered to a site near the school. Suggest that they price enough to cover a garden of 10 m^2 at a thickness of about 10 cm. Have these students report their findings to the class. **learning modality: verbal**

Soil Damage and Loss

Inquiry Challenge

Materials *soil, sod, water, 2 painter's pans*
Time 20 minutes

Ask: **How can plants help reduce loss of soil?** Challenge small groups to form a hypothesis that addresses that question and then design an experiment that can test their hypothesis. A typical experiment might entail comparing the difference in the amount of soil in runoff when water is poured on a slope of bare soil and on a slope of soil covered by sod. Review groups' plans, and then encourage students to carry out their experiments. **cooperative learning**

Using the Visuals: Figure 13

After students have examined the map and key, ask them if they can identify any pattern in the location of areas of high and moderate risk of desertification relative to existing deserts. (Most areas at risk of desertification occur along the borders of existing deserts.) Ask students to hypothesize about why this pattern occurs. *(Possible response: Areas along the borders of existing deserts may already be semi-arid with limited vegetation and thus easily affected by overgrazing and soil erosion.)* **learning modality: visual**

Answers to Self-Assessment

Caption Question

Figure 13 Possible response: Asia and Australia

Checkpoint

The three main kinds of land use are agriculture, development, and mining.

Ongoing Assessment

Writing Have students write a paragraph explaining the causes and effects of desertification.

The Dust Bowl

Using the Visuals: Figure 14

To tie concepts together, have students compare the map in this figure with the map of soil types in Figure 9, as well as the map of landform regions in Figure 3 in Chapter 1. Ask: **In what landform region did the Dust Bowl occur?** *(In the Great Plains landform region)* **What soil types are found in that region?** *(Prairie soils and desert soils)* Point out that there is no exact boundary between the two. Instead, prairie soils gradually become desert soils as you go west. **Why would plowing and drought greatly affect desert soils?** *(They are sandy and thin, with little humus.)* **learning modality: visual**

Language Arts CONNECTION

Woody Guthrie (1912–1967) first became famous as a chronicler of the "Dust Bowl refugees" or "Okies," who fled the devastation of the Dust Bowl for California and other Western states in the 1930s. Many libraries have recordings of his "Dust Bowl Ballads." They include songs of many verses that describe living through dust storms and other hardships. Perhaps the most famous in the collection is "So Long, It's Been Good to Know You." Guthrie's most noted song, "This Land Is Your Land," was written later in his life.

In Your Journal A folk ballad often has four-line verses, with rhymes of the last words of every other line. Encourage students to write two or three verses. Guthrie and other folk balladeers often wrote new words to tunes of popular songs. To give students a structure on which to write their verses, they could write new words to a song they know. **learning modality: verbal**

Figure 14 The Dust Bowl included western Oklahoma and parts of the surrounding states. Wind blew dry particles of soil into great clouds of dust that traveled thousands of kilometers.

Language Arts CONNECTION

Woody Guthrie wrote and sang folk songs. Guthrie lived in Oklahoma and Texas at the time of the Dust Bowl and wrote a series of songs called "Dust Bowl Ballads." (A ballad is a song that tells a story.) One of the ballads describes how

We saw outside our window
Where wheat fields they had grown
Was now a rippling ocean
Of dust the wind had blown.

In Your Journal

Write the words for a ballad that tells the story of a problem in your community and how you think the problem should be solved.

The Dust Bowl

Toward the end of the 1800s, new settlers moved on to the Great Plains. This region sweeps eastward from the base of the Rocky Mountains across the western parts of North and South Dakota, Nebraska, Kansas, Oklahoma, and Texas.

The soil of the Great Plains is fertile. Before the settlers arrived, the soil was covered with short grass that required little moisture. The **sod**—a thick mass of tough roots at the surface of the soil—kept the soil in place and held the moisture. As the settlers plowed the soil to grow crops, the soil was exposed. In times of drought, the topsoil quickly dried out, turned to dust, and blew away.

By 1930, almost all of the Great Plains had been turned into farms or ranches. But after several very dry years in a row, large areas of the soil turned to dust. The wind blew the soil east in great, black clouds. The clouds turned the sky dark as far away as Chicago and even New York City. Eventually the soil blew out over the Atlantic Ocean, where it was lost forever.

The problem was most serious in the southern Plains states. There, the drought and topsoil loss lasted until 1938. This area, shown in Figure 14, was called the **Dust Bowl.** Many people in the Dust Bowl states abandoned their farms and moved away.

Background

Facts and Figures During the dust storms of the 1930's, more than 20 million hectares of land were destroyed in the southern Great Plains alone. A single storm in 1934 dumped more than 300 metric tons of soil as far east as the East Coast of the United States.

In an attempt to deter further soil erosion, President Franklin D. Roosevelt issued an executive order to plant a belt of trees about 160 kilometers wide, stretching from Canada to Texas at about 100° longitude. The belt of trees was intended to serve as a windbreak and to hold moisture in the soil. By 1942, 30,000 kilometers of trees had been planted by the government with the help of farmers in North and South Dakota, Nebraska, Oklahoma, and Texas.

Soil Conservation

After the Dust Bowl, farmers in the United States began to take better care of their land. They adopted methods of farming that helped save the soil. **Soil conservation** is the management of soil to prevent its destruction. **Ways that soil can be conserved include contour plowing, conservation plowing, leaving the soil to lie fallow, and crop rotation.** You can read about some of these methods in *Exploring Soil Conservation.*

Contour plowing is the practice of plowing fields along the curves of a slope. This helps slow the runoff of excess rainfall and prevents it from washing the soil away.

Conservation plowing disturbs the soil and its plant cover as little as possible. Dead weeds and stalks of the previous year's crop are left in the ground to help return soil nutrients, retain moisture, and hold soil in place.

EXPLORING *Soil Conservation*

These farming practices can help reduce soil erosion.

◄ Strip cropping and contour plowing
Farmers alternate strips of tall crops, such as corn, with short crops, such as squash. The short crops prevent soil from washing out of the tall crop rows, which are less protected. Crops are planted in curving rows that follow the slope, or contour, of the land. Contour plowing can reduce soil erosion as much as 50 percent on gently sloping land.

▲ Windbreaks
Rows of trees are planted along the edges of fields. These windbreaks block the wind and also trap eroding soil. Using fruit or nut trees as windbreaks provides an extra benefit for the farmer and wildlife.

Conservation plowing ▼
Rather than plowing fields and leaving them bare, farmers use machines that break up only the subsoil. This method leaves the dead stalks and weeds from the previous year's crop in the ground to hold the topsoil in place.

Terracing ►
Steep hillsides are built up into a series of flat "terraces." The ridges of soil at the edges of the terraces slow down runoff and catch eroding soil.

Media and Technology

Concept Videotape Library
Grade 6, Tape 1 "Is Our Soil Endangered?"

EXPLORING

Soil Conservation

Ask students: **Which of the farming practices pictured would help reduce soil erosion during a drought? Explain your answer.** *(Strip cropping, contour plowing, and terracing are designed to prevent soil loss through runoff, which rarely occurs during a drought. Both windbreaks and conservation plowing would help reduce soil erosion by wind, which is likely to occur during a drought.)* Explain that conservation plowing has drawbacks, since farmers must use chemicals to kill weeds before planting. **learning modality: verbal**

Soil Conservation

Real-Life Learning

Allow students time to observe the schoolyard and surrounding area. Have them point out areas at risk of soil erosion, such as areas of exposed soil or sloping ground. Then, have them suggest strategies for conserving soil in these areas, such as planting ornamental vegetation or windbreaks, or creating terraces. Encourage students to list and present their suggestions to the appropriate school authorities. **cooperative learning**

Ongoing Assessment

Skills Check Have students make a flowchart that shows what caused people to leave the Great Plains in the 1930s.

Restoring the Land

Using the Visuals: Figure 15

After students have examined the photographs and read the caption, have them list the sequence of events that transformed the landscape pictured on the left to that on the right. *(1) Mining cuts were smoothed out. 2) Subsoil and topsoil was replaced. 3) Grass was planted.)* Then ask students to infer why reclamation did not end with the replacement of the soil. *(Exposed soil is more likely to be eroded. Planting grass helps to hold soil in place.)* **learning modality: verbal**

3 Assess

Section 3 Review Answers

1. Development changes Earth's surface by destroying wildlife habitats, reducing the amount of farmland, and covering the surface with structures.
2. Everything that lives on land depends directly or indirectly on soil. Also, soil takes a long time to form; there is a limited supply.
3. Two ways that soil can be conserved include contour plowing—the practice of plowing fields along the curves of a slope—and conservation plowing—a practice that disturbs the soil and its plant cover as little as possible.
4. You would plow the hillside along its curves instead of against its curves.

CHAPTER PROJECT

Check Your Progress

Check to see that all students have made measurements, observations and recorded data. Query students on what they think their data show about soil fertility, and encourage them to begin drawing conclusions and thinking about their presentation.

Performance Assessment

Writing Have students write a short magazine-style article recounting what happened on the Great Plains in the 1930s, describing the causes, and explaining what methods are used today to prevent another Dust Bowl.

Figure 15 When the mining operation (at left) was completed, the mine operators smoothed out the sides of the mining cuts. Then they carefully replaced the subsoil and topsoil that was removed before mining. Finally, they planted grass. The former mine is now agricultural land (at right).

To restore fertility to soil, farmers periodically leave fields **fallow,** or unplanted with crops. A method that helps preserve the soil's fertility is **crop rotation.** In crop rotation, a farmer plants different crops in a field each year. Some crops use less nutrients than others. Certain crops, such as peanuts and other legumes, actually improve soil fertility.

Restoring the Land

It is often possible to restore land damaged by erosion or mining. The process of restoring an area of land to a more natural, productive state is called **land reclamation.** In addition to restoring lands for agriculture, land reclamation can restore habitats for wildlife. Many different types of land reclamation projects are currently underway all over the world. But it is generally more difficult and expensive to restore damaged land and soil than it is to protect them in the first place. Figure 15 shows an example of land reclamation.

Section 3 Review

1. Explain how one of the major kinds of land use can change Earth's surface.
2. Explain the importance of soil as one of Earth's resources.
3. What are some techniques that farmers use to conserve soil?
4. **Thinking Critically Problem Solving** If you had to plant corn on a steep hillside, how would you do it so that rain would not wash the soil away?

CHAPTER PROJECT

Check Your Progress

Check your bean seeds daily and water them as needed. Count and record the number of seeds that sprout. You can also measure the height of each plant, count the number of leaves, and note the leaf color. After about 14 days, you should be able to make comparisons. What differences did you observe in the bean plants grown in the different materials? When did these differences appear? Based on your data, what conclusions can you draw about which material is best for growing bean plants?

Program Resources

- **Unit 2 Resources** 4-3 Review and Reinforce; 4-3 Enrich

Section 4 Waste Disposal and Recycling

DISCOVER ACTIVITY

What's in the Trash?

Your teacher will give you a trash bag. The items in the bag represent the most common categories of household waste in the United States.

1. Before you open the bag, predict what the two most common categories are.
2. Put on some plastic gloves. Open the bag and sort the trash items into categories based on what they are made of.
3. Count the number of trash items in each category. Construct a bar graph showing the number of pieces of trash in each category.

Think It Over

Interpreting Data Based on your graph, what are the two most common types of household waste? Was your prediction correct?

Every year, people in the United States throw away enough white paper to build a wall 4 meters high from coast to coast. People also throw away 1.6 billion pens, 2.9 million tons of paper towels, and 220 million automobile tires. Disposable products can be convenient, but they have created a big problem—what to do with all the trash.

GUIDE FOR READING

- What can be done with solid waste?
- What are the "three R's"?
- What techniques can be used to manage hazardous waste?

Reading Tip Before you read, preview *Exploring a Landfill* on page 116. Make a list of any unfamiliar words in the diagram. Look for the meanings of these words as you read.

The Problem of Waste Disposal

In their daily activities, people generate many types of waste, including used paper, empty packages, and food scraps. **Municipal solid waste** includes all the waste materials produced in homes, businesses, and other places in a community. **Three methods of handling solid waste are to bury it, to burn it, or to recycle it.** Each method has advantages and disadvantages.

Landfills Until fairly recently, people often disposed of waste in open holes in the ground. But these open dumps were dangerous. Rain falling on the wastes dissolved chemicals from the waste, forming a polluted liquid called **leachate.** Leachate could pollute the soil, run off into streams and lakes, or trickle down into the groundwater.

READING STRATEGIES

Reading Tip One word included in *Exploring a Landfill* that may be unfamiliar to students is *groundwater.* Ask students what they think the word means, then let them consult other sources to verify their responses. *(Groundwater refers to fresh water that has seeped down through the soil and collected in permeable rock or soil layers below Earth's surface.)*

Program Resources

- **Unit 2 Resources** 4-4 Lesson Plan; 4-4 Section Summary
- **Guided Reading and Study Workbook** Section 4-4

Section 4 Waste Disposal and Recycling

Objectives

After completing the lesson, students will be able to

- name and describe two ways of dealing with solid waste;
- list the four major types of recyclable waste;
- describe methods for managing solid waste;
- identify methods for managing hazardous wastes;
- list and describe the categories of hazardous wastes;
- explain how hazardous wastes affect human health

Key Terms municipal solid waste, leachate, sanitary landfill, incineration, recycling, hazardous waste

1 Engage/Explore

Activating Prior Knowledge

Ask students: **What kinds of things does your family throw away?** *(Paper, metal cans, glass jars, plastic milk jugs, and so on)* **How does your family get rid of its trash?** *(Trash will likely be collected. Some families may recycle some trash.)*

DISCOVER

Skills Focus interpreting data
Materials *trash bag with household wastes (see Advance Preparation below), plastic gloves, graph paper, ruler*
Time 20 minutes
Advance Preparation For each group, prepare a trash bag containing: 4 paper items; 2 items of yard waste such as leaves; 1 piece of rubber, cloth, or wood waste; 1 soda can or other metal item; 1 glass jar or bottle; 1 plastic item; 1 food-waste item such as an orange peel.
Tips Have students work on the floor so glass containers do not fall and break.
Expected Outcome Students should sort the items into the categories above.
Think It Over Paper and yard waste

2 Facilitate

The Problem of Waste Disposal

Building Inquiry Skills: Making Models

Materials *glass or plastic jar, coffee filter, rubber band, soil, food coloring, beaker, water*
Time 10 minutes

ACTIVITY

Have each group of students make a simple model of leachate, as follows: Put a coffee filter over the mouth of a jar, letting it hang into the jar, and secure it in place with a rubber band. Fill the filter about halfway with soil. Put several drops of food coloring on the soil, then pour water into the jar. When students have finished, ask: **What do you see in the bottom of the jar?** *(Colored water)* **Where did the color come from?** *(The food coloring)* **What does the food coloring represent in this model?** *(Chemicals on the soil's surface)* **In a real landfill, where do chemicals come from?** *(The wastes in the landfill)* **learning modality: kinesthetic**

EXPLORING a Landfill

Ask different volunteers to read the captions aloud. Ask: **What is special about this landfill?** *(It is designed to prevent it from polluting the surrounding environment.)* Then ask: **Why do landfill operators want to reduce the waste's volume before burying it?** *(To keep the landfill from running out of space; to make the landfill last as long as possible.)* **What do you think happens when a town's landfill runs out of space?** *(The town has to build a new landfill; the trash has to be trucked to another town's landfill or maybe even out of state; the town has to find another way to dispose of its trash, perhaps by building an incinerator.)* **learning modality: logical/mathematical**

In 1976, the government banned open dumps. Now much solid waste is buried in landfills that are constructed to hold the wastes more safely. A **sanitary landfill** holds municipal solid waste, construction debris, and some types of agricultural and industrial waste. *Exploring a Landfill* shows the parts of a well-designed sanitary landfill. Once a landfill is full, it is covered with a clay cap to keep rainwater out.

Even well-designed landfills can pollute the soil and groundwater. And while capped landfills can be reused for some purposes, such as parks, they cannot be used for housing or agriculture.

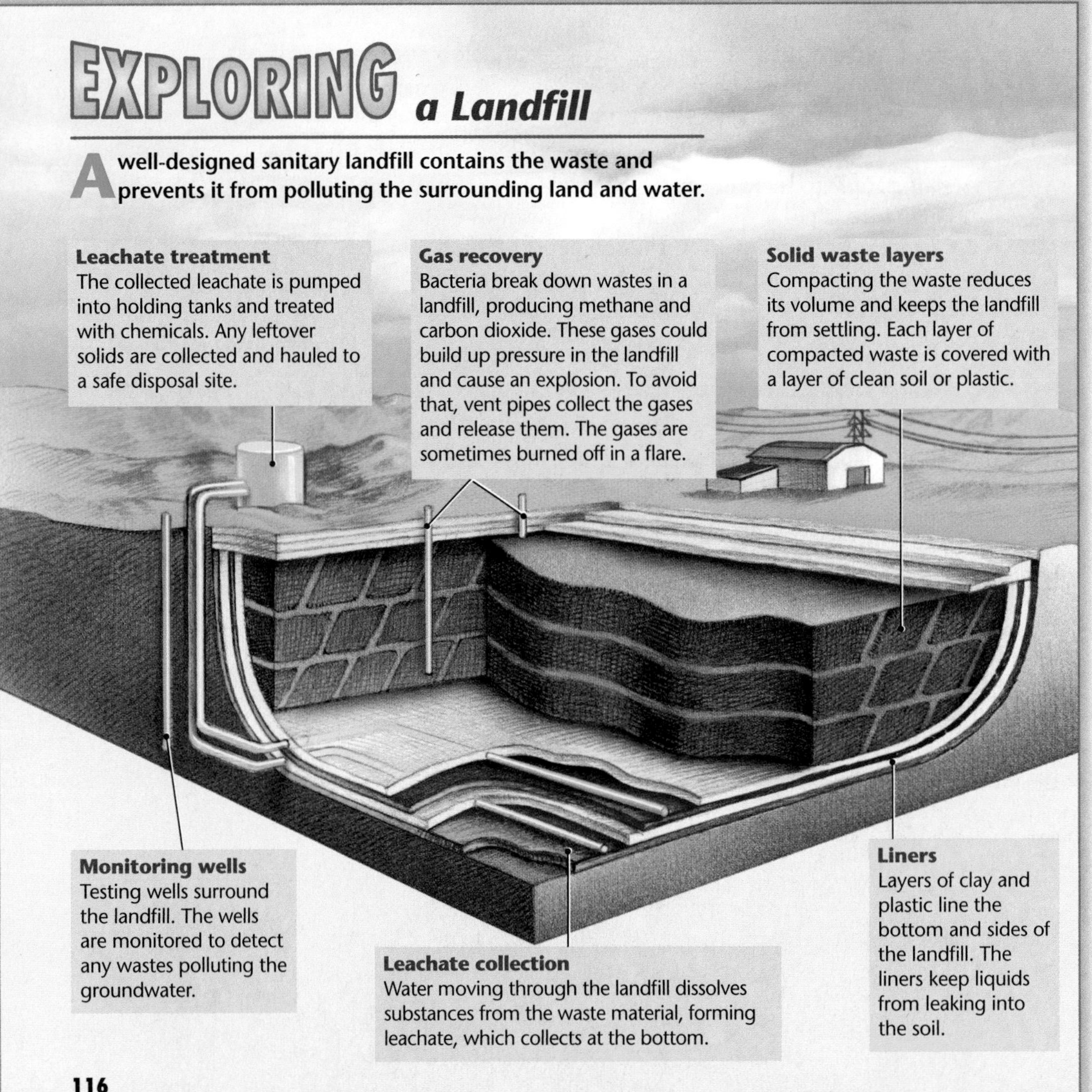

Background

History of Science Sanitary landfills are a vast improvement over open dumps, but they are not an ideal solution. Many of the materials that fill up landfills are organic and could biodegrade. But little of the paper, grass clippings, and food waste in a sanitary landfill actually decomposes. That's because the soil used to cover the landfill limits the availability of the oxygen needed for the organic wastes to decompose.

One solution is municipal solid waste composting. With this technique, all the organic wastes that a community produces can be composted. As much as three fourths of all household waste by weight could be composted. This would dramatically reduce the volume of waste disposed in sanitary landfills. One drawback of this type of composting is that heavy metals and toxic pesticide residues may be left in the compost.

Figure 16 This waste-to-energy plant generates electricity while disposing of municipal solid waste.

Incineration The burning of solid waste is called **incineration** (in sin ur ay shun). Incineration has some advantages over landfills. Incinerators do not take up as much space. They do not pollute groundwater. The heat produced by burning solid waste can be used to generate electricity in "waste-to-energy" plants.

Unfortunately, incinerators have drawbacks. Incinerators release some pollution into the air. And although incinerators reduce the volume of waste by as much as 90 percent, some waste still remains. This waste needs to be disposed of somewhere. Incinerators also cost much more to build than sanitary landfills.

☑ *Checkpoint* *What is a waste-to-energy plant?*

Recycling

INTEGRATING TECHNOLOGY The process of reclaiming raw materials and reusing them is called **recycling.** Recycling reduces the volume of solid waste. Recycling also saves the energy needed to obtain and process raw materials. **Most recycling involves four major categories of products: metal, glass, paper, and plastic.**

Metal Common metals such as iron and aluminum can be melted and reused. The aluminum in soda cans, for example, can be recycled. Recycling metal saves money and causes less pollution than making new metal. With recycling, no ore needs to be mined, transported to factories, or processed. Recycling metals also helps conserve these nonrenewable resources.

Glass Recycling glass is easy and inexpensive. The glass pieces can be melted down over and over to make new glass containers. The recycled pieces melt at a lower temperature than the raw materials. Therefore less energy is required. Recycling glass also reduces the environmental damage caused by mining the raw materials used to make glass.

Sharpen your Skills

Graphing

ACTIVITY

What happens to trash? Use the data in the table below to construct a circle graph of methods of municipal solid waste disposal in the United States. Give your circle graph a title. (For help making a circle graph, see the Skills Handbook.)

Method of Disposal	Percentage of Waste
Landfills	56%
Recycling	27%
Incineration	17%

Sharpen your Skills

Graphing

Materials *protractor, drawing compass*
Time 15 minutes

Students should determine the size of each wedge of the circle graph by multiplying 360° by each percentage. *(Landfills = 202°, Recycling = 97°, Incineration = 61°) Sample title:* Methods of Waste Disposal in the U.S.
Extend Have students make a second circle graph to show what would happen if 15% of the total waste were recycled instead of being sent to landfills. *(Landfills = 148°, Recycling = 151°)* **learning modality: logical/mathematical**

Recycling

Building Inquiry Skills: Calculating

Materials *newspapers, metric ruler, calculator (optional)*
Time 10 minutes

Show students a stack of one week's issues of a major daily newspaper that you have collected. Explain that one tree, 10.5 to 12 m tall, produces a stack of newspapers 1.2 m high. Choose a volunteer to measure the height of your stack of papers. Ask: **How many weeks would it take for me to use up one tree just by reading the newspaper?** *(120 cm ÷ height of your stack)* **How many trees would I use up in a year?** *(52 ÷ weeks to use 1 tree)* **If every one of your families also read the newspaper every day, how many trees would we all use up in a year?** *(above answer × [number of students + yourself])* **learning modality: logical/mathematical**

Media and Technology

Transparencies "Exploring a Landfill," Transparency 11

Concept Videotape Library Grade 6, Tape 1 "Where Does Your Garbage Go?"

Answers to Self-Assessment

☑ *Checkpoint*

A power plant that uses the heat from burning solid waste to generate electricity

Program Resources

- **Product Testing Activities by *Consumer Reports*** "Testing Orange Juice"; "Testing Toilet Paper," pp. 1–8

Ongoing Assessment

Skills Check Have each student construct a compare/contrast table that identifies the advantages and disadvantages of sanitary landfills and incinerators.

Students can save their tables in their portfolios.

TRY THIS

Skills Focus classifying **Materials** *pieces of plastic products (see Advance Preparation below)*
Time 10 minutes
Tips Assemble a set of plastic pieces by selecting several examples from each of these recycling categories: **1** (polyethylene terphthalate), soft-drink bottles; **2** (high-density polyethylene), milk and water jugs; **3** (vinyl), shampoo bottles; **4** (low-density polyethylene), ketchup bottles; **5** (polypropylene), squeeze bottles; **6** (polystyrene), fast-food containers and coffee cups; **7** (all other resins and layered multi-materials). To reduce preparation time, assemble one set of plastic pieces and let students take turns sorting the pieces.
Expected Outcome Students should be able to sort the plastics into at least four or five groups according to the plastics' color/clarity and rigidity.
Extend Have students make a compare/contrast table listing the types, descriptions, and uses of the different groups of plastics. **learning modality: logical/mathematical**

What Can You Do?

Building Inquiry Skills: Communicating

Challenge students individually or in small groups to think of a creative way to communicate the "three R's" to their community. For example, students could create posters, public service announcements, skits, rap songs, or poems. At a specified time, have each student or group present its product to the class for critique. Then after students have made their revisions, let them present their products in a community forum, such as a parent-teacher meeting, parents' night at school, or a community civic association meeting. **learning modality: verbal**

It's in the Numbers

Plastic bottles and other plastic products usually have numbers inside a triangle indicating the type of plastic they are made of. Plastics must be sorted by type before they can be recycled.

Sort pieces of plastic products into groups by their recycling numbers. Compare and contrast the pieces in each group with each other and with those in other groups.

Classifying Write a sentence describing characteristics of the plastics in each group.

Paper About 17 trees are needed to make one metric ton of paper. Paper mills turn wood into a thick liquid called pulp. Pulp is spread out and dried to produce paper. Pulp can also be made from used paper such as old newspapers. Most paper products can only be recycled a few times. Recycled paper is not as smooth or strong as paper made from wood pulp. Each time paper is recycled, the new paper is rougher, weaker, and darker.

Plastic When oil is refined to make gasoline and other petroleum products, solid materials called resins are left over. Resins can be heated, stretched, and molded into plastic products. Common products made from plastic include milk jugs, detergent containers, and soda bottles. When they are recycled, they can take on very different forms: as carpeting, park benches, fiber filling for jackets, and many other things!

Is Recycling Worthwhile? Recycling is not a complete answer to the solid waste problem. Some materials cannot be recycled. There are not enough uses for some recycled products, such as low-quality newspaper. Finally, all recycling processes require energy and create some pollution.

☑ *Checkpoint* ***What are some advantages and disadvantages of recycling?***

What Can You Do?

There are lots of actions individuals can take to help control the solid waste problem. **These actions are sometimes called the "three R's"—reduce, reuse, and recycle.** Reduce means creating less waste in the first place. For example, you can use a cloth shopping bag instead of a disposable paper or plastic bag. Reuse means finding another use for an object instead of discarding it. For example, you could refill plastic drink bottles with drinking water or juice you mix instead of buying drinks in new bottles. Recycle means reclaiming raw materials to create new products. You can make sure you recycle at home, and you can also encourage others to recycle. How about starting a used paper collection and recycling program at your school?

Figure 17 Composting is a form of recycling in which natural processes break down waste such as leaves, grass clippings, and vegetable scraps. Many communities have neighborhood compost bins like this one in Brooklyn, in New York City.

Background

Facts and Figures In the United States and other developed countries, the average computer is replaced every three years—not because it is broken but because rapid technological advances and new generations of software make it obsolete. Although they may still be in working order, old computers have little resale value and are even difficult to give away. As a result, they are frequently discarded in the trash.

According to an estimate by researchers at Carnegie Mellon University, by 2005 there will be 55 million computers discarded in landfills around the world. Nearly 150 million computers will be recycled for their usable components and recyclable materials. These include plastics and metals such as aluminum, copper, tin, nickel, palladium, silver, and gold.

Hazardous Wastes

Many people picture hazardous wastes as bubbling chemicals, thick fumes, or oozing slime. But even some harmless-looking, common materials such as window cleaner, radio batteries, and nail polish remover can become hazardous wastes. **Hazardous waste** is any material that can be harmful to human health or the environment if it is not properly disposed of.

Hazardous wastes are created during the manufacture of many household products. Many more are produced by agriculture and industry.

Types of Hazardous Wastes **There are four categories of hazardous waste: toxic, explosive, flammable, and corrosive.** Toxic, or poisonous, wastes can damage the health of humans and other organisms. Explosive wastes react very quickly when exposed to air or water, or explode when they are dropped. Flammable wastes catch fire easily. Corrosive wastes dissolve or eat through many materials.

Other wastes that require special disposal are radioactive wastes. Radioactive wastes contain unstable atoms. These unstable atoms give off radiation that can cause cancer and other diseases. Radioactive waste can remain dangerous for thousands of years.

Health Effects of Hazardous Wastes A person can be exposed to hazardous wastes by breathing, eating, drinking, or touching them. Many factors determine the effects of a hazardous substance on a person. One factor is how harmful the substance is. Another factor is how much of the substance a person is exposed to. A third factor is how long the exposure lasts. A person may be exposed for only a short time or for many years. Finally, a person's age, weight, and health all influence how a substance affects that person.

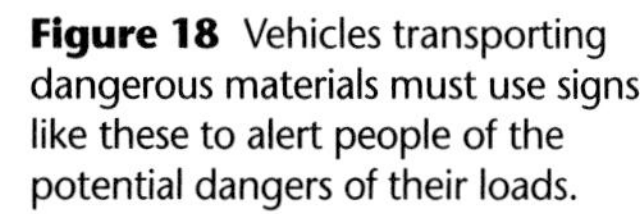

Figure 18 Vehicles transporting dangerous materials must use signs like these to alert people of the potential dangers of their loads.

Category: Radioactive
Examples: Uranium, plutonium

Category: Flammable
Example: Kerosene

Category: Toxic
Examples: Chlorine, PCBs, mercury

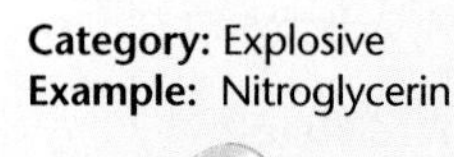

Category: Explosive
Example: Nitroglycerin

Category: Corrosive
Examples: Hydrochloric acid, sodium hydroxide

2 Facilitate

Hazardous Wastes

Building Inquiry Skills: Classifying

Materials *labels from common hazardous household products*
Time 10 minutes

Challenge students to sort the labels into four of the categories described on this page—toxic, explosive, flammable, and corrosive—plus a fifth group for products whose warnings indicate more than one type of hazard. Ask: **How many labels do you have in each group? What kinds of products do those labels represent?** *(Answers will vary, but students may find that many, if not most, hazardous products fall into more than one category.)* **learning modality: verbal**

Real-Life Learning

Time 5 minutes

ACTIVITY

Encourage students to copy the symbols from Figure 18. Then instruct students to cut out the individual symbols and tape the appropriate ones to hazardous products they find in the classroom, other areas of the school (the art room or shop area, for example), and at home. In a follow-up class discussion, ask: **Were you surprised by the number of hazardous products you found?** *(Students may not have realized that so many common, everyday products contain hazardous substances.)* **learning modality: kinesthetic**

Media and Technology

Concept Videotape Library
Grade 6, Tape 1 "It Really Isn't Gargage"

Answers to Self-Assessment

Checkpoint

Reduces need for raw materials and landfill space, saves energy; some products not suitable, some recycled materials not in demand

Ongoing Assessment

Writing Have each student name the categories of hazardous wastes and define each category in his or her own words.

Students can save their work in their portfolios.

3 Assess

Section 4 Review Answers

1. It goes to landfills.
2. *Reduce* means creating less waste in the first place. *Reuse* means finding another use for an object instead of discarding it. *Recycle* means reclaiming raw materials to create new products.
3. Hazardous wastes are materials that can be harmful to human health or the environment if not properly disposed of.
4. One method is to bury hazardous wastes in landfills lined and sealed with plastic and clay. Other disposal methods include incineration at very high temperatures, exposure to organisms that break the wastes down, pumping the wastes deep underground, and recycling them.
5. The recycling of both metals and paper reclaims raw materials for new products. Metals can be recycled many times, whereas paper products can be recycled only a few times before quality is reduced.
6. Workers who clean up hazardous wastes wear protective clothing to avoid exposure by breathing or touching the wastes. Exposure can be damaging to the health of humans.

Science at Home

If students' families already recycle, tell students to weigh the materials being recycled separately from the other materials. Let students report their findings in class.

Performance Assessment

Writing Have each student briefly explain the benefits of recycling compared with discarding waste materials in landfills or burning them in incinerators.

Portfolio Students can save their explanations in their portfolios.

In general, short-term exposure to hazardous wastes may cause irritation or more severe health problems. These health problems can include breathing difficulties, internal bleeding, paralysis, coma, and even death. **Long-term exposure to hazardous wastes may cause diseases such as cancer, and may damage body organs, including the brain, liver, kidneys, and lungs.** These effects may eventually be life threatening.

Figure 19 Hazardous wastes can pollute the soil, water, and air. Environmental scientists in protective gear test the contents of an old storage tank.

Disposal of Hazardous Wastes It is hard to safely dispose of hazardous wastes. Burying them can pollute the soil or groundwater. Releasing wastes into lakes or rivers can pollute surface water. Burning hazardous wastes can pollute the air. You can feel, smell, and see the problem!

Methods of hazardous waste disposal include burial in landfills, incineration, and breakdown by living organisms. Liquid wastes can be stored in deep rock layers. Hazardous wastes are most often disposed of in carefully designed landfills. These landfills are lined with clay and plastic to keep chemicals from leaking into the soil and groundwater. A clay and plastic cover prevents rainwater from seeping into the wastes.

Scientists are still researching methods that will provide safe, permanent disposal of radioactive wastes. Some radioactive wastes are currently stored in vaults dug hundreds of meters underground or in concrete and steel containers above ground.

Reducing Hazardous Wastes The best way to manage hazardous wastes is to produce less of them in the first place. Industries are eager to develop safe alternatives to harmful chemicals. At home, you can find substitutes for some hazardous household chemicals.

Section 4 Review

1. What happens to most solid waste in the United States?
2. Name and define the "three R's" of solid waste management.
3. What are hazardous wastes?
4. Describe one method used to dispose of hazardous waste.
5. **Thinking Critically Comparing and Contrasting** Compare the recycling of metal and paper. How are they similar? How are they different?
6. **Thinking Critically Inferring** Why must the workers who clean up hazardous wastes wear protective clothing? Explain.

Science at Home

Trash Weigh-In For one week, have your family collect their household trash in large bags. Do not include food waste. At the end of the week, hold a trash weigh-in. Multiply the total amount by 52 to show how much trash your family produces in a year. Together, can you suggest any ways to reduce your family trash load?

Program Resources

◆ **Unit 2 Resources** 4-4 Review and Reinforce; 4-4 Enrich

CHAPTER 4 STUDY GUIDE

Rocks and Weathering

Key Ideas

- Rock weathers, or wears down, when it is exposed to air, water, weather, and living things at Earth's surface.
- Mechanical weathering breaks rock into smaller pieces. The agents of mechanical weathering include freezing and thawing, release of pressure, growth of plants, actions of animals, and abrasion.
- Chemical weathering changes the mineral content of rock. The agents of chemical weathering are water, oxygen, carbon dioxide, living organisms, and acid rain.
- Climate and rock type determine how fast weathering occurs.

Key Terms

weathering	ice wedging
erosion	chemical weathering
mechanical weathering	permeable
abrasion	

Soil Formation and Composition

Key Ideas

- Soil is made of small particles of rock mixed with the decaying remains of organisms.
- Soil forms in layers called horizons as bedrock weathers and organic materials build up.
- The three soil horizons are the A horizon, the B horizon, and the C horizon. The A horizon is made up of topsoil, which is rich in humus. The B horizon consists of clay and other particles washed down from the A horizon, but little humus. The C horizon is made up of partly weathered rock without clay or humus.
- Plants and animals break up and mix the soil, and also add the organic materials that form humus.

Key Terms

soil	loam	subsoil
bedrock	soil horizon	litter
humus	topsoil	decomposers

Soil Conservation

Key Ideas

- Land is a limited resource. All the people on Earth must share land for agriculture, development, mining, and other uses.
- Soil can be eroded away and its fertility can be decreased by improper farming practices.
- Soil can be conserved and its fertility can be maintained by using various methods of soil conservation.

Key Terms

development	contour plowing
desertification	conservation plowing
sod	fallow
Dust Bowl	crop rotation
soil conservation	land reclamation

Waste Disposal and Recycling

INTEGRATING ENVIRONMENTAL SCIENCE

Key Ideas

- Three ways of handling solid waste are to bury it, burn it, or recycle it.
- One way to reduce solid waste is to practice the "three R's"—reduce, reuse, and recycle.
- Hazardous wastes are materials that can threaten human health and safety or harm the environment if not properly disposed of.

Key Terms

municipal solid waste	incineration
leachate	recycling
sanitary landfill	hazardous waste

Organizing Information

Compare/Contrast Table On a separate piece of paper, make a table of ways to dispose of municipal solid waste. Your table should compare landfills and incinerators with regard to cost, pollution, attractiveness, and usefulness to a community. Then complete your table and add a title. For tips on compare/contrast tables, see the Skills Handbook.)

Program Resources

- **Unit 2 Resources** Chapter 4 Project Scoring Rubric
- **Performance Assessment** Chapter 4
- **Chapter and Unit Tests** Chapter 4 Test

Media and Technology

Computer Test Bank Chapter 4 Test

Organizing Information

Compare/Contrast Table Sample table:

Solid Waste Disposal Methods

	Landfill	Incinerator
Cost	cheaper to build	more expensive to build
Pollution	can cause pollution of soil and groundwater	can cause air pollution and also create some solid waste that must be disposed of elsewhere
Attractiveness	not attractive while in operation	could be more attractive than an operating landfill
Usefullness to Community	capped landfill can be reused for some purposes and can produce methane that can be captured for use as fuel	could be used to generate electricity

Reviewing Content

Multiple Choice

1. b **2.** b **3.** a **4.** a **5.** d

True or False

6. Erosion **7.** true **8.** humus
9. development **10.** true

Checking Concepts

11. Rapid mechanical weathering is more likely where the temperature shifts back and forth because each time water expands and contracts, ice wedging would widen and deepen cracks in rocks.
12. Soils forms as rock is broken down by weathering and mixes with other materials on the surface.
13. Topsoil contains more humus than subsoil.
14. Plants act as an agent of mechanical weathering when their roots pry apart cracks in rocks and as an agent of chemical weathering when their roots produce a weak acid that slowly dissolves rocks.
15. Conservation plowing disturbs the soil and plant cover as little as possible, thus keeping the soil in place, retaining moisture, and conserving soil nutrients.
16. Individuals can help control the solid waste problem by reducing, or creating less waste in the first place; by reusing, or finding another use for an object instead of discarding it; and by recycling, or reclaiming raw materials to create new products.
17. A typical answer should mention how earthworms break up hard, compacted soil, decompose organic material in soil, mix humus with other materials, enrich soil with their wastes, and aerate the soil.

Thinking Critically

18. Breaking rocks into pieces increases the rate at which the rock will weather chemically because breaking the rock exposes more surface area to weathering agents.
19. a. mechanical weathering
b. chemical weathering **c.** chemical weathering
20. Answers may vary. A typical answer may mention that type of rock and climate determine the rate at which the rock weathers and soil forms. Thus, one or both of those factors may have caused the difference in rate at the two locations.
21. Radioactive waste remains dangerous for thousands of years. Burying it in an open dump or sanitary landfill or burning it in an incinerator would not protect people and other organisms from the hazards of radioactivity. Burning the waste might pollute the air, and burying the waste could pollute the groundwater or incorporate radioactive substances in the food chain.

Applying Skills

22. The sandy soil would lose water more quickly because there is space between the larger, jagged sand particles for water to run through, while clay particles can hold a lot of water.
23. Answers will vary. A typical design might include the following: use two identical flower pots with drain holes; place gravel at the bottom of each pot and cover with equal amounts of the sample soils; suspend the pots

CHAPTER 4 ASSESSMENT

Reviewing Content

Multiple Choice

Choose the letter of the best answer.

1. The most important force of mechanical weathering in cool climates is
a. oxidation.
b. freezing and thawing.
c. animal activity.
d. abrasion.

2. Most chemical weathering is caused by
a. acid rain.
b. water.
c. oxygen.
d. carbon dioxide.

3. The B horizon consists of
a. subsoil. **b.** topsoil.
c. rock particles. **d.** bedrock.

4. The loss of so much topsoil that plants can no longer grow in an area is called
a. desertification.
b. crop rotation.
c. conservation plowing.
d. land reclamation.

5. Hazardous wastes that contain unstable atoms are
a. toxic. **b.** flammable.
c. corrosive. **d.** radioactive.

True or False

If the statement is true, write true. If it is false, change the underlined word or words to make the statement true.

6. Mechanical weathering is the movement of rock particles by wind, water, or ice.
7. Weathering occurs faster in a wet climate.
8. The decayed organic material in soil is called loam.
9. Three types of land use that change Earth's surface are agriculture, recycling, and mining.
10. The bottom of a sanitary landfill is lined with clay and plastic to prevent leachate from polluting groundwater.

Checking Concepts

11. Where is mechanical weathering likely to occur more quickly: where the winter temperature usually stays below freezing, or where it more often shifts back and forth around the freezing point? Explain.
12. Briefly describe how soil is formed.
13. Which contains more humus, topsoil or subsoil?
14. Explain how plants can act as agents of both mechanical and chemical weathering.
15. How does conservation plowing contribute to soil conservation?
16. Explain how individuals can help control the solid waste problem by practicing the "three R's."
17. Writing to Learn Write a description of your life as an earthworm. What would it be like to live in the soil? What would you see? What would you eat? How would you move through the soil? How would you change it?

Thinking Critically

18. Predicting Suppose mechanical weathering breaks a rock into pieces. How would this affect the rate at which the rock weathers chemically?
19. Classifying Classify the following examples as either mechanical weathering or chemical weathering:
a. Cracks appear in a sidewalk next to a large tree.
b. A piece of limestone develops holes like Swiss cheese.
c. A rock exposed at the surface slowly turns reddish brown.
20. Relating Cause and Effect Two rocks, each in a different location, have been weathering for the same amount of time. Mature soil has formed from one rock but only immature soil from the other. What factors might have caused this difference in rate of soil formation?
21. Applying Concepts Why is it unsafe to bury or incinerate radioactive waste?

Applying Skills

Use the following information to answer Questions 22–24. You have two samples of soil. One is mostly sand and one is mostly clay.

22. Developing Hypotheses Which soil sample do you think would lose water more quickly? Why?

23. Designing Experiments Design an experiment to test how quickly water passes through each soil sample.

24. Posing Questions Suppose you are a farmer who wants to grow soybeans in one of these two soils. What questions would you need to answer before choosing where to plant your soybeans?

Performance (Chapter Project) Assessment

Present Your Project You are ready to present your conclusions about what type of material is best for growing bean plants. Decide how to display the data you collected on the different materials. How did your group's results compare with those of the other groups in your class?

Reflect and Record In your journal, describe how well the results of your experiment matched your predictions. What have you learned from this project about soil characteristics that help plants to grow? What improvements could you make to your experiment?

Test Preparation

Use these questions to prepare for standardized tests.

Use the diagram of soil horizons to answer Questions 25–29.

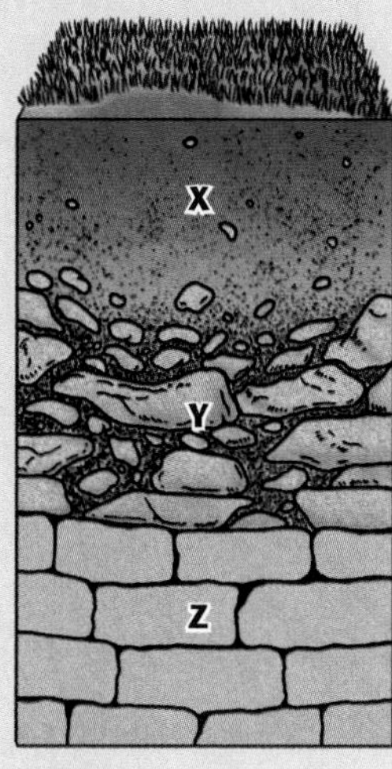

25. Layer X in the diagram consists of a mixture of humus, clay, and other minerals called
a. litter. **b.** gravel.
c. subsoil. **d.** topsoil.

26. Layer Y is made up of partly weathered rock called the
a. C horizon.
b. B horizon.
c. A horizon.
d. humus horizon.

27. One soil horizon, made up of clay and other particles but little humus, has not yet developed in this soil. The missing soil horizon is the
a. A horizon.
b. B horizon.
c. C horizon.
d. bedrock horizon.

28. The missing soil horizon will develop
a. above layer X.
b. below layer Z.
c. between layers X and Y.
d. between layers Y and Z.

29. In which layer or layers would you expect to find the most plant roots, insects, and other soil organisms?
a. layers Y and Z **b.** layer Z
c. layer Y **d.** layer X

over two catch basins and pour equal amounts of water into the pots. Compare the amount of water that passes through the pots.
24. Answers may vary. *Sample questions:* In what kind of soil do soybeans grow best? What needs to be added to either type of soil to make it suitable for growing soybeans?

Program Resources

- **Inquiry Skills Activity Book** Provides teaching and review of all inquiry skills

Performance (Chapter Project) Assessment

Present Your Project As each group presents its results to the class, assess how well students explain the experiment they carried out, including their descriptions of the types of soils used, explanations of the data they collected, and conclusions they have drawn from their data. Also assess the way in which they present their findings, including any visual aids or graphs they use.

Reflect and Record In assessing their work in this project, students should compare the data and conclusions of their group both with their predictions and with the data and conclusions of other groups. Each student should also explain what lessons can be drawn from the project and how the project could have been carried out in a better way.

Test Preparation

25. d **26.** a **27.** b **28.** c **29.** d

CHAPTER 5

Erosion and Deposition

Sections	Time	Student Edition Activities	Other Activities
CHAPTER PROJECT **Changes in the Land** p. 125	Ongoing (2 weeks)	Check Your Progress, pp. 148, 153, 157 Present Your Project, p. 163	
1 Changing Earth's Surface pp. 126–131 ◆ Describe the processes that wear down and build up Earth's surface. ◆ Identify the force that pulls rock and soil down slopes.	2 periods/ 1 blocks	**Discover** How Does Gravity Affect Materials on a Slope?, p. 126 **Sharpen Your Skills** Observing, p. 129 **Science at Home,** p. 129 **Skills Lab: Developing Hypotheses** Sand Hills, pp. 130–131	TE Demonstration, p. 133
2 Water Erosion pp. 132–144 ◆ Explain how water erosion is mainly responsible for shaping Earth's land surface. ◆ Describe some land features formed by water erosion including groundwater erosion. ◆ Describe land features formed when rivers and streams deposit sediment. ◆ Describe the features of a river system.	2 periods/ 1 block	**Discover** How Does Moving Water Wear Away Rocks?, p. 132 **Try This** Raindrops Falling, p. 134 **Science at Home,** p. 141 **Real-World Lab: You and Your Environment** Streams in Action, pp. 142–143	TE Real-Life Learning, pp. 133, 136, 139 TE Building Inquiry Skills: Comparing/Contrasting, p. 133 TE Including All Students, p. 134 TE Inquiry Challenge, pp. 135, 136 TE Using the Visuals: Figure 9, p. 135; Figure 12, p. 137 TE Integrating Chemistry, p. 140
3 *Integrating Physics* **The Force of Moving Water** pp. 145–148 ◆ Describe how water is able to do work. ◆ Explain how sediment enters rivers and streams. ◆ List the factors that affect a river's ability to erode and carry sediment.	1 period/ $\frac{1}{2}$–1 block	**Discover** How Are Sediments Deposited?, p. 145 **Sharpen Your Skills** Developing Hypotheses, p. 147	TE Inquiry Challenge, p. 147 LM 5, "The Daily Grind"
4 Glaciers pp. 149–143 ◆ Name and describe two kinds of glaciers. ◆ Describe two processes by which glaciers erode land. ◆ Explain how glaciers deposit sediments, and the role of the ice ages in glacial erosion.	1 period/ $\frac{1}{2}$ block	**Discover** How Do Glaciers Change the Land?, p. 149	TE Building Inquiry Skills: Designing Experiments, p. 150 TE Building Inquiry Skills: Observing, p. 151 TE Demonstration, p. 152
5 Waves pp. 154–157 ◆ Identify what gives ocean waves their energy. ◆ Describe how waves shape a coast and create landforms.	1 period/ $\frac{1}{2}$ block	**Discover** What Can Be Learned From Beach Sand?, p. 154 **Sharpen Your Skills** Calculating, p. 155	TE Inquiry Challenge, p. 156
6 Wind pp. 158–160 ◆ Describe the process by which wind causes erosion. ◆ Identify the features resulting from erosion and deposition by wind.	1 period/ $\frac{1}{2}$ block	**Discover** How Does Moving Air Affect Sediment?, p. 158 **Science at Home,** p. 160	TE Inquiry Challenge, p. 159 TE Demonstration, p. 159
Study Guide/Chapter Assessment pp. 161–163	1 period/ $\frac{1}{2}$ block		ISAB Provides teaching and review of all inquiry skills

For Standard or Block Schedule The Resource Pro® CD-ROM gives you maximum flexibility for planning your instruction for any type of schedule. Resource Pro® contains Planning Express®, an advanced scheduling program, as well as the entire contents of the Teaching Resources and the Computer Test Bank.

CHAPTER PLANNING GUIDE

Program Resources	Assessment Strategies	Media and Technology
UR Chapter 5 Project Teacher Notes **UR** Chapter 5 Project Overview and Worksheets	**SE** Performance Assessment: Present Your Project, p. 163 **TE** Check Your Progress, pp. 148, 153, 157 **UR** Chapter 5 Project Scoring Rubric	Science Explorer Internet Site at www.phschool.com Student Edition on Audio CD, Chapter 5
UR 5-1 Lesson Plan **UR** 5-1 Section Summary **UR** 5-1 Review and Reinforce **UR** 5-1 Enrich **UR** Chapter 5 Skills Lab	**SE** Section 1 Review, p. 129 **TE** Ongoing Assessment, p. 127 **TE** Performance Assessment, p. 129	Concept Videotape Library, Grade 6, Tape 1, "Flying Over America" Transparency 12, "Landslide, Slump, and Creep" Lab Activity Videotapes, Grade 6 Tape 1
UR 5-2 Lesson Plan **UR** 5-2 Section Summary **UR** 5-2 Review and Reinforce **UR** 5-2 Enrich **UR** Chapter 5 Real-World Lab	**SE** Section 2 Review, p. 141 **TE** Ongoing Assessment, pp. 133, 135, 137, 139 **TE** Performance Assessment, p. 141	Transparency 13, "Exploring the Course of a River", and 14, "Meander Formation" Lab Activity Videotapes, Grade 6 Tape 1
UR 5-3 Lesson Plan **UR** 5-3 Section Summary **UR** 5-3 Review and Reinforce **UR** 5-3 Enrich	**SE** Section 3 Review, p. 148 **TE** Ongoing Assessment, p. 147 **TE** Performance Assessment, p. 148	Transparency 15, "Water Erosion, Deposition, and Movement of Sediment"
UR 5-4 Lesson Plan **UR** 5-4 Section Summary **UR** 5-4 Review and Reinforce **UR** 5-4 Enrich	**SE** Section 4 Review, p. 153 **TE** Ongoing Assessment, p. 151 **TE** Performance Assessment, p. 153	Transparency 16, "Exploring Glacial Landforms"
UR 5-5 Lesson Plan **UR** 5-5 Section Summary **UR** 5-5 Review and Reinforce **UR** 5-5 Enrich	**SE** Section 5 Review, p. 157 **TE** Ongoing Assessment, p. 155 **TE** Performance Assessment, p. 157	Concept Videotape Library, Grade 6, Tape 1, "The Wave" Transparency 17, "Wave Erosion and Wind Erosion"
UR 5-6 Lesson Plan **UR** 5-6 Section Summary **UR** 5-6 Review and Reinforce **UR** 5-6 Enrich	**SE** Section 6 Review, p. 160 **TE** Ongoing Assessment, p. 159 **TE** Performance Assessment, p. 160	Transparency 17, "Wave Erosion and Wind Erosion"
RCA Provides strategies to improve science reading skills **GRSW** Provides worksheets to promote student comprehension of content	**SE** Chapter 5 Study Guide/Assessment, pp. 161–163 **PA** Chapter 5 Performance Assessment **CUT** Chapter 5 Test **CTB** Chapter 5 Test	Computer Test Bank, Chapter 5 Test

Key: **SE** Student Edition
CTB Computer Test Bank
ISAB Inquiry Skills Activity Book
GRSW Guided Reading and Study Workbook
TE Teacher's Edition
PTA Product Testing Activities by *Consumer Reports*
RCA Reading in the Content Area
PA Performance Assessment
UR Unit Resources
LM Laboratory Manual
IES Interdisciplinary Explorations Series
CUT Chapter and Unit Tests

Meeting the National Science Education Standards and AAAS Benchmarks

National Science Education Standards	Benchmarks for Science Literacy	Unifying Themes
Science As Inquiry (Content Standard A) ◆ **Develop descriptions, explanations, predictions, and models using evidence** Students make models to show how erosion and deposition can change a landscape. Students investigate the relationship between the height and width of a hill. Students use a stream table to model how rivers erode the land. *(Chapter Project; Skills Lab; Real-World Lab)* **Physical Science** (Content Standard B) ◆ **Transfer of energy** As gravity pulls water down a slope, the water's potential energy changes to kinetic energy. The energy in waves comes from wind that blows across the water's surface. *(Sections 3, 5)* **Earth and Space Science** (Content Standard D) ◆ **Structure of the Earth system** Weathering, erosion, and deposition act together in a cycle that wears down and builds up Earth's surface. The forces that cause erosion and deposition are gravity, running water, glaciers, waves, and wind. *(Chapter Project; Skills Lab; Real-World Lab)* **Science in Personal and Social Perspectives** (Content Standard F) ◆ **Risks and benefits** Students examine the issue of protecting homes in flood plains. *(Science and Society)*	**1B Scientific Inquiry** Students make models to show how erosion and deposition can change a landscape over time. Students investigate the relationship between the height and width of a hill using a model. Students use a stream table to model how rivers erode the land. *(Chapter Project; Skills Lab; Real-World Lab)* **4B The Earth** Gravity pulls everything toward the center of Earth. *(Section 1)* **4C Processes That Shape the Earth** Weathering, erosion, and deposition act together in a cycle that wears down and builds up Earth's surface. The forces that cause erosion and deposition are gravity, running water, glaciers, waves, and wind. *(Chapter Project; Sections 1, 2, 3, 4, 5, 6; Skills Lab; Real-World Lab)* **4E Energy Transformation** As gravity pulls water down a slope, the water's potential energy changes to kinetic energy that can do work. The energy in waves comes from wind that blows across the water's surface. *(Sections 3, 5)* **7D Social Trade-Offs** Students examine the issue of protecting homes in flood plains. *(Science and Society)*	◆ **Energy** Gravity is the force that pulls rocks and soil down slopes. Moving water is the major agent of erosion. Energy is the ability to do work or cause change. Gravity pulls glaciers downhill. The energy in waves comes from wind that blows across the water's surface. Deflation is the process by which wind removes surface materials. *(Sections 1, 2, 3, 4, 5, 6; Skills Lab; Real-World Lab)* ◆ **Modeling** Students model forces of erosion and deposition. *(Chapter Project; Skills Lab; Real-World Lab)* ◆ **Patterns of Change** Weathering, erosion, and deposition act together in a cycle that wears down and builds up Earth's surface. *(Chapter Project; Sections 1, 2, 3, 4, 5, 6; Skills Lab; Real-World Lab)* ◆ **Scale and Structure** Students investigate the relationship between the height and width of a hill. A drainage basin is the land area from which a river and its tributaries collect their water. *(Skills Lab; Section 2)* ◆ **Stability** Erosion and deposition are at work everywhere on Earth. *(Sections 1, 2, 3, 4, 5, 6)* ◆ **Systems and Interactions** Gravity, running water, glaciers, waves, and wind are the forces that cause erosion and deposition. *(Chapter Project; Sections 1, 2, 3, 4, 5, 6; Skills Lab; Real-World Lab)*

Take It to the Net

Interactive text at www.phschool.com

Science Explorer comes alive with iText.

- **Complete student text** is accessible from any computer with Internet access or a CD-ROM drive.
- **Animations, simulations, and videos** enhance student understanding and retention of concepts.
- **Self-tests and online study tools** assess student understanding.

STAY CURRENT with **SCIENCE NEWS®**

Find out the latest research and information about Earth's Surface: Weathering, Erosion, and Deposition at: **www.phschool.com**

Go to **www.phschool.com** and click on the Science icon.Then click on Science Explorer: Life, Earth, and Physical Science under PH@school.

Student Edition Activities Planner

ACTIVITY	Time *(minutes)*	Materials *Quantities for one work group*	Skills
Section 1			
Discover, p. 126	10	**Nonconsumable** small board, marble, block of wood, sandpaper	Developing Hypotheses
Sharpen Your Skills, p. 129	10	No special materials are required.	Observing
Science at Home, p. 129	home	**Nonconsumable** camera (optional)	Observing
Skills Lab, pp. 130–131	40	**Consumable** cardboard paper tube, sheets of white paper, masking tape **Nonconsumable** 500 mL of dry sand, tray (about 15 × 45 × 60 cm), wooden barbecue skewer, spoon, ruler, pencil or crayon	Developing Hypotheses, Designing Experiments, Creating Data Tables, Graphing, Predicting
Section 2			
Discover, p. 132	15	**Consumable** 2 bars of soap **Nonconsumable** cold-water faucet, watch or clock with second hand	Predicting
Try This, p. 134	15	**Consumable** fine-textured soil, newspaper, water **Nonconsumable** petri dish, plastic dropper, meter stick	Drawing Conclusions
Science at Home, p. 141	home	**Consumable** 27 sugar cubes, paper towel, water **Nonconsumable** small dish	Comparing and Contrasting
Real-World Lab, pp. 142–143	40	**Consumable** blue food coloring, water, 20-gauge wire, 10–12 cm plastic stirrers with two small holes each, plastic foam cup, liquid detergent **Nonconsumable** plastic tub (27 × 40 × 10 cm), diatomaceous earth, spray bottle, watch or clock, metal spoon, scissors, 2 wood blocks about 2.5 cm thick, 2–3 L bucket, plastic measuring cup, hand lens	Making Models, Observing, Predicting
Section 3			
Discover, p. 145	15	**Consumable** fine and coarse sand, soil, clay, small pebbles, water **Nonconsumable** clear plastic jar or bottle with top, plastic beaker	Inferring
Sharpen Your Skills, p. 147	5	No special materials are required.	Developing Hypotheses
Section 4			
Discover, p. 149	5; 10	**Consumable** sand, water, paper towel, bar of soap **Nonconsumable** small plastic container, freezer	Inferring
Section 5			
Discover, p. 154	15	**Nonconsumable** sand from 2 beaches, hand lens	Posing Questions
Sharpen Your Skills, p. 155	10	**Nonconsumable** calculator (optional)	Calculating
Section 6			
Discover, p. 158	10	**Consumable** cornmeal, plastic straw **Nonconsumable** shallow pan	Observing
Science at Home, p. 160	home	**Consumable** flour **Nonconsumable** 1-cm deep pan, plastic straw, several coins	Making Models

A list of all materials required for the Student Edition activities can be found on pages TVA34–TVA40. You can obtain information about ordering materials by calling 1-800-848-9500 or by accessing the Science Explorer Internet site at **www.phschool.com**.

CHAPTER 5 PROJECT

Changes in the Land

Most people think of the land as static—what is here today will be here tomorrow and forever. In the context of a human lifetime, that notion makes some sense. But in the context of the history of Earth, that notion is not valid, since Earth's surface is constantly changing.

Purpose In the Chapter 5 Project, students will make models to show how erosion and deposition change Earth's surface over time. By doing this project, students will gain a better understanding of the processes that change the land and the kinds of landforms that result.

Skills Focus Students will be able to:

- make models of a landscape—an initial basic landscape, and then a second model of the landscape as changed by water erosion and wave erosion;
- predict how the first landscape will be changed by erosion;
- relate cause and effect in making changes to the initial landscape due to erosion;
- communicate the results of the project in a presentation to the class.

Project Time Line The entire project will require about three weeks. Depending on how much time students spend working on the project each day, two or three days will be required for each of the following phases.

- Make a drawing of a landscape that will be changed by erosion.
- Collect and prepare materials for making the model.
- Make a three-dimensional model of the landscape using the drawing as a guide.
- Make a second drawing that predicts the effects of gravity, water erosion, and glacial erosion on the landscape.
- Make a second model using the second sketch as a guide.
- Add the effects of wave erosion to the second model.
- Make a presentation of the two models to the class.

For more detailed information on planning and supervising this project, see Chapter 5 Project Teacher Notes in Unit 2 Resources.

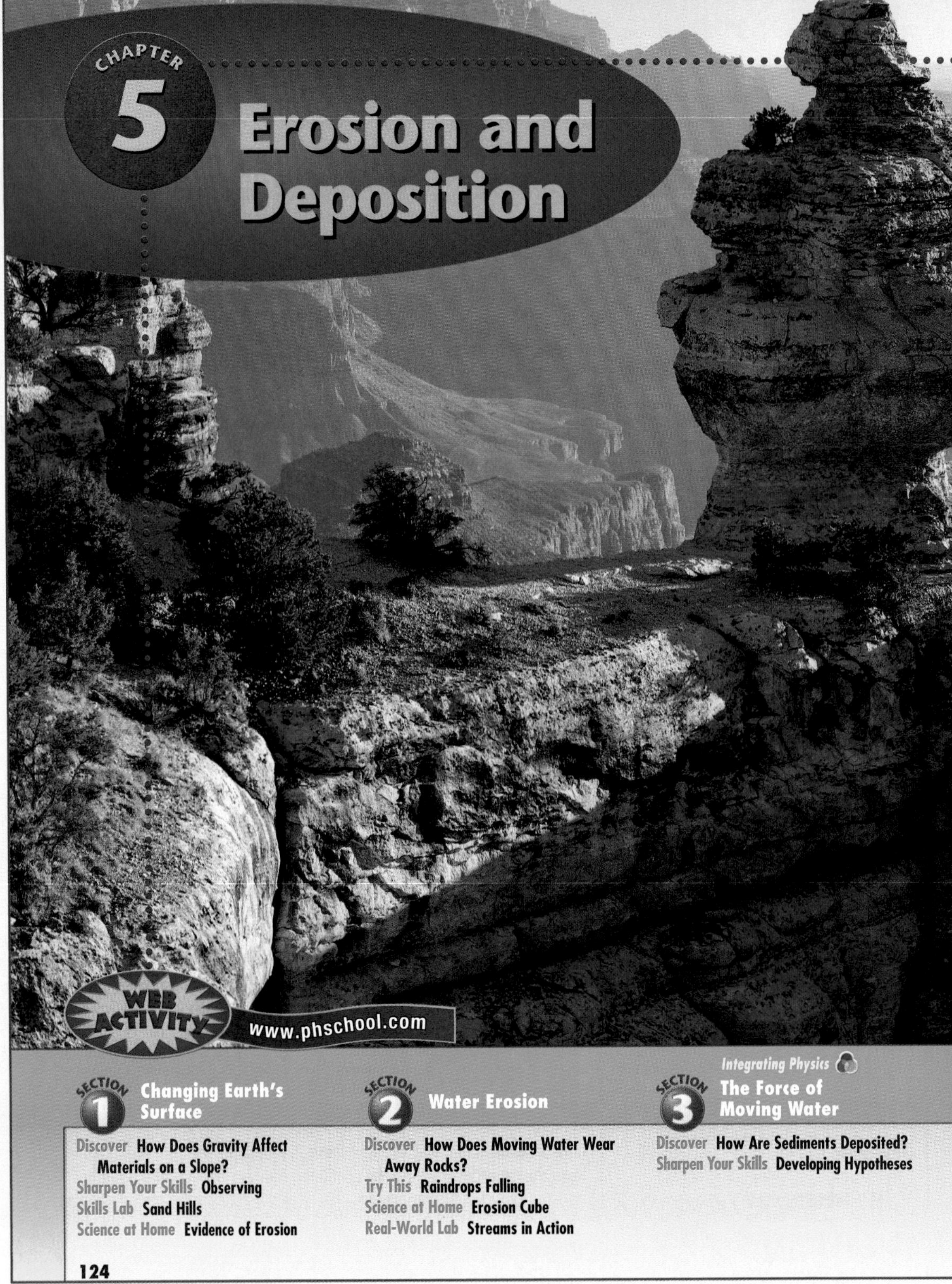

CHAPTER 5 Erosion and Deposition

SECTION 1 Changing Earth's Surface
Discover How Does Gravity Affect Materials on a Slope?
Sharpen Your Skills Observing
Skills Lab Sand Hills
Science at Home Evidence of Erosion

SECTION 2 Water Erosion
Discover How Does Moving Water Wear Away Rocks?
Try This Raindrops Falling
Science at Home Erosion Cube
Real-World Lab Streams in Action

Integrating Physics
SECTION 3 The Force of Moving Water
Discover How Are Sediments Deposited?
Sharpen Your Skills Developing Hypotheses

124

Suggested Shortcuts

- You may wish to divide the class into small groups to carry out the project.
- You can make this project shorter and less involved by having students make the initial drawing of an uneroded landscape but forego making the first model. After each section, students can make new drawings that reflect changes from erosion. Then, about the time students learn about wave erosion, they could begin making a model that reflects all types of erosion. In the presentation, students could show their series of drawings and then present their model.
- For a class project, build one large model on a board covering a large table. Small groups can be in charge of making different sections of the model.

Possible Materials The suggested basic material for making such a model is a mixture of white glue and sand. For each small model, students will need about 20 mL of white glue, 700 mL of sand, and 60 mL of water. This can

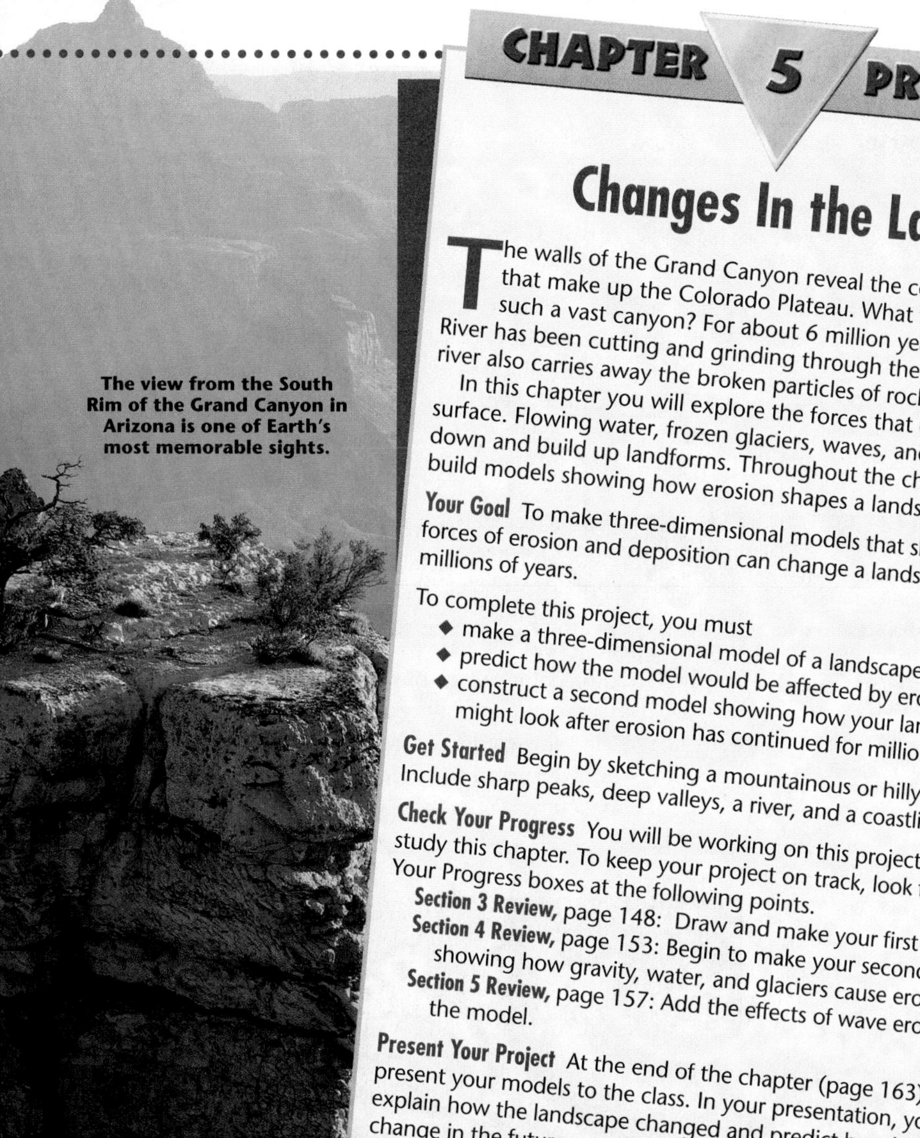

CHAPTER 5 PROJECT

Changes In the Land

The walls of the Grand Canyon reveal the colorful rock layers that make up the Colorado Plateau. What force shaped such a vast canyon? For about 6 million years the Colorado River has been cutting and grinding through the plateau. The river also carries away the broken particles of rock.

In this chapter you will explore the forces that change Earth's surface. Flowing water, frozen glaciers, waves, and wind all wear down and build up landforms. Throughout the chapter, you will build models showing how erosion shapes a landscape.

Your Goal To make three-dimensional models that show how the forces of erosion and deposition can change a landscape over millions of years.

To complete this project, you must

- ◆ make a three-dimensional model of a landscape
- ◆ predict how the model would be affected by erosion
- ◆ construct a second model showing how your landscape might look after erosion has continued for millions of years

Get Started Begin by sketching a mountainous or hilly landscape. Include sharp peaks, deep valleys, a river, and a coastline.

Check Your Progress You will be working on this project as you study this chapter. To keep your project on track, look for Check Your Progress boxes at the following points.

Section 3 Review, page 148: Draw and make your first model.

Section 4 Review, page 153: Begin to make your second model, showing how gravity, water, and glaciers cause erosion.

Section 5 Review, page 157: Add the effects of wave erosion to the model.

Present Your Project At the end of the chapter (page 163), you will present your models to the class. In your presentation, you will explain how the landscape changed and predict how it might change in the future.

The view from the South Rim of the Grand Canyon in Arizona is one of Earth's most memorable sights.

Section 4 Glaciers

Discover **How Do Glaciers Change the Land?**

Section 5 Waves

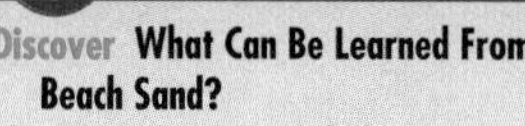

Discover **What Can Be Learned From Beach Sand?**

Sharpen Your Skills **Calculating**

Section 6 Wind

Discover **How Does Moving Air Affect Sediment?**

Science at Home **Modeling Desert Pavement**

125

be mixed in a 4-L plastic bucket. Wear plastic gloves when preparing the mixture. For a base, use either a plastic-coated paper plate, a piece of wood, or a small tray. Students can add any other materials to make their models attractive and realistic. Alternatives to the glue-sand mixture include modeling clay, salt dough, and papier mâché.

Launching the Project To introduce the project, describe the region in which students live, mentioning prominent rivers and landforms. Then ask: **If you could go back a few million years, would this region look the same?** *(Most students will say that changes have occurred in the last million years, though they may lack specifics.)* **What if you could go forward a few million years? What changes in the land would you expect to see?** *(Answers will vary. Students may speculate about added mountains or rivers.)* Explain that in Chapter 5 they will learn about how erosion and deposition make changes in the land, and in the Chapter 5 Project, they will make models that dramatically show such changes. To help students get started, pass out Chapter 5 Project Overview and Worksheets in Unit 2 Resources. You may also wish to pass out the Chapter 5 Project Scoring Rubric at this time.

Program Resources

- ◆ **Unit 2 Resources** Chapter 5 Project Teacher Notes; Chapter 5 Project Overview and Worksheets; Chapter 5 Project Scoring Rubric

www.phschool.com

You will find an Internet activity, chapter self-tests for students, and links to other chapter topics at this site.

Media and Technology

Student Edition on Audio CD
Chapter 5

Performance Assessment

Use the Chapter 5 Project Scoring Rubric to assess students' work. Students will be assessed on

- ◆ how well they make their initial drawings and first model;
- ◆ how effectively and comprehensively they represent the different kinds of erosion in their second model;
- ◆ how well-constructed and attractive their models are;
- ◆ how effectively they present their models and related concepts to the class.

SECTION 1 Changing Earth's Surface

Objectives

After completing the lesson, students will be able to
- ◆ describe the processes that wear down and build up Earth's surface;
- ◆ identify the force that pulls rock and soil down slopes.

Key Terms erosion, sediment, deposition, mass movement

1 Engage/Explore

Activating Prior Knowledge

Encourage students to relate their experiences on a steep path up a hill or mountain. Ask: **What happens when you step on loose rock or dirt?** *(You will slip, and the rock and dirt falls downhill.)* **What could naturally cause a similar movement of sediment downhill?** *(Students might suggest a heavy storm or earthquake.)*

DISCOVER

Skills Focus developing hypotheses
Materials *small board, marble, block of wood, sandpaper*
Time 10 minutes
Tips Precut sandpaper to sizes that can be wrapped around the board and the block of wood. The block of wood should be completely wrapped in sandpaper; the board does not have to be completely wrapped if there is enough overlap.
Think It Over Upon tipping the board, the marble will immediately roll down the slope, while the block of wood will move down when the board is tipped higher. When sandpaper covers the board and the block, the block or wood may move only when the board is tipped up almost to vertical. Hypotheses will vary. A typical hypothesis might suggest that movement downward depends both on the angle of the board and on the type of material on the board.

SECTION 1 Changing Earth's Surface

DISCOVER ACTIVITY

How Does Gravity Affect Materials on a Slope?

1. Place a small board flat on your desk. Place a marble on the board and slowly tip the board up slightly at one end. Observe what happens.
2. Place a block of wood on the board. Slowly lift one end of the board and observe the result.
3. Next, cover the board and the wood block with sandpaper and repeat Step 2.

Think It Over

Developing Hypotheses How do the results of each step compare? Develop a hypothesis to explain the differences in your observations.

GUIDE FOR READING

- ◆ What processes wear down and build up Earth's surface?
- ◆ What force pulls rock and soil down slopes?
- ◆ What are the different types of mass movement?

Reading Tip As you read, make a list of main ideas and supporting details about erosion, deposition, and mass movement.

Madison River Canyon is a quiet wilderness area in the Rocky Mountains of Montana. In 1959, something happened to change the canyon forever. When a strong earthquake jolted nearby Yellowstone National Park, a mountainside along the canyon gave way. In a few seconds, nearly 30 million cubic meters of rock, soil, and trees slid into the canyon. If this much material were in the shape of a cube, then each side of the cube would be three times longer than a football field. Rock and soil from the landslide dammed the Madison River, forming a new lake.

Figure 1 During a landslide, loose rock and soil on the side of a mountain suddenly slide away from underlying bedrock. This landslide in Madison River Canyon, Montana, buried a highway and campground.

READING STRATEGIES

Reading Tip Students should make three lists, one of ideas about erosion, another of ideas about deposition, and a third of ideas about mass movement. Students can use the subheadings as organizers for the third list, listing details about each type of mass movement under the subheadings. Suggest that they use their lists as a study guide for the section.

Student's lists might begin as follows:
Erosion
1. The process by which natural forces move rock and soil
2. Examples include a landslide and rain water carrying soil and gravel down a driveway.
3. Gravity, running water, glaciers, waves, and wind cause erosion.

Wearing Down and Building Up

A landslide like the one in Madison River Canyon is a spectacular example of erosion. **Erosion** is the process by which natural forces move weathered rock and soil from one place to another. A landslide is a very rapid type of erosion. Other types of erosion move soil and rock more slowly. Gravity, running water, glaciers, waves, and wind can all cause erosion. You may have seen water carrying soil and gravel down a driveway after it rains. That's an example of erosion. Erosion also caused the damage to the road in Figure 2.

The material moved by erosion is **sediment.** Both weathering and erosion produce sediment. **Deposition** occurs where the agents of erosion lay down sediment. Deposition changes the shape of the land. You may have watched a playing child who picked up several toys and then carried them across a room and put them down. This child was acting something like an agent of erosion and deposition.

Weathering, erosion, and deposition act together in a cycle that wears down and builds up Earth's surface. Erosion and deposition are at work everywhere on Earth. Sometimes they work slowly. At other times, they work more quickly, such as during a thunderstorm. Then, heavy rain soaks into rock and soil. These water-soaked materials may then come loose suddenly and slide down a mountain. But as a mountain wears down in one place, new landforms build up in other places. Erosion and deposition are never-ending.

Figure 2 Heavy winter rains washed out this California highway. *Relating Cause and Effect What caused the erosion that you can see in the photograph?*

☑ ***Checkpoint*** *What happens to sediment as a result of erosion and deposition?*

Mass Movement

Imagine that you are sitting on a bicycle at the top of a hill. With only a slight push, you can coast down the hill. If the slope of the hill is very steep, you will reach a high speed before reaching the bottom. The force that pulls you and your bicycle downward is gravity. Gravity pulls everything toward the center of Earth.

Gravity is the force that moves rock and other materials downhill. Gravity causes **mass movement,** any one of several processes that move sediment downhill. Mass movement can be rapid or slow. **The different types of mass movement include landslides, mudslides, slump, and creep.**

2 Facilitate

Wearing Down and Building Up

Including All Students

To help students who have limited English proficiency better understand the concept of a cycle, ask: **Can you name other natural cycles?** *(Cycle of day and night, water cycle, rock cycle, oxygen–carbon dioxide cycle)* Emphasize that a cycle has no beginning and no end and that it is continually occurring everywhere on Earth. Ask: **What part of this cycle wears down Earth's surface?** *(weathering)* **What part builds up Earth's surface?** *(deposition)* Point out that erosion acts as a bridge between those two processes. **limited English proficiency**

Mass Movement

Using the Visuals: Figure 1

After students have examined the figure and read the caption, ask: **Have you ever seen a pile of rocks at the bottom of a cliff?** *(Students may mention such sights at roadcuts or at the bottom of cliffs in parks.)* **What type of landform is necessary for such a landslide to occur?** *(A steep slope)* Then have students speculate on what could cause a landslide. Guide them to an understanding that any disturbance can begin one rock rolling, and that rock can cause another to move, and so on until a whole mass moves together down a slope. Ask: **How could mechanical or chemical weathering result in a landslide?** *(A block of rock could break apart due to weathering and then move down a slope because of gravity.)* **learning modality: visual**

Program Resources

- **Unit 2 Resources** 5-1 Lesson Plan; 5-1 Section Summary
- **Guided Reading and Study Workbook** Section 5-1

Media and Technology

Transparencies "Landslide, Slump, and Creep," Transparency 12

Answers to Self-Assessment

Caption Question

Figure 2 Heavy rain caused the erosion in the photograph.

☑ ***Checkpoint***

Erosion moves sediment from one place to another. Deposition lays down sediment in new locations, building new landforms.

Ongoing Assessment

Writing Have students use the key terms *erosion, deposition,* and *mass movement* in sentences.

Mass Movement, continued

Sharpen your Skills

Observing

Time 10 minutes
Expected Outcome Students should construct a table that includes the following: Soil is the primary material involved in both slump and creep. Slump occurs on a steep slope, while creep occurs on a gentle slope. Slump occurs quickly, while creep occurs slowly.
Extend Have students complete their tables by including similar information about landslides and mudflows.
learning modality: visual

Demonstration

Materials *soil, sand, gravel, large plastic tray, water, watering can*
Time 10 minutes

Build a model mountain on the plastic tray using soil, sand, and gravel. Then, as students observe, shake the tray. Ask: **What does the shaking model?** *(An earthquake)* **What does the model earthquake cause?** *(A landslide)* Rebuild the mountain, and then use the watering can to "rain" on the model. Continue this until some movement occurs. Ask: **What did the "rainfall" cause?** *(A mudslide or slump)* **What did the water do to the mountain that caused mass movement to occur?** *(The water added weight to the material. It also caused the soil to become mud, which can flow.)* Students might infer that for a time the added water actually held the "mountain" together, because the addition of water causes cementation. But once a certain amount is reached, the added weight and change to mud causes a downward movement. Ask: **What force is responsible for all these types of mass movement?** *(Gravity)*
learning modality: visual

Figure 3 A mudflow caused by heavy rains raced through the streets of this town in Italy.
Relating Cause and Effect *What characteristic of soil can contribute to a mudflow?*

Landslides The most destructive kind of mass movement is a landslide, which occurs when rock and soil slide quickly down a steep slope. Some landslides may contain huge masses of rock. But many landslides contain only a small amount of rock and soil. Such mass movement is common where road builders have cut highways through hills or mountains.

Mudflows A mudflow is the rapid downhill movement of a mixture of water, rock, and soil. The amount of water in a mudflow can be as high as 60 percent. Mudflows often occur after heavy rains in a normally dry area. In clay soils with a high water content, mudflows may occur even on very gentle slopes. Under certain conditions, clay soils suddenly turn to liquid and begin to flow. For example, an earthquake can trigger both mudflows and landslides. Mudflows like the one in Figure 3 can be very dangerous.

Slump If you slump your shoulders, the entire upper part of your body drops down. In the type of mass movement known as slump, a mass of rock and soil suddenly slips down a slope. Unlike a landslide, the material in slump moves down in one large mass. It looks as if someone pulled the bottom out from under part of the slope. Figure 4 shows an example of slump. Slump often occurs when water soaks the base of a mass of soil that is rich in clay.

Figure 4 Slump can look as if a giant spoon has started to scoop a mass of soil out from a hillside.

128

Background

Facts and Figures Gravity is the force that causes mass movement, but water almost always plays a major role, even in landslides of rock fragments. Water reduces friction, so that during a wet season rocks that previously were stable may suddenly slide over other rocks. In sand or clay, some water may add to stability, just as wet beach sand is used to make a sand castle. But too much water causes flow.

Landslides and mudflows result in 25–50 deaths per year in the United States and an average of 600 deaths per year throughout the world. They are also responsible for huge monetary losses, including more than \$1.5 billion a year in the United States. In earthquakes, damage from mass movement can be more significant than that from the quake itself.

Creep Landscapes affected by creep may have the eerie, out-of-kilter look of a funhouse in an amusement park. Creep is the very slow downhill movement of rock and soil. It can even occur on gentle slopes. Like the movement of an hour hand on a clock, creep is so slow you can barely notice it. But you can see the effects of creep in objects such as telephone poles, gravestones, and fenceposts. Creep may tilt these objects at spooky angles. Creep often results from the freezing and thawing of water in cracked layers of rock beneath the soil. How have the trees in Figure 5 been affected by creep?

Figure 5 Creep has slowly tilted these trees downhill, causing their trunks to grow in a curve. ***Predicting*** *If creep continues, how might it affect the road, the fence, and the electric power lines?*

Sharpen your Skills

Observing ACTIVITY

Compare the examples of mass movement in Figures 4 and 5. Based on your observations, construct a table comparing slump and creep. Include the Earth materials involved, the type of slope, and the speed for each type of mass movement.

Section 1 Review

1. Explain the difference between erosion and deposition.
2. What force causes erosion?
3. What are four types of mass movement?
4. **Thinking Critically Relating Cause and Effect** Why would a landslide be more likely on a steep mountain than on a gently sloping hill?

Science at Home

Evidence of Erosion After a rainstorm, take a walk with an adult family member around your neighborhood. Look for evidence of erosion. Try to find areas where there is loose soil, sand, gravel, or rock. (**CAUTION:** *Stay away from any large pile of loose sand or soil—it may slide without warning.*) Which areas have the most erosion? The least erosion? How does the slope of the ground affect the amount of erosion? Sketch or take photographs of the areas showing evidence of erosion.

Media and Technology

Concept Videotape Library Grade 6, Tape 1 "Flying Over America"

Program Resources

◆ **Unit 2 Resources** 5-1 Review and Reinforce; 5-1 Enrich

Answers to Self-Assessment

Caption Questions

Figure 3 Clay soils with high water content can suddenly turn to liquid.

Figure 5 Students may predict that the road will buckle or even break and the fence and poles will tilt and perhaps fall over.

3 Assess

Section 1 Review Answers

1. Erosion moves sediment from one place to another, while deposition lays down sediment in new locations.

2. The force of gravity and the forces exerted by running water, glaciers, waves, and wind cause erosion.

3. The four types of mass movement are landslides, mudflows, slump, and creep.

4. On a gently sloping hill, the force of gravity cannot pull down rock and soil quickly because of the friction between the hill and the rock and soil. On a steep mountain, though, the force of gravity can much more easily overcome the force of friction.

Science at Home

Tips Encourage students to make this erosion ACTIVITY survey around their neighborhood. They should especially look for evidence of mass movement, such as piles of rock at the bottom of a hill or cliff as well as landscapes affected by creep. Also have students anticipate what they will learn in the next section by looking for evidence of water erosion, especially in places that lack vegetation. Students can bring their drawings and/or photos to class and present interesting examples. Use the best examples to make a bulletin board that focuses on mass movement and water erosion.

Performance Assessment

Drawing Have students make drawings of each of the four types of mass movement, using the block illustrations in Figures 1, 4, and 5 for models of landslide, slump, and creep, respectively. For mudslide, they will have to create their own illustration to represent that type in a similar way. Display the best illustrations on a bulletin board.

Students can keep their drawings in their portfolios.

Skills Lab

Developing Hypotheses

Sand Hills

Preparing for Inquiry

Key Concept Gravity causes mass movement, a process that moves sediment downhill.

Skills Objectives Students will be able to:
- develop a hypothesis about how the height and width of a sand hill will change as more sand is added;
- design an experiment to test the hypothesis;
- create a data table and use the data to make a graph;
- predict what would happen if the experiment were continued.

Time 40 minutes

Advance Planning For the trays, collect either cardboard box tops or plastic trays. Make sure the sand is very dry.

Alternative Materials A fine aquarium gravel could be used in place of the sand. Butcher-block paper cut to fit the tray bottom could be used instead of taping smaller sheets together. If barbecue skewers are unavailable, cut stiff wire to about the same length as a skewer.

Guiding Inquiry

Invitation Focus on the primary skill of the lab—developing hypotheses—by asking: **What is a hypothesis?** *(A hypothesis is a proposed explanation or answer to a question.)* **What do scientists do to support or disprove a hypothesis?** *(They test the hypothesis through an experiment.)* **Why is it better to formulate a hypothesis with specifics rather than generalities?** *(Specifics can be tested with experiments and either confirmed or proved wrong. Generalities are hard to test experimentally.)*

Introducing the Procedure
- Give students time to read through the whole procedure, and then ask: **What sort of mass movement is involved in this lab? Explain.** *(Landslides, because the material pulled down the slope slides quickly and doesn't involve water.)*
- **What is the force that moves material down a slope?** *(Gravity)*

Skills Lab

Developing Hypotheses

Sand Hills

In this lab, you will develop and test a hypothesis about how mass movement affects the size and shape of a sand hill.

Problem

What is the relationship between the height and width of a sand hill?

Materials

dry sand, 500 mL
cardboard tube
tray (about 15 cm × 45 cm × 60 cm)
wooden barbecue skewer
masking tape
spoon
ruler
pencil or crayon
several sheets of white paper

Procedure  

1. Begin by observing how gravity causes mass movement in sand. To start, place the cardboard tube vertically in the center of the tray.
2. Using the spoon, fill the cardboard tube with the dry sand. Take care not to spill the sand around the outside of the tube.
3. Carefully lift the sand-filled tube straight up so that all the sand flows out. As you lift the tube, observe the sand's movement.
4. Develop a hypothesis explaining how you think the width of the sand pile is related to its height for different amounts of sand.
5. Empty the sand in the tray back into a container. Then set up your system for measuring the sand hill.
6. Copy the data table into your lab notebook.
7. Following Steps 1 through 3, make a new sand hill.

How to Measure a Sand Hill

1. Cover the bottom of the tray with unlined white paper and tape it firmly in place.
2. Mark off points 0.5 cm apart along one side of the paper in the tray.
3. Carefully draw the sand hill's outline on the paper. The line should go completely around the base of the hill.
4. Now measure the width of the hill against the marks you made along the edge of the paper.
5. Measure the sand hill's height by inserting a barbecue skewer through its center. Make a mark on the skewer at the top of the hill.
6. Remove the skewer and use the ruler to measure how much of the skewer was buried in the hill. Try not to disturb the sand.

Troubleshooting the Experiment
- Guide students in developing a specific hypothesis that can be tested. A testable hypothesis might be: "As sand is added to the sand hill, the hill's height will increase half as much as its width." Allow students to test any reasonable hypothesis.
- Tell students to fill the cardboard tube carefully so that they don't spill sand outside the tube onto the hill. In filling the tube, one student can hold it while another student pours in the sand.
- The rate of raising the tube will affect how fast the sand flows out, and thus affect how much sand moves down the hill. Students should raise the tube at about the same rate each time.
- Demonstrate how to use the skewer to measure the height of the hill. Caution students to be as gentle as possible when inserting the skewer into the hill so as not to cause mass movement because of the skewer.

DATA TABLE					
Test	1	2	3	4	5
Width					
Height					

8. Measure and record the sand hill's height and width for Test 1. (See the instructions on the bottom of the previous page to help you accurately measure the height and width.)
9. Now test what happens when you add more sand to the sand hill. Place your cardboard tube vertically at the center of the sand hill. Be careful not to push the tube down into the sand hill! Using the spoon, fill the tube with sand as before.
10. Carefully raise the tube and observe the results of the sand's movement.
11. Measure and record the sand hill's height and width for Test 2.
12. Repeat Steps 9 through 11 at least three more times. After each test, record your results. Be sure to number each test.

Analyze and Conclude

1. Make a graph showing how the sand hill's height and width changed with each test. (*Hint:* Use the *x*-axis of the graph for height. Use the *y*-axis of the graph for width.)

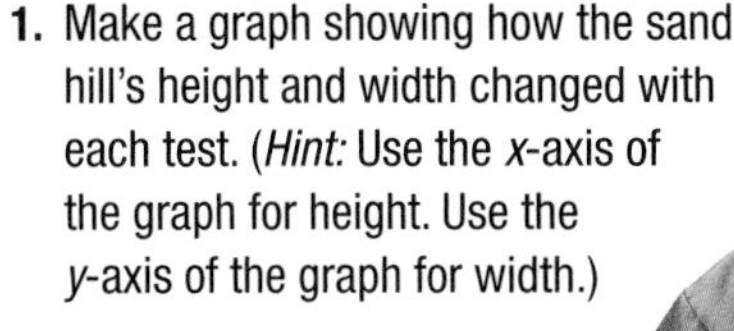

2. What does your graph show about the relationship between the sand hill's height and width?
3. Does your graph support your hypothesis about the sand hill's height and width? Why or why not?
4. How would you revise your original hypothesis after examining your data? Give reasons for your answer.
5. **Think About It** Predict what would happen if you continued the experiment for five more tests. Extend your graph with a dashed line to show your prediction. How could you test your prediction?

Design an Experiment

Do you think the use of different materials, such as wet sand or gravel, would produce different results from dry sand? Make a new hypothesis about the relationship between slope and width in hills made of materials other than dry sand. Design an experiment in which you test how these different materials form hills. Obtain your teacher's approval before you try the experiment.

Program Resources

◆ **Unit 2 Resources** Chapter 5 Skills Lab

Media and Technology

Lab Activity Videotapes
Grade 6, Tape 1

Safety

Students should wear their goggles when working with sand, since dry sand could become lodged in an eye and cause damage. Also, advise students to be careful when handling the skewer, for it could penetrate skin or harm the eyes. Review the safety guidelines in Appendix A.

Expected Outcome

Results may vary depending on several factors, including the type and dryness of the sand, the diameter of the cardboard tube, and the way in which students add sand to the hill. In tests 2 through 5, both height and width will increase, though width will probably increase more. Repeated tests show that the relationship between the sand hill's height and width remains constant (*i.e.,* the points fall approximately along a straight line on the graph). The amount by which the hill's height and width increase depends on the amount of sand added in relation to the total amount of sand in the pile.

Analyze and Conclude

1. Graphs will vary. A typical graph should show a line rising from left to right.
2. Answers will vary. A typical response may suggest that as the height of the sand hill increases, the hill's width increases more.
3. Answers will vary depending on students' hypotheses. Students should compare their original hypothesis with the data collected to determine whether the hypothesis was supported or not.
4. Answers will vary depending on the original hypotheses. Students whose hypotheses were not supported should develop a new hypothesis that would be supported by the data collected.
5. Answers will vary depending on the graphs made from the data of the five tests. Most students should infer from the graph that width will continue to increase more rapidly than height.

Extending the Inquiry

Design an Experiment Hypotheses will vary. Using wet sand would probably increase the height of the hill at the expense of the width; using wet gravel might produce the opposite effect. Encourage students to make a hypothesis about one of the materials and design an experiment. Allow students to carry out the best designs and report their findings to the class.

Section 2 Water Erosion

Objectives

After completing the lesson, students will be able to

- explain how water erosion is mainly responsible for shaping Earth's land surface;
- describe some of the land features formed by water erosion, including groundwater erosion;
- describe land features formed when rivers and streams deposit sediment;
- describe the features of a river system.

Key Terms runoff, rill, gully, stream, river, tributary, drainage basin, divide, flood plain, meander, oxbow lake, alluvial fan, delta, groundwater, stalactite, stalagmite, karst topography

1 Engage/Explore

Activating Prior Knowledge

Elicit students' descriptions of a major river in their region. Then ask: **Where does the river get its water?** *(From smaller rivers and streams)* Keep backtracking until students describe something like a rill or gully.

Discover Activity

Skills Focus predicting
Materials *2 bars of soap, cold- water faucet, watch or clock with second hand*
Time 15 minutes
Tips Before students carry out the experiment, have them read the procedure and identify the variable tested (dripping water) and the control (the bar in the dry place). For Step 2, students should record the number of drops in one minute; for Step 3, they should record a prediction.
Expected Outcome The dripping water will wear a depression in the bar of soap.
Think It Over Predictions may vary. Typical predictions may suggest that the depression will grow larger in another 10 minutes and larger still after an hour. Increasing the flow would speed up the process; decreasing the flow would slow it down.

Section 2 Water Erosion

Discover Activity

How Does Moving Water Wear Away Rocks?

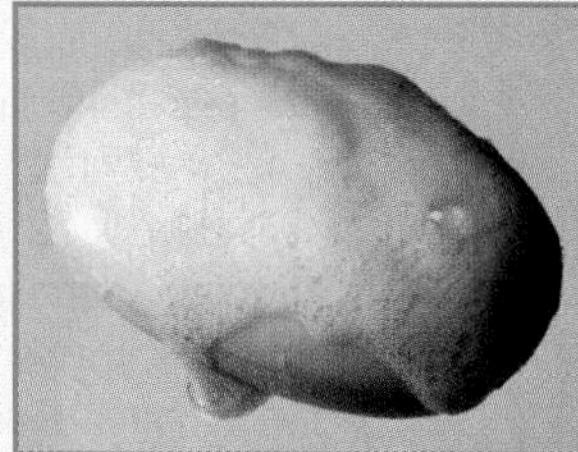

1. Obtain two bars of soap that are the same size and brand.
2. Open a faucet just enough to let the water drip out very slowly. How many drops of water does the faucet release per minute?
3. Place one bar of soap in a dry place. Place the other bar of soap under the faucet. Predict the effect of the dripping water droplets on the soap.
4. Let the faucet drip for 10 minutes.
5. Turn off the faucet and observe both bars of soap. What difference do you observe between them?

Think It Over

Predicting What would the bar of soap under the dripping faucet look like if you left it there for another 10 minutes? For an hour? How could you speed up the process? Slow it down?

Guide for Reading

- What process is mainly responsible for shaping Earth's land surface?
- What features are formed by water erosion?
- What features are formed when rivers and streams deposit sediment?

Reading Tip Before you read, use the headings to make an outline on water erosion and deposition.

Walking in the woods in summer, you can hear the racing water of a stream before you see the stream itself. The water roars as it foams over rock ledges and boulders. When you reach the stream, you see water rushing by. Sand and pebbles tumble along the bottom of the stream. As it swirls downstream, it also carries twigs, leaves, and bits of soil. In sheltered pools, insects such as water striders silently skim the water's calm surface. Beneath the surface, you see a rainbow trout hovering in the clear water.

If you visit the stream at other times of year, it will be very different. In winter, the stream freezes. Chunks of ice scrape and grind away at the stream's bed and banks. In spring, the stream floods. Then the flow of water may be strong enough to move large rocks. But throughout the year, the stream continues to erode its small part of Earth's surface.

A woodland stream ▼

Reading Strategies

Reading Tip If necessary, review with students how to make an outline. Then encourage them to skim the section before beginning their outlines. Suggest students use the subheadings under each main heading for the first two levels of the outline. For example, the next level under "Runoff and Erosion" should include "Rills and Gullies," "Streams and Rivers," and "Amount of Runoff."

Vocabulary Call student's attention to the highlighted sentence on page 133, in which moving water is said to be an "agent" of erosion. Students have learned about "agents" of chemical weathering, and now they study "agents" of erosion. An *agent* in this sense is not a representative, such as in "insurance agent," or a spy, such as in "secret agent." Rather, here *agent* means a "force or substance that causes change."

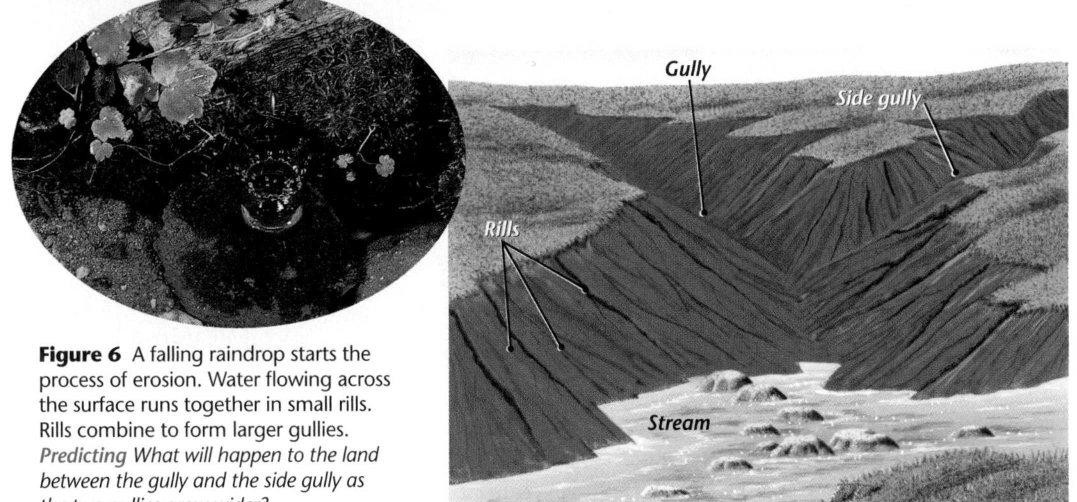

Figure 6 A falling raindrop starts the process of erosion. Water flowing across the surface runs together in small rills. Rills combine to form larger gullies. *Predicting What will happen to the land between the gully and the side gully as the two gullies grow wider?*

Runoff and Erosion

Running water creates many landforms. **Moving water is the major agent of the erosion that has shaped Earth's land surface.**

Erosion by water begins with the splash of rain, as you can see in Figure 6. Some rainfall sinks into the ground. Some evaporates or is taken up by plants. The force of a falling raindrop can loosen and pick up soil particles. As water moves over the land, it carries these particles with it. This moving water is called runoff. **Runoff** is all the remaining water that moves over Earth's surface. When runoff flows in a thin layer over the land, it may cause a type of erosion called sheet erosion.

Rills and Gullies Because of gravity, runoff and the material it contains move downhill. As runoff travels, it forms tiny grooves in the soil called **rills.** As the rills flow into one another, they grow larger, forming gullies. A **gully** is a large groove, or channel, in the soil that carries runoff after a rainstorm. As water flows through gullies, it moves soil and rocks with it, thus enlarging the gullies through erosion. Gullies flow only after it rains.

Program Resources

- **Unit 2 Resources** 5-2 Lesson Plan; 5-2 Section Summary
- **Guided Reading and Study Workbook** Section 5-2

Answers to Self-Assessment

Caption Question

Figure 6 The land between will erode until the gullies run together, lengthening the stream.

2 Facilitate

Runoff and Erosion

Real-Life Learning

Time 15 minutes

ACTIVITY

Most schools have a baseball field on the grounds or nearby. After a rain, take students out to the field and direct their attention to the base paths around the infield, which are usually made of easily eroded sandy soil. There, challenge students to find rills and rills that converge to form gullies. **learning modality: visual**

Building Inquiry Skills: Comparing and Contrasting

Materials *clear plastic or glass jars, samples of runoff from different locations, marker, masking tape*

ACTIVITY

Time 10 minutes

On the day of a heavy rain, encourage students to collect a sample of runoff. They can do this after school, in a location near where they live. To collect a sample, they can dip a jar into a stream of runoff water. Students should use tape and a marker to label the jar as to where the runoff was collected. Then in school the next day, have students examine each sample and note how much sediment it contains. Challenge students to draw conclusions about the locations in which runoff picks up the most sediment particles. **learning modality: kinesthetic**

Ongoing Assessment

Writing Have students explain how rills and gullies become streams.

Runoff and Erosion, continued

Skills Focus drawing conclusions
Materials *petri dish, fine-textured soil, newspaper, plastic dropper, water, meter stick*
Time 15 minutes
Tips To drop water from a height of 2 m, many students will have to climb onto a table or chair. Make sure they can accomplish this safely. An alternative would be to cut the distances in half, dropping water from 0.5 m in the first trials and then 1 m in the second trials.
Expected Outcome Students should observe that the drops from 2 m caused splashes that traveled farther than the splashes from the 1-m drops. Since the drops picked up sediment when they hit the soil, the 2-m drops also caused more erosion. Students should draw the conclusion that the 2-m drops had more force because the water fell a greater distance.
Extend Encourage students to try the same procedure with different materials in the dish, including sand, clayey soil, and gravel, and then compare results.
learning modality: kinesthetic

River Systems

Including All Students

Materials *atlas or encyclopedia*
Time 20 minutes

Pair students with different abilities and assign each pair one of the major rivers of North America, including the Colorado, the Columbia, the Hudson, the Mackenzie, the Mississippi, the Ohio, the Rio Grande, the Sacramento, and the Yukon. Then have students make a labeled map that includes the assigned river and its important tributaries. On this map, students should also show and label states, major cities, and the body of water into which the river flows.
learning modality: visual

Figure 7 As water erodes gullies, soil can be lost.

Raindrops Falling

Find out how the force of falling raindrops affects soil.

1. Fill a petri dish with fine-textured soil to a depth of about 1 cm. Make sure the soil has a smooth flat surface, but do not pack it firmly in the dish.
2. Place the dish in the center of a newspaper.
3. Fill a dropper with water. Squeeze a large water drop from a height of 1 m onto the surface of the soil. Repeat 4 times.
4. Use a meter stick to measure the distance the soil splashed from the dish. Record your observations.
5. Repeat Steps 1 through 4, this time from a height of 2 m. Which traveled farther, the splash from 1 m or the splash from 2 m?

Drawing Conclusions Which test produced the greater amount of erosion? Why?

Streams and Rivers Gullies join together to form a larger channel called a stream. A **stream** is a channel along which water is continually flowing down a slope. Unlike gullies, streams rarely dry up. Small streams are also called creeks or brooks. As streams flow together, they form larger and larger bodies of flowing water. A large stream is often called a **river.**

Amount of Runoff The amount of runoff in an area depends on five main factors. The first factor is the amount of rain an area receives. A second factor is vegetation. Grasses, shrubs, and trees reduce runoff by absorbing water and holding soil in place. A third factor is the type of soil. Some types of soils absorb more water than others. A fourth factor is the shape of the land. Land that is steeply sloped has more runoff than flatter land. Finally, a fifth factor is how people use the land. For instance, a paved parking lot absorbs no water, so all the rain that falls on it becomes runoff. Runoff also increases when a farmer cuts down crops, since this removes vegetation from the land.

Generally, more runoff means more erosion. In contrast, things that reduce runoff, such as plant leaves and roots, will reduce erosion. Even though deserts have little rainfall, they often have high runoff and erosion. This is because deserts usually have few plants. In wet areas, runoff and erosion may be low because there are more plants to protect the soil.

Checkpoint *What factors affect the amount of runoff in a region?*

River Systems

A stream grows into a larger stream or river by receiving water from tributaries. A **tributary** is a stream that flows into a larger stream. A small creek that flows into a large river is a tributary to that river. So too is a large river that adds its water to another large river. For instance, the Missouri River becomes a tributary of the Mississippi River near the city of St. Louis, even though both rivers are about the same size there.

Background

Facts and Figures Urbanization makes a tremendous difference in amount of runoff. When precipitation occurs in a natural area, 80–100% of the water that doesn't evaporate filters through the surface to become groundwater and 0–20% flows as runoff. In an urban area—because of roads, parking lots, and buildings—only 0–10% of water filters into the ground while 90–100% flows as surface runoff.

The Ohio River begins in Pittsburgh, Pennsylvania, at the confluence of the Allegheny and Monongahela rivers and flows 1,579 km before emptying into the Mississippi. The Ohio's drainage basin is about 528,400 km^2, about 16% of the Mississippi River's drainage basin of 3,222,000 km^2. Tributaries other than those shown in Figure 8 include the Kanawha, Scioto, Great Miami, and Green rivers.

Look at Figure 8. Notice all the tributaries to the Ohio River. Together, all these streams—from tiny rills to great rivers—form a system that drains a large part of eastern North America. A **drainage basin** is the land area from which a river and its tributaries collect their water.

If you were to follow a river upstream all the way to its source, you would finally reach a divide. A **divide** is the high ground between two drainage basins. The most famous divide within the United States is the Continental Divide, which follows the high ground of the Rocky Mountains. The Continental Divide separates streams that flow into the Gulf of Mexico from streams that flow into the Great Basin or the Pacific Ocean.

Ohio River Drainage Basin

Figure 8 The drainage basin of the Ohio River drains much of eastern North America. ***Interpreting Maps*** *What are the tributaries of the Ohio River? Could a tributary come from outside the drainage basin?*

Erosion by Rivers

Scientists classify rivers by identifying certain features that form as a result of erosion. **Through erosion, a river creates valleys, waterfalls, flood plains, meanders, and oxbow lakes.**

Rivers often form on steep mountain slopes. Near its source, a river is often fast-flowing and generally follows a straight, narrow course. The steep slopes along the river erode rapidly. The result is a deep, V-shaped valley.

Waterfalls may occur where a river meets an area of rock that is very hard and erodes slowly. The river flows over this rock and then flows over softer rock downstream. The softer rock wears away faster than the harder rock. Eventually a waterfall develops where the softer rock was removed. This process formed Niagara Falls, shown in Figure 9. Areas of rough water called rapids also occur where a river tumbles over hard rock.

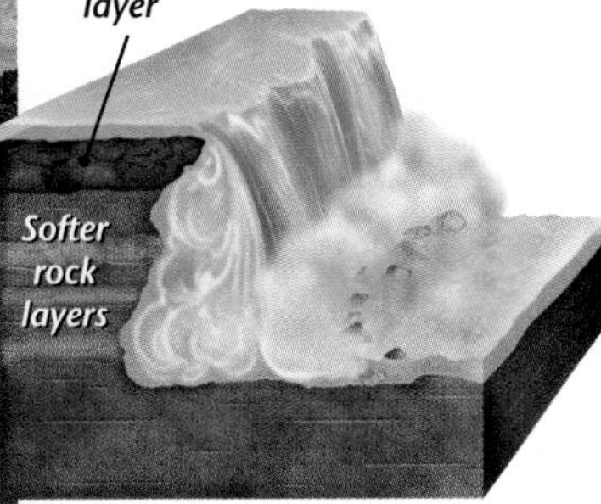

Figure 9 Niagara Falls formed on the Niagara River, which connects Lake Erie and Lake Ontario. A flat layer of tough rock lies over a layer of softer rock that erodes easily. When the softer rock erodes, pieces of the harder rock above break off, creating the waterfall's sharp drop.

Answers to Self-Assessment

Checkpoint

The amount of rain, the vegetation, type of soil, shape of the land, and how people use the land

Caption Question

Figure 8 The Allegheny, Monongahela, Wabash, Kentucky, and Tennessee rivers. A tributary could not come from outside the drainage basin.

Inquiry Challenge

ACTIVITY

Materials *shallow pan (2 cm deep, 10 cm wide, and at least 50 cm long), 2 buckets, rubber tubing (2-cm diameter), screw clamp, bricks, sand, water*
Time 30 minutes for setup

Challenge groups of students to design and build a stream table to study stream erosion and deposition. A typical design using the materials listed above would entail placing the pan on a table, with one end raised by several bricks. A bucket for adding water is then placed on a higher stack of bricks on the high side of the pan. Water is added to the pan by siphoning through rubber tubing and into the pan; a screw clamp on the tubing regulates the flow. The second bucket acts as an overflow reservoir at the low end of the pan. Help students make a notch in the pan to facilitate overflow. Once the stream table is made, groups can investigate whether a drainage basin forms when several small streams are begun at the high end of the table. **cooperative learning**

Erosion by Rivers

Using the Visuals: Figure 9

Materials *stream table, eraser, sand, water*
Time 20 minutes

After students examine the figure and read the caption, ask: **What is necessary for a waterfall to form on a stream?** *(An area of rock that is very hard and erodes much more slowly than the softer rock downstream.)* Then challenge small groups to create a model of the formation of a waterfall in a stream table. Students can use any hard material to model the hard-to-erode rock layer. An eraser, for example, could be placed across the stream in the stream table, stuck into the sand as a barrier. As water flows over the ruler, a "waterfall" will form as the soil downstream erodes. **learning modality: kinesthetic**

Ongoing Assessment

Oral Presentation Call on students to explain how the Ohio River can have its own drainage basin but also be a tributary to the Mississippi River.

Erosion by Rivers, continued

Real-Life Learning

Materials *topographic map*
Time 15 minutes

Provide students with copies of a topographic map that shows a river in their city or region. Then challenge students to use the map to measure and describe the boundaries of the flood plain of that river. Because interpretations will vary, invite selected students to explain to the class what they have found, and help students come to a consensus about the extent of the flood plain. For a definitive statement, have students contact the office of the county engineer. Because counties have rules about building on flood plains, the county engineer usually can give details about the width of the plain. **learning modality: logical/mathematical**

Using the Visuals: Figure 10

Draw students' attention to the photo of meanders. Have each student trace the river onto a clean sheet of paper. Then challenge students to use their tracings to make a labeled diagram of one or more illustrations that shows how an oxbow lake forms. A typical diagram should illustrate the processes of flooding, the river finding a new channel between two meanders, and the isolation of the oxbow lake. **learning modality: visual**

Inquiry Challenge

Materials *stream table, sand, water*
Time 20 minutes

Point out that meanders occur on wide, relatively flat plains rather than in mountainous areas. Challenge groups to form a hypothesis about how steepness of slope is related to development of meanders. After discussing each group's hypothesis, encourage students to test their hypotheses by designing and carrying out an experiment. **cooperative learning**

Figure 10 The oxbow lake (above) was formerly a part of the channel of the Kasanak River in Alaska. These meanders (right) were formed by a river in Australia.

Lower down on its course, a river usually flows over more gently sloping land. The river spreads out and erodes the land, forming a wide river valley. The flat, wide area of land along a river is a **flood plain.** A river often covers its flood plain when it overflows its banks during floods. On a wide flood plain, the valley walls may be kilometers away from the river itself.

A river often develops meanders where it flows through easily eroded rock or sediment. A **meander** is a looplike bend in the course of a river. As the river widens from side to side, it tends to erode the outer bank and deposit sediment on the inner bank of a bend. Over time, the bend—or meander—becomes more and more curved.

When the gently sloping part of a river flows through an area of sediment or soft rock, it can erode a very wide flood plain. Along this part of a river's course, its channel is deep and wide. Meanders are common along this part of a river. The southern stretch of the Mississippi River is one example of a river that meanders on a wide, gently sloping flood plain.

Sometimes a meandering river forms a feature called an oxbow lake. An **oxbow lake** is a meander that has been cut off from the river. An oxbow lake may form when a river floods. During the flood, high water finds a straighter route downstream. As the flood waters fall, sediments dam up the ends of a meander. The meander has become an oxbow lake.

☑ *Checkpoint How does an oxbow lake form?*

136

Background

History of Science The term *delta* as used to describe the landform at the mouth of a river was coined by the ancient Greek historian Herodotus in the fifth century B.C. He noticed that the shape of the area where the Nile River flowed into the Mediterranean Sea was roughly triangular, the same shape as the Greek letter delta.

Facts and Figures The Mississippi Delta is actually a combination of seven lobes, or subdeltas. The river created each subdelta one after another over 5,000 years as it shifted its course six times. The reason for each shift is that deposition fills in a channel over time. When the channel becomes too shallow, the river shifts course by breaking through a natural levee back upstream. Studies show that the Mississippi has flowed through its present course for 500 years.

Deposits by Rivers

Figure 11 This alluvial fan in Death Valley, California, was formed from deposits by streams from the mountains.

As water moves, it carries sediments with it. Any time moving water slows down, it drops, or deposits, some of the sediment. As the water slows down, fine particles fall to the river's bed. Larger stones quit rolling and sliding. **Deposition creates landforms such as alluvial fans and deltas. It can also add soil to a river's flood plain.** In *Exploring the Course of a River* on pages 138–139, you can see these and other features shaped by rivers and streams.

Alluvial Fans Where a stream flows out of a steep, narrow mountain valley, the stream suddenly becomes wider and shallower. The water slows down. Here sediments are deposited in an alluvial fan. An **alluvial fan** is a wide, sloping deposit of sediment formed where a stream leaves a mountain range. As its name suggests, this deposit is shaped like a fan.

Deltas A river ends its journey when it flows into a still body of water, such as an ocean or a lake. Because the river water is no longer flowing downhill, the water slows down. At this point, the sediment in the water drops to the bottom. Sediment deposited where a river flows into an ocean or lake builds up a landform called a **delta.** Deltas can be a variety of shapes: some are arc-shaped, others are triangle-shaped. The delta of the Mississippi River is an example of a type of delta called a "bird's foot" delta.

Soil on Flood Plains Deposition also occurs during floods. *INTEGRATING LIFE SCIENCE* Then heavy rains or melting snow cause a river to rise above its banks and spread out over its flood plain. When the flood water finally retreats, it deposits sediment as new soil. Deposition of new soil over a flood plain is what makes a river valley fertile. Dense forests can grow in the rich soil of a flood plain. The soil is also perfect for growing crops.

Figure 12 This satellite image shows part of the Mississippi River delta, which is always growing and changing. *Observing What happens to the Mississippi River as it flows through its delta? Can you find the river's main channel?*

Answers to Self-Assessment

Caption Question

Figure 12 The river's main channel flows almost to the tip of the delta, where it divides into two or three large channels and many smaller ones.

☑ Checkpoint

An oxbow lake forms when a meander is cut off from the river, such as after flood waters fall.

Deposits by Rivers

Using the Visuals: Figure 12

Materials *world atlas or encyclopedia*
Time 15 minutes

Have pairs of students find maps in an atlas or encyclopedia that show the deltas of these major world rivers: Nile River (Egypt), Niger River (Nigeria), Ganges River (Bangladesh), Mekong River (Vietnam), Mississippi River (Louisiana), Columbia River (Oregon/Washington). Have students make drawings and write descriptions of each delta. In a class discussion, call on students to compare and contrast the deltas. Then ask: **Why do you think the Columbia River has no delta at its end?** *(Some students should infer that the currents of the Pacific Ocean move the sediments away, preventing development of a delta.)* **learning modality: visual**

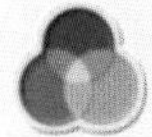

Integrating Life Science

Refer students back to their study of soil composition in Chapter 4. Ask: **What kind of soil composition is good for plant growth?** *(Loam is best, in which sand, silt, and clay are in balance and there is adequate humus content.)* Point out that flooding causes deposits that enrich the soil of a flood plain. Ask: **How could deposits from a river enrich soil?** *(The sediment carried by the river must include the materials that make up good soil, including organic material.)* Explain that this new soil has never held crops or other vegetation and so it contains a lot of nutrients. **learning modality: logical/mathematical**

Ongoing Assessment

Skills Check Have students make two flowcharts, one for the process that results in an alluvial fan and the other for the process that results in a delta.

EXPLORING the Course of a River

After students have examined the feature, display a large map of the United States where all students can see. Then call on students to read the feature's annotations. Begin with the river's beginnings, in the mountains. On the map, point to the source of the Missouri River in the Rocky Mountains of southwestern Montana. Ask: **Why would a river in the mountains have rapids, waterfalls, and a V-shaped valley?** *(In mountains, the slopes are steep and the land is not easily eroded. The river cuts down rather than spreads out.)* Continue examining the course of the river, questioning students about the process that creates each characteristic. Also, keep referring to the map of the Missouri River and the river into which it flows, the Mississippi. Explain that many scientists speak of the Missouri-Mississippi system as one river. On the map, point out meanders, oxbow lakes, and the Mississippi Delta. **limited English proficiency**

Building Inquiry Skills: Predicting

Challenge students to write a prediction about what they would see if they could use a time machine to examine the landscape in *Exploring the Course of a River* a million years from today. *(Predictions will vary. Students might predict that the mountains will be worn down by the river, the meanders will be wider, and the delta will be larger. Students who have an understanding of other Earth processes, such as plate tectonics, may predict more profound changes.)* Have student volunteers read their predictions to the class. Then invite analysis from other students. **learning modality: logical/mathematical**

EXPLORING the Course of a River

The slope and size of a river, as well as the land through which it flows, determine how a river shapes the land.

Background

Facts and Figures A river begins at its *headwaters,* or *head*. This is often in a mountainous region, but not always. The head of the Mississippi River is in the lake region of Minnesota. A river ends at its *mouth*. A delta often forms at a river's mouth, but not always. The Columbia River in the Northwest has no delta because of the strong ocean currents near its mouth at the Pacific Ocean.

The flood plain of the southern stretch of the Mississippi River extends over 1,000 km, from Cairo, Illinois, to its mouth at the Gulf of Mexico. At some places, this flood plain is more than 200 km wide. Throughout, the river meanders back and forth, ever widening its flood plain. Between 1765 and 1932, the river cut off 19 meanders, forming oxbow lakes. Since that time, dams and artificial levees have somewhat stabilized the course.

Waterfalls and rapids Waterfalls and rapids are common where the river passes over harder rock.

V-shaped valley Near its source, a river often flows through a deep, V-shaped valley. As the river flows, it cuts a deeper valley.

Meanders Where a river flows across easily eroded sediment, its channel bends from side to side in a series of meanders.

Oxbow lake

Flood plain A flood plain forms when a river's power of erosion widens its valley rather than deepening it.

Beaches Sand carried downstream by rivers spreads along the coast to form beaches.

Cultural Diversity

Have students use an encyclopedia, library books, or videos to find out about life along a river, using the Missouri-Mississippi rivers as an example. Ask students to write a description of what it would be like to live near the river in Montana, in Missouri, and in the delta region of Louisiana. After students have completed, ask: **If a friend told you she once lived near a river, would you automatically know what her life had been like?** *(No, because life varies along the course of a river.)* Encourage students to share their descriptions and compare life in the three different regions. **learning modality: verbal**

Real-Life Learning

Materials *state map*
Time 15 minutes

Provide maps of your state for students to examine. Then challenge students to plan a canoe or rafting trip along one of the state's major rivers, writing a description of what they could see. Some students might even wish to create a travel-type brochure. Encourage students to share their plans in a class discussion. **learning modality: visual**

Including All Students

Materials *poster board, colored pencils, markers*
Time 30 minutes

Have students who need additional challenges make a bulletin board that shows the course of a river. They can make drawings of river features and add labels with definitions and descriptions of processes. **learning modality: visual**

Media and Technology

Transparencies "Exploring the Course of a River," Transparency 13; "Meander Formation," Transparency 14

Ongoing Assessment

Drawing Have students make their own drawing of the course of a river. In their drawing, students could add the river's origin where two or more streams run together, as well as an alluvial fan as the river leaves the mountains.

Students can keep their drawings in their portfolio.

Groundwater Erosion and Deposition

Addressing Naive Conceptions

Many students may believe that all or most of the groundwater consists of rivers or lakes beneath Earth's surface. Point out that underground caves do sometimes contains streams and lakes, but this is the exception rather than the rule. Groundwater can be found everywhere beneath the surface—even under dry deserts. **learning modality: verbal**

Integrating Chemistry

ACTIVITY

Materials *small pieces of limestone, corrugated cardboard, plastic wrap, books, piece of clear plastic, plastic dropper, vinegar*
Time 10 minutes

Have students observe a model of the weathering of limestone by groundwater. Make a trough of corrugated cardboard, line it with plastic wrap, and elevate one end on a stack of books. Under the low end, place a piece of clear plastic. Spread the limestone pieces along the inside of the trough, and then add drops of vinegar—a weak acid—to the top of the trough. Students will see the water trickling through the limestone pieces. The drops will trickle down to the piece of plastic. Allow the liquid to dry, and have students observe the resulting deposition. **learning modality: visual**

Inquiry Challenge

ACTIVITY

Materials *aluminum cake pan, plaster of Paris, bowl, washcloth, ringstand*
Time 20 minutes a day for 2-3 days

Challenge small groups of students to use the materials above, or other materials of their choosing, to model the formation of stalagmites on a cave floor. A typical setup might involve mixing plaster of Paris in a bowl, saturating a washcloth, hanging the saturated washcloth from a ringstand, and then allowing the washcloth to drip into a cake pan. Students will have to periodically resaturate the washcloth. After 2–3 days, "stalagmites" will have formed in the pan. **learning modality: kinesthetic**

Groundwater Erosion and Deposition

When rain falls and snow melts, not all of the water evaporates or becomes runoff. Some water soaks into the ground. There it fills the openings in the soil and trickles into cracks and spaces in layers of rock. **Groundwater** is the term geologists use for this underground water. Like running water on the surface, groundwater affects the shape of the land.

INTEGRATING CHEMISTRY Groundwater can cause erosion through a process of chemical weathering. When water sinks into the ground, it combines with carbon dioxide to form a weak acid, called carbonic acid. Carbonic acid can break down limestone. Groundwater containing carbonic acid flows into cracks in the limestone. Then some of the limestone changes chemically and is carried away in a solution of water. This gradually hollows out pockets in the rock. Over time, these pockets develop into large holes underground, called caves or caverns.

The action of carbonic acid on limestone can also result in deposition. Inside limestone caves, deposits called stalactites and stalagmites often form. Water containing carbonic acid and calcium from limestone drips from a cave's roof. As the water

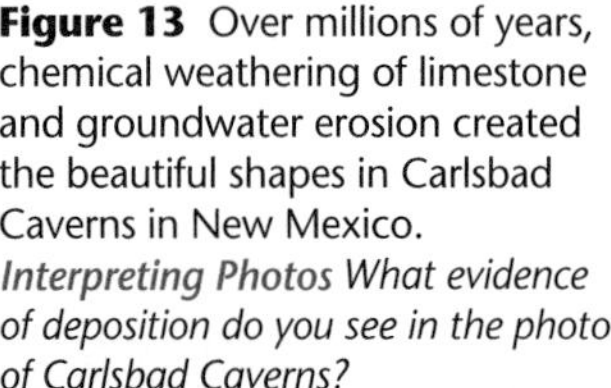

Figure 13 Over millions of years, chemical weathering of limestone and groundwater erosion created the beautiful shapes in Carlsbad Caverns in New Mexico. *Interpreting Photos What evidence of deposition do you see in the photo of Carlsbad Caverns?*

Background

Facts and Figures Carlsbad Caverns, a national park, is located in southeastern New Mexico. These caverns formed 60–70 million years ago when plate movements created cracks in the limestone of the area, allowing groundwater to move into the rock and hollow out the caverns. The largest chamber of the caverns is the Big Room, which is 550 m long, 335 m wide, and 78 m high at its highest.

Mammoth Cave in central Kentucky is also part of the national park system. This cave, created through chemical weathering of limestone, is part of the Flint Ridge cave system. About 550 km of interconnected passageways have been explored in this system, more than anywhere else in the world. Mammoth Cave contains lakes, waterfalls, and rivers, including Echo River, which is as much as 18 m wide.

Figure 14 A sinkhole, such as this one in Florida, is a characteristic feature of karst topography. Sinkholes can pose a hazard for people who live in a karst region.

evaporates, a deposit of calcite forms. A deposit that hangs like an icicle from the roof of a cave is called a **stalactite** (stuh LAK tyt). Slow dripping builds up a cone-shaped **stalagmite** (stuh LAG myt) from the cave floor.

In rainy regions where there is a layer of limestone near the surface, groundwater erosion can significantly change the shape of the land. Surface streams are rare, because water sinks easily down into the weathered limestone. Deep valleys and caverns are common. If the roof of a cave collapses because of the erosion of the underlying limestone, the result is a depression called a sinkhole. This type of landscape is called **karst topography** after a region in Eastern Europe. In the United States, there are regions of karst topography in Florida, Kentucky, and Indiana.

Section 2 Review

1. What is the major cause of erosion on Earth's surface?
2. Briefly describe five features formed by rivers and streams as they erode the land.
3. What are the results of deposition along the course of a stream or river?
4. How can groundwater contribute to erosion?
5. **Thinking Critically Comparing and Contrasting** How is an alluvial fan similar to a delta? How is it different?

Science at Home

Erosion Cube In a small dish, build a cube out of 27 small sugar cubes. Your cube should be three sugar cubes on a side. Fold a square piece of paper towel to fit the top of the cube. Wet the paper towel, place it on the cube, and let it stand for 15 or 20 minutes. Every few minutes, sprinkle a few drops of water on the paper towel to keep it wet. Then remove the paper towel. What happened to your cube? How is the effect of water on a sugar cube similar to groundwater eroding limestone? How is it different?

Program Resources

◆ **Unit 2 Resources** 5-2 Review and Reinforce; 5-2 Enrich

Answers to Self-Assessment

Caption Question

Figure 13 The photo shows both stalactites and stalagmites, which are evidence of deposition.

3 Assess

Section 2 Review Answers

1. Moving water is the major cause of erosion on Earth's surface.
2. Students' descriptions should reflect the section's discussion of valleys, waterfalls, flood plains, meanders, and oxbow lakes.
3. Deposition results in the creation of alluvial fans and deltas, as well as new soil over flood plains.
4. Groundwater can cause erosion through a process of chemical weathering. Carbonic acid in the water breaks down limestone, which is carried away by the water in solution.
5. An alluvial fan is similar to a delta in that both are deposits of sediment that occur when a stream slows down. An alluvial fan is a wide, sloping deposit formed where a stream leaves a mountain range, while a delta is a deposit when a stream flows into an ocean or lake.

Science at Home

Materials *small dish, 27 small sugar cubes, paper towel, water*
Tips Encourage students to carry out this activity and write answers to the questions about what occurred. Students should find that some of the sugar of the large cube will dissolve in the water of the paper towel, and the paper towel will absorb that solution, leaving the cube smaller and misshapen. The purpose of building a large cube with smaller ones is to provide more surface area for water to seep through. The result is analogous to water seeping through cracks in limestone, eroding the rock with carbonic acid, and then carrying the limestone away in solution.

Performance Assessment

Skills Check Have students make a table that compares and contrasts the features created by water erosion and water deposition.

You and Your Environment

Streams in Action

Preparing for Inquiry

Key Concept As water moves over land, it moves soil and rock with it, forming a channel through erosion.

Skills Objectives Students will be able to:

- make a model of a stream;
- observe differences in how time and angle of slope affect how a stream erodes the land;
- predict how increasing the angle of slope will affect how a stream erodes the land.

Time 40 minutes

Advance Planning Diatomaceous earth is a silica material that works well in stream tables. In dry form, though, its dust can cause lung damage and eye irritation. The dust will not be a problem if the material is kept moist.

Wear goggles and plastic gloves when preparing the stream tables. First, place about 1 kg of diatomaceous earth into each tub. Pour water into the tub and allow it to soak through the diatomaceous earth. Agitate the tub slightly to expose all the diatomaceous earth to the water. Drain off any excess water. Then, wearing gloves, form a hill at one end of the tub, sloping the diatomaceous earth from high on one side to the bottom of the tub, leaving about a third of the tub free of the material.

Use plastic stirrers with two holes; straws with only one hole will not work as well. Experiment with making the dripper before the lab so that you can advise students about the procedure.

Alternative Materials The advantage of using diatomaceous earth is that after it dries it can be used again. But local topsoil or commercial soil or sand could be used instead.

Guiding Inquiry

Invitation Help students focus on the key concept by asking: **What is the major agent of erosion that shapes Earth's surface?** *(Moving water)* **How does water cause erosion?** *(The force of moving water picks up soil and rock particles and carries them with it as it moves downhill.)* **What factors affect how much sediment a river can erode?** *(Factors include a river's slope, volume of flow, and shape of its streambed.)*

Introducing the Procedure

- Give students time to read through the whole procedure, and then ask: **What factor are you investigating in Part A?** *(How the amount of runoff affects the amount of erosion.)* **What factor are you investigating in Part B?** *(How the slope of a stream affects its power to erode.)*

Troubleshooting the Experiment

- When starting the dripper, students should see a stream of water forming as the drops accumulate on the diatomaceous earth. If not, the dripper needs to be adjusted to increase the flow.
- Have each group select a time keeper who will keep track of drip time.

Real-World Lab

You and Your Environment

Streams in Action

Erosion can form gullies, wash away topsoil, and pollute rivers with sediment. You can observe the effects of erosion using a stream table.

Problem

How do rivers and streams erode the land?

Skills Focus

making models, observing, predicting

Materials  

plastic tub at least 27 cm × 40 cm × 10 cm
diatomaceous earth
plastic measuring cup
spray bottle
hand lens
watch or clock
water
1 metal spoon
plastic foam cup
blue food coloring
liquid detergent
scissors
2 wood blocks about 2.5 cm thick
bucket to hold 2–3 L of water or a source of tap water
plastic stirrers, 10–12 cm long, with two small holes each
wire 13–15 cm long, 20 gauge

Making the Dripper

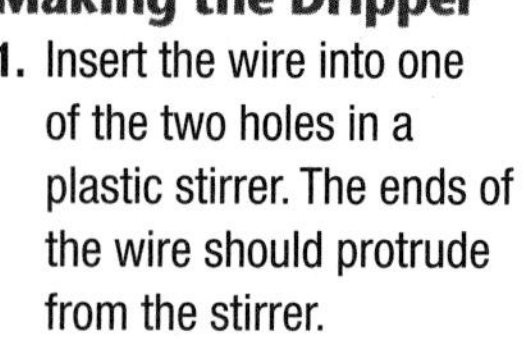

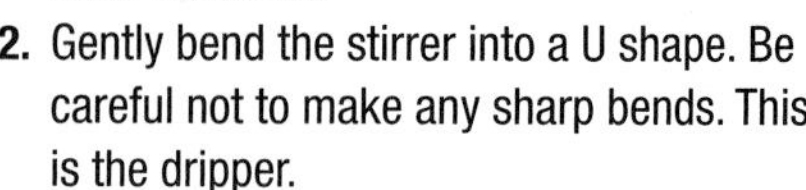

1. Insert the wire into one of the two holes in a plastic stirrer. The ends of the wire should protrude from the stirrer.
2. Gently bend the stirrer into a U shape. Be careful not to make any sharp bends. This is the dripper.
3. With scissors, carefully cut two small notches on opposite sides of the top of the foam cup.
4. Fill the cup to just below the notches with water colored with two drops of blue food coloring. Add more food coloring later as you add more water to the cup.
5. Add one drop of detergent to keep air bubbles out of the dripper and increase flow.
6. To start the dripper, fill it with water. Then quickly tip it and place it in one of the notches in the cup, as shown above.
7. Adjust the flow rate of the dripper to about 2 drips per 1 second. (*Hint:* Bend the dripper into more of a U shape to increase flow. Lessen the curve to reduce flow.)

Procedure

Part A Creating Streams Over Time

1. Your teacher will give you a plastic tub containing diatomaceous earth that has been soaked with water. Place the tub on a level surface. **CAUTION:** *Dry diatomaceous earth produces dust that may be irritating if inhaled. To keep the diatomaceous earth from drying out, spray it lightly with water.*
2. One end of the tub will contain more diatomaceous earth. Use the block of wood to raise this end of the tub 2.5 cm.
3. Place the cup at the upper end of the slope with the notches pointing to the left and right.
4. Press the cup firmly down into the earth to secure its position.
5. Start the dripper (see Step 6 in the box above). Allow the water to drip to the right onto the diatomaceous earth.

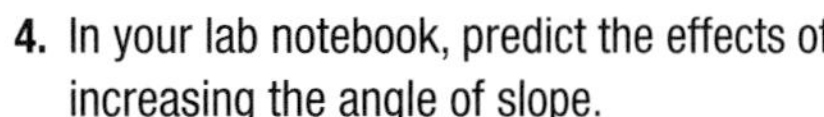

6. Allow the dripper to drip for 5 minutes. (*Hint:* When you need to add more water, be careful not to disturb the dripper.)
7. Observe the flow of water and the changes it makes. Use the hand lens to look closely at the stream bed.
8. After 5 minutes, remove the dripper.
9. In your lab notebook, draw a picture of the resulting stream and label it "5 minutes."
10. Now switch the dripper to the left side of the cup. Restart the dripper and allow it to drip for 10 minutes. Then remove the dripper.
11. Draw a picture and label it "10 minutes."

Part B Changing the Angle of Slope

1. Remove the cup from the stream table.
2. Save the stream bed on the right side of the tub. Using the bowl of the spoon, smooth out the diatomaceous earth on the left side.
3. To increase the angle of slope of your stream table, raise the end of the tub another 2.5 cm.
4. In your lab notebook, predict the effects of increasing the angle of slope.
5. Replace the cup and restart the dripper, placing it in the notch on the left side of the cup. Allow the dripper to drip for 5 minutes. Notice any changes in the new stream bed.
6. At the end of 5 minutes, remove the dripper.
7. Draw a picture of the new stream bed in your lab notebook. Label it "Increased Angle."
8. Follow your teacher's instructions for clean-up after this activity. Wash your hands when you have finished.

Analyze and Conclude

1. Compare the 5-minute stream with the 10-minute stream. How did the length of time that the water flowed affect erosion along the stream bed?
2. Were your predictions about the effects of increasing the angle of slope correct? Explain your answer.
3. What eventually happened to the eroded material that was carried downstream?
4. What other variables besides time and angle of slope might affect the way rivers and streams erode the land?
5. **Apply** Have you ever seen water flowing down a hillside or street after a heavy rain? If so, how much did the land slope in that area? Did you notice anything about the color of the water? Explain.

Design an Experiment

Design a stream table experiment to measure how the amount of sediment carried by a river changes as the volume of flow of the river increases. Obtain your teacher's approval before you try the experiment.

◆ Advise students to have their lab notebooks handy to make their drawings and write their predictions.

Expected Outcome

In Part A, students should observe that the dripping water erodes the diatomaceous earth, moving some of the material from the high end to the low end. The dripping water will form a channel; the 10-minute drip will form a deeper channel than the 5-minute drip. In Part B, increasing the angle of slope will produce a deeper channel and more erosion.

Analyze and Conclude

1. Students should observe that the 10- minute stream produced a deeper channel than the 5-minute stream. Likewise, the 10-minute stream moved more material down the slope.
2. Answers may vary. Most students will have predicted that increasing the angle of slope would result in a deeper channel and more erosion, and their results should have confirmed that prediction.
3. Students should observe that the eroded material moves down the slope and is deposited at the open end of the stream table.
4. Answers may vary. A typical answer might suggest that the volume of flow and the speed of the water affect the way rivers and streams erode the land. Some students might also mention that the kind of material over which the water flows also affects erosion.
5. Answers will vary. A typical answer might mention water flowing down a steeply sloping hillside or street, with the water being cloudy or dirty from eroded soil.

Extending the Inquiry

Design an Experiment Designs will vary. A typical design might investigate volume of flow. Students could suggest pouring water onto opposite sides of the slope from two sizes of plastic straws and comparing the erosion caused by each stream. After reviewing the designs, encourage students to carry out their experiments.

Program Resources

◆ **Unit 2 Resources** Chapter 5 Real-World Lab

Media and Technology

 **Lab Activity Videotapes** Grade 6, Tape 1

Safety

Caution students to wear their goggles at all times when working with diatomaceous earth, since any dust in their eyes could be harmful. Also advise students to wear lab aprons and be careful when using the scissors and wire. Review the safety guidelines in Appendix A.

SCIENCE AND SOCIETY

Protecting Homes in Flood Plains

Purpose

Students will learn about a difficult societal issue related to flooding and water erosion.

Role-Play

Time 40 minutes

- In this activity, students will role-play a town meeting after a major flood has destroyed homes and businesses within a river's flood plain. If there is a major river in your area, students could predict what would be damaged if it flooded and then use those projections in the role-play. You could also develop a flood scenario for any river and give students copies.
- Divide the class into three main groups. Students in one group of four or five will role-play public officials, including a mayor, a Congressperson, the head of a federal agency for flood relief, and so on. This group will run the town meeting. Students in a second group will role-play people affected by the flood. Students in a third group will role-play citizens who oppose public moneys for rebuilding in the flood plain. Give each group 10–15 minutes to discuss within the group positions and arguments to take in the town meeting. Then hold the town meeting, with rules set by the "officials" group. Encourage students to assert their positions respectfully but passionately.

Extend Encourage students to find out what happened in Grand Forks after the 1997 Red River flood. With real data, students can realistically assess positions taken during the role-play.

You Decide

Have students write their speeches after participating in the role-play. A good speech should include a clear description of the problems the flood caused, a list of options, and an argument for one option.

SCIENCE AND SOCIETY

Protecting Homes in Flood Plains

At least ten million American households are located in flood plains. Living near a river is tempting. Riverside land is often flat and easy to build on. Because so many people now live in flood plains, the cost of flood damage has been growing. Communities along rivers want to limit the cost of flooding. They want to know how they can protect the people and buildings already in flood plains. They also want to know how to discourage more people from moving into flood plains.

The Issues

Should the Government Insure People Against Flood Damage? The United States government offers insurance to households in flood plains. The insurance pays part of the cost of repairs after a flood. Insurance helps people, but it is very expensive. Only 17 percent of people who live in flood plains buy the government insurance. Government flood insurance is available only in places that take steps to reduce flood damage. Cities must allow new building only on high ground. The insurance will not pay to rebuild homes that are badly damaged by floodwater. Instead, these people must use the money to find a home somewhere else.

Critics say that insurance just encourages people to move back into areas that flood. Supporters say it rewards towns and cities that make rules to control building on flood plains.

How Much of the Flood Plain Should Be Protected? Government flood insurance is available only in areas where scientists expect flooding about once in 100 years, or once in 500 years. Such figures are just estimates. Three floods occurred in only 12 years in a government flood-insurance area near Sacramento, California.

Should the Government Tell People Where They Can Live? Some programs of flood control forbid all new building. Other programs may also encourage people to move to safer areas. The 1997 flood on the Red River in Grand Forks, North Dakota, is one example. After the flood, the city of Grand Forks offered to buy all the damaged buildings near the river. The city wants to build high walls of earth to protect the rest of the town.

The Grand Forks plan might prevent future damage, but is it fair? Supporters say that since the government has to pay for flood damage, it has the right to make people leave flood plains. Critics of such plans say that people should be free to live where they want, even in risky areas.

Who should decide in which neighborhood no new houses can be built? Who decides which people should be asked to move away from a flood plain? Experts disagree over whether local, state, or United States government officials should decide which areas to include. Some believe scientists should make the decision.

You Decide

1. Identify the Problem
In your own words, describe the controversy surrounding flood plains and housing.

2. Analyze the Options
List several steps that could be taken to reduce the damage done to buildings in flood plains. For each step, include who would benefit from the step, and who would pay the costs.

3. Find a Solution
Your town has to decide what to do about a neighborhood damaged by the worst flood in 50 years. Write a speech that argues for your solution.

Background

Facts and Figures A flood plain might be thought of as a natural safety valve for times when a river's channel can't hold all the runoff. Because the flooding of any particular river is relatively rare, builders often don't take this natural feature into consideration. Geologists try to predict major floods by using the past to calculate a probability. A "50-year flood," for instance, is one that occurs only once every 50 years, *on average*. The problem is that such a flood *can* occur in any year, and even two years in a row.

The 1997 Red River flood was a 500-year flood caused by an ice block to the north that prevented runoff from heavy snows and rains from flowing downstream (north into Canada). Flood waters spread out over the 64-km-wide flood plain, causing catastrophic damage.

INTEGRATING PHYSICS 

SECTION 3 The Force of Moving Water

DISCOVER ACTIVITY

How Are Sediments Deposited?

1. Put on your goggles.
2. Obtain a clear plastic jar or bottle with a top. Fill the jar about two-thirds full with water.
3. Fill a plastic beaker with 200 mL of fine and coarse sand, soil, clay, and small pebbles.
4. Pour the mixture into the jar of water. Screw on the top tightly and shake for two minutes. Be sure to hold onto the jar firmly.
5. Set the jar down and observe it for 10 to 15 minutes.

Think It Over

Inferring In what order are the sediments in the jar deposited? What do you think causes this pattern?

The Merrimack River in New Hampshire and Massachusetts is only 180 kilometers long. But the Merrimack does a great deal of work as it runs from the mountains to the sea. The river's waters fall 82 meters through many rapids and waterfalls. During the 1800s, people harnessed this falling water to run machines. These machines could spin thread and weave cloth very quickly and cheaply. Thanks to water power, the towns along the river grew quickly into cities.

GUIDE FOR READING

- What enables water to do work?
- How does sediment enter rivers and streams?
- What factors affect a river's ability to erode and carry sediment?

Reading Tip Before you read, rewrite the headings of the section as *how, why,* or *what* questions. As you read, look for answers to these questions.

Work and Energy

The waters of the Merrimack River could drive machines because a river's water has energy. **Energy** is the ability to do work or cause change. There are two kinds of energy. **Potential energy** is energy that is stored and waiting to be used later. The Merrimack's waters begin with potential energy due to their position above sea level. **Kinetic energy** is the energy an object has due to its motion. **As gravity pulls water down a slope, the water's potential energy changes to kinetic energy that can do work.**

Figure 15 Dams like this one on the Merrimack River in Lowell, Massachusetts, help to harness the power of flowing water.

READING STRATEGIES

Reading Tip Students should rewrite the headings as questions such as these: "How is work related to energy?" "How does water erode and carry sediment?" and "What is sediment load, and how is it related to erosion?" Suggest that students write answers to each question and use their questions and answers as a study guide for the section.

Program Resources

- **Unit 2 Resources** 5-3 Lesson Plan; 5-3 Section Summary
- **Guided Reading and Study Workbook** Section 5-3

INTEGRATING PHYSICS 

SECTION 3 The Force of Moving Water

Objectives

After completing the lesson, students will be able to

- describe how water is able to do work;
- explain how sediment enters rivers and streams;
- list the factors that affect a river's ability to erode and carry sediment.

Key Terms energy, potential energy, kinetic energy, abrasion, load, friction, turbulence

1 Engage/Explore

Activating Prior Knowledge

Encourage students to describe different rivers they've seen in terms of size and speed. Then ask: **The water in which river moves faster, a narrow river moving down from a steep mountain valley or a large river moving over a wide coastal plain?** *(Most students will say the narrow mountain river moves faster.)* Suggest that they may have to revise their opinions after reading the section.

DISCOVER ACTIVITY

Skills Focus inferring
Materials *clear plastic jar or bottle with top, water, plastic beaker, fine and coarse sand, soil, clay, small pebbles*
Time 15 minutes
Tips To simplify the activity, make the sediment mixtures in advance.
Expected Outcome Students will observe the slow settling of the sediments, with the larger particles settling first and the smaller sizes settling in succession. After 10–15 minutes, most particles will have settled, though the water will remain cloudy due to the suspension of fine particles.
Think It Over The particles are deposited by size, with the largest on the bottom and the smallest on top. Gravity acting on the different weights of the sediment particles causes the pattern.

2 Facilitate

Work and Energy

Social Studies CONNECTION

Throughout the nineteenth century, Lowell was noted for its textile mills, as were other towns in New England. Today, part of the old central city of Lowell is a national historical park, designated as a birthplace of the American industrial revolution. In the twentieth century, the textile industry largely abandoned the Northeast for the South, and then relocated much of its production overseas.

In Your Journal Challenge students to find library books that explore a mill worker's life in the nineteenth century. Books on American life in the 1800s contain such material. Typically, women workers worked over 10 hours a day, six days a week. **learning modality: verbal**

How Water Erodes and Carries Sediment

Using the Visuals: Figure 16

Ask: **What are three main ways that a stream carries sediment?** *(A stream carries sediment in solution, suspended in the water, and by moving it along its bed.)* Explain that scientists divide a stream's load into three parts, called the dissolved load, the suspended load, and the bed load. Ask: **Does a stream move all sediment particles on the bed the same way?** *(No. The way in which sediment moves along the bed depends on the particle size. Smaller particles bounce, while larger particles roll.)* Explain that the bed load is responsible for most of the erosive power of a stream—the cutting down through rock that streams and rivers do. The movement of sand and gravel on the bed wears away the bottom and sides of the channel by abrasion. **learning modality: visual**

Social Studies CONNECTION

The cotton mills in Lowell, Massachusetts, were built in the 1820s. The mills employed young women from the farms and small towns of New England. At that time, it was unusual for women to work outside the home. The hours of work at a mill were long and pay was low. But mill work helped these women to earn and save their own money. Most later returned to their hometowns.

In Your Journal

Use library references to find out more about the daily life of the mill workers. Write a diary entry describing a worker's typical day.

When energy does work, the energy is transferred from one object to another. At the textile mills along the Merrimack River, the kinetic energy of the moving water was transferred to the spinning machines. It became mechanical energy harnessed for a human purpose—making cloth. But all along a river, kinetic energy does other work. A river is always moving sediment from the mountains to the sea. At the same time, a river is also eroding its banks and valley.

☑ *Checkpoint What are potential energy and kinetic energy?*

How Water Erodes and Carries Sediment

Gravity causes the movement of water across Earth's land surface. But how does water cause erosion? In the process of water erosion, water picks up and moves sediment. Sediment includes soil, rock, clay, and sand. Sediment can enter rivers and streams in a number of ways. **Most sediment washes or falls into the river as a result of mass movement and runoff. Other sediment erodes from the bottom or sides of the river.** Wind may also drop sediment into the water.

Abrasion is another process by which a river obtains sediment. **Abrasion** is the wearing away of rock by a grinding action. Abrasion occurs when particles of sediment in flowing water bump into the streambed again and again. Abrasion grinds down sediment particles. For example, boulders become smaller as they are moved down a streambed. Sediments also grind and chip away at the rock of the streambed, deepening and widening the stream's channel.

The amount of sediment that a river carries is its **load.** Gravity and the force of the moving water cause the sediment load to move downstream. Most large sediment falls to the bottom and moves by rolling and sliding. Fast-moving water actually lifts sand and other, smaller, sediment and carries it downstream. Water dissolves some sediment completely. The river carries these dissolved sediments in solution. If you look at Figure 16, you can observe the different ways in which water can carry sediment. Notice for example, how grains of sand or small stones can move by bouncing.

Figure 16 Rivers and streams carry sediment in several ways. *Predicting What will eventually happen to a boulder on the bottom of a river?*

Direction of flow
Dissolved sediment
Suspended sediment
Larger particles pushed or rolled along stream bed
Smaller particles move by bouncing

146

Background

Facts and Figures A typical river transports most sediment in suspension, a lesser amount in solution, and the least amount along its bed. The Mississippi River has a sediment load of about 450 million metric tons of sediment per year.

The bouncing movement of sand particles along the river bed is called saltation. This occurs when a swift-flowing stream becomes turbulent, picking up sand grains and moving them a short distance. When a grain falls back to the bed, it strikes another grain, causing it to jump up into the current.

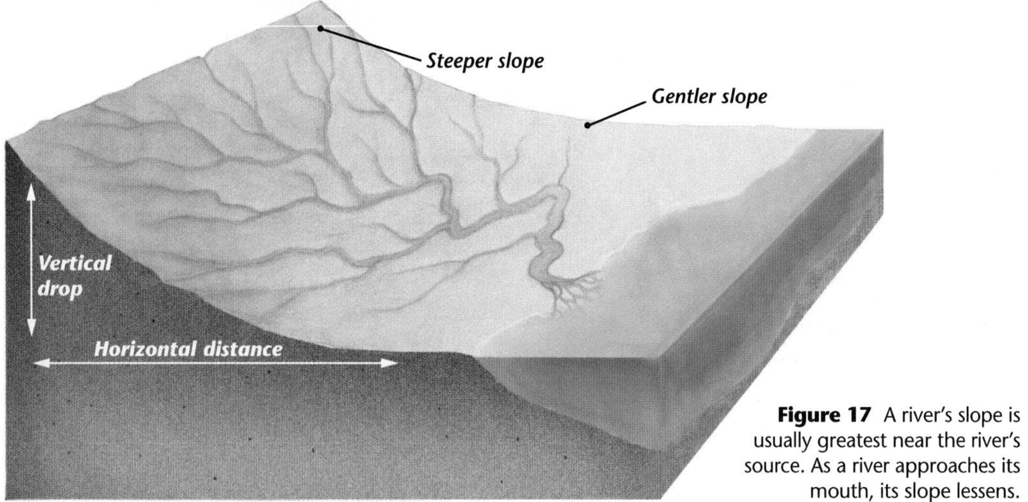

Figure 17 A river's slope is usually greatest near the river's source. As a river approaches its mouth, its slope lessens.

Erosion and Sediment Load

The power of a river to cause erosion and carry sediment depends on several factors. **A river's slope, volume of flow, and the shape of its streambed all affect how fast the river flows and how much sediment it can erode.**

A fast-flowing river carries more and larger particles of sediment. When a river slows down, its sediment load is deposited. The larger particles of sediment are deposited first.

Slope Generally, if a river's slope increases, the water's speed also increases. A river's slope is the amount the river drops toward sea level over a given distance. If a river's speed increases, its sediment load and power to erode may increase. But other factors are also important in determining how much sediment the river erodes and carries.

Volume of Flow A river's flow is the volume of water that moves past a point on the river in a given time. As more water flows through a river, its speed increases. During a flood, the increased volume of water helps the river to cut more deeply into its banks and bed. A flooding river may have hundreds of times more eroding power than the river has at other times. A flooding river can carry huge amounts of sand, soil, and other sediments. It may move giant boulders as if they were pebbles.

Streambed Shape A streambed's shape affects the amount of friction between the water and the streambed. **Friction** is the force that opposes the motion of one surface as it moves across another surface. Friction, in turn, affects a river's speed. Where a river is deep, only a small fraction of the water comes in contact with the

Sharpen your Skills

Developing Hypotheses

A geologist is comparing alluvial fans. One alluvial fan is composed of gravel and small boulders. The other fan is composed of sand and silt. Propose a hypothesis to explain the difference in the size of the particles in the two fans. (*Hint*: Think of the characteristics of the streams that formed each alluvial fan.)

Erosion and Sediment Load

Sharpen your Skills

Developing Hypotheses

Time 5 minutes
Tips Suggest that students reread the description in Section 2 of how an alluvial fan forms and examine the accompanying photo in Figure 11.
Expected Outcome Hypotheses may vary. A typical hypothesis might suggest that the river that produced the gravel-boulder alluvial fan had a greater slope and volume of flow than the river that produced the sand-silt fan, because the heavier sediment could have been carried only by a fast-flowing river.
Extend Challenge students to design an experiment to test their hypotheses using a stream table. After reviewing designs, encourage students to test their hypotheses. **learning modality: logical/mathematical**

Inquiry Challenge

Materials *stream table, sand or diatomaceous earth, water*
Time 30 minutes

Challenge small groups to develop a hypothesis from one of the concepts related to erosion and sediment load. Examples: "A river's sediment load increases as the river's speed increases." "An increase in the river's volume of flow causes its speed to increase." Have students design an experiment to test their hypothesis, designating the variable to be tested. Review groups' designs, and then have each group carry out its design using a stream table. If more than one group does the same experiment, have groups compare results at the end. **cooperative learning**

Media and Technology

Transparencies "Water Erosion, Deposition, and Movement of Sediment," Transparency 15

Answers to Self-Assessment

Caption Question

Figure 16 The boulder will become smaller as it is moved down the streambed due to abrasion.

Checkpoint

Potential energy is energy that is stored and waiting to be used later. Kinetic energy is the energy an object has due to its motion.

Ongoing Assessment

Oral Presentation Call on students at random to explain how a river deepens and widens its channel and how slope and volume of flow affect sediment load.

Erosion and Sediment Load, continued

Using the Visuals: Figure 18

Ask: **Where does the river erode its bank, at point A or B?** *(At B, on the outside of the curve)* **As this process of erosion and deposition continues, what river feature will this curve develop into?** *(A meander)* Emphasize that this is how meanders develop. **learning modality: visual**

3 Assess

Section 3 Review Answers

1. As gravity pulls water down a slope, the water's potential energy changes to kinetic energy that can do work.
2. Most sediment washes or falls into a river as a result of mass movement and runoff. Other sediment erodes from the bottom or sides of a river.
3. Slope, volume of flow, and streambed shape
4. Large sediment moves by rolling or sliding along the streambed. Smaller sediment moves when water lifts it up and carries it downstream. Some sediment is also carried as dissolved sediment in solution.
5. As slope increases, so does a river's speed. And as a river's speed increases, so does its sediment load.

CHAPTER PROJECT

Check Your Progress

Students may have trouble with the scale of their first drawing. Explain that they need to think in terms of a large area, such as a whole state or region. Supply the materials students will need to make their first model.

Performance Assessment

Writing Have students explain the difference in erosive power between a mountain stream and a river with a wide flood plain.

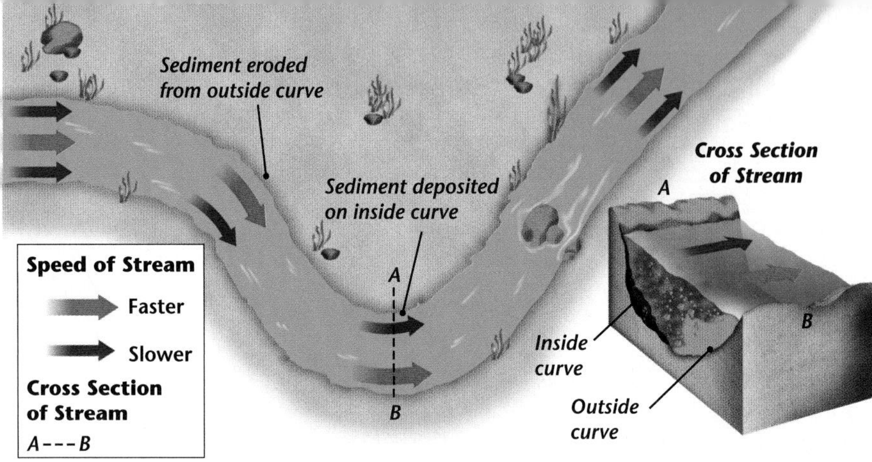

Figure 18 A river erodes sediment from its banks on the outside curve and deposits its sediment on the inside curve.
Relating Cause and Effect Why does a river deposit sediment on the inside of a curve?

streambed. This reduces friction and allows the river to flow faster. In a shallow river, much of the water comes in contact with the streambed. Therefore friction increases, reducing the river's speed.

A streambed is often full of boulders and other obstacles. This roughness prevents the water from flowing smoothly. Roughness thus increases friction and reduces the river's speed. Instead of moving downstream, the water moves every which way in a type of movement called **turbulence.** For example, a stream on a steep slope may flow at a lower speed than a large river on a gentle slope. Friction and turbulence slow the stream's flow. But a turbulent stream or river may have great power to erode.

The shape of a river affects the way it deposits sediment. Where a river flows in a straight line, the water flows faster near the center of the river than along its sides. Deposition occurs along the sides of the river, where the water moves more slowly.

If a river curves, the water moves fastest along the outside of the curve. There, the river tends to cut into its bank. Sediment is deposited on the inside curve, where the water speed is slowest. You can see this process in Figure 18.

Section 3 Review

1. How can moving water on Earth's surface do work?
2. How does a river collect sediment?
3. What are three factors that affect a river's sediment load?
4. Describe three ways that sediment moves in a river.
5. **Thinking Critically Relating Cause and Effect** What effect does increased slope have on a river's speed and sediment load? Explain.

CHAPTER PROJECT

Check Your Progress

Make a drawing of the landscape that you plan to model. This landscape will show the land before erosion. What kinds of landforms will you show in the model? Be sure to include a high mountain and a coastline. Make a list of materials that you will use to build your model. Once your teacher has approved your drawing and your list of materials, you may build your first model.

Answers to Self-Assessment

Caption Question

Figure 18 A river deposits sediment on the inside of a curve because the water speed is slowest there.

Program Resources

- **Unit 2 Resources** 5-3 Review and Reinforce; 5-3 Enrich
- **Laboratory Manual** 5, "The Daily Grind"

Glaciers

Discover Activity

How Do Glaciers Change the Land?

1. Put some sand in a small plastic container.
2. Fill the container with water and place the container in a freezer until the water turns to ice.
3. Remove the block of ice from the container.
4. Holding the ice with paper towels, rub the ice, sand side down, over a bar of soap. Observe what happens to the surface of the soap.

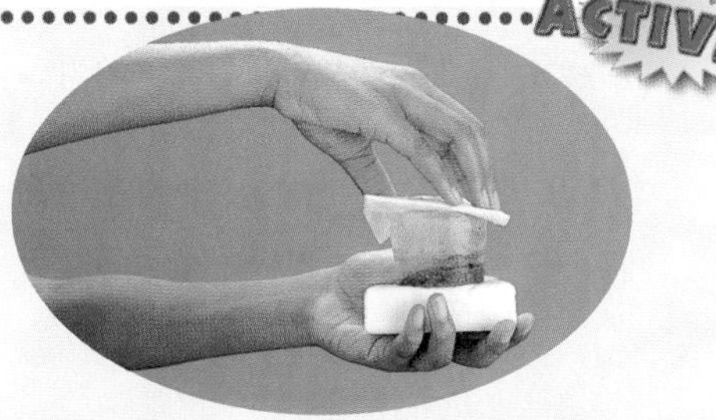

Think It Over

Inferring Based on your observations, how do you think moving ice could change the surface of the land?

You are on a boat trip near the coast of Alaska. You sail by vast evergreen forests and snowcapped mountains. Then, as your boat rounds a point of land, you see an amazing sight. A great mass of ice winds like a river between rows of mountains. Suddenly you hear a noise like thunder. Where the ice meets the sea, a giant chunk of ice breaks off and plunges into the water. Carefully, you pilot your boat around the iceberg and toward the mass of ice. It towers over your boat. You see that it is made up of solid ice that is deep blue and green as well as white. What is this river of ice?

GUIDE FOR READING

- What are the two kinds of glaciers?
- How do glaciers cause erosion and deposition?

Reading Tip Before you read, preview the headings and key terms in the section. Make a list of predictions about the characteristics of glaciers.

Kinds of Glaciers

Geologists define a **glacier** as any large mass of ice that moves slowly over land. **There are two kinds of glaciers—valley glaciers and continental glaciers.**

A **valley glacier** is a long, narrow glacier that forms when snow and ice build up high in a mountain valley. The sides of mountains keep these glaciers from spreading out in all directions. Instead, they usually move down valleys that have already been cut by rivers. Valley glaciers are found on many high mountains.

A **continental glacier** is a glacier that covers much of a continent or large island. Continental glaciers are much larger than

Figure 19 The Mendenhall Glacier in Alaska winds downhill between high mountains.

READING STRATEGIES

Reading Tip After students preview the headings, suggest that they use the headings to make an outline of the section. This will require them to place each vocabulary word under the appropriate heading. Suggest that students include in their outlines the terms introduced in the feature *Exploring Glacial Landforms.* Students should predict that glaciers are made of snow and ice and that they move, causing erosion and deposition.

Program Resources

- **Unit 2 Resources** 5-4 Lesson Plan; 5-4 Section Summary
- **Guided Reading and Study Workbook** Section 5-4

Glaciers

Objectives

After completing the lesson, students will be able to

- name and describe two kinds of glaciers;
- describe the two processes by which glaciers erode the land;
- explain how glaciers deposit sediments, and the role of the ice ages in glacial erosion.

Key Terms glacier, valley glacier, continental glacier, ice age, plucking, till, moraine, kettle

1 Engage/Explore

Activating Prior Knowledge

Encourage students to recall their experiences with packed snow. Ask: **Is there a difference between the snow on top of a mound of snow and the snow on the bottom?** *(The snow is fluffier on top, while it's chunky like ice on the bottom.)* **What causes this difference?** *(The weight of the snow on top compresses the snow on the bottom.)* Explain that huge glaciers form by the same process.

Discover

Skills Focus inferring

Materials *sand, small plastic container, water, freezer, paper towel, bar of soap*

Time 5 minutes for setup; 10 minutes the next day

Tips Make sure the containers are kept in the freezer long enough for the water to freeze solid.

Expected Outcome The sand should have frozen to the bottom of the ice. Rubbing the sand-side of the ice over soap will produce gouges and scratches by abrasion.

Think It Over Answers may vary. A typical answer might suggest that the sediment in ice changes the surface by abrasion, causing scratches and gouges in rock and soil.

2 Facilitate

Kinds of Glaciers

Including All Students

To help students unfamiliar with world geography, use a globe or large world map to point out Antarctica and Greenland. Then ask: **Where would valley glaciers be found?** *(In mountain ranges such as the Rockies, Alps, and Himalayas)* **Do all mountain ranges contain glaciers?** *(No)* Explain that glaciers occur only in mountain ranges where more snow falls than melts each year. For instance, there are no glaciers in the Appalachian Mountains. **learning modality: verbal**

Ice Ages

Using the Visuals: Figure 20

After students have examined the figure, ask: **What could have started and ended the last ice age?** *(A change in climate)* Explain that Earth's climate has changed many times in the past and may change again. **learning modality: logical/mathematical**

How Glaciers Form and Move

Building Inquiry Skills: Designing Experiments

ACTIVITY

Ask: **Since huge glaciers move only very short distances every day, how could you measure the movement of a valley glacier?** Then divide students into small groups and challenge each to design an experiment that would test the hypothesis that valley glaciers move several centimeters to a few meters daily. One way would be to drive stakes into a glacier, record their positions in relation to surrounding landforms, and then check those positions periodically over many years. **learning modality: logical/mathematical**

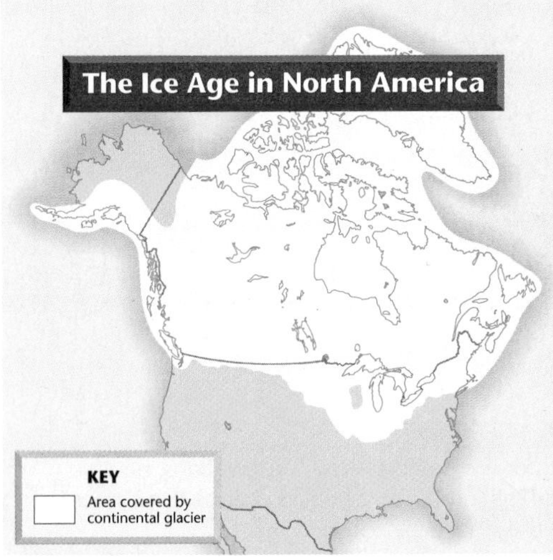

Figure 20 The continental glacier of the last ice age covered most of Canada and Alaska as well as much of the northern United States. The ice age lasted about 70,000 years and ended about 10,000 years ago.

valley glaciers. They spread out over large areas of the land. Today, continental glaciers cover about 10 percent of Earth's land. They cover Antarctica and most of Greenland. The glacier covering Antarctica spreads out over 14 million square kilometers and is over 2 kilometers thick.

Ice Ages

Many times in the past, continental glaciers have covered large parts of Earth's surface. These times are known as **ice ages.** For example, about 9 million years ago, continental glaciers began to form in North America, Europe, and Asia. These glaciers slowly grew and advanced southward. By about 2.5 million years ago, they covered about a third of Earth's land. The glaciers advanced and retreated, or melted back, several times. Figure 20 shows how far south the glaciers came on the North American continent during the most recent ice age. They finally retreated about 10,000 years ago.

How Glaciers Form and Move

Glaciers can form only in an area where more snow falls than melts. High in mountain valleys, temperatures seldom rise above freezing. Snow builds up year after year. The pressure of the weight of more and more snow compacts the snow at the bottom into ice. Once the depth of snow and ice reaches more than 30 to 40 meters, gravity begins to pull the glacier downhill.

Valley glaciers flow at a rate of a few centimeters to a few meters per day. But sometimes a valley glacier slides down more quickly in what is called a surge. A surging glacier can flow as much as 6 kilometers a year. Unlike valley glaciers, continental glaciers can flow in all directions. Continental glaciers spread out much as pancake batter spreads out in a frying pan.

☑ *Checkpoint* *How do glaciers form?*

Glacial Erosion

The movement of a glacier changes the land beneath it. Although glaciers work slowly, they are a major force of erosion. **The two processes by which glaciers erode the land are plucking and abrasion.**

As a glacier flows over the land, it picks up rocks in a process called **plucking.** Beneath a glacier, the weight of the ice can break rocks apart. These rock fragments freeze to the bottom of the

Background

History of Science To the northeast of Juneau, Alaska, is Glacier Bay National Park and Preserve, which includes numerous glaciers. In 1794, the British explorer George Vancouver described an "immense body" of ice that extended from shore to shore. Now, more than two centuries later, the glaciers that composed that ice have retreated 135 km, leaving behind many fiords, including Glacier Bay.

In the last 1 billion years, Earth has had several major ice ages, each lasting generally for millions of years. The last one is often called the Pleistocene Ice Age, or simply the Ice Age. Fluctuations in Earth's climate cause the advance and retreat of glaciers over continents. During the Pleistocene Ice Age, glaciers actually advanced over North America and then melted back several times over periods of about 60,000 years.

glacier. When the glacier moves, it carries the rocks with it. Figure 21 shows plucking by a glacier. Plucking can move even huge boulders.

Many rocks remain on the bottom of the glacier, and the glacier drags them across the land. This process, called abrasion, gouges and scratches the bedrock. You can see the results of erosion by glaciers in *Exploring Glacial Landforms* on pages 152–153.

Figure 21 As a glacier moves downhill, the ice plucks pieces of bedrock from the ground. *Predicting What evidence of plucking might you find after a glacier melts?*

Glacial Deposition

A glacier gathers a huge amount of rock and soil as it erodes the land in its path. **When a glacier melts, it deposits the sediment it eroded from the land, creating various landforms.** These landforms remain for thousands of years after the glacier has melted.

The mixture of sediments that a glacier deposits directly on the surface is called **till.** Till is made up of particles of many different sizes. Clay, silt, sand, gravel, and boulders can all be found in till.

The till deposited at the edges of a glacier forms a ridge called a **moraine.** A terminal moraine is the ridge of till at the farthest point reached by a glacier. Long Island in New York is a terminal moraine from the continental glaciers of the last ice age.

INTEGRATING LIFE SCIENCE Other features left in glacial sediments are prairie potholes. These potholes are shallow depressions in till that were formed by flowing water as the continental glacier melted. Today, prairie potholes contain water for only part of the year. Each prairie pothole is a small oasis for living things. Grasses and moisture-loving plants grow thickly in and around the potholes. In the spring, the potholes brim with water from melting snow or rain. Thousands of migrating ducks and other birds stop off at the potholes to feed and rest on their way north. Some stay to build nests and raise their young.

Figure 22 This prairie pothole in Wisconsin is surrounded by farmland. Prairie potholes were left in till deposited by glaciers.

Answers to Self-Assessment

Caption Question

Figure 21 Evidence includes rocky knobs that are rounded on one side, but steep on the other side, where the glacier plucked away pieces of rock.

✓ Checkpoint

Glaciers form where more snow falls than melts. As snow builds up, its weight compacts the snow beneath into ice.

Glacial Erosion

Using the Visuals: Figure 21

After students have examined the figure, ask: **Why does the rock beneath a glacier crack?** *(The weight of the glacier causes the rock to crack.)* **Is this erosion or weathering?** *(The cracking itself weathers the rock. Erosion occurs when the rock fragments attach to the glacier by freezing and are carried away.)* **How do the rock fragments shown in the figure cause further weathering?** *(They scratch and gouge the land as the glacier moves.)* **learning modality: visual**

Building Inquiry Skills: Observing

Materials *ice cube, modeling compound, sand, cardboard*

Time 10 minutes; observe 1 hour later

Have students make a model landscape by spreading clay over a sheet of cardboard and rubbing sand over the clay. Then invite students to slide an ice cube slowly over the sand. Finally, have them leave the ice cube to melt at the end of the path. Students should sketch and write a description of the model glacial landforms they have made, including till, moraines, and a glacial lake. **learning modality: kinesthetic**

Ongoing Assessment

Writing Have students write an explanation of what a glacier is, how it forms, and how it moves.

Glacial Deposition

EXPLORING Glacial Landforms

Invite volunteers to read the annotations for each of the glacial landforms included in the feature. Then ask: **How is the mountain valley shown in this feature different from the valley shown in Exploring the Course of a River in Section 2?** *(A river makes a V-shaped valley; a glacier makes a U-shaped valley.)* Explain that through erosion, a glacier widens, deepens, and straightens a river-cut valley. Where there was once narrow valley, there is now a trough, or U-shaped valley. A fiord is a glacial trough partly filled with water as a result of rising sea level. **learning modality: visual**

Demonstration

Materials *stream table, sand or soil, water, ice cubes*

Time 10 minutes for setup; 10 minutes for observation on 2 days

As students observe, set up a stream table with a steady stream of water. After 10–15 minutes, discontinue the water. Have students examine the resulting valley and sketch what they observe. Then place ice cubes along the length of the stream-formed valley, moving the cubes in succession down the valley. Allow the ice to melt overnight. Again, have students examine the valley and sketch what they see. Finally, invite students to compare the stream-formed valley with the final valley. They should see that the first was V-shaped, while the second had widened to become more U-shaped. **learning modality: visual**

EXPLORING Glacial Landforms

As glaciers advance and retreat, they sculpt the landscape by erosion and deposition.

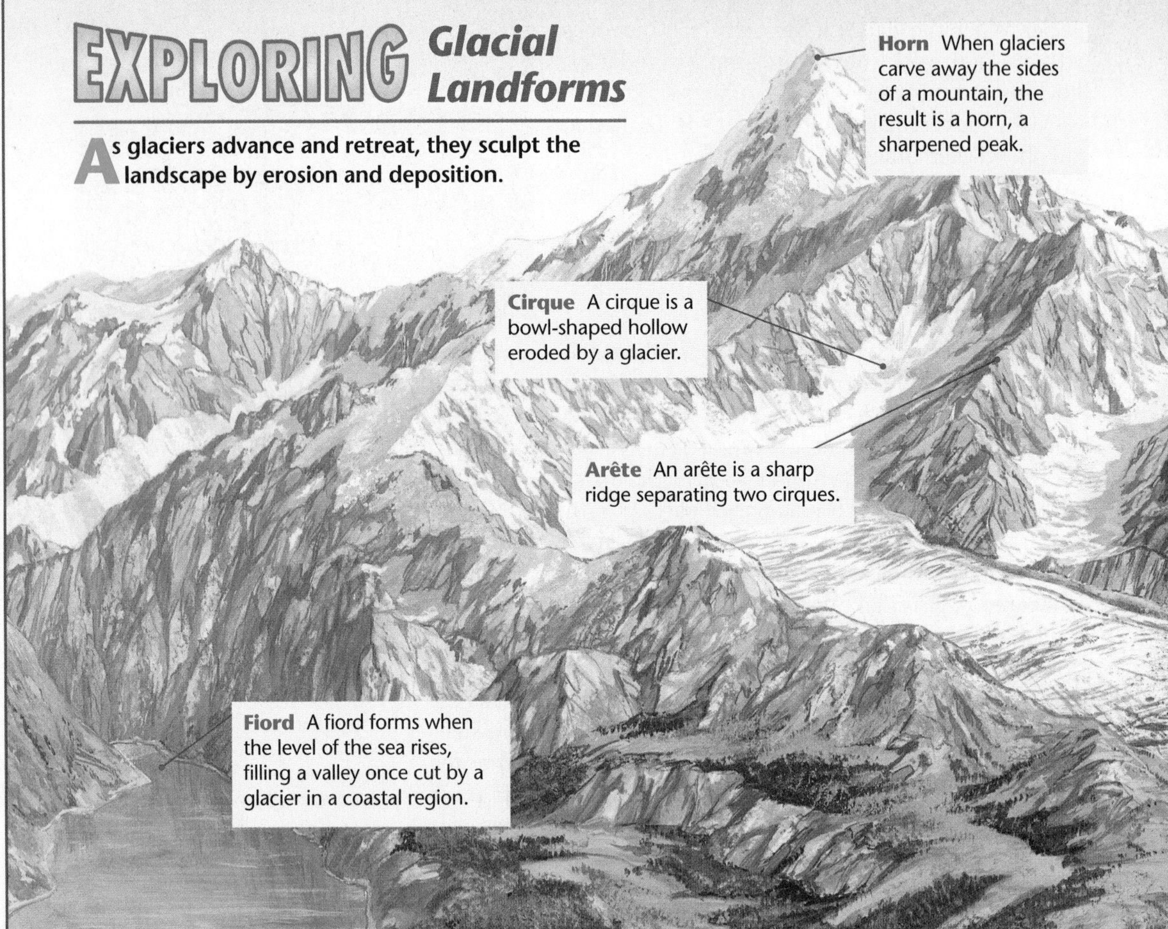

Retreating glaciers also create features called kettles. A **kettle** is a small depression that forms when a chunk of ice is left in glacial till. When the ice melts, the kettle remains. The continental glacier of the last ice age left behind many kettles. Kettles often fill with water, forming small ponds or lakes called kettle lakes. Such lakes are common in areas that were covered with ice.

The continental glacier of the last ice age also formed the Great Lakes. Before the ice age, there were large river valleys in the area now occupied by the lakes. As the ice advanced over these valleys, it scooped out loose sediment and soft rock, forming broad, deep basins. The Great Lakes formed over thousands of years as the glaciers melted and these basins filled with water.

Background

Integrating Science Earth's biosphere extends even into glaciers. Several species of "ice worms," related to earthworms, live in ice. The worms average about 3 mm long and 1 mm in diameter. They thrive at a temperature of about 0°C, so on sunny days, they burrow deeper into the ice. Biologists believe ice worms feed on red algae, also common in glaciers.

Facts and Figures Perhaps the world's most famous glacial landform is the Matterhorn, a spectacular horn on the border of Italy and Switzerland in the Pennine Alps. This extremely steep peak rises to an elevation of 4,478 m and is a favorite of tourists and mountain climbers. The Matterhorn formed as three glaciers carved cirques on different sides of the original larger mountain.

Section 4 Review

1. How are valley glaciers and continental glaciers different?
2. What are two types of glacial erosion?
3. Describe three features formed by glacial deposition.
4. **Thinking Critically Relating Cause and Effect** Driving through the countryside in Michigan, you and your family come upon a series of small, round lakes. Explain the process that formed these features.

CHAPTER PROJECT

Check Your Progress

Now you are ready to begin building your second model. Pattern the model after your drawing that predicts the effects of erosion and deposition. The model will show how gravity, water, and glaciers have changed your model landscape. Where on your model would glaciers be likely to form?

3 Assess

Section 4 Review Answers

1. Valley glaciers are found in high mountains, and the sides of the mountains keep these glaciers from spreading out. Continental glaciers cover much of a continent or large island.
2. Plucking and abrasion
3. Answers will vary. Students should describe a moraine, prairie pothole, kettle, drumlin, or glacial lake
4. These lakes are kettle lakes, which form when a chunk of glacier is left behind in glacial till. When the ice melts, a depression called a kettle remains in the ice. A kettle filled with water is called a kettle lake.

CHAPTER PROJECT

Check Your Progress

Students should make a second drawing that predicts how the second model will look. These drawings should reflect concepts students have learned about mass movement, water erosion and deposition, and glacial erosion and deposition. Advise students to include what they think are the most important changes caused by these processes. For students having trouble, suggest that they use the *Exploring* features in Section 2 and 3 for reference. Students will need more building materials for the second model.

Program Resources

◆ **Unit 2 Resources** 5-4 Review and Reinforce; 5-4 Enrich

Media and Technology

 **Transparencies** "Exploring Glacial Landforms," Transparency 16

Performance Assessment

Skills Check Have students make a table that compares and contrasts the features created by glacial erosion and glacial deposition. The table should include a description of each feature, as well as an explanation of how it forms.

 Students can keep their tables in their portfolios.

Waves

Objectives

After completing the lesson, students will be able to

- ◆ identify what gives ocean waves their energy;
- ◆ describe how ocean waves shape a coast and the landforms waves create.

Key Terms beach, longshore drift, spit

1 Engage/Explore

Activating Prior Knowledge

Encourage students who have been to beaches to share their observations of the sand on the beaches and the waves that flow over the beaches. Elicit descriptions of the color and texture of sand particles, noting any differences among beaches. Then have students describe how they think the waves affect the beaches. Finally, challenge students to develop a hypothesis about how beaches form.

DISCOVER

Skills Focus posing questions
Materials *sand from 2 beaches, hand lens*
Time 15 minutes
Tips Have student volunteers go as a group to collect sand from a nearby lake or ocean beach. If that is impractical, obtain two different kinds of sand commercially. Suggest that students avoid mixing the two samples by completely removing the first sample before examining the second.
Expected Outcome Students should observe differences in the two samples, such as differences in particle shape, size, color, and texture. Specific differences will depend on the samples used.
Think It Over Questions will vary. *Sample questions:* Is beach sand a result of erosion? How is beach sand deposited? What causes differences in samples of beach sand collected at different places?

Waves

DISCOVER ACTIVITY

What Can Be Learned From Beach Sand?

1. Collect a spoonful of sand from each of two different beaches. The two samples also may come from different parts of the same beach.
2. Examine the first sample of beach sand with a hand lens.
3. Record the properties of the sand grains, for example, color and shape. Are the grains smooth and rounded or angular and rough? Are all the grains in the sample the same shape and color?
4. Examine the second sample and repeat Step 3. How do the two samples compare?

Think It Over

Posing Questions What questions do you need to answer to understand beach sand? Use what you know about erosion and deposition to help you think of questions.

GUIDE FOR READING

- ◆ What gives waves their energy?
- ◆ How do waves shape a coast?

Reading Tip **As you read, make a concept map showing features formed by wave erosion and deposition.**

Ocean waves contain energy—sometimes a great deal of energy. The waves that sweep onto the Pacific coast are especially powerful. Created by ocean winds, they carry energy vast distances across the Pacific Ocean. Acting like drills or buzzsaws, the waves erode the solid rock of the coast into cliffs and caves. Waves also carry sediment that forms features such as beaches. But these features do not last long. More waves follow to change the shoreline yet again.

How Waves Form

The energy in waves comes from wind that blows across the water's surface. As the wind makes contact with the water, some of its energy transfers to the water. Large ocean waves are the result of powerful storms far out at sea. But ordinary breezes can produce waves in lakes or small ponds.

The energy that water picks up from the wind causes water particles to move up and down as the wave goes by. But the water particles themselves don't move forward. Only the form of the wave moves. Have you ever watched a wave in a field of tall grass? Each blade of grass moves back and forth but doesn't move from its place. But the energy of the wave moves across the field.

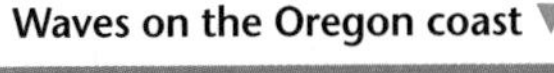

Waves on the Oregon coast ▼

READING STRATEGIES

Reading Tip If necessary, review how to make a concept map. A typical concept map of this section will begin with the general title "Waves." The map can then be divided into "Wave Formation," "Wave Erosion," and "Wave Deposition." Landforms created by wave erosion should fall under "Wave Erosion." Make sure students include linking words between circled words.

Study and Comprehension To help students understand waves, generate a wave in a length of rope. Tie one end of a rope about 2 m long to a pipe, post, or door handle. Then pull the rope straight and, as students observe, flip it with your wrist to make waves that are analogous to ocean waves. Like ocean water, the rope itself does not move forward. Rather, energy moves forward while the rope moves up and down.

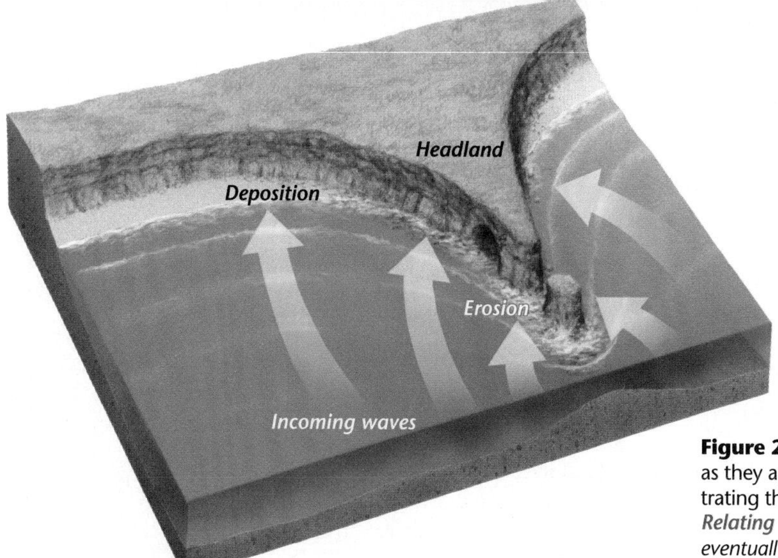

Figure 23 Incoming waves bend as they approach the shore, concentrating their energy on headlands. *Relating Cause and Effect* *What will eventually happen to the headlands?*

A wave changes as it approaches land. In deep water, a wave only affects the water near the surface. But as the wave approaches shallow water, the wave begins to drag the bottom. The friction between the wave and the bottom causes the wave to slow down. Now the water actually does move forward with the wave. This forward-moving water provides the force that shapes the land along the shoreline.

Erosion by Waves

Waves are the major force of erosion along coasts. One way waves erode the land is by impact. Large waves can hit rocks along the shore with great force. This energy in waves can break apart rocks. Over time, waves can make small cracks larger. Eventually, the waves cause pieces of rock to break off.

Waves also erode land by abrasion. As a wave approaches shallow water, it picks up sediment, including sand and gravel. This sediment is carried forward by the wave. When the wave hits land, the sediment wears away rock like sandpaper wearing away wood.

Waves coming to shore gradually change direction. The change in direction occurs as different parts of a wave begin to drag on the bottom. Notice how the waves in Figure 23 change direction as they approach the shore. The energy of these waves is concentrated on headlands. A headland is a part of the shore that sticks out into the ocean. Headlands stand out from the coast because they are made of harder rock that resists the waves. But, over time, waves erode the headlands and even out the shoreline.

☑ *Checkpoint* *What are two of the processes by which waves can cause erosion?*

Sharpen your Skills

Calculating

A sandy coast erodes at a rate of 1.25 meters per year. But a severe storm can erode an additional 3.75 meters from the shore. If 12 severe storms occur during a 50-year period, how much will the coast erode? If you wish, you may use an electronic calculator to find the answer.

2 Facilitate

How Waves Form

Using the Visuals: Figure 23

After students have examined the figure, ask: **Where will an incoming wave first make contact with the bottom as it approaches the shore?** *(Directly in front of the headland)* **What happens when a wave drags the bottom?** *(It slows down.)* Thus, as the wave on either side of the headland continues on, the wave approaching the headland slows down, causing the wave to "wrap" around the headland, as the arrows show. This section of the wave is concentrated in a smaller space, and its energy is concentrated as well. **learning modality: visual**

Erosion by Waves

Sharpen your Skills

Calculating

Time 10 minutes ACTIVITY
Tips Some students may need calculators to do the multiplication required to determine how much the coast will erode.
Expected Outcome In 50 years at the normal 1.25 m/yr, the coast will erode 62.5 m. In addition, each of the 12 storms will cause a further 3.75 m of erosion, or 45 m together. Therefore, the total over the period is 62.5 + 45, or 107.5 m of erosion.
Extend After students have read the rest of the section, have them look again at this problem. Ask: **Since waves steadily erode sandy coasts, and storms erode them even more, why are there any sandy coasts left?** *(Although waves do erode coasts, they also deposit sediments on coasts. Thus, waves both wear down and build up coasts.)* **learning modality: logical/mathematical**

Program Resources

- **Unit 2 Resources** 5-5 Lesson Plan; 5-5 Section Summary
- **Guided Reading and Study Workbook** Summary 5-5

Answers to Self-Assessment

Caption Question

Figure 23 They will erode back, evening out the shoreline.

☑ *Checkpoint*

Waves cause erosion by impact and abrasion.

Ongoing Assessment

Writing Have students explain in their own words how waves erode the land.

Media and Technology

Transparencies "Wave Erosion and Wind Erosion," Transparency 17

Landforms Created by Wave Erosion

Inquiry Challenge

Materials *aluminum baking pan, sand, water, metric ruler, piece of cardboard* ACTIVITY
Time 15 minutes

Ask students: **Do large waves erode more than small waves?** Then challenge students to use the materials to investigate the question and draw a conclusion. A typical experiment will involve building a sand hill on one side of the pan, adding water, and making waves with the piece of cardboard, first small waves and then large waves. Students should observe that the larger the wave, the more the erosion. **learning modality: kinesthetic**

Deposits by Waves

Including All Students

Support students who need more help by first sketching a beach on the board. Then, with an arrow, show an ocean wave hitting the shore diagonally, at about a 30° angle. Explain that waves usually hit shores diagonally because a shoreline's shape varies. Then ask: **What happens to the water that travels onto the beach with the wave?** *(Once the wave's energy is spent, the water runs back down the beach to the ocean.)* **What force causes this "backwash"?** *(Gravity causes the water to run back down the beach.)* Explain that waves often push water up onto a beach at an angle, but gravity pulls it back down the beach perpendicular to the shore, just as gravity pulls sediment down a hill in mass movement. Draw an arrow that shows this perpendicular movement of water. Draw several more pairs of arrows, zigzagging up or down the beach. Ask: **How does this affect particles of sediment on the beach?** *(They move up the beach with the combination of incoming waves and backwash.)* The combination of waves and backwash is responsible for longshore drift. Have students draw a copy of the sketch on the board. **limited English proficiency**

Figure 24 Waves cut these cliffs on the coast of Australia. The blocks of rock offshore are sea stacks. *Developing Hypotheses Develop a hypothesis to explain how these sea stacks formed.*

Landforms Created by Wave Erosion

When waves hit a steep, rocky coast, they strike the area again and again. Think of an ax striking the trunk of a tree. The cut gets bigger and deeper with each strike of the blade. Finally the tree falls. In a similar way, ocean waves erode the base of the land along a steep coast. Where the rock is softer, the waves erode the land faster. Over time the waves may erode a hollow area in the rock called a sea cave.

Eventually, waves may erode the base of a cliff so much that the rock above collapses. The result is a wave-cut cliff. You can see an example of such a cliff in Figure 24.

Another feature created by wave erosion is a sea arch. A sea arch forms when waves erode a layer of softer rock that underlies a layer of harder rock. If an arch collapses, the result might be a sea stack, a pillar of rock rising above the water.

☑ *Checkpoint* *How can waves produce a cliff on a rocky coast?*

Deposits by Waves

Waves not only erode the land, they also deposit sediment. **Waves shape the coast through both erosion and deposition.** Deposition occurs when waves slow down and the water drops its sediment. This process is similar to the deposition that occurs on a river delta when the river slows down and drops its sediment load.

Background

Facts and Figures The difference between rocky and sandy coastlines is a function of how much sediment there is to be deposited. Where sediment is abundant, a beach forms. The sand often originates from far away. Much of the sand on North Carolina's Cape Hatteras, for example, originally came from the Hudson River, Long Island, and southern New England.

Media and Technology

Concept Videotape Library
Grade 6, Tape 1 "The Wave"

As waves reach the shore, they drop the sediment they carry, forming a beach. A **beach** is an area of wave-washed sediment along a coast. The sediment deposited on beaches is usually sand. Most sand comes from rivers that carry eroded particles of rock into the ocean. But not all beaches are made of sand carried by rivers. Some beaches are made of small fragments of coral or sea shells piled up by wave action. Florida has many such beaches.

The sediment on a beach usually moves down the beach after it has been deposited. Waves usually hit the beach at an angle instead of straight on. These angled waves create a current that runs parallel to the coastline. As repeated waves hit the beach, some of the beach sediment moves down the beach with the current, in a process called **longshore drift.**

Figure 25 This satellite image of Cape Cod in Massachusetts shows how longshore drift can carry sand and deposit it to form a spit. ***Observing*** *How many spits can you find in this image?*

One result of longshore drift is the formation of a spit. A **spit** is a beach that projects like a finger out into the water. Spits form as a result of deposition by longshore drift. Spits occur where a headland or other obstacle interrupts longshore drift, or where the coast turns abruptly. Incoming waves carrying sand may build up sandbars, long ridges of sand parallel to the shore.

INTEGRATING ENVIRONMENTAL SCIENCE A barrier beach is similar to a sandbar, but a barrier beach forms when storm waves pile up sand above sea level. Barrier beaches are found in many places along the Atlantic coast of the United States, such as the Outer Banks of North Carolina. People have built homes on many of these barrier beaches. But the storm waves that build up the beaches can also wash them away. Barrier beach communities must be prepared for the damage that hurricanes and other storms can bring.

Section 5 Review

1. How do ocean waves form?
2. Describe two landforms created by wave erosion and two landforms created by wave deposition.
3. Why are headlands eroded faster than the land at the ends of inlets and bays?
4. **Thinking Critically Predicting** You visit a rocky headland by the ocean that has a sea arch and several sea stacks. How might this area change in the next 500 years?

CHAPTER PROJECT

Check Your Progress

Now you are ready to add the effects of wave erosion to your model. What landforms will wave erosion produce along the coastline on your model? What materials will you use to model these landforms? When you have finished your second model, make labels for the landforms on your models.

Program Resources

- **Unit 2 Resources** 5-5 Review and Reinforce; 5-5 Enrich

Answers to Self-Assessment

Caption Questions

Figure 24 *Sample hypothesis:* Sea stacks can form when waves erode a layer of soft rock faster than hard rock.

Figure 25 At least five spits can be seen.

Checkpoint

When they erode the base of the land so much that the rock above collapses.

Integrating Environmental Science

Display a large map of the United States. Direct students' attention to the barrier islands along the Atlantic and Gulf coasts, especially off the North Carolina coast. Ask: **How permanent do you think these barrier beaches are?** *(Ocean waves are constantly eroding and depositing sediment, thus making changes in these beaches every day.)* **learning modality: visual**

3 Assess

Section 5 Review Answers

1. Ocean waves form when wind makes contact with ocean water and transfers some of its energy to the water.
2. Answers will vary. Students should describe any two landforms created by wave erosion: sea cave, wave-cut cliff, sea arch, and sea stack. They should also describe any two landforms created by wave deposition: beach, spit, and barrier beach.
3. Headlands are eroded faster because waves change direction as they approach the shore, thereby concentrating their energy on headlands.
4. In 500 years, the headland may have eroded back, evening out the shore. Erosion by waves may also have caused the sea arch to collapse, creating more sea stacks.

CHAPTER PROJECT

Check Your Progress

At this point, students should be putting the finishing touches on their second models. To add features related to wave erosion, students will need more of the sand-glue mixture, as well as some additional sand or gravel. Help students think ahead to their presentations by questioning them about why they included various features.

Performance Assessment

Drawing Have students make a labeled drawing of the landforms created by wave erosion and deposition.

Wind

Objectives

After completing the lesson, students will be able to

- ◆ describe the process by which wind causes erosion;
- ◆ identify the features resulting from erosion and deposition by wind.

Key Terms sand dune, deflation, loess

1 Engage/Explore

Activating Prior Knowledge

Encourage students who have lived near or visited a desert or have seen deserts in films or books to describe what they've seen. Ask: **Are there any natural landforms that are most common in a sandy desert?** *(Most students will know about sand dunes.)* Have students speculate on how sand dunes form. Then ask: **Are there any other places where you might expect to see sand dunes?** *(beaches)* **What characteristics are common to deserts and sandy areas?** *(Both contain little vegetation, and both are often windy.)*

DISCOVER

Skills Focus observing
Materials *shallow pan, cornmeal, plastic straw*
Time 10 minutes
Tips Caution students to avoid blowing the cornmeal in the direction of another student. Have each student immediately clean up any cornmeal he or she blows out of the pan. Emphasize that students should blow through the straw *gently.*
Think It Over Students should observe that blowing gently through the straw created ripples in the cornmeal or piles that are similar to sand dunes.

Wind

DISCOVER ACTIVITY

How Does Moving Air Affect Sediment?

1. Cover the bottom of a pan with a flat layer of cornmeal 1–2 centimeters deep.
2. Gently blow over the layer of cornmeal using a straw to direct your breath. Observe what happens.

CAUTION: *Do not blow the cornmeal in the direction of another student.*

Think It Over

Observing What changes did the wind you created make in the flat layer of cornmeal?

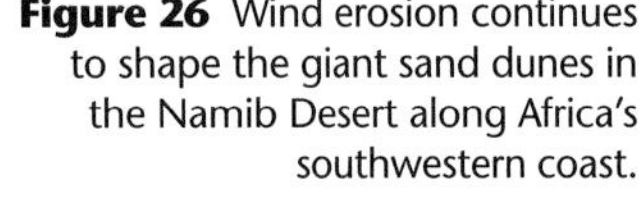

GUIDE FOR READING

- ◆ How does wind cause erosion?
- ◆ What features result from deposition by wind?

Reading Tip Before you read, preview Figure 27. In your notebook, write some predictions about the characteristics of wind erosion.

Imagine a landscape made almost entirely of sand. One such place is the Namib Desert. The desert stretches for about 1,900 kilometers along the coast of Namibia in Africa. In the southern half of the Namib are long rows of giant sand dunes. A **sand dune** is a deposit of windblown sand. Some sand dunes in the Namib are more than 200 meters high and 15 kilometers long. Much of the sand in the dunes originally came from the nearby Orange River. Over thousands of years, wind has swept the sand across the desert, piling up huge, ever-changing dunes.

How Wind Causes Erosion

Wind by itself is the weakest agent of erosion. Water, waves, moving ice, and even mass movement have more effect on the land. Yet wind can be a powerful force in shaping the land in areas where there are few plants to hold the soil in place. As you might guess, wind is very effective in causing erosion in deserts. There, few plants can grow, and wind can easily move the grains of dry, light sand.

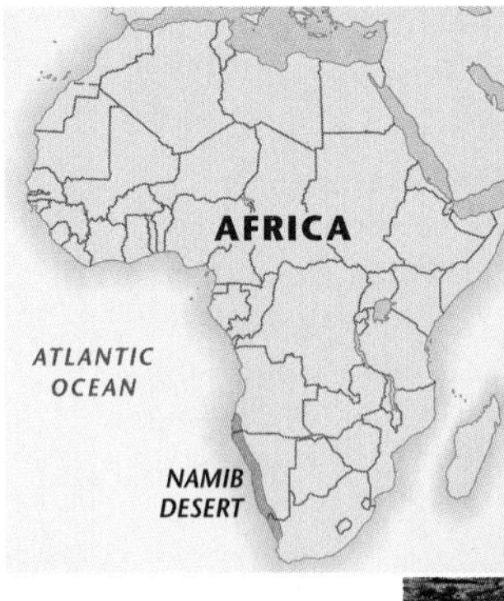

Figure 26 Wind erosion continues to shape the giant sand dunes in the Namib Desert along Africa's southwestern coast.

READING STRATEGIES

Reading Tip Students should predict that wind erosion moves particles of different sizes in different ways. Have them explain in writing how they think different sizes of sediment are affected by wind. Once they have read the section, suggest that they rewrite their explanations to conform to their better understanding of wind erosion.

Vocabulary Call students' attention the key term *deflation.* Explain that it derives from a Latin word meaning "to blow away." Use a balloon to illustrate this meaning. When you blow the balloon up, the balloon "inflates"—air "blows in" the balloon. When you allow the air to escape, the balloon "deflates"—air "blows away" from the balloon. In wind deflation, the wind blows sediment away. Also point out the key term *loess.* Explain that it derives from a German word for "loose."

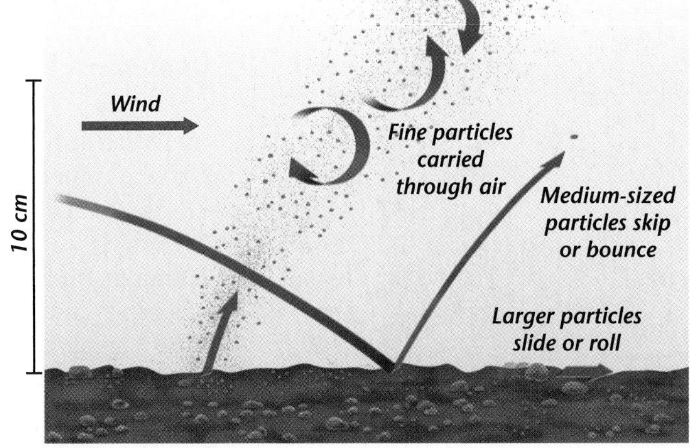

Figure 27 Wind erosion moves sediment particles of different sizes in the three ways shown above. *Comparing and Contrasting Compare the movement of sediment by wind with the movement of sediment by water in Figure 16 on page 146. How are the processes similar? How are they different?*

The main way that wind causes erosion is by deflation. Geologists define **deflation** as the process by which wind removes surface materials. When wind blows over the land, it picks up the smallest particles of sediment. This sediment is made of bits of clay and silt. The stronger the wind, the larger the particles that it can pick up and move through the air. Slightly heavier particles, such as sand, might skip or bounce for a short distance. But sand soon falls back to the ground. Strong winds can even roll heavier sediment particles over the ground. Figure 27 shows how wind erodes by deflation.

Deflation does not usually have a great effect on the land. However, in parts of the Great Plains in the 1930s, deflation caused the loss of about 1 meter of topsoil in just a few years. In deserts, deflation can sometimes create an area of rock fragments called desert pavement. You can see an area of desert pavement in Figure 28. There, wind has blown away the smaller sediment. All that remains are rocky materials that are too large and heavy to be moved. Where there is already a slight depression in the ground, deflation can produce a bowl-shaped hollow called a blowout.

Figure 28 Wind erosion formed this desert pavement in the Arizona desert. Wind-driven sand may polish and shape individual stones.

Abrasion by wind-carried sand can polish rock, but it causes little erosion. At one time, geologists thought that the sediment carried by wind cut the stone shapes seen in deserts. But now evidence shows that most desert landforms are the result of weathering and water erosion.

☑ ***Checkpoint*** *Where would you be most likely to see evidence of wind erosion?*

Program Resources

- **Unit 2 Resources** 5-6 Lesson Plan; 5-6 Section Summary
- **Guided Reading and Study Workbook** Section 5-6

Media and Technology

Transparencies "Wave Erosion and Wind Erosion," Transparency 17

Answers to Self-Assessment

Caption Question

Figure 27 In both, larger particles slide or roll and smaller particles are carried along suspended. One major difference is that, in water, some sediment is transported dissolved in solution.

☑ ***Checkpoint***

Wind erosion is powerful in areas where there are few plants to hold soil in place.

2 Facilitate

How Wind Causes Erosion

Inquiry Challenge

Materials *coarse and fine sand, hair dryer, block of wood, ice-cube tray*
Time 15 minutes

Ask students: **Does wind move different sizes of sediment different distances?** Then have small groups investigate the question by mixing coarse and fine sand together, making a pile of sand on a block of wood, placing an ice-cube tray next to the block, and using a hair dryer on a low setting to blow the sand in the direction of the ice-cube tray. Students should observe that the coarse sand will blow into the near sections of the ice-cube tray, while the fine sand will blow into the far sections. Have students draw a conclusion in writing. (Make sure students wear goggles for this activity. You may want students to put down a plastic dropcloth before beginning the activity.) **learning modality: kinesthetic**

Demonstration

ACTIVITY

Materials *sand, large funnel, sheet of plastic, books, hair dryer, extension cord*
Time 10 minutes

To demonstrate abrasion by wind-carried sediment, set up a table outside and prop a sheet of plastic against a stack of books. Have a student volunteer—wearing goggles—use a hand to cover the bottom of a funnel and fill it with sand. Then, as the class observes, invite the student to release the sand from the funnel 3–4 cm in front of the piece of plastic as you aim a hair dryer on high speed at the plastic. Repeat the process several times. Then have students examine the plastic to observe pits and other signs of abrasion. **learning modality: visual**

Ongoing Assessment

Oral Presentation Call on students at random to explain how wind transports different-sized sediment particles.

Deposits Resulting From Wind Erosion

Using the Visuals: Figure 29

After students have examined the photo, ask: **Which of the three ways shown in Figure 27 would likely have carried the sediment to this loess deposit?** *(By fine particles carried through the air)* Explain that winds can carry fine particles great distances. **learning modality: verbal**

3 Assess

Section 6 Review Answers

1. Wind erodes by deflation. When wind blows over the land, it picks up smaller sediment and bounces or rolls larger sediment over the ground.
2. Sand dunes form when wind carrying sediment strikes an obstacle, such as a boulder or clump of grass, which traps the windblown sediment. Loess deposits form when wind lays down fine sediments in layers.
3. A blowout is a bowl-shaped hollow produced when deflation removes sediment from a slight depression in the ground.
4. The sediment that makes up the sand dune may eventually blow away, since wind is a powerful force where plants don't hold soil in place.

Science at Home

ACTIVITY

Materials *coins, shallow pan, plastic straw, flour*
Tips Encourage students to carry out this demonstration at home. Caution them to make sure family members are far enough away to avoid getting flour in their eyes. Students should be prepared to explain what deflation is and what the coins and flour represent.

Performance Assessment

Writing Have students write a story in which they imagine being a sand particle blown from desert pavement to a sand dune.

Figure 29 Wind carrying fine particles of silt built up this loess deposit near Natchez, Mississippi.

Deposits Resulting From Wind Erosion

All the sediment picked up by wind eventually falls to the ground. This happens when the wind slows down or some obstacle, such as a boulder or a clump of grass, traps the windblown sand and other sediment. **Wind erosion and deposition may form sand dunes and loess deposits.** When the wind strikes an obstacle, the result is usually a sand dune. Sand dunes can be seen on beaches and in deserts where wind-blown sediment has built up.

Sand dunes come in many shapes and sizes. Some are long, with parallel ridges, while others are U-shaped. They can also be very small or very large—some sand dunes in China have grown to heights of 500 meters. Sand dunes move over time. Little by little, the sand shifts with the wind from one side of the dune to the other. Sometimes plants begin growing on a dune. Plant roots can help to anchor the dune in one place.

Sand dunes are most often made of the coarser sediments carried by wind. The finer sediments, including particles of clay and silt, are sometimes deposited in layers far from their source. This fine, wind-deposited sediment is **loess** (LES). Large loess deposits are found in central China and in such states as Nebraska, South Dakota, Iowa, Missouri, and Illinois. Loess helps to form fertile soil. Many areas with thick loess deposits are valuable farmlands.

Section 6 Review

1. Describe how wind erodes the land.
2. How do sand dunes and loess deposits form?
3. What is a blowout and what is the process that produces one?
4. **Thinking Critically Predicting** You visit a beach that has sand dunes covered with dune grass. But where people take a shortcut over one dune, the grass has been worn away. What may eventually happen to the dune if people keep taking this path?

Science at Home

Modeling Desert Pavement Here's how to make a model of desert pavement. Put a few coins in a shallow pan about 1 centimeter deep. Sprinkle enough flour over the coins to bury them beneath a thin layer of flour. Then blow air gently through a straw across the surface of the flour. Be careful not to draw in any flour through the straw. Be certain the blown flour will not get in your or anyone else's eyes. Ask your family to predict what the surface of the pan would look like if the "wind" continued to blow for a long time.

Background

Facts and Figures There are two main sources of the wind-deposited clay and silt that form loess deposits: deserts and glacial meltwater flood plains. The loess deposits of China derived mainly from great desert regions of Asia. The loess deposits of the U.S. Midwest originated in the deflation of the dry flood plains of meltwater rivers as continental glaciers melted back at the end of the Pleistocene Ice Age.

Program Resources

- **Unit 2 Resources** 5-6 Review and Reinforce; 5-6 Enrich

Changing Earth's Surface

Key Ideas

- Weathering, erosion, and deposition act to wear down and build up Earth's surface.
- Gravity pulls sediment downhill in the process of mass movement. There are four main types of mass movement: landslides, mudslides, slump, and creep.

Key Terms

erosion, sediment, deposition, mass movement

Water Erosion

Key Ideas

- Moving water is the major force of erosion that has shaped Earth's land surface.
- A river may form V-shaped valleys, waterfalls, meanders, oxbow lakes, and flood plains.
- When a river slows down, it deposits some of the sediment load it carries, forming features such as alluvial fans and deltas.

Key Terms

runoff	drainage basin	delta
rill	divide	groundwater
gully	flood plain	stalactite
stream	meander	stalagmite
river	oxbow lake	karst topography
tributary	alluvial fan	

The Force of Moving Water

INTEGRATING PHYSICS

Key Ideas

- When gravity pulls water down a slope, water's potential energy changes to kinetic energy, and it does work.
- Most sediment washes or falls into streams, or is eroded from the streambed by abrasion.
- The greater a river's slope or volume of flow, the more sediment it can erode.

Key Terms

energy	abrasion	friction
potential energy	load	turbulence
kinetic energy		

Glaciers

Key Ideas

- The two kinds of glaciers are valley glaciers and continental glaciers.
- Glaciers erode the land through plucking and abrasion. Melting glaciers deposit sediment.

Key Terms

glacier	ice age	moraine
valley glacier	plucking	kettle
continental glacier	till	

Waves

Key Ideas

- The energy of ocean waves comes from wind blowing across the water's surface and transferring energy to the water.
- Ocean waves hitting land cause erosion through impact and abrasion. Waves also move and deposit sediment along the shore.

Key Terms

beach, longshore drift, spit

Wind Erosion

Key Ideas

- Wind causes erosion mainly through deflation, the blowing of surface materials.
- Landforms created by wind deposition include sand dunes and loess deposits.

Key Terms

sand dune, deflation, loess

Organizing Information

Flowchart Make a flowchart showing how a stream forms. Your flowchart should include the following terms in the correct order: rills, runoff, gullies, stream, raindrops. Give your flowchart a title. (For tips on making a flowchart, see the Skills Handbook.)

Program Resources

- **Unit 2 Resources** Chapter 5 Project Scoring Rubric
- **Performance Assessment** Chapter 5
- **Chapter and Unit Tests** Chapter 5 Test

Media and Technology

Computer Test Bank Chapter 5 Test

Organizing Information

Flow Chart Sample flowchart:

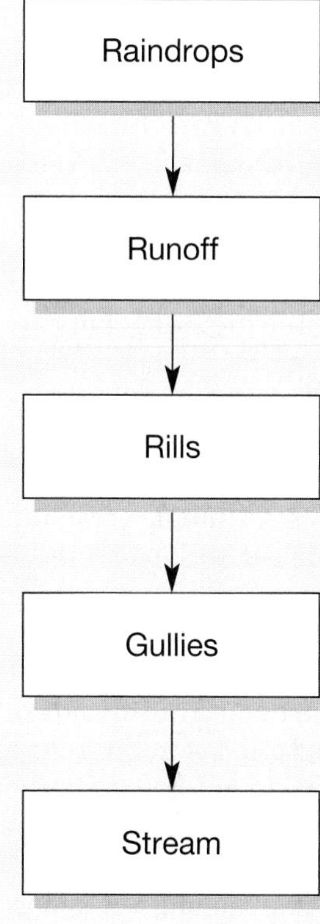

Reviewing Content

Multiple Choice

1. c **2.** a **3.** b **4.** d **5.** b

True or False

6. deposition **7.** karst topography **8.** true **9.** true **10.** moraine

Checking Concepts

11. The agents of erosion that are in part caused by the force of gravity are moving water and glaciers. Gravity itself causes mass movement and is therefore also an agent of erosion.
12. If a river's slope increases, its speed also increases. And the greater the volume of flow, the greater the speed. A fast-flowing river carries more and larger particles of sediment.
13. Where a river bends, the water moves faster along the outside of the curve. There, the river tends to cut into its bank. Sediment is deposited on the inside curve, where the water speed is slowest.
14. Any time moving water slows down, it deposits some of its sediment. When a river flows into a still body of water, such as an ocean or a lake, the sediment in the water drops to the bottom. This deposited sediment builds up a landform called a delta.
15. Erosion occurs when groundwater containing carbonic acid flows into cracks in limestone. The rock changes chemically and some of it gets carried away in solution by water, creating holes and caves. Deposition results when water dripping from a cave's roof evaporates, depositing calcite.
16. Ice ages are times when continental glaciers cover large parts of Earth's surface.
17. Students' letters will vary. An adequate response should describe the features described in *Exploring the Course of a River* on pages 138–139. For each feature, there should be some explanation about how it formed. An excellent response should weave the information together in a creative and interesting way.

Thinking Critically

18. Abrasion occurs when particles of sediment in flowing water bump into the streambed again and again. A very turbulent stream or the fast-flowing water of a flooding river would cause the most erosion of a streambed.
19. Deflation removed all the sand and smaller sediment, leaving behind the rocky materials that were too large and heavy to be moved by wind.
20. Answers may vary. *Sample answer:* You could observe the landforms in front of the glacier. If it is retreating, then the landforms would be those recently sculpted by glacial erosion and deposition.
21. If the house was right on a riverbank, then it would be within the river's flood plain. A family should hesitate because the house might be damaged or destroyed by a flood in the future.
22. The sand came from rivers that carried the particles to the ocean, where waves dropped them to form the beach.

CHAPTER 5 ASSESSMENT

Reviewing Content

Multiple Choice

Choose the answer that best completes the sentence.

1. The eroded materials carried by water or wind are called
a. stalactites.
b. desert pavement.
c. sediment.
d. moraines.

2. The downhill movement of eroded materials is known as
a. mass movement.
b. abrasion.
c. deposition.
d. deflation.

3. A mass of rock and soil deposited directly by a glacier is called
a. load. **b.** till.
c. loess. **d.** erosion.

4. When waves strike a shoreline, they concentrate their energy on
a. beaches.
b. cirques.
c. sand dunes.
d. headlands.

5. The erosion of sediment by wind is
a. deposition. **b.** deflation.
c. plucking. **d.** glaciation.

True or False

If the statement is true, write true. If it is false, change the underlined word or words to make the statement true.

6. The process by which sediment in water settles in new locations is mass movement.
7. An area of alluvial fans may be found where groundwater erodes limestone to form valleys, sinkholes, and caverns.
8. Because it is moving, flowing water has a type of energy called kinetic energy.
9. A looplike bend in the course of a river is a meander.
10. The sediment deposited at the edge of a glacier forms a ridge called a kettle.

Checking Concepts

11. What agents of erosion are in part caused by the force of gravity?
12. How do a river's slope and volume of flow affect the river's sediment load?
13. Describe how the speed of flowing water changes where a river bends. How does this affect a river's deposition of sediment?
14. Why does a delta develop when a river flows into a larger body of water?
15. Describe the process by which groundwater can cause erosion and deposition in limestone beneath Earth's surface.
16. What are ice ages?
17. **Writing to Learn** You go on a rafting journey that takes you down a river from the mountains to the sea. Write a letter to a friend describing the features created by erosion and deposition that you see as you travel down the river. Include features near the river's source, along the middle of its course, and where it reaches the ocean.

Thinking Critically

18. **Applying Concepts** Under what conditions would you expect abrasion to cause the most erosion of a riverbed?
19. **Relating Cause and Effect** In a desert, you see an area that looks as if it were paved with rock fragments. Explain how this situation occurred naturally.
20. **Problem Solving** Suppose you are a geologist studying a valley glacier. What method could you use to tell if it is advancing or retreating?
21. **Making Judgments** A salesperson offers to sell your family a new house right on a riverbank for very little money. Why might your family hesitate to buy this house?
22. **Inferring** You see a sandy beach along a coastline. What can you infer about where the sand came from?
23. **Comparing and Contrasting** How are landslides similar to mudflows? How are they different?

162

Applying Skills

The table below shows how a river's volume of flow and sediment load change over six months. Use the table to answer Questions 24–26.

Month	Volume of Flow (cubic meters/second)	Sediment Load (metric tons/day)
January	1.5	200
February	1.7	320
March	2.6	725
April	4.0	1600
May	3.2	1100
June	2.8	900

24. Graphing Make one graph with the month on the *x*-axis and the volume of flow on the *y*-axis. Make a second graph with the sediment load on the *y*-axis. Compare your two graphs. When were the river's volume of flow and load the greatest? The lowest?

25. Developing Hypotheses Use your graphs to develop a hypothesis about the relationship between volume of flow and sediment load.

26. Relating Cause and Effect What may have occurred in the river's drainage basin in April to cause the changes in volume of flow and sediment load? Explain.

CHAPTER PROJECT Performance Assessment

Present Your Project Now you are ready to explain your models of erosion to your class. Label your models to indicate the features that changed during erosion.

Reflect and Record In your journal, write about the easiest and hardest parts of this project. How would you do each model differently if you did the project again?

Test Preparation

Use these questions to prepare for standardized tests.

Read the passage. Then answer Questions 27–30.

This is the story of a great river. The Missouri River is America's second longest river after the Mississippi River. Its vast drainage basin covers parts of 10 states and 2 Canadian provinces. Early settlers called the Missouri the "Big Muddy" because its waters carry a heavy sediment load.

The Missouri River begins in the Rocky Mountains near Three Forks, Montana, where three small streams join. The upper Missouri flows through a deep valley called the Gates of the Mountains. Then at Great Falls, Montana, it plunges down a series of waterfalls and rapids.

Leaving the mountains, the middle Missouri flows across the Great Plains. Major tributaries, such as the Yellowstone and Platte rivers, flow into it. The Missouri has eroded a wide valley as it winds through the plains. Steep ridges called bluffs sometimes form the edges of the valley.

The Missouri ends just north of St. Louis, Missouri, where it flows into the Mississippi.

27. A good title for this passage is
a. The Rivers of America.
b. Following the Missouri River.
c. Tributaries of the Missouri River.
d. Sedimental Journey.

28. A deep valley, waterfalls, and rapids can be found
a. where the Missouri crosses the Plains.
b. nowhere along the Missouri.
c. on the upper Missouri.
d. on the lower Missouri.

29. Along the middle Missouri's valley are features called
a. gullies. **b.** drainage basins.
c. gates. **d.** bluffs.

30. The nickname "Big Muddy" refers to the Missouri's
a. sediment load.
b. source.
c. meanders.
d. tributaries.

Program Resources

◆ **Inquiry Skills Activity Book** Provides teaching and review of all inquiry skills

23. Both are types of mass movement that result from the rapid downhill movement of earth materials and both can be triggered by an earthquake. Unlike landslides, which are mostly rock and soil, mudslides are up to 60 percent water and can occur on very gentle slopes.

Applying Skills

24. The flow and load were greatest in April. They were lowest in January.
25. A river's load varies directly with its volume of flow.
26. Rainfall or melting snow probably increased throughout the drainage basin in April, creating more runoff and eroding more sediment.

Present Your Project As each student presents his or her models to the class, assess whether the student effectively and comprehensively showed changes from the first to the second model, how well made the model is, and how well-done the presentation is. Students should explain the natural processes that result in the changes shown in their models.
Reflect and Record In judging how they would make the models differently if they could redo the project, students should compare their own models with those of other students. As they assess the results of their presentations, students should mention the benefits of preparing for their talk, since they knew they had to understand erosion in order to explain their models.

Test Preparation

27. b **28.** c **29.** d **30.** a

CHAPTER 6

Earth's Land Resources

Sections	Time	Student Edition Activities	ACTIVITY Other Activities
CHAPTER PROJECT **What's in a Package?** p. 165	Ongoing (2 weeks)	Check Your Progress, p. 172, 185 Present Your Project, p. 189	
1 Exploring Earth's Surface pp. 166–172 ◆ List the factors that determine the topography of Earth's surface. ◆ Name and describe the main types of landforms. ◆ Identify the four "spheres" that make up Earth's surface. ◆ Name and describe the layers that make up Earth's structure.	1 period/ $\frac{1}{2}$ block	**Discover** What Is the Land Like Around Your School?, p. 166	**TE** Building Inquiry Skills: Organizing Information, p. 168 **TE** Exploring Landforms, p. 169 **TE** Building Inquiry Skills: Classifying, p. 169 **TE** Demonstration, p. 171
2 Topographic Maps pp. 173–177 ◆ Describe a topographic map. ◆ Explain how elevation, relief, and slope are shown on topographic maps. ◆ Identify the Global Positioning System.	1 period/ $\frac{1}{2}$ block	**Discover** Can a Map Show Relief?, p. 173 **Sharpen Your Skills** Interpreting Data, p. 175	**TE** Building Inquiry Skills: Making Models, p. 176 **LM** 6, "Using a Topographic Map" **IES** "Wagons West," pp. 22–23
3 Earth's Land Biomes pp. 178–186 ◆ List and describe Earth's major land biomes. ◆ List and descrie Earth's major freshwater and ocean biomes.	2-3 periods/ 1–1$\frac{1}{2}$ blocks	**Discover** How Much Rain Is That?, p. 178 **Try This** Desert Survival, p. 181 **Sharpen Your Skills** Inferring, p. 183 **Skills Lab: Controlling Variables** Save That Soil, p. 186	**TE** Building Inquiry Skills: Communicating, p. 179 **TE** Building Inquiry Skills: Making Models, pp. 180, 182 **TE** Building Inquiry Skills: Inferring, p. 183
Study Guide/Chapter Assessment pp. 187–189	1 period/ $\frac{1}{2}$ block		**ISAB** Provides teaching and review of all inquiry skills

For Standard or Block Schedule The Resource Pro® CD-ROM gives you maximum flexibility for planning your instruction for any type of schedule. Resource Pro® contains Planning Express®, an advanced scheduling program, as well as the entire contents of the Teaching Resources and the Computer Test Bank.

CHAPTER PLANNING GUIDE

Program Resources	Assessment Strategies	Media and Technology
UR Chapter 6 Project Teacher Notes **UR** Chapter 6 Project Overview and Worksheets	**SE** Performance Assessment: Present Your Project, p. 189 **TE** Check Your Progress, pp. 172, 185 **UR** Chapter 6 Project Scoring Rubric	Science Explorer Internet Site at www.phschool.com Student Edition on Audio CD, Chapter 6
UR 6-1 Lesson Plan **UR** 6-1 Section Summary **UR** 6-1 Review and Reinforce **UR** 6-1 Enrich	**SE** Section 1 Review, p. 172 **TE** Ongoing Assessment, pp. 167, 169 **TE** Performance Assessment, p. 172	Concept Videotape Library, Grade 6, Tape 1, "Flying Over America" Transparencies 18, "Landform Regions of the United States"; 19, "Exploring Landforms"
UR 6-2 Lesson Plan **UR** 6-2 Section Summary **UR** 6-2 Review and Reinforce **UR** 6-2 Enrich	**SE** Section 2 Review, p. 177 **TE** Ongoing Assessment, p. 175 **TE** Performance Assessment, p. 177	Transparency 20, "Exploring Topographic Maps"
UR 6-3 Lesson Plan **UR** 6-3 Section Summary **UR** 6-3 Review and Reinforce **UR** 6-3 Enrich **UR** Skills Lab blackline masters	**SE** Section 3 Review, p. 185 **TE** Ongoing Assessment, p. 179, 181, 183 **TE** Performance Assessment, p. 185	Concept Videotape Library, Grade 6, Tape 1, "Earth's Many Biomes" Lab Activity Videotapes, Grade 6 Tape 2
RCA Provides strategies to improve science reading skills **GRSW** Provides worksheets to promote student comprehension of content	**SE** Chapter 6 Study Guide/Assessment, pp. 187–189 **PA** Chapter 6 Performance Assessment **CUT** Chapter 6 Test **CTB** Chapter 6 Test	Computer Test Bank, Chapter 6 Test

Key: **SE** Student Edition
CTB Computer Test Bank
ISAB Inquiry Skills Activity Book
GRSW Guided Reading and Study Workbook
TE Teacher's Edition
PTA Product Testing Activities by *Consumer Reports*
RCA Reading in the Content Area
PA Performance Assessment
UR Unit Resources
LM Laboratory Manual
IES Interdisciplinary Explorations Series
CUT Chapter and Unit Tests

Meeting the National Science Education Standards and AAAS Benchmarks

National Science Education Standards	Benchmarks for Science Literacy	Unifying Themes
Science As Inquiry (Content Standard A) ◆ **Design and conduct a scientific investigation** Students investigate how rainfall can cause erosion. *(Skills Lab)* **Life Science** (Content Standard C) ◆ **Populations and ecosystems** Students observe how climate affects biomes. *(Section 3)* **Earth and Space Science** (Content Standard D) ◆ **Structure of the Earth system** Topography is determined by elevation, relief, and landforms. *(Section 1)* **Science and Technology** (Content Standard E) ◆ **Evaluate completed technological designs or products** Students analyze product packaging. *(Chapter Project)* ◆ **Understandings about science and technology** Topographic maps provide highly accurate information on the elevation, relief, and slope of the ground surface. *(Section 2)* **Science in Personal and Social Perspectives** (Content Standard F) ◆ **Science and technology in society** Solid waste can be buried, burned, or recycled. *(Chapter Project)*	**1B Scientific Inquiry** Students analyze product packing. Students investigate how rainfall can cause erosion. *(Chapter Project, Skills Lab)* **3A Technology and Science** Topographic maps provide highly accurate information on the elevation, relief, and slope of the ground surface. *(Section 2)* **3C Issues in Technology** The basic ways to deal with solid waste are to bury it, burn it, or recycle it. *(Chapter Project)* **4B The Earth** Topography is determined by elevation, relief, and landforms. *(Section 1)*	◆ **Modeling** Topographic maps provide highly accurate information on the elevation, relief, and slope of the ground surface. *(Section 2)* ◆ **Scale and Structure** The three main types of landforms are plains, mountains, and plateaus. *(Section 1)* ◆ **Stability** Biomes are areas with similar climates and organisms. *(Section 3)* ◆ **Systems and Interactions** The basic ways to deal with solid waste are to bury it, burn it, or recycle it. Mapmakers use contour lines to represent elevation, relief, and slope on topographic maps. The types of plants determine the kinds of animals that live in an area. *(Chapter Project, Sections 2, 3)* ◆ **Unity and Diversity** Scientists divide Earth into the lithosphere, hydrosphere, atmosphere, and biosphere. A map is a model of all or part of Earth's surface. Ecologists classify ecosystems into biomes. *(Sections 1, 3)*

Take It to the Net

Interactive text at www.phschool.com

Science Explorer comes alive with iText.

- **Complete student text** is accessible from any computer with Internet access or a CD-ROM drive.
- **Animations, simulations, and videos** enhance student understanding and retention of concepts.
- **Self-tests and online study tools** assess student understanding.

STAY CURRENT with

Find out the latest research and information about The Nature of Science at: **www.phschool.com**

Go to **www.phschool.com** and click on the Science icon.Then click on Science Explorer: Life, Earth, and Physical Science under PH@school.

Student Edition Activities Planner

ACTIVITY	Time (minutes)	Materials *Quantities for one work group*	Skills
Section 1			
Discover, p. 166	10	**Consumable** piece of unlined paper **Nonconsumable** magnetic compass	Forming Operational Definitions
Section 2			
Discover, p. 173	20	**Consumable** 8 pieces of cardboard of increasing dimensions, unlined paper **Nonconsumable** scissors, metric ruler	Making Models
Sharpen Your Skills, p. 175	10	No special materials are required.	Interpreting Data
Section 3			
Discover, p. 178	20	**Consumable** adding-machine paper, masking tape **Nonconsumable** meter stick, scissors	Developing Hypotheses
Try This, p. 181	10	**Nonconsumable** small potted cactus, hand lens, scissors	Observing
Sharpen Your Skills, p. 183	5	No special materials are required.	Inferring
Skills Lab, p. 186	40	**Consumable** newspaper, water, loose soil, sod **Nonconsumable** 2 blocks, 2 unbreakable pans	Developing Hypotheses, Controling Variables, Observing

A list of all materials required for the Student Edition activities can be found on pages TVA34–TVA40. You can obtain information about ordering materials by calling 1-800-848-9500 or by accessing the Science Explorer Internet site at: **www.phschool.com**

CHAPTER 6 PROJECT

What's in a Package?

The Chapter 6 Project provides an opportunity for students to examine product packaging, determine the various materials used and their functions, and investigate what happens to the materials when the packages are discarded.

Purpose Students will identify the materials used in a package; infer the purpose of each material for the product's producers, retailers, and consumers; find out what happens to each type of material in the community's waste-disposal system; and communicate findings in a display.

Skills Focus After completing the Chapter 6 Project, students will be able to

- classify the types of materials used in product packages;
- infer the purpose of each material;
- draw conclusions about what happens to each type of material when it is discarded;
- communicate their findings.

Project Time Line The Chapter 6 Project requires about two weeks to complete. This project is most appropriate as an individual activity, though students could work cooperatively to research what happens to the various materials when they are discarded. As the class studies Section 1, each student should choose a product package and begin analyzing the materials used in it. The major portion of the project involves finding out what happens to each material when the package is discarded and then preparing a class display.

Advance Preparation You may wish to contact the municipal department or private company that handles waste collection and recycling in the students' community, and arrange to have a representative speak to the class when students are ready to research waste disposal. If a visit to the class is not possible, arrange to have a designated representative available to answer students' questions on the phone. Other sources of information include municipal waste department fact sheets and town Web sites.

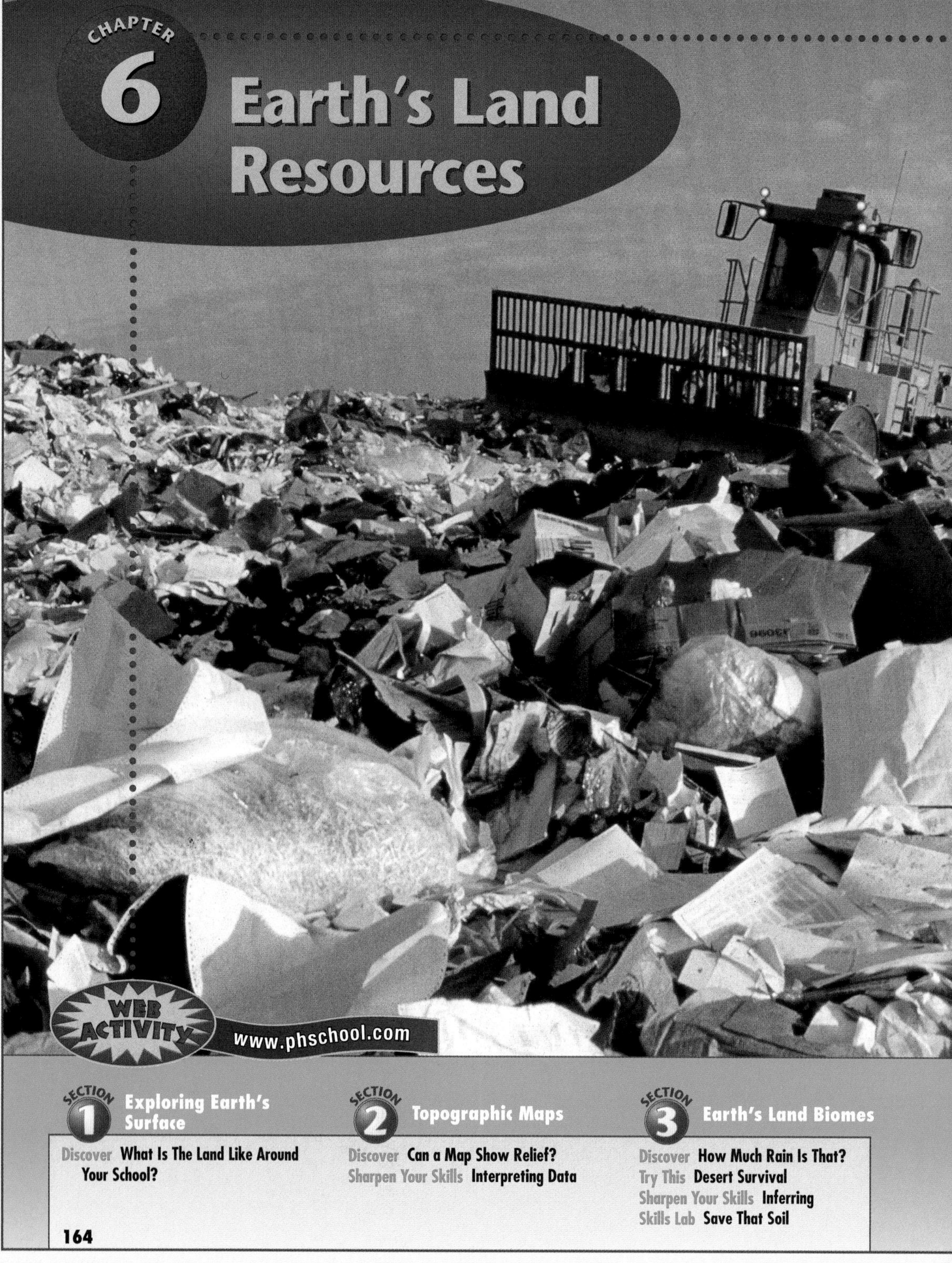

164

Possible Materials

- Let each student choose a package for the project. Encourage students to choose packages that include two or more different materials. Alternatively, you may wish to collect appropriate packages and assign them to students. CAUTION: *Tell students to make sure the packages are empty before they bring them to school. If students select cans, bottles, and plastic containers for foods, advise them to wash the containers thoroughly with hot, soapy water before bringing them to class. Do not allow students to use packaging for raw chicken, ground beef, or any other uncooked meats or fish. Be particularly aware of your school's policy regarding students bringing over-the-counter medicines, vitamin pills, and similar items to school, as empty packages may be misinterpreted by administrators or other teachers.*
- Students will need scissors to take their packages apart.

CHAPTER 6 PROJECT

What's in a Package?

The next time you're in the supermarket, take a look at all the different kinds of packages. There are glass bottles, plastic bottles, metal cans, cardboard boxes, plastic bags, paper wrappers, and more! Different kinds of packages are used for different kinds of products.

Many of these packages are opened and then thrown away. But where is "away"? In this chapter, you will read about what happens to wastes after they are discarded. While you study the chapter, you will be analyzing the anatomy of a package.

Your Goal To analyze and display information about a product package.

Your display must

- Include a cutaway portion of the package with the different materials labeled.
- Identify the purpose of each part of the package.
- Describe what happens to each part of the package after it is thrown away in your community.

Get Started Obtain a product package to study. Empty the package and clean it out.

Check Your Progress You'll be working on this project as you study this chapter. To keep your project on track, look for Check Your Progress boxes at the following points.

Section 1 Review, page 172: Cut the package open and identify the materials from which it is made.

Section 3 Review, page 185: Investigate what happens to the materials that make up the package.

Present Your Project At the end of the chapter (page 189), you will assemble your product display and present it to your class.

A bulldozer climbs a giant pile of trash at a landfill site. Waste disposal is a growing environmental concern.

165

- Provide posterboard, tape, colored markers, and other supplies for product displays.

Launching the Project Invite students to read the Chapter 6 Project description on page 165. Lead the class in brainstorming types of packaging materials they know of, and list their ideas on the board. Ask students how the materials might be grouped.

Discuss some purposes of packaging materials—for example, keeping the product from spoiling, keeping it from breaking or being damaged during shipment, displaying the product attractively, preventing theft, and making the product convenient for consumers to store and use. Ask students to suggest which packaging materials might be best for each purpose.

Distribute Chapter 6 Project Overview in Unit 2 Resources, and have students review the project rules and procedures. Encourage students' questions and comments. Also distribute Worksheet 1 in Unit 2 Resources, which lists a wide variety of possible products.

At the end of Section 1, distribute Worksheet 2 in Unit 2 Resources, which provides a format for analyzing a package's components.

Additional information on guiding the project is provided in Chapter 6 Project Teacher Notes in Unit 2 Resources.

Performance Assessment

The Chapter 6 Project Scoring Rubric in Unit 2 Resources will help you evaluate how well students complete the Chapter 6 Project. You may want to share the scoring rubric with students so they are clear about what will be expected of them. Students will be assessed on

- their completeness and accuracy in classifying the types of materials used in a product package;
- their ability to infer the purpose of each packaging material;
- their thoroughness in researching what happens to each type of material when the package is discarded in their community;
- how well they have communicated their findings to the class.

Program Resources

- **Unit 2 Resources** Chapter 6 Project Teacher Notes; Chapter 6 Project Overview and Worksheets; Chapter 6 Project Scoring Rubric

Media and Technology

Student Edition on Audio CD Chapter 6

You will find an Internet activity, chapter self-tests for students, and links to other chapter topics at this site.

SECTION 1 Exploring Earth's Surface

Objectives

After completing the lesson, students will be able to
- ◆ list the factors that determine the topography of Earth's surface;
- ◆ name and describe the main types of landforms;
- ◆ identify the four "spheres" that make up Earth's surface;
- ◆ name and describe the layers that make up Earth's structure.

Key Terms topography, elevation, relief, landform, landform region, plain, mountain, mountain range, plateau, lithosphere, core, mantle, crust, rock, geology

1 Engage/Explore

Activating Prior Knowledge

Ask students: **When you think of what the land is like in of our part of the state, what comes to mind?** *(Answers will vary. Encourage students to disagree with one another until the class comes to some consensus.)* Then have students describe a place where they've lived or visited that is different from where they live now.

DISCOVER

Skills Focus forming operational definitions
Materials *piece of unlined paper, magnetic compass*
Time 10 minutes
Tips If a compass is unavailable for students to use, point out which way is north of the school. Give students some idea of how far away 1 km is by referring to a local landmark.
Expected Outcome In choosing words to identify local areas, students will construct a simple map of the area's topography.
Think It Over Answers will vary. Students should develop some generalization of the area's topography based on the type of landforms, slopes, and so on.

SECTION 1 Exploring Earth's Surface

DISCOVER — ACTIVITY

What Is the Land Like Around Your School?

1. On a piece of paper, draw a small square to represent your school.
2. Choose a word that describes the type of land near your school, such as flat, hilly, or rolling. Write the word next to the square.
3. Use a magnetic compass to determine the general direction of north. Assume that north is at the top of your piece of paper.
4. If you travel due north 1 kilometer from your school, what type of land do you find? Choose a word to describe the land in this area. Write that word to the north of the square.
5. Repeat Step 4 for areas located 1 kilometer east, south, and west of your school.

Think It Over
Forming Operational Definitions What phrase could you use to describe the land in your area?

GUIDE FOR READING

- ◆ What determines the topography of Earth's surface?
- ◆ What are the main types of landforms?
- ◆ What are the four "spheres" that make up Earth's surface?

Reading Tip Before you read, preview *Exploring Landforms* on page 169. Make a list of questions you have about landforms.

In 1804, an expedition set out from St. Louis to explore the land between the Mississippi River and the Pacific Ocean. The United States had just purchased a part of this vast territory, called Louisiana, from France. Before the Louisiana Purchase, the United States stretched from the Atlantic coast westward to the Mississippi River. Few United States citizens had traveled west of the Mississippi. None had ever traveled over land all the way to the Pacific.

Led by Meriwether Lewis and William Clark, the expedition traveled up the Missouri River, crossed the Rocky Mountains, followed the Columbia River to the Pacific Ocean—and then returned. The purpose of the expedition was to map America's interior and discover resources.

Topography

On the journey to the Pacific, the Lewis and Clark expedition traveled more than 5,000 kilometers across the continent of North America. As they traveled, Lewis and Clark observed many changes in topography. **Topography** is the shape of the land. An area's topography may be flat, sloping, hilly, or mountainous.

Figure 1 While traveling down the Columbia River, the Lewis and Clark expedition met the Chinook people.

READING STRATEGIES

Reading Tip Encourage students to write at least one question for each of the terms described in the feature. An example might be, "How are coastal plains different from interior plains?" In addition, students might write a question such as, "What kinds of landforms are there besides plains, mountains, and plateaus?"

Media and Technology

Transparencies "Landform Regions of the United States," Transparency 18

The topography of an area is determined by the area's elevation, relief, and landforms. The desktop where you do homework probably has piles of books, papers, and other objects of different sizes and shapes. Your desktop has both elevation and relief!

Elevation The height above sea level of a point on Earth's surface is its **elevation.** When Lewis and Clark started in St. Louis, they were about 140 meters above sea level. By the time they reached Lemhi Pass in the Rocky Mountains, they were more than 2,200 meters above sea level.

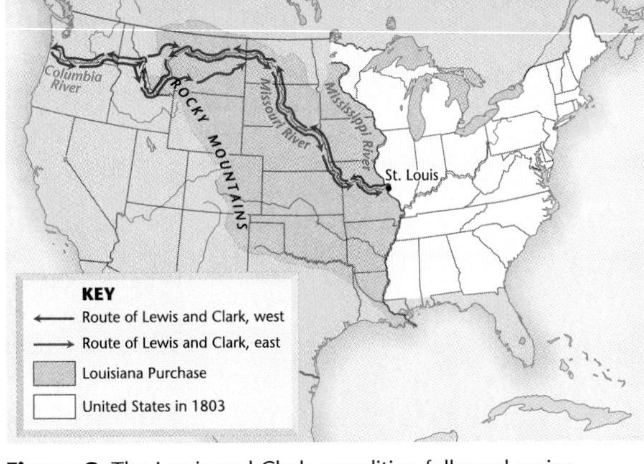

Figure 2 The Lewis and Clark expedition followed major rivers, except when crossing the Rocky Mountains.

Relief The difference in elevation between the highest and lowest parts of an area is its **relief.** As the Lewis and Clark expedition entered the Rocky Mountains, the relief of the land changed from flat or rolling land with low relief to huge mountains with high relief.

Landforms If you followed the route of the Lewis and Clark expedition, you would see many different landforms. A **landform** is a feature of topography formed by the processes that shape Earth's surface. All landforms have elevation and relief. A large area of land where the topography is similar is called a **landform region.** Figure 3 shows the landform regions of the United States, not including Alaska and Hawaii.

☑ *Checkpoint* *What is the difference between elevation and relief?*

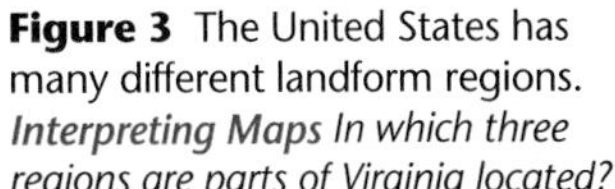

Figure 3 The United States has many different landform regions. *Interpreting Maps In which three regions are parts of Virginia located?*

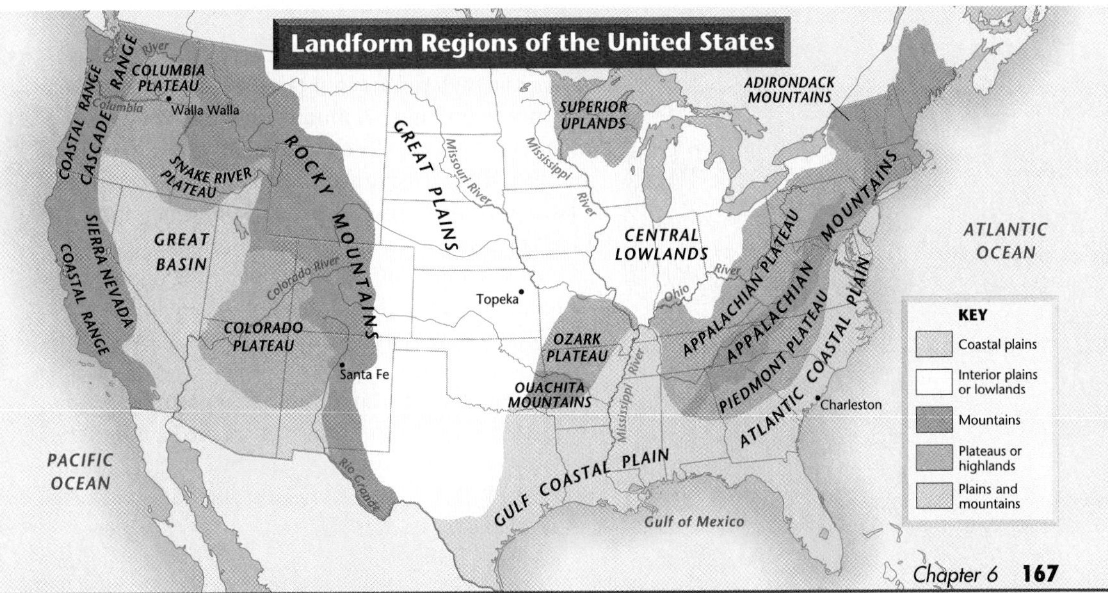

Program Resources

- **Unit 2 Resources** 6-1 Lesson Plan; 6-1 Section Summary
- **Guided Reading and Study Workbook** Section 6-1

Answers to Self-Assessment

Caption Question

Figure 3 Appalachian Mountains, Piedmont Plateau, Atlantic Coastal Plain

☑ Checkpoint

Elevation is the height above sea level of a point on Earth's surface; relief is the difference in elevation between the highest and lowest parts of an area.

2 Facilitate

Topography

Including All Students

Encourage students who need additional challenges to prepare a short presentation to the class about the Lewis and Clark expedition. Students can use reference materials to find out who sent them, how long their expedition lasted, and some of what they saw on their journey. Students may be able to find copies of maps made on this expedition. **learning modality: verbal**

Addressing Naive Conceptions

Many students may have difficulty with the difference between height and elevation. Explain that the height of a cliff, for instance, may be 15 m relative to the ground at the bottom of the cliff. The elevation at the top of the cliff, though, may be 1,500 m, because elevation is height above sea level. Ask: **What is your height above ground as you sit in this classroom?** *(Students might respond with 1 to several meters, depending on the floor they are on.)* **What is your elevation?** *(Students should respond that it is the elevation of the area in which they live.)* Encourage student volunteers to find out the elevation of their area. **learning modality: logical/mathematical**

Using the Visuals: Figure 3

Ask students: **What landform region do you live in?** *(Students should respond with the region on the map that corresponds to their area.)* **What other landform regions shown here have you lived in?** *(Most classes will contain students who have lived in other areas.)* Encourage students who have lived elsewhere to compare and contrast those regions with the local one. **learning modality: visual**

Ongoing Assessment

Writing Have students explain in their own words how elevation and relief help determine an area's topography.

Types of Landforms

Using the Visuals: Figure 4

Ask students: **If you were to visit the Great Plains, how much difference in relief would you expect to see?** *(There is little difference in relief, since a plain has low relief.)* **What do you think the elevation of the area is?** *(The elevation of an interior plain is higher than that of a coastal plain but not as high as a mountainous region.)* **learning modality: verbal**

Building Inquiry Skills: Organizing Information

ACTIVITY

Have students make a Venn diagram that shows the relationships among a mountain, a mountain range, a mountain system, and a mountain belt. *(The diagram should be four increasingly large circles, each successive circle fully encompassing the previous one.)* Then ask: **In what mountain system are the Bitterroot Mountains?** *(Rocky Mountains)* **Challenge students to find out what mountain belt the Rockies are part of.** *(The Rockies are part of the Circum-Pacific mountain belt.)* **learning modality: logical/mathematical**

Including All Students

To help students who have difficulty with written English, write the term *plateau* on the board and call on a student to pronounce the word clearly. Explain that it derives from a French word meaning "flat." Then show students a picture of the Grand Canyon. Have them turn back to the map in Figure 3 and point out that the Grand Canyon is within the Colorado Plateau. Ask: **If a plateau is flat, with low relief, how can the Grand Canyon be part of the Colorado Plateau?** *(A landform region is an area where topography is similar, but that does not mean it is all the same. Streams and rivers may cut a plateau's surface, which is the case with the Grand Canyon. While the surface of a plateau generally has low relief, there is usually a steep slope down to the surrounding land on one or more of the plateau's sides.)* **limited English proficiency**

Figure 4 The Great Plains of western North America include a vast area of flat or rolling land. The Great Plains are interior plains. *Predicting What do you think would be some differences between interior plains and coastal plains?*

Types of Landforms

Landforms can vary greatly in size and shape—from level plains extending as far as the eye can see, to low, rounded hills that you could climb on foot, to jagged mountains that would take you days to walk around. **There are three main types of landforms: plains, mountains, and plateaus.**

Plains A **plain** is a landform made up of flat or gently rolling land with low relief. A plain that lies along a seacoast is called a coastal plain. In North America, a coastal plain wraps like an apron around the continent's eastern and southeastern shores. Coastal plains have both low elevation and low relief.

A plain that lies away from the coast is called an interior plain. Although interior plains have low relief, their elevation can vary. The broad interior plain of North America is called the Great Plains.

The Great Plains extend from Texas north into Canada. From their eastern border in the states of North and South Dakota, Nebraska, Kansas, Oklahoma, and Texas, the Great Plains stretch west to the Rocky Mountains. At the time of the Lewis and Clark expedition, the Great Plains were a vast grassland.

Figure 5 The Bitterroot Mountains in Idaho are part of the Rocky Mountains system.

Mountains A **mountain** is a landform with high elevation and high relief. Mountains usually occur as part of a mountain range. A **mountain range** is a group of mountains that are closely related in shape, structure, and age. After crossing the Great Plains, the Lewis and Clark expedition crossed a rugged mountain range in Idaho now called the Bitterroot Mountains.

The different mountain ranges in a region make up a mountain system. The Bitterroot Mountains are one mountain range in the mountain system known as the Rocky Mountains.

Mountain ranges and mountain systems in a long, connected chain form a larger unit called a mountain belt. The Rocky Mountains are part of a great mountain belt that stretches down the western sides of North America and South America.

Background

Facts and Figures The total area of Earth's surface is about 500 million km^2, of which about 140 million km^2—29 percent—is land area. The average depth of Earth's oceans is 3.8 kilometers. The average elevation of Earth's land surface is 840 m.

Some geographers include hills as a separate type of landform. Hills are less rugged than mountains, with less steep slopes and flatter tops. Interior plains may include extensive areas of hills. And such plains may have much greater elevation than coastal plains, which are often at or near sea level. The High Plains of Colorado rise above 1,500 m. A plateau—sometimes called a tableland—is essentially a high plain that lies above nearby plains.

Plateaus A landform that has high elevation and a more or less level surface is called a **plateau.** A plateau is rarely perfectly smooth on top. Streams and rivers may cut into the plateau's surface. The Columbia Plateau in Washington State is an example. The Columbia River, which the Lewis and Clark expedition followed, slices through this plateau. The many layers of rock that make up the Columbia Plateau are about 1,500 meters thick.

☑ *Checkpoint* *What types of landforms have low relief?*

EXPLORING Landforms

Mountains, plains, and plateaus are just a few of the many landforms that make up the topography of Earth's surface.

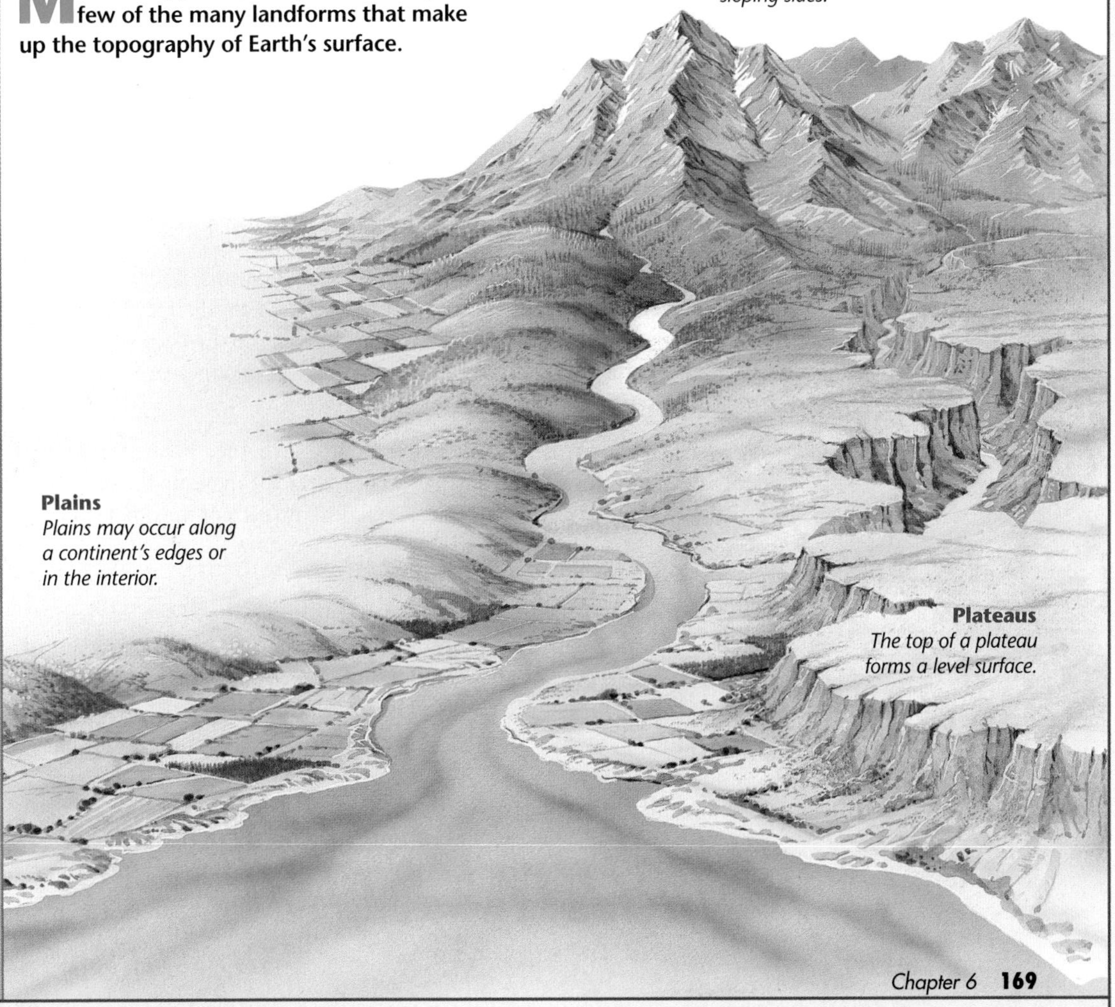

Mountains
A mountain's base usually covers an area of at least several square kilometers, but its peak may rise to a point. Mountains often have steeply sloping sides.

Plains
Plains may occur along a continent's edges or in the interior.

Plateaus
The top of a plateau forms a level surface.

EXPLORING

Landforms

Materials *modeling compound, board*
Time 20 minutes

Call on students to read the annotations for each of the three main types of landforms. Ask other students to identify the elevation and relief of each type of landform. Then divide the class into small groups, and have each group make a clay model of their own design that includes each of the three main landforms.
learning modality: kinesthetic

Addressing Naive Conceptions

Students may believe that classifying landforms is as straightforward as classifying birds or rocks. Point out that Earth's land has an almost infinite variety of landforms. Although there are obvious mountains and plains, there are also transitional areas. Ask: **How would you classify an area between mountains and plains?** *(Most will classify it as foothills.)* Emphasize that classification into three main types of landforms is only a starting point in understanding Earth's surface.
learning modality: verbal

Building Inquiry Skills: Classifying

Materials *raised relief maps*
Time 15 minutes

Raised relief maps, molded in vinyl, are available through science supply catalogs or via the Internet. Some are small-scale maps of the U.S. or the world. Others are regional maps at a scale of 1 : 250,000 based on USGS topographic data. Raised relief maps are excellent tools to use with sight-impaired students. Divide the class into small groups, and assign each group a map. Then challenge group members to collaborate on written descriptions of the landforms and landform regions each map contains. **cooperative learning**

Ongoing Assessment

Skills Check Have students each make a compare/contrast table entitled Main Types of Landforms. They should include elevation, relief, and a description for each landform.

Media and Technology

Transparencies "Exploring Landforms," Transparency 19

Concept Videotape Library Grade 6, Tape 1 "Flying Over America"

Answers to Self-Assessment

Caption Question

Figure 4 Interior plains are generally at a higher elevation as well as drier than coastal plains.

☑ *Checkpoint*

Plains and a plateau's surface have low relief.

Earth's Four Spheres

Including All Students

Write the names of Earth's four spheres on the board. Then, to help students who have trouble with written English, invite all students to play a game of call and response: one student names anything on Earth, and the next student classifies it in one or more of the four spheres. Write the responses underneath the appropriate headings. **learning modality: verbal**

Language Arts CONNECTION

Remind students that a prefix is a word part that appears at the beginning of a word. Point out to students that the names of Earth's four spheres have the same ending with four different prefixes. Ask: **What other words can you think of that start with the prefix *bio-*?** *(Answers will vary, but may include biology, biochemistry, or biotechnology.)* Tell students that the prefix *bio-* refers to life, and that words beginning with *bio-* refer to living tings. Challenge students to use a dictionary to look up the meanings of the prefixes of the names of Earth's other spheres. **learning modality: verbal**

Earth's Four Spheres

Lewis and Clark's two-year journey took them across western North America. Along the way, they observed the land, water, air, and living things. Together, these four things make up everything that is on and around planet Earth. **Scientists divide Earth into four spheres: the lithosphere, atmosphere, hydrosphere, and biosphere.** In this book, you will learn mainly about the lithosphere and how it is affected by each of the other spheres.

Figure 6 A view from space shows all four of Earth's spheres—the atmosphere, hydrosphere, biosphere, and lithosphere. *Observing What evidence of each of the spheres can you see in the photograph?*

The Lithosphere Earth's solid, rocky outer layer is called the **lithosphere** (LITH uh sfeer). The lithosphere is made up of continents as well as smaller landmasses called islands. The lithosphere extends under the entire ocean floor. Its surface varies from place to place. It ranges from smooth plains to wrinkled hills and valleys to jagged mountain peaks.

The Atmosphere The outermost sphere is the atmosphere (AT muh sfeer), the mixture of gases that surrounds the planet. By far the most abundant gases are nitrogen and oxygen, but the atmosphere also contains water vapor, carbon dioxide, and other gases. When water vapor condenses, it forms the droplets that make up clouds.

The Hydrosphere Earth's oceans, lakes, rivers, and ice form the hydrosphere (HY druh sfeer). Most of the hydrosphere consists of the salt water in the oceans, but fresh water is also part of the hydrosphere. Oceans cover more than two thirds of Earth.

The Biosphere All living things—whether in the air, in the oceans, or on and beneath the land surface—make up the biosphere (BY uh sfeer). The biosphere extends into each of the other spheres.

Earth's Structure

You probably know very well the topography of Earth's surface around your home and school. But what do you know about what's inside Earth? Throughout much of human history, Earth's interior was the subject of myths and unsupported theories. In the 1800s, for example, some people actually thought that Earth was hollow! Then, during the 1900s, scientists determined Earth's overall structure.

As you can see in Figure 7, the dense **core** forms the center of Earth. The core is divided into two layers: the solid inner core and the hot, liquid outer core. Surrounding the core is a thick layer called the **mantle.** The mantle is made of hot but solid

Background

Science History The first suggestion that Earth has a solid core was made by a French geologist, Gabriel-August Daubrée. In 1866, he suggested that Earth has a solid core made up of nickel and steel. Around the same time, scientists discovered that earthquakes cause waves that travel through Earth's layers. Since then, earthquake waves have yielded data that have helped scientists understand Earth's core, mantle, and crust.

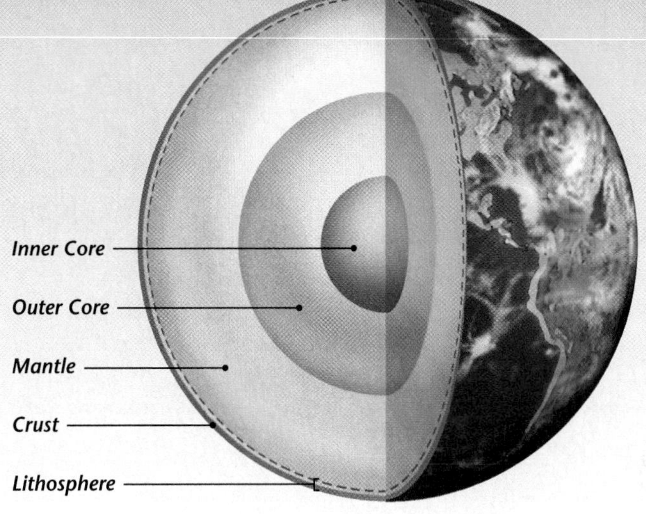

Figure 7 Earth has a layered structure. In this cutaway view, the mantle and core are shown to scale. But the thickness of the crust has been greatly exaggerated.

material that is less dense than the material that makes up the core. Like a giant golf ball, Earth has a rigid outer covering—the lithosphere. The **crust** is the thin, outer layer of the lithosphere that forms Earth's surface. The crust is made up of hard material called **rock.** The lithosphere also includes part of the upper mantle.

The Development of Geology

The modern science of **geology** began in the late 1700s. James Hutton, a Scottish physician and farmer, developed the principle of uniformitarianism. This principle states that the geologic processes that operate today also operated in the past. Thus, ancient rocks can be understood by observing present-day geologic processes. Hutton observed that such processes work very slowly, and inferred that they must have worked over very long spans of time to produce such dramatic features as mountains and canyons. He concluded that Earth must be much older than had been commonly thought at that time.

Although early geologists such as Hutton did not have modern equipment to study Earth, their conclusions were correct. Throughout our planet's long history, its surface has been lifted up, pushed down, bent, and broken by forces beneath the surface. Although the resulting movements of the surface are usually too small and too slow to be directly observed, they are constantly changing Earth's appearance. Thus Earth looks different today from the way it did millions of years ago.

Today, geologists divide the forces that change the surface into two groups: constructive forces and destructive forces. Constructive forces shape the surface by building up mountains and land areas. Destructive forces are those that slowly wear away mountains and, eventually, every other feature on the surface.

Answers to Self-Assessment

Caption Question

Figure 6 The photograph shows green continents of the lithosphere and biosphere, oceans of the hydrosphere, and clouds of the atmosphere.

Earth's Structure

Demonstration

Materials *hard-boiled egg, knife*
Time 5 minutes

Slice a hard-boiled egg in half crosswise. Hold up the cross-section for students to see. Ask students to compare what they see to the layers of earth. Ask: **Which part of the egg is like Earth's core? Mantle? Crust?** *(The yolk is the core; the white is the mantle; the shell is the crust.)* Ask: **How are the layers of the egg different from the layers of Earth?** *(Earth's core has two layers, but you can't see two layers in the egg yolk.)* **learning modality: visual**

Real-Life Learning

Invite a professional geologist to speak to the class about what a geologist does. This could be a teacher from a local university or a geologist from government or private industry. Mining and oil companies often hire geologists to help locate natural resources. Encourage students to make a list of questions to ask before the speaker comes to class. **learning modality: verbal**

Ongoing Assessment

Drawing Have students make a drawing that shows Earth sliced in half to reveal the layers. Students should label inner core, outer core, mantle, and crust.

Earth's Structure, continued

Using the Visuals: Figure 8

Ask students: **Why is this volanic activity an example of Earth's constructive forces?** *(Because it is building up land areas.)* Tell students that, in Icelandic mythology, Surtsey is the god of fire. Ask: **Why do you thing they named the island Surtsey?** *(The smoke and steam from the volcanic eruption make the island look as if it is on fire.)* **learning modality: visual**

3 Assess

Section 1 Review Answers

1. Elevation, relief, and landforms
2. Plains, mountains, and plateaus
3. A mountain belt is larger than a mountain system.
4. The crust, mantle, and core
5. They are similar in that both have a high elevation; they are different in that plateaus have low relief while mountains have high relief.

CHAPTER PROJECT

Check Your Progress

CAUTION: *Make sure students handle scissors carefully. Review the safety guidelines in Appendix A.* Give each student a copy of Chapter 6 Project Worksheet in Unit 2 Resources. Explain that the worksheet will help them analyze the packaging materials and infer the purpose of each one. Remind students to keep a sample of each material for use in their product displays.

Performance Assessment

Writing Have students imagine that they are visiting the United States for the first time and have traveled through every region of the country. Have them write a letter to home describing the landform regions they've seen.

Figure 8 The formation of the island of Surtsey is an example of Earth's constructive forces at work. In 1963, a volcanic eruption began in the ocean near Iceland. Within several years, the volcano added 2.5 square kilometers of new land to Earth's surface—the new island of Surtsey.

Two hundred years ago, the science of geology was young. Then, geologists knew only a few facts about Earth's surface. They knew that Earth is a sphere with a radius at the equator of more than 6,000 kilometers. They knew that there are seven continents surrounded by oceans. They knew that the continents were made up of layers of rock that they could sometimes see on the walls of cliffs and the sides of valleys. They began to explore high mountain ranges. However, many riddles remained: How old is Earth? How has Earth's surface changed over time? Why are there oceans, and how did they form? For the past 200 years, geologists have tried to answer these and other questions about the planet.

Section 1 Review

1. What three factors determine the topography of a region?
2. What are the most common types of landforms?
3. Which is larger, a mountain belt or a mountain system?
4. What are the main layers that form Earth's structure?
5. **Thinking Critically Comparing and Contrasting** How are mountains and plateaus similar? How are they different?

CHAPTER PROJECT

Check Your Progress

Cut your package open so that you can observe its construction. Create a data table identifying each part of the package, the material it is made of, and its purpose. What properties of these materials make them desirable as packaging? (Hint: Packaging benefits include protecting a product from breakage, preventing spoilage, making it more attractive, or making it easier to use. Can you think of other benefits of the materials in your package?)

Program Resources

- **Unit 2 Resources** 6-1 Review and Reinforce; 6-1 Enrich

Section 2 Topographic Maps

DISCOVER

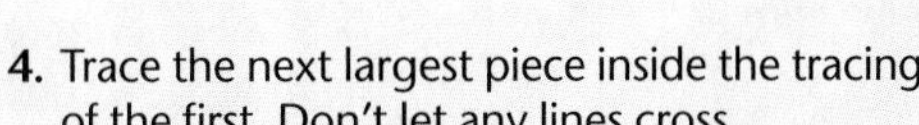

Can a Map Show Relief?

1. Carefully cut the corners off 8 pieces of cardboard so that they look rounded. Each piece should be at least 1 centimeter smaller than the one before.
2. Trim the long sides of the two largest pieces so that the long sides appear wavy. Don't cut any more than one-half centimeter into the cardboard.
3. Trace the largest cardboard piece on a sheet of paper.
4. Trace the next largest piece inside the tracing of the first. Don't let any lines cross.
5. Trace the other cardboard pieces, from largest to smallest, one inside the other, on the same paper.
6. Stack the cardboard pieces in the same order they were traced beside the paper. Compare the stack of cardboard pieces with your drawing. How are they alike? How are they different?

Think It Over

Making Models If the cardboard pieces are a model of a landform, what do the lines on the paper represent?

You are an engineer planning a route for a highway over a mountain pass. To design a safe highway, you need a route that avoids the steepest slopes. To protect the area's water supply, the highway must stay a certain distance from rivers and lakes. You also want to find a route that avoids houses and other buildings. How would you find the best route? You could start by studying a topographic map.

GUIDE FOR READING

- What is a topographic map?
- How do mapmakers represent elevation, relief, and slope?
- What is the Global Positioning System?

Reading Tip As you read, make a list of main ideas and supporting details about topographic maps.

Mapping Earth's Topography

A **map** is a model on a flat surface of all or part of Earth's surface. A **topographic map** is a map showing the surface features of an area. Topographic maps use symbols to portray the land as if you were looking down on it from above. **Topographic maps provide highly accurate information on the elevation, relief, and slope of the ground surface.**

Figure 9 Topographic maps provide the data necessary for the planning of highways, bridges, and other large construction projects.

READING STRATEGIES

Reading Tip Suggest to students that each subsection contains a main idea. Thus, they should write a main idea for each subsection and then support it with details. For example, the main idea of the subsection *Coverage* might be, "The agency responsible for making topographic maps in the United States is the USGS." Any detail in that subsection can be used to support that main idea.

Program Resources

- **Unit 2 Resources** 6-2 Lesson Plan; 6-2 Section Summary
- **Guided Reading and Study Workbook** Section 6-2

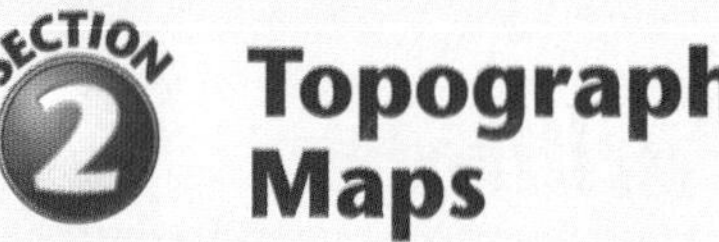

Section 2 Topographic Maps

Objectives

After completing the lesson, students will be able to

- describe a topographic map;
- explain how elevation, relief, and slope are shown on topographic maps;
- identify the Global Positioning System.

Key Terms map, topographic map, scale, symbols, contour line, contour interval, Global Positioning System

1 Engage/Explore

Activating Prior Knowledge

Draw a large circle on the board. Then draw a circle inside the first circle, another circle inside the second circle, and another inside the third circle. Write numbers on the circles: 10 on the outermost, 20 on the circle inside that, and so on. Ask: **What do the numbers suggest about this shape?** *(Many students will infer that the numbers suggest height and thus also infer that the circles represent a hill as seen from above.)*

DISCOVER

Skills Focus making models

Materials *scissors, 8 pieces of cardboard of increasing dimensions, metric ruler, unlined paper*

Time 20 minutes

Tips Cut the cardboard pieces in advance. Suggested sizes of cardboard squares, in centimeters: 4×4, 6×8, 8×10, 10×12, 12×14, 16×18, 18×22, 20×26. The thicker the cardboard, the better.

Expected Outcome Students will trace a series of lines that finally show the "topography" that results when the cardboard pieces are stacked.

Think It Over Answers may vary. A typical answer might suggest that the lines represent lines around the stack at various heights.

2 Facilitate

Mapping Earth's Topography

Math TOOLBOX

Tips Because the figures in the calculation are so large, provide access to a calculator for those students who don't have one. Make sure students understand how to convert between units in the metric system.
Expected Outcome The distance in kilometers is 5,875,000 ÷ 100,000 = 58.75. Have students round to the nearest tenth, or 58.8 km.
Extend Provide problems for students to solve with the scales used by the USGS on topographic maps. *Examples:* **1.** Find the actual distance in kilometers on a map with a scale of 1:24,000 between two points that are 13.2 cm apart. *(1/24,000 = 13.2 cm/d, 1 × d = 24,000 × 13.2, d = 316,800 cm, or 3.2 km)* **2.** Find the actual distance in kilometers on a map with a scale of 1:25,000 between two points that are 25.6 cm apart. *(1/25,000 = 25.6 cm/d, 1 × d = 25,000 × 25.6, d = 640,000 cm, or 6.4 km)* **learning modality: logical/mathematical**

Using the Visuals: Figure 10

After students have examined the symbols, ask: **Which of these symbols could you recognize even without an explanation?** *(Students might mention the symbols for church, campground, divided highway, and railroad tracks.)* Explain that the symbols were created to make sense even to those who have no specialized knowledge. Ask: **Are the symbols for woods and built-up areas always a rectangle?** *(No, these symbols are showing what the colors on the maps mean. Green is used for wooded areas, while gray or pink is used for built-up areas.)* **What can you infer about topographic maps from the last three symbols on the table?** *(Topographic maps are used for watery areas as well as for land.)* **learning modality: visual**

Scale and Ratios

A ratio compares two numbers by division. For example, the scale of a map given as a ratio is 1 : 250,000. At this scale, the distance between two points on the map measures 23.5 cm. How would you find the actual distance? Begin by writing the scale as a fraction.

$$\frac{1}{250{,}000}$$

Next, write a proportion. Let d represent the actual distance between the two points.

$$\frac{1}{250{,}000} = \frac{23.5\text{ cm}}{d}$$

Then write the cross products.

$$1 \times d = 250{,}000 \times 23.5\text{ cm}$$
$$d = 5{,}875{,}000\text{ cm}$$

(*Hint:* To convert cm to km, divide d by 100,000.)

Uses of Topographic Maps People find many uses for topographic maps. Businesses use them to help decide where to build new stores, housing, or factories. Cities and towns use them to decide where to build new schools. If you were planning a bicycle trip, you could use a topographic map to see whether your trip would be flat or hilly.

Scale A map's **scale** relates distance on a map to a distance on Earth's surface. Topographic maps usually are large-scale maps. A large-scale map is one that shows a close-up view of part of Earth's surface. In the United States, most topographic maps are at a scale of 1 : 24,000, or 1 centimeter on the map equals 24,000 centimeters or 0.24 kilometers on the ground. At this scale, a map can show the details of elevation and features such as rivers and coastlines. Large buildings, airports, and major highways appear as outlines at the correct scale.

Coverage Most nations have a government agency that is responsible for making topographic maps. In the United States, that agency is the U. S. Geological Survey, or USGS. The USGS has produced about 57,000 topographic maps at scales of either 1 : 24,000 or 1 : 25,000. The maps cover all of the United States, except for parts of Alaska. Each map covers an area of roughly 145 square kilometers.

Symbols Mapmakers use a great variety of **symbols** to show houses and other small features on topographic maps. If you were drawing a map, what symbols would you use to represent woods, a swamp, or a school? Look at Figure 10 to see the symbols that the USGS uses for these and other features.

***Checkpoint** In the United States, what agency is responsible for producing topographic maps?*

Figure 10 Maps made by the U.S. Geological Survey use more than 150 symbols.

Commonly Used Map Symbols

Feature	Symbol	Feature	Symbol	Feature	Symbol
Contour line: elevation		Primary highway		River	
Contour line: depression		Secondary highway		Stream	
Building		Divided highway		Waterfall or rapids	
School; church		Railroad tracks		Marsh or swamp	
Built-up area		Airport		Rock or coral reef	Reef
Campground; picnic area		Woods		Breakwater; wharf	
Cemetery	Cem	Orchard		Exposed wreck	

Background

Facts and Figures Many USGS topographic maps are at a scale of 1 : 24,000, or 1 in. = 2,000 ft. These maps are known as 7.5-minute quadrangle maps, because each covers a rectangle of 7.5 minutes of latitude and 7.5 minutes of longitude. (There are 60 minutes in each degree of latitude and longitude.) Maps for Alaska cover double that area; the scale is 1 : 63,360, or 1 in. = 1 mi.

The larger the scale of a map, the smaller the area covered. Thus, a large-scale map shows more detail than a small-scale map. Maps with scales larger than 1 : 63,360 are considered large-scale maps; small-scale maps are those with scales smaller than 1 : 1,000,000. Maps with scales in between are called medium-scale maps.

Figure 11 The contour lines on a topographic map represent elevation and relief. *Comparing and Contrasting What information does the topographic map provide that the photograph does not?*

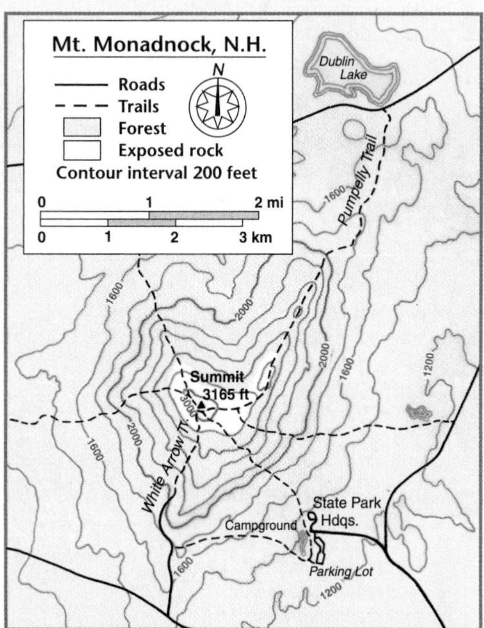

Showing Relief on Topographic Maps

To represent elevation, relief, and slope on topographic maps, mapmakers use contour lines. On a topographic map, a **contour line** connects points of equal elevation.

The change in elevation from contour line to contour line is called the **contour interval.** The contour interval for a given map is always the same. For example, the map in Figure 11 has a contour interval of 200 feet. If you start at one contour line and count up 10 contour lines, you have reached an elevation 2,000 feet above where you started. Usually, every fifth contour line is darker and heavier than the others. These lines are labeled with the elevation in round units, such as 1,600 or 2,000 feet above sea level. Most USGS maps give contour intervals in feet rather than meters.

Looking at a topographic map with many squiggly contour lines, you may feel as if you are gazing into a bowl of spaghetti. But if you follow the rules listed in *Exploring Topographic Maps* on the following page, you can learn to read contour lines. Reading contour lines is the first step toward "seeing" an area's topography by looking at a topographic map.

Interpreting Data

ACTIVITY

You are planning to hike up Mt. Monadnock. Use the topographic map in Figure 11 to determine which route is steeper: the White Arrow Trail or the Pumpelly Trail. What is the difference in elevation between the park headquarters and the summit?

Showing Relief on Topographic Maps

Using the Visuals: Figure 11

Call students's attention to the topographic map and ask: **How are the dark contour lines different from the lighter ones?** *(The dark contour lines are labeled with an elevation, while the lighter ones are not. They are also thicker than the other contour lines.)* **How can you tell what the contour interval is by looking at this map?** *(First, determine the difference in elevation between two dark contour lines. In this case, that is 100 ft. Then divide that number by the number of contour lines from one dark line to the next: 100 ft ÷ 5 = 20 ft.)* **learning modality: logical/ mathematical**

Sharpen your Skills

ACTIVITY

Time 10 minutes
Tips Have students examine the map and ask any initial questions before they try to respond to the problems.
Expected Outcome The White Arrow Trail is steeper. The difference in elevation between the Park Headquarters and the summit is more than 1,600 feet.
Extend Divide the class into small groups, and give each group a topographic map that covers a part of a state park or national park. Then have each group prepare a description of the park, including the highest and lowest points and the difficulty of the park's trails. **learning modality: logical/ mathematical**

Program Resources

- **Interdisciplinary Explorations Series** "Wagons West," pp. 22–23
- **Laboratory Manual** 6, "Using a Topographic Map"

Answers to Self-Assessment

Caption Question

Figure 18 The topographic map provides data on elevation, relief, slope, and the shape of the mountain, while the photograph simply provides a general image.

Checkpoint

The U.S. Geological Survey, or USGS, is responsible for making topographic maps.

Ongoing Assessment

Drawing Have each student use contour lines to show a hill that has a base of 1,000 ft and a top of 1,080 ft.

Showing Relief on Topographic Maps, continued

EXPLORING

Topographic Maps

Call on students to read the descriptions of the various features on the map and explain what the contour interval is. Students should practice finding high and low points on the map, steep and gentle slopes, and ridges and valleys. Also, have students use rulers to measure the scale and determine how much area the map covers. **learning modality: logical/mathematical**

Building Inquiry Skills: Making Models

Materials *topographic map, modeling compound, board*
Time 20 minutes

To reinforce how a topographic map represents elevation and relief, divide students into small groups and provide each group with a topographic map. Then challenge each group to make a three-dimensional model of a section of the map that contains more than one feature. **learning modality: kinesthetic**

Global Positioning System

Integrating Technology

Direct students' attention to Figure 12 and ask: What is the advantage of positioning with three satellites instead of only one? *(Since each satellite is in a different orbit, each has a different angle on Earth's surface. The point at which the different angles intersect pinpoints the location.)* Explain that this is similar to how geologists find the epicenter of an earthquake by using data from three different points. **learning modality: visual**

EXPLORING Topographic Maps

Topographic maps provide data on elevation, relief, slopes, and the shapes of landforms. This USGS map shows part of Tennessee.

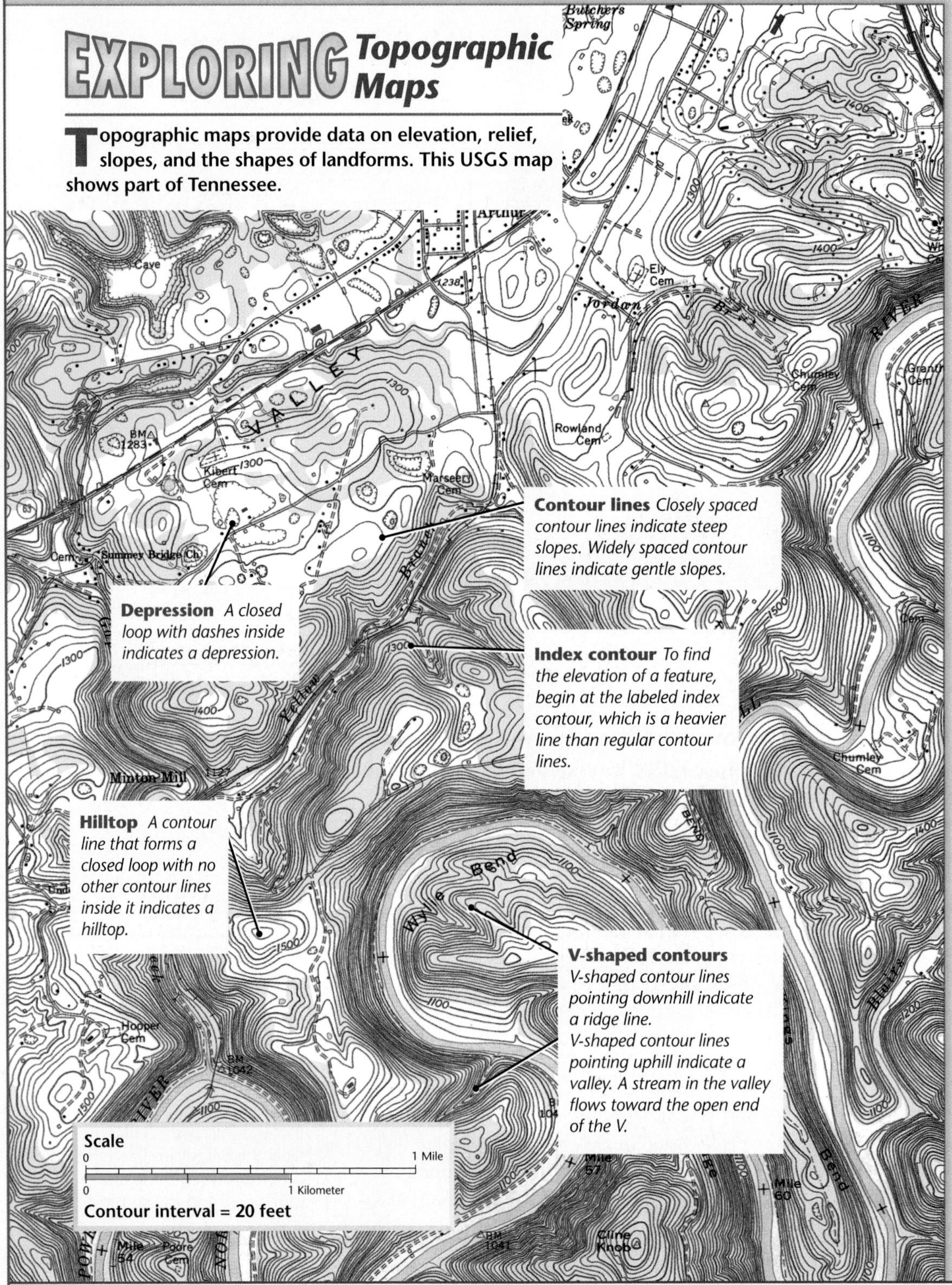

Contour lines *Closely spaced contour lines indicate steep slopes. Widely spaced contour lines indicate gentle slopes.*

Depression *A closed loop with dashes inside indicates a depression.*

Index contour *To find the elevation of a feature, begin at the labeled index contour, which is a heavier line than regular contour lines.*

Hilltop *A contour line that forms a closed loop with no other contour lines inside it indicates a hilltop.*

V-shaped contours *V-shaped contour lines pointing downhill indicate a ridge line. V-shaped contour lines pointing uphill indicate a valley. A stream in the valley flows toward the open end of the V.*

Scale
0 — 1 Mile
0 — 1 Kilometer
Contour interval = 20 feet

Background

History of Science The USGS was founded in 1879. Until the aerial photography of the 1930s, most maps were made using plane table surveying. A topographer would climb to the top of an area's highest point carrying a plane table, a drawing board on a tripod with a sighting device attached. Then, the topographer would sketch any prominent features that could be seen. Since the 1930s, aerial photography has been central to the making of these maps. For each area, two photographs are used, taken from different angles. The planes always fly at a certain altitude to make sure the scale remains the same. But the USGS doesn't rely exclusively on photos. Field workers on the ground carefully determine the position and elevation of particular points on the ground. These control points help mapmakers position map features accurately.

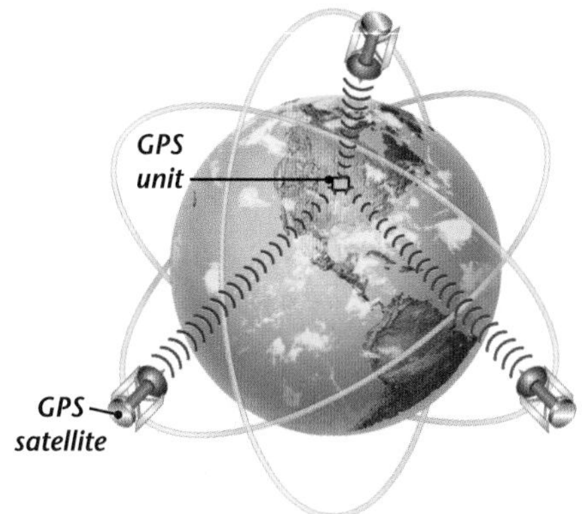

Figure 12 The GPS network includes 24 satellites. Three satellites (left) must be above the horizon to pinpoint the location of the user (right). The user's latitude and longitude appear on the screen of a portable GPS unit like the one in the photograph.

Global Positioning System

INTEGRATING TECHNOLOGY Today, surveyors, pilots, and mapmakers around the world rely on the **Global Positioning System,** or GPS, to determine locations precisely. **The Global Positioning System is a method of finding the precise location of points on Earth's surface using a network of satellites.** At any given moment, there are between five and eight GPS satellites above the horizon in a given area. A hand-held unit the size of a cellular phone picks up signals broadcast by these satellites. A computer inside the GPS unit then calculates the user's location and elevation.

Engineers can use GPS to locate points on the ground for a construction project. Airplanes, ships, and hikers can use GPS to navigate. Some cars now contain both a GPS unit and a digital road map stored in a computer. Using GPS, the computer determines the car's location and suggests a route to your destination.

Section 2 Review

1. What kind of information does a topographic map provide about landforms?
2. How do topographic maps represent elevation and relief?
3. What would the highest and lowest points in an area look like on a topographic map?
4. What is the role of satellites in the Global Positioning System?
5. **Thinking Critically Interpreting Maps** Look at the map on page 176. Where is the highest elevation? Where do you find the steepest slopes? The gentlest slopes?

Science at Home

Maps at Home Maps provide a variety of information you can use every day. With family members look through newspapers, news magazines, and even your car's glove compartment for maps. How many different types of maps can you find? Explain to your family the map's scale and symbols. Compare the main purposes of the maps and the symbols used.

Program Resources

- **Unit 2 Resources** 6-2 Review and Reinforce; 6-2 Enrich

Media and Technology

Transparencies "Exploring Topographic Maps," Transparency 20

3 Assess

Section 2 Review Answers

1. A topographic map provides information on the elevation, relief, and slope of the ground surface of an area.
2. Topographic maps represent elevation and relief with contour lines.
3. The highest point would be a closed loop with no other lines inside it that is surrounded by more contour lines than any other on the map. If the lowest point is a depression, it would be shown as a closed loop with dashes inside. Otherwise, the lowest point would be in the area below the lowest contour line. Often, the lowest point on a map is the surface of a lake, river, or the ocean.
4. A network of satellites broadcast signals that can be picked up by a hand-held unit with a computer inside that can calculate a user's location and elevation.
5. The highest elevation is Cline Knob, at about 1,840 feet, near the bottom of the page. The steepest slopes are the sides of the valley through which the river flows. The gentlest slopes are in the upper left area of the map.

Science at Home

Maps in newspapers and news magazines often use special symbols to show details related to the article they accompany. Maps used for driving show street names and route numbers.

Performance Assessment

Writing Provide each student with a section of a topographic map, then challenge students to describe all the information they can interpret from the map.

Earth's Land Biomes

Objective
After completing the lesson, students will be able to
- ◆ list and describe Earth's major land biomes.

Key Terms biome, canopy, understory, desert, grassland, savanna, deciduous trees, hibernation, coniferous trees, tundra, permafrost

1 Engage/Explore

Activating Prior Knowledge

Ask: **What is the climate like in our area?** *(Students should describe conditions of temperature, precipitation, amount of sunlight during the seasons, and so forth.)* **How do you think our climate affects which organisms live here?** *(Answers will vary depending on the climate of the area. For example, students may say that a warm, humid climate allows a great variety of organisms to live in the area.)*

DISCOVER ACTIVITY

Skills Focus developing hypotheses
Materials *meter stick, adding-machine paper, scissors, marker, tape*
Time 20 minutes

CAUTION: *Hanging the Costa Rican rain forest strip will require the use of a ladder. Choose three reliable students for this task, one to climb the ladder and two to hold the ladder securely. If you are not certain that students can do this task safely, have them hang the strips horizontally.*
Expected Outcome Students should sequence the strips from least to most rainfall, as indicated in the table.
Think It Over The Costa Rican rain forest receives the most precipitation, and the Mojave Desert the least. The amount of rainfall affects what plant species can survive in a particular biome, and the plants in turn determine the consumer species found there.

SECTION 3 Earth's Land Biomes

DISCOVER ACTIVITY

How Much Rain Is That?

The table shows the average amount of rain that falls each year in four different regions. With your classmates, you will create a full-size bar graph on a wall to help you visualize these amounts of rain.

Biome	Rainfall (cm)
Mojave Desert	15
Illinois prairie	70
Smoky Mountains	180
Costa Rican rain forest	350

1. Using a meter stick, measure a strip of adding-machine paper 15 centimeters long. Label this piece of paper "Mojave Desert."
2. Repeat Step 1 for the other three locations. If necessary, tape strips of paper together to make the correct length. Label each strip.
3. Now find a place where you can display the four strips vertically. If the wall of your classroom is not tall enough, you may need to use another wall in your school building. Follow your teacher's instructions to hang your rainfall strips.

Think It Over
Developing Hypotheses Which ecosystem receives the most rain? Which receives the least? What effect do you think the amount of rainfall might have on the types of species that live in these ecosystems?

GUIDE FOR READING
- ◆ **What determines the type of biome found in an area?**
- ◆ **What are Earth's six main land biomes?**

Reading Tip **As you read, make a list of the biomes described in this section. Under each biome name, take notes on the characteristics of that biome.**

Congratulations! You have been selected to join an around-the-world scientific expedition. Your mission is to study the major types of ecosystems on Earth. An ecosystem is all the living and nonliving things that interact in an area. You will be collecting data on the climate conditions and typical organisms found in each of these ecosystems. The result of this expedition will be a database of information on the biomes you visit. A **biome** is a group of ecosystems with similar climates and organisms.

Classifying ecosystems into biomes helps scientists describe the world. As you might expect, not all scientists agree on the exact number and kinds of biomes. The scientists guiding your expedition have chosen to focus on six major land biomes. **The six land biomes are rain forest, desert, grassland, deciduous forest, boreal forest, and tundra.**

During your trip, you will visit places ranging from frozen, windy Arctic plains to steamy tropical jungles. **It is mostly the climate conditions—temperature and rainfall—in an area that determine its biome.** This is because climate limits the distribution of plants in the area. In turn, the types of plants determine the kinds of animals that live there.

178

READING STRATEGIES

Reading Tip Invite students to preview the headings in this section and name the eight major biomes described (rain forest, desert, grassland, deciduous forest, boreal forest, tundra, freshwater, and marine) and the "sub-biomes" or ecosystems within those biomes (for example, tropical rain forests, temperate rain forests). To organize their notes, students can construct a table with the names of the biomes listed in the first column and the characteristics that differentiate biomes labeled across the top of the table—*Temperature, Rainfall, Variety of Species,* and *Typical Organisms,* for example. Students can use their completed biome summaries as a study guide.

Equator

Rain Forest Biomes

Tropical rain forest

Temperate rain forest

Rain Forest Biomes

The first stop on your expedition is a tropical rain forest close to the equator. The rain forest is warm and humid—in fact, it's pouring rain! Fortunately, you remembered to pack a poncho. After just a short shower, the sun reappears. But even though the sun is shining, very little light penetrates the thick vegetation.

Plants are everywhere in the rain forest. Some, such as the ferns, orchids, and vines you observe hanging from tree limbs, even grow on other plants. Among the plants are many species of birds as bright as the numerous flowers all around you.

Tropical Rain Forests Tropical rain forests are found in warm regions close to the equator. Tropical rain forests typically receive a lot of rain. The warm temperatures do not vary much throughout the year, and the sunlight is fairly constant all year.

Tropical rain forests contain an astounding variety of species. For example, scientists studying a 100-square-meter area of one rain forest identified 300 different kinds of trees! These trees form several distinct layers. The tall trees form a leafy roof called the **canopy.** A few giant trees poke out above the canopy. Below the canopy, a second layer of shorter trees and vines form an **understory.** Understory plants grow well in the shade formed by the canopy. Finally, some plants thrive in the near-darkness of the forest floor.

Figure 13 Tropical rain forests contain an amazing variety of plants and other organisms. In the large photo, a river winds through the lush Indonesian rain forest. The top closeup shows a young orangutan swinging from tree limbs. In the bottom closeup, a tarantula climbs over a brightly colored bracket fungus on the forest floor.

2 Facilitate

Rain Forest Biomes

Building Inquiry Skills: Communicating

ACTIVITY

As an ongoing activity throughout this section, encourage students to research additional information about the biomes described in the text. Divide the class into eight groups, and assign one biome to each group. (You may want to use 12 groups and divide the 5 marine habitats among different groups.) Explain that each group should look for additional photographs of the biome and of organisms typically found in it. Students can photocopy (or print out) the pictures and incorporate them into a large poster labeled with the name of the biome. As students read about each biome in the text, call on the group who researched that biome to present its poster to the class. Display the posters in the classroom. **cooperative learning**

Using the Visuals: Figure 13

Display a world map or globe, and have students locate Indonesia. Then have them locate Indonesia on the biome map. Ask: **What do you notice about the locations of the world's tropical rain forests?** *(All are located at or close to the equator.)* **learning modality: visual**

Program Resources

- **Unit 2 Resources** 6-3 Lesson Plan; 6-3 Section Summary
- **Guided Reading and Study Workbook** Section 6-3

Media and Technology

Concept Videotape Library Grade 6, Tape 1 "Earth's Many Biomes"

Ongoing Assessment

Writing Have each student explain how temperature and rainfall determine the types of organisms that live in a particular biome.

Rain Forest Biomes, continued

Cultural Diversity

Have students examine a map of northwestern United States and locate temperate rain forests. They will undoubtedly notice the unusual names of several forests—for example, Tillamook State Forest, Siuslaw National Forest, Siskiyou National Forest (all in Oregon), and Klamath National Forest (California). Ask: **Where do you think those names came from?** *(They are the names of Native American tribes living in those areas.)* Encourage interested students to find out about the history and cultures of indigenous peoples of the American northwest. **learning modality: verbal**

Desert Biomes

Building Inquiry Skills: Making Models

Materials *terrarium with cover; sandy soil; water; desert organisms such as cactus plants, insects, small lizard*
Time 20 minutes

ACTIVITY

Ask students: **If you wanted to build a model of a desert biome in a terrarium, what abiotic materials would you need?** *(Sandy soil; perhaps some gravel and rocks; a source of strong, direct sunlight or artificial light; some water for infrequent watering)* **What organisms would you place in the model biome?** *(Cactus plants, desert insects, a small lizard or other organism)* Encourage a group of volunteers to gather the materials and construct a model desert biome. **learning modality: kinesthetic**

The abundant plant life provides many habitats for animals. A habitat is where an organism lives and gets what it needs. The number of insect species in tropical rain forests is not known, but has been estimated to be in the millions. These in turn feed many bird species, which feed other animals. Although tropical rain forests cover only a small part of the planet, they probably contain more species of plants and animals than all the other land biomes combined.

Temperate Rain Forests The land along the northwestern coast of the United States resembles a tropical rain forest in some ways. This region receives more than 300 centimeters of rain a year. Huge trees grow there, including cedars, redwoods, and Douglas firs. However, it is difficult to classify this region. It is too far north and too cool to be a tropical rain forest. Instead many scientists refer to this ecosystem as a temperate rain forest. The term *temperate* means having moderate temperatures.

Desert Biomes

The next stop on your expedition is a desert. It couldn't be more different from the tropical rain forest you just left. You step off the bus into the searing summer heat. At midday, you cannot even walk into the desert—the sand feels as hot as the hot water that comes from your bathroom faucet at home.

A **desert** is an area that receives less than 25 centimeters of rain per year. The amount of evaporation in a desert is greater than the amount of precipitation, or rain or snow. Some of the driest deserts may not receive any rain at all in a year! Deserts often also undergo large shifts in

Equator

Desert and Grassland Biomes
Desert
Grassland

Figure 14 Desert organisms have adaptations that enable them to live in the harsh conditions of their biome. For example, this shovel-snouted lizard "dances" to avoid burning its feet on the hot sand dunes of the Namib Desert in Africa. *Making Generalizations Describe the climate conditions of a typical desert.*

Background

Facts and Figures The continuing destruction of tropical rain forests around the world may be a factor in climate change. Each year, thousands of square kilometers of rain forest are cut and burned to clear land and access mineral resources. Burning the forests not only kills the unique organisms of the rain forest ecosystem but also releases large quantities of carbon dioxide, contributing to global warming.

Between 1978 and 1996, more than 12.5 percent of the Amazon rain forest was destroyed. In 1998, after analysis of satellite photographs, the Brazilian government reported that rain forest destruction reached a record level of 30,000 square kilometers in 1995. Brazil planned to increase its monitoring and control of the area and implement new measures to protect the rain forest.

temperature during the course of a day. A scorching hot desert like the Namib Desert cools rapidly each night when the sun goes down. Other deserts, such as the Gobi in central Asia, are cooler, even experiencing freezing temperatures in the winter.

The organisms that live in the desert are adapted to the lack of rain and to the extreme temperatures. For example, the trunk of a saguaro cactus has folds that work like the pleats in an accordion. The trunk of the cactus expands to hold more water when it is raining. Many desert animals are most active at night when the temperatures are cooler. A gila monster, for instance, spends much of its time in a cool underground burrow. It may go for weeks without coming up to the surface of the desert.

***Checkpoint** What are some adaptations that help an organism to live in the desert?*

Desert Survival

ACTIVITY

Use a hand lens to carefully observe a small potted cactus. Be careful of the spines! With a pair of scissors, carefully snip a small piece from the tip of the cactus. Observe the inside of the plant. Note any characteristics that seem different from those of other plants.

Observing How is the inside of the cactus different from the outside? Suggest how the features you observe might be related to its desert habitat.

Grassland Biomes

The next stop on the expedition is a grassland called a prairie. The temperature here is much more comfortable than that in the desert. The breeze carries the scent of soil warmed by the sun. This rich soil supports grass as tall as you and your classmates. Sparrows flit among the grass stems, looking for their next meal. Startled by your approach, a rabbit quickly bounds away.

Like some other grasslands, this prairie receives more rain than deserts, but not enough for many trees to grow. A **grassland** receives between 25 and 75 centimeters of rain each year, and is typically populated by grasses and other nonwoody plants. Grasslands that are located closer to the equator than prairies,

Figure 15 Migrating wildebeest make their way across a vast Kenyan savanna.

TRY THIS

Skills Focus observing
Materials *small potted cactus, hand lens, scissors*
Time 10 minutes
Tips Divide the class into small groups and provide a separate cactus plant for each group. Use cactus varieties with narrow tube-shaped or flat segments that will be easy for students to snip through with scissors.
Expected Outcome Students should observe that unlike most other plants, cactuses have sharp spines or other projections, not flat, wide leaves, and they also have a waxy outer covering. The inside of a cactus is fleshy and moist. The lack of wide, flat leaves and the waxy outer covering help conserve water in the hot, dry desert; the fleshy inner core stores moisture for the plant.
Extend Provide books on raising cactuses as houseplants so students can see the wide range of cactus types.
learning modality: visual

Grassland Biomes

Using the Visuals: Figure 15

Begin by having students locate Kenya on a world map or globe. Also have them locate prairie areas in the midwestern United States. **What typical features of grassland biomes are visible in the photograph?** *(tall grass, large herbivores)* **learning modality: visual**

Answers to Self-Assessment

Caption Question

Figure 14 Deserts are typically hot during the day and very dry, receiving less than 25 cm of rain per year.

Checkpoint

Sample answer: The saguaro cactus has folds that allow the trunk to expand and hold more water when it rains.

Ongoing Assessment

Skills Check Have each student create a compare/contrast table showing the temperature and rainfall differences among the three biomes described so far in the text—rain forest, desert, grassland.

Deciduous Forest Biomes

Building Inquiry Skills: Making Models

ACTIVITY Ask students: **Could you build a model of a deciduous forest in a terrarium?** *(No, not of the entire forest, but specific habitats could be modeled in a terrarium.)* **Suppose you want to model a rotting-log habitat on the forest floor. What abiotic materials would you need?** *(Soil, a source of filtered light, water, a rotting log, dead leaves or other plant material)* **What organisms would you place in the model habitat?** *(Mosses, ferns, fungi, earthworms, sowbugs, crickets, toad or salamander)* Encourage volunteers to gather materials and construct a model rotting-log habitat. **learning modality: kinesthetic**

Addressing Naive Conceptions

After students have read about hibernation on the next page, ask: **What animals hibernate during the winter?** *(Students will probably mention bears, among other animals. List responses on the board without commenting on their accuracy.)* Encourage students to find out whether the animals they named do indeed hibernate and what other animals should be added to the list. *(Animals that undergo true hibernation include bats, ground squirrels, chipmunks, groundhogs, frogs, toads, lizards, snakes, and turtles. Students will also discover that some of the animals they named—bears, for example—do not undergo true hibernation, which involves extreme metabolic changes. These animals go through prolonged periods of deep sleep over the winter months but wake up from time to time.)* **learning modality: verbal**

Figure 16 This Michigan forest in autumn is a beautiful example of a deciduous forest. The closeup shows a red fox, a common resident of North American deciduous forests. ***Comparing and Contrasting*** *How do deciduous forests differ from rain forests?*

called **savannas,** receive as much as 120 centimeters of rain each year. Scattered shrubs and small trees grow on savannas along with the grass.

Grasslands are home to many of the largest animals on Earth—plant eaters such as bison, antelopes, zebras, rhinoceros, giraffes, and kangaroos. Grazing by these large plant eaters helps to maintain the grasslands. They keep young trees and bushes from sprouting and competing with the grass for water and sunlight.

Deciduous Forest Biomes

Your trip to the next biome takes you to another forest. It is now late summer. Cool mornings here give way to warm days. Several members of the expedition are busy recording the numerous plant species. Others are looking through their binoculars, trying to identify the songbirds in the trees. You step carefully to avoid a small salamander on the forest floor. Chipmunks chatter at all the disturbance.

You are now visiting the deciduous forest biome. The trees found in this forest, called **deciduous trees** (dee SIJ oo us), shed their leaves and grow new ones each year. Oaks and maples are examples of deciduous trees. Deciduous forests receive enough rain to support the growth of trees and other plants, at least 50 centimeters per year. Temperatures vary during the year. The growing season usually lasts five to six months. As in the rain forest, different plants grow to different heights, ranging from a canopy of tall trees to small ferns and mosses on the forest floor.

Background

Facts and Figures In North America, autumn's shorter days and cooler temperatures cause deciduous trees to drop their leaves. Leaf drop protects trees, which would otherwise dry out during the winter. When the ground is frozen, roots cannot absorb water to replace what is lost by evaporation from leaf surfaces. A leafless tree does not lose as much water in winter as would a tree with leaves.

Conifers' needlelike leaves are also an adaptation to conserve water. For example, a pine needle has a much smaller surface area from which water can evaporate than does a maple leaf. Needles also have a thick, waxy covering that holds in water.

The variety of plants in the forest creates many different habitats. You and your classmates note that different species of birds live at each level, eating the insects and fruits that live and grow there. You observe opossums, mice, and a skunk looking for food in the thick layer of damp leaves on the ground. Other common North American deciduous forest species include wood thrushes, white-tailed deer, and black bears.

If you were to return to this biome in the winter, you would not see much of the wildlife you are now observing. One reason is that many of the bird species migrate to warmer areas. Some of the mammals enter a low-energy state similar to sleep called **hibernation.** During hibernation an animal relies on fat it has stored in its body.

☑ *Checkpoint* *What are deciduous trees?*

Inferring 

Observe the map on the facing page showing the locations of deciduous and boreal forests. How do they compare? Can you suggest a reason why no boreal forests are shown south of the equator?

Boreal Forest Biomes

Now the expedition heads north into a colder climate. The expedition leaders claim they can identify the next biome, a boreal forest, by its smell. When you arrive, you catch a whiff of the spruce and fir trees that blanket the hillsides. Feeling the chilly early fall air, you pull a jacket and hat out of your bag.

This forest contains **coniferous trees** (koh NIF ur us), that produce their seeds in cones and have leaves shaped like needles. The boreal forest is sometimes referred to by its Russian name, the *taiga* (TY guh). Winters in these forests are very cold. The yearly

Figure 17 Common organisms of the boreal forest include moose like this one in Alaska's Denali National Park, and porcupines.

Answers to Self-Assessment

Caption Question

Figure 16 Rain forests get a lot of rain, and the warm temperatures and amount of sunlight are fairly constant year-round. Deciduous forests receive less rainfall, and temperatures vary during the year.

☑ *Checkpoint*

Deciduous trees are trees that shed their leaves and grow new ones each year.

Boreal Forest Biomes

Sharpen your Skills

Inferring

Time 5 minutes 
Expected Outcome
Boreal forests grow in climates that are too cold for deciduous forests. Such climates typically occur in a band at latitudes far from the equator. There are no such areas south of the equator because that hemisphere does not have large continental land areas at the appropriate latitudes. **learning modality: logical/ mathematical**

Building Inquiry Skills: Inferring

Materials *globe, flashlight, masking tape* 
Time 10–15 minutes

Have pairs of students mark the locations of deciduous and boreal forests on a globe with strips of masking tape labeled *D* and *B.* With the room darkened, one student should shine a flashlight at the globe's equator as the other student slowly turns the globe on its axis. Ask: **Which biome, the deciduous forest or the boreal forest, gets stronger [more direct] light?** *(The deciduous forest)* **What do you think this has to do with the climate differences between the deciduous forest and the boreal forest?** *("Stronger" [more-direct] sunlight during the year makes the deciduous forests warmer than the boreal forests.)* **learning modality: kinesthetic**

Ongoing Assessment

Writing Have students describe the differences between deciduous forest and boreal forest biomes.

Tundra Biomes

Using the Visuals: Figure 18

Direct students' attention to the photograph and ask: **What does the land look like in this photograph of the tundra?** *(It is generally flat with low hills.)* Tell students that the term tundra comes from a Lapp word meaning "marshy plain." Ask: **Do you think "marshy plain" is a good description of the tundra?** *(Students may be unsure about the "marshy" part of the description.)* Explain that because the permafrost does not allow water to drain from the soil and because the low temperatures slow evaporation, the tundra's soil is constantly saturated with water, even though the area receives little precipitation. **learning modality: visual**

Cultural Diversity

Ask students: **Do you think any people live in the tundra? If not, why not?** *(Many students may think that people don't live in the tundra because the climate is so harsh.)* Explain that the Lapp people do live in the tundra and that in fact the word "tundra" originally came from a word in their language. Encourage students who need additional challenges to find out more about the Lapp culture and report their findings to the class in posters, displays, or brief oral reports. **learning modality: verbal**

snowfall can reach heights well over your head—or even two or three times your height! Even so, the summers are rainy and warm enough to melt all the snow.

A limited number of trees have adapted to the cold climate of boreal forests. Fir, spruce, and hemlock are the most common species because their thick, waxy needles keep water from evaporating. Since water is frozen for much of the year in these areas, prevention of water loss is a necessary adaptation for trees in the boreal forest.

Many of the animals of the boreal forest eat the seeds produced by the conifers. These animals include red squirrels, insects, and birds such as finches and chickadees. Some of the larger herbivores, such as porcupines, deer, elk, moose, and beavers, eat tree bark and new shoots. This variety of herbivores in the boreal forest supports a variety of large predators, including wolves, bears, wolverines, and lynxes.

Tundra Biomes

The driving wind brings tears to the eyes of the members of the expedition as you arrive at your next stop. It is now fall. The slicing wind gives everyone an immediate feel for this biome, the tundra. The **tundra** is an extremely cold, dry, land biome. Expecting deep snow, many are surprised that the tundra may receive no more precipitation than a desert. Most of the soil in the tundra is frozen all year. This frozen soil is called **permafrost**.

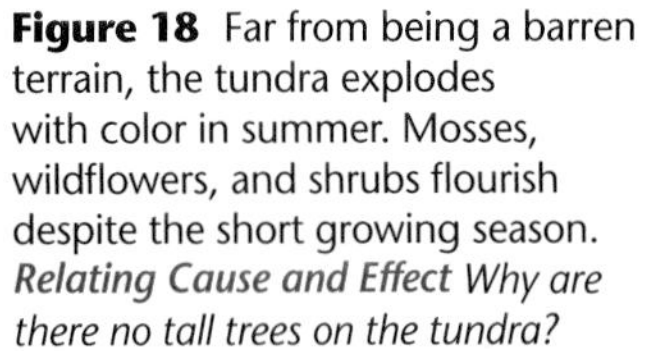

Figure 18 Far from being a barren terrain, the tundra explodes with color in summer. Mosses, wildflowers, and shrubs flourish despite the short growing season. ***Relating Cause and Effect*** *Why are there no tall trees on the tundra?*

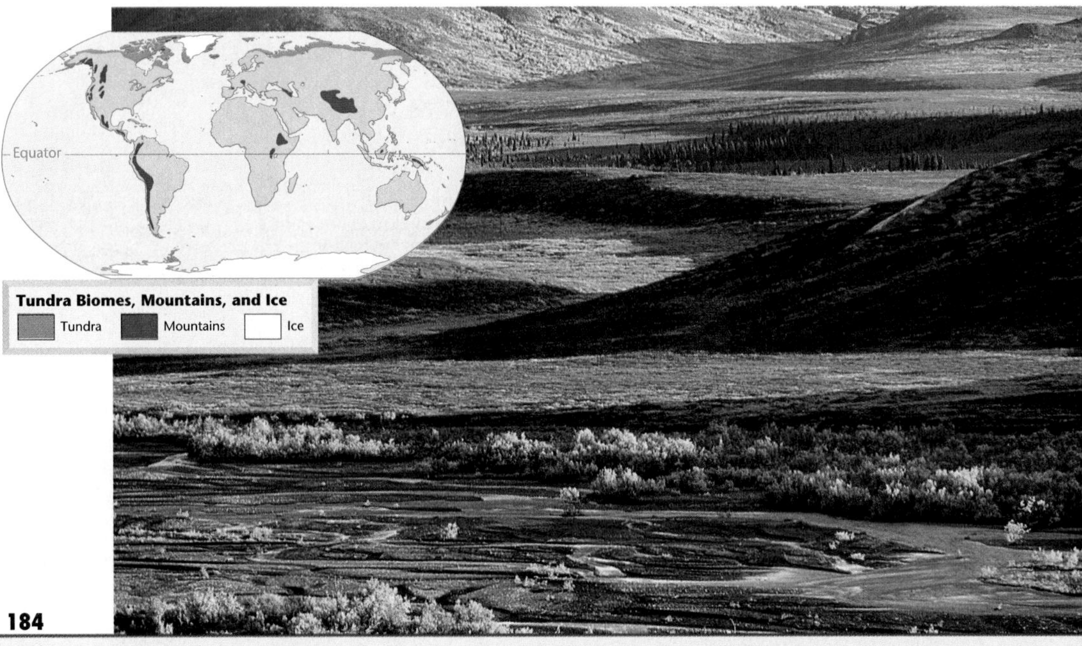

Background

Facts and Figures Tundra generally occurs in the far north, in regions near or above the Arctic Circle, where the snow melts in the summer. In the Southern Hemisphere, tundra occurs on the Antarctic Peninsula, which is the only sizable land area at those latitudes.

Mosses, lichens, grasses and small shrubs carpet the tundra. But life is not easy for tundra plants. Tundra soils are thin, poor in nutrients and humus, and poorly drained. A short distance beneath the surface lies a layer of frozen subsoil called permafrost. Permafrost blocks the downward growth of plant roots. In addition, plants must grow, flower, and produce seeds very quickly during the tundra's short growing season.

During the short summer the top layer of soil on the tundra thaws, but the underlying soil remains frozen.

Plants on the tundra include mosses, grasses, shrubs, and dwarf forms of a few trees, such as willows. Looking across the tundra, you observe that the landscape is already brown and gold. The short growing season is over. Most of the plant growth takes place during the long summer days when many hours of sunshine combine with the warmest temperatures of the year. North of the Arctic Circle the sun does not set during midsummer.

Figure 19 Many waterfowl spend summers on the tundra. This black brant is tending her nest.

If you had visited the tundra during the summer, the animals you might remember most are insects. Swarms of black flies and mosquitos provide food for many birds. The birds take advantage of the plentiful food and long days by eating as much as they can. Then, when winter approaches again, many birds migrate south to warmer climates.

Mammals of the tundra include caribou, foxes, wolves, and hares. The animals that remain in the tundra during the winter grow thick fur coats. What can these animals find to eat on the tundra in winter? The caribou scrape snow away to find lichens, which are fungi and algae that grow together on rocks. Wolves follow the caribou and look for weak members of the herd to prey upon.

The conditions of a mountain change from its base to the top. Conditions at the top of a mountain are often similar to conditions in the tundra.

☑ *Checkpoint* *What are environmental conditions like in the tundra?*

Section 3 Review

1. How does climate determine a biome's characteristics?
2. Which land biome receives the most precipitation? Which two receive the least?
3. In which biome would you find large plant eaters such as antelope and elephants? Explain your answer.
4. **Thinking Critically Comparing and Contrasting** How are the three forest biomes (rain forests, deciduous forests, and boreal forests) alike? How are they different?

CHAPTER PROJECT

Check Your Progress

By now you should be investigating what happens to the different materials in your package when it is thrown away. You will need to find out how your community handles solid waste. (*Hint:* The Department of Public Works may be a good source of this information. Check with your teacher before contacting anyone.)

3 Assess

Section 4 Review Answers

1. Climate limits the types of plants that can survive in the biome, and the types of plants in turn determine the kinds of animals that live there.
2. *Most:* the tropical rain forest (accept also simply rain forest); *least:* the desert and tundra biomes
3. Grassland or savanna; grasslands are home to many large herbivores, which help to maintain the grasslands by keeping young trees and bushes from sprouting.
4. All have tall trees and many habitats for organisms. Students should cite differences in location (latitude), temperature, amount of sunlight, amount of precipitation, and specific types of plants and other organisms.

CHAPTER PROJECT

Check Your Progress

Ask the representative you contracted earlier to present information in a class visit. (See page 164.) If a visit is not possible, designate two or three volunteers to call and collect information for the rest of the class. Remind students to take notes during the visit or phone call so they will have all the information they need for their final presentations and displays.

Answers to Self-Assessment

Caption Question

Figure 18 The short, cool growing season does not allow tall trees to grow.

☑ *Checkpoint*

The tundra is extremely cold during the winter. It receives very little precipitation. Most of the soil is frozen all year long. Days are long in the summer, but the growing season is very short.

Performance Assessment

Skills Check Have students add the tundra biome to the compare/contrast table they created in Ongoing Assessment on page 181.

Skills Lab

Controlling Variables

Save That Soil

Preparing for Inquiry

Key Concept Plants help reduce erosion by holding soil with their roots.

Skills Objectives Students will be able to
- develop a hypothesis about how different land surfaces are affected by rainfall;
- control all variables except land surface;
- observe erosion by water of two different land surfaces.

Time 40 minutes

Advance Planning Purchase enough aluminum or plastic pans for each group to have two. For each group, cut one piece of sod to fit a pan. Obtain enough loose soil for each group to partially fill one pan.

Guiding Inquiry

Troubleshooting the Experiment
- If students have limited experience with controlling variables, discuss what a variable is.
- Some ways students might devise a "rainmaker" are to punch holes in the bottom of a paper cup or to use a sprinkler top for a soda bottle.
- Before Step 4, ask students how they will control the amount and flow of "rainfall."
- In Step 5, remind students to examine not only the soil left at the upper end of each pan but the runoff water at the lower end. Muddier water indicates more erosion.

Expected Outcome

The loose soil will erode easily. The sod will lose very little soil.

Analyze and Conclude

1. "Rain" washed away the loose soil more easily than the soil in the sod.
2. Loose soil erodes more easily than soil growing plants. A farmer can conserve topsoil by keeping the land planted.
3. The amounts of eroded soil can be compared only if the original amounts of soil and "rainfall" were the same.

Skills Lab

Controlling Variables

Save That Soil

In this lab, you'll decide how to control variables as you investigate the way rainfall causes soil erosion.

Problem

How are different types of land surfaces affected by rainfall?

Materials

newspaper
2 blocks
loose soil
water
2 unbreakable pans
sod
"rainmaker"

Procedure

1. Cover a table with newspaper. Obtain two pans. Insert a block under one end of each pan to raise the two ends to the same height.
2. Read over the rest of the lab. Write a hypothesis that you will test. Pay careful attention to the variables you must control.
3. Place loose soil in the raised end of one pan. Place a small square of sod (soil with grass growing in it) in the raised end of the second pan. One variable is the amount of soil in each pan. Find a way to make the two amounts of soil the same. Record your procedures.
4. Create a "rainmaker" that controls the amount of water and the way it falls on the two soil samples. Then use your rainmaker to test the effect of the same amount of "rain" on the two kinds of soil. Record the results.
5. Review your experiment and your results. Do you see any procedure you wish to change? If so, get your teacher's permission to try the lab again with your revised procedures.

Analyze and Conclude

1. What effects did the "rainwater" produce on each type of soil you tested?
2. This experiment models soil erosion. What can you conclude about actual soil erosion caused by rain? How could a farmer use the information gained from this experiment to conserve topsoil?
3. **Think About It** Why was it essential for you to control the amounts of soil and "rainfall" in the two pans?

Design an Experiment

How does soil erosion caused by a gentle, steady rain compare with that caused by a heavy downpour? Design an experiment to find out. Be sure to control the way you imitate the two types of rain. Obtain your teacher's permission before conducting this experiment.

186

Extending the Inquiry

Design an Experiment To compare erosion by different kinds of "rainfall," loose soil should be used in both pans.

Safety

Students should wear safety goggles and lab aprons. Review the safety guidelines in Appendix A.

Program Resources
- **Unit 2 Resources** Skills Lab blackline masters

Media and Technology

Lab Activity Videotape Grade 6, Tape 2

CHAPTER 6 STUDY GUIDE

Exploring Earth's Surface

Key Ideas

- Earth's topography is made up of landforms that have elevation and relief, such as plains, mountains, and plateaus.
- The atmosphere, hydrosphere, and biosphere surround Earth's rocky outer layer, the lithosphere.

Key Terms

topography, elevation, relief, landform, landform region, plain, mountain, mountain range, plateau, lithosphere, core, mantle, crust, rock, geology

Topographic Maps

Key Ideas

- Topographic maps portray the elevation, relief, and slope of the landforms in an area.
- Contour lines are used on a topographic map to show elevation and relief.
- The contour interval of a topographic map is the amount that elevation increases or decreases between contour lines.
- In addition to showing elevation and relief, topographic maps include a variety of other natural and human-made features.

Key Terms

map, topographic map, scale, symbol, contour line, contour interval, Global Positioning System

Earth's Land Biomes

Key Ideas

- Temperature and rainfall mostly determine the biome in an area.
- Land biomes include rain forests, deserts, grasslands, deciduous forests, boreal forests, and tundras.

Key Terms

biome, canopy, understory, desert, grassland, savanna, deciduous tree, hibernation, coniferous tree, tundra, permafrost

Organizing Information

Concept Map Copy the concept map about landforms onto a separate piece of paper. Then complete it and add a title. (For more on concept maps, see the Skills Handbook.)

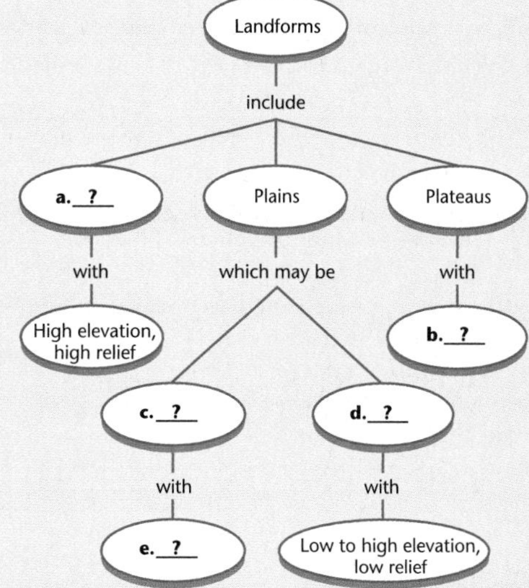

Program Resources

- **Unit 2 Resources** Chapter 6 Project Scoring Rubric
- **Performance Assessment** Chapter 6
- **Chapter and Unit Tests** Chapter 6 Test; Unit 2 Test

Media and Technology

Computer Test Bank Chapter 6 Test

Organizing Information

Concept Map Sample title: *Types of Landforms* **a.** Mountains **b.** High elevation, low relief **c.** Coastal **d.** Interior **e.** Low elevation, low relief

Reviewing Content

Multiple Choice

1. d **2.** c **3.** b **4.** b **5.** d

True or False

6. Elevation **7.** rain forest **8.** true
9. close together **10.** true

Checking Concepts

11. A large area of land where the topography is similar is called a landform region.
12. A mountain range is a series of mountains that have the same general shape and structure.
13. A coastal plain has low elevation, while an interior plain may have high or low elevation.
14. Temperature and precipitation determine an area's biome.
15. Contour lines never cross because a contour line connects points of equal elevation, but they do come together at a perfectly vertical cliff.
16. A 1.5-meter deep depression would not show on a map with a 5-meter contour interval, because that interval shows only changes in elevation greater than 5 meters. The depression would show on a map with a 1-meter contour interval because the depression is greater than the interval.
17. Students should describe the temperature and precipitation conditions, the plants, and the other organisms typically found in the chosen biome.

Thinking Critically

18. The globe has a scale of 1: 26,000,000. A distance of 1 centimeter on the globe would represent 260 kilometers.
19. Both the desert and the tundra are very dry and have extreme living conditions. The desert may be very hot during the day in summer, with large shifts in temperature between day and night; the tundra is cool in summer and bitterly cold in winter. Desert soil is sandy; most of the soil in the tundra is frozen all year long.
20. Students would begin the trip on the Atlantic Coastal Plain. Then they would cross the Piedmont Plateau, the Appalachian Mountains, and the Appalachian Plateau. While traveling across the Gulf Coastal Plain, they would cross the Mississippi River. Then they would cross the flat lands of the Ozark Plateau and Great Plains, followed by the Rocky Mountains, Colorado Plateau. Great Basin, and the Sierra Nevada. They would end their trip by crossing the Coastal Range in California.
21. Mapmakers can go to a site to be mapped and use a GPS unit to find exact locations, which helps them plot the site on a map.
22. Answers will vary. A typical answer might suggest the use of topographic maps to find an area that has a variety of landforms and water environments in a relatively small area in order to accommodate the animals from many regions. In addition, these maps might be used to avoid building in residential areas and other heavily used areas.

CHAPTER 6 ASSESSMENT

Reviewing Content

Multiple Choice

Choose the letter of the best answer.

1. A landform that has high elevation but a mostly flat surface is a
a. coastal plain. **b.** mountain.
c. mountain belt. **d.** plateau.

2. The thin, outer layer of the lithosphere that forms Earth's surface is the
a. outer core. **b.** inner core.
c. crust. **d.** mantle.

3. Much of Canada is covered in pine and spruce forests. The winter is cold and long. What is this biome?
a. tundra **b.** boreal forest
c. deciduous forest **d.** grassland

4. In a tropical rain forest, the leafy roof formed by tall trees is called the
a. understory. **b.** canopy.
c. permafrost. **d.** savanna.

5. On a topographic map, the contour lines form a V at a
a. hilltop. **b.** level area.
c. depression. **d.** valley.

True or False

If the statement is true, write true. If it is false, change the underlined word or words to make the statement true.

6. Relief measures a landform's height above sea level.
7. The land biome that gets the highest average amount of precipitation is the tropical grassland biome.
8. Deciduous trees shed their leaves and grow new ones each year.
9. If contour lines on a slope are spaced wide apart, then the slope is very steep.
10. Contour lines that form a closed loop marked with dashes indicate a depression.

Checking Concepts

11. What do geologists call an area where there is mostly one kind of topography?
12. What is a mountain range?
13. Compare the elevation of a coastal plain to that of an interior plain.
14. What factors determine an area's biome?
15. Could contour lines on a map ever cross? Explain.
16. Which would be more likely to show a shallow, 1.5-meter-deep depression in the ground: a 1-meter contour interval or a 5-meter contour interval? Explain.
17. Writing to Learn Choose any of the biomes described in this chapter. Imagine that you are a typical animal found in that biome. Write a paragraph describing the conditions and other organisms in your animal's biome.

Thinking Critically

18. Applying Concepts Earth's diameter is about 13,000 kilometers. If a globe has a diameter of 0.5 meter, write the globe's scale as a ratio. What distance on Earth would 1 centimeter on the globe represent?
19. Comparing and Contrasting How are the desert biome and the tundra biome similar? How are they different?
20. Observing You and your family make a car trip from the coast of North Carolina west to the coast of California. Use the map in Appendix B to describe what the land is like along your route.
21. Inferring What impact has the development of the Global Positioning System had on mapmaking?
22. Problem Solving Your community has decided to build a zoo for animals from many regions of Earth. How could you use topographic maps of your area to help decide on the best location for the zoo?

Applying Skills

This map shows part of Acadia National Park in Maine. The contour interval is 20 feet. Use the map to answer Questions 23–25.

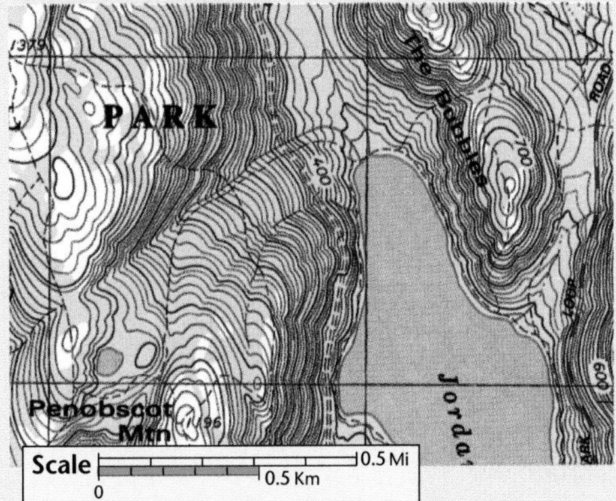

23. Interpreting Maps
  A. What is the elevation of the large lake?
  B. Which of the two Bubbles is higher?

24. Calculating Use the map scale to calculate the distance from the top of Penobscot Mountain to the large lake.

25. Inferring How can you tell whether the streams flow into or out of the large lake?

Performance — CHAPTER PROJECT — Assessment

Present Your Project As you finish work on your project, share it with one or more classmates. Ask: Does the display clearly explain what the package is made of? Are the benefits of the package identified? Does the display describe what happens to each material? If you need to make any revisions to your display, do so now.

Reflect and Record In your project notebook, describe the most surprising information you learned during this project. What questions might you ask before purchasing a product like the one you studied?

Test Preparation

Use these questions to prepare for standardized tests.

The table shows how color is used to help distinguish kinds of features on U.S. Geological Survey topographic maps. Study the table. Then answer Questions 26-29.

Black	Cultural features such as roads and buildings
Blue	Water features such as lakes and rivers
Brown	Topographic features such as contour lines
Green	Vegetation features such as woodlands and orchards
Red	Roads
Purple	Features added from aerial photographs but not checked on the ground

26. On a topographic map, red is used to show
a. vegetation. **b.** water.
c. roads. **d.** buildings.

27. On a map of coastal Virginia, Chesapeake Bay would be
a. brown. **b.** blue.
c. purple. **d.** black.

28. The symbol for a barn would be
a. brown. **b.** black.
c. red. **d.** blue.

29. A large tropical rain forest would most likely appear as a
a. red dashed line. **b.** black rectangle.
c. large blue oval. **d.** large green area.

Program Resources

◆ **Inquiry Skills Activity Book** Provides teaching and review of all inquiry skills

Applying Skills

23. a. between 260 and 280 feet
b. The north Bubble has an elevation of 860 feet, which is higher than the south Bubble's 760 feet.
24. The distance is 0.5 km.
25. Into the large lake; the V-shaped contours point uphill and the streams flow in the opposite direction.

Performance — CHAPTER PROJECT — Assessment

Present Your Project Remind students that their displays should also include a cut-away view of the package and a sample of each material used in it. Having every student present his or her display to the entire class might be time-consuming and tedious. Instead, assign students to small groups or have two poster sessions where half the class displays their projects to the other half.

Reflect and Record Invite students to share their reflections on the project in a class discussion.

Test Preparation

26. c **27.** b **28.** b **29.** d

CHAPTER 7

Fresh Water

Sections	Time	Student Edition Activities	ACTIVITY Other Activities
CHAPTER PROJECT **Build a Watershed** p. 191	Ongoing (2 weeks)	Check Your Progress, pp. 198, 213 Present Your Project, p. 223	
1 The Water Cycle pp. 192–199 ◆ Identify how Earth's water is distributed among saltwater and freshwater sources. ◆ Describe how Earth's water moves through the water cycle. ◆ Give examples of how people and other living things use water.	1 period/ $\frac{1}{2}$ block	**Discover** Where Does the Water Come From?, p. 192 **Sharpen Your Skills** Calculating, p. 193 **Try This** Tabletop Water Cycle, p. 194 **Real-World Lab: You and Your Environment** Water From Trees, p. 199	**TE** Include All Students, p. 194 **TE** Real-Life Learning, p. 195 **TE** Cultural Diversity, p. 196 **TE** Real-Life Learning, p. 197
2 Water on the Surface pp. 200–209 ◆ Describe a river system and how water flows into it. ◆ Identify conditions that cause floods and how floods can be controlled. ◆ Explain how ponds and lakes form. ◆ Describe pond and lake habitats and the process of lake turnover. ◆ Explain how icebergs form and why they are dangerous to ships.	3 periods/ $1\frac{1}{2}$ blocks	**Discover** What's in Pond Water?, p. 200 **Try This** The Knuckle Divide, p. 201 **Science at Home,** p. 209	**TE** Integrating Technology, p. 203 **TE** Building Inquiry Skills: Comparing and Contrasting, p. 204 **TE** Including All Students, p. 205 **TE** Demonstration, p. 206
3 Water Underground pp. 210–215 ◆ Describe springs and how water moves through underground layers of soil and rock. ◆ Explain what an aquifer is and how people obtain water from an aquifer.	2 periods/ $1\frac{1}{2}$ blocks	**Discover** Where Does the Water Go?, p. 210 **Sharpen Your Skills** Drawing Conclusions, p. 211 **Try This** An Artesian Well, p. 212 **Real-World Lab: Careers in Science** Soil Testing, pp. 214–215	**TE** Demonstration, p. 205 **LM** 7, "Field Testing a Body of Fresh Water"
4 INTEGRATING LIFE SCIENCE **Wetland Environments** pp. 216–220 ◆ Identify features of wetlands that make them suitable habitats for living things. ◆ Explain what a wetland is and how wetlands help control flooding.	2 periods/ 1 block	**Discover** Wet or Dry?, p. 216 **Science at Home,** p. 220	**TE** Real-Life Learning, p. 217 **TE** Demonstration, p. 218 **TE** Inquiry Challenge, p. 219
Study Guide/Chapter Assessment pp. 221–223	1 period/ $\frac{1}{2}$ block		**ISAB** Provides teaching and review of all inquiry skills

For Standard or Block Schedule The Resource Pro® CD-ROM gives you maximum flexibility for planning your instruction for any type of schedule. Resource Pro® contains Planning Express®, an advanced scheduling program, as well as the entire contents of the Teaching Resources and the Computer Test Bank.

CHAPTER PLANNING GUIDE

Program Resources	Assessment Strategies	Media and Technology
UR Chapter 7 Project Teacher Notes **UR** Chapter 7 Project Overview and Worksheets	**SE** Performance Assessment: Present Your Project, p. 223 **TE** Check Your Progress, pp. 198, 213 **UR** Chapter 7 Project Scoring Rubric	Science Explorer Internet Site at www.phschool.com Student Edition on Audio CD, Chapter 7
UR 7-1 Lesson Plan **UR** 7-1 Section Summary **UR** 7-1 Review and Reinforce **UR** 7-1 Enrich **UR** Chapter 7 Real-World Lab	**SE** Section 1 Review, p. 198 **TE** Ongoing Assessment, pp. 193, 195, 197 **TE** Performance Assessment, p. 198	Transparency 21, "Exploring the Water Cycle" Lab Activity Videotapes, Grade 6 Tape 2
UR 7-2 Lesson Plan **UR** 7-2 Section Summary **UR** 7-2 Review and Reinforce **UR** 7-2 Enrich	**SE** Section 2 Review, p. 209 **TE** Ongoing Assessment, pp. 201, 203, 205, 209 **TE** Performance Assessment, p. 209	
UR 7-3 Lesson Plan **UR** 7-3 Section Summary **UR** 7-3 Review and Reinforce **UR** 7-3 Enrich **UR** Chapter 7 Real-World Lab	**SE** Section 3 Review, p. 213 **TE** Ongoing Assessment, p. 211 **TE** Performance Assessment, p. 213	Transparency 22, "Underground Zones" Transparency 23, "Wells and Springs" Lab Activity Videotapes, Grade 6 Tape 2
UR 7-4 Lesson Plan **UR** 7-4 Section Summary **UR** 7-4 Review and Reinforce **UR** 7-4 Enrich	**SE** Section 4 Review, p. 220 **TE** Ongoing Assessment, pp. 217, 219 **TE** Performance Assessment, p. 220	
RCA Provides strategies to improve science reading skills **GRSW** Provides worksheets to promote student comprehension of content	**SE** Chapter 7 Study Guide/Assessment, pp. 221–223 **PA** Chapter 7 Performance Assessment **CUT** Chapter 7 Test **CTB** Chapter 7 Test	Computer Test Bank, Chapter 7 Test

Key: **SE** Student Edition
CTB Computer Test Bank
ISAB Inquiry Skills Activity Book
GRSW Guided Reading and Study Workbook
TE Teacher's Edition
PTA Product Testing Activities by *Consumer Reports*
RCA Reading in the Content Area
PA Performance Assessment
UR Unit Resources
LM Laboratory Manual
IES Interdisciplinary Explorations Series
CUT Chapter and Unit Tests

Meeting the National Science Education Standards and AAAS Benchmarks

National Science Education Standards	Benchmarks for Science Literacy	Unifying Themes
Science As Inquiry (Content Standard A) ◆ **Think critically and logically to make the relationships between evidence and explanations** Students relate observations of transpiration to the role of trees in the water cycle. Students compare the water-holding properties of different soil types to determine the best type of soil for a well. *(Real-World Labs)* **Physical Science** (Content Standard B) ◆ **Transfer of energy** The sun is the source of energy that drives the water cycle. *(Sections 1, 2)* **Life Science** (Content Standard C) ◆ **Populations and ecosystems** Rivers, ponds, lakes and wetlands provide habitats for many living things. *(Sections 2, 4)* **Earth and Space Science** (Content Standard D) ◆ **Structure of the Earth system** Oceans cover nearly 71 percent of Earth's surface. Most fresh water is frozen in ice. Water is naturally recycled through the water cycle. Freshwater sources include streams and rivers, ponds and lakes, wetlands, glaciers and icebergs, and groundwater. *(Sections 1, 2, 3, and 4)* **Science in Personal and Social Perspectives** (Content Standard F) ◆ **Science and technology in society** People use water for many purposes. Irrigation is used to supply crops with water. *(Chapter Project; Section 1; Science & History)*	**1B Scientific Inquiry** Students investigate transpiration. Students compare water-holding properties of different soil types. *(Real-World Labs)* **3C Issues in Technology** People use water for household purposes, agriculture, industry, transportation, and recreation. People build dams and levees to control flooding. People obtain groundwater by drilling wells. *(Sections 1, 2, and 3; Science & History)* **4B The Earth** Oceans cover nearly 71 percent of Earth's surface. Most fresh water is frozen in ice. Water is naturally recycled through the water cycle. Freshwater sources include streams and rivers, ponds and lakes, wetlands, glaciers and icebergs, and groundwater. *(Sections 1, 2, 3, and 4)* **5D Interdependence of Life** Rivers, ponds, lakes, and wetlands provide habitats for many living things. *(Sections 1, 2, and 3)* **11B Models** Students design and build a watershed model. Students build a stream trough to investigate stream flow. Students explore the water-holding properties of different soil types. *(Chapter Project; Skills Lab; Real-World Lab)* **12D Communication Skills** Students monitor water use in their homes and community and share their findings. *(Chapter Project)*	◆ **Systems and Interactions** Water is naturally recycled through the water cycle. Plants give off water through the process of transpiration. As fresh water moves over Earth's surface, it forms streams and rivers; collects in ponds, lakes, and wetlands; forms glaciers; and moves underground. *(Sections 1, 2, 3, and 4; Real-World Lab)* ◆ **Modeling** Students design and build a watershed model. Students build a stream trough to investigate stream flow. Students explore the water-holding properties of different soil types. *(Chapter Project; Skills Lab; Real-World Lab)* ◆ **Patterns of Change** Water moves from bodies of water, land, and living things on Earth's surface to the atmosphere and back to Earth's surface in the water cycle. Lake turnover seasonally refreshes the supply of nutrients throughout a lake. Lakes change over time through eutrophication. *(Sections 1, and 2)* ◆ **Unity and Diversity** Rivers, ponds, lakes, and wetlands provide habitats for many living things. *(Sections 1, 2, and 3)* ◆ **Scale and Structure** Water soaks down through permeable materials until it reaches a layer of impermeable materials. *(Section 3; Real-World Lab)*

Take It to the Net

Interactive text at www.phschool.com

Science Explorer comes alive with iText.

- **Complete student text** is accessible from any computer with Internet access or a CD-ROM drive.
- **Animations, simulations, and videos** enhance student understanding and retention of concepts.
- **Self-tests and online study tools** assess student understanding.

STAY CURRENT with **SCIENCE NEWS®**

Find out the latest research and information about Earth's Waters at:
www.phschool.com

Go to **www.phschool.com** and click on the Science icon.Then click on Science Explorer: Life, Earth, and Physical Science under PH@school.

ACTIVITY	Time (minutes)	Materials *Quantities for one work group*	Skills
Section 1			
Discover, p. 192	15	**Consumable** ice, water **Nonconsumable** pitcher, clear drinking glass	Inferring
Sharpen Your Skills, p. 193	20; 20	**Consumable** water **Nonconsumable** 1-liter clear plastic bottle, large bowl, 5 plastic cups, plastic graduated cylinder, calculator, plastic dropper	Calculating
Try This, p. 194	20; 20	**Consumable** water, plastic wrap, sand **Nonconsumable** flat-bottomed clear container, small jar, rubber band, small rock, lamp	Making Models
Real-World Lab, p. 199	20; 20	**Consumable** 3 plastic sandwich bags, 3 twist ties **Nonconsumable** 3 small pebbles, balance	Observing, Calculating, Inferring
Section 2			
Discover, p. 200	20	**Consumable** pond water **Nonconsumable** plastic petri dish, hand lens, microscope, plastic dropper, slide and cover slip	Classifying
Try This, p. 201	10	**Consumable** paper towel, water **Nonconsumable** spoon	Making Models
Science at Home, p. 209	home	**Consumable** milk or juice carton, water, salt **Nonconsumable** large bowl, metric ruler	Making Models
Section 3			
Discover, p. 210	10	**Consumable** water, dry sand **Nonconsumable** pebbles, clear jar, metric ruler	Observing
Sharpen Your Skills, p. 211	10	No specific materials are required	Drawing Conclusions
Try This, p. 212	20	**Consumable** newspaper, plastic straw, modeling clay, water, moist sand **Nonconsumable** loaf pan, funnel, scissors	Making Models
Real-World Lab, pp. 214–215	40	**Consumable** 100 mL powdered potter's clay, 100 mL sand, 3 squares of cheesecloth, 300 mL water **Nonconsumable** hand lens, stopwatch, 3 rubber bands, 3 large plastic funnels or cut-off plastic soda bottle tops, 3 100-mL beakers, 100 mL pebbles	Observing, Measuring, Drawing Conclusions
Section 4			
Discover, p. 216	10–15	**Consumable** water, 2 paper cups **Nonconsumable** 2 dry kitchen sponges, pan	Observing
Science at Home, p. 220	home	**Consumable** water, damp soil **Nonconsumable** loaf pan, watering can, sponge	Observing

A list of all materials required for the Student Edition activities can be found on pages TVA34–TVA40. You can obtain information about ordering materials by calling 1-800-848-9500 or by accessing the Science Explorer Internet site at: **www.phschool.com**

CHAPTER 7 PROJECT

Build a Watershed

The concept of a watershed can be difficult for students to comprehend, since they cannot view an entire river system directly. This project will provide an opportunity for students to make these concepts "real" and observable.

Purpose In this project, students will apply the chapter's concepts and terms to model typical features of a watershed—a main river and its smaller tributaries, the drainage area supplying water to the system, bodies of standing water, various landforms created by the flowing water, and the changes in a river's characteristics as it flows from its headwaters to its mouth.

Skills Focus After completing the Chapter 7 Project, students will be able to
- ◆ create working three-dimensional models of specific watershed and river-system features;
- ◆ identify variables that affect the flow rates of a main river and its tributaries;
- ◆ describe the changes that occur in a river as it flows from its headwaters to its mouth;
- ◆ predict and test the effects of increased rainfall on the river system.

Project Time Line This project requires at least two to three weeks for completion. Only the presentation of the models needs to be done in class. The remaining portions can be done in or out of class, depending on available space and time. Allow at least three days for students to plan their models, including initial sketches and revisions. Building the model will require about one week. Students should complete their models one or two days before they will test and present them, since the materials may require time to dry or set. Before beginning the project, see Chapter 7 Project Teacher Notes in Unit 3 Resources. Also distribute to students Chapter 7 Project Overview, Worksheets, and Scoring Rubric in Unit 3 Resources.

Possible Materials
- ◆ *To form the base:* cookie sheet, roasting pan, aluminum foil baking pan, sheet of corrugated cardboard covered with wax paper or plastic wrap, or sheet of foam core, plywood, or masonite

CHAPTER 7

Fresh Water

WEB ACTIVITY www.phschool.com

SECTION 1 The Water Cycle
Discover Where Does the Water Come From?
Sharpen Your Skills Calculating
Try This Tabletop Water Cycle
Real-World Lab Water from Trees

SECTION 2 Water on the Surface
Discover What's in Pond Water?
Try This The Knuckle Divide
Science at Home Home-made Iceberg

SECTION 3 Water Underground
Discover Where Does the Water Go?
Sharpen Your Skills Drawing Conclusions
Try This Artesian Well
Real-World Lab Soil Testing

190

- ◆ *To shape and form the land:* salt dough or papier mâché (see instructions below), modeling clay, cardboard, or wet paper
  Salt dough: Mix two parts flour to one part salt; add water a little at a time to make a stiff, moldable dough.
  Papier mâché: Mix plaster of paris and water to the consistency of creamed soup; tear plain newsprint paper into thin strips and soak them in the plaster solution.
- ◆ *To waterproof the model:* plastic wrap, clear acrylic spray, or clear waterproof varnish

Launching the Project To introduce the project and motivate student interest, show the class a satellite photograph of a river system without telling students what the subject of the photograph is. Ask: **What do you think this picture shows?** *(Since students have never directly viewed rivers and streams from the photograph's viewpoint, they may at first have difficulty identifying the subject as a river system. Acknowledge all responses but do not comment on their accuracy at this time. When students first identify the subject correctly, confirm this response.)*

CHAPTER 7 PROJECT

Build a Watershed

The bull moose plunges into the stream, sending shimmering drops of water flying in all directions. In addition to a refreshing dip, the stream provides the moose with drinking water and a place to find food.

A stream is one place you can find fresh water on Earth. In this chapter you will explore fresh water as it moves and changes the land, as it collects in lakes and ponds and provides a home for living things, and as it flows underground. Throughout the chapter, you will be making a model showing how water moves over the land.

Your Goal To design and build a three-dimensional model of a watershed and river system.

Your model should
- include a main river and at least two tributaries
- show at least one example of a body of standing water
- be constructed of materials that allow water to run over it
- be built following the safety guidelines in Appendix A

Get Started Begin by previewing Section 1 to see some parts of a river system. Look at the shape of the land surrounding different parts of rivers. Start thinking about materials you could use to make your landscape.

Check Your Progress You'll be working on this project as you study this chapter. To keep your project on track, look for Check Your Progress boxes at the following points.

Section 1 Review, page 198: Sketch a design for your watershed.
Section 3 Review, page 213: Revise your design to include all features.
Section 4 Review, page 220: Build your model watershed.

Present Your Project At the end of the chapter (page 223), you will use a spray bottle to demonstrate your watershed in action!

A bull moose shakes himself off following a dip in an Alaskan stream.

Section 4 Integrating Life Science
Wetlands Environments
Discover **Wet or Dry?**

191

Allow time for students to read the description of the project in their text and in Chapter 7 Project Student Materials in Unit 3 Resources. During this time, pass the photograph around so students can examine it more closely. When students have finished reading the project description, encourage discussion of possible materials to use and any preliminary questions they may have.

Have students work in small groups as a cooperative learning task. To ensure that each group member will have ample opportunity to participate in both the planning and the building of the model, make sure each group consists of no more than three students.

Program Resources

- **Unit 3 Resources** Chapter 7 Project Teacher Notes; Chapter 7 Project Student Materials; Chapter 7 Project Scoring Rubric

Media and Technology

Student Edition on Audio CD Chapter 7

www.phschool.com

You will find an Internet activity, chapter self-tests for students, and links to other chapter topics at this site.

Performance Assessment

The Chapter 7 Project Scoring Rubric in Unit 3 Resources will help you evaluate how well students complete the Chapter 7 Project. Students will be assessed on
- how well they plan their models, including the final sketches, which should include all river-system features identified in the text;
- the accuracy and creativity of their models;
- the organization and thoroughness of their presentation;
- their participation in their groups.

By sharing the Chapter 7 Project Scoring Rubric with students at the beginning of the project, you will make it clear to them what they are expected to do.

The Water Cycle

Objectives

After completing the lesson, students will be able to

- identify how Earth's water is distributed among saltwater and freshwater sources;
- describe how Earth's water moves through the water cycle;
- give examples of how people and other living things use water.

Key Terms water vapor, groundwater, water cycle, evaporation, transpiration, precipitation, irrigation, photosynthesis, habitat

1 Engage/Explore

Activating Prior Knowledge

Invite a student volunteer to describe a rainstorm. Ask: **Where does the water come from that falls as rain?** *(from clouds)* **How does the water get into the clouds?** *(Some students may know that water vapor in the atmosphere condenses to form clouds.)* Continue this line of questioning, guiding students through the water cycle to put the parts together to form a cycle.

DISCOVER

Skills Focus inferring
Materials *ice, water, pitcher, clear drinking glass*
Time 15 minutes
Tips Add enough ice to a pitcher of water to make the water very cold, thus ensuring that droplets will quickly form on the outer surface of the glass. Advise students to be careful not to spill the water onto the outside of the glass when pouring from the pitcher. Once students have completed the activity, you may want to spend time exploring their misconceptions about this phenomenon.
Think It Over Some students may correctly infer that the water droplets come from water vapor in the air condensing on the cold surface of the glass. Some students, however, will propose that the water somehow came from inside the glass.

SECTION 1 The Water Cycle

DISCOVER ACTIVITY

Where Does the Water Come From?

1. Fill a glass with ice cubes and water, being careful not to spill any water. Set the glass aside for 5 minutes.
2. Observe the outside of the glass and the surface it was sitting on.

Think It Over

Inferring Where did the water on the outside of the glass come from? How do you think it got there?

GUIDE FOR READING

- How is Earth's water distributed among saltwater and freshwater sources?
- How does Earth's water move through the water cycle?
- How do people and other living things use water?

Reading Tip As you read, use the headings to make an outline showing how water is important and where it is found.

Why do you think Earth is often called the "water planet"? Perhaps an astronaut suggested this name. From space, an astronaut can see that there is much more water than land on planet Earth. Oceans cover nearly 71 percent of Earth's surface.

Water on Earth

Figure 1 shows how Earth's water is distributed. **Most of Earth's water — roughly 97 percent — is salt water that is found in the oceans. Only 3 percent is fresh water.** Of that 3 percent, about three quarters is found in the huge masses of ice near the North and South Poles. A fraction more is found in the atmosphere. Most water in the atmosphere is invisible **water vapor,** the gaseous form of water. Less than 1 percent of the water on Earth is fresh water that is available for humans to use.

Oceans To explore where Earth's water is found, you can take an imaginary boat trip around the world. Your journey starts in Miami, Florida. From here, you can sail completely around the world without ever going ashore. Although people have given names to regions of the ocean, these regions are all connected, forming a single world ocean.

First you sail southeast across the Atlantic Ocean toward Africa. Swinging around the continent's southern tip, you enter the smaller but deeper Indian Ocean. Next, you head east across the Pacific Ocean, the longest part of your trip. This vast ocean, dotted with islands, covers an area greater than all the land on Earth put together.

READING STRATEGIES

Reading Tip Encourage students to preview the section, noting the two levels of headings that appear. Students can use these headings as the first two levels of their outlines. Student outlines may begin as follows:

I. Water on Earth
  A. Oceans
  B. Ice
  C. Rivers and Lakes
  D. Below Earth's Surface
II. The Water Cycle
  A. Water Evaporates
  B. Clouds Form
  C. Water Falls as Precipitation
III. How Do People Use Water?
  A. Agriculture
  B. Industry
  C. Transportation
  D. Recreation
IV. Water and Living Things

Ice How can you get back to Miami? You could sail all the way around South America. But watch out for icebergs! These floating chunks of ice are made of fresh water. Icebergs in the southern Pacific and Atlantic oceans have broken off the massive sheets of ice that cover most of Antarctica. You would also find icebergs in the Arctic Ocean around the North Pole.

Rivers and Lakes To see examples of fresh water in rivers and lakes, you'll have to make a side trip inland. Sail north past Nova Scotia, Canada, to the beginning of the St. Lawrence Seaway. Navigate through the series of locks along the St. Lawrence River. Suddenly the river widens and you enter Lake Ontario, one of North America's five Great Lakes. Together, the Great Lakes contain nearly 20 percent of all the water in the world's freshwater lakes.

Below Earth's Surface When rain or snow falls, some of the water soaks into the ground. This water trickles down through spaces between the particles of soil and rock. Eventually the water reaches a layer that it cannot move through. Water that fills the cracks and spaces in underground soil and rock layers is called **groundwater.** Far more fresh water is located underground than in all Earth's rivers and lakes. You will learn more about groundwater in Section 3.

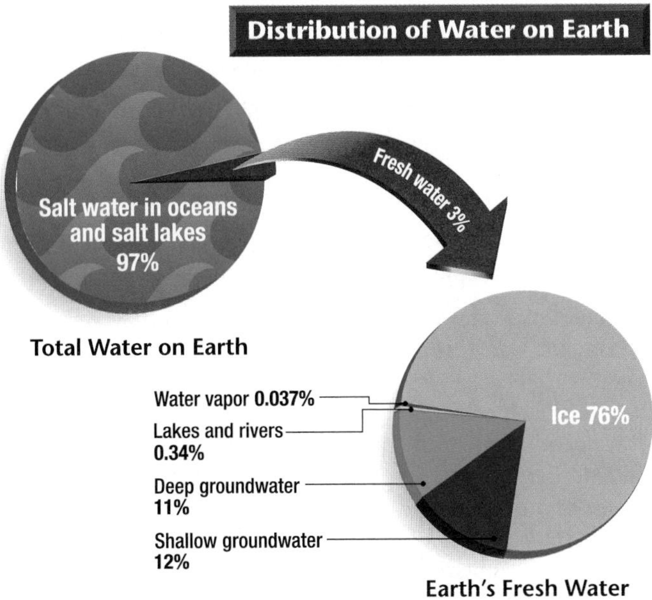

Figure 1 Most of Earth's water is salt water. Of the freshwater sources shown in the bottom circle graph, only the water in lakes, rivers, and shallow groundwater is available for human use.

Sharpen your Skills

Calculating

This activity shows how Earth's water is distributed.

1. Fill a one-liter plastic bottle with water. This represents the total water on Earth.
2. First, measure 97 percent, or 970 milliliters (mL), of the water and pour it into a large bowl. This represents the salt water in Earth's oceans and salt lakes.
3. Next, you will demonstrate how the remaining fresh water is divided. Label five cups to match the freshwater sources in Figure 1. Calculate how much of the remaining 30 mL of water you should pour into each cup to represent the percentage of Earth's fresh water found there.
4. Use a plastic graduated cylinder to measure out the amount of water for each cup. Use a plastic dropper to approximate amounts that are too small to measure accurately.

Which cups contain water that is available for humans to use? How does the amount of water in these cups compare to the original one liter?

Program Resources

- **Unit 3 Resources** 7-1 Lesson Plan; 7-1 Section Summary
- **Guided Reading and Study Workbook** Section 7-1

2 Facilitate

Water on Earth

Using the Visuals: Figure 1

Students may have difficulty interpreting these circle graphs. Focus their attention first on the upper graph. Ask: **What does this circle graph tell you?** *(Salt water makes up almost all of the water on Earth.)* **How is the lower graph related to the upper graph?** *(The lower graph represents all the water in the smaller wedge of the upper graph.)* **learning modality: logical/mathematical**

Sharpen your Skills

Calculating

Materials *water, 1-liter clear plastic bottle, large bowl, 5 cups, plastic graduated cylinder, calculator, plastic dropper*
Time 30 minutes
Tips Students should pour 97% of 1000 mL, or 970 mL, into the bowl. As students proceed, ask them to examine the lower circle graph in Figure 1. Explain that the 3%, or 30 mL, remaining in the bottle represents 100% of the fresh water on Earth. Then have them use the circle graph and a calculator to calculate the amount of water to be placed in each of the five cups. *(Ice: 76% of 30 mL, or about 22 mL; Shallow Groundwater: 3.6 mL; Deep Groundwater: 3.3 mL; Lakes and Rivers: about 0.1 mL; and Water Vapor: about 0.01 mL.)*
Expected Outcome Students should conclude that only the water in the two cups labeled Lakes and Rivers and Shallow Groundwater is available for human use.
Extend Ask students to repeat steps 3 and 4, but this time starting with a full bottle of water that represents Earth's total fresh water. **learning modality: kinesthetic**

Ongoing Assessment

Skills Check Have students make a circle graph of the water available for human use, using Figure 1 as a reference. Students may estimate the relative sizes of the wedges.

Including All Students

To reinforce students' understanding of transpiration, invite students to examine a small plant, such as a geranium, out of soil. Ask: **Through which part does a plant take in water?** *(through its roots)* Help students trace the path that water takes through a plant: from the roots up through the stem and branches to the leaves. Transpiration takes place on the underside of leaves, through openings called stomata. **learning modality: kinesthetic**

TRY THIS

Skills Focus making a model

Materials *flat-bottomed clear container, water, small jar (such as a baby-food jar), sand, plastic wrap, rubber band, small rock, lamp (if direct sunlight is not available)*

Time 20 minutes for setup; 20 minutes an hour later for conclusion

Tips Be sure the top of the jar does not come into contact with the plastic wrap. The plastic wrap should be a little loose and hanging over the edges of the bowl.

Expected Outcome After about one hour, small drops of water should be evident on the inside surface of the plastic wrap. Also, the sand may be moist from drops of water falling from the plastic wrap. Students should infer that they have modeled the processes of evaporation, condensation, and precipitation, as well as land, a body of water, and the atmosphere.

Extend Ask students to make a labeled drawing of their model, using arrows and labels to show the processes that occur and the source of the energy that drives those processes. **learning modality: kinesthetic**

TRY THIS

Tabletop Water Cycle

In this activity you will build a model of the water cycle.

1. Put on your goggles. Pour enough water into a flat-bottomed bowl to cover the bottom. Fill a small jar with sand and place it in the bowl.
2. Loosely cover the top of the bowl with plastic wrap. Secure with a rubber band.
3. Place a rock on top of the plastic, directly over the jar.
4. Place the bowl in direct sunlight or under a lamp. After one hour, observe the bowl and plastic wrap.

Making a Model What features of the water cycle are represented in your model?

The Water Cycle

Water is naturally recycled through the water cycle. The **water cycle** is the continuous process by which water moves through the living and nonliving parts of the environment. **In the water cycle, water moves from bodies of water, land, and living things on Earth's surface to the atmosphere and back to Earth's surface.** The sun is the source of energy that drives the water cycle.

Water Evaporates Water moves continuously through the water cycle. The cycle has no real beginning or end. You can follow a water molecule through one complete cycle in *Exploring the Water Cycle* on the facing page.

Think about a molecule of water floating near the surface of an ocean. The sun is shining and the air is warm. Soon, the molecule has absorbed enough heat energy to change state. It evaporates and becomes water vapor. **Evaporation** is the process by which molecules at the surface of a liquid absorb enough energy to change to the gaseous state. Although the water comes from the salty ocean, it becomes fresh through the process of evaporation. The salt remains in the ocean.

Large amounts of water evaporate constantly from the surfaces of oceans and large lakes. In addition, small amounts evaporate from the soil, puddles, and even from your skin. A significant amount of water is given off by plants. Plants draw in water from the soil through their roots. Eventually the water is given off through the leaves as water vapor in a process called **transpiration.**

Clouds Form Once a water molecule has found its way into the atmosphere, warm air carries it upward. Higher up, the air tends to become much colder. Cold air holds less water vapor than warm air. Some of the water vapor cools and condenses into liquid water. Condensed droplets of water clump together around tiny dust particles in the air, forming clouds.

Water Falls as Precipitation As more water vapor condenses, the water droplets in a cloud eventually become so heavy that they fall back to Earth. Water that falls to Earth as rain, snow, hail, or sleet is called **precipitation.** Most water molecules probably spend only about 10 days in the atmosphere before falling back to Earth. Most precipitation falls directly into the oceans. Water in the ocean may stay there for many years before evaporating, thus continuing the cycle.

When precipitation falls on land, some of the water evaporates again immediately. Some runs off the surface of the land into rivers and lakes. From there, it may eventually evaporate or flow back into the ocean. Some water trickles down into the ground and forms groundwater. Groundwater may move underground

Background

Facts and Figures Within the water cycle, water circulates on land in these three loops: (1) the surface runoff loop, (2) the evaporation-transpiration loop, and (3) the groundwater loop. The last two loops tend to purify water, whereas the first loop does not. The water runs off quickly, instead of filtering through soil and rock.

until it reaches a river, lake, or ocean. Once groundwater reaches the surface, it can continue through the cycle by evaporating again.

Precipitation is the source of all fresh water on and below Earth's surface. The water cycle renews the usable supply of fresh water on Earth. For millions of years, the total amount of water on Earth has remained fairly constant. In the world as a whole, the rates of evaporation and precipitation are balanced.

☑ *Checkpoint* *List three places from which water evaporates.*

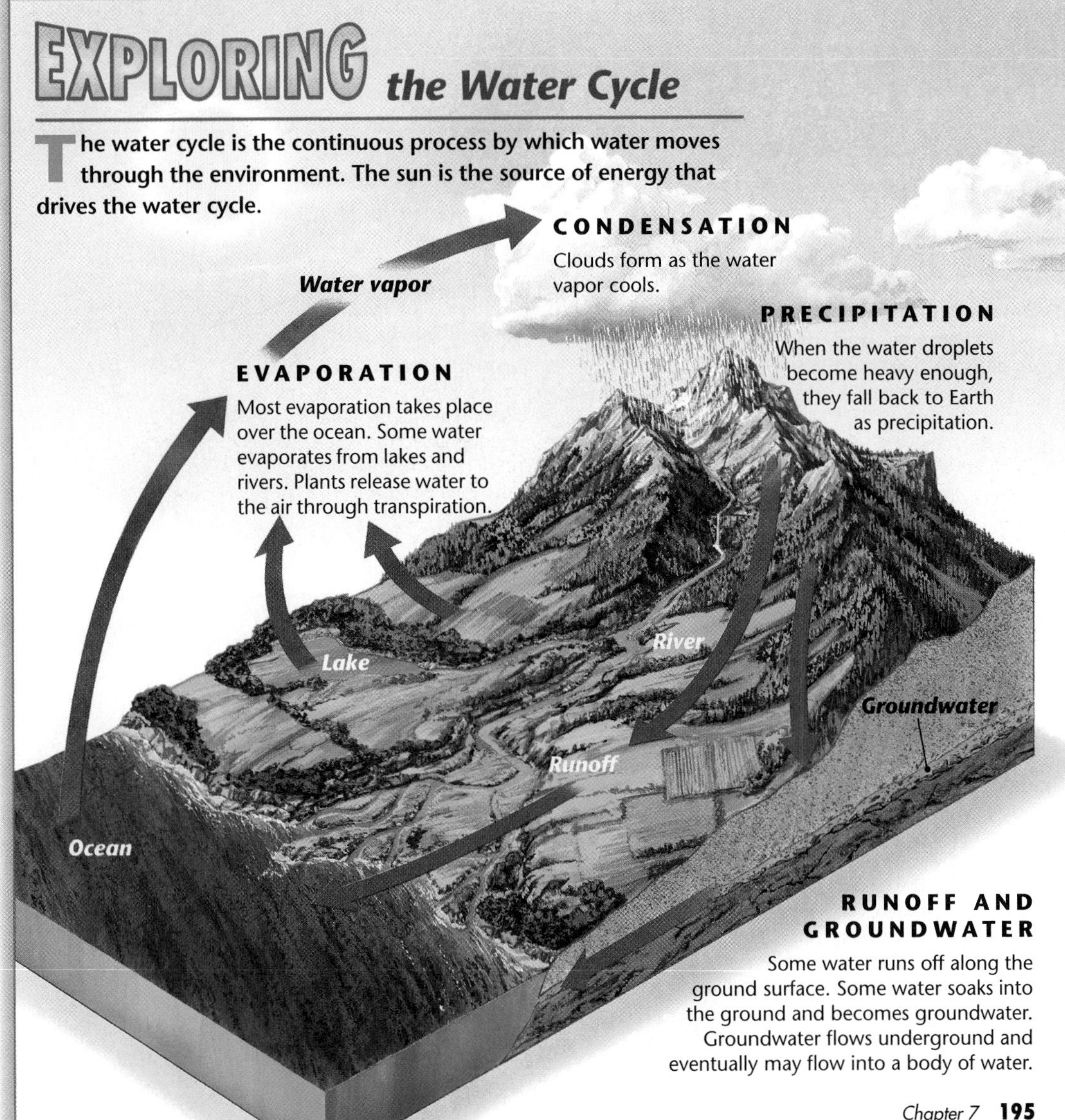

Media and Technology

Transparencies "Exploring the Water Cycle," Transparency 21

Answers to Self-Assessment

☑ *Checkpoint*

Water evaporates from oceans, lakes, and rivers.

EXPLORING the Water Cycle

After students have examined the illustration, ask: **What are the three processes in the water cycle?** *(Evaporation, condensation, and precipitation)* **Which process begins the cycle?** *(Students might mention evaporation, because that is the first shown on the illustration).* Help students understand that a cycle has no beginning or no end, and that one process is no more important than the others. Point out that the water cycle is continuous and has been continuous for billions of years. **learning modality: visual**

Real-Life Learning

To make students aware of where water is found in your local area, give each student an outline map of your state. Then ask students to draw and label any ocean and the major rivers and lakes that are found there. Provide access to almanacs and atlases, and give students one or two days to complete their maps. **learning modality: kinesthetic**

Portfolio Students can save their maps in their portfolios.

Ongoing Assessment

Skills Check Have each student make a cycle diagram that shows the steps in the water cycle.

How Do People Use Water?

SCIENCE & History

Invite student volunteers to read aloud to the class the annotations to the time line. Have a world map available for students to use to locate the various sites. For each method of irrigation, encourage students to draw conclusions about the environment in which it was used and how well the technology worked. Ask: **Do you think all these methods are used somewhere in the world today?** *(Students' responses will vary. Each method is still used today at some place.)*

In Your Journal Give students time to research one of the irrigation techniques discussed in the feature. Students can find out more about the techniques by looking under *irrigation* in an encyclopedia or by doing a library computer search for *irrigation* or *agriculture* and for the various countries listed in the feature. Once students have written their letters, encourage volunteers to read theirs aloud to the class. **learning modality: verbal**

Students can save their letters in their portfolios.

Cultural Diversity

ACTIVITY

Note for students that *paddy* is the Malay word for wet rice. The growing of wet rice, or paddy farming, provides the staple food in much of China and Southeast Asia. Ask some students to prepare a report to the class on this agricultural method, complete with pictures and a flow chart showing the process. **cooperative learning**

How Do People Use Water?

The water people use at home is just a small percentage of all the water used in the United States. **In addition to household purposes, people use water for agriculture, industry, transportation, and recreation.**

Agriculture Has your family ever had a garden? If so, you know that growing fruits and vegetables requires water. On a large farm, a constant supply of fresh water is essential.

However, some parts of the United States don't receive enough regular rainfall for agriculture. In such areas, farmland must be irrigated. **Irrigation** is the process of supplying water to areas of land to make them suitable for growing crops. In the United States, more water is used for irrigating farmland than for any other single purpose.

Water and Agriculture

Plants require a steady supply of water to grow. How have farmers throughout history provided their crops with water? This time line shows some methods developed in different parts of the world.

2000 B.C. Egypt

Egyptian farmers invented a way to raise water from the Nile River. The device, called a *shaduf,* acted as a lever to make lifting a bucket of water easier. The farmers then emptied the water into a network of canals to irrigate their fields. The *shaduf* is still in use in Egypt, India, and other countries.

3000 B.C. | 2000 B.C. | 1000 B.C.

3000 B.C. China

One of the oldest known methods of irrigation was developed for growing rice. Farmers built paddies, or artificial ponds with raised edges. The farmers flooded the paddies with water from a nearby stream. This ancient technique is still widely used throughout Southeast Asia.

700 B.C. Assyria

Sennacherib, king of the ancient nation Assyria, surrounded the capital city of Nineveh with fruit trees, cotton, and exotic plants. To help irrigate the plantations, he built a 10-kilometer canal and a stone aqueduct to transport water from the nearby hills.

Background

Facts and Figures In the early twentieth century, the settlers of the Great Plains used windmills to provide the water to irrigate their crops. But most of those windmills could raise water less than 10 m. With the advent of deep-well drilling and modern pumps, farmers of the 1930s began to reach groundwater much deeper underground. Modern farmers on the Great Plains no longer use ditches in irrigating their fields. That method loses too much water to evaporation, seepage, and runoff—50–60 percent of the total. Instead, many farmers use center-pivot sprinkler systems. The water is pumped underground in pipes to a central pivot and then out through a long, turning "boom" with sprinklers along its length. The result is a circular field of crops. The center-pivot method wastes only 20–30 percent of the water.

Industry Think about the objects in a typical school locker. Did you know that water is needed to produce all these objects? Even though water is not part of the final products, it plays a role in the industrial processes that created them.

Industries use water in many other ways. For example, power plants and steel mills both need huge volumes of water to cool down hot machinery. Water that is used for cooling can often be recycled, or used again for another purpose.

Transportation Oceans and rivers have been used for transporting people and goods since ancient times. If you look at a map of the United States, you will notice that many large cities are located on the coasts. Ocean travel led to the growth of such port cities. In early America, rivers also served as natural highways.

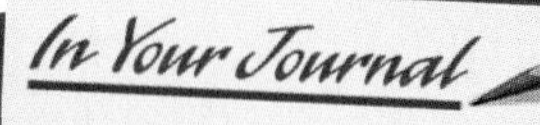

Find out more about one of these agricultural techniques. Imagine that you are a farmer seeing the method in action for the first time. Write a letter to a friend describing the new technique. What problem will it solve? How will it improve your farming?

A.D. 1870 United States

When homesteaders arrived on the dry Great Plains of the central United States, they had to rely on water stored underground. Windmills provided the energy to pump the groundwater to the surface. The farmers dug ditches to carry the water to irrigate their fields.

A.D. 1 | A.D. 1000 | A.D. 2000

A.D. 500 Mexico

To grow crops in areas covered by swampy lakes, the Aztecs built raised plots of farmland called *chinampas*. They grew maize on fertile soil scooped from the lake bottom. A grid of canals kept the crops wet and allowed the farmers to navigate boats between the *chinampas*.

Present Israel

Irrigation is the key to survival in desert regions. Today, methods such as drip irrigation ensure that very little water is wasted when crops are watered. Holes in the pipe allow water to drip directly onto the soil around the roots of each plant.

Real-Life Learning

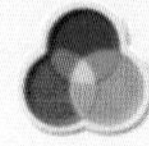

Use magazine pictures of examples of water used in agriculture, household purposes, industry, transportation, and recreation as a starting point for students to brainstorm a list of uses under each category. Then divide the class into five groups, assigning each to one of the five categories. Group members can then work together to make a list of uses in their category and find pictures of those uses in old magazines. Volunteers from each group can then collaborate to prepare a bulletin board that illustrates the five categories of water use. **cooperative learning**

Water and Living Things

Integrating Life Science

To help students better understand water's importance to living things, write these words on the board: *carbon dioxide, food, oxygen, water.* Explain that oxygen is another product of photosynthesis. Then challenge students to write an equation in words that expresses what occurs in photosynthesis. *(carbon dioxide* + *water* = *food* + *oxygen)* Help students understand that the "food" created is in the form of certain molecules (sugars and starches) that plants and other organisms can break down to obtain energy. Ask: **What is one reason a plant dies if it cannot get enough water?** *(It cannot carry out photosynthesis without water, and therefore cannot make food for itself.)* **learning modality: visual**

Ongoing Assessment

Oral Presentation Call on students at random to assess whether they understand the six types of irrigation shown in the Science & History feature. Ask them to explain each method in their own words.

3 Assess

Section 1 Review Answers

1. Most fresh water is found in the huge masses of ice near the poles.
2. Liquid water evaporates from Earth's surface to become water vapor. Clouds form as water vapor rises and cools. Water droplets condense, and then fall back to Earth as precipitation. That water eventually evaporates again, continuing the process.
3. Precipitation is the source of all fresh water on and below Earth's surface. The water cycle renews the supply of fresh water on Earth because when water evaporates, impurities, such as salt, are left behind.
4. The major uses are for household purposes, agriculture, industry, transportation, and recreation.
5. Cutting down trees would reduce the amount of evaporation in an area because trees draw in water from the soil and give it off as water vapor in the process of transpiration.

CHAPTER PROJECT

Check Your Progress

As you review students' drawings, check for their overall understanding. Ask: **Do tributaries flow toward or away from the main river?** *(toward it)* **Are tributaries lower or higher than the main river?** *(higher)* Help them evaluate their choice of materials for cost and practicality.

Performance Assessment

Oral Presentation Divide the class into small groups and challenge each group to list ways people use water locally for one of the water-use categories in the text and report to the class.

Water Used in the Home

Task	Water Used (liters)
Showering for 5 minutes	95
Brushing teeth	10
Washing hands	7.5
Flushing standard toilet	23
Flushing "low-flow" toilet	6
Washing one load of laundry	151
Running dishwasher	19
Washing dishes by hand	114

Figure 2 Many common household activities involve water.

Recreation Do you like to swim in a neighborhood pool? Catch fish from a rowboat in the middle of a lake? Walk along a beach collecting seashells? Or maybe just sit on the edge of a dock and dangle your feet in the water? Then you know some ways that water is used for recreation. And if you brave the winter cold to ski, snowboard, or skate, you are enjoying water in its frozen form.

☑ *Checkpoint* *List an agricultural use, an industrial use, and a household use of water that you relied on today.*

Water and Living Things

INTEGRATING LIFE SCIENCE Here's a riddle for you: What do you and an apple have in common? You both consist mostly of water! In fact, water is a large part of every living thing. Water makes up nearly two thirds of your body. That water is necessary to keep your body functioning.

Water is essential for living things to grow, reproduce, and carry out other important processes. For example, plants use water, plus carbon dioxide and energy from the sun, to make food in a process called **photosynthesis** (foh toh SIN thuh sis). Animals and many other living things depend on the food made by plants. They may eat the plants directly or eat other organisms that eat plants.

Another way that living things use water is as a home. An organism's **habitat** is the place where it lives and that provides the things it needs to survive. Both fresh water and salt water provide habitats for many different types of living things.

Section 1 Review

1. Where is most of the fresh water on Earth found?
2. Describe the general path of water as it moves through the water cycle.
3. How does the water cycle renew Earth's supply of fresh water?
4. What are five major ways that people in the United States use water?
5. **Thinking Critically Relating Cause and Effect** How might cutting down trees affect the amount of evaporation in an area?

CHAPTER PROJECT

Check Your Progress

Begin sketching your model watershed. How will you shape the land to form the main river and tributary? What materials would be easy to shape and allow runoff to occur? Use the sketch to help estimate amounts of materials you will need. (*Hint:* Decide what to use as a base for your model. Draw your sketch on a piece of paper the same size as the base.)

Program Resources

◆ **Unit 3 Resources** 7-1 Review and Reinforce; 7-1 Enrich

Answers to Self-Assessment

☑ *Checkpoint*

Students' responses will vary. A typical response might mention irrigation or watering for an agricultural use, the making of paper for an industrial use, and taking a shower for a household use.

You and Your Environment

Water From Trees

Real-World Lab

Trees play many important roles in the environment—they keep the soil from washing away, remove carbon dioxide from the air, and produce oxygen. Trees are also a vital part of the water cycle. In this lab you will discover how trees help to keep water moving through the cycle.

Problem

How much water do the leaves on a tree give off in a 24-hour period?

Skills Focus

observing, calculating, inferring

Materials

3 plastic sandwich bags
3 small pebbles
balance
3 twist ties

Procedure 

1. Copy the data table into your notebook.
2. Place the sandwich bags, twist ties, and pebbles on a balance. Determine their total mass to the nearest tenth of a gram.
3. Select an outdoor tree or shrub with leaves that are within your reach.
4. Put one pebble into a sandwich bag and place the bag over one of the tree's leaves as shown. Fasten the twist tie around the bag, forming a tight seal around the stem of the leaf.
5. Repeat Step 4 with the other plastic bags on two more leaves. Leave the bags in place on the leaves for 24 hours.
6. The following day, examine the bags and record your observations in your notebook.

DATA TABLE

Starting mass of bags, ties, and pebbles	
Mass of bags, ties, and pebbles after 24 hours	
Difference in mass	

7. Carefully remove the bags from the leaves and refasten each twist tie around its bag so that the bag is closed tightly.
8. Place the three bags, including pebbles and twist ties, on the balance. Determine their total mass to the nearest tenth of a gram.
9. Subtract the original mass of the bags, ties, and pebbles that you found in Step 2 from the mass you found in Step 8.

Analyze and Conclude

1. Based on your observations, how can you account for the difference in mass?
2. What is the name of the process that caused the results you observed? Explain the role of that process in the water cycle.
3. A single birch tree may transpire as much as 260 liters of water in a day. How much water would a grove of 1,000 birch trees return to the atmosphere in a year?
4. **Apply** Based on what you learned from this investigation, what is one reason that people may be concerned about the destruction of forests around the world?

More to Explore

Find another type of tree and repeat this experiment. What might account for any differences in the amount of water the two trees transpire?

Sample Data Table

Starting mass of bags, ties, and pebbles	Mass of bags, ties, and pebbles after 24 hours	Difference in mass
41.3 g	42.9 g	1.6 g

Safety

Caution students to avoid plants such as poison ivy and poison oak. Instruct them to carry out the activity in secure, familiar places. Review the safety guidelines in Appendix A.

Media and Technology

 **Lab Activity Videotapes**
Grade 6, Tape 2

Program Resources

- **Unit 3 Resources** Chapter 7 Real-World Lab blackline master

Real-World Lab

You and Your Environment

Water From Trees

Preparing for Inquiry

Key Concept Plants play an important role in the water cycle through the process of transpiration.

Skills Objectives Students will be able to
- observe the product of transpiration in leaves;
- calculate the mass of the water transpired by leaves in 24 hours;
- infer the important role plants play in the water cycle.

Time 20 minutes for setup; 20 minutes the next day for completion

Advance Planning Ask volunteers to scout around the school for trees or shrubs with large leaves. Make a rough map of the locations of these plants and assign groups to them by writing students' names on the map.

Alternative Materials If no trees or shrubs are available, potted plants such as geraniums can be used in the classroom.

Guiding Inquiry

Invitation To give the lab a context, ask: **How are trees part of the water cycle?** *(Trees draw in water from the soil and give it off as water vapor through the process of transpiration.)* If necessary, review the process of transpiration.

Introducing the Procedure

Have students read through the complete procedure. Then ask: **What is the purpose of determining the mass of the bags, ties, and pebbles in Step 2?** *(Determining that mass provides a basis for comparison after leaving the bags on the leaves for 24 hours.)* **Why should you be sure to make a tight seal around the stem of each leaf?** *(Making a tight seal ensures that nothing can get into or out of the bag during the 24 hours.)*

Water on the Surface

Objectives

After completing the lesson, students will be able to

- ◆ describe a river system and how water flows into it;
- ◆ identify conditions that cause floods and how floods can be controlled;
- ◆ explain how ponds and lakes form;
- ◆ describe pond and lake habitats and the process of lake turnover;
- ◆ explain how icebergs are formed and why they are dangerous to ships.

Key Terms tributary, watershed, divide, levee, reservoir, eutrophication

1 Engage/Explore

Activating Prior Knowledge

Encourage students to describe some of the lakes and ponds they have seen. Ask questions such as, **How large is the lake?** and **What types of plants and animals live in or around it?**

DISCOVER ACTIVITY

Skills Focus classifying
Materials *pond water, plastic petri dish, hand lens, microscope, plastic dropper, slide and cover slip*
Time 20 minutes
Tips Collect water from a local pond, making sure you obtain some bottom mud and suspended particles. (As an alternative, you can prepare a hay infusion or use prepared slides.) *To prepare the slide:* Use a plastic dropper to place a drop of pond water on the slide. Hold one edge of the cover slip on the slide and drag it toward the water drop. Slowly let down the slip's other edge to avoid trapping air bubbles.
Expected Outcome Students should see larger organisms with the hand lens and a greater variety with the microscope.
Think It Over Students could use movement or the consumption of smaller particles as criteria for deciding whether items are alive. Students should recognize that pond water contains a variety of living and nonliving things.

SECTION 2 Water on the Surface

DISCOVER ACTIVITY

What's in Pond Water?

1. Using a hand lens, observe a sample of pond water.

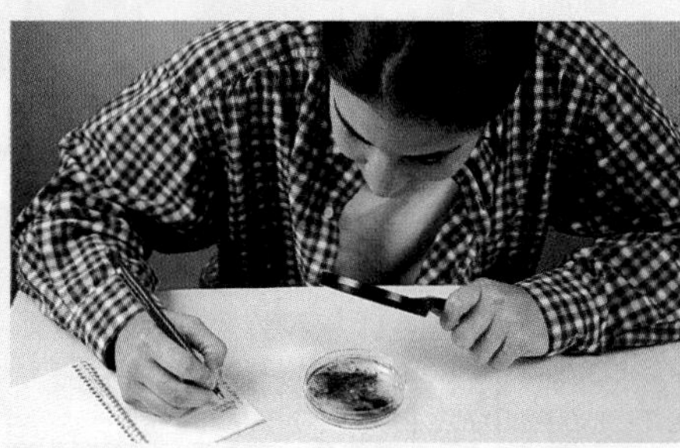

2. Make a list of everything you see in the water. If you don't know the name of something, write a short description or draw a picture.
3. Your teacher has set up a microscope with a slide of pond water. Observe the slide and add any new items to your list. Wash your hands with soap when you are done.

Think It Over

Classifying Use one of these systems to divide the items on your list into two groups: moving/still, living/nonliving, or microscopic/visible without a microscope. What does your classification system tell you about pond water?

GUIDE FOR READING

- ◆ What is a river system?
- ◆ What conditions can cause a flood?
- ◆ How do ponds and lakes form?

Reading Tip Before you read, use the section headings to make an outline. Leave space to take notes as you read.

Standing on a bridge in Albuquerque, New Mexico, you look through your binoculars at the waters of the Rio Grande—the "Big River." The name fits this broad, deep stretch of water. But 700 kilometers upstream, the Rio Grande looks very different. The river begins as trickles of melting snow high in the San Juan Mountains in Colorado. As more water joins the river, it carves deep, narrow canyons out of the rock.

By the time it reaches Albuquerque the river has grown wider. It continues into Texas, winding back and forth across the dusty desert valley. In places, the river is so shallow that it may even dry up during the summer. When the Rio Grande finally empties into the Gulf of Mexico, it is sluggish and heavy with mud.

River Systems

If you were hiking in the San Juan Mountains, you could observe the path of the runoff from melting snow. As you followed one small stream downhill, you would notice that the stream reached a larger stream and joined it. You could then continue along this stream until it flowed into a small river. Eventually this path would lead you to the Rio Grande itself.

Tributaries are the smaller streams and rivers that feed into a main river. **A river and all its tributaries together make up a river system.** The tributaries flow toward the main river following a downhill path due to the pull of gravity.

READING STRATEGIES

Reading Tip On the chalkboard, write *I. River Systems.* Then ask volunteers to find the two headings that would be under this main heading. Student outlines may begin as follows:

I. River Systems
  A. Watersheds
  B. Divides
II. River and Floods

Program Resources

- ◆ **Unit 4 Resources** 7-2 Lesson Plan; 7-2 Summary
- ◆ **Guided Reading and Study Workbook** Section 7-2

Watersheds Just as all the water in a bathtub flows toward the drain, all the water in a river system drains into the main river. The land area that supplies water to a river system is called a **watershed.** Watersheds are also called drainage basins.

A river can flow into another, larger river. When rivers join another river system, the areas they drain become part of the largest river's watershed. You can identify a river's watershed on a map by drawing an imaginary line around the region drained by all its tributaries. Some watersheds are very small. As you can see, the watershed of the Mississippi River is huge. It covers more than 3 million square kilometers!

Virginia's Watersheds As you can see in Figure 4 on the next page, Virginia has many watersheds. The largest is the James River Watershed, which stretches from Chesapeake Bay to Virginia's border with West Virginia. In addition to the James River, this watershed includes the Appomattox River, Maury River, Jackson River, and Rivanna River.

The Yadkin Watershed is the smallest of Virginia's watersheds. Although the map shows how Virginia is divided into different watersheds, it does not show the extension of these watersheds into other states. More of the Yadkin Watershed is in North Carolina.

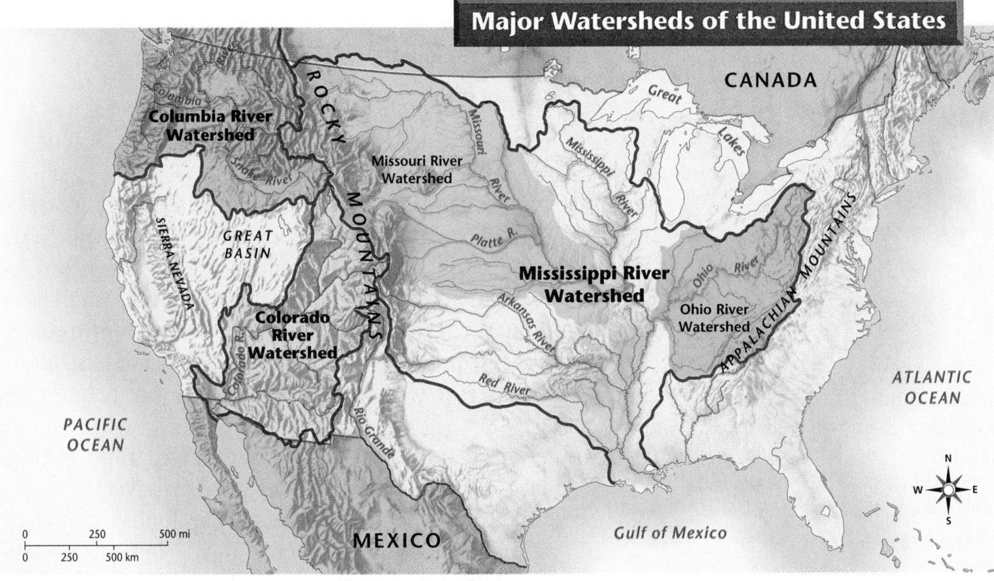

Figure 3 This map shows the watersheds of several large rivers in the United States.
Interpreting Maps Name four tributaries of the Mississippi River. Which tributary has the largest watershed?

Answers to Self-Assessment

Caption Question

Figure 3 Four tributaries of the Mississippi are the Missouri, Arkansas, Red, and Ohio rivers. The Missouri River has the largest watershed.

☑ Checkpoint

Rivers east of the Appalachian Mountains flow into the Atlantic Ocean.

2 Facilitate

River Systems

Using the Visuals: Figure 3

Point out that the map on this page shows *geographic* features such as rivers and mountains, not *political* features such as states, cities, and roads. Display a large political map of the United States. Choose volunteers to come to the large map and locate the rivers and mountain ranges shown on the text map. Ask: **What function do the Rocky Mountains and the Appalachian Mountains play in the major U.S. watersheds?** *(They are the major divides that separate these watersheds.)* Also encourage students to locate on the large map major rivers that are not labeled on the text map—for example, the Connecticut, Hudson, James, Savannah, Rio Grande, and Sacramento rivers—and try to identify their possible watersheds. Ask: **Is our area in any of these rivers' watersheds? Which river?** *(Answers will vary depending on your location.)* **learning modality: visual**

TRY THIS

Skills Focus making models
Materials *paper towel, water, spoon*
Time 10 minutes
Tips Advise students to dribble the water *slowly* and to make sure it falls on the *tops* of their knuckles, not on either side.
Expected Outcome The water will flow from the tops of the knuckles to the hollows between them and to the back of the hand on one side and the spaces between the fingers on the other side. The knuckles are similar to a mountain range in that the water flows downward from them in different directions on two sides. The back of the hand and the fingers represent two different watersheds, and the knuckles represent a divide. **learning modality: kinesthetic**

Ongoing Assessment

Writing Have students briefly describe the terms *watershed* and *divide* in their own words.

River Systems, continued

Using the Visuals: Figure 4

Ask students to look at Figure 4 and identify the watershed in which they live. Then, have students look back at Figure 3. Ask students to identify the divide between the Ohio River Watershed and several of Virginia's watersheds. *(Appalachian Mountains)*

River and Floods

Real-Life Learning

Students who have been personally affected by other floods (such as the Midwest floods of 1997 or flooding in California and the Southeast due to the heavy rains caused by El Niño of 1997-1998) may be uneasy or even upset by the text descriptions on this page and the next. First concentrate objectively on the physical causes of flooding described in the text. Then go on to discuss the safety precautions that should be followed in the event of a flood. Pamphlets with flood-safety guidelines may be available from your state or regional Red Cross chapter or FEMA (Federal Emergency Management Agency) office. Try to obtain such pamphlets for students to review. If students live in a flood-prone area, encourage them to copy the precautions to take home and review with their family members. **learning modality: verbal**

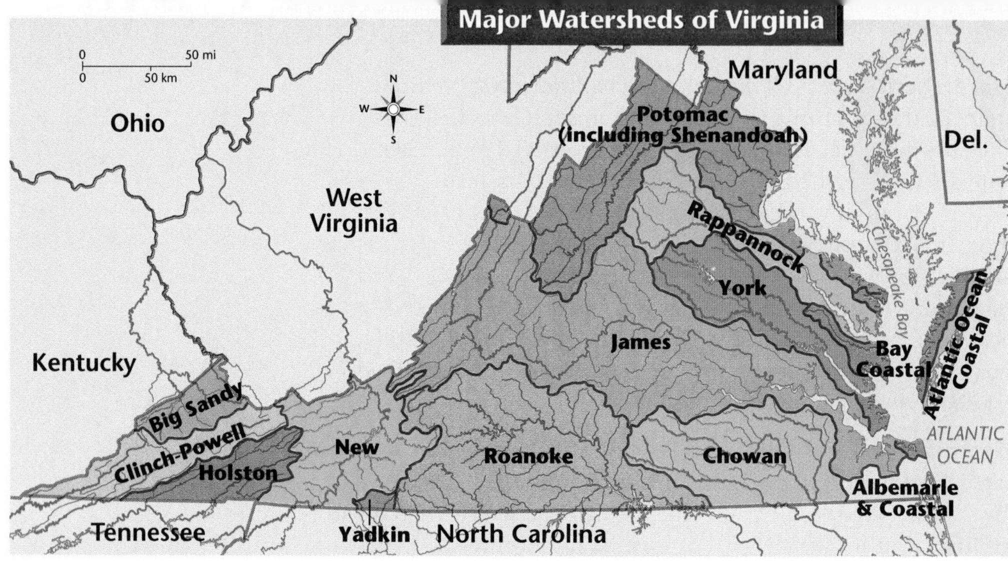

Figure 4 This map shows the main watersheds of Virginia.

Divides One watershed is separated from another by a ridge of land called a **divide.** Streams on each side of the divide flow in different directions. The Continental Divide, the longest divide in North America, follows the line of the Rocky Mountains. West of the Continental Divide, water either flows toward the Pacific Ocean or into the dry Great Basin. Between the Rocky Mountains and the Appalachian Mountains, water flows toward the Mississippi River or directly into the Gulf of Mexico.

☑ *Checkpoint What is a watershed?*

The Knuckle Divide

ACTIVITY

Make your hand into a fist and put it on a paper towel, knuckles facing up. With your other hand, dribble water from a spoon so that it falls onto your knuckles. Observe how the water flows over your hand.

Making a Model How are your knuckles similar to a mountain range on land? What parts of your hand represent a watershed?

Rivers and Floods

A flood occurs when the volume of water in a river increases so much that the river overflows its channel. When heavy rains add more and more water to a river, the river gains speed and strength. Recall that as the speed of a river increases, so does the amount of energy it has. A flooding river can uproot trees and pluck boulders from the ground. As it overflows onto its floodplain, the powerful water can even wash away bridges and houses.

Throughout history, people have both feared and welcomed floods. Ancient Egyptians, for instance, called their fertile cropland "the gift of the Nile." Deposition from regular floods left a layer of rich soil on each side of the river, creating a green strip of good land in the middle of the desert. But floods can also destroy farms, towns, and crops. In the last century, floods have killed millions of people around the world, many of them in the heavily populated flood plains of China, Bangladesh, and India.

Background

Facts and Figures The Red River flooded and devastated parts of North Dakota and Minnesota in the spring of 1997 due to a combination of factors. Throughout the previous winter, 13 massive storms had buried the area with record snowfalls. When the spring thaw arrived, unusually high temperatures melted the snow in days, causing rapid runoff into the Red River and its tributaries. Levees protected some towns but worsened flooding in other towns downriver.

The Red River's valley is one of the flattest on Earth, which allows floodwaters to spread out extensively. In one area close to the Canadian border, the river overflowed its 55-m channel to stretch nearly *65 km* across its valley.

The Red River flows north into Canada. Ice jams in the north slowed water flow, causing river levels to swell further.

Can Floods Be Controlled?

Integrating Technology For as long as people have lived on flood plains, they have tried to control floods. Building dams is one method of flood control. A dam is a barrier across a river that may redirect the flow of a river to other channels or store the water in an artificial lake. Engineers can open the dam's floodgates to release water in dry seasons. Dams work fairly well to control small floods. During severe floods, however, powerful flood waters can wash over the top of a dam or break through it.

Figure 5 These people are working together to protect their community during a flood. *Applying Concepts How do sandbags help control flooding?*

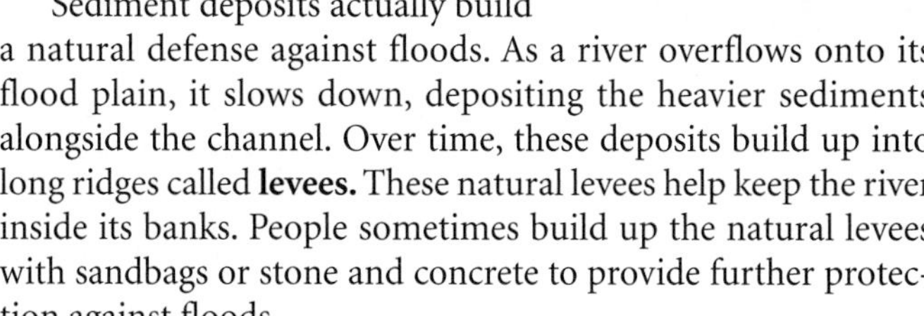

Sediment deposits actually build a natural defense against floods. As a river overflows onto its flood plain, it slows down, depositing the heavier sediments alongside the channel. Over time, these deposits build up into long ridges called **levees.** These natural levees help keep the river inside its banks. People sometimes build up the natural levees with sandbags or stone and concrete to provide further protection against floods.

But building up levees can sometimes backfire. These walls prevent the natural channel-widening process that rivers normally undergo as their volume increases. As a result, during a flood, the water has nowhere to go except downstream. Although built-up levees can work well to prevent small floods, they often make heavy flooding worse for areas farther downstream. The full power of the surge of flood water is passed on to flood the downstream areas.

Bodies of Fresh Water

While water in streams and rivers is always on the move, the water in lakes and ponds is still, or standing, water. Although there is no definite rule to determine whether a body of water is called a pond or a lake, ponds are generally smaller and shallower than lakes. Sunlight usually reaches to the bottom of all parts of a pond. Most lakes have parts where the water is too deep for sunlight to reach all the way to the bottom.

Ponds and lakes form when water collects in hollows and low-lying areas of land. Rainfall, melting snow and ice, and runoff supply water to ponds and lakes. Others are fed by rivers or groundwater. Eventually, water may flow out of a pond or lake into a river, or evaporate from its surface.

Can Floods Be Controlled?

Integrating Technology

Have each group of students set up a stream trough or a long, high-sided tray with a 6-cm-deep layer of mixed sand, gravel, and small pebbles on the bottom. Instruct students to create a narrow, slightly curving river channel about 4 cm deep into the layers. With the trough or tray at a fairly steep angle, students should pour a steady stream of water into the upper end of the river. Ask students: **Does the water stay within the channel?** *(yes)* **What would happen if you had poured more water more quickly?** *(The channel would overflow, causing a flood.)* Invite students to repeat the activity, this time using clay to build levees along the upper and middle sections of the river and pouring more water into the upper end to simulate flood conditions. Ask: **What happened when the water reached the levees?** *(The water flowed downstream, but the water level was very high. Some students may see floods in upper sections if the levee breaks.)* **What happened when the water reached the part of the river that had no levees?** *(The land became flooded.)* **learning modality: kinesthetic**

Bodies of Fresh Water

Real-Life Learning

If there are lakes or ponds in your area, invite volunteers to describe these bodies of water and, if possible, identify the source or sources of water in them.

Answers to Self-Assessment

Caption Questions

Figure 5 Sandbags increase the height of the sides of the river channel, enabling it to hold a larger volume of water.

Ongoing Assessment

Writing Have each student summarize, in a two-column format, the hazards and benefits of flooding described in the text, adding others they think of on their own.

EXPLORING a Pond

After students have read the text in the visual essay, ask: **What are some different habitats that are described?** *(The shore, the shallow water near shore, the bottom of the pond, the surface, and the deeper waters)* Encourage volunteers to summarize how conditions vary in the different habitats. Also encourage students to name other pond organisms they know from personal experience or their reading. **learning modality: verbal**

Building Inquiry Skills: Comparing and Contrasting

Materials *pond algae, pond plants, hand lens*
Time 10 minutes

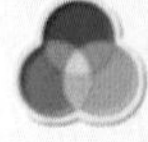

Provide specimens of common pond algae, such as *Spirogyra* or *Cladophora,* and plants, such as pondweeds, for students to examine. Then ask: **How are the algae and plants different?** *(The plants have stems, leaves, and roots, whereas the algae do not have any similar structures.)* **How are they alike?** *(They both are green and able to carry out photosynthesis.)* Emphasize that plants and algae are vital to pond habitats because they produce food and oxygen through photosynthesis. **learning modality: visual**

Integrating Life Science

Point out the text information about temporary ponds that appear in the spring and dry up in the summer. Then ask: **What types of organisms could find temporary homes in a spring pond?** *(Frogs, birds, flying insects, and other animals that could leave the pond when it dried up; plants whose seeds could survive dry conditions)* **What is the importance of temporary ponds?** *(They provide habitats for organisms that require water during part of their lifecycles.)* **learning modality: logical/ mathematical**

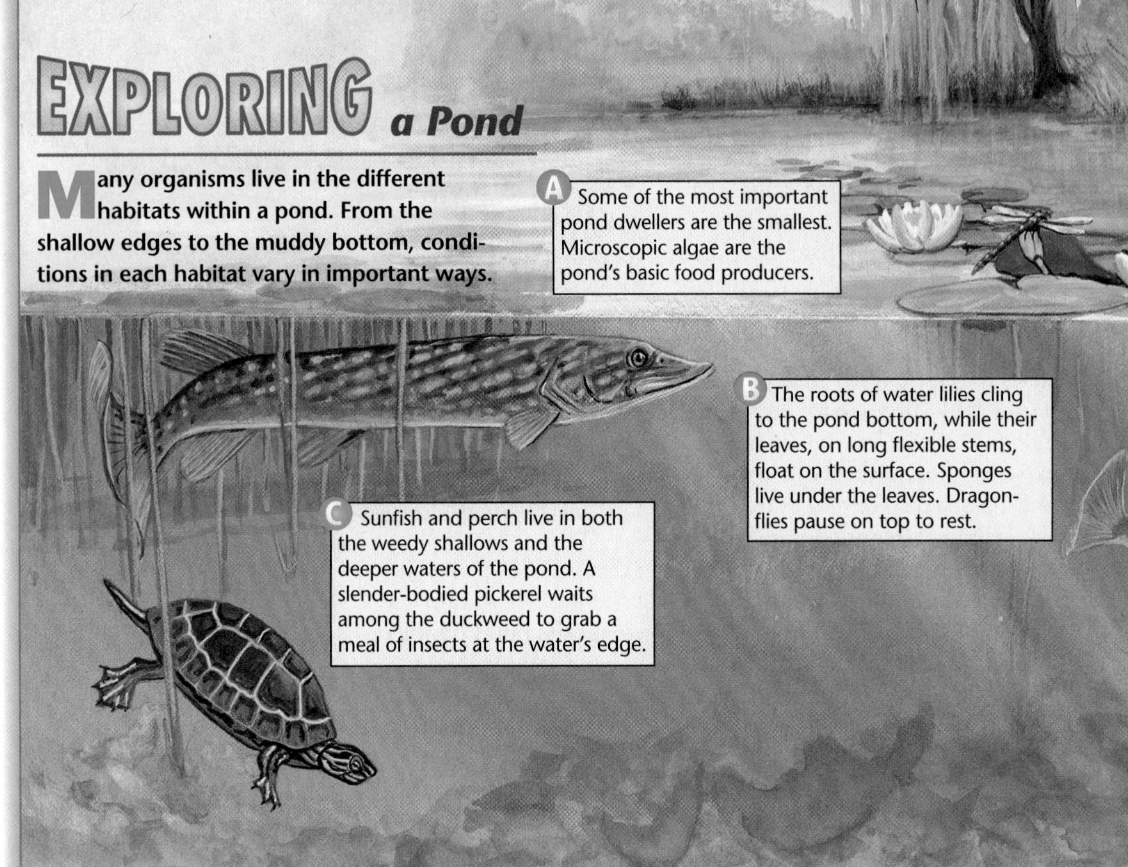

EXPLORING a Pond

Many organisms live in the different habitats within a pond. From the shallow edges to the muddy bottom, conditions in each habitat vary in important ways.

A Some of the most important pond dwellers are the smallest. Microscopic algae are the pond's basic food producers.

B The roots of water lilies cling to the pond bottom, while their leaves, on long flexible stems, float on the surface. Sponges live under the leaves. Dragonflies pause on top to rest.

C Sunfish and perch live in both the weedy shallows and the deeper waters of the pond. A slender-bodied pickerel waits among the duckweed to grab a meal of insects at the water's edge.

Ponds

INTEGRATING LIFE SCIENCE

Compared to a tumbling mountain stream, a pond seems still and peaceful at first glance. Silvery minnows glide smoothly below the surface. A dragonfly touches the water, then whirs away. Lily pads with broad, green leaves and waxy, white blossoms float on the surface. This quiet pond is actually a thriving habitat, supporting a wide diversity of living things.

If you have ever waded in a pond, you know that the muddy bottom is often covered with weeds. Because the water is shallow enough for sunlight to reach the bottom, plants grow throughout a pond. Plantlike organisms called algae also live in the pond. As the plants and algae use sunlight to make food through photosynthesis, they also produce oxygen. Animals in the pond use the oxygen and food provided by plants and algae. You can see some common pond organisms in *Exploring a Pond.*

Background

Integrating Science Lakes and ponds are characterized by specific zones. Lakes have three major zones (see Background, page 206); ponds have two.

The shallow water along the edge of a pond is called the *littoral zone.* More photosynthesis occurs in the littoral zone than anywhere else in the pond, partly because nutrients wash into the pond from the land and feed the algae and plants there.

The open water away from the shore is called the *limnetic zone.* Free-floating photosynthetic bacteria and algae and animallike protists inhabit the limnetic zone, as well as animals, such as fish.

Not all ponds exist year-round. For example, some ponds in the northern and western United States appear only in the spring, when runoff from spring rains and melting snow collects in low areas. The ponds dry up by midsummer as the shallow water quickly evaporates in the heat.

Ponds in colder climates often freeze over during the winter. Ice floats because it is less dense than liquid water. As a result, ice forms on the surface of the pond, while the living things survive in the liquid water below.

☑ *Checkpoint* *Why can plants grow throughout a pond?*

Lakes

Suppose you suddenly found yourself on a sandy beach. Waves break on the shore. The water stretches as far as your eye can see. Gulls screech overhead. Where are you? Although you might think you're at the ocean, this immense body of water could

Lakes

Including All Students

Materials *cup of water, ice cube*
Time 5–10 minutes

Give each student a small cup of water and an ice cube. Ask students to predict what will happen when they put the ice cube in the cup. *(The cube will float.)* Let students test their predictions. Then ask: **What would have happened if ice were more dense than water?** *(The cube would have sunk to the bottom of the cup.)* **How does the lower density of ice enable lake organisms to survive through the winter?** *(Ice that forms on the lake's surface floats on the water, and shields the organisms in the water below from the cold.)*
learning modality: logical/ mathematical

Answers to Self-Assessment

☑ *Checkpoint*

The water in a pond is shallow enough so that sunlight reaches all areas.

Ongoing Assessment

Oral Presentation Have students pretend to be one of the organisms that lives in a pond and describe their habitat and activities.

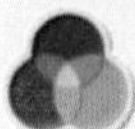

Integrating Life Science

To help students understand the complex relationships among organisms in a lake habitat, ask: **What feeding relationships are identified in the text?** *(Loons and kingfishers eat fish; worms and mollusks feed on food particles that drift down; large, bony fish eat tiny bottom dwellers and fish and birds at the surface.)* **Why are plants and algae important to a lake habitat?** *(They carry out photosynthesis, which produces food and oxygen that other organisms depend on.)* Challenge students to draw a food chain that illustrates one set of feeding relationships that exists in a lake habitat. **learning modality: visual**

Changes in a Lake

Demonstration

Materials *large beaker, cold water, warm water, food coloring, spoon, ice*
Time 10 minutes

Make a working model of lake turnover so students can observe this process. First, fill the beaker about two thirds full of cold water. Tint the warm water with food coloring, and then hold the spoon directly over the cold water and slowly pour the warm water onto the spoon so that it flows gently into the beaker. The warm, tinted water should form a layer on top of the cold water. Next, float ice cubes in the water. The ice will cool the warm water, causing it to sink and mix with the cold water. Ask: **How is this model like lake turnover?** *(Like the model, when the warmer, top layer of a lake cools in the fall, it sinks and causes the waters of the lake to mix together.)* **How does lake turnover cause the minerals and other nutrients to be mixed through the lake?** *(When the warm layer cools and sinks, it pushes up minerals and other nutrients from the lake bottom, causing them to mix through the water.)* **learning modality: visual**

Figure 6 Standing water is found in lakes and ponds. **A.** The cold waters of Crater Lake in Oregon fill the hollow of an ancient volcano. **B.** Water lilies float in a Colorado pond. ***Interpreting Photographs*** *In which of these bodies of water does sunlight reach the bottom? Give evidence to support your answer.*

actually be a lake! You could be on a beach in Indiana, on the shore of Lake Michigan.

Although most lakes are not as large as Lake Michigan, they are generally bigger and deeper than ponds. Most lakes are deep enough that sunlight does not reach all the way to the bottom. A lake bottom may consist of sand, pebbles, or rock. The bottom of a pond is usually covered with mud and algae.

Lake Formation Lakes form in many ways. For example, a cut-off river meander may become an oxbow lake. Ice sheets that melted at the end of the Ice Age created depressions that became lakes. Some lakes were created by movements of Earth's crust. Such movements created the deep valleys in central Africa that lie below Lake Tanganyika and Lake Victoria. Other lakes are the result of volcanoes. An erupting volcano can cause a flow of lava or mud that blocks a river and forms a lake. Some lakes, like the one in Figure 6, form in the empty craters of volcanoes.

People can also create a lake by building a dam across a river. The lake may be used for supplying drinking water, for irrigating fields, and for boating and fishing. A lake that stores water for human use is called a **reservoir.** One of the largest reservoirs in the United States is Lake Mead in Nevada, behind Hoover Dam on the Colorado River.

Lake Habitats Like a pond, a lake provides habitats for many organisms. INTEGRATING LIFE SCIENCE In the shallow water near shore, the wildlife is similar to that in a pond. Water beetles scurry over the slippery, moss-covered rocks. Loons and kingfishers pluck fish from the open water. But unlike

Background

Integrating Science In addition to the two zones described for ponds in the Background on page 204, lakes have an area of deep water called the *profundal zone.* Sunlight does not reach the deeper parts of this zone, so no plants or algae live there.

Particles of food and the remains of dead organisms drift down into the profundal zone. Bacteria decompose the wastes and release the nutrients into the water.

a pond, sunlight does not reach the bottom at the center of a lake. Without sunlight, plants cannot live in the deep water. As a result, fewer other organisms live in the chilly, dark depths of the lake. A few worms and mollusks do live on the bottom. They feed on food particles that drift down from the surface. The deep waters of lakes are also the home of large, bony fish such as pike and sturgeon. These fish eat the tiny bottom dwellers. They also swim to the surface to feed on fish and even small birds.

☑ *Checkpoint* *List four possible ways a lake might form.*

Changes in a Lake

Particularly in cool, northern areas of North America, many lakes undergo changes with the seasons. In the summer, the sun warms the upper layer of water in the lake. The warm water floats on top of the cooler, denser lower layer. But in the fall, the top layer cools off, too. As the water cools, it becomes denser and sinks. This causes the lake waters to mix together. **As the water mixes, minerals, plant matter, and other nutrients rise from the lake bottom to the surface. Called lake turnover, this seasonal change refreshes the supply of nutrients throughout the lake.**

A second type of change that occurs in a lake happens over a long period of time. The organisms in a lake constantly release waste products into the water. The wastes and the remains of dead organisms contain nutrients such as nitrates and phosphates. Algae feed on these nutrients. Over many years, the nutrients build up in the lake in a process called **eutrophication** (you troh fih KAY shuhn). As eutrophication causes more algae to grow, a thick, green scum forms on the surface of the water.

Figure 7 This island floating on Lake Titicaca is woven from totora reeds.

Social Studies CONNECTION

Imagine living on a floating island in the middle of a deep, cold lake. The island is a mat made of thick reeds you have woven tightly together. During a storm, you must anchor your island or it could be swept away. If you were a member of a group of Native Americans who live on Lake Titicaca in South America, such an island might be your home.

Lake Titicaca lies high in the Andes Mountains. Around the edges of the lake grows a hollow reed called totora. The people weave totora reeds together to form "islands" that are strong enough to hold homes and livestock. They also make ropes, boats, tea, and even medicine from the totora reeds.

In Your Journal

How would living on a totora reed island on Lake Titicaca affect your daily routine? Write a journal entry describing what a typical day might be like if you lived on a floating island.

Social Studies CONNECTION

Before students read about the totora reed islands, have them skim the first two paragraphs to find out where these islands are located. *(On Lake Titicaca in the Andes Mountains of South America)* Explain that Lake Titicaca is located on the border between Peru and Bolivia. Display a large map of South America, and have students find Peru (on the west coast), Bolivia (east and south of Peru), the border running north-south between the two countries, and Lake Titicaca itself. Lead students to conclude that this lake is high above sea level since it is in the Andes Mountains.

After students have read the two paragraphs describing the local people's way of life, ask: **Why do you think the local people first started living on reed islands centuries ago?** *(Accept a variety of reasons, and encourage creative thinking. Answers might include to provide protection against enemies, to take advantage of natural resources that were not available on shore, and to escape overcrowded conditions on the lake's shore or elsewhere.)*

In Your Journal Provide time for students to think about their entries before they begin to write. If they have difficulty coming up with ideas, ask: **Do you think the people living on the reed islands have cars? Electricity? How would these things affect your daily routine? learning modality: verbal**

Answers to Self-Assessment

Caption Question

Figure 6 The pond; the water lilies are evidence that the body of water is shallow.

☑ *Checkpoint*

A meander becomes an oxbow lake. Water fills depressions created by melting ice sheets, movements of Earth's crust, or an empty volcanic crater. An erupting volcano blocks a river. People build dams.

Ongoing Assessment

Drawing Have each student draw two simple labeled diagrams, one showing a lake during the summer and the other showing lake turnover in the fall.

Changes in a Lake, continued

Using the Visuals: Figure 8

Emphasize that eutrophication is a natural process, though pollution can speed it up. Ask: **How would the numbers and types of plants and animals change during the process of eutrophication?** *(Gradually the number of animals in a lake would decrease as the numbers of first algae and eventually plants increased. The types of plants and animals would change as the lake became a marsh and then a meadow.)* **learning modality: logical/mathematical**

Icebergs

Including All Students

To reinforce students' understanding of the danger of icebergs to ships, challenge them to write a news report summarizing the sinking of the *Titanic,* focusing on how this "unsinkable" ship was unable to survive a collision with an iceberg. **learning modality: verbal**

Including All Students

Point out the word *calve* used for the breaking-off of icebergs from glaciers. Ask: **What is a calf?** *(A baby cow)* **What does it mean for a cow to calve?** *(To give birth to a calf)* **Why is the word "calve" a good one to use for the process of icebergs forming?** *(The glacier "gives birth" to an iceberg when it breaks off and floats away.)* **limited English proficiency**

A. The process begins as algae and other organisms add nutrients to the lake. These nutrients support more plant growth.

B. Soil, fallen leaves, and decaying matter pile up on the lake bottom. The lake becomes shallower and marshy.

C. Eventually, the plants completely fill the lake, creating a grassy meadow.

Figure 8 A lake environment gradually changes over time. *Predicting Would you expect the water temperature in the lake to be higher in A or B?*

When the algae layer becomes so thick that it begins to block out the sunlight, plants in the lake cannot carry out photosynthesis. They stop producing food and oxygen and die. As dead organisms in the lake decay, the amount of oxygen in the water decreases. The lake environment changes. Many of the fish and other animals no longer have enough oxygen to live. Material from decaying plants and animals piles up on the bottom, and the lake becomes shallower. The sun warms the water to a higher temperature. Now many plants take root in the rich mud on the lake bottom. Eventually, the lake becomes completely filled with plants. The remaining water evaporates, and a grassy meadow takes the place of the former lake.

Icebergs

It was a dark night in the spring of 1912. The gleaming new ocean liner *Titanic* sailed through the North Atlantic on its first voyage, from Southampton, England, to New York City. Suddenly a huge white wall loomed out of the darkness in front of the ship! It was an iceberg, the terror of ships at sea. Underwater, the jagged ice tore a

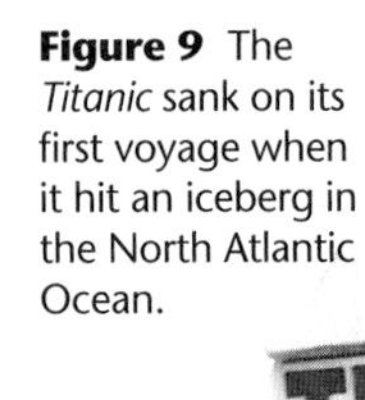

Figure 9 The *Titanic* sank on its first voyage when it hit an iceberg in the North Atlantic Ocean.

Background

Facts and Figures The British ship *Titanic* sank on the night of April 14, 1912, after striking an iceberg off the coast of Newfoundland in the North Atlantic.

Both the sinking of the ship and the devastating death toll could possibly have been avoided. According to some investigations, the ship's speed was too great considering the iceberg warnings that were received. The ship did not have enough lifeboats for the people on board, and a nearby ship, the *Californian,* apparently failed to respond to the *Titanic's* distress signals.

As a result of the *Titanic* disaster, shipping companies took new measures to avoid disaster, including setting up iceberg patrols and radio watches.

series of cuts in the *Titanic's* side. As the ship sank to the bottom of the ocean, more than 1,500 people died.

Recall from Chapter 8 that a glacier is a mass of ice and snow that moves slowly over land. When a glacier reaches the seacoast, icebergs form. With a loud roar, large chunks break off, or calve, and float away. Although icebergs are found in the salty ocean, remember that they consist of fresh water.

In the North Atlantic and Arctic oceans, about 10,000 new icebergs form every year. Many of these icebergs calve from Greenland's continental glacier. As they drift south, the icebergs break into chunks as big as houses. They begin to melt in the warmer water.

The ocean around Antarctica is filled with even larger icebergs. Flat-topped pieces calve from the edges of the glaciers along the coast. In 1995, a giant iceberg broke off Antarctica's Larsen Ice Shelf. Scientists flying over the new iceberg reported that it was about 70 kilometers long and 25 kilometers wide—more than half the size of the state of Rhode Island!

Figure 10 If you could see an entire iceberg at once, how would it look? An artist created this composite photograph to reveal the hidden part of the iceberg. *Applying Concepts What percentage of the ice is underwater?*

The thought of a chunk of floating ice that big is scary enough, but it's more frightening to realize that only about 10 percent of an iceberg is visible above the water. **About 90 percent of an iceberg lies below the surface. The underwater part is a hazard to ships because it is often much wider than the visible part of the iceberg.**

After the *Titanic* disaster, countries involved in Atlantic shipping set up the International Ice Patrol. The Patrol, which is managed by the United States Coast Guard, uses ships, planes, and satellites to track icebergs. The Patrol's warnings have saved many people from disasters like the *Titanic.*

Section 2 Review

1. What bodies of water make up a river system?
2. Explain how ponds and lakes form.
3. Give three examples of typical pond organisms. Describe where in a pond each is found.
4. Where do icebergs form?
5. **Thinking Critically Relating Cause and Effect** How is the depth of the water in the middle of a lake related to the variety of living things there?

Science at Home

Home-made Iceberg With a family member, make a model iceberg. Fill the cut-off bottom of a milk or juice carton with water and freeze. When the water has frozen, peel the carton away from the iceberg. Add salt to a large bowl of water to create an "ocean." Float the iceberg in the bowl. Help your family member use a ruler to measure how much of the iceberg's thickness is above the surface of the water and how much is below. Use these measurements to explain why icebergs can be dangerous to ships.

3 Assess

Section 2 Review Answers

1. A river system is made up of a river and all the smaller rivers and streams that feed into it.
2. Ponds and lakes form when water collects in hollows and low-lying areas.
3. Students may name any three of the organisms and habitats presented in *Exploring a Pond* on pages 204–205.
4. When the end of a glacier reaches the seacoast, large chunks break off and float away as icebregs.
5. The deeper the water is, the smaller the variety is of living things. Plants cannot live in deep water where sunlight does not reach. Without plants, fewer other organisms live in deep water.

Science at Home

ACTIVITY

Materials *empty milk or juice carton, tap water, freezer, large bowl, salt, ruler*
Tips Tell students to use about one teaspoonful of salt for each quart of water to make the "ocean." Students and their family members can calculate the percentages of ice above and below water. These calculations will be easier if the measurements are made in metric units.

Program Resources

- **Unit 3 Resources** 7-2 Review and Reinforce; 7-2 Enrich

Answers to Self-Assessment

Caption Questions
Figure 8 In B, the shallower stage
Figure 10 About 90%

Performance Assessment

Skills Check Have students create a compare/contrast table that summarizes the similarities and differences between a lake and a pond.

SECTION 3 Water Underground

Objectives

After completing the lesson, students will be able to

- ◆ describe springs and how water moves through underground layers of soil and rock;
- ◆ explain what an aquifer is and how people obtain water from an aquifer.

Key Terms pore, permeable, impermeable, saturated zone, water table, unsaturated zone, aquifer, spring, recharge, artesian well

1 Engage/Explore

Activating Prior Knowledge

Show the class a bottle of spring water you have purchased. Ask: **What was the original source of this water?** *(Students may mention wells, springs, or other sources.)* **Where does the water in springs and wells come from?** *(Students may be unsure or may suggest an underground supply; some may know the term "aquifer." Acknowledge all responses without comment at this time.)*

DISCOVER

Skills Focus observing
Materials *pebbles, clear jar, ruler, dry sand, water*
Time 10 minutes
Tips A plastic jar is preferable to avoid the danger of broken glass. Advise students to add the water slowly.
Expected Outcome The water will seep through the sand and collect at the bottom of the jar.
Think It Over The water fills the spaces between the pebbles.

SECTION 3 Water Underground

DISCOVER ACTIVITY

Where Does the Water Go?

1. Add pebbles to a jar to form a layer about 5 centimeters deep. Cover the pebbles with a layer of dry sand about 3 centimeters thick. Pour the sand in slowly to avoid moving the pebbles. These materials represent underground soil layers.
2. Sprinkle water onto the sand to simulate rainfall.
3. Looking through the side of the jar, observe the path of the water as it soaks through the layers. Wash your hands when you are finished with this activity.

Think It Over

Observing Describe what happens when the water reaches the bottom of the jar.

GUIDE FOR READING

- ◆ How does water move through underground layers of soil and rock?
- ◆ How do people obtain water from an aquifer?

Reading Tip As you read, create a flowchart that shows one possible path of water from a rainstorm to a well.

When you were younger, did you ever dig a hole in the ground hoping to find a buried treasure? Though you probably never found a trunk full of gold, you could have found a different kind of treasure without even realizing it. If you continued to dig deeper, past tangled grass roots and small stones, you would have noticed the soil begin to feel heavier and wetter. If you dug deep enough, the bottom of your hole would have started to fill up with water. You would have "struck groundwater!" In the days before pipes and public water systems, such a discovery was like finding a treasure. A usable source of fresh water enabled people to build a house or farm and settle on that land. Today, many people still rely on the water underground to meet their water needs.

Underground Layers

Where does this underground water come from? Like the water in rivers, lakes, and glaciers, it comes from precipitation. Recall what can happen to precipitation when it falls. It can evaporate right away, run off the surface, or soak into the ground. The water that soaks in trickles downward, following the pull of gravity.

If you pour water into a glass full of pebbles, the water trickles down around the pebbles until it reaches the bottom of the glass. Then the water begins to fill up the spaces between the pebbles. **In the same way, water underground trickles down between particles of soil and through cracks and spaces in layers of rock.**

READING STRATEGIES

Reading Tip Point out that many different flowcharts are possible. After students have read the section, encourage them to compare their flowcharts. Sample flowchart steps: raindrop to ground to groundwater to well.

Vocabulary Write the terms *permeable* and *impermeable* on the board. Explain that the root *perme* comes from a Latin word meaning "to pass through." Then ask what the suffix *-able* means. (*"Capable of being" something*) Challenge students to find the meaning of *permeable.* (*"Capable of being passed through"; correct students if they say "capable of passing through."*) Ask what the prefix *im-* means. (*"not"*) Again, challenge students to find the meaning of *impermeable.* (*Not capable of being passed through*)

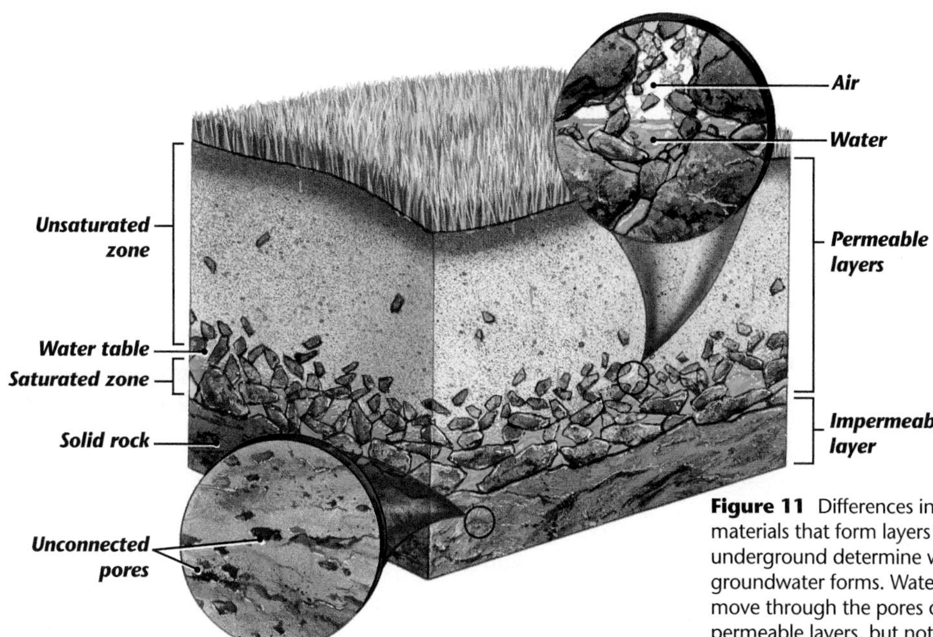

Figure 11 Differences in the materials that form layers underground determine where groundwater forms. Water can move through the pores of permeable layers, but not through impermeable layers. *Interpreting Diagrams What is the difference between the saturated and unsaturated zone?*

Different types of rock and soil have different-sized spaces, or **pores,** between their particles. How easily water moves through the material depends not only on the size of the pores, but also on whether the pores are connected to each other. Materials that allow water to easily pass through, or permeate, are called **permeable.** Sand and gravel are permeable materials.

As water soaks down through permeable rock, it eventually reaches layers of material that it cannot pass through. These materials have few or no pores or cracks for the water to flow through. Materials that water cannot pass through easily are called **impermeable.** Clay and granite are impermeable materials.

Once water reaches an impermeable layer, it is trapped. It can't soak any deeper. Instead, the water begins to fill up the spaces above the impermeable material. The area of permeable rock or soil that is totally filled, or saturated, with water is called the **saturated zone.** The top of the saturated zone is the **water table.** Knowing the depth of the water table in an area tells you how deep you must dig to reach groundwater.

Soil and rock layers above the water table contain some moisture, too. But here the pores contain air as well as water. They are not saturated with water. Therefore, the layer of rocks and soil above the water table is called the **unsaturated zone.**

☑ *Checkpoint* *Give an example of a permeable material other than sand or gravel.*

Sharpen your Skills

Drawing Conclusions

You have just bought some land and need to dig a well. By drilling a number of holes on your property, you learn that there is a layer of impermeable granite rock located approximately 12 meters underground. If the saturated zone is 3 meters thick, how deep should you dig your well? (*Hint:* Drawing a diagram may be helpful.)

2 Facilitate

Underground Layers

Using the Visuals: Figure 11

Point out the two circular insets and ask: **What is different about the pores in the two pictures?** *(The pores in the top-right picture are larger and are connected to one another; the pores in the bottom-left picture are smaller and are not connected.)* **Which picture represents a permeable rock layer?** *(The top-right picture)* **In this picture, how do the pores differ above and below the water table?** *(Above, the pores contain both air and water; below, the pores contain only water.)* **learning modality: visual**

Sharpen your Skills

Drawing Conclusions

Time 10 minutes

ACTIVITY

Tips Before students attempt to solve the problem, ask: **Where is the saturated zone located, on top of the impermeable layer or below it?** *(on top of it)*

Expected Outcome The depth of the well should be at least 9 m. Some students may realize that making it exactly 9 m deep may cause it to run dry in drought conditions or if too much water is withdrawn. Accept answers ranging from somewhat more than 9 m to somewhat less than 12 m.

Extend Encourage students to make a simple three-dimensional model showing the saturated zone, the impermeable layers, and the depth of the well. **learning modality: logical/mathematical**

Program Resources

- **Unit 3 Resources** 7-3 Lesson Plan; 7-3 Section Summary
- **Guided Reading and Study Workbook** Section 7-3

Media and Technology

Transparencies "Underground Zones," Transparency 22

Answers to Self-Assessment

Caption Questions

Figure 11 The pores in the saturated zone are filled with water, whereas in the unsaturated zone, the pores contain air as well as water.

☑ *Checkpoint*

Other permeable materials include soil, porous rock such as sandstone, foam rubber, plastic foam, and cloth.

Ongoing Assessment

Drawing Have each student make a simple sketch of an underground water supply, without referring to Figure 11, and label its features with the terms *pores, permeable materials, impermeable materials, saturated zone, water table,* and *unsaturated zone.*

Aquifers

Skills Focus making models
Materials *newspaper, loaf pan, modeling clay, moist sand, funnel, plastic straw, scissors, water*
Time 20 minutes
Tips Before students begin, slowly add a little water to the sand to moisten it. Make extra clay available for students to stop any leaks that occur. Also provide paper towels so students can remove any water that overflows the funnel.
Expected Outcome Water will flow from the funnel into the sand layer at the high end, downhill through the sand layer, and then up the straw at the low end. The layers of clay and sand represent impermeable and permeable layers under ground. The water represents rain or other precipitation. The flow of the water downhill through the sand layer represents real water movement in an aquifer. The model is like a real aquifer in that water moves through a permeable layer. It is different because water would fall as precipitation and soak through permeable material until it reaches a layer of impermeable rock.
Extend Ask students: **What do you think would happen if you cut the straw below the water level of the funnel?** Suggest that students test their predictions. *(Cutting the straw below the water level will produce a gushing artesian well.)*
learning modality: kinesthetic

Including All Students

Choose a volunteer to find the derivation of the word "aquifer" in a dictionary. *(From the Latin* aqua, *meaning "water")* Ask: **What other English words do you know that have "aqua" in them?** *(Examples include aquarium, the colors aqua and aquamarine, the astrological sign Aquarius, aquatic, and aqueduct.)* **What non-English words for *water* do you know that are similar to *aqua*?** *(Students may suggest the Spanish word* agua.*)*
limited English proficiency

An Artesian Well

In this activity you will build a model of an artesian well. Before you start, cover your desk or table with newspaper.

1. Cover the bottom of a loaf pan with clay. Pile the clay higher at one end.
2. Cover the clay with about 4 cm of moist sand.
3. Cover the sand with a thin sheet of clay. Seal the edges of the clay tightly against the sides of the pan.
4. Push a funnel into the high end so that the bottom of the funnel is in the sand.

5. Insert a short piece of plastic straw through the clay and into the sand layer at the low end. Remove the straw, discard it, and then insert a new piece of straw in the same hole.
6. Slowly pour water into the funnel. Do not let the water overflow the funnel.
7. Observe the level of water in the straw. Wash your hands after this activity.

Making a Model What real-world feature does each part of your model represent? How is your model like a real artesian well? How is it different?

Aquifers

Any underground layer of rock or sediment that holds water is called an **aquifer.** Aquifers can range in size from a small underground patch of permeable material to an area the size of several states. The huge Ogallala aquifer lies beneath the plains of the midwest, stretching from South Dakota to Texas. Millions of people obtain their drinking water from this underground storehouse. The Ogallala aquifer also provides water for crops and livestock.

Maybe you picture groundwater as a large, still pool beneath Earth's surface. In fact, the water is actually in motion, seeping through the layers of rock. How fast it moves depends largely on how steeply the aquifer slopes and how permeable the rocks are. Groundwater in some aquifers moves only a few centimeters a day. At that rate, the water moves about 10 meters a year—less than the length of a typical classroom. Groundwater may travel hundreds of kilometers and stay in an aquifer for thousands of years before coming to the surface again.

☑ *Checkpoint* *What factors affect how fast water moves in an aquifer?*

Bringing Groundwater to the Surface

Look at Figure 12 and notice how the level of the water table generally follows the shape of the underground rock layers. The depth of the water table can vary greatly even over a small area of land. Heavy rain or lots of melting snow raise the level of the water table. The level falls in dry weather.

Where the water table meets the ground surface, groundwater bubbles or flows out of cracks in the rock in places called **springs.** The groundwater may feed a stream or pond, or form a wetland. People can also bring groundwater to the surface.

Wells Since ancient times, people have brought groundwater to the surface for drinking and other everyday uses. **People can obtain groundwater from an aquifer by drilling a well below the water table.** Locate the well near the center of Figure 12. Because the bottom of the well is in the saturated zone, the well contains water. Notice the level of the bottom of the dry well in the diagram. Because this well does not reach below the water table, water cannot be obtained from it.

Long ago, people dug wells by hand. They lined the sides of the well with brick or stone to keep the walls from collapsing. To bring up water, they lowered and raised a bucket. Today, most wells are dug with well-drilling equipment. Pumps bring up the groundwater.

Pumping water out of an aquifer lowers the water level near the well. If too much water is pumped out too fast, the well may

Background

Facts and Figures Taking more groundwater from an aquifer than can be naturally recharged is known as *aquifer depletion.* Wells running dry is not the only serious consequence. When water is depleted from an aquifer, the land above it may settle, a condition called subsidence. In California's San Joaquin Valley, for example, aquifer depletion has caused some land areas to sink nearly 10 meters in a 50-year period. When groundwater is depleted in coastal areas, salt water is drawn into the aquifer. This makes the groundwater salty and unfit for drinking.

Aquifer depletion is due largely to withdrawing water for irrigation. With traditional irrigation methods, more than 50 percent of the water applied to fields simply evaporates. Recent advances in irrigation technology are improving the efficiency of water use.

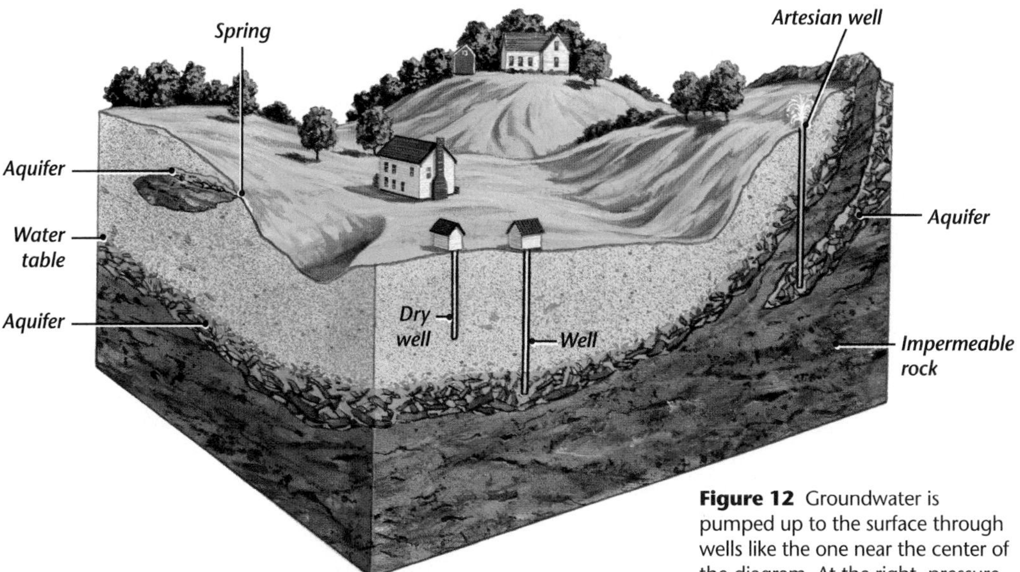

Figure 12 Groundwater is pumped up to the surface through wells like the one near the center of the diagram. At the right, pressure causes water to spurt from an artesian well. Where an aquifer meets the ground surface, at the left, a spring may form. *Interpreting Diagrams Why does the dry well not contain any water?*

run dry. It will be necessary either to dig deeper to reach the lowered water table, or to wait for rainfall to refill the aquifer. New water that enters the aquifer from the surface is called **recharge.**

Artesian Wells In some aquifers, groundwater is trapped between two layers of impermeable rock or sediment. This water is under great pressure from the weight of the water above it. If the top layer of rock is punctured, the pressure sends water spurting up through the hole. Water flows without pumping from a well dug in such an aquifer. A well in which water rises because of pressure within the aquifer is called an **artesian well** (ahr TEEZH uhn well).

Section 3 Review

1. Describe what happens to water that soaks into the ground.
2. Why is it important to know the depth of an aquifer before drilling a well?
3. Draw a cross section of the ground that includes the following labeled features: permeable layer, saturated zone, unsaturated zone, impermeable layer, and water table.
4. **Thinking Critically Inferring** During the winter, a small spring flows on your property. Every summer, the spring dries up. What might be the reason for the change?

CHAPTER PROJECT

Check Your Progress

At this point, add the body of standing water to your watershed sketch. If your model will include any wetland areas, what materials will you use to model them? (*Hint:* Be sure to consider how water will enter and leave the body of water.)

Program Resources

- **Laboratory Manual** 7, "Field Testing a Body of Fresh Water"
- **Unit 3 Resources** 7-3 Review and Reinforce; 7-3 Enrich

Media and Technology

Transparencies "Wells and Springs," Transparency 23

Answers to Self-Assessment

Checkpoint

How fast the water moves in an aquifer depends on how steeply the aquifer slopes and how permeable the rocks are.

Caption Question

Figure 12 The dry well does not reach below the water table.

Bringing Groundwater to the Surface

Using the Visuals: Figure 12

Call students' attention to the two wells in the figure. Ask: **Why is the one well dry?** *(The well does not reach to the water table.)* **How could that well become a working well?** *(It could be dug deeper, or it could pump water if the water table rose.)* **learning modality: visual**

3 Assess

Section 3 Review Answers

1. The pull of gravity causes water to trickle down between particles of soil and through cracks and spaces in rock until it reaches impermeable materials.
2. Without knowing the depth of the aquifer, the drillers don't know how deep they must drill the well to be below the water table.
3. Students' drawings should show the layers in the following sequence from top to bottom: permeable layer; within the permeable layer—unsaturated zone, water table, saturated zone; impermeable layer.
4. The water table must fall below the level of the spring in summer and rise above it in winter. Factors such as precipitation and human water use could also affect the depth of the water table.

CHAPTER PROJECT

Check Your Progress

As you review students' sketches, check to see whether bodies of standing water are located in relatively level areas. Also have students describe the materials they plan to use to represent wetlands, to make sure the materials will show the specific, unique properties of wetlands.

Performance Assessment

Writing or Drawing Have each student write a paragraph or draw and label a sketch to explain why water flows from an artesian well without needing to be pumped.

Real-World Lab

Careers in Science

Soil Testing

Preparing for Inquiry

Key Concept Different soil materials have different permeabilities.

Skills Objectives Students will be able to

- measure how quickly water flows through sand, clay, and pebbles;
- interpret data to conclude that the sizes of a material's particles and the spaces between them determine its permeability.

Time 40 minutes

Advance Planning At least one day before students do the lab, gather sufficient materials for each group. If funnels are not available, cut the tops off plastic soda bottles, or let students do this. Have them cover the rough edge with masking tape to avoid cutting themselves.

Guiding Inquiry

Invitation After distributing the sand, clay, and pebbles, have students look at and feel them. Ask: **Which material would let water pass through it the quickest? Which do you think would hold water best?** Write their hypotheses on the board, and discuss these responses when students complete the lab.

Introducing the Procedure

- After students read the help-wanted ad, ask: **Which would be a good location for a well—in soil that lets water pass through it easily, or in soil that does not let water pass through?** *(Soil that lets water pass through easily)*
- After students read the instructions, ask: **Why should the layers of sand, clay, and pebbles be the same depth?** *(The depth is a variable that should be controlled; making the layers different depths could affect the results.)*

Real-World Lab

Careers in Science

SOIL TESTING

In what type of soil is it best to site a well? This is a question that hydrologists, scientists who study groundwater, need to answer before new houses or other buildings can be constructed. In this lab, you will compare different soil types to learn more about their water-holding properties.

HELP WANTED

Hydrologists to conduct soil tests for new housing development. Homes will have private wells. Engineers must test soil permeability to select best locations. Please send resumé and references to

Problem

How fast does water move through sand, clay, and pebbles?

Skills Focus

observing, measuring, drawing conclusions

Materials (per group)

hand lens
3 100-mL beakers
sand, 100 mL
water, 300 mL
stopwatch
pebbles, 100 mL
3 rubber bands
powdered potter's clay, 100 mL
3 squares of cheesecloth
3 large funnels or cut-off plastic soda bottle tops

Procedure 

1. Copy the data table into your notebook.
2. Use a hand lens to observe each of the three material samples closely. Record your observations in your data table.
3. Place a piece of cheesecloth over the bottom of each funnel or bottle top and secure it with a rubber band.
4. Place the sand in one funnel, the pebbles in another, and the clay in another. Be sure that there is at least 5 cm of space above the material in each funnel.
5. Place each funnel on top of a beaker.
6. Slowly pour 100 mL of water into the funnel containing the sand. Do not let the water overflow the funnel.
7. Start the stopwatch when the water begins to flow or drip out of the bottom of the funnel.

DATA TABLE

Material	Observations	Time for Water to Stop Dripping
Sand		
Clay		
Pebbles		

Program Resources

- **Unit 3 Resources** Chapter 7 Real-World Lab blackline masters

Safety

Have students wear safety goggles. Review the safety guidelines in Appendix A.

Media and Technology

 **Lab Activity Videotapes** Grade 6, Tape 2

8. Stop the stopwatch when the water stops dripping out of the funnel or after 5 minutes. Record the time to the nearest second in your data table.
9. Repeat Steps 6 through 8 with the pebbles and then with the clay. When you are finished with this activity, dispose of your materials according to your teacher's instructions. Wash your hands thoroughly with soap.

Analyze and Conclude

1. Through which material did water move the fastest? The slowest?
2. What can you conclude about the permeability of the three materials?
3. Based on your observations of each sample, suggest an explanation for the differences in their permeability.
4. Based on the results of this lab, would you expect to get more water from a well dug in sand, pebbles, or clay? Explain.
5. **Apply** Why might gardeners and landscapers need to know about the permeability of different soil types?

More to Explore

Which of the soil samples that you tested do you think the soil of the grounds at your school most resembles? Design an experiment to test your hypothesis. With your teacher's permission, carry out your experiment.

Sample Data Table

Material	Observations	Time for Water to Stop Dripping
Sand	small grains, irregular shapes, whitish to brownish	9 minutes
Pebbles	large pieces, smooth shapes, various colors	2 minutes
Clay	tiny particles, regular shapes, tannish color	greater than 15 minutes

Troubleshooting the Experiment

- In Step 1, suggest that students make the Observations section of their tables larger so they have more room to record.
- If necessary, demonstrate how to make sure the beaker is filled exactly to the 100-mL mark in Step 6. Also remind students to stop pouring the water if it comes close to overflowing the funnel.

Expected Outcome

Times will vary. Sample data might show that it takes about 9 minutes for 100 mL of water to flow through sand, 2 minutes to flow through pebbles, and 15 minutes to flow through clay.

Analyze and Conclude

1. The fastest through pebbles, the slowest through clay
2. A layer of pebbles is the most permeable, a layer of clay the least permeable, and a layer of sand somewhere between those two.
3. The sizes of the particles and of the spaces between them determine a material's permeability. Clay is least permeable because it has the smallest particles and the smallest spaces. Pebbles are the most permeable because they are the largest particles and have the largest spaces between them.
4. You would get more water from a well dug in pebbles because there are larger pores that can hold more water, and the water moves through the pebbles faster into the well as water is pumped out.
5. Some plants may survive and grow best in sandy soils that let water drain away from their roots, while other plants grow best in clay soils that hold water.

Extending the Inquiry

More to Explore Students should be able to estimate the soil's permeability by observing whether water is absorbed after a rain or pools on top. Each group could test an actual sample and compare results with the data using sand, pebbles, and clay.

Wetland Environments

Objectives

After completing the lesson, students will be able to

- ◆ identify features of wetlands that make them suitable habitats for living things;
- ◆ explain what a wetland is and how wetlands help control flooding.

Key Term wetland

1 Engage/Explore

Activating Prior Knowledge

Write the terms *marsh, swamp,* and *bog* on the board, and ask: **What is similar about all three of these areas?** *(All are wet—but the water is not as deep as in a pond or lake.)* Then have students define each term in their own words. Encourage responses that identify differences between the three types of wet areas, but do not correct students' definitions or comment on their accuracy at this time.

DISCOVER

Skills Focus observing
Materials *2 dry kitchen sponges, water, pan, 2 paper cups*
Time 10–15 minutes
Tips Make sure sponges are completely dry when students begin.
Expected Outcome The damp sponge will absorb water immediately, whereas water will run off the dry sponge at first.
Think It Over The damp sponge absorbs water faster. The dry sponge models dry land. The damp sponge models the behavior of wetlands: they soak up excess water and help prevent flooding.

INTEGRATING LIFE SCIENCE

Wetland Environments

DISCOVER ACTIVITY

Wet or Dry?

1. Hold a kitchen sponge under water until it is soaked. Then squeeze out the water until the sponge is just damp.
2. Place the damp sponge next to a dry sponge in a pan. The sponges represent areas of wet and dry land.
3. Pour water into two paper cups until each is half full.
4. Hold one cup in each hand so that the cups are about 10 centimeters above the pan. Pour the water onto both sponges at the same time.

Think It Over

Observing Which of the sponges absorbs water faster? How are your observations related to what might happen in areas of wet and dry land?

GUIDE FOR READING

- ◆ What features of wetlands make them good habitats for living things?
- ◆ How do wetlands help control flooding?

Reading Tip **Before you read, write a short description of what you think a wetland is. As you read, add details and examples to your description.**

A **wetland** is an area of land that is covered with a shallow layer of water during some or all of the year. Wetlands form in places where water is trapped in low areas or where groundwater seeps onto the surface of the land. They can range in size from a water-filled roadside ditch to an area covering thousands of square kilometers. Some wetlands fill up during spring rains and dry up over the summer. Others are covered with water year-round.

Marshes, swamps, and bogs are three common types of freshwater wetlands. Marshes generally are grassy areas covered by a shallow layer or stream of water. They contain cattails, rushes, tule, and other tall grass-like plants. Swamps look more like flooded forests, with trees and shrubs growing in the water. In the United States, many swamps are located in the South, where trees grow quickly in the warm, humid climate. Bogs, which are more common in cooler northern states, often form in depressions left by melting ice sheets thousands of years ago. The water in bogs tends to be acidic. Many types of mosses thrive in the conditions found in bogs.

Wetlands along coasts usually contain both fresh and salt water. Coastal wetlands include salt marshes and mangrove forests. Salt marshes are found along both coasts of the United States. They often contain tall, strong grasses growing in a rich, muddy bottom. Mangrove forests, which are found along the

READING STRATEGIES

Reading Tip Students may say that a wetland is a swamp or a place where the land never becomes dry. To provide a structured format for adding details and examples, have students write the description at the top of a sheet of paper and, below that list the following topics in a column, with space between the items for recording additional information as they read: *Definition of wetland, Types of wetlands, Characteristics of wetlands, Importance of wetlands, and Typical organisms.* Encourage students to review their original descriptions after reading the section and revise them, if necessary.

central and southern coasts of Florida, consist of short trees with a thick tangle of roots. The tough roots anchor the mangroves against tropical winds and storms.

☑ *Checkpoint* *Name three types of freshwater wetlands.*

Wetland Habitats

If you've ever enjoyed tart cranberry sauce or crunchy wild rice, you've eaten plants that grow in wetlands. The layer of water covering a wetland can range from several centimeters to a few meters deep. Dead leaves and other plant and animal material serve as natural fertilizer, adding nitrogen, phosphates, and other nutrients to the water and soil. **Because of their sheltered waters and rich supply of nutrients, wetlands provide habitats for many living things.**

Many year-round residents of wetlands are similar to those in other freshwater habitats. As in a pond, frogs, salamanders, turtles, raccoons, muskrats, and many types of insects find food and shelter among the wetland plants. Birds nest in and around the wetlands, feeding on the plants and insects there.

Wetlands also have many temporary residents. Many ducks, geese, and other waterfowl travel from Alaska and Canada to their winter homes in the South along a "flyway." These birds depend on the millions of small, shallow marshes called prairie potholes along their route. Birds stop there to rest, feed, and mate. In the spring, thousands of birds build their nests in the prairie pothole region.

Figure 13 Freshwater wetlands come in many forms. **A.** In Montana, colorful flowers dot a bed of velvety moss in an alpine bog. **B.** Water flows slowly through a marsh in Oregon's Willamette Valley. **C.** Curtains of Spanish moss hang from cypress trees in a Louisiana swamp. ***Comparing and Contrasting*** *How are these three environments similar? How are they different?*

2 Facilitate

Wetland Habitats

Using the Visuals: Figure 13

After students examine the photographs and read the caption and the text describing the three types of wetlands, have students review their earlier definitions (Activating Prior Knowledge on page 216). Suggest that they correct their definitions, if necessary, to reflect the differences shown and discussed here. **learning modality: verbal**

Real-Life Learning

ACTIVITY

Give students an opportunity to examine samples of fresh cranberries, wild rice, blueberries, peat moss, and other products harvested from wetlands. If you wish to allow students to sample any of the foods, prepare them in a nonscience classroom. Wash fruit well, and check for allergies before allowing students to taste any foods. Encourage students to find out if any of these products are commercially harvested in their area and report back to the rest of the class. **learning modality: kinesthetic**

Program Resources

- **Unit 4 Resources** 7-4 Lesson Plan; 7-4 Section Summary
- **Guided Reading and Study Workbook** Section 7-4

Answers to Self-Assessment

Caption Question

Figure 13 The land in all three is covered with shallow water. Swamps are wooded, marshes are grassy, and bogs are mossy. Bogs also have acidic water.

☑ *Checkpoint*

Marshes, swamps, and bogs

Ongoing Assessment

Making Diagrams Have each student draw a Venn diagram to show the similarities and differences among the three types of freshwater wetlands described in this section.

Students can save their diagrams in their portfolios.

The Importance of Wetlands

Including All Students

Let students work in small groups to create public service radio announcements, television spots, newspaper or transit ads, or educational skits designed to increase public awareness of the importance of wetlands—either wetlands in general or a specific wetland in their own community or region. Give each group an opportunity to present its product to the rest of the class. **cooperative learning**

Demonstration

Materials *clean jar with lid, soil, water, cotton batting, beaker*
Time 10 minutes

Point out the text statement that plant roots trap silt and mud in wetlands. Demonstrate this by preparing a very muddy mixture of soil and water in a screw-top jar. Place a layer of cotton batting over the top of a large beaker or other clear container. Shake the jar so the soil mixes well with the water, and ask: **How would you describe this water?** *(Very muddy, cloudy)* Wearing goggles, slowly pour the muddy water on the batting. Ask: **What does the water that collected in the bottom of the container look like?** *(A little muddy, but much clearer than the original mixture)* **What does the cotton represent in this model?** *(The network of plant roots in a wetland.)* **learning modality: visual**

The Importance of Wetlands

Imagine coming home from a long trip, only to find that your house is gone and in its place is a parking lot! That happened to thousands of migrating birds before people began to understand the importance of wetlands. Farmers and builders once considered the soggy soil of wetlands to be "wasteland." This land could not be used unless it was drained and filled in. Thousands of square kilometers of wetlands were developed for farmland or for building homes and businesses. Beginning in the 1970s, however, the government enacted laws to protect wetland habitats.

Wetlands serve important functions for people as well as for wildlife. For example, wetlands provide natural water filtration. As water moves slowly through a wetland, waste materials settle out. The thick network of plant roots traps silt and mud. **Wetlands also help control floods by absorbing extra runoff from heavy rains.** They act like giant sponges, storing water and gradually releasing it as it drains or evaporates. When wetlands are drained or paved over, the water cannot be absorbed. Instead, it runs off the land quickly and can cause floods.

Figure 14 Many unusual species live in the freshwater wetland habitats of the Everglades.

Background

Facts and Figures Since the mid-1980s, the rate of wetland loss in the United States has slowed to less than an estimated 36,000 hectares a year. This is less than a quarter of the rate of loss only a few decades earlier. Wetlands may be developed only if an equal area of wetlands is restored. In addition, there are now many initiatives aimed at increasing the number and quality of wetlands. Many programs offer farmers financial incentives to restore wetlands on their property.

The Everglades: A Unique Environment

Walking down a path in Florida's Everglades National Park, you would feel the ground squish under your feet. Water is the key to the Everglades, a unique region of wetlands. A shallow layer of water moves slowly over the gently sloping land from Lake Okeechobee south to Florida Bay. Tall, sharp-edged blades of sawgrass grow in the water. The thick growth of sawgrass gave this region its Native American name, *Pa-hay-okee*, which means "river of grass." Low islands called hammocks are scattered throughout the sawgrass marsh. Trees like gumbo limbos and palms grow on the hammocks.

Everglades Wildlife As in other wetlands, water means life for many Everglades creatures. Fish and snakes gobble up tiny organisms in the warm, muddy water. Wading birds in a rainbow of colors—pink flamingoes, white egrets, and purple gallinules—stand on skinny legs in the water. A raccoon digs for alligator eggs, unaware of the alligator lying low in the sawgrass nearby.

The Everglades provide habitats for many rare or endangered species. The endangered Florida panther lives deep in the wilderness portions of the Everglades. Many species of birds, such as the wood stork and the roseate spoonbill (named for the unusual

Figure 15 Habitats found in the Everglades include sawgrass marshes, cypress swamps, and mangrove forests. *Interpreting Maps In which area of the park would you expect to find mangrove trees?*

Answers to Self-Assessment

Caption Question

Figure 15 Along the southern and western coasts; mangroves grow in salt water.

The Everglades: A Unique Environment

Using the Visuals: Figure 14

Ask: **What particular *type* of wetland is shown on these pages? How do you know?** *(A marsh; it is covered mostly with grass.)* **Why do you think the Everglades provides a habitat for such a variety of plants and animals?** *(There is a rich supply of nutrients to support the growth of many different plants, which in turn supply food and shelter to many different animals.)* Encourage interested students to find out more about Everglades wildlife and report to the class. **learning modality: visual**

Inquiry Challenge

ACTIVITY

After students have read about the balance of nutrients in wetlands, challenge small groups to design an experiment to answer this question: **What effect do excess fertilizers have on the growth of algae and/or water plants?** Help students recall the major steps to be completed: develop a hypothesis, describe the experiment design, control variables, record and interpret data, and draw a conclusion. Monitor the groups' experimental designs for safety and logic. Then encourage groups to conduct their experiments and report their results and conclusions to the class. **learning modality: logical/mathematical**

Students can save their experiment Portfolio descriptions, data, sketches, and conclusions in their portfolios.

Ongoing Assessment

Writing Have students write a paragraph defining and describing freshwater wetlands.

3 Assess

Section 4 Review Answers

1. Wetlands provide food, shelter, and nesting sites for year-round inhabitants and temporary resting, feeding, and mating sites for migrating birds.
2. By absorbing extra runoff from heavy rains; by acting like giant sponges, storing water, and gradually releasing it
3. The Everglades consist of a shallow layer of water that moves slowly over an enormous area of gently sloping land. Many rare and endangered species make their homes in its many habitats.
4. Answers might include the number of farmers affected and their projected losses, possible commercial uses of the restored Everglades (such as wildlife tours) and their projected revenues, and possible replacements for current agricultural practices or crops.

CHAPTER PROJECT

Check Your Progress

Make sure you give students' sketches a final approval. Consult with students as they build their models to see if they are encountering any problems with the materials and to provide positive feedback, encouragement, and assistance as needed. Establish a plan for students to present their models at the conclusion of the chapter.

Performance Assessment

Oral Presentation Have students give an imaginary tour of a wetland, describing its characteristics, plants and animals, and importance.

shape of its beak), depend on the Everglades as a nesting area. The awkward-looking manatee, or sea cow, lives in the mangrove forests along the coast. Because manatees swim so slowly, they are easily injured by the propellers of powerboats. They have become an endangered species as a result of increased boating.

Figure 16 A manatee floats in the warm waters of Florida Bay. This species is threatened by the increased use of coastal waters around the Everglades.

Threats to the Everglades The Everglades are a fragile environment. Nearby farming has introduced new chemicals into the slow-moving water of the marsh, upsetting the balance of nutrients. Outside the protected limits of the national park, developers have filled in areas of wetland to build new homes and roads. New organisms brought into the area accidentally or for pest control compete with other organisms for space and food.

Water that once flowed into the Everglades from Lake Okeechobee has been diverted for farming. New canals and levees built to provide drinking water and to control flooding have changed the flow of water into and out of the Everglades. Some areas are drying up, while others are flooded.

Preserving the Everglades Scientists and government officials have been trying for many years to develop a plan to preserve the Everglades and save its endangered wildlife. One plan involves building an elaborate system of pipes and canals to refill some drained areas with fresh water. The National Park Service, the State of Florida, and the U.S. Army Corps of Engineers are working together to manage the supply of water to areas around and within the Everglades.

Section 4 Review

1. How are wetlands important to wildlife?
2. Explain how wetlands help control floods.
3. How are the Everglades unusual?
4. **Thinking Critically Making Judgments** Some of the plans to restore the Everglades will require millions of dollars and will negatively affect local farmers. What information would you want to have to help decide what plan of action to take to save the Everglades?

CHAPTER PROJECT

Check Your Progress

Now you are ready to build your model watershed. Be sure to follow the plan you have drawn. When your model is finished, do a practice run of your demonstration. (*Hint:* Some materials need to be worked with quickly before they harden. Others need time to dry before you can pour water over them. Be sure to leave yourself enough time to build your model and let it dry before your presentation.)

Program Resources

- **Unit 3 Resources** 7-4 Review and Reinforce; 7-4 Enrich

CHAPTER 7 STUDY GUIDE

The Water Cycle

Key Ideas

- About 97 percent of Earth's water is salt water stored in the oceans. Less than 1 percent is usable fresh water.
- In the water cycle, water evaporates from Earth's surface into the atmosphere. The water forms clouds, then falls back to Earth as precipitation. Energy from the sun drives the water cycle.
- The water cycle renews Earth's supply of fresh water. In the world as a whole, the rates of evaporation and precipitation balance each other.
- People use water for many purposes, including household use, industry, agriculture, transportation, and recreation.
- All living things need water to carry out their life processes.

Key Terms

water vapor
groundwater
water cycle
evaporation
transpiration
precipitation
irrigation
photosynthesis
habitat

Water on the Surface

Key Ideas

- Runoff from precipitation forms streams, which flow together to form rivers. The area drained by a river system is its watershed.
- Floods occur when a river overflows its channel and spreads out over its floodplain.
- Ponds and lakes are bodies of standing water that form when fresh water collects in depressions in the land.

Key Terms

tributary
watershed
divide
levee
reservoir
eutrophication

Water Underground

Key Ideas

- As water soaks into the ground, it moves through the pores between particles of soil and rock. Water moves easily through permeable materials, but does not move easily through impermeable materials.
- People dig wells to obtain groundwater from aquifers.

Key Terms

pore
permeable
impermeable
saturated zone
water table
unsaturated zone
aquifer
spring
recharge
artesian well

Wetland Environments

INTEGRATING LIFE SCIENCE

Key Ideas

- Wetlands are covered with a shallow layer of water for all or part of the year.
- Wetlands provide nesting and feeding areas for birds and other wildlife. Wetlands also filter water and help control floods.

Key Term

wetland

Organizing Information

Cycle Diagram Copy the cycle diagram about the water cycle onto a separate piece of paper and complete it. (For more on cycle diagrams, see the Skills Handbook.)

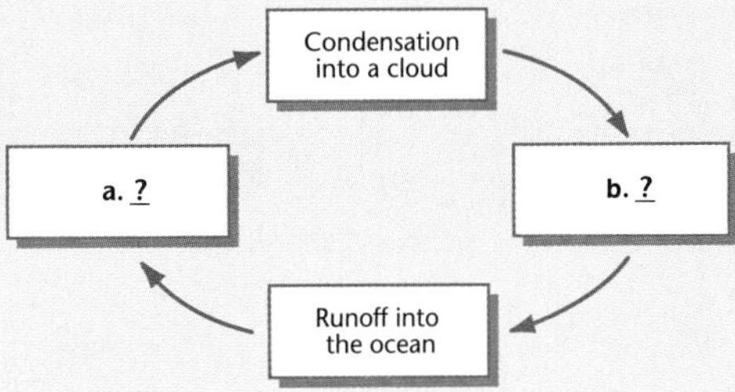

Program Resources

- **Unit 3 Resources** Chapter 7 Project Scoring Rubric
- **Performance Assessment** Chapter 7
- **Chapter and Unit Tests** Chapter 7 Test

Media and Technology

Computer Test Bank Chapter 7 Test

Organizing Information

Cycle Diagram Sample title: Path of a Water Molecule **a.** Evaporation from the ocean **b.** Precipitation onto Earth's surface

Reviewing Content

Multiple Choice

1. c **2.** b **3.** b **4.** d **5.** c

True or False

6. groundwater **7.** fresh **8.** transpiration
9. true **10.** true

Checking Concepts

11. Earth is called the "water planet" because oceans cover nearly 71 percent of Earth's surface.
12. Students should describe the change from liquid to gas involved in evaporation and the change from gas to liquid involved in condensation.
13. More than 97 percent of the total water on Earth is salt water, which is generally not available for human use. About two thirds of the fresh water on Earth is ice, which is mostly unavailable for human use.
14. Plants use the water to make food, and other living things on Earth obtain food either by eating plants or by eating other organisms that eat plants.
15. In the fall, the top layer of water in a lake cools off, becoming denser, and sinks. This causes the lake's layers to mix together. As they mix, minerals, plant matter, and other nutrients are brought from the lake bottom to the surface, refreshing the supply of nutrients throughout the lake.
16. Many migratory waterfowl stop in wetlands to rest, feed, mate, and build nests.
17. Students' descriptions may vary. A typical response might mention that water is a large part of every living thing, that water is essential for living things to grow, reproduce, and carry out other important processes, and that water provides habitats for many organisms.

Thinking Critically

18. Answers may vary. A typical answer might mention the availability of water for industry and transportation of people and goods.
19. The variety of organisms in the center of a pond is much greater because sunlight reaches the bottom. Sunlight does not reach the deep water at the center of a lake, so plants and algae and the organisms that depend on them cannot live there.
20. *Permeable:* cotton, paper towel, bread; *impermeable:* aluminum foil, plastic wrap, glass
21. The sun's heat provides the energy to evaporate water, and the sun's heat is more intense near the equator than at the Arctic Ocean.

Reviewing Content

Multiple Choice

Choose the letter of the best answer.

1. More than 97 percent of Earth's total water supply is found in
   a. ice sheets.
   b. the atmosphere.
   c. the oceans.
   d. groundwater.
2. The energy that drives the water cycle comes from the
   a. Earth. b. sun.
   c. rain. d. ocean.
3. Rain that falls on a steep, paved street during a thunderstorm will most likely become
   a. groundwater. b. runoff.
   c. a spring. d. a reservoir.
4. More than two thirds of Earth's fresh water is found in
   a. rivers and streams.
   b. ponds and lakes.
   c. wetlands.
   d. glaciers and icebergs.
5. Groundwater is stored in
   a. wetlands. b. water tables.
   c. aquifers. d. impermeable layers.

True or False

If the statement is true, write true. If it is false, change the underlined word or words to make the statement true.

6. Most of Earth's liquid fresh water is found in the form of <u>lakes</u>.
7. In the water cycle, precipitation returns <u>salt</u> water to Earth.
8. The process by which the leaves of plants give off water into the atmosphere is <u>condensation</u>.
9. Water moves easily through <u>permeable</u> rock layers.
10. To supply water, the bottom of a well must be located in the <u>saturated zone</u>.

Checking Concepts

11. Explain why Earth is called the "water planet."
12. Describe two changes of state that occur during the water cycle.
13. Explain why so little of Earth's water is available for human use.
14. How is the water supplied to plants important for many other living things on Earth?
15. Describe how temperature changes in the fall and spring can help distribute nutrients throughout a lake.
16. Explain how wetlands are important to migrating birds.
17. **Writing to Learn** As the information officer aboard a starship, you are assigned to write a handbook describing Earth's waters to visitors from other galaxies. Write a description in which you explain how water is important to living things on Earth.

Thinking Critically

18. **Making Generalizations** Explain why towns and cities are often located along bodies of water.
19. **Comparing and Contrasting** How is the variety of organisms you would find in the center of a pond different from those you would find in deep water at the center of a lake?
20. **Classifying** Determine which of the following materials are permeable and which are impermeable: aluminum foil, cotton, plastic wrap, glass, paper towel, and bread.
21. **Relating Cause and Effect** A molecule of water is likely to evaporate more quickly from the Caribbean Sea near the equator than from the Arctic Ocean. Explain why this statement is true.

Applying Skills

Use the diagram of underground layers to answer Questions 22–24.

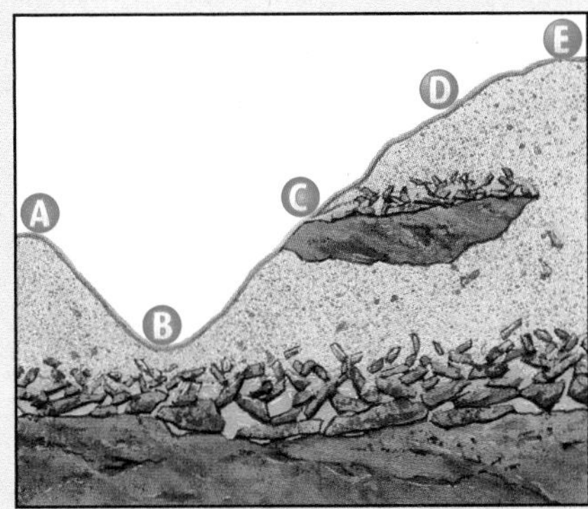

22. **Drawing Conclusions** Would point D or point E be a better location to dig a well? Explain your reasoning.
23. **Inferring** At which location could you obtain groundwater without having to pump it up? What is such a place called?
24. **Predicting** Draw a simple diagram showing how this area might look during a very rainy season.

Performance Assessment — Chapter Project

Present Your Project Before presentation day, show your watershed model to a classmate. Ask your classmate to predict how the water will flow over the model. Can your classmate identify the features of the watershed? If you need to make any final adjustments to your model, do so now. On presentation day, use a spray bottle to spray rain onto your model.

Reflect and Record In your notebook, explain what you would change about your model now that you have demonstrated it. What aspect of freshwater flow was most difficult to model? What other watershed features might you add?

Test Preparation

Use these questions to prepare for standardized tests.

Study the circle graph. Then answer Questions 25–28.

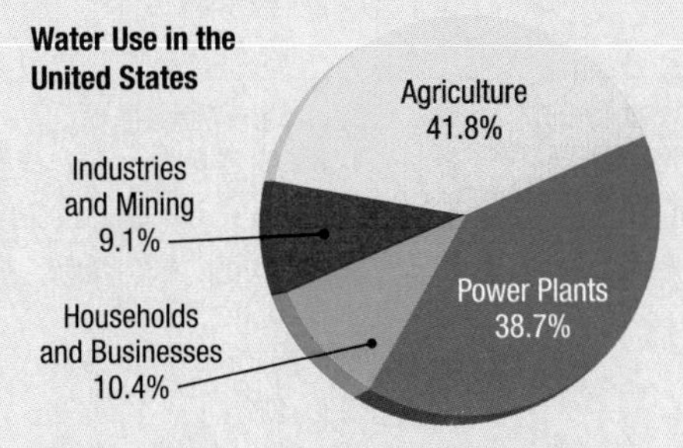

25. Together the two largest categories of water users represent about what percentage of the total water used in the United States?
    a. 19.5 percent b. 49.9 percent
    c. 51.1 percent d. 80.5 percent
26. Which of the four categories of water users shown in the graph represents the largest use of water in the United States?
    a. agriculture
    b. households and businesses
    c. industries and mining
    d. power plants
27. If the total daily usage of water in the United States is 1,280 billion liters, about how many liters are used each day by power plants?
    a. 38.7 billion b. 387 billion
    c. 495 billion d. 49,500 billion
28. If farmers were able to reduce their water use by 10 percent, by about how much would total water use decrease in the United States?
    a. 1.5 percent b. 4.2 percent
    c. 10 percent d. 41.8 percent

Program Resources

◆ **Inquiry Skills Activity Book** Provides teaching and review of all inquiry skills

Applying Skills

22. Accept Point D or Point E: Point D because the distance down to the saturated zone is less, although Point E has a much larger water supply to draw from.
23. Point C; a spring
24. Students' drawings should show a higher water table and thicker saturated zone. They might show a pond at point B.

Performance Assessment — Chapter Project

Present Your Project To maximize sharing of information and to give students an opportunity to compare their models, try to schedule all the presentations in no more than two class periods or one block, allocating a specific maximum amount of time for each model. If possible, arrange the room with the students forming a large circle so everyone can see each model as it is presented.

Prompt students to identify the specific features in the model by name, explain how the features are formed in nature, and describe the role they play in the river system. Encourage the other students to ask questions about each model as it is presented. Make sure you provide all students with positive feedback about their model. Suggest that students save their models for presentation on Parents' Night or at a science fair.

Reflect and Record Encourage students to use the Chapter 7 Project Scoring Rubric to help assess their models. Suggest that they review their sketches to make sure their models accomplished what they planned. Students might also evaluate the materials they used to make the models for their effectiveness to the application.

Test Preparation

25. d **26.** a **27.** c **28.** b

CHAPTER 8 Freshwater Resources

Sections	Time	Student Edition Activities	ACTIVITY Other Activities
CHAPTER PROJECT **A Precious Resource** p. 225	Ongoing (2 weeks)	Check Your Progress, p. 235, 250, 254 Present Your Project, p. 257	
1 Water to Drink pp. 226–235 ◆ Describe sources of drinking water and how it is treated and distributed. ◆ Explain what happens to wastewater.	2–3 periods/ 1–1½ blocks	**Discover** How Hard Is It to Move Water?, p. 226 **Real-World Lab: You, the Consumer** Testing the Waters, pp. 228–229 **Try This** Moving Water Uphill, p. 232	TE Inquiry Challenge, pp. 227, 230 TE Addressing Naive Conceptions, p. 230 TE Building Inquiry Skills: Predicting, p. 231; Controlling Variables, p. 234 TE Integrating Physics, p. 232 TE Real-Life Learning, p. 233 PTA "Testing Shampoos," pp. 1–8
2 Balancing Water Needs pp. 236–242 ◆ Describe conditions that can result in a water shortage and list sources of fresh water for the future. ◆ Explain how water can be conserved.	2 periods/ 1 block	**Discover** Can You Reach a Balance?, p. 236 **Sharpen Your Skills** Predicting, p. 239 **Science at Home,** p. 240 **Skills Lab: Making Models** Getting the Salt Out, p. 241	TE Integrating Technology, p. 237 PTA "Testing Bottled Waters," pp. 1–8
3 Freshwater Pollution pp. 243–250 ◆ Describe what water pollution is and list some of its sources. ◆ Explain how runoff affects ponds and streams. ◆ Describe how pollution can be prevented and how polluted water can be cleaned up.	1 period/ ½ block	**Discover** Will the Pollution Reach Your Wells?, p. 243 **Sharpen Your Skills** Classifying, p. 245 **Try This** How Do Your Algae Grow?, p. 248	TE Using the Visuals, pp. 242, 248 TE Real-Life Learning, p. 245 TE Integrating Chemistry, p. 245 LM 8, "Pollution of a Water Supply" IES "Where River Meets Sea," pp. 28–30
4 *INTEGRATING PHYSICS* **Water As an Energy Resource** pp. 251–254 ◆ Explain how moving water can produce electricity. ◆ Describe the benefits and limitations of hydroelectric power. ◆ Describe the impact of dams.	1 period/ ½ block	**Discover** Can Water Do Work?, p. 251 **Try This** Making a Water Wheel, p. 252	TE Exploring a Hydroelectric Power Plant, p. 253 IES "Mill Life in the 1840s," pp. 12–13 IES "Back to the Thirties," pp. 38–39
Study Guide/Chapter Assessment pp. 255–257	1 period/ ½ block		ISAB Provides teaching and review of all inquiry skills

For Standard or Block Schedule The Resource Pro® CD-ROM gives you maximum flexibility for planning your instruction for any type of schedule. Resource Pro® contains Planning Express®, an advanced scheduling program, as well as the entire contents of the Teaching Resources and the Computer Test Bank.

CHAPTER PLANNING GUIDE

Program Resources	Assessment Strategies	Media and Technology
UR Chapter 8 Project Teacher Notes **UR** Chapter 8 Project Overview and Worksheets	**SE** Performance Assessment: Present Your Project, p. 257 **TE** Check Your Progress, pp. 235, 250, 254 **UR** Chapter 8 Project Scoring Rubric	Science Explorer Internet Site at www.phschool.com Student Edition on Audio CD, Chapter 8
UR 8-1 Lesson Plan **UR** 8-1 Section Summary **UR** 8-1 Review and Reinforce **UR** 8-1 Enrich **UR** Chapter 8 Real-World Lab	**SE** Section 1 Review, p. 235 **TE** Ongoing Assessment, pp. 227, 231, 233 **TE** Performance Assessment, p. 235	Concept Videotape Library, Grade 6, Tape 2, "Positive Bacteria" Lab Activity Videotapes, Grade 6 Tape 2 Transparency 24, "Exploring Drinking-Water Treatment" Transparency 25, "Exploring Wastewater Treatment" Transparency 26, "Cutaway View of a Septic Tank"
UR 8-2 Lesson Plan **UR** 8-2 Section Summary **UR** 8-2 Review and Reinforce **UR** 8-2 Enrich **UR** Chapter 8 Skills Lab	**SE** Section 2 Review, p. 240 **TE** Ongoing Assessment, pp. 237, 239 **TE** Performance Assessment, p. 240	Concept Videotape Library, Grade 6, Tape 2, "Xeriscape" Lab Activity Videotapes, Grade 6 Tape 2
UR 8-3 Lesson Plan **UR** 8-3 Section Summary **UR** 8-3 Review and Reinforce **UR** 8-3 Enrich	**SE** Section 3 Review, p. 250 **TE** Ongoing Assessment, pp. 245, 247, 249 **TE** Performance Assessment, p. 250	Concept Videotape Library, Grade 6, Tape 2, "Rain, Rain, Go Away"
UR 8-4 Lesson Plan **UR** 8-4 Section Summary **UR** 8-4 Review and Reinforce **UR** 8-4 Enrich	**SE** Section 4 Review, p. 254 **TE** Ongoing Assessment, p. 253 **TE** Performance Assessment, p. 254	Concept Videotape Library, Grade 6, Tape 2, "Energy" Transparency 27, "Exploring a Hydroelectric Power Plant"
RCA Provides strategies to improve science reading skills **GRSW** Provides worksheets to promote student comprehension of content	**SE** Chapter 8 Study Guide/Assessment, pp. 255–257 **PA** Chapter 8 Performance Assessment **CUT** Chapter 8 Test **CTB** Chapter 8 Test	Computer Test Bank, Chapter 8 Test

Key: **SE** Student Edition
CTB Computer Test Bank
ISAB Inquiry Skills Activity Book
GRSW Guided Reading and Study Workbook
TE Teacher's Edition
PTA Product Testing Activities by *Consumer Reports*
RCA Reading in the Content Area
PA Performance Assessment
UR Unit Resources
LM Laboratory Manual
IES Interdisciplinary Explorations Series
CUT Chapter and Unit Tests

Meeting the National Science Education Standards and AAAS Benchmarks

National Science Education Standards	Benchmarks for Science Literacy	Unifying Themes
Science As Inquiry (Content Standard A) ◆ **Use appropriate tools and techniques to gather, analyze, and interpret data** Students test and compare various types of water. *(Real-World Lab)* ◆ **Think critically and logically to make the relationships between evidence and explanations** Students investigate desalination. *(Skills Lab)* **Science and Technology** (Content Standard E) ◆ **Design a solution or product** Students design and build a model water treatment system. *(Chapter Project)* ◆ **Understandings about science and technology** Various processes are used to treat drinking water and wastewater. Hydroelectric power plants generate electricity. *(Sections 1, 2 and 4)* **Science in Personal and Social Perspectives** (Content Standard F) ◆ **Personal health** Water supplies often need treatment to make water safe. Water pollution makes water unsafe. *(Sections 1 and 3)* ◆ **Populations, resources, and environments** Water shortages occur due to supply and demand. *(Section 2; Science and Society)* ◆ **Science and technology in society** There are various ways to conserve water. Human activities can cause water pollution. *(Sections 2 and 3)*	**1B Scientific Inquiry** Students test and compare various types of water. Students investigate desalination. *(Real-World Lab; Skills Lab)* **3A Technology and Science** Water undergoes treatment before and after people use it. There are various ways to conserve water. Hydroelectric power plants generate electricity. *(Sections 1, 2, and 4)* **3B Design and Systems** Students build a water treatment system. *(Chapter Project)* **3C Issues in Technology** Water pollution can be caused by human activities. Hydroelectric power plants have both positive and negative effects. *(Sections 3 and 4)* **4B The Earth** Water shortages occur when there is too little water or too great a demand. *(Section 2; Science and Society)* **8C Energy Sources and Use** Hydroelectric power plants change the energy of moving water into electricity. *(Section 4)*	◆ **Systems and Interactions** Various processes are used to treat drinking water and wastewater. Water pollution can affect surface water, groundwater, and even rain. *(Sections 1 and 3)* ◆ **Patterns of Change** Water shortages occur when there is too little water or too great a demand. High demands on the Ogallala Aquifer have caused water levels to drop there. *(Section 2; Science and Society)* ◆ **Modeling** Students design and build a model of a water treatment plant. Students investigate desalination using a distillation model. *(Chapter Project; Skills Lab)* ◆ **Unity and Diversity** Students test and compare various types of water. Sources of water pollution include point and nonpoint sources. *(Real-World Lab; Section 3)* ◆ **Energy** Hydroelectric power plants capture the energy of moving water and change it into electrical energy. *(Section 4)*

Take It to the Net

Interactive text at www.phschool.com

Science Explorer comes alive with iText.

- **Complete student text** is accessible from any computer with Internet access or a CD-ROM drive.
- **Animations, simulations, and videos** enhance student understanding and retention of concepts.
- **Self-tests and online study tools** assess student understanding.

STAY CURRENT with **SCIENCE NEWS®**

Find out the latest research and information about Earth's Waters at: **www.phschool.com**

Go to **www.phschool.com** and click on the Science icon.Then click on Science Explorer: Life, Earth, and Physical Science under PH@school.

Student Edition Activities Planner

ACTIVITY	Time (minutes)	Materials Quantities for one work group	Skills
Section 1			
Discover, p. 226	20	**Consumable** 2 heavy plastic trash bags, water **Nonconsumable** 2 large trash barrels, large plastic pitcher with lid	Calculating
Real-World Lab, pp. 228–229	40	**Consumable** liquid soap, 200 mL tap water, 200 mL distilled water, 200 mL spring water, 200 mL mineral water, 4 pieces of pH paper, 4 paper cups **Nonconsumable** hot plate, ruler, wax pencil, 4 200-mL beakers, 4 test tubes and stoppers, test tube rack, pH indicator chart, 25-mL graduated cylinder	Observing, Inferring, Drawing Conclusions
Try This, p. 232	20	**Consumable** water **Nonconsumable** books, 2 large bowls, pitcher, plastic tubing	Observing
Section 2			
Discover, p. 236	15	**Consumable** water **Nonconsumable** large measuring cup, plastic dropper, 2 small bowls, spoon, stopwatch	Predicting
Sharpen Your Skills, p. 239	5, 5	**Nonconsumable** large measuring cup	Predicting
Science at Home, p. 240	home	**Consumable** toothpaste, water, tape, toothbrush	Comparing and Contrasting
Skills Lab, p. 241	40	**Consumable** aluminum foil, water, ice, salt **Nonconsumable** hot plate, 250-mL beaker, plastic spoon, shallow pan, plastic tube, 500-mL flask, stirring rod, rubber stopper, 50 cm rubber tubing	Making Models
Section 3			
Discover, p. 243	15	**Consumable** coffee filter, paper plate, food coloring **Nonconsumable** permanent marker, wet sponge, plastic dropper	Observing
Sharpen Your Skills, p. 245	10	No special materials required.	Classifying
Try This, p. 248	15, 5	**Consumable** masking tape, tap water, pond or aquarium water, liquid fertilizer **Nonconsumable** 2 wide-mouth jars with tops, permanent marker, graduated cylinder	Drawing Conclusions
Section 4			
Discover, p. 251	10	**Consumable** large plastic trash bag, water **Nonconsumable** various cylindrical objects, plant sprayer	Observing
Try This, p. 252	15	**Consumable** aluminum pie plate, small foam ball, 2 toothpicks, running water **Nonconsumable** tin snips or heavy scissors, metric ruler, marker	Developing Hypotheses

A list of all materials required for the Student Edition activities can be found on pages TVA34–TVA40. You can obtain information about ordering materials by calling 1-800-848-9500 or by accessing the Science Explorer Internet site at: **www.phschool.com**

CHAPTER 8 PROJECT

A Precious Resource

In this chapter, students will be introduced to the concepts that water quality can vary widely and that drinking water must be treated for both safety and taste. This project will give students a tangible sense of what the treatment of water entails.

Purpose In this project, students will design a water treatment system with at least two steps. Then, they will assemble and demonstrate a model water treatment system that cleans and recovers as much of 1 liter of dirty water as possible. In doing so, they will gain a better understanding of the processes involved in water treatment.

Skills Focus Students will be able to

- ◆ observe the characteristics of dirty water;
- ◆ design a model water treatment system;
- ◆ create a flow chart that represents the treatment system;
- ◆ make a working model of a water treatment system;
- ◆ communicate the workings of the treatment system to the class;
- ◆ compare and contrast their design with that of others;
- ◆ draw conclusions from the experiences of their classmates.

Project Timeline The entire project will require at least two weeks. On the first day, distribute Chapter 8 Project Overview in the Unit 3 Resources. Allow class time for students to discuss what the project will entail and the possible materials needed to carry it out. At this time, you may wish to distribute Chapter 8 Project Scoring Rubric in Unit 3 Resources, so students are clear about what will be expected of them. Students will be doing the Chapter 8 Project Worksheet 1 in Unit 3 Resources and Chapter 8 Project Worksheet 2, in Unit 3 Resources.

Once they've completed Worksheet 2, allow class time for students to decide on a design and begin assembling the treatment system model. Students will need more time during the second week to test the model, to make any changes necessary to improve the design, and finally to prepare for the presentation to the class. At least one class period will be needed for students to present their water-treatment models. End with a class discussion that focuses on a comparison of all the models.

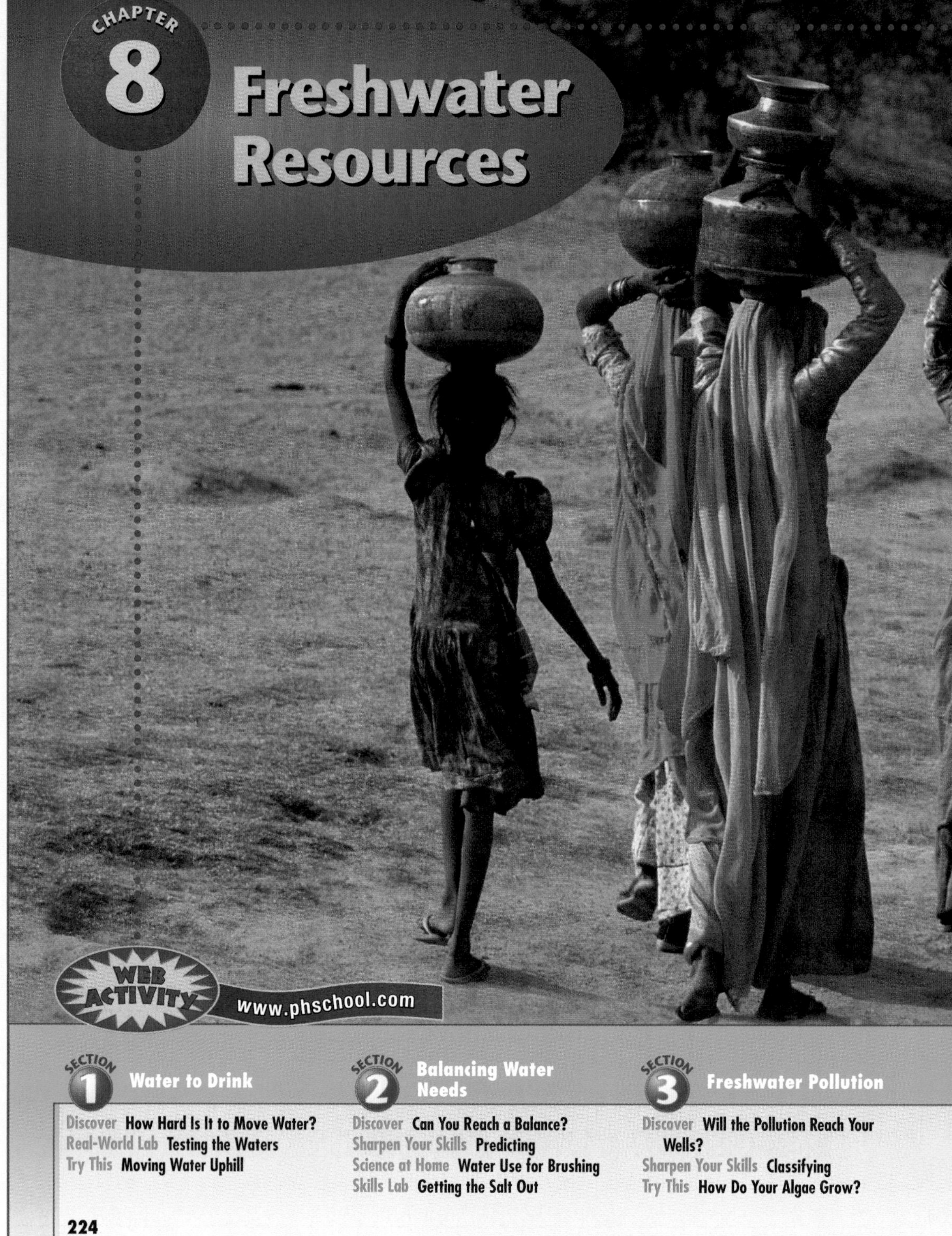

Chapter 8 Freshwater Resources

Suggested Shortcuts You can simplify the project by limiting the model to filtration as the only treatment method. You also may wish to divide students into groups of three or four to design and build their system to save time. Students can complete Chapter 8 Project Worksheet 1 in their groups, and then present their results to the class.

Possible Materials Because students design their own treatment systems, materials may vary widely. In fact, you should encourage students to think of unique materials as long as they are not too difficult to obtain. All students, though, will need certain materials, especially for Chapter 8 Project Worksheet 1, in which they experiment with a variety of filtration materials.

CHAPTER 8 PROJECT

A Precious Resource

If you lived in Rajasthan, India, you might walk two kilometers every morning to collect a heavy bucket of water from a spring-fed oasis. Your family would use this water for breakfast, washing dishes, and laundry. When you came home from school, you would fetch more water for the evening meal and bathing.

In this chapter, you will explore water as a resource. You will discover what happens when water is scarce, and how water can become polluted. You will also learn how people can use freshwater resources more wisely, and how water pollution can be prevented or cleaned up. Throughout the chapter, you will be building your own model water treatment system.

Your Goal To design and build a water treatment system to clean one liter of dirty water.

Your treatment system should

- consist of at least two treatment steps
- be made from materials that have been approved by your teacher
- recover as much of one liter of clean water as possible
- be built following the safety guidelines in Appendix A

Get Started Your teacher will give you a sample of dirty water. Begin now by using your senses to observe your sample. Make a list of all your observations. Think about what types of substances might be present in this water. **CAUTION:** *Never taste or drink the water samples before or after treatment.*

Check Your Progress You'll be working on this project as you study this chapter. To keep your project on track, look for Check Your Progress boxes at the following points.

Section 1 Review, page 235: Plan the steps of your system.
Section 3 Review, page 250: Assemble your treatment system.
Section 4 Review, page 254: Test and modify your system.

Present Your Project At the end of the chapter (page 257), you will demonstrate how well your system cleans up the dirty water sample.

SECTION 4 *Integrating Physics* **Water as an Energy Resource**

Discover **Can Water Do Work?**
Try This **Making a Water Wheel**

These residents of Rajasthan, India, balance steel and brass containers of water on their heads for the walk home from the oasis.

225

All students will need a supply of dirty water. You can make such water by mixing 1 tablespoon of fuller's earth (a highly absorbent, opaque clay) per cup of tap water. You could also use water from a local river or pond, making sure to include mud from the bottom.

Filtration materials include sand, gravel, charcoal or activated charcoal, window screening, various fabrics, and coffee filters or other papers. Each student or group will need a 2-L clear plastic soda bottle with the bottom cut off. The bottles will work as filter supports when held upside down on a ring stand.

If students want to include a coagulation step in the system, they will need alum (aluminum sulfate) or baking soda (sodium bicarbonate).

Launching the Project To introduce this project, show students a container of tap water and a container of dirty water. Ask: **What are some methods by which you could make this dirty water as clean as the tap water?** *(Accept any suggestion. Many students will mention methods of filtration. Some students might suggest a distillation method.)* Write the list on the board. At this point, you might also prepare the "cleanness scale" as described in the Teacher's Notes in Unit 3 Resources. Ask: **Would adding tap water to the dirty water be a way to make the water safe to drink?** *(Some students may correctly suggest that simply diluting the water would not be sufficient.)*

Finally, have students read the description of the project in the text and in the Chapter 8 Project Overview. Encourage them to begin thinking of steps they could include in their water treatment system.

Program Resources

- **Unit 3 Resources** Chapter 8 Project Teacher Notes; Chapter 8 Overview and Worksheets; Chapter 8 Project Scoring Rubric

Media and Technology

Student Edition on Audio CD
Chapter 8

www.phschool.com

You will find an Internet activity, chapter self-tests for students, and links to other chapter topics at this site.

Performance Assessment

To assess students' performance in this project, use the Chapter 8 Project Scoring Rubric Unit 3 Resources. Students will be assessed on

- their treatment system design and flow chart;
- their treatment system model;
- their class presentation;
- their group participation, if they worked in groups.

Water to Drink

Objectives

After completing the lesson, students will be able to
- ◆ describe sources of drinking water and how it is treated and distributed;
- ◆ explain what happens to wastewater.

Key Terms water quality, pH, hardness, concentration, filtration, flocs, coagulation, sewage, sludge, septic tank, leach field

1 Engage/Explore

Activating Prior Knowledge

Display a glass of water, and tell students that it came from a school drinking fountain. Ask: **Where did this water come from before that?** *(Answers will vary. A typical answer might mention a local river or reservoir.)* Have students make a flowchart of a possible route by which the water came to the school, including any treatment the water received on its journey.

Discover Activity

Skills Focus calculating
Materials *2 large trash barrels, 2 heavy plastic trash bags, water, large plastic pitcher with lid*
Time 20 minutes
Tips Spilled water is to be expected in this activity, so it would be best to do this outdoors on a warm day. Bigger pitchers will result in fewer passes. To save time, students could pass multiple pitchers, as long as someone keeps count.
Expected Outcome Students will experience the amount of time and effort needed to move water.
Think It Over Answers will vary depending on the size of the pitcher. Students should make this calculation using the number of passes it took to transfer the 100 L of water. For example, if it took 50 passes to transfer 100 L, then it would take 2.5 times that to transfer 250 L.

Section 1 Water to Drink

Discover Activity

How Hard Is It to Move Water?

1. Line two large trash barrels with heavy plastic bags. Fill one barrel with about 100 liters of water. This is about how much water a person uses during a five-minute shower.
2. Form a line of students between the barrels. Your goal is to transfer all the water from the first barrel to the second barrel. Avoid spilling the water. Be careful of slippery floors if you are doing this activity indoors.
3. The first person in line should fill a large plastic pitcher with water, put the cover on, and hand it to the next person.
4. Pass the pitcher to the end of the line, where the last person should empty it into the second barrel. Hand the empty pitcher back down the line to the first person.
5. Repeat Steps 3 and 4 until all the water has been transferred to the second barrel. How many times did you pass the pitcher down the line?

Think It Over

Calculating Suppose a person uses an average of 250 liters of water a day. How many times would you have to pass the pitcher to move the amount of water this person would use in a day? In a year?

Guide for Reading

- ◆ What is the goal of drinking-water treatment?
- ◆ What happens to wastewater in most large communities?

Reading Tip Before you read, rewrite the section headings as how, why, or what questions. As you read, find answers to these questions.

At first, doctors in Milwaukee, Wisconsin, thought that 1993 was just a bad year for the flu. Patient after patient complained of nausea, fever, and other flulike symptoms. Within just a few weeks, about 400,000 people came down with symptoms of the disease. Public health officials began looking for another explanation for the epidemic.

The investigators discovered that all the victims had drunk water from the same water treatment plant. Tests revealed that the water contained a tiny parasite, a protist called *Cryptosporidium.* One sip of water could contain enough *Cryptosporidium* to make a person ill! This parasite had not been killed by the chemicals used to treat water at the plant. The scientists hypothesized that the *Cryptosporidium* might have come from runoff from fields where cows grazed. Although most of the victims recovered after a few weeks, about 100 deaths were blamed on the contamination.

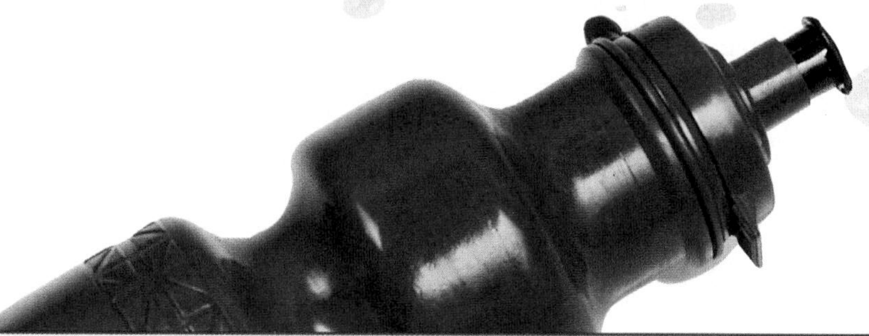

Reading Strategies

Reading Tip Before students write their questions, write *how, why,* and *what* on the chalkboard. Have a volunteer read the first heading and then choose one of these words to turn the heading into a question. Student's questions and answers may vary. Typical questions and answers: What are the sources of drinking water? *(Rivers, lakes, reservoirs, and aquifers)* How is drinking water treated? *(Treatment ranges from a simple filter on a household well to complex processes at public treatment plants.)* What steps does a typical treatment plant carry out? *(First filtration, coagulation, second filtration, chlorination, aeration, and additional treatment.)* What does water distribution involve? *(Water goes from a treatment plant to a central pumping station, where it is pumped through water mains and smaller pipes to houses and buildings.)*

Figure 1 An aqueduct carries water from one place to another. This aqueduct, the Pont du Gard in France, was built by the Romans more than 2,000 years ago. *Inferring Why do you think the Romans found it necessary to construct aqueducts?*

Milwaukee's experience was a reminder of the importance of a safe, clean water supply. In this section, you will follow drinking water on its journey to and from homes, schools, and businesses.

Sources of Drinking Water

Where does the water in your kitchen faucet come from? The first step in tracing the path of your water supply is to identify its source. Recall that Earth's liquid fresh water is found on the surface in rivers, lakes, and reservoirs, and underground in rock layers called aquifers. Most people in the United States get their drinking water from one of these sources.

If you live near a large lake or river, your water may come from that source. A distant lake or reservoir could also supply your drinking water. For instance, the city of Los Angeles draws much of its water from the Sierra Nevada Mountains, halfway across California. Or you may rely on groundwater as a source of drinking water. About half the people in the United States, including most people in rural areas, pump drinking water from aquifers.

Your drinking water comes from either a public or private water supply. Most large communities maintain public water supplies. These communities collect, treat, and distribute water to residents. In smaller communities and rural areas, people rely on private wells that supply water for individual families.

☑ *Checkpoint* *List three possible sources of drinking water.*

Treating Drinking Water

After you have identified the source of your drinking water, what is the next step in its journey to your faucet? **Water from both public and private supplies often needs some treatment to ensure that the water is safe and appealing to drink.** Treatment can range from a simple filter on a household well to complex processes at public treatment plants.

2 Facilitate

Sources of Drinking Water

Real-Life Learning

To familiarize students with the source of their own drinking water, display a large map of your area. Ask: **What bodies of water in our area could be the source of our drinking water?** *(Students should point out any reservoir, lake, or major river in the area.)* **Is there any other possible source of drinking water?** *(groundwater)* Designated students could call the local water department, find out the source of your water, and report to the class. If students live in an area where there is no water department and most people get water from private wells, have students contact a nearby state geological survey office or drilling company to find out about local aquifers. **learning modality: verbal**

Treating Drinking Water

Inquiry Challenge

Materials *lake or river water, slide, plastic dropper, microscope*
Time 15 minutes

Have students examine untreated water from a local surface water source to make inferences about why the water would need to be treated. Place several beakers of this water around the classroom, where students can examine it closely and smell it. Then each student can make a slide to examine under a microscope. Each student should conclude by writing a short description of the water and why they think it is not safe to drink. Caution students never to taste the water and to wash their hands after the activity. **learning modality: visual**

Ongoing Assessment

Oral Presentation Call on students at random to explain why communities treat drinking water and to identify the sources of drinking water.

Program Resources

- **Unit 3 Resources** 8-1 Lesson Plan; 8-1 Section Summary
- **Guided Reading and Study Workbook** Section 8-1
- **Product Testing Activities by *Consumer Reports*** "Testing Shampoos," pp. 1–8

Answers to Self-Assessment

Caption Question

Figure 1 The Romans needed a way to transport water to places where there was not enough water to meet their needs.

☑ *Checkpoint*

A typical answer should include three of the following: rivers, lakes, reservoirs, and aquifers.

Real-World Lab

You, the Consumer

Testing the Waters

Preparing for Inquiry

Key Concept Bottled waters, including distilled water, spring water, and mineral water, differ from tap water and from each other in a number of ways.

Skills Objectives Students will be able to

- observe that samples of different kinds of water differ in a variety of ways;
- infer that dissolved solids may affect other water qualities;
- draw conclusions about the differences among different types of water.

Time 40 minutes

Advance Planning Bring to class unopened bottles of distilled water, spring water, and noncarbonated mineral water. Obtain a pump bottle of liquid soap, such as a nondetergent hand-washing soap. Make sure to have enough unused, small paper cups. Obtain narrow-range (6–8) pH paper, which can detect subtle differences in similar samples.

Alternative Materials Burners and stands can be used in place of hot plates. Use small jars in place of test tubes. Instead of stoppers, use plastic wrap or wax paper held in place with rubber bands.

Guiding Inquiry

Invitation To give the lab a context, ask: **Why do many people buy costly bottled water instead of always using relatively inexpensive tap water?** *(People buy bottled waters for taste, health purposes, use in appliances, and a variety of other reasons.)*

Introducing the Procedure

- Ask students: **Why is it important to use the same amount of water in each beaker when heating the water?** *(The goal is to boil away the same amount in each beaker.)*
- Ask: **What factors might influence the taste test?** *(Dissolved substances in the different waters, individual tastes among students)*

Appearance and Taste Picture a glass of water. What observations would affect whether or not you were willing to take a sip? What if the water were cloudy, or had a funny smell? What if the water were rust-colored? Cloudiness, odor, and color are three factors that affect water quality. **Water quality** is a measurement of the substances in water besides water molecules. Some substances, such as iron, can affect the taste or color of water but are harmless unless present at very high levels. Other

Real-World Lab

You, the Consumer

Testing the Waters

How does the bottled water sold in supermarkets differ from the water that comes out of your kitchen faucet? In this lab, you will discover some differences among various types of water.

Problem

How do distilled water, spring water, and mineral water differ from tap water?

Skills Focus

observing, inferring, drawing conclusions

Materials

hot plate	liquid soap
ruler	wax pencil
tap water, 200 mL	distilled water, 200 mL
spring water, 200 mL	mineral water, 200 mL
4 200-mL beakers	4 test tubes and stoppers
4 pieces of pH paper	test tube rack
25-mL graduated cylinder	pH indicator chart
	4 paper cups per person

Procedure

1. Copy the data table into your notebook.
2. Label the beakers A, B, C, and D. Pour 100 mL of tap water into beaker A. Pour 100 mL of the other water samples into the correct beaker (refer to the data table).
3. Heat each water sample on a hot plate until about 20 mL remains. Do not allow the water to boil completely away. **CAUTION:** *Do not touch the hot plate or beakers.*
4. After the water samples have cooled, look for solids that make the water cloudy. Rank the samples from 1 to 4, where 1 has the fewest visible solids and 4 has the most visible solids. Record your rankings in the data table.
5. Label the test tubes A, B, C, and D. Pour 10 mL of each water sample from the source bottle into the correct test tube.
6. Dip a piece of pH paper into test tube A to measure its acidity. Match the color of the pH paper to a number on the pH indicator chart. Record the pH (0–14) in your data table.

Troubleshooting the Experiment

- Heating the water in Step 3 may take 15–20 minutes, and then cooling may take another 10–15 minutes. During those periods, have students continue with the rest of the steps of the Procedure. That is, after beginning Step 3, they should do Steps 5–12 and then return at the end to do Step 4.
- If wide-opening droppers are available, have students use them to add soap to samples.

Sample Data Table

Water Sample	Visible Solids (1–4)	pH (0–14)	Soap-sud Height (cm)	Taste
A Tap water	2	7.0	11	metallic, refreshing
B Distilled water	1	7.0	10	tasteless, flat
C Spring water	3	7.5	9	refreshing
D Mineral water	4	8.0	8	salty, bitter

substances, such as certain chemicals and microorganisms, can be harmful to your health.

Acidity The **pH** of water is a measurement of how acidic or basic it is, on a scale of 0 to 14. Pure water is neutral, meaning it is neither an acid or a base, and has a pH of 7. The lower the pH, the more acidic the water. Acidic water can cause problems by dissolving lead or other metals from the pipes it passes through. The higher the pH, the more basic the water.

DATA TABLE

Water Sample	Visible Solids (1–4)	pH (0–14)	Soapsud Height (cm)	Taste
A - Tap water				
B - Distilled water				
C - Spring water				
D - Mineral water				

7. Repeat Step 6 for the other samples.
8. Add two drops of liquid soap to test tube A. Put a stopper in the test tube and shake it 30 times. With the ruler, measure the height of the soapsuds in the test tube. Record the measurement in your data table.
9. Repeat Step 8 for the other samples.
10. Label the four cups A, B, C, and D. Write your name on each cup.
11. Pour a little tap water into cup A directly from the original source bottle. Taste the tap water. In your data table, describe the taste using one or more of these words: salty, flat, bitter, metallic, refreshing, tasteless. **CAUTION:** *Do not conduct the taste test in a lab room. Use a clean cup for each sample and discard it after use.*
12. Repeat Step 11 with the other samples.

Analyze and Conclude

1. Review your data table. Compare each of the bottled water samples to the tap water sample. What similarities and differences did you detect?
2. Rank the samples from the one with the fewest soapsuds to the one with the most. Compare this ranking to the one for visible solids. What pattern do you see? What do both of these tests have to do with the hardness of water?
3. What other information about the water samples might you need before deciding which one to drink regularly? Explain.
4. **Apply** Based on your results, which sample would you most want to use for (a) drinking, (b) boiling in a kettle, and (c) washing laundry? Which sample would you least want to use for each purpose? Explain.

Getting Involved

Conduct a survey to find out what percentage of people buy bottled mineral water, distilled water, and spring water. Why do they buy each type of water and how do they use it in their homes?

Program Resources

- **Unit 3 Resources** Chapter 8 Real-World Lab blackline masters

Media and Technology

Lab Activity Videotapes
Grade 6, Tape 2

Safety

Emphasize that in Step 3 students should not let the water boil away completely. Advise that an oven mitt is essential to use when handling hot beakers. Caution students to be careful using the electric hotplates. Students should pour tasting samples only from the original bottles and always use a new cup. Review the safety guidelines in Appendix A.

Expected Outcome

The different kinds of water will differ in amount of dissolved solids, pH value, ability to produce soapsuds, and taste. See Sample Data Table.

Analyze and Conclude

1. Answers may vary. A typical answer: Distilled water has fewer visible solids, lower pH, greater soapsud height than tap water, and flatter taste than tap water. Both spring water and mineral water have more visible solids, higher pH, lower soapsud height, and more salty or refreshing taste than tap water.
2. Answers may vary. See Sample Data Table for typical rankings. Students should observe that the sample with the most visible solids has the fewest soapsuds, and vice versa. Both tests measure the hardness of water. The more visible solids, the harder the water; the fewer soapsuds, the harder the water.
3. Answers may vary. A typical answer may mention testing for the concentrations of other substances, such as lead and nickel, as well as for the coliform count.
4. Answers may vary. A typical answer: (a) The spring water is best for drinking because it tastes best; the distilled water is worst because it is tasteless. (b) The distilled water is best for boiling because it contains the least solids; the mineral water is worst because its minerals leave a residue. (c) The distilled or tap water is best for washing because they produce the most soapsuds; the mineral water is worst because it produces the fewest soapsuds.

Extending the Inquiry

Getting Involved Students could collaborate on constructing a simple survey with such questions as these: Do you ever buy bottled water? What kind? How often? For what use? Several questions could be constructed so that they can be answered with a "yes" or "no." For those questions, students could circle or check the appropriate response. Other questions could elicit short-answer responses. Once students have constructed the survey, help them make copies and decide where they could do the survey. Local grocery stores are good places to begin.

Addressing Naive Conceptions

Materials *noncarbonated mineral water, softened water, 2 beakers, non-detergent soap*
Time 10 minutes

Ask students: **What does the term *hard water* mean?** *(Some students may take the term literally and think it is harder to the touch than soft water.)* Explain that water is called "hard" because minerals are dissolved in it, not because it is harder to the touch. Then give each student the opportunity to compare mineral water and softened water. (Buy commercial mineral water; bring softened water to school from a home that has soft water or a water softener.) Have students pour a sample of each type of water into a beaker. Encourage students to compare the two samples. Then have students add a small amount of soap to each sample, stir, and compare. Students should observe more suds in the soft water. **limited English proficiency**

Inquiry Challenge

Materials *muddy water, large beaker, alum crystals, stirring rod*
Time 20 minutes

Invite students to investigate coagulation. First have them hypothesize what will happen when alum is added to muddy water. Then they can add one tablespoon of alum crystals to a beaker of muddy water and stir slowly for 5 minutes. Students will observe large clumps settle quickly and smaller clumps later. **learning modality: kinesthetic**

Math TOOLBOX

Time 15 minutes
Tips Have students rewrite as fractions the following concentrations:

- 2 ppm of copper *(2/1,000,000)*
- 0.09 ppm of cyanide *(0.09/1,000,000)*
- 0.24 ppb of arsenic *(0.24/1,000,000,000)*

learning modality: logical/mathematical

Math TOOLBOX

Parts per . . .

Concentrations are often measured in parts per million (ppm) or parts per billion (ppb). What do these units mean? If you own one compact disc by your favorite band, and the disc sells one million copies, your disc is one of the one million sold, or one part per million. When you see a concentration written in this form, you can rewrite it as a fraction:

1. Suppose the concentration of iron in a water sample is 500 parts per million.
2. Write this concentration as a fraction by putting the number of parts on top, and the "whole" on the bottom:

$$500 \text{ parts per million} = \frac{500}{1{,}000{,}000}$$

Hardness The level of two minerals—calcium and magnesium—in water is referred to as **hardness.** Hard water contains high levels of these minerals. The minerals come from rocks such as limestone that water flows through. For most people, the main drawback of hard water is that it does not form suds well when mixed with soap. That means that it takes more soap or detergent to get laundry clean in hard water. The minerals in hard water also form deposits that can clog pipes and machinery. Soft water, on the other hand, contains lower levels of calcium and magnesium. Soft water leaves fewer deposits and forms better soapsuds than hard water.

Disease-Causing Organisms Another factor affecting water quality is the presence of disease-causing organisms. The coliform count measures the number of *Escherichia coli* bacteria. Since these bacteria are found in human and animal wastes, their presence in the water shows that it contains waste material. A high coliform count is an indicator, or sign, that the water may also contain other disease-causing organisms.

Standards of Quality The Environmental Protection Agency (EPA), which is responsible for protecting the quality of water and other natural resources in the United States, has developed water-quality standards for drinking water. These standards set concentration limits for certain chemicals, minerals, and bacteria in drinking water. A **concentration** is the amount of one substance in a certain volume of another substance. For example, the concentration of letters in alphabet soup might be written as the number of letters per liter of soup. Figure 2 shows the standards for some different substances.

Checkpoint *List five factors that affect water quality.*

Selected Water-Quality Standards

Substance	Limit
Arsenic	0.05 parts per million (ppm)
Carbon tetrachloride	0.005 ppm
Copper	1.3 ppm
Cyanide	0.2 ppm
Lead	0.015 ppm
Coliform count	No more than 5% of samples taken in a month can be positive.
pH	6.5–8.5

Source: U.S. Environmental Protection Agency, National Primary and Secondary Drinking-Water Standards.

Figure 2 The EPA has set standards for the amounts of various substances in drinking water. ***Interpreting Data*** *Based on this table, is a concentration of 0.09 ppm of arsenic in drinking water acceptable? Is a concentration of 0.05 ppm of cyanide acceptable?*

230

Background

Facts and Figures The standards in Figure 2 represent maximum contaminant levels (MCLs) except for copper and lead, which are action levels requiring treatment. In 1998, the U.S. Environmental Protection Agency announced regulations requiring community water agencies to inform customers of basic facts regarding their drinking water, including: (1) the source of the water, (2) what contaminants were in the water and which exceeded EPA health standards, (3) what health risks were associated with those contaminants that exceeded standards, and (4) any violations and actions that had been taken against the water agency that year.

A Typical Treatment Plant

Follow the water from river to faucet in *Exploring Drinking-Water Treatment* to see what happens in a typical water treatment plant.

The first step in treating water from a lake or river is usually filtration. **Filtration** is the process of passing water through a series of screens that allows the water through, but not larger solid particles. During this first step, trash, leaves, branches, and other large objects are removed from the water.

In the second step, a chemical such as alum is added to cause sticky globs, called **flocs,** to form. Other particles in the water stick to the flocs, a process called **coagulation.** The heavy clumps sink to the bottom in the settling basins. The water is then filtered again.

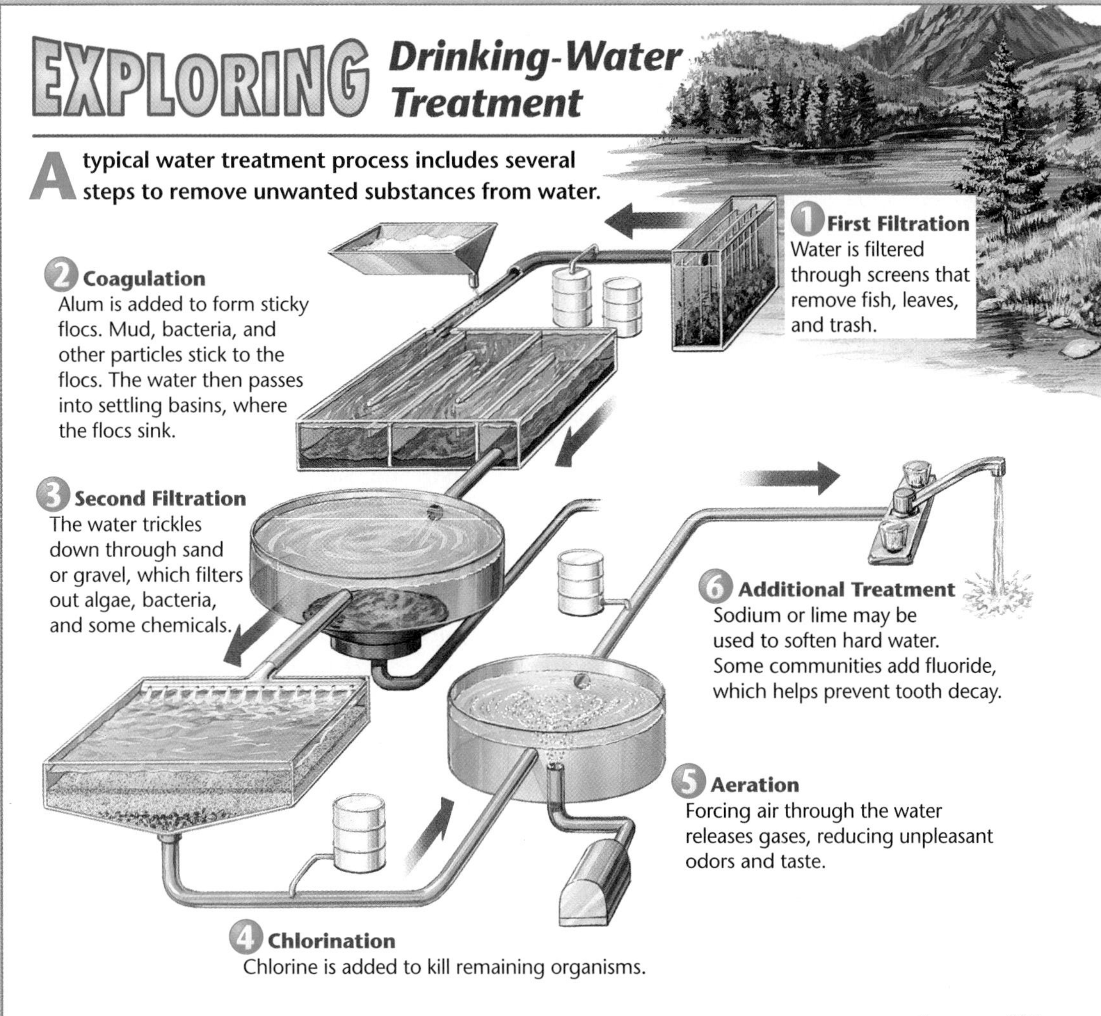

A Typical Treatment Plant

EXPLORING Drinking-Water Treatment

As students read aloud the descriptions of the steps in drinking-water treatment, have other students create a table on the blackboard showing each step and its results. Encourage students to investigate the process used at the local drinking-water treatment plant, if there is one. Students can compare the process shown here with the local process by making flow charts of each. **learning modality: visual**

Building Inquiry Skills: Predicting

Materials *pond water, 2 L plastic bottle with top, funnel, 2 large plastic jars*
Time 15 minutes

Challenge students to model aeration. First, invite them to examine and smell the pond water and predict how the pond water will change after being aerated. To aerate the water, students can pour it through a funnel into a clean, 2-L plastic bottle. Then with the top on, students should shake the bottle vigorously. After shaking, they should pour the water into a jar. Finally, students should pour the water back and forth between that jar and another 10 times. Then have students examine and smell the water to test their predictions. **learning modality: kinesthetic**

Media and Technology

Transparencies "Exploring Drinking-Water Treatment," Transparency 24

Answers to Self-Assessment

Checkpoint

Any five: cloudiness, odor, color, acidity, hardness, and presence of disease-causing organisms

Caption Question

Figure 2 A concentration of 0.09 ppm of arsenic is unacceptable. A concentration of 0.05 ppm of cyanide is acceptable.

Ongoing Assessment

Writing Have students explain in writing how each step in drinking-water treatment affects water quality by describing how the step affects appearance, taste, acidity, hardness, and/or the presence of disease-causing organisms.

Water Distribution

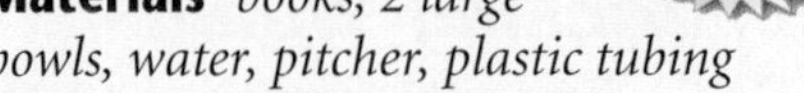

Skills Focus observing

Materials *books, 2 large bowls, water, pitcher, plastic tubing*

Time 20 minutes

Tips Cut lengths of tubing before class, at least 50–60 cm each. Demonstrate how to fill the siphon with water by completely immersing it in the water of the higher bowl. Emphasize that the finger must completely cover the end of the siphon and that no air should be allowed inside the tube. Have students cover their books with paper to protect them during the experiment.

Expected Outcome Water will flow through the siphon from the higher bowl into the lower bowl, eventually emptying the higher bowl.

Extend Students can experiment with longer siphons and circuitous routes, such as holding the middle of the tubing above the higher bowl. **learning modality: kinesthetic**

Integrating Physics

After students have read about water pressure and distribution, divide the class into groups of three or four. Then have each group consider this hypothesis derived from a statement in the text: *In an enclosed space, water exerts pressure in all directions.* Challenge groups to design an experiment that could test this hypothesis. A design should consist of a description and a drawing. Once the designs are finished, groups could evaluate one another's experiments. Finally, encourage students to perform the experiments that seem most likely to test the hypothesis. **cooperative learning**

Moving Water Uphill

In this activity you will see how a device called a siphon can be used to move water.

1. Pile a stack of books on a table. Place one bowl on top of the books and another bowl on the table. Pour water into the higher bowl until it is about half full.

2. Submerge a piece of plastic tubing in the water in the upper bowl. When the tubing is full of water, put a finger over each end.
3. Keeping one end of the tubing underwater, place the other end in the lower, empty bowl. Release both fingers and watch what happens.

Observing In what direction does the water first have to travel to get out of the higher bowl? Can you explain this movement?

The next step is to chlorinate the water. If you have ever been to a public swimming pool, you are familiar with the smell of chlorine. Chlorine is added to drinking water for the same reason it is added to swimming pools—to kill disease-causing microorganisms. At this point, the water is usually ready to be distributed to homes. Sometimes other chemicals are added to kill specific organisms, such as the *Cryptosporidium* you read about earlier.

Water from an aquifer may require less treatment than water from a lake or river. Flowing through the rocks or sand naturally filters and purifies the water. However, most public water supplies that use a groundwater source still add chlorine to kill disease-causing organisms.

Public health officials regularly test samples from water treatment plants to assess water quality. They test for the substances covered by the drinking-water standards, including chemicals, dissolved solids, pH, hardness, and disease-causing organisms. Private well owners should also test their water regularly to make sure no treatment is needed.

✓ *Checkpoint* *What is the goal of most drinking-water treatment systems?*

Water Distribution

INTEGRATING PHYSICS Once it has been treated, the water is ready to be distributed to homes and businesses. From a treatment plant, water goes to a central pumping station. There the water is pumped into an underground network of steel or concrete pipes called water mains. The water mains branch off to smaller pipes. These feed into smaller copper or plastic pipes that carry water into houses and other buildings.

Water pressure causes the water to move through this system of pipes. Whenever water is in an enclosed space, it exerts pressure in all directions. For example, water pressure pushes water through a garden hose. If the hose springs a leak, a jet of water sprays out of the hole into the air. The pressure pushes the water out through the hole.

Pumping stations are designed to keep water pressure steady throughout the system. If there is a leak in one of the pipes, water escapes—just as it did from the garden hose—and the pressure drops. A typical distribution system can push water up against the downward force of gravity about five or six stories. High-rise buildings must use additional pumps to raise the water to higher floors.

Rather than use a central pumping station, some communities store their water high in the air! No, not as clouds or water vapor, but in a water tower or tank on top of a hill. Treated

Background

Facts and Figures The use of chlorine as a disinfectant in drinking-water treatment began in the United States in 1908. Chlorination has proved quite effective in reducing the outbreak of waterborne diseases caused by bacteria and other pathogens, though such diseases still sicken an estimated 940,000 Americans every year. Filtration of the water before chlorination is important. First, it removes organisms that chlorine might not destroy. Second, it removes organic matter that might react with chlorine and form harmful compounds. Because these compounds may cause diseases in humans, treatment plants add as little chlorine as possible. Ozone (O_3) is being used as a disinfectant instead of chlorine in some cities. As it kills microorganisms, it breaks down into oxygen gas, which improves water quality.

Figure 3 These firefighters rely on water pressure to force streams of water through the air. *Predicting If the diameter of the firehose were larger, would the spray be more powerful or less powerful?*

water is pumped up into the water tower. When the water is released, the weight of the water supplies additional pressure that sends the water rushing downward, filling the town's water mains and pipes.

Treating Wastewater

Finally, after a long journey, the water reaches your house. You take a shower, flush the toilet, or wash a load of laundry. What happens now to the used water that goes down the drain? That wastewater and the different kinds of wastes in it are called **sewage.** You might be surprised to learn that this water could someday return as part of your drinking water! No need to worry, however. The wastewater goes through many changes to make this possible.

In many communities, a network of pipes called sanitary sewers carries sewage away from homes. Sanitary sewers are separated from storm sewers, which drain rainwater and runoff from sidewalks, lawns, and parking lots.

Cities and towns have had sanitary sewer systems for only about the last 200 years. Before then, wastewater was often dumped into open gutters and allowed to run directly back into rivers or oceans. Although people eventually realized that this practice helped spread disease, it still occurs in some places, both in the United States and the rest of the world. Coastal cities, in particular, sometimes still pump untreated sewage into the oceans.

Most communities treat their wastewater to make it safe to return to the environment. Different communities may use different treatment processes.

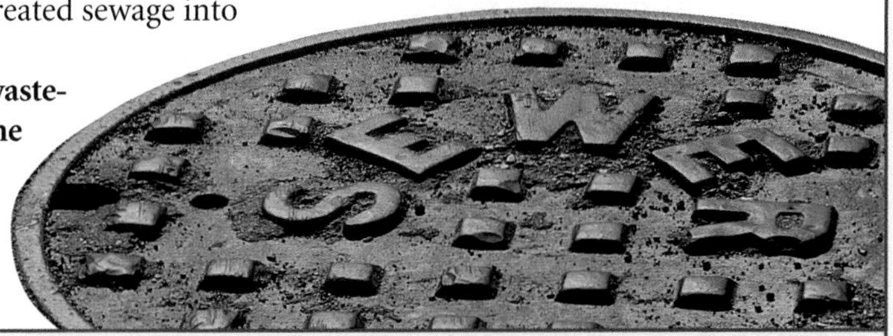

Figure 4 If your community has a sanitary sewer system, you may have seen a sewer cover like this one in the street. Sanitary sewers carry wastewater away from homes and businesses.

Answers to Self-Assessment

☑ Checkpoint

The goal is to make the water safe and appealing to drink.

Caption Question

Figure 3 The spray would be less powerful because water would move more slowly through a hose with a larger diameter.

Treating Wastewater

Real-Life Learning

ACTIVITY

Some students may have little experience or understanding of the plumbing of a building. Have a member of the school's custodial staff lead students on a tour of the separate water and sewage pipes running into and out of the school. This could begin in a school restroom and end in the school basement. Encourage students to develop a list of questions about construction and maintenance before the tour begins. **learning modality: kinesthetic**

Using the Visuals: Figure 4

ACTIVITY

Help students understand that a sewer cover functions as a door into the sanitary sewer system. Ask: **What is the purpose of this removable cover?** *(To function as a point of access for workers to maintain the system.)* Then have students identify the location of such sewer covers on their way home from school or near their homes. In class the next day, make a list on the board of the locations they have found. Then challenge students to use the locations to make inferences about the underground sewer system. **learning modality: visual**

Ongoing Assessment

Skills Check Invite students to predict what would happen if the wastewater that goes down the drain somehow got into the underground network of water mains *without* going to a treatment plant. *(The drinking water would become contaminated with waste material and disease-causing organisms.)*

Treating Wastewater, continued

EXPLORING Wastewater Treatment

Ask volunteers to read aloud the descriptions of the steps in wastewater treatment. Then ask: **In drinking-water treatment, bacteria are eliminated in three of the steps. Why are bacteria used as part of wastewater treatment?** *(In drinking-water treatment, bacteria that could be harmful to health are eliminated. In wastewater treatment, the bacteria serve the beneficial purpose of breaking down sewage.)* Challenge students to find out about the process used at the local wastewater treatment plant. Students can compare the process shown here with the local process by making flowcharts of each. **learning modality: visual**

Building Inquiry Skills: Controlling Variables

ACTIVITY

Materials *2 clear plastic soda bottles with caps, pond water with mud, funnel, permanent marker*

Time 10 minutes for setup; 5 minutes each day for 5 days

Divide students into groups and have each group investigate the settling process. First, have students mark the two bottles as A and B. Next, they should use a funnel to pour pond water into the bottles, making each about half full. Caps should then be screwed tightly onto both bottles. Finally, students should place both bottles on a table for two days. Bottle A should be left undisturbed; bottle B should be shaken three times a day each day. After two days, have students describe the experiment, identify a variable and a control, and draw conclusions about differences in the water of the two bottles. Tell students not to taste the pond water and to wash their hands after handling it. **cooperative learning**

You can follow one typical wastewater treatment process, called a trickling filter system, in *Exploring Wastewater Treatment.*

During primary treatment, deposits of fine solids called **sludge** settle out from the wastewater. Despite its unappetizing name, sludge is a useful material. It can be treated with heat and chemicals and used as fertilizer. Sludge can also be reused in secondary treatment. In one method, bacteria are added to the sludge to create "activated sludge." The activated sludge is mixed into the wastewater. The bacteria then break down the remaining sewage in the water.

If necessary, additional treatment may remove other substances from the water, such as metals and industrial chemicals. Once wastewater has gone through an effective treatment process, it is safe to return to the environment. It may be released

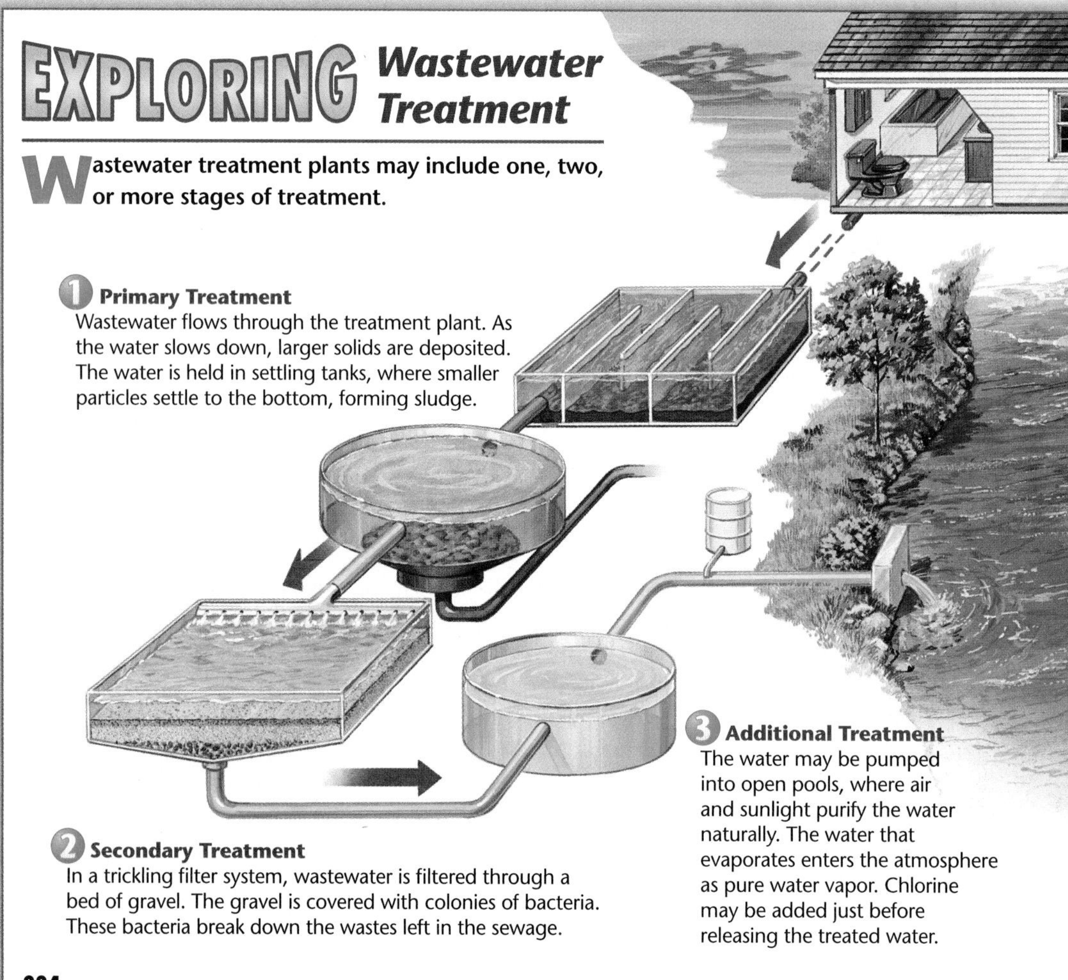

Background

Facts and Figures Raw wastewater is about 1,000 parts water for every 1 part waste; that is, about 99.9 percent of wastewater is water. During primary treatment of wastewater, 30–50 percent of the organic matter present in raw sewage settles to the bottom of the settling tanks. By the end of secondary treatment, as much as 90 percent of the total organic matter has been removed.

Media and Technology

Transparencies "Exploring Wastewater Treatment," Transparency 25; "Cutaway View of a Septic Tank," Transparency 26

Concept Videotape Library Grade 6, Tape 2, "Positive Bacteria"

back into lakes, rivers, and oceans or pumped back into the ground. The water rejoins the water cycle. Eventually, it could return to the same reservoir or aquifer that is the source of your water supply.

Treated wastewater that is not quite clean enough for drinking can still be used in other ways. For instance, some communities use this "gray water" to water the grass on golf courses or public parks. Gray water can also be used for irrigation or as cooling water in factories.

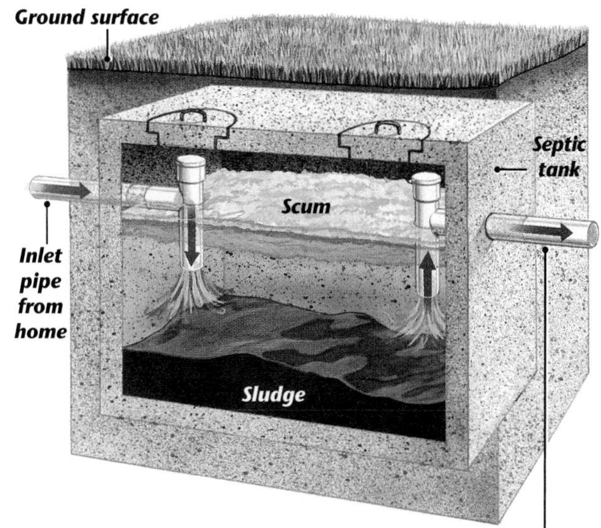

Figure 5 Sewage flows into a septic tank, where bacteria break down the waste material. Cleaner water leaves the tank and flows into a leach field. There, the water slowly releases the remaining dissolved minerals into the soil.

Septic Systems

Just as some people rely on private wells rather than public water supplies, many people are not connected to public sanitary sewer systems. They use other methods to dispose of sewage, such as a septic system. A septic system like the one in Figure 5 includes a **septic tank,** an underground tank containing bacteria that treat wastewater as it passes through. Sludge settles to the bottom of the tank and must be cleaned out regularly so it does not fill up the tank. The remaining water filters out through holes in the septic tank into the ground around it. The area around the septic tank that the water filters through is called a **leach field.** Over time, the remaining wastes break down naturally in the soil of the leach field.

Section 1 Review

1. How does drinking-water treatment improve water quality?
2. What is the goal of wastewater treatment?
3. List the main sources of drinking water. Classify each source as surface water or groundwater.
4. Describe how drinking water is delivered to homes and businesses in a community.
5. **Thinking Critically Inferring** Explain why it is important to know the depth and location of drinking-water wells before deciding where to build a septic tank.

CHAPTER PROJECT

Check Your Progress

Now you are ready to plan the steps of your water treatment system. What will each step accomplish? What materials will you use to perform each step? Draw a diagram of your system and a flowchart showing how it will work. Check your plans with your teacher. (*Hint:* Be sure to consider how your treatment unit will be constructed. How will you hold the pieces in place?)

Program Resources

- **Unit 3 Resources** 8-1 Review and Reinforce; 8-1 Enrich

3 Assess

Section 1 Review Answers

1. Drinking-water treatment removes unwanted substances from the water and makes it safe and appealing to drink.
2. The goal of wastewater treatment is to make it safe to return to the environment.
3. The main sources are rivers, lakes, and reservoirs, which are surface water, and aquifers, which are groundwater.
4. From a treatment plant, water goes to a central pumping station, where it is pumped to homes and businesses through an underground system of pipes.
5. Water from a septic tank flows through holes into a leach field. If a septic tank is built too close to a well, the wastewater from the tank could mix with the water around the well and make the water unsafe to drink.

CHAPTER PROJECT

Check Your Progress

Review each student's flow chart and water-treatment design. Make sure each design has at least two steps. Help students evaluate their designs by asking them to explain what each step is supposed to accomplish. When satisfied that a design has been well thought out, give the go-ahead to begin assembling the system.

Performance Assessment

Drawing Have students make a drawing of a fictional town, focusing on its water source, how its water is treated, how its water is distributed, and how its wastewater is treated. In their drawings, students can use representative illustrations to stand for the various parts, such as a treatment plant, water mains, a home, and so on.

Students can save their drawings in their portfolio.

SECTION 2 Balancing Water Needs

Objectives

After completing the lesson, students will be able to

- ◆ describe conditions that can result in a water shortage and list sources of fresh water for the future;
- ◆ explain how water can be conserved.

Key Terms drought, conservation, desalination

1 Engage/Explore

Activating Prior Knowledge

Begin by eliciting a list of common household uses of water. Write this list on the board. Ask: **How could you use less water for each of these uses?** *(Students should propose ways to conserve water for each use, such as taking shorter showers, not running water while brushing teeth, and not watering the yard in the bright sun.)* Then challenge students to think of reasons why water should not be wasted.

DISCOVER ACTIVITY

Skills Focus predicting
Materials *large measuring cup, water, plastic dropper, 2 small bowls, spoons, stopwatch*
Time 15 minutes
Tips Use a relatively small plastic dropper in order to accentuate the drop in the level of the water in the cup when the rate is increased in Step 4. Tell students to clean up any water spills, using a sponge or paper towel.
Expected Outcome Students should infer that increased demand will diminish the amount of water if the supply is constant over time. They should also infer that decreasing demand is one way to keep the supply at a constant level.
Think It Over Answers may vary. A typical answer might suggest that the water user must decrease the rate of use by removing a spoonful every two or three dropperfuls, depending on dropper size.

SECTION 2 Balancing Water Needs

DISCOVER ACTIVITY

Can You Reach a Balance?

1. Fill a large measuring cup with water to represent a reservoir. Record the level of the water. One partner, the water supplier, should have a plastic dropper and a small bowl of water. The other partner, the water user, should have a spoon and an empty bowl.
2. Start a stopwatch. For two minutes, the water supplier should add water to the measuring cup one dropperful at a time. Each time the water supplier adds a dropperful of water, the water user should remove one spoonful of water from the reservoir.
3. At the end of two minutes, record the level of water in the cup.
4. Now increase the rate of water use by removing two spoonfuls of water for every dropperful added.

5. After another two minutes, record the level of water in the cup again.

Think It Over

Predicting What changes will you need to make so that the water level in the reservoir stays constant?

GUIDE FOR READING

- ◆ What conditions can result in a water shortage?
- ◆ What are some ways industries can conserve water?

Reading Tip Before you read, write an explanation of what you think water conservation means. As you read, add to your explanation.

Has this ever happened to you? You're eating dinner with your family and you ask someone to pass the rolls. As the basket makes its way around the table, each person takes a roll. By the time it gets to you, there's nothing left in the basket but crumbs!

This scenario is an example of a limited resource, the rolls, being used by many people. The same thing can happen to a river! For example, the Colorado River holds a resource that is precious in the Southwest—water. In this desert region there is little precipitation to provide water for people's needs. As the river flows through seven states and into Mexico, it is tapped again and again to provide water for drinking, irrigation, and other uses. The river's mouth at the Gulf of California is now often only a dry riverbed.

Figure 6 Cracks appear in the dry soil of an empty riverbed.

READING STRATEGIES

Reading Tip Ask students to write just one or two sentences about water conservation. Students may say that water conservation means not wasting water or not polluting water. Then ask volunteers to share their ideas with the class. After students have read the section, they can discuss how their ideas have changed.

Vocabulary Call students' attention to the boldface term *desalination* on page 408. Explain that *de* is a word part from Latin that means "away," and *sali* is also from Latin and means "salt." Thus, *desalination* of water is a process that removes salt from water.

Water Supply and Demand

Figure 7 Farmers require large amounts of water to irrigate crops in the dry desert. *Relating Cause and Effect What are two factors that might result in a shortage of water available for irrigation?*

States along a river such as the Colorado have to decide how much water each one can take from the river. The deserts of Nevada and Arizona are home to some of the fastest-growing cities in the country. As more people move to Las Vegas, Phoenix, and Tucson, these cities need more water. They increase their demand on already scarce water supplies. Meanwhile, farmers claim a large share to irrigate their fields. Mining companies use water to cool down machinery and flush out the mines they dig. The cities, farms, and mines compete for water rights—the legal right to take water from a particular source.

The Southwest is just one of many places in the world where there doesn't seem to be enough water to go around. As you know, the water cycle ensures that water is a renewable resource. However, the water supply in a specific area is only renewed when there is enough time for rainfall to replace what has been used. **A water shortage occurs when there is too little water or too great a demand in an area—or both.**

Drought Places that normally get enough precipitation may experience a few years of scarce rainfall, a condition known as a **drought.** A drought affects the supply of groundwater as well as surface water. Without precipitation to recharge the aquifer, the amount of groundwater in the aquifer decreases. What happens to a well as the level of the water table falls? Imagine trying to drink from a tall glass of milk through a straw the length of a toothpick. When the level of the milk falls below the bottom of the straw, you can no longer reach it to drink. In the same way, when the water table falls below the bottom of a well, the well runs dry.

Aquifer Overuse Even without droughts, the demands of growing populations can result in overuse of aquifers. *INTEGRATING TECHNOLOGY* When water is used up faster than the aquifer can be recharged, the aquifer is depleted, or emptied.

When too much water is pumped out of an aquifer, the ground above the aquifer can sink or collapse. The ground is no longer supported by the pressure of the water inside it. To

2 Facilitate

Water Supply and Demand

Using the Visuals: Figure 7

After students have studied this figure, have them turn back to the *Science & History* feature on irrigation in Chapter 7, pages 196–197. Point out that Israel is a desert nation. Ask: **How does the irrigation technique used in Israel take into account that most of the country is very dry?** *(One purpose of the technique described is to waste as little water as possible.)* Help students understand that in Israel, the demand for irrigation water is great because the supply is short. **learning modality: verbal**

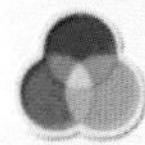

Integrating Technology

Materials *10 2-L plastic soda bottles, box, concrete block, water*
Time 15 minutes

To model how groundwater can support the weight of the land above it, fill a box with empty plastic bottles with caps on. Have students predict what will happen when you place a concrete block on top of the bottles. Then place the block on the bottles. The bottles will collapse under its weight. Next, fill the bottles with water, screw on the caps tightly, and return them to the box. Again ask students to predict what will happen. This time when you place the block on top of the bottles, they will not collapse. **learning modality: logical/mathematical**

Program Resources

- **Unit 3 Resources** 8-2 Lesson Plan; 8-2 Section Summary
- **Guided Reading and Study Workbook** Section 8-2
- **Product Testing Activities by *Consumer Reports*** "Testing Bottled Waters," pp. 1–8

Answers to Self-Assessment

Caption Question

Figure 7 Both too little water and too great a demand in an area could result in a shortage of water available for irrigation.

Ongoing Assessment

Writing Have each student write a TV news reporter's script for each of the following situations: too great a demand for water results in a water shortage, too little water results in a water shortage. Students should make up the details for each situation.

Water Supply and Demand, continued

Social Studies CONNECTION

After students have read the feature, ask: **What is a miller?** *(A person who grinds grain to make flour)* Explain that flowing water can be used to supply energy to run a mill. Then challenge students to come up with their solutions. Students' solutions may vary, but they should each take the following into consideration. Of the four possible uses of water, those of both the fisherman and the miller would not take water from the river. Because the fisherman needs the river to be half full, no more than 5,000 L can be withdrawn per day. The total needed by the grain farmer and the livestock owner add up to 5,100 L per day. Thus, students could assign less water to one or the other of those two in order to keep the river half full or consider reusing the water for washing animals for one of the other purposes.

Extend Students could return to this problem after reading Section 3. In a reconsideration, they could propose ways by which the grain farmer and livestock owner would not return polluted water to the river. **learning modality: logical/mathematical**

Conserving Water

Using the Visuals: Figure 8

After students have considered the conservation suggestions in the figure, have them meet in small groups to brainstorm additional ways to save water. Have groups present their suggestions to the class. **cooperative learning**

Social Studies CONNECTION

Laws regarding the use of water are a very old concept. Nearly 4,000 years ago in ancient Mesopotamia, now modern-day Iraq, a ruler named Hammurabi wrote in his code of laws:

"If a man neglects the canal so that water floods a neighboring field, he shall repay the loss with his own grain."

In Your Journal

A river carries 10,000 liters of water a day through your village. Imagine that you are a member of the village council. Propose a fair way to assign water rights to the following people. (*Hint:* Think about which uses will return water to the river and which will not.)

- Grain farmer, wants 4,000 liters a day for watering crops
- Livestock owner, wants 600 liters a day for washing animals and 500 liters a day for animals to drink
- Fisherman, needs to keep the river at least half full for the fish to survive
- Miller, needs 3,500 liters a day to turn waterwheel

prevent collapse, engineers can artificially recharge an aquifer. One method is to pump water from wastewater treatment plants or industrial cooling water into shallow ponds that feed the aquifer. Another method is to inject water down wells directly into the saturated zone. However, because these techniques require expensive equipment and additional water, it is a better solution not to overuse the aquifer.

☑ *Checkpoint* *How can a drought cause a well to run dry?*

Conserving Water

During a water shortage, people often pay more attention to how they use water. They look for ways to avoid wasting water both at home and at work. Using a resource wisely so that it will not be used up is called **conservation.**

In the Home Most people in the United States have access to as much clean, safe water as they want. As a result, it is often easy to use more water than needed without thinking much about it. But as Figure 8 shows, there are some simple things you can do to help conserve water around your home.

Can these suggestions really make a difference? Figure it out. How long do you stand under the shower? For every minute, you use about 18 liters of water. If you stand under the shower for 10 minutes, that's about 180 liters. But if you showered for 5 minutes instead, you would use only 90 liters. And if each student in a class of 25 showered for 5 minutes instead of 10, they would save a total of 2,250 liters of water—enough to fill 22 trash barrels! As you can see, small efforts by many individuals can add up to a lot of water savings.

In Agriculture As you learned in Chapter 11, the biggest use of water in the United States is for agriculture. In the last few decades, farmers have found new ways to use less water. When water is carried into fields in open canals or ditches, much of it is lost through evaporation. Using pipes to carry water reduces the time that water is exposed to the air. Two such methods are sprinkler irrigation and drip irrigation. Sprinkler irrigation sprays water onto crops from overhead pipes. Drip irrigation distributes water through pipes with tiny holes. The water drips directly onto the soil near the plants' roots so that very little is wasted.

In Industry Paper mills, oil refineries, chemical factories, and other industries have made changes in manufacturing processes to use less water. For example, in the 1950s it took about 227,000 liters of water to make 1,000 kilograms of

Background

Facts and Figures An estimate from the World Resources Institute is that 65–70 percent of water used by people throughout the world is wasted, through leaks, evaporation, runoff, and similar losses. The United States wastes about 50 percent of the water it withdraws. Irrigation accounts for almost 70 percent of world water use; about two-thirds of that is wasted. One way to conserve water is to use treated wastewater for irrigation.

In the typical U.S. home, bathing (including showering), flushing toilets, and washing hands accounts for about 78 percent of water used. Water-saving showerheads and low-flow toilets can prevent a good deal of that waste. In 1994, a federal law mandated that all new toilets sold in the U.S. would use no more than 6 L per flush.

writing paper. By the 1980s, paper mills needed only half that much water to produce the same amount of paper.

New water-saving techniques help industries save money in water costs and meet the requirements of environmental laws. **Reducing water use, recycling water, and reusing water are three major forms of water conservation by industries.** These approaches conserve water while also reducing the amount of wastewater that plants release. For example, some factories that use water to cool machinery are building lagoons on their property. The heated water cools off in the lagoons and then can be used again. Other factories are replacing water-cooling systems with cooling systems that use air. Another change is to use high-pressure water sprays to clean products and equipment instead of dipping the objects in large tanks of water.

Fresh Water for the Future

As the number of people in the world increases, so does the need for water. Where can people find new sources of water for the future? One obvious place would seem to be the other 97 percent of water on Earth—the salt water in the oceans. For thousands

Predicting ACTIVITY

Find a leaking faucet in your school or home, or turn on a faucet just enough to produce a very slow drip. How much water do you think will drip from the faucet in half an hour? Write down your prediction. Place a large measuring cup under the faucet. After half an hour, check the cup. How does the result compare with your prediction? How much water would you save per day if you fixed the leaking faucet?

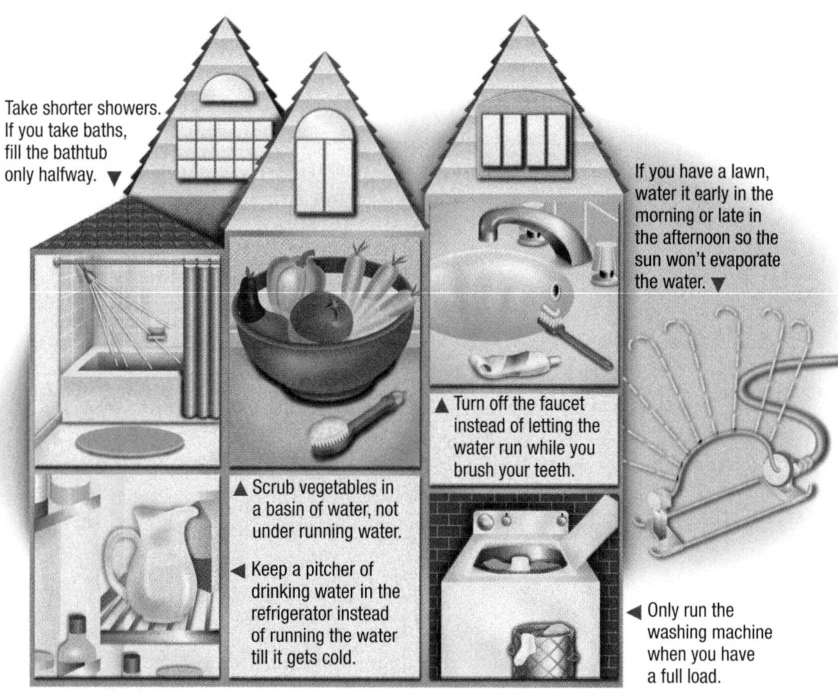

Figure 8 There are many simple ways to conserve water around the home. ***Developing Hypotheses*** *Which of these ideas do you think would save the most water per day in your home? How could you test your hypothesis?*

Media and Technology

 **Concept Videotape Library**
Grade 6, Tape 2 "Xeriscape"

Answers to Self-Assessment

Checkpoint

A drought can cause the water table to fall below the bottom of the well.

Caption Question

Figure 8 Answers may vary. A typical answer: Taking shorter showers would save the most water. This could be tested by measuring the water saved by each idea and then comparing.

Sharpen your Skills

Predicting

Materials *large measuring cup*
Time 5 minutes for setup; 5 minutes for results
Tips Contact a member of your school's custodial staff to find a leaking faucet somewhere in the building. Students can extrapolate from their data how much water would be wasted in a month or year by multiplying by the appropriate number of minutes and days.
Expected Outcome The amount of water that drips into the cup will vary; in general, students will underestimate the amount.
Extend Ask a custodian to fix a leaking school faucet while students watch. Students can then use this knowledge to help fix a leaking faucet at home.
learning modality: logical/mathematical

Fresh Water for the Future

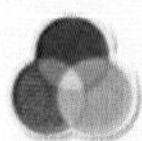

Integrating Chemistry

Ask students: **How does the process of distillation produce fresh water from salt water?** *(The saltwater solution evaporates, leaving the salt behind. When the water condenses, it is pure fresh water.)* **How does distillation compare to the water cycle you studied in Chapter 7?** *(The processes are similar since both include evaporation and condensation.)* Guide students in a comparison of the solar energy that drives the water cycle and the energy used for desalination. Ask: **What is a major drawback in using this method of desalination?** *(The cost of energy, such as electricity, needed to drive the process)* **learning modality: verbal**

Ongoing Assessment

Skills Check Have students make a concept map that includes all the suggestions mentioned in the text for how water can be conserved.

3 Assess

Section 2 Review Answers

1. Answers may vary. A typical answer might describe a drought or a situation in which there is too great a demand for the supply of water.
2. Reducing water use, recycling water, and reusing water are three major forms of water conservation by industries.
3. The aquifer can be depleted if water is used up faster than the aquifer can be recharged. Overpumping can cause the ground above the aquifer to sink or collapse.
4. Tugboats could tow a wrapped iceberg from Antarctica to a coastal region of Africa or South America and the water could be piped to shore as the iceberg melted.
5. Answers may vary. A typical answer: A community should be able to limit water use in times of shortage but not when water is in good supply.

Science at Home

ACTIVITY

Encourage students to introduce this activity at home by explaining to family members that water is a precious resource that should not be wasted. Students might do this with more than one family member, making it into a friendly competition about who can conserve the most water. Tell students that if the tape will not stick to the wet sink, they could mark the levels with bar soap.

Performance Assessment

Writing Challenge each student to assume the role of a government official in a region experiencing a severe drought. Because of the water shortage, the official has been asked to recommend a set of regulations limiting water use by homes and businesses. Students should write a brief introduction to the regulations and then list ten specific recommendations.

Figure 9 The ocean is one possible source of drinking water for the future. ***Applying Concepts*** *How can ocean water be made suitable for drinking?*

of years, people have tried different methods to make salty ocean water drinkable.

Desalination The process of obtaining fresh water from salt water is called **desalination.** One method of desalination, called distillation, is to boil water so that it evaporates, leaving the salt behind. The water vapor is then condensed to produce liquid fresh water. Another method involves freezing the water, which also leaves the salt behind. Still another method is to pump water at high pressure through a very fine filter. The filter separates out pure water and returns saltier water to the ocean.

INTEGRATING CHEMISTRY

Desalination is very expensive because of the energy and equipment it requires. In spite of the cost, however, Saudi Arabia, Kuwait, Israel, and other nations in the dry Middle East depend on this technology. A few cities in the United States, such as Santa Barbara, California, have also built desalination plants.

Icebergs Some people think that icebergs are another possible source of fresh water for dry regions. Tugboats could tow a wrapped iceberg from Antarctica to a coastal area of Africa or South America. An iceberg would provide millions of liters of pure water that could be piped to shore as the iceberg melted. However, such plans raise environmental questions: How would a huge mass of ice offshore affect local weather? What would happen to living things as the ice cooled the water around it? These questions need to be answered before icebergs can be seen as a solution to Earth's future water needs.

Section 2 Review

1. Describe a situation that could lead to a water shortage in a community.
2. Name three ways that industries can conserve water.
3. Describe the possible effects overpumping might have on an aquifer.
4. Explain how an iceberg might provide drinking water in the future.
5. **Thinking Critically Making Judgments** Do you think communities should be able to limit how often people water their lawns or wash their cars? Why or why not?

Science at Home

Water Use for Brushing Place a stopper over the drain in a sink. Ask a family member to brush his or her teeth over the sink, allowing the water to run until he or she is done. Mark the level of the water in the sink with a small piece of tape. Remove the stopper and let the water drain. Replace the stopper and have the person repeat the brushing, this time turning the water on only when needed. Mark the water level with another piece of tape. Point out the difference in the amount of water used in each case.

Answers to Self-Assessment

Caption Question

Figure 9 Various methods of desalination can make ocean water suitable for drinking.

Program Resources

- **Unit 3 Resources** 8-2 Review and Reinforc; 8-2 Enrich

Making Models

Getting the Salt Out

Desalination plants use many methods to produce fresh water from ocean water. In this lab, you will make a model of a desalination plant using the method of distillation.

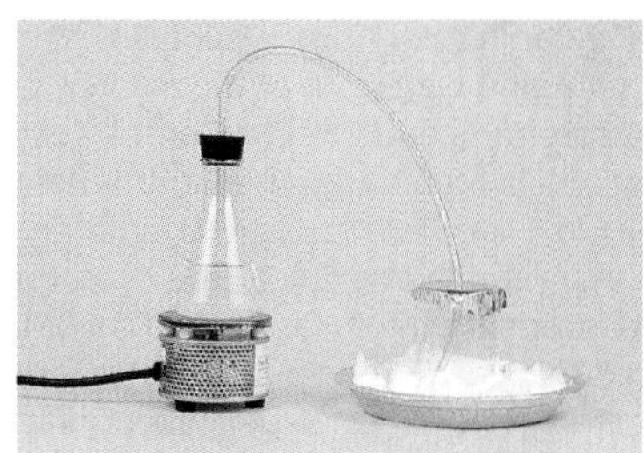

Skills Lab

Problem

How can distillation be used to obtain fresh water from salt water?

Materials

hot plate	aluminum foil	250-mL beaker
plastic spoon	water, 100 mL	shallow pan
ice	plastic tube	500-mL flask
stirring rod	rubber stopper	salt
rubber tubing, 50 cm		

Procedure 

1. Pour 100 mL of water into the flask.
2. Add one spoonful of salt to the water in the flask and stir until dissolved. The solution should not be cloudy.
3. Gently insert the plastic tube through the hole of the rubber stopper. Do not force the tube into the hole; ask your teacher for help if you are having difficulty.
4. Insert one end of the plastic tube into the rubber tubing.
5. Put the rubber stopper in the flask. The bottom of the plastic tube should be above the surface of the solution.
6. Cover the beaker with aluminum foil. Press the edges of the foil against the beaker.
7. Push the free end of the rubber tubing through the center of the aluminum foil covering the top of the beaker.
8. Place the beaker in the pan, surrounded by ice.
9. Put the flask on the hot plate, keeping it away from the pan of ice. Turn the hot plate on. Bring the solution to a boil. **CAUTION:** *Do not touch the hot plate or flask. Do not allow the solution to boil completely away.*
10. Observe what happens in the flask and the beaker. Continue heating the solution until a liquid has accumulated in the beaker.
11. Turn off the hot plate and allow the flask and the beaker to cool. What is left behind in the flask? Record your observations.

Analyze and Conclude

1. What happened to the water in the flask during the boiling process? What happened inside the beaker?
2. How does the liquid collected in the beaker differ from the liquid in the flask?
3. What is the purpose of the ice in this activity?
4. **Think About It** Imagine building a desalination plant that uses the method of distillation to produce water for a city. What difficulties might you encounter in using this process on such a large scale?

More to Explore

How could you change the setup and procedure to recover fresh water from salt water without using the hot plate? Design an experiment to accomplish this goal. Obtain your teacher's permission before carrying out your experiment.

Program Resources

- **Unit 3 Resources** Chapter 8 Skills Lab blackline masters

Media and Technology

Lab Activity Videotapes
Grade 6, Tape 2

Safety

Caution students to wear the oven mitt any time they touch the hot flask. Caution them to keep water away from electrical outlets and the hot plate plug. Do not allow the water to boil completely away. Review the safety guidelines in Appendix A.

Skills Lab

Making Models

Getting the Salt Out

Preparing for Inquiry

Key Concept Distillation is one method that can be used in desalination.

Skills Objective Students will be able to
- make a model of a desalination plant using distillation.

Time 40 minutes

Advance Planning Obtain bags of ice on the morning of the lab. Cut the rubber tubing into 50-cm lengths.

Alternative Materials In place of salt, use "instant seawater," which can be found at pet stores.

Guiding Inquiry

Troubleshooting the Experiment

- Make sure students do not add too much salt to the water in the flask. The solution should not be cloudy.
- Demonstrate how to insert the plastic tube gently through the hole of the rubber stopper. Wetting the tube or rubbing it with glycerin can help.
- Warn students not to tear a large hole in the aluminum foil when they push the rubber tubing through its center.

Expected Outcome

The water in the flask should boil, causing the water to evaporate, leaving the salt behind. The water vapor should move through the tubing and condense in the beaker.

Analyze and Conclude

1. It evaporated; water vapor from the flask condensed in the beaker.
2. It is fresh water; the flask has salt water.
3. The ice served to cool the water vapor, causing it to condense in the beaker.
4. Answers may vary. A typical answer: It would require a lot of heat to boil all the water required for a city. Generating this heat to run the desalination plant might prove too costly.

Extending the Inquiry

More to Explore Designs may vary. A typical design might suggest using the same setup, though with the flask placed in direct sunlight.

SCIENCE AND SOCIETY

The Ogallala Aquifer

Purpose To provide students with an understanding of the problems associated with overuse of water resources.

Role-Play

Time a day to prepare; 30 minutes for role-play

Divide students into four groups: (1) a five-member "fact-finding committee" appointed by Congress, (2) a group to argue for more regulations and charges on water use, (3) a group to argue that different water-saving farming practices should be instituted, and (4) a group to argue that current practices should continue. Tell the first group to work out rules and an agenda for a public meeting on water use on the Great Plains. Students in each of the other groups can work together to prepare a presentation to the committee during the public meeting. Then hold the public meeting, using the rules and agenda worked out by the committee members. Encourage students to act the way they think citizens would act in a real public meeting of this kind.

Extend Challenge students to find out whether water shortages are a problem in your area. Suggest that they contact the local water department to ask what plans are in place in case of a drought or some other water problem.

You Decide

Have students individually complete the first two steps before the role-play as a way of preparing themselves for their participation. After the role-play is concluded, students can complete the last step, using what they learned in the role-play for finding a solution to the problem.

Students can save their letters in their portfolio.

SCIENCE AND SOCIETY

The Ogallala Aquifer

The Ogallala Aquifer lies beneath eight states of the Great Plains. It contains about 4 quadrillion liters of groundwater—about the amount of water in Lake Huron. Rainfall is scarce on the Great Plains. But by pumping water out of the aquifer, farmers can grow cotton, wheat, sorghum, and corn to feed cattle. More than one third of the nation's livestock are raised in this area.

Water in the Ogallala was trapped there during the last Ice Age, about 12,000 years ago. Now, due to the demands of irrigation, water levels are dropping much faster than the aquifer can recharge. In certain parts of the aquifer, water levels have fallen as much as 12 meters since 1980. Farmers recognize that the Ogallala cannot withstand this heavy use for long. However, not all agree on what should be done.

The Issues

Should Water Use Be Regulated? One way to reduce water use might be to charge people for water. But who owns the water and who would determine the cost? In most of the Great Plains, water has been free to anyone who dug a well on their land. To charge for water, local governments would need to construct a public water system as in most cities. This would be a very complex and costly task. Both farmers and consumers would be affected by the charge. Higher costs for growing crops would result in higher supermarket prices for grains and meat.

Should Farmers Change Their Practices? Farmers could switch to crops such as sunflowers and grains that need less water. These crops, however, are less valuable than others for producing food and for feeding livestock. As a result, they would be less profitable than traditional crops. Farmers could use water-saving methods of irrigation. Such methods are expensive to install but eventually save both water and money.

Another possibility is "dryland farming," a method that was used by pioneer farmers. This method involves keeping the soil moist using only rainwater. Because dryland farming depends on the amount of rainfall, it is unpredictable. It may not produce large harvests.

Should Current Use Continue? Many residents of the Great Plains depend on the aquifer for a living. Some people feel that farmers there must continue their present water use in order to compete with farmers elsewhere in the nation and around the world. They feel that people today should not have to suffer in order to preserve the aquifer for future generations. New sources of water may be discovered, or better methods of transporting water to the Great Plains may be developed. Better irrigation techniques that use less water may also be invented. But other people feel that since these possibilities are not certain, water use must be greatly reduced now to save the aquifer.

You Decide

1. **Identify the Problem**
   In your own words, explain the problem facing the farmers on the Great Plains.
2. **Analyze the Options**
   Make a chart of the solutions mentioned. List advantages and drawbacks of each. Who would benefit from each solution? Who would suffer?
3. **Find a Solution**
   As a resident of the Great Plains, write a letter to the newspaper proposing a solution to the Ogallala problem.

Background

The Ogallala is the largest known aquifer in the world. Water from the aquifer is used to irrigate nearly 6 million hectares, or about 20 percent of all cropland in the United States. Each year, about 26 billion m^3 of groundwater are pumped from the aquifer. Since 1950, the water table in the Ogallala has dropped an average of 30 m. In some places, the drop has been much greater. For example, the depth to groundwater in Floyd County, Texas, dropped from about 25 m in 1950 to about 75 m in 1984, despite a significant decrease of irrigated land during that time. Throughout the aquifer, water is being pumped out at about eight times the rate that natural recharge occurs. If all pumping ceased, some scientists have estimated it would take at least 1,000 years for the aquifer to recover to be completely recharged.

Freshwater Pollution

DISCOVER ACTIVITY

Will the Pollution Reach Your Wells?

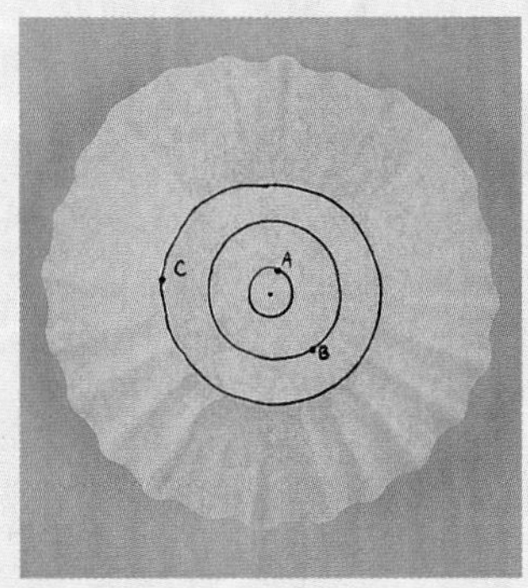

1. With a permanent marker, draw three rings on a coffee filter as shown in the picture. Draw three dots and label them A, B, and C as shown. These dots represent the locations of drinking-water supply wells.
2. Place the coffee filter on a paper plate. Moisten the coffee filter with a wet sponge. The damp coffee filter represents an aquifer.
3. Squirt five drops of food coloring onto the center of the damp coffee filter. Observe how the "pollution" travels.

Think It Over

Observing Which wells are affected by the pollution? Describe the pattern the pollution forms.

The newspaper headlines told an amazing story: "River in Flames!" "Bridges Burn As River Catches Fire!" This really happened to the Cuyahoga River in Cleveland, Ohio, in the summer of 1969. Are you wondering how a river could catch fire? What was in the Cuyahoga that allowed it to burn?

The Cuyahoga flows through a large industrial region on its way to Lake Erie. Factories along its banks used to dump their wastes into the river. Freighters spilled oil and gasoline into the water. Over time, the river became so full of chemicals and sewage that the pollution floating in it could actually burn.

Alarmed by the fire and the destruction it caused, people in Ohio began a massive campaign to clean up the Cuyahoga. Today it is safe to use for boating and fishing. The Cuyahoga River is a dramatic example of how serious water pollution can become—and of how people can work together to undo its damage.

GUIDE FOR READING

- What are some sources of water pollution?
- How does agricultural runoff affect ponds and streams?
- How can living things help clean up polluted water?

Reading Tip As you read, make a list of sources of freshwater pollution. Write one sentence about each source.

What Is Pollution?

If you turned on your faucet and a stream of bright green water came out, you'd be fairly sure that the water contained something it shouldn't. But many things that can make water unsafe to drink don't change its color, taste, or smell. The addition of any substance that has a negative effect on water or the living things that depend on the water is called **water pollution.** Water pollution can affect surface water, groundwater, and even rain. It can result from both natural causes and human activities.

READING STRATEGIES

Reading Tip Point out that the four section heads beginning with "Human Wastes" provide a primary list of sources of freshwater pollution. The subheads under "Industrial Wastes" are specific types of pollution. For each of these heads, students should find a sentence or phrase that explains that source of pollution. For example: *Dumping human wastes into drinking water can spread disease.*

Program Resources

- **Unit 3 Resources** 8-3 Lesson Plan; 8-3 Section Summary
- **Guided Reading and Study Workbook** Section 8-3
- **Laboratory Manual** 8, "Pollution of a Water Supply"

SECTION 3 Freshwater Pollution

Objectives

After completing the lesson, students will be able to

- describe what water pollutuion is and list some of its sources;
- explain how runoff affects ponds and streams;
- describe how pollution can be prevented and how polluted water can be cleaned up.

Key Terms water pollution, point source, nonpoint source, acid rain, pesticide

1 Engage/Explore

Activating Prior Knowledge

Ask students: **What is water pollution?** *(Focus on answers that relate to the addition of any substance that has a negative effect on water or living things in the water.)* Challenge students to brainstorm a list of things that could make water polluted. List their suggestions on the board. Then as students read the section, have them classify the list by the sources of water pollution in the text.

DISCOVER

Skills Focus observing
Materials *permanent marker, coffee filter, paper plate, wet sponge, food coloring, plastic dropper*
Time 15 minutes
Tips Students should allow time for the marker to dry before wetting the coffee filter. Make sure students moisten the filter thoroughly without making it dripping wet.
Expected Outcome Students should infer that aquifer pollution can affect more than just the place at which it first occurs.
Think It Over Answers may vary. A typical answer should mention that the "pollution" spreads out unevenly, following tiny dips and creases in the paper, just as in an aquifer. Wells closer to the center are affected more than wells farther away.

2 Facilitate

What Is Pollution?

Integrating Life Science

Help students recall their knowledge of food chains and food webs by displaying an illustration of a food chain or food web from a life science text. Ask: **If you were to show this food chain as a pyramid, which of the organisms would you place at the top?** *(The large, meat-eating animals)* Challenge students to use the food chain to trace a pollutant from the producers (plants or algae) to the top consumers. **learning modality: visual**

Using the Visuals: Figure 11

ACTIVITY

Ask students: **What can you infer from the pyramid shape of the illustration?** *(The number of organisms that make up each level decreases at each higher level of the pyramid.)* Guide students in understanding that the total mass of the organisms at a level is greater than the total mass of the level above. Thus, if the amount of DDT stays the same as it moves from a lower level to a higher level, the concentration would increase. Have students model this increase in concentration by forming a triangle: 10 students in the first row, 7 students in the next, and so on. Give a paper clip to each student in the first row, and have them pass the clips up the triangle. Students will see that the concentration of paper clips becomes greater at each succeeding level. **learning modality: kinesthetic**

The substances that cause water pollution are called pollutants. Disease-causing organisms such as the *Cryptosporidium* you read about in Section 1 are one form of pollutant. As Figure 10 shows, other types of pollutants include toxic, or poisonous, chemicals and metals, as well as radioactive substances.

INTEGRATING LIFE SCIENCE Some types of pollutants can build up in the bodies of living things. Trace the path of one such pollutant in Figure 11. The pesticide DDT dissolves in water and is absorbed by microscopic algae. The algae, which contain only low levels of the chemical, are eaten by small water animals. When frogs or fish eat these smaller animals, they also consume the chemicals from the algae these animals had eaten. The frogs and fish are in turn eaten by birds or other animals. Each larger organism consumes a greater number of the smaller organisms, and therefore more of the DDT.

When humans eat the fish from such a pond, the toxic chemicals build up in their bodies in the same way. Over a long time, even tiny amounts of certain pollutants can build up to levels that can cause birth defects or illnesses such as cancer. Drinking impure water or eating contaminated fish are not the only ways that pollutants can affect humans. Bathing or swimming in polluted water can irritate the skin or cause more serious problems.

Point and Nonpoint Sources

To clean up a polluted body of water like the Cuyahoga River, people first need to identify the source of the pollution to prevent further damage. **The major sources of water pollution are human wastes, industrial wastes, agricultural chemicals, and runoff from roads.**

Freshwater Pollutants

Kind of Pollutant	Examples	Sources
Disease-causing organisms	*Giardia, Cryptosporidium,* bacteria	Human wastes, runoff from livestock pens
Pesticides and fertilizers	DDT, nitrates, phosphates	Runoff from farm fields, golf courses
Industrial chemicals	PCBs, carbon tetrachloride, dioxin	Factories, industrial waste disposal sites
Metals	Lead, mercury, copper	Factories, waste disposal sites
Radioactive wastes	Uranium, carbon-14	Medical and scientific disposal sites, nuclear power plants
Petroleum products	Oil, gasoline	Road runoff, leaking underground storage tanks

Figure 10 This table lists some examples of the different types of freshwater pollutants. ***Relating Cause and Effect*** *Why might it be helpful to know the source of a particular pollutant detected in a body of water?*

Background

Facts and Figures Examples of point sources of freshwater pollution include factories, mines, and wastewater treatment plants. Because these sources can be identified, they are much easier to control than nonpoint sources. Examples of nonpoint sources include septic tanks, lawns, streets and parking lots, farm fields, pastures, and construction sites. Nonpoint pollution from agriculture is responsible for about 60 percent of all pollutants entering streams and lakes.

Water pollution from the pesticide DDT is an example of a pollutant from a nonpoint source. DDT was once the most-used pesticide in the world. Its use was banned in the United States in 1972, though it is still used in other countries.

Figure 11 A very small amount of the pesticide DDT in water can build up to harmful levels in living things. *Interpreting Diagrams Which organism ends up with the most DDT?*

Each of these sources of pollution can be a point source or a nonpoint source, depending on how the pollution enters a body of water. For example, suppose you notice a pipe gushing white sudsy water into a river. The pipe is a **point source,** a specific source of pollution that can be identified. More often, though, the source of pollution is less obvious. Pollutants may be carried along in runoff from a farm field, a street, or a construction site. The chemicals, sewage, or radioactive materials eventually flow into a lake or river or seep into groundwater and are carried far away. It's hard to trace the exact source of this pollution. A widely spread source of pollution that can't be tied to a specific point of origin is called a **nonpoint source.**

☑ *Checkpoint* *Why are nonpoint sources difficult to identify?*

Classifying

Classify the following as point sources or nonpoint sources of water pollution:

- salt used on icy roads
- an open drain in a sink at a paint factory
- a sanitary sewer pipe with a leak
- fertilizer sprayed onto an orchard

Give a reason why you classified each source as you did.

Human Wastes

Today it seems obvious that dumping human wastes into drinking water can spread disease. But scientists have only understood this connection for the last 150 years.

Dr. Snow's Discovery Cholera is a disease caused by bacteria that live in human wastes. Cholera causes people to become very dehydrated and can be fatal. In 1854, an English doctor named John Snow discovered the cause of a cholera outbreak in London. In the

INTEGRATING HEALTH

Answers to Self-Assessment

Caption Questions

Figure 10 Knowing the source might be necessary to prevent further pollution.

Figure 11 The fish-eating birds

☑ *Checkpoint*

Nonpoint sources can't be tied to specific points of origin. They may come from a widespread area.

Point and Nonpoint Sources

Sharpen your Skills

Classifying

Time 10 minutes

ACTIVITY

Both the salt used on icy roads and fertilizer sprayed onto an orchard are nonpoint sources, because neither can be tied to a specific point of origin. Both the open drain in a sink at a paint factory and a sanitary sewer pipe with a leak are specific sources of pollution, and thus should be classified as point sources.

Extend Have students explain what pollution would result from a leak in a sanitary sewer pipe. Then challenge them to describe how an investigator could identify the point source from a discovery of that pollution. **learning modality: logical/mathematical**

Human Wastes

Integrating Health

To familiarize students with diseases spread in water, or waterborne diseases, assign to each a disease and challenge them to make an information sheet about the disease. This sheet could include facts about the cause of the disease, the way it is spread, its symptoms, and the way it is treated and prevented. Some common waterborne diseases include cholera, typhoid fever, enteritis, bacterial dysentery, amoebic dysentery, giardiasis, schistosomiasis, and infectious hepatitis. Have students share their information sheets with the class. **learning modality: verbal**

Portfolio Students can save their information sheets in their portfolios.

Ongoing Assessment

Drawing Have students make a flow chart showing the path of a pesticide used on a farm field to water birds in a lake some distance away.

Human Wastes, *continued*

Using the Visuals: Figure 12

Ask students: **Where do you think this water tank might have been filled?** *(The water might have come from a well, a river, or a lake away from the city.)* Encourage students to analyze the risk to the people that the water in the tank might also be contaminated, from either human waste or animal waste. Help students understand that people in the past were always at risk because their drinking water was not treated. **learning modality: verbal**

Industrial Wastes

Demonstration

ACTIVITY

Materials *2-L clear plastic soda bottle with top cut off, gravel, sand, pump sprayer from window cleaner bottle, nylon fabric, tape, water, food coloring, 2 beakers, plant sprayer*

Time 30 minutes

To show students how a chemical spill on land can pollute groundwater, make a model of groundwater contamination. Prepare the model by cutting off the top of a 2-L plastic bottle. Tape a piece of nylon fabric over the end of a pump sprayer from a bottle of window cleaner. Fill the 2-L bottle about one third full with rocks, insert the end of the pump sprayer into the rocks, and cover the rocks with an 8-cm layer of sand. Then slowly add water until the "water table" just reaches the layer of sand. Pump water out of the ground to show that the water is clear. Next, model chemical pollution by mixing food coloring with about 200 mL of water and "spilling" it onto the sand. At this point, only a little of the polluted water will seep down into the groundwater. Then model rain by spraying water onto the sand. This will move the pollution down into the groundwater. This time when you pump out groundwater, it will be polluted. Encourage students to comment on the process and the role of rain. **learning modality: visual**

poorer sections of the city, people carried water home in buckets from public wells. After 500 people in one neighborhood died in just ten days, Dr. Snow traced the cholera to a well near a pipe carrying sewage. He ended the epidemic by removing the pump handle so no one could get water from that source. Dr. Snow's work showed the danger of releasing untreated sewage into bodies of water that might be used for drinking water.

Sewage in Cities As you know, today wastewater is usually treated before being released to the environment. However, while water treatment usually kills bacteria, some viruses and parasites are able to resist chlorine and other water treatment processes. Most of these organisms come from human or animal wastes that get into the water supply.

During heavy rains and floods, sanitary sewers sometimes overflow and run into storm sewers. Since the storm sewers generally lead directly into surface water, the sewage from the sanitary sewers can pollute the water. For this reason, people are often told to boil water for drinking and cooking after a flood. The boiling kills many disease-causing organisms.

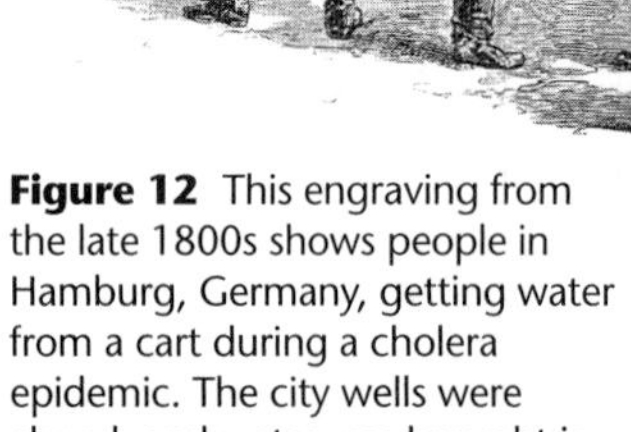

Figure 12 This engraving from the late 1800s shows people in Hamburg, Germany, getting water from a cart during a cholera epidemic. The city wells were closed, and water was brought in from the countryside.

Sewage in Rural Areas Disposing of human waste is not just a problem in big cities. In rural areas, people must be careful where they locate septic tanks. If a tank is too near a stream or on a hill, wastewater can leak into the stream or flow into the area of a well downhill.

Wastes from cattle, pigs, and chickens can also be a problem in rural areas. They contribute disease-causing bacteria and other kinds of pollution to water that runs off from pastures and barnyards.

☑ *Checkpoint* *Why should drinking water and sewage be kept separate?*

Industrial Wastes

Most cities and towns in the United States have wastewater treatment systems that handle sewage effectively. For this reason, water pollution by factories and mines is a more serious problem than sewage in most areas of the country. Chemicals, smoke, and heated water are three types of industrial pollutants.

Background

History of Science For most of human history, people thought diseases were caused by a variety of agents, including swamp vapors and even poisons created by the movement of planets. Although John Snow proved that cholera was associated with sewage-contaminated drinking water, he did not know the actual cause of the disease. The French chemist Louis Pasteur advanced the "germ theory of disease," which states that infectious diseases are caused by specific microorganisms. In 1876, a German physician, Robert Koch, proved that bacteria can cause disease. Since then, scientists have identified the agents of most infectious diseases, including diseases associated with wastewater, such as dysentery, cholera, and typhoid fever.

Chemicals Many factory processes, especially those for making dyes and plastics or treating metals, involve toxic chemicals and strong acids. Other toxic wastes are produced as by-products, or side effects, of manufacturing and mining. Although laws now limit and control chemical pollution, some factories still release toxic chemicals directly into nearby rivers and lakes.

Another problem is leftover wastes. In the past, many industries stored toxic wastes in barrels or other containers buried underground. Over the years, however, many of these containers rusted or broke. The chemicals leaked out, polluting both the soil and the groundwater.

Figure 13 Many lakes and rivers have been polluted by wastes from nearby industries. These environmental scientists are collecting water samples from a pond for testing.

Smoke and Exhaust Many power plants and factories burn coal or oil to fuel their processes. The engines of millions of cars, trucks, and buses burn gasoline. Every day, smoke and exhaust from these sources pour into the air, especially around large cities. When coal, oil, and gasoline are burned, molecules of the gases sulfur dioxide and nitrogen oxide are released into the atmosphere. There the sulfur and nitrogen react with water, forming sulfuric and nitric acids. The result is rain or other forms of precipitation that are more acidic than normal, called **acid rain.** When acid rain falls on lakes and ponds, the water can become so acidic that fish and other wildlife cannot survive. Acid rain also eats away the stone of buildings and statues.

INTEGRATING CHEMISTRY

Heat Pollution Think about how hot a metal slide gets on a sunny day. Imagine borrowing enough water from a swimming pool to cool the slide, and then returning the water to the pool. How would this change the swimming pool? Would you still want to jump in to cool off? The warm water would probably not be very refreshing.

Figure 14 A noisy jumble of taxis, cars, and buses crowds a city street. *Relating Cause and Effect How are these vehicles related to water pollution?*

Real-Life Learning

ACTIVITY

Divide students into small groups and challenge each group to contact a local company to find out how it disposes of chemicals. If the companies use a hazardous waste disposal service, students might inquire about what happens to the chemicals then. Small industries and manufacturing companies might be easiest to contact. Advise groups to write a list of questions before making contact. **cooperative learning**

Integrating Chemistry

ACTIVITY

Materials *2 small potted plants, tape, marker, 2 plant sprayers, distilled water, vinegar, pH paper*
Time 20 minutes; periodic attention for 1–2 weeks

Divide students into small groups and invite each group to investigate the effects of acid rain on plants. First, students should label one plant "Water" and the other plant "Acid Rain." Then they should fill one plant sprayer with distilled water and the other with a half-and-half mixture of distilled water and vinegar. Advise students to test the two solutions with pH paper to determine the acidity of each. Then have students predict how each solution will affect the plants. Students should water each plant by spraying the soil and the plant, using distilled water on the "Water" plant and the water-vinegar mixture on the "Acid Rain" plant. Have students observe the plants for 1–2 weeks. **learning modality: kinesthetic**

Media and Technology

Concept Videotape Library
Grade 6, Tape 2 "Rain, Rain, Go Away"

Answers to Self-Assessment

Checkpoint

Sewage contains bacteria, viruses, and parasites that can cause disease.

Caption Question

Figure 14 Molecules from the exhaust of vehicles pour into the air, react with water in the air to form sulfuric and nitric acids, and fall on lakes and ponds in the form of acid rain.

Ongoing Assessment

Oral Presentation Call on students at random to explain how water can be polluted by sewage contamination, industrial chemicals, smoke and exhaust, and heat.

Agricultural Chemicals

Integrating Life Science

Bring to class several, common garden-store fertilizers. Student volunteers can read appropriate parts of the labels of the products, including the indications for use, instructions for application, and cautions if ingested or otherwise misused. Encourage students to pay special attention to how much of each product should be used and how it affects living things. In each case, ask: **If a consumer does not read the instructions, how might he or she misuse the product?** *(In most cases, consumers overapply these products.)* Have students speculate on the overuse of such products. **learning modality: verbal**

TRY THIS

Skills Focus drawing conclusions
Materials *2 wide-mouth jars with tops, masking tape, permanent marker, tap water, pond or aquarium water, liquid fertilizer, graduated cylinder*
Time 15 minutes for setup; 5 minutes every day for 1 week
Tips Use liquid fertilizer marketed for home use, which is diluted. Otherwise the fertilizer may be too strong.
Expected Outcome The water in both jars will likely show algal growth, but the growth of algae in jar A will be markedly more because of the added fertilizer. Jar B is included as a control in the experiment.
Extend Aquariums often contain various water plants. Students could remove all the animals from an aquarium and add liquid fertilizer to the water, which would again encourage algal growth. That growth will eventually harm the plants, just as it would in a pond or lake. **learning modality: kinesthetic**

How Do Your Algae Grow?

ACTIVITY

In this activity you will observe how fertilizers affect the growth of algae in pond water.

1. Label two jars A and B. Pour tap water into each jar until it is half full.
2. Add water from a pond or aquarium to each jar until it is three-quarters full.

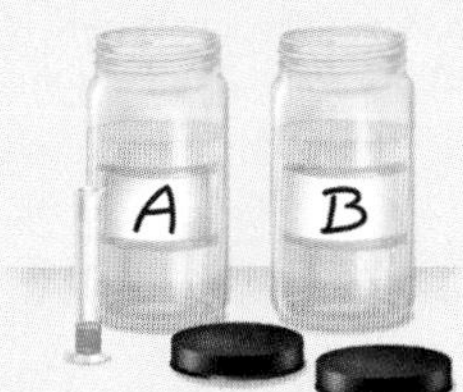

3. Add 5 mL of liquid fertilizer to jar A only.
4. Cover both jars tightly and place them on a windowsill in the sunlight. Wash your hands with soap.
5. Observe the jars every day for a week.

Drawing Conclusions How did the fertilizer affect the growth of the algae in jar A? What was the purpose of jar B in this experiment?

Much of the water in factories is used to cool machinery or metal objects. Even if it contains no chemicals, the warm water alone can act as a pollutant. Many water organisms can live in only a narrow range of temperatures. Warm water released by a factory into a nearby river or pond raises the temperature of the water, sometimes enough to harm the living things there.

Agricultural Chemicals

INTEGRATING LIFE SCIENCE Have you ever "fed" a houseplant with fertilizer to make it grow? On a larger scale, farmers spread or spray fertilizer on their fields to produce better crops. When rain falls on the fields, it washes some of the chemicals away as runoff. Water used for irrigation also creates runoff. The fertilizers in the runoff are a nonpoint source of pollution.

The rich supply of nutrients from fertilizers encourages the growth of plants and algae in and around nearby bodies of water. As you learned in Chapter 7, ponds and lakes naturally change over time due to the process of eutrophication. As more plants grow in the water, dead plant material piles up on the bottom, making the water shallower and warmer. As the plant matter decays, the amount of oxygen in the water decreases. With the addition of fertilizers, this natural process speeds up. A thick, soupy scum of algae forms on top of the water. The scum blocks the sunlight and chokes the flow of water, changing the living conditions for other organisms.

Runoff and irrigation water also carry away other pollutants from farm fields. **Pesticides** are chemicals intended to kill insects and other organisms that damage crops. Pesticides may be sprayed on crops and then run off. Sometimes they are sprayed directly on ponds to kill mosquitoes. But at the same time, these chemicals can harm other insects or the animals that eat them.

☑ *Checkpoint* *How can chemicals used in agriculture reach streams, ponds, and lakes?*

Runoff from Roads

Have you ever noticed an oily sheen on a puddle in a parking lot after a rain shower? The sheen was probably caused by gasoline and motor oil that leaked from cars. When it rains, these oily substances are washed off along with the runoff. During cold winter weather, runoff also picks up the salt that is sprinkled on roads and sidewalks to melt ice. This runoff is a nonpoint source of pollution. Gasoline, oil, and salt pollute rivers and lakes that the runoff enters. These substances can also seep down into groundwater and pollute wells or even an entire aquifer.

Background

Integrating Science Eutrophication of ponds and lakes occurs naturally as nutrients and sediments gradually fill in a body of water. But human activity can greatly increase this process. For example, algal growth markedly increased in Lake Erie from about 1910, as the human population increased near the lake. Such an acceleration of the natural process is called artificial eutrophication.

Program Resources

- **Interdisciplinary Exploration Series** "Where River Meets Sea," pp. 28–30

Figure 15 A thick layer of red algae tints a pond the color of tomato soup. *Inferring What might be the cause of the algae growth in this pond?*

Cleaning Up Polluted Water

Many pollutants are eventually removed from freshwater bodies through natural cleaning processes. **Living things in lakes, streams, and wetlands filter out and break down waste materials.** For example, plant roots filter larger particles from the water. Some plants, such as water hyacinths and duckweed, can absorb metals and chemicals. And just as certain bacteria are used in purifying wastewater, some are also useful in cleaning up toxic chemicals. Bacteria that consume oil have been used to help clean up oil spills. Waste-eating bacteria may also prove to be useful in breaking down toxic chemicals in rivers and lakes.

Pollution clean-up programs can be based on such natural treatment processes. For example, both natural and artificial wetlands are being used to clean up water pollution. Wetlands have been built near coal mines to treat acidic mining runoff before it returns to the environment.

Not only living things can help clean up polluted water. Passing through the sand or rock of an aquifer naturally filters and purifies groundwater. But natural filtering cannot remove or destroy many pollutants, such as metals or manufactured chemicals. Cleaning up this kind of pollution in groundwater is very difficult. One method involves pumping polluted groundwater to the surface, sending it through a treatment plant, and returning it to a nearby lake.

Figure 16 These purple water hyacinths can be an attractive part of a cleanup program. The plants absorb certain metals and chemicals from polluted water.

Preventing Pollution

Despite the successes in cleaning up some water pollution, most pollutants are very difficult to remove. It is often easier to avoid causing the pollution in the first place. In the late 1960s, as

Runoff from Roads

Including All Students

Pair students who are still mastering English with native English speakers. Have each pair create a flow chart to show how gasoline, oil, and salt can travel from the surface of a road to a lake or aquifer that is a source of drinking water. After students have completed their charts, ask: **At what points could this type of pollution be controlled?** *(It could be controlled before it gets on the road by keeping motor vehicles in good running condition and by using sand and cinders on ice instead of salt. It could also be controlled along roads by catching the runoff before it goes farther.)* **limited English proficiency**

Cleaning Up Polluted Water

Building Inquiry Skills: Comparing and Contrasting

Challenge students to compare and contrast the natural process of cleaning water described on this page with wastewater treatment described in Section 1, pages 233–234. Students could describe how settling, filtration, and the breakdown of substances by bacteria are a part of both the natural and the treatment processes. **learning modality: logical/mathematical**

Answers to Self-Assessment

Checkpoint

When rain falls on the fields, it washes some of the chemicals away as runoff. The runoff eventually reaches streams, ponds, and lakes.

Caption Question

Figure 15 Nutrients from fertilizers from the nearby crop field might be the cause of the algae growth in the pond.

Ongoing Assessment

Oral Presentation Have students describe how fertilizers can cause eutrophication and how wetlands help to clean up polluted water.

Preventing Pollution

Using the Visuals: Figure 17

Divide students into small groups and challenge each group to design and create a poster to inform the public about how to prevent pollution. **cooperative learning**

ACTIVITY

3 Assess

Section 3 Review Answers

1. The major sources are human wastes, industrial wastes, agricultural chemicals, and runoff from roads.
2. Rain washes fertilizers from farmers' fields into runoff to become a nonpoint source of pollution. The rich supply of nutrients from fertilizers encourages growth of plants and algae.
3. During floods, sanitary sewers may overflow and run into storm sewers. Since storm sewers generally lead into surface water, sewage from the sanitary sewers can pollute drinking water.
4. Students should not support this change because the industrial wastes pumped into the ground would likely pollute the groundwater.

CHAPTER PROJECT

Check Your Progress

Help students with any difficulties they have in assembling their treatment systems. If students experience difficulties in assembling the system, encourage them to think of alternative ways in which the system could be constructed.

Figure 17 One way you can help prevent water pollution is to educate others about its causes. This student is stenciling a storm drain to remind people of its connection to a nearby river.

people became more aware of the problems of pollution, they urged the government to create laws to control pollution. The goals of those laws include the cleanup of polluted lakes and rivers, better wastewater treatment, and limits on releasing pollutants to the environment. The government also established water-quality standards and programs to clean up waste disposal sites.

Industry and Agriculture Many recycling techniques that help conserve water also help to lessen pollution. For example, factories cool water and reuse it instead of returning it to a river, reducing heat pollution. Industries also look for ways to replace toxic materials with less harmful ones. Printing inks, for instance, can be made with water instead of chemical solvents.

Farmers are trying to reduce the problem of runoff from pastures and barnyards. Some collect and reuse this water for irrigation. Other farmers plant fields of coarse grasses that filter out pollutants before the water reaches a river or pond.

What Can You Do? You can also help keep pollutants from entering the environment. Dispose of toxic substances carefully. For example, chemicals like paint and motor oil should never be poured down the drain, but instead be taken to sites that collect hazardous waste. Avoid overfertilizing lawns or gardens. Form a group of students to educate others in your community about the causes and effects of freshwater pollution. Because many kinds of water pollution are so difficult to clean up, the most important place to stop pollution is at its source.

Section 3 Review

1. List four sources of water pollution.
2. How can fertilizers cause water pollution?
3. Explain why people are often instructed to boil drinking water after a flood.
4. **Thinking Critically Making Judgments** To prevent water pollution, a factory proposes pumping its wastes into the ground instead of into a river. Would you support this change? Why or why not?

CHAPTER PROJECT

Check Your Progress

At this point, you should be ready to assemble your model treatment system. Does the system include at least two treatment steps? Be sure to ask an adult to help you cut materials or assemble them if necessary. *(Hint:* Test your treatment setup for leaks using clean tap water.)

Performance Assessment

Oral Presentation Divide students into small groups and give each group a specific instance of water pollution, such as sewage in the water supply. Groups should analyze the case and prepare a presentation that classifies the pollution, explains the possible consequences, and proposes a solution.

Background

Facts and Figures Since agriculture contributes more than half of the pollution that enters U.S. lakes and streams, control of runoff from fields and feedlots would make the most difference in preventing pollution. The upgrading of sewage systems would also make a big difference. A 1994 EPA report cited 1,100 cities that dump poorly treated sewage into nearby waters. Upgrading inadequate systems could cost $500 billion.

Program Resources

- **Unit 3 Resources** 8-3 Review and Reinforce; 8-3 Enrich

Section 4 Water as an Energy Resource

DISCOVER ACTIVITY

Can Water Do Work?

1. Spread out a large plastic trash bag on the ground. On top of the bag, place several cylindrical objects such as corks, spools, marbles, balls, and empty cans.

2. Fill a plant sprayer with water. Then turn the nozzle to produce a fine mist of water. Try to move the objects with the spray of water. **CAUTION:** *Be careful of slippery wet floors if you are doing this activity indoors.*
3. Now turn the sprayer nozzle to produce a narrower stream of water. Try again to move the objects. Be sure to wipe up any spilled water when you are done.

Think It Over

Observing How does changing the nozzle opening affect the stream of water? At which setting did the objects move more easily? Why?

Picture a curving wall of concrete swooping up nearly 170 meters—taller than a 40-story building. On one side of the wall is a deep reservoir. On the other side, only a narrow river trickles between rocky canyon walls. This is Grand Coulee Dam on the Columbia River in Washington. Completed in 1942, it is still one of the largest dams in the world. Behind Grand Coulee, the water in the reservoir pushes on the concrete dam. The dam's floodgates control that awesome energy. When the gates open to release the water, the water's energy is transformed into enough electricity to light thousands of homes and businesses.

For centuries, people have used the energy of moving water to turn water wheels and run machinery. Today that energy is also a source of electrical power in many parts of the world.

GUIDE FOR READING

- How does moving water produce electricity?
- In what ways is hydroelectric power a good source of energy?

Reading Tip Before you read the section, preview *Exploring a Hydroelectric Power Plant.* Write a list of questions you have about hydroelectric power.

Power from Moving Water

Have you ever seen a fast-moving river propel a kayaker along? If so, you know how much energy moving water can have. It can move boats, carve out canyons, and sweep away cars in a flood. The energy that sends the kayak through the rapids is kinetic

READING STRATEGIES

Reading Tip Suggest that students preview *Exploring a Hydroelectric Power Plant* by reading the labels and skimming the numbered steps. Sample question: How much electricity can a typical hydroelectric power plant generate?

Program Resources

- **Unit 3 Resources** 8-4 Lesson Plan; 8-4 Section Summary
- **Guided Reading and Study Workbook** Section 8-4
- **Interdisciplinary Explorations Series** "Mill Life in the 1840s," pp. 12–13; "Back to the Thirties," pp. 38–39

INTEGRATING PHYSICS

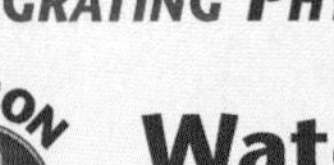

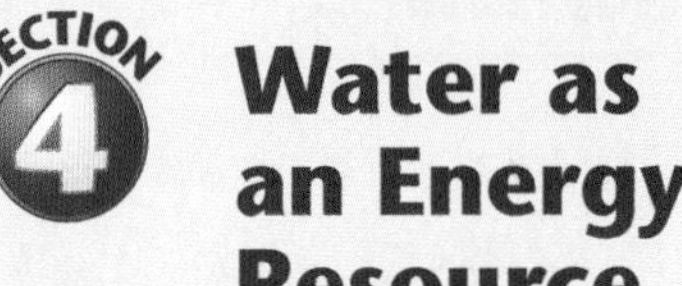

Section 4 Water as an Energy Resource

Objectives

After completing the lesson, students will be able to

- explain how moving water can produce electricity;
- describe the benefits and limitations of hydroelectric power;
- describe the impact of dams.

Key Terms kinetic energy, potential energy, hydroelectric power

1 Engage/Explore

Activating Prior Knowledge

Show students a picture of Niagara Falls or water flowing over a large dam. Ask: **How would you describe the force of this falling water?** *(Students should agree that the water has great force.)* Then encourage students to suggest ways in which that force could be harnessed to power machinery through the production of electricity.

DISCOVER

Skills Focus observing
Materials *large plastic trash bag, various cylindrical objects, plant sprayer, water*
Time 10 minutes
Tips Emphasize to students beforehand not to spray water at each other. This activity may best be done out of doors on a warm day, where spillage is not an issue.
Expected Outcome The narrower stream of water will move the objects farther and more easily than the fine mist.
Think It Over Changing the nozzle opening affects how narrow the stream of water is. The setting that produced the narrower stream moved the objects more easily because the force of the water was more concentrated.

2 Facilitate

Power from Moving Water

Including All Students

To reinforce the difference between potential and kinetic energy for students who need extra help, hold a book in the air above a desk. Ask: **What kind of energy does the book have now?** *(potential energy)* Drop the book and ask: **What kind of energy was this converted into as the book fell from my hand to the desk?** *(potential energy was converted to kinetic energy)* Divide students into groups and challenge them to make a list of as many examples of both kinetic and potential energy as they can. Once their lists are made, have each student read to the class one of the examples. Allow the whole class to come to a consensus on whether the example is one of potential energy, kinetic energy, or both.
learning modality: visual

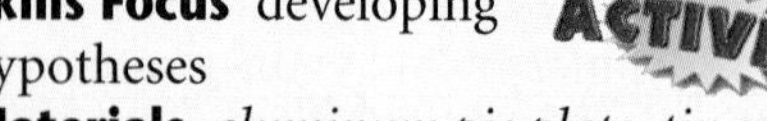

Skills Focus developing hypotheses ACTIVITY
Materials *aluminum pie plate, tin snips, metric ruler, marker, small foam ball, 2 toothpicks, running water*
Time 15 minutes
Tips Students should measure the squares on the plate before beginning to cut, using a marker to draw 5-cm lines. A heavy pair of scissors can be used instead of tin snips. Demonstrate how and where to push the aluminum squares and toothpicks into the ball. Remind students to be very careful of the sharp edges of the pie plate.
Expected Outcome Students' hypotheses will vary. Most will correctly hypothesize that increasing the volume of water will increase the speed of the water wheel.
Extend Students could investigate how the number of blades on the water wheel affects it speed and motion. **learning modality: kinesthetic**

Making a Water Wheel

ACTIVITY

In this activity you will see how the kinetic energy of water can do work.

1. Put on your goggles.
2. Cut an aluminum pie plate into four squares about 5 cm on a side. **CAUTION:** *Be careful not to cut yourself on the sharp edges of the pie plate.*
3. Push the sides of the aluminum squares into a foam ball as shown. Insert two toothpicks into the sides of the ball.

4. Rest the toothpicks on top of your fingers and place the blades under a stream of slowly running water.

Developing Hypotheses How would increasing the volume of water affect the speed of the water wheel? Test your hypothesis. Describe what happens to the speed of the water wheel.

energy. **Kinetic energy** is the form of energy that an object has when it is moving.

Energy can change from one form to another. If the water's movement is stopped, all of its energy becomes potential energy. **Potential energy** is energy that is stored and waiting to be used. To think about potential energy in another way, imagine that you're holding a baseball bat at the top of your swing. The bat at that point has potential energy. As you swing at a ball, the bat's energy becomes kinetic energy. If you hit the ball, the energy is transferred again, becoming the kinetic energy of the ball.

Hydroelectric power is electricity produced by the kinetic energy of water moving over a waterfall or a dam. To generate hydroelectric power (or "hydropower"), engineers build a dam across a river. Water backs up behind the dam, floods the valley, and creates a reservoir. Water stored behind a dam has potential energy, which is changed to kinetic energy when the water is released. **Hydroelectric power plants capture the kinetic energy of moving water and change it into electrical energy.**

How is the kinetic energy of moving water changed into the energy that lights your house and runs your computer? Follow the path of the water in *Exploring a Hydroelectric Power Plant* on the next page to see how these energy changes take place.

☑ ***Checkpoint*** *What type of energy does a diver have while standing at the edge of a diving board?*

The Impact of Dams

In some ways, hydroelectric power seems like an ideal way to produce electricity. **Hydroelectric power is clean, safe, and efficient. Although building a dam is expensive, the water is free and is naturally renewed by the water cycle.** Unlike power plants that burn coal or oil, hydroelectric plants do not contribute to air pollution. In the United States, hydroelectric power accounts for about 8 or 9 percent of electricity produced, while worldwide it generates about 20 percent. Some countries, such as Norway and Brazil, produce almost all their electrical energy through hydropower.

Hydroelectric plants do have limitations, however. Only certain locations are suitable for building a dam. A fast-moving river is necessary, as is an area that can be flooded to create a reservoir.

Dams and the Environment Dams affect all living things in the area around them. Flooding the land behind a dam can destroy wildlife habitats as well as farms and towns. What was once a fast-moving river becomes the still, deep waters of a reservoir. Some organisms

INTEGRATING LIFE SCIENCE

Background

Facts and Figures The Columbia River basin has the largest hydroelectric power system in the world. The system has 100 dams, including the Grand Coulee Dam and 18 other large dams. These dams provide electricity to such large cities as Seattle, Portland, and Boise at a cost 40 percent below the national average. The dams have also reduced the number of salmon from 10–16 million before the dams to about 2.5 million now.

EXPLORING a Hydroelectric Power Plant

Hydroelectric power is generated by changing energy from one form to another.

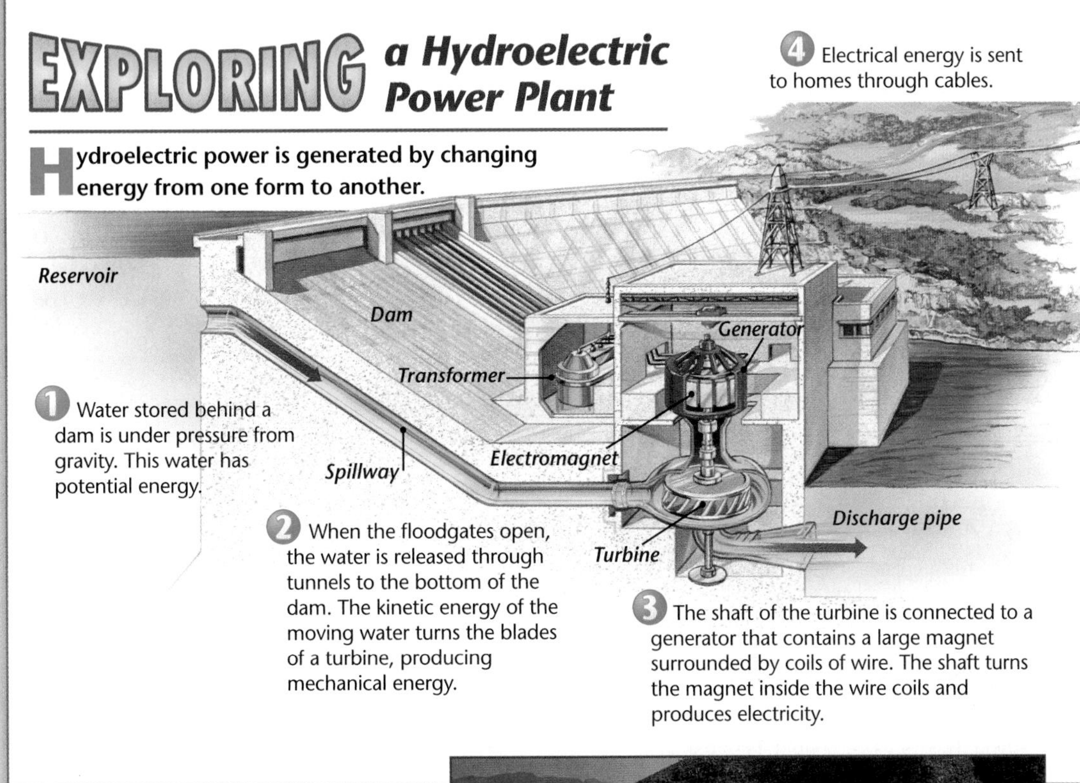

cannot survive the change. In addition, the dam is a barrier across the river. It may prevent fish from traveling to the parts of a river where they usually lay their eggs and young fish are hatched. Dams like Grand Coulee on the Columbia River, for instance, have greatly reduced the population of salmon in the river.

Figure 18 This photograph shows the Theodore Roosevelt Dam in Arizona. ***Interpreting Photographs*** *What natural feature of the river made this a good location to build a dam?*

As a river slows down, it deposits some of the sediments it carries. These deposits can build up behind a dam instead of being carried downstream to enrich the flood plain near the river's mouth. Since the Aswan Dam was built in Egypt, for example, farmlands near the mouth of the Nile River no longer receive the rich load of nutrients the river once brought.

Displaced by a Dam How would you feel if you discovered that your riverside home would soon be dozens of meters under the water of a lake? People whose homes or farms are located

Media and Technology

Transparencies "Exploring a Hydroelectric Power Plant," Transparency 27

Concept Videotape Library Grade 6, Tape 2 "Energy"

Answers to Self-Assessment

Checkpoint

The diver has potential energy.

Caption Question

Figure 18 The banks of the river came close together at this point, making a narrow spot where a dam could be built. Also, the canyon through which the river runs might have been an area that could be flooded to create a reservoir.

EXPLORING

A Hydroelectric Power Plant

Materials *thin insulated wire, strong bar magnet, galvanometer, wire stripper*
Time 10 minutes

Invite students to read aloud the descriptions of the steps in producing hydroelectric power. Then, set up an apparatus that produces electricity from the movement of a magnet. First, remove the insulation from both ends of the insulated wire. Coil the wire into at least seven loops and connect each of the stripped ends to a galvanometer terminal. Finally, move the bar magnet into and out of the coils of wire. Students should observe the needle of the galvanometer move, evidence of an induced electric current. **learning modality: visual**

The Impact of Dams

Integrating Life Science

Ask students: **What is a habitat?** *(The place where an organism lives and that provides it with the things it needs to survive.)* Then call on students to compare and contrast a river habitat with a lake habitat. As they describe characteristics, emphasize that different organisms are adapted to different conditions. Ask: **What happens when the conditions of a habitat change radically?** *(Some organisms disappear while others thrive.)* **learning modality: logical/mathematical**

Ongoing Assessment

Writing Challenge students to classify each of the following as an example of either potential energy, kinetic energy, or both, giving reasons for each: (1) water flowing over a dam *(potential being converted into kinetic)*, (2) water in a reservoir behind a dam *(potential)*, (3) a rubber band stretched to its limit *(potential)*, and (4) a rock rolling down a hill *(potential being converted into kinetic)*.

3 Assess

Section 4 Review Answers

1. Hydroelectric power plants capture the energy of moving water and change it into electrical energy.
2. Students should mention two of these advantages: hydroelectric power is clean, safe, and efficient. The water is free and naturally renewed by the water cycle.
3. Answers may vary. A typical answer: A positive example is the creation of a reservoir where many types of organisms can live. A negative example is the destruction of wildlife habitats.
4. Answers may vary. A typical answer might mention a fast-flowing river, a valley behind the proposed location of the dam, a limited impact on the wildlife of an area, and the need to displace few people in building the dam.

CHAPTER PROJECT

Check Your Progress

Provide dirty water for students to use in testing their systems. Also set up the "cleanness scale" of grades of dirty water to help groups evaluate their results. Help groups whose systems do not yield positive results evaluate their systems and make appropriate changes.

Performance Assessment

Skills Check Have students make a compare/contrast table that lists the benefits and the disadvantages of building a hydroelectric dam. Tell students that they may include what they learned from the text as well as any ideas they have thought of themselves.

Students can save their tables in their portfolio.

Figure 19 Building the Aswan Dam meant flooding the valley that housed these statues of ancient Egyptian rulers. Piece by piece, workers carefully dismantled the great monuments and moved them to higher ground.

where a dam's reservoir is planned have had to face this issue. Large dams flood hundreds or thousands of square kilometers, covering towns and valleys with water. When the Aswan High Dam was built on the Nile, about 80,000 people had to relocate. The ancient monuments of Abu Simbel had to be moved as the water in Lake Nasser rose higher and higher.

One of the largest dams ever built is now under construction on the Yangzi River in China. The Three Gorges Dam, due to be completed in 2009, could displace more than 1.5 million people.

Benefits of Dams For countries that want to build up their industries, hydroelectric power often seems the best way to provide the electricity they need. Water power is the least expensive and least polluting large-scale energy source. Besides electricity, dams can supply water for irrigation and help in flood control.

In some places, people have suggested building small dams to supply power to a local area. Smaller dams uproot fewer people and do less harm to the environment, while still providing energy for a region to grow. However, since dams are expensive to build, small dams may not produce enough power to be worthwhile. Large dams, on the other hand, produce great amounts of power, but they also have a major effect on the land around them.

Section 4 Review

1. How does a hydroelectric plant use moving water to generate electric power?
2. Name two advantages of hydroelectric power.
3. Give one positive example and one negative example of how building a dam could affect wildlife in the area.
4. **Thinking Critically Problem Solving** Suppose you were assigned to choose a site to build a new hydroelectric plant. What features would you look for to find a good site? Be sure to consider the impact on living things as well as the physical characteristics of the site.

CHAPTER PROJECT

Check Your Progress

Now you are ready to test your model system, using the dirty water sample your teacher has provided. Does your treatment unit clean up the water? Measure how much of the original one liter of water is recovered. Based on your results, decide whether you need to redesign any part of your treatment system. (*Hint:* To modify your system, consider changing materials as well as adding more steps.)

Program Resources

◆ **Unit 3 Resources** 8-4 Review and Reinforce; 8-4 Enrich

CHAPTER 8 STUDY GUIDE

Section 1 Water to Drink

Key Ideas

- Sources of drinking water include rivers, lakes, reservoirs, and groundwater.
- Many communities maintain public water supplies to collect, treat, and distribute water to residents. Some homes have private wells.
- Most drinking water is treated to ensure that it is safe and appealing to drink.
- Pumps and gravity are used to increase water pressure and move water through a system of pipes.
- Wastewater and sewage are treated to prevent contamination of drinking water.

Key Terms

water quality, pH, hardness, concentration, filtration, flocs, coagulation, sewage, sludge, septic tank, leach field

Section 2 Balancing Water Needs

Key Ideas

- Water is scarce in many places, leading to competition for limited supplies.
- Water shortage can occur when there is too little water or too much demand in an area.
- Industries can conserve water by reducing water use, recycling water, and reusing water.
- Desalination of ocean water and icebergs are two possible future sources of fresh water.

Key Terms

drought, conservation, desalination

Section 3 Freshwater Pollution

Key Ideas

- Sources of water pollution include human and animal wastes, industrial and agricultural chemicals, and runoff from roads.
- Acid rain is caused by sulfur and nitrogen from smokestacks and car exhausts.

Key Terms

water pollution, point source, nonpoint source, acid rain, pesticide

Section 4 Water as an Energy Resource

Integrating Physics

Key Ideas

- Hydroelectric power plants capture the kinetic energy of moving water and change it into electrical energy.

Key Terms

kinetic energy, potential energy, hydroelectric power

Organizing Information

Concept Map Copy the concept map about freshwater pollution onto a separate sheet of paper. Complete it and add a title.

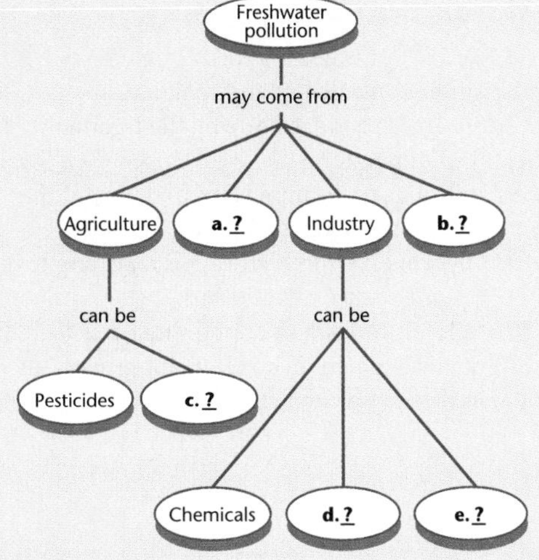

Program Resources

- **Unit 3 Resources** Chapter 8 Project Scoring Rubric
- **Performance Assessment** Chapter 8
- **Chapter and Unit Tests** Chapter 8 Test

Media and Technology

Computer Test Bank Chapter 8 Test

Organizing Information

Concept Map Sample title: Sources of Freshwater Pollution

a., b. Human wastes or sewage, Runoff from roads
c. Fertilizers
d., e. Smoke and exhaust, Heat

Reviewing Content

Multiple Choice

1. b **2.** b **3.** d **4.** a **5.** d

True or False

6. hardness **7.** wastewater **8.** true **9.** nonpoint **10.** fertilizers

Checking Concepts

11. Answers may vary. A typical answer: The water begins in a reservoir, is treated in a treatment plant, and then moves to a pumping station, where it is pumped through water mains to smaller pipes and finally into the home.
12. Sewage flows into a septic tank, where bacteria break it down and sludge settles to the bottom. Cleaner water leaves the tank and flows into a leach field.
13. There is not enough water to go around. Different types of uses must compete for the limited supply.
14. Farmers can use pipes instead of open ditches to carry water into their fields. They can use methods such as drip irrigation that waste little water.
15. Most of the water on Earth is salty and cannot be used for drinking or irrigation. Much of the fresh water on Earth is in the form of ice.
16. Answers may vary. A typical answer should describe the build-up of a pollutant in the bodies of larger organisms that eat smaller organisms in and around a stream.
17. Coal and oil produce nitrogen oxides and sulfur dioxide when they are burned. These gases react with water vapor in the air to form nitric acid and sulfuric acid. These acids return to Earth's surface dissolved in precipitation.
18. It might provide a clean, safe, and efficient way of producing electricity. It also might force people to move.

19. Writing to Learn Answers may vary. A typical answer should mention that a water shortage can occur when there is too little water or too great a demand, and thus people should conserve water. Suggestions of ways to conserve should reflect the ways shown in Figure 8.

CHAPTER 8 ASSESSMENT

Reviewing Content

Multiple Choice

Choose the letter of the best answer.

1. Chlorine is added during water treatment in order to
   a. make particles form flocs.
   b. kill disease-causing organisms.
   c. improve the taste of the water.
   d. remove objects such as fish and trash.
2. Primary treatment of wastewater typically involves
   a. adding chlorine.
   b. filtering out solids.
   c. adding sludge.
   d. adding waste-eating bacteria.
3. One process used to obtain fresh water from salt water is
   a. coagulation. b. filtration.
   c. recharge. d. desalination.
4. The main source of acid precipitation is
   a. smoke from coal-burning factories.
   b. pesticides sprayed in the air.
   c. runoff from farm fields.
   d. toxic chemicals buried underground.
5. Water flowing swiftly possesses
   a. mechanical energy. b. electrical energy.
   c. potential energy. d. kinetic energy.

True or False

If the statement is true, write true. If it is false, change the underlined word or words to make the statement true.

6. The pH of water is a measurement of the amount of calcium and magnesium.
7. Sludge is produced during the treatment of drinking water.
8. A drought can cause wells to dry up if the level of the water table falls.
9. Oily runoff from highways is an example of a point source of pollution.
10. Agricultural runoff containing pesticides often results in increased plant growth in nearby ponds and streams.

Checking Concepts

11. Describe one possible path of drinking water from its source to a home.
12. Explain how a septic system works.
13. Why are water rights an important issue in dry areas?
14. Describe one way that farmers can reduce the amount of water lost during irrigation.
15. Why isn't most of the water on Earth's surface available for people to use?
16. Explain how low levels of a pollutant in a stream can have harmful effects on wildlife in and around the stream.
17. How does acid rain form?
18. How might building a dam affect people living nearby?
19. **Writing to Learn** You have been hired as a public relations specialist for the city water department. Your first assignment is to prepare a brief fact sheet for city residents about the importance of conserving water. The fact sheet should also include some simple suggestions of ways to conserve water at home.

Thinking Critically

20. **Relating Cause and Effect** How can increased demand for water cause the ground above an aquifer to collapse?
21. **Comparing and Contrasting** How is the process of desalination similar to the water cycle? How is it different?
22. **Problem Solving** Explain why finding the source of water pollution can be difficult.
23. **Making Judgments** Do you think that the benefits of hydroelectric power outweigh the disadvantages? Give reasons to support your answer.

256

Thinking Critically

20. When too much water is pumped out of an aquifer, the ground is no longer supported by the pressure of the water inside. As a result, the ground above the aquifer can sink or collapse.
21. Answers may vary. The method of distillation is similar in that it uses evaporation and condensation to obtain fresh water from salt water. It is different in that the water is boiled instead of evaporating naturally.
22. The pollution source may be widespread and/or far away from the polluted water. Pollutants may dissolve and move throughout a body of water. Sources such as gasoline tanks may be hidden underground.
23. Answers may vary. A typical answer should mention the benefits as being a clean, safe, and efficient way to produce electricity; the disadvantages as the destruction of wildlife habitats and the displacement of farms and towns.

Applying Skills

A family had their drinking-water well tested to check the water quality. The test results are shown in the table below. Use the data in the table to answer Questions 24–27.

Drinking Water Sample Test Results

Lead	0.2 parts per million
Copper	0.006 parts per million
pH	5.0
Coliform count	5 out of 5 samples positive

24. Inferring The family suspects that their septic tank is polluting the well. What evidence exists to support this conclusion?

25. Designing Experiments What might be the source of the lead in the water? How could you test your answer?

26. Developing Hypotheses How might the low pH of the water be related to the lead contamination?

27. Predicting The family noticed that their water does not form suds well when mixed with soap. Predict what other substances may be present in high levels in the water.

Performance CHAPTER PROJECT **Assessment**

Present Your Project It's time to put your treatment system to the test! Use your system to clean up the dirty water sample. Measure the volume of water recovered by your system. How can you evaluate your results?

Reflect and Record In your journal, reflect on what you have learned as you built your water treatment system. Explain how the different materials used in your classmates' projects affected their results. How could you improve your process to recover more water or make the water cleaner? What else would you want to know about the treated water before you would consider it drinkable?

Test Preparation

Use these questions to prepare for standardized tests.

A family conducted a survey of their current water use. Study the bar graph below, which shows their average use for one day. Then answer Questions 28–31.

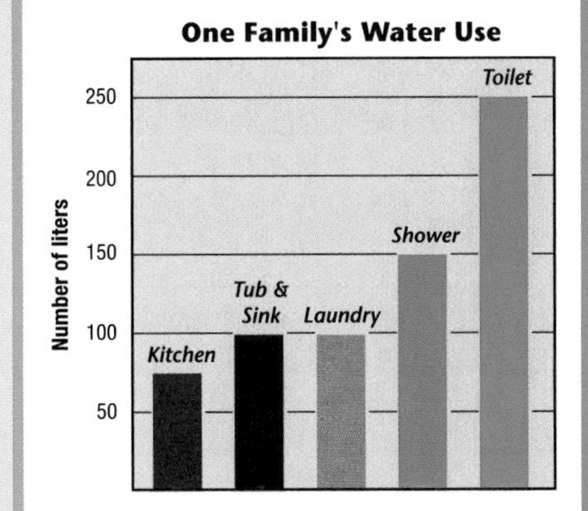

28. Which of the categories represents the family's largest water use?
a. laundry **b.** shower
c. kitchen **d.** toilet

29. If everyone in the family agreed to take 5-minute showers instead of 10-minute showers, about how many liters of water would be saved each day?
a. 5 **b.** 11 **c.** 75 **d.** 150

30. The family found that they used about 675 liters of water per day on average. About what percentage of this is used for the laundry?
a. 10 **b.** 15 **c.** 37 **d.** 100

31. The family decided to try to reduce their water use. Which of the following measures could help them save water?
a. run washing machines only when full
b. repair leaky faucets
c. turn off the tap when brushing their teeth
d. all of the above

Program Resources

◆ **Inquiry Skills Activity Book** Provides teaching and review of all inquiry skills

Applying Skills

24. The coliform count result supports the suspicion, because all 5 of the samples taken contained coliform bacteria. This is evidence that the water has been contaminated with waste material.
25. The source of lead might be from the pipes the water passes through. Students' suggestions for tests may vary. A typical way to test that answer would be to measure the amount of lead in a sample of water collected before the water passes through the pipes.
26. The lower the pH, the more acidic the water. Acidic water can dissolve lead from the pipes it passes through.
27. Calcium and magnesium are probably present in high levels, since hard water does not form suds well when mixed with soap.

Performance CHAPTER PROJECT **Assessment**

Present Your Project As students ready their presentations, field any questions about what they need to present to the class. Encourage students who are having trouble with their models to make last-minute changes, but reassure them that a good effort and clear presentation can make up for disappointing results. Use the Scoring Rubric on page 36 of the Unit 4 Resources to help in assessing the presentations.

Reflect and Record After all presentations have been made, encourage students in a class discussion to evaluate their own designs in light of their classmates' designs. Students can come to a consensus about what steps and materials were most effective in cleaning water. Then have all students write their reflections about the project in their journals.

Test Preparation

28. d **29.** c **30.** b **31.** d

Ocean Motions

Sections	Time	Student Edition Activities	ACTIVITY Other Activities
CHAPTER PROJECT **Protecting a Shoreline** p. 259	Ongoing (1 week)	Check Your Progress, pp. 265, 270, 284 Present Your Project, p. 287	
1 Wave Action pp. 260–265 ◆ Describe the characteristics of waves and explain how they form. ◆ Describe how waves change near the shore. ◆ Identify the effects of waves on beaches and coastlines.	1 period/ $\frac{1}{2}$ block	**Discover** How Do Waves Change a Beach?, p. 260 **Try This** Wave Motion, p. 262	TE Demonstration, p. 261 TE Including All Students, p. 261 TE Including All Students, p. 262 TE Demonstration, p. 263 TE Inquiry Challenge, p. 264 TE Visual Arts Connection, p. 265
2 *Integrating Space Science* **Tides** pp. 266–270 ◆ Explain what causes tides and the daily and monthly tide cycles. ◆ Describe how people use the energy of tides.	1 period/ $\frac{1}{2}$ block	**Discover** When Is High Tide?, p. 266 **Sharpen Your Skills** Graphing, p. 268	TE Including All Students, p. 267 TE Including All Students, p. 266 IES "Where River Meets Sea," pp. 26–27
3 Ocean Water Chemistry pp. 271–277 ◆ Identify the salinity, gas content, and temperature of ocean water. ◆ Describe how ocean conditions change with depth.	1–2 periods/ $\frac{1}{2}$–1 block	**Discover** Will the Eggs Sink or Float?, p. 271 **Science at Home,** p. 275 **Skills Lab: Designing Experiments** Investigating Changes in Density, pp. 276–277	TE Integrating Chemistry, p. 272 TE Including All Students, p. 273 TE Including All Students, p. 274 TE Inquiry Challenge, p. 275 LM Chapter 9, "Density and Salinity" IES "Where River Meets Sea," pp. 15–16, 18–25
4 Currents and Climate pp. 278–284 ◆ Identify the forces that cause surface currents and deep currents. ◆ Describe how surface currents affect climate on land. ◆ Describe deep currents, upwelling, and El Niño.	1–2 periods/ $\frac{1}{2}$–1 block	**Discover** Which Is More Dense?, p. 278 **Sharpen Your Skills** Drawing Conclusions, p. 280 **Real-World Lab: How Things Work** Modeling Ocean Currents, pp. 282–283	TE Demonstration, p. 279 TE Including All Students, p. 280
Study Guide/Chapter Assessment pp. 285–287	1 period/ $\frac{1}{2}$ block		ISAB Provides teaching and review of all inquiry skills

For Standard or Block Schedule The Resource Pro® CD-ROM gives you maximum flexibility for planning your instruction for any type of schedule. Resource Pro® contains Planning Express®, an advanced scheduling program, as well as the entire contents of the Teaching Resources and the Computer Test Bank.

CHAPTER PLANNING GUIDE

Program Resources	Assessment Strategies	Media and Technology
UR Chapter 9 Project Teacher Notes **UR** Chapter 9 Project Student Overview and Worksheets	**SE** Performance Assessment: Present Your Project, p. 287 **TE** Check Your Progress, pp. 265, 270, 284 **UR** Chapter 9 Project Scoring Rubric	Science Explorer Internet Site at www.phschool.com Student Edition on Audio CD, Chapter 9
UR 9-1 Lesson Plan **UR** 9-1 Section Summary **UR** 9-1 Review and Reinforce **UR** 9-1 Enrich	**SE** Section 1 Review, p. 265 **TE** Ongoing Assessment, pp 261, 263, 265 **TE** Performance Assessment, p. 265	Concept Videotape Library, Grade 6, Tape 1, "The Wave" Transparency 28, "Parts of a Wave" Transparency 29, "Longshore Drift and Rip Currents"
UR 9-2 Lesson Plan **UR** 9-2 Section Summary **UR** 9-2 Review and Reinforce **UR** 9-2 Enrich	**SE** Section 2 Review, p. 270 **TE** Ongoing Assessment, pp. 267, 269 **TE** Performance Assessment, p. 270	Transparency 30, "Spring and Neap Tides"
UR 9-3 Lesson Plan **UR** 9-3 Section Summary **UR** 9-3 Review and Reinforce **UR** 9-3 Enrich **UR** Chapter 9 Skills Lab	**SE** Section 3 Review, p. 275 **TE** Ongoing Assessment, p. 273 **TE** Performance Assessment, p. 275	Concept Videotape Library, Grade 6, Tape 2, "Density" Transparency 31, "Exploring the Water Column" Lab Activity Videotapes, Grade 6 Tape 2
UR 9-4 Lesson Plan **UR** 9-4 Section Summary **UR** 9-4 Review and Reinforce **UR** 9-4 Enrich **UR** Chapter 9 Real-World Lab	**SE** Section 4 Review, p. 284 **TE** Ongoing Assessment, pp. 279, 281 **TE** Performance Assessment, p. 284	Transparency 32, "Major Ocean Currents" Lab Activity Videotapes, Grade 6 Tape 2
RCA Provides strategies to improve science reading skills **GRSW** Provides worksheets to promote student comprehension of content	**SE** Chapter 9 Study Guide/Assessment, pp. 285–287 **PA** Chapter 9 Performance Assessment **CUT** Chapter 9 Test **CTB** Chapter 9 Test	Computer Test Bank, Chapter 9 Test

Key: **SE** Student Edition
CTB Computer Test Bank
ISAB Inquiry Skills Activity Book
GRSW Guided Reading and Study Workbook
TE Teacher's Edition
PTA Product Testing Activities by *Consumer Reports*
RCA Reading in the Content Area
PA Performance Assessment
UR Unit Resources
LM Laboratory Manual
IES Interdisciplinary Explorations Series
CUT Chapter and Unit Tests

Meeting the National Science Education Standards and AAAS Benchmarks

National Science Education Standards	Benchmarks for Science Literacy	Unifying Themes
Science As Inquiry (Content Standard A) ◆ **Design and conduct a scientific investigation** Students design an experiment and control variables to investigate density of ocean water. *(Skills Lab)* ◆ **Develop descriptions, explanations, predictions, and models using evidence** Students model ocean currents to gain an understanding of how currents affect climate. *(Real-World Lab)* **Physical Science** (Content Standard B) ◆ **Properties and changes of properties in matter** The total amount of dissolved salts in water is salinity. Water density increases when salinity increases or temperature decreases. *(Section 3; Skills Lab)* ◆ **Transfer of energy** Waves form when winds transmit their energy to water. The movement of water between high and low tide is a source of potential energy. Surface currents are driven mainly by winds. Students model the movement of ocean water due to surface currents. *(Sections 1, 2, and 4; Real-World Lab)* **Earth and Space Science** (Content Standard D) ◆ **Earth in the solar system** Tides are caused by the interaction of Earth, the moon, and the sun. *(Section 2)* **Science and Technology** (Content Standard E) ◆ **Design a solution or product** Students build a model to explore preventing shoreline erosion. *(Chapter Project)*	**1B Scientific Inquiry** Students build a model to explore preventing shoreline erosion. Students design an experiment and control variables to investigate water density. *(Chapter Project; Skills Lab)* **4B The Earth** Tides are caused by interaction of the moon, sun and Earth. Ocean currents affect climate by moving cold and warm water around the globe. *(Sections 2 and 4)* **4C Processes that Shape the Earth** Waves shape a beach through erosion and deposition. *(Section 1)* **4D Structure of Matter** The total amount of dissolved salts in water is called salinity. The density of water increases when salinity increases or temperature decreases. *(Section 3; Skills Lab)* **4E Energy Transformation** Waves form when winds transmit their energy to water. Surface currents are driven mainly by winds. Students model the movement of ocean water due to surface currents. *(Sections 1 and 4; Real-World Lab)* **8C Energy Sources and Use** The movement of water between high and low tide is a source of potential energy. *(Section 2)* **11B Models** Students build an ocean beach model to investigate erosion. Students model ocean currents to gain an understanding of how currents affect climate. *(Chapter Project; Real-World Lab)*	◆ **Energy** Waves form when winds transmit their energy to water. The movement of water between high and low tide is a source of potential energy. Surface currents are driven mainly by winds. *(Sections 1, 2, and 4)* ◆ **Patterns of Change** Pressure increases continuously from the surface to the deepest part of the ocean. The density of water increases when salinity increases or temperature decreases. *(Sections 1 and 3; Skills Lab)* ◆ **Systems and Interactions** Tides are caused by the interaction of Earth, the moon, and the sun. Currents affect climate by moving cold and warm water around the globe. *(Sections 2 and 4)* ◆ **Stability** The daily rise and fall of Earth's waters on shores are called tides. On average, ocean water salinity is about 35 parts per thousand. *(Sections 2 and 3)* ◆ **Modeling** Students build an ocean beach model to investigate erosion. Students model ocean currents to gain an understanding of how currents affect climate. *(Chapter Project; Real-World Lab)*

Take It to the Net

Interactive text at www.phschool.com

Science Explorer comes alive with iText.

- **Complete student text** is accessible from any computer with Internet access or a CD-ROM drive.
- **Animations, simulations, and videos** enhance student understanding and retention of concepts.
- **Self-tests and online study tools** assess student understanding.

STAY CURRENT with **SCIENCE NEWS**®

Find out the latest research and information about Earth's Waters at: **www.phschool.com**

Go to **www.phschool.com** and click on the Science icon.Then click on Science Explorer: Life, Earth, and Physical Science under PH@school.

Student Edition Activities Planner

ACTIVITY	Time (minutes)	Materials *Quantities for one work group*	Skills
Section 1			
Discover, p. 260	15	**Consumable** water, wooden tongue depressor **Nonconsumable** aluminum baking pan, sand, pebbles, book, metric ruler	Observing
Try This, p. 262	20	**Consumable** water, thread **Nonconsumable** large aquarium tank, several metal washers and corks	Observing
Section 2			
Discover, p. 266	15	**Nonconsumable** calculator	Predicting
Sharpen Your Skills, p. 268	20	**Consumable** graph paper **Nonconsumable** calculator, ruler	Graphing
Section 3			
Discover, p. 271	10	**Consumable** tap water, salt, two uncooked eggs **Nonconsumable** two beakers or jars, teaspoon, stirring rod	Observing
Science at Home, p. 275	home	**Consumable** cardboard milk carton, tape, water **Nonconsumable** awl or punch	Applying Concepts
Skills Lab, pp. 276–277	40	**Consumable** table salt, water, ice **Nonconsumable** thumbtacks, thermometer, metric ruler, unsharpened pencil, sharpened pencil, 100- and 250-mL graduated cylinders, 250-mL beaker, balance, hot plate, spoon	Designing Experiments, Controlling Variables, Measuring, Creating Data Tables, Graphing
Section 4			
Discover, p. 278	10	**Consumable** warm and cold water, food coloring **Nonconsumable** plastic bowl, plastic dropper, cup, stirring rod	Inferring
Sharpen Your Skills, p. 280	5	No special materials are required.	Drawing Conclusions
Real-World Lab, pp. 282–283	60	**Consumable** 3 sticks modeling clay, newspaper, blue and red construction paper, jointed drinking straw, 400 mL light-reflecting rheoscopic fluid or water and food coloring, chalk **Nonconsumable** rectangular baking tray, permanent marker, ruler, hole puncher	Making Models, Observing, Inferring

A list of all materials required for the Student Edition activities can be found on pages TVA34–TVA40. You can obtain information about ordering materials by calling 1-800-848-9500 or by accessing the Science Explorer Internet site at **www.phschool.com**.

CHAPTER 9 PROJECT

Protecting a Shoreline

When students think of waves at the beach, they may be more likely to think of surfing than erosion. They may not realize how quickly waves can wash away sand and pebbles, wear away rock, and undermine structures built close to the shore.

Purpose In this project, students will make a model shoreline and lighthouse, generate waves in a wave tank they construct, and measure wave erosion. They will also model and assess ways to prevent wave erosion. By doing this project, students will gain a better understanding of how waves cause erosion and how erosion can be controlled.

Skills Focus After completing the Chapter 9 Project, students will be able to
- ◆ make a model of a beach and lighthouse and generate waves in a wave tank;
- ◆ observe and measure wave erosion of the beach;
- ◆ design and test methods to reduce wave erosion of the beach;
- ◆ demonstrate and explain the best method to the rest of the class.

Project Timeline The entire project will require at least two weeks. Depending on how much class time students can spend working on the project each day, about two days may be required for each of the following phases.
- ◆ Brainstorm a plan and a list of materials for the wave tank and model beach and lighthouse.
- ◆ Make a to-scale sketch of the tank and model and finalize the list of materials.
- ◆ Build the wave tank and model beach and lighthouse.
- ◆ Generate waves and measure erosion of the beach, modifying the model and method of measuring as needed.
- ◆ Brainstorm methods and materials to prevent erosion.
- ◆ Modify the model to introduce erosion-prevention methods and measure how well the methods prevent erosion.
- ◆ Demonstrate and explain to the class the best method(s) of preventing erosion.

For more detailed information on planning and supervising the chapter project, see Chapter 9 Project Teacher Notes in Unit 3 Resources.

Suggested Shortcuts
- ◆ You may wish to divide the class into small groups to carry out the project.
- ◆ You can make this project shorter and less involved by explaining to students how to build a wave tank and model beach and lighthouse and provide them with the necessary materials. You can give students suggestions for measuring and preventing erosion.
- ◆ For a class project, build one wave tank with model beach and lighthouse, and then let groups take turns testing methods to protect the beach from erosion.

Possible Materials Wave tanks can be constructed from large cardboard box tops or plastic under-bed storage boxes. Cardboard boxes must be lined with plastic. See Chapter 9 Project Worksheet 1 in Unit 3 Resources, for more detailed guidelines. A large aluminum baking pan or a paint roller pan can be used for

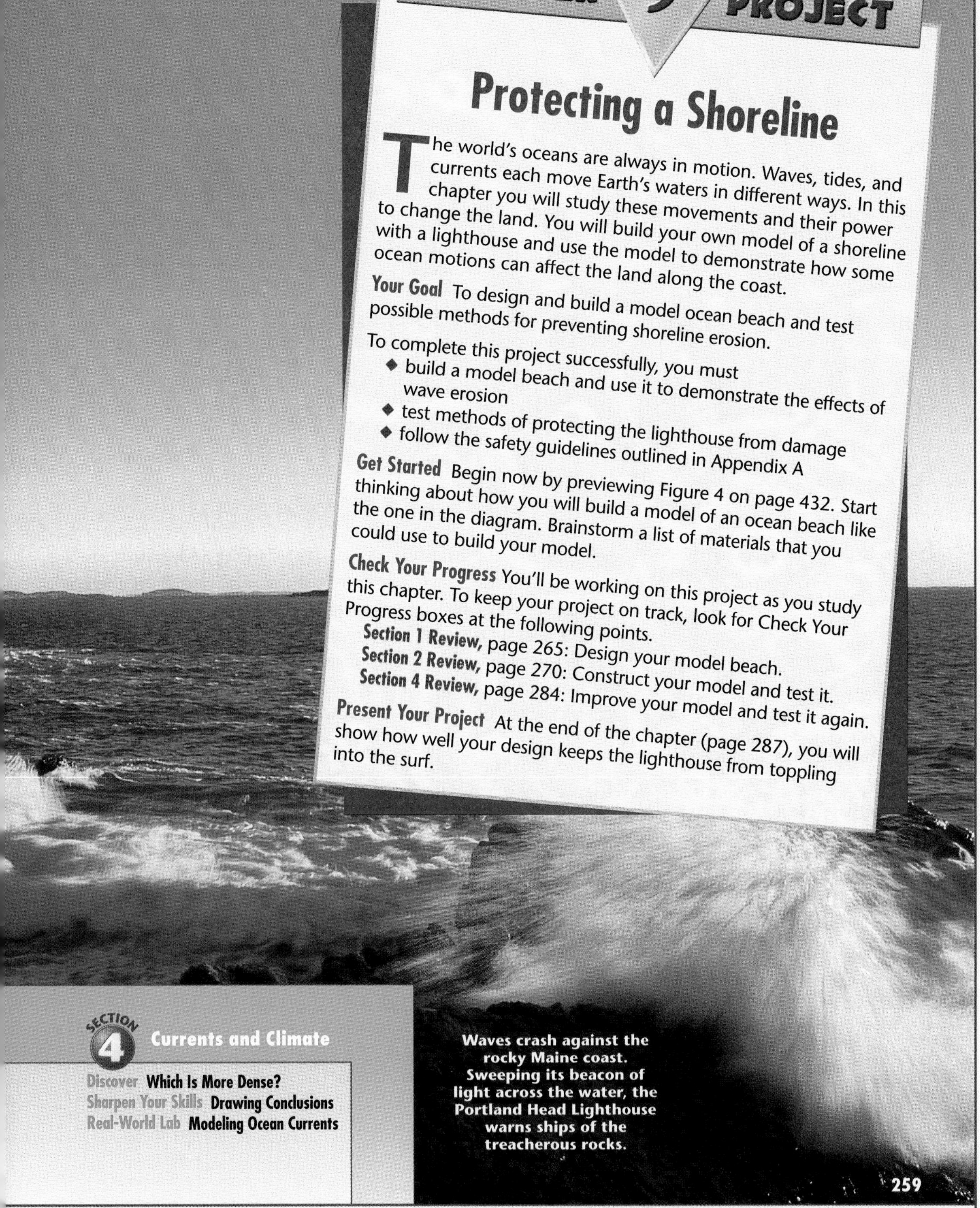

CHAPTER 9 PROJECT

Protecting a Shoreline

The world's oceans are always in motion. Waves, tides, and currents each move Earth's waters in different ways. In this chapter you will study these movements and their power to change the land. You will build your own model of a shoreline with a lighthouse and use the model to demonstrate how some ocean motions can affect the land along the coast.

Your Goal To design and build a model ocean beach and test possible methods for preventing shoreline erosion.

To complete this project successfully, you must

- build a model beach and use it to demonstrate the effects of wave erosion
- test methods of protecting the lighthouse from damage
- follow the safety guidelines outlined in Appendix A

Get Started Begin now by previewing Figure 4 on page 432. Start thinking about how you will build a model of an ocean beach like the one in the diagram. Brainstorm a list of materials that you could use to build your model.

Check Your Progress You'll be working on this project as you study this chapter. To keep your project on track, look for Check Your Progress boxes at the following points.

Section 1 Review, page 265: Design your model beach.
Section 2 Review, page 270: Construct your model and test it.
Section 4 Review, page 284: Improve your model and test it again.

Present Your Project At the end of the chapter (page 287), you will show how well your design keeps the lighthouse from toppling into the surf.

Waves crash against the rocky Maine coast. Sweeping its beacon of light across the water, the Portland Head Lighthouse warns ships of the treacherous rocks.

SECTION 4 Currents and Climate

Discover **Which Is More Dense?**
Sharpen Your Skills **Drawing Conclusions**
Real-World Lab **Modeling Ocean Currents**

a smaller, simpler wave tank. For the beach and gradually sloping ocean bottom, students should use a combination of materials, such as fine sand, silt, and small pebbles. The lighthouse may be constructed of small square or rectangular pieces, such as toy blocks, small flat stones, or sugar cubes, held together with modeling clay. Beach protection materials might include larger stones or wooden blocks held together with modeling clay for seawalls, and craft sticks or toy logs placed perpendicular to the beach for groins. To measure erosion, students can use toothpicks stuck into the beach and labeled with masking tape.

Launching the Project Challenge students to think of kinds of structures commonly built along beaches. *(Students might mention lighthouses, high-rise hotels, restaurants, homes, marinas, and amusement parks.)* Ask: **What are some limitations of building near an ocean coast?** *(Students might mention hurricanes, storms, blowing sand, and erosion.)* Emphasize that the shape of a coast is constantly being altered by wave erosion. Therefore, when structures are built on a coast, methods of controlling erosion often must be adopted to protect these structures. Explain to students that in the Chapter 9 Project, they will devise and test methods to protect a model beach and lighthouse from wave erosion. To help students get started, pass out Chapter 9 Project Overview and Worksheets in Unit 3 Resources. You may also wish to pass out the Chapter 9 Project Scoring Rubric at this time.

Performance Assessment

Use the Chapter 9 Project Scoring Rubric to assess students' work. Students will be assessed on

- how well they plan their wave tank and models and the appropriateness of their materials;
- the accuracy of the models they build and how well they collect and record data;
- how effectively they present their models and explain their results to the class;
- how much they contribute to their group's effort, if they have worked in groups.

Program Resources

- **Unit 3 Resources** Chapter 9 Project Teacher Notes; Chapter 9 Project Overview and Worksheets; Chapter 9 Project Scoring Rubric

You will find an Internet activity, chapter self-tests for students, and links to other chapter topics at this site.

Media and Technology

Student Edition on Audio CD Chapter 9

Wave Action

Objectives

After completing the lesson, students will be able to

- ◆ describe the characteristics of waves and explain how they form;
- ◆ describe how waves change near the shore;
- ◆ identify the effects of waves on beaches and coastlines.

Key Terms wave, crest, wavelength, frequency, trough, wave height, longshore drift, sandbar, rip current, groin

1 Engage/Explore

Activating Prior Knowledge

Encourage students who have been to a beach or wave pool to describe how it feels to stand in the waves. Ask: **What happened to your body when a wave passed by?** *(It bobbed up and down.)* **If you were at the beach, what happened to the sand under your feet as the water flowed back out to sea?** *(It was washed away by the water.)* Ask students to consider how much sand would be washed away after years of wave action.

DISCOVER

Skills Focus observing
Materials *aluminum baking pan, sand, pebbles, book, ruler, water, wooden tongue depressor*
Time 15 minutes
Tips To save time, do the activity as a class demonstration. For a more dramatic effect, raise the pan a few more centimeters and then ask: **Why does raising the pan change how the waves affect the beach?** *(It increases how fast the water flows away from the beach and how much sand it can carry.)*
Expected Outcome Students should observe that as the waves move away from the beach, they carry sand, causing erosion of the beach.
Think It Over The flow of water away from the beach caused the sand to be washed away.

SECTION 1 Wave Action

DISCOVER ACTIVITY

How Do Waves Change a Beach?

1. In one end of an aluminum pan, build a "beach" of sand and pebbles. Put a book under that end of the pan to raise it about 5 centimeters.

2. Pour water slowly into the other end of the pan until it covers the edge of the sand, just as water touches the edge of a beach.
3. Place a wooden tongue depressor in the water. Move it back and forth gently in a regular rhythm to make waves in the pan. Continue for about 2 minutes.
4. Once the water has stopped moving, observe what has happened to the beach. Wash your hands when you are finished with this activity.

Think It Over
Observing How has the motion of the water changed the edge of the beach?

GUIDE FOR READING

- ◆ How does a wave form?
- ◆ How do waves change near the shore?
- ◆ How do waves affect beaches and coastlines?

Reading Tip **Before you read, preview the diagrams and photographs in the section to see different types of wave action. Make a list of questions you have about wave motion.**

Stretched flat on his surfboard, the surfer paddles out into the clear turquoise water. The surfboard bobs up and down as he awaits the perfect surfing wave. After a few minutes, he spots the telltale signs in an approaching wave. At the last possible moment before the wave crashes over him, the surfer jumps into a standing position. He balances skillfully as the energy of the wave sends the surfboard skimming down the smooth front of the curling wave.

If you've ever seen a video of surfers "catching a wave" along a Pacific beach, you know that they make this difficult sport look almost easy. But even experienced surfers can seldom predict when the next good wave will roll into shore. As you will read in this section, many different forces influence the size, shape, and timing of waves.

How Waves Form

When you watch the surfer's wave crash onto the beach, you are seeing the last step in the process of the wave's development. The process begins with wind. Without the energy of wind,

READING STRATEGIES

Reading Tip As students preview the diagrams and photographs in the section, encourage them to ask themselves, "What is happening in this picture?" Asking this question will bring up additional questions. Students' questions may include, "Do waves go up-and-down or back-and-forth?" and "What makes a wave break near the shore?"

Vocabulary Preview the terms with students before they read the section. Give special attention to words that students are probably familiar with, such as *crest, frequency,* and *trough,* but have different meanings in this context. Use students' familiarity with the words to help them understand the new meanings.

the surface of the ocean would be as smooth as a mirror. **Most waves form when winds blowing across the water's surface transmit their energy to the water.** A **wave** is the movement of energy through a body of water.

Waves start in the open ocean. The size of the wave depends on the strength of the wind and on the length of time it blows. A gentle breeze creates small ripples on the surface of the water. Stronger winds create larger waves.

The size of the wave also depends on the distance over which the wind blows. Winds blowing across longer distances build up bigger waves. In the wide Pacific Ocean, a wave might travel a third of the way around the world before reaching the California coast.

Although waves may appear to carry water toward shore, the water does not actually move forward in deep water. If it did, ocean water would eventually pile up on the coasts of every continent! The energy of the wave moves toward shore, but the water itself remains where it was. You can test this for yourself by floating a piece of wood or a cork in a bowl of water. Use a spoon to make a wave in the bowl. As the wave passes, the object lurches forward a little, then bobs backward. It ends up in almost the same spot where it started.

Figure 1 A surfer cruises along the smooth front of this cresting wave. The wave's energy moves along, but the water mostly stays where it is. ***Applying Concepts*** *In which direction is the energy of this wave moving?*

2 Facilitate

How Waves Form

Demonstration

ACTIVITY

To illustrate that it is energy and not water that moves in a wave, tie one end of a piece of rope to a chair or other stationary object and invite a student volunteer to move the other end up and down to generate waves. Students will see that the waves reach the chair but the rope as a whole does not get any closer to it. **learning modality: visual**

Including All Students

ACTIVITY

Help students who are having difficulty understanding ocean waves by encouraging them to brainstorm ways that people make waves in liquids. *(Possible ways might include stepping into a bathtub, jumping into a pool, blowing on hot soup, sloshing soft drink in a can, rowing a boat, and throwing pebbles into a pond.)* Have a volunteer list the ways of making waves on the board. Lead the class in a discussion of how all the ways are similar. *(All involve energy being transferred to a liquid, followed by a ripple-like movement in the liquid as the energy passes through it.)* Invite students to observe this for themselves by blowing through a straw across the surface of water in a bowl. **learning modality: logical/mathematical**

Program Resources

- **Unit 3 Resources** 9-1 Lesson Plan; 9-1 Section Summary
- **Guided Reading and Study Workbook** Section 9-1

Answers to Self-Assessment

Caption Question

Figure 1 The energy of the wave is moving toward the shore, or from the right side of the photograph to the left side.

Ongoing Assessment

Drawing Have students draw a labeled diagram showing how the wind creates waves, with arrows to show the direction of the wind and the energy moving through the water in the wave.

Students can save their drawing in their portfolio.

How Waves Form, continued

Skills Focus observing
Materials *aquarium, water, several metal washers and corks, thread*
Time 20 minutes
Tips The larger the aquarium, the greater the effect. Cover the area with plastic to catch spills. When making waves, students should keep their hands near the surface.
Expected Outcome Students will see that corks near the surface move more in the waves than corks closer to the bottom. They may say that increasing the wave height increases movement of all corks.
Extend Ask: **Do you think you would be more likely to become seasick on a boat or a submarine? Explain.** *(You'd be more likely in a boat, because being at the surface of the water, the boat will move more in the waves.)* **learning modality: visual**

Describing Waves

Including All Students

Materials *spring toy*
Time 5 minutes

Invite two students to hold the opposite ends of a spring toy and take turns moving their end of the toy up and down, first slowly then faster, to generate waves. Ask: **What happens to the waves when you move your hand faster?** *(The waves move faster and get closer together.)* **As the frequency of the waves increases, what happens to the wavelength?** *(It gets shorter.)* **learning modality: kinesthetic**

Using the Visuals: Figure 2

Ask: **What is the name for the distance between the crest and trough of a wave?** *(wave height)* **What is the name for the distance from the crest of one wave to the crest of the next?** *(wavelength)* **How would you describe the movement of the buoy?** *(Up and down in a circular path)* **How would the buoy move if it wasn't tied to a weight?** *(Mostly up and down, but it might also move over the surface of the water because of the wind.)* **learning modality: visual**

Wave Motion

This activity shows how waves formed at the surface affect deeper water.

1. Fill an aquarium about three-quarters full of water.
2. Tie enough metal washers to a cork so that the cork floats about 3 cm from the bottom of the tank.
3. Repeat Step 2 with more corks so that they float 9 cm from the bottom, 15 cm from the bottom, and so on until the last cork floats on the surface.

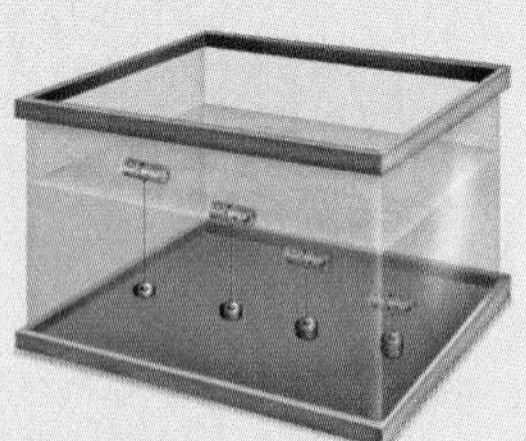

4. Make small, steady waves in the tank by moving your hand up and down in the water. Note what happens to each cork.
5. Repeat Step 4, increasing the height of the waves by moving your hand faster.

Observing How does increasing the wave height affect the motion of each cork?

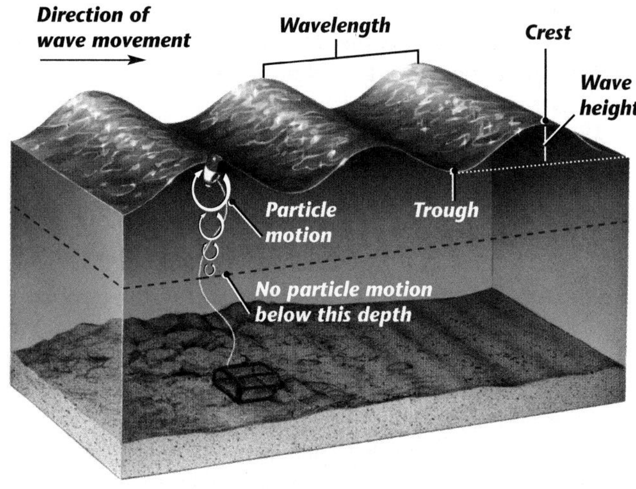

Figure 2 As a wave passes by, the water particles move in a circular motion. The buoy on the surface swings down into the trough of one wave, then back up to the crest of the next wave. Below the surface, the water particles move in smaller circles. At a depth equal to about one half the wavelength, the water particles are not affected by the surface wave.

Figure 2 shows what happens to the water as a wave travels along. As the wave passes, water particles move in a circular path. They swing forward and down with the energy of the wave, then back up to their original position.

Notice that the deeper water particles in Figure 2 move in smaller circles than those near the surface. The wind affects the water at the surface more than the deep water. Below a certain depth, the water does not move at all as the wave passes. If you were inside a submarine in deep water, you would not be able to tell whether the water above you was rough or smooth.

Describing Waves

If you ask a sailor to describe a wave, you might hear some unfamiliar terms. To a sailor, "a following sea" refers to waves traveling in the same direction as the boat. "Combers" are large, cresting waves. And "spindrift" is ocean spray torn by the wind from the surface of the waves.

Scientists have their own vocabulary of terms to describe the size and strength of waves. The name for the highest part of a wave is the **crest.** The horizontal distance between crests is the **wavelength.** Long, rolling waves with lots of space between crests have long wavelengths. Short, choppy waves have shorter wavelengths. Waves are also measured by their **frequency,** the number of waves that pass a point in a certain amount of time.

Background

History of Science The amount of energy in waves is tremendous. A single wave just 1.3 m high moving along 35 m of coast contains enough energy to power a medium-sized city for a day. In the late 1800s, people designed a way to transform the energy of waves to a usable form. A float was used to transfer kinetic wave energy to a piston that operated a siren. Buoys with wave-powered sirens have been used ever since. However, it was not until late in this century before a British scientist, Dr. Stephen Salter, found a way to generate electricity with waves. Now there are wave-generated power stations along the coasts of Britain, Norway, Japan, and India. They are not more common because they are not usually economical and waves as a power source are not consistent.

The name for the lowest part of a wave is the **trough.** The vertical distance from the crest to the trough is the **wave height.** The energy and strength of a wave depend mainly on its wave height. In the open ocean, most waves are between 2 and 5 meters high. During storms, the waves can grow much higher and more powerful.

☑ *Checkpoint Do waves that are close together have a longer or shorter wavelength than waves that are far apart?*

How Waves Change Near Shore

In deep water, waves usually travel as long, low waves called swells. As the waves approach the shore, the water becomes shallower. Follow the waves in Figure 3 as they enter the shallow water. The bottoms of the waves begin to touch the sloping ocean floor. Friction between the ocean floor and the water causes the waves to slow down. As the speed of the waves decrease, their shapes change. **Near shore, the wave height increases and the wavelength decreases.** When the wave reaches a certain height, the crest of the wave topples. The wave breaks onto the shore, forming surf.

At first, the energy of the breaking wave, or breaker, causes the water to surge up the beach. But the force of gravity pulling down on the rising water soon causes it to lose its energy. The water that moves up the beach flows back into the sea. Have you ever stood at the water's edge and felt the pull of the water rushing back out to the ocean? This pull, often called an undertow, carries shells, seaweed, and sand away from the beach. A strong undertow can be dangerous to swimmers.

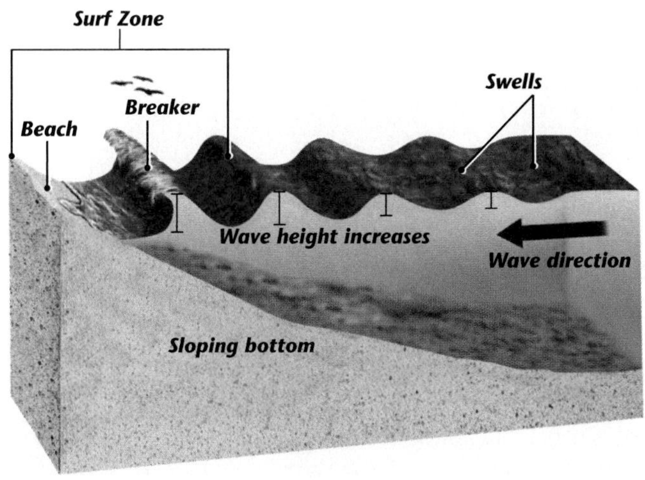

Figure 3 Friction with the ocean floor causes waves to slow down in the shallow water near shore. The wave height increases until the waves break, forming surf. *Interpreting Diagrams What happens to the wavelength as the waves approach shore?*

How Waves Change Near Shore

Using the Visuals: Figure 3

Use the figure to reinforce how a wave changes near shore. Ask: **What happens to the bottoms of waves as the waves near the shore?** *(They touch the ocean floor, causing the waves to slow down.)* **What happens to the tops of waves when the bottoms slow down?** *(They keep moving forward until the waves topple over.)* Encourage students to imagine that they're running and they stop suddenly. Ask: **How does your body react?** *(The top of the body keeps moving forward.)* Point out that in waves when the bottom of one wave slows down, the water in the waves behind it keeps moving forward and piles up, causing the wave height to increase until it breaks. **learning modality: visual**

Demonstration

Materials *manila folder or stiff paper, five marbles*
Time 5 minutes

Open the folder flat on a desk (or crease a piece of stiff paper) and place four marbles in a row down the middle. Place a fifth marble a few cm from the group, and then flick it with your finger so it moves forward and hits the row of marbles. The flicked marble will stop, but its energy will travel through the four marbles, causing the last one to roll away from the others. Ask: **What made the marble on the end roll away?** *(The energy that was transmitted from the flicked marble through the other marbles)* **How is this model like the movement of energy through water as a wave?** *(Energy moves, but particles don't.)* **learning modality: visual**

Media and Technology

Transparencies "Parts of a Wave," Transparency 28

Concept Videotape Library Grade 6, Tape 1 "The Wave"

Answers to Self-Assessment

☑ *Checkpoint*

Waves that are close together have a shorter wavelength than waves that are far apart.

Caption Question

Figure 3 As the waves approach the shore, wavelength decreases.

Ongoing Assessment

Skills Check Point out that much of the damage done by hurricanes is caused by the huge waves they produce. Challenge students to infer why the high winds that occur during hurricanes produce such huge waves.

How Waves Affect the Shore

Using the Visuals: Figure 4

To reinforce longshore drift and rip current, ask: **What does longshore drift move?** *(water and sand)* **Why has the sandbar formed?** *(Because the longshore drift is moving in that direction, and the waves are slowing down, causing sand to be deposited)* **How has the sandbar helped create a rip current?** *(A narrow opening has formed through the sandbar, allowing a rush of water to flow back to the sea.)* **learning modality: visual**

Building Inquiry Skills: Comparing and Contrasting

The term *rip current* is often confused with the term *undertow,* which is also called backwash. To make sure students are not confusing the two terms, ask: **How are rip current and undertow similar and how are they different?** *(Both are movements of water away from the beach after waves break on shore. Undertow is the gradual outflow of water from any wave that breaks on shore. Rip current is the rapid outflow of a narrow stream of trapped water through a break in a sandbar.)* Have students make a Venn diagram showing these differences and similarities. **learning modality: verbal**

Reducing Beach Erosion

Inquiry Challenge

ACTIVITY

Materials *large plastic box or aluminum baking pan, sand, pebbles, books, water*
Time 20 minutes

Challenge students to identify factors that affect the rate of beach erosion. Have them predict what these factors might be, and then decide how they can test for them. For example, students might predict that one factor is slope of the ocean floor. They can test this factor by varying the slope of a beach model and comparing the erosion. Other factors students might identify are size and energy of waves and beach composition. **learning modality: logical/mathematical**

How Waves Affect the Shore

What happens on shore as waves pound the beach? The diagram in Figure 4 shows some of their effects. Since wave direction at sea is determined by the wind, waves usually roll toward shore at an angle. But as they touch bottom, the shallower water slows the shoreward side of the wave first. The rows of waves gradually turn and become more nearly parallel to the shore.

Longshore Drift As the waves come into shore, water washes up the beach at an angle, carrying sand grains with it. The water and sand then run straight back down the beach. This movement of sand along the beach is called **longshore drift.** As the waves slow down, they deposit the sand they are carrying on the shallow, underwater slope in a long ridge called a **sandbar.**

Rip Currents As a sandbar grows, it can trap the water flowing along the shore. In some places, water breaks through the sandbar and begins to flow back down the sloping ocean bottom. This process creates a **rip current,** a rush of water that flows rapidly back to sea through a narrow opening. Rip currents can carry a swimmer out into deep water. Because rip currents are narrow, a strong swimmer can usually escape by swimming across the current, parallel to the beach.

✓ *Checkpoint* *In what direction does a rip current pull a swimmer?*

Figure 4 Waves approach the shore at an angle. This results in a gradual movement of sand along the beach. *Interpreting Diagrams In which direction is longshore drift moving the sand along this beach?*

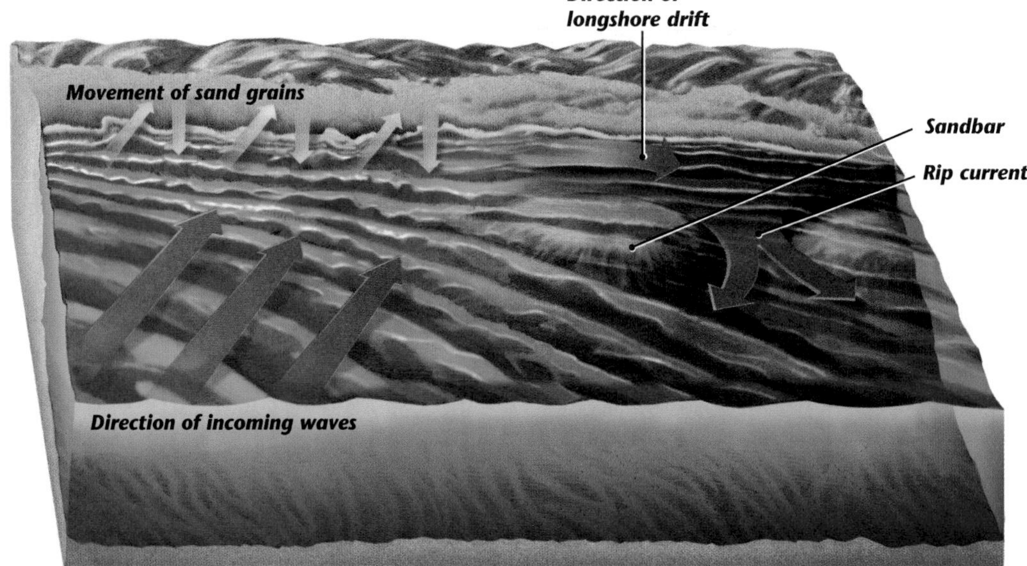

Background

Facts and Figures The erosion and deposition of sand that change the shape of a beach occur in cycles that correspond to the weather. During fair weather, waves generally tend to be low, often under 1 m high, and have little energy. Under these conditions, more sand is deposited on the beach than is eroded away. During stormy weather, in contrast, wave height and power greatly increase. Under these conditions, more sand is eroded from the beach than is deposited. When the storms end, the waves return to fair-weather size and sand builds up on the beach again.

Figure 5 "The Breaking Wave off Kanagawa" is a wood-block print by the Japanese artist Hokusai.

Visual Arts CONNECTION

The Japanese artist Hokusai (1760–1849) is well known for his land and ocean scenes. His print at the left shows a cresting wave with the snow-capped Mt. Fuji in the background.

As a teenager, Hokusai was apprenticed to a wood-block engraver. A wood-block print is made by engraving a separate block of wood for each color ink used in the picture. How many blocks do you think Hokusai needed for this print?

In Your Journal

Imagine you are writing a catalog for a museum exhibit of ocean scenes. Write a brief description of Hokusai's print for the catalog.

Reducing Beach Erosion

Many people like to live near the ocean. But over time, erosion can wear away the beach. This threatens the homes and other buildings. To avoid losing their property, people look for ways to reduce the effect of erosion.

One method of reducing erosion along a stretch of beach is to build a wall of rocks or concrete, called a **groin,** outward from the beach. The sand carried by the water piles up against the groins instead of moving along the shore. However, the groins increase the amount of erosion farther down the beach.

Section 1 Review

1. Describe how ocean waves form.
2. How do wavelength and wave height change as a wave enters shallow water?
3. How do water particles move within a wave?
4. **Thinking Critically Relating Cause and Effect** Explain how building a groin affects the beach on each side of the groin.

CHAPTER PROJECT

Check Your Progress

You are ready to design your model ocean beach. Sketch your design. Be sure to consider what materials you will use for your shoreline and lighthouse. How will you make waves? When your design is finished, you are ready to gather your materials and construct your model. (*Hint:* Design your model, including the lighthouse, to scale.)

Program Resources

◆ **Unit 3 Resources** 9-1 Review and Reinforce; 9-1 Enrich

Media and Technology

Transparencies "Longshore Drift and Rip Currents," Transparency 29

Answers to Self-Assessment

Checkpoint

A rip current pulls a swimmer out to sea, away from shore.

Caption Question

Figure 4 It is moving the sand along the beach from left to right.

Visual Arts CONNECTION

Materials: *potatoes, knife, finger paint*
Time: 10 minutes

Use a potato to model how wood-block prints are made. Cut the potato in half and carve a shape on the cut surface. Explain that the carved surface is a "negative" of the desired image. Invite students to dip the carved potato in finger paint and make a print on a piece of paper. Point out that each color of a wood-block print is done with a separate block.

In Your Journal Before students write their descriptions, encourage them to think about the process of wood-block printing to evaluate Hokusai's print. **learning modality: verbal**

3 Assess

Section 1 Review Answers

1. Most ocean waves form when winds blowing across the ocean transmit their energy to the water.
2. Wavelength decreases and wave height increases.
3. In a circular path
4. Sand piles up on the windward side of the groin, instead of being carried down the beach, while the other side of the groin shows greater erosion.

CHAPTER PROJECT

Check Your Progress

Students should now know how they will construct their wave tank and model beach and lighthouse. Waves can be generated by moving an object or hand up and down in the water of the wave tank.

Performance Assessment

Oral Presentation Have students identify the causes and effects of waves and explain how each cause produces waves and how waves produce each effect.

Tides

Objectives

After completing the lesson, students will be able to

- ◆ explain what causes tides and the daily and monthly tide cycles;
- ◆ describe how people use the energy of tides.

Key Terms tide, spring tide, neap tide

1 Engage/Explore

Activating Prior Knowledge

Encourage students who have been to the ocean to share their observations of tides. For example, ask: **Did the water come farther up the beach at different times of the day? Were there any signs posted about tides? Was there any other evidence of tides?** *(Perhaps students saw sand castles slowly covered over when the tide came in, wet sand exposed when the tide went out, signs posting the times of tides or warnings about high tides, or lines of seaweed and shells marking the farthest reach of tides.)* **Based on these observations, how do tides differ from waves?** *(Tides occur on a regular schedule, not just when the wind blows, and they are the actual movement of water, not just the movement of energy through water.)* Point out that tides differ from waves in these and other ways because they have a different cause, as students will read in this section.

DISCOVER

Skills Focus predicting
Materials *calculator*
Time 15 minutes
Tips Remind students that when subtracting minutes they cannot "borrow" from the hours column.
Think It Over Answers may vary. Students should observe that high tides get earlier as one goes east. Therefore, high tides in Portland should occur at about 4:05 A.M. and 4:50 P.M.

INTEGRATING SPACE SCIENCE

Section 2 Tides

DISCOVER ACTIVITY

When Is High Tide?

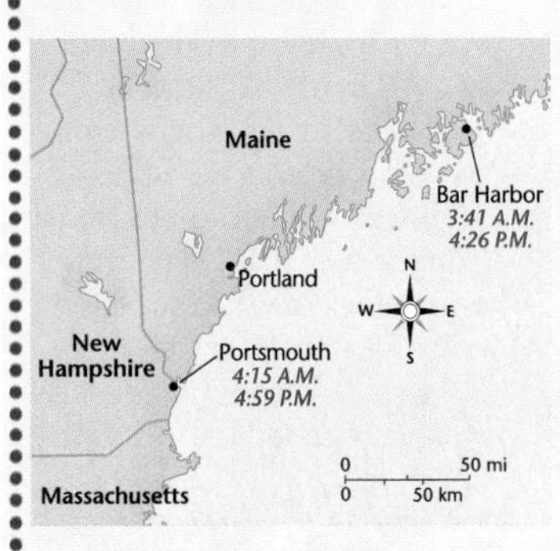

Twice a day, the ocean rises and falls on the New England coast. These daily changes in water level are called tides. The map shows the times of the two high tides in each city on a particular day.

1. Calculate the length of time between the two high tides for each city. Remember to consider both hours and minutes.
2. Look at the times of the high tides in Bar Harbor and in Portsmouth. Is there a pattern in the times of the high tides?

Think It Over

Predicting Notice that the high tides for Portland are not shown. Based on the times of the other high tides on the map, predict when the high tides will occur in Portland.

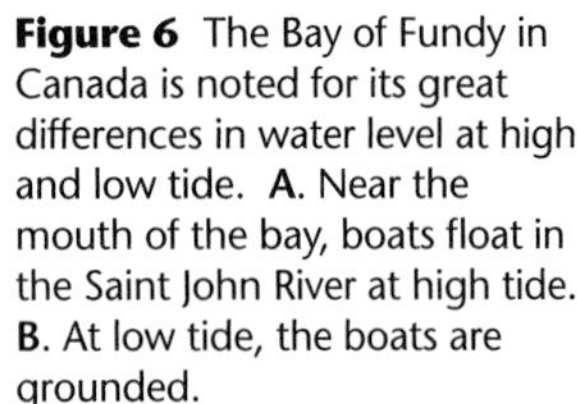

GUIDE FOR READING

- ◆ What causes tides?
- ◆ How are tides a source of energy?

Reading Tip **As you read, use the headings to make an outline about tides.**

You're standing on a riverbank in the town of Saint John, Canada. In the distance there's a loud roaring sound, like a train approaching. Suddenly a wall of water twice your height thunders past. The surge of water rushes up the river channel so fast that it almost looks as if the river is flowing backward!

This thundering wall of water is an everyday event at Saint John. The town is located where the Saint John River enters the Bay of Fundy, an arm of the Atlantic Ocean. The Bay of Fundy is famous for its dramatic daily tides. When the tide comes in, fishing boats float on the water near the piers. But once the tide goes out, so much water flows back to sea that the boats are stranded on the muddy harbor bottom.

Figure 6 The Bay of Fundy in Canada is noted for its great differences in water level at high and low tide. **A.** Near the mouth of the bay, boats float in the Saint John River at high tide. **B.** At low tide, the boats are grounded.

266

READING STRATEGIES

Reading Tip Suggest that students preview the section headings before they begin to read. Student outlines may begin as follows:

I. What Causes Tides?
II. The Daily Tide Cycle
III. The Monthly Tide Cycle
  A. Spring Tides
  B. Neap Tides
  C. Monthly Tide Tables
IV. Energy From Tides

Vocabulary Before students read about spring tides, point out that, in this context, *spring* means "to jump," an indication that spring tides are higher than usual. Stress that spring tides do not occur just in spring but twice a month throughout the year. They are the highest tides each month.

What Causes Tides?

The daily rise and fall of Earth's waters on its coastlines are called **tides.** As the tide comes in, the level of the water on the beach rises gradually. When the water reaches its highest point, it is high tide. Then the tide goes out, flowing back toward the sea. When the water reaches its lowest point, it is low tide. Unlike the surface waves you read about in Section 1, tides happen regularly no matter how the wind blows. Tides occur in all bodies of water, but they are most noticeable in the ocean and large lakes.

Tides are caused by the interaction of Earth, the moon, and the sun. How can distant objects like the moon and sun influence water on Earth? The answer is gravity. Gravity is the force exerted by an object that pulls other objects toward it. Gravity keeps you and everything around you on Earth's surface. As the distance between objects increases, however, gravity's pull grows weaker.

Figure 7 shows the effect of the moon's gravity on the water on Earth's surface. The moon pulls on the water on the side closest to it (point A) more strongly than it pulls on the center of the Earth. This pull creates a bulge of water, called a tidal bulge, on the side of Earth facing the moon. The water at point C is pulled toward the moon less strongly than is Earth as a whole. This water is "left behind," forming a second bulge.

In the places in Figure 7 where there are tidal bulges (points A and C), high tide is occurring along the coastlines. In the places between the bulges (points B and D), low tide is occurring. As Earth rotates, different places on the planet's surface pass through the areas of the tidal bulges and experience the change in water levels.

☑ *Checkpoint* *What force causes the tides to occur on Earth's surface?*

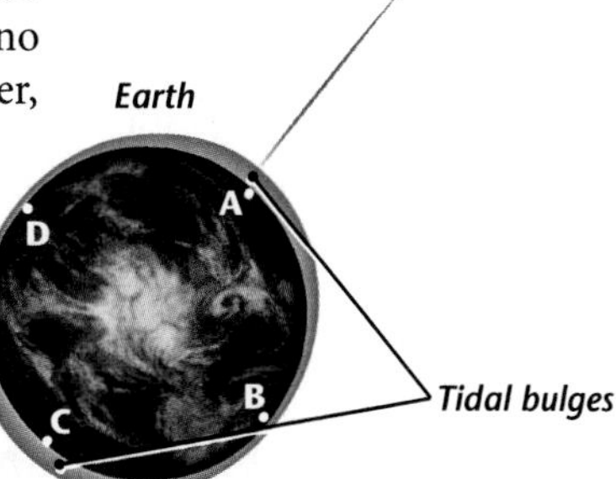

Figure 7 The moon's pull on Earth's water causes tidal bulges to form on the side closest to the moon and the side farthest from the moon. *Comparing and Contrasting Where is the level of the water higher, at point C or point D?*

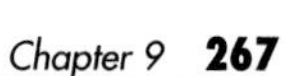

2 Facilitate

What Causes Tides?

Using the Visuals: Figure 6

Use this figure to reinforce the concept of tides. Ask: **Where has the water gone in the right-hand photo?** *(out to sea)* **What is the force that causes tides to rise and fall?** *(The force of gravity between Earth and the moon and sun)* **How do you think tides in the Bay of Fundy affect people's lives?** *(Boaters and fishing crews have to time their departures and arrivals around the tides.)* **learning modality: visual**

Including All Students

ACTIVITY

Materials *small water-filled balloon, piece of string about half a meter long*
Time 5 minutes

To illustrate the pull of gravity on water, give a student a small water-filled balloon attached to a string. Have the student carefully swing the balloon around his or her body at the end of the string. (You may want to have the student do this outside.) Ask: **If you are the sun and the balloon is Earth, what is the string?** *(gravity)* **How does the balloon change shape as you swing it?** *(Its surface bulges where the string pulls it.)* **What does this bulge represent?** *(a tidal bulge)* Guide students in seeing how this is similar to the pull of the sun's gravity on Earth's oceans. Point out that the moon's gravity, though weak, has an even greater pull on Earth's oceans because the moon is so close to Earth. **learning modality: kinesthetic**

Program Resources

- **Unit 3 Resources** 9-2 Lesson Plan; 9-2 Section Summary
- **Guided Study and Reading Workbook** Section 9-2

Answers to Self-Assessment

Caption Question

Figure 7 The level of water is higher at Point C.

☑ *Checkpoint*

The force of gravity; the moon and sun's gravity

Ongoing Assessment

Drawing Have students make a simple labeled diagram to show how the moon causes tides on Earth.

The Daily Tide Cycle

Building Inquiry Skills: Predicting

Challenge students to solve the following problem: While playing frisbee on the beach in the morning, José lost his sunglasses. At 1:00 P.M., he realized they were missing and went back to the beach to look for them. When he got there, he found the beach under water all the way to the high-tide line. When should José go back to look for his sunglasses again? *(In about six hours, or around 7:00 P.M., when it is low tide again)* **learning modality: logical/mathematical**

Graphing

Materials *graph paper, calculator, ruler*
Time 20 minutes
Tips You may need to review graphing negative numbers.
Expected Outcome The high-tide line on the graph should rise steadily while the low-tide line falls, until Day 7 when both trends reverse. Spring tide might be occurring on Day 6 because that is when there is the greatest difference between high and low tides.
Extend Another way to see the relationship between high and low tides is to plot the difference between them. **learning modality: logical/mathematical**

The Monthly Tide Cycle

Including All Students

ACTIVITY

Use students to model spring tides and neap tides. Have students represent the sun, moon, and Earth and demonstrate the correct positions of each of the bodies at the two spring tides and the two neap tides. Challenge the rest of the class to identify each type of tide as it is demonstrated. **learning modality: kinesthetic**

Graphing

ACTIVITY

This table lists the highest high tides and lowest low tides at the mouth of the Savannah River at the Atlantic Ocean in Georgia for one week. Use the data to make a graph.

Day	Highest High Tide (m)	Lowest Low Tide (m)
1	1.9	0.2
2	2.1	0.1
3	2.3	0.0
4	2.4	−0.2
5	2.5	−0.2
6	2.6	−0.3
7	1.9	0.3

1. On the horizontal axis, mark the days.
2. On the vertical axis, mark tide heights ranging from 3.0 to –1.0 meters. (*Hint:* Mark the negative numbers below the horizontal axis.)
3. Plot the tide heights for each day on the graph. Connect the high tide points with one line and the low tide points with another line.

How do the high and low tides change during the week? What type of tide might be occurring on Day 6? Explain.

The Daily Tide Cycle

As Earth turns completely around once each day, people on or near the shore observe the rise and fall of the tides as they reach the area of each tidal bulge. The high tides occur about 12 hours and 25 minutes apart in each location. As Earth rotates, easternmost points pass through the area of the tidal bulge before points farther to the west. Therefore, high tide occurs later the farther west you go along a coastline.

In some places, the two high tides and two low tides are easy to observe each day. But in other places, the range between the water levels is less dramatic. One set of tides may even be so minimal that there appears to be only one high tide and one low tide per day. This situation is common along the coasts of Texas and western Florida, due to the gradual slope of the ocean floor in the Gulf of Mexico.

Several factors affect the height of the tide in any particular location. For example, high tide on a certain day in southern California is not necessarily the same height as high tide farther up the Pacific coast in Oregon. Landforms such as capes, peninsulas, and islands interrupt the water's movements. A basin at the mouth of a river can also increase the range of tides. As you read in Chapter 7, the speed and depth of moving water increases when it flows into a narrower channel. That is what causes the dramatic tides in the mouth of the Saint John River you read about earlier.

☑ ***Checkpoint*** *Describe one factor that affects the height of the tides in a particular area.*

The Monthly Tide Cycle

Even though the sun is 150 million kilometers from Earth, it is so massive that its gravity also affects the tides. The sun pulls the water on Earth's surface toward it. In Figure 8 on the facing page, you can follow the positions of the Earth, moon, and sun at different times during a month. Notice that sometimes the moon and sun pull together on Earth's waters. At other times, they pull in different directions. Changes in the positions of Earth, the moon, and the sun affect the height of the tides during a month.

Spring Tides Twice a month, at the new moon and the full moon, the sun and moon are lined up. Their combined gravitational pull produces the greatest range between high and low tide, called a **spring tide.** These tides get their name not because they occur during the spring season, but from an Old English word, *springen*, which means "to jump."

Background

History of Science The idea of using tides for power is far from new. Water wheels turned by ocean waves were in use along the coast of England as early as the 1100s. In this country, a tide mill was used for grinding corn in Massachusetts as early as 1640.

Integrating Science Some animals depend on tides to survive and reproduce. For example, a kind of fish called the grunion lays its eggs on the beach during spring tide. After the tide goes out, the eggs remain safely buried in the sand to hatch into larvae. Two weeks later, just as the larvae are ready to turn into small fish, the next spring tide comes in and carries them out to sea.

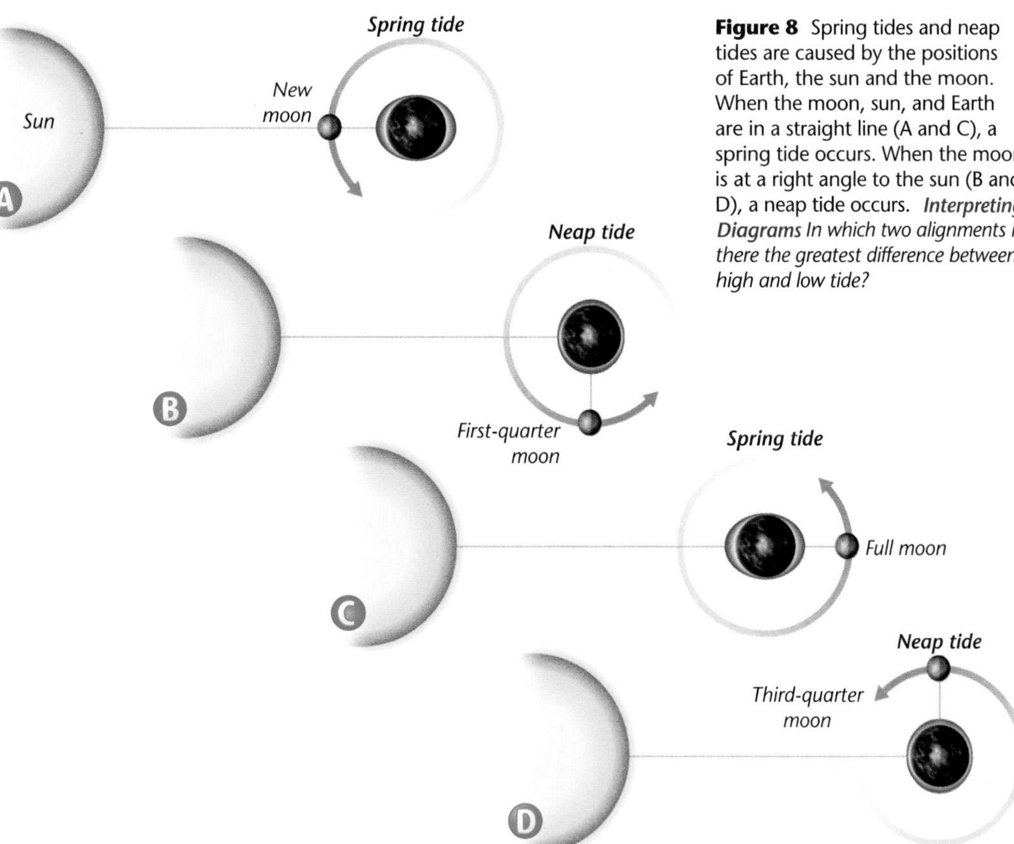

Figure 8 Spring tides and neap tides are caused by the positions of Earth, the sun and the moon. When the moon, sun, and Earth are in a straight line (A and C), a spring tide occurs. When the moon is at a right angle to the sun (B and D), a neap tide occurs. ***Interpreting Diagrams*** *In which two alignments is there the greatest difference between high and low tide?*

Neap Tides In between spring tides, at the first and third quarters of the moon, the sun and moon pull at right angles to each other. This line-up produces a **neap tide,** a tide with the least difference between low and high tide. During a neap tide, the sun's gravity pulls some of the water away from the tidal bulge facing the moon. This acts to "even out" the water level over Earth's surface, reducing the difference between high and low tides.

Monthly Tide Tables Despite the complex factors affecting the tides, scientists can predict tides quite accurately for various locations. They combine knowledge of the movements of the moon and Earth with information about the shape of the coastline and other local conditions. If you live near the coast, your local newspaper probably publishes a tide table. Knowing the times and heights of tides is important to sailors, marine scientists, people who fish, and others who live along a coast.

Using the Visuals: Figure 8

Have students note the alignment of the sun, moon, and Earth in each part of the figure. Then ask: **If the difference between high and low tides in alignment A is 3.0 m and in alignment B is 0.5 m, what would you expect the difference between high and low tides to be in alignment D?** *(The same as in alignment B, or 0.5 m, because this is the other neap tide)* **learning modality: logical/mathematical**

Addressing Naive Conceptions

Because tsunamis are sometimes mistakenly called tidal waves, it is a common misconception that these giant waves are caused by tides. Ask students: **What are tidal waves?** *(Students may not realize that the term tidal wave is a misnomer for tsunami. Explain that tsunamis have nothing to do with tides.)* Ask: **What causes a tsunami?** *(Usually an earthquake beneath the ocean floor. They may also be caused by large undersea landslides.)* **learning modality: verbal**

Program Resources

- **Interdisciplinary Explorations Series** "Where River Meets Sea," pp. 26–27

Media and Technology

 **Transparencies** "Spring and Neap Tides," Transparency 30

Answers to Self-Assessment

✓ Checkpoint

Answers may vary. Factors include landforms—such as capes, peninsulas, and islands, which interrupt the water's movement—and the change in speed and depth of the water as it moves into a narrower channel, such as a river basin.

Caption Question

Figure 8 In alignments A and C

Ongoing Assessment

Writing Have students write a concise paragraph explaining the difference between daily high and low tides, on the one hand, and spring and neap tides on the other.

Students can save their paragraph in their portfolios.

Energy From Tides

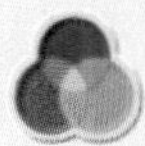

Integrating Technology

Explain that waves as well as tides can be used to generate power. Ask: **Why would tides provide a more dependable power source than waves?** *(Tides occur regularly at a fairly predictable level, whereas the timing and height of waves depend on the wind, which can vary considerably.)* **learning modality: logical/mathematical**

3 Assess

Section 2 Review Answers

1. The moon's gravity pulls on water on the side of Earth facing it more strongly than it pulls on Earth itself. This creates a bulge of water, called a tidal bulge, on the side of Earth closest to the moon.
2. Water can be trapped at high tide. When it is released, gravity pulls it down through tunnels to power electric generators.
3. The sun, moon, and Earth are positioned in a straight line when spring tides occur.
4. Answers may vary. One answer is to prevent being stranded on the beach at low tide.

CHAPTER PROJECT

Check Your Progress

Stress the need for consistency in the size and frequency of waves so their effects on beach erosion can be compared before and after erosion-prevention methods are in place. Suggest that students measure erosion by placing numbered toothpicks at regular intervals along the beach. Students can note which toothpicks have fallen after each wave. This will help them see which part of the beach needs the most protection. Students should refer to the text for methods of controlling erosion.

Performance Assessment

Drawing Have students draw a labeled diagram showing the positions of the sun, moon, and Earth during spring and neap tides.

Figure 9 Pulled by the tide, water rushes through this tidal power plant in France.
Making Generalizations Why are very few locations suitable for building tidal power plants?

Energy From Tides

INTEGRATING TECHNOLOGY **The movement of huge amounts of water between high and low tide are a source of potential energy—energy that is stored and waiting to be used.** Engineers have designed tidal power plants that capture some of this energy as the tide moves in and out.

The first large-scale tidal power plant was built in 1967 on the Rance River in northwestern France. As high tide swirls up the river, the plant's gates open so that the water flows into a basin. As the tide retreats, the gates shut to trap the water. Gravity pulls the water back to sea through tunnels. The energy of the water moving through the tunnels powers generators that produce electricity, just as in a hydroelectric dam on a river.

Although tidal energy is a clean, renewable source of energy, it has several limitations. Harnessing tidal power is practical only where there is a large difference between high and low tides—at least 4 or 5 meters. There are very few places in the world where such a large difference occurs. Daily tides also may not occur at the time when there is a demand for electricity. However, tidal power can be a useful part of an overall plan to generate electricity that also includes other power sources between tides.

Section 2 Review

1. Explain how the moon causes a tidal bulge to form on the side of Earth closest to it.
2. How can tides be used to generate electricity?
3. Describe the positions of the sun and the moon in relation to Earth when spring tides occur.
4. **Thinking Critically Applying Concepts** Imagine that you are the captain of a fishing boat. Why would it be helpful to know the times of the tides?

CHAPTER PROJECT

Check Your Progress

Now that you have built your model, plan an experiment to observe the effects of wave erosion on the shoreline. How will you measure the amount of wave action needed to topple the lighthouse? Once you have observed how waves cause shoreline erosion, repair the beach and design a way to reduce the erosion. Test your method by sending more waves against the shore. (*Hint:* For both tests, place toothpicks at regular intervals on the beach to measure erosion.)

Answers to Self-Assessment

Caption Question

Figure 9 Very few locations are suitable for building tidal power plants because few places in the world have a great enough range between high and low tides.

Program Resources

- **Unit 3 Resources** 9-2 Review and Reinforce; 9-2 Enrich

Ocean Water Chemistry

DISCOVER — ACTIVITY

Will the Eggs Sink or Float?

1. Fill two beakers or jars with tap water.
2. Add three teaspoons of salt to one beaker. Stir until it dissolves.
3. Place a whole, uncooked egg in each jar. Handle the eggs gently to avoid breakage. Observe what happens to each egg.
4. Wash your hands when you are finished with this activity.

Think It Over

Observing Compare what happens to the two eggs. What does this tell you about the difference between salt water and fresh water?

GUIDE FOR READING

- How salty is ocean water?
- How do conditions in the ocean change with depth?

Reading Tip **Before you read, preview the headings in the section. Then write some predictions about the characteristics of ocean water.**

If you've ever been swimming in the ocean and swallowed some water, you know that it is salty. Why? According to an old Swedish legend, it's all because of a magic mill. This mill could grind out anything its owner wanted, such as herring, porridge, or even gold. A greedy sea captain once stole the mill and took it away on his ship, but without finding out how to use it. He asked the mill to grind some salt but then could not stop it. The mill ground more and more salt, until the captain's ship sank from its weight. According to the tale, the mill is still at the bottom of the sea, grinding out salt!

Probably no one ever took this tale seriously, even when it was first told. The scientific explanation for the ocean's saltiness begins with the early stages of Earth's formation, when the ocean covered much of the surface of the planet. Undersea volcanoes erupted, spewing chemicals into the water. Gradually, the lava from these volcanic eruptions built up areas of land. Rain fell on the bare land, washing more chemicals from the rocks into the ocean. Over time, these dissolved substances built up to the levels present in the ocean today.

The Salty Ocean

Just how salty is the ocean? If you boiled a kilogram of seawater in a pot until the water was all gone, there would be about 35 grams of salts left in the bottom of the pot. **On average, one kilogram of ocean water contains about 35 grams of salts—that is, 35 parts per thousand.** The total amount of dissolved salts in water is called **salinity.**

READING STRATEGIES

Reading Tip Before students preview the headings in the section, check that they know which headings are main headings and which are subheadings. Students may predict that ocean water is salty and that its temperature varies with depth and location.

Program Resources

- **Unit 3 Resources** 9-3 Lesson Plan; 9-3 Section Summary

Ocean Water Chemistry

Objectives

After completing the lesson, students will be able to

- identify the salinity, gas content, and temperature of ocean water;
- describe how ocean conditions change with depth.

Key Terms salinity, submersible

1 Engage/Explore

Activating Prior Knowledge

Most students will know that the ocean is salty, but they may not have thought about how this makes ocean water different from fresh water. Ask: **Why is salt often put on icy sidewalks and roads?** *(The salt melts the ice.)* **Which do you think freezes at a lower temperature, salt water or fresh water?** *(salt water)* Guide students in concluding that the salt in ocean water interferes with the formation of ice, making ocean water freeze at a lower temperature than fresh water. Point out that this is just one way salty ocean water differs from fresh water, as students will learn in this section.

DISCOVER

Skills Focus observing
Materials *two beakers or jars, tap water, salt, teaspoon, stirring rod, two uncooked eggs*
Time 10 minutes
Tips The three teaspoons of salt are approximate; students may need to add a little more or less for their egg to float.
Think It Over Students should observe that the egg sinks in fresh water but floats in salt water. Students may infer from their observations that salt water is denser than fresh water.

2 Facilitate

The Salty Ocean

Using the Visuals: Figure 10

Check to see if students understand how the two circle graphs are related by asking: **About what percent of ocean water is chloride?** *(Chloride makes up about half the ions dissolved in ocean water. Therefore, chloride is about half of 3.5 percent, or nearly 2 percent, of ocean water.)* Explain that each wedge of the right-hand graph represents a type of ion. When the salt sodium chloride dissolves, it breaks into sodium and chloride ions. **learning modality: logical/ mathematical**

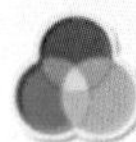

Integrating Chemistry

Materials *small paper cups, water, stirrer, tablespoon, salt*
Time 10 minutes

When class starts, give each student a paper cup one-quarter full of water. Half the students should mix a tablespoon of salt into their cups, then all the students should put their cups in a freezer. When class ends, have students compare cups. They should observe that the plain water is frozen, but the salty water is not. **learning modality: kinesthetic**

Composition of Ocean Water

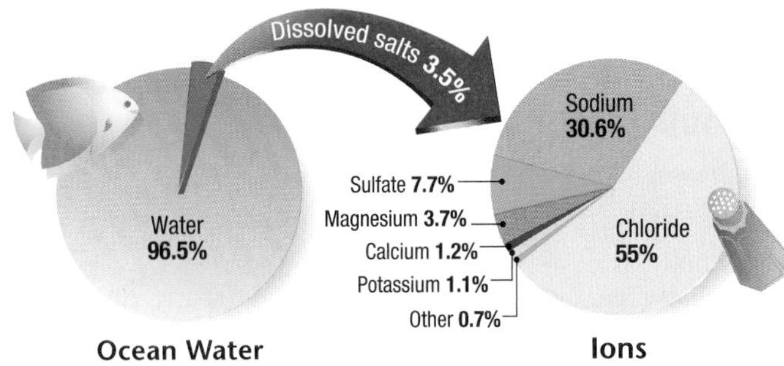

Figure 10 Ocean water contains many different dissolved salts. When salts dissolve, they separate into particles called ions. ***Interpreting Graphs*** *Which ion is most common in ocean water?*

The substance you know as table salt—sodium chloride—is the salt present in the greatest amount in ocean water. When sodium chloride dissolves in water, it separates into sodium and chloride particles called ions. Other salts, such as magnesium chloride, form ions in water in the same way. Together, chloride and sodium make up almost 86 percent of the ions dissolved in ocean water, as shown in Figure 10. Ocean water also contains smaller amounts of about a dozen other ions and other substances that organisms need, such as nitrogen and phosphorus. (See Appendix D for more information on ions.)

Variations in Salinity In most parts of the ocean, the salinity is between 34 and 37 parts per thousand. But near the surface, rain, snow, and melting ice add fresh water to the ocean, lowering the salinity there. Salinity is also lower near the mouths of large rivers. These rivers empty great amounts of fresh water into the ocean. Evaporation, on the other hand, increases salinity, since the salt is left behind as the water evaporates. For example, in the Red Sea, where the climate is hot and dry, the salinity can be as high as 41 parts per thousand. Salinity can also be higher near the poles. As the surface water freezes into ice, the salt is left behind in the remaining water.

Figure 11 These people are relaxing with the paper while floating in the water! The Dead Sea between Israel and Jordan is so salty that people float easily on its surface. ***Relating Cause and Effect*** *How is the area's hot, dry climate related to the Dead Sea's high salinity?*

Background

Facts and Figures Consider these salty facts and figures about Earth's waters.

- There are an estimated 4.5 trillion metric tons of salt dissolved in Earth's oceans and seas. If all this salt was spread out over Earth's surface, it would be as deep as a 15-story building is tall.
- In one small part of the Red Sea, the salinity was recorded to be 270 parts per thousand, or almost eight times that of most ocean water.
- More than 150 km out to sea from the mouth of the Amazon River, the ocean water is still mainly fresh, not salty.
- A few lakes, including the Great Salt Lake in Utah and the Dead Sea, are as salty as, or even saltier than, oceans.

Effects of Salinity Salinity affects several properties of ocean water. INTEGRATING CHEMISTRY For instance, ocean water does not freeze until the temperature drops to about −1.9°C. The salt acts as a kind of antifreeze by interfering with the formation of ice crystals. Salt water also has a higher density than fresh water. That means that the mass of one liter of salt water is greater than the mass of one liter of fresh water. Because its density is greater, seawater has greater buoyancy. It lifts, or buoys up, less dense objects floating in it. This is why an egg floats higher in salt water than in fresh water.

Gases in Ocean Water

Just as land organisms use oxygen and other gases in the air, marine organisms use gases dissolved in ocean water. Two gases found in ocean water that are necessary for living things are oxygen and carbon dioxide.

Oxygen in seawater comes from the atmosphere and from algae in the ocean. Algae use sunlight to carry out photosynthesis, releasing oxygen into the water in the process. Oxygen is scarcer in seawater than in air and is most plentiful near the surface. Carbon dioxide, on the other hand, is about 60 times as plentiful in the oceans as in the atmosphere. Algae need carbon dioxide for photosynthesis. Animals such as corals also use carbon dioxide, which provides the carbon to build their hard skeletons.

Checkpoint *What are two sources of the oxygen in ocean water?*

The Temperature of Ocean Water

In New England, the news reports on New Year's Day often feature the shivering members of a "Polar Bear Club" taking a dip in the icy Atlantic Ocean. Yet on the same day, people enjoy the warm waters of a Puerto Rico beach. Like temperatures on land, temperatures at the surface of the ocean vary with location and the seasons.

The broad surface of the ocean absorbs energy from the sun. Because warm water is less dense than cold water, this warm water stays as a layer on the surface. Near the equator, surface temperatures often reach 25°C, about room temperature. The temperature drops as you travel away from the equator.

The temperature of water affects the amount of dissolved oxygen it can hold. The cold waters in the polar regions contain more dissolved oxygen than warm, tropical waters. But there is still enough oxygen in tropical seas to support a variety of organisms, such as those shown in Figure 12.

Math TOOLBOX

Calculating Density

To calculate the density of a substance, divide the mass of the substance by its volume.

$$\text{density} = \frac{\text{mass}}{\text{volume}}$$

For example, one liter (L) of ocean water has a mass of 1.03 kilograms (kg). Therefore, its density is

$$\frac{1.03 \text{ kg}}{1.00 \text{ L}} = 1.03 \text{ kg/L}$$

Five liters of one type of crude oil has a mass of 4.10 kg. What is its density?

$$\frac{4.10 \text{ kg}}{5.00 \text{ L}} = 0.82 \text{ kg/L}$$

If this oil spilled on the ocean's surface, would it sink or float? Explain your answer in terms of density.

Figure 12 Both this neon-pink basslet and the lacy green sponge depend on the dissolved gases in ocean water.

Math TOOLBOX

Time 10 minutes

Tips The oil will float because of its lower density. Clarify that density is how much mass something has for its volume. For example, an empty soda can that is full of air has less mass than one full of soda because air has a lower density. **learning modality: logical/mathematical**

Gases in Ocean Water

Building Inquiry Skills: Relating Cause and Effect

Point out that the text states oxygen is most plentiful near the surface of the ocean. Ask: **Why is there more oxygen near the surface of the ocean than in deep water?** *(That is where oxygen enters from the atmosphere and where algae, which produce oxygen, live.)* **learning modality: logical/mathematical**

The Temperature of Ocean Water

Including All Students

ACTIVITY

Ask students: **Why are temperatures at the equator higher than those farther away from the equator?** *(Some students may know that one reason is that the sun's rays strike Earth more directly at the equator.)* Have one student shine a flashlight directly onto a piece of graph paper while another student draws around the lighted area. Repeat this process with the light shining at an angle. Then have students estimate the area of each space. Ask: **In which case would the sun's rays provide more heat, and why?** *(Where they shine directly, because they are more concentrated.)* **learning modality: visual**

Media and Technology

Concept Videotape Library
Grade 6, Tape 2 "Density"

Answers to Self-Assessment

Caption Questions

Figure 10 Chloride

Figure 11 The hot, dry climate increases the Dead Sea's salinity by increasing evaporation.

Checkpoint

Oxygen in seawater comes from the atmosphere and from algae in the ocean.

Ongoing Assessment

Oral Presentation Call on students to describe places in the ocean where salinity is very low or very high.

EXPLORING the Water Column

After students have examined the visual essay, have them apply what they learned by describing conditions they would find if they traveled down the water column in a submersible. Divide the class into groups of three and suggest that each group member assume responsibility for determining the brightness, presence or absence of plants, salinity, temperature, and water pressure at one of three depths below the surface: 50 m, 1,500 m, or 4,000 m. Group members should combine their data in a table and then compare their table with those of other groups. Urge groups to resolve any differences in their tables. **cooperative learning**

Including All Students

ACTIVITY

To help students visualize how deep the ocean is at its deepest (about 11,000 m), suggest that they make a to-scale drawing of the three zones, using a scale of 500 m to 1 cm. Remind students to label their drawings with the ocean zones and their depths and to give the scale in a key. **learning modality: logical/ mathematical**

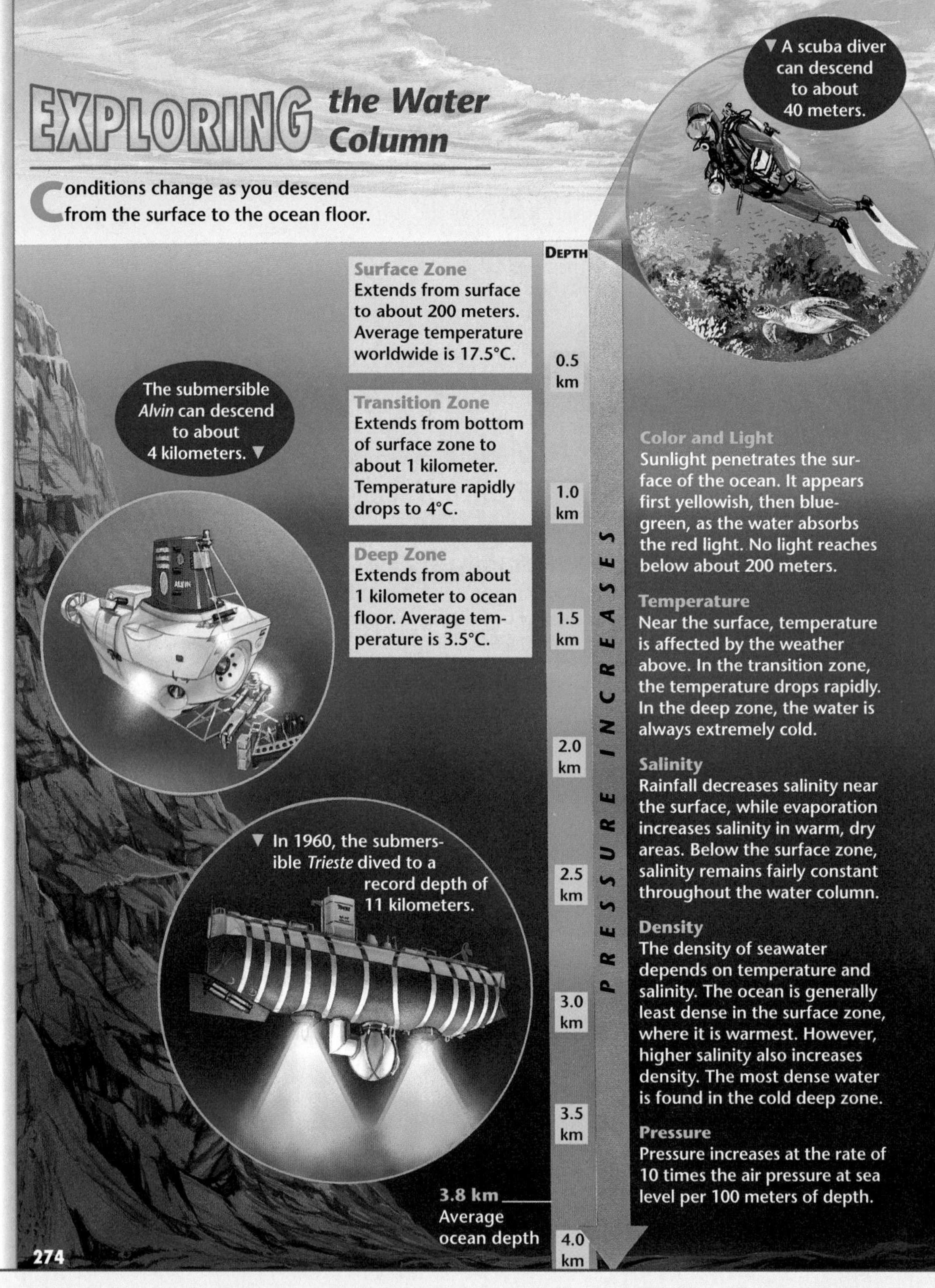

Background

Integrating Science Air contains both oxygen and nitrogen. Under normal pressure nitrogen is not absorbed by the blood. However, when divers are exposed to very high pressure in deep water, their blood absorbs nitrogen as well as oxygen. If they come back up to the surface too quickly, the pressure drops suddenly and the nitrogen dissolved in their blood comes out of solution. This results in bubbles of nitrogen gas in the blood—a very painful, even life-threatening, condition called decompression illness or, more commonly, the bends. To avoid the bends, divers going deeper than about 40 m must return to surface pressure very slowly in a special decompression chamber.

Changes with Depth

Gazing down into the blue-green water from the deck of a ship, you might think that the vast volume of water beneath you is all the same. But in fact, conditions change dramatically from the surface to the depths. If you could descend from the surface to the ocean floor, you would pass through a vertical section of the ocean referred to as the water column. *Exploring the Water Column* shows some of the changes you would observe.

Temperature Decreases If you took temperature readings at different depths, you would observe a pattern. **Temperature decreases as you descend through the water column.** There are three temperature zones in the water column. The first zone, the surface zone, typically extends from the surface to between 100 and 500 meters. Next is the transition zone, which extends from the bottom of the surface zone to about one kilometer. The temperature drops very quickly in the transition zone, to about 4°C. Below the transition zone is the deep zone. The temperature in the deep zone is a constant 3.5°C or colder in most of the ocean.

Pressure Increases Pressure is the force exerted by the weight of water above pressing down. **Pressure increases continuously from the surface to the deepest part of the ocean.** The average depth of the ocean floor is 3.8 kilometers. There the pressure is about 400 times greater than air pressure at Earth's surface.

INTEGRATING TECHNOLOGY Pressure is one obstacle facing scientists who want to study the ocean. A diver can descend safely only to about 40 meters. To survive in deeper water, scientists must use a submersible. A **submersible** is an underwater vehicle built of strong materials to resist pressure. In a submersible, scientists can directly observe the ocean floor, collect samples, and study deep ocean water chemistry.

Section 3 Review

1. What is the salinity of ocean water?
2. How do temperature and pressure change as you descend from the surface to the ocean floor?
3. Describe one factor that increases the salinity of seawater and one factor that decreases salinity.
4. **Thinking Critically Inferring** Would you expect the seawater just below the floating ice in the Arctic Ocean to be higher or lower in salinity than the water in the deep zone there? Explain.

Science at Home

Water Pressure Use a ballpoint pen to poke two holes in a milk carton—one about one third of the way from the bottom and one about two thirds of the way from the bottom. Cover the holes with tape and fill the carton with water. Holding the carton a meter above a sink, remove the tape and observe the streams of water. Explain that increased pressure causes the water to flow out of the bottom hole more quickly. How does this model conditions in the ocean?

Inquiry Challenge

ACTIVITY Challenge students to find a way to demonstrate that water pressure increases with depth. Have students write out their plans, and, after your approval, test their plans. A sample answer might be to push an empty plastic bottle with a lid down into a bucket of water until the bottle begins to collapse. **learning modality: logical/mathematical**

3 Assess

Section 3 Review Answers

1. Salinity is the total amount of dissolved salts it contains, on average 35 parts per thousand.
2. Temperature decreases and pressure increases.
3. Factors increasing salinity include evaporation and freezing; factors decreasing salinity include precipitation and rivers.
4. Salinity would be higher just below the ice because when salt water freezes it leaves the salt behind.

Science at Home

ACTIVITY

Materials *cardboard milk carton, tape, water, awl or punch*

Expected Outcome Students may say that water flows out of the bottom hole with greater force because water is under greater pressure at the bottom of the carton, just as water is under greater pressure at the bottom of the ocean.

Program Resources

- **Unit 3 Resources** 9-3 Review and Reinforce; 9-3 Enrich
- **Interdisciplinary Explorations Series** "Where River Meets Sea," pp. 15–16, 18–25
- **Laboratory Manual** 9, "Density and Salinity"

Media and Technology

Transparencies "Exploring the Water Column," Transparency 31

Performance Assessment

Writing Have students write a paragraph explaining in their own words why it is easier to float in the ocean than in a freshwater lake.

Skills Lab

Designing Experiments

Investigating Changes in Density

Preparing for Inquiry

Key Concept The density of water increases as salinity increases or temperature decreases.

Skills Objectives Students will be able to:

- ◆ design an experiment to determine how a given factor affects the density of ocean water;
- ◆ control the other variables as they measure how their variable affects the density of salt water;
- ◆ measure water density using a hydrometer;
- ◆ create a data table and use the data to make a graph.

Time 40 minutes

Advance Planning You may wish to have students make the hydrometers and practice using them ahead of time. Hydrometers should be calibrated at about 2 cm for fresh, room-temperature water.

Alternative Materials Large clear plastic soda bottles with the tops cut off can be used instead of graduated cylinders. Lumps of clay can be used instead of tacks.

Guiding Inquiry

Invitation Fill a clear, 1- or 2-L soda bottle with ice-cold water and fill another with very warm water to which food coloring has been added. Invite students to touch the sides of the bottles to feel the difference in temperature. Put a file card over the mouth of the warm-water bottle and carefully invert it over the cold-water bottle, making sure to line up the rims of the two bottles. Then, as students observe, gently slide out the file card. Ask: **Why doesn't water in the top bottle mix with water in the bottom bottle?** *(Because it is warmer, which makes it less dense)* **What would have happened if the positions of the two bottles had been reversed?** *(The colder water from the top bottle would sink down and mix with the warmer water in the bottom bottle.)* Reverse the positions of the bottles to demonstrate. Tell students that in this lab they will learn how to measure the density of water that varies in temperature or salinity.

Helping Design a Plan

- ◆ Students should state which variable, such as salinity or temperature, they wish to test. This is the manipulated variable.
- ◆ Then students should explain how they will manipulate that variable. For example, ask: **What different temperatures or concentrations of salt will you use?** *(For best results, the temperatures or salinities should vary as much as possible.)*
- ◆ Then ask: **Which variable will you control, and how will you control it?** *(Either salinity or temperature; by using only water of the same salinity while varying temperature or by using only water of the same temperature while varying salinity)*
- ◆ Finally ask: **How will you measure the responding variable?** *(By measuring the density of water as the manipulated variable takes on different values)*

Skills Lab

Designing Experiments

Investigating Changes in Density

In this lab, you will practice the skill of designing experiments as you learn more about density.

Problem

How do various factors affect the density of ocean water?

Materials

thumbtacks, beaker, 250 mL, water, thermometer, ice, hot plate, table salt, balance, spoon, metric ruler, sharpened pencil, unsharpened pencil with eraser, graduated cylinders, 100 mL and 250 mL

Procedure  

1. Work with your group to brainstorm a list of variables that affect the density of ocean water. Some variables to consider are water temperature and salinity. As a group, choose one variable to test in this investigation.
2. One way to measure density is with a tool called a *hydrometer.* To make a hydrometer, follow the instructions on the facing page.
3. Design an experimental plan to determine how the variable you chose affects density. For example, if you have chosen temperature as your variable, you might decide to start with salt water at 0°C, then heat it to 10°C, 20°C, and 30°C. If salinity is your variable, you might start with 200 mL of tap (fresh) water and add 10 g of salt, then add another 10 g to make 20 g, then add 10 g more to make 30 g. Write out your experimental plan.

DATA TABLE

Manipulated Variable: ______________

Condition Tested	Hydrometer Reading

4. List all the variables you will need to keep constant during your experiment. Revise your experimental plan and add steps to ensure that all other variables remain constant.
5. Review your plan. Make sure it includes the materials you will use and their amounts. Also make sure you have addressed all safety issues. Then check the plan with your teacher.
6. Copy the data table into your notebook.
7. Perform your experiment using the pencil hydrometer.

Analyze and Conclude

1. In your experimental plan, which variable was the manipulated variable, and which was the responding variable? Explain. (Refer to the Skills Handbook if you need more information about these types of variables.)
2. Make a graph of the data you collected in the experiment. Graph the manipulated variable on the horizontal axis. Graph the responding variable on the vertical axis.
3. How do changes in the hydrometer reading relate to density?

Making a Hydrometer

A. Begin with an unsharpened pencil. Starting 1 cm from the unsharpened end, use a second, sharpened pencil to make marks every 0.5 cm along the side of the pencil. Continue making marks until you reach the 4-cm mark.
B. Label each mark, starting at the unsharpened end of the pencil with the label 0.5.
C. Insert 3 thumbtacks as weights into the eraser end of the pencil. **CAUTION:** *Be careful not to cut yourself on the sharp points of the thumbtacks.*
D. Fill the 250-mL graduated cylinder with water at room temperature. Place the pencil in the water, eraser down.
E. Add or remove thumbtacks and adjust their placement in the eraser until the pencil floats upright, with about 2 cm sticking up above the surface of the water.

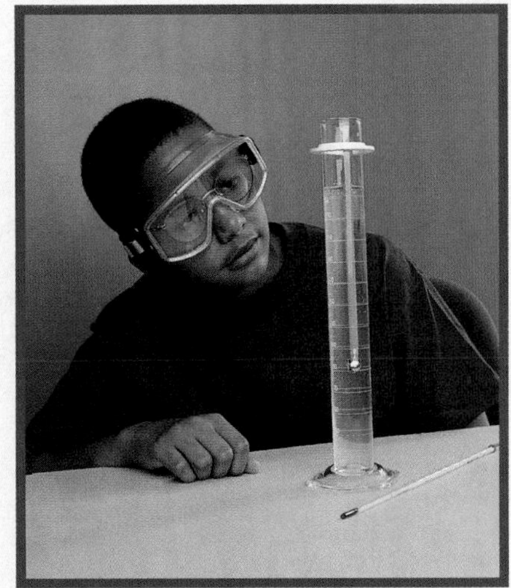

F. In your notebook, record the number next to the mark that is closest to the point where the pencil hydrometer projects from the water. As the density of the water increases, the hydrometer will float above the point you have just marked. If the water becomes less dense, the hydrometer will float below that point.

4. Use the graph to describe the relationship between the manipulated variable you tested and density.
5. Where in Earth's oceans would you find conditions like the ones that you tested?
6. **Think About It** Why is it important to make sure that all conditions other than the manipulated variable are kept constant in an experiment? How well were you able to keep the other variables constant?

More To Explore

In this experiment you observed how manipulating a particular variable affects the density of ocean water. Now conduct a second experiment, this time manipulating a different variable. As you design this experiment, make sure to control all variables except the one you are testing. Be sure to check your experimental plan with your teacher before you begin.

Sample Data Table 1

Manipulated Variable: Salinity

Salinity (g salt/L water)	Hydrometer Reading (cm)
0	2
30	4
60	6

Program Resources

◆ **Unit 3 Resources** Chapter 9 Skills Lab

Safety

Caution students to be careful of the sharp tack points, to use oven mitts or tongs to handle hot items, and to use caution with electricity. Review the safety guidelines in Appendix A.

Sample Data Table 2

Manipulated Variable: Temperature

Temperature (°C)	Hydrometer Reading (cm)
5	4
25	3
45	3

Currents and Climate

Objectives

After completing the lesson, students will be able to

- ◆ identify the forces that cause surface currents and deep currents;
- ◆ describe how surface currents affect climate on land;
- ◆ describe deep currents, upwelling, and El Niño.

Key Terms current, Coriolis effect, climate, upwelling, El Niño

1 Engage/Explore

Activating Prior Knowledge

Elicit descriptions from students of how a river flows. Then ask: **How does the movement of water in a river differ from what you've learned about how ocean water moves?** *(Rivers flow in one direction; waves and tides cause water in oceans to move up and down in deep water and into shore and back to sea in shallow water.)* Explain that there have been instances when someone has sealed a message in a bottle, thrown the bottle into the ocean, and after a time the bottle was found by a person far away. Ask: **How do you think the bottle got there?** *(Some students may know that there are currents in the ocean that could carry the bottle.)* Tell students that they will learn about ocean currents in this section.

DISCOVER ACTIVITY

Skills Focus inferring
Materials *plastic bowl, warm and cold water, food coloring, plastic dropper, cup, stirring rod*
Time 10 minutes
Tips The greater the difference in temperature between the warm and cold water, the more obvious the effect.
Think It Over Students should observe that the cold water settles to the bottom of the bowl. They should conclude that cold water is denser than warm water.

Currents and Climate

DISCOVER ACTIVITY

Which Is More Dense?

1. Fill a plastic container three-quarters full with warm water. Wait for the water to stop moving.
2. Add several drops of food coloring to a cup of ice water and stir.

3. Gently dribble colored water down the inside of the container. Observe.

Think It Over

Inferring Describe what happened to the cold water. Which is more dense, warm water or cold water? Explain.

GUIDE FOR READING

- ◆ What forces cause surface currents and deep currents?
- ◆ How do surface currents affect climate on land?

Reading Tip As you read, make a list of the kinds of ocean currents. Write a sentence describing the causes of each.

People strolling along a Washington beach one May day in 1990 could hardly believe their eyes. Hundreds of sneakers, in all colors and sizes, were washing ashore from the Pacific Ocean. Puzzled, people gathered up the soggy shoes and took them home, wondering where the sneakers had come from. Eventually, the sneaker spill was traced to a cargo ship from South Korea. Containers had washed overboard in a storm and broken open, spilling thousands of shoes into the water.

The sneakers were a ready-made experiment for oceanographers, scientists who study the oceans. From the shoes' drifting, oceanographers could infer both the path and the speed of water movements in the Pacific. Using what they already knew about these movements, scientists made a computer model predicting when and where more sneakers would come ashore. Right on schedule, sneakers washed up in Oregon and British Columbia, Canada. The model also predicted that the shoes would turn back westward across the Pacific. Again it was correct, as some sneakers arrived in Hawaii. The shoes that did not sink could have traveled all the way back to South Korea!

READING STRATEGIES

Reading Tip Encourage students to take notes as they read about ocean currents. After they have finished reading the section, students can use their notes to write their sentences in their own words. Sample sentence: Surface currents are caused by wind and extend down into the water several hundred meters.

Vocabulary The term *El Niño*, which is Spanish for "the child," is applied to the unusual conditions of winds and currents that occur about once every two to seven years in the Pacific. The term is used because the conditions tend to be most pronounced during the Christmas season, when the birth of Jesus is celebrated by Christians.

Earlier in this chapter you learned how the oceans move as a result of wave action and tides. A third type of water movement is currents. A **current** is a large stream of moving water that flows through the oceans. Unlike waves, which do not actually transport water from one place to another, currents carry water great distances. Some currents move water at the surface of the ocean, while other currents move the deep water.

Surface Currents

Figure 16 shows the major surface currents in Earth's oceans. **Surface currents, which affect water to a depth of several hundred meters, are driven mainly by winds.** Following the major wind patterns of the globe, surface currents move in circular patterns in the five major ocean basins. Trace these currents on the map. Notice that most of the currents flow east or west, then double back to complete the circle.

Why do the currents move in these circular patterns? If Earth were standing still, winds and currents would flow in straight lines between the poles and the equator. But as Earth rotates, the paths of the winds and currents curve in relation to Earth's surface. This effect of Earth's rotation on the direction of winds and currents is called the **Coriolis effect** (kawr ee OH lis effect). In the Northern Hemisphere, the Coriolis effect causes the currents to curve to the right. In the Southern Hemisphere, the Coriolis effect causes the currents to curve to the left. You can see the impact of the Coriolis effect by comparing the directions of the currents in the two hemispheres on Figure 13.

Figure 13 Large surface currents generally move in circular patterns in Earth's oceans. *Interpreting Maps Name four currents that flow along the coasts of North America. State whether each current is warm or cold.*

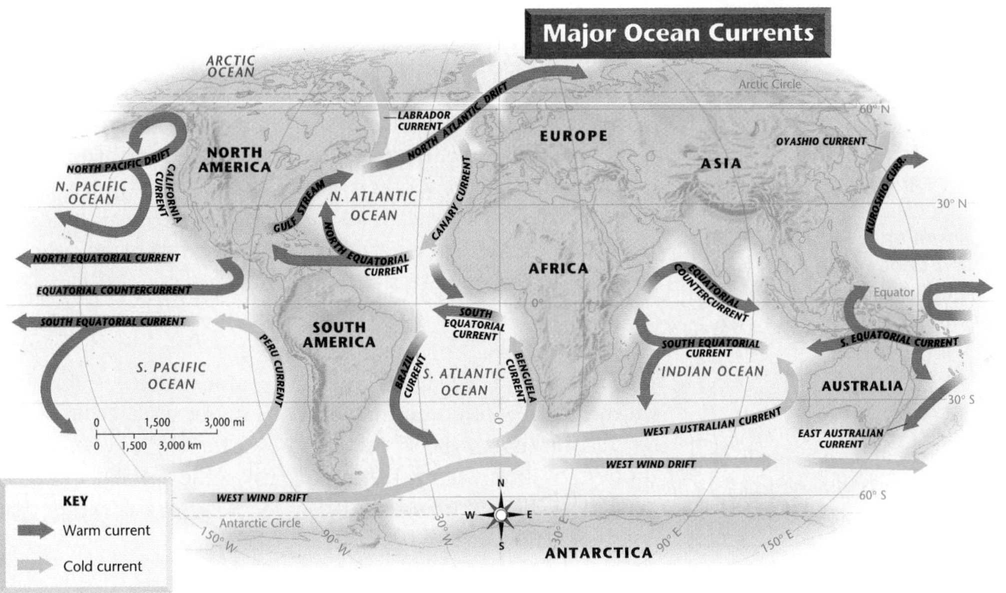

2 Facilitate

Surface Currents

Demonstration

ACTIVITY

Materials *large plastic box or aluminum baking pan, water, ground black pepper, hair dryer*
Time 10 minutes

Fill the box or pan half full of water and sprinkle some pepper on the water at one end. While students observe, use the hair dryer to blow the pepper across the water to the other end of the pan. Then ask: **Why did the pepper move?** *(Students may say that "wind" from the hair dryer moved the pepper.)* Clarify that the pepper moved on a current of water that was put into motion by the flow of air from the hair dryer. Ask: **How is this similar to surface currents in the ocean?** *(The wind blowing across the ocean puts the surface water into motion as currents.)* **learning modality: visual**

Using the Visuals: Figure 13

Call students' attention to the Gulf Stream and have them trace the direction it flows on the map. Ask: **Is the water carried by Gulf Stream warmer or cooler than the water it flows through? Why?** *(Warmer, because it flows from the warm waters of the equator to the north, where the ocean is colder)* **What determines whether a current is cold or warm?** *(It is largely determined by where it originates; warm currents originate near the equator and cold currents originate near the poles.)* **learning modality: visual**

Program Resources

- **Unit 3 Resources** 9-4 Lesson Plan; 9-4 Section Summary
- **Guided Reading and Study Workbook** Section 9-4

Media and Technology

Transparencies "Major Ocean Currents," Transparency 32

Answers to Self-Assessment

Caption Question

Figure 13 The California Current and Labrador Current are cold currents; the North Pacific Drift and Gulf Stream are warm currents.

Ongoing Assessment

Skills Check Have students make a table that compares and contrasts waves, tides, and surface currents in terms of their causes and how they move water.

Students can save their table in their portfolio.

Surface Currents, continued

Including All Students

ACTIVITY To help students better understand the Coriolis effect, have them cut a circle about 20 cm in diameter from a file folder or construction paper and carefully push the point of a pencil through the center. Then they should place a drop of water on top of the circle near the pencil and, holding the pencil between the palms of their hands, twirl it in a counterclockwise direction. Students will see the water appear to swirl around the paper in a clockwise direction. Ask: **How does this demonstrate the Coriolis effect?** *(The rotating Earth, like the spinning paper, moves faster than the water on the surface, causing currents to move in the opposite, or clockwise, direction.)* **learning modality: kinesthetic**

How Surface Currents Affect Climate

Sharpen your Skills

Drawing Conclusions

ACTIVITY

Time 5 minutes
Tips Make sure students know that the Benguela Current is a cold-water current.
Expected Outcome Students should conclude that the Benguela Current brings cool, dry weather to the southwestern coast of Africa.
Extend Encourage students to use an encyclopedia or other reference book to find out about the climate of the southwestern coast of Africa. **learning modality: logical/mathematical**

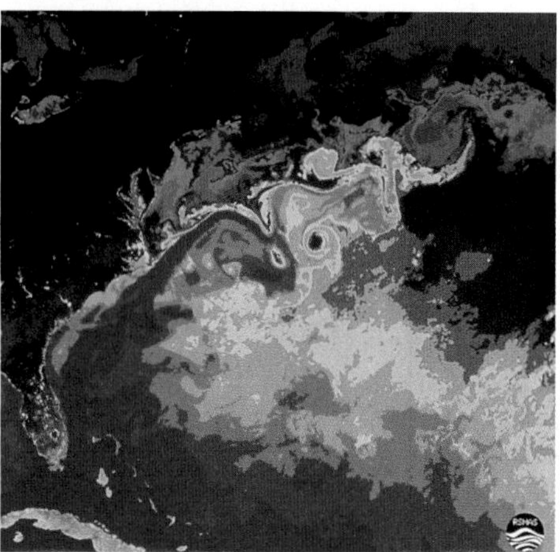

Figure 14 This satellite image of the Atlantic Ocean has been enhanced with colors that show water temperature. Red and orange indicate warmer water, while green and blue indicate colder water. The warm Gulf Stream flows around Florida as you can see in the lower left corner of the image.

The largest and most powerful surface current in the North Atlantic Ocean, the Gulf Stream, is caused by strong winds from the west. The Gulf Stream resembles a fast-moving, deep-blue river within the ocean. It is more than 30 kilometers wide and 300 meters deep, and it carries a volume of water 100 times greater than the Mississippi River. The Gulf Stream carries warm water from the Gulf of Mexico to the Caribbean Sea, then northward along the coast of the United States. Near Cape Hatteras, North Carolina, it curves eastward across the Atlantic, as a result of the Coriolis effect.

☑ *Checkpoint* *Why doesn't the Gulf Stream travel in a straight line?*

How Surface Currents Affect Climate

The Gulf Stream and North Atlantic Drift are very important to people in the city of Trondheim, Norway. Trondheim is located along Norway's western coast. Although it is very close to the Arctic Circle, winter there is fairly mild. Snow melts soon after it falls. And fortunately for the fishing boats, the local harbors are free of ice most of the winter. The two warm currents bring this area of Norway its mild climate. **Climate** is the pattern of temperature and precipitation typical of an area over a long period of time.

Currents affect climate by moving cold and warm water around the globe. In general, currents carry warm water from the tropics toward the poles and bring cold water back toward the equator. **A surface current warms or cools the air above it, influencing the climate of the land near the coast.**

Winds pick up moisture as they blow across warm-water currents. For example, the warm Kuroshio Current brings mild, rainy weather to the southern islands of Japan. In contrast, cold-water currents cool the air above them. Since cold air holds less moisture than warm air, these currents tend to bring cool, dry weather to the land areas in their path.

Drawing Conclusions

ACTIVITY Locate the Benguela Current on Figure 13 on the previous page. Near the southern tip of Africa, the winds blow from west to east. Using what you have learned about surface currents and climate, what can you conclude about the impact of this current on the climate of the southwestern coast of Africa?

Deep Currents

So far you have been reading about currents that move the water in the top few hundred meters of the ocean. Deeper below the surface, another type of current causes the chilly waters at the bottom of the ocean to creep slowly across the ocean floor. **These deep currents are caused by differences in density rather than surface winds.**

Background

History of Science Currents have been studied by seafarers for centuries. In the 1500s, Spanish explorers used the Gulf Stream to speed their ships across the Atlantic from the New World. In the 1700s, Benjamin Franklin published a chart on the Gulf Stream to help ships coming from England avoid its counterflow. As deputy postmaster for the colonies, Franklin recorded how long it took mail ships to cross the Atlantic to the colonies. By the 1800s, the United States Navy was systematically collecting observations on the Gulf Stream and other ocean currents to aid navigation.

As you read in Section 3, the density of water depends on its temperature and its salinity. When a warm-water surface current moves from the equator toward the poles, its water gradually cools off. As ice forms near the poles, the salinity of the water increases from the salt left behind during freezing. As its temperature decreases and salinity increases, the water becomes denser and sinks. Then, the cold water flows back along the ocean floor as a deep current. Deep currents follow the hills and valleys of the ocean floor. Deep ocean currents are also affected by the Coriolis effect, which causes them to curve.

Deep ocean currents move and mix water around the world. They carry cold water from the poles back toward the equator. Deep ocean currents flow much more slowly than surface currents. They may take as long as 1,000 years to make the round trip from the pole to the equator and back again!

Upwelling

In most parts of the ocean, the surface waters do not usually mix with the deep ocean waters. However, some mixing does occur in the polar regions when the surface waters cool, sink, and form deep currents. Mixing also occurs when winds cause upwelling. **Upwelling** is the upward movement of cold water from the ocean depths. As winds blow away the warm surface water, cold water rises to replace it, as shown in Figure 15.

Upwelling brings up tiny ocean organisms, minerals, and other nutrients from the deeper layers of the water. Without this

Figure 15 As cold water rises from the deep ocean, it brings a new supply of nutrients to the surface. The nutrients feed enormous schools of fish such as these anchovies. ***Relating Cause and Effect*** *What causes cold water to rise during upwelling?*

Deep Currents

Building Inquiry Skills: Applying Concepts

Ask students: **Are deep currents cold-water currents or warm-water currents?** *(Deep currents are always cold-water currents)* **Why do cold-water currents mainly flow along the ocean floor?** *(Because cold water is denser than warm water, and this causes it to sink to the bottom)* **learning modality: logical/mathematical**

Building Inquiry Skills: Comparing and Contrasting

Challenge each pair of students to make a table that compares and contrasts surface and deep currents. First, students should decide what headings to use for their table, that is, which aspects of currents to compare and contrast. Then, each partner should be responsible for filling in the cells of the table for one type of current. Urge pairs to share and compare their completed tables. **cooperative learning**

Upwelling

Using the Visuals: Figure 15

Have students use this figure to create a flow chart of the process of upwelling and its effects. Students should infer that events must happen in a certain order for upwelling to occur: first strong winds from the land blow over the ocean, the winds blow away warm surface water, cold water carrying organisms and nutrients rises to take the warm water's place, the nutrients supply food for fish, fishing crews catch the fish. **learning modality: visual**

Answers to Self-Assessment

☑ Checkpoint

The Gulf Stream doesn't travel in a straight line because the Coriolis effect causes it to curve to the right.

Caption Question

Figure 15 Cold water rises to take the place of warm surface water that is blown away.

Ongoing Assessment

Writing In a short paragraph, have students explain in their own words why deep currents originate mainly near the poles.

motion, the surface waters of the open ocean would be very scarce in nutrients. Because of the increased supply of nutrients, zones of upwelling are usually home to enormous schools of fish.

One major area of upwelling lies in the Pacific Ocean off the west coast of South America. Here, upwelling occurs when strong winds from the Andes Mountains sweep across the ocean. Huge schools of silvery anchovies thrive on the nutrients that are brought to the surface. This rich fishing area is important to millions of people who depend on it for food and jobs.

Real-World Lab

How Things Work

Modeling Ocean Currents

Why is the climate in Dublin, Ireland, so different from the climate in St. John's in Newfoundland, Canada? Since both cities are located at the same latitude, you might expect similar climate conditions in the two locations. But when it's 8°C in Dublin in January, it's usually below 0°C in St. John's. This investigation will help you understand why.

Problem

How can you model the movement of ocean water due to surface currents?

Skills Focus

making models, observing, inferring

Materials

rectangular baking tray
chalk
modeling clay, 3 sticks
ruler
permanent marker
hole puncher
newspaper
construction paper, blue and red
jointed drinking straws, one per student
light-reflecting rheoscopic fluid, 400 mL (or water and food coloring)

Procedure

1. Cover your work area with newspaper. Place the baking tray on top of the newspaper.
2. Using the map on the facing page as a guide, draw a chalk outline of the eastern coast of North and South America on the left side of the tray. Draw the outline of the western coast of Europe and Africa on the right side of the tray.
3. Use modeling clay to create the continents, roughly following the chalk outlines you have drawn. Build the continents to a depth of about 3 cm. Press the clay tightly to the pan to form a watertight seal.
4. Fill the ocean area of your model with rheoscopic fluid (or water and food coloring) to a depth of 1 cm.
5. Place 10 blue paper punches in the ocean area marked with a blue X on the map. Place 10 red paper punches in the area marked with a red X.
6. Select a drinking straw and bend it at the joint. Write your initials on the short end of the straw with the marker.

282

Real-World Lab

How Things Work

Modeling Ocean Currents

Preparing for Inquiry

Key Concept Winds blowing across the ocean create surface currents that affect the climate along coasts.

Skills Objectives Students will be able to

- make a model of the Atlantic Ocean and surrounding land masses;
- observe currents flowing around their model ocean;
- infer how currents affect climate on nearby land masses.

Time 60 minutes

Advance Planning Rheoscopic fluid is a liquid that contains light-reflecting particles. It can be ordered from Novo Star Designs, Inc., 317 South Main Street, Burlington, NC 27216–1328. The movement of rheoscopic fluid will be easier to see if the pans are spray-painted with flat black enamel paint. Spray-paint pans with flat white paint if colored water is used instead of rheoscopic fluid. Paint the pans at least one day ahead so the paint will be thoroughly dry. You may wish to make the paper punches yourself before class to save time.

Alternative Materials Cafeteria trays can be used instead of baking trays for this lab. If so, use dark trays for rheoscopic fluid and light trays for colored water. Be sure students build the clay up high enough on the trays to prevent the water from overflowing. You can use water tinted with food coloring instead of rheoscopic fluid.

Guiding Inquiry

Invitation Help students focus on the key concept by asking: **What causes surface currents?** *(Winds blowing across the ocean)* **What determines the direction in which a surface current flows?** *(The direction in which a major wind pattern blows)* **What determines whether a surface current has warm water or cold water?** *(The area from which it originates; currents that start near the equator are warm and currents that start near the poles are cold.)* **How do surface currents affect climate along coasts?** *(They warm or cool the air above them, which influences the climate on nearby land.)*

Introducing the Procedure

- **What is the purpose of the paper punches?** *(They can be used to help track the current.)*
- Give students time to read through the whole procedure, and then ask: **Why does it matter in which direction you blow on the surface of the water to simulate currents?** *(Students are modeling specific winds, because winds almost always blow in a certain direction over a given part of the ocean)*

Troubleshooting the Experiment

- Check students' models of the continents before they add water so they can modify the shapes as necessary.
- Make sure students are blowing in the right direction to create a circular current.

El Niño

Changes in winds and currents can greatly impact the oceans and the neighboring land. One example is **El Niño,** an abnormal climate event that occurs every 2 to 7 years in the Pacific Ocean. El Niño begins when an unusual pattern of winds forms over the western Pacific. This causes a vast sheet of warm water to move eastward toward the South American coast. El Niño conditions can last for one to two years before the usual winds and currents return.

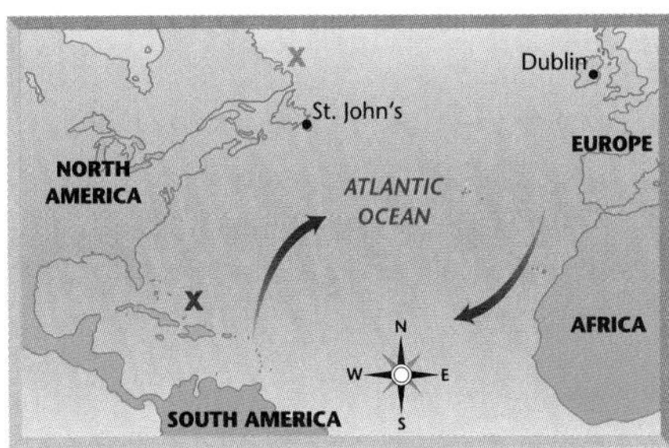

7. With a partner, simulate the pattern of winds that blow in this region of the world. One partner should position his or her straw across the westernmost bulge of Africa and blow toward the west (see arrow on map). The other partner should position his or her straw across the northern end of South America and blow toward the northeast (see arrow on map). Make sure that the straws are bent and that the short ends are parallel to the ocean surface. Both partners should begin blowing gently through the straws at the same time. Try to blow as continuously as possible for one to two minutes.
8. Observe the motion of the fluid and paper punches over the surface of the ocean. Notice what happens when the fluid and punches flow around landmasses.

Analyze and Conclude

1. Draw a map that shows the pattern of ocean currents that was produced in your model. Use red arrows to show the flow of warm water moving north from the equator. Use blue arrows to show the flow of cold water southward from the polar regions.
2. Use Figure 13 to add names to the currents you drew on your map. Which currents are warm-water currents? Which are cold-water currents?
3. Use your model to describe the relationship between winds and surface currents in the ocean.
4. Use your knowledge of ocean currents to explain why the climate in St. John's is different from the climate in Dublin.
5. **Apply** Suppose you wanted to sail to Europe from the east coast of the United States. What two natural factors could help speed up your trip? Explain your answer.

More to Explore

Use your model to simulate an upwelling off the coast of Africa. What conditions cause upwellings to occur? What are the results?

Safety

If you use rheoscopic fluid, you may wish to have students wear safety goggles, even though the fluid is nontoxic. Review the safety guidelines in Appendix A.

Program Resources

- **Unit 3 Resources** Chapter 9 Real-World Lab blackline masters

Media and Technology

Lab Activity Videotapes
Grade 6, Tape 2

Expected Outcome
Students should observe that the paper punches travel roughly clockwise around the model of the ocean.

Analyze and Conclude
1. Students' maps should show that the water current moved in a circular pattern around the Atlantic north of the equator. Red arrows should show that warm water flowed northeast from the Gulf of Mexico toward the northern Atlantic. Blue arrows should show that cold water flowed southwest from the northern Atlantic toward the Caribbean.
2. Warm-water currents include the Gulf Stream, North Atlantic Drift, and North Equatorial Current. Cold-water currents include the Canary Current and the Labrador Current.
3. When students blew through their straws to model winds, they also created surface currents on their model ocean. The surface currents flowed in the same direction as the winds blew.
4. Even though both cities are at the same latitude, the warm waters of the Gulf Stream bring a warm climate to Dublin, Ireland, whereas the cold waters of the Labrador Current bring a cool climate to St. John's, Canada.
5. To sail to Europe from the east coast of the United States, the Gulf Stream and the winds that drive it (the prevailing southwesterlies) could help speed up your trip because both travel from southwest to northeast across the Atlantic Ocean.

Extending the Inquiry

More to Explore Students can simulate an upwelling by modeling a wind blowing off the coast of Africa onto the ocean surface. Upwellings occur when the wind blows away warm surface water. This results in cold water from the bottom of the ocean rising to replace the warm water at the surface.

El Niño

Real-Life Learning

Divide the class into groups and give each group precipitation records for 1980 through the present for a west-coast city (available in *Statistical Abstracts of the United States*). Each group should graph its data and then, based on the level of precipitation, try to identify the years in which the two worst El Niños occurred (1982–1983 and 1997–1998). **learning modality: logical/mathematical**

3 Assess

Section 4 Review Answers

1. They are driven mainly by winds and follow global wind patterns, moving in circular patterns in ocean basins.
2. The water warms the air above it, and winds blow the warmed air over the land.
3. They form when dense ocean water near the poles sinks and flows slowly along the ocean floor toward the equator.
4. Currents in both hemispheres move in the same direction as the major wind patterns, but they move in opposite directions from each other because of the Coriolis effect: clockwise in the North and counterclockwise in the South.

CHAPTER PROJECT

Check Your Progress

Suggest that students consider using more than one method of erosion control. They might try natural methods, such as sand dunes. To determine how much additional wave action their lighthouse can withstand, they should note how many waves it takes and how high the waves must be to topple the lighthouse.

Performance Assessment

Writing Have students imagine that a shipload of rubber ducks spilled off the southern coast of Florida. Challenge them to write a story describing the trip these ducks might take and where they could end up.

Figure 16 Heavy rains caused by El Niño washed out this road in La Honda, California, forcing homes to be evacuated. El Niño can result in severe weather all around the world.

El Niño's Impact El Niño can have disastrous consequences. For example, the arrival of El Niño's warm surface water prevents upwelling off the western coast of South America. Without the nutrients brought by upwelling, fish die or go elsewhere to find food, ruining the fishing catch that season. Seabirds, with no fish to eat, also must leave the area or starve.

El Niño has serious effects on land, too. It causes shifts in weather patterns around the world, bringing unusual and often severe conditions to different areas. For example, El Niño of 1997 and 1998 caused an unusually warm winter in the northeastern United States. However, it was also responsible for heavy rains, flooding, and mudslides in California, as well as a string of deadly tornadoes in Florida.

Forecasting El Niño Although scientists do not fully understand the conditions that create El Niño, they have been able to predict its occurrence using computer models of world climate. Knowing when El Niño will occur can reduce its impact. Scientists and public officials can plan emergency procedures and make changes to protect people and wildlife.

Section 4 Review

1. Describe how surface currents form and travel in the ocean.
2. How is heat transferred from Earth's oceans to land areas?
3. Explain how deep currents form and move in the ocean.
4. **Thinking Critically Comparing and Contrasting** Describe the similarities and differences in the movement of surface currents in the Northern Hemisphere and Southern Hemisphere.

CHAPTER PROJECT

Check Your Progress

This is the time to make final changes to your method of shoreline protection to further decrease erosion. Test your improved method. How much additional wave action does the lighthouse withstand? (*Hint:* Try using a combination of methods to protect the shoreline and lighthouse.)

Background

Facts and Figures One of the largest El Niños on record occurred during the years 1997 to 1998. Although the massive warm-water current was already shrinking by January of 1998, even then it was still 1.5 times the size of the continental United States. Because it was so large, the 1997–1998 El Niño also brought some of the worst—and most unusual—weather that many parts of the world had ever seen. Many places had unusually wet or dry conditions. There were torrential downpours in parts of eastern and central Africa that are usually arid, and drought conditions in northeastern Brazil, Indonesia, and Australia, where it is usually wet. In the United States, El Niño was responsible for unusually wet weather on the West Coast and in the Southeast, and unusually warm weather in the North.

CHAPTER 9 STUDY GUIDE

Section 1 Wave Action

Key Ideas

- Most waves are caused by winds blowing across the surface of the water.
- When waves enter shallow water, the wavelength shortens and wave height increases. The wave becomes unstable and breaks on the shore.
- Waves erode shorelines, carve cliffs, and break up rocks into pebbles and sand.

Key Terms

wave, crest, wavelength, frequency, trough, wave height, longshore drift, sandbar, rip current, groin

Section 2 Tides

Integrating Space Science

Key Ideas

- Tides are caused by the interaction of Earth, the moon, and the sun.
- There are two high tides and two low tides each day in most places.
- The height of tides during a month varies with changes in the positions of Earth, the moon, and the sun.

Key Terms

tide, spring tide, neap tide

Section 3 Ocean Water Chemistry

Key Ideas

- Chloride and sodium are the most abundant ions in ocean water.
- Salinity varies throughout the ocean, depending on the amount of evaporation or freezing, as well as the addition of fresh water from rivers or precipitation.
- Below the ocean surface, the water is divided into layers by temperature, with uniformly cold temperatures in deep water.
- Pressure increases greatly with increasing depth in the ocean.

Key Terms

salinity, submersible

Section 4 Currents and Climate

Key Ideas

- Currents are formed by Earth's rotation, winds, and differences in water temperature.
- The movement of warm-water and cold-water surface currents carries water around the world and influences coastal climates.
- Density differences between warm and cold water cause many deep-water currents in the ocean.
- El Niño changes the pattern of winds and currents and affects Earth's weather.

Key Terms

current, Coriolis effect, climate, upwelling, El Niño

Organizing Information

Flowchart Complete a flowchart about the movement of a wave by putting the following five steps in the correct sequence: *wave travels as low swell; wind creates ripple on ocean surface; wave breaks on shore; wavelength decreases and wave height increases; wave touches bottom in shallow water.* Add a title. (For more on flowcharts, see the Skills Handbook.)

Program Resources

- **Unit 3 Resources** 9-4 Review and Reinforce, p. 79; 9-4 Enrich
- **Unit 3 Resources** Chapter 9 Project Scoring Rubric
- **Performance Assessment** Chapter 9
- **Chapter and Unit Tests** Chapter 9 Test

Media and Technology

Computer Test Bank Chapter 9 Test

Organizing Information

Flowchart Sample flowchart:

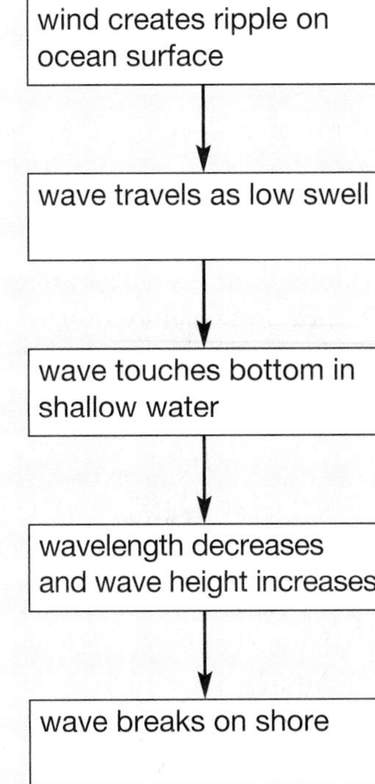

Reviewing Content

Multiple Choice

1. b **2.** b **3.** c **4.** d **5.** a

True or False

6. longshore drift **7.** chloride **8.** true
9. increases **10.** true

Checking Concepts

11. The strength of the wind and the length of time and distance over which the wind blows all influence the size of a wave.
12. As a wave approaches the shore, its bottom begins to make contact with the sloping ocean floor. The friction that results slows down the wave and changes its shape.
13. A rip current forms when water trapped behind a sandbar rushes out from the shore through a narrow opening.
14. There are two high tides a day in most places because, as Earth rotates on its axis once every 24 hours, each place on Earth passes through a tidal bulge two times.
15. A spring tide has the largest difference between high and low tide. It occurs twice a month, when the sun, Earth, and moon are all alligned. A neap tide has the smallest difference between low and high tide. It occurs when the sun and moon pull the tides at right angles to one another.
16. Warm-water currents tend to make the climate milder and wetter on the coasts they pass by because air blowing inland is warmed and moistened by the current.
17. The Coriolis effect is the effect of Earth's rotation on the direction of winds and currents. In the Northern Hemisphere, it causes currents to curve to the right.
18. Upwelling occurs when winds blow away the warm surface water, allowing cold water to rise up to replace it. Upwelling brings up tiny ocean organisms, minerals, and nutrients from the deeper layers of the water, and this attracts large numbers of fish.
19. El Niño is an unusual climate event that occurs every to 2 to 7 years in the Pacific Ocean. It can have many effects, such as preventing the upwelling of nutrients off the western coast of South America and causing shifts in weather patterns around the world.
20. Answers will vary. Students should show that they understand how waves change the shape of the shoreline through erosion and deposition of sand by correctly using terms such as longshore drift and sandbar.

Thinking Critically

21. Movements of water caused at least in part by winds include waves, surface currents, and upwelling. Movements of water not caused by winds include tides and deep currents.
22. You would expect salinity to be low because rain and river water are both fresh, so they dilute ocean water and make it less salty.
23. Compared to the surface, ocean water at 1,000 meters is colder, darker, denser, and at higher pressure. Water at 1,000 meters may also be more or less salty than water at the surface, depending on factors such as precipitation, temperature, and proximity to the mouths of large rivers.

CHAPTER 9 ASSESSMENT

Reviewing Content

Multiple Choice

Choose the letter of the best answer.

1. Rolling waves with a large distance between crests have a long
a. wave height. **b.** wavelength.
c. frequency. **d.** trough.

2. Groins are built to reduce the effect of
a. tsunamis.
b. longshore drift.
c. rip currents.
d. deep currents.

3. At the full moon, the combined gravitational pulls of the sun and moon produce the biggest difference between low and high tide, called a
a. surface current. **b.** neap tide.
c. spring tide. **d.** rip current.

4. Ocean water is more dense than fresh water at the same temperature because of
a. pressure.
b. the Coriolis effect.
c. upwelling.
d. salinity.

5. Winds and currents move in curved paths because of
a. the Coriolis effect. **b.** longshore drift.
c. wave height. **d.** tides.

True or False

If the statement is true, write true. If it is false, change the underlined word or words to make the statement true.

6. Sand is gradually carried down the beach by upwelling.
7. The most common ions dissolved in ocean water are sodium and potassium.
8. Two gases dissolved in ocean water that are important to living things are oxygen and carbon dioxide.
9. As you descend deeper into the ocean, the water gets colder and pressure decreases.
10. Currents carry cold and warm ocean water around the world.

Checking Concepts

11. What factors influence the size of a wave?
12. Explain why the height of a wave changes as it approaches the shore.
13. Explain how a rip current forms.
14. Why are there two high tides a day in most places?
15. What is a spring tide? How does it differ from a neap tide?
16. How do warm-water currents affect climate?
17. What is the Coriolis effect? How does it influence ocean currents?
18. Describe the causes and result of upwelling.
19. What is El Niño? What are some of its effects?
20. **Writing to Learn** Imagine a beach or seashore that you have visited or would like to visit. Using what you know about wave action, write a description of the shape of the beach, sand drift, cliffs, dunes, and other features.

Thinking Critically

21. **Classifying** Classify these different movements of ocean water by whether each is caused by winds or not caused by winds: waves, tides, surface currents, deep currents, upwelling.
22. **Applying Concepts** Would you expect salinity to be high or low in a rainy ocean region near the mouth of a river? Why?
23. **Comparing and Contrasting** In what ways is the ocean at 1,000 meters deep different from the ocean at the surface in the same location?
24. **Relating Cause and Effect** How does the movement of ocean currents explain the fact that much of western Europe has a mild, wet climate?

Applying Skills

The temperature readings in the table were obtained in the Atlantic Ocean near Bermuda. Use the data to answer Questions 25–27.

Depth (m)	Temp. (°C)	Depth (m)	Temp. (°C)
0	19	1,000	9
200	18	1,200	5
400	18	1,400	5
600	16	1,600	4
800	12	1,800	4

25. Graphing Construct a line graph using the data in the table. Plot depth readings on the horizontal axis and temperature readings on the vertical axis.

26. Drawing Conclusions Use your graph to identify the temperature range in the transition zone.

27. Predicting Predict how the ocean temperature at depths of 0 meters and at 1,400 meters would change with the seasons in this location. Explain your reasoning.

Performance  **Assessment**

Present Your Project Use your model to demonstrate your improved method of shoreline protection to the class. If you need to make any final changes to the model, do so before your presentation. Explain to your classmates why you chose this particular method to protect the lighthouse.

Reflect and Record In your project notebook, record the results of your trials. How effective was your method of shoreline protection? How could you improve your model? How well do you think it would perform in the real world?

Test Preparation

Use these questions to prepare for standardized tests.

Read the passage. Then answer Questions 28–30.

Tsunamis are large waves usually caused by earthquakes beneath the ocean floor. They are most common in the Pacific Ocean.

Despite the tremendous amount of energy a tsunami carries, people on a ship at sea may not even realize a tsunami is passing! A tsunami in deep water may have a wavelength of 200 kilometers or more, but a wave height of less than a meter. But when the tsunami reaches shallow water near the coast, friction with the ocean floor causes the tsunami to become a towering wall of water that can exceed 20 meters in height. Tsunamis are capable of causing great damage.

Some nations have developed ways to warn coastal residents and decrease damage from tsunamis, such as barriers designed to break up large waves. Scientists also monitor the ocean floor for earthquakes that may produce tsunamis.

28. Tsunamis are usually caused by
a. huge walls of water.
b. ocean currents.
c. hurricanes.
d. earthquakes.

29. Tsunamis often cause great damage to
a. ships at sea.
b. coastal areas along the Pacific Ocean.
c. the ocean floor.
d. coral reefs in the Atlantic Ocean.

30. One can conclude from the passage that
a. there is no way to reduce the damage caused by tsunamis.
b. given enough warning, the loss of life from tsunamis can be reduced.
c. more damage is caused by hurricanes than tsunamis.
d. an earthquake is just as likely to occur underwater as on land.

24. Much of western Europe has a mild, wet climate because the Gulf Stream brings warm water from the Gulf of Mexico northeast across the Atlantic to the coast of Europe. Winds blowing inland across this warm current make the climate warmer and wetter on the mainland.

Program Resources

- **Inquiry Skills Activity Book** Provides teaching and review of all inquiry skills

Applying Skills

25. Students' graphs should be properly labeled with depth on the x-axis and temperature on the y-axis. The curve should be highest at 0 meters, fall quickly to the right as depth increases beyond 400m, and then level out at about 1,200 meters.

26. The transition zone occurs between about 400 meters and 1,200 meters. Between these depths, the temperature drops from about 18°C to 5°C.

27. Answers may vary. Students may predict that temperature at the surface fluctuates from season to season because the water is warmed by the sun more in summer than in winter. Students should say that temperature at 1,400 meters will not change with the seasons because that is too deep for sunlight to penetrate.

Performance  **Assessment**

Present Your Project As students demonstrate their best methods of erosion control, assess how well the method prevents beach erosion and protects the lighthouse. Students should explain other methods they tried and why they were less successful.

Reflect and Record In assessing the effectiveness of their methods, students should compare them with those of other students. If the methods differ, they should reflect on whether differences in how they built their models or generated waves might have affected the results. In judging how well their methods would perform in the real world, students should consider ways their models and waves differ from real beaches, structures, and waves. For example, their model lighthouses may have weak mortar, or the waves they generated may not have been as high as real waves might be along some parts of the shore.

Test Preparation

28. d **29.** b **30.** b

CHAPTER 10

Ocean Zones

Sections	Time	Student Edition Activities	Other Activities
CHAPTER PROJECT **At Home in the Sea** p. 289	Ongoing (2 weeks)	Check Your Progress, pp. 303, 310 Present Your Project, p. 321	
1 Exploring the Ocean pp. 290–297 ◆ Describe the exploration of the ocean and its floor and identify factors that make ocean-floor research difficult. ◆ Describe features of the ocean floor and the processes that have shaped it.	2 periods/ 1 block	**Discover** What Can You Learn Without Seeing?, p. 290 **Sharpen Your Skills** Interpreting Data, p. 296 **Science at Home,** p. 296 **Skills Lab: Interpreting Data** The Shape of the Ocean Floor, p. 297	TE Including All Students, p. 293 TE Building Inquiry Skills: Making Models, p. 293 TE Building Inquiry Skills: Graphing, p. 295
2 *Integrating Life Science* **Life at the Ocean's Edge** pp. 298 ◆ Describe the factors that affect where ocean organisms live. ◆ Identify the conditions that organisms in the rocky intertidal zone must overcome. ◆ Name and describe the major types of coastal environments.	2 periods/ 1 block	**Discover** Can Your Animal Hold On?, p. 298	TE Addressing Naive Conceptions, p. 299 TE Inquiry Challenge, p. 301 TE Real-Life Learning, p. 302 LM 10, "Microscopic Marine Life" IES "Where River Meets Sea," pp. 6–12
3 *Integrating Life Science* **The Neritic Zone and Open Ocean** pp. 304–310 ◆ Describe conditions in the neritic zone that support organisms and two neritic zone habitats—kelp forests and coral reefs. ◆ Describe conditions in the open ocean and identify where algae live. ◆ Explain how hydrothermal vents support organisms.	1 period/ $\frac{1}{2}$ block	**Discover** How Deep Can You See?, p. 304 **Sharpen Your Skills** Inferring, p. 308	TE Inquiry Challenge, p. 306 TE Building Inquiry Skills: Making Models, p. 309 IES "Where River Meets Sea," pp. 33–34
4 Resources From the Ocean pp. 311–318 ◆ Explain how the supply of fish in a fishery changes from year to year and list sources of water pollution. ◆ Identify the ocean's living and nonliving resources and explain how they can be protected.	2–3 periods/ 1–1$\frac{1}{2}$ blocks	**Discover** Is It From the Ocean?, p. 311 **Try This** Seaweed Candy, p. 313 **Sharpen Your Skills** Observing, p. 314 **Science at Home,** p. 316 **Real-World Lab: You and Your Environment** Cleaning Up an Oil Spill, p. 318	TE Real-Life Learning, p. 312 TE Inquiry Challenge, p. 314 IES "Where River Meets Sea," pp. 35–42
Study Guide/Chapter Assessment pp. 319–321	1 period/ $\frac{1}{2}$ block		ISAB Provides teaching and review of all inquiry skills

For Standard or Block Schedule The Resource Pro® CD-ROM gives you maximum flexibility for planning your instruction for any type of schedule. Resource Pro® contains Planning Express®, an advanced scheduling program, as well as the entire contents of the Teaching Resources and the Computer Test Bank.

CHAPTER PLANNING GUIDE

Program Resources	Assessment Strategies	Media and Technology
UR Chapter 10 Project Teacher Notes **UR** Chapter 10 Project Overview and Worksheets	**SE** Performance Assessment: Present Your Project, p. 321 **TE** Check Your Progress, pp. 303, 310 **UR** Chapter 10 Project Scoring Rubric	Science Explorer Internet Site at www.phschool.com Student Edition on Audio CD, Chapter 10
UR 10-1 Lesson Plan **UR** 10-1 Section Summary **UR** 10-1 Review and Reinforce **UR** 10-1 Enrich **UR** Chapter 10 Skills Lab	**SE** Section 1 Review, p. 296 **TE** Ongoing Assessment, pp. 291, 293, 295 **TE** Performance Assessment, p. 296	Concept Videotape Library, Grade 6, Tape 2, "Journey to the Bottom of the Sea" Transparency 33, "Exploring the Ocean Floor" Lab Activity Videotapes, Grade 6 Tape 2
UR 10-2 Lesson Plan **UR** 10-2 Section Summary **UR** 10-2 Review and Reinforce **UR** 10-2 Enrich	**SE** Section 2 Review, p. 303 **TE** Ongoing Assessment, pp. 299, 301 **TE** Performance Assessment, p. 303	Concept Videotape Library, Grade 6, Tape 2, "Travelin' Along"
UR 10-3 Lesson Plan **UR** 10-3 Section Summary **UR** 10-3 Review and Reinforce **UR** 10-3 Enrich	**SE** Section 3 Review, p. 310 **TE** Ongoing Assessment, pp. 305, 307, 309 **TE** Performance Assessment, p. 310	Transparency 34, "Ocean Zones" Transparency 35, "An Arctic Food Web"
UR 10-4 Lesson Plan **UR** 10-4 Section Summary **UR** 10-4 Review and Reinforce **UR** 10-4 Enrich **UR** Chapter 10 Real-World Lab	**SE** Section 4 Review, p. 316 **TE** Ongoing Assessment, pp. 313, 315 **TE** Performance Assessment, p. 316	Lab Activity Videotapes, Grade 6 Tape 2
RCA Provides strategies to improve science reading skills **GRSW** Provides worksheets to promote student comprehension of content	**SE** Chapter 10 Study Guide/Assessment, pp. 319–321 **PA** Chapter 10 Performance Assessment **CUT** Chapter 10 Test **CTB** Chapter 10 Test	Computer Test Bank, Chapter 10 Test

Key: **SE** Student Edition
CTB Computer Test Bank
ISAB Inquiry Skills Activity Book
GRSW Guided Reading and Study Workbook
TE Teacher's Edition
PTA Product Testing Activities by *Consumer Reports*
RCA Reading in the Content Area
PA Performance Assessment
UR Unit Resources
LM Laboratory Manual
IES Interdisciplinary Explorations Series
CUT Chapter and Unit Tests

Meeting the National Science Education Standards and AAAS Benchmarks

National Science Education Standards	Benchmarks for Science Literacy	Unifying Themes
Science As Inquiry (Content Standard A) ◆ **Use appropriate tools and techniques to gather, analyze, and interpret data** Students graph data to determine the shape of the ocean floor. *(Skills Lab)* ◆ **Develop descriptions, explanations, predictions, and models using evidence** Students create a marine habitat model. Students model oil-spill cleanup. *(Chapter Project; Real-World Lab)* **Life Science** (Content Standard C) ◆ **Populations and ecosystems** The ocean is divided into zones, each characterized by different conditions and organisms. *(Chapter Project; Sections 2 and 3)* **Earth and Space Science** (Content Standard D) ◆ **Structure of the Earth system** The sea floor is made up of many different features. *(Sections 1, 2, and 3)* **Science and Technology** (Content Standard E) ◆ **Understandings about science and technology** Technology has helped in ocean study and in obtaining ocean resources. *(Sections 1 and 4; Science & History)* **Science in Personal and Social Perspectives** (Content Standard F) ◆ **Populations, resources, and environments** Human activities can harm marine environments. *(Section 4; Science and Society)*	**1B Scientific Inquiry** Students explore ways to clean up an oil spill. *(Real-World Lab)* **3A Technology and Science** Technology has helped scientists study the ocean and is used to obtain ocean resources. *(Sections 1 and 4; Science & History)* **3C Issues in Technology** Human activities can harm marine environments. *(Section 4; Science and Society)* **5A Diversity of Life** Different organisms have adapted to living in different parts of the ocean. *(Chapter Project; Sections 2 and 3)* **5D Interdependence of Life** Ocean organisms are connected through complex feeding relationships. *(Sections 2 and 3)* **7D Social Trade-Offs** Students weigh the pros and cons of shrimp farming. *(Science and Society)* **9B Symbolic Relationships** Students graph data to determine the shape of the ocean floor. *(Skills Lab)* **11B Models** Students create a marine habitat model. Students model oil-spill cleanup. *(Chapter Project; Real-World Lab)*	◆ **Scale and Structure** The ocean is divided into zones, each with different habitats. Students graph data to determine the shape of the ocean floor. *(Sections 2 and 3; Chapter Project; Skills Lab)* ◆ **Systems and Interactions** Physical factors determine where marine organisms can live. Human activities can harm marine environments. *(Sections 2, 3, and 4; Science and Society)* ◆ **Energy** The feeding relationships in a habitat make up a food web. Hydrothermal vents supply chemical nutrients that support a unique group of organisms. Oil and natural gas are found in deposits in the ocean floor. *(Sections 2, 3, and 4)* ◆ **Modeling** Students create models of marine habitats and organisms. Students model oil-spill cleanup. *(Chapter Project; Real-World Lab)* ◆ **Unity and Diversity** The ocean floor has features similar to those found on continents. Physical conditions vary between ocean zones. Coastal wetlands include salt marshes and mangrove forests. The neritic zone includes kelp forest and coral reef habitats. The open-ocean zone is divided into the surface zone and the deep zone. *(Sections 1, 2, and 3)*

Take It to the Net

Interactive text at www.phschool.com

Science Explorer comes alive with iText.

- **Complete student text** is accessible from any computer with Internet access or a CD-ROM drive.
- **Animations, simulations, and videos** enhance student understanding and retention of concepts.
- **Self-tests and online study tools** assess student understanding.

STAY CURRENT with **SCIENCE NEWS®**

Find out the latest research and information about Earth's Waters at: **www.phschool.com**

Go to **www.phschool.com** and click on the Science icon. Then click on Science Explorer: Life, Earth, and Physical Science under PH@school.

Student Edition Activities Planner

ACTIVITY	Time (minutes)	Materials *Quantities for one work group*	Skills
Section 1			
Discover, p. 290	15	**Consumable** 10 plastic drinking straws **Nonconsumable** box with mystery object	Inferring
Sharpen Your Skills, p. 296	10	No special materials are required.	Interpreting Data
Science at Home, p. 296	home	**Consumable** graph paper **Nonconsumable** carpenter's measuring tape	Graphing
Skills Lab, p. 297	30	**Consumable** graph paper **Nonconsumable** pencil	Interpreting Data, Graphing, Inferring
Section 2			
Discover, p. 298	15	**Consumable** common materials (such as tape), water **Nonconsumable** ping-pong ball, rock, common materials (such as suction cups), sink or deep pan	Inferring
Section 3			
Discover, p. 304	15	**Consumable** white plastic lid, string, paper clip, tape, water, flour, plastic spoon **Nonconsumable** permanent marker, scissors, meterstick, bucket, stirring rod	Observing
Sharpen Your Skills, p. 308	10	No special materials are required.	Inferring
Section 4			
Discover, p. 311	15	**Consumable** labels from common household products such as thickeners used in cooking, foods, abrasives, polishes, shampoos, and spice mixes containing sea salts	Classifying
Try This, p. 313	20, 5	**Consumable** 2 blocks agar, 1 cup sugar, 4 cups guava or other fruit juice, food coloring, water **Nonconsumable** saucepan, shallow pan, knife	Inferring
Sharpen Your Skills, p. 314	10	No special materials are required.	Observing
Science at Home, p. 316	home	**Consumable** rubber band	Making Models
Real-World Lab, p. 318	40	**Consumable** water, feather, paper towels, paper cup, cotton balls, vegetable oil, wooden sticks **Nonconsumable** graduated cylinder (100 mL), shallow pan, plastic dropper, marking pen	Making Models, Forming Operational Definitions

A list of all materials required for the Student Edition activities can be found on pages TVA34–TVA40. You can obtain information about ordering materials by calling 1-800-848-9500 or by accessing the Science Explorer Internet site at **www.phschool.com**.

CHAPTER 10 PROJECT

At Home in the Sea

Most students do not often have the opportunity to observe marine organisms in their natural habitats. This project will enable students to demonstrate their understanding of marine habitats and organisms in visual form.

Purpose This project is designed to enhance students' knowledge of specific marine habitats and the organisms commonly found there. Students will research and model the habitats' physical features and typical inhabitants and will communicate that knowledge in a class presentation.

Skills Focus Students will be able to
- create three-dimensional models of marine habitats and their typical inhabitants;
- identify adaptations that enable organisms to survive in their habitats;
- represent interactions between organisms and their physical environment.

Project Timeline This project requires about three weeks to complete. During the first week, each group should measure the space available for the habitat model, choose a habitat, research and list its physical features, sketch the planned model for your review, and choose materials for building the model. During the second week, each group should begin building its model habitat. Each group member should choose one organism to model, research its characteristics, and present a plan for your review. During the third week, group members should complete their model organisms, place them in the habitat, and prepare the presentation. See Chapter 10 Project Teacher Notes in Unit 3 Resources for more detailed guidelines on carrying out the project.

Suggested Shortcuts To save time and materials, you could have students create ocean organisms that are smaller than life-size for dioramas, or you could simply have students make a mural rather than three-dimensional models.

Possible Materials Provide a wide variety of materials from which students can choose. Some possibilities are listed below. Encourage students to suggest and use other materials as well.
- *To form the habitat enclosure:* cardboard box, sheets of cardboard or posterboard, chicken wire
- *To shape and form the ocean floor:* brown paper, modeling clay, salt dough or papier mâché, plaster of paris, glue and sand to add texture
- *To make the organism models:* fabric, rolls of brown or white paper, cotton batting or tissue paper for stuffing, construction paper, foam rubber, styrofoam, household sponges, paints or colored markers, pipe cleaners, toothpicks
- *To represent water:* acetate or cellophane
- *To show a food web:* colored yarn to connect organisms

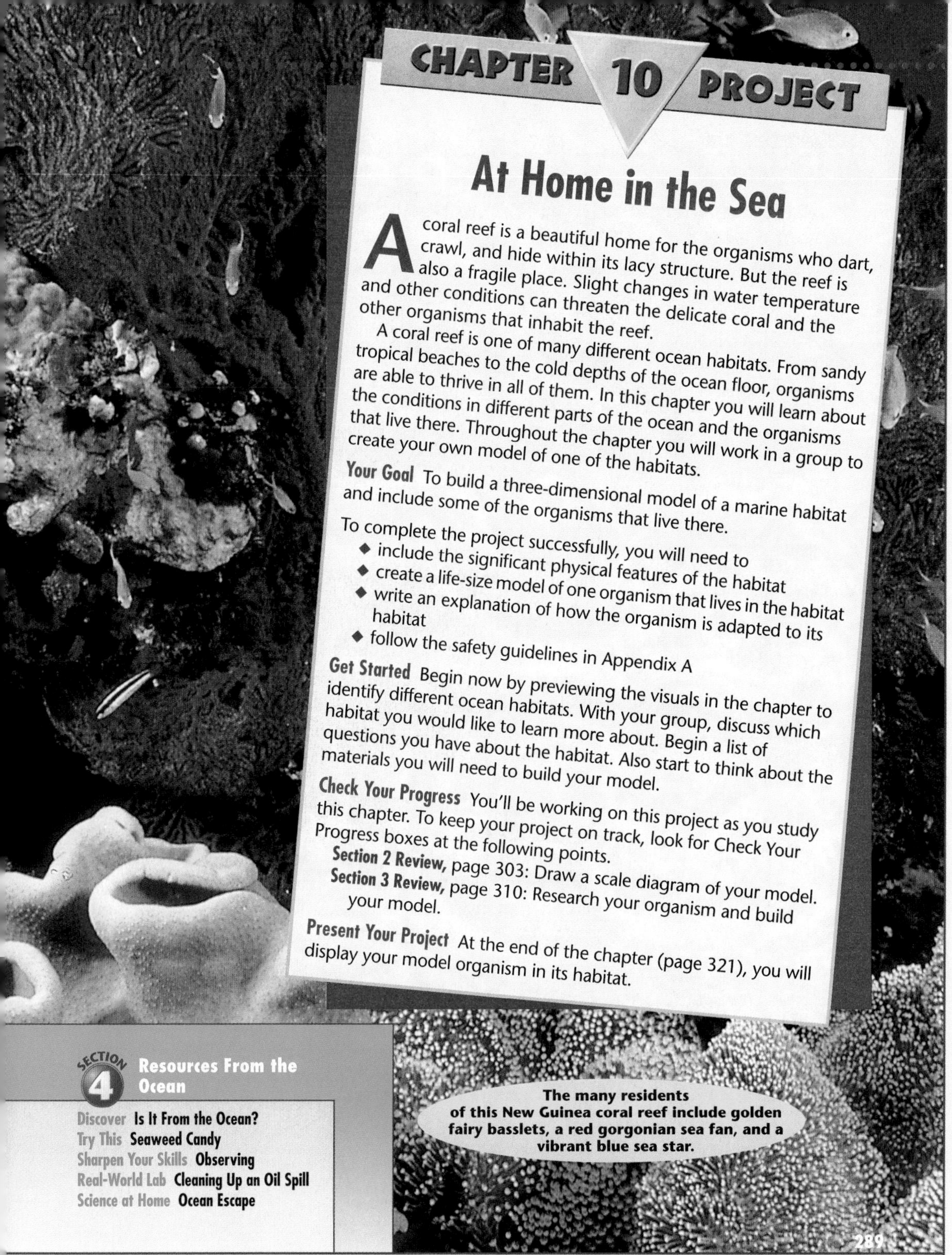

CHAPTER 10 PROJECT

At Home in the Sea

A coral reef is a beautiful home for the organisms who dart, crawl, and hide within its lacy structure. But the reef is also a fragile place. Slight changes in water temperature and other conditions can threaten the delicate coral and the other organisms that inhabit the reef.

A coral reef is one of many different ocean habitats. From sandy tropical beaches to the cold depths of the ocean floor, organisms are able to thrive in all of them. In this chapter you will learn about the conditions in different parts of the ocean and the organisms that live there. Throughout the chapter you will work in a group to create your own model of one of the habitats.

Your Goal To build a three-dimensional model of a marine habitat and include some of the organisms that live there.

To complete the project successfully, you will need to
- include the significant physical features of the habitat
- create a life-size model of one organism that lives in the habitat
- write an explanation of how the organism is adapted to its habitat
- follow the safety guidelines in Appendix A

Get Started Begin now by previewing the visuals in the chapter to identify different ocean habitats. With your group, discuss which habitat you would like to learn more about. Begin a list of questions you have about the habitat. Also start to think about the materials you will need to build your model.

Check Your Progress You'll be working on this project as you study this chapter. To keep your project on track, look for Check Your Progress boxes at the following points.

Section 2 Review, page 303: Draw a scale diagram of your model.

Section 3 Review, page 310: Research your organism and build your model.

Present Your Project At the end of the chapter (page 321), you will display your model organism in its habitat.

The many residents of this New Guinea coral reef include golden fairy basslets, a red gorgonian sea fan, and a vibrant blue sea star.

Launching the Project To introduce the project and motivate student interest, show the class photographs—or a video or CD-ROM—of different marine habitats with their typical organisms. Encourage students to ask questions and offer comments about the environments and organisms they see, but do not attempt to preteach chapter content.

Allow time for students to read the description of the project in their text and the Chapter 10 Project Overview in Unit 3 Resources. Then encourage discussion of the various habitats and organisms that could be modeled, materials that could be used, and any initial questions students may have. Pass out copies of the Chapter 10 Project Worksheets in Unit 3 Resources for students to review.

Have students work in small groups as a cooperative learning task. To ensure that every student will have ample opportunity to participate in planning and building a model habitat, each group should consist of no more than four students. Also emphasize that each student is to build his or her own model organism for the group's habitat.

Performance Assessment

The Chapter 10 Project Scoring Rubric in Unit 3 Resources will help you evaluate how well students complete the Chapter 10 Project. You may wish to share the scoring rubric with your students so they are clear about what will be expected of them. Students will be assessed on
- planning their models, including the completeness and accurateness of their final habitat sketches and the thoroughness of their research on their marine organism model;
- how accurately and neatly they make their models;
- how well they present their models to the class;
- how well they work together in their groups.

Program Resources

- **Unit 3 Resources** Chapter 10 Project Teacher Notes; Chapter 10 Project Overview and Worksheets; Chapter 10 Project Scoring Rubric

www.phschool.com

You will find an Internet activity, chapter self-tests for students, and links to other chapter topics at this site.

Media and Technology

Student Edition on Audio CD Chapter 10

SECTION 1 Exploring the Ocean

Objectives

After completing the lesson, students will be able to

- describe the exploration of the ocean and its floor and identify factors that make ocean-floor research difficult;
- describe features of the ocean floor and the processes that have shaped it.

Key Terms sonar, continental shelf, continental slope, seamount, abyssal plain, mid-ocean ridge, trench

1 Engage/Explore

Activating Prior Knowledge

Ask students: **What does the ocean floor look like?** Encourage them to share what they have seen in books, on television, and in movies. Lead students to understand that the ocean floor has a varied surface, similar to the land's surface.

DISCOVER ACTIVITY

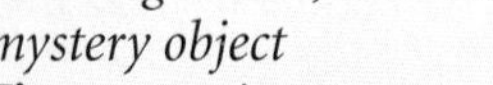

Skills Focus inferring
Materials *10 plastic drinking straws, box with mystery object*
Time 15 minutes
Advance Preparation Obtain as many small cardboard boxes with lids as there will be groups doing the activity. In the bottom of each box, glue or tape an object whose identity could be inferred by determining its contours, such as a ball, small toy, spool, or spoon. Use a different object in each box, making sure each object clears the lid by at least 2 cm. With a sharp pencil or awl, poke 10–15 holes in the lid at various locations.
Tips Students should use the straws as probes, inserting them straight down into the holes and observing how far they stick up.
Expected Outcome Students may not be able to determine the object's identity with certainty, but they should be able to suggest reasonable possibilities.
Think It Over The depths of the straws indicated the object's location, size, and shape.

SECTION 1 Exploring the Ocean

DISCOVER ACTIVITY

What Can You Learn Without Seeing?

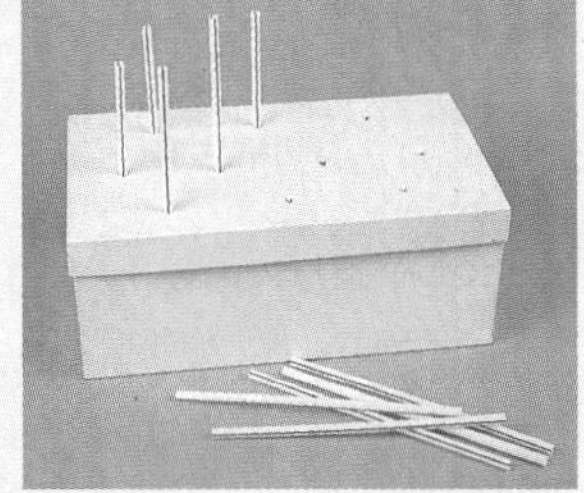

1. Your teacher will provide your group with ten plastic drinking straws and a covered box containing a mystery object. The top of the box has several holes punched in it. Using the straws as probes, try to determine the size, shape, and location of the object inside the box.
2. Based on the information you gathered, describe your object. What can you say about its length, shape, and position? Write down your hypothesis about the identity of the object.
3. Remove the box top to reveal the object.

Think It Over

Inferring Explain how you used the method of indirect observation in this activity to learn about the object.

GUIDE FOR READING

- **What factors make ocean-floor research difficult?**
- **What are some features of the ocean floor?**

Reading Tip **As you read, make a list of features found on the ocean floor. Write one sentence about each feature.**

Imagine going on a voyage around the world lasting three and a half years. Your assignment: to investigate "everything about the sea." Your vessel: a former warship, powered by sails and a steam engine. Its guns have been removed to make room for scientific gear. On board there are thermometers for measuring the temperature of ocean water and hundreds of kilometers of cable for lowering dredges to the bottom of the ocean. With the dredges, you scrape sand, muck, and rock from the ocean floor. You drag trawl nets behind the ship to collect ocean organisms.

The crew of a British ship, HMS *Challenger,* began such a voyage in 1872. By the end of the journey, the scientists had gathered enough data to fill 50 volumes and had collected more than 4,000 new organisms! It took 23 years to publish all the information they learned about oceanwater chemistry, currents, ocean life, and the shape of the ocean floor. The voyage of the *Challenger* was so successful that it became the model for many later ocean expeditions.

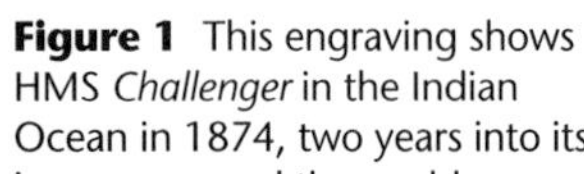

Figure 1 This engraving shows HMS *Challenger* in the Indian Ocean in 1874, two years into its journey around the world.

READING STRATEGIES

Reading Tip Seven ocean-floor features are identified in this section: continental shelf, continental slope, trenches, abyssal plain, mid-ocean ridge, seamounts, and volcanic islands. Suggest that students scan the section first to find and list the names of these features, leaving room after each term to write the sentences later. Encourage students to describe the features in their own words. Sample sentence: The abyssal plain is a part of the ocean floor that is nearly flat.

Voyages of Discovery

For thousands of years before the *Challenger* expedition, people explored the ocean. Knowledge of the ocean has always been important to the people living along its coasts. The ocean has provided food and served as a route for trade and travel to new settlements.

The Phoenicians, who lived along the Mediterranean Sea, were one of the earliest cultures to explore the oceans. By 1200 B.C., they had established sea routes for trade with the other nations around the Mediterranean. After the Phoenicians, people of many European, African, and Asian cultures sailed along the coasts to trade with distant lands.

In the Pacific Ocean around 2,000 years ago, the Polynesians left the safety of the coastline and boldly sailed into the open ocean. Their knowledge of winds and currents enabled the Polynesians to settle the scattered islands of Hawaii, Tahiti, and New Zealand.

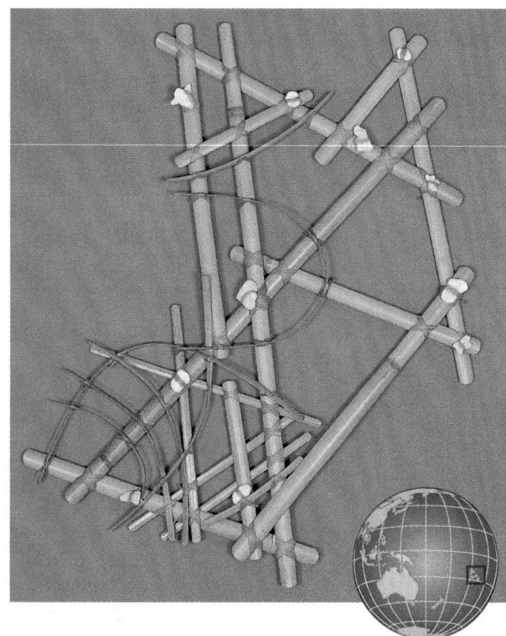

Figure 2 Polynesian sailors used stick charts to navigate the Pacific Ocean. The curved sticks represent currents and winds. The pieces of coral might represent rocks or small islands. *Interpreting Maps Use the map to explain why navigation tools were important to the Polynesians.*

As modern science developed and trade increased, ocean exploration changed. Nations needed accurate maps of the oceans and lands bordering them. Governments also wanted their countries to be known for new scientific discoveries. For example, in the late 1700s, the British government hired Captain James Cook to lead three voyages of exploration. Cook's crew included scientists who studied the stars and collected new species of plants and animals.

Within a century of Cook's voyages, almost all of Earth's coastlines had been mapped. Scientists then turned to the study of the ocean's waters and invented methods to explore its unknown depths. The *Challenger* expedition marked the beginning of the modern science of oceanography.

☑ *Checkpoint* *What are two reasons why people have explored the oceans?*

Exploring the Ocean Floor

INTEGRATING TECHNOLOGY Following the *Challenger*'s example, governments and universities sponsored many other major ocean research expeditions. Until recently, however, the ocean floor was unexplored, and much of the life in the oceans was unknown. Why did it take so long to reach this part of the ocean? Studying the ocean floor is difficult because the

2 Facilitate

Voyages of Discovery

Cultural Diversity

To further students' understanding of the peoples and regions discussed in the text, display a map showing the Pacific Ocean and the coastal areas of the surrounding continents. Explain that Polynesia is a huge area lying within a triangle formed by the Hawaiian Islands (roughly midway between Southeast Asia and Mexico), Easter Island (in the South Pacific, west of Chile), and New Zealand (southeast of Australia). Have volunteers find these three areas on the map and stretch string between them to form a triangle. Ask: **Where do you think the first settlers of Polynesia came from?** *(Some students might infer that the first settlers must have come from Asia.)* Explain that there are still many Asian influences in the cultures of these islands. **learning modality: visual**

Exploring the Ocean Floor

Integrating Technology

Before students read the rest of this section on the next page, ask them to suggest answers to the question at the bottom of this page: **Why did it take so long to reach the ocean floor?** *(Accept all answers without comment.)* Discuss the difficulties of studying the ocean floor after students read the next page. **learning modality: logical/mathematical**

Program Resources

- **Unit 3 Resources** 10-1 Lesson Plan; 10-1 Section Summary
- **Guided Reading and Study Workbook** Section 10-1

Answers to Self-Assessment

Caption Question

Figure 2 They needed to know the locations of and distances between islands so they could travel among them safely.

☑ *Checkpoint*

Any two: To gain scientific information, obtain food, conduct trade, establish new settlements, and gain fame

Ongoing Assessment

Oral Presentation Have students identify some early ocean explorers and describe their voyages.

Exploring the Ocean Floor, continued

SCIENCE & History

Guide students through the sequence of technological developments shown and described on the time line. Then ask: **What is an advantage of having people dive rather than sending a RUM?** *(People can observe things directly rather than just viewing photographs or videotapes.)* **What is an advantage of using a submersible?** *(It can carry people to greater depths than unprotected divers can go.)* **What is a disadvantage of submersibles?** *(The people inside have a limited view and cannot touch underwater objects.)* **Why do you think it is helpful to have a map of the ocean floor that is accurate to within a few centimeters, such as the one created using gravity mapping?** *(Students might suggest that it is important for development of the ocean floor, for defense, to gain a better understanding of Earth processes, or for various other reasons.)*

In Your Journal Students should be able to find out more about the technologies featured on the time line in books on oceanography and ocean exploration. Suggest that they also look in magazines, such as *National Geographic.* In addition to the six technologies shown on these pages, students could research the diving equipment that was used before scuba was invented (including the diving bell and diving helmet) and specific submersibles, such as *Johnson Sea-Link, Deep Rover, Shinkai 6,500, Alvin,* and *Trieste.* Other interesting topics are the atmospheric diving suit known as JIM (see Background) and the deep-diving robot, *Kaiko.* **learning modality: verbal**

ocean is so deep—3.8 kilometers deep on average, more than twice as deep as the Grand Canyon. As you learned in Chapter 4, conditions are very harsh at such depths. First, because sunlight does not penetrate far below the surface, the deep ocean is in total darkness. Second, the water is very cold—only a few degrees above freezing. Finally, there is tremendous pressure due to the mass of water pushing down from above.

Because of the darkness, cold, and extreme pressure, scientists have had to develop new technology to enable them to study the deep ocean floor. Since humans cannot survive these conditions, many of the inventions have involved indirect methods of gathering information. One of the simplest methods, used by the *Challenger*'s crew, was to lower a weight on a long line into the water until the weight touched the bottom. The length of line

Technology and Ocean Exploration

The time line includes several inventions that have helped scientists overcome the challenges of studying the ocean world.

1943 SCUBA

Jacques Cousteau and Emile Gagnan invented SCUBA, which stands for "**s**elf-**c**ontained **u**nderwater **b**reathing **a**pparatus." A tank containing compressed air is strapped to the diver's back and connected by a tube to a mouthpiece. SCUBA enables divers to explore to a depth of 40 meters.

1915 | 1930 | 1945 | 1960

1925 Sonar

Scientists aboard the German ship *Meteor* used sonar to map the ocean floor. They used a device called an echo sounder to produce pulses of sound. The ship's crew then timed the return of the echoes.

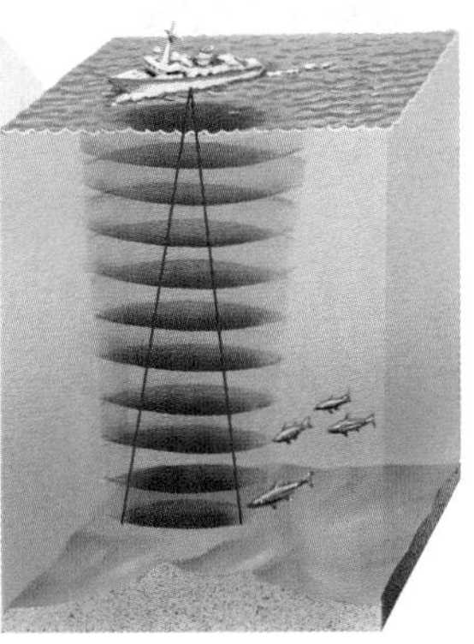

1960 Submersibles

Vehicles with very thick metal hulls protect explorers from extreme pressure and temperature, while enabling them to directly observe the ocean depths.

292

Background

History of Science A significant development in deep-sea diving is the JIM suit, named for Jim Jarratt, its inventor. This diving suit has joints that allow divers to bend their arms and legs. The JIM suit can protect a diver at depths of up to 450 m. Some JIM suits have thrusters that enable the diver to hover in the water. Most importantly, the suit maintains atmospheric pressure so the diver does not need to undergo decompression when resurfacing.

Originally used for work on oil rigs, the JIM suit was first used for scientific research by Sylvia Earle, a marine biologist who has earned international recognition for her deep-sea explorations. Earle's experiences are described in *Window on the Deep* by Andrea Conley (New York: Franklin Watts, 1991).

that got wet was approximately equal to the water's depth at that location. This method was slow and often inaccurate, as the line would descend at an angle. Nevertheless, these depth readings produced the first rough maps of the floor of the North Atlantic.

A major advance in ocean-floor mapping was sonar, a technology invented during World War I to detect submarines. **Sonar**, which stands for **so**und **na**vigation and **r**anging, is a system that uses sound waves to calculate the distance to an object. The sonar equipment on a ship sends out pulses of sound that bounce off the ocean floor. The equipment then measures how quickly the sound waves return to the ship. Sound waves return quickly if the ocean floor is close. Sound waves take longer to return if the ocean floor is farther away.

☑ **Checkpoint** *How is sonar an indirect way of gathering data?*

Each of the inventions shown on these two pages helped solve a problem of ocean exploration. Find out more about one of these inventions. Write a short newspaper article telling the story of its development. Include details about the people who invented it and how it added to people's knowledge of the oceans.

1986

Remote Underwater Manipulator

The Remote Underwater Manipulator, or RUM III, is about the size of a small car. It is controlled by a computer aboard a ship at the surface. Without a crew, the RUM III can collect samples, take photographs, and map the ocean floor.

1975 1990 2005 2020

1978 Satellites

Seasat A was the first satellite in Earth's orbit to study the oceans. Since satellites make millions of observations a day, they provide data on rapidly changing and widespread ocean conditions. Such data include temperatures, algae growth patterns, and even the movement of large schools of fish.

1995

Gravity Mapping

The United States Navy used advanced satellite data to create a new map of the ocean floor. The satellite detected slight changes in gravity related to the shape of the ocean floor, providing accurate measurements within a few centimeters.

Answers to Self-Assessment

☑ **Checkpoint**

Depths are not measured directly but are calculated based on the timing of echoes.

Including All Students

ACTIVITY

Have students do this activity to reinforce the concept of water pressure increasing with depth and to help them understand the problems this causes in underwater exploration. Students should submerge a small, thin, empty plastic bottle with the lid on tightly in a tank or deep sink of water. As they move the bottle lower in the water, they should notice it start to collapse. Ask: **Why is the bottle collapsing?** *(Water pressure is pushing in on all sides of the bottle.)* Point out that at 3.8 km below the ocean's surface, pressure is 400 times greater than it is at sea level. Ask: **What would this kind of pressure do to most hollow objects?** *(It would crush them.)* Help students relate this to the construction of submersibles. **learning modality: kinesthetic**

Building Inquiry Skills: Making Models

ACTIVITY

Explain that the process of using sound waves to determine distance is known as *echolocation.* Let students do the following activity so they can gain a basic understanding of how the process works. Divide the class into pairs, and have the two students in each pair stand facing each other about 1 m apart. One student should hold up a large sheet of cardboard at face level. The other student should close his or her eyes, then walk *slowly* toward the first student while vocalizing sounds (for example, saying "Ah!" repeatedly). Have the partners switch places and repeat. Then ask: **What did you hear as you walked toward the cardboard?** *(Students will hear echoes of their own voices, with the sound changing as they get closer to the cardboard.)* **learning modality: kinesthetic**

Ongoing Assessment

Oral Presentation Have students explain what problems have to be overcome for people to explore the ocean floor.

Features of the Ocean Floor

EXPLORING the Ocean Floor

Point out that the visual essay shows the features described in the text about a journey across the ocean floor. To help students relate the text and essay descriptions, have a different volunteer read each text paragraph aloud, pausing at each boldfaced term to let another volunteer read aloud the related essay caption.

The continental slope is not as steep as it appears in the illustration. It slopes about as much as a theater aisle, dropping an average of 70 m per km. The base of the continental slope generally lies at a depth of 2–3 km. The continental slope ranges from an average of 20–40 km wide up to 200 km wide. Beyond the continental slope, the continental rise (not labeled) gradually descends to the deep ocean floor. Seamounts are volcanic peaks rising 1,000 m or more above the ocean floor.

Students may be able to relate the ocean-floor features to features found on land. For example, students might relate the continental shelf and continental slope on the left in the essay with the foothills of the Rocky Mountains in the western United States, the abyssal plain with the Great Plains, and the continental slope and shelf on the right with the foothills of the Appalachian Mountains in the eastern United States. Students might suggest that the Grand Canyon is like an ocean-floor trench. **learning modality: visual**

Including All Students

Encourage students to imagine what Earth would look like if the oceans dried up. Then show them an illustration showing a "dry Earth" from space (as in Rand McNally's *Atlas of the Oceans,* ©1994, pages 118–119). As an alternative for visually impaired students, use a relief map of the ocean floor. Have students trace the journey from one continent to another, naming each feature as they reach it. **learning modality: visual**

Features of the Ocean Floor

Once scientists were able to map the ocean floor, they discovered something surprising. The bottom of the ocean was not a flat, sandy plain. The deep waters hid mountain ranges bigger than any on Earth's surface, as well as deep canyons reaching into Earth's interior. If you could take a submarine voyage along the ocean floor, what would you see? Trace your journey from the edge of one continent to another in *Exploring the Ocean Floor.*

As you leave the harbor, your submarine first passes over the **continental shelf,** a gently sloping, shallow area of the ocean floor that extends outward from the edge of a continent. At a depth of about 130 meters, the ocean floor begins to slope more steeply. This incline at the edge of the continental shelf is called the **continental slope.** The continental slope marks the true edge of a continent, where the rock that makes up the continent stops and the rock of the ocean floor begins.

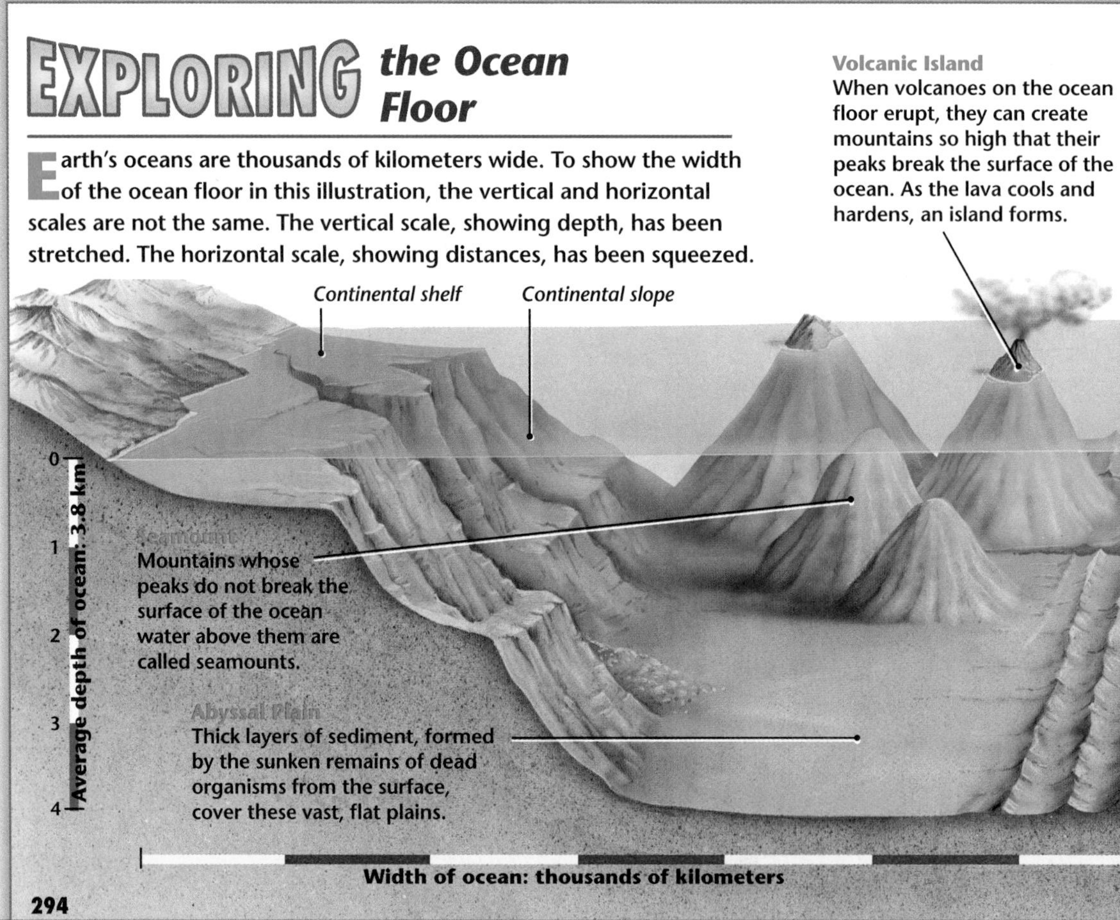

Background

Facts and Figures Sediments on the ocean floor are of two types. One type forms from the remains of organisms that once lived in the ocean's surface waters. The other type forms from material that is eroded from the land.

Very little eroded material reaches the deep ocean basins. Most is deposited on the continental shelves and at the foot of continental slopes. Near the mouth of a large silt-carrying river, the material builds up in a fan-shaped area similar to a delta. Many parts of the deep ocean floor are covered with a sediment ooze made up of organic remains. Sediment thickness varies throughout the ocean. Near the mid-ocean ridge, the newly formed crust has little or no sediment covering it. Moving away from the ridge, the depth increases to hundreds of meters thick.

Your submarine descends more gradually now, following the ocean floor as it slopes toward the deep ocean. After some distance, you encounter a group of mountains. Some are tall enough to break the ocean's surface, forming islands. Others, called **seamounts**, are mountains that are completely underwater. Some seamounts have flat tops because their peaks have eroded away.

Next you cross a broad area covered with thick layers of mud and silt. This smooth, nearly flat region of the ocean floor is called the **abyssal plain** (uh BIHS uhl plain). After gliding over the abyssal plain for many kilometers, you need to steer the submarine sharply upward to avoid a mountain range ahead. The **mid-ocean ridge** is a continuous range of mountains that winds around Earth, much as the line of stitches winds around a baseball. The mid-ocean ridge passes through all of Earth's oceans. Nearly 80,000 kilometers long, it is the longest mountain range on Earth.

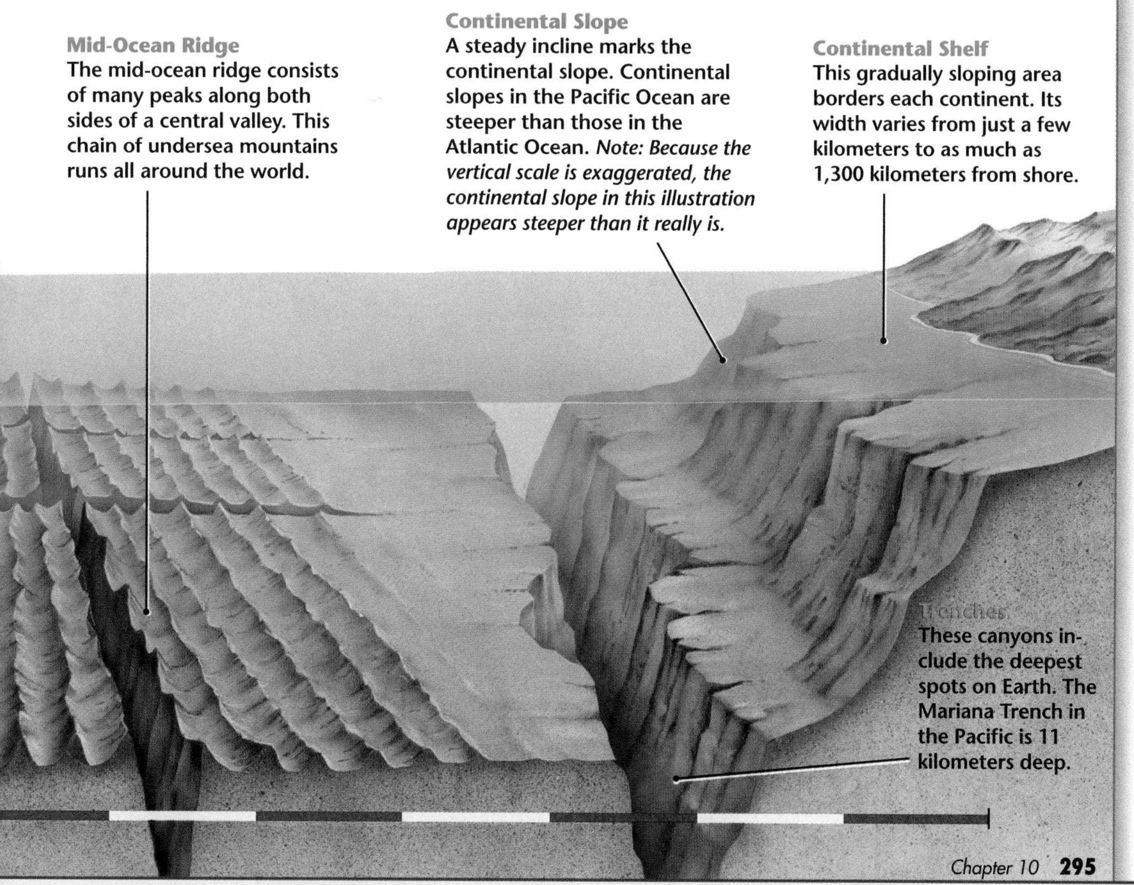

Building Inquiry Skills: Graphing

ACTIVITY

Draw students' attention to the statement in *Exploring the Ocean Floor* that the Mariana Trench is about 11 km deep. To help students appreciate the great depth of this trench, ask: **Which is bigger, Mt. Everest or the Mariana Trench?** *(the Mariana Trench)* Then give each student a copy of the table below and ask: **How many Mt. Everests would fit into the Mariana Trench?** *(about 1.2)* **How many Grand Canyons would fit into it?** *(almost 7)* Finally, suggest that students use the information in the table to make a bar graph comparing the sizes of the objects listed. Make sure students label the vertical axis *Depth or Height (km)* and the horizontal axis with the names of the objects. **learning modality: logical/mathematical**

Object	Depth/Height
Mariana Trench (Pacific)	11.0 km
Mt. Everest (Tibet)	9.0 km
Mt. McKinley (Alaska)	6.0 km
Grand Canyon (Arizona)	1.6 km
Sears Tower (Chicago)	0.5 km
Tallest tree (California)	0.1 km

Including All Students

Urge curious students to consult dictionaries to learn the origin of the word *abyss. (From the Latin* abyssus, *derived from the Greek* abussos, *meaning "bottomless")* Ask: **Why is abyssal plain a good name for that part of the ocean floor?** *(It is flat like a plain on land and, except for the bottom of trenches, is the deepest area of the ocean.)* **limited English proficiency**

Media and Technology

Transparencies "Exploring the Ocean Floor," Transparency 33

Concept Videotape Library Grade 6, Tape 2 "Journey to the Bottom of the Sea"

Ongoing Assessment

Drawing Have each student draw a cross-sectional view of the ocean floor from one continent to another and label at least four different features without referring to *Exploring the Ocean Floor.*

Students can save their drawings in their portfolios.

Features of the Ocean Floor, continued

Sharpen your Skills

Interpreting Data

Time 10 minutes

Tips Tell students that the diagram should compare the total heights from base to summit.

Expected Outcome Mauna Kea is larger than Mt. Everest.

Extend Suggest that students compare Mauna Kea's total height with the depth of the Mariana Trench (about 11 km, or 11,000 m). **learning modality: logical/mathematical**

3 Assess

Section 1 Review Answers

1. Darkness, cold, and extreme pressure
2. Sonar equipment on a ship sends out sound waves that bounce off the ocean floor. The time it takes for the sound waves to return to the ship is used to calculate the depth.
3. Answers may vary. Students could describe the voyage of HMS *Challenger*, Captain Cook's voyages, any of the techniques or equipment presented in *Science & History*, or the tests conducted by scientists aboard the *Glomar Challenger.*
4. A trench
5. Students should infer that the magma contains minerals from Earth's mantle.

Science at Home

Materials *carpenter's measuring tape, graph paper*

Tips To ensure that students understand the procedure, start a graph on the board, using the classroom measurements to show students how to plot the data.

Performance Assessment

Writing Have each student write the script for a tour guide to read to passengers on the imaginary submarine ride on pages 462–464.

Sharpen your Skills

Interpreting Data ACTIVITY

What is Earth's largest mountain? Use the following data to answer the question. Mauna Kea projects about 4,200 meters above sea level. Its base is on the floor of the Pacific Ocean, approximately 5,500 meters below sea level. Mt. Everest rises 8,850 meters from base to summit. Its base is located on land. (*Hint:* Drawing a diagram may be helpful. Start with a line that represents sea level.)

Figure 3 When an undersea volcano reaches above the surface of the water, it forms an island. This peak is Mauna Kea in Hawaii.

At the top of the mid-ocean ridge, your submarine is about two kilometers above the abyssal plain, but you are still at least one kilometer below the surface. From this vantage you can see that the mid-ocean ridge actually consists of two parallel chains of mountains separated by a central valley.

You descend from the mid-ocean ridge to another abyssal plain. Soon your submarine's lights reveal a dark gash in the ocean floor ahead of you. As you pass over it, you look down into a steep-sided canyon in the ocean floor called a **trench.** The trench is so deep you cannot see the bottom.

Your journey is nearly over as your submarine slowly climbs the continental slope. Finally you cross the continental shelf and maneuver the submarine into harbor.

Section 1 Review

1. List three factors that make exploring the deep ocean difficult.
2. Explain how sonar can be used to determine the depth of the ocean.
3. Describe one technique or expedition that has added to people's knowledge of the oceans.
4. Which ocean floor feature makes up the deepest parts of the ocean?
5. **Thinking Critically Inferring** Newly formed volcanic islands have a rich supply of minerals. Explain why this is so.

Science at Home

Make a "Room-Floor" Map With a family member, choose a room in your house and make a "room-floor" map based on depth readings. Imagine that the ceiling is the ocean surface and the floor is the bottom of the ocean. Follow a straight path across the middle of the room from one wall to another. At regular intervals, use a carpenter's measuring tape to take a depth reading from the ceiling to the floor or to the top of any furniture in that spot. Plot the depths on a graph. Then challenge another family member to identify the room by looking at the graph.

Program Resources

- **Unit 3 Resources** 10-1 Review and Reinforce; 10-1 Enrich

Media and Technology

Lab Activity Videotapes
Grade 6, Tape 2

Interpreting Data

THE SHAPE OF THE OCEAN FLOOR

Skills Lab

Imagine you are an oceanographer traveling across the Atlantic along the 45° N latitude line marked on the map. You and your crew are using sonar to gather data on the depth of the ocean between Nova Scotia, Canada, and the town of Soulac on the coast of France. In this lab, you will interpret the data to create a profile of the ocean floor.

Problem

How can you use data about ocean depths to determine the shape of the ocean floor?

Materials

pencil graph paper

Procedure

1. Draw the axes of a graph. Label the horizontal axis Longitude. Mark from 65° W to 0° from left to right. Label the vertical axis Ocean Depth. Mark 0 meters at the top of the vertical axis to represent sea level. Mark –5000 meters at the bottom to represent the depth of 5000 meters below sea level. Mark depths at equal intervals along the vertical axis.
2. Examine the data in the table. The numbers in the Longitude column give the ship's location at 19 points in the Atlantic Ocean. Location 1 is Nova Scotia, and Location 19 is Soulac. The numbers in the Ocean Depth column give the depth measurements recorded at each location. Plot each measurement on your graph. Remember that the depths are represented on your graph as numbers below 0, or sea level.
3. Connect the points you have plotted with a line to create a profile of the ocean floor.

Analyze and Conclude

1. On your graph, identify and label the continental shelf and continental slope.
2. Label the abyssal plain on your graph. How would you expect the ocean floor to look there?
3. Label the mid-ocean ridge on your graph. Describe the process that is occurring there.
4. What might the feature at 10° W be? Explain.
5. **Think About It** How is it helpful to organize data into a data table or graph?

More to Explore

Use the depth measurements in the table to calculate the average depth of the Atlantic Ocean between Nova Scotia and France.

Ocean Depth Sonar Data

Longitude	Ocean Depth (m)
1. 64° W	0
2. 60° W	91
3. 55° W	132
4. 50° W	73
5. 48° W	3512
6. 45° W	4024
7. 40° W	3805
8. 35° W	4171
9. 33° W	3439
10. 30° W	3073
11. 28° W	1756
12. 27° W	2195
13. 25° W	3146
14. 20° W	4244
15. 15° W	4610
16. 10° W	4976
17. 05° W	4317
18. 04° W	146
19. 01° W	0

Skills Lab

Interpreting Data

The Shape of the Ocean Floor

Preparing for Inquiry

Key Concept A profile of the ocean floor can be created by plotting depths on a graph.

Skills Objectives Students will be able to
- graph depth data presented in a table;
- infer the identity of ocean-floor features.

Time 30 minutes

Guiding Inquiry

Introducing the Procedure

- Point out that the voyage from Halifax to Soulac would pass over an ocean-floor landscape similar to the one in *Exploring the Ocean Floor.*
- Show students a large globe or world map and ask: **Which are the longitude lines?** *(The lines running vertically from pole to pole)* Point out that these lines show distances east and west of the Prime Meridian, which passes through Greenwich, England.
- Discuss the graphing procedure. Emphasize that the longitudes listed in the table should be plotted on the graph's horizontal axis and the depths on the vertical axis. Ask: **What would be good intervals to mark on the horizontal axis?** *(Every 5° or 10° from 65°W to 0°W)* What would be good intervals for the vertical axis? *(Every 250 m or 500 m from 0 to −5,000)*

Troubleshooting the Experiment

- The graph works best if students tape two $8\frac{1}{2} \times 11$-inch pieces of graph paper together along the $8\frac{1}{2}$-inch sides so they can spread out the horizontal axis.
- Make sure students label the two axes appropriately. Remind them that they should *not* label the table's exact depths or any "in-between" longitudes on the axes.

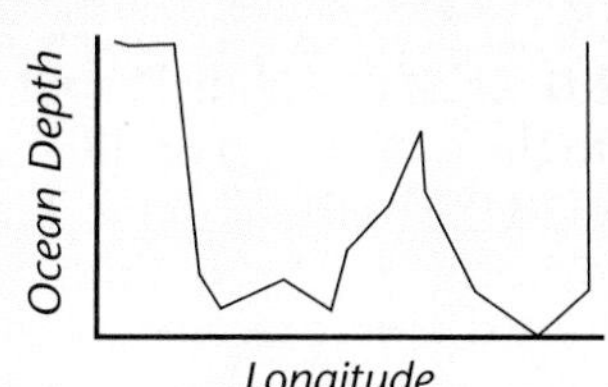

Expected Outcome

Students' graphs may vary slightly; see sample at lower right.

Analyze and Conclude

1. Continental shelf: Locations 1–4 and 18–19; continental slope: Locations 4–5 and 17–18
2. Abyssal plain: Locations 5–9. The ocean floor would look smooth and nearly flat except for seamounts.
3. Mid-ocean ridge: Locations 9–13. Sea-floor spreading; magma squeezes up between two plates, hardens, and adds new rock to the ocean floor.
4. The bottom of a trench; trenches are the deepest parts of the ocean floor.
5. It makes the data easier to understand, compare, and interpret.

Extending the Inquiry

More to Explore 2511 m

Program Resources

- **Unit 3 Resources** Chapter 10 Skills Lab blackline masters

INTEGRATING LIFE SCIENCE 

SECTION 2 Life at the Ocean's Edge

Objectives

After completing the lesson, students will be able to

- describe the factors that affect where ocean organisms live;
- identify the conditions that organisms in the rocky intertidal zone must overcome;
- name and describe the major types of coastal environments.

Key Terms plankton, nekton, benthos, food web, intertidal zone, estuary, brackish

1 Engage/Explore

Activating Prior Knowledge

Encourage students to describe saltwater beaches they have observed either directly or in movies and TV shows. Ask questions such as: **What did the beach look like? What kinds of living things did you see there? What nonliving things had washed up?**

DISCOVER

Skills Focus inferring
Materials *ping-pong ball, rock, box of common materials (such as suction cups, glue, tape, string, rubber bands, plastic wrap, hooks, clay), sink or deep pan, water*
Time 15 minutes
Tips Let each student or group decide whether the animal will cling to the rock permanently (like a sea anemone or sponge) or temporarily (like an octopus). Encourage students to use realistic, animallike structures rather than simply wrapping wire or tape around the ball and rock to hold them together.
Expected Outcome Students' solutions will vary.
Think It Over If the animal could not hold onto the rock, waves or tides would wash it onto the beach or out to sea.

SECTION 2 Life at the Ocean's Edge

DISCOVER ACTIVITY

Can Your Animal Hold On?

1. Your teacher will give you a table-tennis ball, a rock, and a box containing some materials. The ball represents an ocean animal. Use some of the materials to design a way for the animal to cling to the rock.
2. Attach the table-tennis ball to the rock.
3. Place the rock in a sink or deep pan. Run water over the rock from a faucet or pitcher. Observe how well your animal stays in place on the rock.

Think It Over

Inferring How might the ability to "hold on" be important to an animal that lives on the shore?

GUIDE FOR READING

- What factors affect where ocean organisms live?
- What conditions must organisms in the rocky intertidal zone overcome?
- What are the major types of coastal wetlands?

Reading Tip As you read, make a list of the habitats described in this section. Write a sentence or two describing each habitat.

At first glance, a sandy ocean beach may seem lifeless. As you walk along the water's edge in the soft, wet sand, you may notice some dark, tangled seaweed that has washed up on the shore. A crab scuttles away from the pile as you walk by. Seagulls screech and swoop overhead. But for the most part, the beach appears deserted.

If you look more closely at the wet sand, you will see evidence of living things right beneath your feet. Tiny, round holes are signs of burrowing clams. These clams dig down into the sand for protection and to prevent being washed away in the waves. If you wade into the water, you may be able to spot a sand crab taking advantage of the surf to feed. The bottom half of its body buried in the sand, the crab waits for the waves to carry in a fresh supply of food for its next meal.

The organisms on this beach are well suited to the conditions there. In this section, you will learn how marine organisms have adapted to other areas where the land and ocean meet.

Living Conditions

A sandy beach is one type of marine, or ocean, habitat. Remember that an organism's habitat provides the things the organism needs to survive. An organism also must be suited to the physical conditions of the environment it lives in. **Some physical factors that determine where marine organisms can live include salinity, water temperature, light, dissolved gases, nutrients, and wave action.**

As you learned in Chapter 9, these conditions vary in different parts of the ocean. For example, salinity is lower where rivers flow into the ocean, bringing a stream of fresh

READING STRATEGIES

Reading Tip Help students preview the section to identify three major types of habitats: a sandy beach, a rocky shore (which includes tide pools), and coastal wetlands (salt marshes and mangrove forests). Make sure students do not include estuaries as a habitat. Point out that estuaries are a *physical feature*, a "meeting place" of salt and fresh water, and that it is the coastal wetlands found in and around estuaries that are the habitats. Sample sentence: A rocky shore is dry part of the time and pounded by waves part of the time.

Concept Mapping Guide students in making a concept map, with the top circle labeled *Ocean Habitats,* the three major types of habitats in the next level of circles, and specific characteristics of each habitat in the lowest level of circles.

water. Salinity is higher in shallow, warm seas, where more evaporation takes place. Because cold water holds more dissolved gas than warm water, cold ocean waters contain more oxygen than tropical waters. Different organisms are suited to live in these different conditions. As a result, the same organisms do not live in every part of the ocean.

On land, most organisms live on or near the surface. The ocean, on the other hand, is a three-dimensional environment. It is inhabited by organisms at every depth. Scientists classify marine organisms according to where they live and how they move.

Plankton are tiny algae and animals that float in the water and are carried by waves and currents. Algae plankton include geometrically shaped diatoms like those shown in Figure 4. Animal plankton include microscopic crustaceans and fish larvae. **Nekton** are free-swimming animals that can move throughout the water column. Octopus and squid, most fishes, and marine mammals such as whales and dolphins are nekton. **Benthos** are organisms that inhabit the ocean floor. Some benthos, like crabs, sea stars, and lobsters, move from place to place. Others, like sponges and sea anemones, stay in one location.

Plankton, nekton, and benthos are all found in most marine habitats. Many plankton and benthos are algae which, like plants, use sunlight to produce their own food through photosynthesis. Other plankton and benthos, as well as all nekton, are consumers. They eat either the algae or other consumers. Finally, some organisms, including many benthos, are decomposers. They break down wastes and remains of other organisms. These feeding relationships in a habitat make up a **food web.**

Figure 4 Marine organisms can be classified as plankton, nekton, or benthos. **A.** Intricate diatoms, one type of algae plankton, float on the ocean surface. **B.** These microscopic crustaceans, called copepods, are animal plankton. **C.** Free-swimming animals, such as this school of sweetlip fish, are nekton. **D.** Benthos live on the ocean floor. The sea stars and sea anemones in this colorful array are benthos.

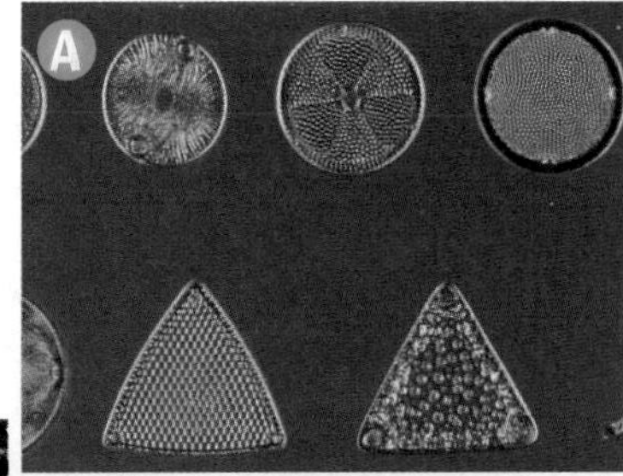

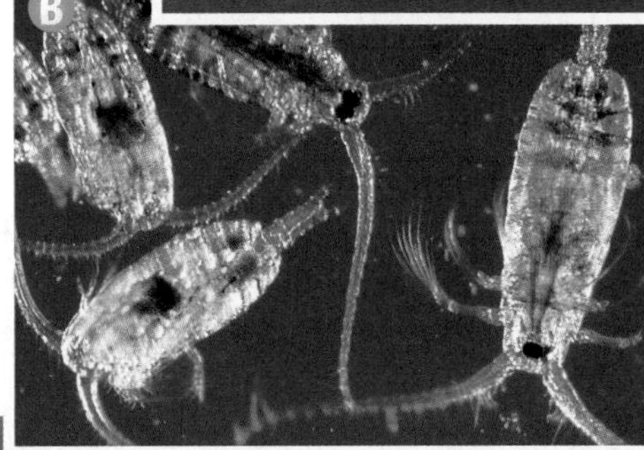

2 Facilitate

Living Conditions

Addressing Naive Conceptions

ACTIVITY

Because students may know that warm water holds more dissolved solids than cold water does, they may find it surprising that the opposite is true for gases. Give two students each a bottle of carbonated water, one warm and one cold. Have both students open the bottles at the same time and compare the amount of gas that fizzes out of solution. Ask: **Which kept the most gas in it—the warm water or the cold water?** *(cold)* **learning modality: visual**

Including All Students

To clarify the text statement that animal plankton include microscopic crustaceans and fish larvae, show students pictures of crustaceans, such as crayfish, crabs, and lobsters. Then ask: **What characteristics do crustaceans appear to have?** *(Hard outer skeleton, a body divided into segments, and jointed legs)* Show pictures of various larvae and ask: **What is a larva?** *(A newly hatched, immature stage of an animal)* **limited English proficiency**

Building Inquiry Skills: Classifying

Name a common marine animal, such as a sea turtle or dolphin, and ask students to identify whether it is an example of nekton or benthos. Let volunteers name other animals for the rest of the students to classify. **learning modality: verbal**

Program Resources

- **Unit 3 Resources** 10-2 Lesson Plan; 10-2 Section Summary
- **Guided Reading and Study Workbook** Section 10-2
- **Laboratory Manual** 10, "Microscopic Marine Life"

Media and Technology

Concept Videotape Library Grade 6, Tape 2 "Travelin' Along"

Ongoing Assessment

Concept Mapping Have each student draw a concept map to show the three main types of marine organisms described on this page, their characteristics, and examples.

Living Conditions, continued

Language Arts CONNECTION

Students can verify that this poem fits the haiku format by counting the syllables on their fingers as they recite the poem quietly or by marking the syllables on a copy of the poem they have made. Emphasize that a haiku is an "in-a-nutshell" description of something, with unnecessary words left out. In this haiku, for example, *is* has been omitted from the last line.

In Your Journal If some students need additional support in writing their own haiku, suggest that they try describing the image in a sentence, then look for alternative words to make the syllable count work.

Students can save their haiku in their portfolios. **learning modality: verbal**

Rocky Shores

Building Inquiry Skills: Predicting

Before students read "Along the Rocks" and "In Tide Pools," ask: **What kinds of body structures would help animals survive in an area that is sometimes underwater and sometimes exposed to sun and air?** *(Shells or other protective coverings, or structures that enable them to hide among rocks or bury themselves in sand when exposed)* Encourage students to keep these ideas in mind as they think about the habitats and organisms they will model for the chapter project. **learning modality: logical/mathematical**

Language Arts CONNECTION

About 350 years ago, a form of poetry called *haiku* grew popular in Japan. Here is an example of a haiku about a beach.

Shining air bubbles
pushing up the hardpacked sand:
a shy clam revealed.

This poem may appear simple, but it follows a strict structure. A haiku is a 17-syllable poem written in 3 lines. There are 5 syllables in the first line, 7 syllables in the second line, and 5 syllables in the third line. A haiku should capture a moment in nature and suggest a mood or feeling.

In Your Journal

Prepare to write your own haiku about the edge of the ocean. Work with a partner to think of what you might see, hear, and feel. Review the habitats in this section for ideas. Then choose one simple, specific subject to write about. Write a draft and exchange it with your partner. After making revisions, illustrate your poem.

The first group of ocean habitats you will learn about are those found at the very edge of the ocean. The sandy beach you read about earlier is one example. Two habitats with a richer variety of life are rocky shores and salt marshes. As you read, think about how conditions in these habitats are similar, and how they are different.

☑ *Checkpoint* *Are sharks plankton, nekton, or benthos? Why?*

Rocky Shores

Imagine if your home had no walls or roof. Twice a day, a huge storm passes through, bringing a drenching downpour and winds so strong you can hardly keep your balance. At other times, the hot sun beats down, leaving you parched and dry. This is what life is like for organisms that live on rocky shores in the intertidal zone. The **intertidal zone** stretches from the highest high-tide line on land out to the point on the continental shelf exposed by the lowest low tide.

Organisms that live in the rocky intertidal zone must be able to tolerate the pounding of the waves and changes in salinity and temperature. They must also withstand periods of being underwater and periods of being exposed to the air. They must avoid drying out, hide from predators, and find food in this harsh setting. How are organisms able to survive?

Along the Rocks Rocky shores are found along much of both coasts of the United States. Figure 5 shows some of the colorful organisms that typically live along the rocky California coast.

The highest rocks, above the highest high-tide line, make up the spray zone. The spray zone is never completely covered with water, but it gets wet as the waves break against the rocks. A stripe of black algae indicates the highest high-tide line. The rocks below this level are encrusted with barnacles. Barnacles can close up their hard shells, trapping a drop of water inside to carry

300

Background

Integrating Science With its regular exposure to waves, air, sunlight, and changes in temperature, the intertidal zone is a stressful habitat for the organisms found there. As noted in the student text, organisms that live along a rocky shore typically have some way of sealing in moisture—a slimy coating, for example, or a shell or case that can be closed.

Unlike the organisms that inhabit a rocky shore, organisms that live on a sandy beach generally do not have adaptations to protect them against drying out. Because the sand is constantly shifting and provides little protection against wave action, most animals living there are active and continuous burrowers. Rather than anchoring themselves in place, many of these animals follow the changing tide line up and down the beach.

them through the dry period until the next high tide. Lower down, clumps of blue and black mussels stick out amidst the algae. The mussels produce sticky threads that harden on contact with the water, attaching the mussels to the rock. The threads are so strong that scientists are studying them as a model for new glues. The rocks are also home to flat mollusks called limpets. Limpets have a large, muscular foot to hold on tightly. They secrete drops of mucus around the edges of their shells to form a tight seal.

Algae that live in the intertidal zone are also adapted to withstand the physical conditions. Rootlike structures anchor the strands of algae firmly to the rocks. Some algae are covered with a thick layer of slime. The slime keeps the algae from drying out during low tide.

In Tide Pools When the tide goes out, some water remains in depressions among the rocks called tide pools. As the water in a tide pool is warmed by the sun, it begins to evaporate. The remaining water becomes saltier. If it rains, however, the salinity quickly decreases. Organisms in the tide pool must be able to withstand these changes in temperature and salinity, as well as the force of the waves when the tide comes in again.

Sea stars cling to the rocks with rows of tiny suction cups on their undersides. Spiny purple sea urchins crawl slowly along the bottom of the tide pool. If the bottom is sandy, sea urchins can use their spines to dig a hole in which to bury themselves during heavy surf. Under shady rock ledges, sponges and sea anemones wait for the incoming tide to bring a fresh supply of plankton and other food particles. A sea anemone may look delicate, but some can survive out of water for over two weeks. When out of the water, the anemone pulls its tentacles inside. It folds up into a round blob, resembling a rolled-up sock.

Figure 5 The constantly changing water level in the intertidal zone creates different habitats along a rocky coast. *Comparing and Contrasting How are conditions different for organisms near the top of the rocks compared to organisms at the bottom?*

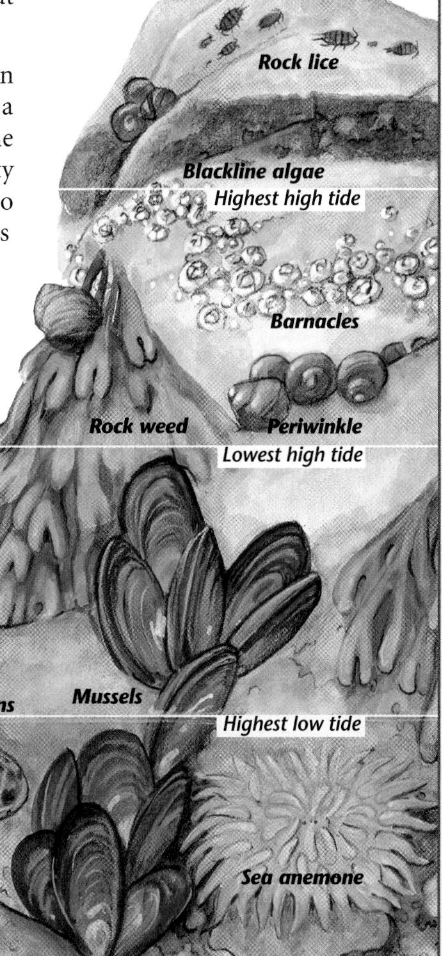

Using the Visuals: Figure 5

Ask students: **Which organisms in this picture live in the spray zone?** *(The rock louse and blackline algae)* **Why do different organisms live in different levels of the intertidal zone?** *(They are adapted for different conditions—greater or lesser wave intensity, more or less exposure to sun and air, and changes in temperature and salinity.)* Have students review the text, this time looking specifically for information about those adaptations, including how organisms hold on to rocks. *(Limpets: large, muscular foot and mucus; mussels: sticky threads; algae: rootlike structures; sea stars: tiny suction cups)* Prompt students to recall the methods and materials they used to attach the ping-pong ball to the rock if they did the Discover activity, and ask: **Were the techniques you used similar to the adaptations of any of these organisms? Which ones?** *(Answers will vary.)* Encourage students to keep the adaptations described on these pages in mind as they plan and build model organisms for the chapter project. **learning modality: visual**

Inquiry Challenge

ACTIVITY

Challenge students to design an experiment that tests how the salinity of a saltwater solution changes as the water evaporates. Students will most likely design tests that involve leaving a saltwater solution in a warm or sunlit place to evaporate. **learning modality: logical/mathematical**

Answers to Self-Assessment

✓ Checkpoint

Sharks are nekton; they can swim freely throughout the water column.

Caption Question

Figure 5 Organisms near the top are never completely covered with water, whereas those at the bottom are always covered with water, though its temperature and salinity may vary widely.

Ongoing Assessment

Oral Presentation Have students identify the physical conditions to which intertidal organisms must be adapted.

Where River Meets Ocean

Using the Visuals: Figure 6

Have students turn back to page 217 in Chapter 7 to compare the photographs of freshwater wetlands with the two pictures of coastal wetlands on this page. Ask: **What is the major difference between the wetlands shown on page 217 and the wetlands shown here?** *(Bogs, marshes, and swamps have fresh water, whereas salt marshes and mangrove forests have a mixture of salty and fresh water.)* **learning modality: logical/ mathematical**

Real-Life Learning

ACTIVITY

If students live in a coastal state, give them copies of their state's map to examine for estuaries. If they do not live in a coastal state, provide maps of Delaware or Maryland. Ask: **What kinds of estuaries are found in this area? What cities are located near the estuaries?** *(Answers will vary, depending on the area.)* **learning modality: visual**

Including All Students

Encourage students who need additional challenges to find out more about the health of the Chesapeake Bay. Much scientific research has been carried out in this area, and there are numerous books and articles that discuss the causes and effects of pollution in the Chesapeake Bay and the results of cleanup efforts. Students can share what they learn with a written report or oral presentation. **learning modality: verbal**

Where River Meets Ocean

Other important environments along the ocean's edge are estuaries. **Estuaries** are coastal inlets or bays where fresh water from rivers mixes with the salty ocean water. Water that is partly salty and partly fresh is **brackish.**

Coastal wetlands are habitats found in and around estuaries. **Along the United States coasts, most coastal wetlands are either salt marshes or mangrove forests.** Salt marshes are especially abundant along the east coast from Massachusetts to Florida. Mangrove forests are found in the tropical waters along the southern coast of Florida and the Gulf of Mexico.

Salt Marshes A salt marsh oozes with smelly mud. Mosquitoes swarm over the water as it flows slowly through the tall, green grasses. The fresh water and tides contribute sediments, animal and plant matter, and other nutrients to the salt marsh, forming a soft, rich mud bottom.

A single plant, cordgrass, dominates the marsh. Unlike most plants, cordgrass can survive in salt water. The plant releases salt through small openings in its long, narrow leaves. The cordgrass that is not eaten by animals breaks down and is decomposed by bacteria and fungi in the water. The decomposed material supplies nutrients to organisms in the marsh.

Tidal channels run through the cordgrass. Waves break up as they enter the channels, so that organisms in the marsh are protected from the surf. Within the shelter of the marsh, fish, crabs, shrimp, and oysters hatch and feed before entering the harsher ocean environment offshore. As the tide retreats, mud flats are exposed. Hordes of crabs search for food in the rich mud. Herons, stilts, and egrets stalk across the mud to prey on the crabs and other benthos exposed by the low tide.

Figure 6 Salt marshes and mangrove forests are two types of coastal wetlands. **A.** Salt water flows through tidal channels in a salt marsh. **B.** Arching prop roots anchor these black mangrove trees firmly in the soft, sandy soil around Florida Bay. ***Making Generalizations*** *How does the plant life in each of these habitats provide shelter for marine organisms?*

Mangrove Forests Mangroves—short, gnarled trees that grow well in brackish water—fringe the coastline of southern Florida. The mangroves'

302

Background

Facts and Figures Estuaries are extremely productive ecosystems. Productivity is a measurement of how quickly carbon and other nutrients are cycled through an ecosystem.

Several factors contribute to the high productivity of estuaries. As rivers flow into estuaries, they carry nutrients washed from the land. The ocean tides help circulate the nutrients and also help remove waste products. The numerous plants that grow in the fertile mud of the estuaries provide shelter and a source of organic matter for other organisms in the estuaries.

prop roots anchor the trees to the land. Mangroves can withstand all but the strongest hurricane winds. Without the mangroves to break the action of winds and waves, the coastline would change dramatically each hurricane season. The prop roots also trap sediment from the land. They create a protected nursery rich in nutrients for many young animals.

Protecting Estuaries The rivers that flow into estuaries can carry harmful substances as well as nutrients. When pollutants such as pesticides, sewage, and industrial waste get into the river water, they end up in the estuary. The pollutants change the water quality in the estuary. In turn, organisms that live in the estuary are affected. It can take many years for ocean tides to flush a heavy load of pollutants out of an estuary.

For example, Chesapeake Bay is a huge estuary located on the mid-Atlantic coast. It has been a rich source of oysters, clams, and blue crabs. However, pollutants from inland sources accumulated in the bay for many years. Their effect was to greatly reduce the number and kinds of organisms in the Chesapeake. When people realized the threat to the estuary, they took action. The water quality of rivers that empty into Chesapeake Bay is now regulated by law. Cleanup efforts have reduced much of the pollution in the bay. Today, organisms like the blue crab are making a comeback.

Figure 7 A crabber in Chesapeake Bay pulls up the last trap of the day. As the health of the estuary improves, the blue crab population is growing again.

Section 2 Review

1. Name five physical factors that affect organisms in marine habitats.
2. Describe conditions in the rocky intertidal zone.
3. List two ways that salt marshes and mangrove forests are alike and two ways they are different.
4. **Thinking Critically Making Judgments** A builder has proposed filling in a salt marsh to create a seaside resort. What positive and negative impacts might this proposal have on wildlife, local residents, and tourists? Would you support the proposal? Why or why not?

CHAPTER PROJECT

Check Your Progress

Your group should now select the marine environment you will create. Measure the space where you will build your model. Make a list of the physical features you will need to represent. Draw a scale diagram of your model and show it to your teacher. Label the different features and note the materials you will use. (*Hint:* Draw your sketch on graph paper to plan its size to fit the space.)

3 Assess

Section 2 Review Answers

1. Any five: Salinity, water temperature, light, dissolved gases, nutrients, wave action, exposure to air

2. Answers should include pounding waves, changes in salinity and water temperature, and exposure to sunlight and air.

3. *Similarities:* Brackish water, shallow water, rich in nutrients, plants break up waves and shelter organisms. *Differences:* Salt marshes have cordgrass and a muddy bottom; mangrove forests have mangrove trees and sandy soil and are located farther south.

4. Accept a variety of responses as long as students support their viewpoints with specific details. *Sample answer:* Filling in the salt marsh would destroy natural habitats and thus eliminate most wildlife. A resort would help people because it would employ local residents and attract tourists who would support other local businesses.

CHAPTER PROJECT

Check Your Progress

Hold a class meeting in the area that will be transformed into a marine environment. Discuss the possible habitats that could be built. Monitor students' choices to avoid repetition and encourage variety. Ask students for their ideas about arranging the habitats in a logical order around the area—for example, from the highest part of the intertidal zone at one end to the deep zone at the other end. Assign a specific amount of space to each group, and let students take measurements.

Program Resources

- **Unit 3 Resources** 10-2 Review and Reinforce; 10-2 Enrich
- **Interdisciplinary Explorations Series** "Where River Meets Sea," pp. 6–12

Answers to Self-Assessment

Caption Question

Figure 6 Thick cordgrass in salt marshes and tree roots in mangrove forests break up ocean waves and provide sheltered places for organisms to hide, feed, and breed.

Performance Assessment

Organizing Information Have each student make a two-column table to summarize and compare the characteristics of the intertidal zone and an estuary.

Section 3 The Neritic Zone and Open Ocean

Objectives

After completing the lesson, students will be able to

- describe conditions in the neritic zone that support organisms and two neritic zone habitats—kelp forests and coral reefs;
- describe conditions in the open ocean and identify where algae live;
- explain how hydrothermal vents support organisms.

Key Terms neritic zone, open-ocean zone, holdfast, atoll, bioluminescence, hydrothermal vent

1 Engage/Explore

Activating Prior Knowledge

Unlike coastal areas, the neritic zone and open ocean are not directly observable by most students. Question students to elicit what they do know about these areas—for example: **What kinds of animals live in the deep ocean? What do those animals feed on? How deep is the water out beyond the continental slope?** *(Accept all responses without comment.)*

DISCOVER ACTIVITY

Skills Focus observing
Materials *permanent marker, white plastic lid, scissors, string, paper clip, tape, meterstick, bucket, tap water, flour, plastic spoon, stirring rod*
Time 15 minutes
Tips You may want to construct one device yourself beforehand so students can use it as a model. Suggest that they record their observations at each depth.
Expected Outcome At some depth, the flour particles suspended in the water will begin to obscure the lid.
Think It Over Students should infer that visibility decreases as water depth increases.

Section 3 The Neritic Zone and Open Ocean

DISCOVER

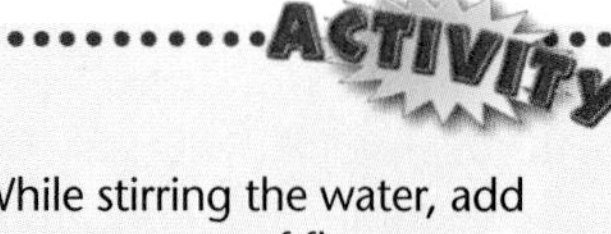

How Deep Can You See?

1. With a permanent marker, divide a white plastic lid into four quarters. Shade in two quarters as shown.
2. Use a pair of scissors to carefully poke a small hole in the center of the lid.
3. Tie a piece of string to a paper clip. Place the clip underneath the lid and thread the string up through the hole.
4. Tape the string tightly to a meterstick so that the lid presses against the bottom of the meterstick.
5. Fill a large, deep bucket with tap water.
6. While stirring the water, add one teaspoon of flour to represent the dissolved substances in seawater. The water should be slightly cloudy.
7. Lower the lid into the water so that it is 5 cm below the surface. Note whether the lid is still visible in the water.
8. Lower the lid 10 cm below the surface, then 15 cm, and so on until the lid is no longer visible.

Think It Over

Observing At what depth could you no longer see the lid? Based on your results, how do you think visibility changes with depth in the ocean?

GUIDE FOR READING

- What conditions in the neritic zone support organisms?
- Where do algae live in the open ocean?
- How do hydrothermal vents support organisms?

Reading Tip Before you read, preview Figure 8 on the facing page. Write some predictions about how the neritic zone and open ocean are similar and how they are different.

Floating mats of golden-brown, leaflike fronds on the ocean surface mark the location of a kelp forest. Diving below the surface, you find yourself surrounded by tall, swaying stalks of giant kelp. Sunlight filters through the water, producing a greenish light. As you pull yourself hand over hand down one of the kelp strands, you notice small bulbs at the base of each frond. You pinch one of the bulbs, and a bubble of gas escapes. These bulbs keep the heavy kelp fronds upright in the water.

The kelp forest is full of life. Bright-orange sheephead fish dart past you. Young sea lions chase one another around the kelp stalks. A sea otter, surrounded by a stream of bubbles, dives past you, down to the rocky bottom. When it rises, the otter is clutching a sea star between its paws. On the surface again, you watch the sea otter as it rolls on to its back among the kelp. The otter deftly uses its paws to scoop out the meat from the soft underside of the sea star.

◀ Sea otter eating a sea star

READING STRATEGIES

Reading Tip Suggest that students set up a two-column table for recording their predictions, with the headings *Similarities* and *Differences* at the top of the table and *Neritic Zone* and *Open Ocean* in the left column (or vice versa). As they read the section, students can cross out any predictions they discover to be incorrect and add other similarities and differences.

Sample Prediction: Both zones will have many kinds of organisms; in the neritic zone, living things will exist all the way to the bottom, but in the open-ocean zone, living things proably won't be found all the away to the bottom.

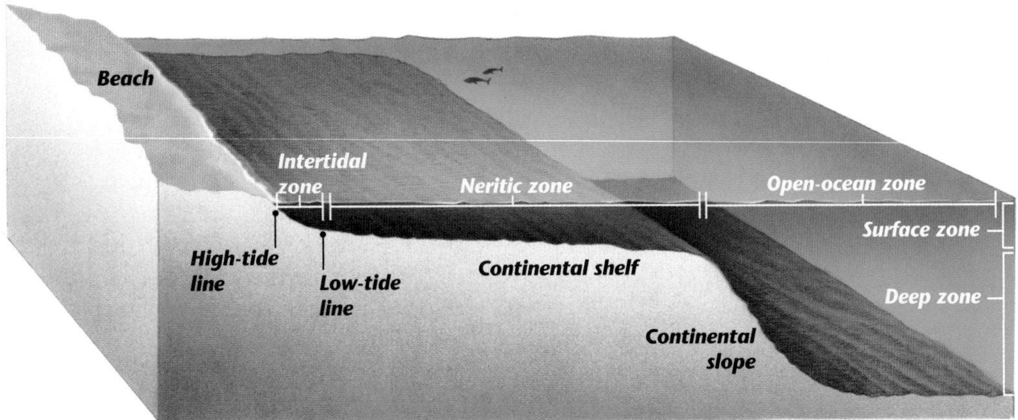

Figure 8 The ocean zone closest to land is the intertidal zone, which is bounded by the high-tide and low-tide lines. Next is the neritic zone, followed by the open-ocean zone, which makes up most of the world's oceans. The open ocean is divided by depth into the surface zone and the deep zone. *Interpreting Diagrams Which zones lie over the continental shelf?*

A kelp forest is one habitat found in the neritic zone. The **neritic zone** is the part of the ocean that extends from the low-tide line out to the edge of the continental shelf. Beyond the edge of the continental shelf lies the **open-ocean zone.** Locate the neritic and open-ocean zones in Figure 8. In this section you will learn how organisms are adapted to the conditions in these zones, from the sunlit surface waters to the coldest depths.

Conditions in the Neritic Zone

A huge variety of organisms are found in the neritic zone, more than in any other area of the ocean. Most of the world's major fishing grounds are found in this zone. What makes the neritic zone home to so many living things? The answer has to do with its location over the continental shelf. **The shallow water over the continental shelf receives sunlight and a steady supply of nutrients washed from the land into the ocean.** The light and nutrients enable large plantlike algae, such as the giant kelp, to grow. These algae serve as a food source and shelter for other organisms.

In many parts of the neritic zone, upwelling currents bring additional nutrients from the bottom to the surface. These nutrients support large numbers of plankton, which form the base of ocean food webs. Schools of fish such as sardines and anchovies feed on the plankton. Major fisheries in upwelling areas include Monterey Canyon off the California coast, Newfoundland's Grand Banks, and Georges Bank off the New England coast.

Two diverse habitats typically found within the neritic zone are kelp forests and coral reefs. As you read about each, think about how they are similar and how they are different.

☑ *Checkpoint* *What are two ways that nutrients may be supplied to the neritic zone?*

2 Facilitate

Conditions in the Neritic Zone

Using the Visuals: Figure 8

Focus students' attention on the intertidal and neritic zones in the illustration. Point out that this figure is not to scale—the deep zone is relatively much deeper than shown here. Then ask: **What is the major difference between these two zones in terms of their water levels?** *(The water level varies at different points in the intertidal zone, while the neritic zone is always underwater.)* **Where does the neritic zone end and the open ocean begin?** *(At the edge of the continental shelf)* **learning modality: visual**

Real-Life Learning

To emphasize the importance of the neritic zone to the nation's economy, urge volunteers to research the types and amounts of fish taken from the neritic zone off U.S. shores by commercial fisheries and the dollar value of those catches each year. Suggest that students begin by looking in *Statistical Abstract of the United States* or *Agricultural Statistics* from the U.S. Department of Agriculture. Let students present their findings in brief oral reports, posters, or illustrated bar graphs. **learning modality: verbal**

Program Resources

- **Unit 3 Resources** 10-3 Lesson Plan; 10-3 Section Summary
- **Guided Reading and Study Workbook** Section 10-3

Media and Technology

Transparencies "Ocean Zones," Transparency 34

Answers to Self-Assessment

Caption Question

Figure 8 The intertidal and neritic zones

☑ *Checkpoint*

Nutrients may be washed into the ocean from the land or brought from the bottom to its surface by upwelling currents.

Ongoing Assessment

Drawing Have each student draw and label a simple diagram showing the intertidal, neritic, and open-ocean zones, without referring to Figure 8.

Students can save their diagrams in their portfolios.

Life in a Kelp Forest

Inquiry Challenge

Materials *string, weight, tape, plastic bucket or aquarium tank, water, balloons, plastic foam balls, clay* **ACTIVITY**
Time 15 minutes

Give each student or small group a piece of string and challenge them to devise a way of making the string float upright in water with its lower end weighted on the bottom of the bucket or tank. Students may use any of the other materials to accomplish this. A typical solution might include tying or taping partially inflated balloons or plastic foam balls at intervals along the string and tying a weight on one end. Ask: **How is your method similar to the structure of giant kelp strands?** *(The balloons or plastic foam balls are like the gas-filled bulbs on a kelp's stalk and the weight is like the holdfast.)* **learning modality: logical/ mathematical**

Coral Reefs

Including All Students

Provide samples of several different types of coral for students to examine. Emphasize that these pieces of coral are not the coral animals, which are soft, but the hard structures they produced and then left behind when they died. Ask: **Where do you think the coral animals lived?** *(In the tiny holes in the coral)* **How do you think this hard structure helps coral animals survive?** *(It provides protection for the animals' soft bodies and anchors them to the ocean floor.)* Encourage students to consider a coral reef as their model habitat for the chapter project. **learning modality: visual**

Figure 9 Light streams through a forest of giant kelp and shadowy rockfish near Monterey, California. The closeup shows the gas-filled bulbs that keep the kelp upright in the water.

Life in a Kelp Forest

Kelp forests grow in cold neritic waters, such as those along the Pacific coast from Alaska to Mexico. These large, heavy algae require a solid, rocky bottom to anchor their stalks. A bundle of rootlike strands called a **holdfast** attaches the algae to the rocks. A stalk of giant kelp can grow to 30 meters in length. The gas-filled bulbs shown in the closeup to the left keep the heavy kelp stalk upright in the water.

The kelp use the sunlight and dissolved gases in the neritic zone to produce their own food. The kelp also provide a habitat for many other organisms. The curtains of kelp hide young gray whales from predators while their mothers are feeding. Sea slugs and snails live amid the tangle of the holdfasts.

Sea otters play a particularly important role in the kelp forest. In addition to eating abalone, sea otters feed on sea urchins, which eat the kelp. In areas where sea otters have disappeared, armies of sea urchins have devoured the kelp. The once-thriving forest has become a barren rocky zone.

Coral Reefs

Although a coral reef may look as if it is made of rock, it is actually made of living things. Coral reefs are created by colonies of tiny coral animals, each of which is not much larger than a pencil eraser. The coral animals produce a hard structure that surrounds their soft bodies. After the coral dies, the empty structure remains. New coral animals attach and grow on top of it. Over many years, a reef is built. Most of the coral reefs that exist today were begun about 5,000 to 10,000 years ago.

Microscopic algae live within the bodies of the coral animals and provide food for them. Because the algae require warm temperatures and sunlight, coral reefs can only form in shallow, tropical ocean waters. The reefs grow above continental shelves or around volcanic islands, where the water is shallow.

In areas where the seafloor is sinking, a reef may develop over time into an atoll. An **atoll** is a ring-shaped reef surrounding a shallow lagoon. Figure 10 shows the development of an atoll. It begins as a fringing reef that closely surrounds the edges of the island. As the reef grows upward, the island sinks, and a barrier reef forms. Water separates the top of the barrier reef from the land. The island continues to sink until it is eventually underwater, forming the atoll.

Background

Facts and Figures In addition to obtaining food from the algae living inside them, coral animals, or polyps, capture prey with stinging tentacles. In fact, some coral species do not contain any symbiotic algae. However, only those with algae build reefs.

In recent years, many tropical reefs have been affected by a mysterious ailment known as "bleaching." The affected corals expel the algae from their tissues and eventually die. Scientists hypothesize that bleaching is triggered by environmental stressors such as elevated ocean temperatures and the higher levels of ultraviolet radiation that have been associated with severe climatic events such as El Niño.

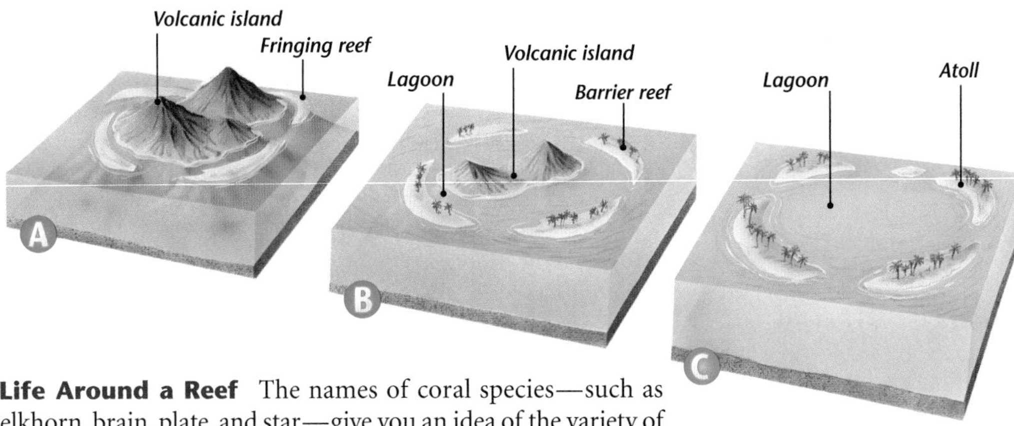

Figure 10 An atoll develops in stages. **A.** A fringing reef closely surrounds an island. **B.** As the island sinks, a lagoon forms inside the barrier reef. **C.** Finally, the island sinks below the surface, leaving a ring-shaped atoll. *Interpreting Diagrams In which stage is the reef the youngest?*

Life Around a Reef The names of coral species—such as elkhorn, brain, plate, and star—give you an idea of the variety of shapes coral can form. Many animals live in and around the crevices of the reef, including octopuses, spiny lobsters, shrimp, toothy moray eels, and fish in all colors and sizes. Parrotfish like the one in Figure 11 scrape coral off the reef to eat. The parrotfish grind up the broken coral inside their bodies, producing the fine, soft sand commonly found around the reef.

Coral Reefs and Humans Coral reefs are natural aquarium exhibits, displaying a colorful diversity of life to be enjoyed and studied. Reefs also protect coastlines during violent storms. The reefs break up the surf, preventing waves from severely eroding the land. However, human activities can harm the fragile reefs. Boat anchors dragging across a reef can damage it. Divers can accidentally break off pieces of the reef. Even brushing against the reef can harm some of the coral animals. Because coral only grows a few millimeters a year, a reef cannot quickly recover.

Changes in water temperature and clarity also affect coral reefs. For example, if the water becomes too warm, the corals release the algae that live inside them. Cloudy water endangers the algae by reducing the amount of light that reaches them. If sediments produced by storms or human activities bury a reef, the algae in the living coral cannot survive. Without the algae, the coral animals do not grow well and eventually die.

Today many people understand the importance of coral reefs and try to protect them. Many reef areas have been designated as marine sanctuaries, which limits the amount of diving and other activity allowed near the reef. Scientists worldwide are also studying the effects of temperature change and pollution on the reefs to better protect them.

☑ ***Checkpoint*** *How can human activities impact a coral reef?*

Figure 11 A parrotfish delicately nibbles away at a coral reef in the Red Sea. Reefs provide a habitat for many fish and other marine organisms.

Using the Visuals: Figure 10

Encourage students to refer to this illustration as they review the stages of atoll development in the last paragraph on page 306. Then ask: **How do you think conditions in the lagoon might be different from conditions outside the reef or atoll?** *(The water in the lagoon is warmer because it is shallower; the lagoon is also protected from ocean waves and currents.)* **How might these differences affect the types of organisms that live in the lagoon?** *(Organisms that could not survive in the deep, dark, cold water of the ocean depths would be able to survive in a lagoon.)* **learning modality: logical/mathematical**

Real-Life Learning

The United States government has designated a number of sites as national marine sanctuaries (NMSs). These include Stellwagen Bank, Monitor, and Gray's Reef in the Atlantic Ocean; Florida Keys and Flower Garden Banks in the Gulf of Mexico; and Olympic Coast, Cordell Bank, Gulf of the Farallones, Monterey Bay, Channel Islands, Humpback Whale, and Fagatele Bay in the Pacific Ocean. Encourage interested students to choose and find out about one or more of these sanctuaries, especially their role in protecting marine environments. Invite students to share what they learn in a class bulletin board display on marine sanctuaries. **learning modality: verbal**

Program Resources

- **Interdisciplinary Explorations Series** "Where River Meets Sea," pp. 33–34

Answers to Self-Assessment

Caption Question

Figure 10 A fringing reef is the youngest.

☑ ***Checkpoint***

Any one: Boat anchors can drag across a reef. Divers may break off pieces accidentally or injure the coral animals by brushing against them. Human activities can make the water cloudy, reducing the amount of sunlight. Chemicals can pollute the water.

Ongoing Assessment

Writing Have each student write a paragraph explaining why coral reefs are fragile.

Students can save their paragraphs in their portfolios.

Conditions in the Open Ocean

Sharpen your Skills

Inferring

Time 10 minutes ACTIVITY
Tips Make sure students note the three major clues needed to solve the problem: (1) more friction is needed to stay afloat in warm water, (2) more streamlined shapes create less friction, and (3) copepod B is more streamlined than copepod A.
Expected Outcome Based on the text and illustration clues, students can infer that copepod A is found in warm, tropical waters and copepod B in cold, polar waters.
Extend Challenge students to devise a model to demonstrate this relationship between friction and water temperature. **learning modality: logical/ mathematical**

Building Inquiry Skills: Applying Concepts

Draw students' attention to the statement that if the water is cloudy, sunlight does not reach as deep. Ask: **Have you ever observed something like this?** *(Students may cite their personal experiences. If necessary, remind them of their observations in the Discover activity at the beginning of this section.)* **In the Discover, why couldn't you see the lid when it was deeper in the water?** *(Students may say that the flour particles blocked the view.)* Explain that when light rays enter clear water and strike a submerged object, they bounce back up and enter our eyes so we see the object. In the cloudy water, however, the light rays bounced off the flour particles and scattered in all directions, so we could not see the submerged lid when it got too deep. **learning modality: verbal**

Inferring

ACTIVITY

To keep from sinking, many plankton rely on the friction between their bodies and the surrounding water. More friction is needed to stay afloat in warm water than in denser cold water. One of the copepods below is found in tropical ocean waters, while the other is found near the poles. Which do you think is which? Explain your reasoning. (*Hint:* More streamlined shapes create less friction with their surroundings.)

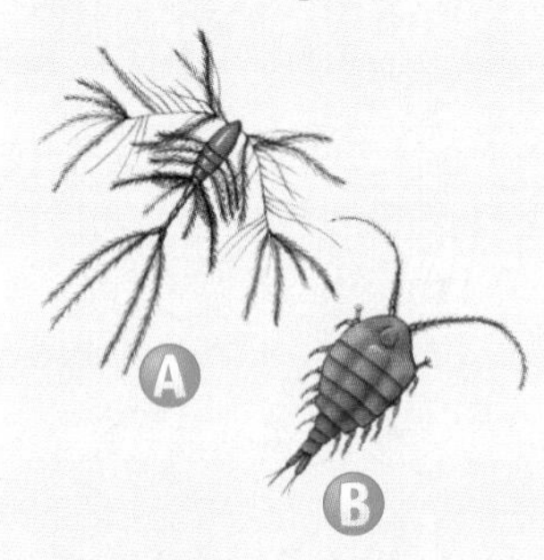

Conditions in the Open Ocean

The open ocean begins where the neritic zone ends, at the edge of the continental shelf. Diving into the open ocean is like descending a long staircase with a light only at the very top. Light from the sun only penetrates a short distance into the water, typically to a depth of less than 200 meters. If the water is cloudy with sediment, sunlight does not reach as deep. In clear tropical waters, on the other hand, some light may reach as deep as a few hundred meters.

The fact that only a small portion of the open ocean receives sunlight is one way it differs from the neritic zone. Another difference is the amount of dissolved nutrients in the water. While the neritic zone receives a constant supply of nutrients from shore, dissolved nutrients are less abundant in the open ocean. As a result, the open ocean zone supports fewer organisms.

The Surface Zone The surface zone extends as far as sunlight reaches below the surface. **The surface zone is the only part of the open ocean that receives enough sunlight to support the growth of algae.** These microscopic algae are the base of open-ocean food webs. Animal plankton that feed on algae include tiny crustaceans called copepods, shrimp-like krill, and the young of many ocean animals such as crabs, mollusks, and fishes.

Figure 13 on the facing page shows an Arctic food web. Each organism in this food web depends either directly or indirectly on the plankton. Throughout the ocean, plankton are a source of food for other organisms of all sizes. If you think of sharks as sharp-toothed, meat-eating hunters, you might be surprised to learn that the biggest sharks of all feed entirely on tiny plankton! Whale sharks, which can grow to more than 10 meters long, strain plankton from the water. Many whales feed only on plankton as well, including Earth's largest animal, the blue whale.

The Deep Zone When you explored the water column in Chapter 9, you observed that the ocean became darker and colder as you descended. Because of its harsh conditions, the deep ocean is often compared to a desert. Compared to other land and ocean environments, few organisms live in the deep zone. But unlike a desert baking under the bright sun, the deep ocean is cold, dark, and wet.

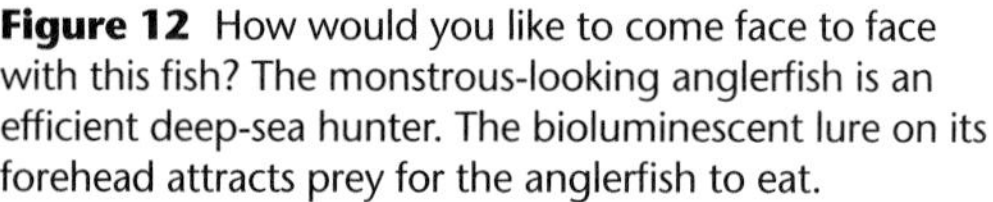

Figure 12 How would you like to come face to face with this fish? The monstrous-looking anglerfish is an efficient deep-sea hunter. The bioluminescent lure on its forehead attracts prey for the anglerfish to eat.

Background

Facts and Figures The deep zone represents more than 90 percent of the water column in most parts of the ocean. This zone is also called the *aphotic zone,* meaning "without light." Most deep-ocean species are dark in color and have few stripes or other markings. Many organisms in the deeper areas have only small, poorly developed eyes or may be completely blind.

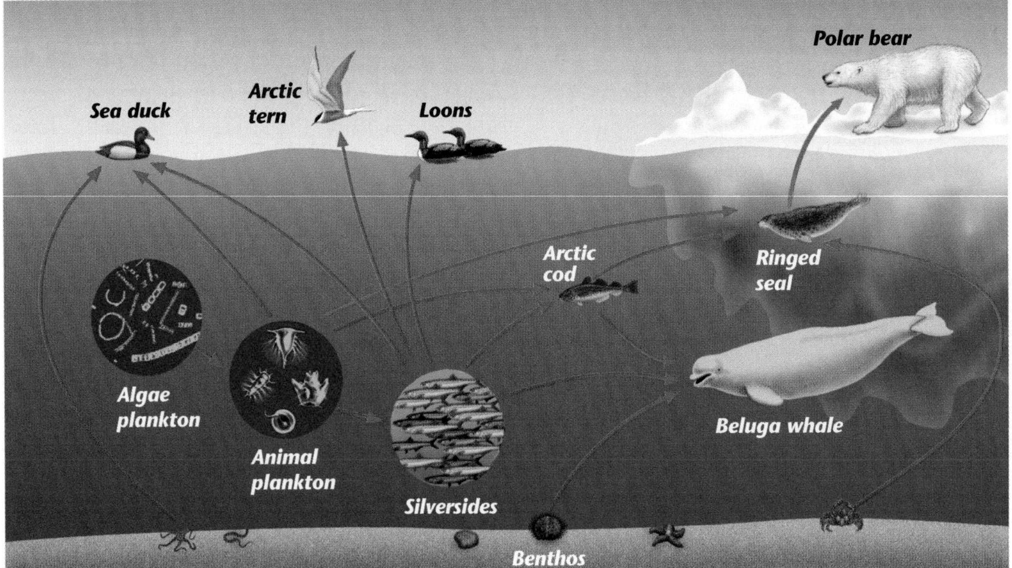

Figure 13 This marine food web includes typical organisms found in the Arctic Ocean. The arrows indicate what each organism eats. *Interpreting Diagrams Which organisms feed directly on the Arctic cod? Which organisms depend indirectly on the cod?*

Finding food in the darkness is a challenge. Many deep-sea fishes produce their own light. The production of light by living things is called **bioluminescence.** Some fishes use chemical reactions to produce their own light, like fireflies on land. Other fishes have colonies of bioluminescent bacteria living in pockets on their bodies. Still others have light-producing organs. The anglerfish, for example, has a light organ on its head. The fish lurks in the shadows below the pool of light. Shrimp and fishes that are attracted to the light become the anglerfish's prey.

Because the food supply in most of the deep ocean is much more limited than in shallower water, animals in this zone must be good hunters to survive. The gaping mouths of many deep-sea fishes are filled with fang-like teeth. Rows of sharp teeth stick out at angles, ensuring that any animal it bites cannot escape.

☑ *Checkpoint* *Why do very few organisms live in the deep zone?*

Hydrothermal Vents

As the submersible *Alvin* descended to a depth of 2,500 meters into the Galápagos Rift in the Pacific Ocean one day in 1977, the scientists aboard could hardly believe their eyes. Outside the submersible, the headlights revealed a bizarre scene. Clouds of black water billowed up from chimney-shaped structures on the ocean floor. Meter-long tubes with gaping, lipstick-red ends swayed in the water. White crabs scuttled over the rocks, crawling around clams as big as dinner plates.

Using the Visuals: Figure 13

Point out that in a diagram of a food web, each arrow points *from* the organism being eaten *to* the organism doing the eating. To make sure students understand this, ask: **Which organisms are eaten by the ringed seal?** *(animal plankton, cod, benthos)* **Which organisms eat the seal?** *(polar bear)* Next, have students recall the definition of *food web* from Section 2. *(The pattern of feeding relationships in a habitat)* Explain that a food web is made up of many separate food chains. A food chain is one series of feeding relationships—one organism being eaten by another, that organism in turn being eaten by another organism, and so on up the "chain." You may want to add that a food-chain diagram shows how energy is transferred in an ecosystem. Ask: **What is one food chain in this web?** *(Example: algae plankton → animal plankton → small fish → arctic cod → beluga whale)* Have students identify other chains in the web. **learning modality: visual**

Building Inquiry Skills: Making Models

ACTIVITY

Assign each student one of the organisms or groups (such as algae plankton or benthos) shown in Figure 13, making sure there are more lower-level organisms than top-level consumers. Have students stand and stretch colored yarn between themselves to indicate the feeding relationships shown in the diagram. For greater challenge, repeat the activity using another habitat, such as a tide pool, and let students figure out the feeding relationships on their own. **learning modality: kinesthetic**

Media and Technology

 **Transparencies** "An Arctic Food Web," Transparency 35

Answers to Self-Assessment

Caption Question

Figure 13 The beluga whale and seal feed directly on the cod. The polar bear depends indirectly on the cod because it eats seals.

☑ *Checkpoint*

Conditions in the deep zone are harsh, with very cold water and no light. Food supplies are very limited.

Ongoing Assessment

Organizing Information Have each student create a two-column table to compare and contrast the characteristics of the surface zone and deep zone.  Students can save their tables in their portfolios.

Hydrothermal Vents

Including All Students

Tell students that hydrothermal vents were first discovered in the late 1970s. Ask: **Why do you think the vents were not discovered before then?** *(Scientists did not have the technology for diving to the deepest parts of the ocean floor.)* If students have difficulty making this association, have them review Science & History on pages 292–293. **learning modality: logical/mathematical**

3 Assess

Section 3 Review Answers

1. Shallow water, sunlight, steady supply of nutrients
2. The depth to which sunlight penetrates
3. The heated water coming from the vent carries gases and minerals from Earth's interior.
4. The light that the fish produce attracts prey animals in the darkness.
5. Eroded soil could wash into the ocean and bury the reef or make the water cloudy. Sunlight would not reach the algae living in the coral, and the algae and coral animals would die.

CHAPTER PROJECT

Check Your Progress

At this point, each group should have completed its plan for the habitat model and chosen the materials to use. Review each group's design to make sure the physical features and organisms to be included are appropriate for that habitat. Encourage each student to draw a sketch of the organism he or she has chosen to model. As students build their models, meet with them regularly to discuss their progress and any problems they may be encountering.

Performance Assessment

Oral Presentation Have each student describe the major characteristics of the neritic zone, surface zone, or deep zone.

Figure 14 Giant tube worms cluster around a hydrothermal vent on the deep ocean floor.

The scientists were surprised not only by the strange appearance of these deep-sea creatures, but also by the fact that they were so abundant. In the deepest parts of the ocean, organisms tend to be very small and slow-moving because food is so rare. The number, size, and variety of organisms were unusually large for such a deep part of the ocean. What could these organisms find to eat so far from sunlight?

The strange community the scientists in *Alvin* observed was located around a hydrothermal vent. A **hydrothermal vent** is an area where ocean water sinks through cracks in the ocean floor, is heated by the underlying magma, and rises again through the cracks. These vents are located along ocean ridges, where the plates are moving apart and new ocean floor is forming.

The heated water coming from a vent carries gases and minerals from Earth's interior. **The chemical nutrients in the heated water support the unique group of organisms that are found around hydrothermal vents.** Bacteria feed directly on the chemical nutrients that are spewed out of the vents. Like the algae in the surface zone that use sunlight to produce food, these bacteria use the chemicals to produce food. They form the base of the food web at a hydrothermal vent.

Other organisms, like the giant clams, feed on the bacteria. The red-tipped tube worms are supplied with food by bacteria living within their tissues. Meanwhile, the scuttling crabs feed on the remains of the other inhabitants in their unusual habitat.

Section 3 Review

1. Describe the physical conditions in the neritic zone.
2. What factor limits where algae are found in the open ocean?
3. What is the source of nutrients for organisms around a hydrothermal vent?
4. Explain how bioluminescence is important to some fish that live in the deep ocean.
5. **Thinking Critically Relating Cause and Effect** When forests on a tropical island are cut down, the soil is more easily eroded. Explain how this could affect a coral reef near the island.

CHAPTER PROJECT

Check Your Progress

By now you should have selected an organism to model. Research your organism to determine its size and other physical characteristics. How does the organism survive in its marine habitat? Check your plan for constructing the organism with your teacher. Your group should also begin building your model habitat. Make sure you have collected all the necessary materials before you begin building.

Program Resources

- **Unit 3 Resources** 10-3 Review and Reinforce; 10-3 Enrich

Resources From the Ocean

DISCOVER — ACTIVITY

Is It From the Ocean?

1. Your teacher will give you some labels from common household products. Read the ingredient information on each label.
2. Divide the products into two piles—those you think include substances that come from the ocean and those that do not.

Think It Over

Classifying For each product that you classified as coming from the ocean, name the item from the ocean that is used to produce it. In what ocean zone is it found?

When European explorers began sailing to North America, they were astounded by the huge number of codfish that lived off its eastern coast. One traveler reported that this area was so "swarming with fish that they could be taken not only with a net but in baskets let down and weighted with a stone." Others reported sailing through schools of cod so thick they slowed the boats down!

This cod fishery stretched from Newfoundland to a hook of land appropriately named Cape Cod. For more than 400 years, the seemingly endless supply of "King Cod" supported a thriving fishing industry. But beginning in the early 1900s, fishing crews had to work harder to catch the same amount of cod. As the fishing grew more difficult each year, it became clear that the cod were disappearing. With the price of cod rising, there was more competition to catch the fewer fish available. In 1992, the Canadian government had to declare the fishery closed.

No one knows for sure how long it will take the cod population to fully recover. Scientists are studying cod and other fisheries to learn how to preserve them for future generations.

GUIDE FOR READING

- How does the supply of fish in a fishery change from year to year?
- Who controls and protects ocean resources?

Reading Tip **Before you read, rewrite the headings in the section as how, why, or what questions. As you read, look for answers to those questions.**

Living Resources

Cod are just one example of a living resource from the ocean. How many other kinds of seafood

Figure 15 Big catches of cod like this one from Georges Bank, off the New England coast, have become less common since the early 1900s.

READING STRATEGIES

Reading Tip Tell students they should use the five main headings from the section. Student questions may include "What are some living resources from the ocean?" and "Where in the ocean are mineral resources found?" At the conclusion of the section, give students an opportunity to share their questions and answers by reading them aloud.

Program Resources

- **Unit 3 Resources** 10-4 Lesson Plan; 10-4 Section Summary
- **Guided Reading and Study Workbook** Section 10-4

Resources From the Ocean

Objectives

After completing the lesson, students will be able to

- explain how the supply of fish in a fishery changes from year to year and list sources of water pollution;
- identify the ocean's living and nonliving resources and how they can be protected.

Key Terms aquaculture, nodules

1 Engage/Explore

Activating Prior Knowledge

Ask: **What kinds of foods do people obtain from the ocean?** *(Students should name a variety of fishes, shellfish, and other marine organisms.)* **Besides food, what other ocean resources do people use?** *(Students may have difficulty naming other resources. Accept all responses without comment.)*

DISCOVER

Skills Focus classifying
Materials *labels from common household products, including thickeners used in cooking, foods, abrasives, polishes, shampoos, and spice mixes containing sea salt*
Time 15 minutes
Tips If students seem confused about which substances come from the ocean, suggest that they consider both the living and nonliving things that can be found in the ocean.
Expected Outcome Students should be able to identify some substances that come from the ocean, especially seafoods and sea salt. They may not be able to identify other substances from the ocean at this time, such as stabilizers made from algae and abrasives made from diatoms.
Think It Over Answers will vary depending on the labels you use. Sample answers of products containing ocean resources: clam chowder—clams, intertidal zone; metal polish—diatoms, neritic and open-ocean zones; chocolate milk—kelp, neritic zone.

2 Facilitate

Living Resources

Real-Life Learning

Suggest that students visit a fish market or the seafood section of a super-market at a time when the store is not busy. Tell them to list the names of all the fish and other food items on display. Also have them interview the manager or clerk to obtain the answers to these questions: **Which of the foods are obtained from the ocean? From what source(s) does the store buy the items? What country or region is each item from originally? Does the store buy each item fresh, frozen, or dried? Are any items hard to obtain, and why?** Encourage students to add questions of their own. Provide an opportunity for students to report and compare their findings in class. **learning modality: verbal**

Using the Visuals: Figure 16

Have students review the map key and look for the locations of the various ocean resources. Then ask: **Where on this map is the cod fishing area you read about on the previous page?** *(Off the northeastern coast of North America)* **Besides fish, what other resources can be found in that area of the ocean?** *(mineral resources/nodule deposits, oil and natural gas)* **What other areas have both fisheries and deposits of oil and gas?** *(Off the coasts of Alaska and California, eastern and southeastern South America, western Africa, Great Britain, Southeast Asia, Indonesia, and western Australia, and in the Gulf of Mexico and the Mediterranean Sea)* **What problems might drilling for oil or gas in the same ocean area where fisheries operate cause?** *(Sample answers: Building and operating the drilling rigs could disturb the fish and frighten them away; oil spills could kill the fish.)* **learning modality: visual**

have you tasted: tuna, shrimp, flounder, lobster, clams, squid, oysters, seaweed, or mussels? These foods and the many others that come from the ocean make up about five percent of the world's total food supply.

Harvesting Fish Just six species make up the majority of fishes harvested for eating: herring, sardine, anchovy, cod, pollock, and mackerel. Locate the world's major fisheries in Figure 16. You can see that they are all located close to coasts. Nearly all fishes caught are harvested from coastal waters or areas of upwelling. These waters contain nutrients and plankton on which they feed.

If used wisely, fisheries naturally renew themselves each year. **New fish are born, replacing those that are caught, but only as long as the fishery is not overfished. Overfishing causes the supply of fish to decrease.** Overfishing has become a problem as better technology has enabled people to catch large numbers of fish very quickly. For example, some fishing fleets have electronic equipment that allows them to locate schools of fish precisely. They can be caught faster than they can reproduce. Once this occurs, it begins a cycle that leads to fewer and fewer fish each season. Eventually, the fishery may be depleted, like the cod fishery you read about earlier.

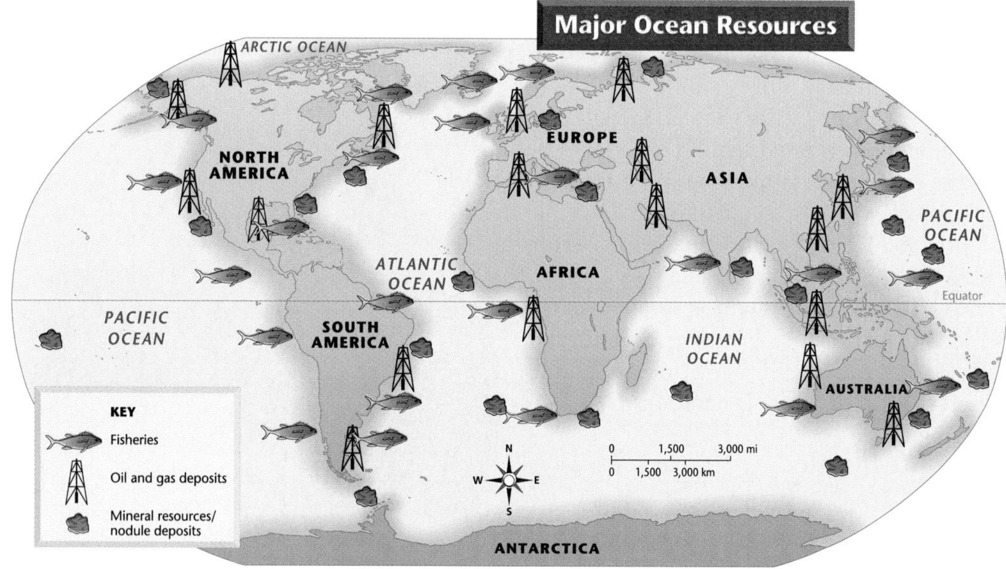

Figure 16 All over the world, the oceans are an important source of food, oil and gas, and minerals. *Interpreting Maps Where are Africa's major fisheries located?*

Background

Facts and Figures Today most of the world's commercial fish harvest is caught with huge nets, of which there are three main types. Seines are used to surround schools of fish. One end of a seine is attached to a large vessel, and the other end is pulled by a small, high-powered boat. After the school is surrounded, the bottom of the net is pulled tight, trapping the fish. Trawls are funnel-shaped nets with a large, open mouth and a small, closed tail. Fish are caught as the trawl is pulled through the water. Gill nets are long, rectangular nets used to form a wall of webbing that entangles fish when they swim into it. A fourth type of net, called a drift net, is about 5.5 km long and used mainly in open waters. Its use is controversial because whales, dolphins, marine birds, sea turtles, and other animals are also sometimes caught.

Aquaculture As fish stocks become depleted, **aquaculture,** the farming of saltwater and freshwater organisms, is likely to become more common. *INTEGRATING TECHNOLOGY* Aquaculture has been practiced in some Asian countries for centuries. This process involves creating an environment for the organisms and controlling nutrient levels, water temperature, light, and other factors to help them thrive. Oysters, abalone, and shrimp have successfully been farmed in artificial saltwater ponds and protected bays. Even landlocked regions can produce seafood using aquaculture. For example, salmon are now being raised in Nebraska fields that once were cattle ranches.

Other Ocean Products People harvest ocean organisms for many purposes besides food. For example, algae is an ingredient in many household products. Its gelatin-like texture makes it an ideal base for detergents, shampoos, cosmetics, paints, and even ice cream! Sediments containing the hard fragments of diatoms are used for abrasives and polishes. Many researchers believe that other marine organisms may be important sources of chemicals for medicines in the future.

Checkpoint How are fisheries naturally renewed each year?

Mineral Resources

In addition to living organisms, the ocean contains valuable nonliving resources. Some of these are found within ocean water itself. Chapter 8 described how fresh water can be extracted from ocean water in the process of desalination. Desalination provides fresh water for many dry areas and islands. When the fresh water is removed from ocean water, the salts that are left behind are also a valuable resource. Over half of the world's supply of magnesium, a strong, light metal, is obtained from seawater in this way.

A second source of nonliving resources is the ocean floor. From the layer of sediments covering the continental shelves, gravel and sand are mined for use in building construction. In some areas of the world diamonds and gold are mined from sand deposits. Metals such as manganese also accumulate on the ocean floor. The metals concentrate around pieces of shell, forming black lumps called **nodules** (NAHJ oolz). Because they sometimes occur in waters as deep as 5,000 meters, recovering the nodules is a difficult process. The technology to gather them is still being developed.

Not all nations have agreed on who owns the rights to nodules and other resources on the deep ocean floor. Some feel the

Seaweed Candy

Make this Asian dessert to discover one way to eat algae. Remember to prepare food only in a non-science classroom. Be sure to get permission before using a stove.

2 blocks of agar (one 0.5-ounce package)
1 cup sugar
4 cups guava juice or other fruit juice
food coloring

1. Rinse the agar, a substance obtained from algae.
2. Break agar into cubes and place them in a saucepan.
3. Put on your goggles. Add the sugar and juice to the pan. Bring the mixture to a boil. Turn down the heat and cook, stirring, until the agar dissolves.
4. Remove pan from heat and stir in a few drops of food coloring. Pour the mixture into a shallow pan. Let cool.
5. Refrigerate candy until firm.
6. Cut into blocks and serve.

Inferring What purpose does the agar serve in this recipe? What purposes do the sugar and juice serve?

Integrating Technology

Explain that oysters are farmed not only for food but for the pearls they produce. Other farmed organisms include mussels, clams, fish, and algae. Encourage interested students to find out more about marine aquaculture and report to the class. **learning modality: verbal**

TRY THIS

Skills Focus inferring
Materials *2 blocks of agar, 1 cup sugar, 4 cups guava juice or other fruit juice, food coloring, water, saucepan, shallow pan, knife*
Time 20 minutes to prepare, several hours to set, 5 minutes to serve
Safety Supervise students closely when they work with the heated mixture. Make sure they wear goggles and mitts. Be careful when slicing the candy into blocks. *CAUTION: Check for food allergies before allowing students to taste the candy.*
Expected Outcome The mixture will set in a gelatinlike consistency.
Answers The agar binds the ingredients together in a smooth gel. The sugar and juice simply add flavor.
Extend Let students make the candy without agar to see what happens.

Mineral Resources

Building Inquiry Skills: Inferring

Explain that nodules were first found by HMS *Challenger.* During the time of HMS *Challenger,* technology did not exist to recover the nodules on a commercial scale. Today, deep-sea robots could be used to collect them. Ask: **Why do you think no companies are recovering the ocean nodules now?** (*Students may infer that existing technology is too expensive or inefficient to recover the nodules profitably.*) **learning modality: logical/mathematical**

Answers to Self-Assessment

Caption Question

Figure 16 Africa's major fisheries are located off its west and southwest coasts.

Checkpoint

New fish are born, replacing the fish that are caught.

Ongoing Assessment

Writing Have each student write a paragraph explaining how overfishing can occur and what its effects are.

Fuels From the Ocean Floor

Sharpen your Skills

Observing

Time 10 minutes

Expected Outcome All oil and gas deposits and all but one fishery (east of the Philippines) are located close to land, whereas mineral deposits are located throughout the ocean.

Extend Ask students: **Why do you think the map does not show any oil and gas deposits in the deepest parts of the ocean?** *(They tend to form on the continental shelves. Also, deposits on the deep-ocean floor may be too deep to extract with current technology.)* **learning modality: visual**

Building Inquiry Skills: Comparing and Contrasting

Tell students that when oil and gas form in rock layers, they seep through layers of permeable rock until they are trapped by a layer of impermeable rock, where they collect to form a reservoir. Ask: **What does this remind you of?** *(Underground water collecting in an aquifer; see Chapter 7, Section 3.)* **learning modality: logical/mathematical**

Ocean Pollution

Inquiry Challenge

Time 15–20 minutes for set-up, several days for follow-up observations

Challenge small groups of students to design an experiment that tests the effects of reduced salinity on brine shrimp. Let each group start with a "normal" culture that you have prepared. *(Possible experiment: Distribute the "normal" culture equally among small, clear vials. Add varying amounts of plain water to all but one vial, keeping that as the control. The more difficult challenge is to devise a method for counting the living brine shrimp in each vial; students may decide to use a sampling method.)* **cooperative learning**

Figure 17 Lit up like a city at night, this Norwegian oil-drilling platform rises above the icy waters of the North Sea. Hundreds of people may live and work aboard such an oil rig.

nations who find and recover the minerals should own them. Others feel that this is unfair to nations that cannot yet afford the technology to obtain a share of these resources.

Fuels From the Ocean Floor

Another type of nonliving resource forms from the remains of dead marine organisms. These remains sink to the bottom of the ocean, where they are buried by sediments. As more sediments accumulate, the buried remains decompose. Over hundreds of thousands of years, the heat and pressure from the overlying layers gradually transform the remains into oil and natural gas.

As you know, many organisms live in the part of the ocean above the continental shelf. The thick sediments on the continental shelves bury the remains of living things. As a result, the richest deposits of oil and gas are often located on the continental shelves.

Oil rigs like the one in Figure 17 drill the rocky ocean floor as much as 300 meters below the surface. Imagine trying to dig a hole in the concrete bottom of a swimming pool, while standing on a raft floating on the surface of the water. You can see why drilling the ocean floor is very difficult! Ocean drilling is made even harder by strong currents, winds, and violent storms.

Sharpen your Skills

Observing ACTIVITY

Refer back to the map of ocean resources in Figure 16. Which resources are located close to land? Which are located throughout the ocean? Can you suggest an explanation for any patterns you observe?

✓ ***Checkpoint*** *What is the source of the oil and gas deposits on the ocean floor?*

Ocean Pollution

It was once thought that the ocean was so vast that people could not damage it by throwing wastes into it. This is partially true—the ocean is a self-cleaning system that can absorb some wastes without permanent damage. But dumping large amounts of wastes into the ocean threatens many marine organisms.

Background

Facts and Figures About 80 percent of ocean pollution comes from the land, while the remaining 20 percent occurs at sea. In recent years international agreements have helped to reduce dumping by ships at sea.

The Ocean Dumping Ban Act of 1988 prohibited ocean dumping of both sewage sludge and industrial waste by coastal cities in the United States.

Recall that water pollution is the addition of any substance that has a negative effect on the living things that depend on the water. Most ocean pollution comes from the land. Although some is the result of natural occurrences, most pollution is related to human activities.

Natural Sources Some pollution is the result of weather. For example, heavy rains wash fresh water into estuaries and out into the water offshore. This surge of fresh water pollutes the ocean by lowering its salinity. A sudden change in salinity may kill ocean animals that are unable to adjust to it.

Human Sources Pollutants related to human activities include sewage, chemicals, and trash dumped into coastal waters. Chemicals that run off fields and roads often end up in the ocean. These substances can harm ocean organisms directly. The pollutants can also build up in their bodies and poison other animals, including people, that feed on them. Trash can cause serious problems, too. Seals, otters, and other marine mammals that need to breathe air can get tangled in old fishing lines or nets and drown. Other animals are harmed when they swallow plastic bags that block their stomachs.

Oil Spills One major threat to ocean life is oil pollution. When an oil tanker or drilling platform is damaged, oil leaks into the surrounding ocean. Oil is harmful to many organisms. It coats the bodies of marine mammals and birds. This destroys their natural insulation and affects their ability to float. The oil is also harmful to animals that swallow it.

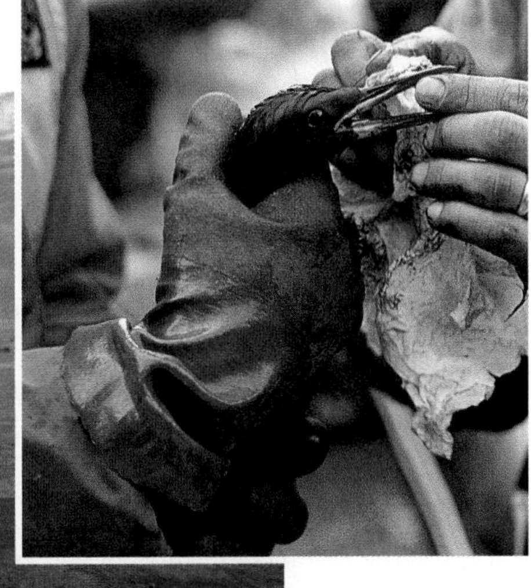

Figure 18 Removing oil from a beach is a difficult, messy chore. This cleanup worker is using absorbent mops to remove oil from the sand. In the closeup, two more workers try to clean oil from a bird's beak and feathers. *Inferring What might have caused this oil pollution?*

Building Inquiry Skills: Applying Concepts

Have students refer back to the Arctic food-web diagram in Figure 13. Then pose the following problem: **Suppose that an oil spill killed many of the plankton in an area of the Arctic Ocean. What effect would this have on the food web in that area?** (*The small fish, which depend entirely on plankton, would die. Without animal plankton and small fish, Arctic cod would die. Arctic terns, which feed on small fish, would not survive. Animals that depend on the cod and small fish—beluga whales and loons—would die if they did not move to another area. Only the seals and sea ducks, which eat benthic invertebrates as well as fish, might survive in the area—but only if there were enough invertebrates to sustain their populations. If the seals did not survive in the area, the polar bears would also have to move to another area.*) **learning modality: logical/mathematical**

Including All Students

Ask students: **What kinds of chemicals might run off fields and roads into coastal waters?** *(Fertilizers, pesticides, and weed killers from fields; salt and oil from roads)* If students have read Chapter 8, ask: **Are these pollutants from point sources or nonpoint sources? Explain.** *(Nonpoint sources, because you cannot pinpoint their origin)* Challenge students to make a flowchart to show how these substances get to the ocean. **learning modality: logical/mathematical**

Program Resources

- **Interdisciplinary Explorations Series** "Where River Meets Sea," pp. 35–42

Answers to Self-Assessment

☑ Checkpoint

The oil and gas deposits were formed from the remains of living organisms.

Caption Question

Figure 18 It probably was spilled by an oil tanker or drilling platform that was damaged.

Ongoing Assessment

Concept Mapping Have each student draw a concept map showing the two major forms of ocean pollution (natural and human), their sources, and examples of the damage they cause.

Protecting Earth's Oceans

Building Inquiry Skills: Communicating

Have students imagine they are delegates to the United Nations, and they are meeting to discuss a major mineral deposit recently discovered in the mid-Atlantic Ocean. Have student teams represent the nation that discovered the deposit, the nation with the technology to mine it, and the closest nations to the deposit. With you serving as moderator, let students debate the issue of who owns the deposit and has the right to mine it. **learning modality: verbal**

3 Assess

Section 4 Review Answers

1. The supply of fish decreases because more fish are harvested than can be naturally replaced.
2. The world ocean is a continuous body of water with no boundaries, so no one nation owns it. All nations have an interest in it.
3. Any one: Fresh water from desalination, magnesium, gravel, sand, shells, diamonds, gold, manganese and other metals, oil, natural gas; answers regarding location and use will vary depending on which resource is chosen.
4. Accept either viewpoint so long as students support it with specific details and reasonable arguments.

Science at Home

ACTIVITY

Materials *rubber band*
Tips Let students do the activity themselves in class before they try it with a family member at home. Give students an opportunity to present their responses to the question in a class discussion.

Performance Assessment

Writing Have each student describe one way that a nation could prevent overfishing in its waters.

Figure 19 Flags fly outside the United Nations headquarters in New York City. The United Nations develops policies on the use of the oceans by countries. *Applying Concepts Why can't each nation make its own laws regarding ocean resources?*

Interestingly, there is a natural cleaning process that slowly takes place after oil spills. Certain bacteria that live in the ocean feed on the oil and multiply. It takes many years, but eventually an oil-covered beach can become clean again. This has happened even in the portions of the Prince William Sound in Alaska that were blanketed with oil from the 1989 wreck of the oil tanker *Exxon Valdez.*

Protecting Earth's Oceans

Who owns the ocean and its resources? Who has the responsibility of protecting them? These are questions that nations have been struggling to answer for hundreds of years. **Because the world ocean is a continuous body of water that has no boundaries, it is difficult to determine who, if anyone, should control portions of it. Nations must cooperate to manage and protect the oceans.**

The United Nations has established different boundaries in the oceans. According to one treaty, a nation now controls the first 22 kilometers out from its coasts. The nation also controls resources in the waters or on the continental shelf within 370 kilometers of shore. This treaty leaves approximately half of the ocean's surface waters as "high seas," owned by no nation. Ownership of the ocean floor beneath the high seas is still under debate.

Other international efforts have resulted in cooperation aimed at reducing ocean pollution. Examples include the establishment of marine refuges and regulations for building safer oil tankers.

Section 4 Review

1. How can overfishing affect a fishery?
2. Explain why international cooperation is necessary to solve many problems related to ocean resources.
3. Name a nonliving resource found in the ocean. Where is it located? How is it obtained and used?
4. **Thinking Critically Making Judgments** Should mineral resources on the ocean floor belong to whoever finds them, or to the closest nation? Consider each position and write a short paragraph stating your opinion.

Science at Home

Ocean Escape Have a family member hook one end of a rubber band around his or her wrist. Stretch the rubber band across the back of the hand and hook the free end over three fingers as shown. Now ask the person to try to remove the rubber band without using the other hand. Explain that this shows how difficult it is for seals or dolphins to free themselves from a plastic beverage ring or piece of net. Can you propose any ways to reduce this threat to marine mammals?

316

Answers to Self-Assessment

Caption Question

Figure 19 Different nations' laws might conflict. No nation owns the "high seas."

Program Resources

- **Unit 3 Resources** 10-4 Review and Reinforce; 10-4 Enrich

SCIENCE AND SOCIETY

Shrimp Farms—At What Cost to the Environment?

About one quarter of the world's shrimp are raised on shrimp farms. Many shrimp farms are created by clearing trees from mangrove forests and digging shallow, fenced-in ponds. Farmers then fill the ponds with ocean water and shrimp larvae. After about six months, when the shrimp are big enough to sell, the farmers drain the pond water back into the ocean.

To grow healthy shrimp, farmers often add fertilizers, medicines, and pesticides to the ponds. When the pond water is released to the ocean, these chemicals can harm other animals. The United Nations has estimated that 25 percent of the world's mangrove forests have been destroyed as a result of shrimp farming. As awareness of the environmental impact of shrimp farms has grown, the industry has come under attack.

▲ Shrimp farmer in Malaysia

The Issues

How Important Is Shrimp Farming? For many people in the world, shrimp is more than luxury food: It is a staple of their diet and their main source of animal protein. The demand for shrimp currently is greater than the natural supply in Earth's oceans. To meet the demand, many countries, including the United States, have turned to shrimp farming. Shrimp farms provide needed food and jobs that some people believe are worth a certain amount of damage to the environment. They feel it is not possible to have shrimp farms that are both highly productive and environmentally safe.

Can the Pollution Be Reduced? Shrimp farmers are exploring ways to reduce the impact of their farms on the coastal environment. Better pond construction can help stop chemicals from leaking into the surrounding waters. Some governments recognize the importance of mangrove forests in providing a habitat for many species and in protecting the shoreline. These governments have passed laws regulating where shrimp farms may be built. Farmers must investigate the impact their ponds will have on nearby mangrove forests and get approval before choosing a location. These methods of reducing environmental damage, however, are expensive and time-consuming for the shrimp farmers.

Should Farmers Use Alternative Methods? In some parts of Asia, a less destructive method of shrimp farming has been practiced for centuries. Raising shrimp in ditches dug around clusters of mangroves provides the young shrimp with a natural nutrient supply that includes debris from the trees. A gate keeps the shrimp from escaping into the ocean and also allows the motion of the tides to replenish the water in the ditches. The disadvantage of this method is that it is much less profitable than the constructed shrimp ponds. Many shrimp farmers could not afford to switch to this method. If they did, the price of shrimp worldwide would rise.

You Decide

1. Identify the Problem

In your own words, summarize the problem facing shrimp farmers.

2. Analyze the Options

Make a list of the solutions mentioned. List the advantages and drawbacks of each. Who would benefit from each plan? Who might suffer?

3. Find a Solution

Write a brochure or pamphlet for shrimp farmers that states your proposed solution to their problem. After you have written the text, illustrate your brochure.

You Decide

- Students' responses to Identify the Problem and Analyze the Options should be based on the concepts and issues presented in the text. In response to Find a Solution, however, students may suggest solutions based on their small-group discussions.
- Students can share their solutions by displaying the brochures or pamphlets on a bulletin board.

SCIENCE AND SOCIETY

Shrimp Farms—At What Cost to the Environment?

Purpose

Identify ways in which shrimp farming affects the environment, and propose a solution that addresses shrimp farmers' needs as well as environmental concerns.

Role-Play

Time 80–90 minutes

- After students have read the introductory text and the three paragraphs under The Issues, ask: **If you were a shrimp farmer who used the usual farming methods, would you want to change your methods? Why or why not?** Let students discuss this question freely until opposing viewpoints are clear.
- Divide the class into small groups, with each group member representing a different viewpoint—for example, a shrimp farmer who does not want to change his or her methods, another farmer who thinks new methods should be tried, an owner of a seafood company that sells shrimp, and a science advisor or government official who wants to protect the mangrove forests. Tell students that each group's goal is to arrive at an *agreement* on how shrimp farming should be done.

Extend Students could survey a local supermarket to see whether fresh, frozen, and/or canned shrimp are available and, if so, how much they cost. Suggest that students talk with the seafood department's manager or clerk to find out whether any fresh shrimp are obtained from shrimp farms in this country or overseas. Students can also check the labels on canned or frozen shrimp to find the country of origin.

Real-World Lab

You and Your Environment

Cleaning Up an Oil Spill

Preparing for Inquiry

Key Concept Oil is difficult to remove from water, beaches, and organisms.

Skills Objectives Students will be able to
- model oil-spill cleanup using a variety of materials;
- form operational definitions of what clean water is and what a clean beach is.

Time 40 minutes

Advance Planning Obtain a feather for each group. Pillow feathers may be used if you cannot obtain larger ones.

Guiding Inquiry

Invitation Give each group a small paper cup containing a little dark molasses. Tell students that molasses is very similar in consistency to crude oil—the type of oil usually carried by tankers. Encourage students to examine the molasses by tilting the cup to see how it coats the sides and by dipping an index finger into it and rubbing it against their thumb to feel its consistency.

Introducing the Procedure
Have students read the newspaper article at the top of the page. Ask: **If you were one of the volunteers, what things would you expect to help clean?** *(Birds, sea otters, and any other animals coated with oil; rocks, sand, gravel, and plants on the beach)* **What kinds of cleanup materials do you think you'd use?** *(Accept all reasonable suggestions.)*

Troubleshooting the Experiment
- If necessary, remind students to record their observations in steps 5 and 6.
- Tell students to put any oil they recover (Step 6) in the clean paper cup.

Real-World Lab

You and Your Environment

CLEANING UP AN OIL SPILL

Oil Spill in Bay

An oil tanker hit a reef yesterday, spilling thousands of barrels of crude oil into the water. Cleanup efforts will begin today. Workers must race against time to save birds and sea otters. With stormy weather forecasted, however, scientists expect considerable damage. Volunteers are needed to help clean up.

Imagine that you are a volunteer helping to clean up an oil spill. In this activity, you will use a variety of materials to remove as much oil as possible from the water and to keep oil from reaching the beach. You will also see how oil affects animals that are exposed to a spill.

Problem

How can an oil spill be cleaned up?

Skills Focus

making models, forming operational definitions

Materials

water	shallow pan	vegetable oil
feather	paper cup	plastic dropper
paper towels	cotton balls	wooden sticks
marking pen	graduated cylinder, 100 mL	

Procedure 

1. Place a pan on a table or desk covered with newspaper. Label one end of the pan "Beach" and the other end "Open Ocean."
2. Pour water into the pan to a depth of 2 cm.
3. Gently pour 20 mL of vegetable oil into the center of the pan. Record your observations.
4. Dip a feather and your finger into the oil. Observe how each is affected by the oil.
5. Try to wipe oil off the feather and your finger using paper towels. Record whether any oil is left on the feather or your skin.
6. Now try to clean up the spill. Record your observations with each step. First, using the wooden sticks, try to keep the oil from reaching the "beach." Next, gently blow across the surface of the water from the "open ocean" side to simulate wind and waves. Then use the cotton balls, paper towels, and dropper to recover as much of the oil as possible.
7. When you are finished, dispose of the oil and used items in the paper cup. Wash your hands.

Analyze and Conclude

1. How successful were you in cleaning up the oil? Is the water as clean as it was at the start?
2. How well were you able to keep the oil from reaching the beach? Describe how useful the different materials were in cleaning up the oil.
3. Describe what happened when you cleaned the feather and your finger. What might happen to fish, birds, and other animals if they were coated with oil as a result of an oil spill?
4. Predict how storms with strong winds and waves would affect the cleanup of an oil spill.
5. **Apply** Look at the used cleanup materials in the paper cup. What additional problems for cleanup crews does this suggest?

Getting Involved

One way to reduce the threat of oil spills is to transport less oil across the oceans. To make that possible, people would need to use less oil in their daily lives. Oil is used to heat homes, to produce gasoline, and to make products such as plastics and textiles. List at least three ways to reduce the amount of oil you and your family use.

318

Safety

Students should wear safety goggles and lab aprons during this lab to protect their eyes and clothing. At the conclusion of the lab, make sure students dispose of all oil and cleanup materials in an appropriate container and wash their hands thoroughly. Review the safety guidelines in Appendix A.

Program Resources

- **Unit 3 Resources** Chapter 10 Real-World Lab blackline masters

Media and Technology

 **Lab Activity Videotapes** Grade 6, Tape 2

CHAPTER 10 STUDY GUIDE

Exploring the Ocean

Key Ideas

- Technology such as sonar enables scientists to study the deep ocean floor despite the darkness, cold, and extreme pressure there.
- The ocean floor has features similar to those found on the continents, including plains, mountain ranges, volcanoes, and trenches.

Key Terms

sonar, seamount, trench, continental shelf, abyssal plain, continental slope, mid-ocean ridge

Life at the Ocean's Edge

Integrating Life Science

Key Ideas

- Physical factors that affect marine organisms include salinity, water temperature, light, dissolved gases, nutrients, and wave action.
- Organisms in the rocky intertidal zone must be able to tolerate the pounding of the waves, as well as being both underwater and exposed to the air for long periods of time.
- Coastal wetlands include salt marshes and mangrove forests.

Key Terms

plankton, food web, brackish, nekton, intertidal zone, benthos, estuary

The Neritic Zone and Open Ocean

Integrating Life Science

Key Ideas

- The neritic zone receives sunlight and nutrients washed from the land. Habitats in this zone include kelp forests and coral reefs.
- The thin layer of sunlit water at the surface is the only part of the open ocean that can support algae, which need the sunlight to produce food. Other marine organisms depend on the food made by algae.
- The chemical nutrients in the hot water around a hydrothermal vent support the organisms that live around the vent.

Key Terms

neritic zone, atoll, open-ocean zone, bioluminescence, holdfast, hydrothermal vent

Resources From the Ocean

Key Ideas

- If used wisely, fisheries are a renewable resource. New fish will replace those that are caught, but only if overfishing does not reduce the population too severely.
- Nonliving resources from the ocean include dissolved substances in seawater and minerals and fuels from the ocean floor.

Key Terms

aquaculture, nodules

Organizing Information

Compare/Contrast Table Make a table about ocean habitats on a separate sheet of paper. Include rows for the following habitats: tide pool, coral reef, surface zone, and hydrothermal vent. For each habitat, fill in the ocean zone where it is found, the conditions (such as sunlight, pressure, and temperature) that exist there, and the types of organisms typically found there. (See the Skills Handbook for more on compare/contrast tables.)

Expected Outcome

Students will be unable to clean all the oil from their fingers and the feather and will be able to recover only a small amount of the oil floating on the water. Remind students that crude oil is much thicker and stickier than cooking oil.

Analyze and Conclude

1. Few, if any, students will be completely successful in cleaning up the oil. An observable film of oil will remain.
2. Students' success in keeping the oil from reaching the beach will vary. The wooden sticks will create barriers to prevent some oil from washing onto the beach. The paper towels and cotton balls will soak up some, but not all of the oil. The dropper will remove some oil but will also suction up water.
3. A light film of oil remains on the finger and feather. Heavily coated animals cannot survive. The insulation that fur and feathers provide is destroyed by the oil coating. Heavily coated birds cannot fly.
4. Winds and waves would wash the oily water onto the beach and would scatter it more widely on the water.
5. Cleanup materials are coated or saturated with oil and have to be disposed of in a way that they will not create more pollution.

Extending the Inquiry

Getting Involved Make sure students understand that they should not consider *vegetable* oil—the type of oil they used in this lab. Suggest that students first determine various uses of petroleum (fuel oil) by their families, then look for ways to reduce uses—for example, turning down the thermostat to use less heating oil and car-pooling to use less gasoline.

Organizing Information

Compare/Contrast Table

See table on the bottom left.

Habitat	Zone	Conditions	Organisms
Tide pool	Intertidal	Varying salinity, exposure, temperature, rough wave action	Barnacles, mussels, sea stars, sea urchins, sea anoemones
Coral reef	Neritic	Shallow water, warm temperatures, sunlight, steady stream of nutrients, may have upwelling currents	Coral, fishes, shrimp, eels
Surface zone	Open ocean	Receives sunlight, dissolved nutrients less abundant than in neritic zone	Microscopic algae, copepods, krill, young of many ocean animals, jellyfish
Hydrothermal vent	Deep	High pressure, dark, warm	Crabs, clams, tubeworms, bacteria

Reviewing Content

Multiple Choice

1. c **2.** c **3.** d **4.** d **5.** b

True or False

6. Nekton **7.** intertidal **8.** true **9.** atoll **10.** true

Checking Concepts

11. Students may cite methods used by the HMS *Challenger* (pp. 290–293) or methods described in the text and the Science & History time line on pages 292–293.
12. Sonar equipment on a ship sends out sound waves that bounce off the ocean floor. By measuring the time that these waves take to return to the ship, it is possible to calculate the depth of the ocean at that point.
13. A typical marine food web consists of producers, consumers, and decomposers. Many plankton and benthos are producers that make their own food through photosynthesis.
14. Any three: They must be able to tolerate the pounding of waves, changes in salinity and temperature, and alternating periods of being underwater and exposed to air.
15. The rivers that flow into estuaries can carry pollutants such as pesticides, sewage, and industrial wastes.
16. An atoll is a ring-shaped coral reef surrounding a shallow lagoon. It starts as a fringing reef around an island and forms when the island sinks and the reef grows upward.
17. Hydrothermal vents occur in the deepest parts of the ocean far from sunlight, where food is scarce and organisms tend to be small, slow-moving, and of limited variety. Around the vents, however, the number, size, and variety of organisms is unusually large.
18. Students' descriptions of the ocean floor should include all the major features identified in the text on pages 294–296 and the accompanying visual essay (continental shelf, continental slope, trenches, abyssal plain, mid-ocean ridge, volcanic island, seamount) and organisms typically found in each area, drawn from Sections 2 and 3.

Thinking Critically

19. *plankton:* microscopic algae *nekton:* squid, whales, sea otters, anglerfish *benthos:* sea stars, giant clams
20. The neritic zone lies above the continental shelf. Here, the water is shallower, warmer, and contains more nutrients than the deep zone. These conditions support a large number and wide variety of fish.
21. Populations of animals that feed directly on plankton would decline as their food supply decreased. In turn, populations of animals that feed on the plankton-eaters would also decline.
22. Runoff on land could wash fertilizers into streams and rivers, which would eventually carry them into the ocean. Near land, the fertilizers would cause excess growth of plants and algae, upsetting the natural balance in coastal habitats.

CHAPTER 10 ASSESSMENT

Reviewing Content

Multiple Choice

Choose the letter of the best answer.

1. A smooth, nearly flat region of the ocean floor is called a(n)
a. trench. **b.** mid-ocean ridge.
c. abyssal plain. **d.** sea mount.

2. An area where rivers flow into the ocean and fresh water and salt water mix is a(n)
a. tide pool.
b. hydrothermal vent.
c. estuary.
d. kelp forest.

3. A tropical ocean community made by tiny animals that have algae growing in their tissues is a(n)
a. mangrove forest. **b.** salt marsh.
c. intertidal zone. **d.** coral reef.

4. In the open-ocean zone, organisms depend directly or indirectly on food that is made by
a. marine mammals.
b. nekton in the water column.
c. plants growing on the deep ocean floor.
d. algae near the surface.

5. Most ocean pollutants come from
a. marine organisms. **b.** the land.
c. the atmosphere. **d.** Earth's core.

True or False

If the statement is true, write true. If it is false, change the underlined word or words to make the statement true.

6. <u>Benthos</u> are free-swimming animals that can move throughout the water column.

7. The area between the high and low tide lines is the <u>neritic</u> zone.

8. Water that is partly salty and partly fresh is <u>brackish</u>.

9. A ring-shaped coral reef surrounding a lagoon is called a(n) <u>seamount</u>.

10. Many deep-sea fishes use their <u>bioluminescence</u> to attract prey.

Checking Concepts

11. Describe one method that has been used to study the ocean floor.

12. How can sonar be used to measure the depth of the ocean?
13. Describe a typical marine food web.
14. Describe three physical factors that organisms in the rocky intertidal zone must overcome.
15. Explain why estuaries are especially vulnerable to pollution.
16. What is an atoll? How is it formed?
17. Explain why scientists were surprised to discover the variety of organisms living around hydrothermal vents.
18. Writing to Learn Imagine that you are an "aquanaut" on a voyage of discovery across the ocean floor. Write a logbook entry that summarizes your observations as you travel from one continent to another. Include details about the shape of the ocean floor, as well as some organisms you encounter along your journey.

Thinking Critically

19. Classifying Classify each of the following organisms as plankton, nekton, or benthos: squid, sea stars, microscopic algae, whales, sea otters, anglerfish, and giant clams.
20. Making Generalizations Explain why many of the world's fisheries are located in the neritic zone.
21. Predicting Suppose the number of plankton in the ocean suddenly decreased to half their current number. Predict how this would affect other marine organisms.
22. Relating Cause and Effect How might fertilizers used on farmland result in ocean pollution near shore?

Applying Skills

Use the diagram of a portion of the ocean floor to answer Questions 23–25.

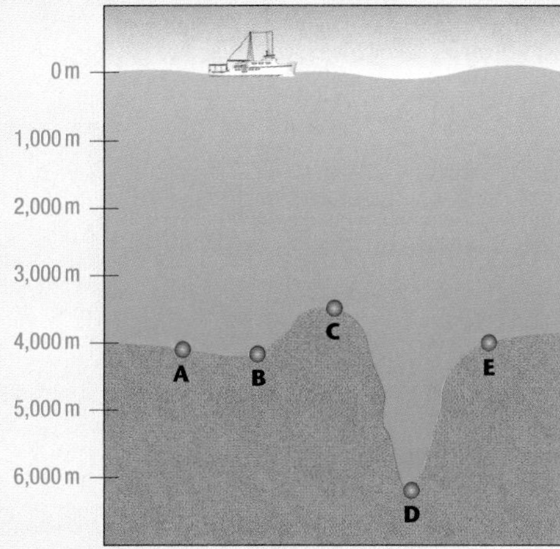

23. **Interpreting Diagrams** What is the approximate depth of the ocean floor at point A? At point C?
24. **Inferring** What might the feature between locations A and B be? The feature at point D?
25. **Posing Questions** What other information would help you determine whether point A or point E is closer to the mid-ocean ridge? Explain.

Performance CHAPTER PROJECT Assessment

Present Your Project With your group, rehearse the guided tour of the environment you will give. As you rehearse, check to see that your marine environment is complete. Make any final changes now.

Reflect and Record In your notebook, write a paragraph summarizing how each organism your group modeled belongs in the habitat you built. What was the most difficult element of the environment to model?

Test Preparation

Use these questions to prepare for standardized tests.

Study the diagram. Then answer Questions 26–29.

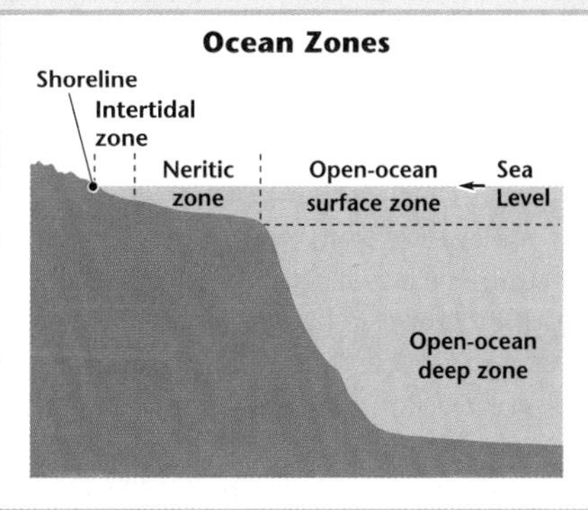

26. Which part of the ocean supports the greatest variety of organisms?
    a. neritic zone
    b. intertidal zone
    c. open-ocean deep zone
    d. open-ocean surface zone
27. Which part of the ocean is in constant darkness and cold, with few organisms?
    a. neritic zone
    b. intertidal zone
    c. open-ocean deep zone
    d. open-ocean surface zone
28. Organisms in this area must be able to survive severe changes in salinity, temperature, and exposure to air.
    a. neritic zone
    b. intertidal zone
    c. open-ocean surface zone
    d. open-ocean deep zone
29. The edge of the continental shelf forms the boundary between which parts of the ocean?
    a. high tide and low tide lines
    b. intertidal zone and neritic zone
    c. neritic zone and open ocean
    d. open-ocean deep zone and hydrothermal vents

Applying Skills

23. *A:* about 4,000 m; *C:* about 3,500 m
24. *Between A and B:* abyssal plain; *at point D:* trench
25. The distance between each point and the closest continental slope or the age of the rock on the seafloor at each point

Performance CHAPTER PROJECT Assessment

Present Your Project Allow 10–15 minutes for each group to give a "guided tour" of its marine habitat. Prompt each group member to express his or her knowledge of the habitat and its inhabitants. Each student should also describe the characteristics of the particular organism that he or she modeled, including its specific physical and behavior adaptations to that habitat and, possibly, the organism's role in the food web. Allow time for questions and discussion after each group's presentation. Be sure to provide all students with positive feedback about their models.

Reflect and Record Emphasize that each group member is responsible for discussing conditions in the group's habitat, as well as his or her own organism. After students have described any difficulties they encountered in building the habitat, ask them to suggest other methods or materials they could have used.

Test Preparation

26. a **27.** c **28.** b **29.** c

Program Resources

- ◆ **Unit 3 Resources** Chapter 10 Project Scoring Rubric
- ◆ **Performance Assessment** Chapter 10
- ◆ **Chapter and Unit Tests** Chapter 10 Test; Unit 3 Test
- ◆ **Inquiry Skills Activity Book** Provides teaching and review of all inquiry skills

Media and Technology

Computer Test Bank
Chapter 10 Test

Chesapeake Bay

This interdisciplinary feature presents the central theme of Chesapeake Bay as a valued resource by connecting three different disciplines: science, social studies, and mathematics. The three explorations are designed to capture students' interest and help them see how the content they are studying in science relates to other school subjects and to real-world events. The unit is particularly suitable for team teaching.

1 Engage/Explore

Activating Prior Knowledge

Help students recall what they learned in previous chapters by writing each of the following terms on the board: estuary, drainage basin, watershed, river, tributary. Then have volunteers write a definition for each of the terms. Ask students: **How do the headwaters and mouth of a body of water compare?** *(The headwaters are the source whereas the mouth is the end, or where the body flows into another body of water.)* **What do you know about Chesapeake Bay?** *(Accept all responses without comment at this time.)*

Introducing the Unit

Display a large map of the eastern United States and invite a volunteer to point out Chesapeake Bay. Ask: **Where does water flow into the bay?** *(at the mouths of rivers)* **Where does it flow out of the bay?** *(at the bay's mouth)* **What body of water does the bay flow into?** *(the Atlantic Ocean)* **How might water in the bay be affected by tides?** *(During rising tides, ocean water flows into the bay, raising the water level.)*

INTERDISCIPLINARY EXPLORATION

CHESAPEAKE BAY

What would you name a body of water that—

- *is the largest estuary in the United States, covering an area of about 18,000 square kilometers (7,000 square miles, with its tidal tributaries),*
- *holds more than 68 trillion liters (18 trillion gallons) of water,*
- *is fed by a drainage basin covering 165,800 square kilometers (64,000 square miles) and parts of six states,*
- *has a length of 322 kilometers (200 miles) and a width between 5.5 and 56 kilometers (3.4 and 35 miles)?*

Native Americans called this body of water *Chesapeake,* meaning "great shellfish bay."

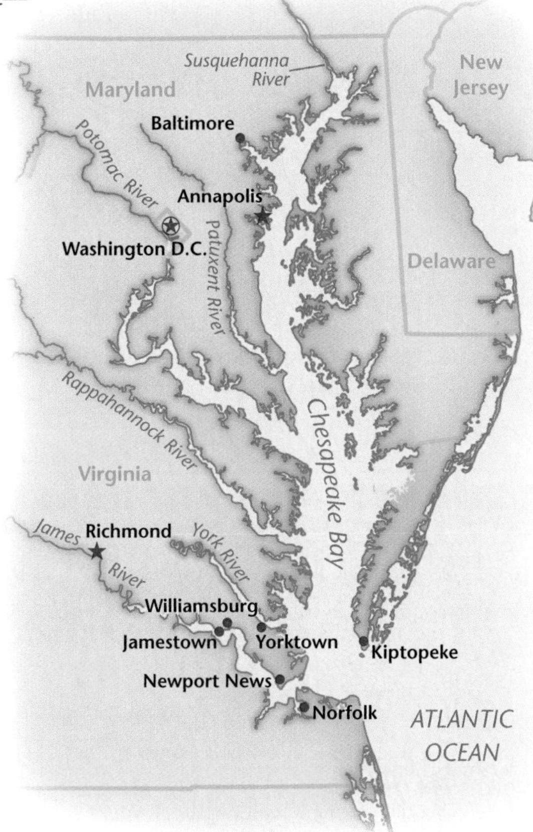

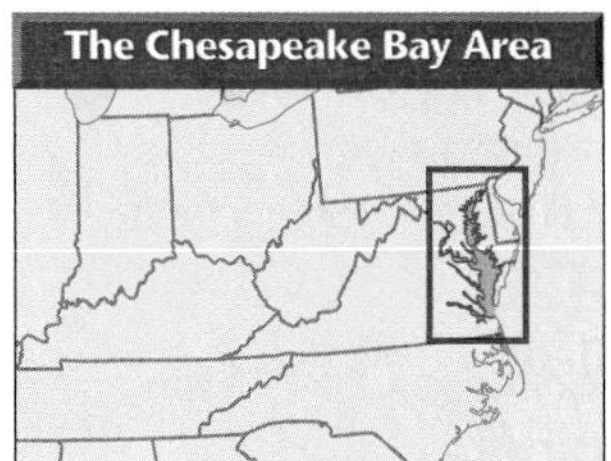

Chances are you or the student next to you has sat down to a meal of shellfish or fish from Chesapeake Bay. The map shows the Chesapeake Bay region, an area once so rich in resources it became known as "the Land of Pleasant Living."

Fresh water from 46 major rivers and six states drains into Chesapeake Bay. Its headwaters are fed by the mighty Susquehanna River, which flows into the bay from the north. The bay's eastern shore is comprised of the Delmarva Peninsula, a tongue of land that, as its name suggests, includes parts of the states of Delaware, Maryland, and Virginia. Along the bay's western shore lie Virginia and Maryland and the mouths of many rivers, such as the wide Potomac. At its south end are the Virginia capes, or headlands, forming Chesapeake Bay's opening to the Atlantic Ocean.

Program Resources

- **Unit 3 Resources** Interdisciplinary Explorations

The Land and Waters of Pleasant Living

Early colonists at Jamestown, Virginia

Who wouldn't be drawn to an area of abundant water and resources? Early settlers to the Chesapeake Bay region relied on the bay for many things, including transportation and food. The bay and the many rivers that feed it, including the Potomac, Rappahannock, York, and James, provided vital waterways for settlers. Native Americans and, later, European settlers who arrived in the1600s used these waterways for transportation, building their communities along the banks.

Chesapeake Bay was home to a wide variety of organisms, so fishing became an important industry in the bay region. Abundant shellfish including blue crabs, clams, and oysters, and fish such as eels, ocean-spawning bluefish, and striped bass were harvested by early settlers.

▲Fishers hauling in a net in Chesapeake Bay

Although the bay continues to be a major waterway, its value as a fishery has declined due to human impact. As the local human population increased, overfishing took place and shellfish habitats were destroyed by pollution and increased sediment accumulation. Recent efforts to reduce pollution and limit habitat destruction have resulted in renewed fish and shellfish populations in Chesapeake Bay.

Social Studies Activity

Use the map to choose a city on Chesapeake Bay to learn more about. Imagine that you are the first mayor of the newly founded city. Write a newspaper advertisement to convince settlers to come to your city. Before writing, learn about the history, founding, and trade of the city. Look for answers to the following questions:

- Who founded the city? When was it founded? Why did settlers decide to move there? Where did they come from?
- What part did Chesapeake Bay play in the city's founding?
- What other physical features were important to the city?
- Where did the city's name come from?
- What were the main products produced in the city?

▲ Blue crabs from Chesapeake Bay

Background

Integrating Science Today's Chesapeake Bay is actually one of many such bays that formed and disappeared over geologic history, expanding and shrinking with sea level's rise and fall. It formed as a result of the waters of the Atlantic Ocean eroding and drowning the mouths of the many rivers that flow into it. Chesapeake Bay did not actually begin as a bay but as the Susquehanna River, which once flowed straight to the sea. About 10,000 years ago at the end of the last ice age, glacial ice melted, raising the level of Earth's oceans. The Atlantic overflowed its ocean basin and flooded the former shoreline, forming Chesapeake Bay. Even today, Atlantic tidal waters rise and backfill the bay, reaching as far north as Havre de Grace, Maryland, to meet the Susquehanna River at its mouth.

Social Studies

2 Facilitate

- Have students refer to the map on page 322 to find the Potomac, Rappahannock, York, and James Rivers. Then have students locate the settlements named or pictured. Ask: **Why do you think people chose these places to settle and build a town?** *(The locations provided easy access to a river or the bay for travel and transportation of goods.)* Ask students how they think motorized transport changed the bay area. *(Possible answers: It made transportation easier, since people no longer had to depend on their own strength to move boats. Since motors burn fuel, it increased pollution and other negative human impacts on the ecosystem.)*
- To extend this exploration, students could construct a time line of important events that have occurred in the Chesapeake Bay region since early times.

Social Studies Activity

Let students work individually. To provide more choices of cities, suggest that they consult other, more detailed maps of the area. Caution students to choose cities that are large enough to merit entries in encyclopedias or other readily available reference books. If time allows, let students read their advertisements aloud.

Unit 3 Resources The following worksheet correlates with this page: Finding Locations on a Map.

3 Assess

Activity Assessment

Evaluate students' research procedures, particularly note-taking and outlining. Make sure their reports are in the form of newspaper advertisements and that they include the type of information that answers the questions on the student page.

Science

2 Facilitate

- Review the diagrams of saltwater intrusion to make sure students understand how an intrusion occurs. Have a volunteer explain what the arrows in the diagrams represent. Help students find the line that separates the salt groundwater from the fresh groundwater. Point out the change in this division as water is removed from the aquifer. Ask: **How does an increase in the population in the area contribute to the problem of saltwater intrusion?** *(People can remove water from the aquifer as long as they don't remove more water than can be replaced by rain. An increase in population means an increase in water use, and more water is removed from the aquifer than is replaced by rain.)*
- To extend this exploration, suggest that students research where their drinking water comes from and how it is treated.

Science

Please, *Don't* Pass the Salt!

The city of Chesapeake, Virginia, had a big problem. At the end of the twentieth century, the city's drinking water tasted so bad that many residents turned to bottled water rather than turning on the tap.

Human population is growing everywhere, including in the Chesapeake Bay region. As the population there grew, a greater demand was placed on groundwater drawn from the local freshwater aquifer for drinking and other uses. As a result, fresh water in the aquifer drained very quickly.

If an aquifer is drained faster than it can be refilled by rainwater or other natural sources of fresh water, the result is called overdraft. In aquifers near Chesapeake Bay, overdraft is an especially serious problem. Normally, the fresh water in the aquifer keeps the salty water of the bay from entering the aquifer, as you can see in Diagram A. When too much freshwater is removed from the pore spaces in the aquifer, salt water moves into these spaces, causing saltwater intrusion, as shown in Diagram B. The water in the aquifer becomes too salty to drink.

Science Activity

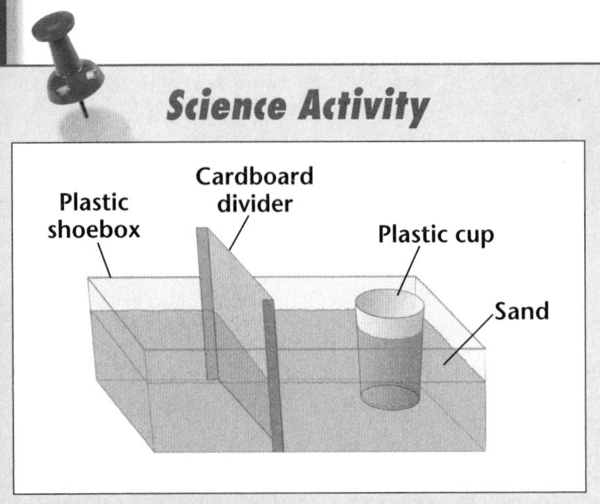

Use a plastic shoebox and sand to model saltwater intrusion in an aquifer. Set up your model following the illustration. Then use a baster to model overdraft and the intrusion of salt water in your aquifer.

Saltwater Intrusion

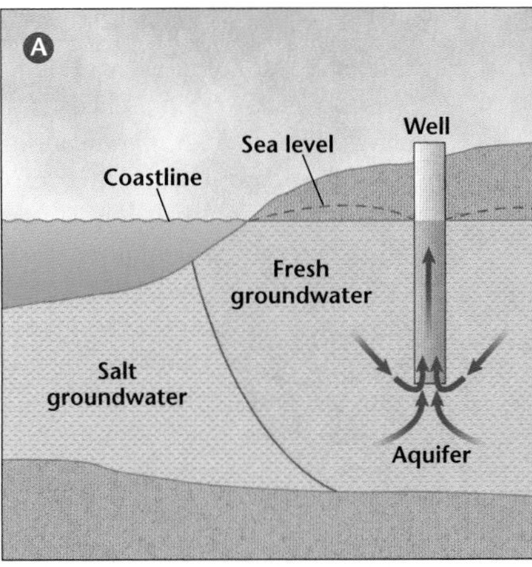

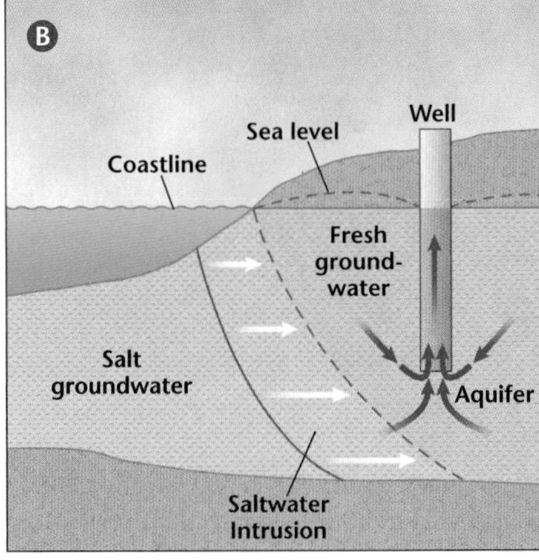

Background

Facts and Figures Saltwater intrusion occurs whenever salt water moves into a freshwater environment, like a freshwater aquifer or freshwater marsh. This intrusion can occur as the result of a natural process, such as a storm surge from a hurricane. More commonly, saltwater intrusion results from human activities such as overdraft or construction. Along the shores of the Gulf of Mexico, the construction of navigation channels and oil field canals provides conduits for salt water to move deep into inland marshes. Water high in salt content can have a negative impact on marsh ecosystems. Most or all native freshwater vegetation can be destroyed, resulting in the loss of plant roots that hold soil in place. This leads to rapid erosion and destruction of the wetland.

Osmosis

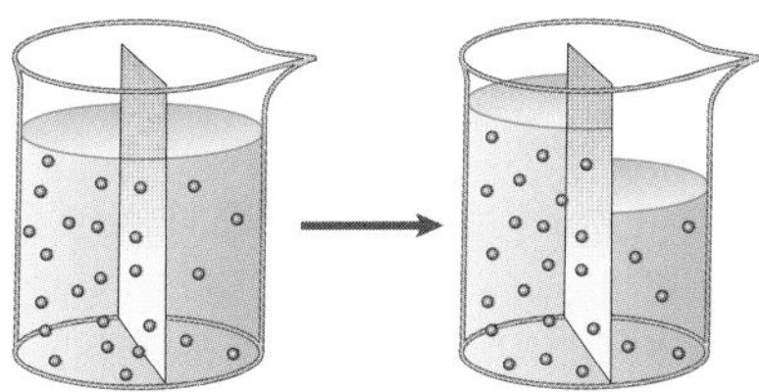

Reverse Osmosis

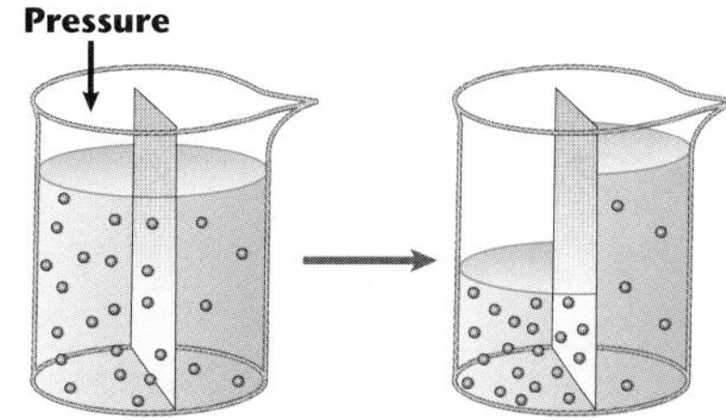

To solve the problem of contaminated drinking water, Chesapeake's Northwest River Water Treatment Plant installed reverse osmosis technology to filter the groundwater water removed from the aquifer.

Osmosis is a natural process in which water moves across a membrane. Suppose two samples of water, one containing more salt than the other, are separated by a membrane that blocks the movement of salt. Water will pass through the membrane, moving from the water that contains less salt to the water that contains more salt. This flow continues until the weight of the higher column of water makes it impossible for more water to move across the membrane.

If the weight of water exerts a force that can stop the process of osmosis, what would a greater force do? Can it reverse the process of osmosis? Yes, it can, as you can see in the second diagram.

In a water treatment plant, reverse osmosis technology involves pumping water at high pressure through a filter, or membrane, that contains tiny pores. The pores are large enough to allow water to pass through them but too small for salt to pass through. The filters are housed in long plastic tubes arranged in a series of banks. Groundwater is pumped through the banks of tubes and filtered for salt, then further treated and stored in tanks to await use by the public.

▲ Reverse osmosis equipment at the Northwest River Water Treatment Facility

Science Activity

Before students do the activity, remind them that an aquifer is an underground layer of rock or soil that holds water. To access water in an aquifer, a well is dug into the aquifer. The Interdisciplinary Explorations worksheet in Unit 3 Resources provides complete instructions for building the model shown in the diagram.

Unit 3 Resources The following worksheet correlates with this page: Modeling Saltwater Intrusion.

3 Assess

Activity Assessment

Schedule time for students to explain their models to the class. During their presentations, focus on evaluating students' understanding of what each feature of the model represents and how saltwater intrusion occurs.

Background

Integrating Science and Technology

A large East Coast sugar and corn syrup distributor uses reverse osmosis technology to turn a wastewater disposal problem into a revenue source. The company transports corn syrup in tanker trucks to various food manufacturers and processors. After delivery, each truck is cleaned and rinsed to remove the sugar syrup. The resulting rinse water contains a 1.5 to 5 percent sugar concentration, which exceeds limits for local sewer disposal. Using reverse osmosis, the distributor is able to concentrate this rinse into a 30 percent sugar solution. This concentrated solution is then sold to an animal feed company, turning what once was waste into a marketable product.

2 Facilitate

- Ask any students who have crossed the Chesapeake Bay Bridge-Tunnel to describe their experience to the class. Ask them how it felt to travel through the tunnels beneath the water of the bay.
- Have students determine the minimum average number of vehicles per year that have used the bridge-tunnel since it was built. (Students should divide 75 million vehicles by the number of years since 1964.)

Math Activity

Let students complete the activity on their own or in pairs. Remind them that 1 kilometer equals 1000 meters. If necessary, guide students to see that in order to determine the length of the causeway, they must first add up the lengths of all other segments, including the total length of trestles, and subtract that sum from the total shore to shore length.

After students have completed the table, have them work through the bulleted questions in the Math Activity as a whole-class activity.

Unit 3 Resources The following worksheets correlate with this page: Calculating Tolls; Graphing Population Changes.

Mathematics

Riding Over (and Under) Chesapeake Bay

The mouth of Chesapeake Bay is home to an engineering marvel that links Virginia Beach on the Bay's south (or west) shore with Cape Charles on the north (or east) shore. Called the Chesapeake Bay Bridge-Tunnel, this modern wonder is both a bridge and a tunnel, crossing both over and under the bay's brackish waters.

Since its opening in 1964, over 75 million vehicles have, for the price of a toll, used the bridge-tunnel to reduce their travel time around Chesapeake Bay. Measuring approximately 28.3 km shore to shore, it is the second largest artificial water crossing in the world (second only to the Lake Pontchartrain Causeway in Louisiana) and the longest bridge in the world over ocean water.

The crossing actually consists of a series of low-level trestles interrupted by two tunnels beneath Thimble Shoals and Chesapeake navigation channels. There are also high level bridges over two other navigation channels. Artificial islands are located at each end of the two tunnels, and at each of the four islands is a rest stop. On the southernmost island there is also a gift shop, restaurant, and fishing pier, making the crossing both a travel convenience and tourist attraction.

Look at the table showing lengths of the various segments making up the Chesapeake Bay Bridge-Tunnel. Segments of the bridge-tunnels are listed in order from Trestle A at the south shore across the bay to Trestle F at the north shore.

CHESAPEAKE BAY BRIDGE—TUNNEL DATA

Segment	Approximate Length in Kilometers	in Meters
Total Shore to Shore	28.3 km	a. ?
Total Trestles (A-F)	19.9 km	b. ?
Trestle A	—	—
Thimble Shoal Tunnel	1.8 km	c. ?
Trestle B	—	—
Chesapeake Tunnel	1.6 km	d. ?
Trestle C	—	—
North Channel Bridge	e. ?	1160 m
Trestle D	—	—
Causeway	f. ?	g. ?
Trestle E	—	-
Fishermans Inlet Bridge	h. ?	140 m
Trestle F	—	—

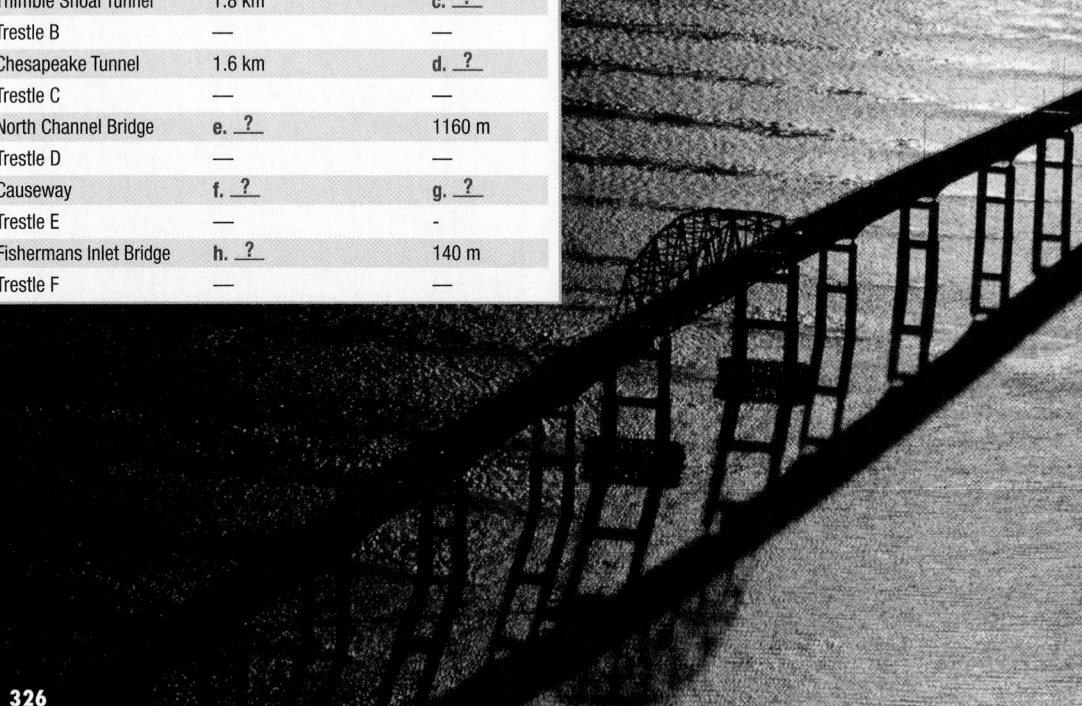

326

Background

History Before the Chesapeake Bay Bridge-Tunnel was built, passengers and vehicles traveled by land around the bay or crossed it by ferry. During the 1930s through 1950s, a privately owned ferry service ran between the Eastern Shore of Virginia and the Norfolk/Virginia Beach area. Demand for the service increased, and in 1956, the local Ferry Commission began exploring the possibility of building a fixed crossing to connect the two shores. Construction of the bridge-tunnel took 42 months, and was accomplished under severe conditions including hurricanes and northeasters. Following its opening on April 15, 1964, it was selected as "One of the Seven Engineering Wonders of the Modern World" in a worldwide competition.

Math Activity

Now complete the table so that each length given appears in both kilometers and meters. Then, use the data in the table on page 326 to calculate the length of the causeway in both kilometers and meters.

- ◆ Which tunnel is longer? By how many kilometers is it longer?
- ◆ Which bridge is longer? By how many meters and kilometers is it longer?
- ◆ What is the approximate average length of the trestles?
- ◆ Which segment of the bridge-tunnel would take the shortest time to cross?

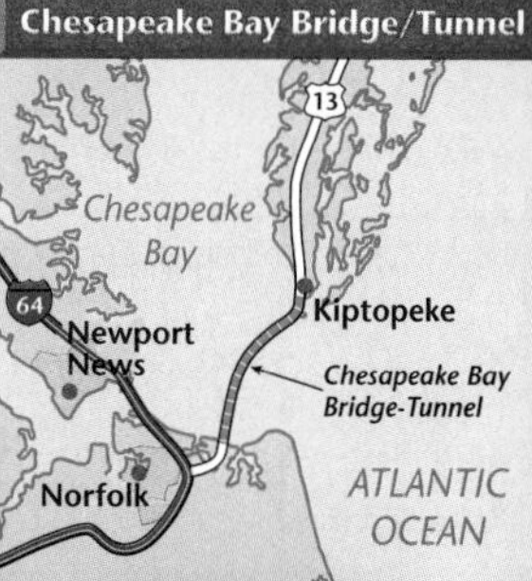

Celebrate the Bay

Plan a class fair featuring cities on Chesapeake Bay today, such as Norfolk (above). Set up a booth for each city and create a travel brochure to persuade people to visit.

As a team, choose a city to represent. Then divide up tasks so different members find information on the following topics:

- ◆ Interesting attractions and events that your city offers—zoos, museums, parks, sports events, music festivals, and so on.
- ◆ Influences of different groups on the city's food, customs, music, and architecture.
- ◆ Physical features of the area around the city.
- ◆ Famous people—writers, political figures, entertainers—who lived there.
- ◆ Historic places to visit, such as monuments, houses, battlefields, and statues.
- ◆ Illustrations and pictures of special attractions.
- ◆ Maps of walking tours and historic areas.
- ◆ Native plants and animals in the area.

Before starting your brochure, decide which attractions to highlight. Think of a slogan for your travel campaign. If you wish, make a poster. Celebrate life on the bay today!

3 Assess

Activity Assessment

a. 28,320 m
b. 19,900 m
c. 1800 m
d. 1600 m
e. 1.16 km
f. 3.7 km
g. 3700 m
h. 0.14 km

- ◆ Thimble Shoal; 0.1 km
- ◆ North Channel Bridge; 1020 m, 1.02 km
- ◆ 3.32 km, 3320 m
- ◆ Fishermans Inlet Bridge

Tie It Together

Time 1 week (2 days for research, 2 days for preparing the brochure and booth, 1 day for the fair)

Tips Have students work in groups of four or five. Encourage groups to choose a city that can be researched easily with readily available resource materials. If necessary, help each group divide up the tasks and work out a plan for researching and compiling information. Guide students through the writing process as follows:

- ◆ In the research stage, suggest that they narrow the topics by listing all their ideas and then selecting the ones that are most interesting.
- ◆ In the drafting stage, remind students to begin the brochure with a general introduction, followed by topic-specific sections such as Key Attractions, Famous People, and Historic Sites.
- ◆ In the editing stage, remind students to read the draft carefully, looking for errors and ways to improve the brochure.

Extend Groups could choose one cultural aspect to research across different cities. For example, one group could find out about (and possibly prepare for class tasting) foods representing different ethnic and regional groups. Another group could research the music in different cities. Still another group could explore various types of arts and crafts characteristic of different cities and regions.

The Atmosphere

Sections	Time	Student Edition Activities	Other Activities
CHAPTER PROJECT **Watching the Weather** p. 329	Ongoing (2 weeks)	Check Your Progress, pp. 333, 356 Present Your Project, p. 359	
1 The Air Around You pp. 330–335 ◆ State how the atmosphere is important to living things. ◆ Identify the gases that are present in Earth's atmosphere.	2 periods/ 1 block	**Discover** How Long Will the Candle Burn?, p. 330 **Try This** Breathe In, Breathe Out, p. 332 **Real-World Lab: You and Your Environment** How Clean Is the Air?, pp. 334–335	TE Building Inquiry Skills: Inferring, p. 500
2 *Integrating Environmental Science* **Air Pollution** pp. 336–343 ◆ Identify and describe outdoor and indoor air pollutants. ◆ Explain the importance of ozone in the upper atmosphere. ◆ Describe the greenhouse effect and explain how it affects climate.	2 periods/ 1 block	**Discover** How Does the Scent Spread?, p. 336 **Try This** How Acid Is Your Rain?, p. 337 **Sharpen Your Skills** Communicating, p. 338 **Science at Home,** p. 341	TE Addressing Naive Conceptions, p. 337 TE Building Inquiry Skills: Observing, p. 338 TE Real-Life Learning, p. 339 TE Math Toolbox, p. 341 TE Inquiry Challenge, p. 341 TE Integrating Earth Science, p. 342 LM 11, "Examining Acid Rain"
3 Air Pressure pp. 345–350 ◆ Identify some of the properties of air. ◆ Name instruments that are used to measure air pressure. ◆ Explain how increasing altitude affects air pressure and density.	2 periods/ 1 block	**Discover** Does Air Have Mass?, p. 345 **Try This** Soda-Bottle Barometer, p. 347 **Skills Lab: Measuring** Working Under Pressure, pp. 348–349 **Science at Home,** p. 350	TE Including All Students, p. 346 TE Including All Students, p. 347 TE Real-Life Learning, p. 346 PTA "Testing Food Wraps," pp. 1–8
4 Layers of the Atmosphere pp. 351–356 ◆ Describe the characteristics of the main layers of the atmosphere.	1–2 periods/ $\frac{1}{2}$–1 block	**Discover** Is Air There?, p. 351	TE Exploring Layers of the Atmosphere, p. 353 TE Building Inquiry Skills: Modeling, p. 355 IES "Wagons West," p. 41
Study Guide/Chapter Assessment pp. 357–359	1 period/ $\frac{1}{2}$ block		ISAB Provides teaching and review of all inquiry skills

For Standard or Block Schedule The Resource Pro® CD-ROM gives you maximum flexibility for planning your instruction for any type of schedule. Resource Pro® contains Planning Express®, an advanced scheduling program, as well as the entire contents of the Teaching Resources and the Computer Test Bank.

CHAPTER PLANNING GUIDE

Program Resources	Assessment Strategies	Media and Technology
UR Chapter 11 Project Teacher Notes **UR** Chapter 11 Project Overview and Worksheets	**SE** Performance Assessment: Present Your Project, p. 359 **TE** Check Your Progress, pp. 333, 356 **UR** Chapter 11 Project Scoring Rubric	Science Explorer Internet Site at www.phschool.com Student Edition on Audio CD, Chapter 11
UR 11-1 Lesson Plan **UR** 11-1 Section Summary **UR** 11-1 Review and Reinforce **UR** 11-1 Enrich **UR** Chapter 11 Real-World Lab	**SE** Section 1 Review, p. 333 **TE** Ongoing Assessment, p. 331 **TE** Performance Assessment, p. 333	Concept Videotape Library, Grade 6, Tape 2, "A Trip Through the Earth"; "Air Today, Gone Tomorrow" Transparency 36, "Gases in Dry Air"
UR 11-2 Lesson Plan **UR** 11-2 Section Summary **UR** 11-2 Review and Reinforce **UR** 11-2 Enrich	**SE** Section 2 Review, p. 343 **TE** Ongoing Assessment, pp. 337, 339, 441 **TE** Performance Assessment, p. 343	Concept Videotape Library, Grade 6, Tape 2, "A Better Cool"; "Our Passion for Driving"; "The Greenhouse Effect" Transparencies 37, "Temperature Inversion"; 38, "The Ozone Cycle"; 39, "The Greenhouse Effect"; 40, "Exploring Climate Predictions" Lab Activity Videotapes, Grade 6 Tape 3
UR 11-3 Lesson Plan **UR** 11-3 Section Summary **UR** 11-3 Review and Reinforce **UR** 11-3 Enrich **UR** Chapter 11 Skills Lab	**SE** Section 3 Review, p. 350 **TE** Ongoing Assessment, p. 347 **TE** Performance Assessment, p. 350	Concept Videotape Library, Grade 6, Tape 2, "Racing Hot Air Balloons" Transparency 41, "Density of Air at Two Altitudes" Lab Activity Videotapes, Grade 6 Tape 3
UR 11-4 Lesson Plan **UR** 11-4 Section Summary **UR** 11-4 Review and Reinforce **UR** 11-4 Enrich	**SE** Section 4 Review, p. 356 **TE** Ongoing Assessment, pp. 353, 355 **TE** Performance Assessment, p. 357	Concept Videotape Library, Grade 6, Tape 2, "A Trip Through the Earth" Transparency 42, "Layers of the Atmosphere"
RCA Provides strategies to improve science reading skills **GRSW** Provides worksheets to promote student comprehension of content	**SE** Chapter 11 Study Guide/Assessment, pp. 357–359 **PA** Chapter 11 Performance Assessment **CUT** Chapter 11 Test **CTB** Chapter 11 Test	Computer Test Bank, Chapter 11 Test

Key: **SE** Student Edition
CTB Computer Test Bank
ISAB Inquiry Skills Activity Book
GRSW Guided Reading and Study Workbook
TE Teacher's Edition
PTA Product Testing Activities by *Consumer Reports*
RCA Reading in the Content Area
PA Performance Assessment
UR Unit Resources
LM Laboratory Manual
IES Interdisciplinary Explorations Series
CUT Chapter and Unit Tests

Meeting the National Science Education Standards and AAAS Benchmarks

National Science Education Standards	Benchmarks for Science Literacy	Unifying Themes
Science As Inquiry (Content Standard A) ◆ **Design and conduct a scientific investigation** Students investigate particles in air. *(Real-World Lab)* ◆ **Use the appropriate tools and techniques to gather, analyze, and interpret data** Students use a barometer to measure air pressure. *(Skills Lab)* ◆ **Develop descriptions, explanations, predictions, and models using evidence** Students gather and interpret weather data and predict weather conditions. *(Chapter Project)* **Physical Science** (Content Standard B) ◆ **Properties and changes of properties in matter** Some gases in air are chemically active. Smog and acid rain form when certain substances in the air combine. Density and pressure are two properties of air. *(Sections 1, 2, 3)* **Earth and Space Science** (Content Standard D) ◆ **Structure of the Earth system** Earth's atmosphere is a mixture of gases and is in four layers. *(Sections 1, 4)* **Science and Technology** (Content Standard E) ◆ **Abilities of technological design** Students consider the issue of air polluted by cars. *(Science and Society)* ◆ **Understandings about science and technology** Technology can help control pollution. *(Section 2)*	**1B Scientific Inquiry** Students gather and interpret weather data and predict weather. Students investigate particles in air. *(Chapter Project; Real-World Lab)* **3A Technology and Science** Students use a barometer to measure air pressure. Technology has helped scientists explore the atmosphere. *(Skills Lab; Science & History)* **3B Designs and Systems** The engines of motor vehicles release emissions into the air. *(Section 1)* **3C Issues in Technology** Some human activities cause air pollution. Students consider the issue of air polluted by cars. *(Section 2; Science and Society)* **4B The Earth** Earth's atmosphere is a mixture of various gases and is divided into four main layers. *(Sections 1, 2, 4)* **4D Structure of Matter** Earth's atmosphere is made up of molecules of various gases. Smog and acid rain form when certain substances in the air combine. Density and pressure are two properties of air. *(Sections 1, 2, 3)* **4E Energy Transformation** Earth's atmosphere is heated by the sun. *(Section 4)* **6E Physical Health** Pollution can affect the health of humans. *(Section 1)* **7D Social Trade-Offs** Pollution can affect the health of humans. *(Section 1)* **8C Energy Sources and Use** Important human activities can cause air and water pollution. *(Section 1)* **12D Communication Skills** Students create drawings, graphs, and tables to summarize their weather observations. *(Chapter Project)*	◆ **Energy** Fossil fuels are an important source of energy. Photochemical smog is caused by the action of sunlight on chemicals. Earth's atmosphere is heated by the sun. *(Sections 2, 4; Science and Society)* ◆ **Patterns of Change** Students use their weather observations to predict weather conditions. Weather factors affect the number of particles in the air. Air pressure and density decrease as altitude increases. Students construct a barometer and use it to measure air pressure. *(Chapter Project; Real-World Lab; Sections 2, 3; Skills Lab)* ◆ **Scale and Structure** Earth's atmosphere is made up of nitrogen, oxygen, and various other gases and is divided into four main layers. *(Sections 1, 4)* ◆ **Stability** The composition of the atmosphere remains fairly constant. The layers of the atmosphere are classified by their characteristic temperatures. *(Sections 1, 4)* ◆ **Systems and Interactions** Earth's atmosphere makes conditions on Earth suitable for living things. Most air pollution is caused by burning fossil fuels. Cars add to air pollution. *(Sections 1, 2; Science and Society)*

Take It to the Net

Interactive text at www.phschool.com

Science Explorer comes alive with iText.

- **Complete student text** is accessible from any computer with Internet access or a CD-ROM drive.
- **Animations, simulations, and videos** enhance student understanding and retention of concepts.
- **Self-tests and online study tools** assess student understanding.

STAY CURRENT with **SCIENCE NEWS®**

Find out the latest research and information about Weather and Climate at: **www.phschool.com**

Go to **www.phschool.com** and click on the Science icon.Then click on Science Explorer: Life, Earth, and Physical Science under PH@school.

Student Edition Activities Planner

ACTIVITY	Time (minutes)	Materials Quantities for one work group	Skills
Section 1			
Discover, p. 330	15	**Consumable** modeling clay, short candle, matches **Nonconsumable** aluminum pie pan, small glass jar, stopwatch or watch with second hand, large glass jar	**Inferring**
Try This, p. 332	10	**Consumable** limewater, straw **Nonconsumable** glass	**Developing Hypotheses**
Real World Lab, pp. 334–335	20,10,10, 10,10	**Consumable** coffee filters **Nonconsumable** vacuum cleaner with intake hose (1 per class), rubber band, thermometer, low-power microscope	**Measuring, Interpreting Data**
Section 2			
Discover, p. 336	5	**Nonconsumable** bottle of perfume (for teacher only)	**Inferring**
Try This, p. 339	10	**Consumable** rainwater, pH paper, pH chart, lemon juice **Nonconsumable** two plastic cups	**Measuring**
Sharpen Your Skills, p. 340	15	No special materials are required.	**Communicating**
Science at Home, p. 343	home	**Consumable** petroleum jelly **Nonconsumable** 2 empty glass jars	**Predicting, Observing**
Section 3			
Discover, p. 345	10	**Consumable** balloon **Nonconsumable** balance	**Drawing Conclusions**
Try This, p. 347	15	**Consumable** water, long straw, modeling clay **Nonconsumable** 2-liter soda bottle	**Inferring**
Skills Lab, pp. 348–349	40,10,10	**Consumable** large rubber balloon, white glue, 12- to 15-cm drinking straw, modeling clay, 10 cm x 25 cm cardboard strip, tape **Nonconsumable** blunt scissors, wide-mouthed glass jar, rubber band, metric ruler, pencil	**Measuring, Observing, Inferring**
Science at Home, p. 350	home	**Consumable** tap water **Nonconsumable** glass, piece of heavy cardboard	**Communicating**
Section 4			
Discover, p. 351	10	**Nonconsumable** heavy rubber band, plastic bag, wide-mouthed glass jar	**Predicting**

A list of all materials required for the Student Edition activities can be found on pages TVA34–TVA40. You can obtain information about ordering materials by calling 1-800-848-9500 or by accessing the Science Explorer internet site at **http://www.phschool.com**.

CHAPTER 11 PROJECT

Watching the Weather

Most people make observations about the weather almost every day of their lives, but they might not be very aware of specific weather conditions and how they change. Of course they notice when a storm is raging, but they might not notice the red clouds at sunset that may indicate a storm is coming. Most students may not think much about the conditions that make up the weather. If they think about the weather at all, they may just think of it as good or bad.

Purpose In this project, students will become more aware of the weather and the variables such as temperature, precipitation, and wind speed that make up weather conditions. Students also will develop ways of observing weather variables.

Skills Focus Students will be able to

- ◆ design and implement a plan for observing and recording daily weather conditions;
- ◆ look for patterns in their observations that will help them understand the weather and how it changes;
- ◆ create data tables and other means of displaying their observations for the rest of the class.

Project Time Line The entire project will take a minimum of two weeks. The longer students make and record weather observations, the more likely they are to see trends in their data. On the first day, allow class time for introducing the project and brainstorming how students can use their senses to describe the weather. Students should decide as soon as possible which weather variables they will observe and how they will observe them. Students also must devise a way to record their observations. Additional class time will be necessary during the two-week period to monitor students' progress and give extra guidance to students who are having difficulty. At the end of the project, students will need time to review and organize their data and present their results to the rest of the class. For more detailed information on planning and supervising the chapter project, see Chapter 11 Project Teacher Notes in Unit 4 Resources.

Suggested Shortcuts To reduce the amount of time students spend on the project, you may assign each student or group of students just one weather variable, such as temperature or precipitation, to monitor. Then, at the end of the project, students can pool their results and the whole class can work together to look for patterns in the data.

Possible Materials Each student will need a log for recording his or her observations, but no other materials or equipment are needed. In fact, you should stress to students that they are to rely only on their senses and not instruments such as thermometers or wind vanes. However, students will need to depend on various materials in their environment, such as the school flag or the clothes people are wearing, to observe weather conditions. Urge students to be creative in the materials they use for their observations. Smoke rising from chimneys, for example, can reveal the direction and speed of the wind as well as flags flying from poles can.

CHAPTER 11 PROJECT

Watching the Weather

The air is cool and clear—just perfect for a trip in a hot-air balloon. As you rise, a fresh breeze begins to move you along. Where will it take you? Hot-air balloon pilots need to know about the weather to plot their course.

In this chapter, you will learn about the air around you. As you learn about the atmosphere, you will use your senses to collect information about weather conditions. Even without scientific instruments it is possible to make many accurate observations about the weather.

Your Goal To observe weather conditions without using instruments and to look for hints about tomorrow's weather in the weather conditions today.

Your completed project must

- include a plan for observing and describing a variety of weather conditions over a period of two to three weeks
- show your observations in a daily weather log
- display your findings about weather conditions

Get Started Begin by discussing what weather conditions you can observe. Brainstorm how to use your senses to describe the weather. For example, can you describe the wind speed by observing the school flag? Can you describe the temperature based on what clothes you need to wear outside? Be creative.

Check Your Progress You'll be working on this project as you study this chapter. To keep your project on track, look for Check Your Progress boxes at the following points.

Section 1 Review, page 333: Collect and record observations.
Section 4 Review, page 356: Look for patterns in your data.

Present Your Project At the end of the chapter (page 359), use your weather observations to prepare a display for the class.

Hot-air balloons soar into the atmosphere at a balloon festival in Snowmass, Colorado.

SECTION 4 Layers of the Atmosphere

Discover **Is Air There?**

329

Launching the Project To help students start thinking of weather variables they might observe, hand out copies of newspaper weather reports. On the chalkboard, have a volunteer list the weather variables given in the reports, such as temperature, humidity, barometric pressure, and wind speed and direction. Then challenge students to think of ways these weather variables could be observed without instruments. For example, ask: **If a thin skin of ice forms on puddles during the day, what does that tell you about the temperature?** *(It has fallen below the freezing point of water.)* **If the school flag is flying straight out from its pole, what does that tell you about the wind?** *(It is blowing at a high speed.)* Urge students to think of other observations that could give them information about weather conditions.

Performance Assessment

The Chapter 11 Project Scoring Rubric in Unit 4 Resources will help you evaluate how well students complete the Chapter 11 Project. You may wish to share the scoring rubric with your students so they know what will be expected of them. Students will be assessed on

- how thoroughly they collect and record observations of a variety of different weather conditions;
- how accurately they interpret their data to predict weather conditions and identify weather trends;
- how complete and creative their presentation of results are;
- if they work in groups, how much they contribute to their group's effort.

Program Resources

- **Unit 4 Resources** Chapter 11 Project Teacher Notes; Chapter 11 Project Overview and Worksheets; Chapter 11 Project Scoring Rubric

Media and Technology

Student Edition on Audio CD Chapter 11

You will find an Internet activity, chapter self-tests for students, and links to other chapter topics at this site.

SECTION 1 The Air Around You

Objectives

After completing the lesson, students will be able to

- ◆ state how the atmosphere is important to living things;
- ◆ identify the gases that are present in Earth's atmosphere.

Key Terms weather, atmosphere, ozone, water vapor

1 Engage/Explore

Activating Prior Knowledge

Ask students to recall the fire triangle, which many will have learned about in fire safety demonstrations. After drawing a large triangle on the chalkboard, ask: **What is the fire triangle?** *(A triangle representing the three components needed for fire to burn: fuel, heat, and air)* As students explain, label the sides of the triangle on the chalkboard. Then relate the fire triangle to the composition of air by asking: **What is in air that fire needs to burn?** *(oxygen)* Point out that living things also need oxygen, and oxygen is just one of the components of air they will learn about in this section.

DISCOVER ACTIVITY

Skills Focus inferring
Materials *modeling clay, aluminum pie pan, short candle, matches, small glass jar, stopwatch or watch with second hand, large glass jar*
Time 15 minutes
Tips You can use beakers instead of jars for this activity. You may wish to have students practice using stopwatches before they begin the activity.
Expected Outcome Students should observe that the candle quickly burns out under the small jar and that it burns somewhat longer under the large jar.
Think It Over The gas needed for the candle to burn is oxygen. The candle burned longer under the large jar because the large jar contained more oxygen.

SECTION 1 The Air Around You

DISCOVER ACTIVITY

How Long Will the Candle Burn?

1. Put on your goggles.
2. Stick a small piece of modeling clay onto an aluminum pie pan. Push a short candle into the clay. Carefully light the candle.
3. Hold a small glass jar by the bottom. Lower the mouth of the jar over the candle until the jar rests on the pie pan. As you do this, start a stopwatch or note where the second hand is on a clock.
4. Watch the candle carefully. How long does the flame burn?
5. Wearing an oven mitt, remove the jar. Relight the candle and then repeat Steps 3 and 4 with a larger jar.

Think It Over

Inferring How would you explain any differences between your results in Steps 4 and 5?

GUIDE FOR READING

- ◆ How is the atmosphere important to living things?
- ◆ What gases are present in Earth's atmosphere?

Reading Tip **Before you read, preview Figure 2. As you read, write a sentence about each of the major gases in the atmosphere.**

As you walk home from school, the air is warm and still. The sky is full of thick, dark clouds. In the distance you see a bright flash. A few seconds later, you hear a crack of thunder. As you turn the corner onto your street, raindrops start to fall. You begin to run and reach your home just as the downpour begins. That was close! From the shelter of the entrance you pause to catch your breath and watch the storm.

Importance of the Atmosphere

Does the weather where you live change frequently, or is it fairly constant from day to day? **Weather** is the condition of Earth's atmosphere at a particular time and place. But what is the atmosphere? Earth's **atmosphere** (AT muh sfeer) is the layer of gases that surrounds the planet. To understand the relative size of the atmosphere, imagine that the planet Earth is the size of an apple.

Figure 1 When seen from space, Earth's atmosphere appears as a thin layer near the horizon. The atmosphere makes life on Earth possible.

READING STRATEGIES

Reading Tip Make sure students understand how the two parts of Figure 2 are related by pointing out that the table shows the gases that make up the tiny wedge of the circle that is not nitrogen or oxygen. After students have read the section and written their sentences, suggest that they form pairs, read their sentences to each other, and try to identify which gas each sentence describes. Also urge them to work together to resolve any factual errors they detect in each other's sentences. Possible student sentences include the following: The most abundant gas in air is nitrogen. Air is 21 percent oxygen.

Study and Comprehension Before students read the section, have them use the main headings and subheadings to make an outline. Then, as they read the section, have them write down at least one important fact under each heading on their outline.

If you breathe on the apple, a thin film of water will form on its surface. Earth's atmosphere is like that water on the apple—a thin layer of gases on Earth's surface.

Earth's atmosphere makes conditions on Earth suitable for living things. The atmosphere contains oxygen and other gases that you and other living things need to live. In turn, living things affect the atmosphere. The atmosphere is constantly changing, with atoms and molecules of gases moving around the globe and in and out of living things, the land, and the water.

Living things also need warmth and liquid water. By trapping energy from the sun, the atmosphere keeps most of Earth's surface warm enough for water to exist as a liquid. In addition, Earth's atmosphere protects living things from dangerous radiation from the sun. It also prevents Earth's surface from being hit by most meteoroids, or chunks of rock from outer space.

☑ *Checkpoint* *What would conditions on Earth be like without the atmosphere?*

Language Arts CONNECTION

The word *atmosphere* comes from two Greek words: *atmos*, meaning "vapor," and *sphaira*, meaning "ball," or "globe." So the atmosphere is the vapors or gases surrounding a globe—in this case, Earth.

In Your Journal

As you read this chapter, write down all the words that end in *-sphere*. Look up the roots of each word in a dictionary. How does knowing the roots of each word help you understand its meaning?

Composition of the Atmosphere

The atmosphere is made up of a mixture of atoms and molecules of different kinds of gases. An atom is the smallest unit of a chemical element that can exist by itself. Molecules are made up of two or more atoms. **Earth's atmosphere is made up of nitrogen, oxygen, carbon dioxide, water vapor, and many other gases, as well as particles of liquids and solids.**

Nitrogen As you can see in Figure 2, nitrogen is the most abundant gas in the atmosphere. It makes up a little more than three fourths of the air we breathe. Each nitrogen molecule consists of two nitrogen atoms.

Gases in Dry Air

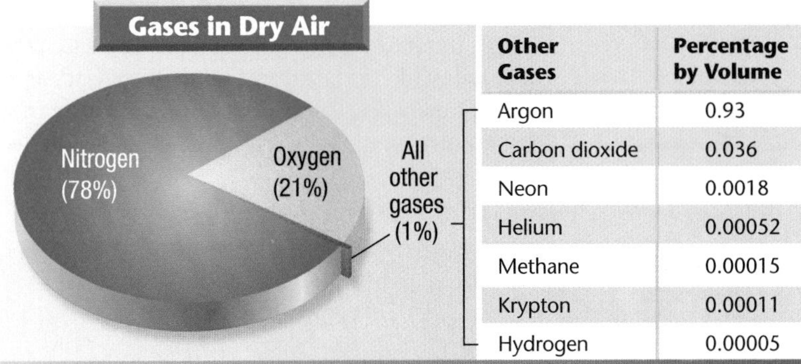

Other Gases	Percentage by Volume
Argon	0.93
Carbon dioxide	0.036
Neon	0.0018
Helium	0.00052
Methane	0.00015
Krypton	0.00011
Hydrogen	0.00005

Figure 2 Dry air in the lower atmosphere always has the same composition of gases. *Interpreting Data* *What two gases make up most of the air?*

2 Facilitate

Importance of the Atmosphere

Language Arts CONNECTION

Point out that many scientific terms are based on Greek words. Ask: **Why do you think English borrowed many scientific terms from Greek?** *(The Greeks were among the first Western people to study and write about the natural world. The words they used were passed on to people throughout Europe.)*

In Your Journal Other words ending in *-sphere* are terms for the layers of the atmosphere. For each term, have students write the meaning of the prefix. **learning modality: verbal**

Composition of the Atmosphere

Building Inquiry Skills: Making Models

Earth's atmosphere is composed largely of just a few gases, but even gases present in small amounts may be important to life. Also, the gases in Earth's atmosphere are present in the same proportions everywhere below an elevation of about 80 km. To reinforce these concepts, invite students to explain how a cake models the composition of the atmosphere. Provide a simple cake recipe first. Ask: **In what ways are the ingredients in a cake like the gases in Earth's atmosphere?** *(A cake is made up largely of just a few ingredients, especially flour. Ingredients, such as baking powder, included in small amounts may be essential for the cake. The ingredients in the cake are usually in the same proportions.)* **learning modality: logical/mathematical**

Ongoing Assessment

Oral Presentation Call on students at random to state ways that the atmosphere contributes to life on Earth.

Program Resources

- **Unit 4 Resources** 11-1 Lesson Plan; 11-1 Section Summary
- **Guided Reading and Study Workbook** Section 11-1

Media and Technology

Transparencies "Gases in Dry Air," Transparency 36

Answers to Self-Assessment

☑ *Checkpoint*

Water could not exist as a liquid on Earth's surface. Earth would also be exposed to meteoroids and dangerous radiation from the sun. There would be no life on Earth without the oxygen and other gases that living things need.

Caption Question

Figure 2 Nitrogen and oxygen

Composition of the Atmosphere, continued

Integrating Life Science

The text gives just a short summary of the nitrogen cycle. Divide the class into groups and challenge each group to research the nitrogen cycle further and then make an illustrated flowchart of it. Each student in the group should take responsibility for learning about and illustrating one part of the cycle. Urge groups to share their flowcharts and work together to resolve any discrepancies. Display their best efforts in the classroom. **cooperative learning**

Building Inquiry Skills: Inferring

Materials *tall glass jar, large cake pan, clean steel wool, water, tape*

Time 5 minutes one day; 5 minutes the next day

Estimate the amount of oxygen in the atmosphere by having students follow these instructions: Fill a cake pan almost full of water. Push steel wool down into the bottom of a tall glass jar so it will not fall out when the jar is turned over. (**CAUTION:** Remind students to handle glass carefully.) Fill the jar with water, cover the mouth with a hand, and place the jar upside down in the cake pan. Remove the hand and tilt the jar slightly to let out enough water so that the water level in the jar is just above the water level in the pan. Mark the water level in the jar with a piece of tape and leave the jar where it is. Have students check the water level the next day. It should be about one fifth higher than it was. Explain that oxygen in the air combines with iron in steel wool to form rust. Ask: **From this experiment, how can you tell how much oxygen there is in air?** *(About one fifth of the air is used up, so the air must be about one fifth oxygen.)* **learning modality: logical/mathematical**

Breathe In, Breathe Out

How can you detect carbon dioxide in the air you exhale?

1. Put on your goggles.
2. Fill a glass or beaker halfway with limewater.

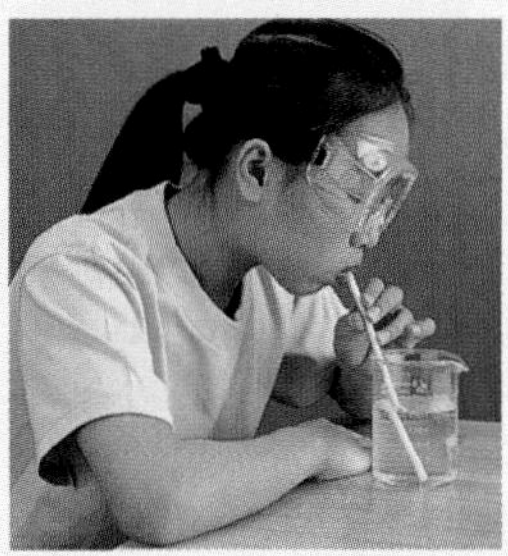

3. Using a straw, slowly blow air through the limewater for about a minute. **CAUTION:** *Do not suck on the straw or drink the limewater.*
4. What happens to the limewater?

Developing Hypotheses What do you think would happen if you did the same experiment after jogging for 10 minutes? If you tried this, what might the results tell you about exercise and carbon dioxide?

INTEGRATING LIFE SCIENCE Nitrogen is essential to living things. Proteins and other complex chemical substances in living things contain nitrogen. You and all other organisms must have nitrogen in order to grow and to repair body cells.

Most living things cannot obtain nitrogen directly from the air. Instead, some bacteria convert nitrogen into substances called nitrates. Plants then absorb the nitrates from the soil and use them to make proteins. To obtain proteins, animals must eat plants or other animals.

Oxygen Most oxygen molecules have two oxygen atoms. Even though oxygen is the second-most abundant gas in the atmosphere, it makes up less than one fourth of the volume. Plants and animals take oxygen directly from the air and use it to release energy from food in a usable form.

Oxygen is also involved in other important processes. Any fuel you can think of, from the gasoline in a car to the candles on a birthday cake, uses oxygen as it burns. Without oxygen, a fire will go out. Burning uses oxygen rapidly. During other processes, oxygen is used slowly. For example, steel in cars and other objects reacts slowly with oxygen to form iron oxide, or rust.

Have you ever noticed a pungent smell in the air after a thunderstorm? This is the odor of ozone, which forms when lightning interacts with oxygen in the air. **Ozone** is a form of oxygen that has three oxygen atoms in each molecule instead of the usual two.

Carbon Dioxide Each molecule of carbon dioxide has one atom of carbon and two atoms of oxygen. Even though the atmosphere contains only a small amount of carbon dioxide, it is essential to life. Plants must have carbon dioxide to produce food. Animals, on the other hand, give off carbon dioxide as a waste product.

When fuels such as coal and gasoline are burned, they release carbon dioxide. Burning these fuels increases the amount of carbon dioxide in the atmosphere. Rising carbon dioxide levels may be raising Earth's temperature. The issue of Earth's rising temperature, or global warming, is discussed in Section 2.

Figure 3 To burn, these candles need oxygen, one of the gases in the atmosphere. *Predicting What would happen if the candles used up all of the oxygen around them?*

Background

History of Science Scientists began searching for the components of air more than 300 years ago. In the 1600s, an English scientist named Robert Boyle discovered that air contains a substance needed for life when he noted that living things died if deprived of air. He called this substance "vital air." We now call it oxygen.

Almost 100 years later, Joseph Black, a Scottish medical student, found that limestone mixed with acid gives off a substance that puts out flames. He called it "fixed air." We now know it as carbon dioxide.

About 15 years later, one of Black's students, Daniel Rutherford, used a liquid to absorb vital air and fixed air. The substance that remained he called "noxious air," because it put out flames and killed living things. We now know it as nitrogen.

Other Gases Oxygen and nitrogen together make up 99 percent of dry air. Carbon dioxide and argon make up most of the other one percent. The remaining gases are called trace gases because only small amounts of them are present.

Water Vapor The composition of the air discussed so far has been for dry air. In reality, air is not dry because it contains water vapor. **Water vapor** is water in the form of a gas. Water vapor is invisible—it is not the same thing as steam, which is made up of tiny droplets of liquid water. Each water molecule contains two atoms of hydrogen and one atom of oxygen.

The amount of water vapor in the air varies greatly from place to place and from time to time. Air above a desert or polar ice sheet may contain almost no water vapor. In tropical rain forests, on the other hand, as much as five percent of the air may be water vapor.

Water vapor plays an important role in Earth's weather. Clouds form when water vapor condenses out of the air to form tiny droplets of liquid water or crystals of ice. If these droplets or crystals become large enough, they can fall as rain or snow.

Figure 4 This lush vegetation grows in a rain forest in Costa Rica. The percentage of water vapor in the air in a rain forest may be as high as five percent.

Particles Pure air contains only gases. But pure air exists only in laboratories. In the real world, air also contains tiny solid and liquid particles of dust, smoke, salt, and other chemicals. Sometimes you can see particles in the air around you, but most of them are too small to see.

Section 1 Review

1. Describe two ways in which the atmosphere is important to life on Earth.
2. What are the four most common gases in dry air?
3. Why are the amounts of gases in the atmosphere usually shown as percentages of dry air?
4. **Thinking Critically Applying Concepts** How would the amount of carbon dioxide in the atmosphere change if there were no plants? If there were no animals?

CHAPTER PROJECT

Check Your Progress

Have you determined *how, where,* and *when,* you will make your observations? Organize a notebook to record them. Think of ways to compare weather conditions from day to day. Make your observations without weather instruments or TV weather reports. (*Hint:* You can estimate how much of the sky is covered by clouds.) For your own safety, do not try to make observations during storms.

Media and Technology

Concept Videotape Library
Grade 6, Tape 2 "A Trip Through the Earth"

Answers to Self-Assessment

Caption Question

Figure 3 Their flames would go out.

Program Resources

◆ **Unit 4 Resources** 11-1 Review and Reinforce; 11-1 Enrich

TRY THIS

Skills Focus developing hypotheses
Materials *glass, limewater, straw*
Time 10 minutes
Tips Make sure students are careful not to splash or ingest any of the limewater.
Expected Outcome Students should observe that the limewater becomes cloudy when they blow into it because of carbon dioxide in their breath. After exercise, more carbon dioxide is exhaled, causing the limewater to get cloudier.
Extend Invite students to detect carbon dioxide in carbonated water by adding some of it to the limewater. **learning modality: kinesthetic**

3 Assess

Section 1 Review Answers

1. *Any two:* Provides oxygen and other gases living things need, traps energy from the sun to keep Earth's surface warm, and protects from meteoroids and radiation from the sun
2. Nitrogen, oxygen, argon, carbon dioxide
3. Because the amount of water vapor in air varies greatly
4. Without plants there would be less oxygen and more carbon dioxide; without animals there would be less carbon dioxide and more oxygen.

CHAPTER PROJECT

Check Your Progress

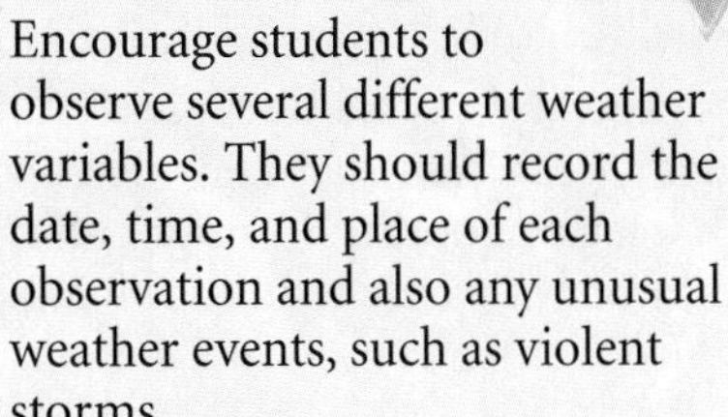

Encourage students to observe several different weather variables. They should record the date, time, and place of each observation and also any unusual weather events, such as violent storms.

Performance Assessment

Writing Have students write a paragraph identifying the three most important gases in air for living things, the percentage of each, and why the gas is important.

Real-World Lab

You and Your Environment

How Clean Is the Air?

Preparing for Inquiry

Key Concept The number of particles in air is affected by the weather.

Skills Objectives Students will be able to

- ◆ measure the number of particles in samples collected from the air;
- ◆ interpret how the number of particles is affected by weather factors.

Time 20 minutes the first day; 10 minutes a day for four days

Advance Planning If possible, students should collect particle samples outside. If they do, the vacuum cleaner may need an extension cord. However, they should not collect samples outside in wet weather. Instead, have students collect the samples as soon as possible after a rainfall. If you use only one vacuum cleaner, plan sufficient time for each group of students to use it.

Alternative Materials A portable vacuum cleaner is easier to carry outside than a regular vacuum cleaner. Instead of coffee filters, you can use paper towels for filters, but they are less effective because they let more particles pass through. Avoid using facial tissues because they are too fragile.

Guiding Inquiry

Invitation To help students focus on the key concept, ask: **What does air contain besides gases?** *(particles)* **How do you think weather conditions might affect the number of particles in the air?** *(Rain might wash particles out of the air, and wind might either stir them up or blow them away.)*

Introducing the Procedure

Ask: **Why do people in some occupations, such as wood-working, wear protective masks?** *(Because they work where there are high levels of particles in the air, and protective masks trap the particles so they do not breathe them in)* Mention some devices students may be familiar with, including motor vehicles and furnaces, that have filters to trap particles in the air that flows through them.

Troubleshooting the Experiment

- ◆ If possible, have students run the vacuum cleaner for 30 minutes each time. However, if the air is very dirty, 20 minutes each time may be enough.
- ◆ Because a vacuum cleaner is noisy, it may be necessary to run it outside of class time.
- ◆ Explain the importance of controlling other variables besides weather conditions that might influence the number of particles collected, such as proximity to a dusty playing field. Stress that samples should be taken in the same place each day to help control these other variables.

Safety

Emphasize the importance of not using the vacuum cleaner around water because of electrical shock. Review the safety guidelines in Appendix A.

Real-World Lab

You and Your Environment

How Clean Is the Air?

Sometimes you can actually see the atmosphere! How? Since air is normally transparent, it can only be visible because it contains particles. In this activity, you will use a vacuum cleaner to gather particles from the air.

Problem

How do weather factors affect the number of particles in the air?

Skills Focus

measuring, interpreting data

Materials

coffee filters
rubber band
thermometer
low-power microscope
vacuum cleaner with intake hose (1 per class)

Procedure

1. Predict what factors will affect the number of particles you collect. How might different weather factors affect your results?
2. In your notebook, make a data table like the one below.
3. Place the coffee filter over the nozzle of the vacuum cleaner hose. Fasten the coffee filter securely to the hose with a rubber band. Make sure the air passes through the coffee filter before entering the vacuum cleaner.
4. You will take air samples in the same place each day for five days. If possible, find a place outdoors. Otherwise, you can run the vacuum cleaner out a classroom window. **CAUTION:** *Do not use the vacuum cleaner outdoors on wet or rainy days.* If it is wet or rainy, collect the sample as soon as possible after it stops raining.
5. Hold the vacuum nozzle at least one meter above the ground each time you use the vacuum. Turn on the vacuum. Run the vacuum for 30 minutes. Shut off the vacuum.

DATA TABLE

Date and Time	Temperature	Amount of Precipitation	Wind Direction	Wind Speed	Number of Particles

334

6. While the vacuum is running, observe the weather conditions. Measure the temperature. Estimate the amount of precipitation, if any, since the previous observation. Note the direction from which the wind, if any, is blowing. Also note whether the wind is heavy, light, or calm. Record your observations.
7. Remove the coffee filter from the nozzle. Label the filter with the place, time, and date. Draw a circle on the filter to show the area that was over the vacuum nozzle.
8. Place the coffee filter on the stage of a microscope (40 power). Be sure that the part of the filter that was over the vacuum nozzle is directly under the microscope lens. Without moving the coffee filter, count all the particles you see. Record the number in your data table.
9. Repeat Steps 3–8 each clear day.

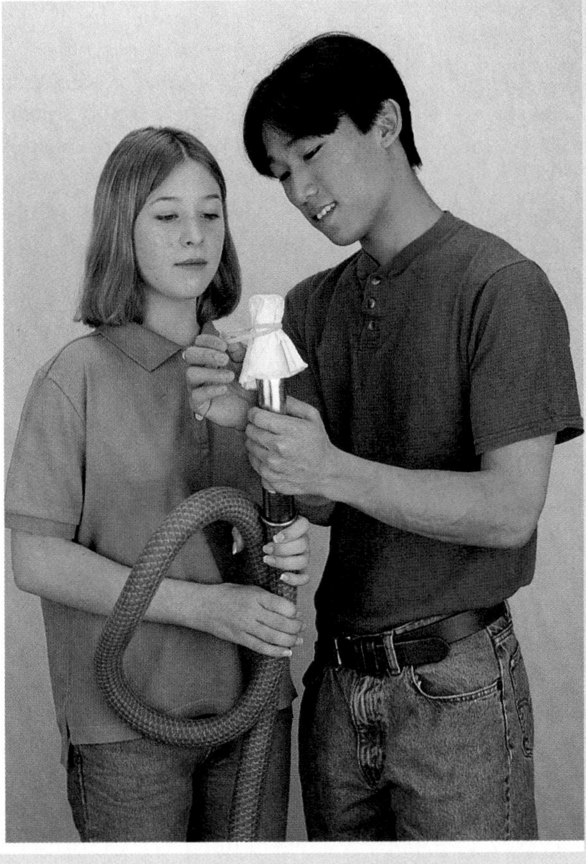

Analyze and Conclude

1. Was there a day of the week when you collected more particles?
2. What factors changed during the week that could have caused changes in the particle count?
3. Did the weather have any effect on your day-to-day results? If so, which weather factor do you think was most important?
4. Make a list of some possible sources of the particles you collected. Are these sources natural, or did the particles come from manufactured products?
5. How could you improve your method to get more particles out of the air?
6. **Apply** Identify areas in or around your school where there may be high levels of dust and other particles. What can people do to protect themselves in these areas?

Design an Experiment

Do you think time of day will affect the number of particles you collect? Develop a hypothesis and a plan for testing it. Could you work with other classes to get data at different times of the day? Before carrying out your plan, get your teacher's approval.

Expected Outcome

Using the microscope, students should be able to see and count the particles collected on the filters. The number of particles may vary greatly from one sample to another.

Analyze and Conclude

1. The particle count may vary from day to day depending on human activities and the weather.
2. The particle count is likely to be higher later in the week as particles given off by motor vehicles and factories and produced by other human activities accumulate in the air. Changing weather conditions also may cause changes in the particle count.
3. Weather factors most likely to affect day-to-day results are wind speed and recent precipitation.
4. Particles can come from many different sources. Natural sources include flowering plants, bare ground, and forest fires. Manufactured products that produce particles include motor vehicles, factories, and power plants.
5. Possible ways to get more particles out of the air include using a more powerful vacuum cleaner or a vacuum cleaner with a wider hose, running the vacuum cleaner longer each time, and using a finer filter.
6. Apply The cafeteria, gymnasium, and shop may have more particles than the classrooms. Playing fields and parking lots may have more particles than lawn areas. Wearing dust masks and using special air filters can help protect people from high levels of particles in the air.

Extending the Inquiry

Design an Experiment Students may hypothesize that more particles will be collected later in the day as particles accumulate in the air during the day as the result of human activity, such as driving vehicles and construction. They can test their hypotheses by comparing samples collected at different times of day.

Sample Data Table

Date and Time	Temp.	Amt. of Precipitation	Wind Direction	Wind Speed	# of Particles
Oct. 1, 2 P.M.	18°C	none	SW	calm	60
Oct. 2, 2 P.M.	19°C	none	SW	light breeze	55
Oct. 3, 2 P.M.	11°C	1 cm	W	moderate wind	18
Oct. 4, 2 P.M.	12°C	5 cm	W	strong wind	10
Oct. 5, 2 P.M.	13°C	5 cm	W	strong wind	11

Program Resources

- **Unit 4 Resources** Chapter 11 Real-World Lab

Media and Technology

Lab Activity Videotapes
Grade 6, Tape 3

INTEGRATING ENVIRONMENTAL SCIENCE

Section 2 Air Pollution

Objectives

After completing the lesson, students will be able to
- ◆ identify and describe outdoor and indoor air pollutants;
- ◆ explain the importance of ozone in the upper atmosphere;
- ◆ describe the greenhouse effect and explain how it affects climate.

Key Terms air pollution, emissions, photochemical smog, ozone, temperature inversion, acid rain, ozone layer, chlorofluorocarbons, greenhouse effect, global warming

1 Engage/Explore

Activating Prior Knowledge

Encourage students to describe specific examples of air pollution that they have seen, such as smog hanging over a city, smoke coming from factory smokestacks, and grime or pollen settling on cars parked outdoors. Ask: **What kinds of materials pollute the air we breathe?** *(Accept all responses without comment at this time.)*

Discover Activity

Skills Focus inferring
Materials *bottle of perfume*
Time 5 minutes
Tips Make sure students are evenly spaced throughout the room so the scent will reach different students at different times.
Expected Outcome Students closest to you will smell the perfume first, and those standing farthest away will smell it last.
Think It Over Students will see a "wave" of raised hands traveling from you to the farthest parts of the room. Students should infer that molecules of perfume traveled across the room in the air.

INTEGRATING ENVIRONMENTAL SCIENCE

Section 2 Air Pollution

Discover Activity

How Does the Scent Spread?

1. Choose a place to stand so that you and your classmates are evenly spread around the room.
2. Your teacher will open a bottle of perfume in one corner of the room.
3. Raise your hand when you first smell the perfume.

Think It Over
Inferring Describe the pattern you observed as people raised their hands. How do you think the smell traveled across the room?

Guide for Reading

- ◆ What causes photochemical smog?
- ◆ How is the ozone layer important?
- ◆ What are climate predictions based on?

Reading Tip As you read, make a list of different types of air pollution. Write a sentence about the effect of each type.

June 25, 1997, began as an ordinary day aboard the Russian space station *Mir.* The three crew members were busy with their usual tasks. One checked on the various scientific experiments. Another was exercising. The third cosmonaut was skillfully guiding a supply ship as it docked with *Mir.*

Suddenly, the crew members heard a frightening sound—the crumpling of collapsing metal. The space station jolted from side to side. The pressure gauges indicated an air leak! One crew member hurried to prepare the emergency evacuation vehicle. Meanwhile, the other two managed to close the airtight door between the damaged area and the rest of the space station. Fortunately, the pressure soon returned to normal. A disaster had been avoided. There was no need to abandon ship.

Closing the door preserved the most valuable resource on *Mir*—the air. Although you probably don't think about the air very often, it is just as important on Earth as it is on a space station. Air is a resource you use every minute of your life.

Figure 1 The air supply aboard the space station *Mir* was threatened by a collision during docking.

What's in the Air?

Though you can't see, taste, or smell it, you are surrounded by air. Air is a mixture of nitrogen, oxygen, carbon dioxide, water vapor, and other gases. Almost all living things depend on these gases to carry out their life processes.

Nitrogen, oxygen, and carbon dioxide cycle between the atmosphere and living things. These cycles ensure that the air supply on Earth will not run out. But they don't guarantee that the air will always be clean. A change to the atmosphere that has harmful effects is called **air pollution.** Substances that cause pollution are called pollutants. Pollutants can be solid particles,

Reading Strategies

Reading Tip Students could list the following types of air pollution: emissions (particles and gases) from factories, power plants, and automobiles; photochemical smog; acid rain; cigarette smoke; carbon monoxide from incomplete burning of fuels; radon; and chlorofluorocarbons. Their sentences should describe or explain the source of each type.

Caption Writing Distribute photocopies of Figure 4, and suggest that each student write a new caption that identifies each source of indoor pollution shown. Then have each student add another source of air pollution to the drawing. Have students exchange cartoons and expand the caption to include the pollution source that was added.

such as ash, or gases, such as chlorine. Air pollution can affect the health of humans and other living things. Pollution can even impact the climate of the whole planet.

What causes air pollution? If you're like many people, you probably picture a factory smokestack, belching thick black smoke into the sky. Until the mid-1900s, factories and power plants that burned coal produced most of the air pollution in the United States. Solid particles and gases that are released into the air are called **emissions.** Today, there is an even larger source of emissions that cause air pollution: motor vehicles such as cars, trucks, and airplanes. The engines of these vehicles release gases such as carbon monoxide, an invisible toxic gas.

Though most air pollution is the result of human activities, there are some natural causes as well. For example, an erupting volcano sends an enormous load of soot, ash, sulfur, and nitrogen oxide gases into the atmosphere.

☑ *Checkpoint* *What are some examples of air pollutants?*

Smog

Have you ever heard a weather forecaster talk about a "smog alert"? A smog alert is a warning about a type of air pollution called photochemical smog. **Photochemical smog** is a thick, brownish haze formed when certain gases in the air react with sunlight. When the smog level is high, it settles as a haze over a city. Smog can make people's eyes burn and irritate their throats.

The major sources of photochemical smog are the gases emitted by automobiles and trucks. Burning gasoline in a car engine releases some gases into the air. These gases include hydrocarbons (compounds containing hydrogen and carbon) and nitrogen oxides. The gases react in the sunlight and produce a form of oxygen called **ozone.** Ozone, which is toxic, is the major chemical found in smog.

Language Arts CONNECTION

People sometimes coin, or invent, a word to express a specific idea. For example, Londoners coined the word *smog* to describe the heavy gray air formed when coal smoke mixed with ocean fog.

In Your Journal

Can you guess the meaning of these coined words?

- brunch
- chortle
- squinched
- liger

Try coining a few descriptive words of your own. Exchange your words with a classmate and see if you can guess the meanings of the other's words.

Figure 2 A haze of photochemical smog hangs over this city's skyline. *Interpreting Photographs What is the source of the smog?*

Program Resources

- **Unit 4 Resources** 11-2 Lesson Plan; 11-2 Section Summary
- **Guided Reading and Study Workbook** Section 11-2

Answers to Self-Assessment

☑ *Checkpoint*

Air pollutants include solid particles such as ash, and gases such as chlorine and carbon monoxide.

Caption Question

Figure 2 The source of smog is the gases emitted by automobiles and trucks in the city.

2 Facilitate

What's in the Air?

Addressing Naive Conceptions

Materials *drawing compass, calculator*
Time 10–15 minutes

Ask: **Which gas do you think is most common in the air we breathe?** *(Accept all responses without comment.)* Then provide the following data: nitrogen 78%; oxygen 21%; argon 0.9%; other gases, including carbon dioxide and water vapor, 0.1%. Ask: **Was your prediction correct, or were you surprised?** *(Students may have thought that oxygen is the most common gas or that carbon dioxide is present in a much higher proportion.)* Challenge each student to use these data to create a circle graph. *(Nitrogen 281°, oxygen 75.5°, argon 3°, other gases 0.5°)* **learning modality: logical/mathematical**

Smog

Language Arts CONNECTION

To clarify how the word smog was created, write *smoke* + *fog* on the board, erase *oke* and *f*, and write = *smog.*

In Your Journal As a class, discuss suggestions for each word. (*Brunch:* a meal midway between breakfast and lunch; *chortle:* to chuckle and snort; *squinch:* to squint or squeeze and pinch; *liger:* the offspring of a lion and a tiger) The word *chortle* was coined by British author Lewis Carroll, who coined many terms in his famous poem "Jabberwocky." Students may enjoy identifying other coined words in the poem. **learning modality: verbal**

Ongoing Assessment

Oral Presentation Call on students to each name one source of particles or gases that contribute to air pollution.

Smog, continued

Integrating Health

Some respiratory problems, such as asthma, bronchitis, and emphysema are caused or worsened by breathing polluted air. A local hospital, nursing association, or pediatric practice may be able to provide pamphlets or a speaker on these topics. Encourage students to use the information they receive to make posters that include a labeled diagram of the respiratory system (or parts of it) and a brief description of how the system is affected. **learning modality: verbal**

Acid Rain

Building Inquiry Skills: Observing

ACTIVITY

Materials *plastic cup, scissors, piece of nylon stocking fabric, tape, hand lens*
Time 10–15 minutes for setup plus follow-up observations

Have students examine nylon stocking fabric with a hand lens and draw what they see. Also have students pull and twist the fabric to test its strength and flexibility. Then have each student make an "acid rain tester" by cutting out the bottom of a plastic cup and taping a piece of stocking over the opening. Take students outdoors to hang the testers where they will be exposed to air and rain. At the end of a week, have students reexamine the fabric, compare it with their original drawings, retest its strength and flexibility, and look for broken fibers and other signs of damage. Encourage students to consider what could have caused any damage. Point out that polluting gases in the air, such as sulfur oxides and nitrogen oxides, also affect the nylon. **learning modality: visual**

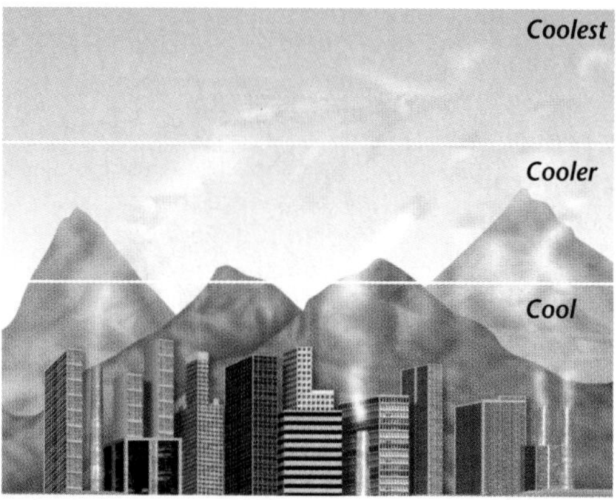

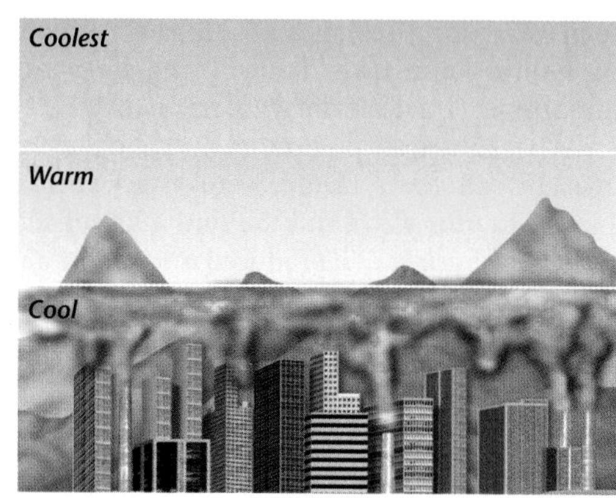

Figure 3 Normally, pollutants rise high in the air and blow away (left). But during a temperature inversion, a layer of warm air traps pollutants close to the ground (right).

Temperature Inversion Pollutants usually blow away from the place where they are produced. Normally, air close to the ground is heated by Earth's surface. As the air warms, it rises into the cooler air above it. The pollutants are carried higher into the atmosphere where they blow away. But certain weather conditions cause a condition known as a temperature inversion. During a **temperature inversion,** a layer of warm air prevents the rising air from escaping. The polluted air is trapped and held close to Earth's surface. The smog becomes more concentrated and dangerous.

Health Effects of Smog The effects of smog can be more serious than itchy, watery eyes and a scratchy throat. The ozone in smog can cause lung problems and harm the body's defenses against infection. When smog levels reach a certain point, a city issues a smog alert. During a smog alert, you should avoid exercising outdoors. People who have asthma or other conditions that affect their breathing should be particularly careful.

INTEGRATING HEALTH

✓ *Checkpoint* *What happens during a temperature inversion?*

Acid Rain

Another type of air pollution is caused by power plants and factories that burn coal and oil. These fuels produce nitrogen oxides and sulfur oxides when they are burned. These gases react with water vapor in the air, forming nitric acid and sulfuric acid. The acids return to Earth's surface dissolved in precipitation. Precipitation that is more acidic than normal is called **acid rain.** Acid rain can be in the form of snow, sleet, or fog as well as rain.

As you can imagine, acid falling from the sky has some negative effects. When acid rain falls into a pond or lake, it changes

Background

Facts and Figures Ordinary rainwater contains dissolved carbon dioxide and other compounds of natural origin that form weak acid solutions. Normally, the pH of rainwater is about 5 to 6. But rain in the northeastern United States usually has a pH of about 4. Sometimes the rain in this region is at least as acidic as vinegar, which has a pH of 3.

One factor that makes acid rain such a complex problem is that it occurs far from the source of the gases that cause it. For example, gases from coal-burning power plants in England are blown eastward and cause acid rain in Sweden and Norway. In the United States, midwestern and eastern states produce much of the acid rain that falls in New England and southeastern Canada.

the conditions there. Many fish, and particularly their eggs, cannot survive in more acidic water. Acid rain that falls on the ground can damage plants by affecting the nutrient levels in the soil. Whole forests have been destroyed by acid rain. Fortunately, some of the effects of acid rain are reversible. Badly damaged lakes have been restored by adding substances such as lime that neutralize the acid.

Acid rain doesn't just affect living things. The acid reacts with stone and metal in buildings and statues. Automobiles rust more quickly in areas with acid rain. These effects are not reversible.

Indoor Air Pollution

You might think that you could avoid air pollution by staying inside. But in fact, the air inside buildings can be polluted, too. Many substances can cause indoor air pollution. Some, such as dust, pet hair, and air fresheners, bother only those people who are allergic to them. Other pollutants have more widespread effects. Asbestos, a building material common in older buildings, can cause lung disease. Products such as oil-based paints, glues, and cleaning supplies may give off toxic fumes. Read the label whenever you use any of these products. You may need to open a window or use the chemical outdoors.

If you have been near someone smoking a cigarette, you know how the smell stays in your clothes and hair even after you leave the room. The smoke reached your lungs every time you inhaled near the smoking person. Research has shown that cigarette smoke can damage the lungs and heart. Now smoking is banned in many places such as restaurants, airports, and stadiums.

How Acid Is Your Rain?

ACTIVITY

In this activity you will test whether rain in your area is more or less acidic than lemon juice (citric acid).

1. Collect some rainwater in a clean plastic cup.
2. Indoors, dip a piece of pH paper into the cup. Compare the color of the paper to the chart on the package to find the pH. (The lower the pH of a substance, the more acidic it is.)
3. Pour a little lemon juice into a plastic cup. Repeat Step 2 with the lemon juice.

Measuring What is the pH of the rainwater? How does it compare to the pH of the lemon juice?

Figure 4 Air inside buildings can be polluted, too. *Observing How many sources of pollution can you spot in this room?*

TRY THIS

ACTIVITY

Skills Focus measuring
Materials *rainwater, 2 plastic cups, pH paper, pH chart, lemon juice*
Time 10 minutes
Tips You might want to collect rainwater ahead of time for this activity.
Expected Outcome Rainwater is normally slightly acidic (pH 5–6); a pH lower than 5 indicates acid rain. Lemon juice's pH is 2.
Extend Have students measure the pH of tap water and compare it with their pH measurements of rainwater and lemon juice. **learning modality: logical/mathematical**

Indoor Air Pollution

Real-Life Learning

ACTIVITY

Materials *containers of various products such as oil-based paints, glues, and cleaning supplies that give off toxic fumes*
Time 10 minutes

Display the products for students to examine their labels. (CAUTION: *Instruct students to not open any container.*) Have volunteers read aloud cautionary statements on the labels. Then ask: **How could you use these products safely?** *(Instructions may vary. Usually such products can be used safely outside or in well-ventilated areas.)* **How should such products be stored?** *(They should be stored in a secure area, away from small children and pets, and the containers should be closed tightly.)* **How should such products be disposed of?** *(Most such products should be taken to a hazardous waste site.)* **learning modality: verbal**

Media and Technology

Transparencies "Temperature Inversion," Transparency 37

Answers to Self-Assessment

Checkpoint

A layer of warm air prevents cooler air below it from rising, trapping polluted air close to Earth's surface.

Caption Question

Figure 4 *Samples:* Smoking, dusting, burning wood in the fireplace, cat hair, bird feathers, flower pollen, carpet fumes

Ongoing Assessment

Drawing Have each student draw and label a diagram to explain how acid rain forms.

Students can save their drawings in their portfolios.

Indoor Air Pollution, continued

Including All Students

For students who need additional help with language skills, write *carbon dioxide* and *carbon monoxide* on the board and ask: **What difference do you see between these terms?** *(The prefixes di- and mon-; draw a box around each prefix.)* **What do these word parts mean?** *(Di- means "two," mon- means "one.")* **What do you think *dioxide* and *monoxide* mean?** *("Two oxygens" and "one oxygen")* Write CO_2 and CO below the terms, and draw a simple diagram of each molecule. Explain that CO_2, a harmless gas, has two oxygen atoms in each molecule, while CO has only one. CO is deadly because it is absorbed by red blood cells more easily than oxygen (O_2) is. When a person breathes CO, it replaces the O_2 in the body, causing suffocation. Stress the value of detectors in preventing CO poisoning. **learning modality: verbal**

Sharpen your Skills

Communicating

Time 15 minutes

ACTIVITY

Tips Have students work in groups of three. Establish a time limit of 30 or 45 seconds for the announcement. Let each group tape-record its announcement.

Expected Outcome Play the announcements in class, and have students assess each one for the elements cited in the text, including "listener appeal."

Extend Let the class choose the most effective announcement. Arrange to have it broadcast over the school's PA system. **learning modality: verbal**

Figure 5 Installing a carbon monoxide detector in a home can save lives. Because carbon monoxide has no color or odor, it cannot be detected by sight or smell.

Carbon Monoxide One particularly dangerous type of indoor air pollution is carbon monoxide. Carbon monoxide is a colorless, odorless gas that forms when wood, coal, oil, or gas are incompletely burned. When carbon monoxide builds up in an enclosed space such as a basement, apartment, or house, it can be deadly. Because carbon monoxide cannot be detected by sight or smell, its victims have no warning that the level is dangerously high. Any home heated by wood, coal, oil, or gas should have a carbon monoxide detector. The detector sounds a warning alarm when the gas is present.

Radon Another type of pollution that is difficult to detect is radon. Radon is a colorless, odorless gas that is radioactive. It is formed naturally by certain types of rocks underground. Radon can enter homes through cracks in basement walls or floors. Research indicates that breathing radon gas over many years may cause lung cancer and other health problems. But the level of radon necessary to cause these effects is unknown. To be safe, many homeowners have installed ventilation systems to prevent radon from building up in their homes.

Communicating

ACTIVITY

Write a radio public service announcement to inform people about either carbon monoxide or radon. Think about how the announcement could catch your listeners' attention. Describe the source and effects of the pollutant. Suggest how listeners can protect themselves.

☑ *Checkpoint* *Why is it important to install carbon monoxide detectors in homes?*

The Ozone Layer

If you have ever had a sunburn, you have experienced the painful effects of the sun's ultraviolet radiation. But did you know that such burns would be even worse without the protection of the ozone layer? The **ozone layer** is a layer of the upper atmosphere about 30 kilometers above Earth's surface. Actually, the concentration of ozone in this layer is very low—only a few parts per million.

Background

Integrating Science The ozone layer is located in the upper atmosphere, in the stratosphere. In 1985, meteorologists brought a strange discovery to the attention of other scientists: there was a "hole" in the ozone layer. They had observed a large area in the stratosphere over Antarctica where the ozone layer had become much thinner. The area of the hole in the mid-1990s was about 23.3 million km^2, roughly as big as North America. There is also evidence of a smaller hole in the ozone layer above the Arctic.

CFCs are the primary cause of the depletion of the stratospheric ozone layer. Ultraviolet radiation from the sun breaks the CFCs apart, forming chlorine. Chlorine reacts with ozone, thereby destroying the ozone molecules.

Yet even the small amount of ozone in the ozone layer protects people from the effects of too much ultraviolet radiation. These effects include sunburn, eye diseases, and skin cancer.

Since you read earlier that ozone is a pollutant, the fact that ozone can be helpful may sound confusing. The difference between ozone as a pollutant and ozone as a helpful gas is its location. Ozone close to Earth's surface in the form of smog is harmful. Higher in the atmosphere, where people cannot breathe it, ozone protects us.

The Source of Ozone Ozone is constantly being made and destroyed. When sunlight strikes an ozone molecule, the energy of the ultraviolet radiation is partly absorbed. This energy causes the molecule to break apart into an oxygen molecule and an oxygen atom, as shown in Figure 6. The oxygen atom soon collides with another oxygen molecule. They react to form a new ozone molecule. Each time this cycle occurs, some ultraviolet energy is absorbed. That energy does not reach Earth's surface.

The Ozone Hole In the late 1970s, scientists observed that the amount of ozone in the ozone layer seemed to be decreasing. What was to blame for this loss of ozone?

One problem was a group of gases containing chlorine and fluorine, called **chlorofluorocarbons,** or "CFCs." CFCs had been used instead of smelly, toxic ammonia in refrigerators and air conditioners. CFCs were also used in fire extinguishers and aerosol spray cans. Then scientists discovered that CFCs react with ozone molecules. The CFCs block the cycle that absorbs ultraviolet radiation. In 1990, many nations signed an agreement to ban the use of almost all CFCs by the year 2000. Unfortunately, the CFC molecules are very stable. They have remained in the atmosphere for a long time. But scientists predict that if the ban is maintained, the ozone layer will gradually recover.

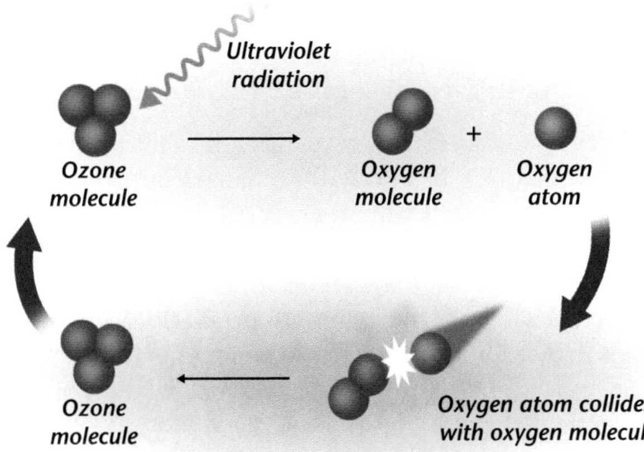

Figure 6 When ultraviolet radiation from the sun strikes an ozone molecule, some energy is absorbed by the ozone molecule. This energy causes the ozone molecule to split into an oxygen molecule and a free oxygen atom. *Interpreting Diagrams What happens when the free oxygen atom collides with an oxygen molecule?*

The Ozone Layer

Inquiry Challenge

Materials *clay or other materials of students' choice; flashlight or lamp*
Time 10 minutes

Challenge pairs of students to create a model to demonstrate the ozone cycle. *(Sample model: Shape three balls from clay to represent oxygen atoms. Stick the three balls together to represent an ozone molecule. Shine light at the ozone molecule and detach one oxygen atom. Then there is an oxygen molecule and a single oxygen atom. To create an ozone molecule, stick the single ball to the two attached balls, returning to the first step in the cycle.)* **cooperative learning**

Media and Technology

Transparencies "The Ozone Cycle," Transparency 38

Answers to Self-Assessment

✓ Checkpoint

Carbon monoxide cannot be seen or smelled, so detectors are needed to warn people when it is present at dangerous levels.

Caption Question

Figure 6 An ozone molecule is formed.

Ongoing Assessment

Writing Have each student explain how ozone forms in the atmosphere and why this process protects organisms on Earth.

Students can save their work in their portfolios.

Global Climate Change

Integrating Earth Science

Materials *2 small glass aquaria; 2 thermometers; 2 rulers; string; paper cup cut in half lengthwise; tape; glass aquarium cover or plastic wrap*
Time 10 minutes

ACTIVITY

Put two glass aquaria on a sunny windowsill, and lay a ruler across each one. Suspend a thermometer from each ruler with the numbered side facing toward the classroom and away from the window. Shade each thermometer by taping a cup half behind it. Ask a volunteer to read both thermometers and record these starting temperatures on the board. Then cover one aquarium with a glass cover or a piece of plastic wrap taped to the sides. At regular intervals, have other volunteers take new readings and record the temperatures and times on the board. In a follow-up class discussion, ask: **What happened to the air temperature in the uncovered aquarium?** *(It should have increased a bit at first, then stayed the same.)* **What happened to the air temperature in the covered aquarium?** *(It kept increasing.)* **What does the air inside the aquaria represent in this model?** *(The air near Earth's surface)* **What does the cover on the aquarium represent?** *(The gases that trap heat and keep it from escaping into space)* **What is this process called?** *(The greenhouse effect)* **learning modality: logical/mathematical**

EXPLORING Climate Predictions

Point out that the questions posed in the captions are ones that scientists ask as they study Earth's climate and try to predict long-term changes. Emphasize that there are no "right" answers to questions such as these. In a class discussion or in small groups, let students offer their own ideas in response to the questions. **learning modality: verbal**

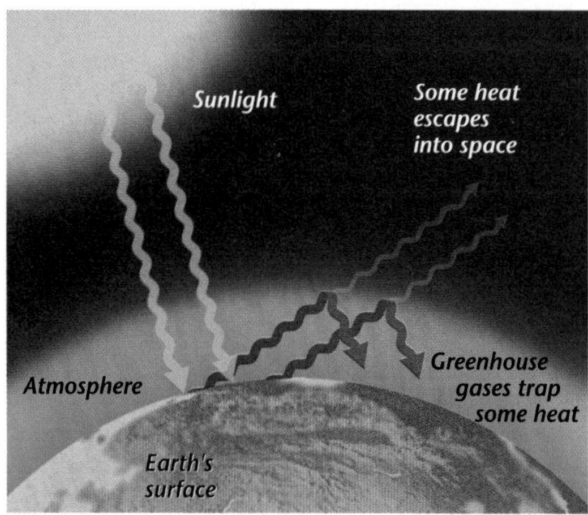

Figure 7 When energy in the form of sunlight strikes Earth's surface, it changes to heat. Certain gases in the atmosphere trap some of the heat, preventing it from escaping back into space. This trapping of heat is known as the greenhouse effect.
Applying Concepts What gases in the atmosphere trap heat near Earth's surface?

Global Climate Change

Some changes to the atmosphere affect the climate of the whole planet. To understand why, you need to know more about the atmosphere.

The Greenhouse Effect Think about the INTEGRATING EARTH SCIENCE sun shining through a window on a cool day. The window lets light enter the room. The light strikes objects in the room and is converted to heat. But the closed windows trap the warm air inside, so the room becomes warmer.

In the atmosphere, water vapor, carbon dioxide, and certain other gases act like windows. These gases allow sunlight to reach Earth's surface, but they prevent the heat from escaping back into space. The trapping of heat near Earth's surface is called the **greenhouse effect**. Without the greenhouse effect, Earth would be much colder—about 33°C colder on average.

Global Warming Since the 1800s, coal and oil have been the main sources of energy in most of the world. As you have read, burning these substances produces carbon dioxide. During this time, the amount of carbon dioxide in the atmosphere has increased from 280 parts per million to 350 parts per million. This amount is increasing more quickly every year.

Does increasing carbon dioxide cause the greenhouse effect to become stronger? One theory, called **global warming,** predicts that the increase in carbon dioxide will cause the average temperature to continue to rise. Scientists have estimated that the increase in the next century could be as much as 3 to 8 Celsius degrees. Although that may not sound like a big change, it could have a huge impact. Parts of the Antarctic ice cap would melt, raising the level of the oceans. The temperature change would affect climate patterns all over the world. This would affect where crops are grown. There might also be more severe storms.

Predicting Climate Change It is difficult to predict how Earth's climate will be affected by changes in the atmosphere. The systems that create climate are very complex. Scientists have studied these systems for less than a century, a very short time to learn about processes that can occur over thousands of years. **Most scientists base their climate predictions on computer models that calculate the effects of changes in the atmosphere.** As *Exploring Climate Predictions* shows, making these predictions requires many types of information.

Background

History of Science In June 1992, the United Nations Conference on Environment and Development met to discuss international environmental problems, including pollution and deterioration of Earth's atmosphere. As a result, more than 165 nations have signed a climate change treaty to curb carbon dioxide emissions and thus reduce the greenhouse effect.

Media and Technology

Concept Videotape Library
Grade 6, Tape 2 "Our Passion for Driving"; "The Greenhouse Effect"

EXPLORING Climate Predictions

Many factors affect the complex systems that create climate. Good predictions must consider as many of these factors as possible.

Emissions
Power plants, factories, and vehicles produce gases that increase the greenhouse effect. Will there be more emissions in the future, or will ways be found to reduce them? Will people change their habits to use less energy?

Oceans
Carbon dioxide cycles between the atmosphere and the oceans, where it dissolves in the water. If ocean temperatures change, will more or less carbon dioxide be dissolved?

Forests
Plants take in carbon dioxide during photosynthesis. As forests are cut down, more carbon dioxide stays in the atmosphere. But if Earth continues to get warmer, more plants may grow. They will remove more carbon dioxide from the air. Which effect will be greater?

Clouds
If Earth gets warmer, more water will evaporate. More water vapor in the air would increase the greenhouse effect. But there would also be more clouds, which reflect sunlight away from Earth's surface. Will the result be warmer or cooler air?

Section 1 Review

1. How does photochemical smog form?
2. How does the ozone layer protect people?
3. How do scientists make climate predictions?
4. Give three examples of indoor air pollutants and list their sources.
5. **Thinking Critically Predicting** One possible result of global warming is that melting ice could cause ocean levels to rise. What effects might this have?

Science at Home

Solids in the Air With a family member, set up two particle collectors. Smear petroleum jelly on the inside of two clean, empty glass jars. Place one inside your home and the other outside. Make sure both jars are in locations where they will not be disturbed. Predict what you will find if you leave the jars in place for a few days. Compare the solid particles in each jar. How similar are they? Can you identify any of the particles?

3 Assess

Section 1 Review Answers

1. Hydrocarbons and nitrogen oxides react in sunlight to produce ozone, the major chemical in photochemical smog.
2. The ozone layer absorbs some of the harmful ultraviolet energy in sunlight and prevents it from reaching Earth's surface.
3. Most scientists base their climate predictions on computer models that calculate the effects of changes in the atmosphere.
4. *Any three:* dust, pet hair, and air fresheners; asbestos from building materials; oil-based products; gases and particles in cigarette smoke; carbon monoxide from burning wood, coal, oil, or gas as fuel; radon gas that enters buildings from rocks underground
5. *Sample answer:* Rising ocean levels would flood coastal areas, destroying cities, farms, and habitats.

Science at Home

Materials *2 clean, empty glass jars; petroleum jelly*

Suggest that students place the inside jar in a busy room, such as the kitchen or living room, and the outside jar in their yard or close to a driveway or street. Depending on the time of year, students may observe pollen grains as well as dust, pet hair, soot, and the like.

Media and Technology

Transparencies "The Greenhouse Effect," 39, and "Exploring Climate Predictions," 40

Concept Videotape Library Grade 6, Tape 2 "A Better Cool"

Answers to Self-Assessment

Caption Question

Figure 7 Water vapor, CO_2, and others

Program Resources

◆ **Unit 4 Resources** 11-2 Review and Reinforce; 11-2 Enrich

Performance Assessment

Drawing Have each student draw and label a diagram to explain one of the following processes: the formation of photochemical smog, the formation of acid rain, the ozone cycle, or the greenhouse effect.

Students can save their diagrams in their portfolios.

SCIENCE AND SOCIETY

Cars and Clean Air

Purpose

To help students learn ways that pollution from cars can be reduced and make a reasonable judgment about the best ways to do this.

Panel Discussion

Time one day to prepare; 30 minutes for panel discussion

After students have read the feature, ask for volunteers to form a panel to discuss the issues. Have each panel member assume one of the following roles: a car manufacturer, a person who commutes 50 miles a day to work, a person who lives near a busy intersection, a lawmaker, and a public health official. Students should take the point of view of the individual they represent and present relevant facts and opinions for that individual. Following the panel discussion, take a class vote on which methods of reducing pollution seem most effective and whether the methods should be voluntary or enforced.

Extend Challenge students to learn about alternative means of transportation in their community and report on the costs and availability of each.

You Decide

1. Even the least polluting cars cause some air pollution, and there are more cars on the road each year. More cars also mean more traffic jams, which produce more pollution than does driving on the open road. Automobiles pollute the air with particles such as soot and gases that contribute to smog and acid rain.
2. Driving cars that are more efficient and produce less pollution, and driving less
3. Students should illustrate more than one way to help reduce pollution from cars. Their captions should demonstrate that they understand how the solutions address the problem.

SCIENCE AND SOCIETY

Cars and Clean Air

New technology and strict laws have brought cleaner air to many American cities. But in some places the air is still polluted. Cars and trucks still cause about half the air pollution in cities. And there are more cars on the road every year!

Worldwide, there are about 500 million cars. More cars will mean more pollution and more traffic jams. Unfortunately, cars stuck in traffic produce three times as much pollution as cars on the open road. What can people do to reduce air pollution by cars?

The Issues

Can Cars Be Made To Pollute Less? In the past 20 years, cars have become more fuel-efficient and pollution levels have been lowered. Now engineers are running out of ways to make cars run more efficiently and produce less pollution. But technology does offer other answers.

Some vehicles use fuels other than gasoline. For instance, natural gas can power cars and trucks. Burning natural gas produces less pollution than burning gasoline.

Battery-powered electric cars produce no air pollution. However, the electricity to charge the batteries often comes from power plants that burn oil or coal. So electric cars still produce some pollution indirectly. Car makers have produced a few electric cars, but they are expensive and can make only fairly short trips.

Should People Drive Less? Many car trips are shorter than a mile—an easy distance for most people to walk. For longer trips, people might consider riding a bicycle. Many cars on the road carry just one person. Some people might consider riding with others in car pools or taking buses or subways.

Are Stricter Standards or Taxes the Answer? Some state governments have led efforts to reduce pollution. The state of California, for example, has strict anti-pollution laws. These laws set standards for gradually reducing pollutants released by cars. Stricter laws might make some old cars illegal.

Another approach is to make driving more expensive so that people use their cars less. That might mean higher gasoline taxes or fees for using the roads at busy times.

You Decide

1. **Identify the Problem** In your own words, explain why automobiles make it hard to improve air quality. What kinds of pollution are caused by automobiles?
2. **Analyze the Options** What are some ways to reduce the pollution caused by cars? Should these actions be voluntary, or should governments require them?
3. **Find a Solution** How would you encourage people to try to reduce the pollution from cars? Create a visual essay from newspaper and magazine clippings. Write captions to explain your solution.

Background

Young teens tend to see things in all-or-nothing terms. They may think that any method of reducing pollution from cars should be adopted and enforced. Help students appreciate that most methods of reducing pollution from cars have drawbacks by citing these two examples.

Catalytic converters convert unburned hydrocarbons in car exhaust into nonpoisonous gases. These devices have been required by law for many years on all new cars sold in the United States. However, catalytic converters also result in a higher production of sulfuric acid, which contributes to acid rain.

Cars that are more fuel-efficient burn less gas and produce fewer pollutants per mile driven. However, the number of cars on the road and the number of miles people drive every year are both increasing.

Section 3 Air Pressure

Discover Activity

Does Air Have Mass?

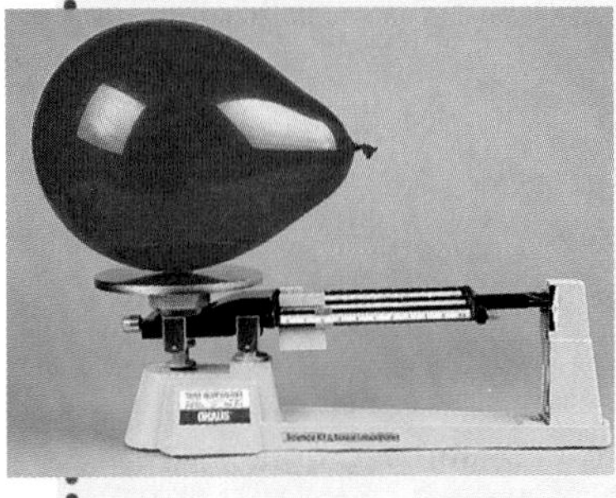

1. Use a balance to find the mass of a deflated balloon.
2. Blow up the balloon and tie the neck closed. Do you think the mass of the inflated balloon will differ from the mass of the deflated balloon?
3. Find the mass of the inflated balloon. Compare this mass to the mass of the deflated balloon. Was your prediction correct?

Think It Over

Drawing Conclusions Did the mass of the balloon change after it was inflated? What can you conclude about whether air has mass?

Guide for Reading

- What are some of the properties of air?
- What instruments are used to measure air pressure?
- How does increasing altitude affect air pressure and density?

Reading Tip As you read this section, use the headings to make an outline about air pressure.

One of the best parts of eating roasted peanuts is opening the jar. When a jar of peanuts is "vacuum packed," most of the air is pumped out, creating low pressure inside. When you break the seal, the "whoosh" you hear is air from the outside rushing into the jar. The "whoosh" is the result of a difference in pressure between the outside of the jar and the inside.

Properties of Air

It may seem to you that air has no mass. However, air consists of atoms and molecules, which have mass. So air must have mass. **Because air has mass, it also has other properties, including density and pressure.**

Density The amount of mass in a given volume of air is its **density**. You can calculate density by dividing mass by volume.

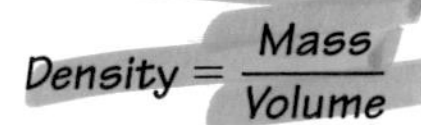

$$\text{Density} = \frac{\text{Mass}}{\text{Volume}}$$

If there are more molecules in a given volume of air, the density is higher. If there are fewer molecules, the density is lower.

Pressure The force pushing on an area or surface is known as **pressure**. A denser substance has more mass per unit volume than a less dense one. So denser air exerts more pressure than less dense air.

To understand pressure, think of carrying a heavy backpack. The weight presses the straps into your shoulders just as the pack does to the hiker in the photo.

Reading Strategies

Reading Tip Suggest to students that they summarize the main points under each heading in a few words and add these to their outline. Student outlines might begin as follows:

I. Properties of Air
   A. Density
   B. Pressure
II. Measuring Air Pressure
   A. Mercury Barometer

Program Resources

- **Unit 4 Resources** 11-3 Lesson Plan; 11-3 Section Summary
- **Guided Reading and Study Workbook** Section 11-3

Section 3 Air Pressure

Objectives

After completing the lesson, students will be able to

- identify some of the properties of air;
- name instruments that are used to measure air pressure;
- explain how increasing altitude affects air pressure and density.

Key Terms density, pressure, air pressure, barometer, mercury barometer, aneroid barometer, altitude

1 Engage/Explore

Activating Prior Knowledge

Introduce students to the concept of air pressure by asking: **Did your ears ever "pop" when you rode in an elevator or airplane?** *(Many students probably have had this experience.)* Explain that as one goes higher, the pressure of the air outside the body decreases while the pressure of the air inside the body, including the ears, stays the same. The popping sensation is air escaping from inside the ears into the throat to even out the pressure. Tell students they will learn more about air pressure and other properties of air in this section.

Discover

Skills Focus drawing conclusions
Materials *balance, balloon*
Time 10 minutes
Tips You may want to review how to use the balance before students begin the activity. The larger the balloon, the greater the difference in mass will be. Inflatable balls may be substituted for balloons.
Expected Outcome The balloon should have a greater mass after it is inflated.
Think It Over Students should say that the mass of the balloon increased after it was inflated and conclude from this that air has mass.

2 Facilitate

Properties of Air

Including All Students

Materials *two sink plungers*

Time 5 minutes

To help students appreciate how much pressure air exerts, give pairs of students two sink plungers and show them how to put the plungers together by matching the ends. Then have the students try to pull the plungers apart. Relate this to air pressure by asking: **Why are the plungers hard to pull apart?** *(Because air is pressing on the outside of the two plungers and holding them together)* **learning modality: kinesthetic**

Measuring Air Pressure

Building Inquiry Skills: Predicting

Reinforce students' understanding of how a mercury barometer works by asking: **Why must there be a vacuum in the tube of a mercury barometer?** *(So the mercury can rise inside the tube)* **What do you predict would happen if the tube was filled with air?** *(The column of mercury would not rise as high because of the pressure from the air in the tube. The barometer would give an incorrect reading.)* **learning modality: verbal**

Real-Life Learning

Materials *copies of newspaper weather reports*

Time 15 minutes

Help students appreciate how barometer readings relate to weather. First, explain that the average air pressure worldwide is 29.9212 inches. A drop of less than an inch can be a sign of a major storm, and a rise of less than an inch a sign of fair weather. Then show students newspaper weather reports for several different days. Have them observe how changes in barometric pressure are related to weather conditions. **learning modality: logical/mathematical**

When you take off a backpack, it feels as if all the pressure has been taken off your shoulders. But has it? The weight of the column of air above you remains, as shown in Figure 10.

Air pressure is the result of the weight of a column of air pushing down on an area. The weight of the column of air above your desk is about the same as the weight of a large school bus! So why doesn't air pressure crush your desk? The reason is that the molecules in air push in all directions—down, up, and sideways. So the air pushing down on the top of your desk is balanced by the air pushing up on the bottom of the desk.

Figure 10 There is a column of air above you all the time. The weight of the air in the atmosphere causes air pressure.

Measuring Air Pressure

Have you ever heard a weather report say that the air pressure is falling? Falling air pressure usually indicates that a storm is approaching. Rising air pressure usually means that the weather is clearing. A **barometer** (buh RAHM uh tur) is an instrument that is used to measure changes in air pressure. **There are two kinds of barometers: mercury barometers and aneroid barometers.**

Mercury Barometers The first barometers invented were mercury barometers. Figure 11 shows how a mercury barometer works. A **mercury barometer** consists of a glass tube open at the bottom end and partially filled with mercury. The space in the tube above the mercury is almost a vacuum—it contains no air. The open end of the tube rests in a dish of mercury. The air pressure pushing down on the surface of the mercury in the dish is equal to the

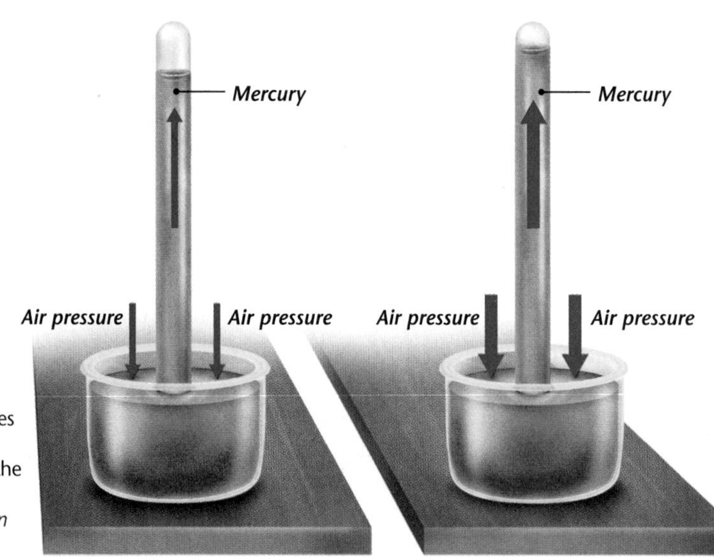

Figure 11 Air pressure pushes down on the surface of the mercury in the dish, causing the mercury in the tube to rise. ***Predicting*** *What happens when the air pressure increases?*

Background

History of Science The first mercury barometer was invented in 1643 by an Italian physicist named Evangelista Torricelli. Torricelli was studying why liquids rise only to a certain height in a column. Because mercury is so heavy, he thought it would rise to a lower height than water and be more convenient to study. He filled a long glass tube with mercury, blocked the open end with his finger, and turned the tube upside down in a container of mercury. The mercury in the glass tube went down to about 76 cm. Torricelli experimented with different-sized tubes, but the height of the mercury stayed the same. From this Torricelli concluded that the height of the mercury in the tube was directly related to the pressure of the air on the mercury in the container. Thus, he had invented a way to measure air pressure.

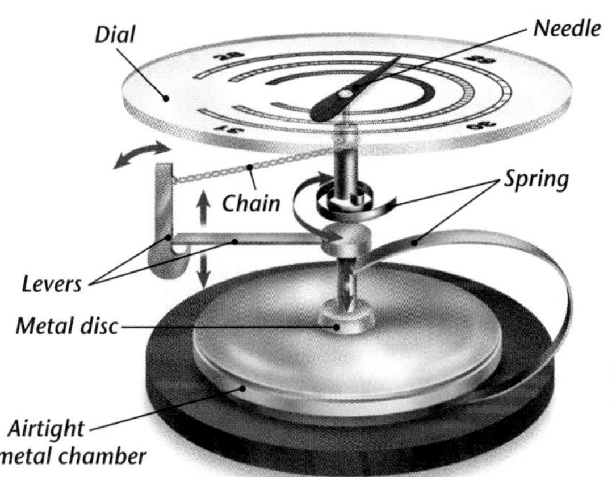

Figure 12 Changes in air pressure cause the walls of the airtight metal chamber to flex in and out. The needle on the dial indicates the air pressure.

weight of the column of mercury in the tube. At sea level the mercury column is about 76 centimeters high, on average.

When the air pressure increases, it presses down more on the surface of the mercury. Greater air pressure forces the column of mercury higher. What will happen to the column of mercury if the air pressure decreases? The column will fall.

Aneroid Barometers If you have a barometer on a desk or wall at home, it is probably an aneroid barometer. The word *aneroid* means "without liquid." An **aneroid barometer** (AN uh royd) has an airtight metal chamber, as shown in Figure 12. The metal chamber is sensitive to changes in air pressure. When air pressure increases, the thin walls of the chamber are pushed in. When the pressure drops, the walls bulge out. The chamber is connected to a dial by a series of springs and levers. As the shape of the chamber changes, the needle on the dial moves.

Aneroid barometers are smaller than mercury barometers and don't contain a liquid. Therefore, they are portable and often more practical for uses such as airplane instrument panels.

Units of Air Pressure Weather reports use several different units for air pressure. Most weather reports for the general public use inches of mercury. For example, if the column of mercury in a mercury barometer is 30 inches high, the air pressure is "30 inches of mercury" or just "30 inches."

National Weather Service maps indicate air pressure in millibars. One inch of mercury equals approximately 33.87 millibars, so 30 inches of mercury is approximately equal to 1,016 millibars.

☑ *Checkpoint* *Name two common units used to measure air pressure.*

Soda-Bottle Barometer

Here's how to build a device that shows changes in air pressure.

1. Fill a 2-liter soda bottle one-half full with water.
2. Lower a long straw into the bottle so that the end of the straw is in the water. Seal the mouth of the bottle around the straw with modeling clay.
3. Squeeze the sides of the bottle. What happens to the level of the water in the straw?
4. Let go of the sides of the bottle. Watch the level of the water in the straw.

Inferring Explain your results in terms of air pressure.

Including All Students

Materials *calculator*
Time 10 minutes

Invite students who need additional challenges to do this activity. It will give them a better appreciation of how air pressure is measured. First, tell students that if you laid a quarter on a table, it would exert a pressure of 0.00013 kg per cm^2. Then say that the pressure exerted by the atmosphere at sea level is 1.03 kg per cm^2. Ask: **How many quarters would you need to stack on top of each other for the quarters to exert the same pressure as the air at sea level?** *(1.03 kg ÷ 0.00013 kg = 7,923)* **If six quarters are about 1 cm thick, how high would the stack of quarters be?** *(7,923 ÷ 6 = 1,321 cm, or about 1.3 km)* **learning modality: logical/mathematical**

Try This

Skills Focus inferring
Materials *2-liter soda bottle, water, long straw, modeling clay*
Time 15 minutes
Tips Before students seal the mouth of the bottle with clay, make sure the straw is in the water but not touching the bottom of the bottle.
Expected Outcome When students squeeze the sides of the bottle, the water level rises in the straw. When they let go of the sides, the water level falls in the straw. Students should infer that the water rises in the straw because air pressure increases in the bottle when the sides of the bottle are squeezed.
Extend Ask: **What do you think would happen if you heated the air in the bottle?** *(The air would expand and make the water rise in the straw.)* **learning modality: logical/mathematical**

Program Resources

- **Product Testing Activities by *Consumer Reports*** "Testing Food Wraps," pp. 1–8

Answers to Self-Assessment

Caption Question

Figure 11 When the air pressure increases, the column of mercury in the tube of a mercury barometer goes up.

☑ *Checkpoint*

Two common units used to measure air pressure are inches and millibars.

Ongoing Assessment

Skills Check Challenge students to make a table comparing and contrasting mercury barometers and aneroid barometers.

Skills Lab

Measuring

Working Under Pressure

Preparing for Inquiry

Key Concept A flexible wall of a sealed container will expand and contract with changes in the pressure of the outside air.

Skills Objectives Students will be able to

- measure air pressure with a simple barometer that they construct;
- observe daily weather conditions;
- infer from their data the kinds of weather conditions that are associated with high and low air pressure.

Time 40 minutes the first day; 10 minutes each day for the next two days

Advance Planning You may wish to have students work in pairs for this activity, because it is easier for two people to assemble the barometer. If possible, bring a commercial aneroid barometer to class to familiarize students with air pressure readings before they begin the activity. You may want to leave the barometer so students can compare their readings with the readings on the commercial barometer. When students record weather conditions during the lab, at a minimum they should record whether the sky is cloudy or fair. You may want them to record additional factors, including temperature. If so, place an outdoor thermometer in a shady location where students can see it from the classroom.

Alternative Materials Students can use beakers instead of wide-mouthed glass jars, rubber dental dams instead of balloons, and rulers instead of cardboard strips.

Guiding Inquiry

Invitation Show students a commercial aneroid barometer and then ask: **How does the aneroid barometer work?** *(Changes in air pressure cause slight movements in or out of the walls of a box, and these movements are measured on a scale.)* Tell students that they will make a barometer that works the same way as a commercial aneroid barometer. However, their barometer will be less accurate.

Increasing Altitude

The air pressure at the top of Alaska's Mount McKinley—more than 6 kilometers above sea level—is less than half the air pressure at sea level. **Altitude,** or elevation, is the distance above sea level, the average level of the surface of the oceans. **Air pressure decreases as altitude increases. As air pressure decreases, so does density.**

Altitude Affects Air Pressure Imagine a stack of ten books. Which book has more weight on it, the second book from the top or the book at the bottom? The second book from the top has only the weight of one book on top of it. The book at the bottom

Skills Lab

Measuring

Working Under Pressure

Air pressure changes are related to changing weather conditions. In this lab, you will build and use your own barometer to measure air pressure.

Problem

How can a barometer detect changes in air pressure?

Materials

modeling clay	scissors
white glue	tape
pencil	wide-mouthed glass jar
metric ruler	rubber band
large rubber balloon	
drinking straw, 12–15 cm long	
cardboard strip, 10 cm x 25 cm	

Procedure

1. Cut off the narrow opening of the balloon.
2. Fold the edges of the balloon outward. Carefully stretch the balloon over the open end of the glass jar. Use a rubber band to hold the balloon on the rim of the glass jar.
3. Place a small amount of glue on the center of the balloon top. Attach one end of the straw to the glue. Allow the other end to extend several centimeters beyond the edge of the glass jar. This is your pointer.

348

Introducing the Procedure

Have students read the entire procedure. Then ask: **What part of your barometer is like the flexible sides of the metal box in a commercial aneroid barometer?** *(The balloon stretched across the jar)* Point out that the balloon will expand when the air pressure falls. Ask: **Why does the expanding balloon make the pointer in your barometer fall?** *(Students may think that the pointer should rise, not fall, as the balloon expands.)* Explain that the pointer resting on the jar is like a seesaw. The rim of the jar acts like a fulcrum, and the clay weights down the free end of the straw. The free end falls when the expanding balloon causes the other end of the straw to rise.

Troubleshooting the Experiment

- Before students cut their balloon, suggest they inflate it to stretch the rubber.
- Caution students to avoid making holes in the balloon when they cut it. Once the balloon is in place, they should make sure it does not leak air.

of the stack has the weight of all the other books pressing on it.

Air at sea level is like the bottom book. Recall that air pressure is the weight of the column of air pushing down on an area. Sea-level air has the weight of the whole atmosphere pressing on it. So air pressure is greatest at sea level. Air near the top of the atmosphere is like the second book from the top. There, the air has less weight pressing on it, and thus has lower air pressure.

DATA TABLE

Date and Time	Air Pressure	Weather Conditions

4. While the glue dries, fold the cardboard strip lengthwise and draw a scale along the edge with marks 0.5 cm apart. Write "High pressure" at the top of your scale and "Low pressure" at the bottom.
5. After the glue dries, add a pea-sized piece of modeling clay to the end of the pointer. Place your barometer and its scale in a location that is as free from temperature changes as possible. Arrange the scale and the barometer as shown in the diagram. Note that the pointer of the straw must just reach the cardboard strip.
6. Tape both the scale and the barometer to a surface so they do not move during your experiment.
7. In your notebook, make a data table like the one at the left. Record the date and time. Note the level of the straw on the cardboard strip.
8. Check the barometer twice a day. Record your observations in your data table.
9. Record the weather conditions for each day.

Analyze and Conclude

1. What change in atmospheric conditions must occur to cause the free end of the straw to rise? What change must occur for it to fall?
2. According to your observations, what kind of weather is usually associated with high air pressure? With low air pressure?
3. If the balloon had a tiny hole in it, what would happen to the accuracy of your barometer?
4. **Think About It** What effect, if any, would a great temperature change have on the accuracy of your barometer?

More to Explore

Compare changes in air pressure shown by your barometer with high and low air pressure readings shown on newspaper weather maps during the same time period. How do your readings compare with the readings in the newspapers?

Expected Outcome

When the air pressure outside is low, the higher air pressure inside the jar pushes up on the balloon, causing the pointer to fall. When the air pressure outside is high, it pushes down on the balloon, causing the pointer to rise. Low air pressure is likely to be followed by cloudy or even stormy weather conditions. High air pressure is likely to be followed by fair weather conditions.

Analyze and Conclude

1. Air pressure must rise for the free end of the straw to rise. Air pressure must fall for the free end of the straw to fall.
2. Clear, dry weather usually is associated with high air pressure. Cloudy, wet, or stormy weather usually is associated with low air pressure.
3. A tiny hole in the balloon would cause the barometer not to work because air would leak in or out to equalize the air pressure inside and outside the jar.
4. Think About It A great increase in temperature would cause the air inside the barometer to expand and a large decrease in temperature would cause it to contract, affecting the readings.

Extending the Inquiry

More to Explore Students' air pressure readings should agree in general with high and low air pressure readings given in the newspaper. If the readings do not agree, it may be because students' barometers are faulty. Balloons may leak air or not be stretchy enough, or the lumps of clay may be too large. Also, students' barometers are not likely to be accurate enough to reflect minor fluctuations in air pressure. In addition, the readings reported in the newspaper may have been taken at a different time of day when air pressure was lower or higher.

Sample Data Table

Date and Time	Air Pressure	Weather Conditions
April 2, 10:00 A.M.	1	rainy, 24°C
April 2, 2:00 P.M.	2	cloudy, 23°C
April 4, 10:00 A.M.	4	sunny, 18°C
April 4, 2:00 P.M.	5	sunny, 19°C

Safety

In Step 2, to reduce chances of the jar breaking, suggest that one student hold the jar while the other stretches the balloon and rubber band over it. Review the safety guidelines in Appendix A.

Media and Technology

Lab Activity Videotapes
Grade 6, Tape 3

Program Resources

- **Unit 4 Resources** Chapter 11 Skills Lab

Increasing Altitude

Integrating Life Science

People who live at high altitudes have developed adaptations to the low pressure and density of oxygen in the air around them. Ask: **What kinds of adaptations would allow people to live successfully at high altitudes?** *(A larger chest and lungs would allow a person to take in more air.)* **learning modality: logical/mathematical**

3 Assess

Section 3 Review Answers

1. It increases its pressure.
2. Air presses down on the mercury in the bottom of the barometer, and this forces the mercury up into the sealed tube. The greater the air pressure, the higher the mercury rises and the higher the air pressure reading.
3. Because it has low pressure and density, there are fewer oxygen molecules in each lungful of air.
4. You would expect to see the air pressure increase because the column of air pressing down on the barometer would be taller.

Science at Home

Materials *glass, tap water, piece of heavy cardboard*
Tips Students should fill the glass until the level of water bulges over the rim and then slide the cardboard *completely* over the rim, being careful not to let any air bubbles under the cardboard. Some water may overflow the glass, so students should do this over a sink.

Performance Assessment

Skills Check Call on volunteers to infer why an inflated balloon flies around the room when it is released. *(The force of the air escaping the balloon propels the balloon.)*

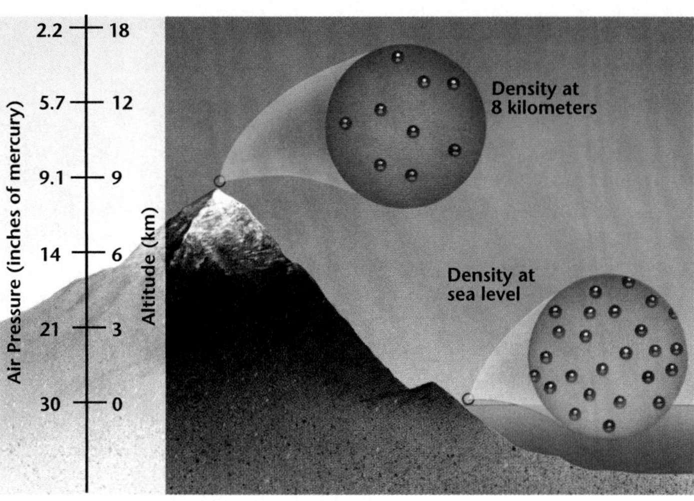

Figure 13 The density of air decreases as altitude increases. Air at sea level has more gas molecules in each cubic meter than air at the top of a mountain.

Altitude Also Affects Density If you were near the top of Mount McKinley and tried to run, you would get out of breath quickly. Why would you have difficulty breathing at high altitudes? *INTEGRATING LIFE SCIENCE*

As you go up through the atmosphere, the air pressure decreases. As air pressure decreases, the density of the air decreases. So density decreases as altitude increases, as shown in Figure 13.

Whether air is at sea level or at 6 kilometers above sea level, the air still contains 21 percent oxygen. However, since the air is less dense at a high altitude, there are fewer oxygen molecules to breathe in each cubic meter of air than there are at sea level. You are taking in less oxygen with each breath. That is why you get out of breath quickly.

Section 3 Review

1. How does increasing the density of a gas affect its pressure?
2. Describe how a mercury barometer measures air pressure.
3. Why is the air at the top of a mountain hard to breathe?
4. **Thinking Critically Predicting** What changes in air pressure would you expect to see if you carried a barometer down a mine shaft? Explain.

Science at Home

Under Pressure Here's how you can show your family that air has pressure. Fill a glass to the brim with water. Place a piece of heavy cardboard over the top of the glass. Hold the cardboard in place with one hand as you turn the glass upside down. **CAUTION:** *Be sure the cardboard does not bend.* Now remove your hand from the cardboard. What happens? Explain to your family that the cardboard doesn't fall because the air pressure pushing up on it is greater than the weight of the water pushing down.

Media and Technology

Transparencies "Density of Air at Two Altitudes," Transparency 41

Concept Videotape Library Grade 6, Tape 2 "Racing Hot Air Balloons"

Program Resources

- **Unit 4 Resources** 11-3 Review and Reinforce; 11-3 Enrich

Layers of the Atmosphere

DISCOVER — ACTIVITY

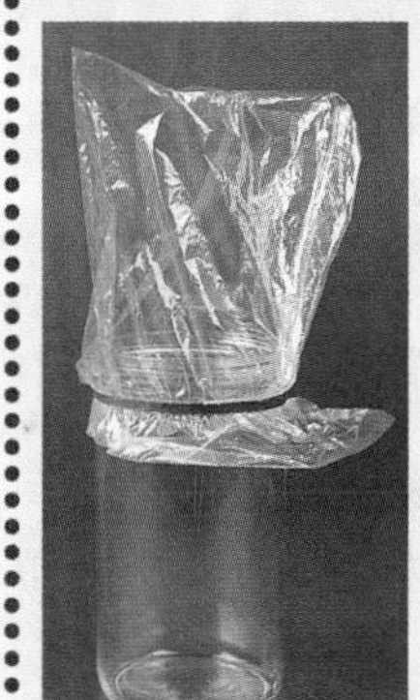

Is Air There?

1. Use a heavy rubber band to tightly secure a plastic bag over the top of a wide-mouthed jar.
2. Gently try to push the bag into the jar. What happens? Is the air pressure higher inside or outside of the bag?
3. Remove the rubber band and line the inside of the jar with the plastic bag. Use the rubber band to tightly secure the edges of the bag over the rim of the jar.
4. Gently try to pull the bag out of the jar with your fingertips. What happens? Is the air pressure higher inside or outside of the bag?

Think It Over

Predicting Explain your observations in terms of air pressure. How do you think differences in air pressure would affect a weather balloon as it traveled up through the atmosphere?

GUIDE FOR READING

- **What are the characteristics of the main layers of the atmosphere?**

Reading Tip **Before you read, preview *Exploring Layers of the Atmosphere.* Make a list of unfamiliar words. Look for the meanings of these words as you read.**

Imagine taking a trip upward into the atmosphere in a hot-air balloon. You begin on a warm beach near the ocean, at an altitude of 0 kilometers.

You hear a roar as the balloon's pilot turns up the burner to heat the air in the balloon. The balloon begins to rise, and Earth's surface gets farther and farther away. As the balloon rises to an altitude of 3 kilometers, you realize that the air is getting colder. As you continue to rise, the air gets colder and colder. At 6 kilometers you begin to have trouble breathing. The air is becoming less dense. It's time to go back down.

What if you could have continued your balloon ride up through the atmosphere? As you rose farther up through the atmosphere, the air pressure and temperature would change dramatically. **The four main layers of the atmosphere are classified according to changes in temperature. These layers are the troposphere, the stratosphere, the mesosphere, and the thermosphere.**

The Troposphere

You live in the inner, or lowest, layer of Earth's atmosphere, the **troposphere** (TROH puh sfeer). **Tropo-** means "turning" or "changing"; conditions in the troposphere are more variable than in the other layers. The troposphere is where Earth's weather occurs.

READING STRATEGIES

Reading Tip Students lists might include the names of the layers of the atmosphere, as well as terms such as *meteoroid* and *aurora borealis*. Suggest that, as they read and encounter the words on their list, students record their meanings.

Program Resources

- **Unit 4 Resources** 11-4 Lesson Plan; 11-4 Section Summary
- **Guided Reading and Study Workbook** Section 11-4

Layers of the Atmosphere

Objectives

After completing this lesson, students will be able to

- describe the characteristics of the main layers of the atmosphere.

Key Terms troposphere, stratosphere, mesosphere, thermosphere, ionosphere, aurora borealis, exosphere

1 Engage/Explore

Activating Prior Knowledge

Ask: **Did you ever see a shooting star?** *(Most students probably will say yes.)* **What is a shooting star?** *(A meteor burning up because of friction as it falls through Earth's atmosphere)* Point out that most shooting stars are visible from about 50 to 80 km above Earth in a layer of the atmosphere called the mesosphere. This layer protects us from being bombarded by shooting stars and other space debris. The mesosphere is just one of four major layers of the atmosphere students will read about in this section.

DISCOVER — ACTIVITY

Skills Focus predicting
Materials *heavy rubber band, plastic bag, wide-mouthed glass jar*
Time 10 minutes
Tips Make sure the rubber band is tight and the plastic bag does not have holes in it. Caution students to push gently on the bag to avoid breaking the bag or the jar.
Expected Outcome Students should find it difficult to push the bag into or pull it out of the jar.
Think It Over Trying to push the bag into the jar decreases the volume and increases the air pressure inside the jar. Trying to pull the bag out of the jar increases the volume and decreases the air pressure inside the jar. As a weather balloon traveled up, it would expand until it burst as the air pressure outside the balloon became lower than the air pressure inside.

2 Facilitate

The Troposphere

Building Inquiry Skills: Graphing

Challenge students to calculate the temperature for every 1,000 m above Earth's surface in the troposphere, starting at sea level and ending at 10,000 m. They should assume that the temperature is 15.0°C at sea level and decreases 6.5 Celsius degrees for each 1,000-m increase in altitude. Then have students draw a graph that shows the relationship between altitude and temperature in the troposphere. **learning modality: logical/mathematical**

The Stratosphere

Addressing Naive Conceptions

In Section 2, students read that ozone is a harmful chemical in smog. In this section, they read that ozone is a natural component of the atmosphere that protects Earth from ultraviolet solar radiation. Students may wonder if ozone is harmful or not. Explain that the ozone in the stratosphere absorbs, and thus protects us from, too much sunlight. Ozone in this layer occurs naturally. However, ozone in the troposphere harms our health and contributes to photochemical smog. Ozone in this layer is caused by pollution. **limited English proficiency**

The Mesosphere

Building Inquiry Skills: Inferring

Challenge students to explain why there is a temperature reversal between the stratosphere and mesosphere. Ask: **Why is the mesosphere generally colder than the stratosphere?** *(Because it contains no ozone molecules to absorb solar radiation and convert the radiation into heat)* **learning modality: logical/mathematical**

Figure 14 This weather balloon will carry a package of instruments to measure weather conditions high in the atmosphere.
Applying Concepts Which is the first layer of the atmosphere the balloon passes through on its way up?

Although hot-air balloons cannot travel very high into the troposphere, other types of balloons can. To measure weather conditions, scientists launch weather balloons that carry instruments up into the atmosphere. The balloons are not fully inflated before they are launched. Recall that air pressure decreases as you rise through the atmosphere. Leaving the balloon only partly inflated gives the gas inside the balloon room to expand as the air pressure outside the balloon decreases.

The depth of the troposphere varies from more than 16 kilometers above the equator to less than 9 kilometers above the North and South Poles. Even though it is the shallowest layer of the atmosphere, the troposphere contains almost all of the mass of the atmosphere.

As altitude increases in the troposphere, the temperature decreases. On average, for every 1-kilometer increase in altitude the air gets about 6.5 Celsius degrees cooler. At the top of the troposphere, the temperature stops decreasing and stays constant at about –60°C. Water here forms thin, feathery clouds of ice.

☑ *Checkpoint* *Why are clouds at the top of the troposphere made of ice crystals instead of drops of water?*

The Stratosphere

The **stratosphere** extends from the top of the troposphere to about 50 kilometers above Earth's surface. *Strato-* is similar to *stratum,* which means "layer" or "spreading out."

The lower stratosphere is cold, about –60°C. You might be surprised to learn that the upper stratosphere is warmer than the lower stratosphere. The upper stratosphere contains a layer of ozone, the three-atom form of oxygen. When the ozone absorbs energy from the sun, the energy is converted into heat, warming the air.

As a weather balloon rises through the stratosphere, the air pressure outside the balloon continues to decrease. The volume of the balloon increases. Finally, the balloon bursts, and the instrument package falls back to Earth's surface.

The Mesosphere

Above the stratosphere, a drop in temperature marks the beginning of the next layer, the **mesosphere.** *Meso-* means "middle," so the mesosphere is the middle layer of the atmosphere. The mesosphere begins 50 kilometers above Earth's surface and ends at 80 kilometers. In the outer mesosphere, temperatures approach –90°C.

Background

Facts and Figures You may wish to share the following facts and figures about the mesosphere with students.

- The mesosphere is the coldest part of the atmosphere. Temperatures there reach lows that are as cold as the lowest temperatures ever recorded anywhere on Earth.
- Oddly, air temperatures in the mesosphere are colder in summer than in winter. Temperatures there also are colder over the equator than over the North and South poles.
- The clouds that form in the mesosphere are unlike any other clouds in the atmosphere. They are formed of ice crystals and are called noctilucent clouds because they are visible only at night.

EXPLORING Layers of the Atmosphere

The atmosphere is divided into four layers: the troposphere, the stratosphere, the mesosphere, and the thermosphere. The thermosphere is further divided into the ionosphere and the exosphere.

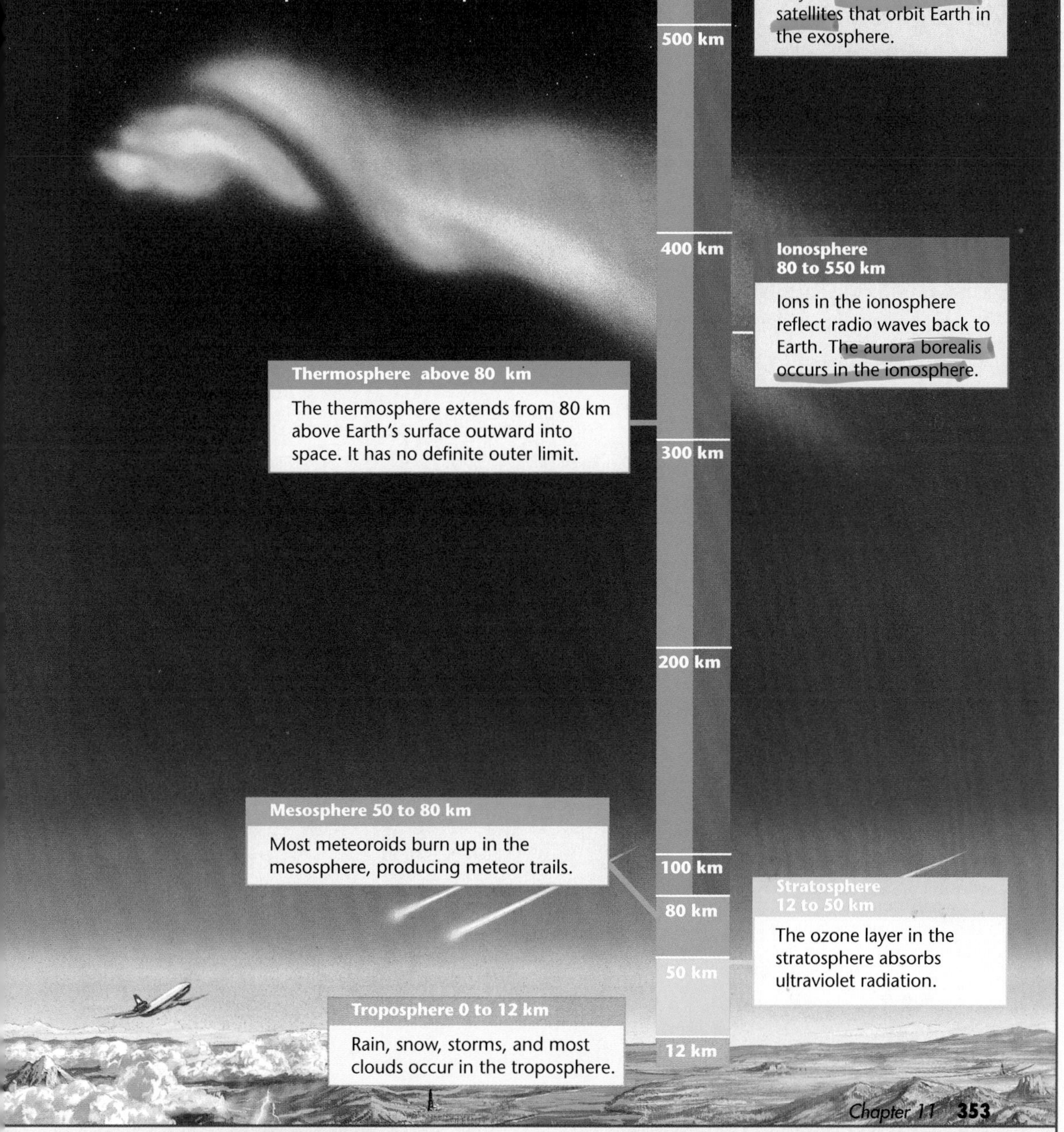

Exosphere above 550 km
Phone calls and television pictures often reach you by way of communications satellites that orbit Earth in the exosphere.

Ionosphere 80 to 550 km
Ions in the ionosphere reflect radio waves back to Earth. The aurora borealis occurs in the ionosphere.

Thermosphere above 80 km
The thermosphere extends from 80 km above Earth's surface outward into space. It has no definite outer limit.

Mesosphere 50 to 80 km
Most meteoroids burn up in the mesosphere, producing meteor trails.

Stratosphere 12 to 50 km
The ozone layer in the stratosphere absorbs ultraviolet radiation.

Troposphere 0 to 12 km
Rain, snow, storms, and most clouds occur in the troposphere.

EXPLORING

Layers of the Atmosphere

ACTIVITY

Materials *posterboard, colored markers, index cards, buttons and other small objects for game pieces*
Time 30 minutes

Divide the class into groups and have each group use the information presented in the feature to create a board game. The object of the game should be to get from the ground to the top of the atmosphere. Reaching the objective might involve overcoming various obstacles in the different layers of the atmosphere, such as clouds and storms in the troposphere, very high temperatures in the stratosphere, meteoroids in the mesosphere, electrically charged ions in the ionosphere, and orbiting satellites in the exosphere. To advance through the layers of the atmosphere, players might be required to correctly answer questions about each layer, such as the layer's temperature or height above Earth's surface. Group members should work together to brainstorm the objectives and rules of the game. The actual work of constructing the game board and other parts of the game should be divided up among individual group members. Suggest that the groups exchange games and try them out. **cooperative learning**

Media and Technology

Concept Videotape Library Grade 6, Tape 2 "A Trip Through the Earth"

Transparencies "Layers of the Atmosphere," Transparency 42

Answers to Self-Assessment

Caption Question

Figure 14 The first layer is the troposphere.

Because the temperature at that altitude is always below the freezing point of water

Ongoing Assessment

Writing Challenge students to write a short story describing their imaginary ascent up through the troposphere and stratosphere in a hydrogen balloon. They should describe the conditions they pass through in each layer.

Students can save their stories in their portfolios.

The Mesosphere, continued

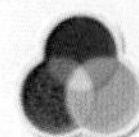

Integrating Space Science

Stress that the mesosphere protects Earth from meteoroids that are pulled toward the planet by gravity. Tell students that the moon has gravity, too, but no atmosphere to protect it from meteoroids. As a result, meteoroids crash on the moon's surface, forming large depressions called craters. Challenge students to draw labeled diagrams showing what happens to meteoroids that fall toward the moon as compared with those that fall toward Earth. **limited English proficiency**

SCIENCE & History

Point out that exploring the atmosphere is difficult because it requires scientists or their instruments to reach high altitudes. Ask: **What are some ways explorers of the atmosphere have made scientific observations at high altitudes?** *(By climbing to the tops of mountains, ascending in hydrogen balloons, flying kites, and attaching instruments to balloons and satellites)* **What have these explorers learned through these means?** *(That air pressure decreases with altitude, that lightning is a form of electricity, how the sun influences the atmosphere, and the temperature, air pressure, and humidity at various altitudes)*

In Your Journal Ask volunteers to read their paragraphs aloud to the class. The items students would take with them should show they understand how the atmosphere changes with altitude. For example, warm clothing would be necessary above an altitude of just a few kilometers because temperature declines steadily with increasing altitude. Also, a supply of oxygen would be needed above about 7 km. Instruments should include at least a thermometer for measuring changes in temperature and a barometer for measuring changes in air pressure. **learning modality: verbal**

INTEGRATING SPACE SCIENCE If you watch a shooting star streak across the night sky, you are seeing a meteoroid burn up as it enters the mesosphere. The mesosphere protects Earth's surface from being hit by most meteoroids, which are chunks of stone and metal from space. What you see as a shooting star, or meteor, is the trail of hot, glowing gases the burning meteoroid leaves behind.

Checkpoint *What is the depth of the mesosphere?*

The Thermosphere

Near the top of the atmosphere, the air is very thin. The air 80 kilometers above Earth's surface is only about 0.001 percent as dense as the air at sea level. It's as though you took a cubic

Explorers of the Atmosphere

The atmosphere has been explored from the ground and from space.

1746

Franklin's Experiment with Electricity

American statesman and inventor Benjamin Franklin and some friends in Philadelphia experimented with electricity in the atmosphere. To demonstrate that lightning is a form of electricity, Franklin flew a kite in a thunderstorm. However, Franklin did not hold the kite string in his hand, as this historical print shows.

1600 **1700** **1800**

1643

Torricelli Invents the Barometer

Italian physicist and mathematician Evangelista Torricelli improved existing scientific instruments and invented some new ones. In 1643 he invented the barometer, using a column of mercury 1.2 meters high.

1804

Gay-Lussac Studies the Upper Troposphere

French chemist Joseph-Louis Gay-Lussac ascended to a height of about 7 kilometers in a hydrogen balloon to study the upper troposphere. Gay-Lussac studied pressure, temperature, and humidity.

354

Background

Facts and Figures At sea level, an air molecule can travel just a fraction of a centimeter before colliding with another, whereas in the upper thermosphere it can travel as far as 10 km before colliding with another. Because of their very high temperatures, air molecules in the upper thermosphere move at speeds of up to 40,000 km per hour, allowing many to escape into outer space. Therefore, where the thermosphere ends and outer space begins is arbitrary. Air molecules become farther and farther apart as you travel higher above Earth's surface until, somewhere thousands of kilometers above the surface, there are no more air molecules.

meter of air at sea level and expanded it into 100,000 cubic meters at the top of the mesosphere. The outermost layer of the atmosphere, the **thermosphere**, extends from 80 kilometers above Earth's surface outward into space. It has no definite outer limit. The atmosphere does not end suddenly at the outer edge of the thermosphere. Gas atoms and molecules there are so far apart that the air blends gradually with outer space.

The **thermo-** in thermosphere means "heat." Even though the air in the thermosphere is thin, it is very hot, up to 1,800°C. The temperature in the thermosphere is actually higher than the temperature in a furnace used to make steel! But why is the thermosphere so hot? Energy coming from the sun strikes the thermosphere first. Nitrogen and oxygen molecules convert energy from the sun into heat.

In Your Journal

Imagine you were one of the first people to go up into the atmosphere in a balloon. What would you need to take? Find out what the early explorers took with them in their balloons. Write at least two paragraphs about what you would take, and why.

1931

Piccard Explores the Stratosphere

Swiss-Belgian physicist Auguste Piccard made the first ascent into the stratosphere. He reached a height of about 16 kilometers in an airtight cabin attached to a huge hydrogen balloon. Piccard is shown here with the cabin.

1900 — 2000

1960

First Weather Satellite Launched

TIROS-1, the first weather satellite equipped with a camera to send data back to Earth, was put into orbit by the United States. As later weather satellites circled Earth, they observed cloud cover and recorded temperatures and air pressures in the atmosphere.

1994

Space Shuttle Investigates the Atmosphere

The NASA space shuttle *Atlantis* traveled to a height of 300 kilometers in the thermosphere. *Atlantis* carried the ATLAS–3 research program, which observed the sun's influence on the atmosphere.

Answers to Self-Assessment

Checkpoint

The mesosphere extends from 50 to 80 km above Earth's surface, so it has a depth of 30 km.

The Thermosphere

Building Inquiry Skills: Modeling

Time 5 minutes

ACTIVITY

Challenge a group of student volunteers to pretend they are atoms and molecules and to demonstrate the density and speed of atoms and molecules in the atmosphere, first at sea level, then in the thermosphere. *(For sea level, students should stand close together and move very slowly. For the thermosphere, they should stand as far apart as possible and move very quickly.)* Point out that the classroom would have to be much larger for them to be as far apart as atoms and molecules really are in the thermosphere. Ask: **How much larger would the classroom have to be?** *(Almost 100,000 times larger)* **learning modality: kinesthetic**

Including All Students

To help students whose native language is not English remember that the defining characteristic of the thermosphere is its high temperature, stress that the prefix *thermo-* means "heat." Ask: **What are some other words that start with this prefix?** *(thermometer, thermostat, thermal, thermos)* Have students explain how each of the terms is related to heat. **limited English proficiency**

Ongoing Assessment

Oral Presentation Call on students to describe density, temperature, and pressure of air in the thermosphere as compared with the troposphere. Call on other students to explain why the thermosphere has these characteristics.

The Thermosphere, continued

Integrating Technology

Help students understand why satellites orbit Earth at such high altitudes. First point out that molecules in air create resistance that can slow down objects orbiting Earth. Then ask: **What happens to the density of molecules in air as you go higher above Earth's surface?** *(It decreases.)* **Why do you think satellites orbit Earth at such high altitudes?** *(The lower density of air molecules creates less resistance to slow down orbiting satellites.)* **learning modality: logical/mathematical**

3 Assess

Section 4 Review Answers

1. Answers may vary. The troposphere is where weather occurs. The stratosphere contains the ozone layer. The mesosphere is where most meteoroids burn up. The thermosphere is very hot.
2. A shooting star, or meteor, is a trail of hot, glowing gas left by a meteoroid as it burns up in the atmosphere. You would see it in the mesosphere.
3. A glowing light display caused when energy from the sun causes gas molecules to become electrically charged; it occurs in the lower layer of the thermosphere.
4. Because it does not absorb much energy from the sun

CHAPTER PROJECT

Check Your Progress

Students may observe such trends in their observations as cooler temperatures after a storm and fair weather after an increase in air pressure. Which weather conditions changed most will depend partly on how precisely the variables were measured. Also, some weather variables, such as temperature and wind speed, have a greater range than others, including air pressure.

Figure 15 The aurora borealis, seen from Fairbanks, Alaska, creates a spectacular display in the night sky.

Despite the high temperature, however, you would not feel warm in the thermosphere. An ordinary thermometer would show a temperature well below 0°C. Why is that? Temperature is the average amount of energy of motion of each molecule of a substance. The gas molecules in the thermosphere move very rapidly, so the temperature is very high. However, the molecules are spaced far apart in the thin air. And there are not enough of them to collide with a thermometer and warm it very much. So an ordinary thermometer would not detect the molecules' energy.

The Ionosphere The thermosphere is divided into two layers. The lower layer of the thermosphere, called the **ionosphere** (eye AHN uh sfeer), begins 80 kilometers above the surface and ends at 550 kilometers. Energy from the sun causes gas molecules in the ionosphere to become electrically charged particles called ions. Radio waves bounce off ions in the ionosphere and then bounce back to Earth's surface.

The brilliant light displays of the **aurora borealis**—the Northern Lights—also occur in the ionosphere. The aurora borealis is caused by particles from the sun that enter the ionosphere near the North Pole. These particles strike oxygen and nitrogen atoms in the ionosphere, causing them to glow.

The Exosphere **Exo-** means "outer," so the **exosphere** is the outer layer of the thermosphere. The exosphere extends from 550 kilometers outward for thousands of kilometers. When you make a long-distance phone call or watch television, the signal may have traveled up to a satellite orbiting in the exosphere and then back down to your home. Satellites are also used for watching the world's weather and carrying telescopes that look deep into space.

INTEGRATING TECHNOLOGY

Section 4 Review

1. Describe one characteristic of each of the four main layers of the atmosphere.
2. What is a shooting star? In which layer of the atmosphere would you see it?
3. What is the aurora borealis? In which layer of the atmosphere does it occur?
4. **Thinking Critically Drawing Conclusions** Why is the mesosphere the coldest part of the atmosphere?

CHAPTER PROJECT

Check Your Progress

At this point, review your weather log. What do you notice about the weather on one day that might allow you to predict the next day's weather? What weather conditions changed the most from day to day? Continue to record your observations and start thinking about how you will present them.

Background

Facts and Figures Another sphere around Earth, called the magnetosphere, extends above the atmosphere to more than 65,000 km above Earth's surface. It is a magnetic field that traps charged particles from the sun. The trapped particles follow the lines of magnetic force and bounce back and forth from one pole to the other, sometimes breaking through into the ionosphere to produce auroras.

Program Resources

- **Unit 4 Resources** 11-4 Review and Reinforce; 11-4 Enrich

CHAPTER 11 STUDY GUIDE

Section 1 The Air Around You

Key Ideas

- Earth's atmosphere makes conditions on Earth suitable for living things.
- Earth's atmosphere is made up of molecules of nitrogen, oxygen, carbon dioxide, and water vapor, as well as some other gases and particles of liquids and solids.

Key Terms

weather
atmosphere
ozone
water vapor

Section 2 Air Pollution

INTEGRATING ENVIRONMENTAL SCIENCE

Key Ideas

- Air pollutants can be in the form of solid particles or gases.
- The major sources of photochemical smog are the gases emitted by motor vehicles.
- Sources of indoor air pollution include smoke, dust, pet hair, asbestos, and other substances. Two dangerous pollutants that are very difficult to detect are carbon monoxide and radon.
- Certain gases in Earth's atmosphere prevent heat from escaping back into space.
- The ozone layer protects people and other living things from the effects of too much ultraviolet radiation.
- Most scientists base their climate predictions on computer models that calculate the effects of changes in the atmosphere.

Key Terms

air pollution
emissions
photochemical smog
ozone
temperature inversion
acid rain
ozone layer
chlorofluorocarbons
greenhouse effect
global warming

Section 3 Air Pressure

Key Ideas

- Properties of air include mass, density, and pressure.
- Air pressure is the result of the weight of a column of air pushing down on an area.
- Air pressure is measured with mercury barometers and aneroid barometers.
- Air pressure decreases as altitude increases. As air pressure decreases, so does density.

Key Terms

density
pressure
air pressure
barometer
mercury barometer
aneroid barometer
altitude

Section 4 Layers of the Atmosphere

Key Ideas

- The four main layers of the atmosphere are classified according to changes in temperature. These layers are the troposphere, the stratosphere, the mesosphere, and the thermosphere.
- Rain, snow, storms, and most clouds occur in the troposphere.
- Ozone in the stratosphere absorbs energy from the sun.
- Most meteoroids burn up in the mesosphere, producing meteor trails.
- The aurora borealis occurs in the ionosphere.
- Communications satellites orbit Earth in the exosphere.

Key Terms

troposphere
stratosphere
mesosphere
thermosphere
ionosphere
aurora borealis
exosphere

Organizing Information

Concept Map On a separate sheet of paper, construct a concept map about air pressure. Be sure to include the following terms: attitude, density, and the two types of barometer. (For more on concept maps, see the Skills Handbook.)

Organizing Information

Concept Map Sample title: Air Pressure

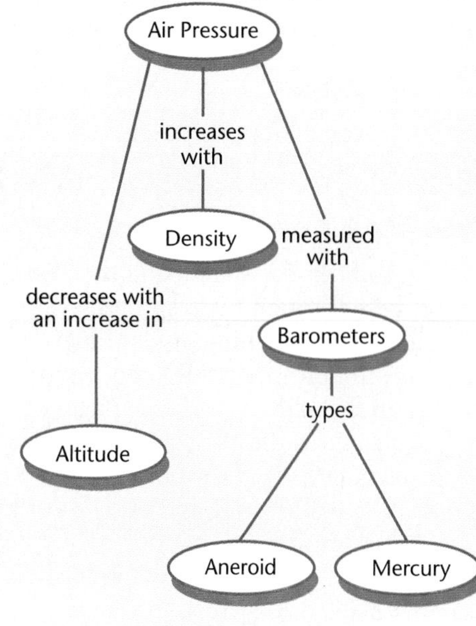

Program Resources

- **Unit 4 Resources** Chapter 11 Project Scoring Rubric
- **Performance Assessment** Chapter 11
- **Chapter and Unit Tests** Chapter 11 Test

Media and Technology

Computer Test Bank Chapter 11 Test

Performance Assessment

Writing Challenge students to write crossword puzzles using all the boldfaced terms in the section. Then have students exchange crossword puzzles and clues with a partner and try to solve their partner's puzzle.

Reviewing Content

Multiple Choice

1. d **2.** b **3.** c **4.** b **5.** b

True or False

6. true **7.** true **8.** upper **9.** more
10. decreases

Checking Concepts

11. Carbon dioxide is added to the atmosphere through the respiration of animals and the burning of fossil fuels.
12. It is difficult to include water vapor in a graph that shows the percentages of different gases in the atmosphere because the percentage of water vapor varies greatly.
13. Photochemical smog can cause breathing and lung problems and harm the body's defenses against infection.
14. Coal and oil produce nitrogen oxides and sulfur oxides when they are burned. These gases react with water vapor in the air to form nitric acid and sulfuric acid. The acids return to Earth's surface dissolved in precipitation.
15. Moving upward from Earth's surface, the layers are troposphere, stratosphere, mesosphere, thermosphere.
16. As you move upward through the troposphere, the temperature decreases by about 6.5°C for each 1,000-meter increase in altitude.
17. Students' letters should demonstrate a thorough understanding of their chosen layer of the atmosphere.

Thinking Critically

18. You would experience a decrease in temperature and also in the pressure and density of the air. You would feel cold unless you dressed appropriately. You would also feel the effects of low oxygen pressure and density. For example, you might be short of breath and tire easily.

CHAPTER 11 ASSESSMENT

Reviewing Content

Multiple Choice

Choose the letter of the answer that best completes each statement.

1. The most abundant gas in the atmosphere is
   a. ozone. **b.** carbon dioxide.
   c. oxygen. **d.** nitrogen.
2. A deadly gas formed when fuels are incompletely burned is
   a. ozone.
   b. carbon monoxide.
   c. photochemical smog.
   d. CFCs.
3. A barometer is used to measure
   a. temperature. **b.** smog.
   c. air pressure **d.** density.
4. The layers of the atmosphere are classified according to changes in
   a. altitude.
   b. temperature.
   c. pressure.
   d. density.
5. The inner layer, or "weather layer," of the atmosphere is called the
   a. mesosphere.
   b. troposphere.
   c. thermosphere.
   d. stratosphere.

True or False

If the statement is true, write true. If it is false, change the underlined word or words to make the statement true.

6. Plants need carbon dioxide from the atmosphere to make food.
7. Most photochemical smog is produced by motor vehicles.
8. Ozone in the lower atmosphere protects people from ultraviolet radiation.
9. If the mass of a fixed volume of air increases, it becomes less dense.
10. Air pressure increases as you climb from land at sea level to the top of a mountain.

Checking Concepts

11. Name two ways in which carbon dioxide is added to the atmosphere.
12. Explain why it is difficult to include water vapor in a graph that shows the percentages of various gases in the atmosphere.
13. Describe some possible health effects of photochemical smog.
14. How does acid rain form?
15. List the following layers of the atmosphere in order moving up from Earth's surface: thermosphere, stratosphere, troposphere, mesosphere.
16. Describe the temperature changes that occur as you move upward through the troposphere.
17. **Writing to Learn** You are a scientist who has a chance to join a research mission to explore the atmosphere. To win a place on this mission, write a persuasive letter telling which layer of the atmosphere you want to research and why you chose it.

Thinking Critically

18. **Predicting** Describe the changes in the atmosphere that you would experience while climbing a mountain four or more kilometers high. How might these changes affect you physically?
19. **Applying Concepts** Why can an aneroid barometer be used to measure elevation as well as air pressure?
20. **Comparing and Contrasting** How are radon and carbon monoxide alike? How are they different?
21. **Predicting** What effect might a sudden increase in the amount of ozone in the ozone layer have?

358

19. Air pressure decreases as elevation or altitude increases. An aneroid barometer can be calibrated to show the change in air pressure as a change in altitude.
20. Both radon and carbon monoxide are gases that pollute indoor air and are difficult to detect. Carbon monoxide forms when wood, coal, oil, or gas is incompletely burned. Radon is formed naturally by certain types of rocks underground and is radioactive. Carbon monoxide can kill people if it reaches certain levels. Radon is thought to cause cancer over long periods of time.
21. More ultraviolet light would be blocked and prevented from reaching Earth's surface. Sunburn and cases of eye diseases and cancer caused by ultraviolet radiation would decrease.

Applying Skills

The table below shows the temperature at various altitudes above Omaha, Nebraska, on a day in January. Use the table to answer the questions that follow.

Altitude (kilometers)	0	1.6	3.2	4.8	6.4	7.2
Temperature (°C)	0	–4	–9	–21	–32	–40

22. Graphing Make a line graph of the data in the table. Put temperature on the horizontal axis and altitude on the vertical axis. Label your graph.

23. Interpreting Graphs At about what height above the ground was the temperature –15°C?

24. Interpreting Graphs What was the approximate temperature 2.4 kilometers over Omaha?

25. Calculating Suppose an airplane was about 6.8 kilometers above Omaha on this day. What was the approximate temperature at 6.8 kilometers? How much colder was the temperature at 6.8 kilometers above the ground than at ground level?

Performance CHAPTER PROJECT Assessment

Present Your Project For your class presentation, prepare a display of your weather observations. Include drawings, graphs, and tables that summarize the weather you observed. Practice presenting your project to your group. Do you need to make any improvements? If so, make them now.

Reflect and Record In your journal, write how you might improve your weather log. What weather conditions would you like to know more about? What factors could you have measured more accurately using instruments?

Test Preparation

Use these questions to prepare for standardized tests.

Study the graph. Then answer Questions 26–29.

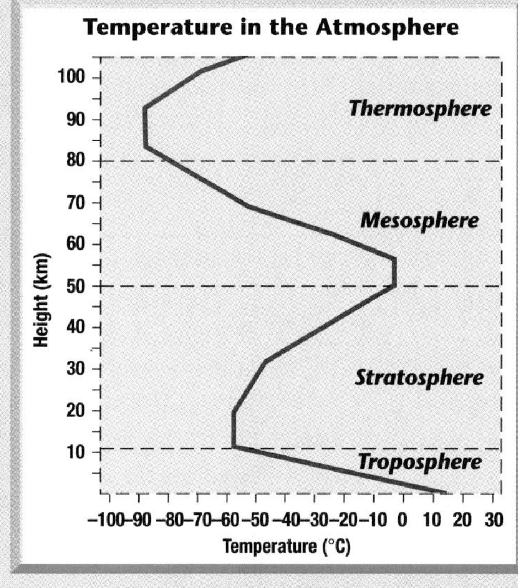

26. Name the layer of the atmosphere that is closest to Earth's surface.
a. thermosphere **b.** troposphere
c. stratosphere **d.** mesosphere

27. Which layer of the atmosphere has the lowest temperature?
a. thermosphere **b.** troposphere
c. stratosphere **d.** mesosphere

28. The range of temperatures found in the stratosphere is about ___ Celsius degrees.
a. 100 **b.** 0
c. 30 **d.** 60

29. Which of the following best describes how temperature changes as altitude increases in the troposphere?
a. steadily increases
b. increases then decreases
c. steadily decreases
d. decreases then increases

Sample Graph for Question 22

Altitude (km): 0, 2, 4, 6, 8
Temperature (°C): –40 –35 –30 –25 –20 –15 –10 –5 0

Program Resources

◆ **Inquiry Skills Activity Book** Provides teaching and review of all inquiry skills

Applying Skills

22. Students' graphs should show a line with a negative slope, that is, a line that slopes downward to the right. See sample graph below.
23. The temperature was -15°C at about 4 kilometers above the ground.
24. At 2.4 kilometers over Omaha, the approximate temperature was -6.5°C.
25. The approximate temperature at 6.8 kilometers above Omaha was -36°C, which was about 36° colder than the temperature at ground level.

Performance  Assessment

Present Your Project Displays should show how, where, and when observations were made and what scale was used to categorize each weather variable. Encourage students to present their observations in creative ways, such as weather centers, bulletin boards, or newspaper or television weather reports. Students should be prepared to discuss any trends they have identified in their observations.

Reflect and Record Students may be able to improve their weather logs by observing more weather variables or making more frequent or detailed observations. Encourage students to look at other students' logs for additional ideas. Weather factors that are not directly observable, such as temperature and air pressure, could be measured more accurately using instruments.

Test Preparation

26. b **27.** a **28.** d **29.** c

CHAPTER 12 Weather Factors

Sections	Time	Student Edition Activities	ACTIVITY Other Activities
CHAPTER PROJECT **Your Own Weather Station** p. 361	Ongoing (2-3 weeks)	Check Your Progress, pp. 371, 380, 390 Present Your Project, p. 393	
1 Energy in the Atmosphere pp. 362–367 ◆ State in what form energy travels from the sun to Earth. ◆ Explain what happens to energy from the sun when it reaches Earth.	2–3 periods/ $1–1\frac{1}{2}$ blocks	**Discover** Does a Plastic Bag Trap Heat?, p. 362 **Science at Home,** p. 365 **Skills Lab: Developing Hypotheses** Heating Earth's Surface, pp. 366–367	TE Integrating Physics, p. 363 TE Exploring Energy in the Atmosphere, p. 364
2 *INTEGRATING PHYSICS* **Heat Transfer** pp. 368–371 ◆ Describe how temperature is measured. ◆ Explain the three ways heat is transferred.	1 period/ $\frac{1}{2}$ block	**Discover** What Happens When Air Is Heated?, p. 368 **Try This** Temperatures at Two Heights, p. 370	TE Demonstration, p. 369 TE Building Inquiry Skills: Calculating, p. 369 TE Inquiry Challenge, p. 370 IES "Wagons West," pp. 31–32 PTA "Testing Disposable Cups," pp. 1–8
3 Winds pp. 372–380 ◆ Explain what causes winds. ◆ Distinguish between local winds and global winds. ◆ Describe the major global wind belts and where they are located.	2 periods/ 1 block	**Discover** Which Way Does the Wind Turn?, p. 372 **Try This** Build a Wind Vane, p. 373 **Real-World Lab: You and Your Community** Where's the Wind?, pp. 374–375	TE Demonstration, p. 373 TE Including All Students, p. 376 TE Demonstration, p. 377 TE Including All Students, p. 378
4 Water in the Atmosphere pp. 381–386 ◆ Describe how relative humidity is measured. ◆ Explain how clouds form. ◆ Describe the main types of clouds.	1–2 periods/ $\frac{1}{2}$–1 block	**Discover** How Does Fog Form?, p. 381 **Sharpen Your Skills** Interpreting Data, p. 383 **Science at Home,** p. 386	TE Inquiry Challenge, p. 382 TE Building Inquiry Skills: Measuring, p. 383 TE Building Inquiry Skills: Inferring, p. 384 LM 12, "Using a Psychrometer to Determine Relative Humidity"
5 Precipitation pp. 387–390 ◆ Identify the main types of precipitation. ◆ Describe how precipitation is measured and ways that it might be controlled.	1–2 periods/ $\frac{1}{2}$–1 block	**Discover** How Can You Make Hail?, p. 387 **Sharpen Your Skills** Calculating, p. 389	TE Building Inquiry Skills: Observing, p. 388 TE Building Inquiry Skills: Measuring, p. 389 IES "Where River Meets Sea," pp. 24–25; "India Beyond the Golden Age," p. 33
Study Guide/Chapter Assessment pp. 391–393	1 period/ $\frac{1}{2}$ block		ISAB Provides teaching and review of all inquiry skills

For Standard or Block Schedule The Resource Pro® CD-ROM gives you maximum flexibility for planning your instruction for any type of schedule. Resource Pro® contains Planning Express®, an advanced scheduling program, as well as the entire contents of the Teaching Resources and the Computer Test Bank.

CHAPTER PLANNING GUIDE

Program Resources	Assessment Strategies	Media and Technology
UR Chapter 12 Project Teacher Notes **UR** Chapter 12 Project Overview and Worksheets	**SE** Performance Assessment: Present Your Project, p. 393 **TE** Check Your Progress, pp. 371, 380, 390 **UR** Chapter 12 Project Scoring Rubric	Science Explorer Internet Site at www.phschool.com Student Edition on Audio CD, Chapter 12
UR 12-1 Lesson Plan **UR** 12-1 Section Summary **UR** 12-1 Review and Reinforce **UR** 12-1 Enrich **UR** Chapter 12 Skills Lab	**SE** Section 1 Review, p. 365 **TE** Ongoing Assessment, p. 363 **TE** Performance Assessment, p. 365	Concept Videotape Library, Grade 6, Tape 2, "The Greenhouse Effect"; Tape 3, "Changes in Climate"; "Never Put Up the Umbrella Until It Starts to Rain"; "Why Is the Sky Blue?" Transparency 43, "Energy in the Atmosphere"
UR 12-2 Lesson Plan **UR** 12-2 Section Summary **UR** 12-2 Review and Reinforce **UR** 12-2 Enrich	**SE** Section 2 Review, p. 371 **TE** Ongoing Assessment, p. 369 **TE** Performance Assessment, p. 371	Concept Videotape Library, Grade 6, Tape 3, "A Wave Is a Wave Is a Wave"; "As Hot As a Desert"; "Hot Is Hot, Cold Is Not" Transparency 44, "Types of Heat Transfer"
UR 12-3 Lesson Plan **UR** 12-3 Section Summary **UR** 12-3 Review and Reinforce **UR** 12-3 Enrich **UR** Chapter 12 Real-World Lab	**SE** Section 3 Review, p. 380 **TE** Ongoing Assessment, pp. 373, 377, 379 **TE** Performance Assessment, p. 380	Lab Activity Videotapes, Grade 6 Tape 3 Transparency 45, "Global Winds"
UR 12-4 Lesson Plan **UR** 12-4 Section Summary **UR** 12-4 Review and Reinforce **UR** 12-4 Enrich	**SE** Section 4 Review, p. 386 **TE** Ongoing Assessment, pp. 383, 385 **TE** Performance Assessment, p. 386	Transparency 46, "Exploring the Water Cycle"; Transparency 47, "Clouds"
UR 12-5 Lesson Plan **UR** 12-5 Section Summary **UR** 12-5 Review and Reinforce **UR** 12-5 Enrich	**SE** Section 5 Review, p. 390 **TE** Ongoing Assessment, p. 389 **TE** Performance Assessment, p. 390	
RCA Provides strategies to improve science reading skills **GRSW** Provides worksheets to promote student comprehension of content	**SE** Chapter 12 Study Guide/Assessment, pp. 391–392 **PA** Chapter 12 Performance Assessment **CUT** Chapter 12 Test **CTB** Chapter 12 Test	Computer Test Bank, Chapter 12 Test

Key: **SE** Student Edition
CTB Computer Test Bank
ISAB Inquiry Skills Activity Book
GRSW Guided Reading and Study Workbook
TE Teacher's Edition
PTA Product Testing Activities by *Consumer Reports*
RCA Reading in the Content Area
PA Performance Assessment
UR Unit Resources
LM Laboratory Manual
IES Interdisciplinary Explorations Series
CUT Chapter and Unit Tests

Meeting the National Science Education Standards and AAAS Benchmarks

National Science Education Standards	Benchmarks for Science Literacy	Unifying Themes
Science As Inquiry (Content Standard A) ◆ **Use appropriate tools and techniques to gather, analyze, and interpret data** Students create a weather station. Students investigate wind patterns. *(Chapter Project; Real-World Lab)* ◆ **Think critically and logically to make the relationships between evidence and explanations** Students compare heating and cooling rates of sand and water. *(Skills Lab)* **Physical Science** (Content Standard B) ◆ **Transfer of energy** Energy travels to Earth from the sun as electromagnetic waves. Different materials absorb radiation at different rates. Heat is transferred by radiation, conduction, and convection. *(Sections 1, 2; Skills Lab)* **Earth and Space Science** (Content Standard D) ◆ **Structure of the Earth system** The movement of air between the equator and the poles produces global winds. Water moves between the atmosphere and Earth's surface in the water cycle. Precipitation is any form of water that falls to Earth. *(Sections 1–5)* ◆ **Earth in the solar system** Nearly all the energy in Earth's atmosphere comes from the sun. Winds are caused by unequal heating of the atmosphere by the sun. As the sun heats Earth's surface, the amount of water in the atmosphere changes. *(Sections 1, 3, 4)*	**1B Scientific Inquiry** Students create a weather station. Students investigate heating and cooling rates of sand and water. Students investigate wind patterns. *(Chapter Project; Skills Lab; Real-World Lab)* **3A Technology and Science** Students use instruments to measure weather conditions. Students measure wind to determine the best location for a door on a building. *(Chapter Project; Real-World Lab)* **4B The Earth** Nearly all the energy in Earth's atmosphere comes from the sun. The movement of air between the equator and the poles produces global winds. Water moves between the atmosphere and Earth's surface in the water cycle. Precipitation is any form of water that falls from clouds to Earth's surface. *(Sections 1, 3, 4, 5)* **4E Energy Transformation** The direct transfer of energy by electromagnetic waves is called radiation. Different materials absorb radiation at different rates. Heat is transferred by radiation, conduction, and convection. Winds are caused by unequal heating of the atmosphere. *(Sections 1, 2, 3; Skills Lab)* **4F Motion** Visible light is a mixture of all the colors of the rainbow. *(Section 1)* **12C Manipulation and Observation** Students measure weather conditions using various instruments. *(Chapter Project)*	◆ **Energy** Nearly all the energy in Earth's atmosphere comes from the sun. Different materials absorb radiation at different rates. The energy transferred from a hotter object to a cooler one is referred to as heat. Wind is the movement of air. *(Sections 1, 2, 3; Skills Lab)* ◆ **Modeling** Students create a weather station. Students make a simple anemometer. *(Chapter Project; Real-World Lab)* ◆ **Patterns of Change** Students look for patterns in their weather data. Monsoons change direction with the seasons. Students investigate wind patterns around a building. *(Chapter Project; Section 3; Real-World Lab)* ◆ **Systems and Interactions** When Earth's surface is heated, it radiates some of the heat back into the atmosphere. Winds are caused by the unequal heating of Earth and its atmosphere. Water moves between the atmosphere and Earth's surface in the water cycle. *(Sections 1, 3, 4)* ◆ **Unity and Diversity** Most light reaches Earth in the form of visible light, infrared radiation, and ultraviolet radiation. Heat is transferred by radiation, conduction, and convection. Both local winds and global winds are caused by differences in air pressure. The three main types of clouds are cumulus, stratus, and cirrus. Rain, sleet, freezing rain, hail, and snow are types of precipitation. *(Sections 1, 2, 3, 4, 5)*

Take It to the Net

Interactive text at www.phschool.com

Science Explorer comes alive with iText.

- **Complete student text** is accessible from any computer with Internet access or a CD-ROM drive.
- **Animations, simulations, and videos** enhance student understanding and retention of concepts.
- **Self-tests and online study tools** assess student understanding.

STAY CURRENT with **SCIENCE NEWS®**

Find out the latest research and information about Weather and Climate at: **www.phschool.com**

Go to **www.phschool.com** and click on the Science icon.Then click on Science Explorer: Life, Earth, and Physical Science under PH@school.

Student Edition Activities Planner

ACTIVITY	Time *(minutes)*	Materials *Quantities for one work group*	Skills
Section 1			
Discover, p. 362	10	**Consumable** plastic bag, 2 small pieces of paper, tape **Nonconsumable** 2 thermometers	Measuring
Science at Home, p. 365	home	No special materials required.	Observing
Skills Lab, pp. 366–367	40	**Consumable** 300 mL water, string, 300 mL sand, graph paper **Nonconsumable** 2 thermometers (or temperature probes), 2 400-mL beakers, metric ruler, ring stand and two ring clamps, lamp with 150-W bulb, clock or stopwatch	Developing Hypotheses, Measuring, Creating Data Tables, Drawing Conclusions
Section 2			
Discover, p. 368	10	**Consumable** aluminum pie plate, thread, candle **Nonconsumable** heavy scissors, hot plate or incandescent light	Inferring
Try This, p. 370	10, 10, 10, 20	**Consumable** graph paper **Nonconsumable** 2 thermometers, metric tape measure, watch or clock	Interpreting Data
Section 3			
Discover, p. 372	10	**Consumable** heavy-duty tape **Nonconsumable** pencil, large smooth ball, marker	Making Models
Try This, p. 373	15	**Consumable** construction paper, soda straw, tape, straight pin **Nonconsumable** scissors, metric ruler, pencil with eraser	Observing
Real-World Lab, pp. 374–375	40	**Consumable** 15 cm x 20 cm corrugated cardboard sheet, round toothpick, 2 wooden coffee stirrers, narrow masking tape **Nonconsumable** pen, wind vane, meter stick	Measuring, Interpreting Data, Drawing Conclusions
Section 4			
Discover, p. 381	10	**Consumable** hot tap water, 2 ice cubes, cold tap water **Nonconsumable** narrow-necked plastic bottle	Developing Hypotheses
Sharpen Your Skills, p. 383	10	No special materials required.	Interpreting Data
Science at Home, p. 386	home	**Consumable** cold water, ice cubes **Nonconsumable** large glass	Communicating
Section 5			
Discover, p. 387	15	**Consumable** 15 g salt, 50 mL water, 15 mL cold water, crushed ice **Nonconsumable** beaker, stirrer, clean test tube, watch or clock	Inferring
Sharpen Your Skills, p. 389	15	**Nonconsumable** funnel, narrow straight-sided glass jar, metric ruler, calculator	Calculating

A list of all materials required for the Student Edition activities can be found on pages TVA34–TVA40. You can obtain information about ordering materials by calling 1-800-848-9500 or by accessing the Science Explorer Internet site at: **www.phschool.com**

CHAPTER 12 PROJECT

Your Own Weather Station

In this chapter, students will learn more about specific weather factors, how they are related, and how they can be measured with instruments. The Chapter 12 Project gives students an opportunity to use instruments to take measurements of each of the weather factors.

Purpose In this project, students will set up a weather station and use instruments to measure weather factors over a two-week period. At the end of the project, students will look for patterns in their data and use them to try to predict the weather. Doing the project will give students a better understanding of weather factors and how they can be used to predict the weather.

Skills Focus After completing this project, students will be able to

- plan and create a model weather station;
- use their weather station to measure weather factors;
- record the data in a weather log;
- graph their data and analyze it for trends;
- use the trends to try to predict the weather;
- compare their predictions with actual weather conditions;
- communicate their findings to the rest of the class.

Project Time Line The entire project will take about three weeks. On the first day, introduce the project and hand out the Chapter 12 Project Overview in Unit 4 Resources. Allow time for class discussion of the project rules and for students to brainstorm weather factors, how they can be measured, and ways to record the measurements. At this time, you may wish to divide the class into small groups for the project.

Distribute the Chapter 12 Project Worksheet 1 in Unit 4 Resources, to help students plan their weather station, and Worksheet 2, in Unit 4 Resources, to show students a way to measure cloud cover. You also may wish to distribute the Chapter 12 Project Scoring Rubric, in Unit 4 Resources, so students will know what is expected of them.

Give students a day or two to plan their weather station and assemble the instruments and other materials they will need. Allow one class period for students to set up their weather station and practice using the instruments. You may wish to give students enough class time each day over the next two weeks to measure and record weather data. At the end of two weeks, give students a day or two to graph and analyze their data. Finally, set aside a class period at the end of the project for students to present and discuss their results.

For more information on supervising the chapter project, see Chapter 12 Project Teacher Notes in Unit 4 Resources.

Suggested Shortcuts You can streamline the project by having students make and share a single weather station. If you assemble the instruments and materials for the shared weather station yourself, you will save another day or two. If you do the project as a class project, assign different students to make the weather observations each day.

CHAPTER 12 PROJECT

Your Own Weather Station

A drenching spring rain is just what the flowers need! As the weather gets warmer, the garden will bloom. Warm days, soft winds, and plenty of rain—all of these are weather factors that affect growing things. In this chapter, you will learn about a variety of weather factors, including air pressure, temperature, wind speed and direction, relative humidity, precipitation, and the amount and types of clouds.

Your Goal To measure and record weather conditions using instruments. You will look for patterns in your data that can be used to predict the next day's weather.

In completing your project, you will
- develop a plan for measuring weather factors
- record your data in a daily log
- display your data in a set of graphs
- use your data and graphs to try to predict the weather
- follow the safety guidelines in Appendix A

Get Started Begin by previewing the chapter to see what weather factors you want to measure. Discuss with a group of your classmates what instruments you might use. Brainstorm what observations you should make each day.

Check Your Progress You'll be working on the project as you study this chapter. To keep your project on track, look for Check Your Progress boxes at the following points.

Section 2 Review, page 371: Prepare to make observations.
Section 3 Review, page 380: Collect and record data.
Section 5 Review, page 390: Graph your data and look for patterns.

Present Your Project At the end of the chapter (page 393), present your weather observations and explain how well you predicted the weather.

Spring rains are an important factor in helping these tulips grow.

Section 4 Water in the Atmosphere

Discover **How Does Fog Form?**
Sharpen Your Skills **Interpreting Data**
Science at Home **Condensation on Glass**

Section 5 Precipitation

Discover **How Can You Make Hail?**
Sharpen Your Skills **Calculating**

361

Possible Materials A weather station requires a sheltered place outdoors, such as the slatted wooden box described in Worksheet 1. Several instruments are needed, including a thermometer, psychrometer, barometer, wind vane, anemometer, and rain gauge. Useful additions are a device for measuring cloud cover (see Worksheet 2) and a chart showing cloud types (or use Exploring Clouds, page 385 in the text).

Students will need commercial thermometers and psychrometers. They can use the barometer they made in the Skills Lab in Chapter 12, pages 348–349 in the text. They also can make their own wind vane (Try This, page 373 in the text), anemometer (Real-World Lab, pages 374–375 in the text), and rain gauge (Sharpen Your Skills, page 389 in the text). However, commercial instruments are more accurate and should be used if possible.

Launching the Project Introduce the project by discussing weather stations. Ask: **If you were going to visit another city, what would you want to know about the weather so you would be prepared?** *(Students may say they would want to know how hot or cold it was and if it was raining or snowing.)* **How could you find out what the weather conditions in the city were?** *(Students may say they would watch a national weather report on television or look at a national weather map in a newspaper.)* Point out that weather information for specific locations is collected and recorded by weather stations. Tell students that in this project they will make a weather station and observe and record weather factors for a location near their school.

Program Resources

- **Unit 4 Resources** Chapter 12 Project Teacher Notes; Chapter 12 Project Overview and Worksheets; Chapter 12 Project Scoring Rubric

Media and Technology

Student Edition on Audio CD
Chapter 12

www.phschool.com

You will find an Internet activity, chapter self-tests for students, and links to other chapter topics at this site.

Performance Assessment

To assess students' performance in this project, use the Chapter 12 Project Scoring Rubric in Unit 4 Resources. Students will be assessed on their
- weather observations and weather log;
- graphical presentation and interpretation of weather data;
- presentation of the results to the class;
- group participation, if they worked in groups.

Energy in the Atmosphere

Objectives

After completing the lesson, students will be able to

- ◆ state in what form energy travels from the sun to Earth;
- ◆ explain what happens to energy from the sun when it reaches Earth.

Key Terms electromagnetic wave, radiation, infrared radiation, ultraviolet radiation, scattering, greenhouse effect

1 Engage/Explore

Activating Prior Knowledge

Encourage students to think about the way the sun heats Earth's surface by asking: **Which is cooler on a hot, sunny day, a lawn or a parking lot?** *(a lawn)* Point out that even without trees, a grass-covered surface stays cooler than a surface covered by blacktop. Ask: **Why doesn't the lawn get as hot as the parking lot?** *(Students may not know.)* Tell students that grass absorbs less light than pavement even when both surfaces receive the same amount of sun. As a result, the grass does not get as hot. Add that such differences in the heating of Earth's surface, on a large scale, are the major cause of Earth's weather.

DISCOVER

Skills Focus measuring
Materials
2 thermometers, plastic bag, 2 small pieces of paper, tape
Time 10 minutes
Tips Make sure the bulbs of both thermometers are shaded by the pieces of paper from direct rays of light or both may show equally high temperatures.
Expected Outcome The thermometer in the bag should show a higher temperature.
Think It Over The plastic bag trapped the heat inside it from the sun, and this caused the thermometer in the bag to show a higher temperature.

Section 1

Energy in the Atmosphere

DISCOVER ACTIVITY

Does a Plastic Bag Trap Heat?

1. Record the initial temperatures on two thermometers. (You should get the same readings.)
2. Place one of the thermometers in a plastic bag. Put a small piece of paper in the bag so that it shades the bulb of the thermometer. Seal the bag.
3. Place both thermometers on a sunny window ledge or near a light bulb. Cover the bulb of the second thermometer with a small piece of paper. Predict what you think will happen.
4. Wait five minutes. Then record the temperatures on the two thermometers.

Think It Over

Measuring Were the two temperatures the same? How could you explain any difference?

GUIDE FOR READING

- ◆ In what form does energy from the sun travel to Earth?
- ◆ What happens to energy from the sun when it reaches Earth?

Reading Tip Before you read, skim the section for boldfaced words that are unfamiliar to you. As you read, find their meanings and write them down in your notebook.

Think of a sunny summer day. When you get up in the morning, the sun is low in the sky and the air is cool. As the sun rises, the temperature increases. By noon it is quite hot. As you will see in this chapter, heat is a major factor in the weather. The movement of heat in the atmosphere causes temperatures to change, winds to blow, and rain to fall.

Energy from the Sun

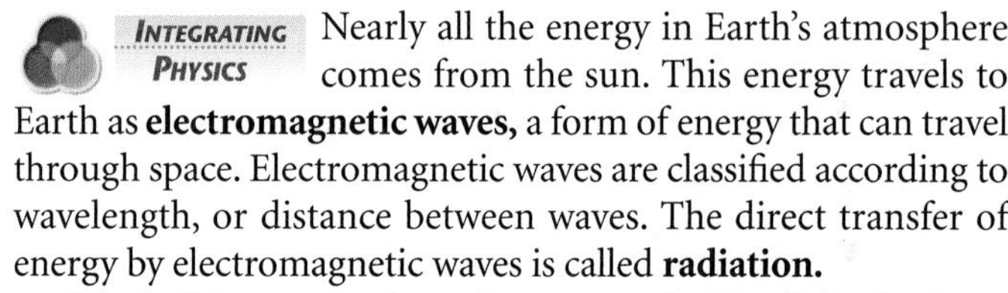

INTEGRATING PHYSICS Nearly all the energy in Earth's atmosphere comes from the sun. This energy travels to Earth as **electromagnetic waves,** a form of energy that can travel through space. Electromagnetic waves are classified according to wavelength, or distance between waves. The direct transfer of energy by electromagnetic waves is called **radiation.**

Most of the energy from the sun reaches Earth in the form of visible light and infrared radiation, and a small amount of ultraviolet radiation. Visible light is a mixture of all of the colors that you see in a rainbow: red, orange, yellow, green, blue, and violet. The different colors are the result of different wavelengths

READING STRATEGIES

Reading Tip Suggest that students make a list of unfamiliar boldfaced words and then fill in their meanings as they read.
Study and Comprehension Suggest that students use ROY G. BV to remember the order of colors in the spectrum of visible light, going from longer to shorter wavelengths. The colors represented by the letters are red, orange, yellow, green, blue, and violet.

Media and Technology

Concept Videotape Library
Grade 6, Tape 2 "The Greenhouse Effect"

Concept Videotape Library
Grade 6, Tape 3 "Changes in Climate"; "Never Put Up the Umbrella Until It Starts to Rain"; "Why Is the Sky Blue?"

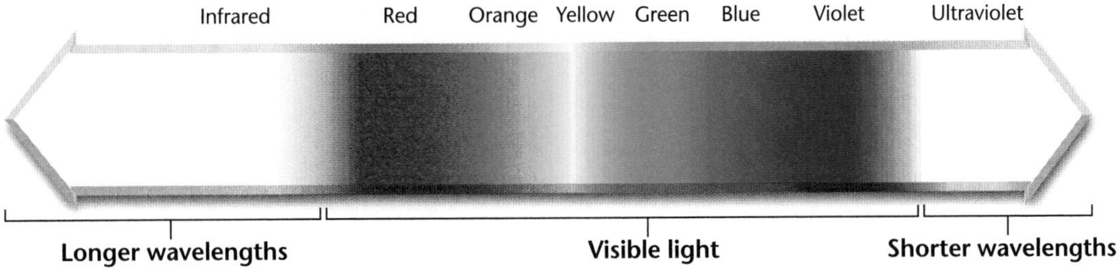

Figure 1 Electromagnetic waves include infrared radiation, visible light, and ultraviolet radiation. *Interpreting Diagrams What type of radiation has wavelengths that are shorter than visible light? What type has wavelengths that are longer?*

of visible light. Red and orange light have the longest wavelengths, while blue and violet light have the shortest wavelengths.

Infrared radiation is a form of energy with wavelengths that are longer than red light. Infrared radiation is not visible, but can be felt as heat. Heat lamps used to keep food warm in restaurants give off both visible red light and invisible infrared radiation. The sun also gives off **ultraviolet radiation,** which has wavelengths that are shorter than violet light. Sunburns are caused by ultraviolet radiation. This radiation can also cause skin cancer and eye damage.

☑ *Checkpoint* *Which color of visible light has the longest wavelengths?*

Energy in the Atmosphere

Before the sun's rays can reach Earth's surface, they must pass through the atmosphere. The path of the sun's rays is shown in *Exploring Energy in the Atmosphere* on the following page.

Some of the energy from the sun is absorbed within the atmosphere. Water vapor and carbon dioxide absorb some infrared radiation. The ozone layer in the stratosphere absorbs most of the ultraviolet radiation. Clouds, dust, and other gases also absorb energy from the sun.

Some of the sun's rays are reflected. Clouds in the atmosphere act like mirrors, reflecting some solar energy back into space. In addition, dust particles and molecules of gases in the atmosphere reflect light from the sun in all directions.

2 Facilitate

Energy from the Sun

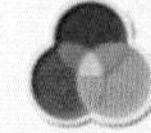

Integrating Physics

Materials *prism*
Time 5 minutes

Show students a prism and explain that its angled sides bend the different colors in sunlight by different amounts, splitting the light into a rainbow. Demonstrate by placing the prism in sunlight. Then ask: **Where does light have the shortest wavelength and where does light have the longest wavelength?** *(The end with violet light is the shortest, and the end with red light is the longest.)* **learning modality: visual**

Energy in the Atmosphere

Building Inquiry Skills: Inferring

Describe the following hypothetical situation to the class. City A is located where the ozone layer of the stratosphere has become very thin. City B is located where the ozone layer is still relatively thick. Ask: **How do you think the two cities compare in terms of the ultraviolet radiation they receive?** *(City A would get more ultraviolet radiation than City B because less of the ultraviolet radiation would be absorbed by ozone in the stratosphere.)* **learning modality: logical/mathematical**

Program Resources

- **Unit 5 Resources** 12-1 Lesson Plan; 12-1 Section Summary
- **Guided Reading and Study Workbook** Section 12-1

Media and Technology

Transparencies "Energy in the Atmosphere," Transparency 43

Answers to Self-Assessment

Caption Question

Figure 1 Ultraviolet radiation has wavelengths that are shorter than visible light. Infrared radiation has wavelengths that are longer than visible light.

☑ *Checkpoint*

Red light has the longest wavelengths.

Ongoing Assessment

Drawing Have students draw a representation of the visible spectrum, showing the different colors of visible light in order by wavelength.

Energy in the Atmosphere, continued

Including All Students

Remind students that the moon, unlike Earth, has no atmosphere. Then ask: **If you were standing on the moon during the day, what color would the sky appear to be?** *(Students may know from photographs that the sky would appear to be black.)* **Why wouldn't the sky appear to be blue?** *(Because without an atmosphere on the moon there are no gas molecules to scatter the light and make it look blue)* **learning modality: logical/mathematical**

EXPLORING

Energy in the Atmosphere

Materials *several sheets of light- and dark-colored construction paper, bandanas or other material for blindfolds* ACTIVITY
Time 10 minutes

Point out to students that all parts of Earth's surface are not heated equally by energy from the sun. Demonstrate this point by placing several pieces of construction paper in direct sunlight. Use white, black, and at least one or two other light and dark colors. After the papers have been in the sun for at least five minutes, ask volunteers to put on blindfolds. Then rearrange the order of the papers and have the volunteers try to tell which papers are light colored and which are dark colored based on how warm or cool they feel to the touch. Ask: **Why do the dark-colored papers feel warmer than the light-colored papers?** *(Dark-colored surfaces absorb more of the light that strikes them, whereas light-colored surfaces reflect more of the light that strikes them.)* **Which surfaces on Earth do you think reflect more of the sun's light back into space?** *(Light-colored surfaces such as sand or snow)* **Which surfaces absorb more of the sun's light?** *(Dark-colored surfaces such as bare soil or blacktop pavement)* **learning modality: kinesthetic**

Reflection of light in all directions is called **scattering.** When you look at the sky, the light you see has been scattered by gas molecules in the atmosphere. Gas molecules scatter short wavelengths of visible light (blue and violet) more than long wavelengths (red and orange). Scattered light is therefore bluer than ordinary sunlight, which is why the daytime sky looks blue.

When the sun is rising or setting, light from the sun passes through a greater thickness of the atmosphere than when the sun is higher in the sky. More light from the blue end of the spectrum is removed by scattering before it reaches your eyes. The remaining light from the sun contains mostly red and orange light. The sun looks red, and clouds around it become very colorful.

☑ *Checkpoint* ***Why would particles from volcanic eruptions make sunsets and sunrises more red?***

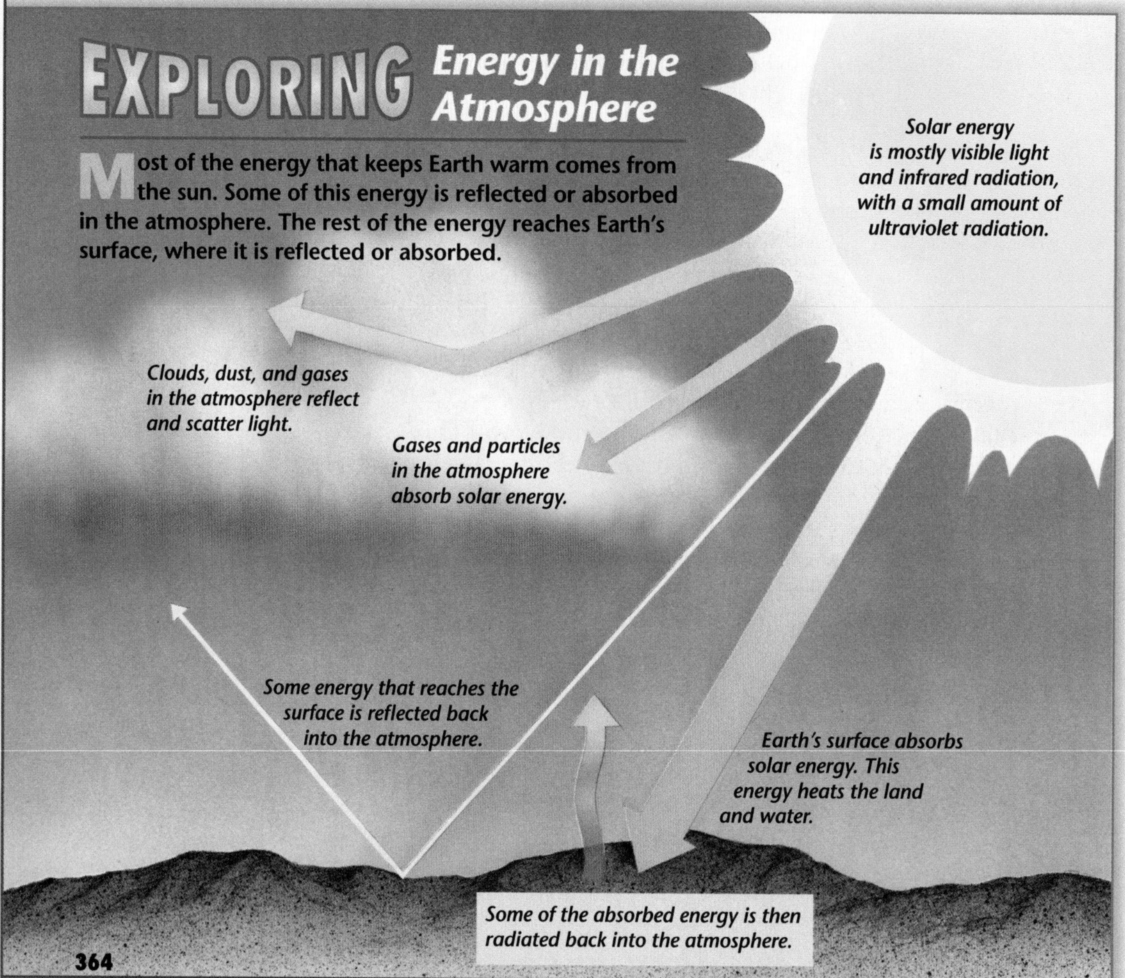

Background

Facts and Figures The amount of energy produced by the sun is amazing. An area of the sun's surface the size of a postage stamp gives off enough energy to power 500 60-watt light bulbs. Although only one part in two billion of the total amount of solar energy reaches Earth, this is still a huge amount. If the amount of solar energy reaching Earth in just one hour could be used, it would meet the world's total energy needs for a year. If the amount of solar energy reaching Earth in a day could be used, it would take 700 billion tons of coal to match it.

A tiny fraction of the sun's energy actually is trapped and used for power. Some solar energy plants collect sunlight with mirrors and focus it with lenses on tubes filled with fluid. The fluid heats up, and the heat is used to boil water into steam that powers electric generators.

Energy at Earth's Surface

Some of the sun's energy reaches Earth's surface and is reflected back into the atmosphere. Some of the energy, however, is absorbed by the land and water and changed into heat.

Different surfaces are affected by the sun's energy differently. If you have walked across a lawn and then crossed a street on a hot sunny day, you know that the street becomes much hotter than the lawn, even though both receive the same amount of sunlight. This is because dark-colored materials absorb more of the sun's energy than light-colored materials do.

If you have been to the beach on a sunny day, you've probably noticed a similar difference in the temperature of the sand and the water. It takes more energy to heat the water than the sand, so the water temperature increases more slowly. As you will learn later in this chapter, uneven heating of surfaces sets winds in motion.

When Earth's surface is heated, some of the energy returns to the atmosphere as infrared radiation. Most of this infrared radiation cannot travel all the way through the atmosphere back into space. Instead, much of it is absorbed by gases in the air. The energy from the absorbed radiation heats the gases in the air. These gases form a "blanket" around Earth that holds heat in the atmosphere. The process by which gases hold heat in the air is called the greenhouse effect.

The greenhouse effect is a natural process that keeps Earth's atmosphere at a temperature that is comfortable for most living things. You will learn more about the greenhouse effect in Chapter 14.

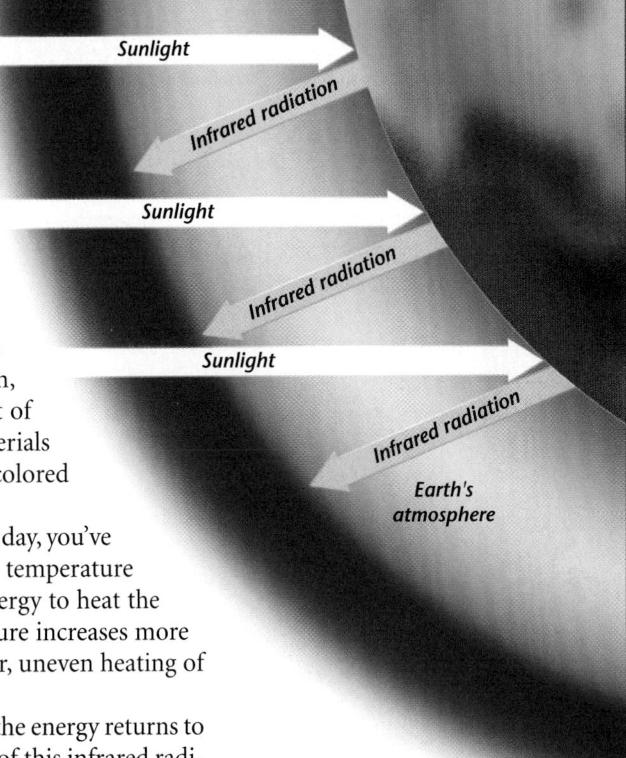

Figure 2 Sunlight travels through the atmosphere to Earth's surface. Earth's surface then gives off infrared radiation. Much of this energy is held by the atmosphere, warming it.

Section 1 Review

1. List three forms of radiation from the sun. How are these alike? How are they different?
2. What happens to the energy from the sun that is absorbed by Earth's surface?
3. Why is the sky blue? Why are sunsets often red?
4. **Thinking Critically Applying Concepts** What might conditions on Earth be like without the greenhouse effect?

Science at Home

Heating by Radiation With an adult family member, explore the role radiation plays in heating your home. Are some rooms warmer and sunnier in the morning? Are other rooms warmer and sunnier in the afternoon? How does opening and closing curtains or blinds affect the temperature of a room? Explain your observations to your family.

3 Assess

Section 1 Review Answers

1. Visible light, infrared radiation, and ultraviolet radiation; they differ in their wavelengths.
2. It is changed into heat.
3. The sky is blue because short-wavelength blue light is scattered more by gas molecules in the atmosphere. Sunsets are often red because the light from the setting sun passes through a greater thickness of the atmosphere than when the sun is higher in the sky, and more blue light is removed by scattering, leaving mostly red light to reach your eyes.
4. Without the greenhouse effect, more infrared radiation radiated back from Earth's surface would escape into space instead of being held in the atmosphere, so Earth's surface would be much colder.

Science at Home

Tips Suggest to students that they try to do this ACTIVITY activity on a sunny day, preferably when the furnace or other source of artificial heat is not operating.

Program Resources

- **Unit 4 Resources** 12-1 Review and Reinforce; 12-1 Enrich

Answers to Self-Assessment

Checkpoint

The particles would scatter more light from the sun. This would remove more light from the blue end of the spectrum, causing the remaining light to look mostly red.

Performance Assessment

Oral Presentation Call on students to explain in their own words one of the various things that can happen to sunlight that reaches Earth's atmosphere.

Skills Lab

Developing Hypotheses

Heating Earth's Surface

Preparing for Inquiry

Key Concept Sand heats and cools more quickly than water.

Skills Objectives Students will be able to
- develop hypotheses about how quickly sand and water heat and cool;
- measure the temperature of sand and water while they are heating and cooling;
- create a data table to record their measurements;
- conclude from their data whether sand or water heats and cools more quickly.

Time 40 minutes

Advance Planning To be sure students have enough class time to record temperatures for a full 30 minutes, you may wish to set up the equipment and measure out the sand and water ahead of time. Make sure the sand is dry. Both sand and water should be at room temperature when the lab begins.

If using probeware, refer to the *Probeware Lab Manual.*

Alternative Materials Students can use small wide-mouthed glass jars instead of beakers, as long as both jars are the same size and shape. They also can substitute sugar for sand. If ring stands and clamps are not available, you can substitute two 2-L soda bottles placed about 30 cm apart and connected by a ruler placed across the tops. The thermometers can be suspended from the ruler.

Guiding Inquiry

Invitation To help students formulate hypotheses about the heating and cooling of sand and water, have them recall walking barefoot on a beach. Ask: **Did you ever walk barefoot on the beach on a sunny day? What was the temperature of the sand like?** *(The sand was probably hot.)* **When you reached the water, how did it feel in comparison to the hot sand?** *(much cooler)* **If you ever walked barefoot on the beach after dark, which felt warmer, the sand or the water?** *(the water)* Challenge students to think of other past observations that might help them formulate their hypotheses.

Skills Lab

Developing Hypotheses

Heating Earth's Surface

In this lab, you will develop and test a hypothesis about how quickly different materials absorb radiation.

Problem

How do the heating and cooling rates of sand and water compare?

Materials 

2 thermometers or temperature probes
2 beakers, 400 mL
sand, 300 mL
water, 300 mL
lamp with 150-W bulb
metric ruler
clock or stopwatch
string
graph paper
ring stand and two ring clamps

Procedure  

1. Do you think sand or water will heat up faster? Record your hypothesis. Then follow these steps to test your hypothesis.
2. Copy the data table into your notebook. Add enough rows to record data for 15 minutes.
3. Fill one beaker with 300 mL of dry sand.
4. Fill the second beaker with 300 mL of water at room temperature.
5. Arrange the beakers beneath the ring stand.
6. Place one thermometer in each beaker. If you are using a temperature probe, see your teacher for instructions.
7. Suspend the thermometers from the ring stand with string. This will hold the thermometers in place so they do not fall.
8. Adjust the height of the clamp so that the bulb of each thermometer is covered by about 0.5 cm of sand or water in a beaker.
9. Position the lamp so that it is about 20 cm above the sand and water. There should be no more than 8 cm between the beakers. **CAUTION:** *Be careful not to splash water onto the hot light bulb.*
10. Record the temperature of the sand and water in your data table.
11. Turn on the lamp. Read the temperature of the sand and water every minute for 15 minutes. Record the temperatures in the Light On column in the data table.
12. Which material do you think will cool off more quickly? Record your hypothesis. Again, give reasons why you think your hypothesis is correct.
13. Turn the light off. Read the temperature of the sand and water every minute for another 15 minutes. Record the temperatures in the Light Off column (16–30 minutes).

DATA TABLE

Temperature with Light On (°C)			Temperature with Light Off (°C)		
Time (min)	Sand	Water	Time (min)	Sand	Water
Start			16		
1			17		
2			18		
3			19		
4			20		
5			21		

Introducing the Procedure

Have students read through the steps of the procedure. Clarify any steps they do not understand. Students should use exactly the same amount of sand as water and place both beakers exactly the same distance from the lamp. Explain that by making these factors the same for both the sand and water, they will be controlling other variables that might affect the outcome of the experiment.

Troubleshooting the Experiment

- To reduce the number of setups needed, divide the class into groups and have each group use one setup.
- Make sure that each lamp is positioned so it shines evenly on the two beakers. If one beaker receives more direct rays than the other, it may bias the results. Also check that both thermometers are positioned the same distance below the surface and held in an upright position by the string.

Analyze and Conclude

1. Draw two line graphs to show the data for the temperature change in sand and water over time. Label the horizontal axis from 0 to 30 minutes and the vertical axis in degrees Celsius. Draw both graphs on the same piece of graph paper. Use a dashed line to show the temperature change in water and a solid line to show the temperature change in sand.
2. Calculate the total change in temperature for each material.
3. Based on your data, which material had the greater increase in temperature?
4. What can you conclude about which material absorbed heat faster? How do your results compare with your hypothesis?
5. Review your data again. In 15 minutes, which material cooled faster?
6. How do these results compare to your second hypothesis?
7. **Think About It** If your results did not support either of your hypotheses, why do you think the results differed from what you expected?
8. **Apply** Based on your results, which do you think will heat up more quickly on a sunny day: the water in a lake or the sand surrounding it? Which will cool off more quickly after dark?

More to Explore

Do you think all solid materials heat up as fast as sand? For example, consider gravel, crushed stone, or different types of soil. Write a hypothesis about their heating rates as an "If . . . then. . ." statement. With the approval and supervision of your teacher, develop a procedure to test your hypothesis. Was your hypothesis correct?

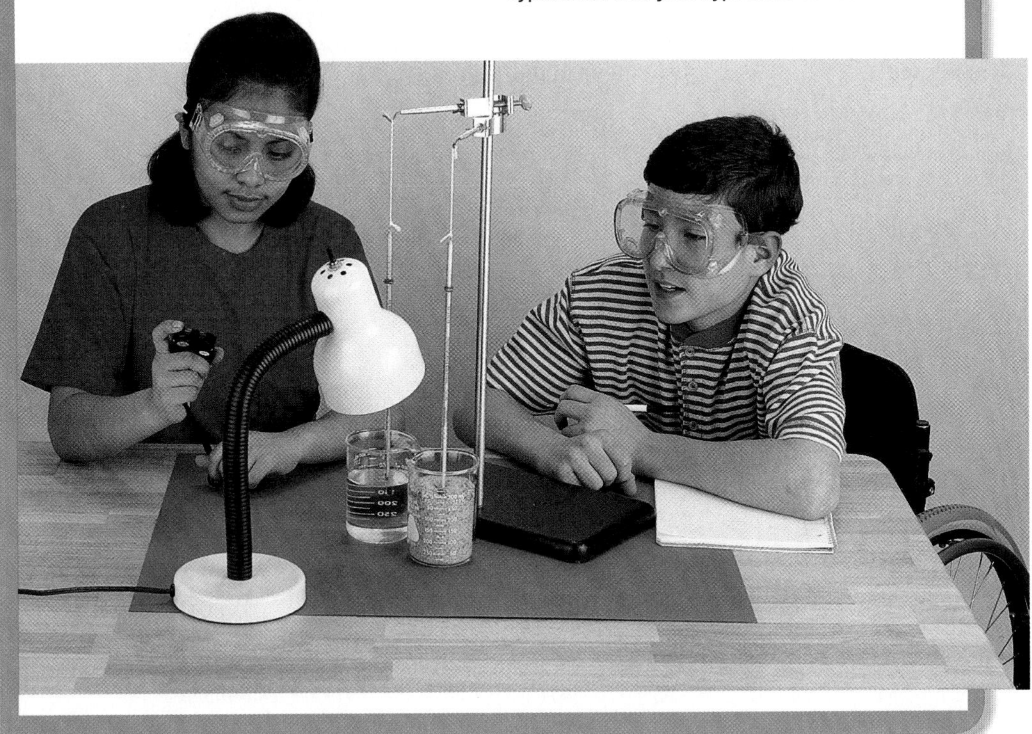

Program Resources

- **Unit 4 Resources** Chapter 12 Skills Lab
- **Probeware Lab Manual** Blackline master

Safety

Caution students to be careful not to touch the light bulb or splash water on it. Review the safety guidelines in Appendix A.

Media and Technology

Lab Activity Videotapes
Grade 6, Tape 3

Expected Outcome
Students should find that the sand heats and cools more quickly than the water.

Analyze and Conclude
1. Both graphs should rise steadily during the first 15 minutes and then decline steadily during the second 15 minutes. The line for sand temperature should rise and fall more steeply than the line for water temperature, indicating a greater rate of change in temperature for sand than water.
2. Exact answers will vary depending on the specific temperatures recorded. However, the sand should show a greater total change in temperature than the water.
3. The data should show that the sand had a greater increase in temperature.
4. Students should conclude that the sand absorbed heat faster than the water. These results may or may not agree with their hypothesis.
5. The data should show that the sand cooled faster.
6. These results may or may not agree with their second hypothesis.
7. Answers may vary. One possible answer is that they expected both the sand and water to heat and cool at the same rate because there were equal amounts of the two substances.
8. Based on their results, students should say that the sand surrounding a lake will heat up more quickly on a sunny day and cool off more quickly after dark than the water in the lake.

Extending the Inquiry

More to Explore Students may think that solids with a different texture, made of different materials, or having different colors might heat up at different rates than sand. For example, students may think that rock would heat up faster than sand because it is more solid. Students may hypothesize that soil will heat up faster than sand because it is darker in color. They can test their hypothesis by repeating the skills lab and substituting soil or other materials for water.

Integrating Physics 

Section 2 Heat Transfer

Objectives

After completing the lesson, students will be able to
- ◆ describe how temperature is measured;
- ◆ explain the three ways heat is transferred.

Key Terms thermal energy, temperature, thermometer, heat, conduction, convection

1 Engage/Explore

Activating Prior Knowledge

Introduce students to the concept of heat transfer by helping them recall the shimmery effect produced by heated air rising from hot pavement. Ask: **On a hot sunny day, did you ever see cars, buildings, or other objects appear to shimmer or waver on the other side of a street or parking lot?** *(Most students probably will say yes.)* **What causes this effect?** *(Hot air rising from the pavement)* Explain that the sun heats up the ground more quickly than the air, especially if the surface of the ground is dark colored. The heated air then rises and bends light waves as they pass through it, making objects on the other side shimmer.

Discover Activity

Skills Focus inferring
Materials *aluminum pie plate, heavy scissors, thread, candle or hot plate or incandescent light*
Time 10 minutes
Tips You may want to poke the holes in the flat parts yourself.
Expected Outcome The spiral will spin.
Think It Over The spiral spun because warm air rose from the heat source and pushed against the spiral.

Integrating Physics 

Section 2 Heat Transfer

Discover Activity

What Happens When Air Is Heated?

1. Use heavy scissors to cut the flat part out of an aluminum pie plate. Use the tip of the scissors to poke a small hole in the middle of the flat part.
2. Cut the part into a spiral shape, as shown in the photo. Tie a 30-centimeter piece of thread to the middle of the spiral.
3. Hold the spiral over a source of heat, such as a candle, hot plate, or incandescent light bulb.

Think It Over
Inferring What happened to the spiral? Why do you think this happened?

Guide for Reading
- ◆ How is temperature measured?
- ◆ In what three ways is heat transferred?

Reading Tip As you read, make a list of the types of heat transfer. Write a sentence about how each type occurs.

You know that energy from the sun is absorbed by Earth's surface. Some energy is then transferred from the surface to the atmosphere in the form of heat. The heat then moves from place to place within the atmosphere. But how does heat move in the atmosphere?

Energy and Temperature

Gases are made up of small particles, called molecules, that are constantly moving. The faster the molecules are moving, the more energy they have. Figure 3 shows how the motion of

Figure 3 The lemonade is cold, so the molecules move slowly. The herbal tea is hot, so the molecules move faster than the molecules in the lemonade. ***Inferring*** *Which liquid has a higher temperature?*

Reading Strategies

Reading Tip Student lists should include radiation, conduction, and convection. Their sentences should explain that radiation occurs by direct transfer of heat by one substance touching another, and that convection occurs as the result of the movement of fluids.

Program Resources
- ◆ **Unit 4 Resources** 12-2 Lesson Plan; 12-2 Section Summary
- ◆ **Guided Reading and Study Workbook** Section 12-2
- ◆ **Product Testing Activities by *Consumer Reports*** "Testing Disposable Cups," pp. 1–8
- ◆ **Interdisciplinary Explorations Series** "Wagons West," pp. 31–33

molecules is related to the amount of energy they hold. The total energy of motion in the molecules of a substance is called **thermal energy.** On the other hand, **temperature** is the *average* amount of energy of motion of each molecule of a substance. That means that temperature is a measure of how hot or cold a substance is.

Measuring Temperature

Ask someone what the weather is like. The answer will probably include the temperature. Temperature is one of the most important elements of weather. **Air temperature is usually measured with a thermometer.** A **thermometer** is a thin glass tube with a bulb on one end that contains a liquid, usually mercury or colored alcohol.

Thermometers work because liquids expand when they are heated and contract when they are cooled. When the air temperature increases, the liquid in the bulb expands and rises up the column. What happens when the temperature decreases? The liquid in the bulb contracts and moves down the tube.

Temperature is measured in units called degrees. The two most common scales are shown in Figure 4. Scientists use the Celsius scale. On the Celsius scale, the freezing point of pure water is 0°C (read "zero degrees Celsius"). The boiling point of pure water is 100°C. Weather reports in the United States use the Fahrenheit scale. On the Fahrenheit scale, the freezing point of water is 32°F and the boiling point is 212°F.

Checkpoint *How many degrees Celsius are there between the freezing point of water and the boiling point of water?*

Figure 4 Scientists use the Celsius scale to measure temperature. However, weather reports use the Fahrenheit scale. *Measuring According to this thermometer, what is the air temperature in degrees Celsius?*

How Heat Is Transferred

The energy transferred from a hotter object to a cooler one is referred to as **heat.** The types of heat transfer are shown in Figure 5 on page 371. **Heat is transferred in three ways: radiation, conduction, and convection.**

Radiation Have you ever felt the warmth of the sun's rays on your face? You were feeling energy coming directly from the sun as radiation. Recall that radiation is the direct transfer of energy by electromagnetic waves. The heat you feel from the sun or a campfire travels directly to you as infrared radiation. You cannot see infrared radiation, but you can feel it as heat.

2 Facilitate

Energy and Temperature

Demonstration

Materials *glass jar with lid, black and white sheets of construction paper, toothpick, thread, glue, tape, scissors*
Time 15 minutes

ACTIVITY

Make a radiometer to show students that heat increases the movement of air molecules. Cut four 2-cm squares from white construction paper and four from black construction paper. Glue each black square to a white square. Holding a toothpick vertically, glue one edge of each square to the shaft of the toothpick, like feathers sticking out from the shaft of an arrow. Arrange the squares so that colors alternate between black and white. Tape the end of a piece of thread to one end of the toothpick. Tape the other end of the thread to the inside of a jar lid. Put the lid on the jar, making sure the toothpick dangles freely, and place the jar in sunlight. Soon the toothpick will start to spin. When it does, ask: **What causes the toothpick to spin?** *(The black squares heat up faster than the white squares, and this heats the air molecules close to them. The heated air molecules bounce off the black squares, pushing the toothpick around in a circle.)* **learning modality: visual**

Measuring Temperature

Building Inquiry Skills: Calculating

Materials *calculator*
Time 10 minutes

Help students become more familiar with the Celsius scale by having them convert several Fahrenheit temperatures to their Celsius equivalents, using the formula °C = (°F - 32) x 5/9. **learning modality: logical/mathematical**

Ongoing Assessment

Skills Check Have students compare and contrast the terms *thermal energy, temperature,* and *heat.*

Media and Technology

Transparencies "Types of Heat Transfer," Transparency 44

Answers to Self-Assessment

Caption Questions

Figure 3 The herbal tea has a higher temperature.
Figure 4 The air temperature is about 20 degrees Celsius.

Checkpoint

Between the freezing point of water and the boiling point of water there are 100 Celsius degrees.

How Heat Is Transferred

Inquiry Challenge

Materials *ball*
Time 5 minutes

Challenge students to model the three different types of heat transfer by using a ball to represent heat and students to represent air molecules. Then have students move the ball around the classroom in different ways to model radiation, conduction, and convection. Ask: **How would you move the ball to represent radiation?** *(Toss or roll it.)* **How would you move the ball to represent conduction?** *(Pass it from one student to another.)* **How would you move the ball to represent convection?** *(Have one student walk with it.)* **learning modality: kinesthetic**

Heat Transfer in the Troposphere

TRY THIS

Skills Focus interpreting data
Materials *2 thermometers, metric tape measure, watch or clock, graph paper*
Time 10 minutes per day for 3 days; 20 minutes to graph and analyze data
Tips Doing this activity on sunny days will lead to greater differences in temperatures at the two heights.
Expected Outcome Students should find that the temperature 1 cm above the ground varies more than the temperature 1.25 m above the ground. The ground heats up during the day as it absorbs sunlight. It cools quickly at night as it radiates the heat back into the air. Heat is not effectively transferred through air, so air close to the ground will be more affected by these variations in ground temperature than air farther above the ground.
Extend Have students repeat the activity in a shady location and then compare the data obtained from the two locations. They should find less variation in the shady-location readings. Challenge students to explain why. **learning modality: logical/mathematical**

Temperatures at Two Heights

ACTIVITY

How much difference do you think there is between air temperatures near the ground and air temperatures higher up? Give reasons for your prediction.

1. Take all of your measurements at a location that is sunny all day.
2. Early in the morning, measure the air temperature 1 cm and 1.25 m above the ground. Record the time of day and the temperature for both locations. Repeat your measurements late in the afternoon.
3. Record these measurements in the morning and afternoon for two more days.
4. Graph your data for each height with temperature on the vertical axis and time on the horizontal axis. Draw both lines on the same piece of graph paper using the same axes. Label both lines.

Interpreting Data At which height did the temperature vary the most? How can you explain the difference?

Conduction Have you ever walked barefoot on hot sand? Your feet felt hot because heat moved directly from the sand into your feet. When a fast-moving molecule bumps into a nearby slower-moving molecule, it transfers some of its energy. The direct transfer of heat from one substance to another substance that it is touching is called **conduction.** The molecules that gain energy can in turn pass the energy along to other nearby molecules. When you walk on hot sand, the fast-moving molecules in the sand transfer heat into the slower-moving molecules in your feet.

The closer together the molecules in a substance are, the more effectively they can conduct heat. Conduction works well in some solids, such as metals, but not as well in liquids and gases. Air and water do not conduct heat very well.

Heat transfer by convection

Convection How can you dry your boots over a hot-air vent, even though the furnace is in another room? Air from the furnace carries the heat to your boots. In fluids (liquids and gases), molecules can move from place to place. As the molecules move, they take their heat along with them. The transfer of heat by the movement of a fluid is called **convection.**

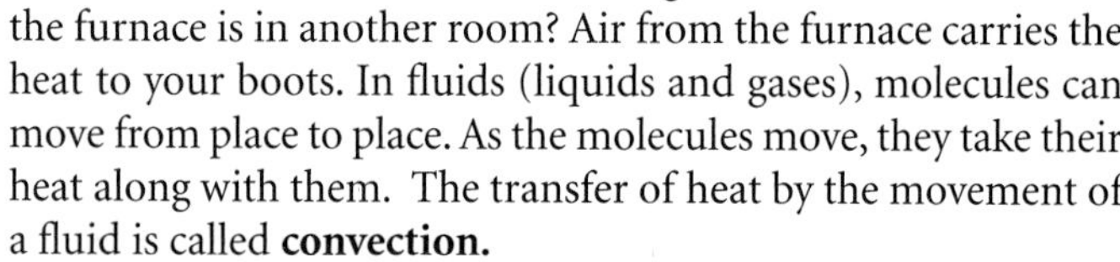

✓ ***Checkpoint*** *Give at least one example each of radiation, conduction, and convection in your daily life.*

Heat Transfer in the Troposphere

Radiation, conduction, and convection work together to heat the troposphere. When Earth's surface absorbs solar energy during the day, the surface of the land becomes warmer than the air. Air near Earth's surface is warmed by radiation and conduction of heat from the surface to the air. However, heat is not easily conducted from one air molecule to another. Only the first few meters of the troposphere are heated by conduction. Thus, the air close to the ground is usually warmer than the air a few meters up.

Convection causes most of the heating of the troposphere. When the air near the ground is heated, the molecules have more energy. Because they have more energy, the molecules move

Background

Facts and Figures The highest air temperature ever recorded near Earth's surface is 58°C (136°F), which was recorded in Libya in northern Africa. The highest average annual air temperature ever recorded is 34°C (94°F), which is the average daytime temperature in Ethiopia in eastern Africa. The highest air temperature ever recorded in the Western Hemisphere is 57°C (134°F), at Death Valley, California.

Program Resources

- **Unit 4 Resources** 12-2 Review and Reinforce; 12-2 Enrich

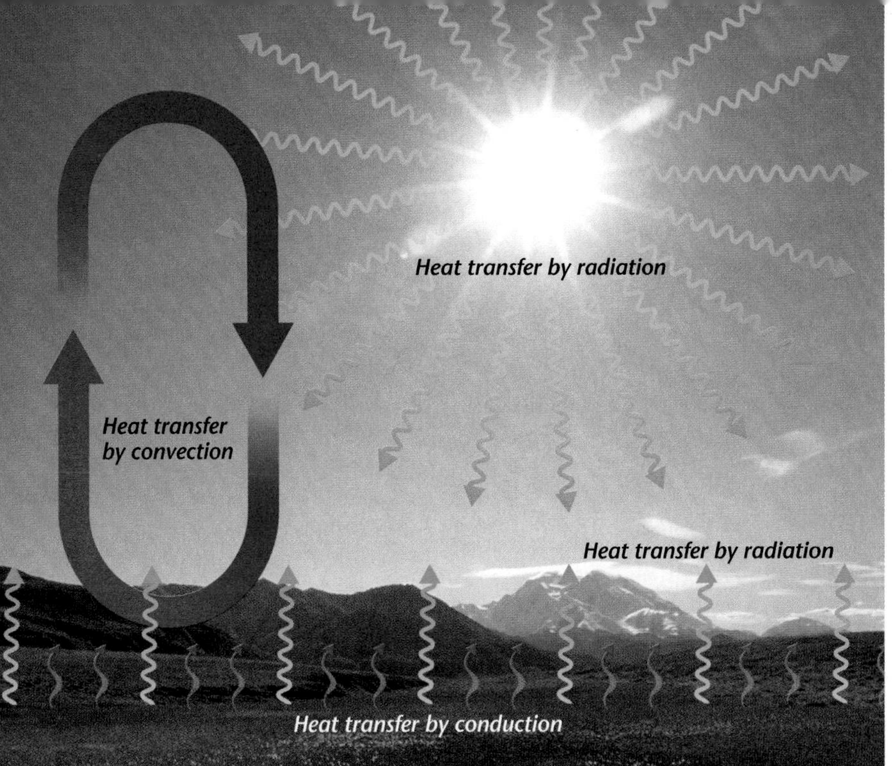

faster. As the molecules in the heated air move, they bump into each other and move farther apart. The air becomes less dense. Cooler, denser air sinks, forcing the warmer, less dense air to rise.

The upward movement of warm air and the downward movement of cool air form convection currents. Convection currents move heat throughout the troposphere.

Figure 5 All three types of heat transfer—radiation, convection, and conduction—occur near Earth's surface.

Section 2 Review

1. What is temperature?
2. Describe how a thermometer works.
3. Name three ways that heat can be transferred. Briefly explain how the three work together to heat the troposphere.
4. **Thinking Critically Applying Concepts** When you light a fire in a fireplace, warm air rises by convection and goes up the chimney. How, then, does a fireplace heat a room? Why do only the people directly in front of the fireplace feel the warmth of the fire?

CHAPTER PROJECT

Check Your Progress

Gather the instruments you will need to measure the weather factors. (*Hint:* Make sure you know how to take accurate measurements.) Plan when and where to measure weather factors. Be sure to take your measurements at the same location and at the same

Answers to Self-Assessment

☑ Checkpoint

Possible examples might include heat radiating from a campfire, heat being conducted through the bottom of a metal pot on a stove, and heat flowing in convection currents through a house heated by a furnace.

Using the Visuals: Figure 5

Call students' attention to the illustration and have them locate the arrows showing each of the three types of heat transfer. Point out that radiation occurs from Earth's surface as well as from the sun. **learning modality: visual**

3 Assess

Section 2 Review Answers

1. The average amount of energy of motion in the molecules of a substance
2. When the air temperature increases, the liquid in the bulb of a thermometer expands and rises up the column. When the air temperature decreases, the liquid contracts and moves down the column.
3. Heat can be transferred by radiation, conduction, and convection. Air near Earth's surface is warmed by radiation and by conduction of heat from the surface to the air. When the air near the ground is heated, it becomes less dense and rises in convection currents.
4. A fireplace heats a room by radiation. Only people sitting directly in front of the fire feel its warmth because radiation is the direct transfer of energy and does not effectively heat areas of the room out of the direct line of the fireplace.

CHAPTER PROJECT

Check Your Progress

Check that students have all the instruments they need and know how to use them. Make sure that the place they plan to take their measurements is suitable. Remind students to take their measurements in the same place and at the same time each day.

Performance Assessment

Drawing Have students draw a diagram to show how heat is transferred from Earth's surface to the atmosphere.

Winds

Objectives

After completing the lesson, students will be able to

- explain what causes winds;
- distinguish between local winds and global winds;
- describe the major global wind belts and where they are located.

Key Terms wind, anemometer, wind-chill factor, local wind, sea breeze, land breeze, monsoons, global wind, Coriolis effect, latitude, jet stream

1 Engage/Explore

Activating Prior Knowledge

Introduce students to winds by helping them recall a time when they flew a kite. Ask: **What made the kite fly in the air?** *(the wind)* **What is wind?** *(the movement of air)*. Then remind students how hard it can be to hold on to a kite against the force of a strong wind. Stress that even though air is an invisible gas, it still consists of molecules, and their movement, especially at high speeds, can exert a lot of force. Tell students they will learn more about wind in this section.

DISCOVER

Skills Focus making models

Materials *heavy-duty tape, pencil, large smooth ball, marker*

Time 10 minutes

Tips Make sure students spin the ball in a counterclockwise direction before their partner draws on it with the marker. You might want to have students also draw a line from the "South Pole" to the "Equator" to see what direction winds blow in the Southern Hemisphere due to Earth's rotation.

Expected Outcome The lines students draw should veer to the west as the marker goes from the "North Pole" to the "Equator" of the ball.

Think It Over The movement of cold air from Canada to the United States would turn toward the west.

Section 3 Winds

DISCOVER ACTIVITY

Which Way Does the Wind Turn?

Do this activity with a partner. Think of the ball as a model of Earth and the marker as representing wind.

1. Using heavy-duty tape, attach a pencil to a large smooth ball so that you can spin the ball from the top without touching it.
2. One partner should hold the pencil. Slowly turn the ball counterclockwise when seen from above.
3. While the ball is turning, the second partner should use a marker to try to draw a straight line from the "North Pole" to the "equator" of the ball. What shape does the line form?

Think It Over

Making Models If cold air were moving south from Canada into the United States, how would its movement be affected by Earth's rotation?

GUIDE FOR READING

- What causes winds?
- What are local winds and global winds?
- Where are the major global wind belts located?

Reading Tip **Before you read, preview the illustrations and read their captions. Write down any questions you have about winds. As you read, look for answers to your questions.**

The highest point in the northeastern United States, at 1,917 meters above sea level, is Mount Washington in New Hampshire. On April 12, 1934, instruments at the weather observatory atop Mount Washington measured a wind speed of 370 kilometers per hour. That's the greatest wind speed ever measured at Earth's surface apart from a fierce storm such as a tornado. What causes this incredible force?

What Causes Winds?

Because air is a fluid, it can move easily from place to place. The force that makes air move is caused by a difference of air pressure. Fluids tend to move from areas of high pressure to areas of low pressure. A **wind** is the horizontal movement of air from an area of high pressure to an area of lower pressure. **All winds are caused by differences in air pressure.**

READING STRATEGIES

Reading Tip Student questions might include: Why does the wind blow? What is a monsoon? How are winds connected to the energy of the sun? Encourage students to record the answers to their questions as they encounter them in their reading.

Vocabulary Urge students to look up the word *doldrums* in a dictionary. In addition to being the name for the equatorial zone of calm winds, students will find that it also means "a period of inactivity or stagnation." Call students' attention to the explanation given in the text for the name *horse latitudes.* Knowing the rather memorable story behind it will help them remember that the *horse latitudes* also are zones of calm.

Most differences in air pressure are caused by unequal heating of the atmosphere. As you learned in the previous section, convection currents form when an area of Earth's surface is heated by the sun's rays. Air over the heated surface expands and becomes less dense. As the air becomes less dense, its air pressure decreases. If a nearby area is not heated as much, the air above the less-heated area will be cooler and denser. The cool, dense air has a higher air pressure so it flows underneath the warm, less dense air. This process forces the warm air to rise.

Measuring Wind

Winds are described by their direction and speed. Wind direction is determined with a wind vane. The wind swings the wind vane so that one end points into the wind. The name of a wind tells you where the wind is coming from. For example, a south wind blows from the south toward the north. A north wind blows to the south.

Wind speed is measured with an **anemometer** (an uh MAHM uh tur). An anemometer has three or four cups mounted at the ends of spokes that spin on an axle. The force of the wind against the cups turns the axle. A speedometer attached to the axle shows the wind speed.

A cool breeze can be very refreshing on a warm day. However, during the winter, a similar breeze can make you feel uncomfortably cold. The wind blowing over your skin removes body heat. The stronger the wind, the colder you feel. The increased cooling that a wind can cause is called the **wind-chill factor.** Thus a weather report may say, "The temperature is 20 degrees Fahrenheit. But with a wind speed of 30 miles per hour, the wind-chill factor makes it feel like 18 degrees below zero."

☑ *Checkpoint* *Toward what direction does a west wind blow?*

Build a Wind Vane

Here's how to build your own wind vane. ACTIVITY

1. Use scissors to cut out a pointer and a slightly larger tail fin from construction paper.
2. Make a slit 1 cm deep in each end of a soda straw.
3. Slide the pointer and tail fin into place on the straw, securing them with small pieces of tape.

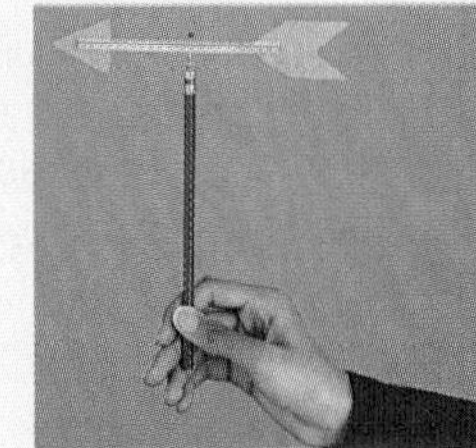

4. Hold the straw on your finger to find the point at which it balances.
5. Carefully push a pin through the balance point and into the eraser of a pencil. Move the wind vane back and forth to make sure it can spin freely.

Observing How can you use your wind vane to tell the direction of the wind?

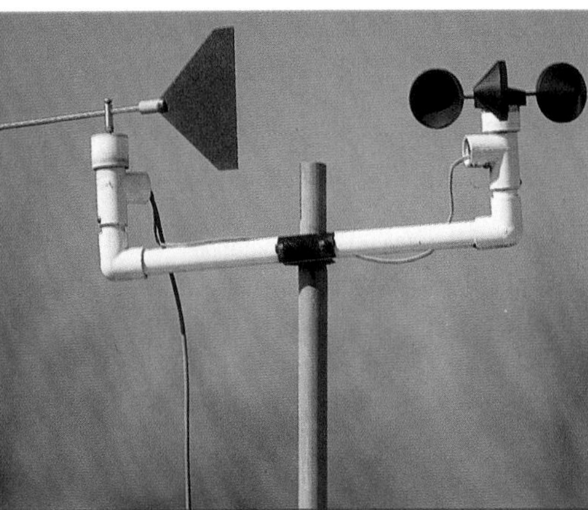

Figure 6 The wind vane on the left points in the direction the wind is blowing from. The anemometer on the right measures wind speed. The cups catch the wind, turning faster when the wind blows faster.

Program Resources

- **Unit 4 Resources** 12-3 Lesson Plan; 12-3 Section Summary
- **Guided Reading and Study Workbook** Section 12-3

Media and Technology

Concept Videotape Library
Grade 6, Tape 3 "A Wave Is a Wave Is a Wave"

Answers to Self-Assessment

☑ *Checkpoint*

A west wind blows toward the east.

2 Facilitate

What Causes Winds?

Demonstration

Materials *pinwheel, lamp with incandescent light bulb*
Time 10 minutes

Show students how differences in temperature cause air movement by holding a pinwheel over a lamp. First hold the pinwheel over the lamp with the light bulb turned off. The pinwheel will remain stationary. Then hold the pinwheel over the lamp with the light bulb turned on. Once the light bulb gets hot, the pinwheel will start to spin. Ask: **Why did the pinwheel start spinning after the lightbulb was turned on?** *(The hot light bulb heated the air around it, which rose and turned the pinwheel.)* **learning modality: visual**

Measuring Wind

TRY THIS

Skills Focus observing
Materials *scissors, construction paper, metric ruler, soda straw, tape, straight pin, pencil with eraser*
Time 15 minutes
Expected Outcome Students should find when they take their wind vane outside in the wind or blow on it that the wind vane points in the direction from which the wind is coming.
Extend If students set their wind vane in the center of a compass, it will show them whether it is an east, west, north, or south wind. Remind students that winds are named for the direction from which they blow. **learning modality: kinesthetic**

Ongoing Assessment

Drawing Have students make a simple drawing with arrows and labels to show how differences in air temperature cause wind.

Students can keep their drawings in their portfolios.

Real-World Lab

You and Your Community

Where's the Wind?

Preparing for Inquiry

Key Concept Obstacles such as buildings can change the speed and direction of the wind.

Skills Objectives Students will be able to

- measure the direction and speed of the wind on all sides of the school building;
- interpret their data to determine which side of the building is less windy than the other sides;
- conclude from the data which side of the building provides the best location for a door.

Time 40 minutes

Advance Planning Follow weather reports when scheduling the lab so students take their measurements on a day when the wind is blowing steadily, not in gusts, and from its usual direction (west in most of the United States). Students can make the anemometers one day and measure wind speed and direction another day. You may want to have a fan or hair dryer for students to use to test their anemometers.

Alternative Materials If you do not have a wind vane, students can measure wind direction by observing the direction that flags are flying or smoke is drifting. Instead of using a corrugated cardboard sheet to make the anemometer, students may use a piece of plastic foam cut from the bottom of a plastic foam plate. Also, wooden craft sticks may be used in place of wooden stirrers. Other types of tape, such as adhesive or electrical tape, will work as well as masking tape.

Guiding Inquiry

Invitation Help students focus on the problem in the lab by asking: **Which two factors do you need to know to determine wind patterns?** *(Wind direction and wind speed)* **How can you measure wind direction?** *(With a wind vane or by observing the direction in which objects are blowing in the wind)* **How can you measure wind speed?** *(With an anemometer)* Point out to students that in this lab they will make a simple anemometer. Then they will use a wind vane to measure wind direction and their anemometer to measure wind speed. Making the measurements on all sides of their school building will let them determine wind patterns around it and from this decide on the best location for a door.

Introducing the Procedure

Explain that the second coffee stirrer added to the anemometer provides a balance for the stirrer that measures wind speed. Point out that the numbers on the dial do not represent actual units, such as kilometers per hour. However, they do allow wind speeds to be compared. Stress the importance of taking all measurements the same distance from the building. Suggest that they select a spot near the middle of each side about 2 to 3 m from the building.

Local Winds

Have you ever flown a kite at the beach on a hot summer day? Even if there is no wind inland, there may be a cool breeze blowing in from the water toward the beach. This breeze is an example of a local wind. **Local winds** are winds that blow over short distances. **Local winds are caused by unequal heating of Earth's surface within a small area.** Local winds form only when no winds are blowing from farther away.

Real-World Lab

You and Your Community

Where's the Wind?

Your city is planning to build a new community center. You and your classmates want to be sure that the doors will not be hard to open or close on windy days. You need to know which side of the building will be sheltered from the wind. You decide to measure wind speeds around a similar building.

Problem

How can you determine wind patterns around a building?

Skills Focus

measuring, interpreting data, drawing conclusions

Materials

pen	round toothpick
wind vane	2 wooden coffee stirrers
meter stick	narrow masking tape

corrugated cardboard sheet, 15 cm x 20 cm

Procedure

1. You'll begin by making a simple anemometer that uses wooden coffee stirrers to indicate wind speed. On your piece of cardboard, draw a curved scale like the one shown in the diagram. Mark it in equal intervals from 0 to 10.
2. Carefully use the pen to make a small hole where the toothpick will go. Insert the toothpick through the hole.
3. Tape the wooden coffee stirrers to the toothpick as shown in the diagram, one on each side of the cardboard.
4. Copy the data table into your notebook.
5. Take your anemometer outside the school. Stand about 2–3 m away from the building and away from any corners or large plants.

374

Unequal heating often occurs on land that is next to a large body of water. It takes more energy to warm up a body of water than it does to warm up an equal area of land. This means that as the sun heats Earth's surface during the day, the land warms up faster than the water. The air over the land becomes warmer than the air over the water. The warm air expands and rises, creating a low-pressure area. Cool air blows inland from the water and moves underneath the warm air. A wind that blows

DATA TABLE

Location	Wind Direction	Wind Speed

6. Use the wind vane to find out what direction the wind is coming from. Hold your anemometer so that the card is straight, vertical, and parallel to the wind direction. Observe which number the wooden stirrer is closest to. Record your data.
7. Repeat your measurements on all the other sides of the building. Record your data.

Analyze and Conclude

1. Was the wind stronger on one side of the school building than the other sides? How can you explain your observation?
2. Do your classmates' results agree with yours? What might account for any differences?
3. **Apply** Based on your data, which side of the building provides the best location for a door?

More to Explore

What effect do plants have on the wind speed in an area? Could bushes and trees be planted so that they reduce the wind speed near the doors? What measurements could you make to find out?

375

Sample Data Table

Location	Wind Direction	Wind Speed
East side of building	W	1
South side of building	NW	4
West side of building	W	3
North side of building	SW	6

Program Resources

- **Unit 4 Resources** Chapter 12 Real-World Lab

Media and Technology

Lab Activity Videotapes
Grade 6, Tape 3

Troubleshooting the Experiment

- Have students test their anemometers before they take them outside to measure wind speed. They can use a fan or hair dryer set on low or simply blow on them. They should make sure the coffee stirrers blow freely in the wind and adjust them if necessary.
- Check that students are holding their anemometers parallel to wind direction. Otherwise, the anemometer will give a reading that is too low.

Safety

Do not do this lab on a day when there is danger of lightning or high winds. Review the safety guidelines in Appendix A.

Expected Outcome

Students will probably find that one side of the building had winds blowing at a lower speed than the other sides. If a west wind was blowing, then the east side of the building probably was the least windy. Students also may find that wind direction is different from one side of the building to another.

Analyze and Conclude

1. Students probably will find that the wind was stronger on the side of the building that the wind was coming from. Students should explain their observations by saying that the building blocked and slowed the wind on the other sides of the building.
2. Classmates' results may or may not agree. Differences could be due to students measuring the wind at somewhat different locations around the building, wind gusts, or slight differences in how the anemometers were made.
3. Students should conclude that the best location is the side of the building that has winds with the lowest speed.

Extending the Inquiry

More to Explore Students may say that bushes and trees can block the wind and reduce its speed near the doors. They could find out by determining wind patterns around bushes and trees, as they did around the school building, to see how these obstacles affect wind direction and speed.

Local Winds

Using the Visuals: Figure 7

Help students analyze the figure's details by asking: **How do the two pictures differ?** *(One shows daytime, the other shows nighttime; warm air is shown rising over the land in the daytime picture and over the water in the nighttime picture.)* **What do the differences tell you about the heating and cooling of land compared with water?** *(Land warms up and cools off more quickly than water.)* **learning modality: visual**

Including All Students

Materials *bubble-blowing kit*
Time 10 minutes

Point out to students that, on a local scale, wind direction can be affected by such features as hills, trees, and buildings. Even bushes and cars can cause the wind to change direction. Help students appreciate this by having them blow soap bubbles outside on a breezy day and observe the bubbles as they go around or over obstacles. Ask: **How did the obstacles affect the direction of the bubbles?** *(Answers will vary depending on local winds and obstacles. One possible answer is that a parked car caused the bubbles to rise over the top of it.)* **learning modality: kinesthetic**

Monsoons

Cultural Diversity

Point out to students that the word *monsoon* comes from an Arabic word meaning "season." It used to mean a wind in South and Southeast Asia that changed direction with the seasons, although now it means *any* wind that changes direction with the seasons. Add that many other local winds also have special names. Have students who need an extra challenge look up the following names for local winds in other parts of the world: *chinook, levanter, mistral, sirocco,* and *Santa Ana.* They should find out what each name means and what type of wind it refers to. Then give the students a chance to share what they learn with the rest of the class. **learning modality: verbal**

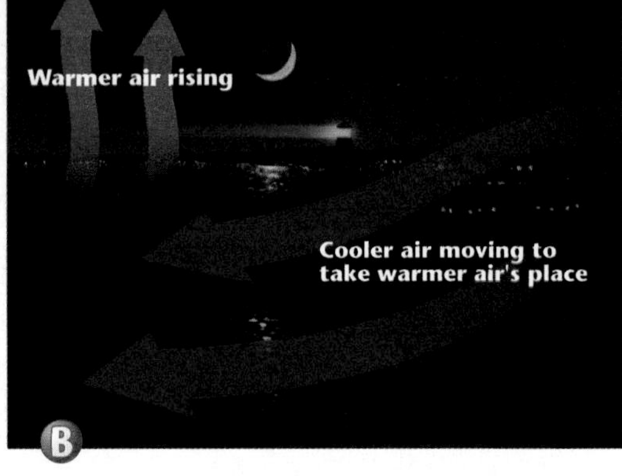

Figure 7 A. During the day, cool air moves from the sea to the land, creating a sea breeze. B. At night, cooler air moves from the land to the sea. *Forming Operational Definitions What type of breeze occurs at night?*

from an ocean or lake onto land is known as a **sea breeze** or a lake breeze. Figure 7A shows a sea breeze.

At night, the situation is reversed. Land cools more quickly than water, so the air over the land becomes cooler than the air over the water. As the warmer air over the water rises, cooler air moves from the land to take its place. The flow of air from land to a body of water is called a **land breeze.**

Monsoons

A process similar to land and sea breezes can occur over wider areas. In the summer in South and Southeast Asia, the land gradually gets warmer than the ocean. A large "sea breeze" blows steadily inland from the ocean all summer, even at night. In the winter, the land cools and becomes colder than the ocean. A "land breeze" blows steadily from the land to the ocean.

Sea and land breezes over a large region that change direction with the seasons are called **monsoons.** The summer monsoon in South Asia and Southeast Asia is very important for the crops grown there. The air blowing from the ocean during the rainy season is very warm and humid. As the humid air rises over the land, the air cools, producing heavy rains that supply the water needed by rice and other crops.

Figure 8 This heavy rain in Nepal is part of the summer monsoon, which blows from the ocean to the land. In the winter, the monsoon reverses and blows from the land to the ocean.

Summer Monsoon

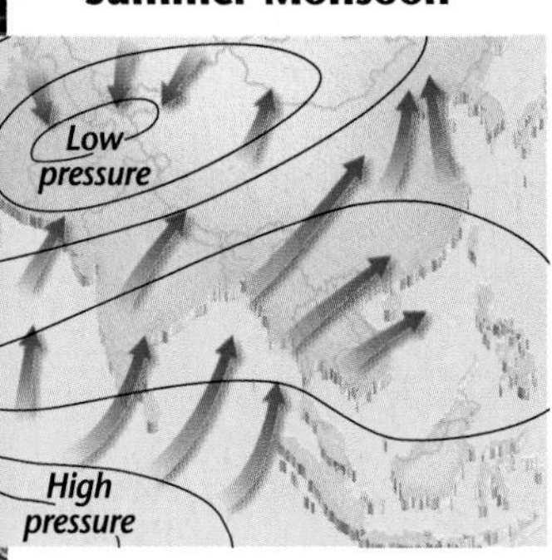

Winter Monsoon

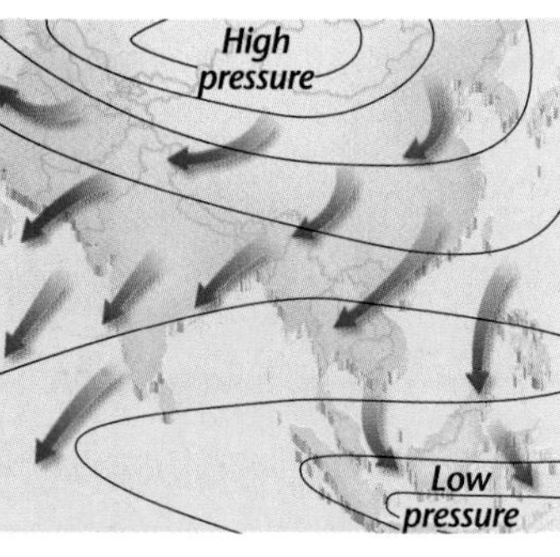

Background

Facts and Figures Mount Washington, New Hampshire, not only has the highest wind speed ever recorded, as stated in the text. It also has the highest average wind speed in the United States, at 56 kilometers per hour. The overall windiest state is not New Hampshire, however, but Alaska, because it holds the most local records for highest average wind speed. Other especially windy places include Amarillo, Texas; Boston, Massachusetts; Wichita, Kansas; Buffalo, New York; and Honolulu, Hawaii.

High wind speeds can make you feel much colder because of wind-chill. For example, if the actual air temperature is 4°C (40°F), a 10-mph wind makes it feel like it's -2°C (28°F). Increase wind speed to 30 mph, and the same 4°C temperature feels like -11°C (13°F). Winds greater than 30 mph cause very little additional chilling.

Global Winds

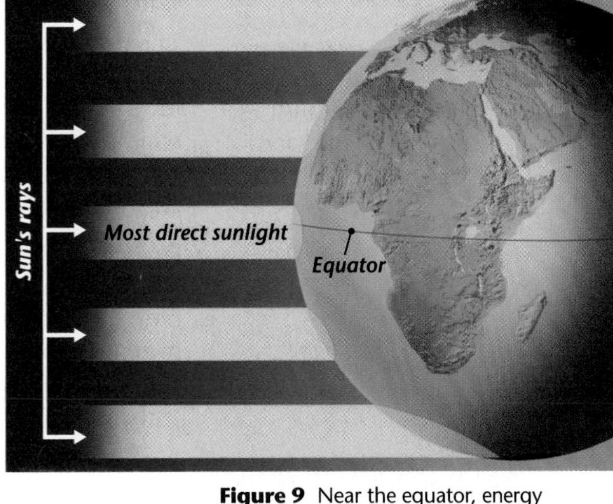

Figure 9 Near the equator, energy from the sun strikes Earth almost directly. Near the poles, the same amount of energy is spread out over a larger area.

Winds that blow steadily from specific directions over long distances are called **global winds.** Like local winds, global winds are created by unequal heating of Earth's surface. Refer to Figure 9 to see how sunlight strikes Earth's surface. In the middle of the day near the equator, the sun is almost directly overhead. The direct rays from the sun heat Earth's surface intensely. Near the North Pole or South Pole, the sun's rays strike Earth's surface at a lower angle, even at noon. The sun's energy is spread out over a larger area, so it heats the surface less. As a result, temperatures near the poles are much lower than they are near the equator.

Global Convection Currents Temperature differences between the equator and the poles produce giant convection currents in the atmosphere. Warm air rises at the equator, and cold air sinks at the poles. Therefore air pressure tends to be lower near the equator and greater near the poles, causing winds at Earth's surface to blow from the poles toward the equator. Higher in the atmosphere, air flows away from the equator toward the poles. **The movement of air between the equator and the poles produces global winds.**

The Coriolis Effect If Earth did not rotate, global winds would blow in a straight line from the poles toward the equator. Because Earth is rotating, global winds do not follow a straight path. As the winds move, Earth rotates from west to east underneath them, making it seem as if the winds have curved. The way Earth's rotation makes winds curve is called the **Coriolis effect** (kawr ee OH lis). It is named for the French mathematician who studied and explained it in 1835.

In the Northern Hemisphere, all global winds gradually turn toward the right. As you can see in Figure 10, a wind blowing toward the north gradually turns toward the northeast. In other words, a south wind gradually changes to a southwest wind. In the Southern Hemisphere, winds curve toward the left. A south wind becomes an southeast wind, and a north wind becomes a northwest wind.

Figure 10 As Earth rotates, the Coriolis effect turns winds in the Northern Hemisphere toward the right. *Interpreting Diagrams Which way do winds turn in the Southern Hemisphere?*

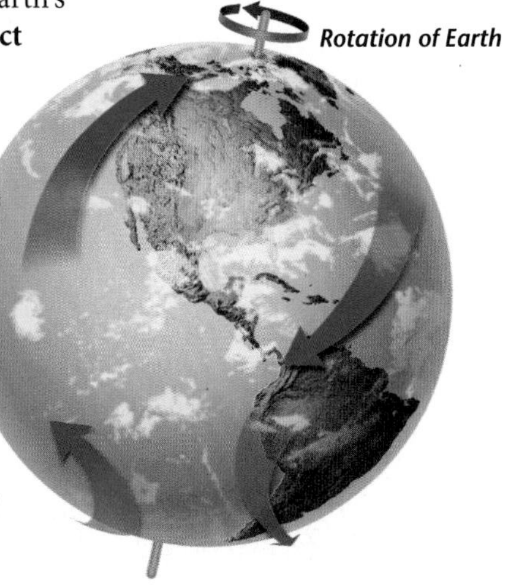

☑ ***Checkpoint*** *What happens to a wind blowing toward the south in the Northern Hemisphere? What would you call this wind?*

Global Winds

Demonstration

Materials *globe, small flashlight*
Time 5 minutes

Challenge a pair of students to model Earth and the sun using a globe and flashlight. *(One student should hold the globe, and the other student should shine the light on the equator, with the room lights dimmed.)* Call students' attention to the fact that the light is direct and bright over the equator but angled and dim at the poles. Ask: **How do these differences in energy cause global winds?** *(The more concentrated energy falling directly on the equator causes air over the equator to be warmer than air over the poles, leading to the convection currents that cause global winds.)* **learning modality: visual**

Media and Technology

Concept Videotape Library
Grade 6, Tape 3 "As Hot As a Desert"; "Hot Is Hot, Cold Is Not"

Answers to Self-Assessment

Caption Questions

Figure 7 A land breeze occurs at night.
Figure 10 In the Southern Hemisphere, winds turn toward the left.

☑ ***Checkpoint***

A wind blowing toward the south in the Northern Hemisphere gradually turns toward the right. You would call it a northeast wind.

Ongoing Assessment

Drawing Have students make a sketch in their journals to show how the Coriolis effect influences global winds.

Global Wind Belts

Including All Students

Materials *globe*
Time 10 minutes

Give students who need extra help a chance to spin a globe in a west to east direction while moving their finger over its surface from north to south. Ask: **How does the path you traced on the globe model global winds?** *(The path of global winds curves to the right in the same way.)* Then have students use the globe to locate a city or country that interests them. Ask: **Which major wind belt flows over that location?** *(Answers will vary depending on locations students choose.)* Suggest that students find the latitude of their location to determine which global wind belt flows over it. **learning modality: kinesthetic**

Social Studies CONNECTION

Make sure students realize that for the time period in question, ships had sails and depended on the wind to move. Suggest that they refer to the illustration on page 379 when doing this feature. From the figure, students should be able to identify which winds they would have used to sail east *(prevailing westerlies)* and which they would have used to sail west *(trade winds).*

In Your Journal Students should see from the figure on page 379 that making use of the trade winds to go west requires a more southern route across the Atlantic. They should write in their letter that the journey west takes almost twice as many weeks because the southern route is less direct and longer. **learning modality: verbal**

Social Studies CONNECTION

From colonial days to the late 1800s, American merchants traded new ships, lumber, cotton, tobacco, and furs for manufactured goods, such as textiles, from England. The eastbound voyage in the early 1800s took about three weeks. However, the westbound passage took almost twice as long—five to six weeks.

In Your Journal

Imagine that you are a sea captain making the voyage to England and back to America. Your family doesn't understand why your journey home takes almost twice as long as your journey to England. Write a letter to your family explaining why you have to travel farther south to take advantage of the prevailing winds on your return voyage.

Global Wind Belts

The Coriolis effect and other factors combine to produce a pattern of calm areas and wind belts around Earth. The calm areas include the doldrums and the horse latitudes. **The major global wind belts are the trade winds, the prevailing westerlies, and the polar easterlies.** As you read about each area, find it in *Exploring Global Winds.*

Doldrums Near the equator, the sun heats the surface strongly. Warm air rises steadily, creating an area of low pressure. Cool air moves into the area, but is warmed rapidly and rises before it moves very far. There is very little horizontal motion, so the winds near the equator are very weak. Regions near the equator with little or no wind are called the doldrums.

Horse Latitudes Warm air that rises at the equator divides and flows both north and south. **Latitude** is the distance from the equator, measured in degrees. At about 30° north and south latitudes, the air stops moving toward the poles and sinks. In each of these regions, another belt of calm air forms. Hundreds of years ago, sailors becalmed in these waters ran out of food and water for their horses and had to throw the horses overboard. Because of this, the latitudes 30° north and south of the equator are called the horse latitudes.

Trade Winds When the cold air over the horse latitudes sinks, it produces a region of high pressure. This high pressure causes surface winds to blow both toward the equator and away from it. The winds that blow toward the equator are turned west by the Coriolis effect. As a result, winds in the Northern Hemisphere between 30° north latitude and the equator blow generally from the northeast. In the Southern Hemisphere between 30° south latitude and the equator, the winds blow from the southeast. These steady easterly winds are called the trade winds. For hundreds of years, sailors relied on them to carry cargoes from Europe to the West Indies and South America.

Figure 11 The bark *Patriot,* built in 1809, carried goods to many parts of the world. ***Applying Concepts*** *How much effect do you think the prevailing winds have on shipping today?*

Background

Integrating Science Like global winds, the surface currents of oceans are deflected by the Coriolis effect. They flow to the right in the Northern Hemisphere and to the left in the Southern Hemisphere.

The prevailing winds blow the surface waters of the oceans and contribute to the deflection of ocean currents caused by the Coriolis effect. For example, the prevailing westerlies, which blow across most of the United States, help make the Gulf Stream the largest, strongest surface current in the North Atlantic Ocean. The Gulf Stream flows from the Caribbean Sea northeast along the east coast of the United States until it reaches North Carolina. Then it veers off into the Atlantic Ocean. Eventually the Gulf Stream reaches the western coast of Europe, where its warm waters bring relatively mild, humid weather.

EXPLORING Global Winds

A series of wind belts circles Earth. Between the wind belts are calm areas where air is rising or falling.

90° N

Polar easterlies

60° N

The horse latitudes are calm areas of falling air.

The prevailing westerlies blow away from the horse latitudes.

Prevailing westerlies

Horse latitudes

30° N

Trade winds

Equator 0°

Doldrums

The doldrums are a calm area where warm air rises.

Trade winds

30° S

Horse latitudes

The trade winds blow from the horse latitudes toward the equator.

Prevailing westerlies

60° S

Polar easterlies

90° S

The cold polar easterlies blow away from the poles.

N W E S

Media and Technology

Transparencies "Global Winds," Transparency 45

Answers to Self-Assessment

Caption Question

Figure 11 Answers may vary. The most likely answer is that prevailing winds have little effect on shipping today because ships no longer depend on the winds to move.

EXPLORING

Global Winds

Make sure students understand that the spin of the planet in the figure is from left to right, or counterclockwise as seen from the North Pole. Check to see that students understand how the two different types of arrows are used in the diagram. Ask: **What do the small blue arrows pointing straight north or straight south represent?** *(The general direction of convection currents in the atmosphere due to unequal heating)* **What do the large red arrows represent?** *(The direction in which global winds blow because of the Coriolis effect)*

Tell students to assume they are planning a sailing trip from California to the tip of South America. Have them use the figure to trace with a finger the route they would take. Ask: **Which winds would help speed you on your way?** *(In the Northern Hemisphere the trade winds and in the Southern Hemisphere the prevailing westerlies)* **Which winds would slow you down?** *(In the Northern Hemisphere the prevailing westerlies and in the Southern Hemisphere the trade winds)*

Students may not understand why the two major global wind belts in each hemisphere blow in opposite north/south directions, even though both are turned in the same east/west direction by Earth's rotation. Explain that they blow in opposite directions because the convection currents that produce them flow in opposite directions. Point out in the figure how, in the Northern Hemisphere, the convection currents in the region of the prevailing westerlies flow to the north, whereas in the region of the trade winds, the convection currents flow to the south. **learning modality: visual**

Ongoing Assessment

Oral Presentation Call on students at random to explain in their own words similarities and differences between the prevailing westerlies and the trade winds.

Jet Streams

Building Inquiry Skills: Inferring

Point out that the jet stream follows the boundary between the prevailing westerlies and polar easterlies. Ask: **Why do you think the jet stream is farther south in the winter?** *(As the sun's direct rays move south, the global wind belts also shift south.)* **learning modality: logical/mathematical**

3 Assess

Section 3 Review Answers

1. Unequal heating of air above Earth's surface causes winds because the warm air rises and cool air moves in to take its place.
2. Both local and global winds are caused by unequal heating of Earth's surface. Local winds cover small areas; global winds circle the globe. Local winds often change direction; global winds do not.
3. The major wind belts are trade winds, prevailing westerlies, and polar easterlies. Students' drawings should show the winds as pictured on page 543
4. The pilot should set a course to the southeast because Earth's rotation will result in the plane going west relative to cities on the ground.

CHAPTER PROJECT

Check Your Progress

Check that students continue to take accurate measurements. Make sure they are recording all the measurements in their weather log, including the units for each measurement.

Figure 12 By traveling east in a jet stream, pilots can save time and fuel. *Predicting What would happen if a plane flew west in a jet stream?*

Prevailing Westerlies In the mid-latitudes, winds that blow toward the poles are turned toward the east by the Coriolis effect. Because they blow from the west to the east, they are called prevailing westerlies. The prevailing westerlies blow generally from the southwest between 30° and 60° north latitudes and from the northwest between 30° and 60° south latitudes. The prevailing westerlies play an important part in the weather of the United States.

Polar Easterlies Cold air near the poles sinks and flows back toward lower latitudes. The Coriolis effect shifts these polar winds to the west, producing winds called the polar easterlies. The polar easterlies meet the prevailing westerlies at about 60° north and 60° south latitudes, along a region called the polar front. The mixing of warm and cold air along the polar front has a major effect on weather changes in the United States.

☑ *Checkpoint* *In what region do the polar easterlies meet the prevailing westerlies?*

Jet Streams

About 10 kilometers above Earth's surface are bands of high-speed winds called **jet streams.** These winds are hundreds of kilometers wide but only a few kilometers deep. Jet streams blow from west to east at speeds of 200 to 400 kilometers per hour. As jet streams travel around Earth, they wander north and south along a wavy path.

Airplanes are aided by a jet stream when traveling east. Pilots can save fuel and time by flying east in a jet stream. However, airplanes flying at jet stream altitudes are slowed down when traveling west against the jet stream winds.

Section 3 Review

1. How does the unequal heating of Earth's surface cause winds?
2. How are local winds and global winds similar? How are they different?
3. Name and draw the three major wind belts.
4. **Thinking Critically Applying Concepts** Imagine you are flying from Seattle to San Francisco, which is almost exactly due south of Seattle. Should the pilot set a course due south? Explain your answer.

CHAPTER PROJECT

Check Your Progress

Check with your teacher to be sure you are using the weather instruments correctly. Are you recording units for each measurement? Collect and record

Performance Assessment

Writing/Drawing Have students write a paragraph explaining what causes global winds and why they flow in the direction they do. Have them accompany their explanation with a clearly labeled diagram.

Answers to Self-Assessment

☑ *Checkpoint*

The polar easterlies meet the prevailing westerlies at about the 60° north and 60° south latitudes.

Caption Question

Figure 12 If a plane flew west in a jet stream, it would be slowed down by the winds flowing east.

Program Resources

◆ **Unit 4 Resources** 12-3 Review and Reinforce; 12-3 Enrich

Water in the Atmosphere

DISCOVER

How Does Fog Form?

1. Fill a narrow-necked plastic bottle with hot tap water. Pour out most of the water, leaving about 3 cm at the bottom. **CAUTION:** *Avoid spilling hot water. Do not use water that is so hot that you cannot safely hold the bottle.*
2. Place an ice cube on the mouth of the bottle. What happens?
3. Repeat Steps 1 and 2 using cold water instead of hot water. What happens?

Think It Over

Developing Hypotheses How can you explain your observations? Why is there a difference between what happens with the hot water and with the cold water?

GUIDE FOR READING

- How is relative humidity measured?
- How do clouds form?
- What are the three main types of clouds?

Reading Tip Before you read, write a definition of "cloud." Revise your definition as you read about clouds.

During a rainstorm, the air feels moist. On a clear, cloudless day, the air may feel dry. As the sun heats the land and oceans, the amount of water in the atmosphere changes. Water is always moving between the atmosphere and Earth's surface.

As you learned in Chapter 11, this movement of water between the atmosphere and Earth's surface is called the water cycle. This cycle is shown in Figure 13. Water vapor enters the air by evaporation from the oceans and other bodies of water. **Evaporation** is the process by which water molecules in liquid water escape into the air as water vapor. Water vapor is also added to the air by living things. Water enters the roots of plants, rises to the leaves, and is released as water vapor.

As part of the water cycle, some of the water vapor in the atmosphere condenses to form clouds. Rain and other forms of precipitation fall from the clouds toward the surface. The water then runs off the surface, or moves through the ground, back into the oceans, lakes, and streams.

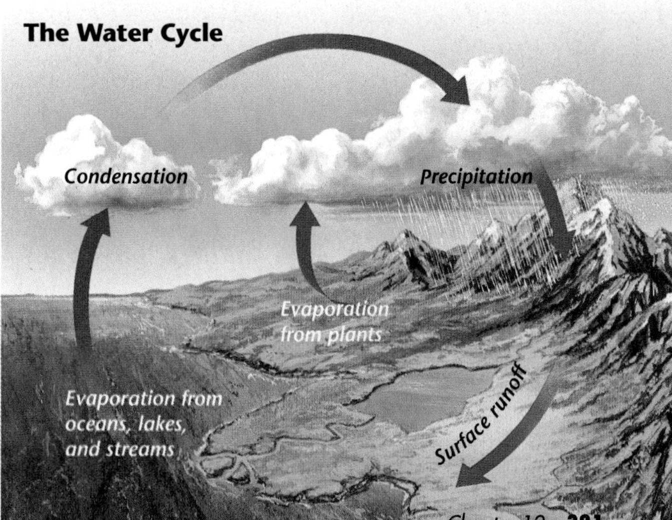

Figure 13 In the water cycle, water moves from lakes and oceans into the atmosphere and falls back to Earth.

READING STRATEGIES

Reading Tip Encourage students to base their initial definition of "cloud" on what they have observed or experienced. Their revised definition should describe a cloud as consisting of drops of liquid water or ice crystals in the air.

Program Resources

- **Unit 4 Resources** 12-4 Lesson Plan; 12-4 Section Summary
- **Guided Reading and Study Workbook** Section 12-4

Media and Technology

Transparencies "Exploring The Water Cycle," Transparency 46

Water in the Atmosphere

Objectives

After completing the lesson, students will be able to

- describe how relative humidity is measured;
- explain how clouds form;
- describe the main types of clouds.

Key Terms evaporation, humidity, relative humidity, psychrometer, condensation, dew point, cumulus, stratus, cirrus

1 Engage/Explore

Activating Prior Knowledge

Help students recall seeing water vapor condense out of the air. Ask: **Have you ever noticed when you take a shower that the bathroom mirror clouds up?** *(Most students will have had this experience.)* **Do you know what causes this?** *(Students may say it is caused by moisture in the air from the shower.)* Explain that when warm moist air from the shower comes into contact with the cool surface of the mirror, the air cools and can hold less water vapor. As a result, water vapor condenses on the mirror. Point out that clouds form the same way: water vapor condenses when warm moist air cools in the atmosphere.

DISCOVER

Skills Focus developing hypotheses

Materials *narrow-necked plastic bottle, hot tap water, 2 ice cubes, cold tap water*

Time 10 minutes

Tips Make sure students let the bottle cool before repeating Steps 1 and 2 with cold water.

Expected Outcome Fog will form in the bottle when it contains hot water but not when it contains cold water.

Think It Over Fog forms in the bottle when warm moist air rises from the surface of the hot water and condenses as it cools near the ice cube. This does not occur when there is cold water in the bottle because the cold water does not produce warm moist air.

2 Facilitate

Humidity

Integrating Life Science

Help students appreciate how evaporation can cool the body by asking: **Did you ever step out of a swimming pool on a hot day and feel cold, even though the air was warmer than the water?** *(Most students will have experienced this.)* **Why did you feel cold?** *(As the water evaporated, it took heat from the body.)* Then help students appreciate the effect of high relative humidity on evaporative cooling. Ask: **What happens when you exercise on a hot, humid day?** *(You get wet with sweat, but the sweat doesn't evaporate and cool you down.)* **learning modality: verbal**

Measuring Relative Humidity

Inquiry Challenge

ACTIVITY

Materials *human hair, drinking straw, tape, glue, clay, shoebox, or other materials of students' choice*

Time 20 minutes for setup; 5 minutes for later observations

Tell students that human hair shrinks when the humidity is low and stretches when the humidity is high. Then challenge students to use a human hair to indicate changes in humidity. One way students might do this is by setting a shoebox on one of its long sides and taping one end of a drinking straw to the inside of this long side. The unattached end of the straw should be close, but not touching, the inside of a short side of the shoebox. Then attach a long human hair to the straw and to the inside of the opposite (top) long side of the shoebox so it suspends the unattached end of the straw, making it a pointer. Plug this end of the straw with a little clay so the hair remains taut. Students can calibrate this hair hygrometer by observing the straw pointer move up and down with changes in humidity. **learning modality: logical/mathematical**

Humidity

Humidity is a measure of the amount of water vapor in the air. The percentage of water vapor in the air compared to the maximum amount the air could hold is called the **relative humidity.** For example, at 10°C, 1 cubic meter of air can hold a maximum of 8 grams of water vapor. If there actually were 8 grams of water vapor in the air, then the relative humidity of the air would be 100 percent. If the air held 4 grams of water vapor, the relative humidity would be half, or 50 percent. The amount of water vapor that the air can hold depends on its temperature. Warm air can hold more water vapor than cool air.

INTEGRATING LIFE SCIENCE "It's not the heat, it's the humidity." What does this common expression mean? Even on a hot day, you can still feel comfortable if the air is dry. Evaporation of moisture from your skin removes heat and helps to keep your body's temperature comfortable. You feel less comfortable on a hot day if the relative humidity is high. When the relative humidity is high, evaporation slows down. Evaporation therefore has less cooling effect on your body.

Measuring Relative Humidity

Relative humidity can be measured with a psychrometer. A **psychrometer** (sy KRAHM uh tur) has two thermometers, a wet-bulb thermometer and a dry-bulb thermometer. The bulb of the wet-bulb thermometer has a cloth covering that is moistened with water. Air is then blown over both thermometers. Because the wet-bulb thermometer is cooled by evaporation, its reading drops below that of the dry-bulb thermometer.

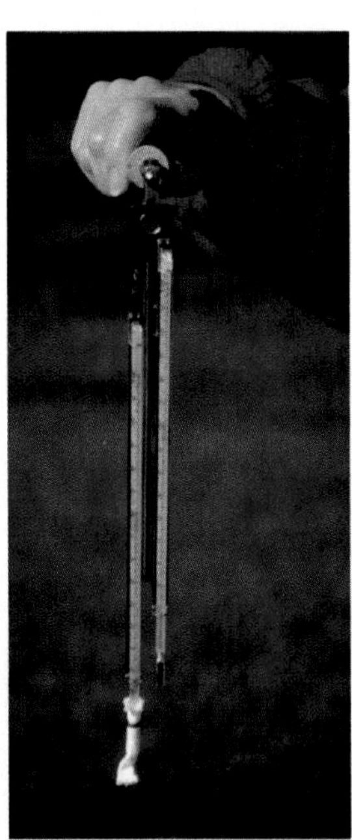

Relative Humidity

Dry-Bulb Reading (°C)	Difference Between Wet- and Dry-Bulb Readings (°C)				
	1	2	3	4	5
10	88	76	65	54	43
12	88	78	67	57	48
14	89	79	69	60	50
16	90	80	71	62	54
18	91	81	72	64	56
20	91	82	74	66	58
22	92	83	75	68	60
24	92	84	76	69	62
26	92	85	77	70	64
28	93	86	78	71	65
30	93	86	79	72	66

Figure 14 A sling psychrometer is used to measure relative humidity. First, find the wet-bulb and dry-bulb temperatures. Then find the dry-bulb temperature in the left column of the table. Find the difference between the wet- and dry-bulb temperatures across the top of the table. The number in the table where these two readings intersect indicates the relative humidity in percent.

Background

Facts and Figures The heat stress index tells you how much hotter it feels because of high humidity. For example, a temperature of 38°C (100°F) combined with a relative humidity of 50% gives a heat stress index of 49°C (120°F). In other words, the humidity makes it feel like it is 11°C (20°F) hotter than it actually is.

The dew point is a good indicator of relative humidity, because the higher the temperature at which water vapor starts condensing out of the air, the more saturated the air must be. When the dew point is 27°C (80°F) or higher, humidity is extremely high. When the dew point is around 10°C (50°F), humidity is moderate. When the dew point is below 4°C (40°F), humidity is very low.

If the relative humidity is high, the water on the wet bulb will evaporate slowly and the wet-bulb temperature will not change much. If the relative humidity is low, the water on the wet bulb will evaporate rapidly and the wet-bulb temperature will drop. The relative humidity can be found by comparing the temperatures of the wet-bulb and dry-bulb thermometers on a table like the one in Figure 14.

☑ *Checkpoint* *What is the difference between humidity and relative humidity?*

How Clouds Form

What do clouds remind you of? They can look like people, animals, countries, and a thousand other fanciful forms. Of course, not all clouds are fluffy and white. Storm clouds can be dark and cover the whole sky.

Clouds of all kinds form when water vapor in the air becomes liquid water or ice crystals. The process by which molecules of water vapor in the air become liquid water is called **condensation.** How does water condense? As you know, cold air can hold less water vapor than warm air. As air cools, the amount of water vapor it can hold decreases. Some of the water vapor in the air condenses to form droplets of liquid water.

The temperature at which condensation begins is called the **dew point.** If the dew point is below the freezing point, the water vapor may change directly into ice crystals. When you look at a cloud, you are seeing millions of tiny ice crystals or water droplets.

For water vapor to condense, tiny particles must be present so the water has a surface on which to condense. Most of these particles are salt crystals, dust from soil, and smoke. Sometimes water vapor condenses onto solid surfaces, such as blades of grass, instead of particles. Water that condenses from the air onto a cold surface is called dew. Frost is ice that has been deposited directly from the air onto a cold surface.

Clouds form whenever air is cooled to its dew point and particles are present. But why does the air cool? If air is warmed near the ground, it

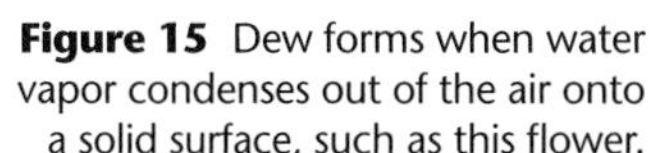

Figure 15 Dew forms when water vapor condenses out of the air onto a solid surface, such as this flower.

Sharpen your Skills

Interpreting Data

ACTIVITY

At lunchtime you use a psychrometer and get readings of 26°C on the dry-bulb thermometer and 21°C on the wet-bulb thermometer. Use Figure 14 to find the relative humidity.

Later in the day you use the psychrometer again and this time get readings of 20°C on the dry-bulb thermometer and 19°C on the wet-bulb thermometer. Find the new relative humidity. Is the relative humidity increasing or decreasing?

Sharpen your Skills

Interpreting Data

ACTIVITY

Time 10 minutes

Tips Remind students to subtract the wet-bulb reading from the dry-bulb reading and then find the difference between the two in the table.

Expected Outcome The first value for relative humidity is 64%, the second is 91%; relative humidity is increasing.

Extend Use the table to help students understand the relationship between temperature and relative humidity. Ask: **When the difference between wet- and dry-bulb readings is small, is the relative humidity high or low?** *(high)* **How is this relationship affected by air temperature?** *(The higher the air temperature, the higher the relative humidity for a given difference between wet- and dry-bulb readings.)* **learning modality: logical-mathematical**

How Clouds Form

Building Inquiry Skills: Measuring

ACTIVITY

Materials *beaker, room-temperature water, ice cubes, stirring rod, thermometer*

Time 10 minutes

Have students find the dew point in the classroom. Have them fill a beaker with room-temperature water and measure and record the water temperature. Then have them add a few ice cubes to the beaker and stir the ice water. As soon as moisture condenses on the outside of the beaker, have students measure and record the temperature of the water again. This temperature represents the dew point in the classroom. Ask: **Would the dew point be the same if you did this experiment on a different day?** *(Probably not, because the dew point depends on the temperature and relative humidity)* **learning modality: logical/mathematical**

Program Resources

- **Laboratory Manual** 12, "Using a Psychrometer to Determine Relative Humidity"

Media and Technology

Concept Videotape Library Grade 6, Tape 3 "The Power of Heat"

Answers to Self-Assessment

☑ *Checkpoint*

Humidity is a measure of the amount of water vapor in the air. Relative humidity is the percentage of water vapor in the air compared to the maximum amount the air could hold.

Ongoing Assessment

Writing Have students explain in their own words how temperature, humidity, and dew point are related.

How Clouds Form, continued

Building Inquiry Skills: Inferring

Materials *water, gallon bottle with cap, bicycle pump*
Time 10 minutes

Show students how clouds form by making a cloud in a bottle. Explain that air gets warmer when compressed and cooler when allowed to expand. Cover the bottom of a gallon bottle with a few centimeters of water. Use a nail to punch holes in the cap, overlapping the holes to make an opening about 0.5 cm in diameter. Place the cap on the bottle and push the nozzle of a bicycle pump into the opening. Have a volunteer push down on the pump two or three times. Quickly release the cap, and a cloud will form inside the bottle. Ask: **Why did a cloud form inside the bottle?** *(Pumping air into the bottle compressed and warmed the air in the bottle, so it picked up moisture from the water. Letting air out of the bottle let the air in the bottle expand and cool, so it could hold less water. Water condensed out of the air, forming a cloud.)* **learning modality: logical/ mathematical**

Types of Clouds

Including All Students

Help students become more familiar with the distinctive shapes of the main cloud types. Find and bring to class several drawings or photographs of different types of clouds. Challenge students to identify the types of clouds shown in the pictures. Ask: **How can you tell which of the three main types a cloud is?** *(by its shape)* **learning modality: visual**

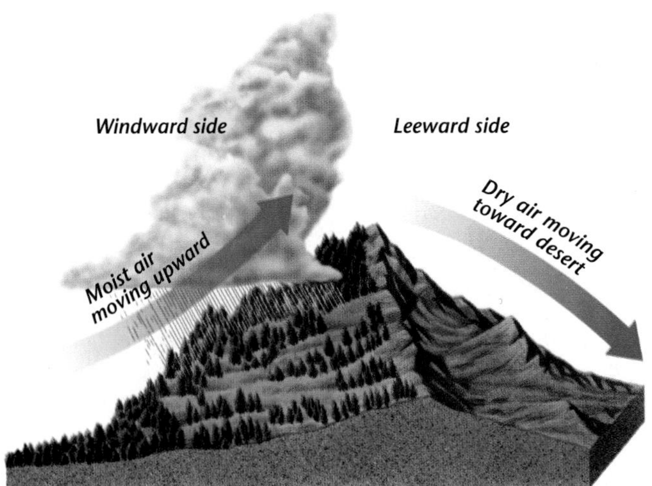

Figure 16 Humid air cools as it is blown up the side of a mountain. *Predicting What happens when water vapor condenses out of the air?*

becomes less dense and rises in a convection current. When the rising air expands and becomes cooler, clouds may form.

When wind strikes the side of a hill or mountain, the air is forced upward. As the air rises along the slope, the air cools. Rain or snow falls on the windward side of the mountains, the side facing the oncoming wind.

By the time the air reaches the other side of the mountains, it has lost much of its water vapor. The air is cool and dry. The land on the leeward side of the mountains—downwind—is in a rain shadow. Just as very little light falls in a sun shadow, very little rain falls in a rain shadow. Not only has the air lost its water vapor while crossing the mountains, but the air has also grown warmer while flowing down the mountainside. This warm, dry air often creates a desert on the leeward side of the mountains.

☑ ***Checkpoint*** *Why are the tops of some mountains almost always covered by clouds?*

Types of Clouds

As you know, clouds come in different shapes. **Meteorologists classify clouds into three main types: cumulus, stratus, and cirrus.** Clouds are also classified by their altitude. Each type of cloud is associated with a different type of weather.

Clouds that look like fluffy, rounded piles of cotton are called **cumulus** (KYOO myuh lus) clouds. The word *cumulus* means "heap" or "mass." Cumulus clouds form less than 2 kilometers above the ground, but may grow in size and height until they extend upward as much as 18 kilometers. Cumulus clouds usually indicate fair weather. Towering clouds with flat tops, called cumulonimbus clouds, often produce thunderstorms. The suffix *-nimbus* comes from a Latin word meaning "rain."

Clouds that form in flat layers are called **stratus** (STRAT us) clouds. *Strato* means "spread out." Stratus clouds usually cover all or most of the sky. As stratus clouds thicken, they may produce drizzle, rain, or snow. They are then called nimbostratus clouds.

Wispy, feathery clouds are called **cirrus** (SEER us) clouds. Cirrus clouds form only at high levels, above about 6 kilometers, where temperatures are very low. As a result, cirrus clouds are made of ice crystals.

Background

Facts and Figures The amount of water contained in a cloud may surprise students. A scientist with the National Center for Atmospheric Research, named Margaret LeMone, actually estimated the weight of a small cumulus cloud. The cloud was about 1,000 m wide, 1,000 m long, and 1,000 m high. Based on other studies of clouds of the same type, LeMone assumed that the cloud contained about 0.5 g of water per cubic meter. Given the size of the cloud, she concluded that it contained a total of 500 million g of water. This is about 550 tons of water, or about 100 tons heavier than a fully loaded jumbo jet.

Did you ever notice a ring around the sun or moon? Called halos, these rings are created when light passes through thin high clouds of ice crystals.

EXPLORING Clouds

The main types of clouds are cumulus, stratus, and cirrus. A cloud's name contains clues about its height and structure.

Cirrus clouds Cirrus, cirrostratus, and cirrocumulus clouds are made up of ice crystals.

Cumulonimbus clouds Thunderstorms come from cumulonimbus clouds. For this reason cumulonimbus clouds are also called thunderheads.

Nimbostratus clouds Nimbostratus clouds may produce rain or snow.

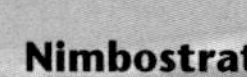

Cumulus clouds Cumulus clouds are usually a sign of fair weather.

EXPLORING Clouds

Extend the information in the Exploring feature by calling students' attention to each of the clouds pictured on the left, starting with cumulus clouds, and explaining how each type of cloud is formed. This will help students understand why the different cloud types have the shapes and other characteristics they do. Explain that cumulus clouds form during clear weather when warm air rises over small regions of Earth, such as plowed fields or paved parking lots, because these areas are heated more by the sun. Nimbostratus clouds are formed by warm air rising over a wide area, so they tend to cover the whole sky. Cumulonimbus clouds are formed when a lot of hot air rises very fast and towers upward for several kilometers. Strong winds at the bottom of the stratosphere flatten the tops of cumulonimbus clouds to give them their characteristic anvil shape. Cirrus clouds are formed high up in the atmosphere where it is very cold and there is little water vapor, making them thin and wispy. **learning modality: visual**

Building Inquiry Skills: Forming Operational Definitions

If students are having difficulty keeping cloud names straight, have them play a quiz game called "Name that Cloud." First have students find and list the definitions of basic cloud names (cumulus, stratus, cirrus, nimbus) and cloud prefixes (alto-, nimbo-, cirro-) on a set of index cards. Then have students use the definitions as the basis for the game. Students should provide a definition of a specific cloud type, and their partner must correctly name the cloud. The person with the most correct responses wins the game. **cooperative learning**

Media and Technology

Transparencies "Clouds," Transparency 47

Answers to Self-Assessment

Caption Question

Figure 16 When water vapor condenses out of the air, clouds form.

☑ Checkpoint

When warm, moist air moves upward over a mountain it cools. This causes water vapor to condense out of the air and form clouds.

Ongoing Assessment

Drawing Have students draw and label each of the three main cloud types.

Types of Clouds, continued

Real-Life Learning

Point out that how large a cloud appears is a good indicator of its altitude. Tell students that in general fist-sized clouds are cumulus clouds, thumb-sized clouds altocumulus, and little-fingernail-sized clouds cirrocumulus. **learning modality: kinesthetic**

3 Assess

Section 4 Review Answers

1. The instrument is a psychrometer. It works by comparing the temperatures on a wet-bulb and a dry-bulb thermometer.
2. For clouds to form, air must be cooled to its dew point and particles must be present in the air.
3. Cumulus clouds look like fluffy, rounded piles of cotton. Stratus clouds form in flat layers. Cirrus clouds are wispy and feathery.
4. Low-level clouds are fog, cumulus, stratus, and nimbostratus. Medium-level clouds are altocumulus and altostratus. High-level clouds are cirrostratus and cirrus.

Science at Home

Materials *large glass, cold water, ice cubes*

Tips Tell students to use cold tap water for the activity, not cold water from the refrigerator, which may be cold enough to make water condense on the outside of the glass without adding ice. Students should explain that the water on the outside of the glass condensed from water vapor in the air. It only appeared after ice was added because water vapor condenses out of the air when the temperature falls below the dew point.

Performance Assessment

Skills Check Have students infer why they can see their breath on a cold day. *(Students should infer that water droplets condense out of their warm, moist breath when it hits the cold air.)*

Figure 17 Fog often forms at night over cool lakes. *Predicting What will happen as the sun rises and warms the air above the lake?*

Cirrus clouds that have feathery "hooked" ends are sometimes called mare's tails. Cirrocumulus clouds, which look like rows of cotton balls, often indicate that a storm is on its way.

Part of a cloud's name may be based on its height. The names of clouds that form between about 2 and 6 kilometers above Earth's surface have the prefix *alto-*, which means "high." The two main types of these clouds are altocumulus and altostratus.

Clouds that form at or near the ground are called fog. Fog often forms when the ground cools at night after a warm, humid day. The ground cools the air just above the ground to the air's dew point. The next day the heat of the morning sun "burns" the fog off as its water droplets evaporate.

Section 4 Review

1. What instrument is used to measure relative humidity? How does it work?
2. What conditions are needed for clouds to form?
3. Describe each of the three main types of clouds.
4. **Thinking Critically Classifying** Classify each of the following cloud types as low-level, medium-level, or high-level: altocumulus, altostratus, cirrostratus, cirrus, cumulus, fog, nimbostratus, and stratus.

Science at Home

Condensation on Glass Fill a large glass half-full with cold water. Show your family members what happens as you add ice cubes to the water. Explain to your family that the water that appears on the outside of the glass comes from water vapor in the atmosphere. Also explain why the water on the outside of the glass only appears after you add ice to the water in the glass.

Answers to Self-Assessment

Caption Question

Figure 17 The fog will "burn" off as its water droplets evaporate.

Program Resources

- **Unit 4 Resources** 12-4 Review and Reinforce; 12-4 Enrich

SECTION 5 Precipitation

DISCOVER ACTIVITY

How Can You Make Hail?

1. Put on your goggles.
2. Put 15 g of salt into a beaker. Add 50 mL of water. Stir the solution until most of the salt is dissolved.
3. Put 15 mL of cold water in a clean test tube.
4. Place the test tube in the beaker.
5. Fill the beaker almost to the top with crushed ice. Stir the ice mixture every minute for six minutes.

6. Remove the test tube from the beaker and drop an ice chip into the test tube. What happens?

Think It Over

Inferring Based on your observation, what conditions are necessary for hail to form?

GUIDE FOR READING

- What are the main types of precipitation?
- How is precipitation measured?

Reading Tip As you read, make a list of the types of precipitation. Write a sentence describing how each type forms.

In Arica, Chile, the average rainfall is less than 1 millimeter per year. Many years pass with no precipitation at all. On the other hand, the average rainfall on Mount Waialeale on the island of Kauai in Hawaii is about 12 meters per year. That's more than enough to cover a three-story house! As you can see, rainfall varies greatly around the world.

Water evaporates into the air from every water surface on Earth and from living things. This water eventually returns to the surface as precipitation. **Precipitation** (pree sip uh TAY shun) is any form of water that falls from clouds and reaches Earth's surface.

Precipitation always comes from clouds. But not all clouds produce precipitation. For precipitation to occur, cloud droplets or ice crystals must grow heavy enough to fall through the air. One way that cloud droplets grow is by colliding and combining with other cloud droplets. As the droplets grow larger, they fall faster and collect more droplets. Finally, the droplets become heavy enough to fall out of the cloud as raindrops.

Types of Precipitation

In warm parts of the world, precipitation is almost always rain or drizzle. In colder regions, precipitation may fall as snow or ice. **Common types of precipitation include rain, sleet, freezing rain, hail, and snow.**

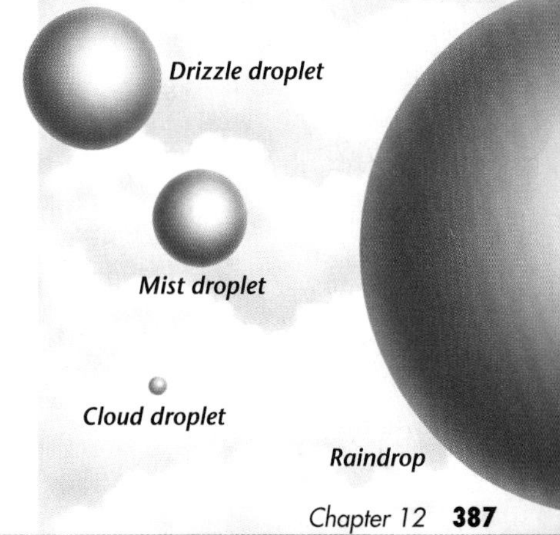

Figure 18 Droplets come in many sizes. Believe it or not, a raindrop has about one million times as much water in it as a cloud droplet.

READING STRATEGIES

Reading Tip Student lists should include rain, sleet, freezing rain, hail, and snow. Suggest to students that they save their sentences and use them as a study guide. Tell students that knowing how each type of precipitation forms will help them understand its characteristics.

Program Resources

- **Unit 4 Resources** 12-5 Lesson Plan; 12-5 Section Summary
- **Guided Reading and Study Workbook** Section 12-5
- **Interdisciplinary Explorations Series** "Where River Meets Sea," pp. 24–25; "India Beyond the Golden Age," p. 33

Precipitation

Objectives

After completing the lesson, students will be able to

- identify the main types of precipitation;
- describe how precipitation is measured and ways that it might be controlled.

Key Terms precipitation, rain gauge, drought

1 Engage/Explore

Activating Prior Knowledge

Stimulate students to think about precipitation by asking: **Did you ever hear the expression, "It's raining cats and dogs"?** *(Most students will say yes.)* **Do you know what it means?** *(That it's raining very hard)* **Where do you think the expression comes from?** *(Students probably will not know.)* Explain that the expression may come from old Norse myths, in which cats were identified with rain and dogs with winds. Tell the class they will learn more about rain and other types of precipitation in this section.

DISCOVER

Skills Focus inferring
Materials *15 g salt, beaker, 50 mL water, stirrer, 15 mL cold water, clean test tube, crushed ice, watch or clock*
Time 15 minutes
Tips The inside of the test tube must be very clean. Have students measure the temperature of the water in the test tube before they add the ice chip. They may be surprised to find it is less than 0°C. (The freezing point of salt water is less than 0°C, the freezing point of fresh water.)
Expected Outcome When the ice chip is dropped into the test tube, the cold water in the test tube will crystalize into ice around it.
Think It Over For hail to form, it must be very cold and there must be particles on which water can crystalize into ice.

2 Facilitate

Types of Precipitation

Building Inquiry Skills: Observing

Materials *transparent plastic lid, dropper, pencil, water*
Time 10 minutes

Have student pairs do this activity to observe how tiny water droplets in clouds merge to form larger drops of water until the drops are heavy enough to fall as precipitation. Students should fill the dropper with water and squeeze many separate drops onto the inside of a transparent plastic lid. Then they should quickly turn the lid over and, holding it in the air by one side, use the point of a pencil from underneath the lid to move the tiny drops of water together. When the drops touch, they will appear to leap together to form larger drops, and when the drops get large enough they will fall like rain. Ask: **What causes the water drops in clouds to move around and bump into each other so they can merge into larger drops?** *(wind and gravity)* **learning modality: kinesthetic**

Using the Visuals: Figure 19

Call students' attention to the devastation caused by freezing rain that is shown in photo B. Ask: **How did freezing rain cause this kind of damage?** *(The weight of the accumulated ice broke tree branches and downed power lines.)* **How would the street pictured in the photo look if, instead of freezing rain, the same amount of snow or hailstones had fallen?** *(Snow is lighter than ice so it probably would not have broken branches or power lines, although it might have blocked the street. Hailstones, depending on their size, might have broken twigs and small branches and even the windshield of the car, but it probably would not have blocked the street with large branches or downed power lines.)* **learning modality: visual**

Figure 19 **A.** Snowflakes form in clouds that are colder than 0°C. **B.** Freezing rain coats objects with a layer of ice. **C.** Hailstones are formed inside clouds during thunderstorms.

Rain The most common kind of precipitation is rain. Drops of water are called rain if they are at least 0.5 millimeter in diameter. Precipitation made up of smaller drops of water is called mist or drizzle. Mist and drizzle usually fall from nimbostratus clouds.

Sleet Sometimes raindrops fall through a layer of air below 0°C, the freezing point of water. As they fall, the raindrops freeze into solid particles of ice. Ice particles smaller than 5 millimeters in diameter are called sleet.

Freezing Rain At other times raindrops falling through cold air near the ground do not freeze in the air. Instead, the raindrops freeze when they touch a cold surface. This is called freezing rain. In an ice storm, a smooth, thick layer of ice builds up on every surface. The weight of the ice may break tree branches onto power lines, causing power failures. Freezing rain and sleet can make sidewalks and roads slippery and dangerous.

Hail Round pellets of ice larger than 5 millimeters in diameter are called hailstones. Hail forms only inside cumulonimbus clouds during thunderstorms. A hailstone starts as an ice pellet inside a cold region of a cloud. Strong updrafts in the cloud carry the hailstone up and down through the cold region many times. Each time the hailstone goes through the cold region, a new layer of ice forms around the hailstone. Eventually the hailstone becomes heavy enough to fall to the ground. If you cut a hailstone in half, you can often see shells of ice, like the layers of an onion. Because hailstones can grow quite large before finally falling to the ground, hail can cause tremendous damage to crops, buildings, and vehicles.

Background

History of Science For centuries people have tried to increase the amount of precipitation that falls. From praying and dancing to sending up explosives into clouds, they have searched for ways to make rain. It wasn't until the 1940s, however, that Vincent Schaefer discovered how to make rain by seeding clouds. He discovered that a grain of dry ice dropped into a cloud led to the formation of millions of ice crystals, often leading to precipitation. Shortly after this discovery, Bernard Vonnegut discovered that silver iodide led to the production of even more ice crystals than dry ice. Since then, no other process has been found that is better at making rain than their cloud-seeding method. Rainmaking companies still use this method in many parts of the world.

Snow Often water vapor in a cloud is converted directly into ice crystals called snowflakes. Snowflakes have an endless number of different shapes and patterns, all with six sides or branches. Snowflakes often join together into larger clumps of snow in which the six-sided crystals are hard to see.

☑ *Checkpoint* *How do hailstones form?*

Measuring Precipitation

Meteorologists measure rainfall with a rain gauge. A **rain gauge** is an open-ended can or tube that collects rainfall. The amount of rainfall is measured by dipping a ruler into the water or by reading a marked scale. To increase the accuracy of the measurement, the top of a rain gauge may have a funnel that collects ten times as much rain as the tube alone. The funnel collects a greater depth of water that is easier to measure. But to get the actual depth of rain, it is necessary to divide by ten.

Snowfall is measured using a ruler or by melting collected snow and measuring the depth of water it produces. On average, 10 centimeters of snow contains about the same amount of water as 1 centimeter of rain. Of course, light, fluffy snow contains far less water than heavy, wet snow.

Figure 20 A rain gauge measures the depth of rain that falls. *Observing How much rain was collected in the measuring tube of this rain gauge?*

Sharpen your Skills

Calculating

ACTIVITY

Make your own rain gauge by putting a funnel into a narrow, straight-sided glass jar. Here's how to calculate how much more rain your funnel collects than the jar alone.

1. First measure the diameter of the top of the funnel and square it.
   Example: 4 × 4 = 16
2. Then measure the diameter of the top of the jar and square it.
   Example: 2 × 2 = 4
3. Divide the first square by the second square.
   Example: $\frac{16}{4} = 4$
4. To find the actual depth of rain that fell, divide the depth of water in the jar by the ratio from Step 3.
   Example: $\frac{8\text{ cm}}{4} = 2\text{ cm}$

Answers to Self-Assessment

☑ *Checkpoint*

Hailstones form when pellets of ice inside cumulonimbus clouds are carried up and down many times, each time adding a new layer of ice, until they become heavy enough to fall to the ground.

Caption Question

Figure 20 Though one cm of rain fell into the gauge, 10 cm were collected.

Building Inquiry Skills: Measuring

Materials *shallow pan, flour, sieve*
Time 10 minutes to collect raindrops; 10 minutes to compare sizes

On a day when it is raining and there is no danger of lightning, challenge students to catch raindrops and estimate their size. Have each student hold a shallow pan containing a smooth layer of flour out in the rain for a second or two, just long enough for several raindrops to land in the pan and form little lumps in the flour. After at least 15-20 minutes when the lumps have dried, have students pour the flour through a sieve to separate the lumps. Ask: **How big are the raindrops you caught?** *(Students should estimate the size of the raindrops from the size of the lumps. The bigger the lumps, the larger the raindrops.)* **learning modality: visual**

Measuring Precipitation

Sharpen your Skills

Calculating

ACTIVITY

Time 15 minutes
Tips Explain that the amount of rain collected in the jar is the amount that fell over an area the size of the funnel opening. The calculations show how much smaller the area of the jar opening is than the area of the funnel opening. The total amount of rain collected must be reduced by this ratio to show how much would have fallen into the jar alone. Note that Figure 20, has a different ratio.
Expected Outcome Students should work through the calculations to make sure they also get a final answer of 2 cm.
Extend Ask: **What is the actual depth of the rain that fell if the diameter of the top of the funnel is 6 cm and the depth of water in the jar is 8 cm?** *(8 cm ÷ (36/4) = 0.89 cm)* **learning modality: logical/mathematical**

Ongoing Assessment

Drawing Have students draw diagrams showing how rain, sleet, and freezing rain form.

Controlling Precipitation

Integrating Technology

Point out that rain-making technology could not be developed until scientists discovered how rain actually forms in clouds. In the early 1900s, a scientist named Alfred Wegener hypothesized that almost all precipitation, even rain, starts out as ice crystals. Explain that the condensation of water alone is a much slower process, and this is why Wegener believed correctly that it could not account for most precipitation. Ask: **How does Wegener's hypothesis relate to the cloud-seeding technology?** *(Clouds are seeded with crystals of dry ice and silver iodide because this quickly leads to the formation of ice crystals large enough to fall as precipitation.)* **learning modality: verbal**

3 Assess

Section 5 Review Answers

1. Rain, sleet, freezing rain, hail, and snow
2. rain gauge
3. Cloud droplets or ice crystals must grow heavy enough to fall through the air.
4. Cumulonimbus clouds produce hail.
5. The can with the larger diameter would collect more rain. However, the depth of the water in the two cans would be the same.

CHAPTER PROJECT

Check Your Progress

Suggest that students experiment with different types of graphs to display their weather data. Also require that they graph all or most of the weather factors on the same graph so they can see how the weather factors change together. This will help them see patterns in the data.

Performance Assessment

Skills Check Have students make a table comparing and contrasting the five common types of precipitation.

Figure 21 The corn in this photo was damaged by a long drought. *Applying Concepts How can cloud seeding be used to reduce the effect of droughts?*

Controlling Precipitation

In some regions, there may be periods that are much drier than usual. Long periods of unusually low precipitation are called **droughts.** Droughts can cause great hardship. In the farming regions of the Midwest, for example, droughts may cause entire crops to fail. The farmers suffer from lost income and consumers suffer from high food prices. In some less-developed countries, droughts can cause widespread hunger, or famine.

INTEGRATING TECHNOLOGY In recent years, scientists have been trying to produce rain during droughts. The most common method is called cloud seeding. In cloud seeding, tiny crystals of dry ice (solid carbon dioxide) and silver iodide are sprinkled into clouds from airplanes. Many clouds contain supercooled water droplets, which are actually below 0°C. The droplets don't freeze because there aren't enough particles around which ice crystals can form. Water vapor can condense on the particles of silver iodide, forming rain or snow. Dry ice works by cooling the droplets even further, so that they will freeze without particles being present.

Cloud seeding has also been used with some success to clear fog from airports. Dry ice is sprinkled into the fog, causing ice crystals to form. This removes some of the fog so pilots can see the runways. Unfortunately, cloud seeding clears only cold fogs, so its use for this purpose is limited.

Section 5 Review

1. Name the five common types of precipitation.
2. What device is used to measure precipitation?
3. What must happen before precipitation can fall from a cloud?
4. What kind of cloud produces hail?
5. **Thinking Critically Applying Concepts** If two open cans of different diameters were left out in the rain, how would the amount of water they collected compare? How would the depth of water in the cans compare?

CHAPTER PROJECT

Check Your Progress

Now you should be ready to begin graphing your weather data. Look for patterns in your graphs. Use your data to predict what the next day's weather will be. Compare your predictions with what actually happens the next day. Are you able to predict the weather with confidence?

Answers to Self-Assessment

Caption Question

Figure 21 Cloud seeding can be used to lessen the effect of droughts by sprinkling clouds with particles around which water droplets can condense to form rain.

Program Resources

- **Unit 4 Resources** 12-5 Review and Reinforce; 12-5 Enrich

CHAPTER 12 STUDY GUIDE

Energy in the Atmosphere

Key Ideas

- Energy from the sun travels to Earth as electromagnetic waves—mostly visible light, infrared radiation, and ultraviolet radiation.
- When Earth's surface is heated, it radiates some of the energy back into the atmosphere in the form of longer-wavelength radiation.

Key Terms

electromagnetic waves
radiation
infrared radiation
ultraviolet radiation
scattering

Heat Transfer

INTEGRATING PHYSICS

Key Ideas

- The energy of motion in the molecules of a substance is called thermal energy.
- Three forms of heat transfer—radiation, conduction, and convection—work together to heat the troposphere.

Key Terms

thermal energy
temperature
thermometer
heat
conduction
convection

Winds

Key Ideas

- All winds are caused by differences in air pressure, which are the result of unequal heating of Earth's surface.
- Local winds are caused by unequal heating of Earth's surface within a small area.
- The movement of air between the equator and the poles produces global winds.

Key Terms

wind
anemometer
wind-chill factor
local wind
sea breeze
land breeze
monsoon
global wind
Coriolis effect
latitude
jet stream

Water in the Atmosphere

Key Ideas

- Relative humidity is the percentage of water vapor in the air compared to the amount of water vapor the air could hold. It can be measured with a psychrometer.
- Clouds of all kinds form when water vapor in the air becomes liquid water or solid ice.
- Meteorologists classify clouds into three main types: cumulus, stratus, and cirrus.

Key Terms

evaporation
humidity
relative humidity
psychrometer
condensation
dew point
cumulus
stratus
cirrus

Precipitation

Key Ideas

- Common types of precipitation include rain, sleet, freezing rain, hail, and snow.
- Rain is measured with a rain gauge.
- Scientists have used cloud seeding to produce rain and to clear fog from airports.

Key Terms

precipitation
rain gauge
drought

Organizing Information

Concept Map Construct a concept map about winds on a separate sheet of paper. Be sure to include the following terms: local winds, global winds, monsoons, sea breezes, land breezes, prevailing westerlies, polar easterlies, tradewinds, and the two types of monsoon. (For more on concept maps, see the Skills Handbook.)

Program Resources

- **Unit 4 Resources** Chapter 12 Project Scoring Rubric
- **Performance Assessment** Chapter 12
- **Chapter and Unit Tests** Chapter 12 Test

Media and Technology

Computer Test Bank
Chapter 12 Test

Organizing Information

Concept Map Answers will vary. A typical concept map is shown below.

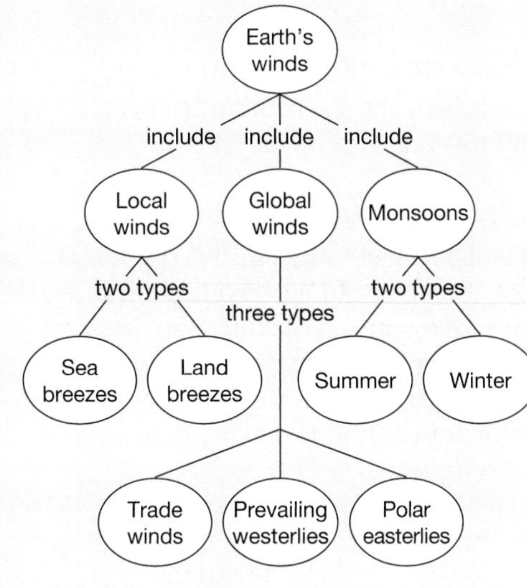

Reviewing Content

Multiple Choice

1. a **2.** b **3.** b **4.** c **5.** c

True or False

6. visible light **7.** greenhouse effect
8. true **9.** anemometer **10.** true

Checking Concepts

11. The greenhouse effect is caused by the absorption of heat from Earth's surface by carbon dioxide, water vapor, and other gases in the atmosphere. It keeps Earth's atmosphere at a temperature that is warmer than it would be otherwise.

12. Convection causes most of the heating of the troposphere as the upward movement of warm air and the downward movement of cool air form convection currents.

13. Like local land and sea breezes, monsoons occur because of unequal heating of land and nearby bodies of water. Unlike local land and sea breezes, monsoons occur over a wide region and change direction with the seasons.

14. Warm air rises at the equator and flows toward the poles. Cold air sinks at the poles and spreads out toward the equator. The movement of air between the equator and the poles produces global winds.

15. When wind strikes the windward side of a mountain range, it is forced upward. As air rises, it becomes cooler. Since cool air can hold less water vapor than warm air, the moisture in the air often precipitates as snow or rain on the windward side of the mountain, leaving little to fall on the leeward side.

16. Clouds usually form high in the air instead of at Earth's surface because the air must be cold for water vapor to condense and form clouds and air at high altitudes usually is colder than air near the surface.

17. Sleet forms when raindrops fall through a layer of air below 0°C and freeze into small particles of ice. Hail forms when an ice pellet in a cumulonimbus cloud is carried up and down through the cold region of the cloud by strong updrafts, each time gathering another layer of ice until the hailstone is heavy enough to fall to the surface. Snow forms when water vapor in a cloud is converted directly into ice crystals.

18. Students' diary entries will vary, but they should reflect students' knowledge of the water cycle and include the terms *evaporation, condensation,* and *precipitation.*

Thinking Critically

19. A nighttime land breeze in a city near the ocean would be caused by the land cooling off more quickly than the water at night so that as warm air rose over the water, cool air would flow from the land to take its place.

20. The relative humidity is 100 percent because since both temperatures were the same, the water on the wet bulb must not have been able to evaporate, which would happen only when the relative humidity is that high.

21. Hail and sleet are both frozen rain. Sleet is smaller than 5 millimeters in diameter, while hail is larger than 5 millimeters in diameter. Sleet forms anytime rain falls through a layer of air below 0°C; hail forms only inside

CHAPTER 12 ASSESSMENT

Reviewing Content

Multiple Choice

Choose the letter of the best answer.

1. Energy from the sun travels to Earth's surface by
a. radiation.
b. convection.
c. evaporation.
d. conduction.

2. Rising warm air transports heat energy by
a. conduction.
b. convection.
c. radiation.
d. condensation.

3. A psychrometer is used to measure
a. rainfall.
b. relative humidity.
c. temperature.
d. humidity.

4. Clouds form because water vapor in the air
a. warms. **b.** conducts.
c. condenses. **d.** evaporates.

5. Rain, sleet, and hail are all forms of
a. evaporation.
b. condensation.
c. precipitation.
d. convection.

True or False

If the statement is true, write true. If it is false, change the underlined word or words to make the statement true.

6. Infrared radiation and ultraviolet radiation make up most of the energy Earth receives from the sun.

7. Reflection of light in all directions is called convection.

8. Water molecules in liquid water escape into the atmosphere as water vapor in the process of evaporation.

9. The instrument used to measure wind speed is a thermometer.

10. Clouds that form near the ground are called fog.

Checking Concepts

11. What causes the greenhouse effect? How does it affect Earth's atmosphere?

12. What form of heat transfer is most important in heating the troposphere?

13. What are monsoons? How are they like land and sea breezes? How are they different?

14. Describe how the movements of hot air at the equator and cold air at the poles produce global wind patterns.

15. Why are deserts often found on the leeward side of mountain ranges?

16. Why do clouds usually form high in the air instead of near Earth's surface?

17. Describe sleet, hail, and snow in terms of how each one forms.

18. **Writing to Learn** Imagine you are a drop of water in the ocean. Write a diary describing your journey through the water cycle. How do you become a cloud? What type of conditions cause you to fall as precipitation? Use descriptive words to describe your journey.

Thinking Critically

19. **Relating Cause and Effect** What circumstances could cause a night-time land breeze in a city near the ocean?

20. **Problem Solving** If you use a psychrometer and get the same reading on both thermometers, what is the relative humidity?

21. **Comparing and Contrasting** How are hail and sleet alike? How are they different?

22. **Classifying** Classify the different types of clouds by the kind of weather associated with each type.

23. **Relating Cause and Effect** What is the source of the energy that powers Earth's winds?

Applying Skills

Use the table below to answer Questions 24–27.

Average Monthly Rainfall

Month	Rainfall	Month	Rainfall
January	1 cm	July	49 cm
February	1 cm	August	57 cm
March	1 cm	September	40 cm
April	2 cm	October	20 cm
May	25 cm	November	4 cm
June	52 cm	December	1 cm

24. Graphing Use the information in the table to draw a bar graph that shows the rainfall each month at this location.

25. Calculating What is the total amount of rainfall each year at this location?

26. Classifying Which months of the year would you classify as "dry"? Which months would you classify as "wet"?

27. Drawing Conclusions The place represented by the rainfall data is in Southeast Asia. What do you think accounts for the extremely heavy rainfall that occurs during some months?

Performance  **Assessment**

Present Your Project Develop a way to present your findings to the class. For example, you could put your graphs and predictions on a poster. Are your graphs neatly drawn and easy to understand? Practice your presentation and make any needed improvements.

Reflect and Record How could you improve the accuracy of your observations? What did you learn about how easy or difficult it is to predict the weather?

Test Preparation

Use these questions to prepare for standardized tests.

Study the graph. Then answer Questions 28–31.

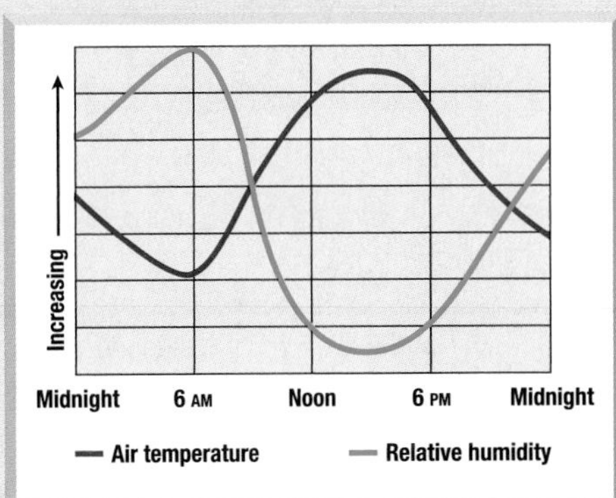

28. The greatest change in air temperature occurred during the period from
a. midnight to 6 A.M.
b. 6 A.M. to noon.
c. noon to 6 P.M.
d. 6 P.M. to midnight.

29. The graph indicates that as air temperature increases, relative humidity
a. increases.
b. sometimes increases and sometimes decreases.
c. decreases.
d. stays about the same.

30. Condensation is most likely to occur at approximately
a. 6 A.M. **b.** noon.
c. 3 P.M. **d.** 6 P.M.

31. Assuming that the amount of water vapor in the air stayed constant through the day, one could infer from the graph that
a. cool air can hold more water vapor than warm air.
b. cool air can hold less water vapor than warm air.
c. cool air and warm air can hold the same amount of water vapor.
d. cool air cannot hold water vapor.

cumulonimbus clouds during thunderstorms when layers of ice form around ice pellets as they are carried up and down through cold regions of a cloud.
22. Cumulus clouds are associated with fair weather. Cumulonimbus clouds are associated with thunderstorms. Nimbostratus clouds are associated with drizzle, mist, rain, or snow.
23. Earth's winds are powered by unequal heating of Earth's atmosphere by the sun.

Program Resources

◆ **Inquiry Skills Activity Book** Provides teaching and review of all inquiry skills

Applying Skills

24. Student's graphs should have one axis labeled "Month" and the other axis labeled "Average Monthly Rainfall (centimeters)." The bars should range from 1 centimeter in height (January, February, March, and December) to 57 centimeters in height (August).
25. 253 centimeters
26. *Dry:* January, February, March, April, November, and December; *Wet:* May, June, July, August, September, and October
27. Monsoons

Performance  **Assessment**

Present Your Project Make sure students have clearly drawn graphs or other visuals to use for their presentations. Advise them to include in their presentations a description of when and where their measurements were made and the instruments that were used. They also should include a discussion of any patterns they see in their data.

Reflect and Record If students used instruments they made themselves, they may be able to improve the accuracy of their observations by using commercial instruments. Students probably will find that it is difficult to predict the weather because some of the patterns they observe in their data may not be significant for prediction. Help students focus on the most significant factors for predicting the weather, including air pressure, clouds, and wind direction.

Test Preparation

28. b **29.** c **30.** a **31.** b

CHAPTER 13

Weather Patterns

Sections	Time	Student Edition Activities	ACTIVITY Other Activities
CHAPTER PROJECT **The Weather Tomorrow** p. 395	Ongoing (2–3 weeks)	Check Your Progress, p. 402, 418, 425 Present Your Project, p. 429	
1 Air Masses and Fronts pp. 396–402 ◆ Identify the major types of air masses that affect the weather in North America. ◆ Name and describe the main types of fronts. ◆ Define cyclones and anticyclones.	1–2 periods/ $\frac{1}{2}$–1 block	**Discover** How Do Fluids of Different Densities Behave?, p. 396 **Sharpen Your Skills** Classifying, p. 401	TE Inquiry Challenge, p. 399 TE Including All Students, p. 399 TE Demonstration, p. 400 TE Including All Students, p. 401
2 Storms pp. 403–414 ◆ List the main kinds of storms and explain how they form. ◆ Describe measures you can take to ensure safety in a storm.	2–3 periods/ 1–1$\frac{1}{2}$ blocks	**Discover** Can You Make a Tornado?, p. 403 **Try This** Lightning Distances, p. 404 **Science at Home,** p. 411 **Real-World Lab: Careers in Science** Tracking a Hurricane, pp. 412–413	TE Demonstration, p. 404 TE Including All Students, p. 405 IES "India Beyond the Golden Age," pp. 31–32 IES "Back to the Thirties," pp. 10–12
3 *INTEGRATING HEALTH* **Floods** pp. 415–418 ◆ Identify the causes of flooding. ◆ Explain how the dangers of floods can be reduced.	1 period/ $\frac{1}{2}$ block	**Discover** What Causes Floods?, p. 415 **Sharpen Your Skills** Communicating, p. 416	TE Using the Visuals: Figure 15, p. 416
4 Predicting the Weather pp. 419–426 ◆ Explain how technology helps forecasters predict the weather. ◆ Describe the types of information shown on weather maps. ◆ Describe El Niño and its effects.	3 periods/ 1$\frac{1}{2}$blocks	**Discover** What's the Weather?, p. 419 **Sharpen Your Skills** Interpreting Data, p. 422 **Skills Lab: Interpreting Data** Reading a Weather Map, p. 426	TE Inquiry Challenge, p. 421 TE Real-Life Learning, p. 424 TE Building Inquiry Skills: Calculating, p. 424 TE Exploring Newspaper Weather Maps, p. 425 LM Chapter 13, "Investigating Weather Maps"
Study Guide/Chapter Assessment pp. 427–429	1 period/ $\frac{1}{2}$ block		ISAB Provides Teaching and review of all inquiry skills

For Standard or Block Schedule The Resource Pro® CD-ROM gives you maximum flexibility for planning your instruction for any type of schedule. Resource Pro® contains Planning Express®, an advanced scheduling program, as well as the entire contents of the Teaching Resources and the Computer Test Bank.

CHAPTER PLANNING GUIDE

Program Resources	Assessment Strategies	Media and Technology
UR Chapter 13 Project Teacher Notes **UR** Chapter 13 Project Student materials	**SE** Performance Assessment: Present Your Project, p. 429 **TE** Check Your Progress, pp. 402, 418, 425 **UR** Chapter 13 Project Scoring Rubric	Science Explorer Internet Site at www.phschool.com Student Edition on Audio CD, Chapter 13
UR 13-1 Lesson Plan **UR** 13-1 Section Summary **UR** 13-1 Review and Reinforce **UR** 13-1 Enrich	**SE** Section 1 Review, p. 402 **TE** Ongoing Assessment, pp. 397, 399, 401 **TE** Performance Assessment, p. 402	Transparencies 48, "North American Air Masses"; 49, "Cold Front"; 50, "Warm Front"; 51, "Occluded Front"
UR 13-2 Lesson Plan **UR** 13-2 Section Summary **UR** 13-2 Review and Reinforce **UR** 13-2 Enrich **UR** Chapter 13 Real-World Lab	**SE** Section 2 Review, p. 411 **TE** Ongoing Assessment, pp. 405, 407, 409 **TE** Performance Assessment, p. 411	Concept Videotape Library, Grade 6, Tape 3, "Violent Storms" Transparency 52, "Clouds and Winds in a Hurricane"
UR 13-3 Lesson Plan **UR** 13-3 Section Summary **UR** 13-3 Review and Reinforce **UR** 13-3 Enrich	**SE** Section 3 Review, p. 418 **TE** Ongoing Assessment, p. 417 **TE** Performance Assessment, p. 418	
UR 13-4 Lesson Plan **UR** 13-4 Section Summary **UR** 13-4 Review and Reinforce **UR** 13-4 Enrich **UR** Chapter 13 Skills Lab	**SE** Section 4 Review, p. 425 **TE** Ongoing Assessment, pp. 421, 423 **TE** Performance Assessment, p. 425	Concept Videotape Library, Grade 6, Tape 3, "Never Put Up the Umbrella Until It Starts to Rain" Transparency 53, "Weather Map"; 54, "Newspaper Weather Map"
RCA Provides strategies to improve science reading skills **GRSW** Provides worksheets to promote student comprehension of content	**SE** Chapter 13 Review, pp. 427–429 **PA** Chapter 13 Performance Assessment **CUT** Chapter 13 Test **CTB** Chapter 13 Test	Computer Test Bank, Chapter 13 Test

Key: **SE** Student Edition
CTB Computer Test Bank
ISAB Inquiry Skills Activity Book
GRSW Guided Reading and Study Workbook
TE Teacher's Edition
PTA Product Testing Activities by *Consumer Reports*
RCA Reading in the Content Area
PA Performance Assessment
UR Unit Resources
LM Laboratory Manual
IES Interdisciplinary Explorations Series
CUT Chapter and Unit Tests

Meeting the National Science Education Standards and AAAS Benchmarks

National Science Education Standards	Benchmarks for Science Literacy	Unifying Themes
Science As Inquiry (Content Standard A) ◆ **Use appropriate tools and techniques to gather, analyze, and interpret data** Students make weather forecasts. Students use data to predict the path of a hurricane. Students interpret a weather map. *(Chapter Project; Real-World Lab; Skills Lab)* **Earth and Space Science** (Content Standard D) ◆ **Structure of the Earth system** An air mass is a huge body of air that has similar temperature, humidity, and air pressure throughout. A storm is a violent disturbance in the atmosphere. Floods occur when so much water pours into a stream or river that it overflows its banks. *(Sections 1, 2, 3)* **Science in Personal and Social Perspectives** (Content Standard F) ◆ **Personal health** There are various measures to take to ensure safety during storms and floods. *(Sections 2, 3)* ◆ **Natural hazards** Unanticipated storms have even changed the course of history. *(Science & History)* ◆ **Risks and benefits** Students analyze the controversy around hurricane evacuations. *(Science and Society)* ◆ **Science and technology in society** Technology helps meteorologists predict the weather. *(Section 4)*	**IB Scientific Inquiry** Students make weather forecasts. Students use data to predict the path of a hurricane. Students interpret a weather map. *(Chapter Project; Real-World Lab; Skills Lab)* **3A Technology and Science** Technology helps meteorologists predict the weather. *(Section 4)* **4B The Earth** An air mass is a huge body of air that has similar temperature, humidity, and air pressure throughout. A storm is a violent disturbance in the atmosphere. Floods occur when so much water pours into a stream or river that it overflows its banks. *(Sections 1, 2, 3)* **6E Physical Health** There are various measures to take to ensure safety during storms and floods. *(Sections 2, 3)* **7C Social Change** Unanticipated storms have even changed the course of history. *(Science & History)* **7D Social Trade-Offs** Students analyze the controversy around hurricane evacuations. *(Science and Society)*	◆ **Energy** A storm is a violent disturbance in the atmosphere. Rushing water in a flood has tremendous power. *(Sections 2, 3)* ◆ **Patterns of Change** Students look for patterns in the weather to make weather forecasts. As an air mass moves into an area, it changes the weather there. Students use data to predict the path of a hurricane. Meteorologists interpret weather data to prepare weather forecasts. *(Chapter Project; Sections 1, 4; Real-World Lab)* ◆ **Scale and Structure** An air mass is a huge body of air that has similar temperature, humidity, and air pressure throughout. A typical hurricane is about 600 kilometers across. *(Sections 1, 2)* ◆ **Systems and Interactions** Four major types of air masses influence the weather in North America. Different atmospheric conditions cause different kinds of storms. A warm-water event, known as El Niño, affects global weather. Students interpret a weather map to describe weather conditions. *(Sections 1, 2, 4; Skills Lab)* ◆ **Unity and Diversity** Air masses are classified as tropical, polar, maritime, or continental and fronts as cold, warm, stationary, or occluded. Four kinds of storms are thunderstorms, tornadoes, hurricanes, and winter storms. *(Sections 1, 2)*

Take It to the Net

Interactive text at www.phschool.com

Science Explorer comes alive with iText.

- **Complete student text** is accessible from any computer with Internet access or a CD-ROM drive.
- **Animations, simulations, and videos** enhance student understanding and retention of concepts.
- **Self-tests and online study tools** assess student understanding.

STAY CURRENT with **SCIENCE NEWS®**

Find out the latest research and information about Weather and Climate at: **www.phschool.com**

Go to **www.phschool.com** and click on the Science icon.Then click on Science Explorer: Life, Earth, and Physical Science under PH@school.

Student Edition Activities Planner

ACTIVITY	Time (minutes)	Materials *Quantities for one work group*	Skills
Section 1			
Discover, p. 396	10	**Consumable** cardboard divider, red food coloring, 1 L warm water, 100 mL table salt, blue food coloring, 1 L cold water **Nonconsumable** plastic shoe box, apron	Developing Hypotheses
Sharpen Your Skills, p. 401	home	No special materials required.	Classifying
Section 2			
Discover, p. 403	10	**Consumable** water, liquid dish detergent **Nonconsumable** large plastic jar with lid, penny or marble	Observing
Try This, p. 404	10	**Nonconsumable** watch or stopwatch, calculator	Calculating
Science at Home, p. 411	home	No special materials required.	Communicating
Real-World Lab, pp. 412–413	40	**Consumable** tracing paper **Nonconsumable** ruler; red, blue, green, and brown pencils	Interpreting Data, Predicting
Section 3			
Discover, p. 415	10	**Consumable** water **Nonconsumable** cup, funnel, basin	Inferring
Sharpen Your Skills, p. 416	10	No special materials required.	Communicating
Section 4			
Discover, p. 419	10	**Nonconsumable** local newspaper weather report	Observing
Sharpen Your Skills, p. 422	10	No special materials required.	Interpreting Data
Skills Lab, p. 426	30	No special materials required.	Interpreting Data, Drawing Conclusions

A list of all materials required for the Student Edition activities can be found on pages TVA34–TVA40. You can obtain information about ordering materials by calling 1-800-848-9500 or by accessing the Science Explorer Internet site at: **www.phschool.com**

CHAPTER 13 PROJECT

The Weather Tomorrow

Predicting the weather is something that interests most people because the weather influences so many things that we do. In this chapter, students will learn what causes changes in the weather and how the information recorded on weather maps can be used to make weather predictions.

Purpose In this project, students will get a chance to predict the weather and then evaluate how well they have done compared with the actual weather and with professional forecasts.

Skills Focus After completing this project, students will be able to

- interpret the symbols in newspaper weather maps;
- compare weather maps from day to day to find patterns in the weather;
- predict the weather for tomorrow based on the weather today;
- draw weather maps to show their weather predictions;
- compare their own predictions with professional forecasts and the next day's weather.

Project Time Line The entire project will take at least two weeks. Students should start collecting newspaper weather maps immediately. They should also read about weather maps in Section 4, paying special attention to *Exploring Newspaper Weather Maps* on page 425. As soon as students have finished reading Section 1 on air masses and fronts, they can start analyzing their weather maps. They should be looking for patterns in the weather by comparing the maps from day to day. Check students' progress at this point and give extra guidance to any students who are having problems.

Students should continue collecting and comparing weather maps over the next week or so. Check their progress when they finish Section 3 by having them predict the next day's weather at their own location and two other locations of their choice that are at least 1,000 km apart. Students should draw a weather map to show their predictions. After a week of predicting the weather, have students

A lightning bolt tears through the dark sky, illuminating a field of wheat.

compare their predictions to the weather maps and professional forecasts.

When students have finished reading the chapter, give them a day or two to organize their presentations. They should display their newspaper weather maps and the weather maps they made to predict the weather. They should also include commentary, written or oral, about the patterns they observed in the weather and how they made their predictions.

For more detailed information on planning and supervising the chapter project, see Chapter 13 Project Teacher Notes, in Unit 4 Resources.

Suggested Shortcuts You can reduce the scope of the project by requiring students to select just one location instead of three. Another shortcut is to have students work in groups. If you do, make sure groups divide tasks in such a way that each student makes a significant contribution. Urge groups to divide tasks according to students' specific abilities and interests, if possible.

This chapter project can also be done as a class project. Spend a few minutes at the beginning of

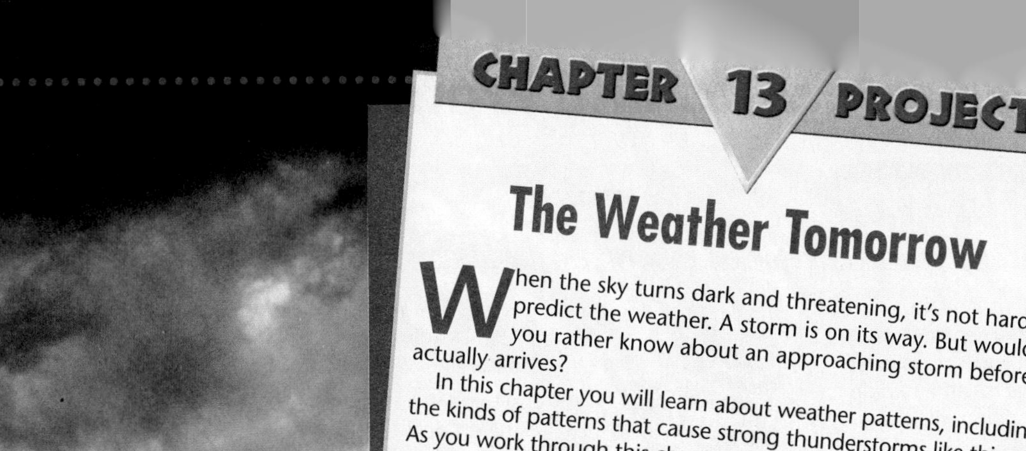

The Weather Tomorrow

When the sky turns dark and threatening, it's not hard to predict the weather. A storm is on its way. But wouldn't you rather know about an approaching storm before it actually arrives?

In this chapter you will learn about weather patterns, including the kinds of patterns that cause strong thunderstorms like this one. As you work through this chapter, you will get a chance to make your own weather forecasts and compare them to the forecasts of professionals. Good luck!

Your Goal To predict the weather for your own community and two other locations in the United States.

To complete the project you will

- compare weather maps for several days at a time
- look for repeating patterns in the weather
- draw maps to show your weather predictions

Get Started Begin by previewing Section 4 to learn about weather maps and symbols. Start a project folder to hold daily national weather maps from your local newspaper and a description of the symbols used on the maps. Choose two locations in the United States that are at least 1,000 kilometers away from your community and from each other.

Check Your Progress You'll be working on this project as you study this chapter. To keep your project on track, look for Check Your Progress boxes at the following points.

Section 1 Review, page 402: Collect weather maps and look for patterns.

Section 3 Review, page 418: Predict the next day's weather.

Section 4 Review, page 425: Compare your predictions to professional forecasts and to the actual weather.

Present Your Project At the end of the chapter (page 429), you will present your weather maps and discuss how well you predicted the weather.

SECTION 4 **Predicting the Weather**

Discover **What's the Weather?**
Sharpen Your Skills **Interpreting Data**
Skills Lab **Reading a Weather Map**

395

make an overhead transp... map so you can point out details on the map as you discuss it. Also spend a few minutes each day comparing that day's weather map with the weather map from the day before. At the end of a week, have students start trying to predict the next day's weather.

Possible Materials Newspaper weather maps are readily available and easy to work with as long as students always use the same source so the maps have the same format. This makes them easier to compare and creates less confusion. A good source for weather maps regardless of where you live is *USA Today.*

Launching the Project Introduce students to weather maps by handing out copies of a national weather map showing today's weather. Have students find their own state on the map, and then challenge them to use the map to learn as much as they can about their state's weather. For example, ask: **What does the map tell you about the temperature in our state today?** Make sure all the students know how to find this and other weather factors for their state on the map. If necessary, call their attention to the map key and point out the relevant symbols and numbers on the map. Tell students they will be collecting and comparing maps like this one for the Chapter 13 Project. They will use the maps to learn how weather changes and how to predict tomorrow's weather from weather conditions today. Point out, however, that students will make their weather predictions without using the weather forecasts that are often included in weather information in newspapers and on radio and television.

Program Resources

- **Unit 4 Resources** Chapter 13 Project Teacher Notes; Chapter 13 Project Overview and Worksheets; Chapter 13 Project Scoring Rubric

Media and Technology

Student Edition on Audio CD
Chapter 13

You will find an Internet activity, chapter self-tests for students, and links to other chapter topics at this site.

Performance Assessment

To assess students' performance in this project, use the Chapter 13 Project Scoring Rubric in Unit 4 Resources. Students will be assessed on

- their collection and interpretation of weather maps;
- their weather predictions;
- their class presentation;
- their group participation, if they worked in groups.

Air Masses and Fronts

Objectives

After completing the lesson, students will be able to

- identify the major types of air masses that affect the weather in North America;
- name and describe the main types of fronts;
- define cyclones and anticyclones.

Key Terms air mass, tropical, polar, maritime, continental, front, occluded, cyclone, anticyclone

1 Engage/Explore

Activating Prior Knowledge

Help students recall the properties of air they learned about in Chapter 16. Ask: **Which is denser, warm air or cold air?** *(cold air)* **What do you think would happen if a large mass of cold air came into contact with a large mass of warm air?** *(The cold air would sink and the warm air would rise.)* Tell students that large masses of cold and warm air often do meet in the atmosphere. Point out that the meeting of large air masses with different temperatures causes most of our weather.

DISCOVER ACTIVITY

Skills Focus developing hypotheses

Materials *cardboard divider, plastic shoe box, red food coloring, 1 L warm water, 100 mL table salt, blue food coloring, 1 L cold water, apron*

Time 10 minutes

Tips The more salt students use, the denser the cold water will be and the more obvious the outcome.

Expected Outcome The red water and the blue water will not mix. Instead, they will form separate layers, with the blue water on the bottom and the red water on top.

Think It Over Students should hypothesize that the cold air mass would move underneath the warm air mass and the warm air mass would rise.

SECTION 1 Air Masses and Fronts

DISCOVER ACTIVITY

How Do Fluids of Different Densities Behave?

1. Put on your apron. Place a cardboard divider across the middle of a plastic shoe box.
2. Add a few drops of red food coloring to a liter of warm water. Pour the red liquid, which represents low-density warm air, into the shoe box on one side of the divider.
3. Add about 100 mL of table salt and a few drops of blue food coloring to a liter of cold water. Pour the blue liquid, which represents high-density cold air, into the shoe box on the other side of the divider.
4. What do you think will happen if you remove the divider?
5. Now quickly remove the divider. Watch carefully from the side. What happens?

Think It Over

Developing Hypotheses Based on this activity, write a hypothesis stating what would happen if a mass of cold air ran into a mass of warm air.

GUIDE FOR READING

- What are the major types of air masses that affect the weather in North America?
- What are the main types of fronts?
- What are cyclones and anticyclones?

Reading Tip Before you read, use the headings to make an outline about air masses and fronts. Leave space to fill in details as you read.

Listen to the evening news and you may hear a weather forecast like this: "A huge mass of Arctic air is moving our way, bringing freezing temperatures." Today's weather is influenced by air from thousands of kilometers away—perhaps from Canada or the Caribbean Sea. A huge body of air that has similar temperature, humidity, and air pressure throughout it is called an **air mass.** A single air mass may spread over an area of millions of square kilometers and be up to 10 kilometers high.

Types of Air Masses

Scientists classify air masses according to two characteristics: temperature and humidity. Whether an air mass is warm or cold depends on the temperature of the region over which the air mass forms. **Tropical,** or warm, air masses form in the tropics and have low air pressure. **Polar,** or cold, air masses form north of 50° north latitude and south of 50° south latitude. Polar air masses have high air pressure.

Whether an air mass is humid or dry depends on whether it forms over water or land. **Maritime** air masses form over oceans. Water evaporates from the oceans, so the air can become very humid. **Continental** air masses form over land, in the middle of continents, and are dry.

READING STRATEGIES

Reading Tip Review with students the outline format. If necessary, provide a model outline on the board to remind students how to arrange numerals and letters. Student outlines might begin as follows:

I. Types of Air Masses
  A. Tropical
    1. Maritime Tropical
    2. Continental Tropical
  B. Polar

Vocabulary Point out to students that the term *cyclone,* as it is used in this section, has a somewhat different meaning than its common usage. Many people use the term *cyclone* to mean a tornado, a type of severe storm students will learn about in Section 2. In this section, the term *cyclone* is used to refer to any large, swirling air mass that has low pressure at the center. Unlike a tornado, a cyclone may cover thousands of kilometers.

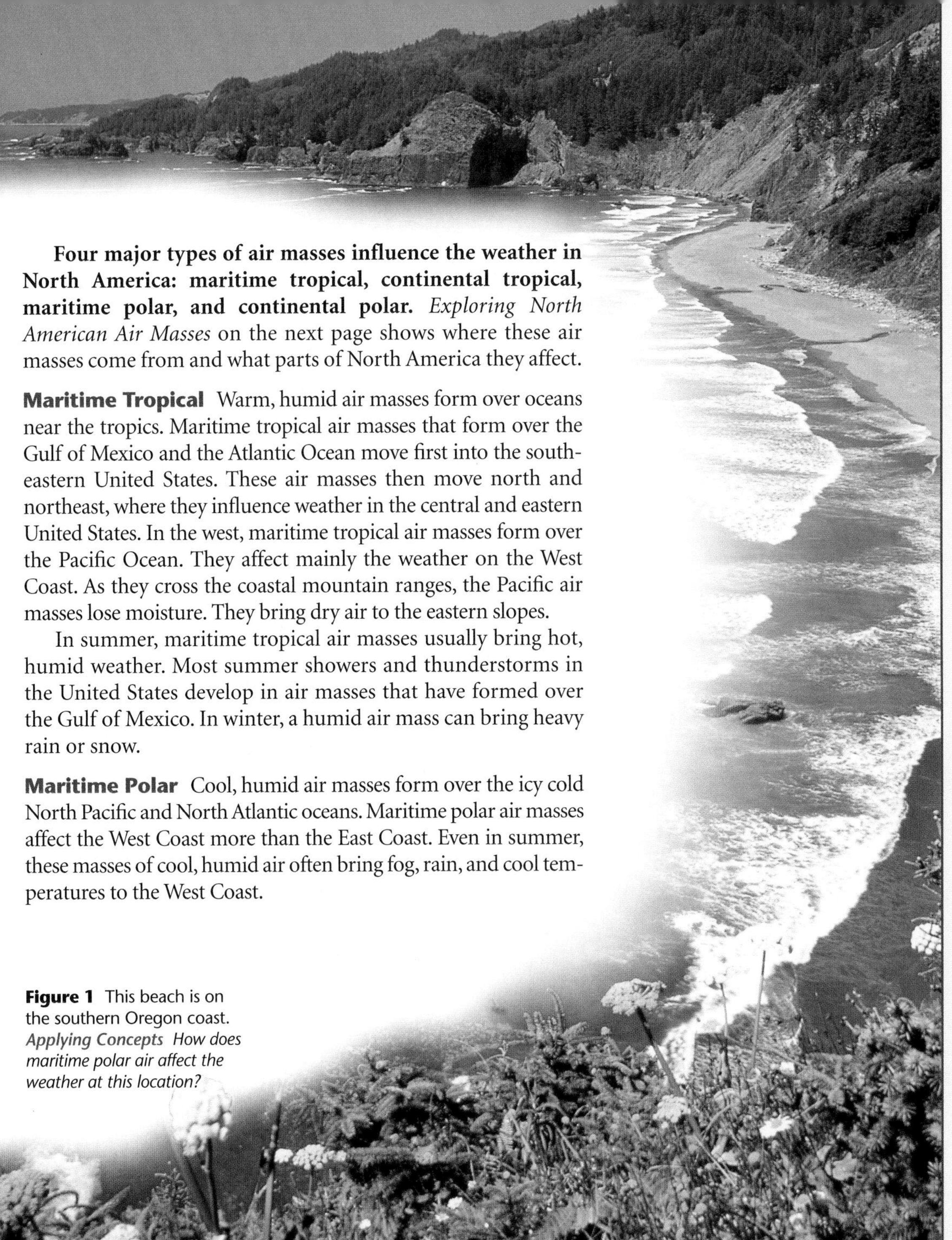

Four major types of air masses influence the weather in North America: maritime tropical, continental tropical, maritime polar, and continental polar. *Exploring North American Air Masses* on the next page shows where these air masses come from and what parts of North America they affect.

Maritime Tropical Warm, humid air masses form over oceans near the tropics. Maritime tropical air masses that form over the Gulf of Mexico and the Atlantic Ocean move first into the southeastern United States. These air masses then move north and northeast, where they influence weather in the central and eastern United States. In the west, maritime tropical air masses form over the Pacific Ocean. They affect mainly the weather on the West Coast. As they cross the coastal mountain ranges, the Pacific air masses lose moisture. They bring dry air to the eastern slopes.

In summer, maritime tropical air masses usually bring hot, humid weather. Most summer showers and thunderstorms in the United States develop in air masses that have formed over the Gulf of Mexico. In winter, a humid air mass can bring heavy rain or snow.

Maritime Polar Cool, humid air masses form over the icy cold North Pacific and North Atlantic oceans. Maritime polar air masses affect the West Coast more than the East Coast. Even in summer, these masses of cool, humid air often bring fog, rain, and cool temperatures to the West Coast.

Figure 1 This beach is on the southern Oregon coast. *Applying Concepts How does maritime polar air affect the weather at this location?*

2 Facilitate

Types of Air Masses

Building Inquiry Skills: Applying Concepts

Some students may need to review concepts covered in earlier chapters to understand the material presented in this section. Check their comprehension of relevant concepts by asking: **How does warm ocean water or a warm land surface heat the air above it?** *(By radiation and conduction of heat from the surface to the air above it and by convection, which carries the heated air high up into the atmosphere in air currents)* **Which type of air mass would you expect to contain more moisture, a maritime air mass or a continental air mass?** *(A maritime air mass, because it forms over the ocean)* **Would a maritime tropical air mass or a maritime polar air mass have more moisture?** *(A maritime tropical air mass, because it is warmer and warm air can hold more moisture than cold air)* **learning modality: verbal**

Including All Students

Help students distinguish among the different types of air masses covered in this section. Challenge them to create crossword puzzles incorporating the terms *tropical, polar, maritime,* and *continental.* After students have created their puzzles, urge them to exchange puzzles with a partner and try to solve them. **learning modality: limited English proficiency**

Program Resources

- **Unit 4 Resources** 13-1 Lesson Plan; 13-1 Section Summary
- **Guided Reading and Study Workbook** Section 13-1

Answers to Self-Assessment

Caption Question

Figure 1 It causes the weather to be cool and humid and often foggy and rainy.

Ongoing Assessment

Writing Have students explain the similarities and differences between polar and tropical air masses and between maritime and continental air masses.

EXPLORING

North American Air Masses

Invite students to apply the information in the feature by having them identify the types of air masses that affect different locations, such as different regions of the United States, different states, or different cities. Include the location where students live. For each location, ask: **What type of air are you likely to find there, and where does it come from?** *(Answers will depend on the locations chosen. For example, northern California receives cool, humid air due to maritime polar air masses from the northern Pacific Ocean.)* **learning modality: visual**

Building Inquiry Skills: Predicting

Point out that when air masses move from where they originate, they tend to be modified by the terrain they pass over. For example, the cold, dry air of continental polar air masses is warmed and moistened when it passes over the Great Lakes. Ask: **How would you predict that the other three North American air masses would be modified by the terrain they usually pass over?** *(Continental tropical air masses would be cooled, maritime polar air masses would be warmed and dried, maritime tropical air masses would be cooled and dried.)* **learning modality: logical/mathematical**

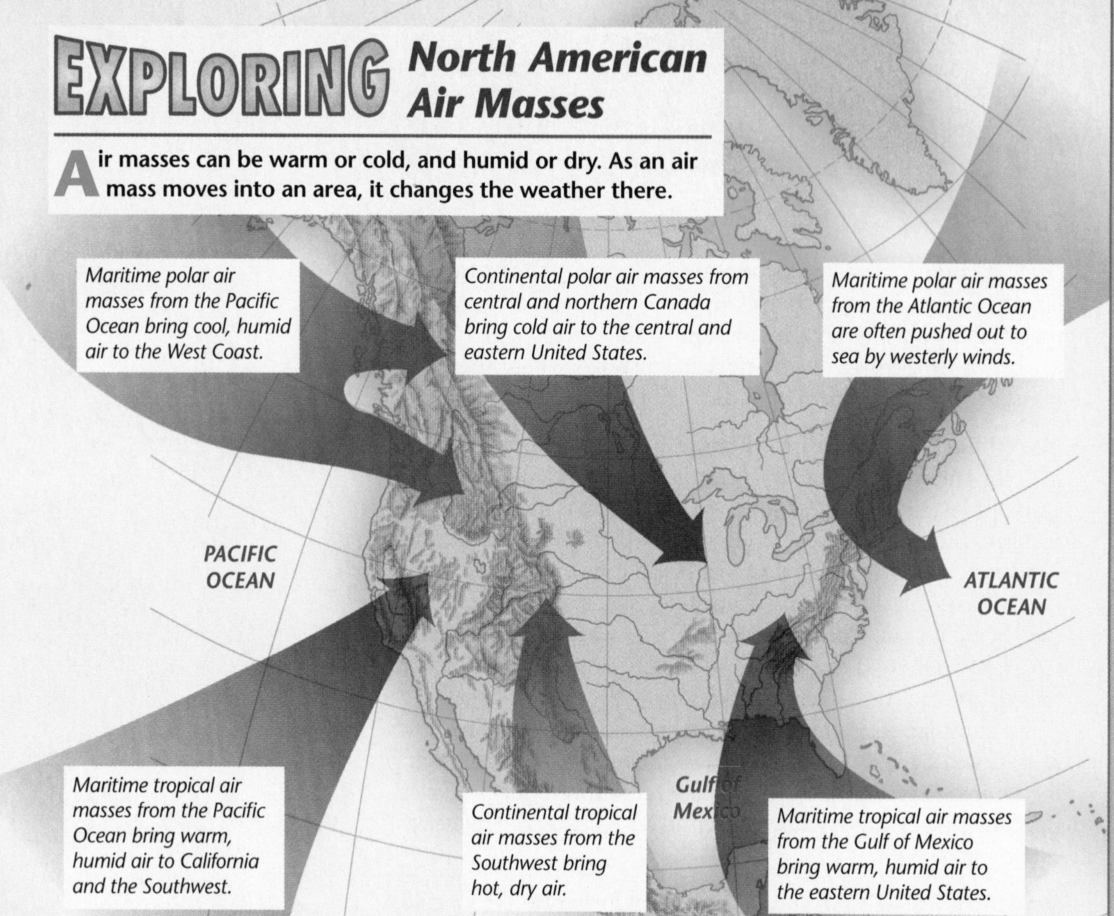

Continental Tropical Hot, dry air masses form only in summer over dry areas of the Southwest and northern Mexico. Continental tropical air masses cover a smaller area than other air masses. They occasionally move northeast, bringing hot, dry weather to the southern Great Plains.

Continental Polar Large continental polar air masses form over central and northern Canada and Alaska. As you would expect, continental polar air masses bring cool or cold air. In winter, continental polar air masses bring clear, cold, dry air to much of North America. Air masses that form near the Arctic Circle can bring bitterly cold weather with very low humidity. In summer, storms may occur when continental polar air masses move south and meet maritime tropical air masses moving north.

☑ *Checkpoint* *Where do continental polar air masses come from?*

Background

History of Science Up until the early 1900s, scientists thought that storms were caused by low air pressure. This conclusion was based on the fact that storms always seemed to occur in low-pressure areas. Then, in the early twentieth century, a Norwegian meteorologist named Vilhelm Bjerknes and a group of his colleagues deduced that storms are caused by the collision of large air masses that differ from one another in temperature and humidity. Although storms do occur in low-pressure areas, the low pressure is not their cause. Rather, low pressure areas, like storms, are a result of the collision of different air masses. This finding is now accepted as one of the most important principles of modern meteorology, and it is the basic principle underlying weather forecasting today.

How Air Masses Move

Recall that the prevailing westerlies are the major wind belts in the continental United States. The prevailing westerlies generally push air masses from west to east. For example, maritime polar air masses from the Pacific Ocean are blown onto the West Coast, bringing heavy rain or snow. Continental polar air masses from central Canada enter the United States between the Rocky Mountains and the Great Lakes. These cold, dry air masses are then blown east, where they affect the weather of the central and eastern United States.

Fronts

As huge masses of air move across the land and the oceans, they bump into each other. But the air masses do not easily mix. Why don't they? Think about a bottle of oil-and-vinegar salad dressing. The less dense oil floats on top of the more dense vinegar.

Something similar happens when two air masses with different temperatures and densities collide. The area where the air masses meet and do not mix becomes a **front.** The term *front,* which is borrowed from military language, means a battle area where opposing armies meet to fight. When air masses meet at a front, the collision often causes storms and changeable weather. A front may be 15 to 200 kilometers wide and extend as much as 10 kilometers up into the troposphere.

There are four types of fronts: cold fronts, warm fronts, stationary fronts, and occluded fronts. The kind of front that develops depends on the characteristics of the air masses and how they are moving. How does each type of front affect your local weather?

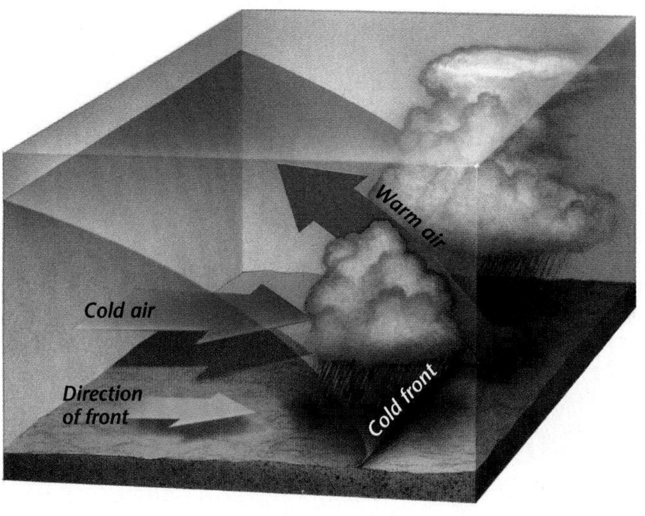

Figure 2 A cold front forms when cold air moves underneath warm air, forcing the warm air to rise.

How Air Masses Move

Inquiry Challenge

Material *world map or globe*
Time 10 minutes

Based on what they have just learned about the movement of air masses in North America, challenge students to infer which types of air masses are likely to affect the weather of Europe. First provide students with a world map or globe, and then ask: **Where do you think air masses come from that move over the European continent?** *(The Atlantic Ocean, northern Eurasia, and the African continent)* **What type of air do you think they bring to Europe?** *(Cool humid air from the Atlantic Ocean, cold dry air from northern Eurasia, and hot dry air from Africa)* **learning modality: logical/mathematical**

Fronts

Including All Students

Materials *red and blue modeling clay*
Time 5 minutes

Give hands-on learners an opportunity to model the formation of warm and cold fronts using wedges of red and blue modeling clay to represent warm and cold air masses, respectively. For each type of front that students model, ask: **In which direction is the front moving?** *(For the cold front, toward the warm air mass; for the warm front, toward the cold air mass)* **learning modality: kinesthetic**

Media and Technology

Transparencies "North American Air Masses," Transparency 48; "Cold Front," Transparency 49

Answers to Self-Assessment

Checkpoint

Continental polar air masses come from central and northern Canada and Alaska.

Ongoing Assessment

Oral Presentation Call on students to name the four types of air masses that influence weather in North America. Then call on other students to state where each type of air mass forms, whether it is warm or cold, and whether it is humid or dry.

Using the Visuals: Figure 3

Help students understand the similarities and differences between warm and cold fronts by having them compare and contrast illustrations of each type of front. Ask: **How does Figures 3, which shows the formation of a warm front, differ from Figure 2, which shows the formation of a cold front?** *(In Figure 3, the warm air mass moves up over the cold air mass; in Figure 2, the cold air mass moves underneath the warm air mass.)* **How are the two figures similar?** *(In both cases, the warm air rises and cools, causing water vapor to condense out of it and form clouds.)* **learning modality: visual**

Demonstration

ACTIVITY

Materials *tall heat-resistant jar or beaker, cold water, pepper, stirrer, container of hot water, food coloring, candle, matches*
Time 15 minutes

Do this demonstration to show students how fronts form. Half-fill a tall, heat-resistant jar or beaker with cold water. Stir pepper into the water until it is mixed throughout. Add food coloring to a container of hot water, mix well, and then gently pour the hot water into the jar of cold water. The two layers of water should remain separate and mix only slightly. Light a candle and hold the jar above it. As the cold water in the bottom of the jar heats up, the pepper will move upward due to convection. However, the pepper will not penetrate the top layer of colored water but instead collect at the "front" between the two layers of water. Ask: **Why doesn't the pepper rise up through the top layer of water?** *(Because the top layer of water is warmer and will not mix with the cooler layer of water containing the pepper)* **learning modality: visual**

Cold Fronts As you know, cold air is dense and tends to sink. Warm air is less dense and tends to rise. When a rapidly moving cold air mass runs into a slowly moving warm air mass, the denser cold air slides under the lighter warm air. The warm air is pushed upward, as shown in Figure 2. The front that forms is called a cold front.

As the warm air rises, it cools. Remember that warm air can hold more water vapor than cool air. The rising air soon reaches the dew point, the temperature at which the water vapor in the air condenses into droplets of liquid water. Clouds form. If there is a lot of water vapor in the warm air, heavy rain or snow may fall. What will happen if the warm air mass contains only a little water vapor? In this case, the cold front may be accompanied by only cloudy skies.

Cold fronts move quickly, so they can cause abrupt weather changes, including violent thunderstorms. After a cold front passes through an area, cool, dry air moves in, often bringing clear skies and cooler temperatures.

Warm Fronts Clouds, storms, and rain also accompany warm fronts. At a warm front, a moving warm air mass collides with a slowly moving cold air mass. Because cold air is more dense than warm air, the warm air moves over the cold air, as shown in Figure 3. If the warm air is humid, showers and light rain fall along the front where the warm and cold air meet. If the warm air is dry, scattered clouds form. Because warm fronts move more slowly than cold fronts, the weather may be rainy or foggy for several days. After a warm front passes through an area, the weather is likely to be warm and humid. In winter, warm fronts bring snow.

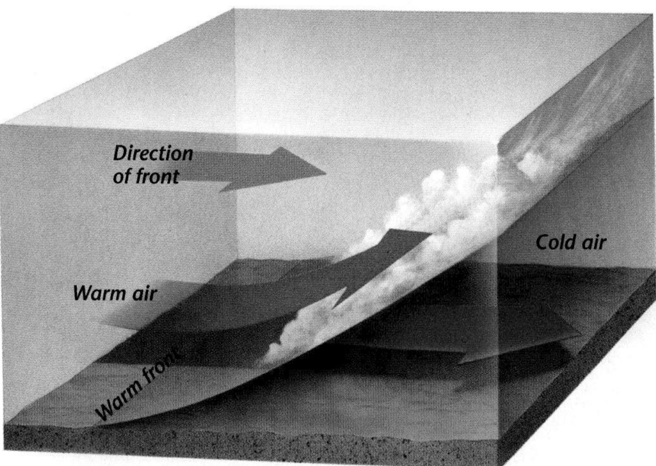

Figure 3 A warm front forms when warm air moves over cold air. *Interpreting Diagrams What kind of weather forms at a warm front?*

Background

Facts and Figures Like fingerprints or snowflakes, no two fronts are exactly alike. For example, the slope of a front can vary considerably, from about 1:100 (1 km of vertical distance covers 100 km of horizontal distance) for a cold front to about 1:200 for a warm front.

The slope of a front is an important determinant of the type of weather the front brings. A cold front with a very steep slope is likely to bring a narrow band of violent storms extending less than 100 km. A warm front with a very gradual slope, on the other hand, is likely to bring cloudy weather but no storms. However, the area affected by the cloudy weather may extend for many hundreds of kilometers.

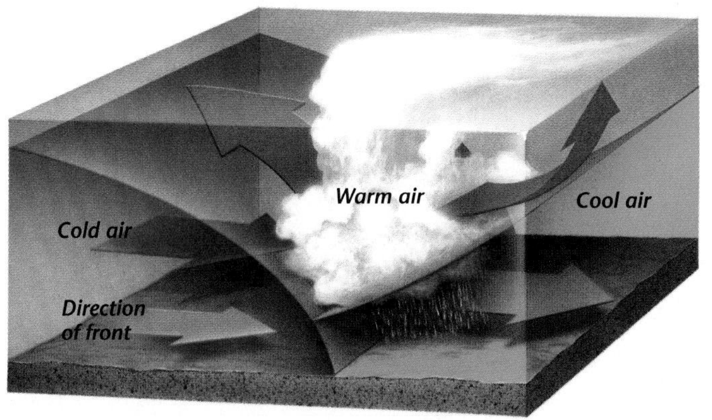

Figure 4 When a cold air mass and a cool air mass come together, the warm air caught between them is forced upward. The result is an occluded front.

Stationary Fronts Sometimes cold and warm air masses meet, but neither one has enough force to move the other. The two air masses face each other in a "standoff." In this case, the front is called a stationary front. Where the warm and cool air meet, water vapor in the warm air condenses into rain, snow, fog, or clouds. If a stationary front remains stalled over an area, it may bring many days of clouds and precipitation.

Occluded Fronts The most complex weather situation occurs at an occluded front, shown in Figure 4. At an occluded front, a warm air mass is caught between two cooler air masses. The denser cool air masses move underneath the less dense warm air mass and push it upward. The two cooler air masses meet in the middle and may mix. The temperature near the ground becomes cooler. The warm air mass is cut off, or **occluded,** from the ground. As the warm air cools and its water vapor condenses, the weather may turn cloudy and rainy or snowy.

Checkpoint What type of front forms when two air masses meet and neither one can move?

Cyclones and Anticyclones

If you look at a weather map, you will see areas marked with an L. The L is short for "low," and indicates an area of relatively low air pressure. A swirling center of low air pressure is called a **cyclone,** from a Greek word meaning "wheel."

As warm air at the center of a cyclone rises, the air pressure decreases. Cooler air blows toward this low-pressure area from nearby areas where the air pressure is higher. Winds spiral inward toward the center of the system. Recall that in the Northern Hemisphere the Coriolis effect deflects winds to the right.

Classifying

At home, watch the weather forecast on television. Make a note of each time the weather reporter mentions a front. Classify the fronts mentioned or shown as cold, warm, stationary, or occluded. Also, note what type of weather is predicted to occur when the front arrives. Is each type of front always associated with the same type of weather?

Sharpen your Skills

Classifying

Tips Have students continue this activity over several days in order to observe at least three different types of fronts.

Expected Outcome Students should find that all types of fronts are associated with clouds and precipitation. However, cold fronts tend to be associated with more abrupt changes in the weather.

Extend Have students continue to monitor weather changes after the fronts pass through their area. Ask: **What type of weather follows each type of front?** *(Cold and occluded fronts are followed by cool, clear weather, warm fronts by warm, humid weather.)* **learning modality: logical/mathematical**

Cyclones and Anticyclones

Including All Students

Materials *two balloons, pencil, thread, ruler*
Time 5 minutes

Instruct students to inflate two balloons to 10 cm in diameter and tie them to the opposite ends of a pencil with pieces of thread 30 cm long. Then have them hold the pencil level, with the balloons 8 cm from their faces, and blow gently between the balloons. Ask: **Why did the balloons move closer together?** *(Blowing away the air between the balloons decreased the air pressure between them. The higher air pressure on the opposite side of the balloons then pushed the two balloons closer together.)* Ask: **How is this like a cyclone?** *(In a cyclone, winds blow in toward the center because there is low pressure there.)* **learning modality: kinesthetic**

Media and Technology

Transparencies "Warm Front," Transparency 50; "Occluded Front," Transparency 51

Answers to Self-Assessment

Caption Question

Figure 3 Clouds, storms, and precipitation form at a warm front.

Checkpoint

A stationary front forms when two air masses meet and neither one can move.

Ongoing Assessment

Drawing Have students create drawings to represent a warm front and a cold front. They should label the air masses as "cold" or "warm" and use arrows to indicate the direction the air masses are moving.

3 Assess

Section 1 Review Answers

1. temperature and humidity
2. A front is the area where two air masses meet and do not mix. A cold front forms when cold air moves underneath warm air. A warm front forms when warm air moves over cold air. A stationary front forms when a warm and a cold air mass meet but neither can move the other. An occluded front forms when a warm air mass is caught between two cool air masses and cut off from the ground.
3. A swirling center of low air pressure; storms and precipitation
4. Because East Coast maritime polar air masses are blown out to sea by prevailing westerlies
5. Maritime tropical and polar air masses are humid; continental tropical and polar air masses are dry.

CHAPTER PROJECT

Check Your Progress

Check that each student has started to collect weather maps. Comparisons of weather in the three locations should include all the weather factors represented on the maps.

Performance Assessment

Skills Check Have students describe the direction of winds in cyclones and anticyclones in the Southern Hemisphere.

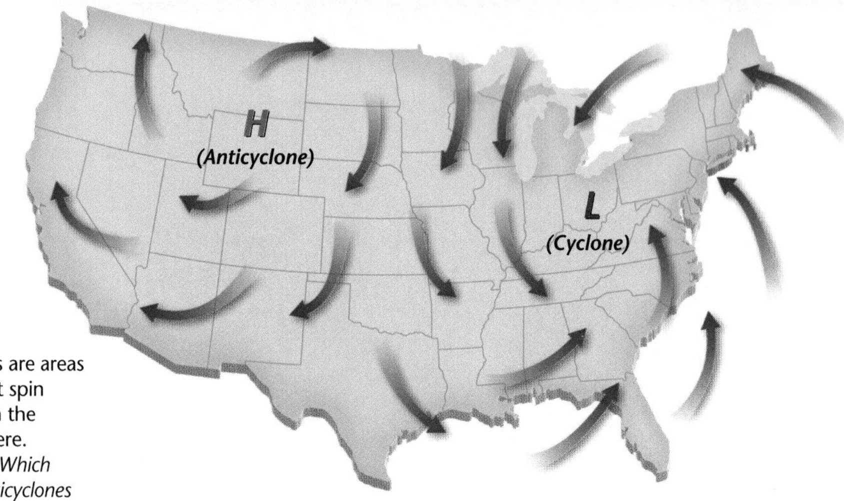

Figure 5 Cyclones are areas of low pressure that spin counterclockwise in the Northern Hemisphere. ***Interpreting Maps*** *Which way do winds in anticyclones spin?*

Because of this, winds in a cyclone spin counterclockwise in the Northern Hemisphere, as shown in Figure 5.

Cyclones play a large part in the weather of the United States. As air rises in a cyclone, the air cools, forming clouds and precipitation. **Cyclones and decreasing air pressure are associated with storms and precipitation.**

As its name suggests, an anticyclone is the opposite of a cyclone in most ways. **Anticyclones** are high-pressure centers of dry air. Anticyclones are also called "highs"—H on a weather map. Winds spiral outward from the center of an anticyclone, moving toward areas of lower pressure. Because of the Coriolis effect, winds in an anticyclone spin clockwise in the Northern Hemisphere. Because air moves out from the center of the anticyclone, cool air moves downward from higher in the troposphere. As the cool air falls, it warms up, so its relative humidity drops. The descending air in an anticyclone causes dry, clear weather.

Section 1 Review

1. What two main characteristics are used to classify air masses?
2. What is a front? Name and describe four types of fronts.
3. What is a cyclone? What type of weather does it bring?
4. Why do maritime polar air masses have more effect on the West Coast than the East Coast?
5. **Thinking Critically Classifying** Classify the four major types of air masses according to whether they are dry or humid.

CHAPTER PROJECT

Check Your Progress

Collect newspaper weather maps for about a week, and arrange them in order. Look carefully at how symbols on the map have moved from one day to the next. What patterns do you see from day to day in different weather factors? How does the weather in your community differ from the weather in the two other locations you selected?

Answers to Self-Assessment

Caption Question

Figure 5 Winds in anticyclones spin clockwise in the Northern Hemisphere.

Program Resources

◆ **Unit 4 Resources** 13-1 Review and Reinforce; 13-1 Enrich

Storms

DISCOVER ACTIVITY

Can You Make a Tornado?

1. Fill a large jar three-quarters full with water. Add a drop of liquid dish detergent and a penny or marble.
2. Put the lid on the jar tightly. Now move the jar in a circle until the water inside begins to spin.

Think It Over

Observing What happens to the water in the jar? Describe the pattern that forms. How is it like a tornado? Unlike a tornado?

GUIDE FOR READING

- What are the main kinds of storms? How do they form?
- What measures can you take to ensure safety in a storm?

Reading Tip As you read, create a table comparing thunderstorms, tornadoes, hurricanes, and snowstorms. Include temperature, precipitation, and safety rules.

Early in 1998, a series of powerful tornadoes roared through central Florida. With winds as high as 210 miles per hour, the tornadoes dropped cars into living rooms, crumpled trailers, and destroyed businesses and school buildings. They were the deadliest tornadoes ever to hit Florida. These tornadoes were not the only violent weather that year. In California the problem was rain. Record rainfalls brought devastating floods and mudslides.

What was causing these disasters? Meteorologists had an answer: El Niño. El Niño is a weather pattern related to the temperature of the water in the tropical Pacific Ocean. When temperatures there rise, they set off a series of events that can influence weather half a world away.

Have you ever experienced a tornado, hurricane, or other severe storm? When rain pours down, thunder crashes, or snowdrifts pile up, it may be hard to think about the actions of air pressure and air masses. Yet these are the causes of severe storms as well as the weather you experience every day.

A **storm** is a violent disturbance in the atmosphere. Storms involve sudden changes in air pressure, which in turn cause rapid air movements. Conditions that bring one kind of storm often cause other kinds of storms in the same area. For example, the conditions that cause thunderstorms can also cause tornadoes.

Figure 6 Tornadoes caused tremendous damage in Florida and other parts of the southeastern United States in 1998.

READING STRATEGIES

Reading Tip There should be a column for each kind of storm. In addition to rows for temperature, precipitation, and safety, students may add rows to their tables for recording such factors as wind speed, size of storm, length of time the storm lasts, and the type of damage it does. Have students save their tables for review.

Program Resources

- **Unit 4 Resources** 13-2 Lesson Plan; 13-2 Section Summary

Storms

Objectives

After completing the lesson, students will be able to

- list the main kinds of storms and explain how they form;
- describe measures they can take to ensure safety in a storm.

Key Terms storm, lightning, tornado, hurricane, storm surge, evacuate

1 Engage/Explore

Activating Prior Knowledge

Introduce students to tornadoes and other storms by asking: **Did you ever see a dust devil, a spinning wind that picks up and carries dust, dead leaves, and other debris?** *(Most students probably will say "yes.")* **What did it look like?** *(a funnel)* **What do think causes dust devils?** *(Air swirling in a circle)* Point out that dust devils resemble small tornadoes. Explain that they are caused by hot air rising rapidly from the heated ground. As the hot air rises, the wind blows it into a spinning motion and it picks up loose material. Add that most dust devils last just a few seconds, rise only a few meters, and cause no damage. Tell students that a similar type of air movement also causes tornadoes, as they will learn in this section.

DISCOVER ACTIVITY

Skills Focus observing
Materials *large plastic jar with lid, water, liquid dish detergent, penny or marble*
Time 10 minutes
Tips Tell students not to shake the jar or slosh the water back and forth to create bubbles. Instead, they should swirl the water gently with a circular motion.
Expected Outcome The water should swirl around in the jar like a tornado.
Think It Over Students should say that the water swirls in a funnel-shaped spiral. It is like a tornado because the water spins around in a circle. It is unlike a tornado because it occurs in water instead of air.

2 Facilitate

Thunderstorms

Demonstration

Materials *bottle with plastic cap, copper wire, aluminum foil, plastic comb, wool fabric*
Time 10 minutes

Show the class how lightning occurs with this demonstration. Push a short piece of copper wire through a small hole in the cap of a bottle. Form the bottom end of the wire into a hook and hang a small strip of aluminum foil over it. Put the cap on the bottle with the hook and foil inside. Rub a comb on wool fabric to give it an electrical charge and then touch the comb to the end of the wire protruding from the top of the bottle cap. Students will see the ends of the foil strip move apart from one another. Ask: **Why did the ends of the foil strip move?** *(Students may not know.)* Explain that the foil became charged with electricity, which was transmitted through the wire from the comb, causing the two ends of the foil strip to repel each other. Ask: **How is this like lightning?** *(A charge is built up when particles in clouds rub together, and when the electricity is discharged from one part of the cloud to another or to the ground, lightning occurs.)* **learning modality: visual**

TRY THIS

Skills Focus calculating
Materials *watch with second hand*
Time 10 minutes
Expected Outcome The number of seconds between the lightning flash and the sound of the thunder will depend on how far away the lightning is. If the lightning is very close, the thunder will occur just a split second later. If the lightning is very far away, the thunder may not even be audible. If the length of time between the lightning and thunder is increasing, the storm is moving away from you. If the length of time is decreasing, the storm is moving toward you. **learning modality: logical/mathematical**

Figure 7 The anvil shape of this cloud is typical of cumulonimbus clouds that produce thunderstorms. *Applying Concepts Why do cumulonimbus clouds often form along cold fronts?*

Lightning Distances

ACTIVITY

Because light travels faster than sound, you see a lightning flash before you hear the clap of thunder. Here's how to calculate your distance from a thunderstorm.

CAUTION: *Do this activity inside a building only.*

1. Count the number of seconds between the moment when you see the lightning and when you hear the thunder.
2. Divide the number of seconds you counted by three to get the distance in kilometers. Example:

$$\frac{15 \text{ s}}{3 \text{ s/km}} = 5 \text{ km}$$

Calculating Wait for another flash of lightning and calculate the distance again. How can you tell whether a thunderstorm is moving toward you or away from you?

Thunderstorms

Do you find thunderstorms frightening? Exciting? A little of both? As you watch the brilliant flashes of lightning and listen to long rolls of thunder, you have probably wondered what caused them.

How Thunderstorms Form Thunderstorms are heavy rainstorms accompanied by thunder and lightning. **Thunderstorms form within large cumulonimbus clouds, or thunderheads.** Most cumulonimbus clouds and thunderstorms form when warm air is forced upward at a cold front. Cumulonimbus clouds also form on hot, humid afternoons in the spring and summer. In both cases, the warm, humid air rises rapidly. As the air rises, it cools, forming dense thunderheads. Heavy rain falls, sometimes along with hail.

Thunderstorms produce strong upward and downward winds—updrafts and downdrafts—inside clouds. When a downdraft strikes the ground, the air spreads out in all directions, producing bursts of wind called wind shear. Wind shear has caused a number of airplane accidents during takeoff or landing.

Lightning and Thunder During a thunderstorm, areas of positive and negative electrical charges build up in the storm clouds. **Lightning** is a sudden spark, or energy discharge, as these charges jump between parts of a cloud, between nearby clouds, or between the cloud and the ground. Lightning is similar to the shocks you sometimes feel when you touch a metal object on a very dry day, but on a much larger scale.

What causes thunder? A lightning bolt can heat the air near it to as much as 30,000°C, much hotter than the surface of the sun. The rapidly heated air expands suddenly and explosively. Thunder is the sound of the explosion. Because light travels faster than sound, you see lightning before you hear thunder.

Background

Facts and Figures Just how serious a threat do thunderstorms pose? At any given moment, about 1,800 thunderstorms are occurring somewhere on Earth. That's a total of 16 million thunderstorms a year worldwide, of which an estimated 100,000 occur in the United States. Every second about 100 bolts of lightning strike Earth's surface. About 80 people in the United States are killed by lightning each year (more than are typically killed each year by tornadoes.) Over the last 10 years, lightning started more than 15,000 fires in the United States and caused hundreds of millions of dollars in damage each year and the destruction of two million acres of forest. The high winds that often accompany thunderstorms can be even more damaging. Thunderstorm winds can exceed 160 km/h, which is as fast as the winds of a hurricane.

Thunderstorm Safety When lightning strikes INTEGRATING HEALTH the ground, the hot, expanding air can start forest fires. When lightning strikes people or animals, it acts like a powerful electric shock. Being struck by lightning can cause unconsciousness, serious burns, or even heart failure.

What should you do to remain safe if you are caught outside during a thunderstorm? **During thunderstorms, avoid touching metal objects because they can conduct electricity from lightning into your body.** Lightning usually strikes the tallest nearby object, such as a tree, house, or flagpole. To protect buildings from lightning, people install metal lightning rods at the highest point on a roof. Lightning rods intercept a lightning stroke and conduct the electricity through cables safely into the ground.

In open spaces, such as a golf course, people can be in danger because they are the tallest objects in the area. It is equally dangerous to seek shelter under a tree, because lightning may strike the tree and you at the same time. Instead, find a low area away from trees, fences, and poles. Crouch with your head down and your hands on your knees. If you are swimming or in a boat, get to shore and find shelter away from the water.

If you are inside a house during a thunderstorm, avoid touching telephones, electrical appliances, or plumbing fixtures, all of which can conduct electricity into the house. It is usually safe to stay in a car with a hard top during a thunderstorm because the electricity will move along the metal skin of the car and jump to the ground. However, do not touch any metal inside the car.

Figure 8 Lightning occurs when electricity jumps within clouds, between clouds, or between a cloud and the ground.

☑ *Checkpoint* *Why is lightning dangerous?*

Tornadoes

A tornado is one of the most frightening and destructive types of storms. A **tornado** is a rapidly whirling, funnel-shaped cloud that reaches down from a storm cloud to touch Earth's surface. If a tornado occurs over a lake or ocean, it is known as a waterspout. Tornadoes are usually brief, but can be deadly. They may touch the ground for 15 minutes or less and be only a few hundred meters across, but wind speeds may approach 480 kilometers per hour.

Integrating Health

There are many naive conceptions about lightning that may cause people to take needless risks in thunderstorms. Address some of these naive conceptions by first asking: **Do you think the old saying is true that lightning never strikes twice in the same place?** *(Students may say "yes".)* Tell students that the chance of lightning striking the same place twice is very small, but there is no reason it cannot happen. In fact, some buildings and even people have been struck by lightning repeatedly. Other myths about lightning include that there is no danger from lightning if it is not raining and that rubber-soled shoes will protect you from being struck by lightning.
learning modality: verbal

Tornadoes

Including All Students

Materials *raw potato, plastic drinking straw*
Time 5 minutes

Tell students that the force of the wind in a tornado may be great enough to drive a drinking straw through a board. If students find this hard to believe, this activity will help them appreciate just how strong the wind can be. Have students place the end of a plastic drinking straw against a raw potato and push as hard as they can. The straw will bend and scarcely penetrate the potato. Now have students hold the straw at least half a meter away from the potato and drive it into the potato as fast as possible. This time the straw will penetrate the potato without bending. Ask: **Why did the straw go through the potato when you drove it in from a distance?** *(It was pushed harder.)* Add that winds in a tornado can push with such force that a blade of grass may be driven into a tree trunk.
learning modality: kinesthetic

Ongoing Assessment

Writing Challenge students to write a public service announcement for television or radio that spells out the precautions people should take to remain safe in a thunderstorm.

Media and Technology

Concept Videotape Library
Grade 6, Tape 3 "Violent Storms"

Answers to Self-Assessment

Caption Question

Figure 7 Cumulonimbus clouds often form along cold fronts because warm air is forced upward. As the warm air rises, it cools, forming dense thunderheads.

☑ *Checkpoint*

Lightning acts like a powerful shock and can cause unconsciousness, serious burns, or even heart failure.

SCIENCE & History

Call students' attention to the feature and then ask: **What types of storms are described in the feature?** *(Thunderstorms and hurricanes)* Point out that tornadoes are not included, and then ask: **Why might tornadoes have less impact on history?** *(A tornado's path of destruction tends to be narrow and short lived.)* Inform students that there are some notable exceptions to the brief, local nature of most tornadoes. For example, the Great Tri-State Tornado of March 18, 1925, killed almost 700 people in three states, and the Superoutbreak Tornadoes of April 3–4, 1974, killed more than 300 people and injured over 5,500 others in 12 states in 24 hours. Add that, unlike thunderstorms and hurricanes, exactly when and where a tornado will touch down is still difficult to predict. Suggest to students who need an extra challenge that they research other examples of tornadoes, thunderstorms, and hurricanes that had an impact, great or small, on the course of history. Urge them to share what they learn with the rest of the class.

In Your Journal Students' paragraphs will vary depending on the specific event they choose. If they choose the storms that affected the *Mayflower*, for example, they may say that, with advance warning, the settlers might have delayed their landing until the storms had passed and then settled in what is now New York City instead of Plymouth. **learning modality: verbal**

How Tornadoes Form **Tornadoes develop in low, heavy cumulonimbus clouds—the same clouds that bring thunderstorms.** Tornadoes are most likely to occur when thunderstorms are likely—in spring and early summer, often late in the afternoon when the ground is warm. The Great Plains often have the kind of weather pattern that is likely to create tornadoes: a warm, humid air mass moves north from the Gulf of Mexico into the lower Great Plains. A cold, dry air mass moves south from Canada. When the air masses meet, the cold air moves under the warm air, which rises. A squall line of thunderstorms is likely to form, with storms traveling from southwest to northeast. A single squall line can cause 10 or more tornadoes.

Tornadoes occur more often in the United States than in any other country. About 800 tornadoes occur in the United States

SCIENCE & History

Weather That Changed History

Unanticipated storms have caused incredible damage, killed numbers of people, and even changed the course of history.

1281 Japan

In an attempt to conquer Japan, Kublai Khan, the Mongol emperor of China, sent a fleet of ships carrying a huge army. A hurricane from the Pacific brought high winds and towering waves that sank the ships. The Japanese named the storm *kamikaze,* meaning "divine wind."

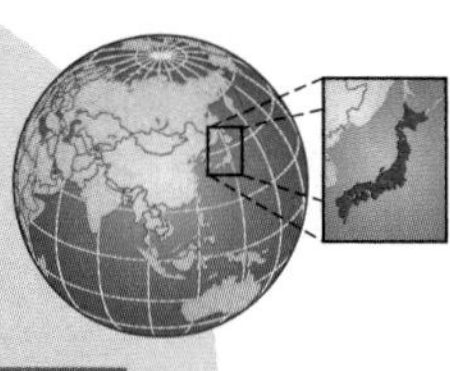

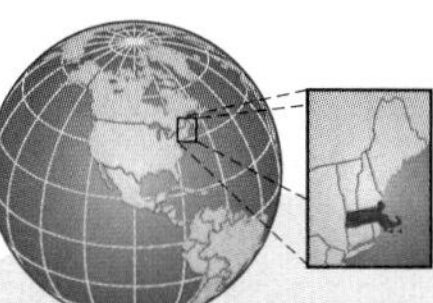

1620 Massachusetts

English Pilgrims set sail for the Americas in the *Mayflower.* They had planned to land near the mouth of the Hudson River, but turned back north because of rough seas and storms. When the Pilgrims landed farther north, they decided to stay and so established Plymouth Colony.

1300 | 1400 | 1500 | 1600

1588 England

King Philip II of Spain sent the Spanish Armada, a fleet of 130 ships, to invade England. Strong winds in the English Channel trapped the Armada near shore. Some Spanish ships escaped, but storms wrecked most of them.

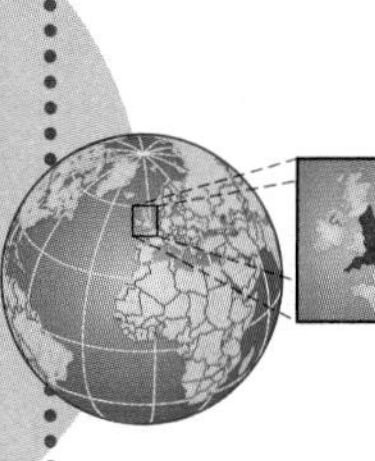

Background

Facts and Figures Tornadoes are commonly classified according to the following scale, which is called the Fujita-Pearson Tornado Intensity Scale after its inventors:

F0 Light (under 116 km/h)
F1 Moderate (116–180 km/h)
F2 Considerable (181–253 km/h)
F3 Severe (254–332 km/h)
F4 Devastating (333–419 km/h)
F5 Incredible (over 419 km/h)

The winds of tornadoes have done some amazing things. In Bedfordshire, England, in May of 1950, a tornado is reported to have plucked the feathers off several chickens, who amazingly were otherwise unharmed. Tornadoes also have lifted frogs and fish from ponds and then dropped them elsewhere, leading to the saying, "a tornado may rain frogs."

every year. Weather patterns on the Great Plains result in a "tornado alley," shown in Figure 9, that runs from north-central Texas across central Oklahoma, Kansas, and Nebraska. However, tornadoes can and do occur in nearly every part of the United States.

☑ ***Checkpoint*** *Where do tornadoes form?*

Tornado Safety A tornado can level houses on one street, but leave neighboring houses standing. INTEGRATING HEALTH Tornado damage comes from both strong winds and flying debris. The low pressure inside the tornado sucks up dust and other objects into the funnel. Tornadoes can move large objects—sheds, trailers, cars—and scatter debris many miles away. One tornado tore off a motel sign in Broken Bow, Oklahoma, and dropped it 30 miles away in Arkansas!

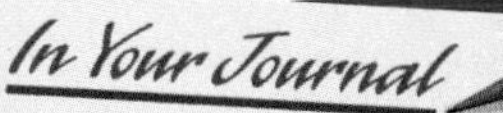

Some of these events happened before forecasters had the equipment to predict weather scientifically. Choose one of the events in the time line. Write a paragraph describing how history might have been different if the people involved had had accurate weather predictions.

1870 Great Lakes

Learning that more than 1,900 boats had sunk in storms on the Great Lakes in 1869, Congress decided to set up a national weather service, the Army Signal Corps. In 1891 the job of issuing weather warnings and forecasts went to a new agency, the U.S. Weather Bureau.

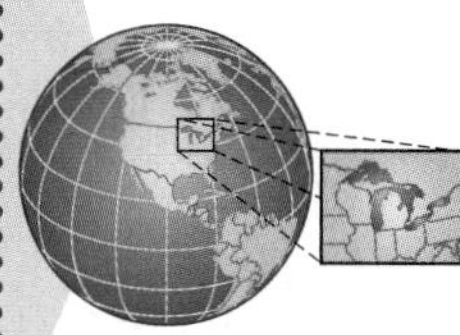

1700 **1800** **1900**

1837 North Carolina

The steamship *Home* sank during a hurricane off Ocracoke, North Carolina. In one of the worst storm-caused disasters at sea, 90 people died. In response, the U.S. Congress passed a law requiring seagoing ships to carry a life preserver for every passenger.

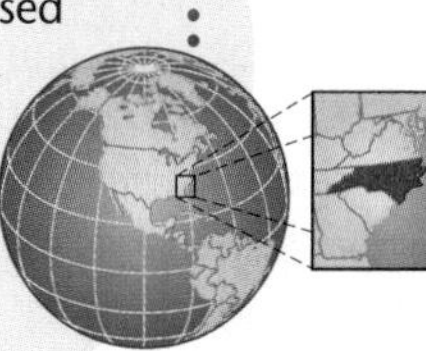

1915 Texas

When a hurricane struck the port city of Galveston in 1900, it killed 6,000 people and destroyed much of the city. As a result, a seawall 5 meters high and 16 kilometers long was built. When another hurricane struck in 1915, the seawall greatly reduced the amount of damage.

Answers to Self-Assessment

☑ ***Checkpoint***

Tornadoes form in low, heavy cumulonimbus clouds.

Integrating Health

To help students take the danger of tornadoes seriously, tell them that tornadoes cause damage and take lives in three ways: the direct force of the wind, the twisting force of the wind, and the lift and drop force at the center of the tornado. Ask a volunteer to record ideas as students brainstorm specific ways that these three tornado forces can cause damage and claim lives. *(Possible ways might include: the direct force of the wind can turn over cars, knock down buildings, and blow debris that smashes windows and kills people; the twisting force of the wind can twist signs off buildings and twist trees and power poles out of the ground; and the lift and drop force at the center of the tornado can suck people and objects high into the air and drop them down elsewhere.)* **cooperative learning**

Ongoing Assessment

Skills Check Have students compare and contrast tornadoes and thunderstorms.

Tornadoes, continued

Using the Visuals: Figure 9

Use the map in Figure 9 to help students understand why the central part of the United States has so many tornadoes. Ask: **What is the reddish shaded area called?** *(Tornado Alley)* **Why is it called that?** *(More tornadoes occur there than anywhere else in the United States.)* **Why do you think so many tornadoes occur there?** *(Because cold and warm air masses meet there)* **learning modality: visual**

Addressing Naive Conceptions

Ask students if the following statements are true or false: **If you don't have a basement, the safest place in your home in the event of a tornado is the southwest corner.** *(False. The safest place is a small windowless room or closet in the center of the house.)* **If a tornado catches you on the road, it is best to stay in your car.** *(False. A tornado can overturn a car or pick it up and drop it elsewhere. You should leave the car and go to a well-built building or lie flat in a low place with your head covered.)* Based on how students respond, discuss any misconceptions they may hold. For example, if students believe that the safest place in a home without a basement is an outside corner, explain that an outside room is more at risk of damage from the wind, and windows in outside rooms put you at risk of flying glass. **learning modality: verbal**

Hurricanes

Including All Students

Explain to students that hurricanes are given names according to certain rules. They are named alphabetically, alternating between masculine and feminine names. For example, in 1999, the first storm of the season was named Arlene, the second Bret, the third Cindy, and so on. Challenge the class to come up with their own list of names for 15 hurricanes. Give each student a number from 1 to 15 and have the student apply the rules to name the hurricane of that number. **limited English proficiency**

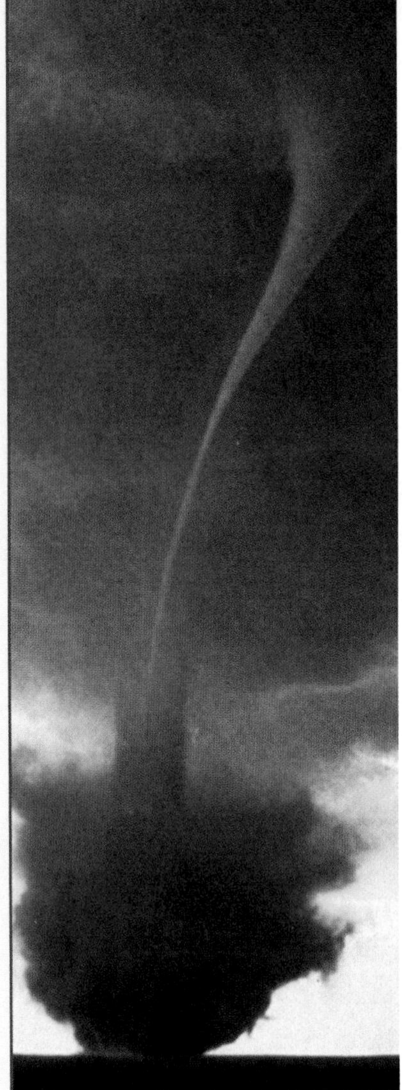

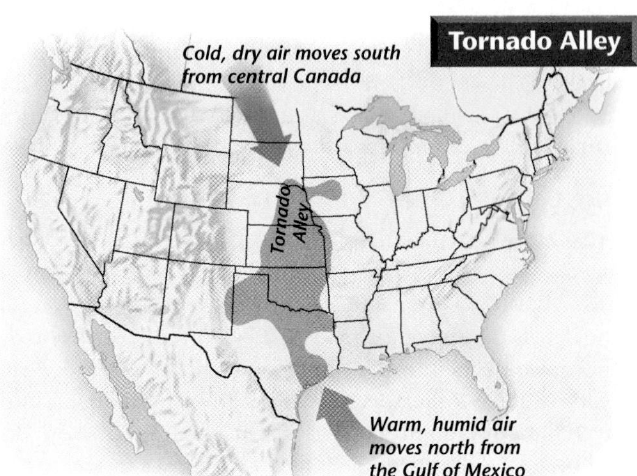

Figure 9 A tornado can cause a lot of damage in a short period of time. The map shows where tornadoes are most likely to occur in the United States.
Interpreting Maps Which states are partially located in "tornado alley"?

What should you do if a tornado is predicted in your area? A "tornado watch" is an announcement that tornadoes are possible in your area. Watch for approaching thunderstorms. A "tornado warning" is an announcement that a tornado has been seen in the sky or on weather radar. If you hear a tornado warning, move to a safe area as soon as you can. Do not wait until you actually see the tornado.

The safest place to be during a tornado is in the basement of a well-built building. If the building you are in does not have a basement, move to the middle of the ground floor. Stay away from windows and doors that could break and fly through the air. Lie on the floor under a sturdy piece of furniture, such as a large table. If you are outdoors or in a car or mobile home, move to a building or lie flat in a ditch.

☑ *Checkpoint* ***What is the difference between a tornado watch and a tornado warning?***

Hurricanes

Between June and November, people who live in the eastern United States hear weather reports much like this: "A hurricane warning has been issued for the Atlantic coast from Florida to North Carolina. Hurricane Michael has winds of over 160 kilometers per hour and is moving north at about 65 kilometers per hour." A **hurricane** is a tropical storm that has winds of 119 kilometers per hour or higher. A typical hurricane is about 600 kilometers across.

Hurricanes also form in the Pacific and Indian oceans. In the western Pacific Ocean, hurricanes are called typhoons. Although hurricanes may be destructive, they bring much-needed rainfall to South Asia and Southeast Asia.

Background

Facts and Figures Hurricanes are ranked on a scale called the Saffir-Simpson Scale, which is based on maximum wind speed:

1 Minimal (119–153 km/h)
2 Moderate (154–177 km/h)
3 Extensive (178–209 km/h)
4 Extreme (210–250 km/h)
5 Catastrophic (over 250 km/h)

Two recent devastating hurricanes were Agnes and Andrew. Agnes, which occurred in June of 1972, caused severe flooding from North Carolina to New York and spawned 17 tornadoes in Florida and Georgia. Andrew, which occurred in August of 1992, caused over $25 billion worth of damage, making it the most expensive hurricane in the history of the United States up to that date.

How Hurricanes Form A typical hurricane that strikes the United States forms in the Atlantic Ocean north of the equator in August, September, or October. **A hurricane begins over warm water as a low-pressure area, or tropical disturbance.** If the tropical disturbance grows in size and strength, it becomes a tropical storm, which may then become a hurricane.

A hurricane gets its energy from the warm, humid air at the ocean's surface. As this air rises and forms clouds, more air is drawn into the system. As with other storm systems, winds spiral inward toward the areas of low pressure. Inside the storm are bands of very high winds and heavy rains. The lowest air pressure and warmest temperatures are at the center of the hurricane. The lower the air pressure at the center of a storm, the faster the winds blow toward the center. Hurricane winds may be as strong as 320 kilometers per hour.

The Eye of the Hurricane The center of a hurricane is a ring of clouds surrounding a quiet "eye," as shown in Figure 10. If you were in the path of a hurricane, you would notice that the wind gets stronger as the eye approaches. When the eye arrives, the weather changes suddenly. The winds grow calm and the sky may clear. After the eye passes, the storm resumes, but the wind blows from the opposite direction.

How Hurricanes Move Hurricanes last longer than other storms, usually a week or more. Hurricanes that form in the Atlantic Ocean are steered by easterly trade winds toward the Caribbean islands and the southeastern United States. After a hurricane passes over land, it no longer has warm, moist air to draw energy from. The hurricane gradually slows down and loses strength, although heavy rainfall may continue for a number of days.

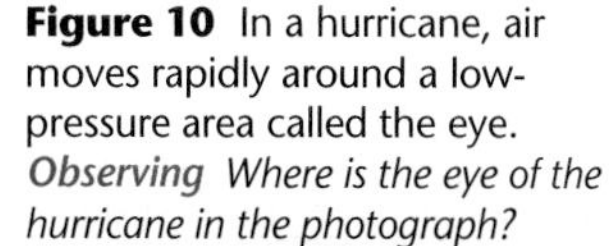

Figure 10 In a hurricane, air moves rapidly around a low-pressure area called the eye. *Observing* *Where is the eye of the hurricane in the photograph?*

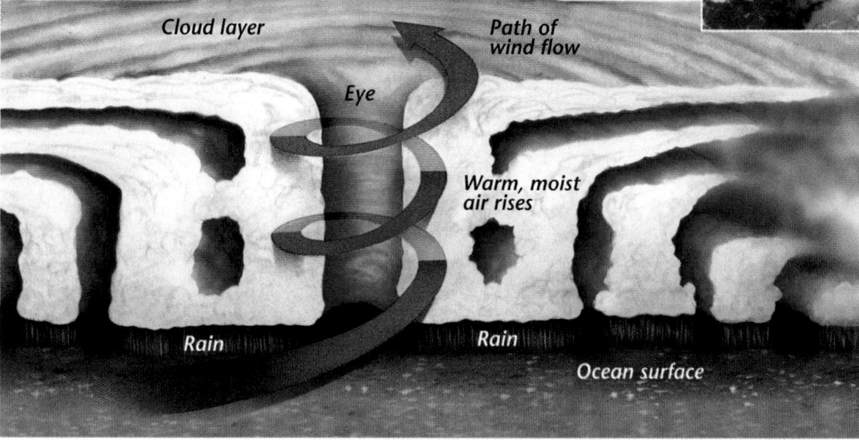

Media and Technology

Transparencies "Clouds and Winds in a Hurricane," Transparency 52

Answers to Self-Assessment

☑ Checkpoint

Tornado watch: tornadoes are possible. Tornado warning: a tornado has been seen in the sky or on weather radar.

Caption Questions

Figure 9 South Dakota, Iowa, Nebraska, Kansas, Missouri, Oklahoma, Texas, New Mexico, Arkansas
Figure 10 In the center of the clouds

Real-Life Learning

If it is hurricane season, have groups of students monitor tropical disturbances, watch for those that develop into hurricanes, and note where the hurricanes reach land. Groups should gather information from newspapers, television, or the Internet and, at the end of hurricane season, present the information to the class. Challenge groups to use a diversity of ways to record and present the information. **cooperative learning**

Using the Visuals: Figure 10

Call students' attention to the figure, then check to be sure that they understand how the two parts of the figure are related, by asking: **In which illustration are you looking down at a hurricane from above?** *(The photograph on the right)* **From which direction are you looking at the hurricane in the drawing?** *(From the side)* **In which direction is the wind blowing in both illustrations?** *(Counterclockwise around the eye of the hurricane)* **learning modality: visual**

Building Inquiry Skills: Problem Solving

Challenge students to solve the following problem. Tell them to assume they have been caught in the path of a hurricane and the eye of the storm is predicted to pass over their town. Now, after two days of high winds and waves and severe thunderstorms with torrential rain, the storm has died down and the sky has cleared. Ask: **Should you assume the storm has passed and start unboarding the windows and cleaning up the debris? Why or why not?** *(No, because this may be a temporary calm due to the eye of the storm. If so, after the eye passes, the storm will return.)* **How could you find out?** *(Listen to weather bulletins on radio or television)* **learning modality: logical/mathematical**

Ongoing Assessment

Oral Presentation Call on students at random to name the parts of the country where hurricanes occur. Call on other students to explain in their own words why hurricanes occur only in those places.

Hurricanes, continued

Integrating Health

Divide the class into groups and challenge the groups to brainstorm a list of actions people in hurricane-prone areas should take: (1) at the beginning of hurricane season *(Trim dead branches from trees, learn safe routes inland)*; (2) if a hurricane watch is issued *(Keep tuned to radio or television for storm updates, check radio and flashlight for batteries, stock up on canned food)*; and (3) if a hurricane warning is issued *(Leave mobile homes, unplug appliances and turn off gas tanks, board up glass windows and doors, listen to radio or television for orders to evacuate and do so immediately when instructed)*. When groups have completed their lists, have them share their ideas with the class. **cooperative learning**

Winter Storms

Visual Arts CONNECTION

Challenge students talented in art to create their own artwork depicting a snowstorm or other storm. Invite them to share their artwork with the class.

In Your Journal Students should comment on how well the words made them see, hear, and feel a snowstorm. **learning modality: visual**

Building Inquiry Skills: Inferring

Towns in the Rocky Mountains get even more snow than Buffalo and Rochester, New York. **Why do you think the high mountain areas of the West receive so much snow?** *(Because warm, moist air from the Pacific Ocean is cooled and drops its moisture as snow when it rises up over the Rocky Mountains)* **How are the Rocky Mountains similar to areas bordering the Great Lakes that receive lake-effect snow?** *(Both areas receive warm, moist west winds that are cooled to produce large amounts of snow.)* **learning modality: logical/mathematical**

Visual Arts CONNECTION

Weather and storms are favorite subjects for artists. "Snow Storm" is an oil painting by English artist J.M.W. Turner (1775–1851). To convey a mood or feeling, artists choose certain colors and textures. How does Turner's choice of colors enhance the mood of the painting? What texture do you see in the sea and sky? How does the texture support the feeling of the painting?

In Your Journal

Write a paragraph or two about the mood of this painting. Describe how you would feel being out in the wind and waves. Before you begin writing, jot down words that describe what you would see, hear, touch, taste, and smell. Exchange your descriptive writing with a partner to get feedback.

Hurricane Damage When a hurricane comes ashore, it brings high waves and severe flooding as well as wind damage. Hurricanes uproot trees, smash buildings, and destroy power lines. Heavy rains flood roads.

One of the most dangerous features of a hurricane is the storm surge. The low pressure and high winds of the hurricane over the ocean raise the level of the water up to six meters above normal sea level. The result is a **storm surge,** a "dome" of water that sweeps across the coast where the hurricane lands. As the hurricane comes onshore, the water comes with it. Storm surges can cause great damage, washing away beaches and destroying buildings along the coast.

Hurricane Safety Until the 1950s, a fast-moving hurricane could strike with little warning. Since then, advances in communications and satellite tracking have made hurricanes less deadly. People now receive information well in advance of an approaching hurricane.

INTEGRATING HEALTH

A "hurricane watch" is an announcement that hurricane conditions are *possible* in your area within the next 36 hours. People should be prepared to **evacuate** (ee VAK yoo ayt), or move away temporarily.

A "hurricane warning" means that hurricane conditions are *expected* within 24 hours. **If you hear a hurricane warning and are told to evacuate, leave the area immediately.** If you must stay in a house, move to the interior of the building, away from windows.

☑ *Checkpoint* *What is a storm surge?*

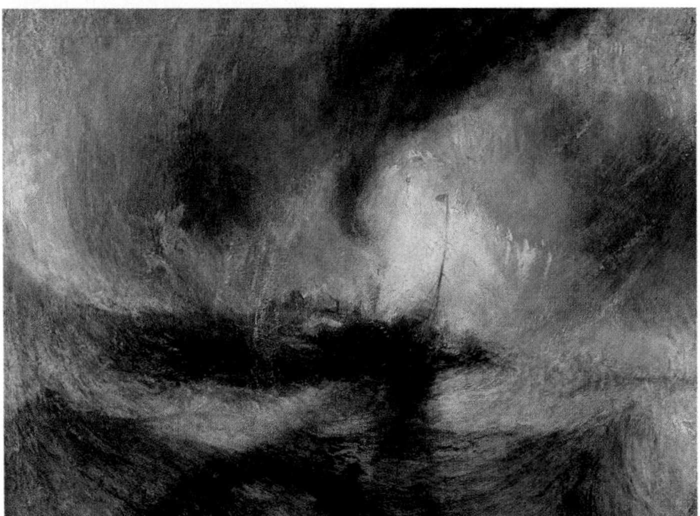

Figure 11 The British artist J.M.W. Turner painted "Snow Storm" in 1842.

Winter Storms

In the winter in the northern United States, much precipitation falls as snow. **Snow falls when humid air cools below 0°C.** Heavy snowfalls can block roads, trapping people in their homes and making it hard for emergency vehicles to move. Extreme cold can damage crops and cause water pipes to freeze and burst.

Background

Integrating Science Two serious health dangers of winter storms are frostbite and hypothermia. Frostbite is damage to body tissue, usually in the nose, ears, fingers, or toes, due to freezing of the tissue. Symptoms include a loss of feeling and a white appearance in the affected area. If you think you have frostbite, slowly rewarm the affected area and get medical help right away.

Hypothermia is a fall in body temperature below normal. Symptoms include shivering, disorientation, slurred speech, and drowsiness. Hypothermia is a life-threatening emergency. If someone shows signs of hypothermia, seek medical help immediately.

Lake-effect Snow Two of the snowiest cities in the United States are Buffalo and Rochester in upstate New York. On average, nearly three meters of snow falls on each of these cities every winter. Why do Buffalo and Rochester get so much snow?

Study Figure 12. Notice that Buffalo is located to the east of Lake Erie, and Rochester is located to the south of Lake Ontario. In the fall and winter, the land near these lakes cools much more rapidly than the water in the lakes. Although the water in these lakes is cold, it is still much warmer than the surrounding land and air. When a cold, dry air mass moves from central Canada southeast across one of the Great Lakes, it picks up water vapor and heat from the lake. As soon as the air mass reaches the other side of the lake, the air rises and cools again. The water vapor condenses and falls as snow, usually within 40 kilometers of the lake.

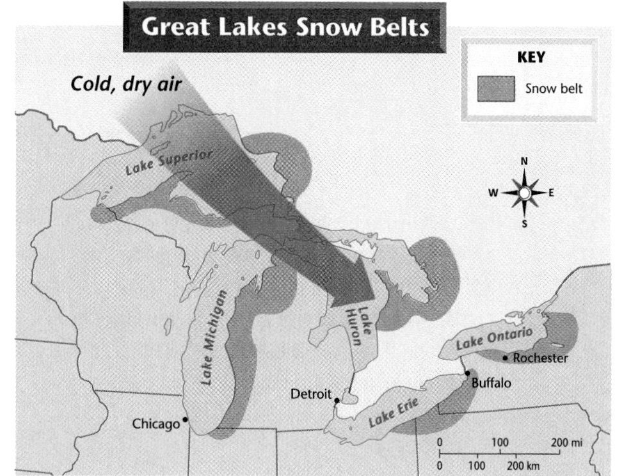

Figure 12 As cold dry air moves across the warmer water, it picks up water vapor. When the air reaches land and cools, lake-effect snow falls. ***Interpreting Maps*** *Which two cities receive large amounts of snow?*

Snowstorm Safety Imagine being out in a snowstorm when *INTEGRATING HEALTH* the wind suddenly picks up. High winds can blow falling snow sideways or pick up snow from the ground and suspend it in the air. This situation can be extremely dangerous because the blowing snow makes it easy to get lost. Also, strong winds cool a person's body rapidly. **If you are caught in a snowstorm, try to find shelter from the wind.** Cover exposed parts of your body and try to stay dry. If you are in a car, the driver should keep the engine running only if the exhaust pipe is clear of snow.

Section 2 Review

1. What weather conditions are most likely to cause thunderstorms and tornadoes?
2. What is the most common path for the hurricanes that strike the United States?
3. What safety precautions should you take if a tornado is predicted in your area? If a hurricane is predicted?
4. **Thinking Critically Applying Concepts** In the winter, cool, humid air from the Pacific Ocean blows across the cold land of southern Alaska. What kind of storm do you think this causes?

Science at Home

Storm Experiences Interview a family member or other adult about a dramatic storm that he or she has experienced. Before the interview, make a list of questions you would like to ask. For example, how old was the person when the storm occurred? When and where did the storm occur? Write up your interview in a question-and-answer format, beginning with a short introduction.

Program Resources

- **Unit 4 Resources** 13-2 Review and Reinforce; 13-2 Enrich
- **Interdisciplinary Exploration Series** "India Beyond the Golden Age," pp. 31–32; "Back to the Thirties," pp. 10–12

Answers to Self-Assessment

Checkpoint

A storm surge is a "dome" of water that sweeps across the coast where a hurricane lands.

Caption Question

Figure 12 Buffalo and Rochester in upstate New York receive large amounts of snow.

Integrating Health

Tell students that the winds of snowstorms make them even more dangerous because they lead to low wind-chill temperatures. Wind chill is how cold it feels because of the wind. For example, if the air temperature is -8°C and the wind is blowing at 50 km/h, the wind-chill temperature is -31°C. Ask: **Why does the wind make you feel colder than the cold air temperature alone?** *(Because it blows the heat away from your body)* **learning modality: logical/mathematical**

3 Assess

Section 2 Review Answers

1. Warm air being forced upward at a cold front to form large cumulonimbus clouds
2. From the Atlantic Ocean westward toward the Caribbean islands and the southeastern United States
3. If a tornado is predicted, go to the basement of a well-built building. If a hurricane is predicted, leave the area immediately.
4. A heavy snowstorm, because the moisture in the cool humid air from the Pacific would condense and fall as snow when it reached the cold land of southern Alaska

Science at Home

Tips Encourage students to tape record or videotape their interview. They might want to present it to the class in the form of a newspaper article or television news report. Suggest that they use drawings or photographs to illustrate their presentation. ACTIVITY

Performance Assessment

Skills Check Have students make a table comparing and contrasting thunderstorms, tornadoes, hurricanes, and snowstorms.

Real-World Lab

Careers in Science

Tracking a Hurricane

Preparing for Inquiry

Key Concept The path of a hurricane is not always easy to predict, making it difficult to issue hurricane warnings.

Skills Objectives Students will be able to

- interpret data on a map representing the location of a hurricane at repeated intervals;
- interpret additional data in tables to plot the continued path of the hurricane;
- use the data to predict when and where the hurricane will come ashore;
- make a judgement about when and for what area a hurricane warning should be issued.

Time 40 minutes

Advance Planning Students will have to press down hard to mark clearly on the tracing paper with the colored pencils, so have a pencil sharpener and extra pencils on hand. Students may need to trace additional maps, so have extra sheets of tracing paper on hand as well. You may wish to make a copy of the map from the student text as an overhead transparency. Use it to show students how to read latitude and longitude and plot the path of the hurricane.

Alternative Materials Instead of having students use tracing paper to trace the map in their text, you may want to provide each student with a photocopy of the map to mark on directly. If so, make copies of the map in advance.

Guiding Inquiry

Invitation To give the lab a context, point out that today hurricanes cause an average of only 17 deaths each year in the United States. Explain that the relatively low death rate is due to early warnings of when and where hurricanes are coming ashore. Earlier in this century, before the knowledge and technology needed for early warnings were available, the death rate from hurricanes was much higher. Add that one of the main jobs of some meteorologists during hurricane season is to track the storms so warnings can be issued in time to save lives.

Introducing the Procedure

Have students read through the steps of the procedure. Clear up any questions they may have. If necessary, review how to find latitude and longitude. Emphasize to students that they will be plotting the eye of the hurricane as it travels across the water. Ask: **How far on either side of the eye of the hurricane is the storm likely to extend?** *(A typical hurricane is 600 km wide, so the storm may extend 300 km on either side of the eye.)* **Why is this important to know for issuing a hurricane warning?** *(The area affected by the hurricane when it comes ashore will be as wide as the storm, and this is the area for which a hurricane warning should be issued.)*

Real-World Lab

Careers in Science

Tracking a Hurricane

Hurricane alert! You work at the National Hurricane Center. It is your job to track the paths of hurricanes and try to predict when and where a hurricane is likely to strike land. Then you must decide whether to warn people in the area to evacuate.

Problem

How can you predict when and where a hurricane will come ashore?

Skills Focus

interpreting data, predicting

Materials

ruler

red, blue, green, and brown pencils

tracing paper

Procedure

1. Look at the plotted path of the hurricane on the map. Each dot represents the location of the eye of the hurricane at six-hour intervals. The last dot shows where the hurricane was located at noon on August 30.
2. Predict the path you think the hurricane will take. Place tracing paper over the map below. Using a red pencil, place an X on your tracing paper where you think the hurricane will first reach land. Next to your X, write the date and time you think the hurricane will come ashore.

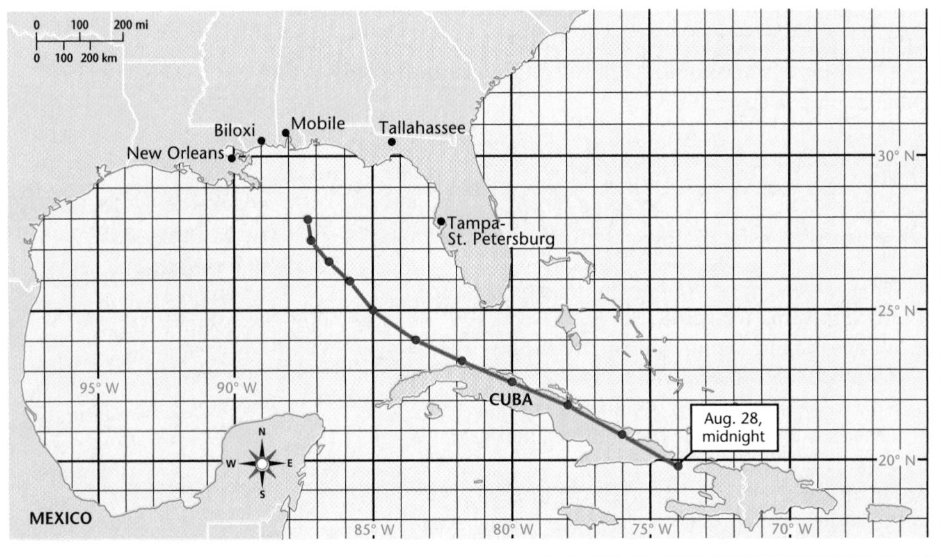

412

3. Hurricane warnings are issued for an area that is likely to experience a hurricane within 24 hours. On your tracing paper, shade in red the area for which you would issue a hurricane warning.
4. Using the following data table, plot the next five positions for the storm using a blue pencil. Use your ruler to connect the dots to show the hurricane's path.

Date and Time	Latitude	Longitude
August 30, 6:00 P.M.	28.3° N	86.8° W
August 31, midnight	28.4° N	86.0° W
August 31, 6:00 A.M.	28.6° N	85.3° W
August 31, noon	28.8° N	84.4° W
August 31, 6:00 P.M.	28.8° N	84.0° W

5. Based on the new data, decide if you need to change your prediction of where and when the hurricane will come ashore. Mark your new predictions in blue pencil on your tracing paper.
6. During September 1, you obtain four more positions. (Plot these points only after you have completed Step 5.) Based on these new data, mark in green pencil when and where you now think the hurricane will come ashore.

Date and Time	Latitude	Longitude
September 1, midnight	28.8° N	83.8° W
September 1, 6:00 A.M.	28.6° N	83.9° W
September 1, noon	28.6° N	84.2° W
September 1, 6:00 P.M.	28.9° N	84.8° W

7. The next day, September 2, you plot four more positions using a brown pencil. (Plot these points only after you have completed Step 6.)

Date and Time	Latitude	Longitude
September 2, midnight	29.4° N	85.9° W
September 2, 6:00 A.M.	29.7° N	87.3° W
September 2, noon	30.2° N	88.8° W
September 2, 6:00 P.M.	31.0° N	90.4° W

Analyze and Conclude

1. Describe in detail the complete path of the hurricane you tracked. Include where it came ashore and identify any cities that were in the vicinity.
2. How did your predictions in Steps 2, 5, and 6 compare to what actually happened?
3. What was unusual about your hurricane's path?
4. How do you think hurricanes with a path like this one affect the issuing of hurricane warnings?
5. Why do you have to be so careful when issuing warnings? What problems might be caused if you issued an unnecessary hurricane warning? What might happen if a hurricane warning were issued too late?
6. **Think About It** In this activity you only had data for the hurricane's position. If you were tracking a hurricane and issuing warnings, what other types of information would help you make decisions about the hurricane's path?

More to Explore

With your teacher's help, search the Internet for more hurricane tracking data. Map the data and try to predict where the hurricane will come ashore.

Troubleshooting the Experiment

- Point out to students that the lines of latitude and longitude on the map are in one-degree increments. Therefore, students will have to estimate where to plot the points because these are given in tenths of a degree of latitude or longitude.
- Use an overhead transparency of the map to show students how to plot the first point in the table as an example.
- If students think they are plotting incorrectly, advise them that hurricanes can change direction.
- As the hurricane changes direction, students' maps may become too crowded and difficult to read. If so, suggest that they trace a new map.

Program Resources

- **Unit 4 Resources** Chapter 13 Real-World Lab

Media and Technology

Lab Activity Videotapes
Grade 6, Tape 3

Expected Outcome

Students' maps should show that the hurricane changed direction twice, once to the east and then to the west, before finally coming ashore near Biloxi, Mississippi, on September 2.

Analyze and Conclude

1. The hurricane first appeared to be moving north toward southern Louisiana. It then turned east toward central Florida, before reversing direction and heading northwest toward the panhandle of Florida. It continued to move west or northwest until it came ashore near Biloxi, Mississippi.
2. Students' predictions will vary. They are likely to have predicted that the storm would come ashore near Mobile in Step 2, between Tallahassee and Tampa-St. Petersburg in Step 5, and near New Orleans in Step 6. The hurricane actually came ashore somewhat east of New Orleans at Biloxi.
3. The path of the hurricane was unusual because it reversed direction.
4. Hurricanes with a path like this one make it difficult to issue accurate warnings because where the hurricane actually comes ashore is different from where it appears to be headed.
5. You have to be careful when you issue hurricane warnings because unnecessary warnings can disrupt lives, put people in danger, and cause economic losses, whereas warnings that come too late can result in needless loss of life and damage to property.
6. Other types of information that would help you make decisions about the hurricane's path and when and where to issue hurricane warnings would include how fast the hurricane is moving, the speed of its winds, and other indicators of the severity of the storm.

Extending the Inquiry

More to Explore A good Internet site for hurricane tracking data is the National Hurricane Center at: **www.nhc.noaa.gov**

SCIENCE AND SOCIETY

Hurricane Alert: To Stay or Not To Stay?

Purpose To inform students of the pros and cons of evacuation in a hurricane and help them decide whether or not the government should have the power to force people to evacuate.

Role-Play

Time a day to prepare; 15 minutes for role-play

Choose several students to role-play a family discussion in which family members argue over whether or not they should evacuate after a hurricane warning has been issued. Instruct some of the students to take the position that the family should evacuate and others to take the opposite position. Urge students to support their arguments with facts from the feature.

Extend Before the role-play is presented to the class, take a poll of students to see how many would and how many would not evacuate in a hurricane. After the role-play has been presented, take the poll again. Call on any students who changed their minds to explain why.

You Decide

1. The government can order but not enforce evacuations in a hurricane. Some people do not want to evacuate. Other people believe that the government should have the right to force people to evacuate for public safety.
2. Forcing people to evacuate may prevent injuries and save lives by getting people to safety. People who benefit are those who would have been killed or injured had they not been evacuated. People who might be harmed include people who need to protect their homes, businesses, or animals. Government officials might try to increase public awareness of the dangers of not evacuating. Citizens could become better informed about the reasons for evacuating.
3. Make sure students' arguments are well reasoned.

SCIENCE AND SOCIETY

Hurricane Alert: To Stay or Not To Stay?

When a hurricane sweeps in from the ocean, the National Hurricane Center tracks the storm's course. Radio stations broadcast warnings. Sirens blow, and people in the storm path take steps to protect their homes and families.

State and local governments may try to keep people safe by closing state offices, setting up emergency shelters, and alerting the National Guard. As the danger increases, a state's governor can order the evacuation of people from dangerous areas. These actions are meant to protect public safety.

But not everyone wants to evacuate. Some people believe they have the right to stay. And officials cannot make people obey an evacuation order. How much can—or should—the government do to keep people safe?

The Issues

Why Play It Safe? Hurricanes can be extremely dangerous. High winds blow off roofs and shatter windows. Flash floods and storm surges can wash away houses. Even after the storm blows away, officials may need to keep people from returning home because of flooded sewers or broken power lines and gas mains.

In recent years, earlier and more accurate forecasts have saved lives. People now have time to prepare and to get out of the hurricane's path. Emergency officials urge people—especially the elderly, sick, or disabled—to leave early while the weather is still good. Most casualties happen when people are taken by surprise or ignore warnings. Those who decide to stay may later have to be rescued by boat or helicopter. These rescues add to the expense of the storm and may put the lives of rescuers in danger.

Why Ride Out the Storm? People have different reasons for not wanting to evacuate. Some want to protect their homes or businesses. Others don't want to leave pets or farm animals or go to public shelters. Store owners may stay open to sell disaster supplies. In addition, warnings may exaggerate the potential danger, urging people to leave when they might actually be safe. Since leaving can be expensive and disruptive, residents have to carefully evaluate the risks.

Is It a Matter of Rights? Should a government have the power to make people evacuate? Some citizens argue that the government should not tell them what to do as long as they are not harming others. They believe that individuals should have the right to decide for themselves. What do you think?

You Decide

1. Identify the Problem
In your own words, explain the controversy around hurricane evacuations.

2. Analyze the Options
Review and list the pros and cons of forcing people to evacuate. What people benefit? Who might be harmed? What more, if anything, should government officials do? What more could citizens do?

3. Find a Solution
Imagine that the radio has broadcast a hurricane warning. Write a dialogue in which you and members of your family discuss the options and decide whether or not to evacuate.

Background

Many of the severe hurricanes that struck the United States earlier in the twentieth century had high fatality rates. For example, in 1900, a hurricane that struck Texas killed 6,000 people. In 1919, a hurricane that struck the Florida Keys killed 900 people. More recent hurricanes have led to less loss of life, primarily because of early warnings. For example, in 1989, hurricane Hugo killed fewer than 30 people in the United States, even though it was a severe storm. However, recent hurricanes have caused huge amounts of property damage. Hugo, for example, caused an estimated $10.5 billion worth of damage. The increased cost of hurricanes is partly due to an influx of population to the coast. With more houses, businesses, and other types of property along the shore, there is much greater potential for property damage due to hurricanes.

Floods

Discover — Activity

What Causes Floods?

1. Fill a cup with water. Hold a funnel above a basin and pour the water very slowly into the funnel.
2. Refill the cup with the same amount of water you used in Step 1. Hold the funnel above the basin and this time pour the water rapidly into the funnel. What happens?

Think It Over

Inferring How is a funnel like a river valley? What do you think would happen if a large amount of water entered a river valley in a short period of time?

Guide for Reading

- What causes flooding?
- How can the dangers of floods be reduced?

Reading Tip **As you read, draw a flowchart showing what can happen during a flood and how people should respond to it.**

Antelope Canyon in the northern Arizona desert is only a few meters wide in places. On August 12, 1997, a group of 12 hikers entered the dry, narrow canyon. That afternoon a severe thunderstorm dropped several inches of rain on the Kaibeto Plateau, 24 kilometers away. Dry stream channels that drain into Antelope Canyon quickly filled with rainwater. The water rushed into the canyon, creating a wall of water over 3 meters high. Tourists at the top of the canyon watched in horror as the water swept the hikers away. Only one hiker survived.

Are you surprised that floods can occur in a desert? Actually, floods like this are more common in the dry Southwest than in areas with more rain.

Figure 13 From the top, Antelope Canyon looks like a narrow slit in the ground.

Reading Strategies

Reading Tip A sample flowchart is: rain falls→river rises→land floods→people evacuate. You might want to have students add the words *dam* and *ice jam* to their flowcharts as additional causes of floods.

Study and Comprehension As students read the last two pages of the section, have them summarize flood safety rules in two brief lists, one a list of what *to* do, the other a list of what *not* to do, in a flood.

Program Resources

- **Unit 4 Resources** 13-3 Lesson Plan; 13-3 Section Summary
- **Guided Reading and Study Workbook** Section 13-3

Integrating Health

Section 3 Floods

Objectives

After completing the lesson, students will be able to

- identify the causes of flooding;
- explain how the dangers of floods can be reduced.

Key Term flash flood

1 Engage/Explore

Activating Prior Knowledge

Introduce the section by having students apply what they know about watches and warnings to floods. Ask: **What do you think is the difference between a flood watch and a flood warning?** *(Students may say a flood watch means floods are possible and a flood warning means floods have already started to occur.)* **What should people do if a flood watch has been issued?** *(Stay tuned to radio or television.)* **What should people do if a flood warning has been issued?** *(Listen for further instructions, evacuate if ordered to do so.)*

Discover

Skills Focus inferring
Materials *cup, water, funnel, basin*
Time 10 minutes
Tips The funnel should be smaller than the cup so it overflows when students fill it rapidly.
Expected Outcome In Step 1, all the water will flow through the funnel. In Step 2, some of the water will overflow the funnel.
Think It Over The top of the funnel is like a river valley in that it drains a large area. The neck of the funnel is much smaller, like the river channel through which the valley's water flows. The river might overflow its banks, similar to the way the water overflowed the funnel, and this would create a flood.

2 Facilitate

Flash Floods

Building Inquiry Skills: Inferring

Point out that flash floods are more likely in hilly areas, such as Antelope Canyon in Arizona, which is described in the text. Ask: **Why do you think flash floods are more likely in hilly areas?** *(Rain water quickly runs off hills and is channeled into narrow valleys and canyons that cannot hold all the water.)* **learning modality: logical/ mathematical**

Flood Safety Measures

Sharpen your Skills

Skills Focus communicating
ACTIVITY
Time 10 minutes
Tips Invite students to read their announcements to the class.
Expected Outcome Dangers include high rushing water, uprooted power poles, landslides, mudslides, washed out roads, and contaminated food and drinking water. Steps to follow in case of a flood include moving to higher ground, staying away from flood waters, leaving a flooded car, and boiling water before drinking.
Extend Have interested students use the Internet to contact the National Weather Service at **www.nws.noaa.gov/er/nerfc/ floodinfo.html** for more information on flood safety. **learning modality: verbal**

Figure 14 Flash floods occur when large amounts of rain are funneled into a narrow valley. This drawing shows what happened in the Antelope Canyon flood.

Flash Floods

Although movies feature the violent winds of tornadoes and hurricanes, floods are the most dangerous weather-related events in the United States. **Floods occur when so much water pours into a stream or river that it overflows its banks and covers the land on either side of the channel.** People who live along certain rivers know that melting snow and spring rains are likely to bring floods.

Unexpected floods are the most dangerous. Floods like the Antelope Canyon flood are called flash floods because the water rises very rapidly—"in a flash"—after it begins to rain heavily. A **flash flood** is a sudden, violent flood that occurs within a few hours, or even minutes, of a storm.

Most flash floods are due to large amounts of rain. For example, a line of thunderstorms may remain over an area, dropping heavy rain for several hours or days. Hurricanes or tropical storms bring downpours that quickly fill stream channels. A flash flood can also be caused by a dam breaking, releasing millions of liters of water all at once. Similarly, if ice that has jammed a river breaks free, the sudden rush of water can cause a flash flood.

☑ *Checkpoint* *Why are flash floods so dangerous?*

Communicating

Write a script for a 30-second public service radio announcement in which you tell about the dangers of floods. Include recommended safety steps to follow in case of a flood.

ACTIVITY

Flood Safety Measures

If you've never been in a flood, it's hard to imagine the awesome power of rushing water. What can people do to protect themselves and their homes?

Predicting Floods Advance warnings can help reduce flood damage and loss of life. Weather satellites supply information about snow cover so that scientists can estimate how much water will run into rivers when the snow melts. Radar can track and measure the size of an approaching rainstorm. Scientists check river gauges that measure water levels. With this information, forecasters can predict flood heights at different points along a river. Their goal is to issue warnings early enough to help people prepare and evacuate if necessary.

Background

Facts and Figures Flooding causes almost half of all weather fatalities, and most flood fatalities occur during flash floods. The worst flash flood in United States history was caused by a dam break in Johnstown, Pennsylvania, in May of 1889. A wall of water 12 m high washed over the city, killing 2,200 people.

It isn't dam breaks that cause most flash floods, but heavy rains. One of the worst flash floods in United States history due to heavy rain occurred in Rapid City, South Dakota, in June of 1972. About 38 cm of rain fell in five hours, and the resulting flood killed 238 people. More recently, Shadyside, Ohio, received 10 cm of rain in just two hours. A torrent 12 m high flooded the town, leaving 26 people dead.

The car stalls in the water.

Moving water pushes against the car.

As the water rises, the car begins to float.

Sixty centimeters of water can wash a car away.

Figure 15 These drawings show what can happen to a car in a flood. *Applying Concepts Why is it dangerous to stay in a car in a flood?*

A "flood watch" is an announcement describing the area in which flooding is possible. Stay alert for more news. A "flood warning" is an announcement that floods have already been reported or are about to occur. It's time to take action!

Emergency Safety What should *you* do in case of a flood? When the danger becomes too great or the water rises too high, people are usually evacuated. **The first rule of flood safety: Move to higher ground and stay away from flood waters.** Don't try to cross streams and rivers that look as if they're flooded. Playing in flood waters may look like fun, but it's dangerous. A few centimeters of fast-moving water can sweep you off your feet. Even the storm drain on a city street can draw you in.

If your family is in a car, the driver shouldn't try to drive on a flooded road. Sometimes less than 60 centimeters of fast-moving water can sweep a car away, as shown in Figure 15. Everyone should leave the car and move to higher ground.

Using the Visuals: Figure 15

ACTIVITY

Materials *small watertight metal container, pebbles or gravel, basin, water*
Time 5 minutes

Point out that a car, like the one pictured in the figure, can float in about 60 cm of water, even though it may have a mass of more than 1,000 kg. The car displaces more and more water as the water rises, until it has displaced its own weight in water. When that occurs, the car floats. To convince students how little water is needed for a car to float, simulate the sequence of events shown in the figure. To model the car, use a small, rectangular, watertight metal container, weighted down with a few pieces of gravel. Place the container in a basin and slowly add water to the basin. By the time the water level is about halfway up the side of the container, the container should start to float. Ask: **What do you think would happen if the water in the basin had a current?** *(The current would push against the container and sweep it away as soon as it floated.)* **learning modality: visual**

Real-Life Learning

Point out that floods can be a big problem in urban areas. Ask: **Why do you think cities might be especially prone to flooding when heavy rains occur?** *(Much of the surface is covered with buildings and pavement that cannot absorb water, so there is a lot of run off, all of which is channeled into drains and sewers. They may not be able to hold all the water when the rain is unusually heavy.)* **Why are urban areas likely to suffer a greater loss of life and property due to floods?** *(Because they have a greater concentration of people, cars, and buildings and other structures)* **learning modality: logical/mathematical**

Answers to Self-Assessment

☑ Checkpoint

Flash floods are so dangerous because the water rises very rapidly in a sudden violent flood.

Caption Question

Figure 15 It is dangerous to stay in a car in a flood because the water can wash the car away.

Ongoing Assessment

Oral Presentation Call on various students to describe in their own words one of the ways that flash floods can occur.

3 Assess

Section 3 Review Answers

1. By pouring so much water into a stream or river that it overflows its banks and covers the land on either side of the channel
2. Move to higher ground, stay away from flood waters, do not try to cross streams and rivers that look flooded, do not play in flood waters, avoid driving on flooded roads, abandon a flooded car and move to higher ground, be careful with food and water that flood waters have touched, and boil water before drinking it to be sure it is safe.
3. A flood watch means flooding is possible, whereas a flood warning means floods have already been reported or are about to occur.
4. Weather satellites, radar, and river gauges
5. Possible answers include a hurricane or tropical storm, a very heavy rain, or melting spring snow.

CHAPTER PROJECT

Make sure students use standard weather symbols on their maps. Remind them to include air masses and fronts and to keep in mind the type of weather usually associated with each kind of front.

Performance Assessment

Writing Have students write a list of rules people should follow to ensure safety in a flood.

Students can save their list of rules in their portfolio.

Figure 16 In the spring of 1997, the Red River of the North flooded regions of North Dakota and Minnesota. A large part of flooded downtown Grand Forks burned down because fire trucks could not get to the scene of the fire or connect to any fire hydrants.

Other Flood Hazards High water is not the only hazard in a flood. Floods can knock down electrical poles and wires, cutting off power supplies. Flood waters can also saturate soil, causing landslides or mudslides. If roads have been flooded or washed away, emergency vehicles such as fire trucks and ambulances may not be able to get through.

Flood waters can wash into wells and water treatment plants, polluting the water. Therefore, be careful with food and water that flood waters have touched. Boil water before drinking it to be sure it is safe.

Section 3 Review

1. How can precipitation cause flooding?
2. What should you do to stay safe during a flood?
3. What is the difference between a flood watch and a flood warning?
4. Name three tools that supply information used in forecasting floods and providing flood information.
5. **Thinking Critically Predicting** Describe two weather situations in which you would expect floods to occur.

CHAPTER PROJECT

Check Your Progress

Now you are ready to predict tomorrow's weather. Look at today's weather map. Then predict tomorrow's weather both where you live and in the two other locations you selected. (*Project Hint:* Refer to the weather patterns you have been observing.) Decide what symbols you will need to use. Then, on an outline map of the United States, draw symbols to show what you think tomorrow's weather will be. Continue to make predictions every day for at least a week.

Program Resources

- **Unit 4 Resources** 13-3 Review and Reinforce; 13-3 Enrich

418

Predicting the Weather

DISCOVER

What's the Weather?

1. Look at the weather report in your local newspaper. Note what weather conditions are predicted for your area today, including temperature, precipitation, and wind speed.
2. Look out the window or think about what it was like the last time you were outside. Write down the actual weather conditions where you are.

Think It Over

Observing Does the weather report match what you observe? What is the same? What is different?

For centuries, people have tried to predict the weather. Every nation's folklore includes weather sayings. Many of these sayings are based on long-term observations. Sailors, pilots, farmers, and others who work outdoors are usually careful observers of clouds, winds, and other signs of coming changes in the weather. Here are two examples:

GUIDE FOR READING

- **How does technology help forecasters predict the weather?**
- **What types of information are shown on weather maps?**

Reading Tip **Before you read, preview Figure 19 and *Exploring Newspaper Weather Maps.* Write a list of any questions you have about weather maps.**

Evening red and morning gray
Will send the traveler on his way;
Evening gray and morning red
Will bring down rain upon his head.

Red sky in the morning,
sailors take warning;
Red sky at night, sailor's delight.

Why do these two weather sayings agree that a red morning sky means bad weather? Recall that in the United States storms usually move from west to east. Clouds in the west may indicate an advancing low-pressure area, bringing stormy weather. If there are high clouds in the west in the morning, the rising sun in the east turns these clouds red. The reverse is true at sunset. As the sun sets in the west, it turns clouds in the east red. Clouds in the east may indicate that a storm is moving away to the east.

READING STRATEGIES

Reading Tip Urge students to answer their own questions as they read. A sample question might be: How is data on weather maps gathered?

Vocabulary Help students understand the terms *isobar* and *isotherm* by explaining that the prefix *iso-* means "the same", the root *-bar* means "air pressure" (as in *barometer*), and the root *-therm* means "temperature" (as in *thermometer*).

Program Resources

- **Unit 4 Resources** 13-4 Lesson Plan; 13-4 Section Summary
- **Guided Reading and Study Workbook** Section 13-4

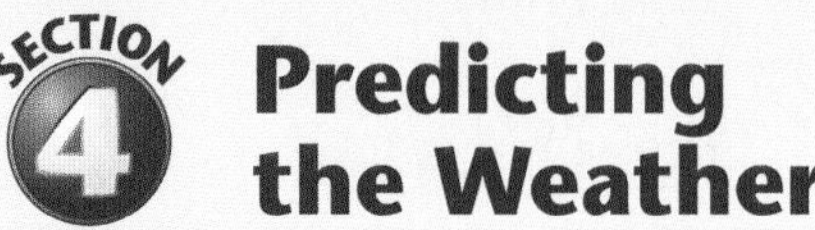

Objectives

After completing the lesson, students will be able to

- explain how technology helps forecasters predict the weather;
- describe the types of information shown on weather maps;
- describe El Niño and its effects.

Key Terms meteorologist, El Niño, isobar, isotherm

1 Engage/Explore

Activating Prior Knowledge

Help students recall occasions when they wanted to know what the next day's or the weekend's weather would be. Ask: **Did you ever wonder how warm or cold it would be the next day so you could plan what to wear to school, or whether it would rain on Saturday and wash out your ball game?** *(Most students will say "yes.")* Point out that the major job of meteorologists, or weather scientists, is predicting the weather. Add that, with modern technology, meteorologists can now predict the weather in the near future quite accurately. Tell students that, in this section, they will learn tips that will also help them predict the weather.

DISCOVER

Skills Focus observing
Materials *local newspaper weather report*
Time 10 minutes
Tips Suggest to students that they consider each of the weather factors reported on in the newspaper before deciding whether or not the actual weather matches the predicted weather.
Expected Outcome The newspaper weather report may or may not match actual conditions, but it probably will be close.
Think It Over The newspaper weather report may match the actual weather in general but not in every detail. For example, the actual temperature may differ from the predicted temperature by a few degrees or showers may be light instead of moderate.

2 Facilitate

Weather Forecasting

Real-Life Learning

Call students' attention to the example of weather folklore given in the opening paragraph of the section. Ask: **Do you know any other weather folklore?** *(Students may give familiar examples, such as a groundhog seeing its shadow meaning that there will be six more weeks of winter.)* Point out that long-term weather predictions, such as a groundhog's shadow predicting a longer winter, usually are unreliable. However, short-term predictions, such as the ones in the text, often are reliable because they are based on scientifically valid observations about the weather. Share other examples of reliable weather folklore with students such as the following: "Mackerel sky, mackerel sky, not long wet, not long dry." (High cirrus clouds that look like fish scales usually mean a change in the weather.) "When the sun or moon is in its house, it will rain soon." (The "house" refers to a ring around the sun or moon, which means clouds are thickening and rain is near.) "The north wind does blow, and we will have snow." (A north wind usually brings cold weather and thus a chance for snow.) **learning modality: verbal**

Building Inquiry Skills: Controlling Variables

Stress that today meteorologists rely on information from many different sources to predict the weather. Therefore, it is important to have standard ways of measuring weather factors. For example, wind speed varies with height, so meteorologists set a standard of 10 m above the ground for recording winds. Ask: **How do you think temperature might be standardized?** *(Students may say that temperature varies by time of day so it should be measured at the same time.)* Inform students that the lowest temperature of the day usually occurs near sunrise and the highest temperature between 1:00 and 4:00 p.m. **learning modality: logical/mathematical**

Weather Forecasting

You can make many predictions from your own observations. For example, if a barometer shows that the air pressure is falling, you can expect a change in the weather. Falling air pressure usually indicates an approaching low-pressure area, possibly bringing rain or snow.

You can read weather signs in the clouds, too. Cumulus clouds often form on warm afternoons when warm air rises. If you see these clouds growing larger and taller, you can expect them to become cumulonimbus clouds, which may bring a thunderstorm. If you see thin cirrus clouds high in the sky, a low-pressure area may be approaching.

Even careful weather observers often turn to professional meteorologists for television weather information. You may hear the person who gives the television weather report referred to as a meteorologist. Despite their name, meteorologists don't study meteors. **Meteorologists** (mee tee uh RAWL uh jists) are scientists who study the causes of weather and try to predict it.

Figure 17 These meteorologists are releasing a weather balloon. The box attached to the balloon contains instruments that will record weather data—such as temperature, pressure, and humidity—high in the troposphere.

Meteorologists interpret information from a variety of sources, including local weather observers, instruments carried by balloons, satellites, and weather stations around the world. They use maps, charts, and computers to analyze the data and to prepare weather forecasts. Meteorologists use radar to track areas of rain or snow, so that forecasters can follow the path of a storm system.

Where do television and radio weather reporters get their information? A lot of weather information comes from the National Weather Service. However, weather forecasts for the general public may not have enough detail to be useful to farmers and pilots. There are also private weather-forecasting services, many of which use advanced, high-technology equipment. Private forecasting services are useful to people who need to answer questions like these: "Will the frost hurt the oranges in my orchard?" "Will the airport be fogged in?" "Will the trucks need to spread sand on the roads today?"

☑ *Checkpoint* ***Where do meteorologists get weather information?***

Background

History of Science Samuel Morse's invention of the telegraph in 1844 revolutionized meteorology. By 1849, scientists at the Smithsonian Institute started gathering weather reports from telegraph operators around the country, and soon the first national weather service was set up. The first weather map showing current conditions based on telegraphed information was published in England in 1851, and the first telegraph system for forecasting severe weather was established in France in 1854.

The United States published its first official weather forecast in 1870. Early weather forecasts were highly inaccurate because they were based on conditions on the ground and not on air masses and fronts.

Figure 18 This satellite photo shows an intense storm over the North Atlantic Ocean.
Observing What weather-related information can you see in the photo?

Weather Technology

Techniques for predicting weather have changed rapidly in recent years. Short-range forecasts—forecasts for up to five days—are now fairly reliable. Meteorologists can also make long-range predictions that were once impossible. **Changes in technology have occurred in two areas: gathering weather data and using computers to make forecasts.**

Weather Balloons and Satellites As you learned in Chapter 15, weather balloons carry instruments high into the troposphere and stratosphere. The instruments measure temperature, air pressure, and humidity.

The first weather satellite was launched in 1960. Cameras on weather satellites in the exosphere can photograph Earth's surface, clouds, storms, and ice and snow cover. These images are then transmitted to meteorologists on Earth, who interpret the information.

Computer Forecasts Computers are widely used to help  INTEGRATING TECHNOLOGY forecast weather. Instruments can now gather thousands of bits of data about temperature, air pressure, wind speed, and other factors. Computers process large amounts of information quickly to help forecasters make predictions. To make a forecast, the computer starts with weather conditions reported from weather stations over a large area. Conditions reported include wind speed and direction, humidity, sunlight, temperature, and air pressure. Then the computer works through thousands of calculations and makes forecasts for 12 hours, 24 hours, 36 hours, and so on. Each forecast builds on the previous forecast. When new weather data come in, the computer revises its forecasts.

Media and Technology

Concept Videotape Library
Grade 6, Tape 3 "Never Put Up the Umbrella Until It Starts to Rain"

Answers to Self-Assessment

Checkpoint

Meteorologists get weather information from local weather observers, instruments carried by balloons, satellites, and weather stations around the world.

Caption Question

Figure 18 You can see temperature, cloud cover, and the location of a storm.

Weather Technology

Inquiry Challenge

Materials *globe, two small balls*
Time 10 minutes

Explain to students that there are two kinds of weather satellites. Geostationary satellites orbit Earth from west to east at a height of about 39,500 km. They always stay above the same spot on Earth's surface. Polar satellites orbit Earth from north to south at a height of about 850 km. They fly over both poles twice a day. Challenge small groups of students to use a globe and two balls, each ball representing one kind of weather satellite, to model how weather satellites orbit Earth. Then ask: **Which type of satellite do you think gets clearer pictures of clouds and other weather factors? Why?** *(Polar satellites, because they orbit at a lower altitude)* **Which type of satellite do you think gets a broader picture of clouds and other weather factors? Why?** *(Geostationary satellites, because they orbit at a higher altitude)* **learning modality: logical/mathematical**

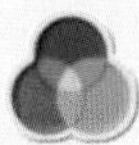

Integrating Technology

Help students appreciate the role computers play in weather forecasting. Inform students that meteorologists divide the troposphere into about 3,000 grids, and weather data for each grid arrives at the National Weather Service twice a day. Managing all that data to track and forecast the weather requires billions of calculations. The computer used by the National Weather Service can perform over two billion calculations per second. If that work had to be done by hand, it would require more than 123,000 people. Ask: **What is the major role played by computers in weather forecasting?** *(Analyzing huge amounts of information quickly)* **learning modality: verbal**

Ongoing Assessment

Oral Presentation Call on various students to explain in their own words how advances in technology have led to more accurate weather forecasts.

El Niño

Building Inquiry Skills: Communicating

Tell students that weather prediction has become more accurate now that scientists understand how global winds and ocean currents influence weather. Explain that periodic changes in highs and lows over the southern Pacific Ocean modify the trade winds, and changes in the trade winds, in turn, influence ocean currents, leading to an increase in the temperature of the water off the coast of South America. The warm ocean water causes unusually rainy weather along the coast of South America and also, by influencing other ocean currents, indirectly causes unusual weather conditions all over the world. Check students' understanding of the widespread influence of El Niño by asking: **How does understanding El Niño help meteorologists predict the weather?** *(Meteorologists can look for changes in ocean currents and, if they occur, anticipate certain unusual weather conditions over a wide area.)* **learning modality: verbal**

Reading Weather Maps

Sharpen your Skills

Interpreting Data

ACTIVITY

Time 10 minutes

Tips Make sure students understand how to read the symbol for wind direction. Explain that when the shaft points down the wind is from the south, when it points left the wind is from the west, and so on.

Expected Outcome Temperature 30°F, wind speed 26–31 mph, wind blowing from the south, air pressure 1016 millibars, 70–80 percent of the sky covered by clouds, snow falling

Extend Ask: **How would you show the same station with a temperature of 34°F, wind direction from the southeast, and sleet falling?** *(Replace 30 with 34, point the shaft halfway between down and right, and replace the star with a triangle containing a solid circle.)* **learning modality: logical/mathematical**

El Niño

Some long-term weather patterns may be caused by changes in ocean currents and global winds. Periodically, a warm-water event known as **El Niño** occurs in the tropical Pacific Ocean. During an El Niño event, winds shift and push warm surface water toward the west coast of South America. The warm water replaces the cold water that usually rises from the deep ocean near the coast.

El Niño events occur once every two to seven years. They can cause dramatic climate changes around the Pacific Ocean and in other places. In the winter of 1997 and 1998, a strong El Niño current caused droughts in Asia and Brazil, heavy rains and floods in California and Peru, and tornadoes in Florida and other parts of the southeastern United States.

Scientists have looked for clues and warnings to help predict the return of El Niño. One signal is rising surface temperatures in the tropical part of the Pacific Ocean. Using data gathered during past El Niño events, scientists were able to predict many of the results of the 1997–1998 El Niño.

☑ **Checkpoint** *What evidence do scientists use to predict an El Niño?*

Sharpen your Skills

Interpreting Data

ACTIVITY

Use the key to Figure 19 to help you answer the questions about this weather station data.

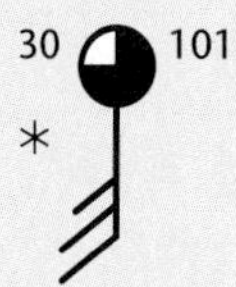

1. What is the temperature at this station?
2. What is the wind speed?
3. Which way is the wind blowing?
4. What is the air pressure?
5. What percent of the sky is covered by clouds?
6. What type of precipitation, if any, is falling?

Reading Weather Maps

A weather map is a "snapshot" of conditions at a particular time over a large area. There are many different types of weather maps. Television forecasters often present maps generated by computers from radar information.

Weather Service Maps Data from more than 300 local weather stations all over the country are assembled into weather maps at the National Weather Service. The information collected by a typical reporting station is summarized in the key to Figure 19. The weather map, which has been simplified, includes most of the weather station data shown in the key.

On some weather maps, you see curved lines. These lines connect places where certain conditions—temperature or air pressure—are the same. **Isobars** are lines joining places on the map that have the same air pressure. (*Iso* means "equal" and *bar* means "pressure.") The numbers on the isobars are the pressure readings. Air pressure readings may be given in inches of mercury or in millibars or both. Figure 19 has isobars.

Isotherms are lines joining places that have the same temperature. The isotherm may be labeled with the temperature in degrees Fahrenheit, degrees Celsius, or both.

Background

Facts and Figures There are three different methods of forecasting weather: the analog, numeric, and synoptic methods. The analog method, also called statistical forecasting, uses mathematical equations based on past weather patterns to forecast future weather. The numeric method uses mathematical equations based on the laws of physics, especially fluid dynamics, to forecast weather. The synoptic method uses a synopsis, or summary, of the total weather picture right now to predict what the weather will be like in the future. Using the synoptic method, the movement of weather systems is shown on a series of weather maps, like the one in Figure 19, which are called synoptic charts. The synoptic method is the most commonly used method of weather forecasting, by both professional and amateur meteorologists.

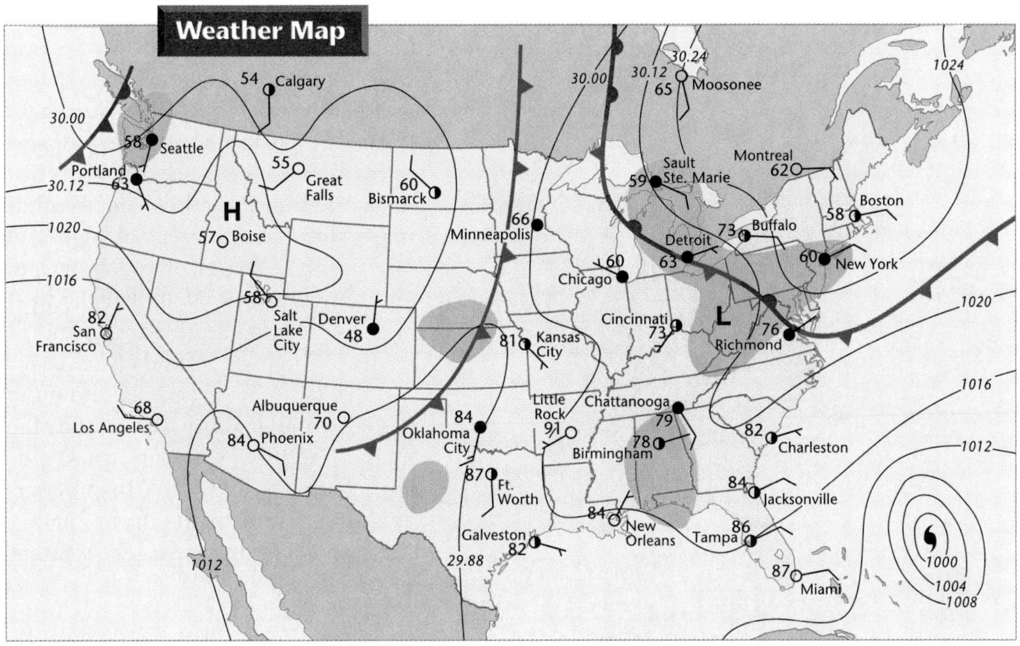

EXPLANATION OF FRONTS

Cold Front
Boundary between a cold air mass and a warm air mass. Brings brief storms and cooler weather.

Warm Front
Boundary between a warm air mass and a cold air mass. Usually accompanied by precipitation.

Stationary Front
Boundary between a warm air mass and a cold air mass when no movement occurs. Brings long periods of precipitation.

Occluded Front
Boundary on which a warm front has been overtaken by a cold front. Brings precipitation.

Weather	Symbol
Drizzle	
Fog	≡
Hail	△
Haze	∞
Rain	•
Shower	▽
Sleet	
Smoke	
Snow	*
Thunderstorm	
Hurricane	

Wind Speed (mph)	Symbol
1–2	
3–8	
9–14	
15–20	
21–25	
26–31	
32–37	
38–43	
44–49	
50–54	
55–60	
61–66	
67–71	
72–77	

Cloud Cover (%)	Symbol
0	
10	
20–30	
40	
50	
60	
70–80	
90	
100	

How Symbols Are Used on a Weather Map

Amount of cloud cover (100%)
Atmospheric pressure (millibars)
Temperature (°F)
38
1018
Wind direction (from the southwest)
Wind speed (21–25mph)

Figure 19 This weather map shows data collected from weather stations all over the country. Below the map is an explanation of what the symbols at each city mean.

Using the Visuals: Figure 19

Have students choose partners and quiz each other on the conditions represented by the symbols at several different weather stations shown in the figure. For example, a student might ask his or her partner from which direction the wind is blowing in Miami *(east)*, how much cloud cover there is in Seattle *(100%)*, or how fast the wind is blowing in Los Angeles *(9–14 mph)*. **cooperative learning**

Real-Life Learning

Challenge students to use the symbols in Figure 19 to summarize actual weather conditions in their location. You may either provide students with the relevant data on temperature, wind direction, and other weather factors for your local area or have students read the data from instruments. Ask: **What, if any, weather factors are not included in the key?** *(relative humidity, dew point, and cloud type)* **How could you represent them on a weather map?** *(Students may say that relative humidity and dew point could be represented by numbers placed near the weather station and cloud type by a symbol placed near the weather station.)* **learning modality: visual**

Building Inquiry Skills: Predicting

Call students' attention to the map in Figure 19 and challenge them to locate the longest cold front. Ask: **Where do you think the cold front will be in a few days?** *(Most likely it will have moved east.)* **As the cold front travels across the country, how do you think it will change the weather?** *(The cold front is likely to bring cloudy, wet, or even stormy weather.)* **learning modality: logical/mathematical**

Program Resources

- **Laboratory Manual** 13, "Investigating Weather Maps"

Media and Technology

Transparencies "Weather Map," Transparency 53

Answers to Self-Assessment

Checkpoint

To predict an El Niño, scientists look for evidence of rising surface temperatures in the tropical part of the Pacific Ocean.

Ongoing Assessment

Skills Check Have students interpret data in Figure 19 to find the following weather information: the air pressure in Tampa, Florida *(1016 millibars)*; a cyclone, or low pressure system *(between Ohio and West Virginia)*; a stationary front *(from Wisconsin to Virginia)*; a hurricane *(east of Florida)*.

Reading Weather Maps, continued

Using the Visuals: Figure 20

Make sure students understand how the three maps in the figure are related, then ask: **If you had a weather map for Day 4, how do you predict it would differ from the map for Day 3?** *(Chances are the weather systems would be farther east by Day 4.)* **learning modality: logical/mathematical**

Real-Life Learning

Time 20 minutes

Point out that even very detailed weather maps cannot give the precise weather conditions for every location because there are many factors that can modify local conditions. For example, the south side of a hill is likely to be warmer than the north side and an open area is likely to be windier than a wooded area. Ask: **What factors do you think might influence local weather conditions at our school?** *(Factors might include large buildings, open grassy areas, forests, hills or mountains, rivers or lakes.)* **learning modality: visual**

The Butterfly Effect

Building Inquiry Skills: Calculating

Materials *calculator*
Time 5 minutes

Help students appreciate how the butterfly effect works with this simple activity. Have students add three numbers, divide the sum by a fourth number, multiply the quotient by a fifth number, and then square the result. Give half the class five numbers written out to three decimal places and give the other half the same numbers rounded to the nearest whole number. Have students compare their results. They will find that answers based on the different sets of numbers diverge more and more with each step in the calculations. Ask: **How does this demonstrate the butterfly effect?** *(Tiny differences in the numbers accumulate into larger differences.)* **learning modality: logical/mathematical**

Newspaper Weather Maps Maps in newspapers are simplified versions of maps produced by the National Weather Service. *Exploring Newspaper Weather Maps* shows a typical newspaper weather map. From what you have learned in this chapter, you can probably interpret most of the symbols on this map. **Standard symbols on weather maps show fronts, areas of high and low pressure, types of precipitation, and temperatures.** Note that the high and low temperatures are given in degrees Fahrenheit instead of Celsius.

The maps in Figure 20 show the path of a winter storm. If you study the maps carefully, you can track this storm and its effects. With practice, you can use information from weather maps to help you predict the weather in your area.

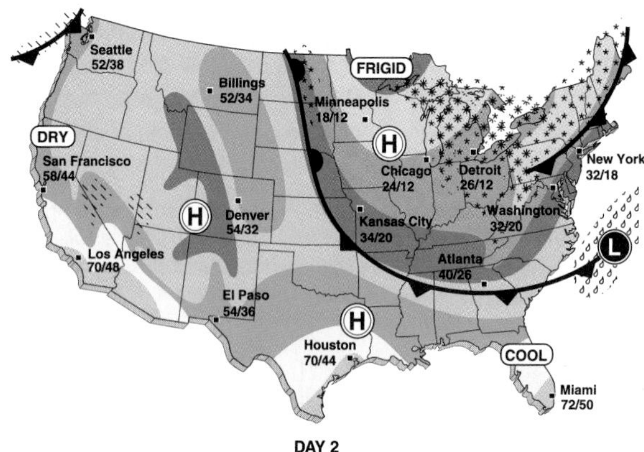

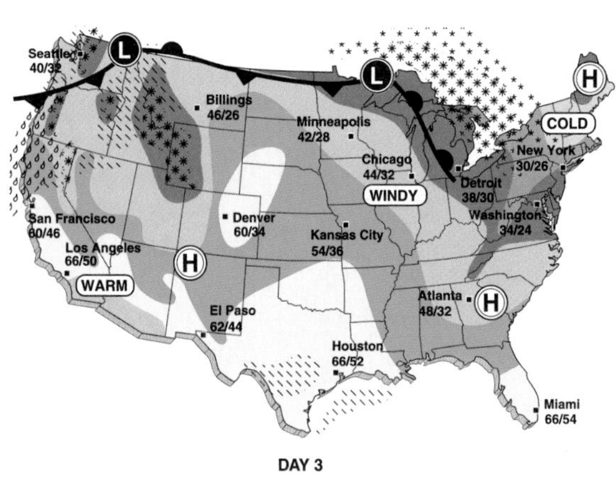

Figure 20 These weather maps show a storm moving from west to east over a three-day period.
Interpreting Diagrams *What were the high and low temperatures in Chicago on Day 2? On Day 3?*

The Butterfly Effect

Even with current technology, weather forecasting is tricky. The main reason is that weather patterns do not follow an orderly, step-by-step process.

A forecast for the weather six days from now is based on forecasts for all the days between now and then. A small change in the weather today can mean a larger change in the weather a week later! This is the so-called butterfly effect. The name refers to a scientist's suggestion that even the flapping of a butterfly's wings causes a tiny disturbance in the atmosphere. This tiny event might cause a larger disturbance that could—eventually—grow into a hurricane.

Background

History of Science The butterfly effect was discovered by a theoretical meteorologist at the Massachusetts Institute of Technology named Edward Lorenz. One day in 1961, Lorenz decided to rerun a computer program for weather forecasting that he had been working on. Rather than enter all the numbers to six decimal places, he took a shortcut and entered the numbers to just three decimal places. After many computer calculations, Lorenz was surprised to discover that the results were very different from the results he had obtained earlier using numbers to six decimal places. This showed Lorenz that weather systems and other complex systems are very sensitive to tiny changes in initial conditions. Lorenz's work was the beginning of the mathematical theory of chaos, which is now important in most sciences, in addition to meteorology.

EXPLORING Newspaper Weather Maps

Weather maps in newspapers use symbols to show fronts, high and low pressure areas, and precipitation. Color bands indicate different temperatures.

Areas in the same temperature range are shown in the same color. For example, light green areas have high temperatures in the 40's.

Major low-pressure areas are shown with an L. High-pressure areas are shown with an H.

COLD
CHILLY
WINDY
Seattle 45/37
Billings 38/25
Minneapolis 32/26
Chicago 36/28
Detroit 37/26
New York 44/34
Washington 48/33
San Francisco 55/42
Denver 40/22
Kansas City 34/30
Los Angeles 60/48
DFW Metroplex 66/46
Atlanta 42/38
El Paso 58/40
Houston 70/50
Miami 74/60

Symbols that look like raindrops or snowflakes show precipitation.

The triangles showing a cold front point in the direction the cold air is moving. The half-circles indicating a warm front show the direction the warm air is moving.

Section 4 Review

1. What kinds of technology do meteorologists use to help predict the weather?
2. Name at least three types of information you could get from a weather map of your area.
3. What lines on a weather map connect points that have the same temperature?
4. **Thinking Critically Predicting** If you observe that air pressure is rising, what kind of weather do you think is coming?

Check Your Progress

CHAPTER PROJECT

After a week of predicting the weather, you are ready to compare your predictions to the actual weather that occurred. Then compare your predictions with those made by professional meteorologists. How accurate were your predictions? How accurate were the predictions made by professional meteorologists?

Program Resources

◆ **Unit 4 Resources** 13-4 Review and Reinforce; 13-4 Enrich

Media and Technology

Transparencies "Newspaper Weather Map," Transparency 54

Answers to Self-Assessment

Caption Question

Figure 20 The high temperature in Chicago on Day 2 was 24°F; low was 12°F. On Day 3 the high was 44°F; the low was 32°F.

EXPLORING

Newspaper Weather Maps

Materials *poster board, colored markers*
Time 30 minutes

Challenge pairs of students to produce a brief national television weather report based on the weather map shown in the feature. Each pair should interpret the symbols on the map, write a script, and create graphics. Invite pairs to present their reports to the class. **cooperative learning**

3 Assess

Section 4 Review Answers

1. Meteorologists use weather balloons, weather satellites, and computers.
2. Temperature, air pressure, wind speed, wind direction, percent cloud cover, and type of precipitation.
3. isotherms
4. fair weather

Check Your Progress

CHAPTER PROJECT

To compare their predictions with the weather that occurs at each of their three locations, student should compare their own weather maps with the newspaper weather maps showing actual weather conditions for the same days. Most newspaper weather reports also give weather predictions that students can use to compare their own predictions with those made by professional meteorologists.

Performance Assessment

Skills Check Have students interpret the weather map in the Exploring feature on this page to find out weather conditions in Atlanta. Then have them describe Atlanta's weather using the symbols in the key to Figure 19.

Skills Lab

Interpreting Data

Reading a Weather Map

Preparing for Inquiry

Key Concept The symbols on weather maps communicate information about weather factors and systems.

Skills Objectives Students will be able to

- interpret data on a weather map;
- draw conclusions about the type of weather affecting different places.

Time 30 minutes

Advance Planning Make an overhead transparency of the map in the lab to use in class.

Alternative Materials You can use an actual weather map from a newspaper.

Guiding Inquiry

Troubleshooting the Experiment

- Make sure students realize how the front changes as it goes across the top of the map.
- Explain why two temperatures are given for each city on the map.

Expected Outcome

Students should use the map on page 425 to interpret the map in the lab. In Step 3, the symbols that look like snowflakes represent snow and those that look like raindrops represent rain. In Step 4, half-circles indicate warm fronts and triangles represent cold fronts. In Step 5, H is the symbol for high pressure and L is the symbol for low pressure.

Analyze and Conclude

1. Orange represents the highest temperatures and light purple represents the lowest temperatures.
2. Miami the highest, Billings the lowest
3. It is raining in California and snowing in parts of the Northwest.
4. Three—warm front, cold front, stationary front
5. Two areas of low pressure and two areas of high pressure
6. It is probably winter. The temperatures are fairly low.
7. A cold front; clouds and snow followed by cold, dry weather

Skills Lab

Interpreting Data

Reading a Weather Map

In this lab, you will interpret data from a weather map to describe weather conditions in various places.

Problem

How does a weather map communicate data?

Procedure

1. Examine the symbols on the weather map below. For more information about the symbols used on the map, refer to Figure 19 on page 423 and to *Exploring Newspaper Weather Maps* on page 425.
2. Observe the different colors on the weather map.
3. Find the symbols for snow and rain.
4. Locate the warm fronts and cold fronts.
5. Locate the symbols for high and low pressure.

Analyze and Conclude

1. What color represents the highest temperatures? What color represents the lowest temperatures?
2. What city has the highest temperature? What city has the lowest temperature?
3. Where on the map is it raining? Where on the map is it snowing?
4. How many different kinds of fronts are shown on the map?
5. How many areas of low pressure are shown on the map? How many areas of high pressure are shown on the map?
6. What season does this map represent? How do you know?
7. **Think About It** The triangles and semicircles on the front lines show which way the front is moving. What front is moving toward Minneapolis? What kind of weather do you think it will bring?

More to Explore

Compare this weather map with the weather map shown in a television news report. Which symbols on these maps are similar? Which symbols are different?

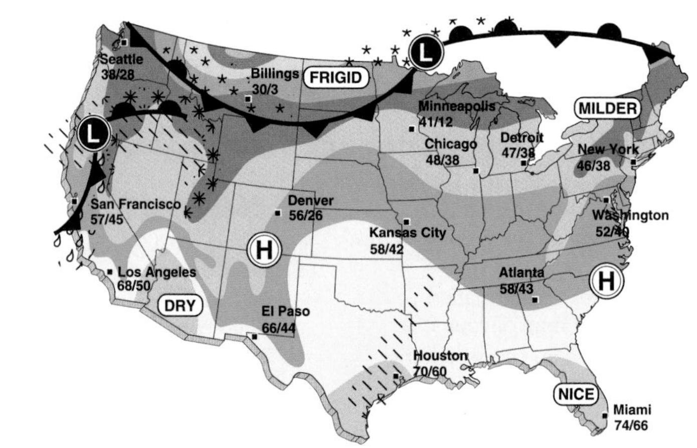

426

Extending the Inquiry

More to Explore Television weather maps use somewhat different symbols, but students should be able to interpret them with their knowledge of newspaper weather maps.

Program Resources

- **Unit 4 Resources** Chapter 13 Skills Lab

Media and Technology

 **Lab Activity Videotapes** Grade 6, Tape 3

Air Masses and Fronts

Key Ideas

- Four major types of air masses influence the weather in North America: maritime tropical, continental tropical, maritime polar, and continental polar.
- When air masses collide, they form four types of fronts: cold fronts, warm fronts, stationary fronts, and occluded fronts.
- Cyclones and decreasing air pressure are associated with storms and precipitation.

Key Terms

air mass, tropical, polar, maritime, continental, front, occluded, cyclone, anticyclone

Storms

Key Ideas

- Thunderstorms and tornadoes form within large cumulonimbus clouds. During thunderstorms, avoid touching metal objects.
- A hurricane begins over warm water as a low-pressure area. If you hear a hurricane warning and are told to evacuate, leave the area immediately.
- Snow falls when humid air cools below 0°C. If you are caught in a snowstorm, try to find shelter from the wind.

Key Terms

storm, lightning, tornado, hurricane, storm surge, evacuate

Floods

Integrating Health 

Key Ideas

- Floods occur when so much water pours into a stream or river that it overflows its banks on either side of the channel.
- The first rule of flood safety: Move to higher ground and stay away from flood waters.

Key Term

flash flood

Section 4 Predicting the Weather

Key Ideas

- Meteorologists interpret weather information from local weather observers, instruments carried by balloons, satellites, and weather stations around the world.
- Changes in weather technology have occurred in two areas: gathering weather data and using computers to make forecasts.
- Standard symbols on weather maps show fronts, areas of high and low pressure, types of precipitation, and temperatures.

Key Terms

meteorologist, El Niño, isobar, isotherm

Organizing Information

Compare/Contrast Table Copy the compare/contrast table about hurricanes and tornadoes onto a separate sheet of paper. Then fill in the empty spaces and add a title. (For more on compare/contrast tables, see the Skills Handbook.)

Type of Storm	Hurricane	Tornado
Where storm forms	Over warm ocean water	**a.** ?
Size of storm	**b.** ?	Several hundred meters
How long storm lasts	A week or more	**c.** ?
Time of year	**d.** ?	Spring, early summer
Safety rules	Evacuate or move inside a well-built building	**e.** ?

Program Resources

- **Unit 4 Resources** Chapter 13 Project Scoring Rubric
- **Performance Assessment** Chapter 13
- **Chapter and Unit Tests** Chapter 13 Test

Media and Technology

Computer Test Bank Chapter 13 Test

Organizing Information

Compare/Contrast Table Sample title: Comparing Hurricanes and Tornadoes **a.** In cumulonimbus clouds **b.** Around 600 kilometers **c.** 15 minutes or less **d.** Summer, early fall **e.** Move to the basement of a well-built building

Reviewing Content

Multiple Choice

1. c **2.** b **3.** d **4.** a **5.** b

True or False

6. continental tropical **7.** stationary front **8.** true **9.** true **10.** isotherms

Checking Concepts

11. temperature and humidity
12. The prevailing westerlies generally push air masses from west to east in the continental United States.
13. A cold front forms when a cold air mass moves underneath a warm air mass, forcing the warm air to rise.
14. Answers may vary. In addition to the dangers of high water to lives and property, floods can knock down electrical poles and cut off power supplies, cause landslides or mudslides, block or wash away roads, pollute drinking water and food.
15. Sources of information that meteorologists use to predict the weather include local weather observers, instruments carried by balloons, satellites, and weather stations around the world.
16. El Niño is a periodic warm water event in which winds shift and push warm water toward the west coast of South America. El Niño can cause dramatic weather changes, including floods, droughts, and tornadoes, over a wide region.
17. Writing to Learn Students' descriptions should show that they are familiar with the characteristics of hurricanes, including the heavy rains and high winds that swirl around the calm eye at the center of the hurricane. Their descriptions also should show that they know hurricanes may cover hundreds of kilometers.

Thinking Critically

18. Warm air masses that influence weather in the United States include maritime tropical air masses from the Gulf of Mexico and the Pacific Ocean and continental tropical air masses from the Southwest. Cold air masses that influence weather in the United States include maritime polar air masses from the Atlantic and Pacific Oceans and continental polar air masses from central and northern Canada. Air masses that form over the water include maritime polar and maritime tropical air masses. Air masses that form over land include continental polar and continental tropical air masses.
19. Cyclones are swirling centers of low pressure air that rotate counterclockwise in the Northern Hemisphere. Anticyclones are swirling centers of high pressure air that rotate clockwise in the Northern Hemisphere. Cyclones are associated with storms and precipitation whereas anticyclones are associated with dry, clear weather.
20. You would not expect hurricanes to form over the oceans off the northeast and northwest coasts of the United States because the temperature of the water is too cold to provide energy for a hurricane.
21. Warm air is less dense than cold air. When a cold front moves through, it flows underneath warm air. When a warm front moves through, it rises up over cold air.

CHAPTER 13 ASSESSMENT

Reviewing Content

Multiple Choice

Choose the letter of the answer that best completes each statement.

1. An air mass that forms over an ocean is called
a. tropical.
b. continental.
c. maritime.
d. polar.

2. Cool, clear weather is usually brought by a
a. warm front.
b. cold front.
c. stationary front.
d. occluded front.

3. Winds spiraling inward toward a center of low pressure form a(n)
a. anticyclone.
b. front.
c. isobar.
d. cyclone.

4. Very large tropical storms with high winds are called
a. hurricanes. **b.** tornadoes.
c. thunderstorms. **d.** blizzards.

5. Most flash floods are caused by
a. hailstorms. **b.** heavy rainfall.
c. high winds. **d.** melting snow.

True or False

If the statement is true, write true. If it is false, change the underlined word or words to make it true.

6. Summers in the Southwest are hot and dry because of maritime tropical air masses.
7. A cold front over an area will bring many days of cloudy weather.
8. Foggy, rainy, or humid weather usually follows the passage of a warm front through an area.
9. Low cumulonimbus clouds may bring both thunderstorms and tornadoes.
10. On a weather map, isobars join places on the map with the same temperature.

Checking Concepts

11. What are the basic characteristics used to describe air masses?
12. Describe how wind patterns affect the movement of air masses in North America.
13. How does a cold front form?
14. Describe three hazards associated with floods.
15. What are some of the sources of information that meteorologists use to predict the weather?
16. What is El Niño? How does it influence the weather in certain regions?
17. Writing to Learn Imagine you are a meteorologist. Your assignment is to investigate a hurricane by flying into it with a large plane. Describe your experiences in a journal entry. Be sure to include descriptive words. How did the hurricane look? Sound? Feel?

Thinking Critically

18. Classifying Classify the major types of air masses that influence weather in the United States in two ways: by temperature and by where they form.
19. Comparing and Contrasting Compare and contrast cyclones and anticyclones. What type of weather is associated with each?
20. Applying Concepts Would you expect hurricanes to form over the oceans off the northeast and northwest coasts of the United States? Explain.
21. Relating Cause and Effect How do differences in air density influence the movement of cold and warm fronts?
22. Making Judgments What do you think is the most important thing people should do to reduce the dangers of storms?

428

Applying Skills

Use the map to answer Questions 23–26.

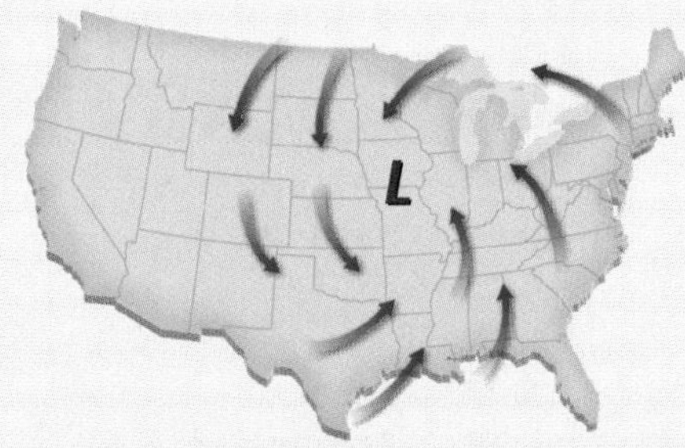

23. **Interpreting Maps** Does the map show a cyclone or an anticyclone? How can you tell?
24. **Interpreting Data** What do the arrows show about the movement of the winds in this pressure center? What else indicates wind direction?
25. **Making Models** Using this diagram as an example, draw a similar diagram to illustrate a high pressure area. Remember to indicate wind direction in your diagram.
26. **Posing Questions** If you saw a pressure center like this on a weather map, what prediction could you make about the weather? What questions would you need to ask in order to make a better prediction?

Performance CHAPTER PROJECT Assessment

Present Your Project Prepare your final report and arrange your maps for presentation. You may want to display each of your maps next to the actual newspaper weather map for that day. Practice your presentation, make any needed changes, and then present your report.

Reflect and Record In your journal, describe what you learned. Are there weather factors on the maps to which you should have paid more attention? Do meteorologists have information that isn't in the newspaper? How could you gather more information to improve your forecasting?

Test Preparation

Use these questions to prepare for standardized tests.

Read the passage. Then answer Questions 27–30.

As Hurricane Andrew roared toward the southern Florida coastline, millions of Florida residents evacuated the area, heading toward safety. It was 1992, and forecasters predicted that Andrew would make landfall sometime in the early morning of August 24. Andrew had been rapidly building speed and strength since it was first classified as a tropical storm on August 17. Andrew quickly advanced to a fierce Category 4 hurricane, with sustained wind speeds estimated at 145 m.p.h. The only type of hurricane that is stronger is a Category 5 hurricane—a very rare event.

Andrew pounded South Florida for several hours. In the end, this hurricane caused over $20 billion in damage to Florida, becoming the most expensive natural disaster in U.S. history up to that date.

27. What is the best title for this selection?
    a. Category 4 Hurricanes
    b. August 24, 1992
    c. Hurricane Andrew Pounds Florida
    d. Hurricane Andrew Heads North
28. What kind of storm was Andrew before it was classified as a hurricane?
    a. tropical storm
    b. thunderstorm
    c. rainstorm
    d. monsoon
29. Which category of hurricanes has the greatest wind speed?
    a. category 1
    b. category 4
    c. category 5
    d. none of the above
30. Why did Andrew cause so much damage?
    a. because it traveled so fast
    b. because it traveled in a northward direction
    c. because it had very strong wind speed
    d. because it traveled over water

22. Answers may vary. Many students will state the importance of staying informed about conditions during storms by listening to weather reports on radio or television.

Program Resources

- **Inquiry Skills Activity Book** Provides teaching and review of all inquiry skills

Applying Skills

23. The map shows a cyclone. You can tell because the air pressure at the center is low and the air is spinning counterclockwise.
24. The winds are spinning in a counterclockwise direction. The low pressure area at the center indicates the winds are spinning inward toward the center.
25. Students' drawings should show a high pressure area surrounded by winds flowing outward from the center in a clockwise direction.
26. If you saw a pressure center like the one depicted on the map on a weather map, you would predict stormy, wet weather. To make a better prediction, you would need to ask about the direction and rate of movement of the pressure center.

Performance Assessment

Present Your Project Encourage students to use a variety of formats for presenting their projects, such as television weather reports and bulletin board displays. Advise students to be prepared to explain the patterns they observed in the weather and how they made their predictions.

Reflect and Record Students may find that they should have paid more attention to the movement of air masses and fronts. They probably learned that it is difficult to predict weather accurately. Meteorologists have a great deal more information than what appears in newspapers, including information from weather radar. To improve their forecasting accuracy, students might consider gathering information from local and national television weather reports. These reports may show weather radar images and other information not found in newspapers.

Test Preparation

27. c **28.** a **29.** c **30.** c

Climate and Climate Change

Sections	Time	Student Edition Activities	Other Activities
CHAPTER PROJECT **Investigating Microclimates** p. 431	Ongoing (3 weeks)	Check Your Progress, p. 439, 458 Present Your Project, p. 465	
1 What Causes Climate? pp. 432–441 ◆ Identify the factors that influence temperature and precipitation. ◆ Explain what causes the seasons.	3 periods/ $1\frac{1}{2}$ blocks	**Discover** How Does Earth's Shape Affect Climate Zones?, p. 432 **Sharpen Your Skills** Inferring, p. 435 **Skills Lab: Controlling Variables** Sunny Rays and Angles, pp. 440–441	**TE** Demonstration, p. 434 **TE** Inquiry Challenge, p. 434 **TE** Building Inquiry Skills: Observing, p. 435 **TE** Including All Students, pp. 436, 437 **TE** Building Inquiry Skills: Inferring, p. 436 **TE** Exploring the Seasons, p. 438
2 Climate Regions pp. 442–453 ◆ Identify factors used to define climates. ◆ Describe the different types of climate regions.	3 periods/ $1\frac{1}{2}$ blocks	**Discover** What Are Different Climate Types?, p. 442 **Try This** Modeling a Humid Climate, p. 447 **Sharpen Your Skills** Classifying, p. 449 **Science at Home,** p. 451 **Real-World Lab: Careers** Cool Climate Graphs, pp. 452–453	**TE** Real-Life Learning, p. 445 **TE** Inquiry Challenge, p. 447 **TE** Including All Students, p. 450 **LM** 14, "Investigating Differences in Climate"
3 Long-Term Changes in Climate pp. 454–458 ◆ Identify how scientists can learn about ancient climates. ◆ Describe how Earth's surface changes during an ice age. ◆ Explain the theories that have been proposed to explain natural climate change.	1 period/ $\frac{1}{2}$ block	**Discover** What Story Can Tree Rings Tell?, p. 454	**TE** Including All Students, p. 456 **TE** Demonstration, p. 457 **TE** Including All Students, p. 458
4 *Integrating Environmental Science* **Global Changes in the Atmosphere** pp. 459–462 ◆ Describe the greenhouse effect and how human activities may be affecting the temperature of Earth's atmosphere. ◆ Describe how human activities have affected the ozone layer.	2 periods/ 1 block	**Discover** What Is the Greenhouse Effect?, p. 459 **Try This** It's Your Skin!, p. 461 **Science at Home,** p. 462	**TE** Demonstration, p. 460
Study Guide/Chapter Assessment pp. 463–465	1 period/ $\frac{1}{2}$ block		**ISAB** Provides teaching and review of all inquiry skills

For Standard or Block Schedule The Resource Pro® CD-ROM gives you maximum flexibility for planning your instruction for any type of schedule. Resource Pro® contains Planning Express®, an advanced scheduling program, as well as the entire contents of the Teaching Resources and the Computer Test Bank.

CHAPTER PLANNING GUIDE

Program Resources	Assessment Strategies	Media and Technology
UR Chapter 14 Project Teacher Notes **UR** Chapter 14 Project Overview and Worksheets	**SE** Performance Assessment: Present Your Project, p. 465 **TE** Check Your Progress, pp. 439, 458 **UR** Chapter 14 Project Scoring Rubric	Science Explorer Internet Site at www.phschool.com Student Edition on Audio CD, Chapter 14
UR 14-1 Lesson Plan **UR** 14-1 Section Summary **UR** 14-1 Review and Reinforce **UR** 14-1 Enrich **UR** Chapter 14 Skills Lab	**SE** Section 1 Review, p. 439 **TE** Ongoing Assessment, pp. 433, 435, 437 **TE** Performance Assessment, p. 439	Concept Videotape Library, Grade 6, Tape 3, "Sunny Days" Transparency 55, "The Seasons"
UR 14-2 Lesson Plan **UR** 14-2 Section Summary **UR** 14-2 Review and Reinforce **UR** 14-2 Enrich **UR** Chapter 14 Real-World Lab	**SE** Section 2 Review, p. 451 **TE** Ongoing Assessment, pp. 443, 445, 447, 449 **TE** Performance Assessment, p. 451	Concept Videotape Library, Grade 6, Tape 3, "Climate in the U.S." Transparencies 56, "World Climate Regions"; 57, "Climate Graph for Washington, D.C."
UR 14-3 Lesson Plan **UR** 14-3 Section Summary **UR** 14-3 Review and Reinforce **UR** 14-3 Enrich	**SE** Section 3 Review, p. 458 **TE** Ongoing Assessment, pp. 455, 457 **TE** Performance Assessment, p. 458	Concept Videotape Library, Grade 6, Tape 3, "Changes in Climate" Transparency 58, "Extent of Northern Hemisphere Glaciation"
UR 14-4 Lesson Plan **UR** 14-4 Section Summary **UR** 14-4 Review and Reinforce **UR** 14-4 Enrich	**SE** Section 4 Review p. 462 **TE** Ongoing Assessment, p. 461 **TE** Performance Assessment, p. 462	Concept Videotape Library, Grade 6, Tape 2, "The Greenhouse Effect" Concept Videotape Library, Grade 6, Tape 2, "Our Passion for Driving"
RCA Provides strategies to improve science reading skills **GRSW** Provides worksheets to promote student comprehension of content	**SE** Chapter 14 Study Guide/Chapter Assessment, pp. 463–465 **PA** Chapter 14 Performance Assessment **CUT** Chapter 14 Test **CTB** Chapter 14 Test	Computer Test Bank, Chapter 14 Test

Key: **SE** Student Edition
CTB Computer Test Bank
ISAB Inquiry Skills Activity Book
GRSW Guided Reading and Study Workbook
TE Teacher's Edition
PTA Product Testing Activities by *Consumer Reports*
RCA Reading in the Content Area
PA Performance Assessment
UR Unit Resources
LM Laboratory Manual
IES Interdisciplinary Explorations Series
CUT Chapter and Unit Tests

Meeting the National Science Education Standards and AAAS Benchmarks

National Science Education Standards	Benchmarks for Science Literacy	Unifying Themes
Science As Inquiry (Content Standard A) ◆ **Design and conduct a scientific investigation** Students investigate how the angle of a light source affects the rate of temperature change on a surface. *(Chapter Project, Skills Lab)* ◆ **Use appropriate tools and techniques to gather, analyze, and interpret data** Students investigate microclimates. Students analyze climate graphs. *(Chapter Project; Real-World Lab)* **Life Science** (Content Standard C) ◆ **Populations and ecosystems** There are five main climate regions, each with typical plants and animals. *(Section 2)* **Earth and Space Science** (Content Standard D) ◆ **Structure of the Earth system** The climate of a region is determined mainly by temperature and precipitation. *(Sections 1, 2, 3, 4)* ◆ **Earth's history** Scientists study fossils, tree rings, and pollen records to learn about ancient climates. *(Section 3)* ◆ **Earth in the solar system** The seasons are caused by the tilt of Earth's axis. *(Section 1)* **Science in Personal and Social Perspectives** (Content Standard F) ◆ **Science and technology in society** Human activities are affecting Earth's climate and atmosphere. *(Section 4)*	**1B Scientific Inquiry** Students investigate microclimates. Students examine how the angle of a light source affects the rate of temperature change of a surface. *(Chapter Project; Skills Lab)* **3C Issues in Technology** Two important worldwide issues are global warming and thinning of the ozone layer. *(Section 4)* **4B The Earth** The seasons are caused by the tilt of Earth's axis. Scientists classify climates according to temperature and precipitation. Throughout Earth's history, climates have gradually changed. *(Sections 1, 2, 4)* **4C Processes That Shape the Earth** Human activities have had an effect on Earth's climate and atmosphere. *(Section 4)* **5D Interdependence of Life** There are five main climate regions, each with its own particular plants and animals. *(Section 2)* **9B Symbolic Relationships** Students compare climate data for four cities. *(Real-World Lab)* **12D Communication Skills** Students present data on the microclimates they studied. *(Chapter Project)*	◆ **Energy** Latitude, altitude, distance from large bodies of water, and ocean currents influence temperature. Students investigate how the angle of a light source affects the rate of temperature change. Global warming is a gradual increase in the temperature of Earth's atmosphere. *(Sections 1, 4; Skills Lab)* ◆ **Scale and Structure** A small area with its own climate is a microclimate. Earth has three main temperature zones. Earth has five main climate regions. *(Chapter Project; Sections 1, 2)* ◆ **Stability** Climate regions are determined on the basis of average temperature and precipitation. Although weather can vary from day to day, climates change more slowly. *(Sections 2, 3)* ◆ **Systems and Interactions** Students relate microclimates to the plants and animals found there. The seasons are caused by the tilt of Earth's axis. Students investigate how the angle of the sun's rays affects the amount of energy absorbed by different parts of Earth's surface. Human activities have had an effect on Earth's climate and atmosphere. *(Chapter Project; Sections 1, 4; Skills Lab)* ◆ **Unity and Diversity** Each hemisphere has a polar zone, temperate zone, and tropical zone. Each climate region has a characteristic average temperature and precipitation. Students compare climate data for four cities. *(Sections 1, 2; Real-World Lab)*

Take It to the Net

Interactive text at www.phschool.com

Science Explorer comes alive with iText.

- **Complete student text** is accessible from any computer with Internet access or a CD-ROM drive.
- **Animations, simulations, and videos** enhance student understanding and retention of concepts.
- **Self-tests and online study tools** assess student understanding.

STAY CURRENT with **SCIENCE NEWS**®

Find out the latest research and information about Weather and Climate at: **www.phschool.com**

Go to **www.phschool.com** and click on the Science icon.Then click on Science Explorer: Life, Earth, and Physical Science under PH@school.

Student Edition Activities Planner

Activity	Time (minutes)	Materials *Quantities for one work group*	Skills
Section 1			
Discover, p. 432	15	**Consumable** cash register or adding machine paper, clear tape, empty toilet paper roll **Nonconsumable** globe, pencil, flashlight, metric ruler	Observing
Sharpen Your Skills, p. 435	10	No special materials required.	Inferring
Skills Lab, pp. 440–441	40	**Consumable** black construction paper, clear tape, graph paper **Nonconsumable** scissors, ruler, 3 thermometers or temperature probes, protractor, books, 100-W incandescent lamp, watch or clock, pencil	Designing Experiments, Controlling Variables, Collecting Data, Graphing, Inferring
Section 2			
Discover, p. 442	15	**Consumable** newspapers or magazines **Nonconsumable** scissors	Forming Operational Definitions
Try This, p. 447	10, 5	**Consumable** water, clear plastic wrap **Nonconsumable** 2 small plastic bowls, 2 rubber bands	Inferring
Sharpen Your Skills, p. 449	10	No special materials required.	Classifying
Science at Home, p. 451	home	No special materials required.	Classifying
Real-World Lab, pp. 452–453	40	**Consumable** 3 pieces of graph paper **Nonconsumable** calculator, ruler, black pencil, blue pencil, red pencil, green pencil, climate map on pages 658–659, U.S. map with city names and latitude lines	Graphing, Interpreting Data, Drawing Conclusions
Section 3			
Discover, p. 454	10	**Nonconsumable** Figure 16 on page 455, magnifying lens	Inferring
Section 4			
Discover, p. 459	15, 5	**Consumable** 2 pieces of black construction paper, 2 shoe boxes, clear plastic wrap, masking tape **Nonconsumable** 2 thermometers, lamp	Inferring
Try This, p. 461	15	**Consumable** ultraviolet-sensitive paper, 3 plastic sandwich bags, 2 sunscreens with different SPF numbers **Nonconsumable** black marking pen	Drawing Conclusions
Science at Home, p. 462	home	**Nonconsumable** calculator	Comparing and Contrasting

A list of all materials required for the Student Edition activities can be found on pages TVA34–TVA40. You can obtain information about ordering materials by calling 1-800-848-9500 or by accessing the Science Explorer Internet site at: **www.phschool.com**

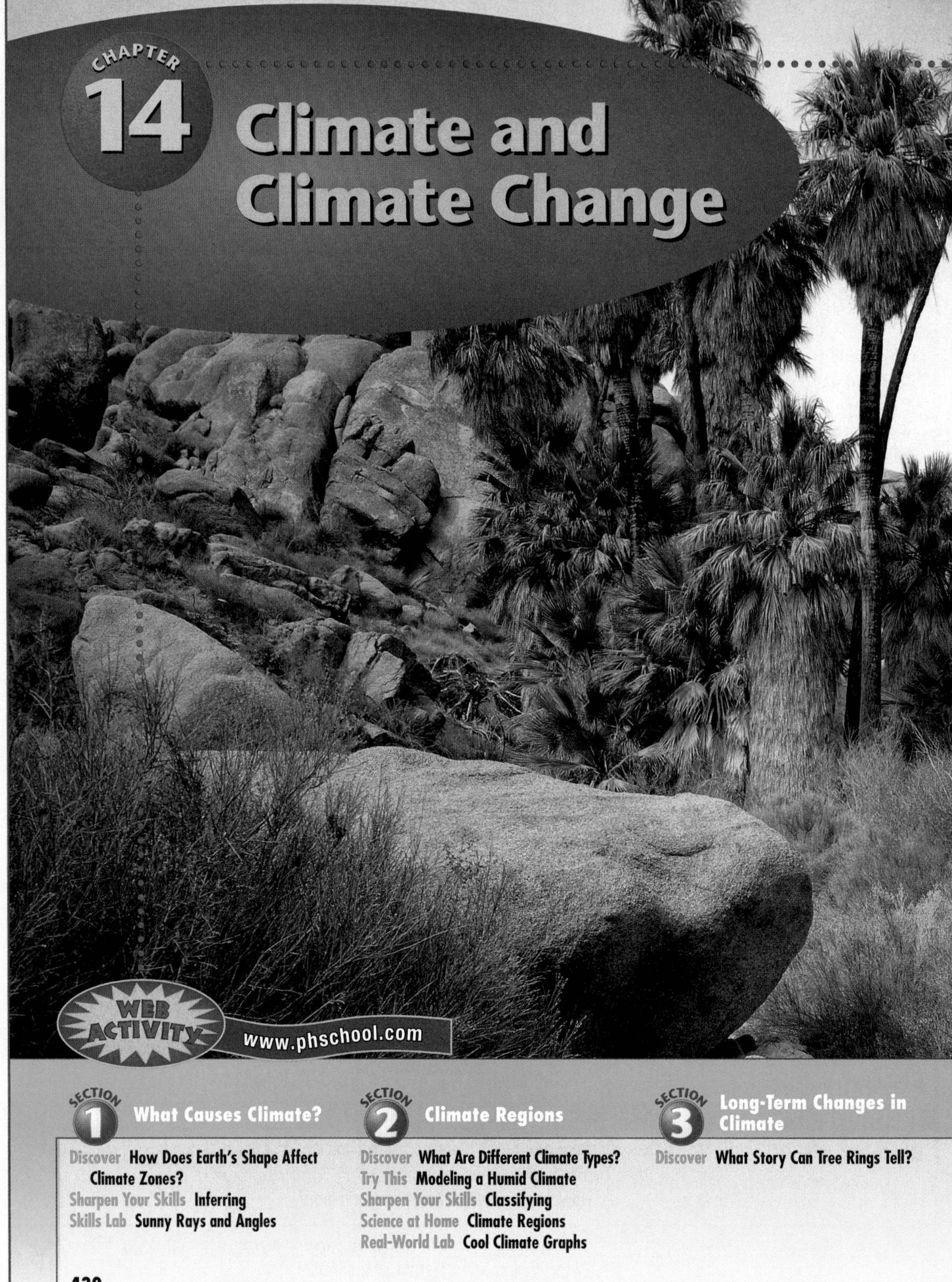

Chapter 14 Climate and Climate Change

www.phschool.com

Section 1 What Causes Climate?
Discover How Does Earth's Shape Affect Climate Zones?
Sharpen Your Skills Inferring
Skills Lab Sunny Rays and Angles

Section 2 Climate Regions
Discover What Are Different Climate Types?
Try This Modeling a Humid Climate
Sharpen Your Skills Classifying
Science at Home Climate Regions
Real-World Lab Cool Climate Graphs

Section 3 Long-Term Changes in Climate
Discover What Story Can Tree Rings Tell?

430

CHAPTER 14 PROJECT

Investigating Microclimates

All students notice daily weather conditions, but many are not aware that these daily patterns determine the climate in which they live. Even more subtle are the various microclimates located in an area. These microclimates support different organisms based on slightly different daily weather conditions.

Purpose In this project, students will gather weather data and observe the organisms living in three different areas to determine their microclimates. In doing so, they will be able to conclude that climates in very small areas can be different from each other, even though these areas are located near each other.

Skills Focus After completing the Chapter 14 Project, students will be able to
- develop hypotheses about how microclimates in three areas will differ;
- create data tables for weather data and environmental factors;
- graph weather data and analyze the data for patterns;
- relate each microclimate to the plants and animals found there;
- communicate the project results in a class presentation.

Project Time Line The entire project will require about three weeks. Begin by distributing Chapter 14 Project Student Materials and Scoring Rubric in Unit 4 Resources. See Chapter 14 Project Teacher Notes in Unit 4 Resources for more information.

Divide the class into groups and allow time for them to choose their three microclimates. For convenience, these areas should be relatively close to the school. Make sure each group chooses areas that have different environmental conditions.

At this point, students can use Worksheet 1 to help them organize their group logbook. Review how to use various weather instruments, if necessary. Students can use Worksheet 2 to practice analyzing weather data. Then students will be ready to gather data in each area for two weeks. Students should collect data from the same location at the same time each day for consistent results. Students will also need time to prepare graphs for their class presentations.

Suggested Shortcuts You can simplify this project by asking each student group to collect data from only one microclimate. The entire class can compare and contrast the data collected by each group. Students could also collect data for only one week instead of two.

Possible Materials Students will need instruments that measure weather data such as thermometers, anemometers, wind vanes, wet and dry bulb thermometers, rain gauges, and light meters. If you don't have class sets of these instruments, schedule their use for each group throughout the day, or students can use their weather instruments from Chapter 12. Students will also need hand lenses to observe organisms and field guides to identify them, a logbook, and graph paper.

CHAPTER 14 PROJECT

Investigating Microclimates

Most of the Mojave Desert is too dry for trees. Only cactus, shrubs, and other hardy plants are able to survive in the parched land. So if you see palm trees, you know there must be water nearby.

Palm trees in the desert grow only in a small area with its own climate—a microclimate. As you work through this chapter, you will investigate microclimates in your community.

Your Goal To compare weather conditions from at least three microclimates.

To complete your project, you must

- hypothesize how the microclimates in three areas will differ from one another
- collect data at the same places and times each day
- relate each microclimate to the plants and animals found there
- follow the safety guidelines in Appendix A

Get Started Begin by brainstorming a list of nearby places that may have different microclimates. How are the places different? Keep in mind weather factors such as temperature, precipitation, humidity, wind direction, and wind speed. Consider areas that are grassy, sandy, sunny, or shaded. Start thinking about what instruments you will need to do your investigation.

Check Your Progress You'll be working on this project as you study this chapter. To keep your project on track, look for Check Your Progress boxes at the following points.

Section 1 Review, page 439: Measure and record weather data.
Section 3 Review, page 458: Graph your data and look for patterns.

Present Your Project At the end of the chapter (page 465), you will present the data you collected about your microclimates. Include any patterns you observed.

Even in a desert, palm trees can survive if they have enough water.

Integrating Environmental Science

SECTION 4 Global Changes in the Atmosphere

Discover **What Is the Greenhouse Effect?**
Try This **It's Your Skin!**
Science at Home **Compare Sunscreens**

431

Launching the Project To introduce this project, take the class on a walk around the school grounds or neighborhood. Call students' attention to the plants and animals found in specific places. Focus on the environmental conditions these organisms need to survive. For example, moss grows only in moist areas. Encourage students to offer comments and to ask questions about the organisms and the environmental conditions that they observe.

Give students time to read the description of the Chapter 14 Project in their text and in the Chapter 14 Project Overview in Unit 4 Resources. Encourage students to begin thinking of nearby places with different microclimates and the conditions that make each place different.

Program Resources

- **Unit 4 Resources** Chapter 14 Project Teacher Notes; Chapter 14 Project Overview and Worksheets; Chapter 14 Project Scoring Rubric

Media and Technology

Student Edition on Audio CD Chapter 14

You will find an Internet activity, chapter self-tests for students, and links to other chapter topics at this site.

Performance Assessment

The Chapter 14 Project Scoring Rubric in Unit 4 Resources will help you evaluate how well students complete the Chapter 14 Project. Students will be assessed on

- how completely and accurately they collect data from their microclimate areas,
- how neat, thorough, and accurate their logbooks are,
- how thorough and interesting their class presentations are,
- how well they worked together in their groups.

By sharing the Chapter 14 Project Scoring Rubric with students at the beginning of the project, you will make it clear to them what they are expected to do.

SECTION 1 What Causes Climate?

Objectives

After completing the lesson, students will be able to
- ◆ identify the factors that influence temperature and precipitation;
- ◆ explain what causes the seasons.

Key Terms climate, tropical zone, polar zone, temperate zone, marine climate, continental climate, windward, leeward, microclimate

1 Engage/Explore

Activating Prior Knowledge

Ask students: **What is the weather like today?** Then ask: **Is today's weather typical of the weather we usually have at this time of year?** *(Accept all answers without comment.)* Explain that the average, year-after-year weather conditions is climate.

DISCOVER ACTIVITY

Skills Focus observing
Materials *globe, cash register or adding machine paper, clear tape, pencil, flashlight, empty toilet paper roll, metric ruler*
Time 15 minutes
Advance Preparation Cut the cash register paper into lengths that are slightly longer than the distance between the equator and the North Pole on the globe.
Tips Have students label the paper before they tape it to the globe. One student should hold the flashlight the same distance from the globe, but move it up in a straight line perpendicular to the globe for each drawing.
Expected Outcome The shapes will change from a perfect circle at the equator to an elongated oval at the North Pole.
Think It Over The shape is a perfect circle at the equator, an oval at the mid-latitudes, and an elongated, faded oval at the poles. The sun's rays heat Earth unevenly because the light rays from the sun hit Earth's surface at different angles.

SECTION 1 What Causes Climate?

DISCOVER ACTIVITY

How Does Earth's Shape Affect Climate Zones?

1. On a globe, tape a strip of cash register paper from the equator to the North Pole. Divide the tape into three equal parts. Label the section near the North Pole *poles,* the section near the equator *equator,* and the middle section *mid-latitudes.*
2. Tape the end of an empty toilet paper roll to the end of a flashlight. Hold the flashlight about 30 cm from the equator. Turn on the flashlight to represent the sun. On the paper strip, have a partner draw the shape of the area the light shines on.
3. Move the flashlight up slightly to aim at the section of the paper marked "mid-latitudes." Keep the flashlight horizontal and at the same distance from the globe. Again have a partner draw the shape of the area that the light shines on.

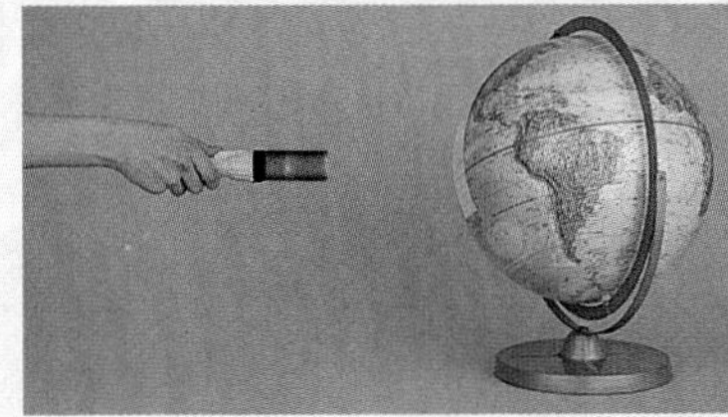

4. Move the flashlight up again to shine on the section of the paper marked "poles." Keep the flashlight horizontal and at the same distance from the globe. Draw the shape of the area that the light shines on.

Think It Over

Observing How does the shape of the area that is illuminated change? Do you think the sun's rays heat Earth's surface evenly?

GUIDE FOR READING

- ◆ **What are the factors that influence temperature and precipitation?**
- ◆ **What causes the seasons?**

Reading Tip **As you read, use the headings to make an outline of the factors that affect climate.**

If you telephone a friend in another state and ask, "What's the weather there today?" she might answer: "It's gray, cool, and rainy. It's usually like that this time of year." Your friend has told you something about both weather and climate.

Weather is day-to-day events. The weather may be cloudy and rainy one day and clear and sunny the next. Weather refers to the condition of the atmosphere at a particular place and time. **Climate,** on the other hand, refers to the average, year-after-year conditions of temperature, precipitation, winds, and clouds in an area. How would you describe the climate where you live?

Two main factors—temperature and precipitation—determine the climate of a region. A climate region is a large area with similar climate conditions throughout. For example, the climate in the southeastern United States is humid, with moderate temperatures.

◀ These polar bears—two males and their mother—are taking it easy in the polar zone.

READING STRATEGIES

Reading Tip Suggest to students that they skim the section first before making their outlines. Students should use the section title as the title for their outlines. They should use the main heads of the section as the main headings in their outlines and the section subheads as the subheadings. Students can fill in details under outline headings as they read the section. Students can use their outlines as study aids.

Student outlines might begin as follows:

I. Factors Affecting Temperature
   A. Latitude
   B. Altitude
   C. Distance from Large Bodies of Water
   D. Ocean Currents
II. Factors Affecting Precipitation
   A. Prevailing Winds
   B. Mountain Ranges

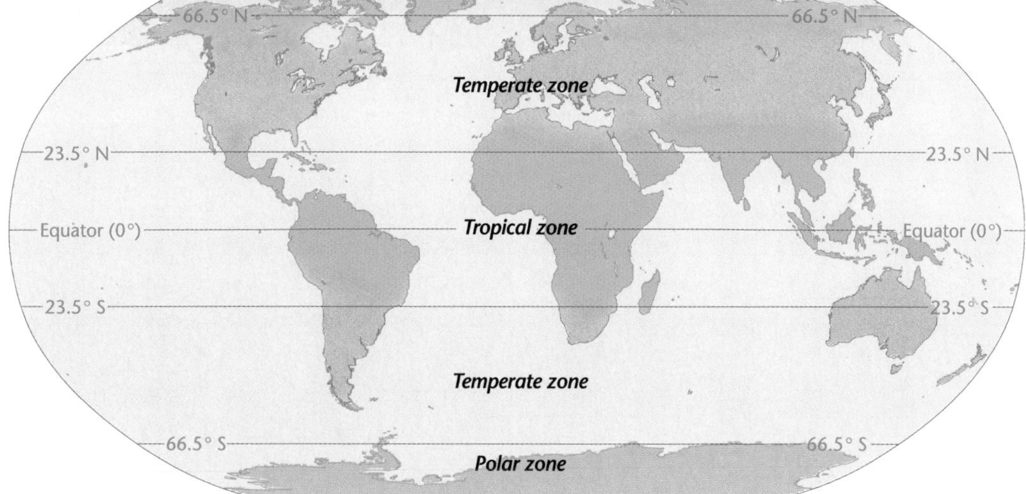

Figure 1 Earth has three main temperature zones.
Interpreting Maps In which temperature zone is most of the United States located?

Factors Affecting Temperature

Tropical countries, such as Panama, are usually hot. Northern countries, such as Finland, are usually cold. Why are some places warm and others cold? **The main factors that influence temperature are latitude, altitude, distance from large bodies of water, and ocean currents.**

Latitude In general, climates of locations farther from the equator are cooler than climates of areas closer to the equator. Why is this? As you found out if you tried the Discover activity, the sun's rays hit Earth's surface most directly at the equator. At the poles, the same amount of solar radiation is spread out over a larger area, and therefore brings less warmth.

Recall that latitude is the distance from the equator, measured in degrees. Based on latitude, Earth's surface can be divided into the three temperature zones shown in Figure 1. The **tropical zone** is the area near the equator, between about 23.5° north latitude and 23.5° south latitude. The tropical zone receives direct or nearly direct sunlight all year round, making climates there warm.

In contrast, the sun's rays always strike at a lower angle near the North and South poles. As a result, the areas near both poles have cold climates. These **polar zones** extend from about 66.5° to 90° north and 66.5° to 90° south latitudes.

The **temperate zones** are between the tropical and the polar zones—from about 23.5° to 66.5° north and 23.5° to 66.5° south latitudes. In summer, the sun's rays strike the temperate zones more directly. In winter, the sun's rays strike at a lower angle. As a result, the weather in the temperate zones ranges from warm or hot in summer to cool or cold in winter.

2 Facilitate

Factors Affecting Temperature

Using the Visuals: Figure 1

Review latitude with students. Ask: **What does latitude measure?** *(The distance from the equator)* Instruct students to find the equator in Figure 1. Then ask: **At what degree of latitude is the North Pole?** *(90° north latitude)* Draw a circle on the board and show students that 360° is a full circle and 180° is a half circle. Ask: **How many degrees are equal to one-fourth of a circle?** *(90°)* Relate these measurements of a circle to degrees of latitude. **learning modality: logical/ mathematical**

Cultural Diversity

Students can learn how climate affects the culture of a group of people by comparing and contrasting types of clothing, housing, and customs of people living in different temperature zones. Encourage groups of students to choose a group of people to study. Groups may choose native cultures or modern cultures from around the world or from different areas of the United States. Monitor the groups' choices so that each is studying a different culture. Groups should divide the research tasks and the preparation for a class presentation. Challenge students to find creative ways to present the culture of the people they studied. **cooperative learning**

Program Resources

- **Unit 5 Resources** 14-1 Lesson Plan; 14-1 Section Summary
- **Guided Reading and Study Workbook** Section 14-1

Media and Technology

 **Concept Videotape Library**
Grade 6, Tape 3 "Sunny Days"

Answers to Self-Assessment

Caption Question

Figure 1 the temperate zone

Ongoing Assessment

Drawing Instruct students to make a diagram that shows the different angles at which the sun's rays strike Earth in each temperature zone.

 Students can save their diagrams in their portfolios.

Factors Affecting Temperature, continued

Demonstration

Materials *small black mat, desk lamp with high intensity bulb, 2 thermometers, 2 ring stands with clamps for thermometers*

ACTIVITY

Time 15–20 minutes

To demonstrate why air temperature is colder at higher altitudes, shine the light directly on the black mat for 10 minutes. During this time, set up the ring stands so that one holds the bulb of one thermometer 5 cm above the mat and the other holds the thermometer 20 cm above the mat. When you turn out the light, place the thermometers over the black mat. Read the thermometers right away, then every minute until the temperature stops rising. Encourage students to infer why the lower thermometer had a higher temperature reading than the higher thermometer. *(The black mat absorbed the light energy from the light as heat, then radiated the heat into the air above it.)* **learning modality: visual**

Inquiry Challenge

ACTIVITY

With the knowledge that large bodies of water greatly moderate the temperatures of nearby land, challenge small groups of students to devise a plan that would help them cool off on a hot summer day. After checking each group's plan, help them gather the materials they will need to implement it. *(One possible plan: set up a fan so that it blows across ice water.)* **cooperative learning**

Figure 2 Mount Kilimanjaro in Tanzania, Africa, is near the equator. *Applying Concepts Why is there snow on top of the mountain?*

Altitude The peak of Mount Kilimanjaro towers high above the African plains. At nearly 6 kilometers above sea level, Kilimanjaro is covered in snow all year round. Yet it is located near the equator, at 3° south latitude. Why is Mount Kilimanjaro so cold?

In the case of high mountains, altitude is a more important climate factor than latitude. Recall from Chapter 1 that the temperature of the troposphere decreases about 6.5 Celsius degrees for every 1-kilometer increase in altitude. As a result, highland areas everywhere have cool climates, no matter what their latitude. At nearly 6 kilometers, the air at the top of Mount Kilimanjaro is about 39 Celsius degrees colder than the air at sea level at the same latitude.

Distance From Large Bodies of Water Oceans or large lakes can also affect temperatures. Oceans greatly moderate, or make less extreme, the temperatures of nearby land. Water heats up more slowly than land; it also cools down more slowly. Therefore, winds from the ocean keep coastal regions from reaching extremes of hot and cold. Much of the west coasts of North America, South America, and Europe have mild **marine climates,** with relatively warm winters and cool summers.

The centers of North America and Asia are too far inland to be warmed or cooled by the oceans. Most of Canada and Russia, as well as the central United States, have **continental climates.** Continental climates have more extreme temperatures than marine climates. Winters are cold, while summers are warm or hot.

Background

Facts and Figures Like altitude, large bodies of water and ocean currents can be as important in influencing the temperature of a location as latitude. For example, Bergen, Norway, is a coastal city located over 2,000 km north of Omaha, Nebraska. Based only on latitude, one would assume that Bergen would have a colder climate. However, the average January temperature in Bergen is higher than that in Omaha, and on average, Bergen is cooler than Omaha in July.

The seasonal temperatures in Bergen are directly influenced by its proximity to the ocean and the North Atlantic Drift. The ocean acts as a huge reservoir of heat energy due to its great depth and volume, and its ability to absorb large amounts of solar radiation.

Ocean Currents Many marine climates are influenced by ocean currents, streams of water within the oceans that move in regular patterns. In general, warm ocean currents carry warm water from the tropics toward the poles. Cold currents bring cold water from the polar zones toward the equator. The surface of the water warms or cools the air above it. The warmed or cooled air then moves over the nearby land. So a warm current brings warm air to the land it touches. A cold current brings cool air.

As you read about the following currents, trace their paths on the map in Figure 3. The best-known warm-water current is the Gulf Stream. The Gulf Stream begins in the Gulf of Mexico, then flows north along the east coast of the United States. When it crosses the North Atlantic, it becomes the North Atlantic Drift. This warm current gives Ireland and southern England a mild, wet climate despite their relatively high latitude.

In contrast, the cool California Current flows from Alaska southward down the West Coast. The California Current makes climates of places along the West Coast cooler than you would expect at their latitudes.

☑ *Checkpoint* *What effect do oceans have on the temperatures of nearby land areas?*

Inferring ACTIVITY

Look at the currents in the South Pacific, South Atlantic, and Indian oceans. What pattern can you observe? Now compare currents in the South Atlantic to those in the North Atlantic. What might be responsible for differences in the current patterns?

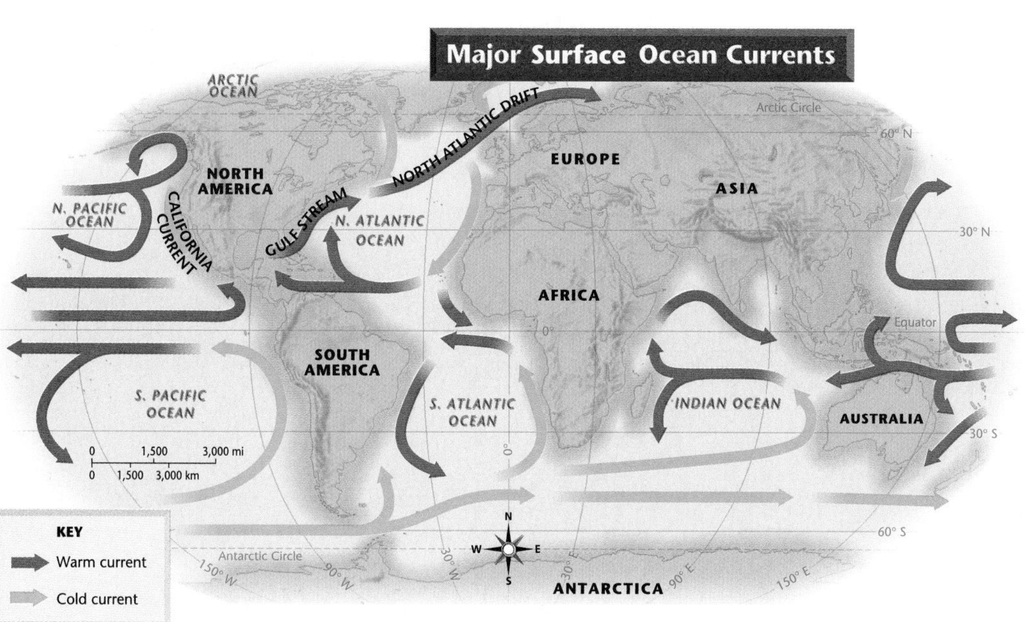

Figure 3 On this map, warm currents are shown in red and cold currents in blue.

Building Inquiry Skills: Observing

ACTIVITY

Materials *heat-resistant pan, water, ice, bricks, bunsen burner or candle, food coloring*
Time 15 minutes

Have students observe how differences in water temperature cause currents. First, they should fill a shallow pan with water and place ice cubes in the center of the pan. Then they should elevate the pan with bricks so that a bunsen burner or candle will fit under the pan. They should heat one side of the pan and place a few drops of food coloring in the water. Students should observe the movement of the colored water in the pan. Ask: **What is causing the water to move?** *(As the water warms, it becomes less dense and rises. The cold water, which is denser, sinks and pushes the warmer water out of the way.)* Encourage students to relate their observations to the movement of ocean currents. **learning modality: kinesthetic**

Sharpen your Skills

Inferring ACTIVITY

Time 10 minutes
Students should observe that the currents in the South Pacific, South Atlantic, and Indian oceans move south toward Antarctica. Students should infer that movement of cold water from the poles toward the equator pushes warm water at the equator toward the poles. Wind direction and land location also affect the direction of currents.
Extend Students may also note the clockwise rotation of currents in the Northern Hemisphere and the counter clockwise rotation in the Southern Hemisphere. Challenge students to trace the changes in Figure 3 when an El Niño occurs. **learning modality: visual**

Answers to Self-Assessment

Caption Question

Figure 2 The top of the mountain is at a higher altitude, so the air there is much cooler than the air at the bottom.

☑ *Checkpoint*

The surface of the water warms or cools the air above it. The warmed or cooled air then moves over nearby land, affecting the temperatures there.

Ongoing Assessment

Writing Instruct students to write a description of how the temperature of a climate is affected by altitude, distance from large bodies of water, and ocean currents.

Factors Affecting Precipitation

Including All Students

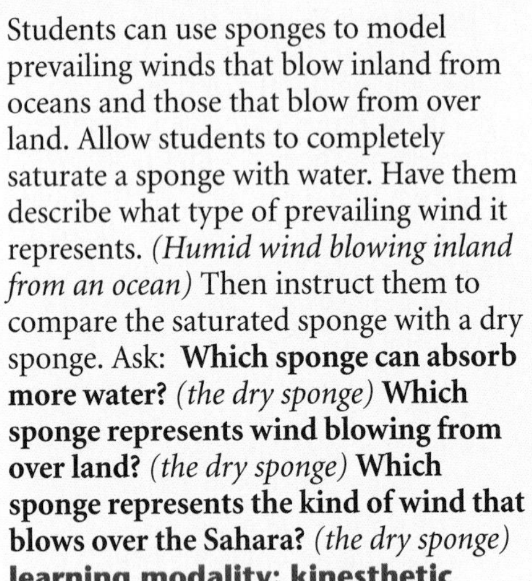

Materials *2 sponges, water*
Time 10 minutes

Students can use sponges to model prevailing winds that blow inland from oceans and those that blow from over land. Allow students to completely saturate a sponge with water. Have them describe what type of prevailing wind it represents. *(Humid wind blowing inland from an ocean)* Then instruct them to compare the saturated sponge with a dry sponge. Ask: **Which sponge can absorb more water?** *(the dry sponge)* **Which sponge represents wind blowing from over land?** *(the dry sponge)* **Which sponge represents the kind of wind that blows over the Sahara?** *(the dry sponge)* **learning modality: kinesthetic**

Building Inquiry Skills: Inferring

Materials *physical map of the United States, map of global wind patterns*
Time 20 minutes

Challenge students to work together in small groups to make inferences about the amount of precipitation in different regions of the United States. Groups can compare wind patterns with topography. Invite groups to share their inferences with the rest of the class. You might wish to record each group's inferences and revisit them as you study climate regions in the next section. Help students determine why they might have inferred incorrectly. **cooperative learning**

Factors Affecting Precipitation

The amount of rain and snow that falls in an area each year determines how wet or dry its climate is. But what determines how much precipitation an area gets? **The main factors that affect precipitation are prevailing winds and the presence of mountains.**

Prevailing Winds As you know, weather patterns depend on the movement of huge air masses. Air masses are moved from place to place by prevailing winds, the directional winds that usually blow in a region. Air masses can be warm or cool, dry or humid. The amount of water vapor in the air mass influences how much rain or snow will fall.

Warm air can carry more water vapor than cold air can. When warm air rises and cools, water comes out of the air as precipitation. For example, surface air near the equator is generally hot and humid. As the air rises and cools, heavy rains fall, nourishing thick tropical forests. In contrast, sinking cold air is usually dry. Because the air becomes warmer as it sinks, it can hold more water vapor. The water vapor stays in the air and little or no rain falls. The result may be a desert.

The amount of water vapor in prevailing winds also depends on where the winds come from. Winds that blow inland from oceans carry more water vapor than winds that blow from over land. For example, the Sahara in Africa is near both the Atlantic Ocean and the Mediterranean Sea. Yet the Sahara is very dry. This is because few winds blow from the oceans toward this area. Instead, the prevailing winds are the dry northeast trade winds. The source of these winds is cool, sinking air from southwest Asia.

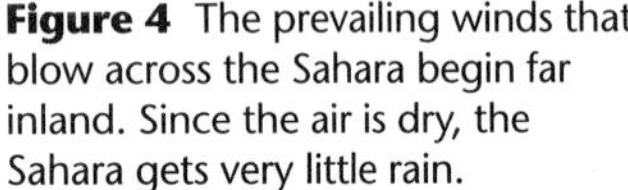

Figure 4 The prevailing winds that blow across the Sahara begin far inland. Since the air is dry, the Sahara gets very little rain.

436

Background

Facts and Figures The dry prevailing winds that blow across the Sahara absorb any water that is present on land, rather than bring rain. Because of this, these winds are sometimes called evaporating winds.

An evaporating wind in northwestern United States, called a chinook, is a westerly wind that blows down the eastern slope of the Rocky Mountains. This wind is made up of warm Pacific air that has lost much of its water vapor on the western slope of the Rockies. It is so warm and dry that it melts snow in the valleys during winter.

Mountain Ranges A mountain range in the path of prevailing winds can also influence where precipitation falls. As you have learned, when humid winds blow from the ocean toward coastal mountains, they are forced to rise up to pass over the mountains. The rising warm air cools and its water vapor condenses, forming clouds. Rain or snow falls on the **windward** side of the mountains, the side the oncoming wind hits.

By the time the air reaches the other side of the mountains, it has lost much of its water vapor, so it is cool and dry. The land on the **leeward** side of the mountains—downwind—is in a rain shadow.

The Owens Valley in California, shown in Figure 5, is in the rain shadow of the Sierra Nevada, about 80 kilometers west of Death Valley. Humid winds blow eastward from the Pacific Ocean. In the photo, you can see that this humid air has left snow on top of the mountains. Then the air flowed down the leeward side of the mountains. As it moved downward, the air became warmer. The desert in the Owens Valley, on the eastern side of the Sierra Nevada, was formed by this hot, dry air.

☑ *Checkpoint* *Why does precipitation fall mainly on the windward sides of mountains?*

Figure 5 The Sierra Nevada runs through eastern California, parallel to the Pacific coast. To the east of the Sierras is the Owens Valley, shown above. *Inferring Is the Owens Valley on the windward or leeward side of the mountains?*

Microclimates

Have you ever noticed that it is cooler and more humid in a grove of trees than in an open field? The same factors that affect large climate regions also affect smaller areas. A small area with specific climate conditions may have its own **microclimate.** Inland mountains, lakes, forests, and other natural features can influence climate nearby, resulting in a microclimate.

You might find a microclimate in a downtown area with clusters of tall buildings, or on a windy peninsula jutting out into the ocean. Even a small park, if it is usually sunnier or windier than nearby areas, may have its own microclimate. The grass on a lawn can be covered in dew and produce conditions like a rain forest, while the pavement in the parking lot is dry, like a desert.

Including All Students

ACTIVITY

Allow students to make shadows on the wall with a flashlight in the darkened classroom or outside on a sunny day. Then ask: **What is a shadow?** *(An area that doesn't receive light because something is blocking the light)* Relate this idea to a rain shadow by explaining that a rain shadow is an area that doesn't receive rain because a mountain range is blocking the rain. Ask: **Which side of a mountain is in a rain shadow?** *(the leeward side)* **limited English proficiency**

Microclimates

Real-Life Learning

Challenge students to identify the locations of microclimates around the school grounds. Lead them to identify microclimates as small as the north side of the school building compared to the south side. They should compare the climates of the microclimates they identify. Ask: **What climate factors cause the microclimates to exist?** *(Students should explain how the amount of precipitation and the temperature are affected in the microclimates.)* **learning modality: logical/mathematical**

Answers to Self-Assessment

Caption Question

Figure 5 the leeward side

☑ *Checkpoint*

Winds are forced to rise up and over mountains. As the air rises it cools, and the water vapor condenses and falls as rain or snow. When the air drops down the leeward side, it's dry because it lost most of its water vapor.

Ongoing Assessment

Oral Presentation Have several students describe the factors that affect the amount of precipitation in an area, and challenge others to relate temperature and precipitation to microclimates.

The Seasons

Integrating Space Science

Draw on the chalkboard Earth's orbit around the sun. Draw Earth so that its poles are perpendicular to its orbit. Ask students: **How long does it take Earth to revolve around the sun?** *(365 days, or one year)* Remind students that Earth spins on its axis, or rotates, once every 24 hours. Explain that the hours of daylight would equal the hours of nighttime if Earth had a straight axis. Then draw Earth with a tilted axis. Ask: **How does the tilted axis affect the length of day and night on Earth?** *(The tilt causes the length of day and night to be different, depending on where Earth is in its orbit.)* **How does the tilted axis affect how the sun's rays strike different parts of Earth?** *(The tilt causes the sun's rays to strike one hemisphere more directly at the equator than the other at different times of the year.)* **learning modality: visual**

Math TOOLBOX

Time 10 minutes
Tips Have students set up the fraction by writing 23.5/90. When students divide the numbers, they should find that Earth's tilt is about 0.26, or just over one quarter, of a right angle. **learning modality: logical/mathematical**

EXPLORING the Seasons

Materials *flashlight, balloon, marker*
Time 10 minutes

Challenge students to use a flashlight and a balloon to observe the effect of Earth's tilted axis on the seasons. One student should hold a round balloon at a tilt similar to Earth's axis while another student shines a flashlight on it. A third student can use a permanent marker to outline the darkened area of the balloon and label the dark side, the light side, the North Pole, the South Pole, and the equator. Then have students compare their balloons to the diagram in *Exploring the Seasons.* **learning modality: kinesthetic**

Math TOOLBOX

Angles

Light from the sun strikes Earth's surface at different angles. An angle is made up of two lines that meet at a point. Angles are measured in degrees. A full circle has 360 degrees.

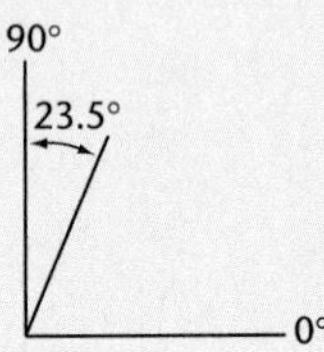

When the sun is directly overhead near the equator, it is at an angle of 90° to Earth's surface. A 90° angle is called a right angle. It is one fourth of a circle.

When the sun is near the horizon, it is at an angle of close to 0° to Earth's surface.

Earth's axis is tilted at an angle of 23.5°. About what fraction of a right angle is this?

The Seasons

INTEGRATING SPACE SCIENCE Although you can describe the average weather conditions of a climate region, these conditions are not constant all year long. Instead, most places on Earth outside the tropics have four seasons: winter, spring, summer, and autumn.

You might think that Earth is closer to the sun during the summer and farther away during winter. If this were true, every place on Earth would have summer at the same time. Actually, when it is summer in the Northern Hemisphere it is winter in the Southern Hemisphere. So the seasons are *not* a result of changes in the distance between Earth and the sun.

Tilted Axis *Exploring the Seasons* on page 603 shows how Earth's axis is tilted in relation to the sun. **The seasons are caused by the tilt of Earth's axis as Earth travels around the sun.** The axis is an imaginary line through Earth's center that passes through both poles. Earth turns, or rotates, around this axis once each day. Earth's axis is not straight up and down, but is tilted at an angle of 23.5°. The axis always points in the same direction—toward the North Star. As Earth travels around the sun, the north end of the axis is pointed away from the sun for part of the year and toward the sun for part of the year.

Winter or Summer Look at *Exploring the Seasons* on the next page. Which way is the north end of Earth's axis tilted in June? Notice that the Northern Hemisphere receives more direct rays from the sun. Also, in June the days in the Northern Hemisphere are longer than the nights. The combination of more direct rays and longer days makes Earth's surface warmer in the Northern Hemisphere than at any other time of the year. It is summer.

In June, when the north end of Earth's axis is tilted toward the sun, the south end of the axis is tilted away from the sun. The Southern Hemisphere receives fewer direct rays from the sun. The days are shorter than the nights. As a result, the Southern Hemisphere is experiencing winter.

Now look at the situation in December, six months later. Which way is the north end of Earth's axis tilted now? The Northern Hemisphere receives fewer direct rays from the sun and has shorter days. It is winter in the Northern Hemisphere and summer in the Southern Hemisphere.

Twice during the year, in March and September, neither end of Earth's axis is tilted toward the sun. At both of these times, one hemisphere has spring while the other has autumn.

Background

Facts and Figures The equator does not have the same seasonal changes as other latitudes because the length of day at the equator changes very little through the year and the sun's rays always hit the equator fairly directly. Because of this, the equator receives about the same amount of energy from the sun all year long. At higher latitudes, the length of day changes because of Earth's tilted axis. This is seen in the extreme at the poles, where six months of continuous daylight are followed by six months of continuous darkness. Even during continuous daylight, temperatures at the poles are very cold because the poles do not receive much of the sun's energy. The sun's energy that reaches the poles is spread over a larger area than at the equator, and much of that sunlight is reflected off the ice and snow near the poles.

EXPLORING the Seasons

The seasons are a result of Earth's tilted axis. The seasons change as the amount of energy each hemisphere receives from the sun changes.

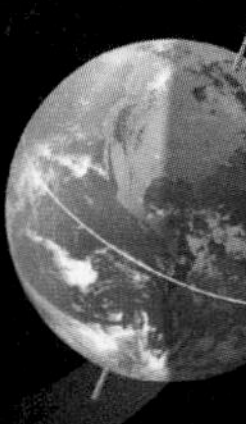
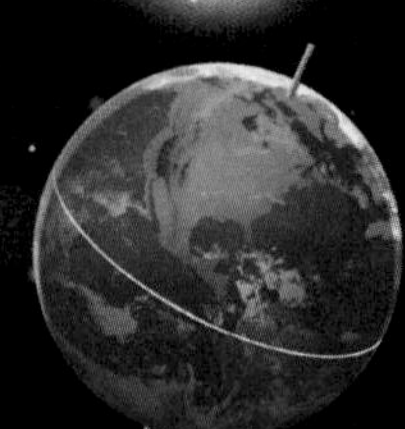

December
The south end of Earth's axis is tilted toward the sun. The Southern Hemisphere receives more energy from the sun. It is summer in the Southern Hemisphere and winter in the Northern Hemisphere.

June
As the north end of Earth's axis is tilted toward the sun, the Northern Hemisphere receives more energy. It is summer in the Northern Hemisphere and winter in the Southern Hemisphere.

March and September
Neither end of Earth's axis is tilted toward the sun. Both hemispheres receive the same amounts of energy.

Section 1 Review

1. Name the four main factors that influence the temperature of an area.
2. How do prevailing winds affect the amount of precipitation an area receives?
3. On which side of mountains—leeward or windward—does precipitation fall?
4. How does the tilt of Earth's axis cause the seasons?
5. **Thinking Critically Developing Hypotheses** How might Earth's climates be different if Earth were not tilted on its axis?

CHAPTER PROJECT

Check Your Progress

Have you chosen your microclimate study sites? If your sites are on private property, get permission. Set up a logbook so that you can record your data. How do you think the conditions in these sites will differ? Write down your hypotheses. Now you are ready to measure daily weather conditions for your microclimates. (*Hint:* Be sure to take your measurements at the same time each day.)

Program Resources

- **Unit 4 Resources** 14-1 Review and Reinforce; 14-1 Enrich

Media and Technology

Transparencies "The Seasons," Transparency 55

3 Assess

Section 1 Review Answers

1. Latitude, altitude, distance from large bodies of water, and ocean currents
2. Prevailing winds that carry more water vapor will cause more precipitation in an area. Prevailing winds that carry warmer air will also cause more precipitation than winds carrying cooler air.
3. windward
4. As Earth travels around the sun, the north end of the axis points toward the sun for part of the year and away from the sun for part of the year. When the north end points toward the sun, the Northern Hemisphere receives more energy than the Southern Hemisphere receives. The seasons change as the amount of energy each hemisphere receives from the sun changes.
5. There would not be seasons, so there would not be the seasonal changes in the climate that many parts of Earth experience now.

CHAPTER PROJECT

Check Your Progress

Meet with each group and review their chosen study sites. If they have chosen a site located on private property, make sure they have permission from the property owners. Review their logbooks. Find out when they plan to measure the daily weather conditions at their study sites. Remind them to take measurements at the same time each day. Invite students to demonstrate how to operate the weather instruments they plan to use. Correct their techniques if necessary.

Performance Assessment

Drawing Challenge students to draw a diagram or map that shows how the factors that affect climate affect their local climate. Students should include all the factors that affect temperature and precipitation that are appropriate.

Skills Lab

Designing Experiments

Sunny Rays and Angles

Preparing for Inquiry

Key Concept The angle at which the sun's rays hit Earth affects the amount of energy absorbed by Earth's surface.

Skills Objectives Students will be able to

- control variables to determine the effect of the angle of light rays on temperature;
- collect temperature data by reading thermometers;
- graph temperature data that they collected;
- infer which thermometer or temperature probe represents certain regions of Earth's surface;
- design an experiment to determine the effect of distance from a light source on temperature.

Time 40 minutes

Alternative Materials If you wish to save time, you can make the construction paper pockets for students ahead of time. If using probeware, refer to the *Probeware Lab Manual.*

Guided Inquiry

Invitation Remind students of their results from the Discover activity. Ask: **On what part of Earth's surface do the sun's rays hit straight on?** *(at the equator)* **Where do the sun's rays hit Earth at the lowest angle?** *(at the poles)* Challenge students to explain how the angle at which the sun's rays hit Earth affects the temperature of each climate zone.

Introducing the Procedure

- Have students read the entire procedure. Then ask: **What part of the experimental setup represents the sun?** *(the lamp)* **What represents Earth's surface?** *(the paper pockets)*
- Point out in the photo how the books are used to hold the thermometers at a 45° and a 90° angle. Demonstrate how to use the protractor.

Skills Lab

Controlling Variables

Sunny Rays and Angles

In this lab, you will investigate how the angle of the sun's rays affects the amount of energy absorbed by different parts of Earth's surface.

Problem

How does the angle of a light source affect the rate of temperature change of a surface?

Materials

books, graph paper, pencil, watch or clock, ruler, clear tape, 3 thermometers or temperature probes, protractor, 100-W incandescent lamp, scissors, black construction paper

Procedure

1. Cut a strip of black construction paper 5 cm by 10 cm. Fold the paper in half and tape two sides to form a pocket.
2. Repeat Step 1 to make two more pockets.
3. Place the bulb of a thermometer inside each pocket. If you're using a temperature probe, see your teacher for instructions.
4. Place the pockets with thermometers close together, as shown in the photo. Place one thermometer in a vertical position (90° angle), one at a 45° angle, and the third one in a horizontal position (0° angle). Use a protractor to measure the angles. Support the thermometers with books.
5. Position the lamp so that it is 30 cm from each of the thermometer bulbs. Make sure the lamp will not move during the activity.
6. Copy a data table like the one below into your notebook.
7. In your data table, record the temperatures on all three thermometers. (All three temperatures should be the same.)
8. Switch on the lamp. In your data table, record the temperature on each thermometer every minute for 15 minutes. **CAUTION:** *Be careful not to touch the hot lampshade.*
9. After 15 minutes, switch off the lamp.

Analyze and Conclude

1. In this experiment, what was the manipulated variable? What was the responding variable? How do you know which is which?
2. Graph your data. Label the horizontal axis and vertical axis of your graph as shown on the sample graph. Use solid, dashed, and dotted lines to show the results from each thermometer, as shown in the key.
3. Based on your data, at which angle did the temperature increase the most?
4. At which angle did the temperature increase the least?

DATA TABLE

	Temperature (°C)		
Time (min.)	0° Angle	45° Angle	90° Angle
Start			
1			
2			
3			
4			
5			

440

Troubleshooting the Experiment

- Show students one completed thermometer pocket to help them construct the pockets properly.
- Make sure students place all three of the thermometer bulbs near each other so that each one is the same distance from the lamp.
- Remind students to record the temperature from each thermometer before they turn on the lamp.

Expected Outcome

The thermometer at the 0° angle will show the highest increase in temperature. The thermometer at the 90° angle will show the lowest increase in temperature. The thermometer at the 45° angle will show a moderate temperature increase.

5. What part of Earth's surface does each thermometer represent?
6. Why is air at the North Pole still very cold in the summer even though the Northern Hemisphere is tilted toward the sun?
7. **Think About It** In this experiment, what variables were held constant?

Design an Experiment

Design an experiment to find out how the results of this investigation would change if the lamp were placed farther from the thermometers. Then design another experiment to find out what would happen if the lamp were placed closer to the thermometers.

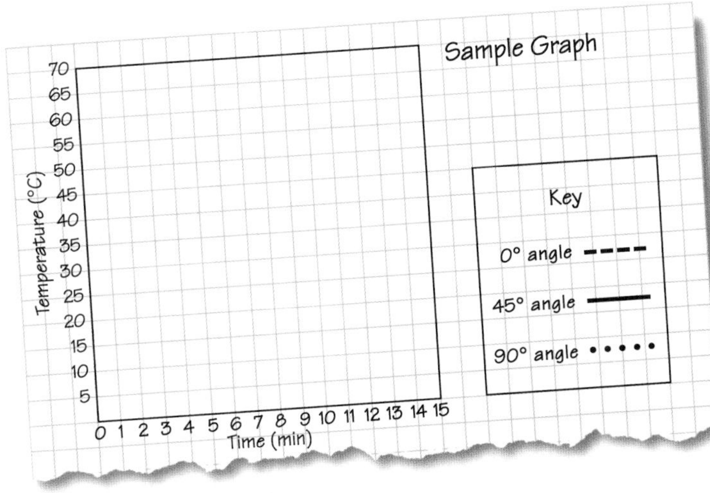

Program Resources

- **Unit 4 Resources** Chapter 18 Skills Lab
- **Probeware Lab Manual** Blackline masters

Media and Technology

Lab Activity Videotapes
Grade 6, Tape 3

Safety

Caution students to be careful when handling the lamp because the light bulb and the lampshade get hot. Review the safety guidelines in Appendix A.

Analyze and Conclude

1. The manipulated variable is the angle of the thermometer. The responding variable is the rate of temperature change. The responding variable is affected by the changes in the manipulated variable.
2. All three lines of the graph should show an increase in temperature over time. However, the line for the thermometer at 0° should show a greater temperature increase than the thermometer at 45°, which should show a greater temperature increase than the thermometer at 90°.
3. at the 0° angle
4. at the 90° angle
5. The thermometer at 0° represents the tropical zone, the thermometer at 45° represents the temperate zone, and the thermometer at 90° represents the polar zone.
6. Because the angle at which the sun's rays strike the North Pole in summer is still very low
7. Variables that were held constant include the thermometers, the heat source, the distance of the heat source from the thermometer bulbs, and the type of heat-absorbing material that enclosed the thermometer bulbs.

Extending the Inquiry

Design an Experiment Students should use the same procedure, except they should change the distances between the thermometers and the lamp.

Section 2 Climate Regions

Objectives

After completing the lesson, students will be able to

- identify factors used to define climates;
- describe the different types of climate regions.

Key Terms rain forest, savanna, desert, steppe, humid subtropical, subarctic, tundra, permafrost

1 Engage/Explore

Activating Prior Knowledge

Invite students to describe places to which they have traveled, read about, or seen in movies. Elicit details about the weather and the kinds of plants and animals that live there. Challenge students to compare the climate and the plants and animals of these places and their home. Ask: **What climate factors cause the climate at home to be different from the places you visited or learned about?** *(Any of the climate factors from Section 1 will cause places to have different climates and organisms.)*

Discover

Skills Focus forming operational definitions
Materials *magazines or newspapers, scissors*
Time 15 minutes
Tips To save class time, assign students to collect magazine pictures for homework, or you could provide the pictures. Before students look at the pictures, encourage them to list some characteristics of various climates.
Expected Outcome Students should sort the pictures into categories such as desert, forest, mountain, and prairie. However, students might sort the pictures based on other climate factors.
Think It Over Accept all answers that are based on some logical classification system. Some students might use actual climate names to describe their pictures.

Section 2 Climate Regions

Discover Activity

What Are Different Climate Types?

1. Collect pictures from magazines and newspapers of a variety of land areas around the world.
2. Sort the pictures into categories according to common weather characteristics.

Think It Over

Forming Operational Definitions Choose several words that describe the typical weather for each of your categories. What words would you use to describe the typical weather where you live?

Guide for Reading

- What factors are used to define climates?
- What are the five main climate regions?

Reading Tip Before you read, preview *Exploring Climate Regions.* Write a list of any questions you have about climate regions.

When the Spanish settlers came to California in the 1700s, they brought with them plants from home. The padres, or priests, who established missions planted vineyards and orchards. They found that grapes, figs, and olives grew as well in California as they had in Spain. What do Spain and California have in common? They have similar climates.

Classifying Climates

The Spanish padres traveled a long distance but found a familiar climate. Suppose you traveled from your home to a place where the weather, the sunlight, and even the plants and trees were very different from what you are used to. Would you know what caused those differences?

Scientists classify climates according to two major factors: temperature and precipitation. They use a system developed around 1900 by Wladimir Köppen (KEP un). This system identifies broad climate regions, each of which has smaller subdivisions.

There are five main climate regions: tropical rainy, dry, temperate marine, temperate continental, and polar. Note that there is only one category of dry climates, whether hot or cold. These climate regions are shown in *Exploring Climate Regions* on pages 444–445.

Olive trees

Reading Strategies

Reading Tip Encourage students to use what they learned in the first section as a basis for writing questions about climate regions. Some questions that students might ask: **How are climate regions defined?** *(By temperature and precipitation)* **How many climate regions are there?** *(Five in the Köppen system, six including highlands)* **Do certain plants and animals live in certain climate regions?** *(Yes, climate regions have very different plants and animals that are especially adapted to living there.)*

Vocabulary Show students that in the word *permafrost,* the prefix *perma* is short for *permanent.* Explain that permafrost is soil that is permanently frozen.

Exploring Climate Regions also shows a sixth type of climate: highlands. Recall that temperatures are cooler at the tops of mountains than in the surrounding areas. So a highland climate can occur within any of the other zones.

Maps show boundaries between the climate regions. In the real world, of course, no clear boundaries mark where one climate region ends and another begins. Each region blends gradually into the next.

☑ *Checkpoint* *What are the five main climate regions?*

Tropical Rainy Climates

The tropics have two types of rainy climates: tropical wet and tropical wet-and-dry. Trace the equator on *Exploring Climate Regions* with your finger. Tropical wet climates are found in low-lying lands near the equator. If you look north and south of tropical wet climates on the map, you can see two bands of tropical wet-and-dry climates.

Tropical Wet In areas that have a tropical wet climate, many days are rainy, often with afternoon thunderstorms. With year-round heat and heavy rainfall, vegetation grows lush and green. Dense rain forests grow in these rainy climates. **Rain forests** are forests in which plenty of rain falls all year-round. Tall trees such as teak and mahogany form the top layer, or canopy, while smaller bushes and vines grow near the ground. There are also many animals in the rain forest, including colorful parrots and toucans, bats, insects, frogs, and snakes.

In the United States, only the windward sides of the Hawaiian islands have a tropical wet climate. Rainfall is very heavy—over 10 meters per year on the windward side of the Hawaiian island of Kauai. The rain forests in Hawaii have a large variety of plants, including ferns, orchids, and many types of vines and trees.

Figure 6 Lush tropical rain forests grow in the tropical wet climate. ***Relating Cause and Effect*** *What climate factors encourage this growth?*

2 Facilitate

Classifying Climates

Addressing Naive Conceptions

Question students to find out what ideas they have about climates in other parts of the world. Ask: **Do you think that other parts of the world have similar climates to areas of the United States?** *(Some students may not think so.)* To make sure students understand that many parts of the world have similar climates, direct them to study the map in *Exploring Climate Regions.* Challenge them to find different countries that share similar climates. Ask: **What factors cause these different regions of the world to have similar climates?** *(These regions share similar factors that affect temperature and precipitation. Such factors include latitude, altitude, prevailing winds, and distance from large bodies of water.)* **learning modality: visual**

Tropical Rainy Climates

Using the Visuals: Figure 6

Direct students to study the plants in the photo and ask: **How do you know this photo shows a tropical wet climate?** *(the lush vegetation)* **How would you describe the temperature of this climate region** *(warm all year long)* **The precipitation?** *(a large amount of precipitation)* Challenge students to identify the climate factors that affect precipitation and temperature in a tropical wet climate. *(Low altitude, near the equator, windward side of mountains, warm and moist prevailing winds)* **learning modality: visual**

Program Resources

- **Unit 4 Resources** 14-2 Lesson Plan; 14-2 Section Summary

Answers to Self-Assessment

☑ *Checkpoint*

Tropical rainy, dry, temperate marine, temperate continental, and polar

Caption Question

Figure 6 Large amounts of rain and warm temperatures

Ongoing Assessment

Writing Instruct students to list the six climate regions. Then have them write a description of a tropical wet climate that includes temperature and precipitation.

Tropical Rainy Climates, continued

EXPLORING

Climate Regions

Instruct student pairs to read aloud the map key and the descriptions of the climate regions to each other. Encourage them to talk about how the climate region definitions on the map are similar to and different from the Köppen system. *(Highland region added and more detailed divisions of the five climate regions)* Then have pairs identify the climate region they live in and the climate region in which their family originated, if they know where. Challenge them to find other places that have the same climates. **learning modality: verbal**

Including All Students

Have students make a flip book of the climate regions using index cards held together with string or a binder ring. This activity will be especially helpful to students with limited English proficiency. Instruct students to write the name of each climate region on one index card. Then have students write a brief description of each region. These descriptions should include precipitation and temperature information. Encourage students with limited English to add illustrations or words from their native language to help them understand the terms. **limited English proficiency**

Students can save their flip books in their portfolios.

EXPLORING Climate Regions

Climate regions are classified according to a combination of temperature and precipitation. Climates in highland regions change rapidly as altitude changes.

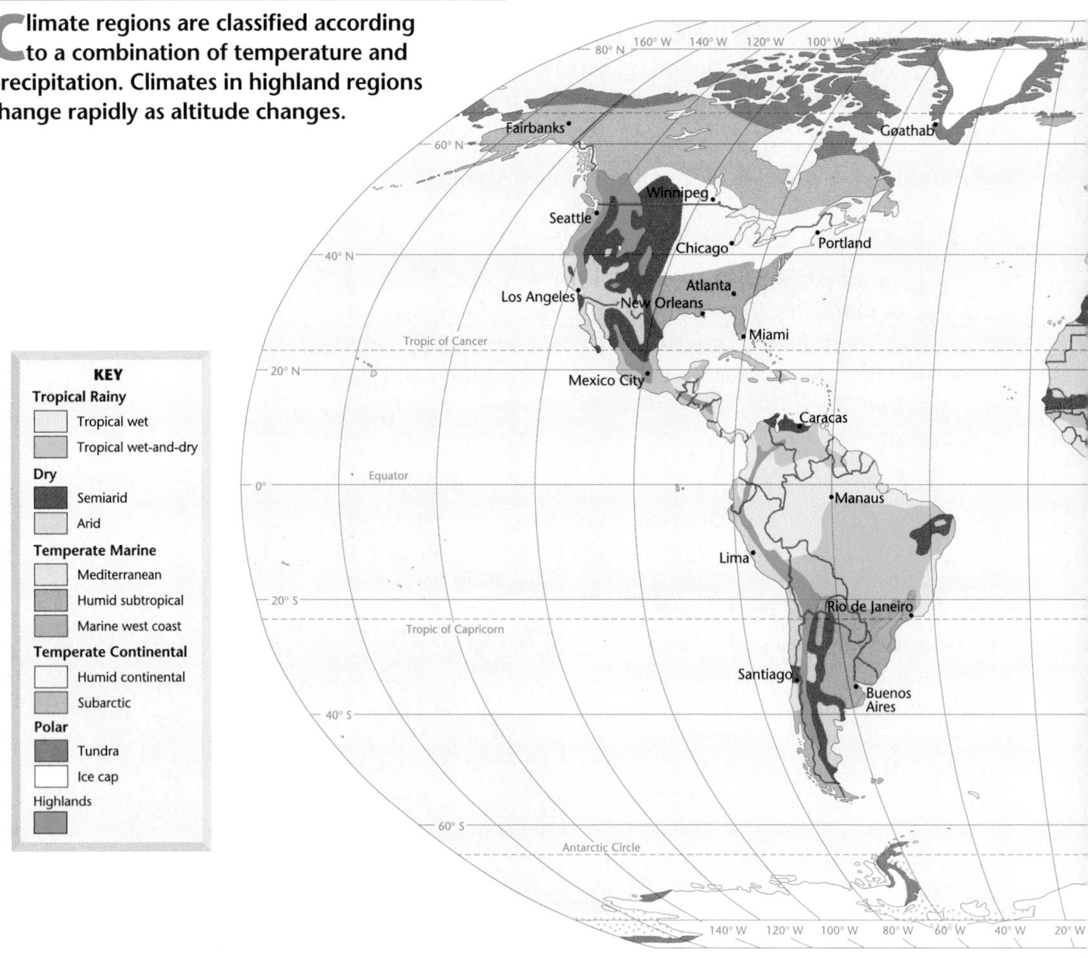

Tropical Rainy
Temperature always 18°C or above.

Tropical wet *Always hot and humid, with heavy rainfall (at least 6 centimeters a month) all year round.*
Tropical wet-and-dry *Always hot, with alternating wet and dry seasons; heavy rainfall in the wet season.*

Dry
Occurs wherever potential evaporation is greater than precipitation. May be hot or cold.

Arid *Desert, with little precipitation, usually less than 25 centimeters a year.*
Semiarid *Dry but receives about 25 to 50 centimeters of precipitation a year.*

Temperate Marine
Average temperature 10°C or above in the warmest month, between –3° and 18°C in the coldest month.

Mediterranean *Warm, dry summers and rainy winters.*
Humid subtropical *Hot summers and cool winters.*
Marine west coast *Mild winters and cool summers, with moderate precipitation year round.*

Background

Integrating Science Plant growth is influenced by genetics and the environment. All plants have different requirements for growth, based on their genetic makeup. Environmental requirements include sunlight, climate, and soil condition. Some plants grow best in sun, others in shade. Plants also differ in the amount of light and water they require for growth.

Wladimir Peter Köppen became interested in the influence of climate on plants while he was a student. He recognized that plants required more rainfall at higher temperatures. From these observations of plants and his knowledge as a meteorologist, Köppen introduced a system to classify climates based on rainfall and temperature. He used monthly rainfall amounts and average monthly temperatures to define the five major climate regions.

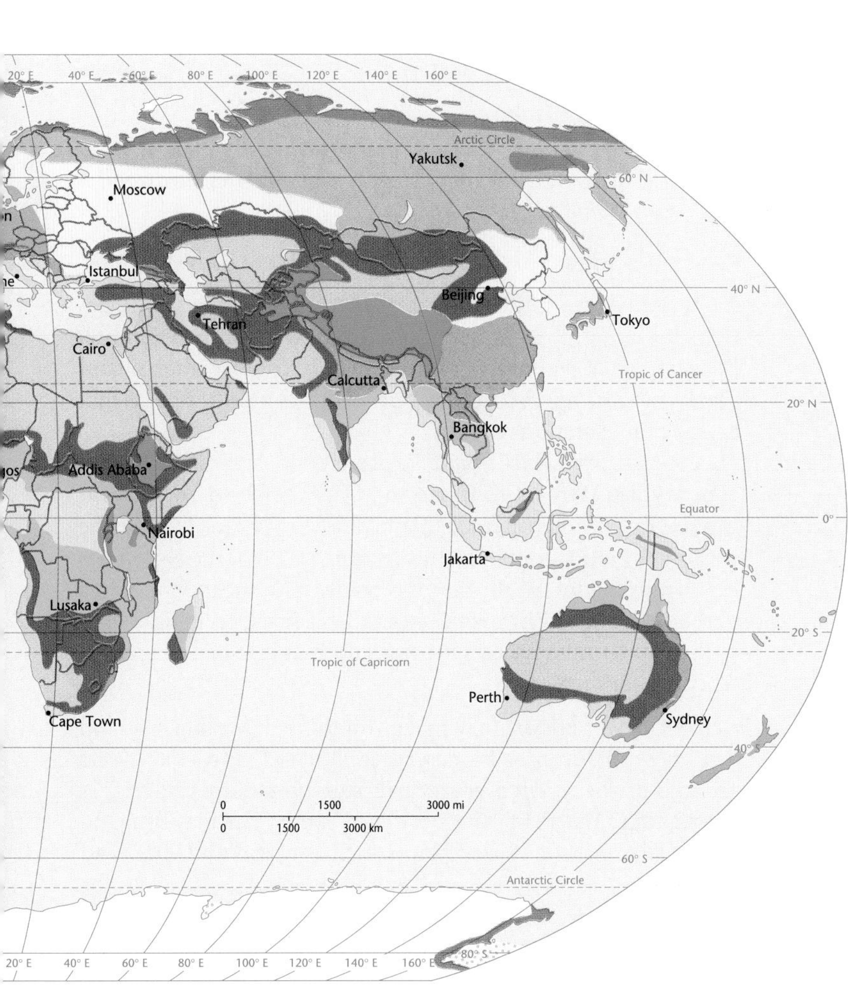

Temperate Continental
Average temperature 10°C or above in the warmest month, –3°C or below in the coldest month.

Humid continental *Hot, humid summers and cold winters, with moderate precipitation year round.*
Subarctic *Short, cool summers and long, cold winters. Light precipitation, mainly in summer.*

Polar
Average temperature below 10°C in the warmest month.

Tundra *Always cold with a short, cool summer—warmest temperature about 10°C.*
Ice cap *Always cold, average temperature at or below 0°C.*

Highlands
Generally cooler and wetter than nearby lowlands, temperature decreasing with altitude.

Real-Life Learning

ACTIVITY

Challenge small student groups to assume the role of a travel agency. Groups should choose one destination and use the climate regions map to identify its climate. Then have groups assemble a travel brochure that describes the destination, its climate, and what travelers would expect to see there. Display actual travel brochures to give students ideas about what to include in their own brochures. Invite groups to share their brochures with the class. You might wish to use the brochures for a bulletin board display. **cooperative learning**

Building Inquiry Skills: Creating Data Tables

As students continue this section, they will learn more about the different climate regions. To help them organize this information, instruct students to create a data table or chart in which they record the characteristics of each climate region. Encourage students to identify climate factors that they will use to organize their tables. Explain that these factors will help them classify each climate region. Students can use the information in *Exploring Climate Regions* to help them organize their tables. **learning modality: logical/mathematical**

Portfolio Students can save their data tables in their portfolios.

Program Resources

- **Laboratory Manual** 14, "Investigating Differences in Climate"

Media and Technology

Transparencies "World Climate Regions," Transparency 56

Concept Videotape Library Grade 6, Tape 3 "Climate in the U.S."

Ongoing Assessment

Writing Challenge students to write an outline about the climate regions. In the outline, they should include the temperature and precipitation factors that are used to classify each climate region.

Tropical Rainy Climates, continued

Using the Visuals: Figure 7

Instruct students to compare the photo in Figure 7 with the one in Figure 6. Ask: **What climate factor do both climate regions have in common?** *(hot temperatures)* **What climate factor differs in these climate regions?** *(the amount and frequency of precipitation)* Challenge students to infer how the difference in the amounts of precipitation can have such a visible affect on a climate. *(Plants with different water requirements live in each climate region. A rain forest plant would not survive in a savanna because there is not enough precipitation.)* **learning modality: visual**

Dry Climates

Including All Students

To help students with the vocabulary terms, invite them to write each of the words, *rain forest, savanna, steppe,* and *desert* on separate index cards. Suggest that students write the definitions of the words on the cards and any other words, phrases, or illustrations that will help them to remember the meanings of the words. Some students might also find it helpful to write the phonetic pronunciation of the words. Students can add their cards to their flip books. **limited English proficiency**

Figure 7 A reticulated giraffe gazes across the grasses and shrubby trees of the African savanna. Savannas are found in tropical wet-and-dry climates.

Tropical Wet-and-Dry Tropical wet-and-dry climates get slightly less rain than tropical climates and have distinct dry and rainy seasons. Instead of rain forests, there are tropical grasslands called **savannas.** Scattered clumps of trees that can survive the dry season dot the coarse grasses. Only a small part of the United States—the southern tip of Florida—has a tropical wet-and-dry climate.

☑ *Checkpoint What parts of the United States have tropical rainy climates?*

Dry Climates

A climate is "dry" if the amount of precipitation that falls is less than the amount of water that could potentially evaporate. Because water evaporates more slowly in cool weather, a cool place with low rainfall may not be as dry as a hotter place that gets the same amount of rain.

Look at *Exploring Climate Regions.* What part of the United States is dry? Why is precipitation in this region so low? As you can see, dry regions often lie inland, far from oceans that are the source of humid air masses. In addition, much of the region lies in the rain shadow of the Sierra Nevadas and Rocky Mountains to the west. Humid air masses from the Pacific Ocean lose much of their water as they cross the mountains. Little rain or snow is carried to dry regions.

Arid The word *desert* may make you think of blazing heat and drifting sand dunes. Some deserts are hot and sandy, but others are cold or rocky. On average, arid regions, or **deserts,** get less than 25 centimeters of rain every year. Some years may bring no rain at all. Only specialized plants such as cactus and yucca can survive the desert's dryness and extremes of hot and cold. In the United States there are arid climates in portions of California, the Great Basin, and the southwest.

Figure 8 Dry-land wheat farming is common in the steppe region of the Great Plains. *Comparing and Contrasting How are steppes similar to savannas, shown in Figure 7? How are they different?*

Background

Integrating Science Plants adapted to living in dry climates have special ways to collect and store water. Desert plants are spread apart so that they don't compete for the small amount of water available. Many cactus plants have roots that spread over a large area just below the surface to capture as much rainwater as possible. The mesquite tree has very deep roots that absorb water from sources deep below the surface.

Plants also store water in their roots, stems, and leaves. A barrel cactus swells after a rainfall because of the water it stores in its stem. Jade plants store water in their leaves. Many desert cacti and succulents open their pores only at night, when the air is cool and less water can evaporate.

Semiarid Locate the semiarid regions on *Exploring Climate Regions.* As you can see, large semiarid areas are usually located on the edges of deserts. A steppe is dry but gets enough rainfall for short grasses and low bushes to grow. For this reason, a **steppe** may also be called a prairie or grassland.

The Great Plains are the steppe region of the United States. Many kinds of short grasses and wildflowers grow here, along with scattered forests. Livestock grazing is an important part of the economy of the Great Plains. Beef cattle, sheep, and goats graze on the short grasses of the region. Farm crops include grains, such as wheat and oats, and sunflowers.

Temperate Marine Climates

Look at *Exploring Climate Regions,* along the coasts of continents in the temperate zones. You will find the third main climate region, temperate marine. There are three kinds of temperate marine climates. Because of the moderating influence of oceans, all three are humid and have mild winters.

Marine West Coast The coolest temperate marine climates are found on the west coasts of continents north of 40° north latitude and south of 40° south latitude. Humid ocean air brings cool, rainy summers and mild, rainy winters.

In North America, the marine west coast climate extends from northern California to southern Alaska. In the Pacific Northwest of the United States, humid air from the Pacific Ocean rises as it hits the western slopes of the Coastal Ranges. As the air cools, large amounts of rain or snow fall on the western slopes.

Because of the heavy precipitation, thick forests of tall trees grow in this region, including coniferous, or cone-bearing, trees such as Sitka spruce, Douglas fir, redwoods, and Western red cedar. One of the main industries of this region is harvesting and processing wood for lumber, paper, and furniture.

Modeling a Humid Climate

ACTIVITY

Here's how you can create humidity.

1. Put the same amount of water in each of two small plastic bowls.
2. Place a sheet of transparent plastic wrap over each bowl. Secure each sheet with a rubber band.
3. Place one bowl on a warm, sunny windowsill or near a radiator. Put the other bowl in a cool location.
4. Wait a day and then look at the two bowls. What do you see on the plastic wrap over each bowl?

Inferring Would you expect to find more water vapor in the air in a warm climate or in a cool one? Why? Explain your results in terms of solar energy.

Figure 9 Seattle, Washington, is in the marine west coast climate region. Here the summers are cool and rainy, and winters are wet and mild.

Answers to Self-Assessment

Checkpoint

The windward sides of the Hawaiian Islands and the southern tip of Florida have tropical rainy climates.

Caption Question

Figure 8 Both steppes and savannas are flat regions where grasses grow. Savannas have clumps of trees while steppes do not.

Inquiry Challenge

Materials *cactus plant, jade plant, various grasses, magnifying lens, forceps*
Time 20 minutes

Challenge students to identify the adaptations that enable these plants to live in a desert or steppe. Encourage students to use a magnifying lens to examine all parts of the plants, including the roots, stems, and leaves. You can use a scalpel or razor blade to slice some cross-sections of leaves, stems, and roots for students to examine. Then have students explain how such adaptations allow the plants to survive in their climates. **learning modality: logical/mathematical**

Temperate Marine Climates

TRY THIS

Skills Focus inferring
Materials *2 small plastic bowls, water, clear plastic wrap, 2 rubber bands*
Time 10 minutes for set up, 5 minutes for later observation
Tips Have students find their own locations to place the bowls. Or, to save time, choose the locations yourself.
Expected Outcome Students will observe more water drops on the plastic wrap of the warm bowl than on the plastic wrap of the cool bowl.

More water vapor is present in the air of warm climates because solar energy warms water, causing it to evaporate into the air.

Extend Instruct students to keep the bowls in the same places, but remove the plastic wrap. Have them check the bowls everyday for one week to find out which bowl has less water at the end of the week. **learning modality: visual**

Ongoing Assessment

Writing Have students describe an air mass in a dry climate and one in a temperate marine climate. *(Air masses in dry climates have little water vapor and air masses in temperate marine climates have a lot of water vapor.)*

Temperate Marine Climates, continued

Including All Students

Give each student a blank map of the United States that has the state borders indicated. Instruct students to shade in the climate regions using a different colored pencil for each climate region. Also have students make a map key. **learning modality: kinesthetic**

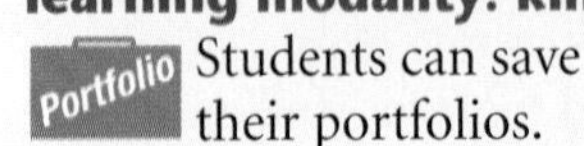

Students can save their maps in their portfolios.

Real-Life Learning

Help students relate the economy of a region to its climate by asking: **How does the climate of each temperate marine climate affect the industry of that region?** *(The climate enables certain plants to grow that have either an agricultural use or are used for lumber, paper, or furniture.)* Challenge students to infer how these industries are affected in a year when the weather is extreme. *(Farmers may lose money because the weather doesn't permit the usual crops to grow, or the crops are damaged.)* **learning modality: logical/mathematical**

Building Inquiry Skills: Comparing and Contrasting

Reinforce that the marine west coast climate, the Mediterranean climate, and the humid subtropical climate are three kinds of temperate marine climates. Have students compare and contrast the three kinds of temperate marine climates. Then challenge students to devise a means of presenting this information. Students might create a table, a map, a diagram, or even a poem. Encourage students to be creative. Invite them to present their comparisons to the class. **learning modality: logical/mathematical**

Figure 10 A. Much of Italy has a Mediterranean climate, with warm, dry summers and cool, rainy winters. B. Rice is a major food crop in places with a humid subtropical climate, as in parts of China. ***Comparing and Contrasting*** *How are Mediterranean and humid subtropical climates similar? How do they differ?*

Mediterranean A coastal climate that is drier and warmer than west coast marine is known as Mediterranean. Find the Mediterranean climates in *Exploring Climate Regions.* In the United States, the southern coast of California has a Mediterranean climate. This climate is mild, with two seasons. In winter, marine air masses bring cool, rainy weather. Summers are somewhat warmer, with little rain.

Mediterranean climates have two main vegetation types. One is made up of dense shrubs and small trees, called chaparral (chap uh RAL). The other vegetation type includes grasses with a few oak trees.

Agriculture is an important part of the economy of California's Mediterranean climate region. Some crops, including olives and grapes, were originally introduced by Spanish settlers. With the help of irrigation, farmers grow many different crops, including rice, oranges, and many vegetables, fruits, and nuts.

Humid Subtropical The warmest temperate marine climates are on the edges of the tropics. **Humid subtropical** climates are wet and warm, but not as constantly hot as the tropics. Locate the humid subtropical climates in *Exploring Climate Regions.*

The southeastern United States has a humid subtropical climate. Summers are hot, with much more rainfall than in winter. Maritime tropical air masses move inland, bringing tropical weather conditions, including thunderstorms and occasional hurricanes, to southern cities such as Houston, New Orleans, and Atlanta. Winters are cool to mild, with more rain than snow. However, polar air masses moving in from the north can bring freezing temperatures and severe frosts.

Mixed forests of oak, ash, hickory, and pines grow in the humid subtropical region of the United States. Cotton was once the most important crop grown in this region. Other crops, including oranges, grapefruits, peaches, peanuts, sugar cane, and rice, are now more important to the economy.

Checkpoint ***What is the main difference between a humid subtropical climate and a tropical climate?***

Background

Facts and Figures The chaparral biome, or plant and animal community, is very typical of Mediterranean climates. The chaparral is characterized by dense growth of evergreen shrubs and small trees. Chaparral plants have small, thick, waxy leaves. These plants are dormant in the hot, dry summer and spring to life with the first rainfall in winter.

The chaparral is a fire-dependent biome. Fires wipe out dead plant material, recycle nutrients, thin old growth, and stimulate new growth from seeds and sprouts. Chaparral plants have adapted to fire by producing seeds early in their life cycles that are either resistant to fire or require fire for germination. Many chaparral plants also produce volatile oils that are highly flammable.

Temperate Continental Climates

Temperate continental climates are found on continents in the Northern Hemisphere. Because they are not influenced very much by oceans, temperate continental climates have extremes of temperature. Why do continental climates occur only in the Northern Hemisphere? The parts of continents in the Southern Hemisphere south of 40° south latitude are not far enough from oceans for dry continental air masses to form.

Humid Continental Shifting tropical and polar air masses bring constantly changing weather to humid continental climates. In winter, continental polar air masses move south, bringing bitterly cold weather. In summer, tropical air masses move north, bringing heat and high humidity. Humid continental climates receive moderate amounts of rain in the summer. Smaller amounts of rain or snow fall in winter.

What parts of the United States have a humid continental climate? The eastern part of the region—the Northeast—has a range of forest types, from mixed forests in the south to coniferous forests in the north. Much of the western part of this region—the Midwest—was once tall grasslands, but is now farmland. Farmers in the Midwest grow wheat, corn, other grains, and soybeans. These crops are used as food for people and for hogs, poultry, and beef cattle.

Subarctic The **subarctic** climates lie north of the humid continental climates. The world's largest subarctic regions are in Russia, Canada, and Alaska. Summers in the subarctic are short and cool. Winters are long and bitterly cold.

In North America, coniferous trees such as spruce and fir make up a huge northern forest that stretches from Alaska to Canada's east coast. Many large mammals, including bears, wolves, and moose, live in the forest. Small mammals such as beavers, porcupines, and red squirrels, and birds such as grouse and owls also live in the forest. Wood products from the northern forest are an important part of the economy.

Sharpen your Skills

Classifying

ACTIVITY

The table shows some climate data for three cities.

	City A	City B	City C
Average January Temperature (°C)	12.8	18.9	–5.6
Average July Temperature (°C)	21.1	27.2	20
Annual Precipitation (cm)	33	152	109

Describe the climate you would expect each city to have. Identify which city is Miami, which is Los Angeles, and which is Portland, Maine. Use *Exploring Climate Regions* on pages 608–609 to help identify each city's climate.

Figure 11 Subarctic climates have cool summers and cold winters. Parts of this region are called "spruce-moose belts."

Temperate Continental Climates

Building Inquiry Skills: Applying Concepts

Invite students to compare and contrast the characteristics of humid continental and subarctic climates. List their similarities and differences on the board. Then ask: **What factor or factors affecting climate causes the differences between subarctic and humid continental climates?** *(primarily latitude)* **What climate factor or factors causes the similarities between these two climates?** *(Distance from large bodies of water and prevailing winds)* **learning modality: logical/mathematical**

Sharpen your Skills

Classifying

Time 10 minutes

Expected Outcome City A is Los Angeles. Its warm and dry climate is a Mediterranean climate. City B is Miami. Its hot and humid climate is a tropical wet-and-dry climate. City C is Portland, Maine. With hot summers and cool winters, it is a humid continental climate.

Extend Challenge students to classify the climates of Seattle, Atlanta, and Chicago. Ask: **Which of these cities has climates similar to City A, City B, or City C?** *(Chicago is like City C, Portland, Maine.)* **Which do not?** *(Seattle has a marine west coast climate, and Atlanta has a humid subtropical climate.)* **learning modality: logical/mathematical**

Answers to Self-Assessment

Caption Question

Figure 10 Both climates are humid with hot summers and mild winters. The Mediterranean climate has dry summers and the humid subtropical climate has wet summers.

Checkpoint

A humid subtropical climate is not as constantly hot as a tropical climate.

Ongoing Assessment

Writing Have students summarize the differences between a temperate continental climate and a temperate marine climate.

Polar Climates

Cultural Diversity

The Inuit and the Pueblo are two Native American groups that live in extreme climates. Show students pictures of the climates these groups live in. Help students locate where these groups live on the map in *Exploring Climate Regions* on pages 444–445. Then challenge student groups to learn how these two groups adapted to their environments. You might assign groups to study one aspect of their traditional cultures, such as housing, food, dress, customs, social structure, communication, and art. Have groups present their findings to the class. **cooperative learning**

Highlands

Including All Students

ACTIVITY

Students can make models of a highland climate using salt dough or papier-mâché. They may base their models on the description of the Rocky Mountains in the text, or they can choose a different mountain range. Their models should show how the climate changes as altitude increases. Encourage students to be creative. Not only could they color-code the various climate regions on the mountain, but they could also add models of the plants and animals that live there. **learning modality: kinesthetic**

Figure 12 Emperor penguins live on the ice cap of Antarctica.

Polar Climates

The polar climate is the coldest climate region. Ice cap and tundra climates are found only in the far north and south, near the North and South poles.

Ice Cap As you can see in *Exploring Climate Regions*, ice cap climates are found mainly on Greenland and in Antarctica. With average temperatures always at or below freezing, the land in ice cap climate regions is covered with ice and snow. Intense cold makes the air dry. Lichens and a few low plants may grow on the rocks.

Tundra The **tundra** climate region stretches across northern Alaska, Canada, and Russia. Short, cool summers follow bitterly cold winters. Because of the cold, some layers of the tundra soil are always frozen. This permanently frozen tundra soil is called **permafrost.** Because of the permafrost, water cannot drain away, so the soil is wet and boggy in summer.

It is too cold on the tundra for trees to grow. Despite the harsh climate, during the short summers the tundra is filled with life. Mosquitoes and other insects hatch in the ponds and marshes above the frozen permafrost. Mosses, grasses, lichens, wildflowers, and shrubs grow quickly during the short summers. Herds of caribou and musk oxen eat the vegetation and are in turn preyed upon by wolves. Some birds, such as the white-tailed ptarmigan, live on the tundra year-round. Others, such as the arctic tern and many waterfowl, spend only the summer there.

☑ *Checkpoint What type of vegetation is found on the tundra?*

Figure 13 The tundra is often very cold, but still many plants and animals live there. ***Observing*** *How are these musk oxen adapted to the cold climate?*

Background

Facts and Figures The alpine tundra, which is the tundra found in a highland climate, is somewhat different from the arctic tundra of a polar climate. The main differences are that the alpine tundra does not have permafrost and receives much more precipitation. Most alpine tundra has well-drained soil. However, bare rock-covered ground is also very common. Low-growing plants, mosses, and lichens characterize both the arctic and the alpine tundras. The alpine tundra plants include more mat-growing plants that are adapted to the gusty winds, heavy snowfalls, and fluctuating temperatures found at mountaintops. Common alpine tundra animals include mountain goats, big-horned sheep, pikas, and marmots. Butterflies, beetles, and grasshoppers are also common, whereas flies and mosquitoes are more rare.

Highlands

Why are highlands a distinct climate region? Remember that temperature falls as altitude increases, so highland regions are colder than the regions that surround them. Increasing altitude produces climate changes similar to the climate changes you would expect with increasing latitude. In the tropics, highlands are like cold islands overlooking the warm lowlands.

The climate on the lower slopes of a mountain range is like that of the surrounding countryside. The foothills of the Rocky Mountains, for instance, share the semiarid climate of the Great Plains. But as you go higher up into the mountains, temperatures become lower. Climbing 1,000 meters up in elevation is like traveling 1,200 kilometers north. The climate higher in the mountains is like that of the subarctic: cool with coniferous trees. Animals typical of the subarctic zone—such as moose and porcupines—live in the mountain forest.

Above a certain elevation—the tree line—no trees can grow. The climate above the tree line is like that of the tundra. Only low plants, mosses, and lichens can grow there.

Figure 14 The top of this mountain is too cold and windy for trees to grow. *Classifying What climate zone does this mountaintop resemble?*

Section 2 Review

1. What two factors are used to classify climates?
2. Briefly describe each of the five main climate types.
3. Give three examples of how the climate of a region affects what plants and animals can live there.
4. **Thinking Critically Applying Concepts** Which of these two places has more severe winters—central Russia or the west coast of France? Why?
5. **Thinking Critically Classifying** Classify the main climate regions according to whether or not trees usually grow in each one.

Science at Home

Climate Regions Describe to your family the characteristics of each of the climate regions found in the United States. Which climate region does your family live in? What plants and animals live in your climate region? What characteristics do these plants and animals have that make them well-adapted to living in your climate region?

3 Assess

Section 2 Review Answers

1. Temperature and precipitation
2. Tropical: hot and rainy; dry: little precipitation; temperate marine: humid with mild winters; temperate continental: warm or cool summers and cold winters, moderate precipitation; polar: cool summers and very cold winters, little precipitation
3. Answers may vary. Students should give examples that show how the climate affects what plants or animals live in a region or what types of farming, ranching, or forestry are important.
4. Central Russia has more severe winters because it is at a higher latitude than France in the center of the continent and has a continental climate; the climate of the coast of France is west coast marine and is more moderate.
5. Trees: tropical rainy, temperate marine, temperate continental, highlands; no trees: dry, polar

Science at Home

ACTIVITY

To ensure students identify their climate correctly, encourage volunteers to identify your climate region and explain what climate factors your community has. Help students identify the special factors of your climate to which plants and animals must adapt. For example, in a temperate continental climate, animals need some kind of adaptation to survive the change of seasons. Encourage students to interview family members about other climate regions they have visited.

Program Resources

- **Unit 4 Resources** 14-2 Review and Reinforce; 14-2 Enrich

Answers to Self-Assessment

Caption Question

Figure 13 They have thick, long coats.
Figure 14 tundra

Checkpoint

Mosses, grasses, lichens, wildflowers, and shrubs

Performance Assessment

Organizing Information Instruct students to make a table in which they list the climate factors and types of living things for each of the six climate regions they studied. Students should also include in their tables information about the subtypes of climate regions, such as ice cap and tundra climates.

Real-World Lab

Careers in Science

Cool Climate Graphs

Preparing for Inquiry

Key Concept Factors in addition to latitude, such as the proximity of large bodies of water, altitude, and the presence of mountains, also help to determine the climate of a region.

Skills Objectives Students will be able to

- ◆ graph the monthly average precipitation, high temperature, and low temperature for three different cities;
- ◆ interpret data to determine which city matches which climate graph;
- ◆ draw conclusions about which city has the best climate for different types of recreational facilities.

Time 40 minutes

Advance Planning Depending on the level of your students, you may want to distribute copies of graphs with the axes already marked. An overhead transparency of a climate graph will help instruct students on making their own.

Guided Inquiry

Invitation To help students relate to the lab, ask: **How does climate affect your life?** *(Students should explain how they have to change their lifestyle based on the yearly weather changes.)* Discuss what kinds of activities students can or cannot do because of the climate.

Introducing the Procedure

Instruct students to look over the climate graph shown in their text. Discuss what kinds of information are being graphed. Ask: **Why is this type of graph useful?** *(A visual picture of monthly temperatures and precipitation makes it easier to compare the climates among different cities.)*

Real-World Lab

Careers in Science

Cool Climate Graphs

You are a land-use planner who has been hired by a company that builds recreational facilities. Your company is considering buying land near at least one of four cities, all at about the same latitude. Your job is to decide which of the cities would be the best place to build a water park and which is the best place to build a ski-touring center.

Problem

Based on climate data, which city is the best place for each type of recreational facility?

Skills Focus

graphing, interpreting data, drawing conclusions

Materials

calculator
ruler
3 pieces of graph paper
black, blue, red, and green pencils
climate map on pages 608–609
U.S. map with city names and latitude lines

Procedure

1. Work in groups of three. Each person should graph the data for a different city, A, B, or C.
2. On graph paper, use a black pencil to label the axes as on the climate graph below. Title your climate graph City A, City B, or City C.
3. Use your green pencil to make a bar graph of the monthly average amount of precipitation. Place a star below the name of each month that has more than a trace of snow.
4. Use a red pencil to plot the average monthly maximum temperature. Make a dot for the temperature in the middle of each space for the month. When you have plotted data for all 12 months, connect the points into a smooth curved line.
5. Use a blue pencil to plot the average monthly minimum temperature for your city. Use the same procedure as in Step 4.
6. Calculate the total average annual precipitation for this city and include it in your observations. Do this by adding the average precipitation for each month.

Washington, D.C., Climate Averages

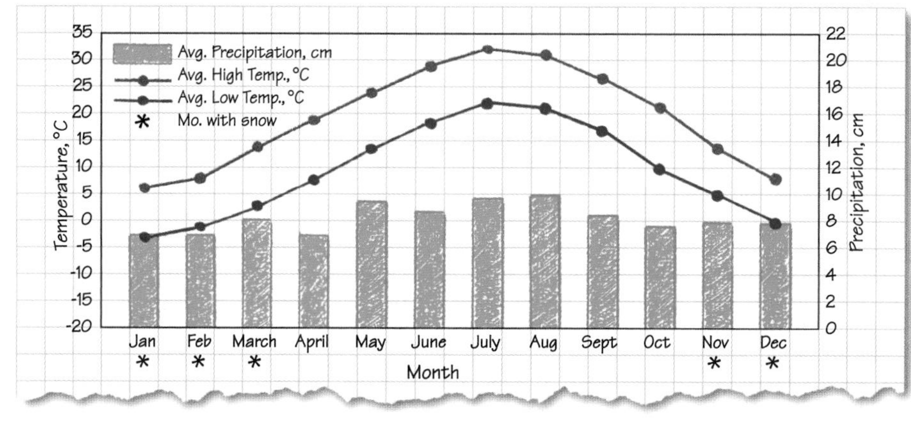

Troubleshooting the Experiment

- ◆ If necessary, review with students the factors that affect climate from Section 1.
- ◆ Walk around the room as students are graphing to help with any problems they might be having.
- ◆ Using maps that show the names of cities and the physical geography will help students match their climate graphs with the proper cities.
- ◆ Encourage students to list the climate criteria for a water-slide park and a cross-country ski touring center.

Expected Outcome

Students should determine the climate type of each city and the identity of each city based on their climate graphs and their U.S. maps.

Climate Data

Washington, D.C.	Jan	Feb	Mar	April	May	June	July	Aug	Sept	Oct	Nov	Dec
Average High Temp. (°C)	6	8	14	19	24	29	32	31	27	21	14	8
Average Low Temp. (°C)	-3	-2	3	8	14	19	22	21	17	10	5	0
Average Precipitation (cm)	6.9	6.9	8.1	6.9	9.4	8.6	9.7	9.9	8.4	7.6	7.9	7.9
Months With Snow	*	*	*	trace	—	—	—	—	—	trace	*	*
City A	**Jan**	**Feb**	**Mar**	**Apr**	**May**	**Jun**	**July**	**Aug**	**Sept**	**Oct**	**Nov**	**Dec**
Average High Temp. (°C)	13	16	16	17	17	18	18	19	21	21	17	13
Average Low Temp. (°C)	8	9	9	10	11.	12	12	13	13	13	11	8
Average Precipitation (cm)	10.4	7.6	7.9	3.3	0.8	0.5	0.3	0.3	0.8	3.3	8.1	7.9
Months With Snow	trace	trace	trace	—	—	—	—	—	—	—	—	trace
City B	**Jan**	**Feb**	**Mar**	**Apr**	**May**	**Jun**	**July**	**Aug**	**Sept**	**Oct**	**Nov**	**Dec**
Average High Temp. (°C)	5	7	10	16	21	26	29	27	23	18	11	6
Average Low Temp. (°C)	–9	–7	–4	1	6	11	14	13	8	2	–4	–8
Average Precipitation (cm)	0.8	1.0	2.3	3.0	5.6	5.8	7.4	7.6	3.3	2.0	1.3	1.3
Months With Snow	*	*	*	*	*	—	—	—	trace	*	*	*
City C	**Jan**	**Feb**	**Mar**	**Apr**	**May**	**Jun**	**July**	**Aug**	**Sept**	**Oct**	**Nov**	**Dec**
Average High Temp. (°C)	7	11	13	18	23	28	33	32	27	21	12	8
Average Low Temp. (°C)	–6	–4	–2	1	4	8	11	10	5	1	–3	–7
Average Precipitation (cm)	2.5	2.3	1.8	1.3	1.8	1	0.8	0.5	0.8	1	2	2.5
Months With Snow	*	*	*	*	*	trace	—	—	trace	trace	*	*

Analyze and Conclude

Compare your climate graphs and observations. Use all three climate graphs, plus the graph for Washington, D.C., to answer these questions.

1. Which of the four cities has the least change in average temperatures during the year?
2. In which climate region is each city located?
3. Which of the cities listed below matches each climate graph?

Colorado Springs, Colorado	latitude 39° N
San Francisco, California	latitude 38° N
Reno, Nevada	latitude 40° N
Washington, D.C.	latitude 39° N

4. Even though these cities are at approximately the same latitude, why are their climate graphs so different?
5. **Apply** Which city would be the best location for a water slide park? For a cross-country ski touring center? What other factors should you consider when deciding where to build each type of recreational facility? Explain.

More to Explore

What type of climate does the area where you live have? Find out what outdoor recreational facilities your community has. How is each one particularly suited to the climate of *your* area?

Analyze and Conclude

1. City A

2. Washington, D.C.: humid subtropical; City A: Mediterranean; City B: semiarid; City C: arid

3. Colorado Springs: City B; San Francisco: City A; Reno: City C

4. Other climate factors, such as distance from large bodies of water, altitude, and mountain ranges, affect the climate of these cities.

5. Washington, D.C., would be the best choice for a water-slide park because it has fewer months with snow and very warm summertime temperatures, even though it has relatively high amounts of precipitation. Colorado Springs would be the best choice for a cross-country ski touring center because it has the most months with enough snow. Other factors to consider include water supply, local economy, building sites, numbers of tourists, roads, and the amount of taxes. These factors will affect the cost of building and maintaining the facility and whether there are enough people to use the facility so that it will make money.

Extending the Inquiry

More to Explore Help students identify and list the recreational facilities in and around your community. Some facilities in your community might include parks, ice skating rinks, pools, amusement parks, water slide parks, ski hills, golf courses, and toboggan runs. Students should describe how the climate requirements of the recreation facilities match the climate factors in your community.

Program Resources

- **Unit 4 Resources** Chapter 14 Real-World Lab

Media and Technology

Transparencies "Climate Graph for Washington, D.C.," Transparency 57

Lab Activity Videotapes Grade 6, Tape 3

Section 3 Long-Term Changes in Climate

Objectives

After completing the lesson, students will be able to

- ◆ identify how scientists can learn about ancient climates;
- ◆ describe how Earth's surface changes during an ice age;
- ◆ explain the theories that have been proposed to explain natural climate change.

Key Terms ice age, sunspot

1 Engage/Explore

Activating Prior Knowledge

To find out what students know about ancient climates ask: **What do you know about climate changes in Earth's past?** *(Some students might mention past ice ages or climate changes that might have caused the extinction of dinosaurs.)* **How do you think these climate changes might have affected plants and animals?** *(Students might mention that plants and animals would die out if they couldn't move or adapt to the climate changes. Accept all answers without comment.)*

Discover Activity

Skills Focus inferring
Materials *Figure 16 from student text, magnifying lens*
Time 10 minutes
Tips Make a photocopy of Figure 16 and enlarge the photo of the tree rings. Students can label on the photocopy thick and thin tree rings. If possible, provide students with cross-sections of tree trunks to examine.
Expected Outcome Students should observe that tree rings are not all the same thickness. Students might infer that temperature and precipitation affect the thickness of tree rings.
Think It Over Students should infer that the relative thickness of tree rings tells about weather conditions in the past.

Section 3 Long-Term Changes in Climate

Discover Activity

What Story Can Tree Rings Tell?

1. Look at the photo of tree rings on page 619. Tree rings are the layers of new wood that form as a tree grows each year.
2. Look closely at the tree rings. Note whether they are all the same thickness.
3. What weather conditions might cause a tree to form thicker or thinner tree rings?

Think It Over

Inferring How could you use tree rings to tell you about weather in the past?

Guide for Reading

- ◆ What principle do scientists follow in studying ancient climates?
- ◆ What changes occur on Earth's surface during an ice age?
- ◆ What theories have been proposed to explain natural climate change?

Reading Tip Before you read, preview the art and photos and read the captions. Write a prediction about how Earth's climate has changed through time.

One of the greatest Native American cultures in the American Southwest was the Ancestral Pueblos. These farming people built great pueblos, or "apartment houses," of stone and sun-baked clay, with hundreds of rooms. By about the year 1000, the Ancestral Pueblos were flourishing. They grew crops of corn, beans, and squash and traded extensively with other groups of people. But in the late 1200s, the climate became drier, reducing the size of their crops. After a long period of drought, the Ancestral Pueblos migrated to other areas.

Although weather can vary from day to day, climates usually change more slowly. But climates do change, both in small areas and throughout the world. Although climate change is usually slow, its consequences are great. Climate changes have affected many civilizations, including the Ancestral Pueblos.

Figure 15 The Ancestral Pueblos lived in these buildings, now in Mesa Verde National Park in southwestern Colorado, about 1,000 years ago.

Reading Strategies

Study and Comprehension Encourage students to look over the section before they read it to identify the main topics. Suggest that they use the topic heads from the section to organize an outline. Then students can use their completed outlines as a study guide. After previewing the art and photos, students may predict that Earth's climate is warmer than it once was.

Studying Climate Change

In studying ancient climates, scientists follow an important principle: If plants or animals today need certain conditions to live, then similar plants and animals in the past also required those conditions. For example, today magnolia and palm trees grow only in warm, moist climates. Scientists assume that the ancestors of these trees required similar conditions. Thus, 80-million-year-old fossils of these trees in Greenland are good evidence that the climate of Greenland was warm and moist 80 million years ago.

Tree rings can also be used to learn about ancient climates. Every summer, a tree grows a new layer of wood under its bark. These layers form rings when seen in a cross section, as shown in Figure 16. In cool climates, the amount the tree grows—the thickness of a ring—depends on the length of the warm growing season. In dry climates, the thickness of each ring depends on the amount of rainfall. By looking at cross sections of trees, scientists can count backward from the outer ring to see whether previous years were warm or cool, wet or dry. A thin ring indicates that the year was cool or dry. A thick ring indicates that the year was warm or wet.

A third source of information about ancient climates is pollen records. Each type of plant has a particular type of pollen. The bottoms of some lakes are covered with thick layers of mud and plant material, including pollen, that fell to the bottom of the lake over thousands of years. Scientists can drill down into these layers and bring up cores to examine. By looking at the pollen present in each layer, scientists can tell what types of plants lived in the area. The scientists can then infer that the climate that existed when the pollen was deposited was similar to the climate where the same plants grow today.

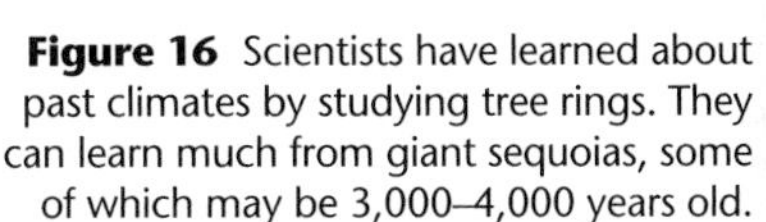

Figure 16 Scientists have learned about past climates by studying tree rings. They can learn much from giant sequoias, some of which may be 3,000–4,000 years old.

2 Facilitate

Studying Climate Change

Including All Students

Help students organize the information in the text by asking: **What three sources of information do scientists use in studying ancient climates?** *(Fossil evidence, tree rings, pollen records)* **What important principle do scientists follow while studying ancient climates?** *(Ancient plants and animals probably required similar living conditions to those required by today's plants and animals.)* **learning modality: verbal**

Building Inquiry Skills: Drawing Conclusions

Explain to students that scientists have found fossils of brachiopods and trilobites in southeastern Wisconsin. These fossils are about 400 million years old. Encourage students to use encyclopedias to learn more about trilobites and brachiopods, or display pictures or fossils of these organisms and help students infer their habitats. Challenge students to use this information to draw a conclusion about the climate of southeastern Wisconsin about 400 million years ago. *(Brachiopods and trilobites are organisms that lived on the bottom of warm, shallow seas. The presence of these fossils in southeastern Wisconsin indicates that this area was covered by warm, shallow seas about 400 million years ago.)* **learning modality: logical/mathematical**

Program Resources

- **Unit 4 Resources** 14-3 Lesson Plan, 14-3 Section Summary
- **Guided Reading and Study Workbook** Section 14-3

Ongoing Assessment

Oral Presentation Call on various students to describe the three sources of information that scientists use to study ancient climates.

Ice Ages

Using the Visuals: Figure 17

Invite students to use Figure 17 to determine whether your area was covered by glaciers 18,000 years ago. Ask: **What could you conclude if a fossil of a mammoth were found north of the mammoth steppe region shown on the map?** *(That the size of the glaciers changed over time, and the mammoth steppe region changed accordingly.)* Elicit suggestions about why woolly mammoths and scimitar-toothed cats are extinct. Discuss how the changing climate might have affected these animals. **learning modality: visual**

Building Inquiry Skills: Inferring

Challenge students to infer what your community might have looked like during the last ice age. Then have students draw a picture showing how the street on which they live might have looked about 18,000 years ago. **learning modality: visual**

Including All Students

Materials *shallow pan, damp sand, ice cubes or crushed ice, water, toothpicks*
Time 20 minutes, 5 minutes

Students can construct models to show why the ocean level rises as ice sheets melt. Instruct students to use the damp sand to mold a land mass in the shallow pan. Suggest that they include depressions, mountains, and coastal areas. Students should add water to the pan to simulate the ocean. Then they can pack the ice on the land masses to represent glaciers and ice sheets. Have students mark the water level at various places on their land masses with toothpicks. Ask students to predict what will happen to the ice sheets and oceans in their models. *(The ice sheets will melt, and the ocean level will rise.)* (Note: Keep pans in a cool, shady area overnight to minimize evaporation.) The next day, have students observe the changes in ice and water in their models. Discuss why oceans are lower during the ice ages than they are now. **learning modality: kinesthetic**

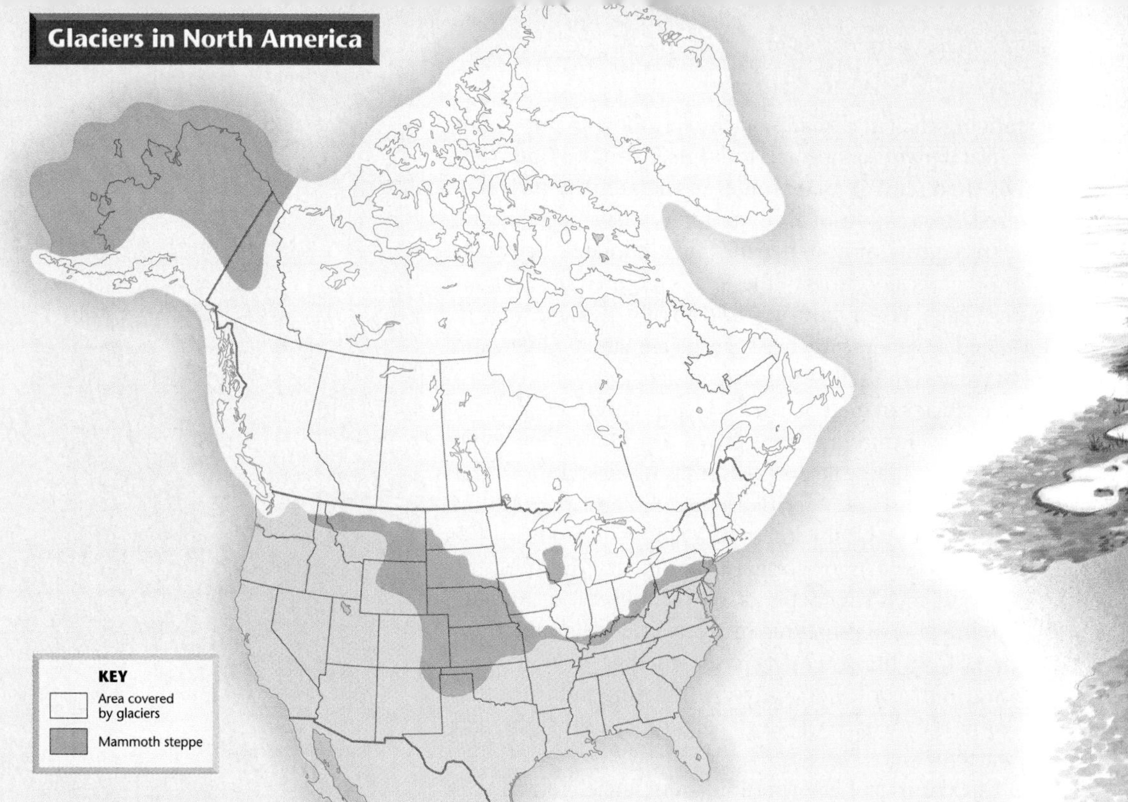

Figure 17 The map shows the parts of North America that were covered by glaciers 18,000 years ago. On the steppe near the glaciers lived many mammals that are now extinct, including woolly mammoths and scimitar-toothed cats.

Ice Ages

Throughout Earth's history, climates have gradually changed. Over millions of years, warm periods have alternated with cold periods known as **ice ages,** or glacial episodes. **During each ice age, huge sheets of ice called glaciers covered large parts of Earth's surface.**

From fossils and other evidence, scientists have concluded that in the past two million years there have been at least four major ice ages. Each one lasted 100,000 years or longer. Long, warmer periods known as interglacials occurred between the ice ages. Some scientists think that we are now in a warm period between ice ages.

The most recent major ice age ended only about 10,500 years ago. Ice sheets covered much of northern Europe and North America, reaching as far south as present-day Iowa and Nebraska. In some places, the ice was more than 3 kilometers thick. So much water was frozen in the ice sheets that the average sea level was much lower than it is today. When the ice sheets melted, the rising oceans flooded coastal areas. Inland, large lakes formed.

☑ *Checkpoint* *Why were the oceans lower during the ice ages than they are now?*

Background

Integrating Science All planets, including Earth, revolve around the sun in elliptical orbits. Because its orbit is not circular, Earth is not the same distance from the sun at all points in its orbit. About January 3, Earth is nearest the sun at a point called the perihelion. About July 4, Earth is farthest from the sun at the aphelion. Since planets move faster when they are closer to the sun, the time interval from the March equinox to the September equinox is longer than the interval between September and March. If Earth's orbit shifts so that its perihelion is in July, the winter season in the Northern Hemisphere will be longer because Earth will be moving more slowly between September and March. This could cause the climate to become cooler, setting the stage for an ice age.

Causes of Climate Change

Why do climates change? Scientists have formed several hypotheses. **Possible explanations for major climate changes include variations in the position of Earth relative to the sun, changes in the sun's energy output, and the movement of continents.**

Earth's Position Changes in Earth's position relative to the sun may have affected climates. According to one hypothesis, as Earth revolves around the sun, the time of year when Earth is closest to the sun shifts from January to July and back again over a period of about 26,000 years.

The angle at which Earth's axis tilts and the shape of Earth's orbit around the sun also change slightly over long periods of time. The combined effects of these changes in Earth's movements may be the main cause of ice ages.

INTEGRATING SPACE SCIENCE **Solar Energy** Short-term changes in climate have been linked to changes in the number of **sunspots**—dark, cooler regions on the surface of the sun. Sunspots increase and decrease in regular 11-year cycles. Sunspot cycles could in turn be caused by changes in the sun's energy output.

Social Studies CONNECTION

Prehistoric people who lived during the last ice age faced a harsh environment. To endure the cold, they learned to make clothing from animal skins. They also used fires for warmth and cooking.

In Your Journal

Make a list of five ways your life would change if the climate suddenly became colder.

Causes of Climate Change

Social Studies CONNECTION

To help students think about how their lives might change, ask: **How would a colder climate affect the plants and animals living in our environment?** *(Some plants might not survive. Animals that depend on them for food also might not survive. Some animals might migrate.)* Explain that the climate in an ice age would be similar to subarctic, tundra, or ice cap climates. Discuss how these climates are different from your current climate.

In Your Journal Provide time for students to make their lists. Encourage students to share their lists in a class discussion. **learning modality: verbal**

Media and Technology

Transparencies "Extent of Northern Hemisphere Glaciation," Transparency 58

Concept Videotape Library Grade 6, Tape 3 "Changes in Climate"

Answers to Self-Assessment

Much of the water on Earth was frozen in ice sheets that covered the land.

Ongoing Assessment

Writing Have students explain what an ice age is and how one might occur.

Causes of Climate Change, continued

Including All Students

ACTIVITY

Give students a photocopied map of the world. Tell them to cut out the continents and India, but leave Europe and Asia together as one continent. Then challenge them to fit the continents together to form Pangaea. **learning modality: kinesthetic**

3 Assess

Section 3 Review Answers

1. Fossil evidence, tree rings, and pollen records
2. The temperature was colder and huge sheets of ice covered large parts of Earth.
3. Earth's position relative to the sun, changes in the sun's energy output, and the movement of continents
4. A volcanic eruption would send ash and other particles into the air that would block the sun's energy from Earth's surface. The climate would become cool, but the change would not be permanent. Over time, the volcanic ash and dust would settle out of the air.

CHAPTER PROJECT

Check Your Progress

Groups should be finished collecting weather data and starting to graph the data. Encourage students to look critically at the data for any similarities and differences. Besides graphing their data, suggest that students construct tables or charts to help them compare and contrast their observations. Encourage students to think about which climate factors caused the weather data to be different in each microclimate.

Performance Assessment

Skills Check Have students make a cause and effect table showing causes for climate change and the effects.

Figure 18 The continents have moved over millions of years. *Interpreting Maps Which present-day continents broke away from Gondwanaland? Which broke away from Laurasia?*

Recently, satellite measurements have shown that the amount of energy the sun produces increases and decreases slightly from year to year. These changes may cause Earth's temperature to increase and decrease. More observations are needed to test this hypothesis.

Movement of Continents Earth's continents have not always been located where they are now. About 225 million years ago, most of the land on Earth was part of a single continent called Pangaea (pan JEE uh).

As Figure 18 shows, most continents were far from their present positions. Continents that are now in the polar zones were once near the equator. This movement explains how tropical plants such as magnolias and palm trees could once have grown in Greenland.

Over millions of years, the continents broke away and gradually moved to their present positions. The movements of continents over time changed the locations of land and sea. These changes affected the global patterns of winds and ocean currents, which in turn slowly changed climates. And as the continents continue to move, climates will continue to change.

Section 3 Review

1. What types of evidence do scientists use to study changes in climate?
2. How was the climate during an ice age different from the climate today?
3. List three factors that could be responsible for changing Earth's climates.
4. **Thinking Critically Predicting** What kinds of climate changes might be caused by a volcanic eruption? Would these changes be permanent? Explain.

CHAPTER PROJECT

Check Your Progress

What types of weather conditions have you measured at each site? Have you been recording all the data in your logbook? You should now be ready to graph and analyze your data. Are the weather conditions at all of your test areas similar, or do you see differences? What do you think causes the different conditions? What organisms did you observe at your sites?

Answers to Self-Assessment

Caption Question

Figure 18 South America, Africa, Australia, and Antarctica broke away from Gondwanaland; North America, Europe, and Asia broke away from Laurasia.

Program Resources

- **Unit 4 Resources** 14-3 Review and Reinforce; 14-3 Enrich

Global Changes in the Atmosphere

DISCOVER ACTIVITY

What Is the Greenhouse Effect?

1. Cut two pieces of black construction paper to fit the bottoms of two shoe boxes.
2. Place a thermometer in one end of each box. Read the temperatures on the thermometers. (They should be the same.) Cover one box with plastic wrap.
3. Place the boxes together where sunlight or a light bulb can shine on them equally. Make sure the thermometers are shaded by the sides of the boxes.
4. What do think will happen to the temperatures on the thermometers? Wait 15 minutes and read the thermometers again. Record the temperatures.

Think It Over

Inferring How can you explain the temperature difference between the box with the plastic wrap and the open box? Why does the inside of a car left in direct sunlight get so warm?

Have you ever seen a headline like the one below? If you hate cold winters and love summer sports, you may wonder what would be wrong with a slightly warmer world. Some experts agree with you, but many scientists are worried about such climate change.

GUIDE FOR READING

- **How might human activities be affecting the temperature of Earth's atmosphere?**
- **How have human activities affected the ozone layer?**

Reading Tip **As you read, draw a concept map showing how human activities can cause changes in the atmosphere and climate.**

ANYWHERE U.S.A. DAILY NEWS

Earth's Average Temperature Expected to Increase by 3 Celsius Degrees

Most changes in world climates are caused by natural factors. In the last hundred years, however, human activities have also had an effect on Earth's climate and atmosphere. Two of the most important worldwide issues are global warming and thinning of the ozone layer.

Global Warming

Over the last 120 years, the average temperature of the troposphere has risen by about 0.5 Celsius degree. Was this increase part of natural variations, or was it caused by human activities? What effects could higher temperatures have? Scientists have done a great deal of research to try to answer these questions.

READING STRATEGIES

Reading Tip Suggest that students look over the section before they read it so they can choose a title and the major concepts for their concept maps. Concept maps might begin as follows:

human activities
can add to the atmosphere
greenhouse gases
CFCs

Program Resources

- **Unit 4 Resources** 14-4 Lesson Plan; 14-4 Section Summary
- **Guided Reading and Study Workbook** Section 14-4

INTEGRATING ENVIRONMENTAL SCIENCE

Global Changes in the Atmosphere

Objectives

After completing the lesson, students will be able to

- describe the greenhouse effect and how human activities may be affecting the temperature of Earth's atmosphere;
- describe how human activities have affected the ozone layer.

Key Terms greenhouse gas, global warming, chlorofluorocarbon

1 Engage/Explore

Activating Prior Knowledge

Invite students to explain what they think of when they hear about global warming and the depletion of the ozone layer. Then elicit their ideas of how the actions of people might affect climate. Record students' remarks on the board. As they study this section, refer to these comments and encourage students to modify the remarks, if necessary.

DISCOVER

Skills Focus inferring
Materials *2 pieces of black construction paper, 2 shoe boxes, 2 thermometers, plastic wrap, masking tape, source of sunlight or lamp*
Time 15 minutes, 5 minutes
Tips Tape the plastic wrap tightly to the box so that the box is air tight. The thermometers must be shaded. If not, they will give artificially high readings.
Expected Outcome The box covered with plastic wrap will be warmer.
Think It Over Light rays that enter both boxes radiate as heat from the box bottom. Heat is trapped inside the box with plastic wrap; heat escapes from the box without. The temperature inside a car increases as the heat from sunlight entering the car builds up and cannot escape.

2 Facilitate

Global Warming

Using the Visuals: Figure 19

If students have done the Discover activity, encourage them to compare their plastic covered box with the greenhouse in Figure 19. Then help students understand the analogy of a greenhouse to the greenhouse effect. Ask: **What part of Earth's atmosphere acts like a greenhouse roof?** *(Certain gases in the atmosphere—water vapor, carbon dioxide, and methane)* **What affect do these gases have on Earth's atmosphere?** *(They trap energy in the atmosphere.)* **Why are some scientists concerned about greenhouse gases?** *(As these gases increase in the atmosphere, they may trap more energy and cause global temperatures to increase.)* **learning modality: verbal**

Figure 19 Sunlight enters the greenhouse and is absorbed. The interior of the greenhouse radiates back energy in the form of infrared radiation, or heat. The heat is trapped and held inside the greenhouse, warming it. *Applying Concepts What gases in Earth's atmosphere can trap heat like a greenhouse?*

The Greenhouse Effect Recall that gases in Earth's atmosphere hold in heat from the sun, keeping the atmosphere at a comfortable temperature for living things. The process by which gases in Earth's atmosphere trap solar energy is called the greenhouse effect.

Gases in the atmosphere that trap solar energy are called **greenhouse gases.** Water vapor, carbon dioxide, and methane are some of the greenhouse gases. **Human activities that add greenhouse gases to the atmosphere may be warming Earth's atmosphere.** For example, the burning of wood, coal, oil, and natural gas adds carbon dioxide to the air. If the increased carbon dioxide traps more heat, the result could be **global warming,** a gradual increase in the temperature of Earth's atmosphere.

The amount of carbon dioxide in the atmosphere has been steadily increasing. Some scientists predict that if the level of carbon dioxide doubles by the year 2100, the average global temperature could go up by 1.5 to 3.5 Celsius degrees.

Another Hypothesis Not everyone agrees about the causes of global warming. Some scientists think that the 0.5 Celsius degree rise in global temperatures over the past 120 years may be part of natural variations in climate rather than a result of increases in carbon dioxide.

Background

Facts and Figures Much of the carbon dioxide produced by burning fossil fuels is absorbed instead of staying in the atmosphere. Plants absorb carbon dioxide from the air and use it to make food in the process of photosynthesis. Rain forests absorb large amounts of carbon dioxide from the atmosphere. Not only is the destruction of rain forests reducing the amount of carbon dioxide that can be absorbed from the atmosphere, but burning them also increases the amount of carbon dioxide added to it.

Earth's oceans also absorb much of the extra carbon dioxide in the atmosphere. Carbon dioxide from the air enters water by simple diffusion. As long as the concentration of carbon dioxide in ocean water is less than that of the air, carbon dioxide gas will diffuse into the water.

As you learned in Section 3, satellite measurements have shown that the amount of energy the sun produces increases and decreases from year to year. These changes in solar energy could be causing periods of warmer and cooler climates. Or climate change could be a result of changes in both carbon dioxide levels and amounts of solar energy.

Possible Effects Global warming has some potential advantages. Farmers in cool areas could plant two crops a year. Places that are too cold for farming today could become farmland. However, many effects of global warming are likely to be less positive. Higher temperatures would cause water to evaporate from exposed soil, such as plowed farmland. Dry soil blows away easily. Thus some fertile fields might become "dust bowls."

A rise in temperatures of even a few degrees could warm up water in the oceans. As ocean surface temperatures increased, the number of hurricanes might increase.

As the water warmed, it would expand, raising sea levels around the world. Glaciers and polar ice caps might partially melt, which would also increase sea levels. Sea levels have already risen by 10 to 20 centimeters over the last 100 years, and could rise another 25 to 80 centimeters by the year 2100. Even such a small rise in sea levels would flood low-lying coastal areas.

☑ *Checkpoint* *What are three possible effects of global warming?*

Ozone Depletion

Another global change in the atmosphere involves the ozone layer, which you learned about in Chapter 11. Ozone in the stratosphere filters out much of the harmful ultraviolet radiation from the sun.

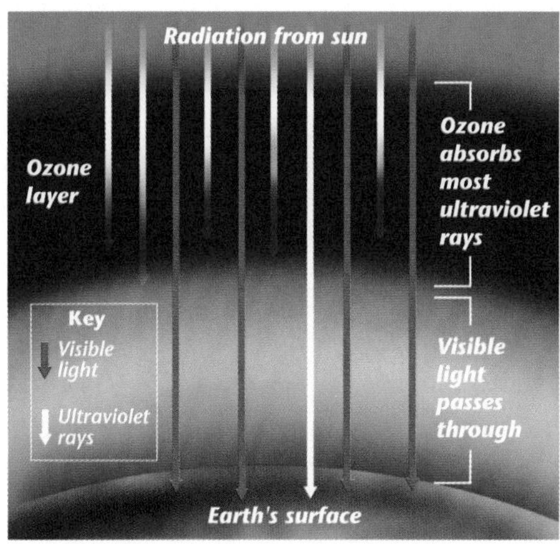

Figure 20 The ozone layer blocks much of the ultraviolet radiation coming from the sun. Visible light can pass through the ozone layer.

TRY THIS

It's Your Skin!

ACTIVITY

How well do sunscreens block out ultraviolet rays? Here's how to compare sunscreens.

1. Close the blinds or curtains in the room. Place one square of sun-sensitive paper inside each of three plastic sandwich bags.
2. Place three drops of one sunscreen on the outside of one bag. Spread the sunscreen as evenly as possible. Label this bag with the SPF number of the sunscreen.
3. On another bag, repeat Step 2 using a sunscreen with a different SPF. Wash your hands after spreading the sunscreen. Leave the third bag untreated as a control.
4. Place the bags outside in direct sunlight. Bring them back inside after 3 minutes or after one of the squares of paper has turned completely white.

Drawing Conclusions Did both of the sunscreens block ultraviolet radiation? Did one of the sunscreens block more ultraviolet radiation than the other one? Explain your results.

Media and Technology

Concept Videotape Library
Grade 6, Tape 2 "The Greenhouse Effect"

Answers to Self-Assessment

Caption Question

Figure 19 Water vapor, carbon dioxide, methane

☑ *Checkpoint*

Areas too cold for farming today could become farmland, some fertile fields could become "dust bowls," the number of hurricanes could increase, and sea levels could rise and flood low-lying coastal areas.

Real-Life Learning

Challenge student groups to make a plan for personally reducing carbon dioxide. Direct groups to first brainstorm a list of sources of carbon dioxide. (You might provide various resources to help groups identify these sources.) Then groups should identify the carbon-dioxide producing activities in which they are involved. Finally, groups should formulate a plan to reduce their carbon dioxide output. Encourage groups to present their plans to the class. **cooperative learning**

Ozone Depletion

TRY THIS

Skills Focus drawing conclusions

Materials *ultraviolet-sensitive paper, 3 plastic sandwich bags, 2 sunscreens with different SPF numbers, black marking pen*

Time 15 minutes

Tips Results will be more obvious if students use sunscreens with highly different SPF numbers. Obtain ultraviolet-sensitive paper from toy or craft stores (called "Sunprint Kit"). Save class time by precutting the paper.

Expected Outcome The paper without sunscreen will show the most color change, and the paper covered with the higher SPF sunscreen will show the least.

Answers Since the untreated paper showed the most color change, the sunscreens did block ultraviolet radiation. The sunscreen with the lower SPF number blocked less ultraviolet radiation because it showed more color change than the paper covered with the higher SPF sunscreen.

Extend Encourage students to return the bags with sunscreen to direct sunlight and monitor them to find out how long the sunscreen is effective. **learning modality: kinesthetic**

Ongoing Assessment

Drawing Challenge students to draw their own diagrams showing how greenhouse gases trap heat energy from sunlight in Earth's atmosphere.

Students can save their diagrams in their portfolios.

Ozone Depletion, continued

Addressing Naive Conceptions

Some students might be confused about why the depletion of the ozone layer is harmful when many metropolitan areas have Ozone Action Days to reduce air pollution. Ask: **Do you know why ozone is harmful to people?** *(Some students may not.)* Explain that ozone is part of smog. Ozone forms when sunlight irradiates the emissions from gasoline engines. Smog reduces visibility, irritates the respiratory system, causes eye irritations, and can damage plants. Point out that the concentration of ozone found in the ozone layer would be harmful for people to breathe. However, the ozone layer protects us from the ultraviolet radiation from the sun. **learning modality: verbal**

3 Assess

Section 4 Review Answers

1. The burning of wood, coal, oil, and natural gas
2. More carbon dioxide in the air traps more heat in the atmosphere, which causes a gradual increase in global temperatures.
3. chlorofluorocarbons
4. Depending on where they live, students might mention milder winters, longer growing seasons, coastal flooding, more hurricanes, and heat waves.

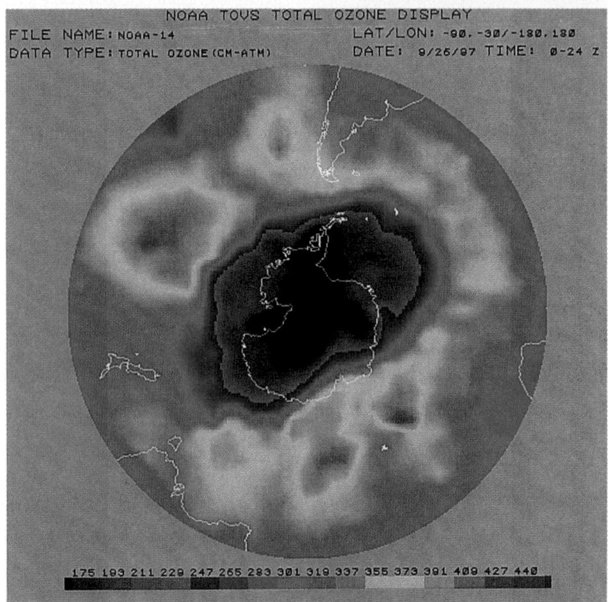

Figure 21 This satellite image shows the concentration of ozone in the air over the South Pole. The dark area shows where the ozone layer is the thinnest.

In the 1970s, scientists noticed that the ozone layer over Antarctica was growing thinner each spring. By 1992, the area of thinner ozone was more than twice as large as the continental United States. What created the ozone hole? **Chemicals produced by humans have been damaging the ozone layer.**

The main cause of ozone depletion is a group of chlorine compounds called **chlorofluorocarbons,** or CFCs. CFCs were used in air conditioners and refrigerators, as cleaners for electronic parts, and in spray cans. Most chemical compounds released into the air eventually break down. CFCs, however, can last for decades and rise all the way to the stratosphere. In the stratosphere, ultraviolet radiation breaks down the CFC molecules into atoms, including chlorine. The chlorine atoms then break ozone down into oxygen atoms.

Because ozone blocks ultraviolet radiation, a decrease in ozone means an increase in the amount of ultraviolet radiation that reaches Earth's surface. If you have ever been sunburned, you can understand one effect of stronger ultraviolet radiation! Ultraviolet radiation can also cause eye damage and several kinds of skin cancer.

In the late 1970s, the United States and many other countries banned the use of CFCs in spray cans. In 1990, many nations signed an agreement to end the production and use of almost all CFCs by 2000. Because ozone depletion affects the whole world, such agreements must be international to be effective.

Section 4 Review

1. What human actions increase the amount of carbon dioxide in Earth's atmosphere?
2. How could increases in carbon dioxide in the air affect world temperatures?
3. What chemicals are the major cause of ozone depletion in the stratosphere?
4. **Thinking Critically Predicting** How might global warming change conditions where you live? How would this affect your life?

Science at Home

Compare Sunscreens Visit a drugstore with your family. Compare the SPF (sun protection factor) of the various sunscreens for sale. Explain why it is important to protect your skin from ultraviolet radiation. Ask your family members to determine the best value for their money in terms of SPF rating and price.

Performance Assessment

Writing Challenge students to write a news article that describes what global warming and ozone depletion are and how human activities have affected the atmosphere.

 Students can save their news articles in their portfolios.

Media and Technology

 **Concept Videotape Library**
Grade 6, Tape 2 "Our Passion for Driving"

Program Resources

- **Unit 4 Resources** 14-4 Review and Reinforce; 14-4 Enrich

What Causes Climate?

Key Ideas

- The climate of a region is determined by its temperature and precipitation.
- The main factors that influence temperature are latitude, altitude, distance from large bodies of water, and ocean currents.
- The main factors that affect precipitation are prevailing winds and the presence of mountains.
- The different seasons are a result of the tilt of Earth's axis as Earth travels around the sun.

Key Terms

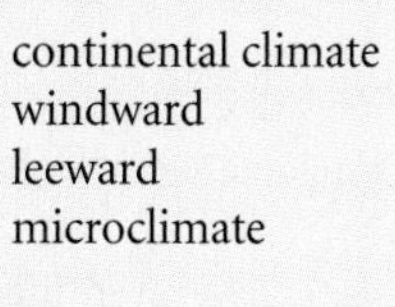

climate
tropical zone
polar zone
temperate zone
marine climate
continental climate
windward
leeward
microclimate

Climate Regions

Key Ideas

- Climates are classified according to temperature and precipitation.
- There are five main climate regions: tropical rainy, dry, temperate marine, temperate continental, and polar. Highlands are often considered to be a sixth climate region.

Key Terms

rain forest
savanna
desert
steppe
humid subtropical
subarctic
tundra
permafrost

Long-Term Changes in Climate

Key Ideas

- During each ice age, huge sheets of ice covered much of Earth's surface.
- Possible explanations for major climate changes include movement of continents, variations in the position of Earth relative to the sun, and changes in the sun's energy output.

Key Terms

ice age
sunspot

Global Changes in the Atmosphere

INTEGRATING ENVIRONMENTAL SCIENCE

Key Ideas

- Human activities that add greenhouse gases to the atmosphere may be warming Earth's atmosphere.
- Chemicals produced by humans have been damaging the ozone layer.

Key Terms

greenhouse gas
global warming
chlorofluorocarbons

Organizing Information

Concept Map Copy the concept map about climate onto a separate sheet of paper. Then complete it and add a title. (For more on concept maps, see the Skills Handbook.)

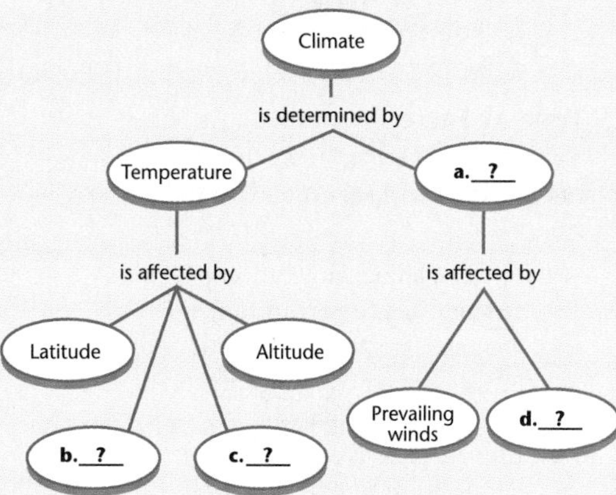

Program Resources

- **Unit 4 Resources** Chapter 14 Project Scoring Rubric
- **Performance Assessment** Chapter 14
- **Chapter and Unit Tests** Chapter 14 Test; Unit 4 Test

Media and Technology

Computer Test Bank Chapter 14 Test

Science at Home

ACTIVITY

To make sure that students can explain to their families the importance of using sunscreen, ask: **Why is it important to protect your skin from ultraviolet radiation?** *(Ultraviolet radiation can cause sunburn and several kinds of skin cancer.)* To help prepare students for comparison shopping, suggest that they take calculators with them to the drugstore and calculate the price per ounce of the sunscreens they are comparing. After they compare the prices of equal quantities, then they can begin to determine which sunscreens are a better value based on their SPF numbers.

Organizing Information

Concept Map Sample Title: *Factors Affecting Climate* **a.** Precipitation **b.** or **c.** Distance from large bodies of water or ocean currents **d.** Mountain ranges

Reviewing Content

Multiple Choice

1. b **2.** c **3.** b **4.** d **5.** a

True or False

6. precipitation **7.** winter **8.** true **9.** true
10. carbon dioxide

Checking Concepts

11. Water heats up and cools down more slowly than land. Oceans and other large bodies of water generally moderate the temperature of nearby land areas.
12. The seasons are caused by the tilt of Earth's axis.
13. Most of the United States is in the temperate zone; Hawaii and southern Florida are in the tropical zone; much of Alaska is in the polar zone.
14. Dry climates occur where potential evaporation is greater than precipitation. The two types of dry climates differ in the amount of precipitation they receive. Steppes get more precipitation than deserts.
15. Present-day continents were once at different latitudes and had different climates. As the continents moved from their original positions, their latitudes changed, global patterns of wind and ocean currents changed, and mountains formed, all of which affect climate.
16. Ozone depletion affects the whole world, and the actions of people around the world affect the ozone. For this reason, everyone around the world must work together to prevent ozone depletion.
17. Answers should show that students have accurately observed their local climate factors and have successfully related them to the concepts in the chapter.

Thinking Critically

18. Answers may vary. *Sample answer:* Large bodies of water moderate the climates of nearby land; warm and cold ocean currents influence the climate of coastal areas; the amount of precipitation is a factor in wet and dry climates.
19. Global warming caused by an increase in greenhouse gases is the result of human activities and can be controlled. Earlier changes in climate were the result of natural forces.

CHAPTER 14 ASSESSMENT

Reviewing Content

Multiple Choice

Choose the letter of the best answer.

1. Temperatures are highest in the tropical zone because
a. the land is flat.
b. the sun's rays strike most directly.
c. Earth's axis is tilted toward the sun.
d. ocean currents warm the region.

2. Continental climates are found
a. on every continent.
b. only near the equator.
c. only in the Northern Hemisphere.
d. only in the Southern Hemisphere.

3. In a wet-and-dry tropical climate, the most common vegetation is
a. coniferous forests.
b. savanna grasslands.
c. tropical rain forest.
d. steppe grasslands.

4. Extremely cold periods in Earth's history have resulted in huge
a. tree rings.
b. sunspots.
c. pollen deposits.
d. glaciers.

5. Chlorofluorocarbons, or CFCs, are the main cause of
a. ozone depletion.
b. global warming.
c. the greenhouse effect.
d. ice ages.

True or False

If the statement is true, write true. If it is false, change the underlined word or words to make it true.

6. The prevailing winds affect how much <u>sunlight</u> falls on an area.
7. When the north end of Earth's axis is tilted toward the sun, it is <u>summer</u> in the Southern Hemisphere.
8. Climate regions are classified according to temperature and <u>precipitation</u>.
9. A <u>thin</u> tree ring indicates that a year was cool or dry.
10. An increase in <u>nitrogen</u> in the atmosphere may be making world temperatures increase.

Checking Concepts

11. Explain how distance from large bodies of water can affect the temperature of nearby land areas.
12. What causes Earth's seasons?
13. Identify the parts of the United States that are located in each of the three temperature zones.
14. How are "dry" climates defined? How do the two types of dry climate differ?
15. How does the movement of continents explain major changes in climate over time?
16. To be effective, why must agreements aimed at preventing or reducing ozone depletion be international?
17. Writing to Learn In what climate region do you live? Write a description of your local climate and identify some of the things—such as latitude, bodies of water, or wind patterns—that affect the climate.

Thinking Critically

18. Relating Cause and Effect Describe three ways in which water influences climate.
19. Comparing and Contrasting How is global warming different from earlier changes in Earth's climate?
20. Making Judgments What is the most important thing that needs to be done about global warming?
21. Relating Cause and Effect Why do parts of the United States have a semiarid climate while neighboring areas have a humid continental climate?

20. Answers may vary. Some students might suggest the most important thing to do is to study the problem more to find definitive answers. Other students might say reduce the amount of carbon dioxide released into the atmosphere.
21. Air that passes over the steppe in a semiarid climate has lost its water vapor as it passed over mountain ranges, so the air is drier. Some of the air that passes over humid continental areas comes from the oceans and doesn't cross mountain ranges, so the air carries more moisture.

Applying Skills

22. Zone A, polar zone; Zone B, temperate zone; Zone C, tropical zone; Zone D, temperate zone; Zone E, polar zone
23. tropical zone; 47 degrees of latitude
24. Zone B

Applying Skills

Use the map of world temperature zones to answer Questions 22–24.

22. **Interpreting Maps** Name each of the five zones shown on the map.
23. **Measuring** What is the name of the temperature zone that includes the equator? How many degrees of latitude does this zone cover?

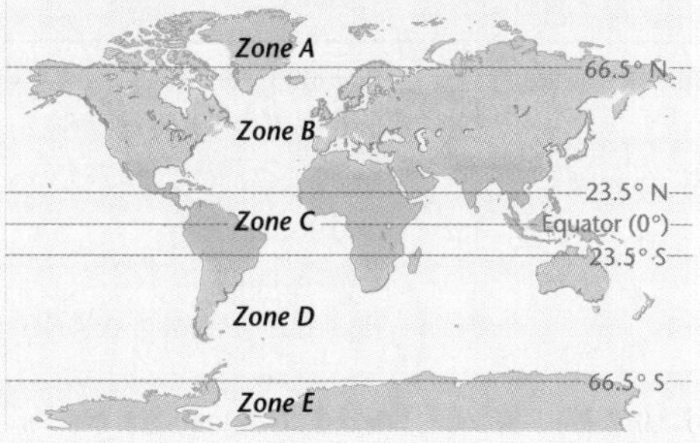

24. **Interpreting Data** Which of the five zones shown on the map has the greatest amount of land area suitable for people to live?

Performance CHAPTER PROJECT Assessment

Present Your Project Decide how to present your project. You could use a written report, oral presentation, or a bulletin board. Do your graphs compare the conditions in the different microclimates? What conditions favor plants or animals in some areas? After you present your project to the class, discuss what you think causes different microclimates.

Reflect and Record In your journal, describe how you could improve your investigation. Are there factors you did not study? Did you notice any organisms that live only in certain microclimates? What additional information about microclimates would you like to find?

Test Preparation

Use these questions to prepare for standardized tests.

Study the graph. Then answer Questions 25–30.

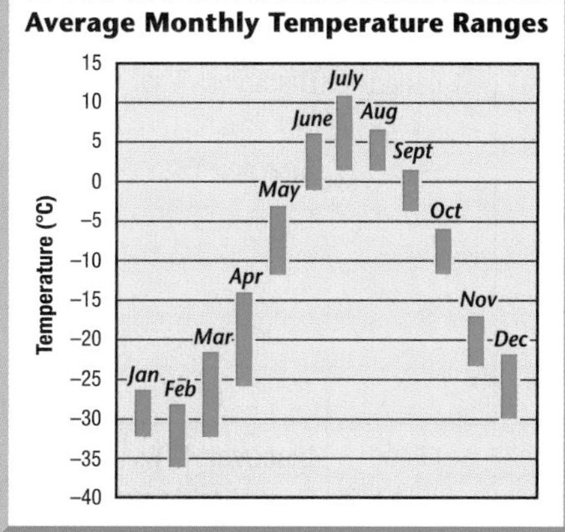

25. Which of the following months has the widest range of temperatures during the year?
    a. September **b.** June
    c. May **d.** April
26. Which month shown on the graph is the warmest on average?
    a. August **b.** June
    c. July **d.** May
27. Which month is the coldest on average?
    a. January **b.** December
    c. March **d.** February
28. What is the average temperature in April?
    a. about −21°C **b.** about −17°C
    c. about 0°C **d.** about −30°C
29. What is the average temperature in December?
    a. about −20°C **b.** about −26°C
    c. about 0°C **d.** about −30°C
30. What kind of climate is indicated by the graph?
    a. polar
    b. temperate continental
    c. temperate marine
    d. tropical rainy

Performance CHAPTER PROJECT Assessment

Present Your Project Find out from groups how they intend to present their projects. Have bulletin board space available for those groups who choose to use it. Groups giving oral presentations could use an overhead projector to display their graphs. Each group should present graphs that compare the weather conditions in the different microclimates they studied. In their presentations, groups should draw conclusions about the kinds of conditions that favor certain plants and animals. After groups have presented their reports, discuss the factors that cause different microclimates. Begin by prompting students to recall the climate factors that affect temperature and precipitation.

Reflect and Record Encourage students to be objective as they evaluate their investigations. For their journals, suggest that they reflect on the concepts they learned in this chapter and what they could have added to their investigation.

Test Preparation

25. d **26.** c **27.** d **28.** a **29.** b **30.** a

Program Resources

◆ **Inquiry Skills Activity Book** Provides teaching and review of all inquiry skills

CHAPTER 15

Energy and Power

Sections	Time	Student Edition Activities	Other Activities
CHAPTER PROJECT **Roller Coaster!** p. 467	Ongoing (1 week)	Check Your Progress, pp. 473, 489, 494 Present Your Project, p. 497	
1 The Nature of Energy pp. 468–475 ◆ Describe the relationship between work and energy. ◆ Define and calculate potential and kinetic energy. ◆ List different forms of energy.	2 periods/ 1 block	**Discover** How High Does a Ball Bounce?, p. 468 **Skills Lab: Designing Experiments** Soaring Straws, pp. 474–475	**TE** Including All Students, p. 469 **TE** Inquiry Challenge, p. 469 **TE** Demonstration, p. 471 **TE** Addressing Naive Conceptions, p. 472 **TE** Real Life Learning, p. 472
2 Energy Conversion and Conservation pp. 476–481 ◆ Describe the conversions between different forms of energy. ◆ State the law of conservation of energy.	1 period/ $\frac{1}{2}$ block	**Discover** What Would Make a Card Jump?, p. 476 **Try This** Pendulum Swing, p. 479 **Science at Home,** p. 481	**TE** Building Inquiry Skills: Applying Concepts, p. 477; Predicting, p. 478 **TE** Including All Students, p. 479 **TE** Demonstration, pp. 478, 480
3 INTEGRATING LIFE SCIENCE **Photosynthesis and Fossil Fuels** pp. 482–489 ◆ Describe the energy conversion that occurs during photosynthesis. ◆ Explain how fossil fuels contain energy that came from the sun.	1 period/ $\frac{1}{2}$ block	**Discover** What Is a Fuel?, p. 482 **Try This** Go for the Green, p. 484 **Sharpen Your Skills** Graphing, p. 487	**TE** Demonstration, pp. 483, 485, 486 **TE** Integrating Physics, p. 483 **TE** Building Inquiry Skills: Inferring, p. 485 **TE** Including All Students, p. 488
4 INTEGRATING MATHEMATICS **Power** pp. 490–494 ◆ Define and calculate power. ◆ Compare energy and power.	1 period/ $\frac{1}{2}$ block	**Discover** Is Work Always the Same?, p. 490 **Real-World Lab: Careers in Science** Can You Feel the Power?, pp. 492–493	**TE** Inquiry Challenge, p. 491 **TE** Building Inquiry Skills: Observing, p. 491 **LM** 15, "Winding Up With Wind"
Study Guide/Chapter Assessment pp. 495–497	1 period/ $\frac{1}{2}$ block		**ISAB** Provides teaching and review of all inquiry skills

For Standard or Block Schedule The Resource Pro® CD-ROM gives you maximum flexibility for planning your instruction for any type of schedule. Resource Pro® contains Planning Express®, an advanced scheduling program, as well as the entire contents of the Teaching Resources and the Computer Test Bank.

CHAPTER PLANNING GUIDE

Program Resources	Assessment Strategies	Media and Technology
UR Chapter 15 Project Teacher Notes **UR** Chapter 15 Project Overview and Worksheets	**SE** Performance Assessment: Present Your Project, p. 497 **TE** Check Your Progress, pp. 473, 489, 494 **UR** Chapter 15 Project Scoring Rubric	Science Explorer Internet Site at www.phschool.com Student Edition on Audio CD, Chapter 15
UR 15-1 Section Lesson Plan **UR** 15-1 Section Summary **UR** 15-1 Review and Reinforce **UR** 15-1 Enrich **UR** Skills Lab blackline masters	**SE** Section 1 Review, p. 473 **TE** Ongoing Assessment, pp. 469, 471 **TE** Performance Assessment, p. 473	Concept Videotape Library, Grade 6, Tape 4, "Energy" Lab Activity Videotapes, Grade 6 Tape 3 Transparency 59, "Kinetic Energy"
UR 15-2 Section Lesson Plan **UR** 15-2 Section Summary **UR** 15-2 Review and Reinforce **UR** 15-2 Enrich	**SE** Section 2 Review, p. 481 **TE** Ongoing Assessment, pp. 477, 479 **TE** Performance Assessment, p. 481	Transparencies 60, "Energy Conversions"; 61, "The Pendulum"
UR 15-3 Section Lesson Plan **UR** 15-3 Section Summary **UR** 15-3 Review and Reinforce **UR** 15-3 Enrich	**SE** Section 3 Review, p. 489 **TE** Ongoing Assessment, pp. 483, 485, 487 **TE** Performance Assessment, p. 489	Concept Videotape Library, Grade 6, Tape 4, "Power for the People" Transparency 62, "Exploring Energy Conversions"
UR 15-4 Section Lesson Plan **UR** 15-4 Section Summary **UR** 15-4 Review and Reinforce **UR** 15-4 Enrich **UR** Real-World Lab blackline masters	**SE** Section 4 Review, p. 494 **TE** Ongoing Assessment, p. 491 **TE** Performance Assessment, p. 494	Lab Activity Videotapes, Grade 6 Tape 3
RCA Provides strategies to improve science reading skills **GRSW** Provides worksheets to promote student comprehension of content	**SE** Chapter 15 Study Guide/Assessment, pp. 495, 497 **PA** Chapter 15 Performance Assessment **CUT** Chapter 15 Test **CTB** Chapter 15 Test	Computer Test Bank, Chapter 15 Test

Key: **SE** Student Edition
CTB Computer Test Bank
ISAB Inquiry Skills Activity Book
GRSW Guided Reading and Study Workbook
TE Teacher's Edition
PTA Product Testing Activities by *Consumer Reports*
RCA Reading in the Content Area
PA Performance Assessment
UR Unit Resources
LM Laboratory Manual
IES Interdisciplinary Explorations Series
CUT Chapter and Unit Tests

Meeting the National Science Education Standards and AAAS Benchmarks

National Science Education Standards	Benchmarks for Science Literacy	Unifying Themes
Science as Inquiry (Content Standard A) ◆ **Design and conduct a scientific investigation** Students examine how to alter power while doing exercise. *(Real-World Lab)* ◆ **Use mathematics in all aspects of scientific inquiry** Students calculate kinetic and potential energy and power. *(Sections 1, 4; Skills Lab; Real-World Lab)* **Physical Science** (Content Standard B) ◆ **Transfer of energy** Energy is transferred in many ways and energy changes form. Energy cannot be created or destroyed. The sun's energy is stored as different forms on Earth. *(Sections 1, 2, 3; Chapter Project; Skills Lab)* **Science and Technology** (Content Standard E) ◆ **Design a solution or a product** Students design a roller coaster powered by potential energy. *(Chapter Project)* ◆ **Implement a proposed design** Roller coaster designs are tested. *(Chapter Project)* Students investigate how gravitational potential energy and elastic potential energy are related in a rubber band launcher. *(Skills Lab)* ◆ **Understandings about science and technology** The reciprocal nature of science and technology are explored as students learn about Watt's steam engine and the value of horsepower. *(Section 4)*	**1B Scientific Inquiry** Students control variables as they build a roller coaster and investigate the relationship between the height reached by a rocket and the amount of stretch in a rubber band launcher. *(Chapter Project; Skills Lab)* **3B Design and Systems** Students design a roller coaster to detailed specifications. *(Chapter Project)* **4B The Earth** Gravity gives objects gravitational potential energy. Some of Earth's resources, including fossil fuels, are limited and can be depleted. *(Sections 2, 3)* **4E Energy Transformations** Energy is conserved. When work is done or change takes place, energy is transferred and transformed. Energy appears in many different forms. *(Sections 1, 2, 3; Chapter Project; Skills Lab)* **5E Flow of Matter and Energy** The sun produces electromagnetic energy that plants and animals store as chemical energy. Fossil fuels are the result of energy stored millions of years ago. *(Sections 2, 3)* **8C Energy Sources and Use** Energy changes form; some energy is converted to thermal energy. Electrical energy can be produced from different energy sources, including fossil fuels. *(Sections 1, 2, 3)* **9B Symbolic Relationships** Equations can be used to calculate energy and power. *(Sections 2, 4; Skills Lab, Real-World Lab)* **10J Harnessing Power** James Watt created the unit horsepower to describe the energy used by machines. *(Section 4)*	◆ **Energy** Energy is defined as the ability to do work or cause change. Energy conversions occur when work is done or energy is transformed. Power is the rate at which energy is transferred or converted. *(Sections 1, 2, 3, 4; Chapter Project; Skills Lab; Real-World Lab)* ◆ **Patterns of Change** Energy converts from one form to another when work is done or energy is transferred. Kinetic energy can be stored as potential energy and potential energy can be released as kinetic energy. *(Sections 1, 2, 3; Chapter Project; Skills Lab; Real-World Lab)* ◆ **Systems and Interactions** An object that has energy can do work. Work is the transfer of energy from one object to another or transforming energy from one form to another. *(Sections 1–4; Chapter Project; Skills Lab)* ◆ **Unity and Diversity** Energy has many different forms. Any form of energy can be converted to another form. *(Sections 1, 2, 3; Chapter Project; Skills Lab)*

Take It to the Net

Interactive text at www.phschool.com

Science Explorer comes alive with iText.

- **Complete student text** is accessible from any computer with Internet access or a CD-ROM drive.
- **Animations, simulations, and videos** enhance student understanding and retention of concepts.
- **Self-tests and online study tools** assess student understanding.

STAY CURRENT with **SCIENCE NEWS®**

Find out the latest research and information about Energy and Energy Resources at: **www.phschool.com**

Go to **www.phschool.com** and click on the Science icon.Then click on Science Explorer: Life, Earth, and Physical Science under PH@school.

Student Edition Activities Planner

ACTIVITY	Time *(minutes)*	Materials *Quantities for one work group*	Skills
Section 1			
Discover, p. 468	10	**Nonconsumable** meter stick, tennis ball	**Observing**
Skills Lab, pp. 474–475	40	**Consumable** 3 plastic straws, empty toilet paper tube, rubber band, masking tape **Nonconsumable** scissors, marker, balance, meter stick, metric ruler, computer and graphing program (optional)	**Controlling Variables**
Section 2			
Discover, p. 476	10	**Consumable** 3 x 5 index card **Nonconsumable** rubber band, scissors	**Forming Operational Definitions**
Try This, p. 479	15	**Nonconsumable** washers or rubber stoppers, string, ring stand, 2 clamps, meter stick	**Observing**
Science at Home, p. 481	home	**Consumable** wire hanger	**Observing**
Section 3			
Discover, p. 482	20	**Consumable** water, wooden coffee stirrer, matches **Nonconsumable** flask, ring stand, clamp, thermometer, small aluminum pan, safety goggles	**Forming Operational Definitions**
Try This, p. 484	15	**Nonconsumable** microscope, prepared slides of at least three different kinds of green leaves	**Observing**
Sharpen your Skills, p. 487	15	**Nonconsumable** compass, protractor	**Graphing**
Section 4			
Discover, p. 490	10	**Nonconsumable** pinwheel, hair dryer with two settings	**Inferring**
Real-World Lab, pp. 492–493	45	**Nonconsumable** calculator; meter stick; stopwatch or clock with a second hand; board, about 2.5 cm x 30 cm x 120 cm; 8–10 books, each about 2 cm thick	**Measuring, Calculating, Interpreting Data**

A list of all materials required for the Student Edition activities can be found on pages TVA34–TVA40. You can obtain information about ordering materials by calling 1-800-848-9500 or by accessing the Science Explorer Internet site at **www.phschool.com**.

CHAPTER 15 PROJECT

Roller Coaster

Students may not realize that all motion can be described in terms of energy. This project will provide students with an opportunity to evaluate motion in terms of kinetic and potential energy.

Purpose In this project, students will have the opportunity to create a roller coaster so that they can gain hands-on experience with the conversion of potential energy into kinetic energy. Students will be able to use energy conversions as criteria for modifying the designs of their models.

Skills Focus After completing the Chapter 15 project, students will be able to

- ◆ create working models of roller coasters in accordance with the specifications;
- ◆ control variables as they experiment with different hill heights and add turns and loops to their roller coasters;
- ◆ evaluate their models in terms of kinetic energy, potential energy, and the law of conservation of energy.

Project Time Line This project will take approximately two weeks to complete. During the first week, students will begin experimenting with different materials to determine how they will construct their tracks and vehicles. Once they determine what materials to use, students may begin to build the tracks, experimenting with hills of different heights. During the second week, students should modify their tracks to include turns and/or vertical loops. They should apply key terms such as friction, kinetic energy, potential energy, acceleration, and velocity to their descriptions of the roller coasters. Finally, students will present their roller coasters to the class. Before beginning the project, see the Chapter 15 Project Teacher Notes in Unit 5 Resources for more details on carrying out the project. Also distribute to students the Chapter 15 Project Overview, Worksheets, and Scoring Rubric in Unit 5 Resources.

466

Possible Materials Students may use cardboard, posterboard, garden hoses, rubber or vinyl tubing, foam pipe insulation, drinking straws, or other materials. Marbles, ball bearings, rubber balls, or toy cars can be used as vehicles. Students may also need additional materials including string, tape, glue, paper clips, bricks, shoe boxes, blocks of wood, stopwatches, cups, or buckets. Encourage students to suggest and use other materials as well, but make sure that they choose materials that are readily available.

Launching the Project To introduce the project, begin a class discussion about roller coasters. Ask students: **Have you ever ridden a roller coaster?** Have them describe their experiences. Did they feel fear or excitement? Why? What happened as the roller coaster rushed down a hill, climbed a hill, or went around a corner? Did it speed up or slow down? Why? Get them involved in a discussion about the hills, speed, and turns of a roller

CHAPTER 15 PROJECT

Roller Coaster!

Slowly, but steadily, you climb the mighty hill. Up, up, up, and then whoosh—you plunge swiftly down the other side. You curve left, then right, and then up again.

This thrilling roller coaster ride is brought to you courtesy of energy. In this chapter you will learn about energy, the forms it takes, and how it is transformed and conserved. You will use what you learn to design and construct your own roller coaster.

Your Goal To design and construct a roller coaster that uses kinetic and potential energy to move.

Your project must

- be no wider than 2 meters and be easily disassembled and reassembled
- have a first hill with a height of 1 meter and have at least two additional hills
- have a car that moves along the entire track without stopping
- follow the safety guidelines in Appendix A

Get Started If you or any of your classmates have ridden a roller coaster, share your experiences. Brainstorm the characteristics of a good roller coaster. Consider how fast the roller coaster moves and how its speed changes throughout the ride.

Check Your Progress You'll be working on this project as you study this chapter. To keep your project on track, look for Check Your Progress boxes at the following points.

Section 1 Review, page 473: Experiment with different hill heights and inclines.

Section 3 Review, page 489: Describe how your vehicle moves along its tracks in terms of potential and kinetic energy.

Section 4 Review, page 494: Add turns and loops to determine their effect.

Present Your Project At the end of the chapter (page 497), you will show how your roller coaster car can move up and down at least three hills once you release it.

The cars on a roller coaster like this one may reach speeds of more than 100 kilometers per hour.

SECTION 4 *Integrating Mathematics* **Power**

Discover **Is Work Always the Same?**
Real-World Lab **Can You Feel the Power?**

467

coaster. Ask students: **What features of a roller coaster would you include if you were going to build one? What materials and knowledge would you need?**

Allow time for students to read the description of the project in the text and the Chapter Project Overview in Unit 5 Resources. Then encourage students to discuss potential and kinetic energy as they relate to a roller coaster. Distribute copies of the Chapter 15 Project Worksheets in Unit 5 Resources for students to review.

Performance Assessment

The Chapter 15 Project Scoring Rubric in Unit 5 Resources will help you evaluate how well students complete the Chapter 15 Project. Students will be assessed on whether

- their roller coaster is no wider than 2 meters and has three hills, the first of which is 1 meter high; and the vehicle successfully completes the entire track without stopping;
- modifications are made to the roller coaster based on the results of experiments and the application of concepts involving energy conversions;
- they are able to apply concepts such as kinetic energy, potential energy, and the law of conservation of energy to the description of their roller coaster;
- their presentation and written analysis are thorough and well-organized.

By sharing the Chapter 15 Project Scoring Rubric with students at the beginning of the project, you will make it clear to them what they are expected to do.

Program Resources

- **Unit 5 Resources** Chapter 15 Project Teacher Notes; Chapter 15 Project Overview and Worksheets; Chapter 15 Project Scoring Rubric

www.phschool.com

You will find an Internet activity, chapter self-tests for students, and links to other chapter topics at this site.

Media and Technology

Student Edition on Audio CD Chapter 15

SECTION 1 The Nature of Energy

Objectives

After completing the lesson, students will be able to

- ◆ describe the relationship between work and energy;
- ◆ define and calculate potential and kinetic energy;
- ◆ list different forms of energy.

Key Terms work, energy, force, kinetic energy, potential energy, elastic potential energy, gravitational potential energy, radiant energy

1 Engage/Explore

Activating Prior Knowledge

Ask students: **What do you mean when you say that someone has "a lot of energy"?** *(Answers will vary, but should include the idea that the person is very active and gets many things done.)* Help students connect this everyday use of *energy* with the scientific definitions.

DISCOVER

Skills Focus observing
Materials *meter stick, tennis ball*
Time 10 minutes
Tips Students should work in pairs or small groups. Suggest that students perform several trials at each position and find the average height. Encourage students to use the same method of observation in every trial.
Expected Outcome The ball bounces the highest when it is dropped from the greatest height.
Think It Over The greater the height from which the ball is dropped, the higher the ball bounces.
Extend Have students repeat the experiment using several different balls, such as hard rubber balls, golf balls, and baseballs.

SECTION 1 The Nature of Energy

How High Does a Ball Bounce?

1. Hold a meter stick vertically, with the zero end on the ground.
2. Drop a tennis ball from the 50-centimeter mark and record the height to which it bounces.
3. Drop the tennis ball from the 100-centimeter mark and record the height to which it bounces.
4. Predict how high the ball will bounce if dropped from the 75-centimeter mark. Test your prediction.

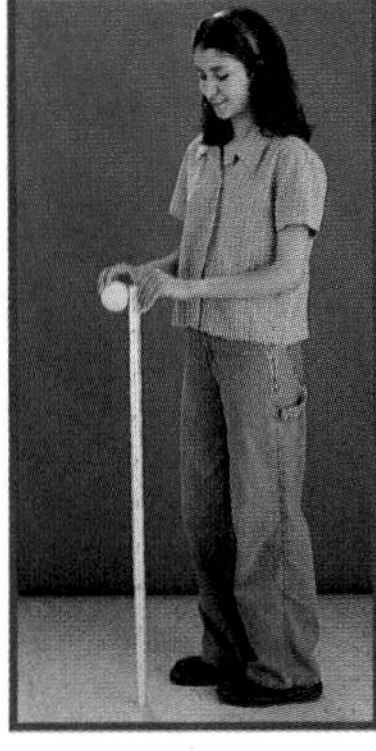

Think It Over
Observing How does the height from which you drop the ball relate to the height to which the ball bounces?

GUIDE FOR READING

- ◆ How are work and energy related?
- ◆ What are the two basic kinds of energy?
- ◆ What are some of the different forms of energy?

Reading Tip Before you read, list some examples of energy. As you read, add to your list.

Brilliant streaks of lightning flash across the night sky. The howling of the wind and the crashing of thunder drown out the sound of falling rain. Then a sound like a railroad locomotive approaches. As the sound grows louder, a small town experiences the power and fury of a tornado. Whirling winds of more than 250 kilometers per hour blow through the town. Roofs are lifted off of buildings. Cars are thrown about like toys. Then, in minutes, the tornado is gone.

The next morning, as rescuers survey the damage, a light breeze delicately carries falling leaves past the debris. How strange it is that the wind is violent enough to destroy buildings one night and barely strong enough to carry a leaf the next morning. Wind is just moving air, but it possesses energy. As you read on, you'll find out what energy is.

What Is Energy?

When wind moves a leaf, or even a house, it causes a change. In the case of the leaf or house, the change is in the position of the object. **Work** is done when a force moves an object through a distance. The ability to do work or cause change is called **energy.** So the wind has energy. It can exert a **force,** a push or pull.

Figure 1 The energy of a tornado can devastate a town in minutes.

READING STRATEGIES

Reading Tip Students may list electricity and nuclear energy. Have them review their lists to see if the examples can be arranged in categories. Ask students to write the categories as column headings on a new sheet of paper and place items in the categories. As students read the section, have them place more examples in the categories and rename or add categories as necessary.

Study and Comprehension Instruct students to write a brief definition of each form of energy in their own words and to include examples from their experience.

Concept Mapping Have students create concepts maps to organize information about the six major forms of energy presented in the section.

Figure 2 A bowling ball can do work because it is moving. *Applying Concepts What is the ability to do work called?*

When an object or organism does work on another object, some of its energy is transferred to that object. **You can think of work, then, as the transfer of energy.** When energy is transferred, the object upon which the work is done gains energy. Energy is measured in joules—the same units as work.

Kinetic Energy

There are two general kinds of energy. **The two kinds of energy are kinetic energy and potential energy.** Whether energy is kinetic or potential depends on whether an object is moving or not.

The examples you have read about so far have involved things that were moving. A moving object can collide with another object and move it some distance. In that way, the moving object does work. For example, a bowling ball knocks over a bowling pin.

Because the moving object can do work, it must have energy. The energy of motion is called **kinetic energy.** The word kinetic comes from the Greek word *kinetos,* which means "moving."

Mass and Velocity The kinetic energy of an object depends on both its mass and its velocity, or how fast the object moves. Think about rolling a golf ball and a bowling ball so that they travel at the same velocity. Which ball would you have to roll more forcefully? You would have to exert a greater force on the bowling ball because it has more mass than the golf ball.

Since energy is transferred during work, the more work you do, the more energy you give to the ball. So a bowling ball has more kinetic energy than a golf ball traveling at the same velocity. Kinetic energy increases as mass increases.

What would you have to do to make the bowling ball move faster? You would have to throw it harder, or use a greater force.

2 Facilitate

What Is Energy?

Including All Students

Materials *sponge, balloon, tuning fork, wood block*
Time 10 minutes

Have small groups of students, including those who are visually impaired, perform these activities and identify the energy source and the object that gains energy as a result.

- blow up a balloon *(energy source—diaphragm and chest muscles; object—the stretched balloon)*
- strike a tuning fork on a table *(energy source—hand or arm; object—the vibrating tuning fork)*
- compress a large soft sponge with a brick or wood block *(energy source—weight of the brick; object—the compressed sponge)*

learning modality: kinesthetic

Kinetic Energy

Inquiry Challenge

ACTIVITY

Materials *skateboards or toy trucks, meter stick, 3 heavy books, large rubber ball*
Time 20 minutes

Arrange the class into cooperative groups. Ask groups to hypothesize how adding mass to an object affects the distance the object moves after being pushed with the same force. Students should design an experiment to test their hypothesis. Remind students that, in a controlled experiment, only one variable should change. After you approve their plans, students should carry them out. **cooperative learning**

Program Resources

- **Unit 5 Resources** 15-1 Lesson Plan; 15-1 Section Summary
- **Guided Reading and Study Workbook** Section 15-1

Answers to Self-Assessment

Caption Question

Figure 2 The ability to do work is called energy.

Ongoing Assessment

Writing Have students list three examples where energy is transferred or stored. For each example, have them explain whether the energy involved is kinetic, potential, or both.

Kinetic Energy, continued

Building Inquiry Skills: Calculating

Have students find the kinetic energy for the following wagons: a 10-kg wagon moving at 5 m/s *(125 kg•m²/s²)*, a 10-kg wagon moving at 10 m/s *(500 kg•m²/s²)*, and a 20-kg wagon moving at 5 m/s *(250 kg•m²/s²)*. Visual learners may benefit from having the wagons drawn on the board to show the difference in their sizes, with arrows to show their velocities. Ask: **Which has the greatest kinetic energy?** *(The 10-kg wagon moving at 10 m/s)* Then ask students to infer how to increase a moving object's kinetic energy. *(Increase its velocity, or its mass)* **learning modality: logical/mathematical**

Math TOOLBOX

Ask students: **What is the exponent in the number 9^2?** *(2)* **What is the value of 9^2?** *(81)* If students incorrectly give the value as 18 (9 × 2), clarify that the square of a number is the number multiplied by itself. Have students write the numbers 1 through 20 on flash cards with their squares on the back. Pair students and have them take turns testing each other. **learning modality: logical/mathematical**

Potential Energy

Building Inquiry Skills: Classifying

Ask students to find, describe, and classify two things with gravitational and two things with elastic potential energy. **learning modality: verbal**

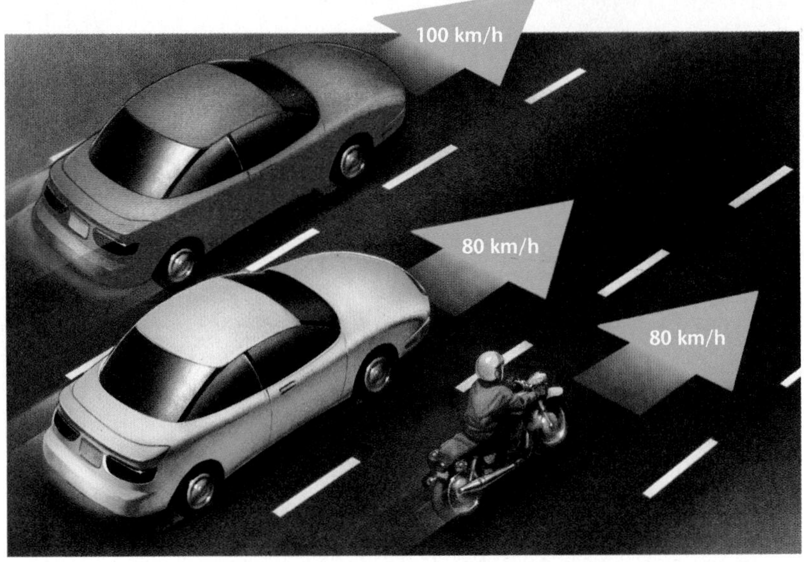

Figure 3 Kinetic energy increases as mass and velocity increase. ***Interpreting Diagrams*** *List the three vehicles in order of increasing kinetic energy.*

In other words, you have to do more work on the bowling ball to give it a greater velocity. Kinetic energy increases when velocity increases.

Calculating Kinetic Energy Kinetic energy depends on both mass and velocity. The mathematical relationship between kinetic energy, mass, and velocity is written as follows.

$$\text{Kinetic energy} = \frac{\text{Mass} \times \text{Velocity}^2}{2}$$

Do changes in velocity and mass have the same effect on kinetic energy? No—changing the velocity of an object will have a greater effect on its kinetic energy than changing its mass. This is because velocity is squared in the energy equation. For instance, doubling the mass of an object will double its kinetic energy. But doubling its velocity will quadruple its kinetic energy.

Checkpoint *What is kinetic energy?*

Math TOOLBOX

Squared Numbers

A squared number is written with an exponent of 2. For example, you can write 2^2, 3^2, or 4^2. To find the value of a squared number, multiply the number by itself.

$2^2 = 2 \times 2 = 4$

$3^2 = 3 \times 3 = 9$

$4^2 = 4 \times 4 = 16$

Notice how fast the squared numbers increase. For example, although the numbers 2 and 3 only differ by one, their squares differ by five.

Potential Energy

Sometimes when you transfer energy to an object, you change its position or shape. For example, you exert a force to lift a book up to your desk or to compress a spring to wind a toy. Unlike kinetic energy, which is the energy of motion, potential energy is stored energy. It might be used later on when the book falls to the floor or when the toy's spring unwinds. Energy that is stored and held in readiness is called **potential energy.** This type of energy has the *potential* to do work.

Background

Integrating Science As the sun warms Earth's land and water, water evaporates and thermal energy is stored in the air containing the evaporated water. When this stored thermal energy is released, it can cause violent storms. The thermal energy is released when warm air cools and condenses, forming liquid water. An average thunderstorm releases about 36 terajoules of energy. Severe storms can release up to 100 times more energy.

The thermal energy stored in warm air also forms tornadoes and hurricanes. A tornado may have wind speeds that exceed 800 km per hour. Hurricanes, which are much larger than tornadoes, release even more energy. They form over warm ocean waters where evaporation takes place. Winds near the eye may be as high as 300 kilometers per hour, and a hurricane may be over 2,000 km in diameter.

An archer gives potential energy to a bow by pulling it back. The stored energy can send an arrow whistling to its target. The potential energy associated with objects that can be stretched or compressed is called **elastic potential energy.**

You give a different type of potential energy to an object when you lift it. Potential energy that depends on height is **gravitational potential energy.**

The gravitational potential energy of an object is equal to the work done to lift it. You can calculate Work = Force × Distance. The force is the force you use to lift the object, or its weight. The distance is the distance the object moves, or its height. This gives you the following formula.

Gravitational potential energy = Weight × Height

When weight is measured in newtons and height is measured in meters, the unit of energy is the newton-meter. This unit is also known as the joule (J). A joule is the amount of work you do when you exert a force of 1 newton to move an object a distance of 1 meter. Work and energy share the same unit because energy and work are so closely related.

Once you know weight and height, you can calculate gravitational potential energy. Suppose that a hiker climbs 40 meters up a hill and that he weighs 680 newtons. The hiker has gained 27,200 joules (680 newtons × 40 meters) of gravitational potential energy at the top of the climb.

The greater the weight of an object or the greater the height it is lifted, the greater its gravitational potential energy. The hiker would gain more gravitational potential energy by climbing to a greater height or by increasing weight, maybe by wearing a backpack.

What if you know the mass of an object instead of its weight? Then you multiply the mass of the object (in kilograms) by the acceleration of gravity (9.8 m/s^2) to find its weight in newtons. Now you can write a second formula for gravitational potential energy.

Gravitational potential energy = Mass × Gravitational acceleration × Height

Again, the unit of measure is the joule.

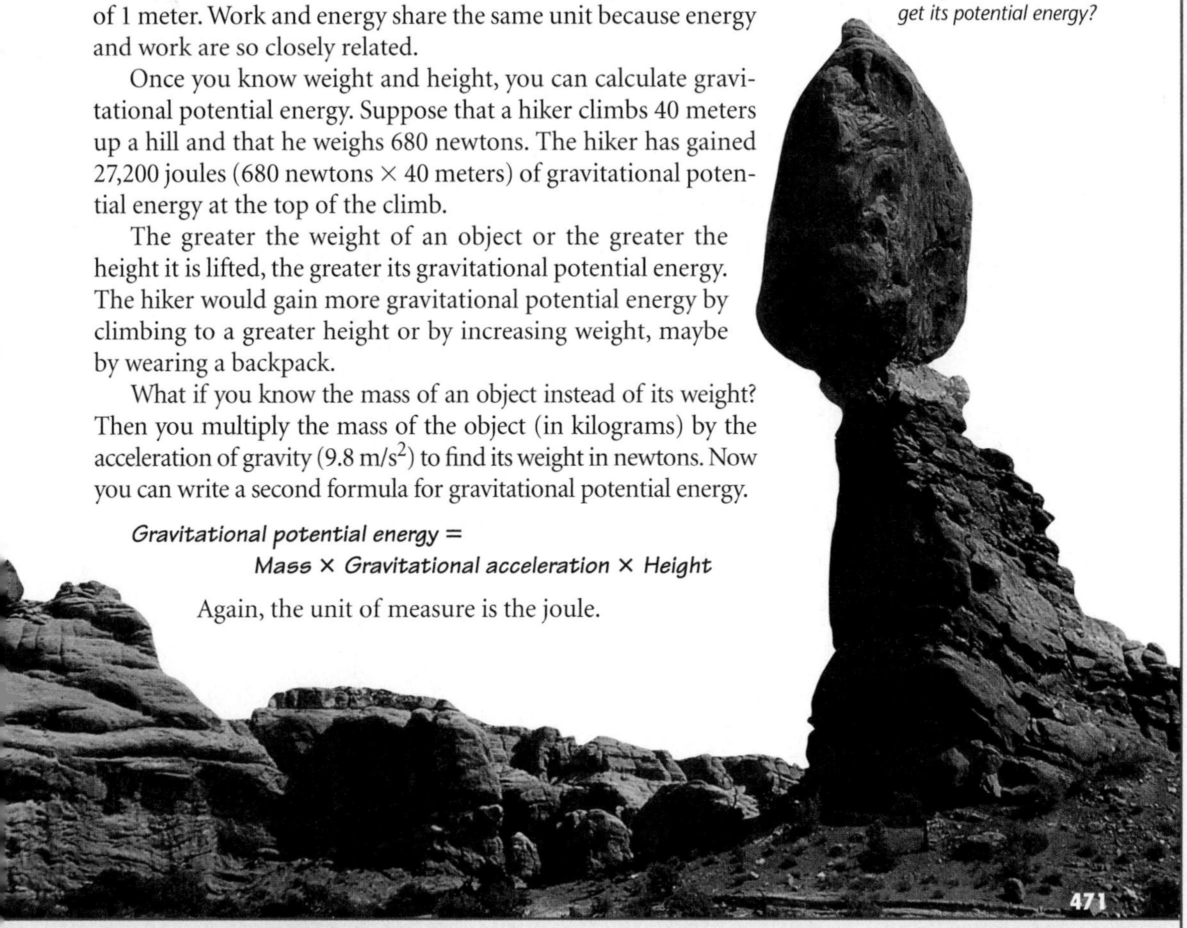

Figure 4 A rock poised for a fall has potential energy. *Inferring* *How did the rock get its potential energy?*

Including All Students

There are many new and confusingly similar terms in these sections: energy, potential, kinetic, chemical, elastic, gravitational. Have students who are still mastering English compile a list of these terms with definitions written out in their own words. Refer to the **ELL Handbook** for additional teaching strategies. **limited English proficiency**

Demonstration

ACTIVITY

Materials *4 identical aluminum pans such as disposable pie pans, 4 marbles of different masses, meter stick, metric ruler, balance. five sheets of corrugated cardboard*
Time 15 minutes

Determine the mass of each marble and record the mass in a data table on the board. Place an aluminum pan on a stack of five sheets of corrugated cardboard. Explain that you are going to test the hypothesis that gravitational potential energy depends on mass and that you will be determining energy by measuring the size of the dent produced in the pan. Ask: **What variable must be controlled?** *(The height)* CAUTION: Have students wear safety goggles or stand clear. Drop the marbles one at a time from a height of 1 m. After each drop, pick up the pan, turn it over, and measure the depth of the dent. Record this in the table. Replace the pans as necessary. Ask: **Which marble had the most energy?** *(The one that made the deepest dent)* Discuss with students whether the hypothesis was verified. *(Yes, the marble with the most mass made the deepest dent.)* **learning modality: visual**

Media and Technology

Transparencies "Kinetic Energy," Transparency 59

Concept Videotape Library Grade 6, Tape 4 "Energy"

Answers to Self-Assessment

Caption Questions

Figure 3 The motorcycle, the car moving at 80 km/h, then the car moving at 100 km/h

Figure 4 Erosion of land around the rock left the rock in a position to fall. Its potential energy depends on its weight and height.

✓ Checkpoint

Kinetic energy is the energy of motion.

Ongoing Assessment

Skills Check Ask students to explain which has the greatest kinetic energy: a motorcycle moving at 30 km/h, a four-door car moving at 30 km/h. or a truck sitting on top of a hill. *(A four-door car moving at 30 km/h has more kinetic energy than the motorcycle because it has more mass. The truck has no kinetic energy because it is not moving.)*

Different Forms of Energy

Addressing Naive Conceptions

Some students may believe that energy cannot change form. Show students a flashlight with the batteries next to it. Ask them to identify the form of energy stored in the batteries. *(chemical or potential)* Then place the batteries in the flashlight and turn it on. Ask: **What form of energy do you see?** *(electromagnetic)* Allow students to place their hands near the bulb of the flashlight. Ask: **What form of energy do you feel?** *(thermal)* **learning modality: tactile/kinesthetic**

Building Inquiry Skills: Applying Concepts

Encourage students to describe each type of energy in their own words. Challenge students to think of one or two examples of each type of energy. **limited English proficiency**

Real Life Learning

ACTIVITY

Materials *wintergreen candies, small mirrors*
Time 15 minutes

Not all wintergreen candies work. Test different brands to see which do work.

CAUTION: *Since small pieces of candy can stick in the throat, give students access to a water fountain. Some students may find the wintergreen flavor unpleasant.* Pass out candies to each student. Darken the room. (Note: The room must be very dark and time must be allowed for eyes to adjust.) Have students chew the candies with their lips open as they watch themselves in the mirrors. As each piece of candy is crushed, they will see tiny flashes of white or bluish-white light. Ask: **What kind of energy did the mints have?** *(chemical)* **What kind of energy did your teeth add?** *(mechanical)* **What kind of energy did you see?** *(electromagnetic)* Explain that this is an example of triboluminescence, luminescence induced by friction. **learning modality: visual**

Figure 5 Energy is all around you in many different forms. The leaping frog is an example of mechanical energy, and the melting ice is an example of thermal energy. *Observing Which forms of energy are shown in the photographs of the sparkler, the sun, and the lightning?*

Different Forms of Energy

The examples of energy you have read about so far involve objects being moved or physically changed. But both kinetic energy and potential energy have a variety of different forms. **Some of the major forms of energy are mechanical energy, thermal energy, chemical energy, electrical energy, electromagnetic energy, and nuclear energy.**

Mechanical Energy The school bus you ride in, a frog leaping through the air, and even the sounds you hear all have mechanical energy. Mechanical energy is the energy associated with the motion or position of an object. Mechanical energy can occur as kinetic energy or potential energy.

Thermal Energy All matter is made up of small particles, called atoms and molecules. These particles have both potential energy and kinetic energy due to their arrangement and motion. Thermal energy is a measure of the energy of the particles in an object. When the thermal energy of an object increases, its particles move faster, making it feel warm to the touch. Ice cream melts when its thermal energy increases.

Chemical Energy Chemical compounds, such as chocolate, wood, and wax, store chemical energy. Chemical energy is potential energy stored in chemical bonds that hold chemical compounds together. Chemical energy is stored in the foods you eat and in a match that is used to light a candle. Chemical energy is even stored in the cells of your body.

Background

Integrating Science Energy is stored as chemical energy in the foods we eat. While energy is often measured in joules, stored food energy is generally measured in kilocalories. Kilocalories are commonly called Calories (with a capital "C"), so that if a serving of skim milk has 86 Calories, it really has 86 kilocalories. The caloric content of a food depends on the quantity of fat, protein, and carbohydrate. A gram of fat provides 9 kcal of energy, a gram of protein provides 4 kcal, and a gram of carbohydrate provides 4 kcal. Whether from fat, protein, or carbohydrate, one calorie represents the same amount of food energy.

For proper nutrition, scientists recommend that less than 30% of kilocalories come from fat, about 15% come from protein, and about 60% come from carbohydrate.

Electrical Energy When you receive a shock from a metal doorknob, you experience electrical energy. Moving electric charges produce electricity, and electrical energy is the energy they carry. You rely on electrical energy from batteries or power lines to run electrical devices such as radios, lights, and computers.

Electromagnetic Energy The light that you see each day is electromagnetic energy. Electromagnetic energy is a form of radiant energy. **Radiant energy** is energy that travels in waves. These waves have some electrical properties and some magnetic properties. In addition to visible light, ultraviolet radiation, microwaves, and infrared radiation are all examples of electromagnetic energy.

Nuclear Energy Another type of potential energy, called nuclear energy, is stored in the nucleus of an atom and is released during nuclear reactions. One of these reactions occurs when a nucleus splits (nuclear fission). Another reaction occurs when nuclei join together (nuclear fusion). Nuclear power plants use fission reactions to produce electricity. Nuclear fusion occurs in the sun and other stars.

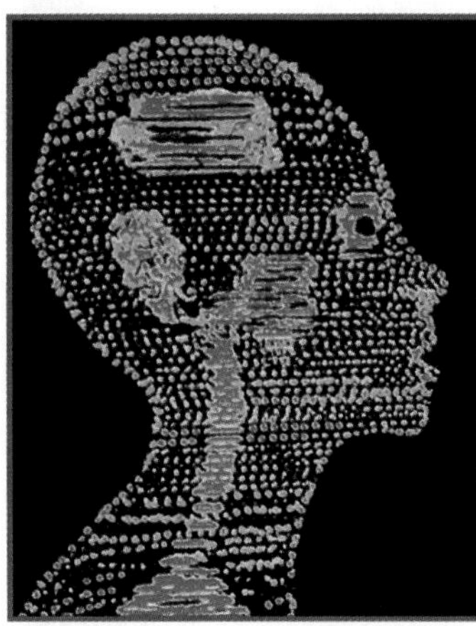

Figure 6 Electromagnetic energy is used to take a CT scan.

Section 1 Review

1. Are energy and work the same thing? Explain.
2. How are kinetic and potential energy different?
3. List the forms of energy and give an example of each.
4. **Thinking Critically Problem Solving** A boulder that weighs 200 N is poised at the edge of a 100-meter cliff. What is its gravitational potential energy? Draw a diagram showing how its potential energy changes as it falls to 50 m, 20 m, and 10 m.

CHAPTER PROJECT

Check Your Progress

Some materials that you can use to build a roller coaster track and car include marbles, rubber tubing, cardboard, and string. Experiment with different hill heights and inclines. (*Hint:* See how high you can make the second and third hills before the roller coaster car can no longer climb up the hills.) Think about how you can explain the types of energy involved as the roller coaster car moves.

3 Assess

Section 1 Review Answers

1. Work and energy are not the same thing, even though they are measured in the same units. Energy is the ability to do work. As work is done, energy is transferred from one object to another.
2. Kinetic energy is the energy of motion. Potential energy is stored energy; it has the potential to do work.
3. The five forms of energy and an example of each are: mechanical—riding a bicycle; thermal—hot water; chemical—food energy; electrical—batteries; electromagnetic energy—sunlight; nuclear energy—fusion in a star
4. Gravitational potential energy = 200 N × 100 m = 20,000 J. At 50 m, 10,000 J. At 20 m, 4,000 J. At 10 m, 2,000 J. Diagrams should be labeled with correct values.

CHAPTER PROJECT

Check Your Progress

You may wish to show students a simple model of a roller-coaster track with one hill. When students have selected their materials, they should begin to experiment by trying different hills. Students should understand that the roller coaster car has the greatest potential energy at the top of the hill. As the car moves down the hill, potential energy is gradually converted into kinetic energy.

Program Resources

◆ **Unit 5 Resources** 15-1 Review and Reinforce; 15-1 Enrich

Answers to Self-Assessment

Caption Question

Figure 5 Sparkler—chemical, thermal, electromagnetic; sun—nuclear, thermal, electromagnetic; lightning—electrical, thermal, electromagnetic

Performance Assessment

Drawing Have students draw a sketch or diagram of playground equipment and label positions where a child would have potential energy and kinetic energy. Diagrams may include a slide, a merry-go-round, a see-saw, climbing equipment, or a swing.

Students can keep their diagrams in their portfolios.

Skills Lab

Designing Experiments

Soaring Straws

Preparing for Inquiry

Key Concept As the amount of stretch (related to elastic potential energy) in a rocket launcher increases, the subsequent height that the rocket attains (related to gravitational potential energy) increases.

Skills Objective Students will be able to

- control variables in an experiment to find the relationship between elastic potential energy and gravitational potential energy.

Time 40 minutes

Advance Planning Collect sufficient toilet paper tubes or ask students to bring them from home. Purchase rubber bands and straws if necessary.

Alternative Materials Any short tube will do for a launcher, for example, a 10 cm–15 cm piece of 5-cm diameter plastic or PVC pipe. Any size rubber bands can be used. ***Computer use is optional.***

Guiding Inquiry

Invitation Shoot a straw into the air with the launcher. The students will immediately want to try it themselves. Tell them that they can try it if they can describe what just occurred in terms of energy. *(The potential energy of the rubber band was transformed into the kinetic energy and then the gravitational potential energy of the rocket.)*

Introducing the Procedure

- Demonstrate the construction of the rocket and launcher using the instructions provided.

Skills Lab

Controlling Variables

SOARING STRAWS

In this lab you will use the skill of controlling variables. You will investigate the relationship between the height reached by a rocket and the amount of stretch in a rubber band.

Problem

How does the gravitational potential energy of a straw rocket depend on the elastic potential energy of the rubber band launcher?

Materials

scissors	rubber band
3 plastic straws	meter stick
marker	metric ruler
balance	masking tape
empty toilet paper tube	
computer and graphing program (optional)	

Procedure

1. Construct the rocket and launcher following the instructions below. Use a balance to find the mass of the rocket in grams. Record the mass.
2. Hold the launcher in one hand with your fingers over the ends of the rubber band. Load the launcher by placing the straw rocket on the rubber band and pulling down from the other end as shown in the photograph. Let go and launch the rocket straight up. **CAUTION:** *Be sure to aim the straw rocket into the air, not at classmates.*
3. In your notebook, make a data table similar to the one on the next page.
4. Have your partner hold a meter stick, or tape it to the wall, so that its zero end is even with the top of the rocket launcher. Measure the height, in meters, to which the rocket rises. If the rocket goes higher than a single meter stick, use two meter sticks.
5. You can measure the amount of stretch of the rubber band by noting where the markings on the rocket line up with the bottom of the launching cylinder. Launch the rocket using three different amounts of stretch. Record your measurements.

MAKING A ROCKET AND LAUNCHER

A. Cut a rubber band and tape it across the open end of a hollow cylinder, such as a toilet paper tube. The rubber band should be taut, but only stretched a tiny amount. This is the launcher.

B. Cut about 3 cm off a plastic straw.

C. Lay 2 full-length straws side by side on a flat surface with the 3-cm piece of straw between them. Arrange the straws so that their ends are even.

D. Tape the straws together side by side.

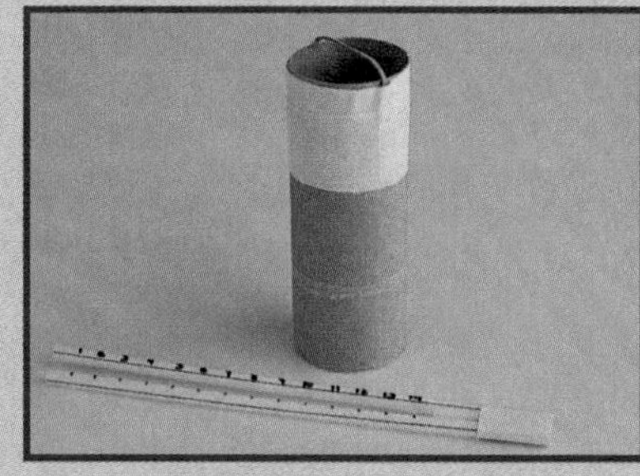

E. Starting from the untaped end, make marks every centimeter on one of the long straws. This is the rocket.

474

- Explain to students that to find the amount of stretch in Step 5 they will have to subtract.
- Warn students not to twist the straw rocket as they read the stretch markings. Instead, they should rotate the entire launcher and rocket assembly to see the marks.

Troubleshooting the Experiment

- For accurate and repeatable results, the straw rocket should be put on the rubber band the same way each time, centered along the elastic and perpendicular to it. The ends of the straws must be kept parallel when the straw rocket is pulled down.
- If a toilet paper tube is used, it may begin to collapse slightly with repeated stretches and affect the results. Offer students a fresh tube if this happens.

Media and Technology

Lab Activity Videotapes
Grade 6, Tape 3

Safety

Warn students not to point or shoot their rockets at another person. Students should wear safety goggles at all times. A straw rocket is usually harmless, but a direct hit in the eye could do considerable harm. Review the safety guidelines in Appendix A.

Program Resources

- **Unit 5 Resources** Chapter 15 Skills Lab blackline masters

DATA TABLE					
Amount of Stretch (cm)	Height (Trial 1) (m)	Height (Trial 2) (m)	Height (Trial 3) (m)	Average Height (m)	Gravitational Potential Energy (mJ)

6. For each amount of stretch, find the average height to which the rocket rises. Record the height in your data table.
7. Find the gravitational potential energy for each amount of stretch:

   Gravitational potential energy =
   Mass × Gravitational acceleration × Height

   You have measured the mass in grams. So the unit of energy is the millijoule (mJ), which is one thousandth of a joule. Record the results in your data table.

Analyze and Conclude

1. Which variable in your data table is the manipulated variable? The responding variable? How do you know?
2. Graph your results in your notebook or on a computer. Show gravitational potential energy on the vertical axis and amount of stretch on the horizontal axis.
3. What measurement is related to the elastic potential energy in this experiment?
4. Look at the shape of the graph. What conclusions can you reach about the relationship between the gravitational potential energy of the rocket and the elastic potential energy of the rubber band?
5. How do you think the amount of energy before the rocket was released compares to the amount of energy after the rocket was released? Explain any difference.
6. **Think About It** Besides the amount of stretch, what other variables might affect the height to which the straw rocket rises? Have you been able to control these variables in your experiment? Explain why or why not.

More to Explore

Use your launcher to investigate launches at angles other than straight up. Instead of manipulating the amount of stretch, hold that variable constant and manipulate the angle of launch. Measure both the heights and distances of the rocket. **CAUTION:** *Be careful not to aim the rocket toward any of your classmates.*

Sample Data Table

Mass of rocket : 1.4 g

Amount of Stretch (cm)	Height (Trial 1) (m)	Height (Trial 2) (m)	Height (Trial 3) (m)	Average Height (m)	Gravitational Potential Energy (mJ)
1.0	0.18	0.23	0.17	0.193	2.6
2.0	0.52	0.46	0.55	0.51	7.0
3.0	0.96	0.94	1.13	1.01	14.1
4.0	1.90	2.12	1.88	1.967	27.0
5.0	2.25	2.44	2.19	2.293	31.5

Expected Outcome
As the elastic potential energy of the rubber band increases, the subsequent gravitational potential energy of the rocket increases. However, the relationship between the two is complex. If the band is stretched very tight, more stretching may have a progressively smaller effect.

Analyze and Conclude
1. Manipulated variable—the amount of stretch of the elastic; responding variable—the height that the rocket reached. The elastic was stretched to various lengths and the height was measured in response to the stretch.
2. The curve should point up and to the right.
3. Amount of stretch
4. As the elastic potential energy of the rubber band increases, the gravitational potential energy increases.
5. Before the rocket was released, elastic potential energy was stored in the stretched rubber band. That energy was converted into a combination of kinetic energy and gravitational potential energy as the rocket moved. Some of the energy was converted to kinetic energy of the rubber band and some was converted to thermal energy of the rubber band by friction. Taking all of these into account, the total amount of energy before the rocket was released equals the total amount of energy after.
6. The height is also affected by the weight of the rocket, the type of rubber band, the diameter of the tube, the air drafts in the room, and the angle of launch. Most of these variables were controlled by performing every trial the same way.

Extending the Inquiry

More to Explore The expected results are that the maximum distance occurs at 45° and the maximum height occurs at 90°. However, air resistance and the aerodynamic characteristics of the rocket will affect the results for maximum distance.

Energy Conversion and Conservation

Objectives

After completing the lesson, students will be able to

- ◆ describe the conversions between different forms of energy;
- ◆ state the law of conservation of energy.

Key Terms energy conversion, law of conservation of energy

1 Engage/Explore

Activating Prior Knowledge

Ask students: **What happens when you rub your hands together?** *(They feel warm.)* Ask: **When you're cold, what are some other ways you can get warm?** *(Jump up and down, stay in heated areas, use electric blankets, stand in the sunlight.)*

DISCOVER ACTIVITY

Skills Focus forming operational definitions
Materials *3 x 5 index card, scissors, rubber band*
Time 10 minutes
Tips Make sure students use a rubber band just large enough to stretch out when the card is flattened. Make sure students wear safety goggles during this activity.
Think It Over As students push down on the card, they stretch the rubber band and give it potential energy. When they release the card, the potential energy changes into kinetic energy as the rubber band snaps back and pulls the card with it.
Extend Ask students to describe any other observations they made during the activity and to identify what kind of energy was involved in each. *(Sample: When the rubber band snapped back, it vibrated and made a sound, an example of mechanical energy.)*

SECTION 2 Energy Conversion and Conservation

DISCOVER ACTIVITY

What Would Make a Card Jump?

1. Fold an index card in half as shown.
2. In the edge opposite the fold, cut two slits that are about 2 cm long and 2 cm apart.
3. Open the card a little, and loop a rubber band through all four slits. Keeping the fold upward, flatten the card and hold it flat as shown.
4. Predict what will happen to the card if you let go. Then test your prediction.

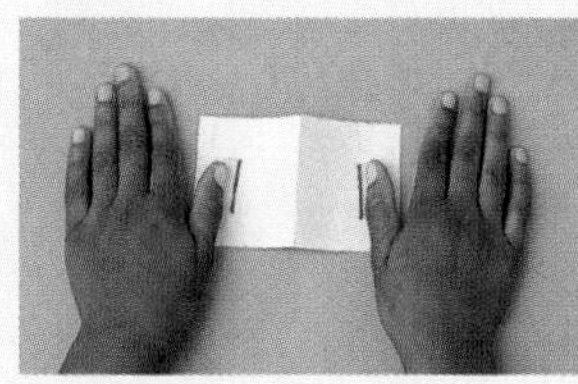

Think It Over
Forming Operational Definitions Describe what happened to the card. Define potential and kinetic energy in terms of the card and the rubber band.

GUIDE FOR READING

- ◆ How are different forms of energy related by energy conversions?
- ◆ What is the law of conservation of energy?

Reading Tip As you read, draw a flowchart to show each example of energy conversions.

The spray of water bounces off your raincoat as you look up at the millions of liters of water plunging toward you. The roar of water is deafening. You hold on to the rail as you are rocked back and forth by the rough waves. Are you doomed? Fortunately not—you are on a sightseeing boat at the foot of the mighty Niagara Falls, located on the border between the United States and Canada. The waterfall carries the huge amount of water that drains from the upper Great Lakes. It is an awesome sight that has attracted visitors from all over the world for hundreds of years.

What many visitors don't know, however, is that Niagara Falls serves as much more than just a spectacular view. The Niagara Falls area is the center of a network of electrical power lines. Water that is diverted above the falls is used to generate electricity for much of the neighboring region.

Figure 7 Niagara Falls is more than 50 meters high.

READING STRATEGIES

Reading Tip Draw a flowchart on the board. As a class, complete the chart for the example of the energy conversion involved in juggling. Then have students work on their own to complete flowcharts for the remaining examples.

Energy Conversion in Juggling
As the orange rises, it slows down.
↓
Kinetic energy decreases.
↓
Potential energy increases.
↓
Orange stops moving.

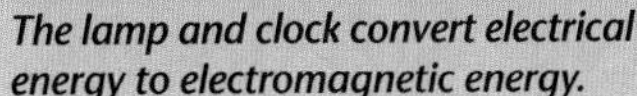

The lamp and clock convert electrical energy to electromagnetic energy.

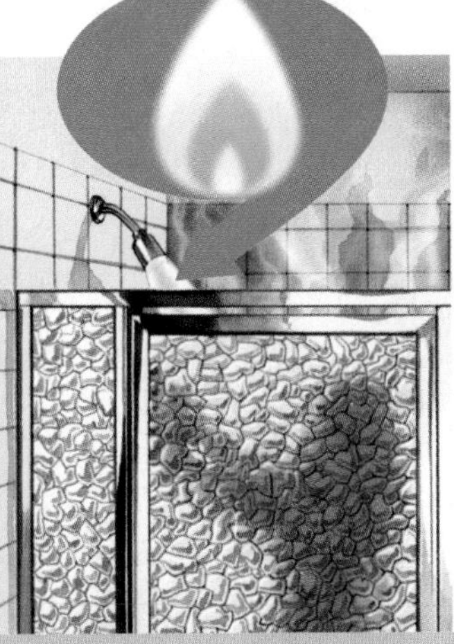

A water heater converts chemical energy in natural gas to thermal energy.

The student's body converts chemical energy in food to mechanical energy.

Figure 8 In just the first few minutes of the morning, this student experiences numerous energy conversions. Imagine how many more can be identified throughout the course of a single day!

Conversions Between Forms of Energy

What does water have to do with electricity? You may already know that the mechanical energy of moving water can be converted, or transformed, into electrical energy. A change from one form of energy to another is called an **energy conversion,** or an energy transformation. **Most forms of energy can be converted into any other form.**

You encounter energy conversions frequently. A toaster, for example, converts electrical energy to thermal energy. In an electric motor, electrical energy is converted to mechanical energy that can be used to run a machine.

Your body converts the chemical energy in the food you eat to the mechanical energy you need to move your muscles. Chemical energy in food is also converted to the thermal energy your body uses to maintain its temperature. Chemical energy is even converted to the electrical energy your brain uses to think.

Often a series of energy conversions is needed to do a task. Strike a match, for example, and the mechanical energy used to move the match is converted to thermal energy. The thermal energy causes the match to release stored chemical energy, which is converted to thermal energy and to the energy you see as light.

A series of conversions occurs in a car engine. Electrical energy produces a spark. The spark's thermal energy causes the fuel to burn, which releases its chemical energy. When the fuel burns, this chemical energy in turn becomes thermal energy. Thermal energy is converted to mechanical energy used to move the car, and to electrical energy that produces more sparks.

☑ *Checkpoint* *Give an example of an energy conversion.*

2 Facilitate

Conversions Between Forms of Energy

Building Inquiry Skills: Applying Concepts

ACTIVITY

Materials *flashlight, electric pencil sharpener, heating pad, potted plant*
Time 15 minutes
Tips CAUTION: *Do not use electrical appliances near water. Make sure students do not trip or pull on cords or plugs.* Place the objects at stations around the room. As students move from station to station, they should identify and record the energy conversions that take place in each object. *(Flashlight—chemical to electrical to thermal and electromagnetic energy; pencil sharpener—electrical to mechanical energy; heating pad—electrical to thermal energy; potted plant—electromagnetic to chemical energy)*
learning modality: kinesthetic

Building Inquiry Skills: Applying Concepts

Help students recognize the variety and number of energy conversions taking place around them. Assign each student an everyday activity, such as cooking dinner, playing ball, riding a bicycle, doing homework, or washing dishes. Students should then give brief oral presentations and describe the energy conversions that took place during the activity. **learning modality: auditory/verbal**

Program Resources

- **Unit 5 Resources** 15-2 Lesson Plan; 15-2 Section Summary
- **Guided Reading and Study Workbook** Section 15-2

Media and Technology

Transparencies "Energy Conversions," Transparency 60

Answers to Self-Assessment

☑ *Checkpoint*

Sample: An electric stove converts electrical energy to thermal energy.

Ongoing Assessment

Drawing Ask students to draw or illustrate an example of one of these energy conversions: mechanical to thermal energy, radiant to thermal energy, or electrical to mechanical energy.

Students can save their drawings in their portfolios.

Kinetic and Potential Energy

Demonstration

Some students may not grasp that energy can be transformed from kinetic to potential. Raise an object above your head, and ask students to identify the kind of energy it has while you are moving it upward. *(Kinetic)* When it is at rest above your head, ask: **What kind of energy does the object have now?** *(It has potential energy.)* Throw a ball into the air above your head with one hand and catch it with the other hand. Make a diagram of the moving ball on the chalkboard. At each position of the ball, from the bottom to the top and then back down, have students compare the kinetic energy and the potential energy. Ask: **How does the speed of the ball change as moves toward the top?** *(It slows down.)* **What happens to the kinetic energy?** *(It decreases, and the potential energy increases.)* **How does the kinetic and potential energy change as the ball falls?** *(The kinetic energy increases as the potential energy decreases.)* **learning modality: visual**

Building Inquiry Skills: Predicting

Challenge students to compare potential energy and kinetic energy as they examine a windup toy. Ask them to predict how increasing the elastic potential energy stored in the toy's spring will affect the length of time the toy runs. Then have students test their predictions by comparing how long the toy runs when wound one, two, or three turns. Ask: **How do you increase the toy's potential energy?** *(Wind it more.)* **How does increased potential energy affect the toy's kinetic energy? How can you tell?** *(There is more potential energy to convert into kinetic energy. You can tell the toy had more potential energy because it ran longer.)* **limited English proficiency**

Figure 9 Energy conversions enable this athlete to vault more than six meters into the air. *Predicting What energy conversions will occur after the vaulter falls over the bar?*

Kinetic and Potential Energy

One of the most common conversions is the conversion of potential energy to kinetic energy. When you jump on a trampoline, your kinetic energy stretches the trampoline, giving it elastic potential energy. When the trampoline snaps back, its potential energy is converted to kinetic energy as it moves upward, lifting you and giving you kinetic energy.

Energy Conversion in an Earthquake A conversion of potential energy to kinetic energy during an earthquake caused the damage you see in Figure 10. The land on Earth's surface is broken into several plates that move slowly in different directions. The movements of the plates produce most earthquakes. For example, when two plates try to move past one another, the friction between them opposes their motion. As a result, potential energy builds up. Eventually, the potential energy is converted to kinetic energy, and the plates suddenly move, causing an earthquake.

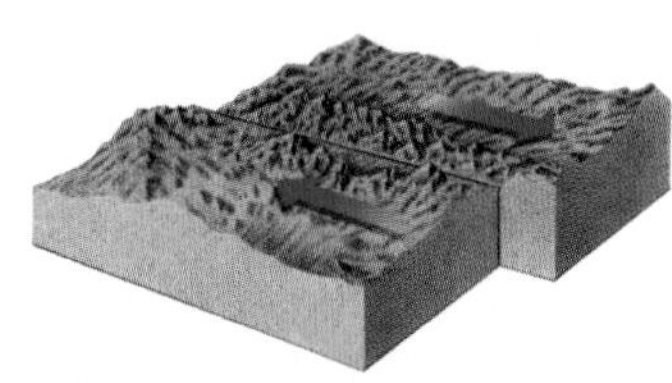

Figure 10 An earthquake converts the potential energy stored in Earth to kinetic energy at Earth's surface.

Energy Conversion in a Waterfall Any matter that rises or falls undergoes a change in its kinetic energy and its potential energy. Consider Niagara Falls, which you read about earlier.

Background

Facts and Figures Hydroelectric power plants convert the kinetic energy of falling water into electric current that can be used to power computers, televisions, and other appliances. One of the nation's best-known hydroelectric power plants is the Hoover Dam on the Colorado River between Nevada and Arizona. The water for the Hoover Dam is stored in Lake Mead, one of the world's largest artificial lakes. Falling water from the reservoir runs through pipes and spins turbines in generating stations on each side of the river. The turbines spin a shaft that turns a large electromagnet. The Hoover power plant generates enough electrical energy to serve 1.3 million people, over 4 billion kilowatt-hours per year. Communities in Arizona, California and Nevada—including Las Vegas—buy the electricity, and the money is used to maintain and operate the dam, reservoir, and electrical generating stations.

The water at the top of the falls has gravitational potential energy because it is higher than at the bottom. But as the water falls, its height decreases, and it loses potential energy. At the same time, its kinetic energy increases because its velocity increases. Thus potential energy is converted into kinetic energy.

Energy Conversion in a Pole Vault As a pole vaulter runs, he has kinetic energy because he is moving. When he plants his pole to jump, the pole bends. His kinetic energy is converted to elastic potential energy in the pole. As the pole straightens out, the vaulter is lifted high into the air. The elastic potential energy of the pole is converted to the gravitational potential energy of the pole vaulter. Once over the bar, the vaulter's gravitational potential energy is converted into kinetic energy as he falls.

Energy Conversion in a Pendulum A continuous conversion between kinetic energy and potential energy takes place in a pendulum. At the highest point in its swing, the pendulum in Figure 11 has only gravitational potential energy. As the pendulum starts to swing downward, it speeds up and its gravitational potential energy changes to kinetic energy. At the bottom of its swing, all its energy is kinetic energy. Then as it swings to the other side and slows down, it regains gravitational potential energy, and at the same time loses kinetic energy. At the top of its swing on the other side it again has only gravitational potential energy. And so the pattern of energy conversion continues.

☑ *Checkpoint* *What energy change occurs when an object falls?*

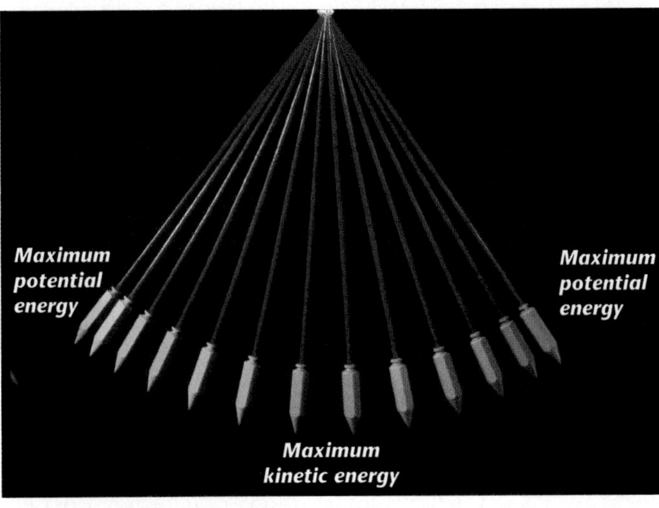

Figure 11 Conversions between kinetic energy and potential energy take place in a pendulum.

Pendulum Swing

ACTIVITY

1. Set up a pendulum using washers or a rubber stopper, string, a ring stand, and a clamp.
2. Pull the pendulum back so that it makes a 45° angle with the vertical. Measure the height of the stopper. Then set it in motion and observe the height to which it swings.
3. Use a second clamp to reduce the length of the pendulum as shown. The pendulum will run into the second clamp at the bottom of its swing.

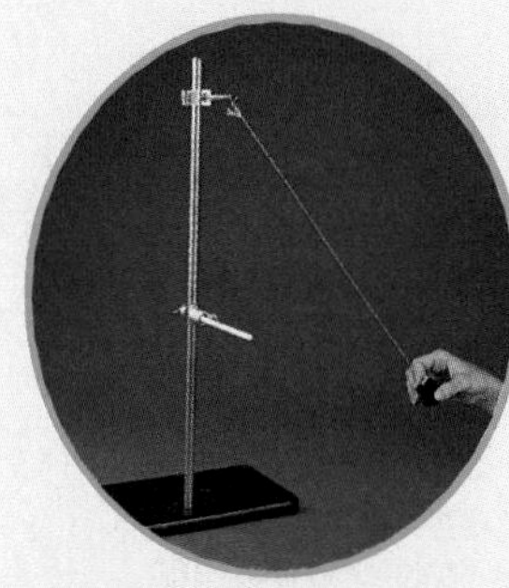

4. Pull the pendulum back to the same height as you did the first time. Predict the height to which the pendulum will swing. Then set it in motion and observe it.

Observing How high did the pendulum swing in each case? Explain your observations.

Including All Students

ACTIVITY

Students who have difficulty connecting the photo in Figure 9 with the text can build a small model. Give students a flexible plastic drinking straw and some modeling clay. Tell them to put one end of the straw in the clay and then gently push down on the other end. Ask: **What happens to the straw?** *(It bends.)* Then ask: **What happens if you release the straw?** *(It straightens.)* Help students recognize that the pole stores energy in the same way as the drinking straw. **learning modality: tactile/ kinesthetic**

TRY THIS

ACTIVITY

Skills Focus Observing
Materials *washers or rubber stoppers, string, ring stand, 2 clamps, meter stick*
Time 15 minutes
Tips Suggest students practice several times so they can get an accurate measurement of the height.
Observing In Step 2, the pendulum swings to almost the same height it was released from. In Step 3, the pendulum will swing through a larger angle but will still reach almost the same height above the table it had when released. The gravitational potential energy it gains is equal to the amount of kinetic energy it has at the bottom of the swing and to the gravitational potential energy it started with. The original amount of potential energy is not affected by changing the length of the pendulum in mid-swing.
Extend Have students test how increasing mass affects the swing of the pendulum. **learning modality: kinesthetic**

Media and Technology

Transparencies "The Pendulum," Transparency 61

Answers to Self-Assessment

Caption Questions

Figure 9 Gravitational potential energy is converted to kinetic energy as the pole vaulter falls.

☑ *Checkpoint*

The gravitational potential energy of the object decreases, and the kinetic energy of the object increases.

Ongoing Assessment

Oral Presentation Have students describe the energy conversions that take place as they swing on a swing. *(Swinging upward—kinetic energy is converted to potential energy; top of the swing— maximum potential energy, kinetic energy is zero. Swinging down—potential energy is converted to kinetic energy.)*

Conservation of Energy

Demonstration

Materials *hammer, nail, wood block*
Time 10 minutes
Tips Have students consider the law of conservation of energy as they predict what happens to the energy applied to a hammer when it hits a nail. Then allow them to observe as you hammer a nail into a wood block. Tell students to touch the top of the nail after you finish. Ask: **What form of energy do you feel?** *(Thermal)* Point out that the law of conservation of energy says in part that energy cannot be created. Ask: **Where did the thermal energy come from?** *(Some of the mechanical energy of the hammer was converted into thermal energy.)* Then ask: **Where did the rest of the energy go?** *(It was used to do work on the nail by forcing it into the wood.)* **learning modality: tactile/kinesthetic**

Visual Arts CONNECTION

Have students look at the drawing and ask: **Where does the water have the maximum potential energy? Kinetic energy?** *(Students may answer that potential energy is greatest at the top of the fall and kinetic energy is greatest at the bottom of the fall.)* Now have students trace the path of the water with one finger. As they attempt to trace the path they should recognize the optical illusions Escher has created by distorting perspective. If perspective were followed correctly, the "top" of the waterfall would be at the same elevation as the "bottom."

In Your Journal Encourage students to use simple, precise terms to describe the drawing. Students should recognize that Escher's drawing does not follow the law of conservation of energy. **learning modality: visual**

Students can save their descriptions in their portfolios.

Figure 12 M. C. Escher's print "Waterfall" was done in 1961.

Visual Arts CONNECTION

The Dutch artist M. C. Escher produced many intriguing illustrations. Escher, who lived from 1898 to 1972, was most recognized for his use of illusions and repeating geometric patterns.

In Your Journal

Look at Escher's "Waterfall." Then look again. In your journal, write a description of the illustration. Did you see anything in the art during your second look that you didn't see at first glance? Is the law of conservation of energy followed or violated in the art? Explain your answer.

Conservation of Energy

If you set a pendulum in motion, will it remain in motion forever? No, it will not. Does that mean that energy is destroyed over time? The answer is no. The **law of conservation of energy** states that when one form of energy is converted to another, no energy is destroyed in the process. **According to the law of conservation of energy, energy cannot be created or destroyed.** So the total amount of energy is the same before and after any process. All energy can be accounted for.

Energy and Friction So what happens to the kinetic energy of the pendulum? As the pendulum moves, it encounters friction at the pivot of the string and from the air through which it moves. When an object experiences friction, the motion (and thus the kinetic energy) of the atoms or molecules increases. This means its thermal energy increases. So the mechanical energy of the moving pendulum is converted to thermal energy. The pendulum slows down, but its energy is not destroyed.

The fact that friction converts mechanical energy to thermal energy should not surprise you. You often take advantage of this.

Background

History of Science When he was 21, M.C. Escher was an architecture student at the School of Architecture and Decorative Arts in Haarlem, Holland. He decided to study graphic art instead of architecture, and he traveled throughout Europe, studying and creating strange landscapes.

In 1936, Escher visited the Alhambra in Spain to study the geometrical tiles used as decoration there and he began to study mathematical papers about geometry and symmetry. Escher corresponded with several mathematicians about his work. He developed a complex system of designing the figures in his art, using a mathematical style of notation that he invented. Escher's unique perspectives and designs have influenced the work of scientists, mathematicians, and cognitive psychologists, as well as interesting the general public.

When you rub your cold hands together to warm them up, you use thermal energy. The fact that energy is converted to thermal energy because of friction explains why no machine is 100 percent efficient. The work you do when you use simple machines like gears is always more than the work the machine does for you.

Energy and Matter You might have heard of Albert Einstein's theory of relativity. Einstein's theory included a small change to the law of conservation of energy. He explained that energy can sometimes be created—by destroying matter! This process is not important for most of the energy conversions described in this chapter. But it is important in nuclear reactions, where huge amounts of energy are produced by destroying tiny amounts of matter. This discovery means that in some situations it appears that energy alone is not conserved. But scientists say that matter and energy together are always conserved. Just as different forms of energy can be converted to one another, matter and energy can be converted back and forth.

Figure 13 Albert Einstein published his theory of special relativity in 1905.

Conserving Energy

INTEGRATING ENVIRONMENTAL SCIENCE When you hear or read about conserving energy, don't get confused with the law of conservation of energy. Conserving energy means saving energy, or not wasting it. In other words, conserving energy means we should not waste fuels, such as gasoline, or our resources will be used up quickly. You will learn more about conserving energy in Chapter 16. The law of conservation of energy in physical science, however, refers to a quantity that remains constant. In science, energy is always conserved because its total quantity does not change.

Section 2 Review

1. What is an energy conversion?
2. State the law of conservation of energy in your own words.
3. Describe the energy conversions that occur when a ball is dropped and bounces back up. Why do you think the ball bounces a little lower each time?
4. **Thinking Critically Applying Concepts** A roller coaster car with a mass of 500 kg is at the top of a hill that is 30 m high. Without friction, what would its kinetic energy be as it reached the bottom of the hill?

Science at Home

Hot Wire Straighten a wire hanger. Have your family members feel the wire and observe whether it feels cool or warm. Then hold the ends of the wire and bend it several times. **CAUTION:** *If the wire breaks, the ends can be sharp. Do not bend it more than a few times.* After bending the wire, have your family members feel it again. Ask them to explain how energy conversions can produce a change in temperature.

Program Resources

◆ **Unit 5 Resources** 15-2 Review and Reinforce; 15-2 Enrich

Conserving Energy

Integrating Environmental Science

Make sure students understand the difference between conservation of energy and conserving an energy resource. Ask students to name an energy resource and describe the conversions that take place when it is used. *(Gasoline—chemical energy from the fuel is converted into thermal and mechanical energy.)* **learning modality: verbal**

3 Assess

Section 2 Review Answers

1. A change from one form of energy to another or an energy transformation.
2. The total energy before a process is the same as the total energy after.
3. As it falls, potential energy changes to kinetic energy. As it bounces back up, kinetic energy is converted to potential energy. The ball does not bounce as high because some energy escapes as thermal energy or sound when the ball hits the ground.
4. Without friction, kinetic energy would be equal to the gravitational potential energy, 500 kg $\times$ 9.8 m/s^2 $\times$ 30 m = 147,000 J.

Science at Home

ACTIVITY

Materials *wire hanger*
Tips Students should find that the wire feels warm after it has been bent. Some of the energy used to bend the wire is converted into thermal energy, so the wire feels warm.

Performance Assessment

Organizing Information Have students make flowcharts to show the energy conversions made by an electric fan.

SECTION 3 Photosynthesis and Fossil Fuels

Objectives

After completing the lesson, students will be able to

- ◆ describe the energy conversion that occurs during photosynthesis;
- ◆ explain how fossil fuels contain energy that came from the sun.

Key Terms photosynthesis, pigment, chlorophyll, chloroplast, respiration, fuel, fossil fuel, combustion

1 Engage/Explore

Activating Prior Knowledge

Show students a piece of coal. Ask: **What is this and what is it used for?** *(Coal: providing thermal energy)* Ask students to describe what happens when the coal is burned. *(The coal produces light and thermal energy.)* Ask: **What does this tell you about the coal?** *(Sample: It contains potential energy.)*

DISCOVER

Skills Focus forming operational definitions
Materials *flask, ring stand, clamp, thermometer, water, wooden coffee stirrer, small aluminum pan, matches, safety goggles*
Time 20 minutes
Tips Caution students to use care when using matches and to keep loose hair and clothing away from the burning wood. The flask will be hot. Also, try to do this activity as far away from smoke alarms as possible.
Expected Outcome The temperature of the water is higher after the coffee stirrer is burned.
Think It Over A fuel is a substance that stores energy.

INTEGRATING LIFE SCIENCE

SECTION 3 Photosynthesis and Fossil Fuels

DISCOVER ACTIVITY

What Is a Fuel?

1. Put on your goggles. Attach a flask to a ring stand with a clamp. Then place a thermometer in the flask.
2. Add enough water to the flask to cover the thermometer bulb. Record the temperature of the water. Then remove the thermometer.
3. Bend a wooden coffee stirrer in three places to look like a W.
4. Stand the bent coffee stirrer in a small aluminum pan so the W is right-side up. Position the pan 4–5 cm directly below the flask.
5. Ignite the coffee stirrer at the center. **CAUTION:** *Be careful when using matches.*
6. When the coffee stirrer has stopped burning, find the temperature of the water again. Wait until the flask has cooled before cleaning up.

Think It Over
Forming Operational Definitions A piece of wood, the gasoline in a car, and kerosene in a lantern are all fuels. How would you define a fuel?

GUIDE FOR READING

- ◆ What type of energy conversion occurs during photosynthesis?
- ◆ What is the source of the energy stored in fossil fuels?

Reading Tip Before you read, preview *Exploring Energy Conversions* on page 488. Write down any questions that you may have. Then look for answers as you read.

Envision a lush, green, swampy forest. Ferns as tall as trees block the view as they rise up to 30 meters. Enormous dragonflies buzz through the warm, moist air. And huge cockroaches, some longer than your finger, crawl across the ground. Where is it? Actually, the question should be, When is it? The time is over 400 million years ago. That's even before the dinosaurs lived! What does this ancient forest have to do with you? You might be surprised to find out just how important this forest is to you.

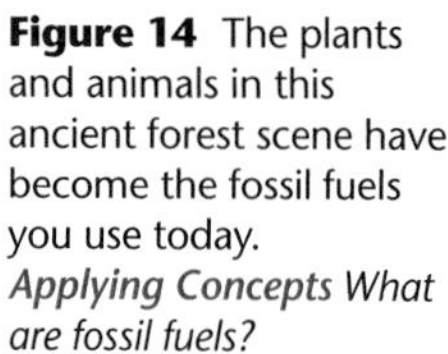

Figure 14 The plants and animals in this ancient forest scene have become the fossil fuels you use today. *Applying Concepts What are fossil fuels?*

482

READING STRATEGIES

Reading Tip Have a volunteer read aloud the sentence that introduces the visual essay *Exploring Energy Conversions.* Before students look at the visual essay, ask volunteers to suggest what the statement might mean. Then have students write their questions. Students' questions might include, "How does steam turn a turbine?"

Program Resources

- ◆ **Unit 5 Resources** 15-3 Lesson Plan; 15-3 Section Summary
- ◆ **Guided Reading and Study Workbook** Section 15-3

Figure 15 When sunlight passes through a prism, it separates into its parts—the colors of the rainbow.

Photosynthesis

This ancient forest is important because plants lived and died there. Plants, including those of this ancient forest, can make their own food. The process through which plants make food is known as **photosynthesis** (foh toh SIN thuh sis). The term *photosynthesis* comes from the two root words *photo,* which means "light," and *synthesis,* which means "putting together." Most organisms around you need photosynthesis to exist. They need the energy in the food produced during photosynthesis to live.

Plants use white light to power photosynthesis. White light, which is electromagnetic energy, is the light you can see. White light is converted into the chemical energy of food during photosynthesis. To understand how this energy conversion occurs, you need to learn more about white light.

The Nature of Light

INTEGRATING PHYSICS The sun is the source of energy on Earth. If you take a walk outside on a sunny day, you feel the sun's radiant energy heat your skin. You see the energy as light on objects around you. But when white light passes through a prism, you can see that it is made up of the colors of the rainbow—red, orange, yellow, green, blue, and violet. Scientists call these colors the visible spectrum.

In addition to prisms, white light strikes many other objects. Some materials such as glass transmit light, or allow the light to pass through. Shiny surfaces such as mirrors reflect, or bounce back, light. Dark objects, such as street pavements, absorb, or take in, light.

Most objects, however, reflect some colors of the visible spectrum while they absorb other colors. For example, when white light strikes a red shirt, the shirt absorbs most of the light's colors. However, the shirt reflects red light. The shirt looks red because your eyes see the reflected color.

Answers to Self-Assessment

Caption Question

Figure 14 Fossil fuels, such as coal, petroleum, and natural gas, are energy sources that store energy from the sun.

2 Facilitate

Photosynthesis

Demonstration

Materials *two seedlings, cups, water, potting soil*
Time 5 minutes a day for several days

Place two similar seedlings in the classroom, one near a window where it receives ample light, and one in a dark corner. Allow students to observe the plants for several days. Ask students to explain any differences in terms of the energy from the sun. **learning modality: visual**

The Nature of Light

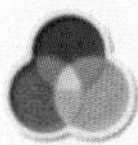

Integrating Physics

Materials *4-inch paper circle, colored markers, flat-head nail, glue, hand drill*
Time 10 minutes

Make a color wheel by coloring six equal sections of a 4-inch circle red, orange, yellow, green, blue, and violet. Place a flat-head nail through the center of the color wheel and glue it in place. When the glue is dry, insert the nail into a hand drill. Turn the drill slowly at first, so students can see all six colors individually. Increase the speed. When you are turning the drill fast enough, students should see what appears to be a white circle, rather than a color wheel. Explain that the circle appears white because the different colors are reaching their eyes so quickly that the brain cannot interpret them as separate colors, but interprets them together as white light, like the light that comes from the sun. **learning modality: visual**

Ongoing Assessment

Oral Presentation Have students tell what energy conversion occurs during photosynthesis. *(During photosynthesis, electromagnetic energy of white light is converted into chemical energy of food.)*

Plants and Light

Skills Focus Observing

Materials *microscope, prepared slides of at least three different kinds of green leaves*

Time 15 minutes

Observing Depending upon the leaves observed, the chloroplasts may differ in number, but the chloroplasts will all be green and oval in shape.

Extend Have students try to identify stomata and their surrounding guard cells on each leaf slide. **learning modality: kinesthetic**

Energy Conversion in Photosynthesis

Building Inquiry Skills: Inferring

Materials *solar-powered calculator that does not run on batteries*

Time 5 minutes

Place the calculator in direct light. Cover the solar cells with your finger. Have students observe how this action affects the number display. Uncover the solar cells. Again, have students observe how the display is affected. Perform similar actions, covering all but one of the solar cells. Ask: **From your observations, what can you infer about the energy that powers the calculator?** *(The energy comes from sunlight.)* **learning modality: visual**

Go for the Green

With a microscope, look for chloroplasts in a prepared slide of a green leaf.

1. Get prepared slides of at least three different kinds of green leaves from your teacher.
2. Study each leaf slide with the microscope.
3. Look for the chloroplasts in each leaf slide. If necessary, move the slide so you can see the chloroplasts clearly.

Observing

How do the chloroplasts differ from one leaf slide to the next? How are the chloroplasts alike?

Plants and Light

Like red shirts and most other objects around you, plants absorb some colors of the visible spectrum and reflect others. When white light strikes the green parts of plants, most of the green light is reflected. Most of the other colors of light are absorbed. Chemical compounds in the plants called **pigments** absorb different colors of light.

The pigment called **chlorophyll** is the most abundant pigment in most plants. Chlorophyll is found in the microscopic plant structures called **chloroplasts.** Chlorophyll absorbs most blue light and red light. Green light, on the other hand, is reflected rather than absorbed. This is why chlorophyll appears green in color, and why plants appear green.

Other plant pigments, called accessory pigments, are yellow, orange, and red. These pigments absorb colors of light that chlorophyll does not. They reflect yellow light, orange light, and red light. Most accessory pigments are usually not visible in plants because they are masked by the chlorophyll.

☑ *Checkpoint* *What colors of light does chlorophyll absorb?*

Energy Conversion in Photosynthesis

Through the process of photosynthesis, plants and some other organisms convert the sun's radiant energy into chemical energy. They use the radiant energy in white light to combine carbon dioxide and water into oxygen and a kind of sugar called glucose. As you know, sugar is a food.

You can think of photosynthesis as taking place in two stages: capturing the sun's energy and producing sugars. You're probably familiar with many two-stage processes. To make a cake, for example, the first stage is to combine the ingredients to make the batter. The second stage is to bake the batter in an oven. To get the desired result—the cake—both stages must occur in the correct order.

Figure 16 In some areas during the fall season, the colors of the accessory pigments in leaves become visible. They produce the beautiful colors of fall leaves.

Background

Integrating Life Science Leaves are green because of the green chlorophyll in their chloroplasts. During autumn, the chlorophyll in deciduous broad leaves breaks down as nights get longer (and days get shorter) and cooler. This allows other pigments that had been hidden by the more plentiful chlorophyll to show their colors. The color of the leaves on each tree depends upon which pigments are now most plentiful.

After the chlorophyll in a leaf breaks down, the leaf is no longer able to make food. Tiny tubes within the stem of the leaf that had carried water to the leaf and food to the plant become clogged. Cells in the stem near the twig separate or dissolve. As the wind blows, the dead leaf easily breaks off the twig.

Capturing the Sun's Energy During the first stage of photosynthesis, plants capture radiant energy in white light. Because white light is electromagnetic energy, a substance that absorbs light also absorbs energy. In plants, the process of capturing energy occurs mainly in the leaves and other green parts of the plants. When light strikes a plant, the plant's chlorophyll absorbs most of the energy. In addition, other plant pigments also absorb some radiant energy. Photosynthesis begins when chlorophyll and the other pigments capture the sun's radiant energy.

Chlorophyll and many other pigments function in a manner similar to that of the solar "cells" in a solar calculator. Solar cells capture the energy in light and use it to power the calculator. Similarly, the pigments in plants absorb light energy and use it to power the second stage of photosynthesis.

Using Energy to Make Food In the second stage of photosynthesis, the captured energy is used to produce sugar. The plant needs two raw materials for this stage: water (H_2O) and carbon dioxide (CO_2). In most plants, the roots absorb water from the soil. The water then moves upwards through the plant's stem to the leaves in tiny tubelike structures. Carbon dioxide is one of the gases that make up air. Carbon dioxide enters the plant through small openings on the undersides of the leaves. These openings are called stomata (STOH mah tuh) (singular *stoma*). Once in the leaves, the water and carbon dioxide gas move into the chloroplasts.

INTEGRATING CHEMISTRY Inside the chloroplasts, water and carbon dioxide undergo a complex series of chemical reactions. The reactions are powered by the radiant energy that was captured during the first stage of photosynthesis. Oxygen gas (O_2) is one important product of the reactions. The other product is a sugar often called glucose ($C_6H_{12}O_6$). Glucose stores the sun's radiant energy as chemical energy.

Figure 17 Photosynthesis occurs inside chloroplasts in the cells of plants and some other organisms. The chloroplasts are the green structures in the cell in the inset.
Applying Concepts Where in a plant are cells with many chloroplasts found?

Building Inquiry Skills: Inferring

ACTIVITY

Materials *4 healthy houseplants of the same variety, masking tape, marker, petroleum jelly, soft cloth*
Time 10 minutes the first day, 5 minutes a day for several days

Apply a thin layer of petroleum jelly to the undersides of two leaves of one plant, four leaves of a second plant, and all leaves of a third plant. Label the pots "Two leaves blocked," "Four leaves blocked," and "All leaves blocked," respectively. Do nothing to the leaves of the fourth plant, labeling it "Control plant." Observe the plants for several days. Ask: **From your observations, why are some of the plants wilted and dying?** *(The leaves coated with the petroleum jelly had blocked stomata, and were unable to obtain the carbon dioxide needed for photosynthesis and food production.)* Use warm water and a soft cloth to remove the petroleum jelly from the leaves. **learning modality: visual**

Demonstration

ACTIVITY

Materials *green plant that lives under water, wide-mouth glass jar, water, glass funnel, test tube, wooden coffee stirrer, match*
Time 10 minutes each day

Put the plant in the jar of water and place the jar in a sunny window. Place the funnel over the plant. The funnel must be completely submerged. Fill the test tube with water and invert it over the narrow end of the funnel, letting no water escape. In several days, students should observe the gas in the test tube and gas bubbles on the upper surfaces of the leaves. To prove that the gas that formed is oxygen, light one end of the stirrer. Blow it out leaving a glowing end. Remove the test tube from the funnel and immediately put the glowing end of the stirrer in the tube. CAUTION: *Do not have the mouth of the tube facing yourself or your students.* The splint should momentarily burst into flame. **learning modality: visual**

Answers to Self-Assessment

Caption Question

Figure 17 Cells with many chloroplasts are found in the leaves.

☑ *Checkpoint*

Chlorophyll absorbs blue light and red light

Ongoing Assessment

Writing Have students make flowcharts to show the steps of photosynthesis.

Energy Conversion in Photosynthesis, continued

Integrating Chemistry

Point out to students that, like mathematical equations, chemical equations must balance. That is, the number of atoms of each element must be the same on both sides of the equation. The subscript numerals tell the number of atoms in one molecule, and the numerals in front of the compounds tells the number of molecules of that compound. Challenge students to show that the chemical equation for photosynthesis balances. **learning modality: logical/mathematical**

Glucose—Stored Energy

Demonstration

ACTIVITY

Materials *houseplant, foil or black paper, paper clips, jar, rubbing alcohol, paper towel, shallow dish, iodine solution*

Time 5 minutes one day, 10 minutes several days later

Demonstrate to students that, in green leaves, starch is produced from sugars that were produced by photosynthesis. Clip a strip of foil or black paper to a leaf of the plant. Place the plant in a sunny location for several days. Remove the strip from the leaf, and place the leaf in a jar of rubbing alcohol overnight to remove its waxy coating and most of its chlorophyll. The next day, blot the leaf dry and place it in a dish. Cover the leaf with iodine solution. Have students observe how the parts of the leaf that were not covered turned purple because iodine turns purple when it comes into contact with starch. **learning modality: visual**

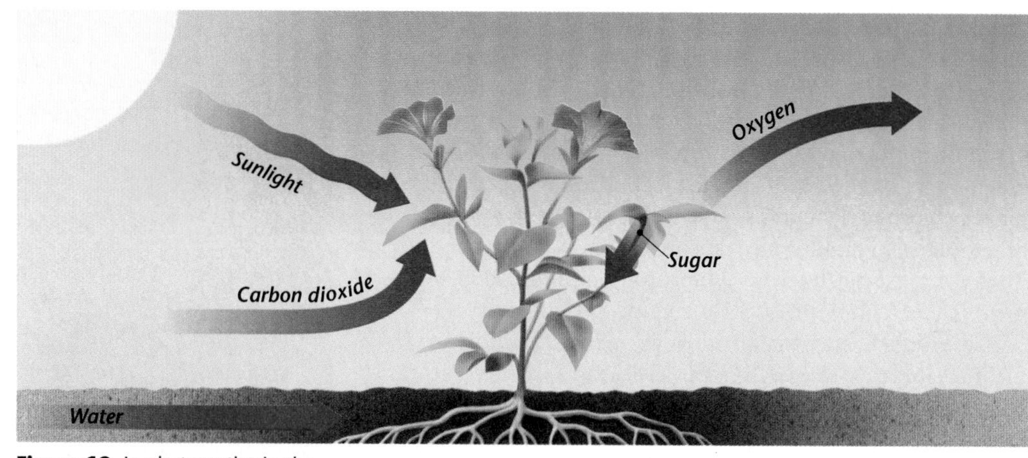

Figure 18 In photosynthesis, the energy in sunlight is used to make sugar and oxygen from carbon dioxide and water.
Classifying Which substances are the raw materials of photosynthesis? Which are the products?

Scientists use a chemical equation to sum up what occurs during photosynthesis. Recall that a chemical equation is a shorthand way of describing a chemical reaction. It shows the raw materials and the products of the reaction it describes. The raw materials are on the left side of the arrow, and the products are on the right side of the arrow. The following equation summarizes the chemical reactions of photosynthesis.

$$\text{carbon dioxide} + \text{water} \xrightarrow{\text{light energy}} \text{glucose} + \text{oxygen}$$
$$6\,CO_2 \quad 6\,H_2O \qquad C_6H_{12}O_6 \quad 6\,O_2$$

The equation reads: carbon dioxide and water combine in the presence of light energy to produce glucose and oxygen.

Glucose and Stored Energy

When a plant breaks down glucose, chemical energy is released. The process by which glucose is broken down is called **respiration.** During respiration, the chemical energy stored in glucose is converted into other forms of energy, such as mechanical energy or thermal energy. Plants use some of this energy to grow, reproduce, and perform other life functions. Plants store unused energy as food.

Humans and many other organisms cannot produce glucose through photosynthesis. Instead, they obtain energy from stored plant food by eating plants or animals that have eaten plants. Animals use the energy in these foods to move, maintain their body temperature, and perform their life functions.

☑ *Checkpoint* ***How are photosynthesis and respiration related?***

Background

History of Science The Dutch physician Jan Ingenhousz has been credited with the discovery of photosynthesis in 1779, when he demonstrated that plants need sunlight to replenish air.

Fossil Fuels

The plants that lived in the ancient forests made their food through photosynthesis. Like plants today, they stored some food. When the ancient plants and the animals that ate the plants died, their remains formed thick layers in swamps and marshes. Clay and sand sediments covered the remains. Over time, more and more sediment piled up. The resulting pressure, along with high temperatures, turned the animal and plant remains into coal.

Coal is a fuel. A **fuel** is a material that releases energy when it burns. Fuels contain potential chemical energy. You probably know about many fuels, such as the gasoline that powers some school buses, the propane used in a gas barbecue grill, and the natural gas that heats some schools and homes. These fuels are **fossil fuels**—energy-rich substances formed from the remains of organisms.

The source of both the energy stored in fossil fuels and the energy stored in food is the same. **The potential chemical energy in fossil fuels and food was stored by plants that converted the sun's radiant energy into chemical energy.** But unlike the food you eat, the fossil fuels you use formed hundreds of millions of years ago.

Like coal, the fossil fuels petroleum and natural gas were also formed from ancient organisms. But these fuels were formed in shallow water, where the remains mixed with mud and sand in layers. Over a long time, the layers were changed into rock. The remains of these organisms gradually formed petroleum and natural gas. Petroleum is refined into a variety of products including gasoline, heating oil, and diesel fuel. You will learn more about how fossil fuels form and are used in Chapter 16.

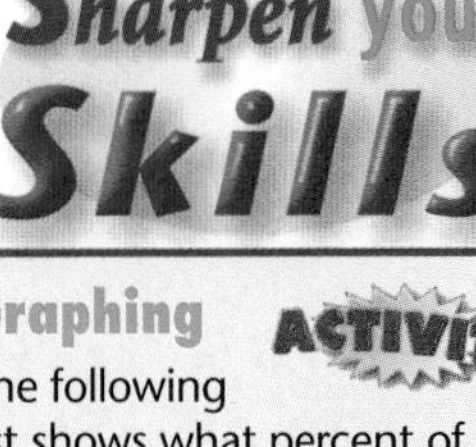

Graphing

The following list shows what percent of power used in a recent year in the United States came from each power source: coal, 23%; nuclear, 8%; petroleum, 39%; natural gas, 24%; water, 3%; and biomass fuels, 3%. Prepare a circle graph that presents these data. (See the Skills Handbook for more on circle graphs.)

What fuel source does the United States rely on most? What percent of total energy needs is met by coal, petroleum, and natural gas combined?

Figure 19 The natural gas burning at the top of this oil well is composed of hydrogen and carbon compounds.

Fossil Fuels

Addressing Naive Conceptions

Some students may think that fossil fuels are made from fossils such as dinosaur bones. Explain that the term *fossil* refers to any remains of an organism from an earlier geological age formed through a geological process. Fossil fuels are made from the remains of plants or diatoms. **learning modality: verbal**

Sharpen your Skills

Graphing

Materials *compass, protractor*
Time 15 minutes
Tips Demonstrate for students how to use the compass and protractor to complete the circle graph.
Expected Outcome Students will find that the United States relies mostly on oil. Together, coal, oil, and natural gas meet 86% of the total energy needs.
Extend Ask students to find out what fuel resources provide the energy they use in their homes.

Media and Technology

Concept Videotape Library
Grade 6, Tape 4 "Power for the People"

Answers to Self-Assessment

Caption Question

Figure 18 The raw materials of photosynthesis are carbon dioxide and water. The products are glucose and oxygen.

☑ Checkpoint

Glucose is a product of photosynthesis and is stored in a plant. During respiration, the glucose is broken down and converted into other forms of energy.

Ongoing Assessment

Writing Have students write paragraphs to describe how ancient plants were converted into a fossil fuel.

Students can save their paragraphs in their portfolios.

EXPLORING

Energy Conversions

Invite students to trace the flow of energy from the sun to the toaster; as they examine the picture, encourage them to find the source of electrical energy. Then guide their analysis further using the following questions: **What kind of energy is in coal? Where did it come from?** *(The chemical energy in coal is the stored chemical energy from plants and animals.)* **When is electromagnetic energy transferred to potential energy?** *(When plants and animals convert light into stored chemical energy)* **When is potential energy converted into electromagnetic energy?** *(When nuclear fusion occurs and the sun converts nuclear energy to electromagnetic energy; when chemical energy in coal is burned and converted to light and thermal energy, and when electrical energy is converted to light and thermal energy.)*

Extend Assign students a different process and challenge them to create a flowchart that shows the energy conversions starting with fusion in the core of the sun. Refer to the **ELL Handbook** for additional teaching strategies.
learning modality: visual

Including All Students

ACTIVITY

For students who need additional challenges, ask: **Are fossil fuels a renewable or non-renewable energy resource?** Have students find a definition for *renewable energy resource.* Organize the class into two teams. Have one team prepare an argument in favor of reducing U.S. dependence on fossil fuels while the other team prepares an opposing argument. Then allow students to debate the issue. **learning modality: verbal**

EXPLORING Energy Conversions

The energy you use to toast your bread may have had a very long history—hundreds of millions of years worth.

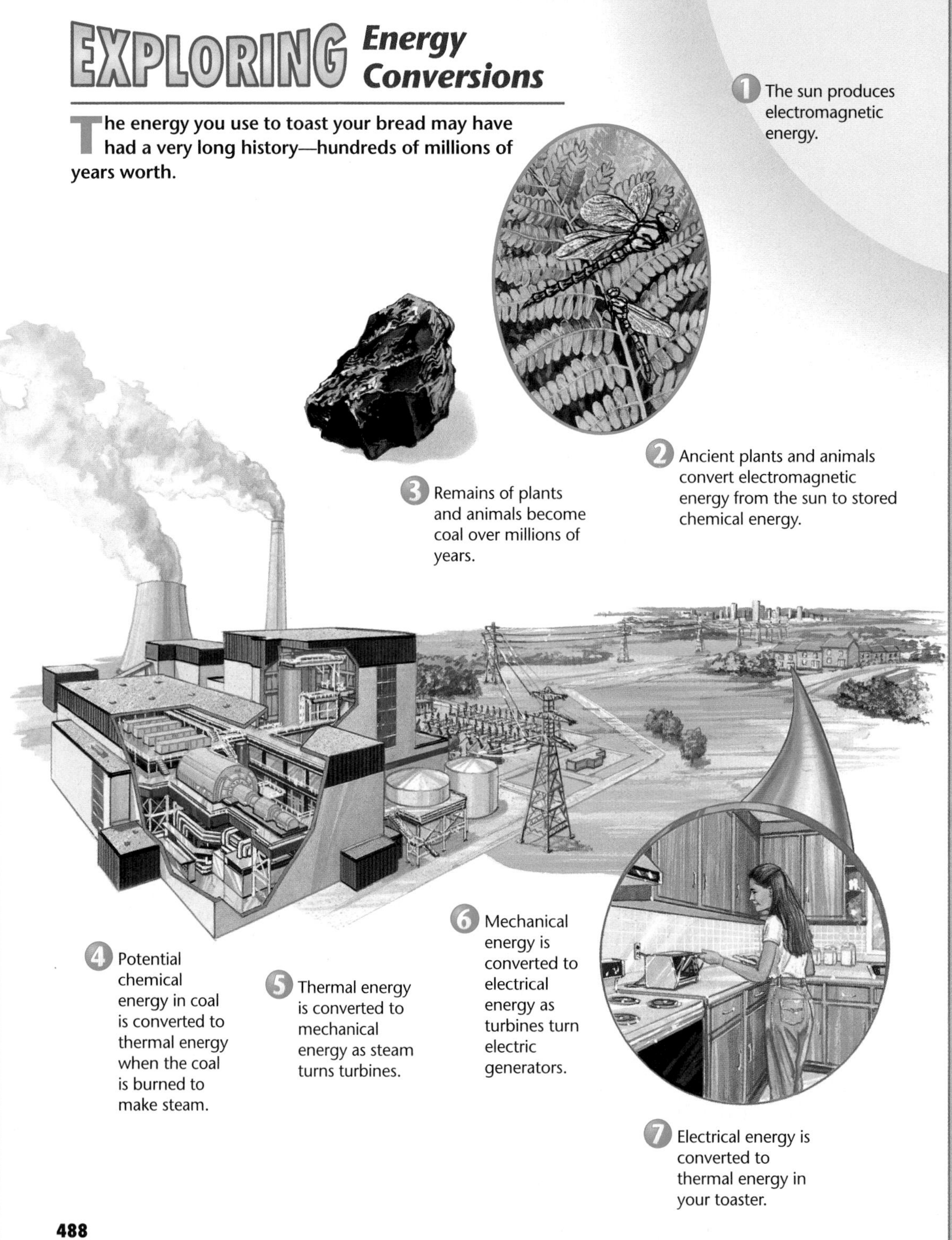

488

Background

Facts and Figures Early fuels included wood, straw, dried dung, and dried peat. There are also a few references to early uses of coal. For example, Aristotle referred to "bodies which have more of earth than of smoke." He called these substances coal.

Archaeologists have found coal dust and coal cinders in Roman ruins in Europe dating back to A.D. 400. However, the first written record of coal mined in Europe was a document written by a monk in Liège about A.D. 1200 that included a reference to "black earth."

Coal mining exploded into prominence in the early 18th century when coke (almost pure carbon made from coal heated in the absence of air) was first used in blast furnaces to smelt iron and make steel. The invention of the steam engine and the beginnings of the industrial age created a huge demand for coal.

Using Fossil Fuels

When you eat, your body stores the energy from the food. That stored energy is converted into other forms of energy during the process of respiration. In a similar way, the potential chemical energy stored in fossil fuels millions of years ago can be converted to other forms of energy by burning, as you can see in *Exploring Energy Conversions.*

The process of burning fuels is known as **combustion**. During combustion, the fuel's potential chemical energy is converted to thermal energy. This thermal energy can be used to heat water until it boils and produces steam.

In modern coal-fired power plants, the steam is raised to a very high temperature in a boiler. As its temperature increases, so does its pressure. When it leaves the boiler it has enough pressure to exert a force on a turbine. A turbine is like a fan, with blades attached to a shaft. The pressure of the steam on the blades causes the turbine to spin very fast. In this process, the thermal energy of the steam is converted to the mechanical energy of the moving turbine. Turbines are connected to generators, which are like electric motors made to run backward. When the generators are spun by turbines, they produce electricity.

Let's summarize the energy conversions and transfers in a power plant. Chemical energy is converted to thermal energy, which is converted to mechanical energy, which is converted to electrical energy. This electrical energy can then be used to light your home and run other electrical devices, such as a toaster.

Section 3 Review

1. Describe the energy changes that occur during photosynthesis.
2. How is the chemical energy in fossil fuels related to the sun's radiant energy?
3. How is the energy of coal released?
4. **Thinking Critically Applying Concepts** What general statement can you make about the supply of fossil fuels, given what you know about their formation?

CHAPTER PROJECT

Check Your Progress

Experiment with different design ideas for your roller coaster vehicle. What variables affect how fast your vehicle moves? How do potential and kinetic energy change as you make modifications to your design? At what point does the vehicle have the greatest kinetic energy? The greatest potential energy? How does friction affect the performance of your roller coaster? How can you relate the law of conservation of energy to your design?

3 Assess

Section 3 Review Answers

1. In the first stage of photosynthesis, the radiant energy in white light is captured by the plant. In the second stage, the captured energy powers chemical reactions that result in the formation of glucose and oxygen. The radiant energy is stored as chemical energy in the glucose.
2. Fossil fuels store the sun's energy. The sun's energy is first converted and stored in plants and in animals that eat plants. The remains of the plants and animals become fossil fuels over millions of years.
3. The energy of coal is released by combustion, when its potential chemical energy is converted to thermal energy.
4. Because fossil fuels are formed much more slowly than we are using them, they may become increasingly scarce.

CHAPTER PROJECT

Check Your Progress

As you review students' designs, make sure they are practical and meet the guidelines established for this project. Encourage students to answer the questions in the text by pointing to specific examples from their design. For example, students should recognize that the car will have the greatest potential energy when it is at the top of the 1-m hill. The car probably has the greatest kinetic energy at the bottom of the first hill or at the lowest point on the track.

Program Resources

◆ **Unit 5 Resources** 15-3 Review and Reinforce; 15-3 Enrich

Media and Technology

 **Transparencies** "Exploring Energy Conversions," Transparency 62

Performance Assessment

Organizing Information Have students construct concept maps starting with the terms: *potential chemical energy, electromagnetic energy, ancient plants and animals, gasoline* and adding other terms of their own.

Power

Objectives

After completing the lesson, students will be able to
- ◆ define and calculate power;
- ◆ compare energy and power.

Key Term power

1 Engage/Explore

Activating Prior Knowledge

Ask students to brainstorm a list of people or things they describe as powerful. *(Samples: computers, car engines, a smell, an athlete's legs, stereo speakers, a superhero)* Ask students to think about what all these things have in common, and how they compare to less powerful things. Explain that the term power has a special meaning in science that is different from its meaning in everyday language.

DISCOVER

Skills Focus inferring
Materials *pinwheel, hair dryer with two settings*
Time 10 minutes
Tips CAUTION: *Make sure students' work areas are dry before they use the hair dryer.* Perform this activity as a demonstration if you do not have enough hair dryers for all students.
Expected Outcome The pinwheel spins faster when blown by a hairdryer at its highest setting.
Think It Over Work is done because air from the dryer exerts a force on the pinwheel and causes it to move. Work is force times distance. It requires more force to make the pinwheel spin at a higher speed. Thus, more work is done at the higher setting.

Power

DISCOVER ACTIVITY

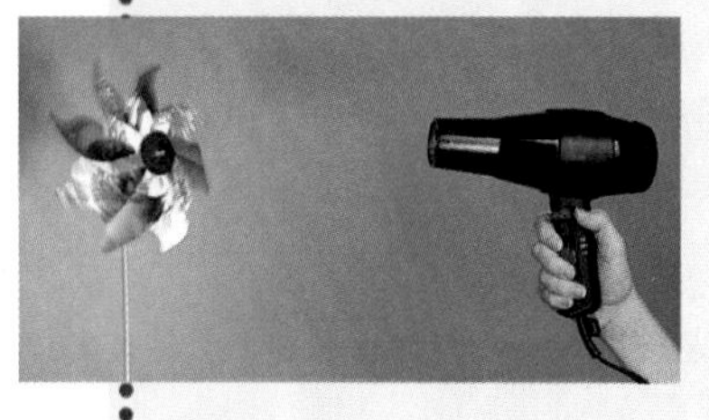

Is Work Always the Same?

1. Obtain a pinwheel and a hair dryer with at least two different power settings.
2. Set the dryer on its lowest setting. Use it to blow the pinwheel. Observe the pinwheel's motion.
3. Set the dryer on its highest setting. Again, use it to blow the pinwheel. Observe the pinwheel's motion.

Think It Over

Inferring Explain why work is done in spinning the pinwheel. What differences can you identify between the two situations? Is the amount of work greater for the high or low speed?

GUIDE FOR READING
- ◆ How do you calculate power?
- ◆ What is the difference between power and energy?

Reading Tip As you read, use your own words to describe the relationship among work, power, and energy.

The ad for a sleek new sports car catches your eye as you read a magazine. Its manufacturer boasts that the car can go from 0 to 100 km/h in 5 seconds because it has a 320-horsepower engine. But what does a car have to do with horses? You may find the answer is more than you think.

What Is Power?

A car does work to accelerate from rest. Some car engines do this work rapidly, while others do it more slowly. The faster an engine can do an amount of work, the more power the engine has. **Power** is the rate at which work is done or the amount of work done in a unit of time.

When you carry an object up some stairs, you do the same amount of work whether you walk or run up the stairs. (Work is the weight of the object times the height of the stairs.) But you exert more power when you run because you are doing the work faster.

You can think of power in another way. A device that is twice as powerful as another can do the same amount of work in half the time. Or it can do twice the work in the same time.

Calculating Power Whenever you know how fast work is done, you can calculate power. **Power is calculated by dividing the amount of work done by the amount of time taken to do the work.** This can be written as the following formula.

$$Power = \frac{Work}{Time}$$

READING STRATEGIES

Reading Tip Have students write the terms *work, power,* and *energy* on a sheet of paper so that they form the points of a large triangle. As they discover the relationships between terms, students should write these relationship as the legs of the triangle. For example, work and power can be connected by the statement, "Power is the amount of work done in a certain amount of time."

Study and Comprehension Encourage students to write a definition of the word *power* using their own words before they study the section. Have students consider the way they use this word in everyday situations. As they read, students should compare the descriptions in the section to their definitions to help them understand the scientific meaning of the word.

Since work is equal to force times distance, you can rewrite the equation for power as follows.

$$Power = \frac{Force \times Distance}{Time}$$

When work is measured in joules and time in seconds, the unit of power is the joule per second (J/s). This unit is also known as the watt (W), in honor of James Watt, who made great improvements to the steam engine. One watt of power is produced when one joule of work is done in one second. In other words, 1 watt = 1 J/s.

A watt is a relatively small unit of power. For example, you produce about one watt of power if you raise a glass of water to your mouth in one second. Because a watt is so small, power is often measured in larger units. One kilowatt (kW) equals 1,000 watts. A washing machine uses about one kilowatt when it is running. An electric power plant can produce a million kilowatts.

☑ *Checkpoint* *What is power?*

Sample Problem

A crane lifts an 8,000-N beam 75 m to the top of a building in 30 s. How much power does the crane use?

Analyze. The force needed to lift the beam will be equal to its weight, 8,000 N. The distance and time are given, so the formula for power can be used.

Write the formula.

$$Power = \frac{Force \times Distance}{Time}$$

Substitute and solve.

$$Power = \frac{8{,}000\ N \times 75\ m}{30\ s}$$

$$Power = \frac{600{,}000\ N\cdot m}{30\ s} \text{ or } \frac{600{,}000\ J}{30\ s}$$

$$Power = 20{,}000\ J/s = 20{,}000\ W \text{ or } 20\ kW$$

Think about it. The answer tells you that the crane used 20,000 W to lift the beam. That equals 20 kW.

Practice Problems

1. A motor exerts a force of 10,000 N to lift an elevator 6 m in 5 s. What is the power produced by the motor?
2. A tow truck exerts a force of 9,000 N to pull a car out of a ditch. It moves the car a distance of 6 m in 25 s. What is the power of the tow truck?

Program Resources

- **Unit 5 Resources** 15-4 Lesson Plan; 15-4 Section Summary
- **Guided Reading and Study Workbook** Section 15-4
- **Laboratory Manual** 15, "Winding Up With Wind"

Answers to Self-Assessment

☑ *Checkpoint*

Power is the rate at which work is done, or the amount of work done in a unit of time.

2 Facilitate

What Is Power?

Inquiry Challenge

ACTIVITY

Materials *various objects that may be comfortably lifted, such as paint cans, small barbells*
Time 20 minutes

Have groups of students design experiments to test whether it is more tiring to do work quickly or slowly. CAUTION: *Review all plans for safety.* Ask: **How can you do the same work at different rates?** *(Lift or push the object at different speeds.)* Help students analyze their results. **cooperative learning**

Sample Problem

Be sure students include the proper units in their calculations. Point out that a newton × meter is a joule and that a joule per second is a watt.

So, $\frac{N \cdot m}{s} = \frac{J}{s} = W$

Practice Problems

1. (10,000 N × 6 m)/ 5 s = 12,000 W
2. (9,000 N × 6 m)/ 25 s = 2,160 W

Power and Energy

Building Inquiry Skills: Observing

Materials *15-W lamp, 40-W lamp, 100-W lamp*
Time 10 minutes

In a darkened room, have students record observations about the energy released by the light bulbs. Caution students not to touch the hot bulbs. Ask: **Why does the 15-W bulb look much dimmer than the 100-W bulb?** *(It converts less electrical energy per second.)* **learning modality: visual**

Ongoing Assessment

Skills Check Ask students what quantities they must measure to find the power of an elevator that travels to the top of a building 15 m tall.

Real-World Lab

Careers in Science

Can You Feel the Power?

Preparing for Inquiry

Key Concept Power is the rate of doing work and depends on force, distance and time.

Skills Objectives Students will
- measure distance and time;
- calculate work and power;
- interpret data.

Time 45 minutes

Advance Planning Have boards, stopwatches, and meter sticks ready. Tell students to bring calculators and 2 cm-thick books to class on lab day. You may want to review using the calculator to calculate rates before the lab.

Alternative Methods If possible, try to borrow several aerobic "steps" to be used in the experiment. They will be easier to set up and be more stable. Aerobic steps are available in several heights.

Guiding Inquiry

Invitation Ask students if they are familiar with aerobics classes. Most will be at least familiar. Some may even take classes. Point out that in some classes students repeatedly step up onto a low platform to increase the effectiveness of the workout. Ask: **How does this increase the effectiveness?** *(By increasing the total distance, total work is increased. By increasing the speed of doing the exercise, power is increased.)*

Introducing the Procedure

- Divide the class into groups of three students each.
- Ask students why the body weights are given in newtons and why the distance is measured in meters. *(Work is measured in joules, which are newton-meters.)*

Troubleshooting the Experiment

- Students should recognize that the work done during the downward motion is done by gravity and cannot be counted as work done by the student. A complete up and down cycle is counted as one repetition, not two.

Power and Energy

Recall that work is the transfer of energy. Thus power can be defined in another way. **Power is the rate at which energy is transferred from one object to another or converted from one form to another.** For this reason, power is not limited to situations in which objects are moved. Power can be found whenever energy is being transferred or converted.

Real-World Lab

Careers in Science

Can You Feel the Power?

Imagine you are a physical therapist who wants to increase the power output of her patients. In this lab, you will simulate a simple exercise using a step.

Problem

How can you change how much power you expended while doing an exercise?

Skills Focus

measuring, calculating, interpreting data

Materials

calculator
meter stick
stopwatch or clock with a second hand
board, about 2.5 cm × 30 cm × 120 cm
8–10 books, each about 2 cm thick

Procedure 

1. Construct a step by making two identical stacks of books. Each stack should be about 20 cm high. Place a board securely on top of the stacks of books so that the ends of the board are even with the outside edges of the books. **CAUTION:** *Be sure to have your partners hold the board steady and level throughout the procedure.*
2. Copy the data table into your notebook.
3. You do work every time you take a step.
   Work = Weight × Height
   a. Assume your weight is 400 N, and your partners' weights are 425 N and 450 N.
   b. Measure the vertical distance in centimeters from the floor to the top of the board. Convert to meters by dividing by 100 and record this height in the data table.
4. Calculate the work you do in stepping up onto the board once. Then calculate the work you do in stepping up onto the board 20 times. Record both answers in your data table.
5. Step up onto the board with both feet and then step backwards off the board onto the floor. This up and down motion is one repetition. Make sure you are comfortable with the motion.
6. Have one partner time how long it takes you to do 20 repetitions performed at a constant speed. Count out loud to help the timer keep track of the number of repetitions. Record the time in your data table.
7. Calculate the power you expended to do 20 repetitions. (Power = Work ÷ Time.) Predict how your results will change if you step up at different speeds.

492

Safety

Falling hazard Be sure partners hold the board steady and level throughout the investigation. Partners should "spot" for the steppers.

Program Resources

- **Unit 5 Resources** Chapter 15 Real-World Lab blackline masters

Media and Technology

Lab Activity Videotapes Grade 6, Tape 3

You know that a 100-watt light bulb is much brighter than a 40-watt light bulb. The wattage printed on a light bulb tells you its power. The power of a light bulb is the rate at which electrical energy is converted into electromagnetic energy (light) and thermal energy. A 100-watt light bulb converts electrical energy at a rate of 100 joules each second. A 100-watt bulb is brighter because it gives off more energy per second than a 40-watt bulb.

DATA TABLE

	Weight (N)	Height of Board (m)	Time for 20 Repetitions (s)	Work for 1 Repetition (J)	Work for 20 Repetitions (J)	Power (W)
Student 1 Trial 1						
Student 1 Trial 2						

8. Repeat Steps 6 and 7, but climb the step more slowly than you did the first time. Record the new data in the Trial 2 row of your data table.
9. Switch roles with your partners and repeat Steps 3 through 8.

Analyze and Conclude

1. Compare the amount of work you did during your first and second trials.
2. Compare the amount of power you produced during your first and second trials.
3. Did you and your partners all do the same amount of work? Explain your answer.
4. Did you and your partners all produce the same power during your trials? Explain your answer.
5. **Apply** Suggest how a physical therapist could use music to change the power output of her patients. Why would a therapist want to change power outputs?

Design an Experiment

Design an experiment to test two other ways a physical therapist could change the power output of her patients. Get your teacher's approval before beginning your experiment.

Sample Data Table

	Weight (N)	Height of Board (m)	Time for 20 Repetitions (s)	Work for 1 Repetition (J)	Work for 20 Repetitions (J)	Power (W)
Student 1 Trial 1	400	0.2	20	80	1600	80
Student 1 Trial 2	400	0.2	30	80	1600	53.3

Expected Outcome

- Students' results should show that, for a given student, the work done for each repetition is the same because the step is the same height. However, slower repetitions mean lower power.
- Students' results should show that the student with a weight of 400 N does less work for each repetition than the heavier students.

Analyze and Conclude

1. The amount of work is the same.
2. The power is greater for the first trial, because it was faster.
3. No. Partners with greater weight do more work.
4. No. The power depended on the student's weight and how long it took to do 20 repetitions.
5. The beat of the music helps participants maintain the rate at which exercises are performed. Students who exercise to music with a faster beat will move faster and produce more power. By increasing the power of their workout, students will burn more calories and increase their overall strength and muscle tone.

Extending the Inquiry

Design an Experiment Other ways to change the power include using handheld or ankle weights, using higher steps, or increasing the speed. Students should test only one variable at a time and should never work unsupervised in the lab.

Horsepower

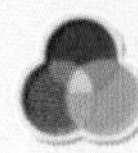

Integrating Technology

Have students find out the horsepower of a vehicle advertised in a newspaper or magazine. Then have them convert its horsepower to watts. **learning modality: logical/mathematical**

3 Assess

Section 4 Review Answers

1. Power = Work/Time
2. Power is the rate of doing work. Because work is the transfer of energy, power is the rate of transferring or converting energy from one form to another.
3. Work = 40 N × 18 m = 720 J; Power = 720 J ÷ 4 s = 180 J/s or 180 W
4. 24,000 J ÷ 60 s = 400 J/s or 400 W
5. The 40-horsepower engine converts energy twice as fast as the 20-horsepower engine and it also produces energy twice as fast as a 20-horsepower engine and has twice as much power as a 20-horsepower engine.

CHAPTER PROJECT

Check Your Progress

Make sure students can describe how the results of their trials helped them find the best place for the features on their roller coasters. Some students may be having trouble with the performance of their roller coasters. Encourage them to simplify their designs until they find one that works, and then add more detail slowly. Students may have difficulty getting vertical loops to work properly.

Performance Assessment

Writing Have students write advertisements for James Watt's steam engine. They should include a definition of power and its relationship to work.

Figure 20 One of Watt's engines (next to the chimney) is shown at work at a coal mine.

Horsepower

When people talk about engines for automobiles, they use another power unit instead of the watt. This unit is the horsepower. One horsepower is equal to 746 watts. (The horsepower is not an SI unit.)

The word horsepower was used by James Watt to advertise the advantages of his improved steam engine of 1769. Watt decided to relate his engine to the common source of power in his day—horse power. He compared the amount of work his steam engine could do to the amount of work a horse could do hauling coal. He defined one horsepower as the amount of work a horse does to lift a 33,000-pound weight a distance of one foot in one minute.

Section 4 Review

1. State the formula for calculating power.
2. How are power and energy related?
3. Find the work you do when you exert a force of 40 N to run a distance of 18 m in 4 seconds. Then find the power you expend.
4. **Thinking Critically Problem Solving** The motor of an electric fan converts 24,000 J of electrical energy every minute (60 s). What is the power of the fan's motor?
5. **Thinking Critically Comparing and Contrasting** A 40-horsepower engine burns twice as much fuel each hour as a 20-horsepower engine. Explain this in terms of power and energy.

CHAPTER PROJECT

Check Your Progress

Add turns to the tracks on your roller coaster. What happens to the speed of the car as it rounds a turn? Are there certain locations along the tracks that are better for turns? Experiment with putting a vertical loop in the tracks. Where is the best place to put a loop? You can say that the roller coaster produces power because it converts gravitational potential energy to kinetic energy. At what point in the car's trip is this rate of conversion greatest?

Program Resources

- **Unit 5 Resources** 15-4 Review and Reinforce; 15-4 Enrich

The Nature of Energy

Key Ideas

- Energy is the ability to do work or produce change.
- Energy is transferred from one object to another when work is done.
- Kinetic energy is the energy that an object has because of its motion. Potential energy is the energy an object has because of its position or condition.
- Six forms of energy are mechanical energy, thermal energy, chemical energy, electric energy, electromagnetic energy, and nuclear energy.

Key Terms

work	potential energy
energy	elastic potential energy
force	gravitational potential energy
kinetic energy	radiant energy

Energy Conversion and Conservation

Key Ideas

- An energy conversion or transformation occurs when energy changes from one form to another.
- In any process, no energy is lost. This is the law of conservation of energy.

Key Terms

energy conversion   law of conservation of energy

Photosynthesis and Fossil Fuels

INTEGRATING LIFE SCIENCE

Key Ideas

- Radiant energy from the sun is transferred to chemical energy in plants during photosynthesis.
- The potential chemical energy in fossil fuels results from photosynthesis in plants.

Key Term

photosynthesis	respiration
pigment	fuel
chlorophyll	fossil fuel
chloroplast	combustion

Power

INTEGRATING MATHEMATICS

Key Ideas

- Power is calculated by dividing the amount of work done (or energy converted) by the time it took. The unit of power is the watt: 1 W = 1 J/s.
- Power is the rate at which work is done, or the rate at which energy is transformed.

Key Term

power

Organizing Information

Concept Map Copy the concept map about energy onto a separate sheet of paper. Then complete it and add a title. (For more on concept maps, see the Skills Handbook.)

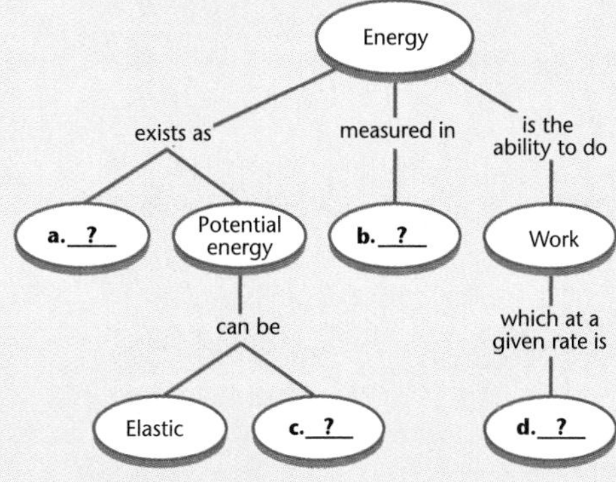

Program Resources

- **Unit 5 Resources** Chapter 15 Project Scoring Rubric
- **Performance Assessment** Chapter 15
- **Chapter and Unit Tests** Chapter 15 Test

Media and Technology

Computer Test Bank Chapter 15 Test

Organizing Information

Concept Map Sample title: What is Energy? **a.** kinetic energy **b.** joules **c.** gravitational **d.** power

Reviewing Content

Multiple Choice

1. b **2.** b **3.** c **4.** a **5.** c

True or False

6. motion **7.** true **8.** chemical
9. work or energy **10.** true

Checking Concepts

11. Kinetic energy is the energy possessed by a moving object, while potential energy is stored energy, due to an object's position or condition. Potential energy can be converted into kinetic energy and vice versa.
12. Mechanical (kinetic energy and gravitational potential energy); thermal, electromagnetic, and chemical energy; elastic potential energy
13. On the perch, the eagle has gravitational potential energy. Halfway to the ground, half the gravitational potential energy has become kinetic energy. When it reaches its prey, all its mechanical energy is kinetic energy. The eagle also converts chemical energy from its food to mechanical energy when it flies.
14. In the first step of photosynthesis, the pigments in plants absorb radiant energy from the sun. Carbon dioxide from the air and water are also absorbed by the plant. In the second step, the captured energy powers chemical reactions that produce glucose and oxygen.
15. The energy is the same in both cases, but the power is double in the second case because the same energy transfer was done twice as fast.
16. Students' biographies should creatively demonstrate that energy is present in every aspect of life.

Thinking Critically

17. kinetic energy $= 0.5 \times 1300 \text{ kg} \times (11 \text{ m/s})^2 = 78{,}650 \text{ J}$
18. Her final potential energy is less because she walked to a lower level. $500 \text{ N} \times (3 \text{ m}) = 1500 \text{ J}$. So her potential energy decreased by 1500 J.
19. Energy conversion occurs in a plant in both photosynthesis and respiration. In photosynthesis, radiant energy is converted into chemical energy which is stored in glucose. In respiration, the glucose is broken down and the energy is converted into mechanical or thermal energy or is restored as chemical energy for future use by the plant.
20. The motorcycle has the least kinetic energy, while the bus has the greatest kinetic energy. Kinetic energy $= 1/2(\text{mass} \times \text{velocity}^2)$. Kinetic energy increases as mass increases.

Applying Skills

21. The club has the greatest potential energy at B and D. It has the greatest kinetic energy at C.
22. At A, the club has no potential or kinetic energy. At B, it has maximum gravitational potential energy and no kinetic energy. At C, it has maximum kinetic energy and no potential energy. At D, it has maximum potential energy and no kinetic energy. At E, when it is brought to rest, it has no potential or kinetic energy.
23. No. The man adds energy as he swings the club. Therefore, energy is conserved.

CHAPTER 15 ASSESSMENT

Reviewing Content

Multiple Choice

Choose the letter of the answer that best completes each statement.

1. Energy of motion is called
   a. elastic potential energy.
   b. kinetic energy.
   c. gravitational potential energy.
   d. chemical energy.
2. When you stretch a rubber band you give it
   a. kinetic energy.
   b. elastic potential energy.
   c. gravitational potential energy.
   d. power.
3. Whenever energy is transferred, some energy is converted to
   a. nuclear energy.
   b. electrical energy.
   c. thermal energy.
   d. mechanical energy.
4. Coal stores energy from the sun as
   a. chemical energy.
   b. electromagnetic energy.
   c. mechanical energy.
   d. electrical energy.
5. The rate at which work is done is called
   a. energy. b. force.
   c. power. d. conservation.

True or False

If the statement is true, write true. If it is false, change the underlined word or words to make the statement true.

6. Kinetic energy is due to the position of an object.
7. Gravitational potential energy depends on weight and height.
8. Green plants convert the electromagnetic energy of the sun into mechanical energy.
9. The SI unit of power is the joule.
10. A device that has three times the power of another can do the same amount of work in one third the time.

Checking Concepts

11. Describe the difference between kinetic energy and potential energy.
12. For each of the following, decide which forms of energy are present: a leaf falls from a tree; a candle burns; a rubber band is wrapped around a newspaper.
13. An eagle flies from its perch in a tree to the ground to capture its prey. Describe its energy transformations as it descends.
14. Explain the two steps in the process of photosynthesis.
15. One chef places a pie in the oven at a low setting so that it is baked in one hour. Another chef places a pie in the oven at a high setting so that the pie bakes in half an hour. Is the amount of transformed energy the same in each case? Is the power the same?
16. **Writing to Learn** As you saw in the figures on pages 472 and 473, you can find different forms of energy all around you. Imagine you are writing your own biography. Pick three major events in your life. Write a paragraph about the form of energy that was most important in each event.

Thinking Critically

17. **Calculating** A 1,300-kg car travels at 11 m/s. What is its kinetic energy?
18. **Problem Solving** A 500-N girl walks down a flight of stairs so that she is 3 m below her starting level. What is the change in the girl's gravitational potential energy?
19. **Applying Concepts** Explain how photosynthesis and respiration are alike and different. Describe the energy conversions involved in each process.
20. **Relating Cause and Effect** A motorcycle, an automobile, and a bus are all traveling at the same velocity. Which has the least kinetic energy? The greatest kinetic energy? Explain your answer.

496

Applying Skills

Use the illustration of a golfer taking a swing to answer the Questions 21–23. The golf club starts at point A and ends at point E.

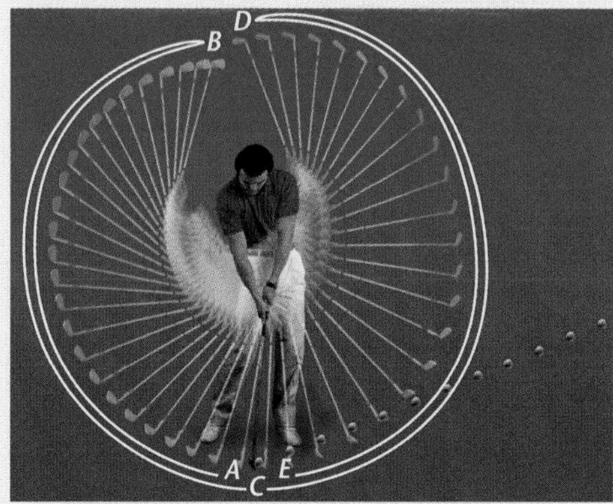

21. **Inferring** At which point(s) does the golf club have the greatest potential energy? At which point(s) does it have the greatest kinetic energy?
22. **Communication** Describe the energy conversions from point *A* to point *E*.
23. **Drawing Conclusions** The kinetic energy of the club at point *C* is more than the potential energy of the club at point *B*. Does this mean that the law of conservation of energy is violated?

Performance Assessment (Chapter Project)

Present Your Project Present your roller coaster to the class. Explain how you selected your materials, as well as the effect of hill height, incline, turns, and loops on the motion of the roller coaster. You should also explain how energy is converted as the roller coaster moves along the tracks. Point out an interesting feature of your roller coaster.

Reflect and Record In your journal, explain how you might improve your roller coaster. Think about what you knew about kinetic and potential energy before the project began, and what you know now. Which features would you change? Which would you keep the same?

Test Preparation

Use these questions to prepare for standardized tests.

Read the passage. Then answer Questions 24–26.

It's the day of the big archery competition. Suki is the first contestant. She steps up to the line, raises her bow and pulls her arrow back. The bow bends and she lets go of the arrow. The bow returns to its original shape as the arrow flies through the air toward the target. However, her arrow falls to the ground before it reaches the target.

24. What type of energy did the arrow have as it moved through the air?
    - **a.** potential energy
    - **b.** kinetic energy
    - **c.** electromagnetic energy
    - **d.** chemical energy
25. Where did the energy of the arrow come from?
    - **a.** It always had the energy.
    - **b.** It gained energy from the air as it moved.
    - **c.** Energy was stored in the arrow when the bow was pulled back.
    - **d.** Energy transferred to the bow as it was pulled back was transferred to the arrow.
26. What caused the arrow to fall short?
    - **a.** It did not have enough energy because Suki did not pull the bow back far enough.
    - **b.** It had too much energy because Suki pulled the bow back too far.
    - **c.** Its kinetic energy was converted to gravitational potential energy as it moved.
    - **d.** Its kinetic energy was converted to potential energy as it moved.

Program Resources

- **Inquiry Skills Activity Book** Provides teaching and review of all inquiry skills

Performance Assessment (Chapter Project)

Present Your Project Students should present their roller coasters to the class either in an oral presentation with demonstrations or as a class exhibit. An exhibit may allow students to interact and test each others' roller coasters. Ask the students to demonstrate how their roller coasters convert potential to kinetic energy.

Reflect and Record Encourage students to concentrate on ways to reduce air resistance and friction so that more gravitational potential energy is converted to kinetic energy.

Test Preparation

24. b **25.** d **26.** a

CHAPTER 16 Energy Resources

Sections	Time	Student Edition Activities	ACTIVITY Other Activities
CHAPTER PROJECT **Energy Audit** p. 499	Ongoing (2–3 weeks)	Check Your Progress, pp. 506, 572, 519 Present Your Project, p. 527	
1 Energy From Fossil Fuels pp. 500–506 ◆ Explain how fuels provide energy. ◆ List the three major fossil fuels. ◆ Explain why fossil fuels are considered nonrenewable resources.	2 periods/ 1 block	**Discover** What's in a Piece of Coal?, p. 500 **Sharpen Your Skills** Graphing, p. 502	TE Inquiry Challenge, p. 502 TE Building Inquiry Skills: Classifying, p. 503 TE Building Inquiry Skills: Observing, p. 504 TE Building Inquiry Skills: Calculating, p. 505
2 Renewable Sources of Energy pp. 507–514 ◆ Explain how the sun provides energy and describe ways to collect this energy. ◆ Identify and describe various sources of renewable energy.	2 periods/ 1 blocks	**Discover** Can You Capture Solar Energy?, p. 507 **Real-World Lab: How It Works** Cooking With Sunshine, p. 513	TE Integrating Technology, p. 508 TE Real-Life Learning, p. 509 TE Demonstration, p. 511 LM 16, "Solar Heating"
3 *Integrating Chemistry* **Nuclear Energy** pp. 515–519 ◆ Describe nuclear fission and nuclear fusion reactions. ◆ Explain how a nuclear power plant produces electricity.	1 period/ $\frac{1}{2}$ block	**Discover** Why Do They Fall?, p. 515 **Try This** Shoot the Nucleus, p. 516 **Sharpen Your Skills** Calculating, p. 517	TE Building Inquiry Skills: Making Models, p. 516 TE Real-Life Learning, p. 518 TE Inquiry Challenge, p. 518
4 Conserving Energy pp. 520–524 ◆ List two ways to ensure that there will be enough energy for the future. ◆ Identify things that individuals can do to conserve energy.	2 periods/ 1 block	**Skills Lab: Designing Experiments** Keeping Comfortable, p. 520 **Discover** Which Bulb Is More Efficient?, p. 521 **Science at Home,** p. 524	TE Building Inquiry Skills: Calculating, p. 522 TE Building Inquiry Skills: Observing, p. 523
Study Guide/Chapter Assessment pp. 525–527	1 period/ $\frac{1}{2}$ block		ISAB Provides teaching and review of all inquiry skills

For Standard or Block Schedule The Resource Pro® CD-ROM gives you maximum flexibility for planning your instruction for any type of schedule. Resource Pro® contains Planning Express®, an advanced scheduling program, as well as the entire contents of the Teaching Resources and the Computer Test Bank.

CHAPTER PLANNING GUIDE

Program Resources	Assessment Strategies	Media and Technology
UR Chapter 16 Project Teacher Notes **UR** Chapter 16 Project Overview and Worksheet	**SE** Performance Assessment: Present Your Project, p. 527 **TE** Check Your Progress, pp. 506, 572, 519 **UR** Chapter 16 Project Scoring Rubric	Science Explorer Internet Site at www.phschool.com Student Edition on Audio CD, Chapter 16
UR 16-1 Lesson Plan **UR** 16-1 Section Summary **UR** 16-1 Review and Reinforce **UR** 16-1 Enrich	**SE** Section 1 Review, p. 506 **TE** Ongoing Assessment, pp. 501, 503, 505 **TE** Performance Assessment, p. 506	Concept Videotape Library, Grade 6, Tape 2, "Our Passion for Driving"; Tape 4 "Power for the People" Transparency 63, "An Electric Power Plant"
UR 16-2 Lesson Plan **UR** 16-2 Section Summary **UR** 16-2 Review and Reinforce **UR** 16-2 Enrich **UR** Chapter 16 Real-World Lab	**SE** Section 2 Review, p. 512 **TE** Ongoing Assessment, pp. 509, 511 **TE** Performance Assessment, p. 512	Concept Videotape Library, Grade 6, Tape 4, "Wired to the Sun" Transparencies 64, "Exploring a Solar House"; 65, "A Geothermal Power Plant" Lab Activity Videotapes, Grade 6 Tape 4
UR 16-3 Lesson Plan **UR** 16-3 Section Summary **UR** 16-3 Review and Reinforce **UR** 16-3 Enrich	**SE** Section 3 Review, p. 519 **TE** Ongoing Assessment, p. 517 **TE** Performance Assessment, p. 519	Transparencies 66, "Nuclear Fission"; 67, "A Nuclear Power Plant"; 68, "Nuclear Fusion" Lab Activity Videotapes, Grade 6 Tape 4
UR Chapter 16 Skills Lab **UR** 16-4 Lesson Plan **UR** 16-4 Section Summary **UR** 16-4 Review and Reinforce **UR** 16-4 Enrich	**SE** Section 4 Review, p. 524 **TE** Ongoing Assessment, p. 523 **TE** Performance Assessment, p. 524	
RCA Provides strategies to improve science reading skills **GRSW** Provides worksheets to promote student comprehension of content	**SE** Chapter 16 Study Guide/Assessment, pp. 525–527 **PA** Chapter 16 Performance Assessment **CUT** Chapter 16 Test **CTB** Chapter 16 Test	Computer Test Bank, Chapter 16 Test

Key: **SE** Student Edition
CTB Computer Test Bank
ISAB Inquiry Skills Activity Book
GRSW Guided Reading and Study Workbook
TE Teacher's Edition
PTA Product Testing Activities by *Consumer Reports*
RCA Reading in the Content Area
PA Performance Assessment
UR Unit Resources
LM Laboratory Manual
IES Interdisciplinary Explorations Series
CUT Chapter and Unit Tests

Meeting the National Science Education Standards and AAAS Benchmarks

National Science Education Standards	Benchmarks for Science Literacy	Unifying Themes
Science As Inquiry (Content Standard A) ◆ **Design and conduct a scientific investigation** Students investigate how solar energy can be used to cook food and compare how well different materials stop heat transfer. *(Real-World Lab; Skills Lab)* ◆ **Use appropriate tools and techniques to gather, analyze, and interpret data** Students evaluate energy use in their school. *(Chapter Project)* **Physical Science** (Content Standard B) ◆ **Transfer of energy** Fuel provides energy as the result of a chemical change. Nuclear reactions convert matter into energy. Certain materials can slow the transfer of heat. *(Sections 1, 3, 4; Skills Lab)* **Science and Technology** (Content Standard E) ◆ **Understandings about science and technology** The energy stored in fuels can be used to generate electricity. Technologies to capture and use solar energy, wind and water power, and alternative fuels help meet energy needs. Nuclear fission can be used to generate electricity. People have developed technologies that improve efficiency and reduce energy use. *(Sections 1, 2, 3, 4; Science & History)* **Science in Personal and Social Perspectives** (Content Standard F) ◆ **Science and technology in society** Students evaluate the benefits and costs of hydroelectric dams. *(Science and Society)*	**1B Scientific Inquiry** Students evaluate energy use in their school, investigate how solar energy can be used to cook food, and compare how well different materials stop heat transfer. *(Chapter Project; Real-World Lab; Skills Lab)* **3A Technology and Science** People have developed technologies that improve energy efficiency and reduce energy use. *(Section 4; Science & History)* **3B Designs and Systems** Control rods are used to control fission reactions in nuclear reactors. Certain materials can slow the transfer of heat. *(Section 3; Skills Lab)* **3C Issues in Technology** Students suggest ways to save energy in their school. Students evaluate the benefits and costs of hydroelectric dams. Reducing energy use is called energy conservation. *(Chapter Project; Science and Society; Section 4)* **8C Energy Sources and Use** The three major fossil fuels are coal, oil, and natural gas. The sun, wind, water, tides, biomass material, Earth's interior, and hydrogen are renewable sources of energy. Controlled nuclear fission reactions can be used to generate electricity. *(Sections 1, 2, 3; Real-World Lab)*	◆ **Energy** Students evaluate energy use in their school. A fuel is a substance that provides a form of energy as the result of a chemical reaction. The sun, wind, water, tides, biomass material, Earth's interior, and hydrogen are renewable sources of energy. Nuclear reactions convert matter into energy. Reducing energy use is called energy conservation. *(Chapter Project; Sections 1, 2, 3, 4; Real-World Lab; Skills Lab; Science & History)* ◆ **Patterns of Change** Over time, heat and pressure changed dead organisms into fossil fuels. When a neutron hits a nucleus, the nucleus splits apart into two smaller nuclei and three neutrons. *(Sections 1, 3)* ◆ **Scale and Structure** Hydrocarbons are energy-rich chemical compounds that contain carbon and hydrogen atoms. The central core of an atom that contains protons and neutrons is called a nucleus. *(Sections 1, 3)* ◆ **Stability** A renewable source of energy is one that is constantly being supplied. Radioactive wastes remain dangerous for many thousands of years. *(Sections 2, 3)* ◆ **Systems and Interactions** Electric power plants generate electricity by converting energy from one form to another. People have developed technologies that improve energy efficiency and reduce energy use. *(Sections 1, 4; Science and Society)* ◆ **Unity and Diversity** Energy sources can be renewable or nonrenewable. Fission and fusion are two types of nuclear reactions. *(Sections 1, 2, 3)*

Take It to the Net

Interactive text at www.phschool.com

Science Explorer comes alive with iText.

- **Complete student text** is accessible from any computer with Internet access or a CD-ROM drive.
- **Animations, simulations, and videos** enhance student understanding and retention of concepts.
- **Self-tests and online study tools** assess student understanding.

STAY CURRENT with **SCIENCE NEWS®**

Find out the latest research and information about Energy and Energy Resources at: **www.phschool.com**

Go to **www.phschool.com** and click on the Science icon.Then click on Science Explorer: Life, Earth, and Physical Science under PH@school.

Student Edition Activities Planner

ACTIVITY	Time *(minutes)*	Materials *Quantities for one work group*	Skills
Section 1			
Discover, p. 500	10	**Nonconsumable** lignite coal, hand lens	Observing
Sharpen Your Skills, p. 502	15	**Nonconsumable** drawing compass, protractor, calculator (optional)	Graphing
Section 2			
Discover, p. 507	10; 5	**Consumable** 500 mL water **Nonconsumable** 2 sealable clear plastic bags, 2 thermometers	Developing Hypotheses
Real-World Lab, p. 513	40	**Consumable** glue, tape, marshmallows, 3 sheets aluminum foil, 3 sheets oaktag paper **Nonconsumable** scissors, 3 thermometers, 3 dowels or pencils, clock or watch	Predicting, Designing Experiments, Forming Operational Definitions
Section 3			
Discover, p. 515	10	**Nonconsumable** 15 dominoes	Inferring
Try This, p. 516	10	**Nonconsumable** 12 marbles	Making Models
Sharpen Your Skills, p. 517	5	**Nonconsumable** calculator (optional)	Calculating
Section 4			
Skills Lab, p. 520	40	**Consumable** ice water, hot water **Nonconsumable** thermometers, beakers, watch or clock, containers and lids made of paper, plastic foam, plastic, glass, and metal	Measuring, Designing Experiments
Discover, p. 521	20	**Nonconsumable** 60-watt incandescent light bulb and 15-watt compact fluorescent light bulb in packages, lamp, thermometer, clock or watch	Inferring
Science at Home, p. 524	home	No special materials are required.	Observing

A list of all materials required for the Student Edition activities can be found on pages TVA34–TVA40. You can obtain information about ordering materials by calling 1-800-848-9500 or by accessing the Science Explorer Internet site at **www.phschool.com**.

CHAPTER 16 PROJECT

Energy Audit

Chapter 16 covers the sources and uses of energy and ways to conserve energy. The Chapter 16 Project is designed to provide real-life application of chapter concepts.

Purpose The Chapter 16 Project will give students an opportunity to examine energy uses in their school and suggest ways to reduce the school's energy consumption. Each student group will choose one area of the school to study, identify the types of energy used in that area, and determine the amount of each type of energy used. As students collect and record data, they will consider ways to reduce each type of energy use. Each group will prepare a written report that describes the students' findings and lists their ideas for reducing energy uses in the area they studied. The class as a whole will then prepare a proposal for conserving energy throughout the school.

Skills Focus After completing the Chapter 16 Project, students will be able to

- create a data table for recording the types and amounts of energy uses in the area selected for study;
- make observations and record data;
- interpret data and draw conclusions as the basis for recommending ways to reduce energy use;
- communicate findings and recommendations in a written report.

Project Time Line The Chapter 16 Project requires two to three weeks to complete, depending on how long a period of time you want to have students collect and evaluate numerical data, including the school's utility bills and readings of electric meters and fuel gauges. Most observations can be made during a class period. For purposes of comparison, making observations of the same area on different days and at different times of day should help students detect average and unusual uses, such as increased use of heating fuel during a cold spell.

Possible Materials
No special materials are required. Students will find it helpful to use calculators.

Chapter 16 Energy Resources

Integrating Chemistry

Section 1 Energy From Fossil Fuels
Discover What's in a Piece of Coal?
Sharpen Your Skills Graphing

Section 2 Renewable Sources of Energy
Discover Can You Capture Solar Energy?
Real-World Lab Cooking With Sunshine

Section 3 Nuclear Energy
Discover Why Do They Fall?
Try This Shoot the Nucleus
Sharpen Your Skills Calculating

498

Advance Preparation

- Discuss with your school principal what students will be doing in this project, and obtain approval for students to enter areas that are usually off-limits to them, such as the utility room, or the cafeteria's kitchen. If necessary, arrange to have the school custodian or another adult accompany students to these areas.
- Obtain copies of the school's utility and fuel bills for students' use in determining the amounts of energy used.

Launching the Project Invite students to read the Chapter 16 Project description on page 499. Lead students in brainstorming a list of areas in the school that they could study.

Take the class on a tour of the school building and grounds. Encourage students to keep track of the different energy uses they observe—electricity for lighting, fuel oil or natural gas for heating, electricity or natural gas for cooking, gasoline for the school buses, and the like.

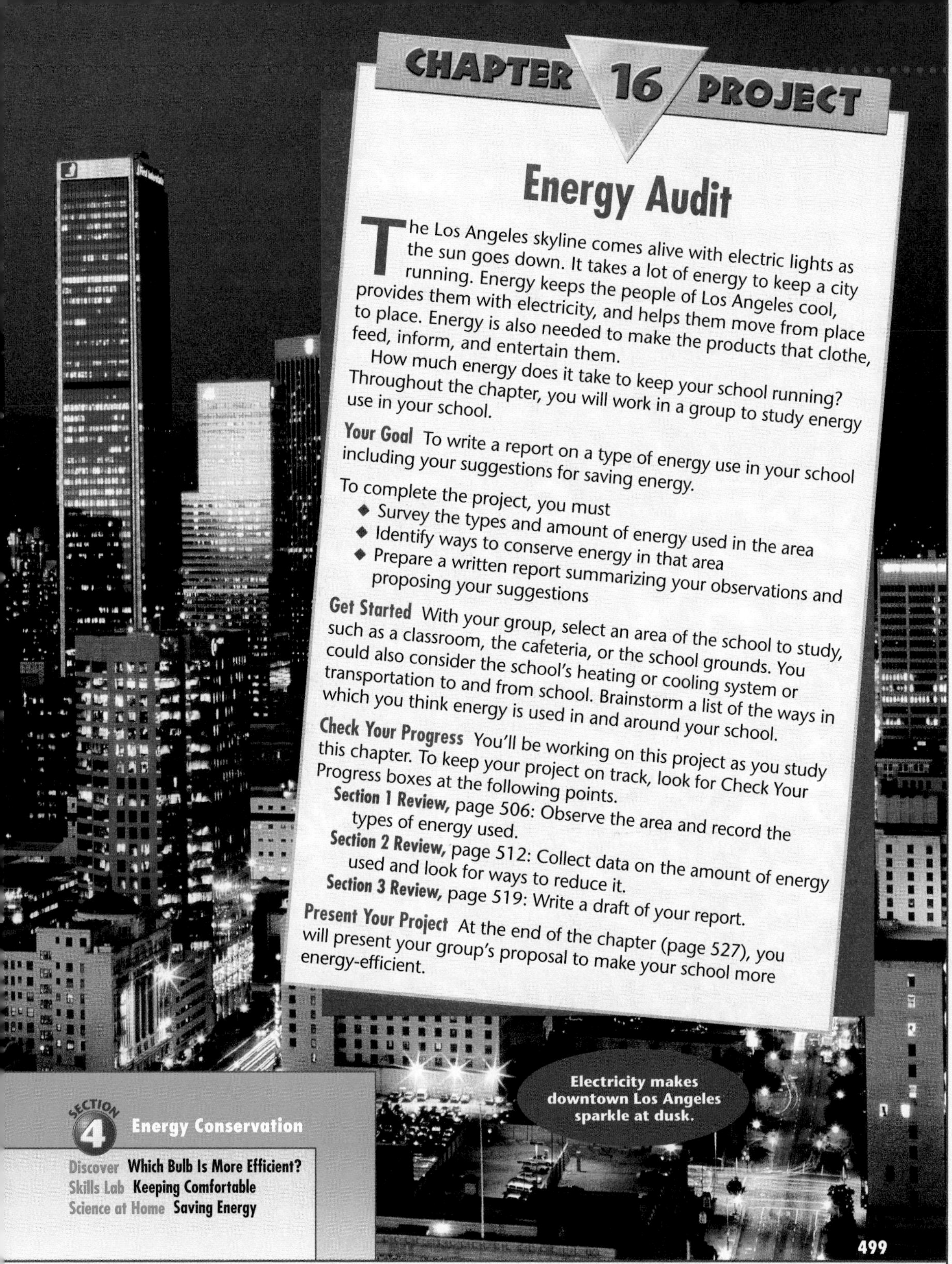

CHAPTER 16 PROJECT

Energy Audit

The Los Angeles skyline comes alive with electric lights as the sun goes down. It takes a lot of energy to keep a city running. Energy keeps the people of Los Angeles cool, provides them with electricity, and helps them move from place to place. Energy is also needed to make the products that clothe, feed, inform, and entertain them.

How much energy does it take to keep your school running? Throughout the chapter, you will work in a group to study energy use in your school.

Your Goal To write a report on a type of energy use in your school including your suggestions for saving energy.

To complete the project, you must

- ◆ Survey the types and amount of energy used in the area
- ◆ Identify ways to conserve energy in that area
- ◆ Prepare a written report summarizing your observations and proposing your suggestions

Get Started With your group, select an area of the school to study, such as a classroom, the cafeteria, or the school grounds. You could also consider the school's heating or cooling system or transportation to and from school. Brainstorm a list of the ways in which you think energy is used in and around your school.

Check Your Progress You'll be working on this project as you study this chapter. To keep your project on track, look for Check Your Progress boxes at the following points.

Section 1 Review, page 506: Observe the area and record the types of energy used.

Section 2 Review, page 512: Collect data on the amount of energy used and look for ways to reduce it.

Section 3 Review, page 519: Write a draft of your report.

Present Your Project At the end of the chapter (page 527), you will present your group's proposal to make your school more energy-efficient.

Electricity makes downtown Los Angeles sparkle at dusk.

SECTION 4 **Energy Conservation**

Discover **Which Bulb Is More Efficient?**
Skills Lab **Keeping Comfortable**
Science at Home **Saving Energy**

Distribute Chapter 16 Project Overview in Unit 5 Resources, and have students review the project rules and procedures. Also distribute Chapter 16 Project Worksheet in Unit 5 Resources. This worksheet provides instructions on how to read electric and gas meters and provides equivalents for converting different energy units (kilowatt-hours, gallons, and so forth) into the common unit of BTUs.

Divide the class into groups of three or four, and let the groups meet briefly to choose areas to study. Monitor the groups' choices to avoid duplication. As an alternative, you could assign an area to each group.

Tell students that each group's members may divide the project responsibilities among themselves in any way they wish. However, emphasize that *every* group member should take part in identifying the types and amounts of energy uses in the area the group has chosen, recording and analyzing data, and developing the written report, and should be prepared to answer questions about the project.

Additional information on guiding the project is provided in Chapter 16 Project Teacher Notes in Unit 5 Resources.

Program Resources

- ◆ **Unit 5 Resources** Chapter 16 Project Teacher Notes; Chapter 16 Project Overview and Worksheet; Chapter 16 Project Scoring Rubric

Media and Technology

Student Edition on Audio CD Chapter 16

You will find an Internet activity, chapter self-tests for students, and links to other chapter topics at this site.

Performance Assessment

The Chapter 16 Project Scoring Rubric in Unit 5 Resources will help you evaluate how well students complete the Chapter 16 Project. You may want to share the scoring rubric with students so they are clear about what will be expected of them. Students will be assessed on

- ◆ their ability to identify and evaluate all the types of energy used in the area studied;
- ◆ their ability to make recommendations for reducing those energy uses and to communicate their findings and recommendations to others;
- ◆ their participation in their group.

SECTION 1 Energy From Fossil Fuels

Objectives

After completing the lesson, students will be able to
- ◆ explain how fuels provide energy;
- ◆ list the three major fossil fuels;
- ◆ explain why fossil fuels are considered nonrenewable resources.

Key Terms hydrocarbons, reserves, petroleum, refinery, petrochemicals, nonrenewable resource

1 Engage/Explore

Activating Prior Knowledge

Ask students: **What is energy?** *(Answers will vary depending on students' prior science learning. Responses may include "strength," "power," "something that makes something else happen," and the like. If necessary, point out that the scientific definition of energy is "the capacity to do work.")*

DISCOVER

Skills Focus observing
Materials *lignite coal, hand lens*
Time 10 minutes
Tips Lignite—the second stage of coal formation after peat—is the only form of coal that may contain recognizable plant remains.
Expected Outcome Students may or may not find fossils of plant remains in the coal samples. If fossils are present, they will be more noticeable with a hand lens.
Think It Over The lignite's texture, layering, and fossils (if present) can be seen more clearly with a hand lens. If fossils are visible, students should be able to infer that coal is made of plant remains.

SECTION 1 Energy From Fossil Fuels

DISCOVER ACTIVITY

What's in a Piece of Coal?

1. Observe a chunk of coal. Record your observations in as much detail as possible, including color, texture, and shape.
2. Now use a hand lens to observe the coal more closely.
3. Examine your coal for fossils, imprints of plant or animal remains.

Think It Over
Observing What did you notice when you used the hand lens compared to your first observations? What do you think coal is made of?

GUIDE FOR READING
- ◆ How do fuels provide energy?
- ◆ What are the three fossil fuels?
- ◆ Why are fossil fuels considered nonrenewable resources?

Reading Tip As you read, make a table comparing coal, oil, and natural gas. Describe each fuel and note how it is obtained and used.

The blackout happened on a November afternoon in 1965, just as evening rush hour was beginning. One small part in one power plant stopped working. To replace the lost power, the automatic controls shifted electricity from another source. This overloaded another part of the system, causing it to shut down. The problem kept growing. Within minutes, much of the Northeast was without electricity! Lights went out, plunging buildings into darkness. Thousands of people were trapped in dark elevators. Traffic signals stopped working, causing huge traffic jams. Electric stoves, radios, clocks—nothing worked. It took 13 hours to restore the power. During that time, more than 30 million people were reminded just how much their lives depended on electricity.

◀ Electric power lines stretch against the evening sky.

Producing electricity is an important use of energy resources. Other uses include transportation and heating. As you read about Earth's energy resources, think about how each is used to meet people's energy needs.

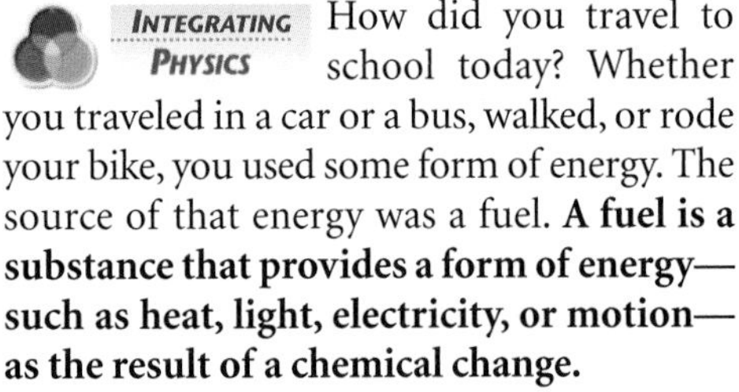

Fuels and Energy

INTEGRATING PHYSICS How did you travel to school today? Whether you traveled in a car or a bus, walked, or rode your bike, you used some form of energy. The source of that energy was a fuel. **A fuel is a substance that provides a form of energy—such as heat, light, electricity, or motion—as the result of a chemical change.**

READING STRATEGIES

Reading Tip Help students set up their tables before they begin to read. Students' tables should consist of columns for coal, oil, and natural gas. The rows should consist of: description, method of obtaining fuel, and use. Encourage students to leave space for additional rows. Students may wish to add further rows to compare advantages and disadvantages or other criteria.

Caption Writing Distribute photocopies of Figure 1. Have each student number the steps shown in the diagram based on the caption description, then write an accompanying key that briefly explains what happens in each numbered step.

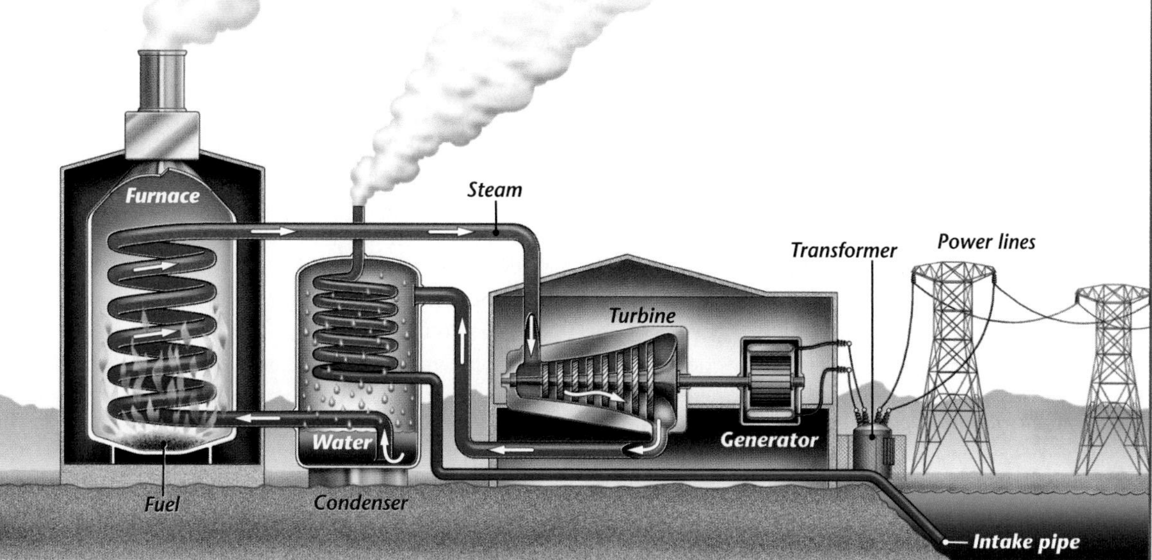

Figure 1 Electric power plants generate electricity by converting energy from one form to another. In the furnace, fuel is burned, releasing thermal energy. This energy is used to boil water and make steam. The mechanical energy of the moving steam turns the blades of a turbine. The turbine turns the shaft of the generator, producing an electric current.

Recall that energy can be converted from one form to another. To see how, rub your hands together quickly for several seconds. Did you feel them become warmer? When you moved your hands, they had mechanical energy, the energy of motion. The friction of your hands rubbing together converted some of this mechanical energy to thermal energy, which you felt as heat.

Combustion Fuels contain stored chemical energy, which can be released by burning. The process of burning a fuel is called combustion. For example, the fuel used by most cars is gasoline. When gasoline is burned in a car engine, it undergoes a chemical change. The gasoline combines with oxygen, producing carbon dioxide and water. The combustion of gasoline also converts some of the stored chemical energy into thermal energy. This thermal energy is converted to mechanical energy that moves the car.

Production of Electricity The energy stored in fuels can be used to generate electricty. In most power plants, the thermal energy produced by burning fuel is used to boil water, making steam, as shown in Figure 1. The mechanical energy of the steam turns the blades of a turbine. The shaft of the turbine is connected to a generator. The generator consists of powerful magnets surrounded by coils of copper wire. As the shaft rotates, the magnets turn inside the wire coil, producing an electric current. The electric current flows through power lines to homes and industries.

☑ *Checkpoint* *What are three energy conversions that might occur in a power plant?*

2 Facilitate

Fuels and Energy

Integrating Physics

After students have read about energy conversion and rubbed their hands together, give some other examples of energy conversions and challenge students to infer the energy changes that are occurring. Some examples include a toaster *(Electrical energy is changed to heat energy.)*, light bulb *(Electrical energy is changed to light and heat energy.)*, power saw *(Electrical energy is changed to mechanical and heat energy.)*, and candle *(Chemical energy is changed to light and heat energy.)*. **learning modality: logical/mathematical**

Real-Life Learning

Invite a local auto mechanic or students who are particularly interested in automobiles to bring in and explain diagrams showing how an internal combustion engine works. Suggest that students who need an additional challenge create posters based on the diagrams. Ask: **Besides cars, trucks, buses, and other automobiles, what other devices contain an internal combustion engine?** *(Gasoline-powered lawnmowers, snowblowers, chainsaws, portable generators, and the like)* **learning modality: visual**

Program Resources

- **Unit 5 Resources** 16-1 Lesson Plan; 16-1 Section Summary
- **Guided Reading and Study Workbook** Section 16-1

Media and Technology

Transparencies "An Electric Power Plant," Transparency 63

Answers to Self-Assessment

☑ *Checkpoint*

When fuel is burned, chemical energy is converted to thermal energy (heat). Some of the thermal energy is converted to the mechanical energy of moving steam. In a power plant, the mechanical energy is then converted to electrical energy.

Ongoing Assessment

Oral Presentation Call on students at random to identify the energy conversions shown in Figure 1 in the order in which they occur.

Sharpen your Skills

Graphing

Materials *drawing compass, protractor, calculator (optional)*
Time 15 minutes
Tips To determine the number of degrees for each use, students should first divide each percentage by 100. Then they should multiply each of those numbers by 360° and round off so the three sections total 360°.
Expected Outcome *Transportation* 96°; *Industry* 137°; *Homes and businesses* 127°

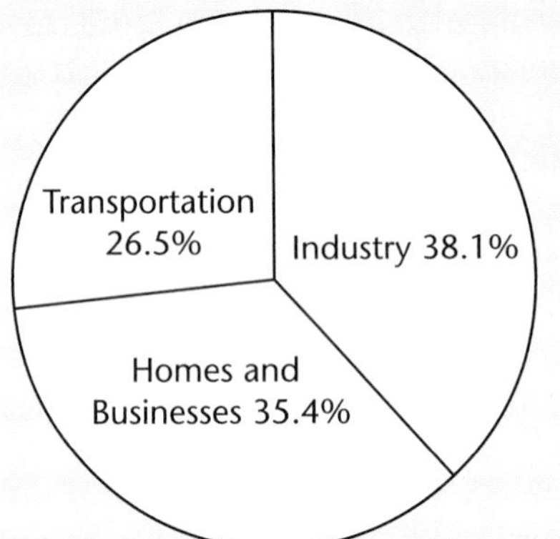

Extend Let students brainstorm specific types of energy uses included in each "end use" category—for example, oil for heating, electricity for refrigeration and lighting, gasoline for automobiles, and so on. **learning modality: logical/mathematical**

Inquiry Challenge

ACTIVITY

Materials *clay, soil, sand, pebbles, leaves, colored paper, books or heavy weights*
Time 20 minutes

Challenge students to devise a model showing how fossil fuels form over time. *(Models might include trapping materials such as leaves or pieces of colored paper in layers of soft material such as clay or soil, and then compressing the materials under heavy weights.)* Ask: **What happens to buried materials to turn them into fossil fuels?** *(Over time, heat and pressure change the materials into hydrocarbons.)* **learning modality: kinesthetic**

Graphing

ACTIVITY

Use the data in the table below to make a circle graph showing the uses of energy in the United States. (To review circle graphs, see the Skills Handbook.)

End Use of Energy	Percent of Total Energy
Transportation	26.5
Industry	38.1
Homes and businesses	35.4

What Are Fossil Fuels?

Most of the energy used today comes from organisms that lived hundreds of millions of years ago. As these plants, animals, and other organisms died, their remains piled up. Layers of sand, rock, and mud buried the dead organisms. Over time, heat and pressure changed the material into other substances. Fossil fuels are the energy-rich substances formed from the remains of once-living organisms. **The three fossil fuels are coal, oil, and natural gas.**

Fossil fuels are made of hydrocarbons. **Hydrocarbons** are energy-rich chemical compounds that contain carbon and hydrogen atoms. During combustion, the carbon and hydrogen combine with oxygen in the air to form carbon dioxide and water. This process releases energy in the forms of heat and light.

Fossil fuels have more hydrocarbons per kilogram than most other fuels. For this reason, they are an excellent source of energy. Combustion of one kilogram of coal, for example, provides twice as much heat as burning one kilogram of wood. Oil and natural gas provide three times the energy of wood.

☑ ***Checkpoint*** *Why do fossil fuels yield more energy than other fuels?*

Figure 2 In the photo, a farmer in Ireland turns over blocks of soft peat. Peat is formed from the remains of plants in the early stages of coal formation. As these remains are more and more deeply buried, peat changes to lignite, then to bituminous coal, and then to anthracite.

Coal

Coal is a solid fossil fuel formed from plant remains. People have burned coal to produce heat for thousands of years. But coal was only a minor source of energy compared to wood until the 1800s. As Europe and the United States entered the Industrial Revolution, the need for fuel increased rapidly. As forests were cut down, firewood became more expensive.

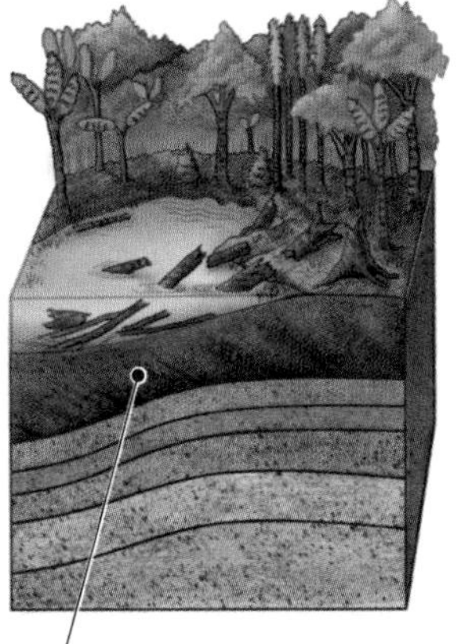

Peat
A. Layers of dead plant material build up to form peat.

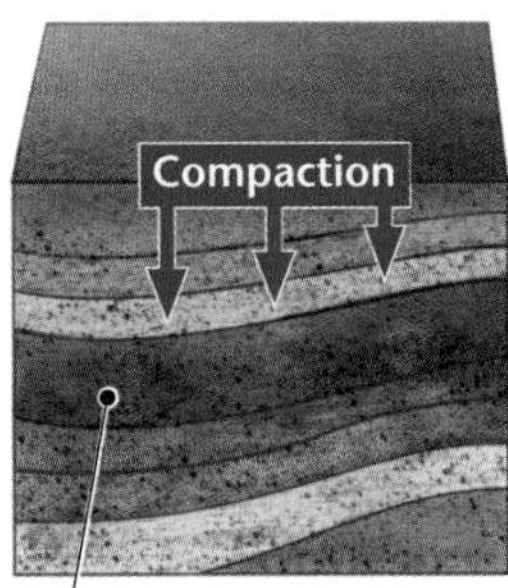

Lignite
B. Lignite is soft brown coal.

Background

Integrating Science "Black lung"—a form of pneumoconiosis (a general term for lung disease caused by breathing dust)—is caused by breathing coal dust over many years. The buildup of dust in the lungs damages the lungs' air sacs where gas exchange occurs. Scarring reduces the elasticity of lung tissue and makes it less able to absorb oxygen. As a result, the heart must pump harder, which damages the heart and can lead to death from heart failure. Black lung causes permanent damage to the lungs and is incurable.

In the early 1900s, scientists established the link between coal dust levels in mines and black lung disease. Continuing efforts to reduce coal dust levels in mines led to a reduction in the number of cases of black lung. The level of coal dust allowed in mines is now limited by federal law.

It became worthwhile to find, mine, and transport coal. Coal fueled the huge steam engines that powered trains, ships, and factories during the Industrial Revolution.

Today, coal provides 23 percent of the energy used in the United States. The major use of coal is to fuel electric power plants.

Coal Mining Before it can be used to produce energy, coal has to be removed from the ground, or mined. INTEGRATING TECHNOLOGY Some coal is located very deep underground or is mixed with other materials, making it too difficult to obtain. Known deposits of coal (and other fossil fuels) that can be obtained using current technology are called **reserves.**

A century ago, miners had to break the coal apart with hand tools. Today they use machines to chop the coal into chunks and lift it to the surface. The coal is then cleaned to remove rocks, sand, and other materials that do not burn. Removing them also makes the coal lighter, reducing the cost of transporting it.

Figure 3 A miner obtains hard coal from a shaft deep underground.

Coal as an Energy Source Coal is the most plentiful fossil fuel in the United States. It is fairly easy to transport, and provides a lot of energy when burned. But coal also has some disadvantages. Coal mining can increase erosion. Runoff from mines can cause water pollution. Finally, burning most types of coal results in more air pollution than other fossil fuels.

In addition, coal mining can be a dangerous job. Thousands of miners have been killed or injured in accidents in the mines. Many more suffer from "black lung," a disease caused by years of breathing coal dust. Fortunately, the mining industry has been working hard to improve conditions. New safety procedures and better equipment, including robots and drills that produce less coal dust, have made coal mining safer.

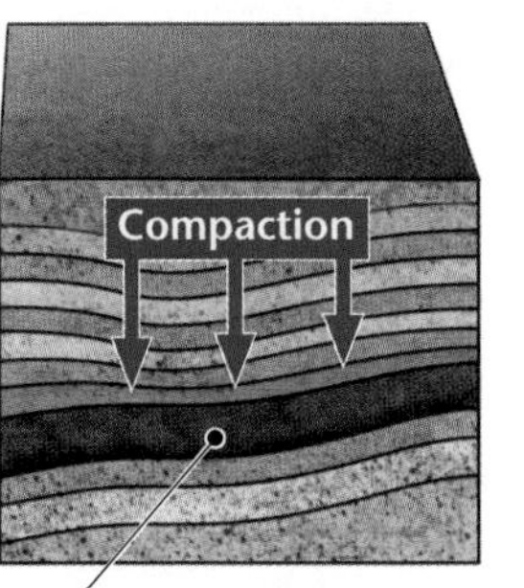

Bituminous coal

C. Bituminous coal is harder than lignite.

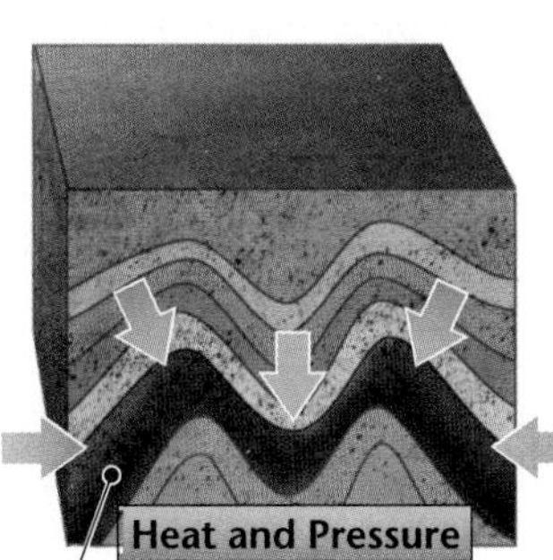

Anthracite

D. Heat and pressure deep beneath the surface produce anthracite, hard coal.

Coal

Building Inquiry Skills: Classifying

ACTIVITY

Materials *samples of peat moss, lignite, bituminous coal, and anthracite; 2 small plastic bags; hand lenses*
Time 10 minutes

CAUTION: *Rinse the coal thoroughly to remove any dust. Make sure students wash their hands after handling the samples.* Give each group hand lenses, a plastic bag containing a sample of peat moss, and a second bag containing the three types of coal. Let students examine the samples, noting similarities and differences between them. Explain that peat is the decayed remains of plants—the early stage of coal formation. Then list the following names and characteristics on the board, and challenge students to identify each coal sample.
Lignite: dark brown; layered; may contain recognizable fragments of plant remains
Bituminous coal: denser than lignite; black; may have bands
Anthracite: the hardest of all coal types; black; shiny **learning modality: kinesthetic**

Integrating Technology

Encourage students to look closely at the photographs on this page. You may wish to show some pictures of coal miners in the past and the labor-intensive methods and equipment they used. Point out that many years ago, young people students' own age—and even younger—worked in coal mines. Encourage students to describe what they think it was like to work in a coal mine years ago. **learning modality: visual**

Media and Technology

Concept Videotape Library
Grade 6, Tape 2 "Our Passion for Driving"

Answers to Self-Assessment

☑ *Checkpoint*

Fossil fuels contain hydrocarbons, which release more energy than other substances when they are burned.

Ongoing Assessment

Skills Check Have each student create a flowchart showing how fossil fuels are formed.

Students can save their flowcharts in their portfolios.

Oil

Building Inquiry Skills: Observing

Materials *2 small paper cups, 30 mL dark molasses, paper towel, aluminum pan*
Time 10 minutes

CAUTION: *If you are concerned about spills, have a few volunteers perform this activity as a demonstration for the other students.* Give each student or group a paper towel, a small paper cup containing about 30 mL of dark molasses, and an empty cup. Explain that molasses is very similar to crude oil in consistency. Invite students to pour the molasses from one cup to the other over the pan, try to pick some up with the paper towel, and touch some between the thumb and index finger. Students will find that the molasses is too thick to pour readily, is not absorbed by the towel, and is sticky. Ask: **How easy do you think it would be to clean up crude oil that spilled on a beach?** *(Extremely difficult)* **learning modality: kinesthetic**

Using the Visuals: Figure 4

Let students answer the caption question, then ask: **Which of the named nations has the smallest oil reserve?** *(United States)* **Does this mean the United States is the nation with the smallest oil reserves in the world?** *(No, it has the eleventh largest. All nations other than those named have smaller reserves than the United States.)* **learning modality: logical/mathematical**

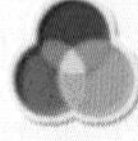

Integrating Technology

Ask students: **Do you know of any other examples where sound waves are used to locate objects or materials?** *(Students may know how sonar is used to map the ocean floor.)* **learning modality: verbal**

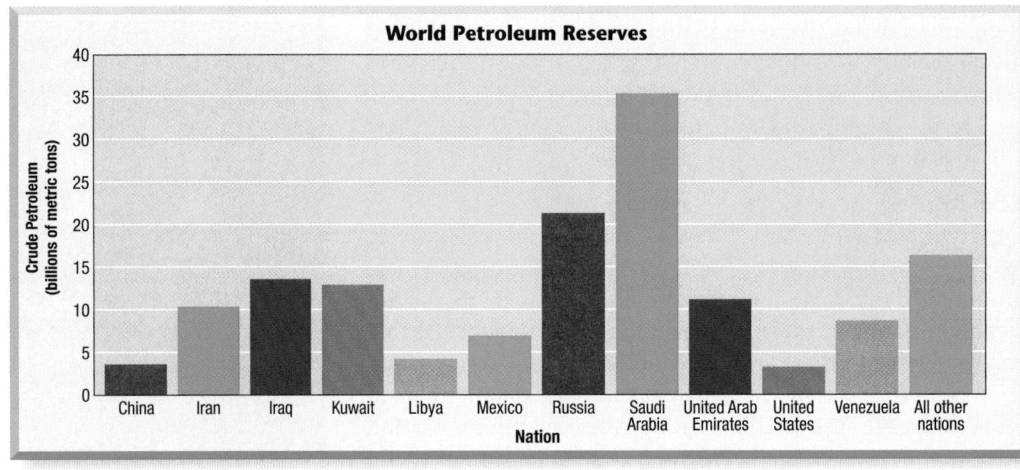

Figure 4 Known petroleum deposits, called reserves, are located in many parts of the world. *Interpreting Graphs Which two nations have the largest reserves?*

Oil

Oil is a thick, black, liquid fossil fuel. It formed from the remains of small animals, algae, and protists that lived in oceans and shallow inland seas hundreds of millions of years ago. **Petroleum** is another name for oil, from the Latin words *petra* (rock) and *oleum* (oil). Most oil deposits are located underground in tiny holes in sandstone or limestone. The oil fills the holes somewhat like water trapped in the holes of a sponge.

Petroleum accounts for more than one third of the energy produced in the world. Fuel for most cars, airplanes, trains, and ships comes from petroleum. Many homes are heated by oil.

The United States consumes about one third of all the oil produced in the world. But only three percent of the world's supply is located in this country. The difference must be purchased from countries with large oil supplies.

Locating Oil Deposits Because it is usually located deep below the surface, finding oil is difficult. Scientists *INTEGRATING TECHNOLOGY* can use sound waves to test an area for oil without drilling. This technique relies on the fact that sound waves bounce off objects and return as echoes. Scientists send pulses of sound down into the rocks below ground. Then they measure how long it takes the echoes to return. The amount of time depends on whether the sound waves must travel through solid rock or liquid oils. This information can indicate the most likely places to find oil. However, only about one out of every six wells drilled produces a usable amount of oil.

Figure 5 An oil rig bobs up and down as it pumps oil from a Texas oil field.

504

Background

Facts and Figures In addition to refined petroleum, gasoline contains many different additives. These include antiknock compounds, metal deactivators and antioxidants, antirust and anti-icing agents, detergents, lubricants, and dyes.

For many years, tetraethyl lead was added to gasoline to improve its combustion characteristics. Lead reduces or eliminates "knocking" caused by premature ignition in high-compression engines and lubricates close-fitting engine parts where oil tends to wash away or burn off. However, because lead is highly toxic, the government phased out and finally banned the use of lead as a gasoline additive. As a result, the amount of lead in the atmosphere decreased by about 98 percent between 1970 and 1996.

Refining Oil When oil is first pumped out of the ground, it is called crude oil. Crude oil can be a runny or a thick liquid. In order to be made into useful products, crude oil must undergo a process called refining. A factory where crude oil is separated into fuels and other products by heating is called a **refinery.**

In addition to gasoline and heating oil, many products you use every day are made from crude oil. **Petrochemicals** are compounds that are made from oil. Petrochemicals are used in plastics, paints, medicines, and cosmetics.

☑ *Checkpoint* *How is petroleum used?*

Natural Gas

The third fossil fuel is natural gas, a mixture of methane and other gases. Natural gas forms from the same organisms as petroleum. Because it is less dense than oil, natural gas often rises above an oil deposit, forming a pocket of gas in the rock.

Pipelines transport the gas from its source to the places where it is used. If all the gas pipelines in the United States were connected, they would reach to the moon and back—twice! Natural gas can also be compressed into a liquid and stored in tanks as fuel for trucks and buses.

Natural gas has several advantages. It produces large amounts of energy, but lower levels of many air pollutants than coal or oil. It is also easy to transport once the network of pipelines is built. One disadvantage of natural gas is that it is highly flammable. A gas leak can cause a violent explosion and fire.

Gas companies help to prevent dangerous explosions from leaks. If you use natural gas in your home, you probably are familiar with the "gas" smell that alerts you whenever there is unburned gas in the air. You may be surprised to learn that natural gas actually has no odor at all. What causes the strong smell? The gas companies add a chemical with a distinct smell to the gas before it is piped to homes and businesses so that any leaks will be noticed.

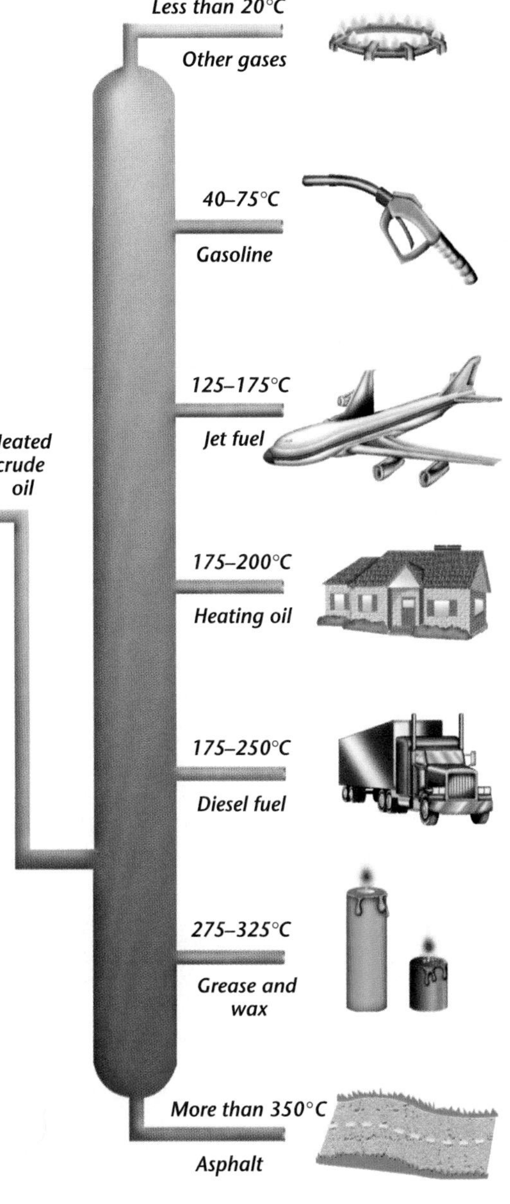

Figure 6 Crude oil is refined to make many different products. In the refining process, heat causes the different molecules in crude oil to separate. Different substances vaporize at specific temperatures.

Natural Gas

Building Inquiry Skills: Calculating

Materials *calculator*
Time 5 minutes

Point out the text statement "If all the gas pipelines in the United States were connected, they would reach to the moon and back—twice!" Have students use the moon's average distance from Earth *(384,392 km)* to calculate the total length of U.S. gas pipelines. *(384,392 × 4 = 1,537,568 km)* They can extend this activity by comparing this distance to another reference, such as the width of their state. **learning modality: logical/mathematical**

Real-Life Learning

Companies that supply natural gas usually publish materials to teach customers about safety issues when dealing with gas appliances and gas lines. Some companies also can provide a representative to speak to your class about gas safety. Contact your local gas company to request materials and, if available, a speaker. **learning modality: verbal**

Fuel Supply and Demand

Building Inquiry Skills: Inferring

Tell students that in 1973, 36 percent of all the oil used in the United States was imported from other countries; in 1993, 51 percent of the oil used was imported. Ask: **What do those percentages tell you?** *(The United States became more dependent on imported oil.)* **Why do you think that happened?** *(The country's oil consumption increased, but production did not increase enough to keep up with the demand.)* **learning modality: logical/mathematical**

Media and Technology

Concept Videotape Library
Grade 6, Tape 4 "Power for the People"

Answers to Self-Assessment

Caption Question

Figure 4 Saudi Arabia and Russia

☑ *Checkpoint*

Petroleum is refined to make fuels and other products, including plastics.

Ongoing Assessment

Skills Check Have each student create a simple, three-column table listing the advantages and disadvantages of each type of fossil fuel.

Students can save their tables in their portfolios.

3 Assess

Section 1 Review Answers

1. Fuels contain stored chemical energy. When they are burned, the chemical energy is converted into other forms of energy.
2. *Coal* is a solid fossil fuel formed from decaying plant matter that was changed by heat and pressure. *Oil* is a thick, black liquid fossil fuel formed from the remains of small animals, algae, and protists. *Natural gas* is a mixture of methane and other gases formed from the same organisms as oil.
3. Because fossil fuels take hundreds of millions of years to form, they can be easily used up faster than they can be replaced.
4. *Advantages:* produces lower levels of many air pollutants; is easy to transport. *Disadvantage:* is highly flammable, so a leak can cause a violent explosion and fire.
5. *Sample answers:* Not all oil deposits have been located; countries may not want to reveal the size of their oil reserves.

CHAPTER PROJECT

Check Your Progress

Point out that the school's meters and gauges show the amount of fuel used for the entire building. To estimate the amount used in each area, students can count the number of rooms in the school (including the cafeteria, gym, auditorium, and so forth) and divide the total amount of fuel used by the number of rooms. Students should suggest whether energy use in this area is above or below average.

Performance Assessment

Writing Have each student explain why it is important for the United States to become less dependent on fossil fuels.

Figure 7 During the gasoline crisis, people frequently had to wait in long lines to buy gas. This shortage reminded Americans of their dependence on oil imported from other nations.
Relating Cause and Effect What caused the gasoline shortage?

Fuel Supply and Demand

Fossil fuels have become essential to modern life. **But remember that fossil fuels take hundreds of millions of years to form. For this reason, fossil fuels are considered a nonrenewable resource.** Anything in the environment that is used by people is a natural resource. **Nonrenewable resources** are natural resources that are not replaced as they are used. For example, Earth's known oil reserves took 500 million years to form. One fourth of this oil has already been used. If fossil fuels continue to be used more rapidly than they are formed, the reserves will eventually be used up.

Many of the nations that consume large amounts of fuel have very limited reserves of their own. They have to buy oil, natural gas, and coal from the regions that have large supplies. The uneven distribution of fossil fuel reserves has often been a cause of political problems in the world. For example, in the 1970s, a group of oil-exporting nations decided to reduce their oil exports to the United States. As the supply of gasoline fell, prices rose very rapidly. People sometimes waited in line for hours to buy gasoline.

New sources of energy are needed to replace the decreasing fossil fuel reserves. The rest of this chapter will describe some other sources of energy, as well as ways to make current fuel resources last longer.

Section 1 Review

1. Explain how fuels provide energy.
2. Name the three fossil fuels and briefly describe each.
3. Explain why fossil fuels are classified as nonrenewable resources.
4. List two advantages and one disadvantage of natural gas as an energy source.
5. **Thinking Critically Applying Concepts** Why is it impossible to know exactly how large the world's oil reserves are?

CHAPTER PROJECT

Check Your Progress

With your team, observe your selected area of the school. Determine which types of energy use take place in this area: heating, cooling, lighting, mechanical devices, electronic equipment, or moving vehicles. Record the specific types and amounts of energy use in a data table. To find the amounts, you will need to collect data from electric meters or fuel gauges. (*Hint:* Observe your area at several different times of the day, since the pattern of energy use may vary.)

506

Program Resources

- **Unit 5 Resources** 16-1 Review and Reinforce; 16-1 Enrich

Answers to Self-Assessment

Caption Question

Figure 7 A group of oil-exporting nations reduced oil exports to the United States.

Renewable Sources of Energy

DISCOVER ACTIVITY

Can You Capture Solar Energy?

1. Pour 250 milliliters of water into each of two sealable, clear plastic bags.
2. Measure and record the water temperature in each bag. Seal the bags.
3. Put one bag in a dark or shady place. Put the other bag in a place where it will receive direct sunlight.
4. Predict what the temperature of the water in each bag will be after 30 minutes.
5. Measure and record the ending temperatures.

Think It Over

Developing Hypotheses How did the water temperature in each bag change? What could account for these results?

GUIDE FOR READING

- How does the sun provide energy?
- What are some renewable sources of energy?

Reading Tip **Before you read, preview the headings in this section. Predict some sources of energy that are renewable.**

As the sun rises over the rim of the canyon where your family is camping, you feel its warmth on your face. The night's chill disappears quickly. A breeze stirs, carrying with it the smell of the campfire. Maybe you'll take a morning dip in the warm water of a nearby hot spring.

This relaxing scene is far from the city, with its bustling cars and trucks, factories and power plants. But there are energy resources all around you here, too. The sun warms the air, the wind blows, and heat from inside Earth warms the waters of the spring. These sources of energy are all **renewable resources**—that is, they are constantly being supplied. Renewable resources, such as sunlight, wind, and trees, are naturally replaced in a short period of time. As you read about each source of renewable energy, think about how it could help meet people's energy needs.

Energy From the Sun

The warmth you feel on a sunny day is **solar energy,** energy from the sun. **The sun constantly gives off energy in the form of light and heat.** Solar energy is the source, directly or indirectly, of most other renewable energy resources. In one day, Earth receives enough solar energy to meet the energy needs of the entire world for 40 years. Solar energy does not cause pollution, and it will not run out for billions of years.

So why hasn't solar energy replaced fossil fuels? One reason is that solar energy is available only when the sun is shining. A backup energy source must be available on cloudy days and at night. Another problem is that

READING STRATEGIES

Reading Tip Based on the headings, students should predict that the sun, wind, flowing water, biomass, and hydrogen are renewable energy sources.

Study and Comprehension Have each student set up a table for taking notes on the advantages and disadvantages of each type of renewable energy source as they read this section.

Program Resources

- **Unit 5 Resources** 16-2 Lesson Plan; 16-2 Section Summary
- **Guided Reading and Study Workbook** Section 16-2

Renewable Sources of Energy

Objectives

After completing the lesson, students will be able to

- explain how the sun provides energy and describe ways to collect this energy;
- identify and describe various sources of renewable energy.

Key Terms renewable resource, solar energy, passive solar system, active solar system, hydroelectric power, biomass fuel, gasohol, geothermal energy

1 Engage/Explore

Activating Prior Knowledge

Ask: **Besides coal, oil, and natural gas, what other sources of energy do you know of?** *(Answers will depend on students' prior learning. They may mention the renewable resources covered in this section and "atomic" [nuclear] energy, covered in the next section.)*

DISCOVER

Skills Focus developing hypotheses

Materials *500 mL water, 2 sealable clear plastic bags, 2 thermometers*

Time 10 minutes for setup; 5 minutes for follow-up

Tips Provide room-temperature water for Step 1. If your classroom does not have a sunny window, arrange to place bags in another location where there is direct sunlight.

Expected Outcome Specific temperatures will vary.

Think It Over The water temperature stayed the same in the dark/shaded bag, while the water temperature increased in the bag placed in sunlight. The water in that bag absorbed heat energy from the sun.

2 Facilitate

Solar Technologies

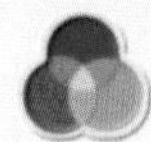

Integrating Technology

Materials *several examples of solar cells and small solar-powered motors (available from home-electronics stores)* **ACTIVITY**

Let students examine the solar cells and motors. Encourage them to use the cells and motors to make simple devices that will operate when placed in sunlight—for example, a solar-powered toy boat or car. Ask: **What energy conversions are taking place?** *(Solar energy to electrical energy to mechanical energy)* **learning modality: kinesthetic**

Figure 8 Aimed at the sun, these mirrors provide power to an electric plant in New South Wales, Australia. *Inferring How does the shape of these mirrors make them more effective?*

although Earth receives a lot of energy from the sun every day, this energy is very spread out. To obtain enough power, it is necessary to collect this energy from a huge area.

Solar Technologies

INTEGRATING TECHNOLOGY Improving technologies to capture and use solar energy will help meet future energy needs. Some current solar technologies are described below.

Solar Plants One way to capture the sun's energy involves using giant mirrors. In a solar plant, rows of mirrors focus the sun's rays to heat a tank of water. The water boils, making steam that can be used to generate electricity.

Solar Cells Solar energy can be converted directly into electricity in a solar cell. A solar cell consists of a "sandwich" of very thin layers of the element silicon and other materials. The upper and lower parts of the sandwich have a negative and a positive terminal, like a battery. When light hits the cell, electrons move across the layers, producing an electric current.

The amount of electricity produced by solar cells depends on the area of the cell and the amount of light available. Solar cells are used to power calculators, lights, telephones, and other small devices. However, it would take more than 5,000 solar cells the size of your palm to produce enough electricity for a typical American home. Building solar cells on a large scale is very expensive. As a result, solar cells are used mostly in areas where fossil fuels are difficult to transport.

☑ *Checkpoint What are solar cells made of and how do they work?*

Background

Integrating Science The solar cells described in the student text are made of crystalline silicon and are also known as photovoltaic (PV) cells. Although suitable for use in calculators and watches, these cells are not very efficient at converting solar energy to electricity and are expensive to produce. A new kind of solar cell made from a thin film of semiconductor material may prove to be more efficient and less expensive.

Media and Technology

Transparencies "Exploring a Solar Home," Transparency 64

Concept Videotape Library Grade 6, Tape 4 "Wired to the Sun"

Solar Heating Systems Solar energy can be used to heat buildings. As shown in *Exploring a Solar House,* there are two types of solar heating systems: passive and active.

A **passive solar system** converts sunlight into thermal energy without using pumps or fans. If you have ever stepped into a car on a sunny day, you have experienced passive solar heating. Solar energy passes through the car's windows as light. The sun's rays heat the seats and other parts of the car, which then transfer heat to the air. The heated air is trapped inside, so the car gets warmer. The same principle can be used to heat a home.

An **active solar system** captures the sun's energy, then uses fans and pumps to distribute the heat. Light strikes the black metal surface of a solar collector. There, it is converted to thermal energy. Water is pumped through pipes in the solar collector to absorb the thermal energy. The heated water flows to a storage tank. Pumps and fans distribute the heat throughout the building.

EXPLORING a Solar House

This solar house uses passive and active heating systems and solar cells to convert solar energy into heat and electricity.

EXPLORING a Solar House

After students have reviewed the figure, ask: **Which of these solar systems do you have in your own home?** *(Most students will probably identify the two passive systems, passive interior heating and window design.)* If any students say that their homes are equipped with active solar systems, invite those students to describe the devices and their operation to the rest of the class. **learning modality: verbal**

Real-Life Learning

Materials *2 thermometers, large glass jar*
Time 10 minutes

Give students an opportunity to directly observe passive solar heating. On a sunny day, take the class outdoors to a place that receives direct sunlight, but away from pavement. Have students read the two thermometers and note the temperatures. Then put one thermometer in an upside-down glass jar and the other thermometer in open air. Have students compare the temperatures after several minutes. Ask: **Why is the temperature higher inside the glass jar?** *(The glass allows light to pass into the jar but traps heat inside the jar.)* **learning modality: logical/mathematical**

Program Resources

◆ **Laboratory Manual** 16, "Solar Heating"

Answers to Self-Assessment

Caption Question

Figure 8 The curved shape concentrates the sun's rays by reflecting them toward the center of the dish.

✓ Checkpoint

They are made of layers of silicon and other materials. When light hits the cell, electrons move across the layers, producing an electric current.

Ongoing Assessment

Oral Presentation Call on students at random to each describe one example of technology that captures solar energy for use by people.

Other Sources of Renewable Energy

Using the Visuals: Figure 9

Tell students that people have used windmills for over a thousand years. Display a photograph of a large "old-fashioned" windmill, and have students compare it with the modern windmills shown in the photograph. Ask: **How are modern windmills different from old windmills?** *(Modern windmills are more streamlined, do not have a building as the base, have fewer blades, and the blades are metal instead of wood.)* **Why do you think wind farms use streamlined windmills like these instead of the old-fashioned type?** *(Modern windmills are stronger and also more sensitive to light winds.)* Encourage interested students to find out about the history and technology of windmills. **learning modality: visual**

Building Inquiry Skills: Predicting

Ask students: **Would burning wood or plant wastes in an open fire be a good way to make use of biomass fuels? Why, or why not?** *(No; open burning allows heat to escape and releases pollutants into the atmosphere.)* **How do you think biomass materials must be burned in order to be efficient and nonpolluting fuels?** *(In some sort of closed incinerator that captures harmful waste products and captures all or most of the heat)* **What else would have to be part of the equipment to generate electricity with the heat of the burning fuel?** *(Water to make steam to drive a turbine)* **learning modality: logical/mathematical**

Including All Students

For students who need help with language skills, write the two words on the board, draw boxes around *gas* in *gasoline* and *ohol* in *alcohol,* draw a plus sign between the two boxes, and ask: **What word do these two parts make when you put them together?** *(gasohol)* **limited English proficiency**

Figure 9 This wind farm in the Mojave Desert is one of many in the state of California. *Making Generalizations What are some advantages of wind power?*

Other Sources of Renewable Energy

The sun is one source of renewable energy. Other renewable energy sources include wind, water, biomass materials, Earth's interior, and hydrogen.

Wind Wind can be used to turn a turbine and generate electricity. Wind power plants or "wind farms" consist of many windmills. Together, the windmills generate large amounts of electric power.

Although wind now provides less than one percent of the world's electricity, it is the fastest-growing energy source. Wind energy is free and does not cause pollution.

Wind energy is not ideal for all locations. Few places have winds that blow steadily enough to be a worthwhile energy source. But as fossil fuels become more scarce and expensive, wind generators will become more important.

Flowing Water As water flows over the land into lakes and oceans, it provides another source of energy. Flowing water can turn a turbine and generate electricity in the same way as steam or wind. A dam across a river blocks the flow of water, creating an artificial lake called a reservoir. Water flows through tunnels at the bottom of the dam. As the water moves through the tunnels, it turns turbines connected to a generator.

Hydroelectric power is electricity produced by flowing water. This type of power is the most widely used source of renewable energy in the world today. Hydroelectric power is inexpensive and does not create air pollution. But hydroelectric power does have drawbacks. In the United States, for example, most suitable rivers have already been dammed. And dams can have negative effects on the environment.

Background

Facts and Figures Besides reducing our dependence on fossil fuels, using biomass fuels helps reduce our waste-disposal problems. In one case in California, the Mesquite Lake Resource Recovery Project, an electric power plant burns cow manure to produce enough electricity for thousands of homes. The manure would otherwise pose a disposal problem because of its high salt content and the presence of seeds that make it undesirable for use as fertilizer.

Some problems are associated with the use of biomass materials. Growing the crops often used as biomass fuels takes up land that could be used for growing other crops. And removing all the stalks, leaves, and roots from a field for use as biomass fuel means that these crop wastes will not decay and enrich the soil. Unprotected soil is also more susceptible to erosion.

Biomass Fuels Wood is one of a group of fuels, called **biomass fuels,** which are fuels made from things that were once alive. Other biomass fuels include leaves, food wastes, and even manure. Burning breaks down complicated molecules in these fuels, releasing energy.

Biomass materials also can be converted into other fuels. For example, corn, sugar cane, and other crops can be used to make alcohol. Adding the alcohol to gasoline forms a mixture called gasohol. Gasohol can be used as fuel for cars and trucks. When bacteria decompose waste materials, they convert the waste into methane gas. The methane produced in some landfills is used for heating buildings.

Biomass fuels are not widely used today. Producing alcohol and methane in large quantities can be expensive. And although wood is renewable, it takes time for new trees to grow. But in the future, biomass fuels may play a larger role in meeting energy needs.

☑ *Checkpoint* *What are the advantages and disadvantages of biomass fuels?*

Geothermal Energy In certain regions, such as Iceland and New Zealand, magma heats underground water to the boiling point. The hot water and steam are valuable sources of **geothermal energy.** In Reykjavik, Iceland, 90 percent of homes are heated by water warmed underground in this way. Geothermal energy can also be used to generate electricity.

Geothermal energy is an unlimited source of cheap energy. Unfortunately, there are only a few places where magma comes close to Earth's surface. Elsewhere, very expensive, deep wells must be drilled to tap this energy. Although it can be costly, geothermal energy is likely to play a part in meeting energy needs in the future.

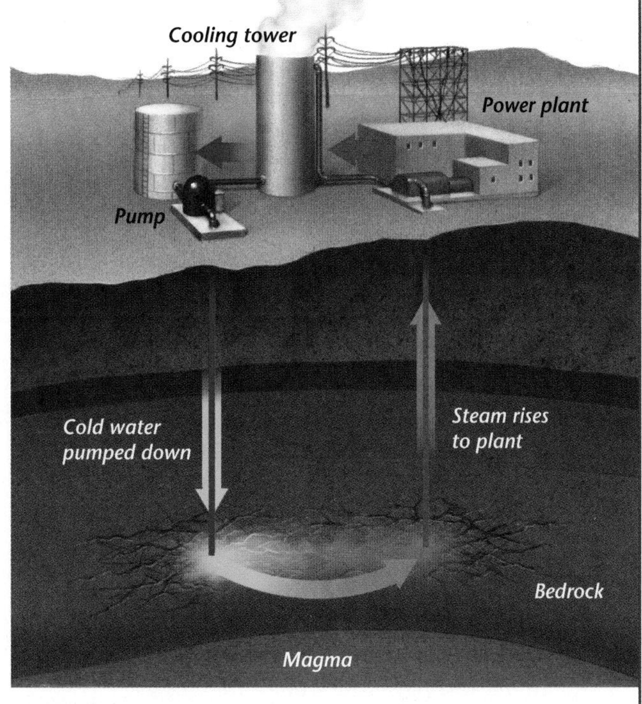

Figure 10 A geothermal power plant uses heat from Earth's interior as an energy source. Cold water is piped deep into the ground, where it is heated by melted rock, called magma. The resulting steam can be used for heat or to generate electricity.

Using the Visuals: Figure 10

Have students work in pairs to create cycle diagrams of the process shown in the figure. Ask: **What do you think the cooling tower is used for?** *(After the steam has been used to turn turbines in the power plant, it is cooled to turn it into liquid water.)* **learning modality: visual**

Including All Students

Support students who need more help in comprehending the term *geothermal.* Write the term *geothermal* on the board and draw a vertical line between the two word parts. Invite volunteers to look up the meaning of each part in a dictionary and read the meanings aloud (*geo,* "Earth"; *thermal,* "heat"). Ask: **What does "geothermal" mean?** *(Earth-heat, or heat inside Earth)* **limited English proficiency**

Hydrogen Power

Demonstration

Materials *electrolysis apparatus, matches*
Time 10 minutes

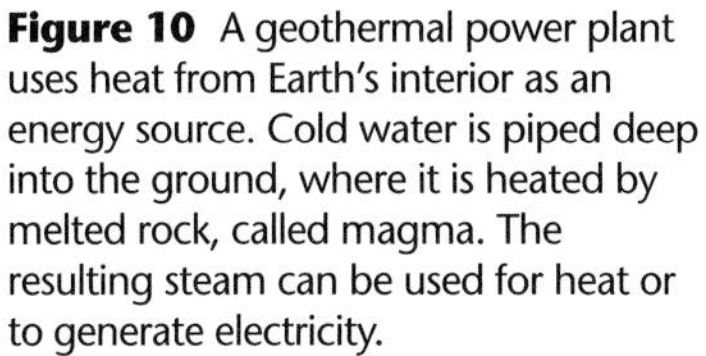

Use an electrolysis apparatus to show students that hydrogen can be obtained by passing an electric current through water. (If you are not familiar with the electrolysis setup and procedure, ask a physical science teacher to show you or to do the demonstration for the class.) At the end of the demonstration, emphasize that more energy is used in producing the electricity needed for electrolysis than is provided by the hydrogen. **learning modality: visual**

Media and Technology

Transparencies "A Geothermal Power Plant," Transparency 65

Answers to Self-Assessment

Caption Question

Figure 9 The wind itself doesn't cost anything and is renewable; wind power does not cause pollution.

☑ *Checkpoint*

Biomass fuels are renewable and can be used to make other fuels. Using biomass materials to produce alcohol and methane can be expensive, and though they are renewable, it takes time for them to grow.

Ongoing Assessment

Writing Have each student briefly describe the two different ways in which biomass materials can be used as fuels.

Students can save their work in their portfolios.

3 Assess

Section 2 Review Answers

1. Energy from the sun
2. Two advantages of solar energy are that it does not cause pollution and that it is renewable. One disadvantage is that it is available only during the day or when the sun is shining. Another problem is that solar energy is spread out over Earth's surface, so energy for power must be collected over a wide area.
3. Active solar systems convert solar energy to thermal energy and then use fans and pumps to distribute the heat. Passive solar systems convert solar energy to thermal energy but do not distribute it.
4. *Any three:* wood, leaves, food wastes, manure, sugar-cane wastes, corn, alcohol, methane
5. Geothermal energy is available only where magma is close to Earth's surface.
6. Accept a variety of responses. Students should support their answers with reasons that take into account the geographic features of their area.

CHAPTER PROJECT

Check Your Progress

Check each group's data table to make sure students are collecting and recording data. Provide some copies of the school's fuel and utility bills so students can determine the amount and actual cost of each type of energy used. If a group is studying energy used for transportation, encourage them to survey other students about transportation to school. They also may need to contact your district's central office or the private company that owns and operates the school buses for information.

Performance Assessment

Skills Check Have each student create a compare/contrast table that includes at least five of the renewable energy sources discussed in this section and identifies one advantage and one disadvantage of each source.

Students can save their tables in their portfolios.

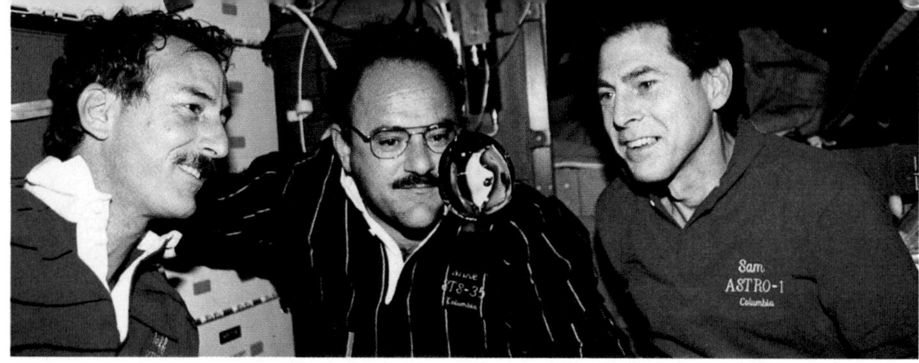

Figure 11 The object fascinating these three astronauts is a bubble of water—the harmless by-product of the hydrogen fuel cells used on the space shuttle.

Hydrogen Power

Now that you have read about so many energy sources, consider a fuel with this description: It burns cleanly, forming only water as a by-product. It creates no smoke, smog, or acid rain. It can be handled and transported through pipelines, much like natural gas. This fuel exists on Earth in large supply.

This ideal-sounding fuel is real—it's hydrogen. However, there is an obstacle. Almost all the hydrogen on Earth is combined with oxygen in the form of water. Pure hydrogen can be obtained by passing an electric current through water. But it takes more energy to obtain the hydrogen than is produced by burning it again.

Scientists aren't ruling out hydrogen as a good fuel for the future. At present, hydroelectric plants decrease their activity when the demand for electricity is low. Instead, they could run at full power all the time, using the excess electricity to produce hydrogen. Similarly, solar power plants often generate more electricity than is needed during the day. This extra electricity could be used to produce hydrogen. If a way can be found to produce hydrogen cheaply, it could someday be an important source of energy.

Section 2 Review

1. What is solar energy?
2. What are some advantages and disadvantages of solar energy?
3. How are active and passive solar heating systems different?
4. List three examples of biomass fuels.
5. What limits the use of geothermal energy?
6. **Thinking Critically Predicting** Which of the renewable sources of energy do you think is most likely to be used in your community in 100 years? Give reasons to support your answer.

CHAPTER PROJECT

Check Your Progress

Continue to collect data on how much energy is used in your group's area of the school. Begin to brainstorm ideas for reducing energy usage in this area. For example, is there a way to use some electrical devices for shorter periods of time? (*Hint:* Interviewing some adults who are responsible for the operation of the school building may give you some good ideas. Be sure to check with your teacher before interviewing anyone.)

Program Resources

- **Unit 5 Resources** 16-2 Review and Reinforce; 16-2 Enrich

How It Works

In the future, will you cook your meals with sunshine instead of electricity? That's certainly a possibility. In this lab, you'll investigate how solar energy can be used to cook food.

Real-World Lab

Problem

What is the best shape for a solar cooker?

Skills Focus

predicting, designing experiments, forming operational definitions

Suggested Materials

scissors	glue	3 thermometers
3 dowels	tape	marshmallows
3 sheets of aluminum foil		clock or watch
3 sheets of oaktag paper		

Procedure

Part 1 Capturing Solar Energy

1. Read over the entire lab. Then predict which shape will produce the largest temperature increase when placed in the sun.
2. Glue a sheet of aluminum foil, shiny side up, to each sheet of oaktag paper. Before the glue dries, gently smooth out any wrinkles in the foil.
3. Bend one sheet into a V shape. Bend another sheet into a U shape. Leave the last sheet flat.
4. Place the aluminum sheets in direct sunlight, using wood blocks or books to hold the U- and V-shapes in position.
5. Tape a dowel to each thermometer. Record the starting temperature on each thermometer.
6. Use the dowels to hold the thermometer bulbs in the center of the aluminum shapes. After 15 minutes, record the final temperature on each thermometer.

Part 2 Designing a Solar Cooker

7. Use the results from Step 6 to design a solar cooker that can toast a marshmallow. Prepare a written description of your plan for your teacher's approval. Include an operational definition of a "well-toasted" marshmallow.
8. After your teacher has approved your plan, test your design by placing a marshmallow on a wooden dowel. Record the time it takes to toast the marshmallow.

Analyze and Conclude

1. What was the role of the aluminum foil in this investigation? What other materials could you have used instead? Explain.
2. Which of the three shapes—V, U, or flat—produced the largest increase in temperature? Propose an explanation for this result.
3. What other variables might have affected your results? Explain.
4. **Apply** What are some possible advantages of a solar cooker based on this design? What are some possible disadvantages?

More to Explore

Try adapting your design to heat water. Show your new design to your teacher before trying it.

Extending the Inquiry

More to Explore Have students use a small volume of water. Encourage them to consider the kind of material to use for the water container.

Media and Technology

 **Lab Activity Videotapes**
Grade 6, Tape 4

Program Resources

- **Unit 5 Resources** Chapter 16 Real-World Lab

Safety

Students should wear safety goggles and use caution in handling glass thermometers. Review the safety guidelines in Appendix A.

Real-World Lab

How It Works

Cooking With Sunshine

Preparing for Inquiry

Key Concept A solar cooker that focuses the sun's rays in its center works best.

Skills Objectives Students will be able to

- predict which of three designs will produce the greatest temperature increase in a solar cooker;
- design an experiment to test how the shape of a solar cooker affects how it functions;
- form an operational definition of a "well-toasted" marshmallow.

Time 40 minutes

Advance Planning Identify a sunny area for the solar cookers.

Guiding Inquiry

Introducing the Procedure

- Have students work in groups of three.
- If needed, review the meaning of "operational definition."

Troubleshooting the Experiment

- In Step 3, make sure students have the foil side on the inside of the U or V.
- In Step 6, make sure students hold the thermometers with their bulbs at the same distance from the foil.

Expected Outcome

Specific temperatures will vary, but the U-shaped cooker should produce the largest temperature increase and the flat cooker the smallest increase.

Analyze and Conclude

1. The foil reflected the sun's rays. Other reflective materials such as mirrors or shiny metal could be used.
2. The U shape; it reflects the sun's rays into the center of the cooker.
3. Variables include time of day, distance between the thermometer bulbs and the cookers' surface, and air movement.
4. *Advantages:* simple design, ease of use, inexpensive, no polluting fumes. *Disadvantages:* cannot be used on a cloudy day or at night; slow; not efficient for cooking large items.

Science and Society

Hydroelectric Dams: Are They All Here to Stay?

Purpose

Evaluate the benefits and costs of removing hydroelectric dams, and recommend removing, adapting, or relicensing a dam.

Role-Play

Time 40 minutes

- After students have read the feature, ask: **Why should people try to protect fish species?** *(Accept a variety of reasons, including the economic value of commercial fishing.)* **Why are hydroelectric dams an important source of energy?** *(They reduce use of fossil fuels, produce electricity at low cost, and don't cause pollution.)*
- Point out that there are *three* possible recommendations: relicense the dam, remove it, or find ways to enable fish to bypass it. Let students discuss the issue freely.
- Divide the class into small groups, with each group member representing a different viewpoint—for example, the company that owns the dam, local industries that rely on the electricity produced by the dam, fisheries, ecologists, and citizens. Provide time for the groups to discuss the options.

Extend Suggest that students research the costs of electricity produced by hydroelectric dams and by burning fossil fuels. They could also investigate the effectiveness of fish ladders.

You Decide

- Students' answers to Identify the Problem and Analyze the Options should use the points in the text.
- In response to Find a Solution, students may rely on issues raised in their discussions or present new ideas. Each student should give a well-reasoned rationale for his or her recommendation.

Science and Society

Hydroelectric Dams: Are They All Here to Stay?

There are hundreds of hydroelectric dams on United States rivers. These dams provide electricity for millions of people. Hydroelectric dams provide clean, inexpensive, and renewable energy. They are a good source of power.

Recently, however, people have learned that dams can have negative effects on river ecosystems. Some people have even suggested removing certain dams. But is this wise? When do the benefits of dams outweigh the problems?

The Issues

How Do Dams Affect the Environment? Because dams change water depth and flow, they can alter the temperature of a river. The water may become too cold or too warm for fish that normally live there. A change in temperature can also reduce the number of algae in a river. This affects other organisms in the river food web.

Some species of fish, such as salmon, herring, and menhaden, hatch in rivers but then travel to the ocean. To breed, they must return to the river. Dams can block the movement of these fish populations. For example, the Columbia River Basin, which has more than 50 dams, once contained more than 10 million salmon. Today it is home to only 2 million salmon.

What Are the Effects of Removing Dams? Some people say that the only way to restore ecosystems is to remove dams. However, these dams supply a small but important part of the nation's electricity. Removing them could force the United States to use more nonrenewable fossil fuels. Fossil fuels also produce more pollution than hydroelectric plants.

The reservoirs behind hydroelectric dams supply water for irrigation and drinking. These supplies would be difficult to replace. In addition, a series of dams on a river can reduce flooding downstream during heavy rains.

What Can People Do? Removing dams might restore some river ecosystems. For example, Edwards Dam on the Kennebec River in Maine was removed in 1999 to allow several threatened fish species to spawn. Edwards Dam provided only a small percent of Maine's electric power. This small amount was easier to replace than the power provided by a much larger dam.

There are other ways to protect migrating fish. Fish ladders, for example, are step-like waterways that help fish pass over dams. Fish can even be carried around dams in trucks. Still, these methods are costly and not always successful.

The government issues licenses for hydroelectric dams. In considering license renewals, officials examine environmental impact as well as energy production.

You Decide

1. Identify the Problem
In your own words, explain some of the major issues surrounding hydroelectric dams.

2. Analyze the Options
Examine the pros and cons of removing dams. What are the benefits? What are the costs? Who will be affected by the change?

3. Find a Solution
The license of a nearby dam is up for review. The dam provides electricity, but also blocks the migration of fish. What do you recommend? Explain.

Background

History of Science In November 1997, the Federal Energy Regulatory Commission for the first time refused to renew the license for a hydroelectric dam—the Edwards Dam on the Kennebec River in Maine. The dam produced only a very small amount of electricity, but prevented salmon and other anadromous fish from spawning in the river.

The owners of hydroelectric dams upstream on the Kennebec contributed millions of dollars toward the costs of removing the dam and restoring 17 miles of spawning grounds in exchange for having their deadlines extended to install fish ladders on the upstream dams.

SECTION 3 Nuclear Energy

DISCOVER ACTIVITY

Why Do They Fall?

1. Line up 15 dominoes to form a triangle, as shown.
2. Knock over the first domino so that it falls against the second row of dominoes. Observe the results.
3. Set up the dominoes again, but then remove the dominoes in the third row from the lineup.
4. Knock over the first domino again. Observe what happens.

Think It Over

Inferring Suppose each domino produced a large amount of energy when it fell over. Why might it be helpful to remove the dominoes as you did in Step 3?

Wouldn't it be great if people could use the same method as the sun to produce energy? In a way, they can! The kind of reactions that power the sun involve the central cores of atoms. The central core of an atom that contains the protons and neutrons is called the **nucleus** (plural nuclei). The reactions that involve nuclei, called nuclear reactions, involve tremendous amounts of energy. Two types of nuclear reactions are fission and fusion.

GUIDE FOR READING

- What happens during fission and fusion reactions?
- How does a nuclear power plant produce electricity?

Reading Tip As you read, create a Venn diagram to compare and contrast nuclear fission and nuclear fusion.

Fission Reactions and Energy

Nuclear reactions convert matter into energy. In 1905, Albert Einstein developed a formula that described the relationship between energy and matter. You have probably seen this famous equation, $E = mc^2$. In the equation, the E represents energy and the m represents mass. The c, which represents the speed of light, is a very large number. This equation states that when matter is changed into energy, an enormous amount of energy is released.

Nuclear fission is the splitting of an atom's nucleus into two smaller nuclei. The fuel for the reaction is a large atom that has an unstable nucleus, such as uranium-235 (U-235). A neutron is shot at the U-235 atom at high speed. **When the neutron hits the U-235 nucleus, the nucleus splits apart into two smaller nuclei and two or more neutrons.** The total mass of all these particles is a bit less than the mass of the original nucleus. The small amount of mass that makes up the difference has been converted into energy—a lot of energy, as described by Einstein's equation.

Figure 12 Albert Einstein, shown here in 1930, described the relationship between energy and matter.

READING STRATEGIES

Reading Tip Review the format of a Venn diagram: two overlapping circles with likenesses noted in the overlap area and differences noted in the outer areas. Likenesses should include the use of atomic nuclei to produce energy; differences should include how the nuclei are affected, the amount of energy produced, fuel availability, safety, and pollution produced.

Program Resources

- **Unit 5 Resources** 16-3 Lesson Plan; 16-3 Section Summary
- **Guided Reading and Study Workbook** Section 16-3

SECTION 3 Nuclear Energy

Objectives

After completing the lesson, students will be able to

- describe nuclear fission and nuclear fusion reactions;
- explain how a nuclear power plant produces electricity.

Key Terms nucleus, nuclear fission, reactor vessel, fuel rods, control rods, meltdown, nuclear fusion

1 Engage/Explore

Activating Prior Knowledge

Ask several students to come to the board, draw what they think an atom looks like, and label its parts. Encourage the rest of the class to discuss the drawings and suggest corrections or additions. You can return to the diagrams later in the section.

DISCOVER

Skills Focus inferring
Materials *15 dominoes*
Time 10 minutes
Tips Make sure students place the dominoes with less than a domino-length space between rows.
Expected Outcome In Step 2, all 15 dominoes will topple as those in one row fall back against those in the next row. With the third row removed in Step 4, the last two rows will remain standing.
Think It Over Removing the third row would stop the production of energy after a certain point.

2 Facilitate

Fission Reactions and Energy

Building Inquiry Skills: Making Models

Materials *sheet of paper*
Time 5 minutes

Give each student a sheet of paper, and tell the class to think of the paper as the nucleus of a U-235 atom. To model the nucleus splitting into two smaller nuclei and three neutrons, have students tear the paper into five pieces—two larger and three smaller—and label the two larger pieces "smaller nucleus" and the three smaller pieces "neutron." Then have students tear a tiny piece off each "smaller nucleus" and set these tiny pieces aside. Explain that the tiny pieces represent the tiny amount of matter that is converted into energy in a fission reaction. **learning modality: kinesthetic**

Try This

Skills Focus making models
Materials *12 marbles*
Time 10 minutes

Tips Caution students not to walk around during this activity so they do not step on the marbles.
Expected Outcome The single marble represents a neutron being shot at an atom's nucleus. When it strikes the cluster, it scatters the marbles, similar to the breaking apart of the nucleus when it is struck by a neutron.
Extend After students have read about nuclear fusion on pages 518–519, challenge them to adapt this activity to model fusion. **learning modality: kinesthetic**

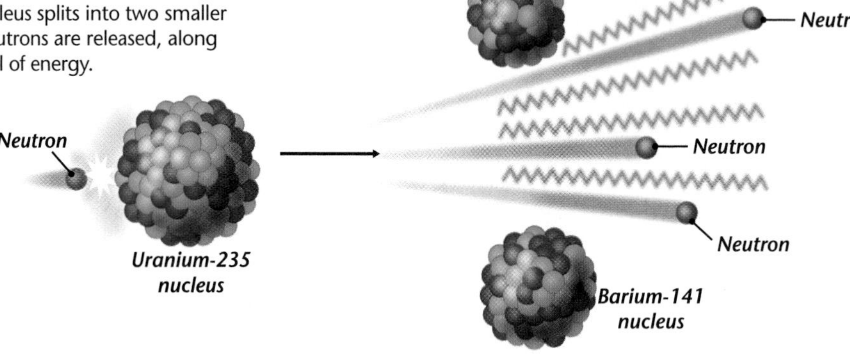

Figure 13 In a nuclear fission reaction, a neutron "bullet" strikes a U-235 nucleus. As a result, the nucleus splits into two smaller nuclei. More neutrons are released, along with a great deal of energy.

Meanwhile, the fission reaction has produced three more neutrons. If any of these neutrons strikes another nucleus, the fission reaction is repeated. More neutrons and more energy are released. If there are enough nuclei nearby, the process continues over and over in a chain reaction, just like a row of dominoes falling. In a nuclear chain reaction, the amount of energy released increases rapidly with each step in the chain.

What happens to all the energy released by these fission reactions? If a nuclear chain reaction is not controlled, the released energy causes a huge explosion. The explosion of an atomic bomb is an uncontrolled nuclear reaction. A few kilograms of matter explode with more force than several thousand tons of a nonnuclear explosive such as dynamite. However, if the chain reaction is controlled, the energy is released as heat, which can be used to generate electricity.

Shoot the Nucleus

In an open area of your classroom, make a model of a nuclear fission reaction. Place a handful of marbles on the floor in a tight cluster, so that they touch one another. Step back about a half-meter from the marbles. Shoot another marble at the cluster.

Making Models What does the marble you shot at the cluster represent? What effect did the marble have on the cluster? How is this similar to a nuclear fission reaction?

Nuclear Power Plants

Controlled nuclear fission reactions take place inside nuclear power plants. **In a nuclear power plant, the heat released from the reactions is used to change water into steam. As in other types of power plants, the steam then turns the blades of a turbine to generate electricity.** Look at the diagram of a nuclear power plant in Figure 14. In addition to the generator, it has two main parts: the reactor vessel and the heat exchanger.

Reactor Vessel The **reactor vessel** is the section of a nuclear reactor where nuclear fission occurs. The reactor contains rods of U-235, called **fuel rods.** When several fuel rods are placed close together, a series of fission reactions occurs. The reactions are controlled by placing **control rods** made of the metal cadmium between the fuel rods. The cadmium absorbs the neutrons

Background

Integrating Science Investigation of the Chernobyl accident revealed two basic causes. First, the reactor was not housed in a containment building and was extremely unstable at low power. This type of reactor is not used commercially in North America or Western Europe because nuclear engineers consider it too unsafe. Second, many of the plant's operators lacked scientific or technical expertise and made major errors when dealing with the initial problem.

The long-term health effects of the Chernobyl disaster are still being studied. Increases in birth defects and thyroid cancer in children have been documented. Other cancers are not expected to increase until 20 or more years after the accident.

released during the fission reactions. As the cadmium control rods are removed, the fission reactions speed up. If the reactor vessel starts to get too hot, the control rods are moved back in place to slow the chain reaction.

Heat Exchanger Heat is removed from the reactor vessel by water or another fluid that is pumped through the reactor. This fluid passes through a heat exchanger. There, the fluid boils water to produce steam, which runs the electrical generator. The steam is condensed again and pumped back to the heat exchanger.

☑ *Checkpoint* *How are fission reactions controlled?*

The Risks of Nuclear Fission

When it was first demonstrated, people thought that nuclear fission would provide an almost unlimited source of clean, safe energy. Today nuclear power plants generate much of the world's electricity—about 20 percent in the United States and more than 70 percent in France. But these plants have some problems.

In 1986, in Chernobyl, Ukraine, the reactor vessel in a nuclear power plant overheated. The fuel rods started to melt, a condition called a **meltdown.** The excess heat increased the steam pressure in the generator. A series of explosions blew parts of the roof off and injured or killed dozens of plant workers and firefighters. Radioactive materials escaped into the environment. Today, the soil in an area the size of Florida remains contaminated with radioactive waste. Atoms that are unstable and release

Calculating

ACTIVITY

A single pellet of U-235 the size of a breath mint can produce as much energy as 615 liters of fuel oil. An average home uses 5,000 liters of oil a year. How many U-235 pellets would be needed to supply the same amount of energy?

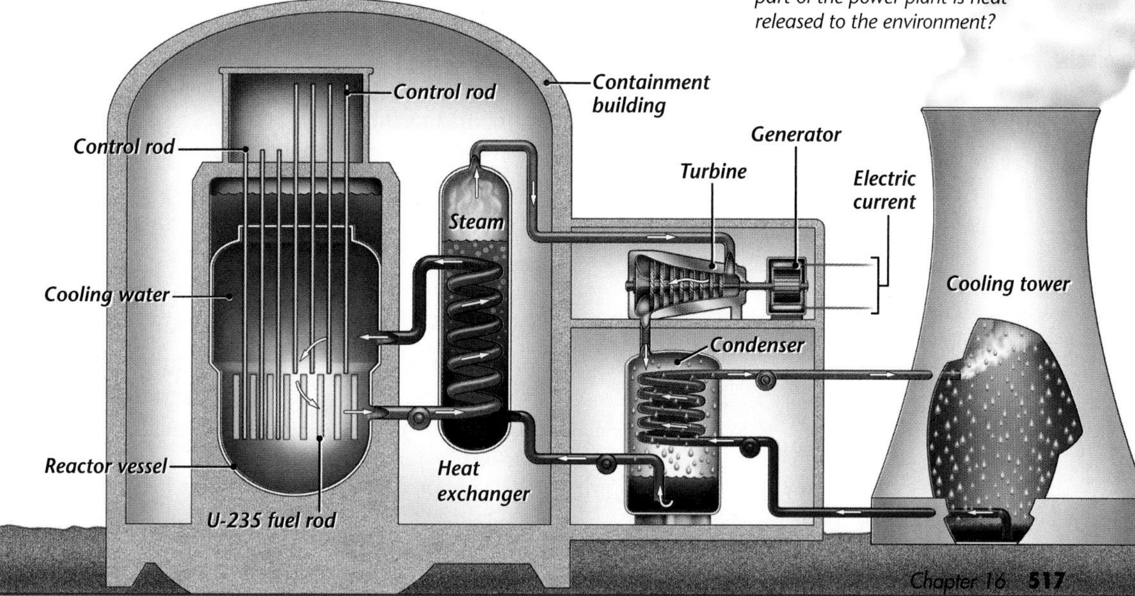

Figure 14 In a nuclear plant, uranium fuel undergoes fission, producing heat. The heat boils water, and the resulting steam drives the turbines that generate electricity. *Interpreting Diagrams From which part of the power plant is heat released to the environment?*

Nuclear Power Plants

Sharpen your Skills

Calculating

Materials *calculator (optional)*
Time 5 minutes
Tips If needed, help students determine how to calculate the answer (divide 5,000 by 615).
Expected Outcome About 8 (8.13) pellets would be needed.
Extend Suggest that each student estimate how many homes are in his or her neighborhood, then calculate how many pellets would be needed to supply energy to all those homes for a year.
learning modality: logical/ mathematical

The Risks of Nuclear Fission

Building Inquiry Skills: Inferring

Display a large world map, and let volunteers locate Chernobyl (51°N, 30°E, about 130 km north of Kiev). Tell students that the force of the 1986 explosion carried radioactive materials high into the atmosphere, where they spread across the Northern Hemisphere and then settled back to Earth in what is called "fallout." The heaviest fallout occurred in Ukraine, Belarus, Sweden, Norway, Denmark, France, and Switzerland. In addition, Finland, Lithuania, Germany, Poland, the Czech Republic, Slovakia, Austria, Hungary, Italy, and Great Britain suffered moderate fallout. Let students find all these countries on the map. Ask: **What does this tell you about the dangers of nuclear power plants?** *(An accident can affect a huge area.)* **learning modality: visual**

Media and Technology

Transparencies "Nuclear Fission," Transparency 66; "A Nuclear Power Plant," Transparency 67

Answers to Self-Assessment

☑ *Checkpoint*

Fission reactions are controlled by placing cadmium control rods between the fuel rods to absorb neutrons.

Caption Question

Figure 14 The cooling tower

Ongoing Assessment

Oral Presentation Call on students at random to each explain a step in the process of how a nuclear power plant converts nuclear energy to electricity.

The Risks of Nuclear Fission, continued

Real-Life Learning

Time 15 minutes

Point out the text statement about the difficulty of finding places to safely store radioactive wastes. Ask students if they would be for or against a nuclear-waste dump being created in their community. Then divide the class into small groups, and allow time for students to debate the issue from opposing viewpoints. As a follow-up, ask a volunteer from each group to summarize the group's discussion and the major points that were made both for and against the new nuclear-waste dump. **learning modality: verbal**

The Quest to Control Fusion

Inquiry Challenge

Materials *two colors of clay or other materials of students' choice*
Time 10 minutes

After students have read about nuclear fusion and examined Figure 16, challenge pairs of students to create a model demonstrating the fusion process. *(Sample model: Shape five small balls from two colors of clay. Stick three balls of one color together to represent a hydrogen-3 nucleus and two balls of another color together to represent a hydrogen-2 nucleus. Then push the two "nuclei" together, leaving four balls adhering to one another to represent a helium nucleus and the fifth ball free—minus a tiny piece—to represent the "neutron plus energy.")* **cooperative learning**

Figure 15 One problem with nuclear power is disposal of the used radioactive fuel rods. In this plant in France, the fuel rods are stored in a deep pool of water.

fast-moving particles and energy from their nuclei are said to be radioactive. Radioactive materials can be damaging to living things. Chernobyl and less serious accidents at other nuclear power plants have led to concerns about nuclear plant safety.

The danger of a meltdown is a serious concern. However, a meltdown can be avoided by careful planning. A more difficult problem is the disposal of radioactive wastes produced by power plants. Radioactive wastes remain dangerous for many thousands of years. Scientists must find a way to safely store these wastes for a long period of time. Finally, nuclear power has turned out to be a much more costly source of power than was originally expected. The safety features required make nuclear plants expensive.

☑ ***Checkpoint*** *What are three problems with using nuclear fission as an energy source?*

The Quest to Control Fusion

A second type of nuclear reaction is fusion. **Nuclear fusion** is the combining of two atomic nuclei to produce a single larger nucleus. **As shown in Figure 16, two kinds of hydrogen nuclei are forced together in a fusion reaction.** One kind (hydrogen-2) has one proton and one neutron, and the other kind (hydrogen-3) has one proton and two neutrons. The tremendous heat and pressure

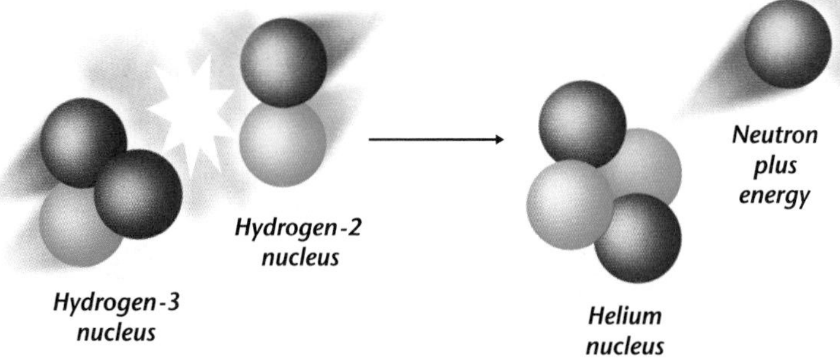

Figure 16 In a nuclear fusion reaction, two nuclei combine to form a single larger nucleus. *Interpreting Diagrams What is released during a fusion reaction?*

Background

Facts and Figures One misconception about nuclear reactors is that they can explode like nuclear bombs. The fuel in a nuclear reactor is not packed densely enough to produce a nuclear explosion. The explosions at Chernobyl were not nuclear explosions. Instead, they were caused by steam from the reactor leaking into the building that housed the reactor. The steam expanded so rapidly that it blew out parts of the building. As the steam escaped from the building, it carried radioactive materials from the reactor into the atmosphere.

cause them to combine and create a helium nucleus with two protons and two neutrons. This helium nucleus has slightly less mass than the total mass of the two hydrogen nuclei. The difference is converted to energy.

Nuclear fusion would have many advantages as an energy source. Fusion can produce much more energy per atom than nuclear fission. The fuel for a nuclear fusion reactor is also readily available. Water, which is plentiful in Earth's oceans, contains one of the kinds of hydrogen needed for fusion. Fusion should be safer and less polluting than nuclear fission. You can see why scientists are eager to find a way to build a nuclear fusion reactor!

Although some fusion bombs have been exploded, scientists have not yet been able to control a large-scale fusion reaction. The biggest problem is temperature. In the sun, nuclear fusion occurs at 15 million degrees Celsius. Such conditions are almost impossible to control on Earth. No material has been found that can serve as a reactor vessel under the high temperature and pressure of a nuclear fusion reaction. Extremely powerful magnetic fields can contain a fusion reaction. However, it takes more energy to generate these fields than the fusion reaction produces.

Although many more years of research are expected, some scientists believe that they will eventually be able to control fusion reactions. If they succeed, the quest for a clean, cheap energy source may be over at last.

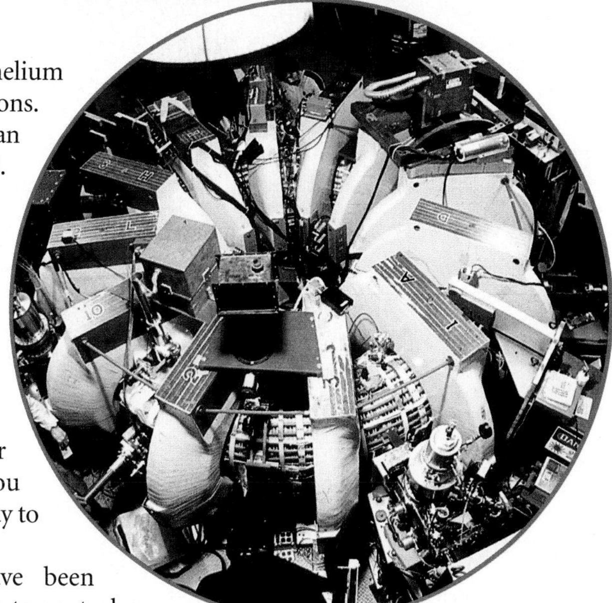

Figure 17 Researchers at Los Alamos National Laboratory in New Mexico are studying fusion as an energy source. This machine creates strong magnetic fields that allow fusion to occur for short periods of time.

Section 3 Review

1. Draw and label a simple diagram of a nuclear fission reaction. Include the following labels: U-235 nucleus, neutrons, smaller nuclei, and energy.
2. How can the energy released in a fission reaction be used to produce electricity?
3. Explain the purpose of control rods.
4. Give two reasons that people have not been able to use nuclear fusion as an energy source.
5. **Thinking Critically Classifying** Is nuclear fission a renewable or nonrenewable energy source? Is nuclear fusion renewable or nonrenewable? Explain.

CHAPTER PROJECT

Check Your Progress

By now you should begin preparing the written report of your findings about energy use in your group's area of the school. Your report should include the major ways energy is used in your chosen area. You should also include recommendations on how energy use might be reduced.

3 Assess

Section 3 Review Answers

1. Students' diagrams should show the U-235 nucleus being struck by one neutron, then splitting to form two smaller nuclei, three neutrons, and energy. (See Figure 16.)
2. The heat energy released by a fission reaction can be used to boil water, producing steam that turns the blades of a turbine to generate electricity.
3. Control rods absorb excess neutrons and control the fission reactions.
4. Fusion reactions cannot be controlled; more energy is needed to produce a fusion reaction than is produced by the reaction itself.
5. Nuclear fission is considered a nonrenewable resource because it depends on uranium, which is a nonrenewable element. Nuclear fusion is considered a renewable resource because Earth's water is abundant and is renewed in natural processes.

CHAPTER PROJECT

Check Your Progress

Encourage students to make their reports concise, focusing on the major points and, when appropriate, using visual displays (such as a neat copy of the data table). Also suggest that they explain how each recommendation would reduce energy use.

Program Resources

- **Unit 5 Resources** 16-3 Review and Reinforce; 16-3 Enrich

Media and Technology

Transparencies Transparencies "Nuclear Fusion," Transparency 68

Answers to Self-Assessment

Checkpoint

An accident can cause serious damage, injury, and death. Radioactive wastes are difficult to dispose of safely. Nuclear power is costly.

Caption Question

Figure 16 A neutron plus energy

Performance Assessment

Skills Check Have each student create a table that compares the advantages and disadvantages of nuclear fission and nuclear fusion as energy sources.

Portfolio Students can save their tables in their portfolios.

Skills Lab

Designing Experiments

Keeping Comfortable

NOTE: This lab is placed before its related section to allow enough time for students to conduct the test in Part 1, then design and carry out their own experiments.

Preparing for Inquiry

Key Concept Different materials lessen the transfer of heat to different degrees.

Skills Objectives Students will be able to

- measure temperature changes of water in a paper cup for use as a baseline;
- design an experiment to compare how well different materials maintain water temperature by slowing heat transfer.

Time 40 minutes

Advance Planning Prepare hot water and ice water ahead of time, and keep them in insulated containers. CAUTION: *Do not use water hot enough to cause scalding.*

If using probeware, refer to the *Probeware Lab Manual.*

Guiding Inquiry

Helping Design a Plan

- Ask: **What is the purpose of doing Part 1 with a paper cup first?** *(To determine a standard for comparing materials)*

Troubleshooting the Experiment

- Have students discuss the questions in Step 5 before writing their plans.
- Make sure students control all variables and record temperatures at regular intervals.

Expected Outcome

The most effective material for stopping heat transfer is plastic foam; the least effective is metal.

Analyze and Conclude

1. Temperatures will vary. Heat flowed from the hot water to the cold water, as shown by the temperature changes.
2. *Rooms:* cold water; *outdoor weather:* hot water; *walls:* paper cup
3. *Most effective:* plastic foam. *Least effective:* metal. Plastic foam kept the cold water close to its starting temperature for the longest time, while metal let the starting temperature increase the most.
4. Students should realize that other issues, such as the materials' strength, durability, and cost, must be considered.

Extending the Inquiry

Design an Experiment Students' experiments should be similar to those they developed in Part 2.

Program Resources

- **Unit 5 Resources** Chapter 16 Skills Lab
- **Probeware Lab Manual** Blackline masters

Safety

Students should use caution in handling the thermometers, hot water, and glass. Review the safety guidelines in Appendix A.

Skills Lab

Designing Experiments

Keeping Comfortable

Two ways to use less energy are to keep heat *out* of your home during hot weather, and *in* during cold weather. In this lab, you will investigate how to do this.

Problem

How well do different materials stop heat transfer?

Suggested Materials

watch or clock
beakers
ice water
hot water
thermometers or temperature probes
containers and lids made of paper, plastic foam, plastic, glass, and metal

Design a Plan

Part 1 Measuring Temperature Changes

1. Use a pencil to poke a hole in the lid of a paper cup. Fill the cup about halfway with cold water.
2. Put the lid on the cup. Insert a thermometer into the water through the hole. (If you are using a temperature probe, see your teacher for instructions.) When the temperature stops dropping, place the cup in a beaker. Add hot water to the beaker until the water level is about 1 cm below the lid.
3. Record the water temperature once every minute until it has increased by 5°C. Use the time it takes for the temperature to increase 1°C as a measure of the effectiveness of the paper cup in preventing heat transfer.

Part 2 Comparing Materials

4. Use the ideas from Part 1 to design a controlled experiment to rank the effectiveness of different materials in preventing heat transfer.
5. Use these questions to help you plan your experiment:
   - What hypothesis will you test?
   - Which materials do you predict will be the best and worst at preventing heat transfer?
   - What will your manipulated, responding, and controlled variables be?
   - What step-by-step procedures will you use?
   - What kind of data table will you use?
6. After your teacher has reviewed your plans, make any necessary changes in your design. Then perform your experiment.

Analyze and Conclude

1. In Part 1, what was the starting temperature of the hot water? What was the starting temperature of the cold water? In which direction did the heat flow? How do you know?
2. If the materials in Part 1 are used to represent your home in very hot weather, which material would represent the rooms in your home? The outdoor weather? The building walls?
3. Which material was most effective at preventing the transfer of heat? Which was the least effective? Explain.
4. **Think About It** Would experiments similar to this one provide you with enough information to choose materials to build a home? Explain.

Design an Experiment

Design an experiment to compare how well the materials would work if the hot water were inside the cup and the cold water were outside. With your teacher's permission, carry out your experiment.

Conserving Energy

DISCOVER — ACTIVITY

Which Bulb Is More Efficient?

1. Record the light output (listed in lumens) from the packages of a 60-watt incandescent light bulb and a 15-watt compact fluorescent bulb.
2. Place the fluorescent bulb in a lamp socket. **CAUTION:** *Make sure the lamp is unplugged.*
3. Plug in the lamp and turn it on. Hold the end of a thermometer about 8 centimeters from the bulb.
4. Record the temperature after 5 minutes.
5. Turn off and unplug the lamp. When the bulb is cool, remove it. Repeat Steps 2, 3, and 4 with the incandescent light bulb.

Think It Over

Inferring Based on the number of lumens, what is the difference between the amount of light given off by the two types of bulbs? The incandescent bulb uses 4 times as much electricity. Why do you think this might be?

GUIDE FOR READING

- What are two ways to make sure there will be enough energy for the future?
- How does insulation help conserve energy?

Reading Tip Before you read, list ways to conserve energy. As you read, add to the list.

Imagine what would happen if the world ran out of fossil fuels today. Much of the electric power that people depend on would disappear. Most buildings would lose their heating and cooling. Forests would disappear as people began to burn wood for heat and cooking. Almost all transportation would stop. Cars, buses, trains, airplanes, and ships would be stranded wherever they ran out of fuel. Since radios, televisions, computers, and telephones depend on electricity, communication would be greatly reduced.

Although fossil fuels won't run out immediately, they also won't last forever. Most people think that it makes sense to start planning now to avoid a fuel shortage in the future. **One approach to the problem is to find new sources of energy. The second way is to make the fuels that are available now last as long as possible while other solutions are being developed.**

Conservation and Efficiency

Reducing energy use is called **energy conservation.** For example, if you walk to the store instead of getting a ride, you are conserving the gasoline needed to drive to the store. Reducing energy use is a solution to energy problems that will help no matter what form of energy is used in the future.

Electricity Production by Energy Source

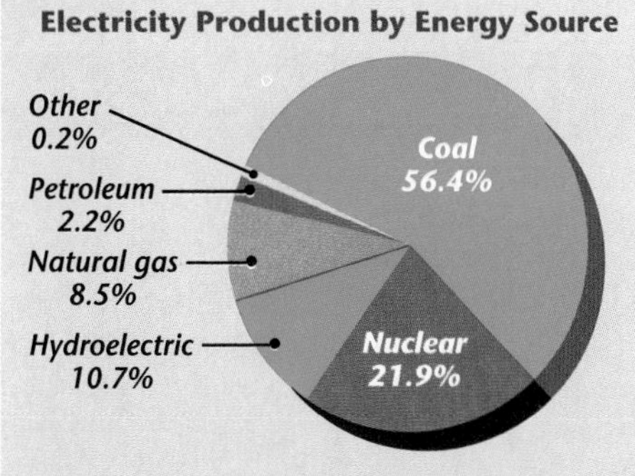

Figure 18 Nonrenewable fossil fuels generate over two thirds of the nation's electricity.

Background

Reading Tip To provide structure and prompt students' thinking, suggest that they list types of energy uses (electricity for lights and appliances, oil or natural gas for heating, gasoline for cars, and so forth) as headings across the top of a page and then list ways to reduce each use below the headings (such as turning off lights and appliances not in use).

Program Resources

- **Unit 5 Resources** 16-4 Lesson Plan; 16-4 Section Summary
- **Guided Reading and Study Workbook** Section 16-4

Conserving Energy

Objectives

After completing the lesson, students will be able to

- list two ways to ensure that there will be enough energy for the future;
- identify things that individuals can do to conserve energy.

Key Terms energy conservation, efficiency, insulation

1 Engage/Explore

Activating Prior Knowledge

Point out the section's title and ask: **What does the term energy conservation mean?** *(Accept all reasonable responses, such as "not wasting energy.")* **What are some examples of wasting energy?** *(Setting a thermostat too high, leaving lights on in an unoccupied room, running a dishwasher with only a small load, and the like.)*

DISCOVER

Skills Focus inferring
Materials *60-watt incandescent light bulb and 15-watt compact fluorescent light bulb in packages, lamp, thermometer, clock or watch*
Time 20 minutes
CAUTION: *Students should use caution when handling the bulbs and lamp plug.*
Tips Compact fluorescent bulbs, widely available in supermarkets and hardware stores, screw into a regular bulb socket.
Expected Outcome The fluorescent bulb will not produce as high a temperature as the incandescent bulb because it uses electricity more efficiently, converting more to light and less to heat.
Think It Over Lumens may vary among bulb brands. Based on 900 lumens for a 60-watt incandescent bulb and 825 lumens for a 15-watt compact fluorescent bulb, the difference is 75 lumens. The incandescent bulb uses more electricity because so much is converted to heat.

2 Facilitate

Conservation and Efficiency

Building Inquiry Skills: Calculating

Materials *packages from 60-watt incandescent light bulb and 15-watt compact fluorescent light bulb, calculator (optional)*
ACTIVITY
Time 10 minutes

Explain that the number of watts printed on a light bulb and its package tells how much electrical energy is needed to light the bulb for one second (1 watt = 1 joule per second). Have students examine the packages and identify the wattage of each bulb. *(Incandescent bulb 60 watts, fluorescent bulb 15 watts)* Ask: **How many times more electrical energy does the incandescent bulb use to produce the same amount of light as the fluorescent bulb?** *(4 times as much)* **What is the expected life of each bulb?** *(Answers will depend on brands of bulbs used; examples: incandescent bulb 1,000 hours, fluorescent bulb 10,000 hours)* **How many incandescent bulbs would you need to equal the life of one fluorescent bulb?** *(10)* **How much would 10 incandescent bulbs cost compared with the cost of one fluorescent bulb?** *($7.50 [10 × 75¢] compared with $20.00; prices may vary)* **How much more than 10 incandescent bulbs would the fluorescent bulb cost over its life?** *($12.50)* **Do you think the fluorescent bulb is worth its higher cost?** *(Accept all answers at this point.)* **According to the fluorescent bulb's package, how much would you save in electricity costs by using that one bulb instead of 10 incandescent bulbs for 10,000 hours?** *($45.00)* **What would your total savings be over the life of the fluorescent bulb?** *($45.00 – $12.50, or $32.50)* **So which type of bulb is better, and why?** *(The fluorescent bulb, because it costs less in the long term and conserves electricity.)* **learning modality: logical/mathematical**

A way to get as much work as possible out of fuels is to use them efficiently. **Efficiency** is the percentage of energy that is actually used to perform work. The rest of the energy is "lost" to the surroundings, usually as heat. People have developed many ways to increase energy efficiency.

Lighting Lights can use as much as 10 percent of the electricity in your home, but much of that electricity is wasted. An incandescent light bulb converts less than 10 percent of the electricity it uses into light. The rest is given off as heat. You can prove this to yourself by holding your hand close to an incandescent light bulb. But don't touch it! Compact fluorescent bulbs, on the other hand, use only about one fourth as much energy to provide the same amount of light.

☑ *Checkpoint* *Which type of light bulb is more energy-efficient?*

Energy-Efficient Devices

Scientists and engineers have developed many technologies that improve energy efficiency and reduce energy use.

1932
Fiberglass Insulation

Long strands of glass fibers trap air and keep buildings from losing heat. Less fuel is used for heating.

1958
Solar Cells

More than 150 years ago, scientists discovered that silicon can convert light into electricity. The first useful application of solar cells was to power the radio on a satellite. Now solar cells are even used on experimental cars like the one below.

1930 | 1940 | 1950

1936
Fluorescent Lighting

Fluorescent bulbs were introduced to the public at the 100th anniversary celebration of the United States Patent Office. Because these bulbs use less energy than incandescent bulbs, most offices and schools use fluorescent lights.

Background

Facts and Figures Energy-efficient devices like those shown in the timeline have helped conserve energy. For example, "superinsulated" homes can use from 70 to 95 percent less energy for heating than homes with conventional insulation. These homes are surrounded by an "envelope" of insulation and have airtight construction.

Because of lighter materials and designs that reduce air drag, the fuel efficiency of passenger cars has improved dramatically, from an average of 6.8 km/L in 1981 to 9.1 km/L in 1994.

The National Appliance Energy Conservation Act sets energy-efficiency standards for refrigerators, washing machines, water heaters, and other appliances. As a result of this law, refrigerators built in the mid-1990s use more than 80 percent less energy than those built in the early 1980s.

Heating and Cooling One method of increasing the efficiency of heating and cooling systems is insulation. **Insulation** is a layer of material that helps block the transfer of heat between the air inside and outside a building. You have probably seen insulation made of fiberglass, which looks like fluffy pink cotton candy. The mat of thin glass fibers trap air. **This layer of trapped air helps keep the building from losing or gaining heat from the outside.** A layer of fiberglass 15 centimeters thick insulates a room as well as a brick wall 2 meters thick or a stone wall almost 6 meters thick!

Buildings lose a lot of heat around the windows. Look at the windows in your school or home. Was the building built after 1980? Have the windows been replaced recently? If so, you will most likely see two panes of glass with space between them. The air between the panes of glass acts as insulation.

In Your Journal

Design an advertisement for one of the energy-saving inventions described in this time line. The advertisement may be a print, radio, or television ad. Be sure that your advertisement clearly explains the benefits of the invention.

1967
Microwave Ovens
The first countertop microwave oven for the home was introduced. Microwaves cook food by heating the water the food contains. The microwave oven heats only the food, not the air, racks, and oven walls as in a conventional oven. Preheating is also not required, saving even more energy.

1997
Smart Roads
The Department of Transportation demonstrated that cars can be controlled by computers. Sensors built into the road control all the cars, making traffic flow more smoothly. This uses less energy.

1970 1980 1990 2000

1981
High-Efficiency Window Coatings
Materials that reflect sunlight were first used to coat windows in the early 1980s. This coating reduces the air conditioning needed to keep the inside of the building cool.

Answers to Self-Assessment

Checkpoint

A compact fluorescent bulb is more energy-efficient.

Building Inquiry Skills: Observing

ACTIVITY

Materials *piece of fiberglass insulation batting sealed in plastic bag, hand lens*
Time 10 minutes

CAUTION: *Wear gloves when you handle the fiberglass batting, and warn students not to remove the batting from the sealed bag, as the glass fibers irritate the skin.* Let students examine the batting inside the bag, paying particular attention to the air spaces between the fibers. Then ask: **What other kinds of materials have spaces to trap air and provide insulation?** *(Examples include the feathers or fibrous material used in the linings of winter jackets, the fuzzy wool or acrylic material in sweaters and mittens, and the plastic-foam material used to insulate hot-water pipes.)* If students did the Skills Lab on page 346, remind them of the containers they tested, and ask: **Which container material was most like fiberglass insulation?** *(plastic foam)* **learning modality: visual**

SCIENCE & History

Call on volunteers to read the time-line annotations. Encourage students to share their experiences with any of the technologies described. Ask students to predict how "smart roads" could affect their lives.

In Your Journal You may wish to let students work in small groups. Encourage them to research the devices shown and incorporate their findings into the advertisements. Provide tape recorders and video cameras so students can create radio and television ads. Allow time for each group to present its ad to the class. **cooperative learning**

Ongoing Assessment

Drawing Have each student draw and label a diagram to explain how insulation conserves energy.

Students can save their drawings in their portfolios.

What You Can Do

Real-Life Learning

Create a class list on the board from students' lists they started if they did the Reading Tip on page 347. Pay particular attention to any ideas that are not covered in the text. Encourage students to copy the list so they can use it in the Science at Home activity below.
learning modality: verbal

3 Assess

Section 4 Review Answers

1. Find new sources of energy, and make the fuels we have now last as long as possible.
2. Insulation traps air so heat is not lost to the outside in cold weather and is kept outside in hot weather, reducing use of the building's heating and cooling systems.
3. Several people sharing one car uses less fuel than each person driving separately.
4. The building with only incandescent lights has higher energy bills because incandescent bulbs are less energy-efficient than fluorescent bulbs; most of the electrical energy used by incandescent bulbs is converted to heat, not light.

Science at Home

Encourage students to look for simple energy-saving ideas that they and their family members can implement easily and inexpensively—for example, wrapping an older, less efficient water heater with an insulating material rather than replacing the heater.

Performance Assessment

Oral Presentation Have each student describe one energy-saving idea that he or she will take responsibility for implementing at home.

Figure 19 A single city bus can transport dozens of people, reducing the number of cars on the roads and saving energy. *Applying Concepts How does riding a bus conserve energy?*

Transportation Engineers have improved the energy efficiency of cars by designing better engines and tires. Another way to save energy is to reduce the number of cars on the road. In many communities, public transit systems provide an alternative to driving. Other cities encourage car-pooling. If four people travel together in one car, they use much less energy than they would by driving separately. Many cities now set aside lanes for cars containing two or more people.

In the future, cars that run on electricity may provide the most energy savings of all. Electric power plants can convert fuel into electricity more efficiently than a car engine converts gasoline into motion. Therefore, a car that runs on electricity is more energy-efficient than one that runs directly on fuel.

What You Can Do

You can reduce your personal energy use by changing your behavior in some simple ways.

- Keep your home cooler in winter and warmer in summer. Instead of turning up the heat, put on a sweater. Use fans instead of air conditioners.
- Use natural lighting instead of electric lights when possible.
- Turn off the lights or television when you leave a room.
- Walk or ride a bike for short trips. Ride buses and trains.
- Recycle, especially metal products. Recycling an aluminum can uses only 5 percent of the energy making a new can uses!

The items in this list are small things, but multiplied by millions of people they add up to a lot of energy saved for the future.

Section 4 Review

1. What are two ways to make energy resources last longer?
2. Explain how putting insulation in a building conserves energy.
3. How does carpooling conserve energy?
4. **Thinking Critically Predicting** An office building contains only incandescent lights. The building next door contains fluorescent lights. Predict which building has higher energy bills. Explain your answer.

Science at Home

Saving Energy With an adult family member, conduct an energy audit of your home. Look for places where energy is being lost, such as cracks around windows and doors. Also look for ways to reduce energy use, such as running the dishwasher only when it is full. Together, create a list of energy-saving suggestions for your family. Post the list where everyone can see it.

Program Resources

- **Unit 5 Resources** 16-4 Review and Reinforce; 16-4 Enrich

Answers to Self-Assessment

Caption Question

Figure 19 A bus uses less fuel than all the individual cars that would be driven by the bus passengers.

CHAPTER 16 STUDY GUIDE

Section 1 Energy From Fossil Fuels

Key Ideas

- A fuel is a substance that provides a form of energy as a result of a chemical change.
- Energy can be converted from one form to another.
- The three major fossil fuels are coal, oil, and natural gas. These fuels release more energy when they are burned than most other substances do.
- Because fossil fuels take hundreds of millions of years to form, they are considered nonrenewable resources.

Key Terms

hydrocarbons
reserves
petroleum
refinery
petrochemicals
nonrenewable resources

Section 2 Renewable Sources of Energy

Key Ideas

- Solar energy is plentiful and renewable, and does not cause pollution. However, a backup energy source is needed.
- Because the sun causes winds and drives the water cycle, wind power and water power are considered indirect forms of solar energy.
- Biomass fuels, geothermal energy, and hydrogen power are other renewable energy sources that are currently in limited use.

Key Terms

renewable resources
solar energy
passive solar system
active solar system
hydroelectric power
biomass fuels
gasohol
geothermal energy

Section 3 Nuclear Energy

INTEGRATING CHEMISTRY

Key Ideas

- Nuclear reactions include fission reactions and fusion reactions.
- In a fission reaction, the impact of a neutron splits an atom's nucleus into two smaller nuclei and two or more neutrons. A large amount of energy is released in the process.
- In a nuclear power plant, the thermal energy released from controlled fission reactions is used to generate electricity.
- Disadvantages of nuclear power include the risk of a meltdown and radioactive waste.

Key Terms

nucleus
nuclear fission
reactor vessel
fuel rods
control rods
meltdown
nuclear fusion

Section 4 Conserving Energy

Key Ideas

- To avoid an energy shortage in the future, people must find new sources of energy and conserve the fuels that are available now.
- Insulation keeps a building from losing heat to, or gaining heat from, the outside.
- Ways to conserve energy use in transportation include making more efficient vehicles, carpooling, and using public transit.

Key Terms

energy conservation
insulation
efficiency

Organizing Information

Compare/Contrast Table Make a table listing an advantage and a disadvantage for each of the following types of energy: coal, petroleum, solar, wind, water, geothermal, nuclear. For example, advantages of coal include the fact that it produces a large amount of energy and is easy to transport. Can you recall any disadvantages of using coal as an energy source? (For tips on making compare/contrast tables see the Skills Handbook.)

Program Resources

- **Unit 5 Resources** Chapter 16 Project Scoring Rubric
- **Performance Assessment** Chapter 16
- **Chapter and Unit Tests** Chapter 16 Test

Media and Technology

Computer Test Bank
Chapter 16 Test

Organizing Information

Compare/Contrast Table
Students' tables should include a single advantage and disadvantage for each energy type similar to the examples in the following:

Advantages and Disadvantages of Energy Sources

Energy Type	Advantage	Disadvantage
Coal	Produces large amount of energy; easy to transport	Causes air pollution when burned; difficult to mine
Petroleum	Produces large amount of energy; can be used to produce plastics and other products	Causes air pollution when burned, difficult to find, must be refined
Solar	Free, renewable, does not cause pollution	Not available on cloudy days or at night, is very spread out
Wind	Free, renewable, does not cause pollution	Not available in many places
Water	Free, renewable, does not cause pollution	Most of the suitable rivers in the United States have already been dammed, dams can have negative effct on the environment
Geothermal	Free, renewable, cheap, does not cause pollution	Available in only a few places, drilling deep wells is expensive
Nuclear	Produces huge amount of energy	Creates radioactive waste, risk of meltdown, costly

CHAPTER 16 ASSESSMENT

Reviewing Content

Multiple Choice

1. b **2.** c **3.** c **4.** a **5.** d

True or False

6. petrochemicals **7.** true **8.** renewable
9. solar cells **10.** true

Checking Concepts

11. The coal must be broken out of the surrounding rock and transported to the surface, often from deep underground. Coal creates dust that is unhealthy to breathe.
12. As plants die and decay, their remains pile up and are buried by layers of sand, rock, and mud. Over millions of years, heat and pressure change the decaying remains into coal.
13. Advantages include production of large amounts of energy and ease of transport; disadvantages include taking a long time to form and being highly flammable.
14. Possible answers include overhangs to shade the windows in summer, positioning the house to receive maximum sunlight in winter, solar cells on the roof to provide electricity, and a backup energy source.
15. Wind can turn a turbine, which rotates an electromagnet to create electricity.
16. Very few locations have tides that are large enough to provide a power source.
17. Advantages include burning cleanly; creating no smoke, smog, or acid rain; ease of handling and transport; and large fuel supply. Disadvantages include taking more energy to obtain the fuel than is produced by burning it.
18. By placing control rods made of cadmium between the fuel rods to limit chain reactions
19. Energy efficiency is the percentage of energy actually used to perform work; *examples:* insulation, fluorescent light bulbs, window coatings, microwave ovens
20. Responses will vary but should include ways of traveling, preparing meals, and obtaining light and heat.

Critical Thinking

21. *Likenesses:* All form from the remains of organisms, contain hydrocarbons, and produce a large amount of energy when burned. *Differences:* Coal forms from plant remains; oil and natural gas form from the remains of small animals, algae, and protists. Coal is solid, oil is liquid, and natural gas is a gas. Natural gas causes less air pollution than coal and oil.
22. Coal is nonrenewable because it takes so long to form. Solar power is renewable because its supply is unlimited. Methane is renewable because it is produced as wastes decompose. Hydrogen is renewable because it can be obtained from water, which is abundant on Earth.
23. Accept both "agree" and "disagree" responses. Students should support their views with explanations that cite the advantages and disadvantages of nuclear power as an energy source.
24. In a furnace, fossil fuel is burned and thermal energy is released. This energy is used to boil water and make steam. The mechanical energy of moving steam turns turbine blades. The turbine turns the shaft of a generator, producing an electric current.

CHAPTER 16 ASSESSMENT

Reviewing Content

Multiple Choice

Choose the letter of the best answer.

1. Which of the following is *not* a fossil fuel?
a. coal **b.** wood
c. oil **d.** natural gas

2. Wind and water energy are both indirect forms of
a. nuclear energy.
b. electrical energy.
c. solar energy.
d. geothermal energy.

3. Which of the following is *not* a biomass fuel?
a. methane
b. gasohol
c. hydrogen
d. sugar-cane wastes

4. The particle used to start a nuclear fission reaction is a(n)
a. neutron.
b. nucleus.
c. proton.
d. atom.

5. A part of a nuclear power plant that undergoes a fission reaction is called a
a. turbine.
b. control rod.
c. heat exchanger.
d. fuel rod.

True or False

If the statement is true, write true. If it is false, change the underlined word or words to make the statement true.

6. Products made from petroleum are called hydrocarbons.
7. The process of burning a fuel for energy is combustion.
8. Geothermal energy is an example of a nonrenewable energy source.
9. Solar energy is harnessed to run calculators using solar satellites.
10. Most of the energy used in the United States today comes from fossil fuels.

Checking Concepts

11. Explain why coal mining is a difficult task.
12. Describe how coal forms.
13. What are some advantages and disadvantages of natural gas as an energy source?
14. Describe three features of a solar home. (Your answer may include passive or active solar systems.)
15. Explain how wind can be used to generate electricity.
16. What factors limit the use of biomass fuels as an energy source?
17. Describe the advantages and disadvantages that hydrogen power would have as a source of energy.
18. How is a nuclear fission reaction controlled in a nuclear power plant?
19. Define *energy efficiency.* Give three examples of inventions that increase energy efficiency.
20. Writing to Learn Suppose you had no electricity. Write a journal entry describing a typical weekday, including your meals, classes, and after-school activities. Explain how you might get things done without electricity.

Critical Thinking

21. Comparing and Contrasting Discuss how the three fossil fuels are alike and how they are different.
22. Classifying State whether each of the following energy sources is renewable or nonrenewable: coal, solar power, methane, hydrogen. Give a reason for each answer.
23. Making Judgments Write a short paragraph explaining why you agree or disagree with the following statement: "The United States should build more nuclear power plants to prepare for the future shortage of fossil fuels."
24. Relating Cause and Effect Explain the steps in which an electric power plant generates electricity by burning a fossil fuel.

Applying Skills

The table below shows how the world's energy production changed between 1973 and 1995. Use the information in the table to answer Questions 25–28.

Source of Energy	Energy Units Produced 1973	Energy Units Produced 1995
Coal	1,498	2,179
Gas	964	1,775
Hydroelectric	107	242
Nuclear	54	646
Oil	2,730	3,228
TOTAL Energy Units	5,353	8,070

25. Interpreting Data How did total energy production change from 1973 to 1995?

26. Calculating What percentage of total world energy production did nuclear power provide in 1973? In 1995?

27. Classifying Classify the different types of energy as renewable or nonrenewable. How important was renewable energy in 1995?

28. Drawing Conclusions Which energy source was the most important in 1995?

Performance (CHAPTER PROJECT) Assessment

Present Your Project Have another group review your report for clarity, organization, and detail. Make revisions based on feedback from the other group. As a class, discuss each group's findings. Make a list of suggestions for conserving energy in your school.

Reflect and Record In your project notebook, explain what types of energy use were the hardest to measure. What other information would you have liked to have when making your recommendations? Record your overall opinion of energy efficiency in your school.

Test Preparation

Use these questions to prepare for standardized tests.

Read the passage. Then answer Questions 29–33.

Tides are a source of renewable energy. Along some coasts, great amounts of water move into bays at high tide and flow out to sea again as the tide falls.

A few tidal power plants have been built to take advantage of this regular motion. A low dam across the entrance to a shallow bay holds water in the bay at high tide. As the tide goes out, water flowing past turbines in the dam generates electricity, as in a hydroelectric power plant.

Tidal power will probably never become a major source of energy because only a few coastal areas in the world are suitable for building tidal power plants. Also, a dam across a bay blocks boats and fish from traveling up the river.

29. How many tidal power plants are now in use?
a. only a few
b. several dozen
c. zero
d. several hundred

30. Tides are an energy source that is
a. widely used throughout the world.
b. renewable.
c. nonrenewable.
d. impossible to use in generating power.

31. Tidal power plants most resemble
a. geothermal power plants.
b. windmills.
c. hydroelectric power plants.
d. water-cooled nuclear power plants.

32. The selection concludes that tidal power
a. will replace other types of power.
b. already produces too much energy.
c. can be developed wherever the tide rises.
d. won't become a major source of energy.

33. A good title for this reading selection would be
a. The Limitless Power of Tides.
b. Tidal Power Blocks Boats.
c. A Minor Source of Renewable Energy.
d. A Major Source of Energy.

Program Resources

◆ **Inquiry Skills Activity Book** Provides teaching and review of all inquiry skills

Applying Skills

25. It increased from 5,353 units to 8,070 units.
26. *1973:* 1%; *1995:* 8%
27. *Renewable:* hydroelectric; *nonrenewable:* coal, gas, nuclear, oil. Renewable energy (hydroelectric power) was not very important to the world's energy production in 1995, representing only 3% of the total energy units produced.
28. oil

Performance (CHAPTER PROJECT) Assessment

Present Your Project Encourage groups to give each other specific suggestions for improving the reports and to avoid making overly general criticisms. In the whole-class discussion, give each group an opportunity to summarize its findings, then focus on the group's suggestions for reducing energy use. Ask students for their ideas about how the proposal should be organized and presented. You may want to have a group of volunteers compile the final proposal and present it to the entire class for further discussion.

Reflect and Record Specific responses to the questions and issues raised in this paragraph will vary. Allow time for students to share the answers and ideas they recorded.

Test Preparation

29. a **30.** b **31.** c **32.** d **33.** c

Chapter 17 Living Resources

Sections	Time	Student Edition Activities	Other Activities
Chapter Project **Variety Show** p. 529	Ongoing ($1\frac{1}{2}$ weeks)	Check Your Progress, pp. 535, 554 Present Your Project, p. 557	
1 Recognizing Environmental Issues pp. 530–536 ◆ Identify the main types of environmental issues. ◆ Define environmental science. ◆ Describe how decision makers balance different needs and concerns related to environmental issues.	2 periods/ 1 block	**Discover** How Do You Decide?, p. 530 **Sharpen Your Skills** Communicating, p. 535 **Real-World Lab: You and Your Environment** Is Paper a Renewable Resource?, p. 536	**TE** Building Inquiry Skills: Graphing, p. 531 **TE** Including All Students, p. 532 **TE** Science and History, p. 533
2 Forests and Fisheries pp. 537–542 ◆ Describe different ways that forests can be managed to provide resources. ◆ Describe different ways that fisheries can be managed to provide resources.	2 periods/ 1 block	**Discover** What Happened to the Tuna?, p. 537 **Sharpen Your Skills** Calculating, p. 540 **Science at Home,** p. 541 **Skills Lab: Interpreting Data** Tree Cookie Tales, p. 542	**TE** Inquiry Challenge, p. 539 **TE** Real-Life Learning, p. 540 **LM** 17, "Managing Fisheries"
3 Biodiversity pp. 543–551 ◆ Identify the factors that affect biodiversity. ◆ Explain the value of biodiversity. ◆ List some ways that biodiversity can be protected. ◆ Name some human activities that threaten biodiversity.	1 period/ $\frac{1}{2}$ block	**Discover** How Much Variety Is There?, p. 543 **Science at Home,** p. 551	**TE** Building Inquiry Skills: Observing, pp. 544, 553; Communicating, pp. 545, 550; Making Models, p. 547 **TE** Demonstration, pp. 545, 550 **TE** Addressing Naive Conceptions, p. 546 **TE** Inquiry Challenge, p. 549 **TE** Real-Life Learning, p. 553
4 *Integrating Health* **The Search for New Medicines** pp. 552–554 ◆ Explain why many rain forest plants are sources of medicines.	1 period/ $\frac{1}{2}$ block	**Discover** How Are Plant Chemicals Separated?, p. 552	**TE** Building Inquiry Skills: Observing, p. 553
Study Guide/Assessment pp. 555–557	1 period/ $\frac{1}{2}$ block		**ISAB** Provides teaching and review of all inquiry skills

For Standard or Block Schedule The Resource Pro® CD-ROM gives you maximum flexibility for planning your instruction for any type of schedule. Resource Pro® contains Planning Express®, an advanced scheduling program, as well as the entire contents of the Teaching Resources and the Computer Test Bank.

CHAPTER PLANNING GUIDE

Program Resources	Assessment Strategies	Media and Technology
UR Chapter 17 Project Teacher Notes **UR** Chapter 17 Project Overview and Worksheets	**SE** Performance Assessment: Present Your Project, p. 557 **TE** Check Your Progress, pp. 535, 554 **UR** Chapter 17 Project Scoring Rubric	Science Explorer Internet Site at www.phschool.com Student Edition on Audio CD, Chapter 17
UR 17-1 Lesson Plan **UR** 17-1 Section Summary **UR** 17-1 Review and Reinforce **UR** 17-1 Enrich **UR** Real-World Lab blackline masters	**SE** Section 1 Review, p. 535 **SE** Analyze and Conclude, p. 536 **TE** Ongoing Assessment, pp. 531, 533 **TE** Performance Assessment, p. 535	Concept Videotape Library, Grade 6, Tape 4, "Can We Still Get What We Need?" Lab Activity Videotapes, Grade 6 Tape 4
UR 17-2 Lesson Plan **UR** 17-2 Section Summary **UR** 17-2 Review and Reinforce **UR** 17-2 Enrich **UR** Skills Lab blackline masters	**SE** Section 2 Review, p. 541 **SE** Analyze and Conclude, p. 542 **TE** Ongoing Assessment, p. 539 **TE** Performance Assessment, p. 541	Lab Activity Videotapes, Grade 6 Tape 4 Transparencies 69, "Logging Methods"
UR 17-3 Lesson Plan **UR** 17-3 Section Summary **UR** 17-3 Review and Reinforce **UR** 17-3 Enrich	**SE** Section 3 Review, p. 551 **TE** Ongoing Assessment, pp. 545, 547, 549 **TE** Performance Assessment, p. 551	Concept Videotape Library, Grade 6, Tape 4, "Can We Save the Tigers?"; "It's All Happening at the Zoo"
UR 17-4 Lesson Plan **UR** 17-4 Section Summary **UR** 17-4 Review and Reinforce **UR** 17-4 Enrich	**SE** Section 4 Review, p. 554 **TE** Ongoing Assessment, p. 553 **TE** Performance Assessment, p. 555	Concept Videotape Library, Grade 6, Tape 4, "A Question of Balance"
RCA Provides strategies to improve science reading skills **GRSW** Provides worksheets to promote student comprehension of content	**SE** Chapter 17 Study Guide/Assessment, pp. 566–567 **PA** Chapter 17 Performance Assessment **CUT** Chapter 17 Test **CTB** Chapter 17 Test	Computer Test Bank, Chapter 17 Test

Key: **SE** Student Edition
CTB Computer Test Bank
ISAB Inquiry Skills Activity Book
GRSW Guided Reading and Study Workbook
TE Teacher's Edition
PTA Product Testing Activities by *Consumer Reports*
RCA Reading in the Content Area
PA Performance Assessment
UR Unit Resources
LM Laboratory Manual
IES Interdisciplinary Explorations Series
CUT Chapter and Unit Tests

Meeting the National Science Education Standards and AAAS Benchmarks

National Science Education Standards	Benchmarks for Science Literacy	Unifying Themes
Science as Inquiry (Content Standard A) ◆ **Design and conduct an investigation** Students observe diversity of organisms. *(Chapter Project)* ◆ **Develop descriptions, explanations, predictions, and models using evidence** Students model paper recycling. Students observe a tree cross section to draw conclusions about how the tree grew. *(Real-World Lab; Skills Lab)* **Life Science** (Content Standard C) ◆ **Diversity and adaptions of organisms** The number of different species in an area is called biodiversity. Plants in many ecosystems produce chemicals that protect them. *(Chapter Project; Sections 3, 4)* **Science in Personal and Social Perspectives** (Content Standard F) ◆ **Populations, resources, and environments** Human activities can threaten biodiversity. *(Section 3)* ◆ **Science and technology in society** Environmental issues include resource management, population growth, and pollution. *(Section 1)* **History and Nature of Science** (Content Standard G) ◆ **History of science** Certain individuals have influenced the viewpoints of others toward the environment. *(Science & History)*	**1B Scientific Inquiry** Students survey a plot of land to observe the diversity of organisms, model paper recycling, and observe a tree cross section to draw conclusions about the conditions in which the tree grew. *(Chapter Project; Real-World Lab; Skills Lab)* **1C The Scientific Enterprise** Certain individuals have influenced the viewpoints of many others toward environmental issues. *(Science & History)* **3A Technology and Society** Students model the process of recycling paper. Some chemicals rainforest plants produce to protect their leaves and bark can also be used to fight human diseases. *(Real-World Lab; Section 4)* **3C Issues in Technology** The three main types of environmental issues are resource management, population growth, and pollution. Some methods of logging and fishing are harmful to the environment. Human activities can threaten biodiversity. *(Sections 1, 2, 3)* **4B The Earth** Forests and fisheries are renewable resources if managed properly. *(Section 2)* **5A Diversity of Life** The number of different species in an area is called biodiversity. Many plants produce chemicals that protect them from predators, parasites, and disease. *(Chapter Project; Sections 3, 4)*	◆ **Evolution** Extinction is the disappearance of all members of a species from Earth. *(Section 3)* ◆ **Modeling** Students model paper recycling. *(Real-World Lab)* ◆ **Patterns of Change** Any change to the environment that has a negative effect on the environment is called pollution. If fish are caught at a faster rate than they can breed, the population of a fishery decreases. *(Sections 1, 2)* ◆ **Scale and Structure** Each pair of light and dark rings in a tree cross section represents one year's growth. *(Skills Lab)* ◆ **Stability** Managing forests and fisheries helps conserve these living resources for the future. *(Section 2)* ◆ **Systems and Interactions** Environmental science is the study of the natural processes that occur in the environment and how humans can affect them. Factors that affect biodiversity in an ecosystem include area, climate, and diversity of niches. Some plants produce chemicals that protect them from predators, parasites, and diseases. *(Sections 1, 3, 4)* ◆ **Unity and Diversity** The three main types of environmental issues are resource management, population growth, and pollution. *(Section 1)*

Take It to the Net

Interactive text at www.phschool.com

Science Explorer comes alive with iText.

- **Complete student text** is accessible from any computer with Internet access or a CD-ROM drive.
- **Animations, simulations, and videos** enhance student understanding and retention of concepts.
- **Self-tests and online study tools** assess student understanding.

STAY CURRENT with **SCIENCE NEWS®**

Find out the latest research and information about Ecology at:
www.phschool.com

Go to **www.phschool.com** and click on the Science icon.Then click on Science Explorer: Life, Earth, and Physical Science under PH@school.

Student Edition Activities Planner

ACTIVITY	Time (minutes)	Materials Quantities for one work group	Skills
Section 1			
Discover, p. 530	15	No special materials are required.	Forming Operational Definitions
Sharpen Your Skills, p. 535	20	No special materials are required.	Communicating
Real-World Lab, p. 536	15; 40; 10	**Consumable** newspaper, water, plastic wrap **Nonconsumable** microscope, microscope slide, eggbeater, square pan, screen, heavy book, mixing bowl	Observing, Designing Experiments
Section 2			
Discover, p. 537	15	**Consumable** graph paper **Nonconsumable** ruler, pencil	Inferring
Sharpen Your Skills, p. 540	15	**Nonconsumable** calculator	Calculating
Science at Home, p. 541	home	No special materials are required.	Classifying
Skills Lab, p. 542	40	**Nonconsumable** tree cookie (tree cross section), metric ruler, hand lens, colored pencils, calculator (optional)	Observing, Measuring, Drawing Conclusions
Section 3			
Discover, p. 543	20	**Nonconsumable** two different birdseed or dried bean mixtures, two cups, paper plate	Inferring
Science at Home, p. 551	home	**Nonconsumable** map of community or state	Communicating
Section 4			
Discover, p. 552	15	**Consumable** strip of filter paper, water, tape **Nonconsumable** black marking pen, clear plastic cup, pencil	Observing

A list of all materials required for the Student Edition activities can be found on pages TVA34–TVA40. You can obtain information about ordering materials by calling 1-800-848-9500 or by accessing the Science Explorer Internet site at: **www.phschool.com**

CHAPTER 17 PROJECT

Variety Show

The Chapter 17 Project is designed to develop students' appreciation for the rich diversity of living things that can be found in even a very small plot of land. The project also provides an opportunity for students to apply methods and skills that are used by field biologists.

Purpose After marking study plots of land, students will observe their plots regularly and record observations and data in a notebook. To conclude the project, students will communicate their findings in a class presentation.

Skills Focus After completing the Chapter 17 Project, students will be able to

- observe, compare and contrast, and classify organisms;
- infer relationships among organisms and between organisms and the abiotic factors in their environment;
- create a data table for recording observations;
- communicate observations and conclusions to others.

Project Time Line The Chapter 17 Project requires two to three weeks to complete. Each small group of students will begin by staking out a 1.5-by-1.5 meter plot of land and preparing a notebook for recording observations, including notes and drawings of the organisms observed, and the date, time, air temperature, and weather conditions during each observation. The major portion of the project involves making regular observations and recording data. During this time, students can use field guides to identify organisms. At the conclusion of the observation period, each group will prepare a class presentation that may include support materials such as photographs, drawings, videos, or computer displays.

Possible Materials

- To mark the plot, each group will need a meter stick or metric tape measure, four small stakes, a hammer, surveyor's tape or sturdy string, and a directional compass.
- When students observe their plots, each group will need a thermometer, hand lenses, rulers, and trowels.

- Provide a variety of field guides so students can research the names and classification of any unfamiliar organisms they observe. A field guide to animal tracks will also be helpful for students who find trace evidence of organisms that have visited the plot.
- When students are ready to prepare their class presentations, provide art supplies and audiovisual equipment such as cameras and videocassette recorders, if available.

Advance Preparation Before introducing the Chapter 17 Project, survey the grounds around your school so that you can guide students to areas where they are likely to find a good variety of organisms. If the school grounds are not appropriate, locate a nearby field, park, vacant lot, or other natural area to which you can take the class during school hours. Obtain permission to use the land, if necessary.

Launching the Project Invite students to read the project description on page 529. Then guide a class brainstorming session about nearby areas that might be good for setting up the study plots. Share what you know about

CHAPTER 17 PROJECT

Variety Show

Can you imagine what this scene would look like if there were no houses? When people move into an environment, they change it in many ways. When trees are cut down and streams are re-routed into underground pipes, it affects the organisms that live there. Development of an area often decreases the diversity, or variety, of species that remain. In the development shown here, many trees were left standing, preserving the homes of organisms that lived here before people moved in. In this chapter's project, you will study the diversity of life in your area.

Your Goal To observe the diversity of organisms in a plot of land.

To complete this project you must

- stake out a 1.5 meter-by-1.5 meter plot of ground
- keep a record of your observations of the abiotic conditions
- identify the species of organisms you observe
- follow the safety guidelines in Appendix A

Get Started Read over the project and prepare a notebook in which to record your observations. Include places to record the date, time, air temperature, and other weather conditions during each observation. Leave space for drawings or photographs of the organisms in your plot.

Check Your Progress You'll be working on this project as you study this chapter. To keep your project on track, look for Check Your Progress boxes at the following points.

Section 1 Review, page 535: Stake out your plot, and begin to observe it.

Section 4 Review, page 554: Identify the organisms in your plot. Begin to prepare your presentation.

Present Your Project At the end of the chapter (page 557), you will present your findings to the class. You will describe your observations and share the diversity of life in your plot.

Housing development in Loudoun County Virginia

SECTION 4 Integrating Health **The Search for New Medicines**

Discover **How Are Plant Chemicals Separated?**

529

possible areas. Help students agree on appropriate areas. Suggest that students may select an area near their homes where they can carry out observations.

Distribute Chapter 17 Project Overview in Unit 5 Resources. Have students review the project rules and procedures. Encourage students' questions. Clarify whether students will be given class time for observing the plots or they must carry out the observations on their own time.

Divide the class into groups of four to six students each. Explain that each group's members may divide the project responsibilities among themselves. However, every member should help plan the notebook, stake out the plot, make and record observations, and develop the group's presentation and be prepared to answer questions. You may also wish to offer the option for students to work alone near their homes if space in the schoolyard is an issue.

To get students started, allow time for groups to meet and begin planning the project notebook. Distribute Worksheet 1, which provides instructions and a grid for making a scale drawing of the study plot. At the end of Section 1, distribute Worksheet 2, which provides guidance for recording information about the organisms that students observe.

Additional information on guiding the project is provided in Chapter 17 Project Teacher Notes in Unit 5 Resources.

Program Resources

- **Unit 5 Resources** Chapter 17 Project Teacher Notes; Chapter 17 Overview and Worksheets; Chapter 17 Project Scoring Rubric

Media and Technology

Student Edition on Audio CD Chapter 17

You will find an Internet activity, chapter self-tests for students, and links to other chapter topics at this site.

Performance Assessment

The Chapter 17 Project Scoring Rubric in Unit 5 Resources will help you evaluate how well students complete the Chapter 17 Project. You may want to share the scoring rubric with students so they are clear about what will be expected of them. Students will be assessed on

- their completeness and accuracy in making observations and recording data;
- their ability to use previous knowledge and reference sources to identify and classify organisms;
- how well they have communicated their findings to the rest of the class;
- participation in their groups.

SECTION 1 Recognizing Environmental Issues

Objectives

After completing the lesson, students will be able to
- ◆ identify the main types of environmental issues;
- ◆ define environmental science;
- ◆ describe how decision makers balance different needs and concerns related to environmental issues.

Key Terms pollution, development viewpoint, preservation viewpoint, conservation viewpoint

1 Engage/Explore

Activating Prior Knowledge

Ask students: **What is an "issue"?** *(Students' responses should include the idea of a problem or question on which people have different viewpoints.)* **What are some examples of issues that you've heard about?** *(Sample answers: Should a run-down historic building in town be restored or demolished? Should owners of beachfront property be allowed to restrict public access to beaches? Should the federal government fund daycare facilities?)*

DISCOVER

Skills Focus forming operational definitions
Time 15 minutes
Tips As students identify general issues such as "air pollution," encourage them to think of specific, *debatable* questions such as "Should car manufacturers be forced to build more efficient engines so our air is cleaner?"
Expected Outcome Decisions regarding the most important issue will vary.
Think It Over Students' definitions will vary but should include the idea of environment-related questions or problems on which people have different viewpoints.

SECTION 1 Recognizing Environmental Issues

DISCOVER ACTIVITY

How Do You Decide?

1. On a sheet of paper, list the three environmental issues you think are most important.
2. Form a group with three other classmates. Share your lists. As a group decide which one of the issues is the most important.

Think It Over
Forming Operational Definitions Based on your group's discussion, how would you define the term *environmental issue?*

GUIDE FOR READING

- ◆ What are the main types of environmental issues?
- ◆ What is environmental science?
- ◆ How do decision makers balance different needs and concerns?

Reading Tip **Before you read, make a list of ways that humans depend on the environment. As you read, add examples from the text.**

Here's a puzzle for you: What is bigger than the United States and Mexico combined; is covered with two kilometers of ice; is a source of oil, coal, and iron; and is a unique habitat for many animals? The answer is Antarctica. People once thought of Antarctica as a useless, icy wasteland. But when explorers told of its huge populations of seals and whales, hunters began going to Antarctica. Then scientists set up research stations to study the unique conditions there. They soon discovered valuable minerals beneath the thick ice.

Now the puzzle is what to do with Antarctica. Many people want its rich deposits of minerals and oil. Others worry that mining will harm the delicate ecosystems there. An ecosystem is all the living and nonliving things that interact in an area. Should Antarctica's ecosystems remain undisturbed? It is not even obvious who should decide Antarctica's fate.

In 1998, 26 nations agreed to ban mining and oil exploration in Antarctica for at least 50 years. As resources become more scarce elsewhere in the world, the debate will surely continue.

Types of Environmental Issues

People have always used Earth's resources. But as the human population has grown, so has its effect on the environment. People compete with each other and with other living things for Earth's limited resources. Disposing of wastes created by people can change ecosystems. And while people are continuing to take resources from the environment, many resources cannot be replaced. These resources could eventually run out.

Figure 1 This leopard seal's habitat could be affected if oil drilling is allowed in Antarctica. This tradeoff is an example of an environmental issue.

530

READING STRATEGIES

Reading Tip Students will likely list air, water, and food. If they do not include shelter, point out that homes and other buildings are constructed from materials taken from the environment.

Paraphrasing This section includes many abstract concepts that some students may find difficult to comprehend or to relate directly to their own experience. To ensure understanding as students read the section, have different volunteers summarize the text under each heading and subheading in their own words. Encourage the rest of the class to suggest additions and improvements to the volunteers' summaries and to offer specific examples of the concepts based on their own experience.

Figure 2 Cherries are a renewable resource. After they are harvested, new cherries will grow in their place. In contrast, the aluminum and iron used to make these kitchen tools are nonrenewable resources.

The three main types of environmental issues are resource use, population growth, and pollution. These issues are all connected, making them very difficult to solve.

Resource Use Recall from Chapter 15 that anything in the environment that is used by people is a natural resource. Some natural resources, called renewable resources, are naturally replaced in a relatively short time. Renewable resources include sunlight, wind, and trees. But it is possible to use up some renewable resources. For example, if people cut down trees faster than they can grow back, the supply of this resource will decrease.

Natural resources that are not replaced as they are used are nonrenewable resources. Most nonrenewable resources, such as coal and oil, exist in a limited supply. As nonrenewable resources are used, the supply may eventually be depleted.

Population Growth Figure 3 shows how the human population has changed in the last 3,000 years. You can see that the population grew very slowly until about A.D. 1650. Around that time, improvements in medicine, agriculture, and sanitation enabled people to live longer. The death rate decreased. But as the population has continued to grow, the demand for resources has also grown.

Pollution Any change to the environment that has a negative effect on living things is called **pollution.** Pollution is an issue because it is often the result of an activity that benefits humans. For example, generating electricity by burning coal can result in air pollution. Some pesticides used to kill insects that eat crops are harmful to other animals.

☑ *Checkpoint* *What is a natural resource?*

Figure 3 If two's company, six billion is certainly a crowd! The human population has grown rapidly in the last few centuries. *Calculating How much has the population grown since 1650?*

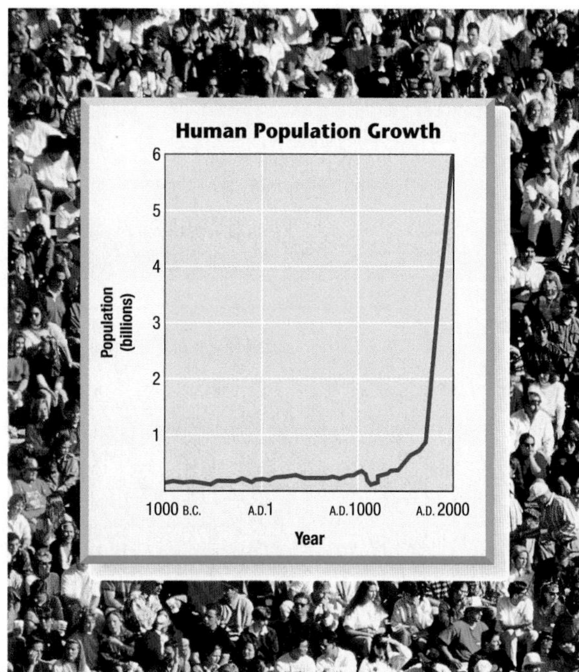

2 Facilitate

Types of Environmental Issues

Building Inquiry Skills: Graphing

Materials *graph paper, ruler, pencil, world map*
Time 15 minutes

Point out that Figure 3 shows the entire world population and that growth rates and population sizes vary among different regions and countries of the world. Give students the current populations of several countries listed below, and have each student make a bar graph to compare the population sizes. Then have students use their graphs to answer the following questions: **Which country has the largest population?** *(China)* **The next largest?** *(India)* **How many times larger than Japan's population is the U.S. population?** *(About twice as large)* Have students compare the United States' and Japan's land areas on a world map, and ask: **Which country has a higher population density?** *(Japan; if needed, help students recall the term* population density *from Chapter 1.)* **learning modality: logical/mathematical**

1998 Population of Selected Countries	
Brazil	165,200,000
China	1,255,100,000
Great Britain	58,200,000
India	975,800,000
Indonesia	207,400,000
Japan	125,900,000
Mexico	95,800,000
Nigeria	121,800,000
Russia	147,200,000
United States	270,000,000

Program Resources

- **Unit 5 Resources** 17-1 Lesson Plan; 17-1 Section Summary
- **Guided Reading and Study Workbook** Section 17-1

Answers to Self-Assessment

Caption Question

Figure 3 By more than 5 million people (from about 750 thousand to about 6 million)

☑ *Checkpoint*

A natural resource is anything in the environment that is used by people.

Ongoing Assessment

Writing Have each student explain why the world's human population has grown so dramatically in the past 350 years.

Approaches to Environmental Issues

Real-Life Learning

Ask students: **What things that you do now or could start doing would help protect the environment if a lot of other people did them, too?** *(Accept all reasonable responses, such as recycling soft-drink cans instead of throwing them in the trash or putting on a sweater instead of turning up the heat at home.)* As students suggest actions, list each one on the board and ask: **How does this help solve environmental problems?** *(Sample answers: Recycling cans reduces our need to mine more aluminum, which is a nonrenewable resource. Putting on a sweater instead of turning up the heat reduces our use of heating fuel, another nonrenewable resource, and the air pollution that is released when fuels are burned.)* **learning modality: logical/mathematical**

Including All Students

ACTIVITY

Materials *current newspapers and magazines, scissors, large sheet of construction paper, tape or glue, markers*
Time 20–40 minutes

For students who need additional challenges, provide a variety of magazines and local and national newspapers. Let students work in groups of two or three to look through the sources and find articles about environmental issues in their community, state, or region. Suggest that each group choose one issue to use as the subject of a poster that summarizes the problem in the students' own words, briefly describes different viewpoints on or proposed solutions to the problem, and includes a photograph, graph, or other visual related to the issue. Display the completed posters in the classroom. Allow time for students to review one another's posters and discuss their ideas and views about the issues. **learning modality: verbal**

Approaches to Environmental Issues

Dealing with environmental issues means making choices. These choices can be made at personal, local, national, or global levels. Whether to ride in a car, take a bus, or ride your bicycle to the mall is an example of a personal choice. Whether to build a landfill or an incinerator for disposing of a town's wastes is a local choice. Whether the United States should allow oil drilling in a wildlife refuge is a national choice. How to protect Earth's atmosphere is a global choice.

Choices that seem personal are often part of much larger issues. Choices of what you eat, what you wear, and how you travel all affect the environment in a small way. When the choices made by millions of people are added together, each person's actions can make a difference.

Making a Difference

Can one individual change the way people think? The leaders featured in this time line have influenced the way that many people think about environmental issues.

1892
California writer John Muir founds the Sierra Club. The group promotes the setting aside of wild areas as national parks. Muir's actions lead to the establishment of Yosemite National Park.

1905
Forestry scientist Gifford Pinchot is appointed the first director of the United States Forest Service. His goal is to manage forests scientifically to meet current and future lumber needs.

1875 — **1900** — **1925**

Theodore Roosevelt (left) and John Muir (right)

1903
President Theodore Roosevelt establishes the first National Wildlife Refuge on Pelican Island, Florida, to protect the brown pelican.

532

Background

History of Science Students could also research these people for *In Your Journal.*

- **Jacques Cousteau** Through his many TV films, marine explorer Cousteau educated millions about ocean life and environmental damage caused by humans.
- **Dian Fossey** A zoologist known for her field studies of the rare mountain gorilla in east-central Africa, Fossey urged the preservation of this endangered species.
- **Jane Goodall** This animal behaviorist's multigenerational studies discovered meat eating and tool use among wild chimpanzees and increased our knowledge of the ecology of nonhuman primates.
- **Chico Mendes** Brazilian rubber tapper Mendes fought to prevent the destruction of rain forests and to establish extractive reserves where products could be harvested without causing ecological damage.

The first step in making environmental decisions is to understand how humans interact with the environment. **Environmental science is the study of the natural processes that occur in the environment and how humans can affect them.**

When people make decisions about environmental issues, the information provided by environmental scientists is a starting point. The next step is to decide what to do with the information. But environmental decisions also involve discussions of values, not just facts and figures. Environmental decisions usually require considering many different points of view. Most of these viewpoints fall into one of these three categories: development, preservation, or conservation.

☑ *Checkpoint* *What is an example of a local choice about an environmental issue?*

In Your Journal

Find out more about one of the people featured in this time line. Write a short biography of the person's life explaining how he or she became involved in environmental issues. What obstacles did the person overcome to accomplish his or her goal?

1949

Naturalist Aldo Leopold publishes *A Sand County Almanac.* This classic book links wildlife management to the science of ecology.

1969

At the age of 79, journalist Marjory Stoneman Douglas founds Friends of the Everglades. This grassroots organization is dedicated to preserving the unique Florida ecosystem. She continues to work for the Everglades until her death in 1998.

1950 **1975** **2000**

1962

Biologist Rachel Carson writes *Silent Spring,* which describes the harmful effects of pesticides on the environment. The book raises awareness of how human activities can affect the environment.

1977

Biologist Wangari Maathai founds the Green Belt Movement. This organization encourages restoring forests in Kenya and other African nations.

Media and Technology

Concept Videotape Library
Grade 6, Tape 4 "Can We Still Get What We Need"

Answers to Self-Assessment

☑ *Checkpoint*

Answers will vary. *Sample answer:* Whether to build a landfill or an incinerator for disposing of a town's wastes

Building Inquiry Skills: Inferring

Point out the text statement that making decisions about environmental issues involves values, and ask: **What is a value?** *(An idea or standard that people think is important or worthwhile)* **What are some examples of values?** *(People should be honest, fair, reliable, and so forth.)* Draw students' attention to an environmental issue discussed in the text, and ask: **How would people's values affect their opinions and decisions about this issue?** *(Sample answer: Government decision makers might decide that wildlife refuges are too important to the survival of certain species to risk damaging them by oil drilling.)* **learning modality: verbal**

SCIENCE & History

ACTIVITY

Call on volunteers to read the entries on the time line. Provide a U.S. and world map and ask other volunteers to locate the places mentioned in the entries. Ask students to share any experiences or information that they have about the featured people or places. Ask students to consider which of these people they would like to learn more about.

In Your Journal Provide a variety of source materials for students' research. After students have written their biographical sketches, encourage them work in small groups to create short skits based on their research, with one member of each group playing the role of the historical person. Encourage students to make their skits fun and interesting by using costumes and props in their portrayal of the person. Also suggest that they incorporate quotations taken from the person's writings, speeches, or interviews. **learning modality: verbal**

Ongoing Assessment

Writing Have each student explain how the actions of individuals can have a large effect on environmental issues.

Students can save their explanations in their portfolios.

Approaches to Environmental Issues, continued

Building Inquiry Skills: Classifying

After students have read about development, preservation, and conservation viewpoints, direct their attention to an environmental issue in the text or from your local area, and ask: **What would be the development viewpoint on this issue?** *(Wildlife refuge example: We need to use all possible new sources of oil in the United States.)* **The preservation viewpoint?** *(Wildlife refuges must be kept natural and unspoiled by human activity.)* **The conservation viewpoint?** *(We need to find ways to use less oil in this country so we don't have to risk damaging natural areas to get it.)* Continue the same procedure using several other issues as examples.
learning modality: logical/mathematical

Weighing Costs and Benefits

Sharpen your Skills

Communicating

ACTIVITY

Time 20 minutes
Tips The three students in each group should represent the development, preservation, and conservation viewpoints.
Expected Outcome *Similarities:* All three viewpoints recognize that Antarctica has valuable resources and unique conditions. *Differences:* The development viewpoint gives priority to people's need for Antarctica's rich supply of oil and mineral resources; the preservation viewpoint gives priority to the needs of the organisms that live in Antarctica; the conservation viewpoint tries to strike a balance between the other two viewpoints.
Extend Let each group choose a local issue and create a compare/contrast table from the same three viewpoints.
learning modality: verbal

Figure 4 The environment is valued for many different reasons. *Applying Concepts In what other ways might this area be valuable?*

Development The belief that humans should be able to freely use and benefit from all of Earth's resources is referred to as the **development viewpoint.** This viewpoint considers the environment in terms of economics. Economics involves business, money, and jobs. According to the development viewpoint, the most valuable parts of the environment are those resources that are most useful to human beings.

Preservation The belief that all parts of the environment are equally important, no matter how useful they are to humans, is the **preservation viewpoint.** This viewpoint considers humans to be the caretakers of nature. Preservationists feel that Earth and its resources should be a source of beauty, comfort, and recreation. The preservation viewpoint is that living things and ecosystems should not be disturbed for the benefit of people.

Conservation The **conservation viewpoint** is the belief that people should use resources from the environment as long as they do not destroy those resources. Conservationists feel that people must balance development and preservation. The conservation viewpoint is that people should manage Earth's resources for the future, not just for today.

✓ ***Checkpoint*** ***What are three viewpoints about how humans should interact with the environment?***

Background

History of Science Should oil exploration be allowed in the Arctic National Wildlife Refuge? Visitors to this vast preserve of boreal forest and tundra in northeastern Alaska can see wildlife ranging from polar bears and musk oxen to arctic foxes and caribou. Opponents of exploration worry that oil exploration and production could damage the refuge's fragile ecosystems. Proponents argue that the United States needs to produce more oil domestically, rather than import it from other countries, to meet the nation's energy needs. In 1995, the Department of the Interior issued a study concluding that oil drilling would adversely affect the refuge's ecosystems. Nonetheless, Congress passed a bill to permit oil exploration there. President Clinton vetoed that measure, but the controversy over the refuge continues.

Weighing Costs and Benefits

Lawmakers work with many different government agencies to make environmental decisions. Together they must consider the needs and concerns of people with many different viewpoints. **To help balance these different opinions, decision makers weigh the costs and benefits of a proposal.**

Costs and benefits are often economic. Will a proposal provide jobs? Will it cost too much money? But costs and benefits are not only measured in terms of money. For example, building an incinerator might reduce the beauty of a natural landscape (a scenic cost). But the incinerator might be safer than an existing open dump site (a health benefit). It is also important to consider short-term and long-term effects. A proposal's short-term costs might be outweighed by its long-term benefits.

Consider the costs and benefits of drilling for oil in Antarctica. Drilling for oil would have many costs. It would be very expensive to set up a drilling operation in such a cold and distant place. Transporting the oil would be difficult and costly. An oil spill in the seas around Antarctica could harm the fish, penguins, and seals there.

On the other hand, there would be many benefits to drilling in Antarctica. A new supply of oil would provide fuel for heat, electricity, and transportation. The plan would create many new jobs. There would be a greater opportunity to study Antarctica's ecosystems. Do the benefits of drilling outweigh the costs? This is the kind of question lawmakers ask when they make environmental decisions.

Communicating

ACTIVITY

Form a group with two other students. Each person will be assigned a different viewpoint toward the environment. Hold a panel discussion in which each person proposes how the continent of Antarctica should be used. What similarities and differences are there among your responses?

Section 1 Review

1. List the three main types of environmental issues.
2. Define environmental science.
3. What is one way to balance different viewpoints on an environmental issue?
4. How has the growth of the human population affected the environment?
5. List three costs and three benefits of drilling for oil on Antarctica.
6. **Thinking Critically Comparing and Contrasting** Compare renewable and nonrenewable resources. Give an example of each type of resource.

Check Your Progress CHAPTER PROJECT

Stake out a square plot measuring 1.5 meters on each side. Record the date, time, temperature, and weather. Observe the organisms in your plot, and record them with notes and drawings. Include enough detail so that you can identify any unfamiliar organisms later. (*Hint:* Also note evidence such as feathers or footprints that shows that other organisms may have visited the plot.)

Program Resources

- **Unit 5 Resources** 17-1 Review and Reinforce; 17-1 Enrich

Answers to Self-Assessment

Caption Question

Figure 4 Accept all reasonable responses. *Sample answer:* The valley might be the source of fish or other animals used for food.

Checkpoint

The three viewpoints are development, preservation, and conservation.

3 Assess

Section 1 Review Answers

1. Resource management, population growth, pollution
2. The study of natural processes that occur in the environment and how humans can affect those processes
3. Weigh the costs and benefits of a proposal
4. As the population grew, people used more and more of Earth's resources. They also produced more wastes.
5. *Costs:* Setting up drilling operations and transporting the oil would be difficult and expensive. Oil spills could damage ecosystems. *Benefits:* New oil supplies would provide fuel for heating, generating electricity, and transportation. Drilling for and transporting the oil would provide new jobs. Setting up oil operations in Antarctica would allow people to study its ecosystems and plan ways to protect its wildlife.
6. Renewable resources are those that are replaced naturally within a fairly short time as they are used, such as trees, sunlight, and wind. Nonrenewable resources are those that are not replaced within a short time as they are used, such as coal and oil.

Check Your Progress CHAPTER PROJECT

If students' plots are grouped in the same area, make sure they leave enough space between the plots so they can move around without walking on another group's plot. In this and subsequent observation sessions, encourage students to note any animal behaviors they see, such as feeding, fighting, or cooperating in some way—for example, ants collecting food.

Performance Assessment

Skills Check Have each student choose one action related to an environmental issue and create a table with the costs of the action listed in one column and its benefits in a second column.

Real-World Lab

You and Your Community

Is Paper a Renewable Resource?

Preparing for Inquiry

Key Concept Paper is a renewable resource because it can be recycled.
Skills Objectives Students will be able to
- observe and compare dry newspaper and recycled paper made from newspaper pulp;
- design an experiment to recycle other types of paper.

Time *Day 1:* 15 minutes; *Day 2:* 40 minutes; *Day 3:* 10 minutes
Advance Planning Gather an ample supply of old newspapers.

Guiding Inquiry

Introducing the Procedure
- Have students read the entire procedure. Clarify that they will do the lab on three different days: Steps 1–2 on Day 1, Steps 3–6 on Day 2, and Step 7 on Day 3.

Troubleshooting the Experiment
- *Day 1:* In Step 1, ask: What do you see in the paper? (*fibers*)
- *Day 2:* Have students reread Steps 3–6. Remind them to replace the newspaper under the screen each day if it is wet.
- *Day 3:* Make sure the pulp is completely dry before handling it.

Expected Outcome
The dried pulp will be rough, stiff, and grayish—like cardboard egg cartons. Cellulose fibers will be visible.

Analyze and Conclude
1. Fibers; they are made of plant material and come from the plants used to make the paper.
2. When the paper is soaked and mashed, the fibers are broken up. When the pulp is flattened and dried, the fibers intertwine again.
3. After two or three recyclings, the fibers become too short or too fragile to intertwine again.
4. Renewable; paper can be recycled, and new trees can be planted.

Extending the Inquiry

Design an Experiment Students' plans should be similar to the lab procedure.

Safety

Students should handle the microscope slide carefully to avoid breakage. Review the safety guidelines in Appendix A.

Real-World Lab

You and Your Community

Is Paper a Renewable Resource?

Recycling is a common local environmental issue. In this lab, you will explore how well paper can be recycled.

Problem

What happens when paper is recycled?

Skills Focus

observing, designing experiments

Materials

newspaper	microscope	water
eggbeater	square pan	screen
plastic wrap	mixing bowl	heavy book
microscope slide		

Procedure 

1. Tear off a small piece of newspaper. Place the paper on a microscope slide and examine it under a microscope. Record your observations.
2. Tear a sheet of newspaper into pieces about the size of postage stamps. Place the pieces in the mixing bowl. Add enough water to cover the newspaper. Cover the bowl and let the mixture stand overnight.
3. The next day, add more water to cover the paper if necessary. Use the eggbeater to mix the wet paper until it is smooth. This thick liquid is called paper pulp.
4. Place the screen in the bottom of the pan. Pour the pulp onto the screen, spreading it out evenly. Then lift the screen above the pan, allowing most of the water to drip into the pan.
5. Place the screen and pulp on several layers of newspaper to absorb the rest of the water. Lay a sheet of plastic wrap over the pulp. Place a heavy book on top of the plastic wrap to press more water out of the pulp.
6. After 30 minutes, remove the book. Carefully turn over the screen, plastic wrap, and pulp. Remove the screen and plastic wrap. Let the pulp sit on the newspaper for one or two more days to dry. Replace the newspaper layers if necessary.
7. When the pulp is dry, observe it closely. Record your observations.

Analyze and Conclude

1. What kind of structures did you observe when you examined torn newspaper under a microscope? What are these structures made of? Where do they come from?
2. What do you think happens to the structures you observed when paper is recycled?
3. Based on your results, predict how many times a sheet of newspaper can be recycled.
4. **Apply** Should paper be classified as a renewable or nonrenewable resource? Explain.

Design an Experiment

Using procedures like those in this lab, design an experiment to recycle three different types of paper, such as shiny magazine paper, paper towels, and cardboard. Find out how the resulting papers differ. Obtain your teacher's approval for your plans before you try your experiment.

536

Program Resources
- **Unit 5 Resources** Real-World Lab blackline masters

Media and Technology

 **Lab Activity Videotapes** Grade 6, Tape 4

Forests and Fisheries

DISCOVER ACTIVITY

What Happened to the Tuna?

1. Use the data in the table to make a line graph. Label the axes of the graph and add a title. (To review graphing, see the Skills Handbook.)
2. Mark the high and low points on the graph.

Year	Western Atlantic Bluefin Tuna Population
1970	240,000
1975	190,000
1980	90,000
1985	60,000
1990	45,000
1994	60,000

Think It Over

Inferring How did the tuna population change during this period? Can you suggest a possible reason for this change?

GUIDE FOR READING

◆ How can forests and fisheries be managed?

Reading Tip As you read, make a list of ways to conserve forests and fisheries.

At first glance, a bluefin tuna and a pine tree may not seem to have much in common. One is an animal and the other is a plant. One lives in the ocean and the other lives on land. However, tuna and pine trees are both living resources. Tuna are a source of food for people. People don't eat pine trees, but they do use them to make lumber, paper, and turpentine. People also use pine needles as mulch in gardens.

Every day you use many different products that are made from living organisms. In this section, you will read about two major types of living resources: forests and fisheries. As you read, think about how they are similar and how they are different.

Forest Resources

Forests are a resource because they contain valuable materials. Many products are made from the flowers, fruits, seeds, and other parts of forest plants. Some of these products, such as maple syrup, rubber, and nuts, come from living trees. Other products, such as lumber and pulp for paper, require cutting trees down. Conifers, including pine and spruce, are used for construction and for making paper. Hardwoods, such as oak, cherry, and maple, are used for furniture because of their strength and beauty.

Trees and other plants produce oxygen that other organisms need to survive. They also absorb carbon dioxide and many pollutants from the air. Trees also help prevent flooding and control soil erosion. Their roots absorb rainwater and hold the soil together.

Figure 5 One important use of forest resources is for building housing.

READING STRATEGIES

Reading Tip Students' lists may vary. *Sample lists of ways to conserve forests:* selective cutting, replanting trees, plan frequency of cutting, log small patches of forest in stages. *Sample list of ways to conserve fisheries:* set fishing limits, control size of fish harvested, close fishery until it recovers, regulate fishing methods, develop aquaculture techniques, fish for new species.

Program Resources

- **Unit 5 Resources** 17-2 Lesson Plan; 17-2 Section Summary
- **Guided Reading and Study Workbook** Section 17-2

Forests and Fisheries

Objectives

After completing the lesson, students will be able to

◆ describe different ways that forests can be managed to provide resources;
◆ describe ways that fisheries can be managed to provide resources.

Key Terms clear-cutting, selective cutting, sustainable yield, fishery, aquaculture

1 Engage/Explore

Activating Prior Knowledge

Invite students to look around the classroom and identify as many products as they can that are derived from trees. *(Examples include writing paper, cardboard, posterboard, paper towels, wood furniture, pencils, rulers, and plywood.)*

DISCOVER

Skills Focus inferring
Materials *graph paper, ruler, pencil*
Time 15 minutes
Expected Outcome Increments used for the vertical axis may vary.
Sample Graph

Changes in Western Atlantic Bluefin Tuna Population

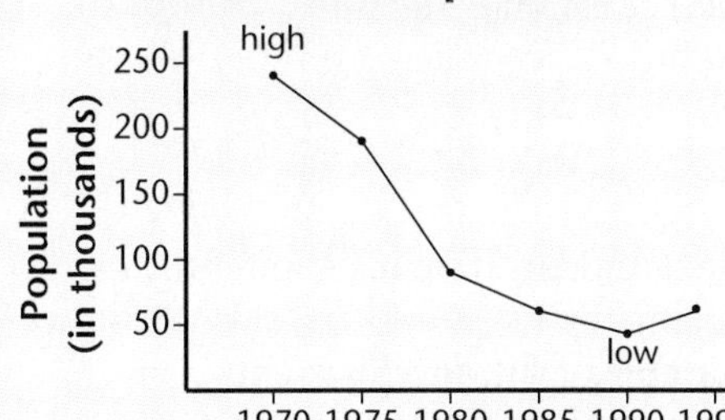

Year

Think It Over The tuna population declined steadily from 1970 to 1990, then increased from 1990 to 1994. The decline was probably due to overfishing of tuna; the rebound may have resulted from limits on tuna fishing.

2 Facilitate

Forest Resources

Including All Students

Review for students who need more help the amount of land area on Earth suitable for forests. Have students look back at the following biome maps in Chapter 6: page 179, tropical and temperate rain forests and page 182, deciduous and boreal forests. Trace each map onto an overhead transparency. Overlay the maps while projecting them so students can see the total land area where forests can grow. **learning modality: visual**

Managing Forests

Social Studies CONNECTION

Provide a picture of a small village with a commons, such as ones found in England or New England. To help students understand how this problem could arise, ask them to put themselves in the place of the local people. Would they stop bringing their cattle to the commons for the greater good, or would they expect others to stop?

In Your Journal Volunteers can share their ideas in a class discussion. Encourage students to comment on each idea's feasibility. **learning modality: verbal**

Building Inquiry Skills: Classifying

After students have read about the two logging methods, ask: **Is clear-cutting an example of the development, preservation, or conservation viewpoint toward the environment?** *(development)* **Which viewpoint does selective cutting represent?** *(conservation)* **What would represent the preservation viewpoint?** *(Not cutting the forest at all)* **learning modality: logical/mathematical**

Figure 6 Clear-cutting has left large portions of these hillsides bare. *Interpreting Photographs What problems might clear-cutting cause?*

Social Studies CONNECTION

Many of the world's living resources are owned by no one—they are shared by everyone. A word that is sometimes used to describe such a shared resource is a "commons." This word comes from a time when villages were built around common areas of open land. All the town's residents grazed their cattle on the commons. This worked well as long as there weren't too many people. But as more and more people brought their cattle to the commons, the area would become overgrazed. There would not be enough pasture to feed even one cow—the "tragedy of the commons."

In Your Journal

Suppose you live in a farming community with a central commons. Propose a solution that will allow residents to use the commons while protecting it from overuse.

Managing Forests

There are about 300 million hectares of forests in the United States. That's nearly a third of the nation's area! Many forests are located on publicly owned land. Others are owned by private timber and paper companies or by individuals. Forest industries provide jobs for 1.5 million people.

Because new trees can be planted to replace trees that are cut down, forests can be renewable resources. The United States Forest Service and environmental organizations work with forestry companies to conserve forest resources. They try to develop logging methods that maintain forests as renewable resources.

Logging Methods There are two major methods of logging: clear-cutting and selective cutting. **Clear-cutting** is the process of cutting down all the trees in an area at once. Cutting down only some trees in a forest and leaving a mix of tree sizes and species behind is called **selective cutting.**

Each logging method has advantages and disadvantages. Clear-cutting is usually quicker and cheaper than selective cutting. It may also be safer for the loggers. In selective cutting, the loggers must move the heavy equipment and logs around the remaining trees in the forest. But selective cutting is usually less damaging to the forest environment than clear-cutting. When an area of forest is clear-cut, conditions change. Clear-cutting exposes the soil to wind and rain. Without the protection of the tree roots, the soil is more easily blown or washed away. Soil washed into streams may harm the fish and other organisms that live there.

Sustainable Forestry Forests can be managed to provide a sustained yield. A **sustainable yield** is a regular amount of a renewable resource such as trees that can be harvested without

Background

Integrating Science Forests can have a profound effect on climate. Scientists think that deforestation contributes to changes in climate at regional and global scales. Through transpiration, trees add huge amounts of water vapor to the atmosphere. In fact, a tree returns to the air about 97 percent of the water that the tree's roots absorb from the ground. This water eventually falls back to Earth through the water cycle. Removal of a forest may cause the rainfall in a region to decline and increase the frequency of droughts.

The deforestation of tropical rain forests, so prevalent in recent years, may contribute to an increase in global temperatures. Burning the felled trees adds carbon dioxide to the atmosphere. The higher the concentration of CO_2 in the atmosphere, the more heat the atmosphere holds in and does not radiate back into space.

reducing the future supply. This works sort of like a book swap: as long as you donate a book each time you borrow one, the total supply of books will not be affected. Planting a tree to replace one being cut down is like donating a book to replace a borrowed one.

Part of forest management is planning how frequently the trees must be replanted to keep a constant supply. Different species grow at different rates. Trees with softer woods, such as pines, usually mature faster than trees with harder woods, such as hickory, oak, and cherry. Forests containing faster-growing trees can be harvested and replanted more often. For example, pine forests may be harvested every 20 to 30 years. On the other hand, some hardwood forests may be harvested only every 40 to 100 years. One sustainable approach is to log small patches of forest. This way, different sections of forest can be harvested every year.

Certified Wood Forests that are managed in a sustainable way can be certified by the Forest Stewardship Council. Once a forest is certified, all wood logged from that forest may carry a "well-managed" label. This label allows businesses and individuals to select wood from forests that are managed for sustainable yields.

☑ *Checkpoint* *What is a sustainable yield?*

Figure 7 Two logging methods are clear-cutting and selective cutting. **A.** After clear-cutting, the new trees are usually all the same age and species. **B.** Selective cutting results in a more diverse forest.

Original forest *Clear-cutting* *Replanted growth*

Original forest *Selective cutting* *Diverse regrowth*

Inquiry Challenge

Materials *colored plastic chips, construction paper squares, or similar objects*
Time 15 minutes

Tell students that another sustainable forestry practice is to harvest all the mature trees in an area at intervals—a practice known as shelterwood cutting. In the first harvest, all the unwanted tree species and dead or diseased trees are cut down. The forest is then left alone so the remaining trees can continue to grow and new seedlings can become established. After a period of time, many of the mature trees are removed in a second harvest, and the forest is again left alone to grow. In a third harvest, the remaining mature trees are cut down. By this time, though, the seedlings have grown into young trees, and more new seedlings are growing. Challenge small groups of students to devise a simple model of shelterwood cutting. Team students who have difficulty seeing or whose movements are limited with students who do not have these disabilities. *(Sample model: Use green paper squares to represent mature trees and brown squares to represent unwanted trees. For the "first harvest," remove all brown squares. Add red squares to represent seedlings. In the "second harvest," remove some of the green squares. Replace the red squares with yellow squares to represent the growth of the seedlings into young trees, and add more red squares. In the "third harvest," remove the remaining green squares, replace the yellow squares with green squares and the red squares with yellow squares, and add more red squares.)* Have each group describe their model in writing. Ask: **How does shelterwood cutting provide a sustainable yield?** *(The forest constantly replenishes itself.)* **learning modality: kinesthetic**

Media and Technology

Transparencies "Logging Methods," Transparency 69

Answers to Self-Assessment

Caption Question

Figure 6 The soil on the hill may erode, and silt may clog streams. Without tree roots to absorb water, areas may flood. Many organisms would lose their habitat.

☑ *Checkpoint*

A regular amount of a renewable resource that can be harvested without reducing the future supply

Ongoing Assessment

Skills Check Have each student construct a table comparing the advantages and disadvantages of clear-cutting and selective cutting.

Students could save their tables in their portfolios.

Fisheries

Calculating

Materials *calculator*
Time 15 minutes
Expected Outcome China–21.6%, Japan–6.0%, United States–5.0%, Peru–7.9%
Extend Have students devise a way of visually comparing these amounts (such as a circle graph or bar graph). **learning modality: logical/mathematical**

Real-Life Learning

Suggest that students visit a fish market or the seafood and canned-fish sections of a supermarket and list the names of all the fish and seafoods they see on display. Encourage students to interview store personnel and examine labels to determine each food's country of origin. Which foods are obtained locally? Which are shipped in from other parts of the country? Which are imported from other countries? Have students report and compare their findings in class. (As an alternative, you could bring supermarket flyers and cookbooks to class and have students make a list of all the fish and seafood they find.) **learning modality: visual**

Calculating

In a recent year, the total catch of fish in the world was 112.9 million metric tons. Based on the data below, calculate the percent of this total each country caught.

Country	Catch (millions of metric tons)
China	24.4
Japan	6.8
United States	5.6
Peru	8.9

Fisheries

Until recently, the oceans seemed like an unlimited resource. The waters held such huge schools of fish, it seemed impossible that they could ever disappear. And fish reproduce in incredible numbers. A single codfish can lay as many as nine million eggs in a single year! But people have discovered that this resource has limits. After many years of big catches, the number of sardines off the California coast suddenly declined. The same thing happened to the huge schools of cod off the New England coast. What caused these changes?

An area with a large population of valuable ocean organisms is called a **fishery.** Some major fisheries include the Grand Banks off Newfoundland, Georges Bank off New England, and Monterey Canyon off California. Fisheries like these are valuable renewable resources. But if fish are caught at a faster rate than they can breed, the population decreases. This situation is known as overfishing.

Scientists estimate that 70 percent of the world's major fisheries have been overfished. But if those fish populations are allowed to recover, a sustainable yield of fish can once again be harvested. **Managing fisheries for a sustainable yield includes setting fishing limits, changing fishing methods, developing aquaculture techniques, and finding new resources.**

Fishing Limits Laws can help protect individual fish species. Laws may also limit the amount that can be caught or require that fish be at least a certain size. This ensures that young fish

Figure 8 A fishing boat returns to harbor at the end of a long day. Overfishing has forced the crews of many boats to find other work until the fisheries recover.

Background

History of Science In 1994, a section of the Georges Bank fishery was closed because of overfishing. A 1998 study of the area found that there were more than three times the number of scallops there than in areas where fishing had continued. Based on these findings, scallopers wanted regulators to let them back into the closed area. However, scallopers can catch 70 to 80 percent of the scallops in areas that are open to fishing. Taking this many scallops could swiftly decimate the scallop population on Georges Bank again. Scallopers' dredges also catch groundfish, endangering those populations.

Some scallop researchers advocate another approach: closing selected scallop beds from time to time to let the scallop populations regenerate, much as areas of forest are allowed to regrow after being cut.

survive long enough to reproduce. Also, setting an upper limit on the size of fish caught ensures that breeding fish remain in the population. But if a fishery has been severely overfished, the government may need to completely ban fishing until the populations can recover.

Fishing Methods Today fishing practices are regulated by laws. Some fishing crews now use nets with a larger mesh size to allow small, young fish to escape. Some methods have been outlawed. These methods include poisoning fish with cyanide and stunning them by exploding dynamite underwater. These techniques kill all the fish in an area rather than selecting certain fish.

Aquaculture The practice of raising fish and other water-dwelling organisms for food is called **aquaculture.** The fish may be raised in artificial ponds or bays. Salmon, catfish, and shrimp are farmed in this way in the United States.

However, aquaculture is not a perfect solution. The artificial ponds and bays often replace natural habitats such as salt marshes. Maintaining the farms can cause pollution and spread diseases into wild fish populations.

New Resources Today about 9,000 different fish species are harvested for food. More than half the animal protein eaten by people throughout the world comes from fish. One way to help feed a growing human population is to fish for new species. Scientists and chefs are working together to introduce people to deep-water species such as monkfish and tile fish, as well as easy-to-farm freshwater fish such as tilapia.

Figure 9 As fishing limits become stricter, aquaculture is playing a larger role in meeting the worldwide demand for fish. This fish farm in Hawaii raises tilapia.

Section 2 Review

1. Describe one example of a sustainable forestry practice.
2. What are three ways fisheries can be managed so that they will continue to provide fish for the future?
3. Why are forests considered renewable resources?
4. **Thinking Critically Comparing and Contrasting** Describe the advantages and disadvantages of clear-cutting and selective cutting.

Science at Home

Forests and Fish With a family member, conduct a "Forest and Fishery" survey of your home. Make a list of all the things that are made from either forest or fishery products. Then ask other family members to predict how many items are on the list. Are they surprised by the answer?

Program Resources

- **Unit 5 Resources** 17-2 Review and Reinforce; 17-2 Enrich
- **Laboratory Manual** 17, "Managing Fisheries"

3 Assess

Section 2 Review Answers

1. *Any one:* replant trees, plan frequency of cutting, log small patches of forest in stages
2. *Any three:* Fishing limits can be imposed; nets with a larger mesh size can be used; dynamiting, poisoning, and other fishing methods that kill all the fish in an area can be outlawed; aquaculture can replace fishing in natural areas.
3. New trees can be planted to replace trees that are cut down.
4. Clear-cutting is quicker, cheaper, and may be safer for loggers, but selective cutting is less damaging to the environment.

Science at Home

ACTIVITY

Encourage students to look beyond the most obvious products, such as wood and paper from forests, and salt and seafood from oceans, and check labels closely to see if they can find the names of other items. Examples include nuts, spices, tree bark and salt hay for mulch, seaweeds (used both as food and in shampoos and other products), and cuttlebone for pet birds.

Performance Assessment

Oral Presentation Call on students at random to name a way to conserve forests or fisheries.

Skills Lab

Interpreting Data

Tree Cookie Tales

Preparing for Inquiry

Key Concept Growth rings provide information about a tree's age and the growing conditions during its life.

Skills Objectives Students will be able to
- observe growth rings in a tree cookie to determine a tree's age;
- draw conclusions from their observations about conditions that affected the tree's growth.

Time 40 minutes

Advance Planning Purchase or prepare a tree cookie for each group. Inexpensive classroom sets of tree cookies are available from biological supply houses. The tree cookies should come from trees that were more than 10 years old. You can also make tree cookies by sawing a tree trunk into cross sections 1.5–2.5 cm thick. To preserve homemade tree cookies, spray or paint all surfaces with clear polyurethane or other clear sealant.

Guiding Inquiry

Troubleshooting the Experiment

Clarify that each year's growth is shown by a pair of rings—a light ring for spring and a dark ring for summer.

Expected Outcome

Results will vary depending on the particular tree cookies used.

Analyze and Conclude

1. Ages will vary. The tree's age is equal to the number of annual rings.
2. Answers will vary. The largest proportion of tree growth usually occurs during a tree's early years.
3. Observations may vary. Spring rings are usually wider, as trees undergo a burst of new growth in the spring when it is usually wetter followed by slower growth in the summer when it is usually drier.
4. Growth rings reflect weather conditions. Generally, rings are wider during years when temperatures are warmer and rainfall is plentiful.
5. Answers will vary. In addition to the tree's age and weather-related growth patterns, students may note holes made by insects or birds, blackening due to fire or lightning, a hollow pith due to disease, or cracks or gashes from tools.
6. You could look for annual growth patterns indicating the weather conditions and additional evidence of fire, disease, or other environmental conditions.

Extending the Inquiry

More to Explore Answers will depend on the specific tree cookies used.

Skills Lab

Interpreting Data

Tree Cookie Tales

Tree cookies aren't snacks! They're slices of a tree trunk that contain clues about the tree's age, past weather conditions, and fires that occurred during its life. In this lab, you'll interpret the data hidden in a tree cookie.

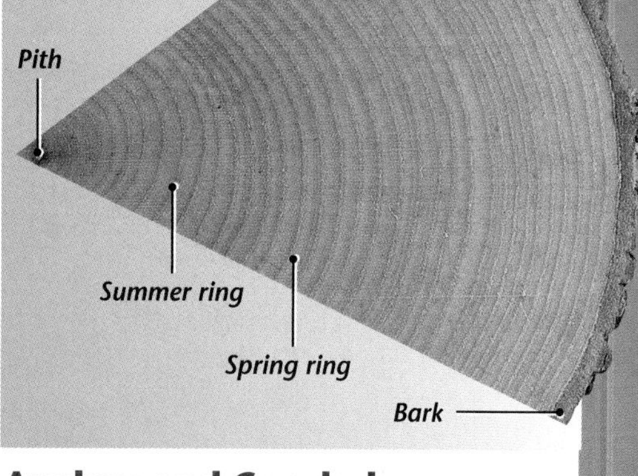

Problem

What can tree cookies reveal about the past?

Materials

tree cookie
metric ruler
hand lens
colored pencils
calculator (optional)

Procedure

1. Use a hand lens to examine your tree cookie. Draw a simple diagram of your tree cookie. Label the bark, tree rings, and center, or pith.
2. Notice the light-colored and dark-colored rings. The light ring results from fast springtime growth. The dark ring, where the cells are smaller, results from slower summertime growth. Each pair of light and dark rings represents one year's growth, so the pair is called an annual ring. Observe and count the annual rings.
3. Compare the spring and summer portions of the annual rings. Identify the thinnest and thickest rings.
4. Measure the distance from the center to the outermost edge of the last summer growth ring. This is the radius of your tree cookie. Record your measurement.
5. Measure the distance from the center to the outermost edge of the 10th summer growth ring. Record your measurement.
6. Examine your tree cookie for any other evidence of its history, such as damaged bark or burn marks. Record your observations.

Analyze and Conclude

1. How old was your tree? How do you know?
2. What percent of the tree's growth took place during the first 10 years of its life? (*Hint:* Divide the distance from the center to the 10th growth ring by the radius. Then multiply by 100. This gives you the percent of growth that occurred during the tree's first 10 years.)
3. How did the spring rings compare to the summer rings for the same year? Suggest a reason.
4. Why might the annual rings be narrower for some years than for others?
5. Using evidence from your tree cookie, summarize the history of the tree.
6. **Think About It** Suppose you had cookies from two other trees of the same species that grew near your tree. How could you verify the interpretations you made in this lab?

More to Explore

Examine and compare several tree cookies. Record any similarities and differences you observe. Do you think any of the tree cookies came from trees growing in the same area? Support your answer with specific evidence.

Program Resources

- **Unit 5 Resources** Skills Lab blackline masters

Media and Technology

Lab Activity Videotapes Grade 6, Tape 4

Section 3 Biodiversity

Discover Activity

How Much Variety Is There?

1. You will be given two cups of seeds and a paper plate. The seeds in Cup A represent the trees in a section of tropical rain forest. The seeds in Cup B represent the trees in a section of deciduous forest.
2. Pour the seeds from Cup A onto the plate. Sort the seeds by type. Count the different types of seeds. This number represents the number of different kinds of trees in that type of forest.
3. Pour the seeds back into Cup A.
4. Repeat Steps 2 and 3 with the seeds in Cup B.
5. Share your results with your class. Use the class results to calculate the average number of different kinds of seeds in each type of forest.

Think It Over

Inferring How does the variety of trees in the tropical rain forest compare with the variety of trees in a deciduous forest? Can you suggest any advantages of having a wide variety of species?

GUIDE FOR READING

- What factors affect an area's biodiversity?
- Which human activities threaten biodiversity?
- How can biodiversity be protected?

Reading Tip Before you read, use the headings to make an outline on biodiversity.

No one knows exactly how many species live on Earth. So far, more than 1.7 million species have been identified. The number of different species in an area is called its **biodiversity.** It is difficult to estimate the total biodiversity on Earth because many areas of the planet have not been thoroughly studied. Some experts think that the deep oceans alone could contain 10 million new species! Protecting this diversity is a major environmental issue today.

Factors Affecting Biodiversity

Biodiversity varies from place to place on Earth. **Factors that affect biodiversity in an ecosystem include area, climate, and diversity of niches.**

Area Within an ecosystem, a large area will contain more species than a small area. For example, suppose you were counting tree species in a forest. You would find far more tree species in a 10-square-meter area than in a 1-square-meter area.

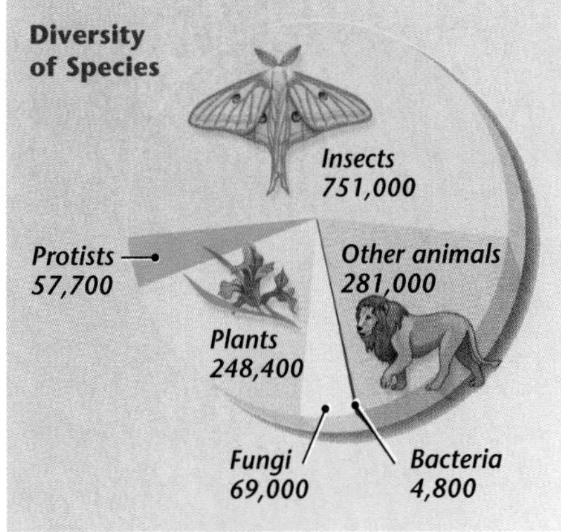

Figure 10 Organisms of many kinds are part of Earth's biodiversity. *Interpreting Graphs Which group of organisms has the greatest number of species?*

Reading Strategies

Reading Tip Suggest that students use the teal headings for the main outline headings and list the purple headings under them. Outlines may begin as shown below.

I. Factors Affecting Biodiversity
   A. Area
   B. Climate
   C. Niche Diversity
II. The Value of Biodiversity

Answers to Self-Assessment

Caption Question

Figure 10 insects

Program Resources

- **Unit 5 Resources** 17-3 Lesson Plan; 17-3 Section Summary
- **Guided Reading and Study Workbook** Section 17-3

Section 3 Biodiversity

Objectives

After completing the lesson, students will be able to

- identify the factors that affect biodiversity;
- explain the value of biodiversity;
- name some human activities that threaten biodiversity;
- list some ways that biodiversity can be protected.

Key Terms biodiversity, keystone species, genes, extinction, endangered species, threatened species, habitat destruction, habitat fragmentation, poaching, captive breeding

1 Engage/Explore

Activating Prior Knowledge

Ask students: **What organisms are native to our area?** *(Answers will vary. Encourage students to consider a wide variety of organism types, including insects, worms, mosses, algae, and bacteria, as well as mammals, birds, fish, reptiles, and amphibians.)* Write the name of each organism on the chalkboard, and after students have finished naming organisms, ask: **Would you say there is very much diversity of species living here?** *(Answers may vary, but in most cases students will say there is.)*

Discover

Skills Focus inferring

Materials *two labeled cups containing different seed mixtures, paper plate*

Time 20 minutes

Advance Preparation Use a mixture of at least ten types of seeds for Cup A and four or five types for Cup B.

Expected Outcome The average number of different kinds of seeds should be greater for the tropical rain forest.

Think It Over The tropical rain forest has a greater variety of trees than the deciduous forest. The wider variety of tree species supports a wider variety of other organisms that depend on the trees for habitat and food.

2 Facilitate

Factors Affecting Biodiversity

Including All Students

For students who need more help, review the meanings of the terms *area* (length times width) and *climate* (the typical weather pattern in an area over a long period of time). If students have difficulty defining *climate* correctly, let them look back at the discussions of climate in Unit 4. **learning modality: verbal**

Building Inquiry Skills: Observing

Materials *books and magazines with photographs of coral reefs*
Time 15 minutes

To illustrate the rich diversity of life on coral reefs, encourage small groups of students to examine other photographs similar to Figure 12, choose a "favorite" photo, and list all the organisms shown in the photo and named in its caption or accompanying text. In a follow-up class discussion, list the number of species on the board for each group. **learning modality: visual**

How Diverse Are Tropical Ecosystems?

In Costa Rica, which is half the size of Tennessee, there are 850 species of birds—200 more than in all the rest of North America.

A 10-hectare area of forest in Borneo contains 700 species of trees, as many as all of North America.

A single river in Brazil contains more species than all of the rivers in the United States combined.

Figure 11 Tropical ecosystems tend to be more diverse than those further from the equator.

Climate In general, the number of species increases from the poles toward the equator. The tropical rain forests of Latin America, southeast Asia, and central Africa are the most diverse ecosystems in the world. These forests cover about 7 percent of Earth's land surface and contain over half of the world's species.

The reason for the great biodiversity in the tropics is not fully understood. Many scientists hypothesize that it has to do with climate. For example, tropical rain forests have fairly constant temperatures and large amounts of rainfall throughout the year. Many plants in these regions have year-round growing seasons. This means that food is available for other organisms year-round.

Figure 12 Coral reefs are the second most diverse ecosystems. *Applying Concepts What is one reason why coral reefs are so diverse?*

Niche Diversity Coral reefs make up less than 1 percent of the oceans' area. But reefs are home to 20 percent of the world's saltwater fish species. Coral reefs are the second most diverse ecosystems in the world. Found only in shallow, warm waters, coral reefs are often called the rain forests of the sea. A reef supports many different niches or roles, for organisms that live under, on, and among the coral. This enables more species to live in the reef than in a more uniform habitat such as a flat sandbar.

☑ *Checkpoint* ***What is one possible reason that tropical regions have the greatest biodiversity?***

The Value of Biodiversity

Perhaps you are wondering how biodiversity is important. Does it matter whether there are 50 or 5,000 species of ferns in some faraway rain forest? Is it necessary to protect every one of these species?

Background

Facts and Figures Scientists have not yet studied most species of plants, animals, fungi, and microorganisms to determine whether they might be useful to humans. Of approximately 250,000 known plant species, only about 25,000 have been investigated.

Insects are one example of an often overlooked biological resource. Insects play a major role in pollinating crops, controlling weeds, and even in controlling some insects that are pests. And other insects produce unusual chemical compounds for which humans may find some use. For example, scientists have found a compound made by fireflies that has potential as an antiviral agent in humans. A fungicide produced by centipedes to protect their eggs might also protect crops from fungus attack.

Figure 13 Ecosystem tours such as safaris can provide income for local people. These tourists are observing giraffes in Botswana.

There are many reasons why preserving biodiversity is important. The simplest reason is that wild organisms and ecosystems are a source of beauty and recreation.

Economic Value Many plants, animals, and other organisms are essential for human survival. In addition to providing food and oxygen, these organisms supply raw materials for clothing, medicine, and other products. No one knows how many other useful species have not yet been identified.

Ecosystems are economically valuable, too. For example, many companies now run wildlife tours in rain forests, savannas, mountain ranges, and other locations. This ecosystem tourism, or "ecotourism," is an important source of jobs and money for nations such as Brazil, Costa Rica, and Kenya.

Value to the Ecosystem All the species in an ecosystem are connected to one another. Species may depend on each other for food and shelter. A change that affects one species will surely affect all the others.

Some species play a particularly important role. A species that influences the survival of many other species in an ecosystem is called a **keystone species.** If a keystone species disappears, the entire ecosystem may change. For example, the sea stars in Figure 14 are a keystone species in their ecosystem. The sea stars prey mostly on the mussels that live in tide pools. When researchers removed the sea stars from an area, the mussels began to outcompete many of the other species in the tide pool. The sea star predators had kept the population of mussels in check, allowing other species to live. When the keystone species disappeared, the balance in the ecosystem was destroyed.

Figure 14 These sea stars on the Washington coast are an example of a keystone species. By preying on mussels, the sea stars keep the mussels from taking over the ecosystem.

The Value of Biodiversity

Building Inquiry Skills: Communicating

Time 20 minutes

ACTIVITY

Divide the class into small groups, and pose the following hypothetical environmental issue for each group to debate: **A chemical for making a new drug has been discovered in a plant species growing in the Amazon rain forest. Several rare species of butterflies depend on the plant for food. To harvest the chemical for human use, the plants have to be cut down and removed from the forest. Should people make use of this new resource, and if so, how?** Encourage each group to try to reach consensus on the issue. After students have debated for a time, let each group report its decision and the reasoning behind it to the rest of the class. **learning modality: verbal**

Demonstration

Materials *model architectural building blocks or photo of arch with keystone*

ACTIVITY

Time 5–10 minutes

Use model architectural building blocks to construct an arch with a keystone. (If such blocks are not available, use a photo of an arch with a keystone.) Point to the keystone, and ask: **What do you predict will happen if I remove this block?** *(Some may predict the arch will fall.)* Remove the keystone to confirm students' predictions. Explain that the block you removed is called a keystone. Ask: **Why is a keystone a good analogy for a keystone species?** *(Because when a keystone species is removed, the entire ecosystem may collapse)* **learning modality: visual**

Answers to Self-Assessment

Caption Question

Figure 12 A coral reef provides many different niches, which enables a wide variety of species to live there.

Checkpoint

Because of its unique climate, the tropical rain forest provides food year-round.

Ongoing Assessment

Writing Have each student identify and briefly explain the three major factors that affect an ecosystem's biodiversity.

Students can save their work in their portfolios.

Gene Pool Diversity

Building Inquiry Skills: Predicting

Ask students: **What is cloning?** *(Making an exact duplicate of an organism—more precisely, using genes taken from an organism's cells to create a new individual that is genetically identical to the original organism)* Pose the following question: **Suppose scientists found an easy and inexpensive way to create large herds of sheep, cattle, and other domestic animals through cloning. Do you think this would be a good idea? Why or why not?** *(Some students may say that cloned herds could have traits that increase our supply of meat, milk, wool, leather, and other products. However, students should realize that entire herds of genetically identical animals could increase susceptibility to disease.)* **learning modality: logical/mathematical**

Extinction of Species

Addressing Naive Conceptions

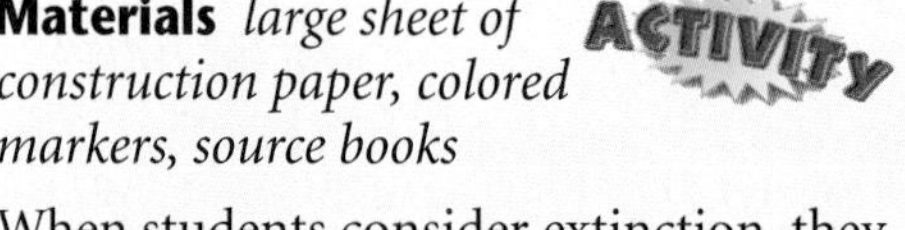

Materials *large sheet of construction paper, colored markers, source books*

When students consider extinction, they usually think of dinosaurs and other species that became extinct in the distant past. Explain that many species have become extinct in relatively recent times. Let each pair of students research one species that became extinct in the past 300 years. Examples include the quagga, dodo, moa, Tasmanian wolf (thylacine), dusky seaside sparrow, Santa Barbara song sparrow, Greek auk, Hawaii oo, passenger pigeon, Abingdon tortoise, blue pike, Tecopa pupfish, and Sampson's pearly mussel. Suggest that one student in each pair draw a picture of the organism and the other student write a brief, first-person description of it—for example, *I'm a quagga, a variety of zebra. I used to live in huge, wild herds in South Africa, but I was hunted for my hide. I became extinct in 1883.* **learning modality: verbal**

Figure 15 Just as diversity of species is important to an ecosystem, diversity of genes is important within a species. Diverse genes give these potatoes their rainbow of colors.

Gene Pool Diversity

The organisms in a healthy population have a diversity of traits. These traits are determined by genes. **Genes** are the structures in an organism's cells that carry its hereditary information. Every organism receives a combination of genes from its parents. Genes determine the organism's characteristics, from its size and appearance to its ability to fight disease. The organisms in one species share many genes. But each organism also has some genes that differ from those of other individuals. These individual differences make up the total gene "pool" of that species.

Species that lack a diverse gene pool are less able to adapt to disease, parasites, or drought. For example, most agricultural crops, such as wheat and corn, have very little diversity. These species are bred to be very uniform. If a disease or parasite attacks, the whole population could be affected. A fungus once wiped out much of the corn crop in the United States in this way. Fortunately, there are many wild varieties of corn that have slightly different genes. At least some of these plants contain genes that make them more resistant to the fungus. Scientists were able to breed corn that was not affected by the fungus. Keeping a diverse gene pool helps ensure that crop species can survive such problems.

☑ *Checkpoint* *What do an organism's genes determine?*

Extinction of Species

The disappearance of all members of a species from Earth is called **extinction.** Extinction is a natural process. Many species that once lived on Earth, from dinosaurs to dodos, are now extinct. But in the last few centuries, the number of species becoming extinct has increased dramatically.

Once a population drops below a certain level, the species may not be able to recover. For example, millions of passenger pigeons once darkened the skies in the United States. People hunted the birds for sport and food, killing many hundreds of thousands. This was only part of the total population of passenger pigeons. But at some point, there were not enough birds to reproduce and increase the population. Only after the birds disappeared did people realize that the species could not survive without its enormous numbers.

Species in danger of becoming extinct in the near future are considered **endangered species.** Species that could become endangered in the near future are considered **threatened species.**

Background

History of Science In the past 100 years, scientists have greatly increased the yields of crops such as corn and wheat by creating highly productive but genetically uniform varieties. With genetic uniformity, however, goes decreased resistance to certain diseases and pests. To restore resistance to these crop varieties, scientists cross them with other, often wild, varieties that retain genetic diversity. Scientists used this approach to create a type of corn that could resist the corn blight fungus described in the student text. They crossed genetically uniform varieties susceptible to the blight with Mexican varieties that possessed the genes needed to be blight resistant. Because the cultivation and domestication of corn (or maize) began in Mexico thousands of years ago, Mexican varieties are ancestral to modern varieties and have greater genetic diversity.

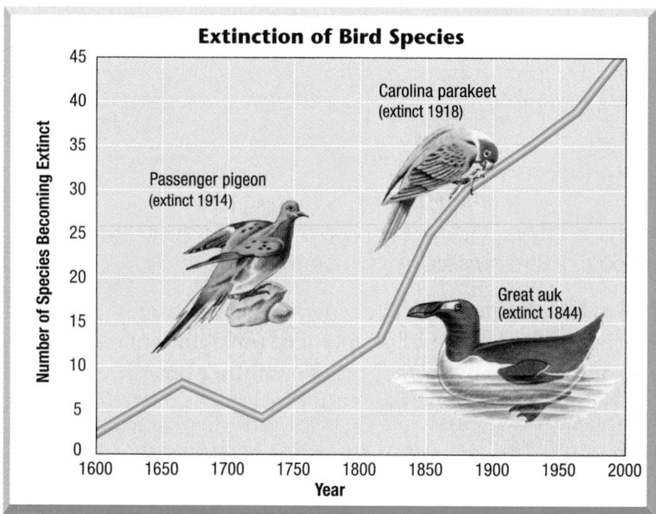

Figure 16 This graph shows the rate of extinction of bird species in the last 400 years. *Interpreting Graphs How many bird species became extinct in 1750? In 1850? In 1950?*

Threatened and endangered species are found on every continent and in every ocean. Some are well-known animals such as Africa's black rhinoceros. Others are little known, such as hutias, rodents that live on only a few Caribbean islands. Ensuring that these species survive is one way to protect Earth's biodiversity.

Causes of Extinction

A natural event, such as an earthquake or volcano, can damage an ecosystem, wiping out populations. **Human activities can also threaten biodiversity. These activities include habitat destruction, poaching, pollution, and introduction of exotic species.**

Habitat Destruction A living thing's habitat is where it lives and gets what it needs to survive. The major cause of extinction is **habitat destruction,** the loss of a natural habitat. This can occur when forests are cleared to build towns or create grazing land. Plowing grasslands or filling in wetlands greatly changes those ecosystems. Some species may not be able to survive such changes to their habitats.

Breaking larger habitats into smaller, isolated pieces, or fragments, is called **habitat fragmentation.** For example, building a road through a forest disrupts habitats. This makes trees more vulnerable to wind damage. Plants may be less likely to successfully disperse their seeds. Habitat fragmentation is also very harmful to large mammals. These animals usually need large areas of land to find enough food to survive. They may not be able to obtain enough resources in a small area. They may also be injured trying to cross to another area.

Figure 17 Building this subdivision caused the habitats in the area to change. Open land was replaced by houses, streets, and yards. *Inferring How would these changes affect species in this area?*

Causes of Extinction

Building Inquiry Skills: Making Models

Materials *sheet of graph paper ruled in centimeters, pencil, calculator (optional)*
Time 10–15 minutes

Use the following activity to demonstrate habitat fragmentation. Have each student draw a rounded rectangle, roughly 20 by 25 cm, on a sheet of graph paper. Explain that the rectangle represents a rain forest in Indonesia and that each centimeter on the graph paper represents 10 m on the actual land. Ask: **How much land does each square centimeter represent?** *(100 m²)* Have students calculate the forest's approximate area. *(50,000 m²)* Next, have students draw a 9-cm by 8-cm rectangle in the middle of one side of the forest, to represent land that was cleared for farming, and a 1-cm-wide "road" through the middle of the forest along the cleared area, dividing the forest into three smaller pieces. Let students calculate the area of each smaller piece and the total area remaining. *(6,300 m² + 4,500 m² + 30,000 m² = 40,800 m²)* Pose the following question: **Suppose orangutans live in this rain forest. Each one needs 10,000 m² of land area to survive. How many orangutans could have lived in the original forest?** *(5)* **How many can live in the remaining forest?** *(3)* **Why not four?** *(The two smaller pieces of forest are too small to support any orangutans at all.)* **learning modality: logical/mathematical**

Answers to Self-Assessment

Checkpoint

Genes determine an organism's traits.

Caption Questions

Figure 16 1750–6; 1850–24; 1950–37
Figure 17 Organisms could no longer meet their food and shelter needs from their surroundings. The number of species probably decreased.

Ongoing Assessment

Writing Have students explain why gene pool diversity is so important to a species' survival.

Causes of Extinction, continued

EXPLORING Endangered Species

Make sure students realize that all of the species shown in this feature are native to the United States. Locate and label the area where each species is found on a large wall map. (Grizzly bear–northern and western U.S.; piping plover–east coastal areas; Eureka Valley primrose–Oregon; whooping crane–central and southwestern U.S.) Encourage interested students to research the names and locations of other endangered species in the United States and add them to the map. Then challenge students to create a large table on the chalkboard listing all the endangered species and the reason why each is endangered. **learning modality: visual**

Real-Life Learning

Point out to students that the tropical fish and parrots sold in reputable pet shops in this country are specifically bred for the pet trade, not imported illegally. Invite a local pet store owner or manager to speak to students about obtaining fish, parrots and other birds, exotic reptiles, and other nonnative species. **learning modality: verbal**

Poaching The illegal killing or removal of wildlife species is called **poaching.** Many endangered animals are hunted for their skin, fur, teeth, horns, or claws. These things are used for making medicines, jewelry, coats, belts, and shoes.

People illegally remove organisms from their habitats to sell them as exotic pets. Tropical fish, tortoises, and parrots are very popular pets, making them valuable to poachers. Endangered plants may be illegally dug up and sold as houseplants. Others are poached to be used as medicines.

Pollution Some species are endangered because of pollution. Substances that cause pollution, called pollutants, may reach animals through the water they drink or air they breathe. Pollutants

Grizzly bear This mammal needs a large area to obtain food. Shrinking wilderness areas have limited its numbers.

Piping plover The population of this tiny, active, coastal bird is recovering as a result of increased protection of its sand dune nesting sites.

Eureka valley evening primrose This flower, which blooms for only one night, must compete for water with exotic plants.

Background

Facts and Figures According to Worldwatch, a research institute that monitors environmental issues, primates are one of the most threatened groups of species on Earth today. Almost half of the world's more than 200 primate species are in danger of extinction.

The declines are due largely to human activity, as forests are lost through logging and clearing for building homes and agriculture. In Malaysia and Indonesia, nearly 80 percent of the forests used by orangutans have been cut down. Japan's macaques are losing living space to cities. Primates are also hunted in various places. Orangutans, gorillas, gibbons, and chimps are trapped for the pet trade.

may also settle in the soil. From there they are absorbed by plants, and build up in other organisms through the food chain. Pollutants may kill or weaken organisms or cause birth defects.

Exotic Species Introducing exotic species into an ecosystem can threaten biodiversity. When European sailors began visiting Hawaii hundreds of years ago, rats from their ships escaped onto the islands. Without any predators in Hawaii, the rats multiplied quickly. They ate the eggs of the nene goose. To protect the geese, people brought the rat-eating mongoose from India to help control the rat population. Unfortunately, the mongooses preferred eating eggs to rats. With both the rats and the mongoose eating its eggs, the nene goose is now endangered.

◀ **Steller's sea lion** This mammal competes with fishermen for its prey along the Pacific coast.

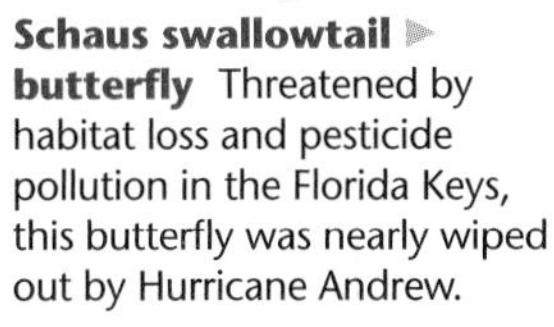

Schaus swallowtail ▶ **butterfly** Threatened by habitat loss and pesticide pollution in the Florida Keys, this butterfly was nearly wiped out by Hurricane Andrew.

▲ **Whooping crane** Threatened by habitat destruction and disease, half of the remaining population of this wading bird is in captivity. The species seems to be recovering well since its lowest point in the 1940s.

◀ **New Mexico ridgenose rattlesnake** Illegal collectors have reduced the population of this rare snake, the largest known group of which lives in a single canyon.

Inquiry Challenge

Materials *plastic chips or paper squares*
Time 10 minutes

Challenge students to work together to devise a model showing how pollutants build up as organisms feed on each other in a food chain. *(Sample model: One student represents a top-level consumer such as a hawk, five students represent first-level consumers such as rabbits, and the rest of the students represent producers such as clover plants. Each "clover plant" holds a plastic chip representing a unit of a toxic chemical sprayed on a field. Each "rabbit" eats several clover plants by taking their chips. Then each "hawk" eats two or three rabbits by taking all of the chips they collected from the clover plants. The two hawks between them will have all of the toxic chemical chips.)* Ask: **Why do you think pollutants build up in organisms?** *(Their bodies cannot break the pollutants down into harmless materials or get rid of them as waste products.)* **cooperative learning**

Including All Students

Encourage students who need additional challenges to research other examples of exotic species that have been introduced to the United States that compete with native species, and what has happened to the native species as a result. Examples include the blue water hyacinth, purple loosestrife, kudzu, leafy spurge, Eurasian milfoil, tamarisk tree, flathead catfish, sea lamprey, green crab, zebra mussel, gypsy moth, brown tree snake, and starling. Let students share their findings in a class discussion. **learning modality: verbal**

Media and Technology

Concept Videotape Library
Grade 6, Tape 4 "Can We Save the Tigers?"

Ongoing Assessment

Skills Check Have each student draw a concept map identifying and explaining the four human causes of extinction described in the text.

Students can save their concept maps in their portfolios.

Protecting Biodiversity

Real-Life Learning

Take the class on a field trip to visit a zoo with a captive-breeding program or invite a zoologist to speak to the class. Before students visit the zoo or listen to the speaker, instruct them to write down two or three questions about captive breeding and endangered species. **learning modality: verbal**

Building Inquiry Skills: Communicating

Time 15 minutes

ACTIVITY

After students read about the California condor, share the following information: In 1973, the federal government listed the gray wolf (timber wolf) as endangered after its population dropped to a few hundred in Minnesota and almost zero in the other lower-48 states. This protected gray wolves from hunting and trapping. In addition, captive breeding programs released more gray wolves into the wild. Biologists estimate that there are now 2,380 wolves in Minnesota and Wisconsin. In 1998 the government recommended removing the gray wolf from the endangered species list. Divide the class into groups to debate the issue of hunting and trapping bans from two viewpoints—that of farmers and ranchers who are losing animals to gray wolf predation, and that of people who support continued protection of the species. **learning modality: verbal**

Demonstration

Materials *aquarium, sand, water, 2 crayfish, several cans and/or boards*

ACTIVITY

Time 15 minutes for initial set-up

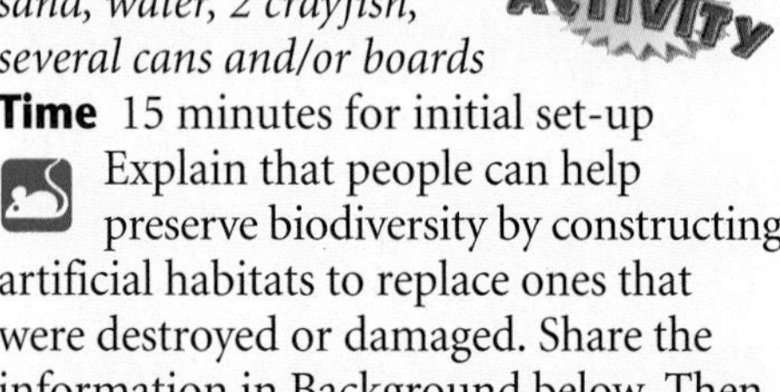

Explain that people can help preserve biodiversity by constructing artificial habitats to replace ones that were destroyed or damaged. Share the information in Background below. Then let students help you create an "artificial" habitat: Set up an aquarium with only sand in the bottom, and add two crayfish. Have students observe the crayfish for a day or two. Then add several and/or boards to the aquarium to provide hiding places. Let students continue to observe the crayfish. **learning modality: visual**

Protecting Biodiversity

Many people are working to preserve the world's biodiversity. Some focus on protecting individual endangered species, such as the giant panda or the Florida panther. Others try to protect entire ecosystems, such as the Great Barrier Reef in Australia. **Many programs to protect biodiversity combine scientific and legal approaches.**

Captive Breeding One scientific approach to protecting severely endangered species is captive breeding. **Captive breeding** is the mating of animals in zoos or wildlife preserves. Scientists care for the young to increase their chance of survival. These offspring are then released back into the wild.

A captive breeding program was the only hope for the California condor. California condors are the largest birds in North America. They became endangered as a result of habitat destruction, poaching, and pollution. By the mid-1980s there were fewer than ten California condors in the wild. Fewer than 30 were in zoos. Scientists captured all the wild condors and brought them to the zoos. Soon afterward, the first California condor chick was successfully bred in captivity. Today, there are more than 100 California condors in zoos. Some condors have even been returned to the wild. Though successful, this program has cost more than $20 million. It is not possible to save many species in this costly way.

Laws and Treaties Laws can help protect individual species. Some nations have made it illegal to sell endangered species or products made from them. In the United States, the Endangered Species Act of 1973 prohibits importing or trading products made from threatened or endangered species. This law also requires the development of plans to save endangered species.

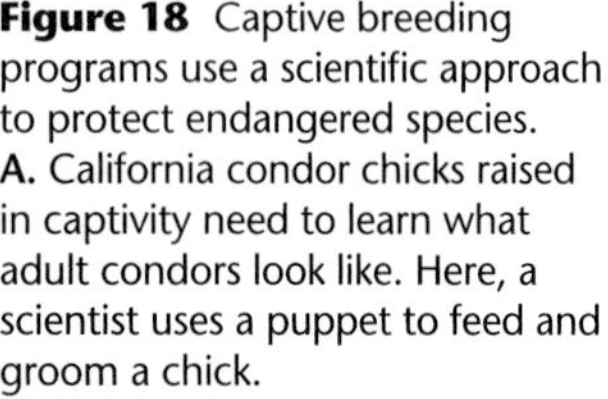

Figure 18 Captive breeding programs use a scientific approach to protect endangered species.
A. California condor chicks raised in captivity need to learn what adult condors look like. Here, a scientist uses a puppet to feed and groom a chick.
B. These young green turtles were hatched in the laboratory. Now a researcher is releasing the turtles into their natural ocean habitat.

550

American alligators, Pacific gray whales, and green sea turtles are just a few of the species that have begun to recover as a result of legal protection.

The most important international treaty protecting wildlife is the Convention on International Trade in Endangered Species. Eighty nations signed this treaty in 1973. This treaty lists nearly 700 threatened and endangered species that cannot be traded for profit. Laws like these are difficult to enforce. Even so, they have helped to reduce the poaching of many endangered species, including African elephants, snow leopards, sperm whales, and mountain gorillas.

Habitat Preservation The most effective way to preserve biodiversity is to protect whole ecosystems. Preserving whole habitats saves not only endangered species, but also other species that depend on them.

Figure 19 Preserving whole habitats is probably the most effective way to protect biodiversity.

Beginning in 1872 with Yellowstone National Park, the world's first national park, many countries have set aside wildlife habitats as parks and refuges. In addition, private organizations have purchased millions of hectares of endangered habitats throughout the world. Today, there are about 7,000 nature parks, reserves, and refuges in the world.

To be most effective, reserves must have the characteristics of diverse ecosystems. For example, they must be large enough to support the populations that live there. The reserves must contain a variety of niches. And of course, it is still necessary to keep the air, land, and water clean, remove exotic species, and control poaching.

Section 3 Review

1. What are three factors that affect biodiversity?
2. List four possible causes of extinction.
3. Give an example of a legal approach and a scientific approach to preventing extinction.
4. Which are the most diverse ecosystems on Earth?
5. Identify three ways in which biodiversity is important.
6. **Thinking Critically Making Generalizations** Explain how the statement "In the web of life, all things are connected" relates to keystone species.

Science at Home

Habitat Brochure Obtain a map of your community or state. With a family member, identify any city, state, or national parks, reserves, or refuges in your area. Create a travel brochure highlighting one of these areas. Describe the habitats there. Find out whether any endangered or threatened species live in the park. Include their pictures in your brochure.

Program Resources

- **Unit 5 Resources** 17-3 Review and Reinforce; 17-3 Enrich

Media and Technology

Concept Videotape Library
Grade 6, Tape 4 "It's All Happening at the Zoo"

3 Assess

Section 3 Review Answers

1. Area, climate, and diversity of niches
2. Habitat destruction, poaching, pollution, and exotic species
3. *Legal approach:* Laws such as the Endangered Species Act and the Convention on International Trade in Endangered Species; *Scientific approach:* captive breeding in zoos or wildlife preserves, habitat preservation
4. Tropical rain forests and coral reefs
5. Biodiversity is important for beauty and recreation, economic reasons, the health of ecosystems, and genetic diversity.
6. A keystone species is one that influences the survival of many other species in an ecosystem. If something happens to the keystone species, all other species in the ecosystem are affected.

Science at Home

ACTIVITY

Besides looking at maps, students can contact their state's Environmental Protection Agency, a local chapter of the National Audubon Society, or their town's parks department. Students' brochures should describe the habitats of endangered or threatened species in the area.

Performance Assessment

Writing Have each student identify and briefly describe the four causes of extinction presented in the text.

Students can save their work in their portfolios.

INTEGRATING HEALTH

Section 4 The Search for New Medicines

Objective

After completing the lesson, students will be able to
◆ explain why many rain forest plants are sources of medicines.

Key Term taxol

1 Engage/Explore

Activating Prior Knowledge

Before students read the introductory text on this page, ask: **Where are temperate rain forests located?** *(Along the northwest coast of the United States)* If students have difficulty recalling this information, have them look back at the biome map on page 179 in Chapter 6.

DISCOVER ACTIVITY

Skills Focus observing
Materials *black marking pen, strip of filter paper, water, clear plastic cup, tape, pencil*
Time 15 minutes
Tips If filter paper is not available, use paper towels cut into strips.
Expected Outcome Water will carry the dissolved black ink up the strip, where the individual colors will separate out.
Think It Over The specific colors that separate from the black ink will depend on the marker used. Different colors will advance up the strip at different rates: blue the fastest, yellow slightly slower, and red much slower.

INTEGRATING HEALTH 

Section 4 The Search for New Medicines

DISCOVER ACTIVITY

How Are Plant Chemicals Separated?

1. Using a black marking pen, draw a dot about 2 centimeters from the end of a strip of filter paper.
2. Pour a few centimeters of water into a clear plastic cup.
3. Tape the top edge of the filter paper strip to a pencil. Place the pencil across the top of the cup so that the ink dot hangs just below the water surface. If necessary, turn the pencil to adjust the length of the paper.

4. Observe what happens to the black dot.

Think It Over
Observing How many different colors of ink did you separate from the black ink? This process models one method of separating individual chemicals contained in plants.

GUIDE FOR READING

◆ Why are many rain forest plants sources of medicines?

Reading Tip **As you read, identify statements that show how biodiversity is related to human health.**

You lace up your hiking boots, and sling your collecting bag over your shoulder. It's time to head out for another day of searching in the cool, damp forest. Stepping carefully to avoid mud, you walk beneath the giant evergreens. Their needle-covered branches form a thick roof above your head. Rotting logs covered with ferns, seedlings, and brightly colored fungi line your path. You scan the ground for telltale signs of the object of your search. What are you looking for in this forest? A plant that can save lives!

Pacific yew tree

This ancient forest is the temperate rain forest of the Pacific Northwest. Many of its giant trees are more than 200 years old. Like tropical rain forests, temperate rain forests are diverse ecosystems. They contain many species that are found nowhere else. Some of these species are threatened or endangered, including the bull trout, Olympic salamander, and the life-saving plant you are looking for—the Pacific yew tree.

Plants and Medicines

People have always valued plants for their ability to heal wounds and fight diseases. For example, aspirin was originally made from the bark of the willow tree. The active chemical in aspirin can now be made in a laboratory.

READING STRATEGIES

Reading Tip Some statements that show how biodiversity is related to human health that students might identify include: *People have always valued plants for their ability to heal wounds and fight diseases. Some chemicals rain forest plants produce to protect their leaves and bark can also be used to fight human diseases. Almost half of all medicines sold today contain chemicals originally found in wild organisms.*

Summarizing To ensure that students understand the sequence of events in the development of taxol as an anticancer drug, have them summarize the text in The Story of Taxol and A Threatened Supply of Taxol on pages 553–554. Tell students to write one sentence that summarizes the main idea of each paragraph. When the sentences are read in order, they will provide a summary of the text.

Figure 20 Scientists studied Pacific yew tree seedlings to learn more about the cancer-fighting substance taxol. In the closeup, a researcher examines taxol crystals.

The ability to fight disease is a result of the plants' adaptations to their environment. Plants in many ecosystems produce chemicals that protect them from predators, parasites, and diseases. This is particularly true in rain forests, where so many organisms make their living by eating plants. **Some chemicals that rain forest plants produce to protect their leaves and bark can also be used to fight human diseases.**

The Story of Taxol

The Pacific yew tree is very resistant to diseases and insects. Scientists began studying the bark of the Pacific yew to find out why it was so hardy. They separated chemicals from the bark. During this analysis, the scientists discovered unusual crystals in the bark. These crystals are made from a chemical called **taxol,** the substance that protects the Pacific yew tree.

Scientists next experimented with taxol in the laboratory. They discovered that taxol crystals affect cancer cells in an unusual way. Typically, cancer cells grow and divide very rapidly. This quick growth forms a mass of cells called a tumor. When cancer cells are exposed to taxol, the taxol forms structures that look like tiny cages around each cancer cell. These structures prevent the cancer cells from dividing. As a result, the cancer cannot grow and spread.

After more research, doctors were ready to test taxol on cancer patients. The taxol treatments often were able to shrink certain types of tumors. Sometimes they even stopped the cancer from spreading in the body. Taxol is now used to treat more than 12,000 cancer patients each year.

✓ *Checkpoint* *How is taxol helpful to Pacific yew trees?*

2 Facilitate

Plants and Medicines

Real-Life Learning

Materials *packages from herbal teas and dietary supplements*
Time 15 minutes

Tell students that many traditional folk remedies are still used today. As examples, supply empty packages from a variety of herbal teas and dietary supplements such as chamomile, St. John's wort, ginseng, kava kava, echinacea, ginkgo biloba, goldenseal, and cat's claw. Let students examine the labels and identify the herb each product contains and its purported benefits. Point out the notice on each supplement's label that the product is not approved by the FDA for medical use. Also encourage students to ask older family members about traditional remedies that were commonly used in the past. **learning modality: verbal**

Building Inquiry Skills: Observing

Materials *small branches from yew shrubs*
Time 10 minutes

Provide each pair or small group of students with a small branch clipped from a variety of yew (*Taxus*) that is commonly used for landscaping. Let students examine the needles and the thin, scaly bark. Explain that the Pacific yew is related to these shrubs but is a large tree that grows up to 14 m tall with a wide trunk. Before taxol was discovered, wood from the Pacific yew was used to build furniture. **learning modality: kinesthetic**

Program Resources

- **Unit 5 Resources** 17-4 Lesson Plan; 17-4 Section Summary
- **Guided Reading and Study Workbook** Section 17-4

Media and Technology

Concept Videotape Library Grade 6, Tape 4 "A Question of Balance"

Answers to Self-Assessment

✓ *Checkpoint*

Taxol makes the trees resistant to diseases and insects.

Ongoing Assessment

Writing Have each student explain how protective chemicals are helpful to plants.

A Threatened Supply of Taxol

Building Inquiry Skills: Calculating

Point out that the text says more than 12,000 cancer patients are treated with taxol each year. Ask: **How many yew trees would have to be cut down to supply the drug to those people?** *(36,000 per year)* **learning modality: logical/mathematical**

Biodiversity and Medicine

Cultural Diversity

Explain that many scientists are learning about the medicinal qualities of wild organisms from native peoples. These groups often still depend on plants and animals for medicines. For example, cat's claw (Uña de Gato), a traditional herbal medicine in Peru, has a high alkaloid content. Limited studies have found that alkaloids may help bolster the disease-fighting function of white blood cells. **learning modality: verbal**

3 Assess

Section 4 Review Answers

1. Many of these plants produce chemicals that protect them against predators, parasites, and diseases.
2. Temperate rain forests, which are cool, damp, and heavily shaded
3. Taxol encloses each cancer cell in a cage that keeps the cell from dividing.
4. The company would be interested in testing new species to determine whether they might have any medical uses.

CHAPTER PROJECT

Check Your Progress

As students observe their plots, encourage them to draw the organisms in detail so they can identify them later using field guides. Remind students to make notes about abiotic factors as well. Check each group's notebook occasionally to make sure students are recording data.

Figure 21 This researcher is pressing leaves as part of a species survey in a forest reserve.

A Threatened Supply of Taxol

The demand for taxol as a cancer treatment has grown rapidly. Now many scientists have become concerned about the supply of Pacific yew trees. It takes the bark of three Pacific yew trees to produce enough pure taxol for one cancer patient's treatment. If the bark is removed from a yew tree, the tree cannot survive. And by the time researchers discovered taxol's value as a cancer-fighting drug, a large portion of the yew trees' temperate rain forests were gone.

Taxol has a very complex chemical structure. Chemists have been working for many years to reproduce this structure. In 1996, chemists successfully created taxol in the laboratory for the first time. This discovery could help protect the remaining Pacific yew trees for future generations.

Biodiversity and Medicine

Almost half of all medicines sold today contain chemicals originally found in wild organisms. What other medicines are growing undiscovered in the forests of the world? So far, only about 2 percent of the world's known plant species have been studied for possible medical use. In 1995 the American Medical Association called for the protection of Earth's biodiversity. Their goal was to preserve the undiscovered medicines that may exist in nature. Governments, scientists, and private companies are working together to find new species all over the world. Perhaps they will find new sources of cancer-fighting drugs.

Section 4 Review

1. What adaptations of rain forest plants make them a likely source of medicines?
2. Describe the ecosystem in which Pacific yew trees are found.
3. How does taxol affect cancer cells?
4. **Thinking Critically Inferring** Suppose a group of scientists is planning an expedition to identify new species in the South American rain forest. Why might a company that manufactures medicines be interested in supporting their expedition?

CHAPTER PROJECT

Check Your Progress

Visit your plot regularly to make observations. Use field guides to identify the plants, animals, and other organisms you observe. Record their locations within your plot along with their common and scientific names. By now you should also be planning how to present your findings. Consider using a series of drawings, a flip chart, a computer presentation, or a video of your plot with closeups of the species you have identified. (*Hint:* Be sure to include the data you collected on abiotic factors.)

Background

Integrating Science Taxol was first tested in women with severe ovarian cancer that had not responded to chemotherapy and radiation. Ovarian tumors in 40 percent of the women shrank to half their original size. When taxol was later given to women with breast cancer, more than half the patients experienced partial remission.

Program Resources

- **Unit 5 Resources** 17-4 Review and Reinforce; 17-4 Enrich

Section 1 Recognizing Environmental Issues

Key Ideas
- Three types of environmental issues are resource use, population growth, and pollution.
- Making environmental decisions requires balancing different viewpoints and weighing the costs and benefits of proposals.

Key Terms
pollution
development viewpoint
preservation viewpoint
conservation viewpoint

Section 2 Forests and Fisheries

Key Ideas
- Because new trees can be planted to replace those that are cut down, forests can be renewable resources.
- Managing fisheries involves setting fishing limits, changing fishing methods, using aquaculture, and finding new resources.

Key Terms
clear-cutting
selective cutting
sustainable yield
fishery
aquaculture

Section 3 Biodiversity

Key Ideas
- Factors that affect biodiversity include area, climate, and diversity of niches.
- Human activities that threaten biodiversity include habitat destruction, poaching, pollution, and introduction of exotic species.
- Three techniques for protecting biodiversity are regulating capture and trade, captive breeding, and habitat preservation.

Key Terms
biodiversity
keystone species
genes
extinction
endangered species
threatened species
habitat destruction
habitat fragmentation
poaching
captive breeding

Section 4 The Search for New Medicines

Integrating Health

Key Ideas
- Many plants make chemicals that protect them from predators, parasites, and disease. These chemicals may fight human diseases.
- The cancer-fighting drug taxol comes from Pacific yew trees, which have been affected by logging of the forests where they grow.
- The possible discovery of other medicines is one reason to protect biodiversity.

Key Term
taxol

Organizing Information

Concept Map Copy the biodiversity concept map below onto a sheet of paper. Complete it and add a title. (For more on concept maps, see the Skills Handbook.)

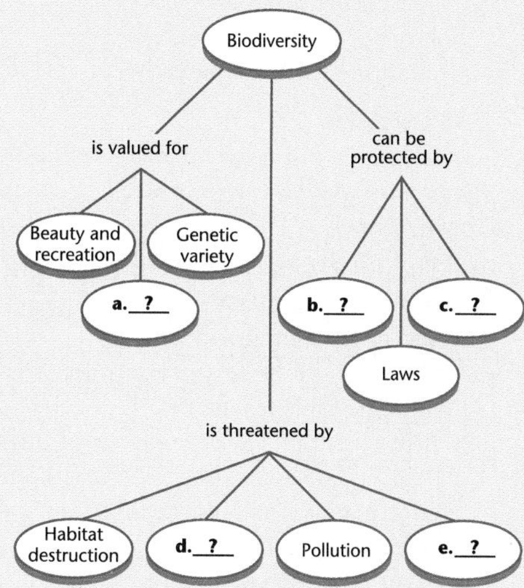

Program Resources
- **Unit 5 Resources** Chapter 17 Project Scoring Rubric
- **Performance Assessment** Chapter 17
- **Chapter and Unit Tests** Chapter 17 Test; Unit 5 Test

Media and Technology

Computer Test Bank Chapter 17 Test

Organizing Information

Concept Map **a.** Economic value; **b., c.** Captive breeding, Habitat preservation; **d., e.** Poaching, Exotic species. Sample title: Facts About Biodiversity

Performance Assessment

Writing Have students explain why it is important to be able to duplicate taxol in a laboratory.

Reviewing Content

Multiple Choice

1. b **2.** d **3.** a **4.** b **5.** b

True or False

6. true **7.** renewable **8.** true **9.** keystone **10.** preservation

Checking Concepts

11. *Sample answers: personal/local issue*—deciding whether to recycle materials; *national/global issue*—setting aside land for wildlife refuges

12. By considering the viewpoints of many different people and weighing the costs and benefits of different solutions

13. Clear-cutting exposes soil to erosion by wind and water, damages streams with eroded silt, and destroys forest habitats. Selective cutting is less damaging to the forest environment and maintains diversity.

14. *Any one:* Set limits on the amount and/or size of fish that can be caught; use nets with a larger mesh size; outlaw fishing methods that kill all the fish in an area rather than selected species; raise fish on farms (aquaculture)

15. Species lose the places where they feed, breed, and nest. If they cannot find a substitute niche, they must move to a new location to survive. If they cannot relocate, they will not survive.

16. Each student's editorial should demonstrate understanding of the viewpoint he or she has chosen: development (using resources freely to benefit people), preservation (not disturbing the environment), or conservation (using resources without destroying them).

Thinking Critically

17. As the number of humans increases, they compete with other species for space, food, water, and other resources. More humans also create more pollution and develop more land, which in turn destroys natural habitats. Pollution and habitat destruction can threaten the survival of some species.

18. An exotic species may compete with native species for limited resources. If the exotic species has no natural predators in its new habitat, it may outcompete the native species.

CHAPTER 17 ASSESSMENT

Reviewing Content

Multiple Choice

Choose the letter of the best answer.

1. The viewpoint that humans should be able to benefit from all of Earth's resources is the
a. conservation viewpoint.
b. development viewpoint.
c. scientific viewpoint.
d. preservation viewpoint.

2. The most diverse ecosystems in the world are
a. coral reefs. **b.** deserts.
c. grasslands. **d.** tropical rain forests.

3. If all members of a species disappear from Earth, that species is
a. extinct. **b.** endangered.
c. nonrenewable. **d.** threatened.

4. The illegal removal from the wild or the killing of an endangered species is called
a. habitat destruction.
b. poaching.
c. pollution.
d. captive breeding.

5. Taxol, which comes from Pacific yew trees, is a medicine that is used to fight
a. heart disease. **b.** cancer.
c. lung disease. **d.** diabetes.

True or False

If the statement is true, write true. If it is false, change the underlined word or words to make the statement true.

6. The three main types of environmental issues today are resource use, pollution, and population growth.

7. Forests and fisheries are examples of nonrenewable resources.

8. A sustainable yield is a number of trees that can be regularly harvested without affecting the health of the forest.

9. A species that influences the survival of many other species in an ecosystem is called a(n) endangered species.

10. The most effective way to protect biodiversity is through habitat fragmentation.

Checking Concepts

11. Give an example of a personal or local environmental issue and an example of a national or global environmental issue.

12. Describe how environmental decisions are made.

13. Compare the effects of clear-cutting and selective cutting on forest ecosystems.

14. Describe one way that overfishing can be prevented.

15. Explain how habitat destruction affects species.

16. Writing to Learn You are a member of the county land use commission. Hundreds of people are moving to your county every day. You must make a decision regarding how to manage a 5,000-hectare woodland area in your county. Choose one point of view: development, preservation, or conservation. Write an editorial for a newspaper explaining your position.

Thinking Critically

17. Relating Cause and Effect Explain how human population growth affects other species on Earth.

18. Making Generalizations Describe how an exotic species can threaten other species in an ecosystem.

19. Predicting How could the extinction of a species today affect your life 20 years from now?

20. Making Judgments Suppose you were given a million dollars toward saving an endangered turtle species. You could use the money to start a captive breeding program for the turtles. Or you could use the money to purchase and protect part of the turtle's habitat. How would you spend the money? Explain your answer.

21. Relating Cause and Effect Explain why many human medicines are made from chemicals that come from plants.

556

19. *Sample answers:* The species might have been the source of a medicine or had another use that is unknown today. The species might have been the source of genes for rare traits that could help other species survive.

20. Accept all reasonable responses so long as students support their choices with well-reasoned arguments that include why the method has a greater chance of success or can achieve more for the money invested.

21. Many plants produce chemicals that ward off disease and parasites. These chemicals often have disease-fighting properties in humans.

Applying Skills

One study identifies the reasons that mammal and bird species are endangered or threatened. Use the table to answer Questions 22–24.

Reason	Mammals	Birds
Poaching	31%	20%
Habitat loss	32%	60%
Exotic species	17%	12%
Other causes	20%	8%

22. **Graphing** Make a bar graph comparing the reasons that mammals and birds are endangered and threatened. Show percents for each animal group on the vertical axis and reasons on the horizontal axis.
23. **Interpreting Data** What is the major reason that mammals become endangered or threatened? What mainly endangers or threatens birds?
24. **Developing Hypotheses** Suggest explanations for the differences between the data for mammals and birds.

CHAPTER PROJECT — Performance Assessment

Present Your Project In your presentation, describe the biodiversity in your plot. Suggest an explanation for any patterns you observed. Make sure each person in your group has a role in the presentation. Before the presentation day, brainstorm questions your classmates might ask. Then prepare answers for them.

Reflect and Record In your journal, write what you learned from observing a single location. Which of your findings were surprising? What was the hardest part of this project? What would you do differently if you did this project again?

Test Preparation

Use these questions to prepare for standardized tests.

Read the passage. Then answer Questions 25–27.

Starting in the late 1940s, the pesticide DDT was used to kill insects that spread disease and damaged crops. At first, DDT seemed to have no effect on other organisms. Over time, however, people noticed that the numbers of bald eagles and other large fish-eating birds were declining.

Ecologists discovered that DDT settled into the soil and eventually found its way into rivers and lakes. The DDT contaminated tiny organisms in the water, which were then eaten by small fishes. As bigger fishes ate the small fishes, and large birds ate the bigger fishes, they took the DDT into their bodies at higher and higher concentrations.

The DDT caused the eagles to lay eggs with very thin shells, which broke before hatching. Eagle populations began to decline steadily. In the 1970s, the use of DDT was banned in the United States. Since then, the populations of bald eagles and other affected birds have begun to recover.

25. What is the main idea of this passage?
    a. DDT has been used to kill harmful insects.
    b. The use of DDT was banned in the 1970s.
    c. The use of DDT led to a decline in the number of bald eagles.
    d. DDT found its way into rivers and lakes.
26. According to this passage, what effect does DDT have on bald eagles?
    a. DDT kills adult bald eagles.
    b. DDT affects the formation of eggshells, so fewer young are hatched.
    c. DDT kills the organisms that bald eagles prey upon.
    d. DDT has no effect on bald eagles.
27. Based on this passage, predict what might have happened if DDT had not been banned.
    a. Crop damage might have increased.
    b. Bald eagle populations might have increased.
    c. DDT might have stopped flowing into rivers and lakes.
    d. Bald eagles might have become endangered.

Applying Skills

22.

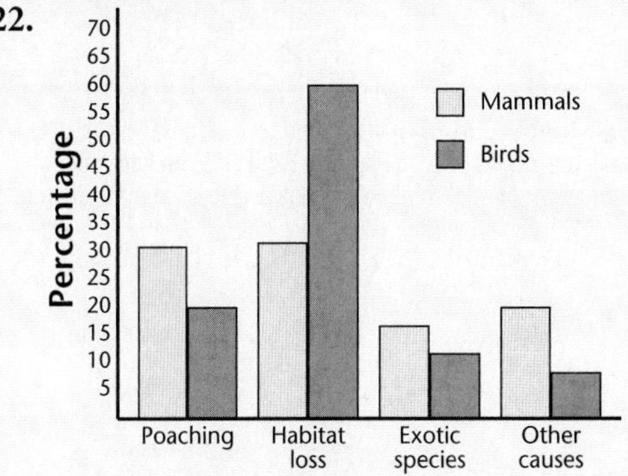

Program Resources

- **Inquiry Skills Activity Book** Provides teaching and review of all inquiry skills

Applying Skills

22. See bottom left.
23. Habitat loss is the major cause for both birds and mammals. Poaching is almost as significant for mammals.
24. *Sample answer:* Areas where birds tend to nest and breed, such as wetlands, are particularly threatened by habitat destruction.

Performance Assessment

Present Your Project Before groups give their presentations to the entire class, meet with each group briefly to review students' plans. Suggest any questions that may not have occurred to them.
Reflect and Record Let each group reconvene to discuss their answers to these questions, then encourage all groups to share their ideas in a class discussion.

Test Preparation

25. c **26.** b **27.** d

CHAPTER 18

Earth, Moon, and Sun

Sections	Time	Student Edition Activities	Other Activities
CHAPTER PROJECT **Where's the Moon?** p. 559	Ongoing (2 weeks)	Check Your Progress, pp. 567, 578, 588 Present Your Project, p. 591	
1 Earth in Space pp. 560–569 ◆ Identify the effects of Earth's rotation and revolution. ◆ Explain the causes of the seasons on Earth.	2 periods/ 1 block	**Discover** Why Does Earth Have Day and Night?, p. 560 **Sharpen Your Skills** Calculating, p. 561 **Skills Lab: Observing** Reasons For The Seasons, pp. 568–569	**TE** Building Inquiry Skills: Comparing and Contrasting, p. 564 **TE** Demonstrations, pp. 562, 565 **TE** Inquiry Challenge, p. 566 **IES** "Riddles of the Pharaohs," pp. 12-13 **LM** 18, "Constructing a Foucalt Pendulum"
2 Phases, Eclipses, and Tides pp. 570–578 ◆ Describe the causes of the the moon's phases. ◆ Describe what causes solar and lunar eclipses. ◆ Identify the cause of the tides.	3 periods/ $1\frac{1}{2}$ blocks	**Discover** How Does the Moon Move?, p. 570 **Sharpen Your Skills** Making Models, p. 574 **Skills Lab: Making Models** A "Moonth" of Phases, pp. 572–573	**TE** Inquiry Challenges, p. 572 **TE** Building Inquiry Skills: Making Models, p. 578 **IES** "Where River Meets Sea," pp. 26-27
3 *Integrating Technology* **Rockets and Satellites** pp. 579–582 ◆ Explain how rockets travel in space. ◆ List the uses for satellites, space stations, and the Space Shuttle.	2 periods/ 1 block	**Discover** How Do Rockets Work?, p. 579 **Try This** Be a Rocket Scientist, p. 581 **Science at Home,** p. 582	**TE** Demonstration, p. 580 **TE** Inquiry Challenge, p. 581 **IES** "Mars the Next Frontier," pp. 14-15, 20-21
4 Earth's Moon pp. 583–588 ◆ Describe how scientists have used the telescope to study the moon. ◆ Explain what scientists learned about the moon from space exploration. ◆ Describe the origin and structure of the moon.	2 periods/ 1 block	**Discover** Why Do Craters Look Different From Each Other?, p. 583 **Sharpen Your Skills** Calculating, p. 587	**TE** Building Inquiry Skills: Interpreting Data, p. 584 **IES** "Riddles of the Pharaohs," pp. 12-13
Study Guide/Chapter Assessment pp. 589–591	1 period/ $\frac{1}{2}$ block		**ISAB** Provides teaching and review of all inquiry skills

For Standard or Block Schedule The Resource Pro® CD-ROM gives you maximum flexibility for planning your instruction for any type of schedule. Resource Pro® contains Planning Express®, an advanced scheduling program, as well as the entire contents of the Teaching Resources and the Computer Test Bank.

CHAPTER PLANNING GUIDE

Program Resources	Assessment Strategies	Media and Technology
UR Chapter 18 Project Teacher Notes **UR** Chapter 18 Project Overview and Worksheets	**SE** Performance Assessment: Present Your Project, p. 591 **TE** Check Your Progress, pp. 567, 578, 588	Science Explorer Internet Site at www.phschool.com Student Edition on Audio CD, Chapter 18
UR 18-1 Lesson Plan **UR** 18-1 Section Summary **UR** 18-1 Review and Reinforce **UR** 18-1 Enrich **UR** Chapter 18 Skills Lab 1	**SE** Section 1 Review, p. 567 **TE** Ongoing Assessment, pp. 563, 565 **TE** Performance Assessment, p. 567	Transparency 70, "Exploring the Seasons" Lab Activity Videotapes, Grade 6 Tape 4
UR 18-2 Lesson Plan **UR** 18-2 Section Summary **UR** 18-2 Review and Reinforce **UR** 18-2 Enrich **UR** Chapter 18 Skills Lab 2	**SE** Section 2 Review, p. 578 **TE** Ongoing Assessment, pp. 571, 573, 575 **TE** Performance Assessment, p. 578	Transparencies 71, "Exploring Solstices and Equinoxes"; 72, "Solar Eclipse"; 73, "Lunar Eclipse"; 74, "High and Low Tides" Lab Activity Videotapes, Grade 6 Tape 4
UR 18-3 Lesson Plan **UR** 18-3 Section Summary **UR** 18-3 Review and Reinforce **UR** 18-3 Enrich	**SE** Section 3 Review, p. 582 **TE** Ongoing Assessment, p. 581 **TE** Performance Assessment, p. 582	Concept Videotape Library, Grade 6, Tape 4, "The Cray Computer" Concept Videotape Library, Grade 6, Tape 4, "Then and Now"
UR 18-4 Lesson Plan **UR** 18-4 Section Summary **UR** 18-4 Review and Reinforce **UR** 18-4 Enrich	**SE** Section 4 Review, p. 588 **TE** Ongoing Assessment, p. 585, 587 **TE** Performance Assessment, p. 588	Transparency 75, "Collision Theory of the Moon's Origin"
RCA Provides strategies to improve science reading skills **GRSW** Provides worksheets to promote student comprehension of content	**SE** Chapter 18 Study Guide/Assessment, pp. 589–591 **PA** Chapter 18 Performance Assessment **CUT** Chapter 18 Test **CTB** Chapter 18 Test	Computer Test Bank, Chapter 18 Test

Key: **SE** Student Edition
CTB Computer Test Bank
ISAB Inquiry Skills Activity Book
GRSW Guided Reading and Study Workbook
TE Teacher's Edition
PTA Product Testing Activities by *Consumer Reports*
RCA Reading in the Content Area
PA Performance Assessment
UR Unit Resources
LM Laboratory Manual
IES Interdisciplinary Explorations Series
CUT Chapter and Unit Tests

Meeting the National Science Education Standards and AAAS Benchmarks

National Science Education Standards	Benchmarks for Science Literacy	Unifying Themes
Science as Inquiry (Content Standard A) ◆ **Communicate scientific procedures and explanations** Students present their observations of the moon using words, charts, and drawings. *(Chapter Project)* ◆ **Identify questions that can be answered through scientific investigations** Students observe the moon and look for patterns in its motions and changing appearance. *(Chapter Project)* **Earth and Space Science** (Content Standard D) ◆ **Earth in the solar system** Earth has day and night and the moon has phases because of relative motions of Earth and the moon in the Solar System. *(Sections 1, 2 and 4)* ◆ **Earth's history** Cratering on the moon and the composition of moon rocks adds to our knowledge of the history of the formation of Earth. *(Section 4)* **Science and Technology** (Content Standard E) ◆ **Abilities of technological design** The space program includes many examples of both the successes and limitations of technology. *(Section 3)*	**3A Technology and Science** The space program includes many examples of both the successes and limitations of technology. *(Section 3)* **3B Design and Systems** Spacecraft are complex systems of many parts that must work together. *(Section 3)* **4B The Earth** Earth has day and night and the moon has phases because of relative motions of Earth and the moon in the Solar System. Cratering on the moon and the composition of moon rocks adds to our knowledge of the history of the formation of Earth. *(Sections 1, 2, and 4)* **4C Processes That Shape the Earth** Cratering on the moon and the composition of moon rocks adds to our knowledge of the history of the formation of Earth. *(Sections 1, 2, and 4)* **4F Motion** Newton's laws govern the motion of rockets and satellites as well as the motion of Earth and the moon. *(Section 3)* **8D Communication** Geosynchronous satellites and other communications satellites have made global communication possible. *(Section 3)* **11C Constancy and Change** Cratering on the moon, and the composition of moon and Earth rocks tell us that Earth and the moon have undergone dramatic changes in their history. *(Section 4)*	◆ **Energy** Energy constraints limit the design of rockets and force the use of multistage rockets to achieve orbital speeds. *(Section 3)* ◆ **Evolution** Cratering on the moon, and the composition of moon and Earth rocks tell us that Earth and the moon have undergone dramatic changes in their history. *(Section 4)* ◆ **Patterns of Change** Earth has day and night and the moon has phases because of relative motions of Earth and the moon in the Solar System. The seasons on Earth are caused by the revolution of Earth and the tilt of Earth's axis. Tides are caused by relative motions of Earth and the Moon *(Sections 1 and 2)* ◆ **Scale and Structure** The moon has one-fourth the radius and one-eightieth the mass of Earth. *(Section 4)* ◆ **Unity and Diversity** The composition of rocks on the moon is similar to the composition of rocks on Earth. But the moon has no air and no liquid water. *(Section 4)* ◆ **Stability** Earth has two high tides and two low tides every day, due to the moon's gravitational pull. The moon's period of rotation and its period of revolution are the same, so it always keeps the same face toward Earth. *(Section 2)*

Take It to the Net

Interactive text at www.phschool.com

Science Explorer comes alive with iText.

- **Complete student text** is accessible from any computer with Internet access or a CD-ROM drive.
- **Animations, simulations, and videos** enhance student understanding and retention of concepts.
- **Self-tests and online study tools** assess student understanding.

STAY CURRENT with **SCIENCE NEWS**®

Find out the latest research and information about The Solar System at: **www.phschool.com**

Go to **www.phschool.com** and click on the Science icon.Then click on Science Explorer: Life, Earth, and Physical Science under PH@school.

ACTIVITY	Time (minutes)	Materials Quantities for one work group	Skills
Section 1			
Discover, p. 560	15	**Nonconsumable** lamp, light bulb, globe	Making Models
Sharpen your Skills, p. 561	10	**Consumable** paper **Nonconsumable** pencil, calculator	Calculating
Skills Lab, pp. 568–569	40	**Consumable** paper **Nonconsumable** books, pencil, acetate sheet with thick grid lines drawn on it, plastic foam ball marked with poles and equator, flashlight, protractor, toothpick	Observing
Section 2			
Discover, p. 570	10	**Nonconsumable** quarters, pennies	Inferring
Sharpen your Skills, p. 574	15	**Consumable** paper **Nonconsumable** rulers, calculators	Making Models
Skills Lab, pp. 576–577	40	**Nonconsumable** floor lamp with 150-watt bulb, pencils, plastic foam balls	Making Models
Section 3			
Discover, p. 581	10	**Nonconsumable** balloons, safety goggles	Observing
Try This, p. 583	20	**Consumable** plastic or paper cup, paper, tape, film canister with a lid that snaps on inside the canister, water, fizzing antacid tablet **Nonconsumable** safety goggles	Observing
Science at Home, p. 584	home	No special materials are required.	Communicating
Section 4			
Discover, p. 585	20	**Nonconsumable** plastic mixing bowl about 25 cm across, sand, 3 marbles of different masses, meter stick	Developing Hypotheses
Sharpen your Skills, p. 589	10	No special materials are required.	Calculating

A list of all materials required for the Student Edition activities can be found on pages TVA34–TVA40. You can obtain information about ordering materials by calling 1-800-848-9500 or by accessing the Science Explorer Internet site at: **www.phschool.com**

CHAPTER 18 PROJECT

Where's the Moon?

Students have probably seen the moon in different phases, and at various times of day, throughout their lives without giving any thought to the patterns of the moon's light and motions. They may not realize that the moon's phases are a predictable cycle based on the positions of the sun, moon, and Earth.

Purpose In this project, students will make daily observations of the moon and will keep track of the moon's appearance and position in the sky. After collecting this information, students will analyze the data and look for patterns.

Skills Focus Students will be able to
- observe the phases of the moon;
- measure the direction and altitude of the moon in the sky;
- interpret data to explain why the moon has phases;
- predict when and where one would expect to see the moon based on rules developed from interpreting the data.

Project Time Line This project requires at least one month to observe all of the phases of the moon. Ideally, the project will last long enough for students to see the moon cycle begin to repeat itself. If cloudy weather makes observations difficult, you may wish to extend the observation time.

Suggested Shortcuts If the time available is less than one month, starting near a new moon should give usable results in about two to three weeks. The moon is most visible in the early evening sky between the new moon and the full moon. Before beginning the project, see Chapter 18 Project Teacher Notes in Unit 6 Resources for more details on carrying out the project.

Possible Materials This project requires few materials. A sample observation sheet is included in the resource materials. Students can determine directions using the eight major compass directions: N, NE, E, SE, S, SW, W, NW. If students do not have a compass, tell them to borrow one and use it to record certain landmarks around their house in each of the eight directions. They can then use these landmarks to orient themselves.

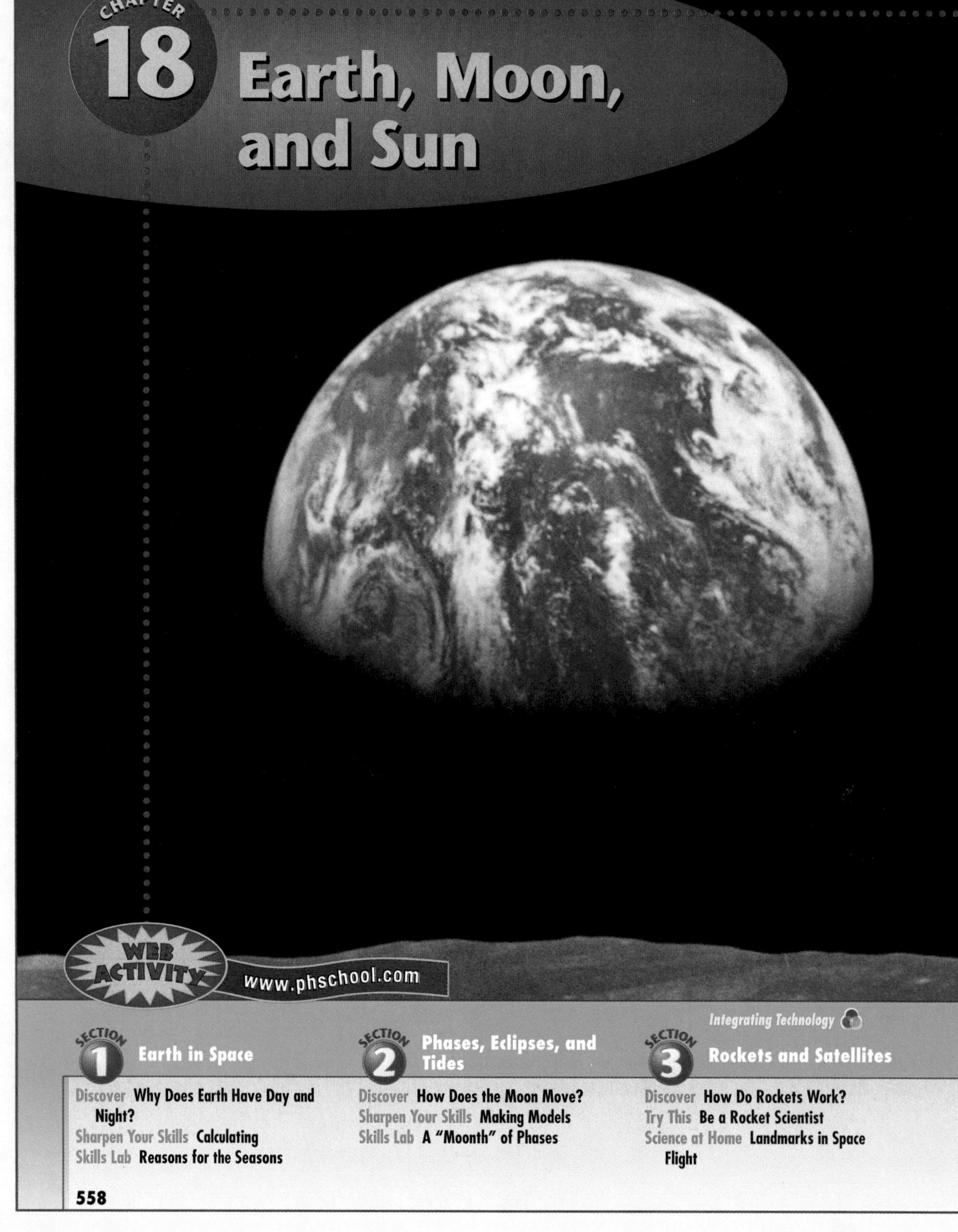

Launching the Project Ask: **When is it possible to see the moon?** If students respond that the moon is only visible at night, ask: **On a clear evening, can you always see the moon in the sky?** *(no)* **Can you ever see the moon during the day?** *(yes)* Encourage students to discuss whether they have seen a relationship between the phase of the moon, such as full or quarter, and how high it is in the sky at a particular time of night, such as 8 P.M. *(Most students will not have noticed a relationship.)* Tell students that in this project they will investigate this relationship.

Emphasize the importance of recording data at least three times per day. Explain that it is easier to monitor movement of the moon by noting its position several times a day rather than just once. To help students get started, pass out copies of the Chapter 18 Project Worksheets in Unit 6 Resources. You may wish to share the Chapter 18 Project Scoring Rubric with your students at this time.

CHAPTER 18 PROJECT

Where's the Moon?

What a view! Though you would have to be in orbit around the moon to see this kind of Earthrise, you don't have to travel at all to see the moonrise from Earth. All you have to do is look in the right direction at the right time and you will see the moon rise in front of you!

In this chapter, you will explore relationships among Earth, the moon, and the sun. In your project, you will observe the position of the moon in the sky every day. These observations will show you the changing positions of Earth and the moon with respect to each other and to the sun.

Your Goal To observe the shape of the moon and its position in the sky every day for one month.

To complete the project you will

- observe and record every day the compass direction in which you see the moon and its height above the horizon
- use your observations to explain the phases of the moon
- develop rules you can use to predict where and when you might see the moon each day throughout a month

Get Started Begin by preparing an observation log. You will want to record the date and time of each observation, the direction and height of the moon, a sketch of its shape, and notes about the cloud cover or other conditions. You can also keep track of the time of moonrise each day.

Check Your Progress You'll be working on this project as you study this chapter. To keep your project on track, look for Check Your Progress boxes at the following points.

Section 1 Review, page 567: Make a map to help you determine the direction of the moon.

Section 2 Review, page 578: Observe the moon every day.

Section 4 Review, page 588: Look for patterns in your observations.

Present Your Project At the end of the chapter (page 591), you will present your observations of the moon using words, drawings, and graphs.

...fferent

...rces

...Chapter 18 Project
...apter 18 Project
...rksheets; Chapter 18
...ubric

...chnology

...ion on Audio CD

You will find an Internet activity, chapter self-tests for students, and links to other chapter topics at this site.

Performance Assessment

Use the Chapter 18 Project Scoring Rubric in Unit 6 Resources to assess students' work. Students will be assessed on

- the quality and consistency of their daily record keeping;
- the quality of their graphs and drawings and their analysis of the data;
- their ability to find patterns in the data and use these to make predictions;
- the level of their understanding as demonstrated in the presentation of their conclusions or their participation in discussion.

Earth in Space

Objectives

After completing the lesson, students will be able to

- ◆ identify the effects of Earth's rotation and revolution;
- ◆ explain the causes of the seasons on Earth.

Key Terms astronomy, axis, rotation, revolution, orbit, latitude, solstice, equinox, vernal equinox, autumnal equinox

1 Engage/Explore

Activating Prior Knowledge

Ask students to estimate what time the sun rises in the morning and sets at night. Then, have them consult a daily newspaper to check their estimates. Next, ask students to describe how the number of hours of daylight each day change during the winter and summer. *(Students should note that there are fewer hours of daylight each day in winter than in summer.)*

DISCOVER

ACTIVITY

Skills Focus making models
Materials *lamp, light bulb, globe*
Time 15 minutes
Tips Place the bulb at a height approximately level with the globe's equator. Alternatively, use flashlights and have students work in pairs. One student can hold the flashlight steady while the other turns the globe.
Expected Outcome The half of the globe facing the bulb will be lit and will move into shadow as the globe rotates.
Think It Over A complete spin of the globe represents one rotation of Earth on its axis, which equals one day. In the model, one day is 5 seconds. To model a year, students can carry the spinning globe in a circle around the bulb.

SECTION 1 Earth in Space

DISCOVER ACTIVITY

Why Does Earth Have Day and Night?

1. Place a lamp with a bare bulb in the middle of a table to represent the sun. Put a globe at the end of the table about 1 meter away to represent Earth.
2. Turn the lamp on and darken the room. Which parts of the globe have light shining on them? Which parts are in shadow?
3. Find your location on the globe. Take about 5 seconds to turn the globe once. Notice when it is lit—day—at your location and when it is dark—night.

Think It Over

Making Models How does one complete turn of the globe represent one day? In this model, how many seconds represent one day? How could you use the model to represent a year?

GUIDE FOR READING

- ◆ What causes day and night?
- ◆ What causes the cycle of seasons on Earth?

Reading Tip Before you read, preview the figures and captions in the section. List any terms that are not familiar to you. Then write their definitions as you read about them.

Ancient Egyptian farmers eagerly awaited the annual spring flood of the Nile River. For thousands of years, their planting was ruled by it. As soon as the Nile's floodwaters withdrew, the farmers had to be ready to plow and plant their fields along the banks of the river. Because of this, the Egyptians wanted to predict when the flood would occur. Around 3000 B.C., people noticed that the bright star Sirius first became visible in the early morning sky every year shortly before the flood began. The Egyptians used this knowledge to predict each year's flood.

Egyptian farmers ▶

READING STRATEGIES

Reading Tip Unfamiliar terms may include *solstice* and *equinox*. Students are likely to recognize *rotation* and *revolution* as words related to turning, but may not know exactly what these terms mean. As students preview each figure and caption, suggest they ask themselves questions such as these:

- ◆ What is being shown in this picture?
- ◆ What is the main idea of the picture?
- ◆ What new information did I learn from the caption?

Vocabulary Point out that the term *revolution* has several meanings in addition to its scientific meaning. Provide student groups with dictionaries and challenge them to look up the meanings of *revolution.*

Rotation
N
S
Axis
Earth

Revolution
Sun
Earth

Figure 1 Earth rotates on its axis and revolves around the sun.
Applying Concepts What is one full rotation called? What is one complete revolution called?

Days and Years

The ancient Egyptians were among the first people to study the stars. The study of the moon, stars, and other objects in space is called **astronomy.**

Ancient astronomers also studied the movements of the sun and the moon as they appeared to travel across the sky. It seemed to them as though Earth were standing still and the sun and moon were moving around it. Actually, the sun and moon seem to move across the sky each day mainly because Earth is rotating on its axis.

Rotation The imaginary line that passes through Earth's center and the North and South poles is called Earth's **axis.** The north end of the axis currently points toward a point in space near Polaris, the North Star. Earth's spinning on its axis is called its **rotation.** A point on the equator rotates at about 1,600 kilometers per hour. Even most commercial jet planes can't fly this fast!

Earth's rotation on its axis causes day and night. As Earth rotates eastward, the sun appears to move westward across the sky. It is day on the side of Earth facing the sun. As Earth continues to turn to the east, the sun appears to set in the west. Sunlight can't reach the side of Earth facing away from the sun, so it is night there. It takes Earth about 24 hours to rotate once on its axis. As you know, each 24-hour cycle of day and night is called a day.

Revolution In addition to rotating on its axis, Earth travels around the sun. The movement of one object around another object is called **revolution.** One complete revolution around the sun is called a year. Earth's path as it revolves around the sun is called its **orbit.** As it travels around the sun, Earth's orbit is not quite a circle. It is a slightly flattened circle, or oval shape.

☑ *Checkpoint* *Why do the sun and moon seem to move each day?*

Calculating

ACTIVITY

Earth moves at a speed of about 30 km/sec as it travels around the sun. What distance, in kilometers, does Earth travel in a minute? An hour? A day? A year?

Program Resources

- **Unit 6 Resources** 18-1 Lesson Plan; 18-1 Section Summary
- **Guided Reading and Study Workbook** Section 18-1
- **Interdisciplinary Explorations Series** "Riddles of the Pharaohs," pp. 12–13

Answers to Self-Assessment

Caption Question

Figure 1 One full rotation is a called a day. One complete revolution is called a year.

☑ *Checkpoint*

The sun and moon seem to move each day mainly because Earth is rotating on its axis.

2 Facilitate

Days and Years

Sharpen your Skills

Skills Focus calculating
Materials *paper, pencil, calculator*
Time 10 minutes
Tips Suggest students set up the problems on paper to make sure units cancel out.
Expected Outcome In 1 min, 1,800 km; in 1 h, 108,000 km; in 1 day, 2,592,000 km; in 1 yr, 946,728,000 km
Extend Students can calculate the distance Earth travels in a decade or century. **learning modality: logical/mathematical**

Ongoing Assessment

Writing Ask students to write short paragraphs describing either the Earth's rotation or the Earth's revolution around the sun.

Days and Years, continued

Demonstration

Materials *turntable such as a lazy Susan, string, weight, ring stand, tape*
Time 15 minutes
Tips Tell students that in 1851 a French physicist named Jean Foucault used a pendulum to prove that Earth rotates. To model his pendulum, hang a small weight from the arm of a ring stand. Swing the pendulum and ask students to describe what happens. *(The weight swings back and forth in one plane.)* Place the pendulum in the center of the turntable. Mark one side of the turntable with a piece of tape. Swing the pendulum and turn the turntable slowly. Challenge students to explain how this models a pendulum at the North Pole and to explain how an experiment could prove that Earth rotates. *(The turntable is like Earth rotating around its axis. The tape mark represents a place on Earth. If a pendulum were swinging above the North Pole, the direction of its swing would appear to make one complete rotation in 24 hours.)* **learning modality: visual**

Real-Life Learning

Materials *old set of Yellow Pages separated into sections*
Time 10 minutes

Many professions or cultures require people to live by a calendar that is determined by seasonal events other than the movements of stars or planets. Assign students to small groups and have each group examine a portion of the Yellow Pages to identify occupations whose work is primarily seasonal. *(Samples: lifeguards, ski instructors, landscapers, and snow plow operators.)* **learning modality: verbal**

SCIENCE & History

Calendars The Egyptian astronomers counted the number of days between each first appearance of the star Sirius in the morning sky. In this way, they found that there were about 365 days in each year. By dividing the year into 365 days, the ancient Egyptians had created one of the first calendars.

People of many different cultures have struggled to come up with workable calendars. Earth's orbit around the sun takes about $365\frac{1}{4}$ days. Four years of about $365\frac{1}{4}$ days each can be approximated by taking 3 years of 365 days and a fourth year of 366 days. You know this fourth year as a "leap year." During a leap year, an extra day is added to February, giving it 29 days instead of its usual 28.

Tracking the Cycle of the Year

For thousands of years, people have used observations of the sky to keep track of the time of year.

1500 B.C.
British Isles
Ancient peoples complete Stonehenge, a monument with giant stones that mark the directions in which the sun rises and sets on the longest day of the year.

1500 B.C. — 900 B.C. — 300 B.C.

1300 B.C.
China
During the Shang dynasty, Chinese astronomers made detailed observations of the sun, planets, and other objects they saw in the night sky. Chinese astronomers calculated that the length of a year is 365.25 days.

300 B.C.
Egypt
Astronomers in Alexandria, Egypt, learned to use an instrument called an astrolabe. Astrolabes were used to find the positions of stars and planets.

Background

Facts and Figures Stonehenge was built over three main periods. The first period began about 3100 B.C., and included the digging of the circular ditch and a ring of 56 pits. During the second period, about 2100 B.C., huge pillars of rock were erected in concentric circles around the center of the site. The 35-ton heel stone may have been placed during this building period. The placement of this stone was one of the most sophisticated accomplishments of the time. On the morning of the summer solstice, a person standing in the center of the circle can see the sun rising directly over this stone. During the third period, the monument was remodeled, and a circle of 30 upright stones, each weighing up to 50 tons was erected. The final phase ended around 1500 B.C.

Dividing the year into smaller parts was difficult also. Early people used moon cycles as a sort of calendar. The time between one full moon and the next one is about $29\frac{1}{2}$ days. A year of 12 of these "moonths" only adds up to 354 days. The ancient Egyptians worked out a calendar that had 12 months of 30 days each, with an extra 5 days that were not part of any month. The Romans borrowed this calendar and made changes to it. With more changes, it eventually became the calendar we know: 11 months having 30 or 31 days each, plus one month (February) having 28 or 29 days.

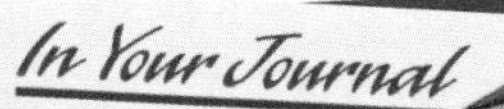

Research one of the accomplishments discussed in the time line. Write a dialogue in which two people from the culture that made the discovery or observation discuss its importance in their lives.

A.D. 1450

Wyoming

The Big Horn Medicine Wheel was built by Native Americans. Individual stones are aligned with the rising and setting sun and several bright stars. The rising of these specific stars may have indicated to people when it was time to move south for the winter.

A.D. 300 **A.D. 900** **A.D. 1500**

A.D. 900

Mexico

The Mayas studied the movement of the sun, the moon, and the planet Venus. They had two different calendars, one with 365 days for everyday use and the other with 260 days for religious uses. These calendars combined to make a 52-year cycle. The Mayas were able to predict astronomical events 3,000 years into the future.

SCIENCE & History

Encourage students to discuss how the peoples in the time line used their astronomical observations. Tell students that anything used to keep track of days, months, and year and the events that occur at those times can be a calendar. Challenge students to think about how the physical structures shown could serve as calendars. *(The giant stones at Stonehenge marked sunrise and sunset on the longest day of the year. The Big Horn Medicine Wheel marked the rising and setting of the sun and other stars.)*

In Your Journal Students should be able to research the accomplishments described in the time line in the library or on the Internet. Suggest they also look in magazines such as *Astronomy, Discover, National Geographic,* and *Natural History.* After they write their dialogues, students can perform them and record them using video or tape recorders. **learning modality: verbal**

Students can save their recordings in their portfolios.

Program Resources

- **Laboratory Manual** 18, "Constructing a Foucault Pendulum"

Ongoing Assessment

Writing Have students write brief paragraphs to explain why it was difficult for ancient peoples to come up with workable calendars. *(It was difficult to reconcile all the events—Earth's orbit around the sun takes $365\frac{1}{4}$ days, and it takes $29\frac{1}{2}$ days from one full moon to the next.)*

Seasons on Earth

Using the Visuals: Figure 2

On Figure 2, guide students to compare the area of Earth's surface covered by the sun's rays at the equator and the surface covered by the same amount of light at the poles. *(At the poles, it is much larger.)* Ask students to infer how this affects the climates at those places. *(The sunlight is more spread out at the poles so it is colder. The sunlight is more concentrated at the equator, so it is warmer.)* **learning modality: visual**

Building Inquiry Skills: Comparing and Contrasting

ACTIVITY

To help students who are still mastering English understand the difference between sunlight at the equator and the poles, give small groups of students flashlights and large sheets of graph paper. Students can shine a flashlight directly above the paper and trace around the lighted area. Then they can shine the flashlight at an angle and trace around the lighted area. Guide students to determine which area represents sunlight at the equator and at the poles. *(The larger area represents the poles.)* Then ask: **Does each square receive more energy when the light shines directly or at an angle?** *(directly)* **limited English proficiency**

Math TOOLBOX

Time 15 minutes
Tips On the chalkboard, draw a small circle to represent Earth. Well above the circle, draw a point to represent Polaris. To show that Polaris is directly overhead at the North Pole, draw a stick figure at the top of the circle. Ask: **If you were standing at the North Pole, where would you see Polaris?** *(Directly overhead)* **What angle is that above the horizon?** *(90°)* **What is the latitude of the North Pole?** *(90° north)* If you see Polaris at an angle of 41° above the horizon, your latitude is 41° north. **learning modality: logical/mathematical**

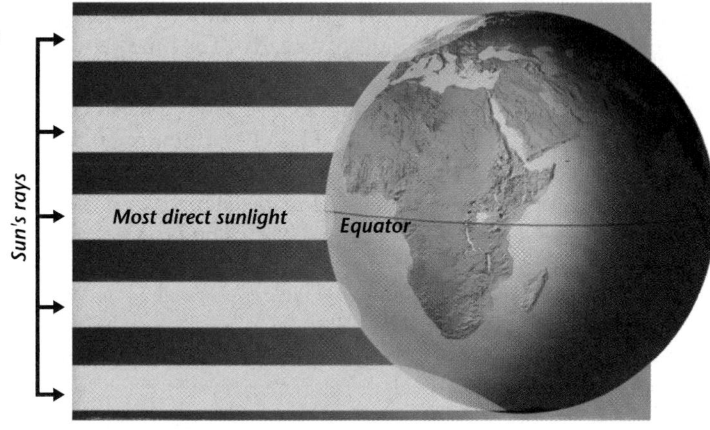

Figure 2 It is warm near the equator because sunlight hits Earth's surface more directly and is less spread out.
Interpreting Diagrams Why is it colder near the poles?

Seasons on Earth

Most places outside the tropics have four distinct seasons: winter, spring, summer, and autumn. But there are great differences in temperature from place to place. For instance, it is warmer near the equator than near the poles. Why is this so?

How Sunlight Hits Earth Figure 2 shows how sunlight hits Earth's surface. Notice that at the equator, sunlight hits Earth's surface more directly. Closer to the poles, sunlight hits Earth's surface at an angle. Near the poles, energy from the sun is spread out over a greater area. That is why it is warmer near the equator than near the poles.

Earth's Tilted Axis If Earth's axis were straight up and down relative to the sun, as in Figure 2, temperatures would remain constant year-round. There would be no seasons. **Earth has seasons because its axis is tilted as it moves around the sun.**

Look at Earth's position in space in *Exploring the Seasons* on the next page. Notice that Earth's axis is tilted at an angle of 23.5° from the vertical. As Earth revolves around the sun, its axis is tilted away from the sun for part of the year and toward the sun for part of the year.

When the north end of Earth's axis is tilted toward the sun, the Northern Hemisphere has summer. At the same time, the south end of Earth's axis is tilted away from the sun. As a result, the Southern Hemisphere has winter.

Summer and winter are not affected by changes in Earth's distance from the sun. In fact, when the Northern Hemisphere is having summer, Earth is at its greatest distance from the sun.

☑ *Checkpoint How is Earth's axis tilted when the Northern Hemisphere has summer?*

Math TOOLBOX

What's Your Angle?

An angle is formed when two lines meet at a point. Angles are measured in degrees (symbol°).

Earth's axis currently points near Polaris, the North Star. As a result, the angle of the North Star above the horizon at any point in the Northern Hemisphere equals the latitude of a person observing from that point. For example, at the equator, which has a latitude of 0°, Polaris would be seen at an angle of 0°, which is on the horizon. What is your latitude if you observe that Polaris is 41° above the horizon? If Polaris is directly overhead?

Background

History of Science Early peoples such as the Sumerians of Babylon used the phases of the moon to make a calendar, counting 12 lunar months a year. The Egyptians later worked out a calendar that corresponded almost exactly to the seasons. The early Romans also used a calendar that was based on the moon. Their calendar had 355 days. An extra month was added about every fourth year. These calendars were regulated by the high priests. However, this calendar was not very accurate. As a result, by Julius Caesar's time, the summer months were coming in springtime. Early calendars such as the Julian calendar also allowed for corrections in time. For example, the correction of one day every four years caused the calendar year to be longer than the year as measured by the seasons. As a result, the vernal equinox in 1582 occurred on March 11, instead of on March 21.

EXPLORING *Solstices and Equinoxes*

The yearly cycle of the seasons is caused by the tilt of Earth's axis as it revolves around the sun.

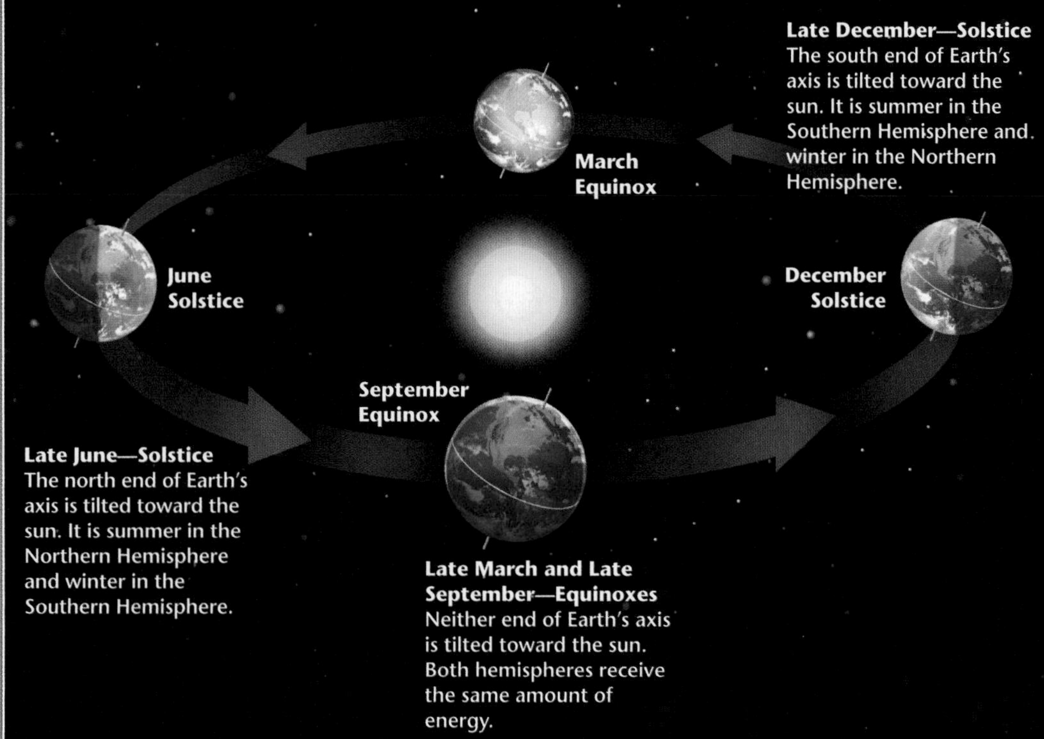

Late December—Solstice
The south end of Earth's axis is tilted toward the sun. It is summer in the Southern Hemisphere and winter in the Northern Hemisphere.

March Equinox

June Solstice

December Solstice

September Equinox

Late June—Solstice
The north end of Earth's axis is tilted toward the sun. It is summer in the Northern Hemisphere and winter in the Southern Hemisphere.

Late March and Late September—Equinoxes
Neither end of Earth's axis is tilted toward the sun. Both hemispheres receive the same amount of energy.

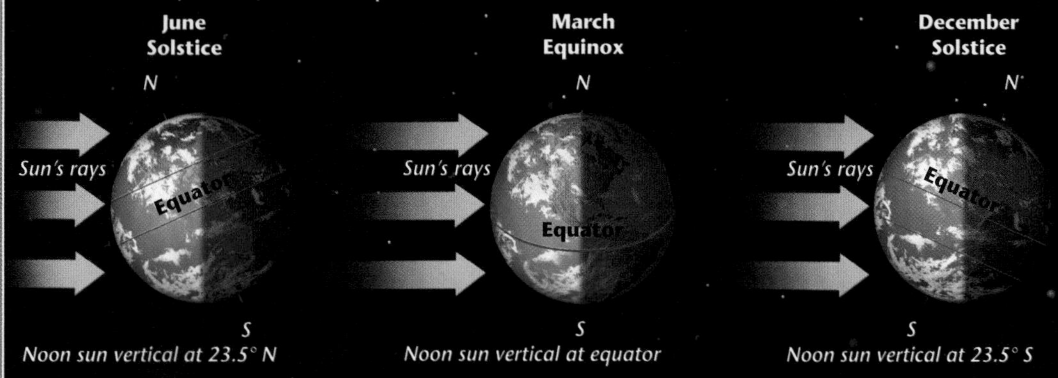

June Solstice
N
Sun's rays
Equator
S
Noon sun vertical at 23.5° N

March Equinox
N
Sun's rays
Equator
S
Noon sun vertical at equator

December Solstice
N
Sun's rays
Equator
S
Noon sun vertical at 23.5° S

EXPLORING

Solstices and Equinoxes

Point out the lines showing Earth's axis and ask students what they notice about them. *(They are all tilted.)* Ask students whether the tilt is different at different points in Earth's revolution. *(The tilt is the same.)* Direct students' attention to the figure in the lower left. Ask them to list two things that cause it to be summer in the Northern Hemisphere. *(In June, the sun shines more directly on the surface. The sun is above the horizon for a longer period each day.)* Now have them look at the lower right. Ask them to list two things that cause it to be winter in the Northern Hemisphere. *(In December, the sun shines less directly on the surface. The sun is above the horizon for a shorter period each day.)* **learning modality: visual**

Demonstration

ACTIVITY

To show students how the tilt of the Earth's axis affects the seasons, place a lamp with a bare bulb on a desk. Tilt a globe so that the Northern Hemisphere is tilted toward the lamp (sun). This represents Earth's position at the June solstice. Walk around the lamp in a circle but keep the tilt the same relative to the room, not the lamp. As you walk, stop every 90° to represent Earth's position at the equinoxes and the winter solstice. Turn the globe so the United States is facing the sun. At each position, ask students to describe the conditions in the United States. *(Sample: In December, the United States is tilted away from the sun so it is cooler.)* **learning modality: visual**

Media and Technology

Transparencies "Exploring Solstices and Equinoxes," Transparency 70

Answers to Self-Assessment

Caption Question

Figure 2 It is colder near the poles because the sunlight hits Earth at an angle and the sun's rays are spread out over a larger area.

Ongoing Assessment

Writing Have students describe the seasons in your area, when they normally occur, and why spring and fall often have similar conditions.

Students can save their descriptions in their portfolios.

Seasons on Earth, continued

Inquiry Challenge

Time 30 minutes

Materials *lamp with bare bulb, plastic foam ball, modeling clay, thin wooden dowel rod*

Tips Challenge small groups of students to make models to test this hypothesis: *If Earth were not tilted, the length of the days would not change.* Once groups set up their models, turn off the lights in the room so they can demonstrate them. *(Place the lamp in the center of a desk. Insert a dowel through the center of each ball and stick each dowel into a lump of clay. Make sure the dowel is vertical. Then turn on the lamp and move the model to several positions. around the lamp. At each position, rotate the ball and observe the light and shadow on the ball. Groups should conclude that the ball is always illuminated the same, with the line between light and shadow going through each pole.)* **cooperative learning**

Addressing Naive Conceptions

Some students may think that the days seem longer in summer because of daylight-savings time. Point out that the total number of daylight hours in the Northern Hemisphere actually is greater in summer. Daylight savings time simply moves the starting time for work and school earlier in the day, so more daylight hours are available after work or school. **learning modality: verbal**

Integrating Life Science

Encourage students to think about how the change in the length of days affects humans. *(Sample: In winter, people go to bed earlier and stay inside more.)* Brainstorm a list of animals or events that are unique to each season. **learning modality: verbal**

Earth in June In June, the north end of Earth's axis is tilted toward the sun. The noon sun is directly overhead at 23.5° north latitude. **Latitude** is a measurement of distance from the equator, expressed in degrees north or south. (The equator has latitude 0° and the North Pole has latitude 90° north.)

The hemisphere that is tilted toward the sun also has more hours of daylight than the hemisphere that is tilted away from the sun. The combination of direct rays and more hours of sunlight heats the surface more than at any other time of the year. It is summer in the Northern Hemisphere.

At the same time, for any place on Earth south of the equator, the sun's energy is spread over a large area. There are also fewer hours of daylight. The combination of indirect rays and fewer hours of sunlight heats Earth's surface less than at any other time of the year. It is winter in the Southern Hemisphere.

Earth in December Look again at *Exploring the Seasons.* Around December 21, the noon sun is overhead at 23.5° south latitude. People in the Southern Hemisphere receive the most direct sunlight, so it is summer there. At the same time, the sun's rays in the Northern Hemisphere are indirect and there are fewer hours of daylight. So it is winter in the Northern Hemisphere.

Both June and December On two days each year, the noon sun is overhead at either 23.5° south or 23.5° north. Each of these days is known as a **solstice** (SAHL stis). The day when the noon sun is overhead at 23.5° south is the winter solstice in the Northern Hemisphere. It is the summer solstice in the Southern Hemisphere. This solstice occurs around December 21 each year, and is the shortest day of the year in the Northern Hemisphere. At

Figure 3 Spring is the season between the vernal equinox and the summer solstice. The warming temperatures of spring make it the best time to plant flowers like these pansies.

Background

History of Science Before calendars, some early peoples may have kept records of passing time by etching notches on sticks, or by tying knots in cords for every passing day. People also observed the changing habits of animals. A Greek epic poem from around 700 B.C. explains that people knew it was time to stop digging in their vineyards when they saw snails climb up plants. On an island near Taiwan, the Yami fisherman still use animal behavior to help them determine the seasons with their lunar-based calendar. Sometime around the month of March, the fishermen light flares and go out in their boats to look for flying fish. If the fish appear, it is time for fishing season to begin. If they do not appear, the Yami know that it is time to insert an extra month to correct their calendar. Fishing season begins the following month, and that year has 13 months instead of 12.

the same time, it is close to the longest day of the year in the Southern Hemisphere.

Similarly, around June 21, the noon sun is overhead at 23.5° north. This is the summer solstice in the Northern Hemisphere and the winter solstice in the Southern Hemisphere.

Earth in March and September Halfway between the solstices, neither hemisphere is tilted toward or away from the sun. This situation occurs on only two days of the year. On these days, the noon sun is directly overhead at the equator.

Each of these days is known as an **equinox,** which means "equal night." During an equinox, the lengths of nighttime and daytime are about the same. The **vernal equinox,** or spring equinox, occurs around March 21, and marks the beginning of spring in the Northern Hemisphere. The **autumnal equinox** occurs around September 23. It marks the beginning of fall in the Northern Hemisphere.

Figure 4 This hungry bear has spent the long winter in a dormant state in a cave in Alaska. *Applying Concepts Why didn't this bear remain active all winter?*

INTEGRATING LIFE SCIENCE In much of the United States, seasonal changes affect living things. In spring and summer, the sun shines for more hours each day and is higher in the sky. The warmer days and additional sunlight allow many plants to begin growing leaves and flowers. Because plants grow more, animals that feed on the plants, from tiny insects to large deer, get more food.

In the fall, the nights get longer, signaling the plants to stop growing and some plants to lose their leaves. With less food available, black bears and some other animals go into a dormant state in which they use very little energy. Others, like many songbirds and waterfowl, travel to warmer climates where food is still available.

Section 1 Review

1. Explain the process that causes day and night.
2. What two factors cause the cycle of the seasons?
3. Compare rotation and revolution.
4. What do the words *solstice* and *equinox* mean? How are they related to the position of Earth's axis?
5. **Thinking Critically Relating Cause and Effect** Are changes in the distance between Earth and the sun important in causing the cycle of the seasons? Explain.

CHAPTER PROJECT

Check Your Progress

Begin recording your daily observations of the moon. Sketch a map of the site from which you will be making observations. Which way is north? East? South? West? Each night, observe and record the moon's direction. You should also estimate the moon's altitude, or height in degrees from the horizon. You can do this by making a fist and holding it at arm's length. One fist above the horizon is 10°, two fists are 20°, and so on.

3 Assess

Section 1 Review Answers

1. Earth rotates on its axis once per day. As Earth rotates, half its surface is facing the sun (day) and half is facing away from the sun (night).
2. The cycle of the seasons is caused by Earth's revolution around the sun and the tilt of Earth's axis.
3. Rotation is turning around a point or an axis; revolution is movement around another object.
4. A solstice is a day when the noon sun is overhead at 23.5° south or 23.5° north. This occurs when one end of Earth's axis is tilted most directly toward the sun. *Equinox* means "equal night," and occurs when neither pole of Earth's axis is tilted toward the sun.
5. The tilt of Earth's axis, not its distance from the sun, is the cause of the cycle of seasons. During the summer months in the Northern Hemisphere, Earth is actually at its farthest point from the sun. During winter in the Northern Hemisphere, Earth is at its closest point to the sun.

CHAPTER PROJECT

Check Your Progress

Students should be ready to begin making observations of the moon. Remind students to draw maps of their observation sites. You might want to give a brief lesson on map-making skills such as defining coordinate systems and making map keys. Make sure students have developed a method for measuring altitude. Instead of the "fist" method, you may want to have students construct astrolabes to measure the altitude of the moon.

Program Resources

◆ **Unit 6 Resources** 18-1 Review and Reinforce; 18-1 Enrich

Answers to Self-Assessment

Caption Question

Figure 4 The amount of available food decreases in the winter season. Bears use less energy when they are dormant.

Performance Assessment

Writing Challenge students to choose a place on the globe they are not familiar with and write descriptions of the amount of sunlight received there throughout the year.

Skills Lab

Observing

Reasons for the Seasons

Preparing for Inquiry

Key Concept The seasons are determined by the tilt of Earth's axis as Earth revolves around the sun.

Skills Objectives Students will be able to

- make an Earth/sun model to observe the effect of the tilt of Earth's axis on the seasons;
- measure and calculate light angle and area.

Time 40 minutes

Advance Planning Make sure the flashlights are working properly. Have extra batteries on hand. The room must be dim enough for the light from the flashlights to be seen. One acetate sheet can be cut into six grids.

Alternative Materials Balls with smooth, unmarked surfaces work best.

Guiding Inquiry

Invitation Ask students: **Why is it warmer in the summer?** *(Many students will hold the common misconception that Earth is closer to the sun.)* Tell students that Earth is actually a bit farther from the sun during the Northern hemisphere summer. In this activity, they will relate the tilt of Earth's axis to the seasons.

Introducing the Procedure

- Tell students the ball must be close enough to the flashlight so that several grid squares can be seen on the ball.
- Make sure students know how to use the protractor to measure the angle of Earth's axis.

Troubleshooting the Experiment

- Students may have difficulty maintaining the tilt of the ball at 23.5° as they move the ball. Have the partner measure the angle before recording information on the size and shape of the grid squares.
- Tell students to keep the axis of Earth tilted towards the same wall as the ball revolves around the light.

Skills Lab

Observing

REASONS FOR THE SEASONS

In this lab, you will use an Earth-sun model to make observations about factors that contribute to the seasons.

Problem

What effect does the tilt of Earth's axis have on the heat and light received by Earth as it revolves around the sun?

Materials (per pair of students)

books	flashlight	paper
pencil	protractor	toothpick

acetate sheet with thick grid lines drawn on it
plastic foam ball marked with poles and equator

Procedure

1. Make a pile of books about 15 cm high.
2. Tape the acetate sheet to the head of the flashlight. Place the flashlight on the pile of books.
3. Carefully push a pencil into the South Pole of the plastic foam ball, which represents Earth.
4. Use the protractor to measure a 23.5° tilt of the axis of your Earth away from your "flashlight sun," as shown in the first diagram. This represents winter.
5. Hold the pencil so that Earth is steady at this 23.5° angle and about 15 cm from the flashlight head. Turn the flashlight on. Dim the room lights.
6. The squares on the acetate should show up on your model Earth. Move the ball closer if necessary or dim the room lights more. Observe and record the shape of the squares at the equator and at the poles.
7. Carefully stick the toothpick straight into your model Earth about halfway between the equator and the North Pole. Observe and record the length of the shadow.
8. Without changing the tilt, turn the pencil to rotate the model Earth once on its axis. Observe and record how the shadow of the toothpick changes.
9. Tilt your model Earth 23.5° toward the flashlight, as shown in the second diagram. This is summer. Observe and record the shape of the squares at the equator and at the poles. Observe how the toothpick's shadow changes.
10. Rotate the model Earth and note the shadow pattern.

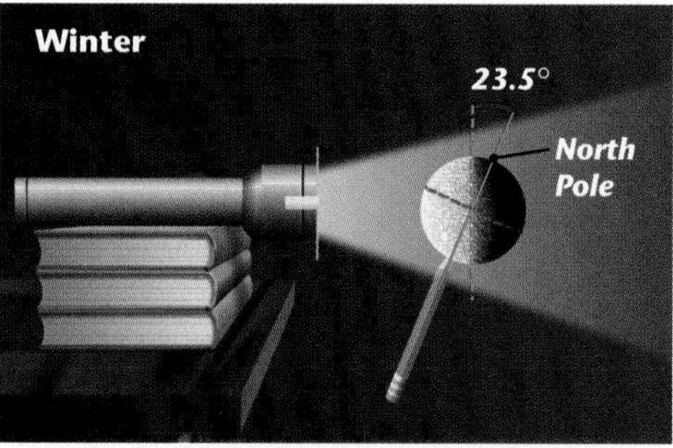

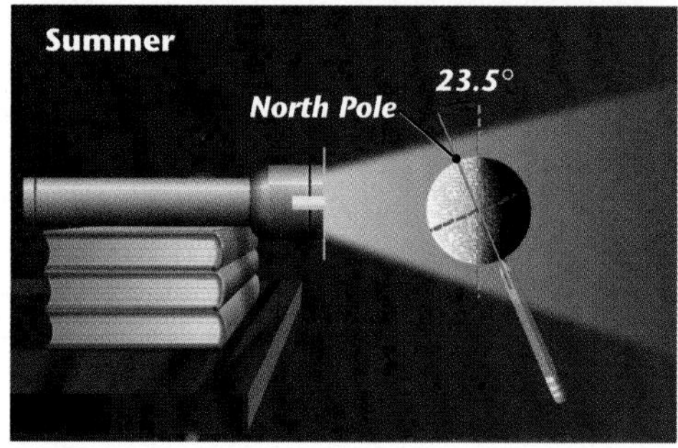

568

Expected Outcome

- The grid squares will be smaller and more square in the region of the ball where the light hits directly.
- The grid squares will be larger and more lengthened where the light hits at an angle.

Analyze and Conclude

1. During winter, the area near 23.5° south latitude; in summer, the region near 23.5° north latitude gets the most concentrated light.

2. Light is more concentrated in the middle zone during the summer, and more spread out during the winter.

3. The same amount of heat is spread out over a larger area.

4. The poles are consistently coolest because the energy is the most spread out there. The equator is warmest because the energy is most concentrated there.

5. The shadow will be longest during winter and shortest during summer.

Analyze and Conclude

1. When it is winter in the Northern Hemisphere, which areas on Earth get the most concentrated amount of light? Which areas get the most concentrated light when it is summer in the Northern Hemisphere?
2. Compare your observations of how the light hits the area halfway between the equator and the North Pole during winter (Step 6) and during summer (Step 9).
3. If the squares projected on the ball from the acetate become larger, what can you conclude about the amount of heat distributed in each square?
4. According to your observations, which areas on Earth are consistently coolest? Which areas are consistently warmest? Why?
5. What time of year will the toothpick's shadow be longest? When will the shadow be shortest?
6. How are the amounts of heat and light received in a square related to the angle of the sun's rays?

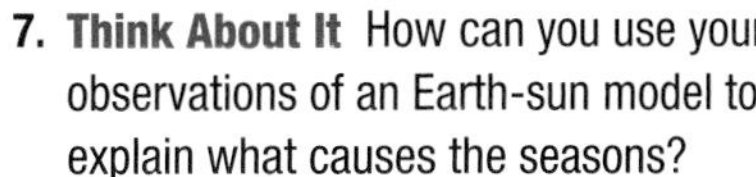

7. **Think About It** How can you use your observations of an Earth-sun model to explain what causes the seasons?

More to Explore

You can measure how directly light from the sun hits Earth's surface by making a shadow stick. You need a stick or pole about 1 m long. With the help of your teacher, push the stick partway into the ground where it will not be disturbed. Make sure the stick stays vertical. At noon on the first day of every month, measure the length of the stick's shadow. The shorter the shadow, the more directly the sun's rays are hitting Earth. At what time of the year are the shadows longest? Shortest? How do your observations help explain the seasons?

6. As the angle increases, the light and heat become less concentrated and spread out over a larger area. Each square receives a smaller portion of light and heat.

7. Think About It During summer in the Northern Hemisphere, the rays hit the Northern Hemisphere directly. The heating effect is greater and the Northern Hemisphere is warmed. During winter the rays hit the Northern Hemisphere at an angle, so the heating effect is less.

Program Resources

◆ **Unit 6 Resources** Chapter 18 Skills Lab

Media and Technology

Lab Activity Videotapes
Grade 6, Tape 4

Extending the Inquiry

More to Explore Over the course of time, students should notice that the length of the shadow at noon varies. The shadow grows longer and longer until the December solstice, around December 21. Then the shadow grows progressively shorter until the June solstice, on or near June 21. When the shadow is longest, the sun's rays are the most spread out and are the least effective at heating the surface.

Section 2 Phases, Eclipses, and Tides

Objectives

After completing the lesson, students will be able to

- describe the causes of the moon's phases;
- explain what causes solar and lunar eclipses;
- identify the cause of the tides.

Key Terms phase, eclipse, solar eclipse, umbra, penumbra, lunar eclipse, tide, gravity

1 Engage/Explore

Activating Prior Knowledge

Ask students to describe observations they have made of the moon. Encourage students to use descriptive language. Prompt students to recall as many things about the moon as possible by asking questions. For example, ask them if they have ever seen the moon low on the horizon, if it was full when it was low on the horizon, and if the moon is ever up in the daytime. Encourage students to think about their observations as they read this section.

Discover

Skills Focus inferring
Materials *quarters, pennies*
Time 10 minutes
Tips Before students try the activity, have them predict how many times the penny will rotate during its revolution around the quarter.
Expected Outcome The penny makes one complete rotation on its axis as it revolves around the quarter.
Think It Over The moon does not appear to rotate when seen from Earth because the same face is always visible from Earth.

Section 2 Phases, Eclipses, and Tides

Discover — Activity

How Does the Moon Move?

1. Put a quarter flat on your desk to represent Earth. Use a penny flat on your desk to represent the moon.
2. One side of the moon always faces Earth. Move the moon through one revolution around Earth, keeping Lincoln's face always looking at Earth. How many times did the penny make one complete rotation?

Think It Over

Inferring From the point of view of someone on Earth, does the moon seem to rotate? Explain your answer.

GUIDE FOR READING

- What causes the phases of the moon?
- What causes solar and lunar eclipses?
- What causes the tides?

Reading Tip **As you read, write a sentence to describe what causes each of the following: phases, solar eclipses, lunar eclipses, tides.**

The moon is Earth's closest neighbor in space—much closer than any planet. In fact, the average distance from Earth to the moon is only about 30 times Earth's diameter. Even so, it is quite far away. On average, the moon is 384,400 kilometers from Earth. If there were a highway to the moon and you could travel at 100 kilometers per hour, it would take you more than five months to get there.

The moon moves in space just as Earth does. As the moon revolves around Earth and Earth revolves around the sun, the relative positions of the moon, Earth, and sun change. **The positions of the moon, Earth, and the sun cause the phases of the moon, eclipses, and tides.**

Crescent moon over Fire Island, New York

Motions of the Moon

The moon revolves around Earth and rotates on its own axis. It takes the moon about 27.3 days to revolve around Earth. Like Earth's orbit around the sun, the moon's orbit around Earth is a flattened circle or oval shape.

The moon rotates slowly on its own axis once every 27.3 days. Because the moon also revolves around Earth every 27.3 days, a "day" and a "year" on the moon are the same length. As you saw if you

Reading Strategies

Reading Tip Suggest students use charts like the one shown to make notes as they read. Then have them use their notes to write the sentences. For example, students may write that phases are caused by the amount of the sunlit side of the moon that faces Earth.

What causes ___ ?	
Moon phases	
Solar eclipse	
Lunar eclipse	
Tides	

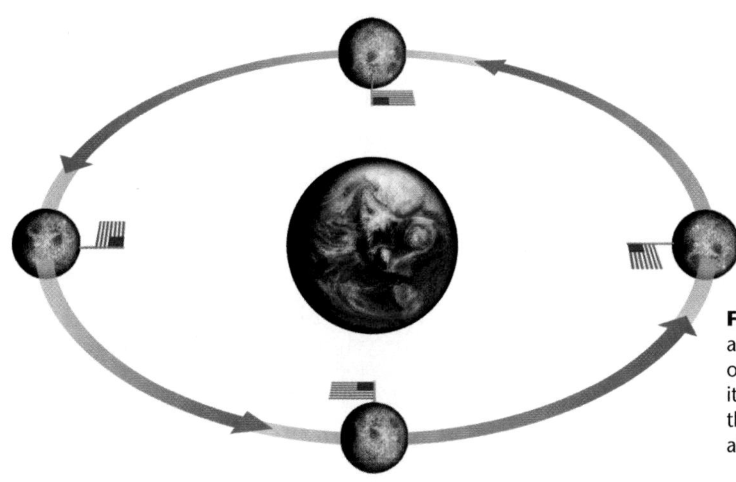

Figure 5 The moon revolves around Earth in the same amount of time the moon takes to rotate on its axis. As a result, the near side of the moon (shown with a flag) always faces Earth.

tried the Discover activity, the same side of the moon, the "near side," always faces Earth. The "far side" of the moon always faces away from Earth, so you never see it from Earth.

☑ *Checkpoint* *How many days does it take the moon to revolve once around Earth?*

Phases of the Moon

On a clear night when the moon is full, the bright moonlight can keep you awake. But the moon does not produce the light you see. Instead, it reflects light from the sun. Imagine taking a flashlight into a dark room. If you were to shine the flashlight on a chair, you would see the chair because the light from your flashlight would bounce, or reflect, off the chair. In the same way that the chair wouldn't shine by itself, the moon doesn't give off light by itself. You see the moon because sunlight reflects off it.

When you see the moon in the sky, sometimes it appears round. Other times you see only a thin sliver, or crescent. The different shapes of the moon you see from Earth are called **phases.** The moon goes through its whole set of phases each time it revolves around Earth, that is, about once a month.

What Causes Phases? Phases are caused by changes in the relative positions of the moon, Earth, and the sun. Because the sun lights the moon, half the moon is almost always in sunlight. However, since the moon revolves around Earth, you see the moon from different angles. The half of the moon that faces Earth is not always the half that is sunlit. **The phase of the moon you see depends on how much of the sunlit side of the moon faces Earth.** To understand the changing phases, refer to *Exploring Phases of the Moon* on the next page.

Social Studies CONNECTION

Before there was artificial lighting, the phases of the moon were important in planning activities. For example, the full moon nearest the autumnal equinox is called the harvest moon, and the following full moon is called the hunter's moon.

In Your Journal

Find out about an event that is determined by the phases of the moon, such as the Jewish Passover, the Christian Easter, or the Islamic fast of Ramadan. How is the date of the event calculated?

2 Facilitate

Motions of the Moon

Including All Students

Students who are not visually oriented may need extra help understanding why the flags in Figure 5 indicate that the moon is rotating. Draw a figure similar to Figure 5 on the board. Ask: **Which way would the flags be pointing if the moon was *not* rotating?** If students have difficulty answering, draw flags on the moons to show that if the moon was not rotating, the flag at only one position would point toward Earth. **learning modality: logical/mathematical**

Phases of the Moon

Social Studies CONNECTION

A harvest moon rises at almost the same time for several nights in a row. Like all full moons, it rises at about the same time the sun sets. Ask: **Why do you think this is called the harvest moon?** *(This full moon provides extra light during the early evening hours to help farmers gather their crops.)*

In Your Journal The dates for these holidays are set using lunar references systems, and students may need additional help to calculate their dates. For example, Easter is the first Sunday after the first full moon that occurs on or after March 21. Ramadan begins and ends one month later when the authorities decree that the twelfth new moon has been sighted by a reliable witness. Passover is from 14 to 22 Nisan. **learning modality: verbal**

Program Resources

- **Unit 6 Resources** 18-2 Lesson Plan; 18-2 Section Summary
- **Guided Reading and Study Workbook** Section 18-2
- **Interdisciplinary Explorations Series** "Where River Meets Sea," pp. 26–27

Answers to Self-Assessment

☑ *Checkpoint*

It takes the moon 27.3 days to revolve around Earth.

Ongoing Assessment

Oral Presentation Have students describe what causes the phases of the moon.

EXPLORING

Phases of the Moon

Some students may think that the far side of the moon is the same as the dark side of the moon. Explain to students that although the same side of the moon always faces Earth, the moon's position in relation to the sun is not fixed. As the moon revolves around Earth, sunlight shines on the near and far sides of the moon at different times. Point out that the diagram and the photographs are taken from different viewpoints. Direct the student's attention to the pictures of the waxing crescent moon. Ask: **If you had been observing for several days, how could you tell whether the moon was waxing or waning?** *(The waxing moon gets larger over time, while a waning moon gets smaller.)* **Where is the moon in its orbit when it is waxing?** *(On the top half of the diagram)*

Extend Ask students to find the origins of the terms *gibbous* and *waxing.* *(*Gibbous *is from the Latin* gibbosus *meaning "humpbacked."* Waxing *is from Old English* weaxan *meaning "to grow.")* **learning modality: visual**

Inquiry Challenge

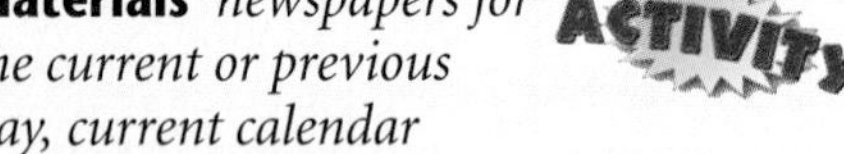

Materials *newspapers for the current or previous day, current calendar*

Time 20 minutes

Tips Invite students to predict the number of days between the new moon, first quarter, full moon, and third quarter. Have groups of students use the weather report from the newspaper to find the dates for each phase, then mark the dates and draw the moon phases on their calendars. Students can compare the data with their predictions. Ask questions such as: **How long does it take for the new moon to reach the first quarter?** *(About one week)* **Why do you think this is called a "quarter moon?"** *(One week is about one-quarter of the complete cycle of phases.)* **learning modality: logical/mathematical**

EXPLORING Phases of the Moon

The diagram in the center shows a view of Earth and the moon phases from above. The sun is shining from the right. The outer ring of photos shows the different amounts of the sunlit side of the moon that an observer on Earth sees as the moon revolves around Earth.

First Quarter
You see half of the lighted side of the moon.

Waxing Crescent
You see more and more of the lighted side of the moon. This is called a waxing crescent moon.

Waxing Gibbous
The moon continues to wax. The moon is called gibbous.

New Moon
The sun lights the side of the moon facing away from Earth. The side of the moon that faces Earth is dark.

Full Moon
You see the whole lighted side of the moon.

Waning Gibbous
The fraction of the lighted side of the moon that you see gets smaller each day.

Third Quarter
You can see half of the moon's lighted side.

Waning Crescent
You see a crescent again.

572

Background

Facts and Figures Consider these facts about the moon.

- In 1959, the Soviet Luna 3 spacecraft photographed the hidden 41% of the moon. Until then, the far side of the moon had never been seen by anyone on Earth.
- Seen from the moon, Earth also goes through a complete cycle of phases. When an observer on Earth sees a new moon, an observer on the dark side of the moon would see a full Earth shining.
- During the first, or waxing, crescent moon, observers can often see a faint glow from the unlit part of the moon. This is caused by the light from the bright Earth being reflected off the moon.

The Cycle of the Phases During the new moon, the side of the moon facing Earth is not lit. As the moon revolves around Earth, you see more and more of the lighted side of the moon every day, until the side of the moon you see is fully lit. As the moon continues in its orbit, you see less and less of the lighted side of the moon. About 29.5 days after the last new moon, the cycle is complete, and you see a new moon again.

Checkpoint *Since the moon does not produce light, how can you see it?*

Eclipses

What would you think if you were walking home from school on a sunny afternoon and the sun began to disappear? Would you be frightened? On rare occasions, the moon completely blocks the sun. The sky grows as dark as night even in the middle of a clear day. The air gets cool and the sky becomes an eerie color. If you don't know what is happening, you can become very frightened.

The moon doesn't usually go directly between Earth and the sun or directly behind Earth. As Figure 6 shows, the moon's orbit around Earth is slightly tilted with respect to Earth's orbit around the sun. As a result, in most months the moon revolves completely around Earth without the moon moving into Earth's shadow or the moon's shadow hitting Earth.

When the moon's shadow hits Earth or Earth's shadow hits the moon, an eclipse occurs. An **eclipse** (ih KLIPS) occurs when an object in space comes between the sun and a third object, and casts a shadow on that object. There are two types of eclipses: solar eclipses and lunar eclipses. (The words *solar* and *lunar* come from the Latin words for "sun" and "moon.")

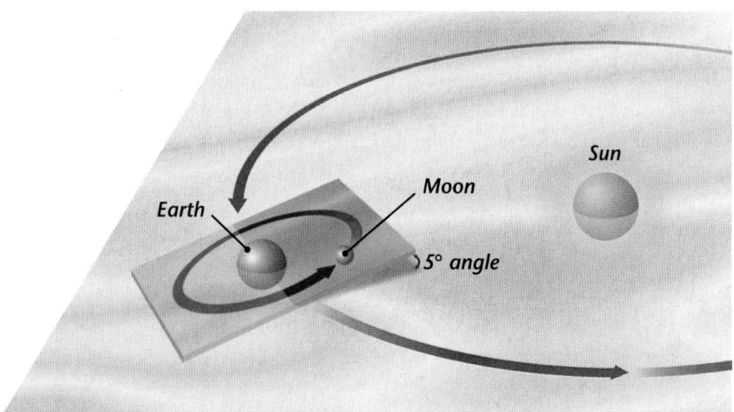

Figure 6 The moon's orbit is tilted with respect to Earth's orbit. So the moon rarely goes directly between Earth and the sun. *Interpreting Diagrams How large is the angle between Earth's orbit and the moon's orbit?*

Building Inquiry Skills: Comparing and Contrasting

The term *phase* is used in many different ways in science. This can be confusing to students whose native language is not English. Have all students list three ways *phase* is used in science (phases of the moon, phases of matter, color phases in a species of animal or plant) and give the appropriate definition for each one. **limited English proficiency**

Eclipses

Using the Visuals: Figure 6

What phase of the moon is shown in the figure? *(Waning crescent)* Point out that around new moon the near side of the moon is the dark side and the far side is lit because the moon is between Earth and the sun. The opposite is true for the full moon. Ask students to explain what phase the moon must be in for a solar eclipse to occur and for a lunar eclipse to occur. **learning modality: visual**

Language Arts Connection

In *A Connecticut Yankee in King Arthur's Court* by Mark Twain, the main character travels back in time to the court of King Arthur. There, his knowledge of eclipses saves him from execution. Have students read the passage from Chapter 5 of the novel in which the Yankee remembers the date on which a solar eclipse occurs. Then challenge students to write journal or diary entries about how a lack of scientific explanations might encourage superstitious beliefs. **learning modality: verbal**

Media and Technology

Transparencies "Exploring Phases of the Moon," Transparency 71

Answers to Self-Assessment

Checkpoint

Light from the sun reflects off the moon, enabling it to be seen from Earth.

Caption Question

Figure 6 The angle between Earth's orbit and that of the moon is about 5°.

Ongoing Assessment

Drawing Have students sketch the position of the moon relative to Earth and the sun at the time of new moon, first quarter, full moon, and third-quarter moon, and write brief explanations for how these phases occur.

Solar Eclipses

Cultural Diversity

Students whose native language is not English may be able to help native speakers understand some of the terms in this section. The words *solar, lunar, umbra,* and *penumbra* are derived from Latin and have cognates in languages based on Latin, such as Spanish. Ask: **What are the names for the sun and moon in other languages?** *(Sample: Spanish—*el sol *and* la luna*)* Tell students that the Latin word *umbra* means "shadow," and *penumbra* means "almost shadow." Ask: **What other words can you think of that might come from these words?** *(Sample: English—*umbrella; *Spanish—*umbroso *and* umbrio *mean "shady,"* sombra *means "shadow.")* **learning modality: verbal**

Sharpen your Skills

Making Models

Materials *paper, metric rulers, calculators*
Time 15 minutes
Tips Guide students to find the other distances in terms of Earth's diameter.
Expected Outcome With Earth as 1 cm in diameter, the moon will be 2.5 mm in diameter, 30 cm away in the opposite corner of the page.
Extend Challenge students to find the distance from Earth to the sun and then estimate the distance where they would place the sun in their scale drawings. *(At about 11,725 cm)* **learning modality: logical/mathematical**

Using the Visuals: Figure 7

Ask students which side of the moon receives the light of the sun during a solar eclipse. *(Far side)* Ask: **Would people in the moon's penumbra experience a total or a partial eclipse?** *(Partial)* **learning modality: visual**

Making Models
Here is how you can draw a scale model of a solar eclipse. The moon's diameter is about one fourth Earth's diameter. The distance from Earth to the moon is about 30 times Earth's diameter. Make a scale drawing of the moon, Earth, and the distance between them. (*Hint:* Draw Earth 1 cm in diameter in one corner of the paper.) From the edges of the moon, draw and shade in a triangle just touching Earth to show the moon's umbra during a solar eclipse.

Solar Eclipses

During a new moon, the moon is almost exactly between Earth and the sun. But most months, as you have seen, the moon travels a little above or below the sun in the sky. A **solar eclipse** occurs when the moon passes between Earth and the sun, blocking the sunlight from reaching Earth. The moon's shadow then hits Earth, as shown in Figure 7. So a solar eclipse is really just a new moon in which the moon blocks your view of the sun.

Total Solar Eclipses The darkest part of the moon's shadow, the **umbra** (UM bruh), is cone-shaped. From any point in the umbra, light from the sun is completely blocked by the moon. The moon's umbra happens to be long enough so that the point of the cone can just reach a small part of Earth's surface. Only the people within the umbra experience a total solar eclipse. During a total solar eclipse, the sky is dark. You can see the stars and the solar corona, which is the faint outer atmosphere of the sun.

Partial Solar Eclipses In Figure 7, you can see that the moon casts another shadow that is less dark than the umbra. In this larger part of the shadow, called the **penumbra** (pih NUM bruh), part of the sun is visible from Earth. During a solar eclipse, people in the penumbra see only a partial eclipse. Since part of the sun remains visible, it is not safe to look directly at the sun during a partial solar eclipse (just as you wouldn't look directly at the sun at any other time).

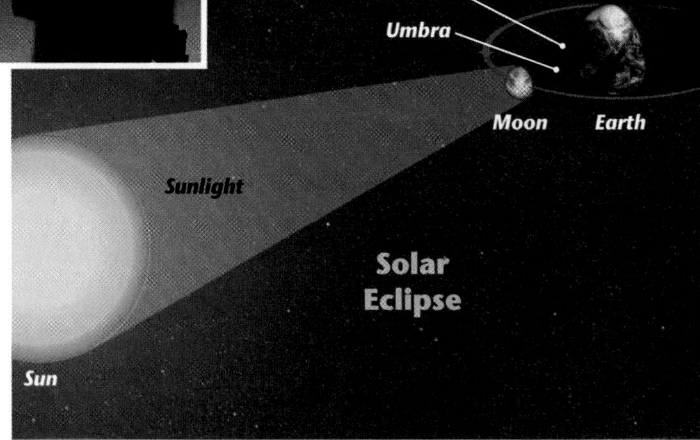

Figure 7 During a solar eclipse, right, the moon blocks light from the sun, preventing the light from reaching Earth's surface. The solar corona, which surrounds the dark disk of the moon, above, is visible during a solar eclipse.

Background

Facts and Figures Many people have seen total lunar eclipses, but few people have the opportunity to view the total solar eclipses. The reason is that a total lunar eclipse is visible over at least half of Earth. A total solar eclipse can only be seen along a narrow path up to a few hundred miles wide and a few thousand miles long.

Astronomers can accurately predict the dates and times of future eclipses. Because a solar eclipse occurs when the new moon is near the plane of Earth's orbit, a lunar eclipse frequently occurs two weeks before and two weeks after a solar eclipse. Six and a half lunar months later, the full moon may be near the plane of Earth's orbit so more lunar and solar eclipses can occur. These periods, when the new moon or full moon is near the plane of Earth's orbit, are called eclipse seasons.

Figure 8 A. During a lunar eclipse, Earth blocks sunlight from reaching the moon's surface. B. This photo of the moon was taken during a total lunar eclipse. C. This photo was taken during a partial lunar eclipse. *Interpreting Diagrams What is the difference between Earth's umbra and penumbra?*

Lunar Eclipses

During most months, the moon goes near Earth's shadow but not quite into it. A **lunar eclipse** occurs at a full moon when Earth is directly between the moon and the sun. You can see a lunar eclipse in Figure 8. During a lunar eclipse, Earth blocks sunlight from reaching the moon. The moon is then in Earth's shadow and looks dark from Earth. Because the moon is closest to Earth's shadow during the full moon, lunar eclipses occur only at full moon.

Total Lunar Eclipses Like the moon's shadow, Earth's shadow has an umbra and a penumbra. When the moon is in Earth's umbra, you see a total lunar eclipse. You can see Earth's shadow on the moon before and after the total part of a lunar eclipse.

Unlike a solar eclipse, a lunar eclipse can be seen anywhere on Earth that the moon is visible. So you are more likely to see a total lunar eclipse than a total solar eclipse.

Partial Lunar Eclipses For most lunar eclipses, Earth, the moon, and the sun are not quite in line, and a partial lunar eclipse results. A partial lunar eclipse occurs when the moon passes partly into the umbra of Earth's shadow. The edge of the umbra appears blurry, and you can watch it pass across the moon for up to two or three hours.

✓ *Checkpoint* *Why do lunar eclipses occur only at full moon?*

Lunar Eclipses

Using the Visuals: Figure 8

Have students compare the images in B and C. Ask: **What phase is the moon in during a lunar eclipse?** *(Full moon)* Ask students to describe what happens when the moon passes into Earth's penumbra. *(Earth's shadow covers a part of the moon as shown in Figure C.)* Then ask: **Why don't we have a lunar eclipse during every full moon?** *(Because the orbit of the moon is tilted 5° to the orbit of Earth, so Earth, the moon, and the sun don't always line up.)* **Why does the moon appear reddish during a lunar eclipse?** *(The reddish color results when sunlight is bent as it passes through Earth's atmosphere and then strikes the moon).* **learning modality: visual**

Building Inquiry Skills: Comparing and Contrasting

You may wish to have students work in groups of three or four to make a table that compares and contrasts the umbra and penumbra of the moon during a total and partial solar eclipse with the umbra and penumbra of Earth during a total and partial lunar eclipse. Members should first decide what headings to use for their table, that is, which aspects of the umbra and penumbra to compare and contrast. Suggested headings could include: "portion of the surface covered by the umbra," "phase of moon when the eclipse occurs," and "portion of Earth from which eclipse is visible." Then the group can fill in the cells of the table for a solar or lunar eclipse. **cooperative learning**

Media and Technology

Transparencies "Solar Eclipse," Transparency 72, "Lunar Eclipse," Transparency 73

Answers to Self-Assessment

Caption Question

Figure 8 The umbra is the area of total darkness, the penumbra is the area of partial darkness.

✓ *Checkpoint*

Earth must come between the sun and the moon during a lunar eclipse; this only happens during the full moon phase.

Ongoing Assessment

Drawing Have students sketch the positions of the sun, moon, and Earth during a solar eclipse and a lunar eclipse.

Students can save their drawings in their portfolios.

Skills Lab

Making Models

A "Moonth" of Phases

Preparing for Inquiry

Key Concept The phases of the moon are caused by the moon's position relative to Earth and the sun.

Skills Objective Students will be able to
- make a model of the Earth-moon-sun system to explore the phases of the moon;
- observe and record the phases of the model system.

Time 40 minutes

Advance Planning Collect lamps (one per group), extra bulbs (150 W bulbs work best), extension cords as needed, and plastic foam balls (one per student pair).

Guiding Inquiry

Invitation Have students think about how the moon varies in appearance in the night sky. Ask volunteers to describe variations they have seen. *(Sample: The moon may appear round (full moon), sometimes the moon can not be seen at all (new moon), or only part of the moon may visible such as a crescent moon.)*

Introducing the Procedure

- Review the photograph to make sure students understand how to position themselves.
- Suggest students make a sketch of their predictions of what they will see at each turn.

Troubleshooting the Experiment

- To model the full moon, make sure students hold the ball slightly above their heads, so the ball is not in their shadow.
- Be sure the student doing the drawing stands directly behind the one with the ball so that they get the same view.

Expected Outcome

Students should be able to identify the eight phases of the moon: new moon, waxing crescent, first quarter, waxing gibbous, full moon, waning gibbous, last quarter, waning crescent.

Skills Lab

Making Models

A "Moonth" of Phases

In this lab, you will use a model of the Earth-moon-sun system to explore how the phases of the moon occur.

Problem

What causes the phases of the moon?

Materials

floor lamp with 150-watt bulb
pencils
plastic foam balls

Procedure

1. Place a lamp in the center of the room. Remove the lampshade.
2. Close the doors and shades to darken the room, and switch on the lamp.
3. Carefully stick the point of a pencil into the plastic foam ball so that the pencil can be used as a "handle."
4. Draw 8 circles on a sheet of paper. Number them 1–8.
5. Have your partner hold the plastic foam ball at arm's length in front and slightly above his or her head so that the ball is between him or her and the lamp. **CAUTION:** *Do not look directly at the bulb.*
6. The ball should be about 1 to 1.5 m away from the lamp. Adjust the distance between the ball and the lamp so that the light shines brightly on the ball.
7. Stand directly behind your partner and observe what part of the ball facing you is lit by the lamp. If light is visible on the ball, draw the shape of the lighted part of the ball in the first circle.
8. Have your partner turn 45° to the left while keeping the ball in front and at arm's length.
9. Repeat Step 7. Be sure you are standing directly behind your partner.
10. Repeat Steps 8 and 9 six more times until your partner is facing the lamp again. See the photograph for the 8 positions.
11. Change places and repeat Steps 4–10.

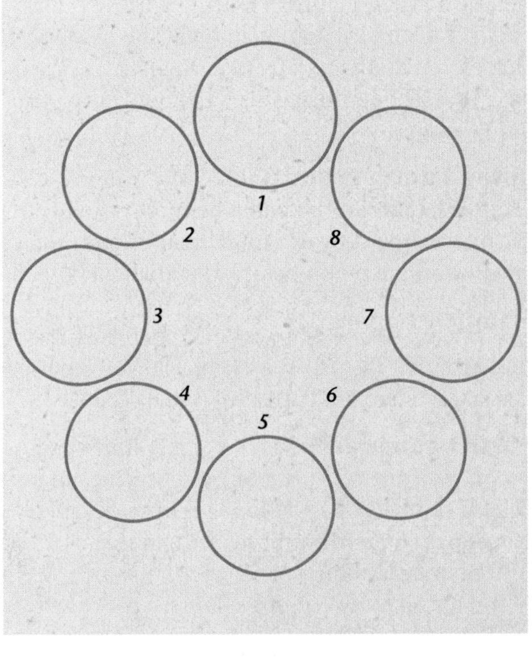

576

Analyze and Conclude

1. The student holding the ball represents Earth. The lamp represents the sun, and the plastic foam ball represents the moon.
2. No part
3. Position 1—new moon, position 2—waxing crescent, position 3—first quarter, position 4—waxing gibbous, position 5—full moon, position 6—waning gibbous, position 7—third quarter, position 8—waning crescent
4. For the first four turns, about 25% more of the lighted part of the ball was visible with each turn until the lighted part of the ball was completely visible (full moon). For the next four turns, about 25% less of the lighted part was visible with each turn until the dark part of the ball was completely visible (new moon) again.
5. One-half of the ball was always lit. An eclipse occurs when the moon's shadow hits Earth or Earth's shadow hits the moon. Neither of these events caused the darkness of a new moon. When the moon is between Earth and the sun, we are looking at the moon's dark side.

Analyze and Conclude

1. In your model, what represents Earth? The sun? The moon?
2. Refer back to your 8 circles. How much of the lighted part of the ball did you see when facing the lamp?
3. Label your drawings with the names of the phases of the moon. Which drawing represents a full moon? A new moon? Which represents a waxing crescent? A waning crescent?
4. How much of the lighted part of the ball did you see after each turn?
5. Whether you could see it or not, how much of the ball's surface was always lit by the lamp? Was the darkness of the new moon caused by an eclipse? Explain your answer.
6. **Think It Over** How did making a model help you understand the phases of the moon? What are some disadvantages of using models? What is another way to make a model to represent the moon's phases?

More to Explore

Design a model to show a lunar eclipse and a solar eclipse. What objects would you use for Earth, the sun, and the moon? Use the model to demonstrate why there isn't an eclipse every full moon and new moon.

Extending the Inquiry

More to Explore A solar eclipse occurs when the moon (plastic foam ball) is directly between the sun (lamp) and Earth (partner holding the ball). In this position, the new moon casts a total eclipse (shadow) on one part of Earth and a partial eclipse on another part. A lunar eclipse appears during a full moon when the moon (plastic foam ball) passes through Earth's (partner holding the ball) shadow. The moon's orbit is tilted slightly with respect to Earth's orbit around the sun.

Safety

Remind students to be careful around the lamps and extension cords. Tell them not to look directly into the lights. Review the safety guidelines in Appendix A.

6. The model speeds up phases so you can see them in a shorter time than watching the phases for a month. The disadvantage of a model is that it does not always show the true size, measurements, or color of the real item. Another model could use a ball painted black on one hemisphere and white on the other. The white half would represent the sunlit side of the moon. A student could walk around the ball to view it from different angles and see the different phases.

Program Resources

- **Unit 6 Resources** Chapter 19 Skills Lab, pp. 28–29

Media and Technology

Lab Activity Videotapes
Grade 6, Tape 4

Tides

Building Inquiry Skills: Making Models

Have students partially blow up round balloons and knot the stems. Instruct them to hold the balloons securely at the stems and the opposite ends and pull on the knotted ends. Have students draw diagrams to show what happens to the balloons when they are being pulled. *(Diagrams should show that the knotted ends and the opposite ends bulged, while the sides between flattened.)* **learning modality: kinesthetic**

3 Assess

Section 2 Review Answers

1. As the moon revolves around Earth, phases are produced by the changing position of the moon relative to Earth and the sun.
2. During a solar eclipse, the moon is between the sun and Earth. During a lunar eclipse, Earth is between the sun and the moon.
3. A "day" and a "year" on the moon are the same length because the moon revolves around Earth at the same rate that it rotates on its axis.
4. Drawings should show that during a lunar eclipse the moon is full and on the opposite side of Earth from the sun.

CHAPTER PROJECT

Check Your Progress

Provide newspapers in the classroom so that students can check the times of moonrise and moonset each day. Encourage students to draw the phase and orientation of the moon in the log along with their daily observations.

Performance Assessment

Oral Presentation Organize the class into small groups to demonstrate the positions of Earth, the sun, and the moon either during a solar eclipse or a lunar eclipse.

Figure 9 The Hopewell Rocks in New Brunswick, Canada, are partly covered at high tide. At low tide, people can walk along the beach between the rocks. *Predicting What would happen if these people stayed on the beach too long?*

Tides

Have you ever built a sand castle at an ocean beach? Was it washed away by the rising water? People who spend time near the ocean see the effects of **tides,** the rise and fall of water, every 12.5 hours or so. The water rises for about six hours, then falls for about six hours, in a regular cycle.

The force of **gravity** pulls the moon and Earth (including the water on Earth's surface) toward each other. The force of gravity between two objects depends on the masses of the objects and the distance between them. **Tides occur mainly because of differences in how much the moon pulls on different parts of Earth.** As discussed in Chapter 9, the position of the sun also influences the height of the tides.

As Earth rotates, the moon's gravity pulls water toward the point on Earth's surface closest to the moon. If that were the only cause, there would be only one high tide at a time, at the point on Earth closest to the moon. Actually, there is a second high tide on the opposite side of Earth, so the explanation must be more complex. The two high tides occur because of the difference in the force of gravity between one place and another. There are also two low tides on Earth located halfway between the high tides. As Earth rotates, tides occur in a 25-hour cycle.

Not every place on Earth has two regular tides every day. The shapes of bays, inlets, and the ocean floor can affect the flow of water, so that the height and timing of the tides can vary even in places that are close to each other.

Section 2 Review

1. Why does the moon change its phases as the month progresses?
2. Describe the relative positions of Earth, the sun, and the moon during a solar eclipse and during a lunar eclipse.
3. Why are a "day" and a "year" on the moon the same length?
4. **Thinking Critically Interpreting Diagrams** Make a diagram to show what phase the moon is in during a lunar eclipse.

CHAPTER PROJECT

Check Your Progress

Bring your log sheet to class so you can share your observations with classmates. Check the newspaper every day to find the times of moonrise and moonset and record this information. If you can, look for the moon at moonrise or moonset, even during daylight hours. Use your map to keep track of the direction in which you can see the moon.

Program Resources

◆ **Unit 6 Resources** 18-2 Review and Reinforce; 18-2 Enrich

Media and Technology

Transparencies "High and Low Tides," Transparency 74

Answers to Self-Assessment

Caption Question

Figure 9 They could get trapped on the beach by high tide.

SECTION 3 Rockets and Satellites

DISCOVER — ACTIVITY

How Do Rockets Work?

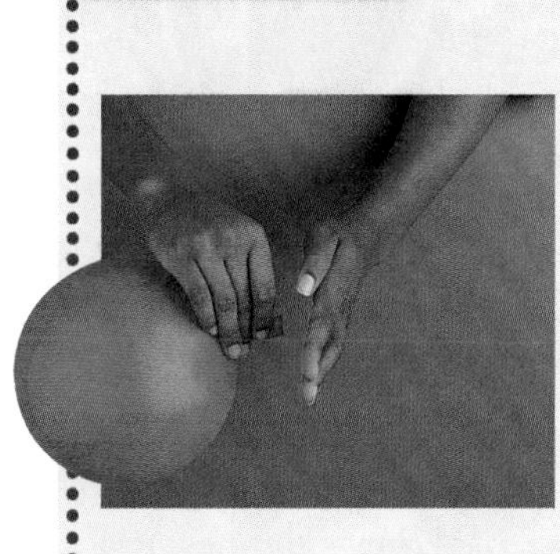

1. Put on your goggles. Blow up a balloon and hold its neck closed with your fingers.
2. Point the balloon toward an area where there are no people. Put your free hand behind the neck of the balloon, so the air will push against your hand. Let go of the balloon.
3. Repeat Steps 1 and 2 without your free hand behind the balloon.

Think It Over

Observing In which direction does the air rush out? In which direction does the balloon go? Does the balloon need to push against something in order to move? Explain your answer.

Curiosity about Earth's "neighborhood" in space has led to moon missions, space shuttle missions, space stations, and Mars missions. But without rockets, none of these accomplishments would have been possible.

GUIDE FOR READING

- How do rockets travel in space?
- What are satellites and space stations used for?

Reading Tip Before you read, rewrite the headings in the section as *how, why,* or *what* questions. As you read, look for answers to those questions.

How Rockets Work

A rocket works in much the way that a balloon is propelled through the air by releasing gas. **A rocket moves forward when gases expelled from the rear of the rocket push it in the opposite direction.** It's a basic law of physics that for every force, or action, there is an equal and opposite force, or reaction. For example, the force of the air going out the back of a balloon is an action force. An equal force, the reaction, pushes the balloon forward.

In a rocket, fuel is burned to make a hot gas. This hot gas is forced out of narrow nozzles in the back of the rocket, propelling the rocket forward.

Figure 10 Hot gas is propelled out of the back of a rocket engine. The force of the gas in one direction (action) produces an opposing force (reaction) that propels the rocket forward.

READING STRATEGIES

Reading Tip Suggest students write their how, why, and what questions in columns under those headings. Encourage them to answer the questions based on what they already know, and revise their answers as they read. Questions may include "How do rockets work?" and "What are multistage rockets?"

Program Resources

- **Unit 6 Resources** 18-3 Lesson Plan; 18-3 Section Summary
- **Guided Reading and Study Workbook** Section Summary 18-3
- **Interdisciplinary Explorations Series** "Mars The Next Frontier", pp. 14–15

SECTION 3 Rockets and Satellites

Objectives

After completing the lesson, students will be able to

- explain how rockets travel in space;
- list the uses for satellites, space stations, and the Space Shuttle.

Key Terms satellite, geosynchronous orbit

1 Engage/Explore

Activating Prior Knowledge

Many students will have watched a space shuttle launch on television or will have seen rockets being launched in news specials, documentaries, or movies. Invite volunteers to describe what happens when a rocket is launched. Ask them to consider the motion of the rocket in their responses. *(Sample: Engines are fired, large clouds of gas come from the rocket boosters, the rocket or space shuttle pulls away from Earth.)* Ask students what forces are at work when a rocket lifts off from the ground. *(Gas pushed out the bottom of the rocket pushes against the rocket.)*

DISCOVER

Skills Focus observing

Materials *balloons, safety goggles*

Time 10 minutes

Tips Remind students to try to blow up the balloons to the same size each time so they can compare their results.

Expected Outcome The balloons will move across the room in both trials.

Think It Over The air rushes out the neck of the balloon, and the balloon goes in the opposite direction. The balloon does not need to push against something to move, because it is the action-reaction pair of forces that makes it move, not the push of air off your hand.

2 Facilitate

How Rockets Work

Using the Visuals: Figure 11

Explain that the force of gases expelled by the rocket boosters creates a thrust or push that causes the rocket to move away. Ask: **What action is shown in the diagram?** *(The force of the gas coming from the back of the rocket engine)* **What reaction?** *(The force making the rocket move away in the opposite direction)* **learning modality: visual**

Multistage Rockets

Demonstration

ACTIVITY

Time 15 minutes
Materials *2 long balloons, nylon fishing line, 2 plastic drinking straws, plastic foam cup, masking tape, scissors*
Tips Thread the straws on the fishing line and tie the line securely across the room. Cut the top off a cup ring. Inflate one balloon about three quarters full and hold the neck tight so no air can escape. Do not tie the neck. Have a volunteer help you place the neck of the balloon through the plastic foam ring and hold it tightly closed. Inflate the second balloon so that the round end extends a short way through the ring. After some practice, you will be able to inflate the second balloon so it presses the neck of the first balloon against the ring and holds it shut. Hold the neck of the second balloon firmly, and tape each balloon to one of the straws on the line. When you release the balloon, the escaping air will propel the balloons down the line. When the first balloon runs out of air, it will release the other. **learning modality: kinesthetic**

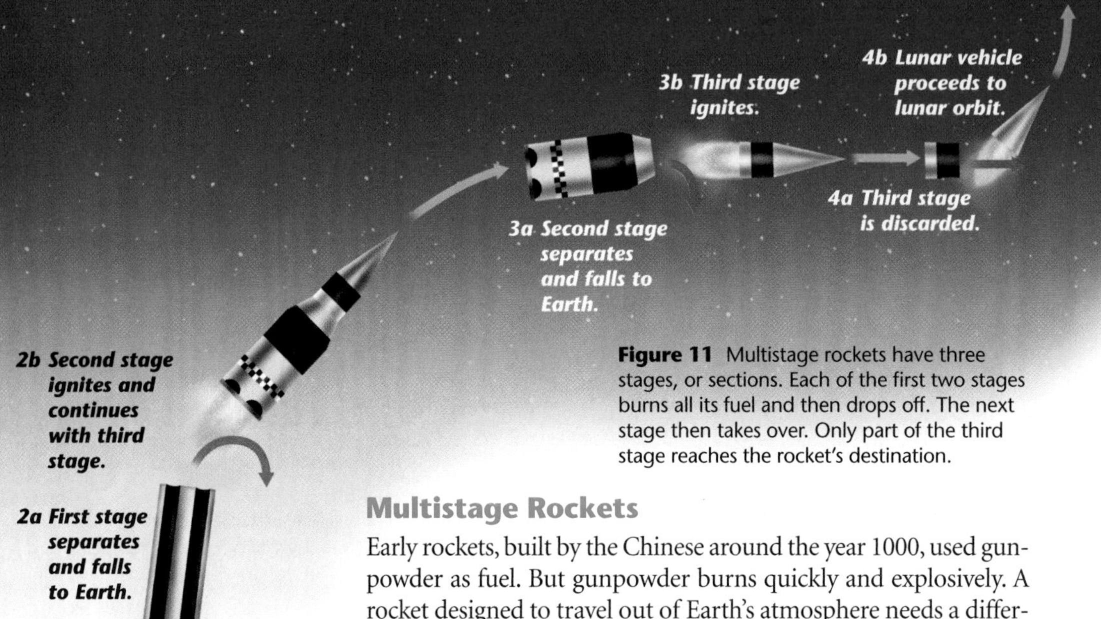

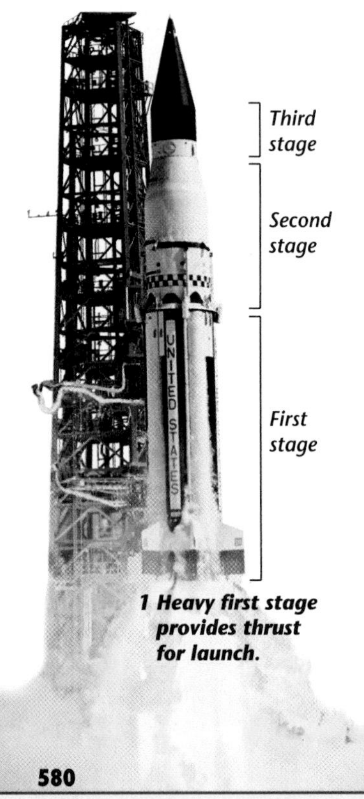

Figure 11 Multistage rockets have three stages, or sections. Each of the first two stages burns all its fuel and then drops off. The next stage then takes over. Only part of the third stage reaches the rocket's destination.

Multistage Rockets

Early rockets, built by the Chinese around the year 1000, used gunpowder as fuel. But gunpowder burns quickly and explosively. A rocket designed to travel out of Earth's atmosphere needs a different sort of fuel that burns slowly and continuously. The American scientist Robert H. Goddard experimented with liquid fuels in the 1920s. He showed that a liquid fuel can provide continuous power. Some solid fuels also burn slowly and continuously.

Another problem remained, however. A rocket can carry only so much fuel. Once the fuel is used up, the rocket falls back to Earth. In 1903, a Russian named Konstantin Tsiolkovsky came up with the idea of multistage rockets. As each stage, or section, of a rocket uses up its fuel, the empty fuel container drops off. Then the next stage ignites and continues up toward the rocket's destination.

The development of powerful multistage rockets in the 1950s and 1960s made it possible to send rockets to the moon and farther into space. Figure 11 shows a rocket similar to the Saturn V that carried the astronauts to the moon. You will learn more about the moon landings in Section 4.

Artificial Satellites

The world was astounded on October 4, 1957, when the Soviet Union launched the first artificial satellite into orbit around Earth. A **satellite** is any natural or artificial object that revolves around an object in space, just as the moon revolves around Earth. This satellite, *Sputnik 1,* revolved around Earth every 96 minutes. Three months later, the United States launched *Explorer 1* into orbit. On April 12, 1961, Yuri Gagarin, a Soviet cosmonaut, orbited Earth, becoming the first person in space.

Background

History of Science Artificial satellites used for communications are generally very reliable. However, on May 19, 1998, a satellite called *Galaxy 4* went out of service when its onboard control system failed and the satellite rolled out of position. Its failure interrupted communications systems all over the United States and the Caribbean.

Because a majority of pager companies in the United States relied on *Galaxy 4,* approximately 40 million pager users lost service. In addition, television and radio networks used *Galaxy 4* to transmit feeds to their stations, so these transmissions were interrupted too. The problem also halted the operation of bank automated teller machines and the systems customers use at gas stations to pay with credit cards. To reestablish service, the company that owns *Galaxy 4* had to reposition another satellite.

Since 1957, thousands of artificial satellites, including space stations, have been launched into orbit. **Satellites and space stations are used for communications, navigation, collecting weather data, and research.**

Satellites Artificial satellites are used to relay telephone calls, to measure Earth's atmosphere, and to photograph weather systems, crops, troops, and ships. In addition, two dozen Global Positioning Satellites give off signals that can be picked up by small receivers on Earth. The receiver can then tell you where you are on Earth's surface.

Some satellites are in **geosynchronous orbits,** which means they revolve around Earth at the same rate that Earth rotates. Geosynchronous satellites above the equator seem to hover over a given point on Earth. Geosynchronous satellites are used to relay television signals and to map weather patterns.

Space Stations A space station is a large satellite in which people can live for long periods. The first space station, the Soviet Union's *Salyut,* was launched in 1971. In 1973, the United States launched *Skylab,* which carried a series of telescopes and scientific experiments. The former Soviet Union, of which Russia was part, launched the *Mir* space station in 1986. Astronauts from many countries, including Americans, visited *Mir*. Sixteen countries, including the United States and Russia, are cooperating on the International Space Station, which is now being built in orbit and will eventually provide living quarters and labs for up to seven astronauts.

☑ *Checkpoint* *What is a geosynchronous orbit?*

Be a Rocket Scientist

You can build a rocket. 

1. Use a plastic or paper cup as the rocket body. Cut out a paper nose cone and tape it to the closed end of the cup.
2. Obtain an empty film canister with a lid that snaps on inside the canister. Go outside to do Steps 3–5.
3. Fill the canister about one-quarter full with water.
4. Put on your goggles. Now add half of a fizzing antacid tablet to the film canister and quickly snap on the lid.
5. Place the canister on the ground with the lid down. Place your rocket over the canister and stand back.

Observing What action happened inside the film canister? What was the reaction of the rocket?

Figure 12 The International Space Station is a cooperative project involving 16 countries, including the United States, Russia, Japan, and Canada. This is an artist's conception of the station in orbit.

Artificial Satellites

TRY THIS

Skills Focus observing
Materials *plastic or paper cup, paper, tape, film canister with a lid that snaps on inside the canister, water, fizzing antacid tablet, safety goggles*
Time 20 minutes
Tips Caution students not to place sharp objects on the rocket.
Expected Outcome The rocket will lift off and shoot 2 to 5 meters into the air.
Observing Gas pressure builds up inside the canister due to the reaction of the antacid and water. Pressure continues to build until it blows off the lid of the canister and launches the rocket.
Extend Challenge students to design and launch rockets powered by two, three, or more film canisters. **learning modality: logical/mathematical**

Inquiry Challenge

ACTIVITY

Pair students and have them use physical activity to model how a satellite with a geosynchronous orbit can stay above the same point on Earth. One student turns very slowly in place at about one turn per minute, while the partner walks around the first student in a circle at a rate of one step per second so that the turning student always faces the walking student. There will be only one radius where this will happen. Ask the students to describe what is happening. Now have the walking student move faster and walk in a smaller circle while the turning student turns at the same rate. Ask the students to describe what happens. *(The first case models a geosynchronous orbit. The second case models a low Earth orbit.)* **learning modality: kinesthetic**

Program Resources

- **Unit 6 Resources** 18-3 Review and Reinforce; 18-3 Enrich
- **Interdisciplinary Exploration Series** "Mars the Next Frontier," pp. 20–21

Answers to Self-Assessment

☑ *Checkpoint*

A geosynchronous orbit is one in which the satellite revolves around Earth at the same rate that Earth rotates on its axis.

Ongoing Assessment

Oral Presentation Ask students to describe how satellites are launched into orbit.

Space Shuttles

Addressing Naive Conceptions

Many students may think that the shuttle is far from Earth when in orbit. In fact, the shuttle was designed for low-Earth orbits of less than 480 km. To help students visualize this, use a paper ruler to measure a distance on the surface of a globe approximately 480 km from your location. Mark the ruler and hold it perpendicular to the globe to show the highest altitude of the orbiting shuttle. **learning modality: visual**

3 Assess

Section 3 Review Answers

1. The rocket's exhaust gases go in one direction and the rocket moves in the opposite direction.
2. Any three: Communications, weather monitoring, navigation, and research
3. Only part of the third stage of the rocket reaches the final destination.
4. Space shuttles cost less than the *Saturn V* rockets and can be reused.

Science at Home

Students may be able to interview their parents or grandparents about the first moon landing. Encourage students to prepare a list of who, what, when, where, why, and how questions before the interview. Students could also write their interviews as magazine articles. Provide examples of interviews from newspapers and magazines for students to use as a style guide.

Performance Assessment

Drawing Create a poster showing how a space station or satellite is launched into orbit and then used for practical applications on Earth.

Portfolio Students can save their posters in their portfolios.

Figure 13 The Space Shuttle *Discovery* is launched into space by its own rockets as well as by rockets attached to it. *Inferring What is one advantage of a reusable space vehicle?*

Space Shuttles

The Saturn V rockets that carried astronauts to the moon in the 1960s and 1970s were very expensive. In addition, they could not be reused because each stage burned up as it fell back through Earth's atmosphere. In the late 1970s, the National Aeronautics and Space Administration (NASA) developed the reusable space shuttles. They are called shuttles because they can go back and forth, or shuttle, between Earth and space. Since the first shuttle was launched in 1981, space shuttles have been the main way that the United States launches astronauts and equipment into space.

NASA is studying several ideas for building better and less expensive ways of launching people and cargo into space. The ideal vehicle would be an aerospace plane that could take off from a runway, travel into space, and land again on a runway.

Section 3 Review

1. How does a rocket work?
2. Describe three uses of satellites and space stations.
3. Which stage of a multistage rocket reaches the final destination?
4. **Thinking Critically Comparing and Contrasting** What is one way that Saturn V rockets and space shuttles are different?

Science at Home

Landmarks in Space Flight Interview someone who remembers the space programs of the 1950s and 1960s. Prepare your questions in advance, such as: How did you feel when you heard that *Sputnik* was in orbit? How did you feel when the first Americans went into space? Did you watch any of the space flights on television? You may want to record your interview, then write it out in a question-and-answer format.

Media and Technology

Concept Videotape Library
Grade 6, Tape 4 "The Cray Computer"; "Then and Now"

Answers to Self-Assessment

Caption Question

Figure 13 Reusable vehicles are less expensive.

Earth's Moon

DISCOVER ACTIVITY

Why Do Craters Look Different From One Another?

The moon's surface has pits in it, called craters.

1. Put on your goggles. Fill a large plastic basin with 2 cm of sand.
2. Drop marbles of different masses from about 20 cm high. Take the marbles out and view the craters they left.
3. Predict what will happen if you drop marbles from a higher point. Smooth out the sand. Now drop marbles of different masses from about 50 cm high.
4. Take the marbles out and view the craters they left.

Think It Over

Developing Hypotheses In which step do you think the marbles were moving faster when they hit the sand? If objects hitting the moon caused craters, how did the speeds of the objects affect the sizes of the craters? How did the masses of the objects affect the sizes of the craters?

GUIDE FOR READING

- **What features of the moon can be seen with a telescope?**
- **How did the Apollo landings help scientists learn about the moon?**

Reading Tip **As you read, write down ways in which the moon's surface is similar to Earth's surface.**

Would you want to take a vacation on the moon? Before you answer, think about these facts. There is no air or liquid water on the moon. Temperatures on the moon's surface range from 100°C, the boiling point of water, to –170°C, well below freezing.

To stay at a comfortable temperature and carry an air supply, the astronauts who landed on the moon had to wear bulky spacesuits. Each spacesuit had a mass of 90 kilograms, about as much as the astronaut himself! Because the moon's gravity is only about one-sixth as strong as Earth's, however, the astronauts were able to leap about like basketball stars despite their heavy spacesuits. What do you think now? Do you still want to go?

Figure 14 Astronaut John W. Young jumps up from the moon's surface as he salutes the flag on April 21, 1972. The machine on the left is the *Apollo 16* lunar lander.

READING STRATEGIES

Reading Tip Have students fill in a Venn diagram that compares the moon's surface and Earth's surface. Remind students to list shared features in the area where the two circles overlap. One shared characteristic is that the moon's average density is similar to the density of Earth's outer layers.

Program Resources

- **Unit 6 Resources** 18-4 Lesson Plan; 18-4 Section Summary
- **Guided Reading and Study Workbook** Section 18-4

Earth's Moon

Objectives

After completing the lesson, students will be able to

- describe how scientists have used the telescope to study the moon;
- explain what scientists learned about the moon from space exploration;
- describe the origin and structure of the moon.

Key Terms telescope, crater, maria

1 Engage/Explore

Activating Prior Knowledge

Hold up a rock. Tell students to imagine that the rock is as large as a building and is traveling through space. Ask them to imagine the rock falling through Earth's atmosphere and landing in an open desert. Ask: **What do you think would happen?** *(Sample: The rock would leave a large depression in the desert sand or explode on impact.)*

DISCOVER

Skills Focus developing hypotheses

Materials *plastic basin or mixing bowl about 25 cm across, sand, 3 marbles of different masses, meter stick*

Time 20 minutes

Tips After Step 2, have students measure the depth and diameter of the craters made.

Expected Outcome The size of the craters will increase with mass and with height.

Think It Over The marbles are moving faster in Step 3. The more massive the impacting object or the faster it hits, the larger the resulting crater will be.

2 Facilitate

The Structure and Origin of the Moon

Using the Visuals: Figure 16

Explain that computer simulations are visual representations of information that are created by computers. Have students organize the information in the figure into a flowchart. Ask: **According to this theory, what is the moon made of?** *(Material from the object that collided with Earth and the material that was broken off Earth)* **learning modality: logical/mathematical**

Building Inquiry Skills: Interpreting Data

ACTIVITY

Pair students and have them measure the diameter of a quarter. Students should then measure the distance from the classroom clock to a position on the opposite side of the room. From that position, one student can hold the quarter at arm's length and close one eye, then move the coin closer until it appears to completely cover the clock. The other student can measure the distance from the partner's eye to the coin. Have students convert their measurements to a common unit, then use the following proportion to calculate the diameter of the clock:

$$\frac{\text{diameter of coin}}{\text{diameter of clock}} = \frac{\text{distance from eye to coin}}{\text{distance from eye to clock}}$$

Ask students how scientists could use this method to find the diameter of the moon. **learning modality: logical/mathematical**

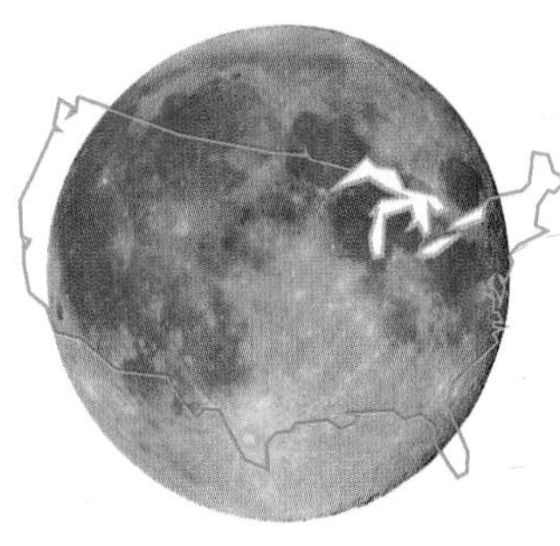

Figure 15 The diameter of the moon is a little less than the distance across the United States.

The Structure and Origin of the Moon

The moon is 3,476 kilometers in diameter, a little less than the distance across the United States. This diameter is only one fourth Earth's diameter. However, the moon contains only one-eightieth as much mass as Earth. Though Earth has a very dense core, the outer layers are less dense. The moon's average density is about the same as the density of Earth's outer layers.

People have long wondered how the moon formed. Scientists have suggested many possible hypotheses. For example, did Earth at one time spin so fast that the material the moon is made of was thrown off? Was the moon formed elsewhere in the solar system and captured by Earth's gravitational pull as it came near? Was the moon formed near Earth at the same time that Earth formed? Scientists have found reasons to reject all of these ideas.

The theory of the moon's origin that best fits the evidence is called the collision theory. It is illustrated in Figure 16. About 4.5 billion years ago, when Earth was very young, an object at least as large as Mars collided with Earth. Material from the object and Earth's outer layers was thrown into orbit around Earth. Eventually, this material combined to form the moon.

Looking at the Moon From Earth

For thousands of years, people could see shapes on the surface of the moon, but didn't know what caused them. The ancient Greeks thought that the moon was perfectly smooth. It was not until about 400 years ago that scientists could study the moon more closely.

Figure 16 This computer simulation shows the collision theory of the moon's origin. In this theory, a large object struck Earth. The resulting debris formed the moon.

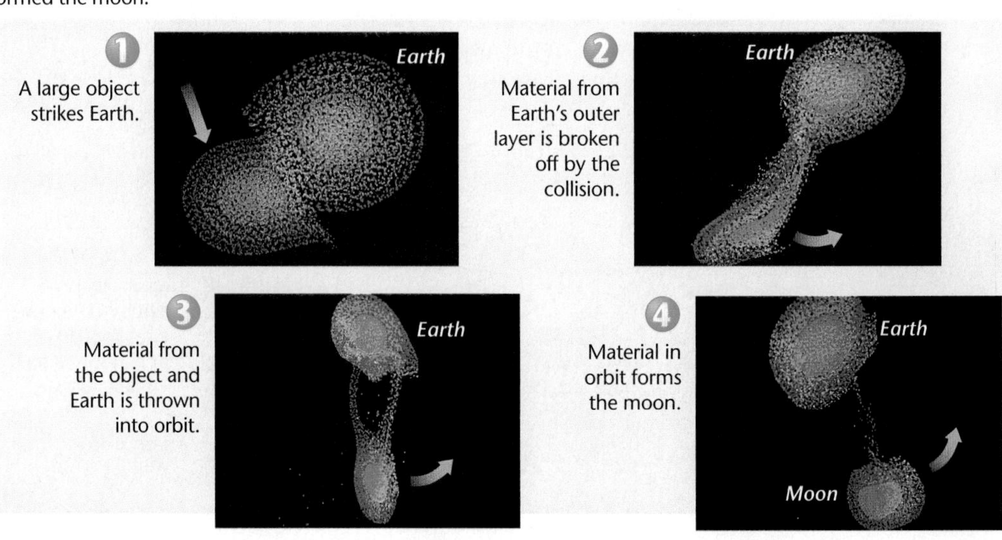

Background

Facts and Figures Inspired by the moon's maria and craters, many science fiction writers have written about travel to the Moon. In 1865, Jules Verne wrote an account of one such journey, *From the Earth to the Moon.* Although this story was fictional, Verne based it on the latest scientific understanding of his day. Written almost 100 years before scientists began to send rockets to the moon, Verne's account closely matches actual events. For example, Verne sited his launch near Cape Canaveral, Florida. He also gave the correct *escape velocity,* the velocity required for an object to escape Earth's gravitational field. In a later book called *Around the Moon,* Verne accurately described the effects of weightlessness that would be experienced by future astronauts.

Figure 17 Astronomers have given names to many of the moon's craters and maria. Copernicus, named after the 16th-century astronomer, is one of the largest craters.

In 1609, the Italian astronomer Galileo Galilei heard about a device that made distant objects appear closer. Galileo soon made his own **telescope** by putting two lenses in a wooden tube. The lenses focused the light coming through the tube, making distant objects seem closer. When Galileo pointed his telescope at the moon, he was able to see much more detail than anyone had ever seen before. **Features on the moon's surface include craters, highlands, and maria.**

Galileo saw that much of the moon's surface is covered with round pits called **craters.** Some craters are hundreds of kilometers across. For 300 years, scientists thought that the craters on the moon had been made by volcanoes. But about 50 years ago, scientists concluded that the craters on the moon were caused by the impacts of meteoroids, rocks from space.

Galileo inferred that some of the other features he saw were highlands, or mountains. The peaks of the highlands and the rims of the craters cast dark shadows, which Galileo could see.

The moon's surface also has dark, flat areas, which Galileo called **maria** (MAH ree uh), the Latin word for "seas." Each one is a "mare" (MAH ray). Galileo thought that the maria might be oceans. Scientists now know that there are no oceans on the moon. The maria are low, dry areas that were flooded with molten material billions of years ago. Since you always see the same maria and craters from Earth, you can tell that the moon always shows the same face to Earth.

Checkpoint *What are maria?*

Visual Arts CONNECTION

When Galileo observed the moon, he drew pictures like the one below. Galileo had been trained as an artist, so he interpreted his observations as an artist would. Light and shadow are used in art to create the appearance of three-dimensional forms.

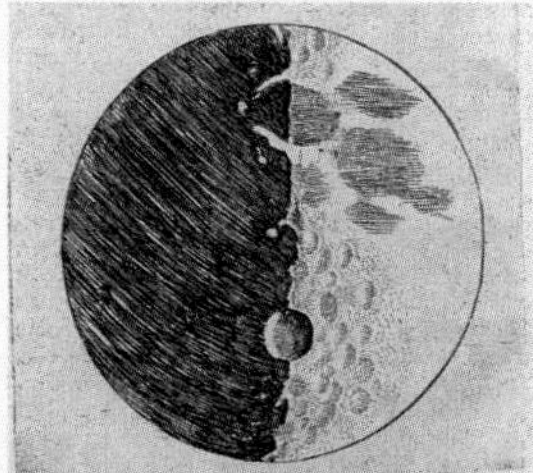

Galileo saw the areas of light and shadow on the moon and concluded that the surface of the moon was not smooth.

In Your Journal

Under a bright light, set up an arrangement of objects. Sketch the outline of the objects. Then observe where the shadows fall. Shade in those areas. Notice how adding shading makes your drawing look more real.

Looking at the Moon from Earth

Including All Students

Students who are mastering English may need extra help using the text to identify the features in Figure 17. Choose one feature in the figure and have a volunteer read its description from the text. Then ask questions such as: **Is the Sea of Tranquillity really an ocean?** *(no)* **What is it?** *(It is one of the maria, dark, flat parts of the moon's surface.)* Repeat for the other labeled features. **limited English proficiency**

Visual Arts CONNECTION

Tell students that although Galileo did not invent the telescope, he constructed the first refracting telescope designed for viewing features in space. Refracting telescopes use a combination of lenses to magnify an image. In addition to the moon's features, Galileo was able to view and sketch the moons of Jupiter, the Milky Way, sunspots, and the shape of Saturn and its rings. Ask students why they think that Galileo's observations were of such great historical importance. *(Sample: No one had ever viewed these features before.)*

In Your Journal Show students examples of paintings that use light and shadow to produce three-dimensional effects. Provide a variety of objects with interesting shapes such as bottles, fruit, models, toys, or carvings with relief for students to sketch. **learning modality: visual**

Program Resources

- **Interdisciplinary Exploration Series** "Riddles of the Pharaohs," pp. 12–13

Media and Technology

 **Transparencies** "Collision Theory of the Moon's Origin," Transparency 75

Answers to Self-Assessment

Checkpoint

Maria are large flat plains on the moon's surface.

Ongoing Assessment

Writing Ask students to explain how scientists think the moon was formed.

Missions to the Moon

Building Inquiry Skills: Applying Concepts

Divide students into small groups of three or four. Tell them they are going to pretend they are NASA scientists during the early 1960s, when President Kennedy made his famous challenge to the nation. Have students brainstorm a list of factors that they, as scientists, need to consider when landing a human on the moon. Encourage students to consider requirements for survival, landing safely, and returning to Earth. Ask: **What five items would you bring with you to the moon?** *(Sample: oxygen, water, spacesuit to wear on the moon, fuel for return trip, books)* Have students share their lists and discuss their reasons for selecting the items. **cooperative learning**

Social Studies Connection

Students may enjoy watching or listening to the first moon landing. Many recordings are available at local libraries, on the Internet (visit the Science Explorer website for information **www.phschool.com**) and also on many multimedia encyclopedias. Encourage students to listen and imagine they are back in the year 1969, watching or listening to the moon landing for the first time. Ask students to describe how they would have felt during the tense last moments of the landing. **learning modality: verbal**

Using the Visuals: Figure 19

Ask students to describe the lunar surface shown in the photograph. Then ask them to describe challenges they think NASA scientists had to consider when creating a vehicle that could explore the moon's terrain. Ask: **Why does the lunar buggy need such large soft wheels?** *(To go over rocks and through small craters)* **learning modality: visual**

Missions to the Moon

"I believe that this nation should commit itself to achieving the goal, before this decade is out, of landing a man on the moon and returning him safely to Earth." With these words from a May 1961 speech, President John F. Kennedy launched an enormous program of space exploration and scientific research.

Exploring the Moon Between 1964 and 1972, the United States and the Soviet Union sent dozens of rockets to explore the moon. Until spacecraft went to the moon, no one knew what its surface was like. Would spacecraft landing on the moon sink deep into thick dust and be lost? When *Surveyor* spacecraft landed on the moon, they didn't sink in, thus showing that the surface was solid. Lunar orbiters then photographed the moon's surface, so scientists could find a flat, safe spot for a rocket to land.

The Moon Landings In July 1969 three astronauts circled the moon in *Apollo 11*. Once in orbit around the moon, Neil Armstrong and Buzz Aldrin got into a tiny Lunar Module called *Eagle*, leaving Michael Collins in orbit in the Command Module. On July 20, 1969, the *Eagle* descended toward a flat area on the moon's surface called the Sea of Tranquillity. Armstrong and Aldrin were running out of fuel, so they had to find a safe landing spot fast. Billions of people held their breaths as they waited to learn if the astronauts had landed safely on the moon. Finally, a red light flashed on the control panel. "Contact light! Houston, Tranquillity Base here. The *Eagle* has landed," Armstrong radioed to Earth.

After the landing, Armstrong and Aldrin left the *Eagle* to explore the moon. When Armstrong first set foot on the moon, he said, "That's one small step for man, one giant leap for mankind." Armstrong meant to say "That's one small step for *a* man," meaning himself, but in his excitement he never said the "a."

Figure 18 On July 20, 1969, *Apollo 11* astronaut Neil Armstrong became the first person to walk on the moon. He took this photo of Buzz Aldrin, the second person to walk on the moon. ***Inferring*** *Why was it important for the lunar module to land on a flat spot?*

Background

History of Science Each Apollo project had a three-passenger Command Module (CM) and a two-passenger Lunar Module (LM). *Apollo 13* was launched at 13:13 on April 11, 1970. It looked like it was going to be the smoothest flight of the program, but two days into the flight, at 21:08 on April 13, an oxygen tank blew up. The CM's supply of electricity, light, and water was lost. The crew decided to use the LM to pilot the crippled CM around the moon and back to Earth. Astronauts had enough oxygen, but they had to conserve water, power, and food. They also had to find a way to remove carbon dioxide from the spacecraft. Mission Control found a way to do this using materials on board. On April 17, after surviving 3.6°C cold and losing a total of almost 15 kg through dehydration, the crew in the LM landed in the Pacific Ocean near Samoa.

Figure 19 Astronauts on later missions had a lunar buggy to help them explore the moon's surface.

On the Surface of the Moon Everything the *Apollo 11* astronauts found was new and exciting. Even looking at their footprints taught the astronauts lessons about the moon's soil. The astronauts bounded around the surface, picking up samples of rocks to bring back to Earth for scientists to study.

In later missions, the astronauts were able to stay on the moon for days instead of hours. They even had a lunar buggy to ride around in. The astronauts were also able to land near the highlands, which were more interesting to study than the flat mare where *Apollo 11* landed.

Moon Rocks and Moonquakes The astronauts brought back to Earth 382 kilograms of moon rocks, about half the mass of a small car. **Much of what scientists have learned about the moon came from detailed study of the moon rocks gathered by astronauts.** Almost all of the rocks were formed from the cooling of molten material, so the moon's surface must once have been very hot. Some of the rocks showed that they had been broken apart by impacts and then reformed. So scientists concluded that meteoroids had bombarded the moon's surface.

The astronauts brought measuring instruments to the moon to record some of the meteoroid impacts. One type of device, known as a seismometer, is used to detect earthquakes on Earth. The seismometers on the moon detected extremely weak moonquakes, the result of changes deep under the moon's surface.

Until the *Apollo* astronauts landed, scientists knew very little about the moon's interior. Another kind of instrument the astronauts left behind measured the amount of heat flowing out from the moon's interior, in order to study what the inside of the moon is like. This instrument showed that the moon has cooled almost completely since it was formed.

☑ *Checkpoint* *What did scientists discover about the interior of the moon as a result of the moon landings?*

Sharpen your Skills

Calculating ACTIVITY

If you went to the moon for a vacation, your weight would only be about one sixth of your weight on Earth. To find your weight on the moon, divide your weight by 6.

If you had to wear a spacesuit that weighed as much as you do, what would be your total weight on the moon?

Building Inquiry Skills: Developing a Hypothesis

Remind students of the collision theory of the moon's origin. One way to test the hypothesis is to compare rocks on Earth and the moon. Tell students that many of the moon rocks contained the mineral feldspar and other minerals, which are also found on Earth. Ask: **How could you use the rocks on Earth to test the theory that the moon was formed when an object collided with Earth?** *(If the moon was ever part of Earth, then the composition of feldspar on the moon should be similar to feldspar found on Earth.)* **learning modality: verbal**

Sharpen your Skills

Calculating

Time 10 minutes ACTIVITY

Tips Some students may be sensitive about their weight. You may wish to have students calculate the weights of some common items such as a car or a boat.

Extend Tell students that density is calculated by dividing the mass of an object by its volume. Ask students to hypothesize whether the density of a solid object would be affected on the moon. *(Its density would not change since its mass and volume would be the same.)* Have students investigate to confirm or reject their hypotheses. **learning modality: logical/mathematical**

Answers to Self-Assessment

Caption Question

Figure 18 Landing on a flat spot allowed the astronauts and the landing gear outside the craft to land safely.

☑ *Checkpoint*

Scientists discovered that the interior of the moon has cooled almost completely since it was formed.

Ongoing Assessment

Writing Have students write a paragraph where they imagine they were the first astronaut to step on the surface of the moon. What would they say? What would they write in their diaries?

Students can save their paragraphs in their portfolios.

3 Assess

Section 4 Review Answers

1. Craters, highlands, and maria
2. The Apollo astronauts collected moon rocks, brought seismometers to detect moon quakes, and measured heat flow in the moon's interior.
3. The craters were formed by the impact of meteoroids on the moon's surface.
4. Scientists once thought that some of the moon's craters were formed by volcanoes because they resembled volcanic craters. The Apollo astronauts measured the heat flow beneath the moon's surface and found that the moon has cooled almost completely since it was formed, so the presence of volcanoes seems unlikely.

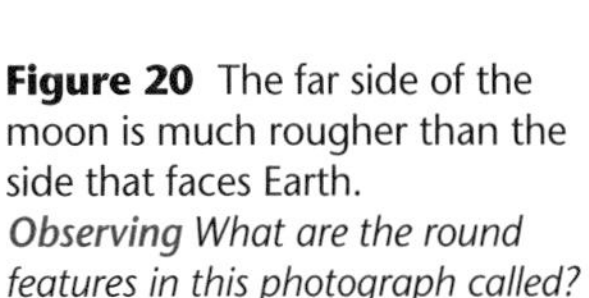

Check Your Progress

At this stage, students will be looking for patterns in their observational data. Encourage them to look for changes throughout the day in addition to comparing their observations over the course of the project. Suggest they look for some of the surface features that they studied in Section 4. Provide moon maps and charts showing what features are likely to be visible. Binoculars will help students spot the highlands, craters, and maria. The elevated walls of craters are most likely to be visible during the crescent and quarter phases.

Performance Assessment

Drawing Have students make a diagram of the moon using shadows to indicate the presence of craters and other features. Students may label the features and write a brief caption to go with each feature.

Students can save their sketches in their portfolios.

Figure 20 The far side of the moon is much rougher than the side that faces Earth.
Observing What are the round features in this photograph called?

Photographs of the Moon The *Apollo* astronauts circled the moon by rocket and photographed its surface. The pictures show that the far side of the moon is rougher than the near side and has very few maria.

The American *Clementine* spacecraft went to the moon in 1994. It took photographs of the moon through different filters chosen to show what types of minerals are on the moon. The name *Clementine* was chosen because it is the name of the prospector's daughter in the old song "My Darlin' Clementine."

In 1998, the American *Lunar Prospector* spacecraft went to the moon. *Lunar Prospector* mapped the entire moon from an altitude of only 100 kilometers. *Lunar Prospector* found evidence that there is ice frozen into the lunar soil near the moon's poles.

Section 4 Review

1. Name the three kinds of features that Galileo saw on the moon's surface.
2. What did the *Apollo* astronauts do on the moon?
3. How did the craters form on the moon?
4. **Thinking Critically Inferring** Why did scientists once think there were volcanoes on the moon? What evidence from the *Apollo* landings makes this unlikely?

CHAPTER PROJECT

Check Your Progress

Compare your observations of the moon early in the day with observations later that day. How does the moon appear to move in the sky during the course of the day? What happens to the appearance of the moon between earlier and later observations? Is there a pattern for each day? (*Hint:* See whether the same pattern holds true for observations later in the month.)

Program Resources

- **Unit 6 Resources** 18-4 Review and Reinforce; 18-4 Enrich

Answers to Self-Assessment

Caption Question

Figure 20 The round features are craters.

CHAPTER 18 STUDY GUIDE

Earth in Space

Key Ideas

- Astronomy is the study of the moon, stars, and other objects in space.
- Earth's rotation on its axis causes day and night.
- One complete revolution of Earth around the sun is called a year.
- Earth has seasons because its axis is tilted as it revolves around the sun.

Key Terms

astronomy	latitude
axis	solstice
rotation	equinox
revolution	vernal equinox
orbit	autumnal equinox

Phases, Eclipses, and Tides

Key Ideas

- The moon revolves around Earth and rotates on its own axis.
- The phase of the moon you see depends on how much of the sunlit side of the moon faces Earth.
- A solar eclipse occurs when the moon passes between Earth and the sun, blocking the sunlight from reaching Earth.
- A lunar eclipse occurs when Earth is directly between the moon and the sun, blocking the sunlight from reaching the moon.
- Tides occur mainly because of differences in how much the moon pulls on different parts of Earth.

Key Terms

phase	penumbra
eclipse	lunar eclipse
solar eclipse	tide
umbra	gravity

Rockets and Satellites

INTEGRATING TECHNOLOGY

Key Ideas

- A rocket moves in one direction when gases are expelled from it in the opposite direction.
- Satellites and space stations are used for communications, navigation, collecting weather data, and research.

Key Terms

satellite   geosynchronous orbit

Earth's Moon

Key Ideas

- Features on the moon's surface include craters, highlands, and maria.
- Much of what scientists have learned about the moon came from detailed study of the moon rocks.

Key Terms

telescope   crater   maria

Organizing Information

Concept Map Copy the concept map about how Earth moves in space onto a sheet of paper. Then complete it and add a title. (For more on concept maps, see the Skills Handbook.)

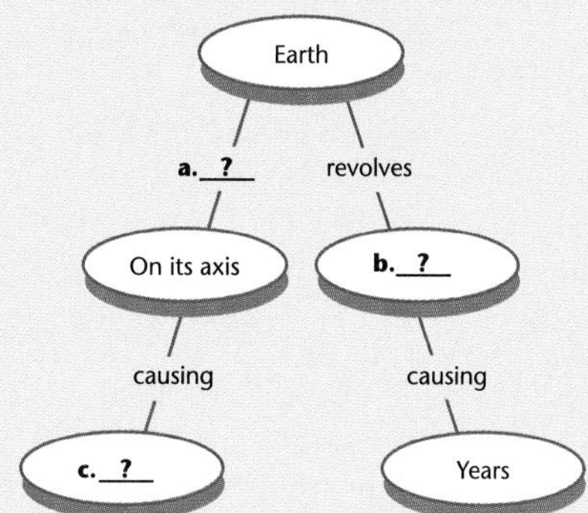

Media and Technology

Computer Test Bank Chapter 18 Test

Program Resources

- **Unit 6 Resources** Chapter 18 Project Scoring Rubric
- **Performance Assessment** Chapter 18
- **Chapter and Unit Tests** Chapter 18 Test

Organizing Information

Concept Map Sample title: *How Earth Moves;* **a.** rotates **b.** around the sun **c.** day and night

Reviewing Content

Multiple Choice

1. c **2.** a **3.** d **4.** d **5.** c

True or False

6. rotation **7.** seasons **8.** true **9.** true
10. lunar seas or maria

Checking Concepts

11. A flattened oval
12. Yes, because seasons are caused by sunlight hitting different hemispheres of a planet at different angles over the year.
13. They are the same.
14. The moon must enter Earth's shadow for a lunar eclipse to take place. In most months, when the moon is full it is near Earth's shadow but not in it. This is because the moon's orbit is slightly tilted relative to the plane of Earth's orbit around the sun.
15. Everyone who can see the moon can see a lunar eclipse, in which the moon goes into Earth's shadow, while only those in a narrow band on Earth's surface can see a total solar eclipse.
16. Closest to the moon, the moon's gravitational pull on water at Earth's surface is stronger than its pull on Earth as a whole, and water flows toward that point. Furthest from the moon, the moon pulls more strongly on Earth as a whole than on water at Earth's surface, creating a high tide at that point as well.
17. Rockets work on the law of action and reaction.
18. A large object collides with Earth, material from Earth's outer layer breaks off, material from Earth and the object are thrown into orbit, the material combines to form the moon.
19. Scientists learned that the moon's surface was once very hot and that it had been bombarded by meteoroids.
20. Students should give detailed descriptions of the surface of the moon, and of objects they would see in the sky (including Earth). New rock samples might tell whether the rocks contain minerals that could be mined.

Reviewing Content

Multiple Choice

Choose the letter of the answer that best completes each statement.

1. The movement of Earth around the sun once a year is Earth's
  a. orbit.
  b. rotation.
  c. revolution.
  d. axis.

2. The darkest part of a shadow is the
  a. umbra.
  b. penumbra.
  c. eclipse.
  d. phase.

3. When Earth's shadow falls on the moon, the shadow causes a
  a. new moon.
  b. solar eclipse.
  c. full moon.
  d. lunar eclipse.

4. A satellite in geosynchronous orbit revolves around Earth once each
  a. hour.
  b. week.
  c. month.
  d. day.

5. The craters on the moon were caused by
  a. highlands. **b.** volcanoes.
  c. meteoroid impacts. **d.** maria.

True or False

If the statement is true, write true. If it is false, change the underlined word or words to make the statement true.

6. Earth's spinning on its axis is called revolution.
7. The tilt of Earth's axis as Earth revolves around the sun causes eclipses.
8. A total eclipse of the sun occurs only during a new moon.
9. Many artificial satellites orbit Earth.
10. The cooling of molten material on the moon formed the craters.

Checking Concepts

11. Describe the shape of Earth's orbit.
12. Mars's axis is tilted at about the same angle as Earth's axis. Do you think Mars has seasons? Explain your answer.
13. How does the time it takes the moon to rotate on its axis compare with the time it takes the moon to revolve around Earth?
14. Why isn't there a lunar eclipse every month?
15. Why do more people see a total lunar eclipse than a total solar eclipse?
16. Why is there a high tide on the side of Earth closest to the moon? On the side of Earth furthest from the moon?
17. What basic law of physics explains how a rocket moves forward?
18. Describe the events that formed the moon, according to the collision theory.
19. What did scientists learn by studying the rocks astronauts brought back from the moon?
20. **Writing to Learn** Imagine that trips to the moon are resuming. You are an astronaut going to the moon. Write a paragraph describing what you see as you arrive. What does the sky look like? What could the rocks you find help scientists learn?

Thinking Critically

21. **Relating Cause and Effect** How does the position of the moon cause high and low tides on Earth?
22. **Applying Concepts** At what time does the full moon rise? Is it visible in the eastern sky or the western sky?
23. **Posing Questions** Suppose you were assigned to design a spacesuit for astronauts to wear on the moon. What questions about the moon would you need to have answered in order to design the spacesuit?

Thinking Critically

21. Tides result mainly from differences in the moon's gravitational pull on different parts of Earth. High tides occur on the side of Earth that is closest to the moon and on the side of Earth that is farthest from the moon. Low tides occur on Earth midway between these two high tides.
22. The full moon rises at sunset because it has to be opposite the sun in the sky for the face we see to be fully lighted. It therefore rises in the east as the sun sets in the west.
23. Sample questions: What are the temperatures like? What kinds of terrain will the astronauts have to cover? Is there any air to breathe or will we need to bring our own?

Applying Skills

Use the illustration below to answer Questions 24–26. (Hint: The tilt of the Earth's axis is 23.5°.)

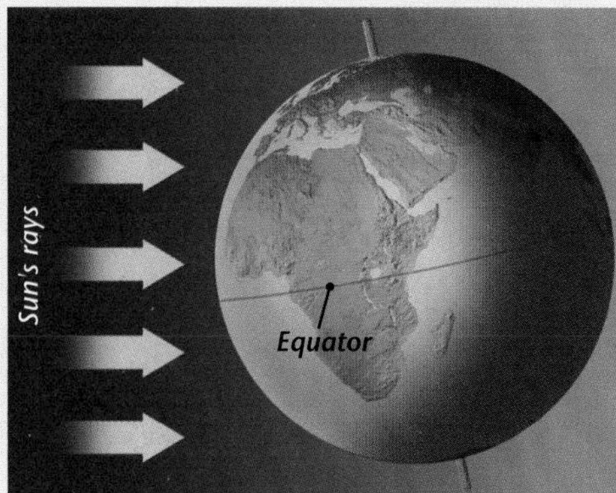

24. Interpreting Diagrams On which hemisphere are the sun's rays falling most directly?

25. Inferring In the Northern Hemisphere, is it the summer solstice, winter solstice, or one of the equinoxes? How do you know?

26. Predicting Six months after this illustration, Earth will have revolved halfway around the sun. Show in a sketch which end of Earth's axis will be tilted toward the sun.

Performance Assessment (Chapter Project)

Present Your Project Now you are ready to present your log, map, and drawings. Here are some ways you can graph your data: time of moonrise for each date; how often you saw the moon at each compass direction; how often you saw the moon at a specific time. Display your graphs. Discuss any patterns you discovered with your classmates. With your classmates, predict when and where you can see the moon.

Reflect and Record In your journal, write about the easiest and hardest parts of this project. What would you do differently if you observed the moon for another month? What observation(s) surprised you? Why?

Test Preparation

Use these questions to prepare for standardized tests.

Study the diagram. Then answer Questions 27–30. Numbers 1, 2, 3, and 4 on the diagram indicate locations of the moon in its orbit around Earth.

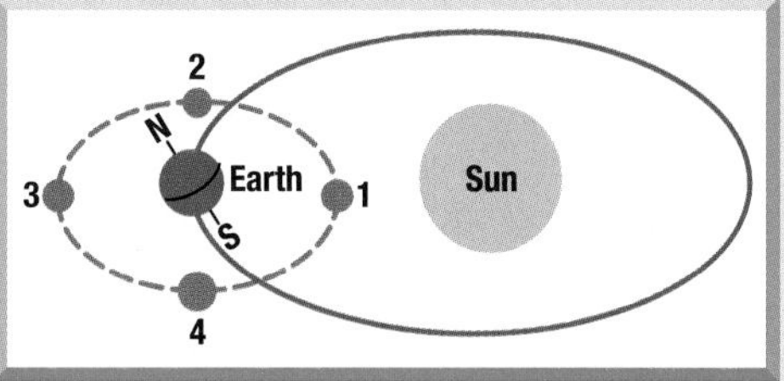

27. About how much time does it take the moon to revolve once around Earth?
- **a.** one day
- **b.** 7 days
- **c.** 27 days
- **d.** one year

28. Which of the following phases is the moon in at location 1?
- **a.** new
- **b.** crescent
- **c.** half
- **d.** full

29. At which location(s) could a lunar eclipse occur?
- **a.** 1 only
- **b.** 3 only
- **c.** 1 and 3
- **d.** 2 and 4

30. Only one side of the moon is visible from Earth because
- **a.** the moon does not rotate on its axis.
- **b.** the moon does not revolve around Earth.
- **c.** the moon is in a geosynchronous orbit around Earth.
- **d.** the moon revolves once and rotates once in the same period of time.

Program Resources

- **Inquiry Skills Activity Book** Provides teaching and review of all inquiry skills

Applying Skills

24. Northern Hemisphere
25. Summer solstice. The north end of Earth's axis is tilted toward the sun.
26. Students' sketches should show the southern end of Earth's axis tilted toward the sun.

Performance Assessment (Chapter Project)

Present Your Project Have students make graphs showing the different patterns, so all information is available for the class. Encourage students to discuss the patterns they see in the graphs. Emphasize these patterns:
- In the course of a day, the moon position changes from the eastern sky, through southern, to western. (Because of Earth's rotation).
- Moonrise gets progressively later throughout the cycle.
- The moon will be seen mostly in the southern half of the sky, rising more easterly and setting more westerly.
- The lit portion of the moon starts on the right side and waxes until full; as it wanes, the right side becomes slowly dark.

Reflect and Record Students may have had trouble determining compass direction or altitude. It may have been frustrating not to see the moon when they looked for it. Students might be surprised to discover that their results confirm that the full moon always rises at about the same time as sunset.

Test Preparation

27. c **28.** a **29.** b **30.** d

CHAPTER

19 The Solar System

Sections	Time	Student Edition Activities	ACTIVITY Other Activities
CHAPTER PROJECT **Model of the Solar System** p. 593	Ongoing (2 weeks)	Check Your Progress, pp. 599, 613, 621 Present Your Project, p. 635	
1 Observing the Solar System pp. 594–599 ◆ Explain how the heliocentric and geocentric models of the solar system differ. ◆ Explain how the observations and views of scientists such as Kepler and Copernicus contributed to the current understanding of the solar system. ◆ Explain the two factors that keep planets in their orbits.	1 period/ $\frac{1}{2}$ block	**Discover** How Do Mass and Speed Affect an Object's Motion?, p. 594 **Try This** A Loopy Ellipse, p. 597	**TE** Building Inquiry Skills: Comparing and Contrasting, p. 596; Modeling, p. 596 **TE** Including All Students, p. 596 **IES** "Mars the Next Frontier," pp. 22–23, 26–27
2 The Sun pp. 600–605 ◆ Describe how the sun produces energy. ◆ List and describe the layers of the sun's atmosphere. ◆ Identify features of the sun's surface.	1–2 periods/ $\frac{1}{2}$–1 block	**Discover** How Can You Safely Observe the Sun?, p. 600 **Try This** Viewing Sunspots, p. 602 **Science at Home,** p. 604 **Real-World Lab: You and Your Environment** Stormy Sunspots, p. 605	**TE** Demonstration, p. 601 **LM** 19, "Measuring the Diameter of the Sun"
3 The Inner Planets pp. 606–613 ◆ Identify the main characteristics of the inner planets.	2 periods/ 1 block	**Discover** How Does Mars Look From Earth?, p. 606 **Sharpen Your Skills** Graphing, p. 609 **Try This** Remote Control, p. 612	**TE** Integrating Earth Science, p. 607 **TE** Building Inquiry Skills: Observing, p. 608, p. 612 **TE** Demonstration, p. 609
4 The Outer Planets pp. 614–623 ◆ Identify the main characteristics of the gas giant planets. ◆ Compare Pluto with the other planets.	3 periods/ $1\frac{1}{2}$ blocks	**Discover** How Large Are the Outer Planets?, p. 614 **Try This** Model Saturn, p. 617 **Skills Lab: Developing Hypotheses** Speeding Around the Sun, pp. 622–623	**TE** Building Inquiry Skills: Making Models, p. 616; Relating Cause and Effect, p. 620 **TE** Using the Visuals, p. 618 **TE** Language Arts, p. 619
5 Comets, Asteroids, and Meteors pp. 624–627 ◆ Identify the characteristics of comets and asteroids. ◆ Describe the formation of meteoroids.	2 periods/ 1 block	**Discover** Which Way Do Comet Tails Point?, p. 624 **Science at Home,** p. 627	**TE** Building Inquiry Skills: Inferring, p. 625; Predicting, p. 625; Hypothesizing, p. 626
6 INTEGRATING LIFE SCIENCE **Is There Life Beyond Earth?** pp. 628–632 ◆ Identify the conditions needed for living things on Earth. ◆ State why Mars and Europa are thought to be good places to look for signs of life.	1 period/ $\frac{1}{2}$ block	**Discover** Is Yeast Alive or Not?, p. 628 **Sharpen Your Skills** Communicating, p. 629 **Science at Home,** p. 631	**TE** Cultural Diversity, p. 629 **TE** Building Inquiry Skills: Making Judgments, p. 630 **TE** Including All Students, p. 630 **IES** "Mars the Next Frontier," pp. 8–11, 38–39
Study Guide/Chapter Assessment pp. 633–635	1 period/ $\frac{1}{2}$ block		**ISAB** Provides teaching and review of all inquiry skills

For Standard or Block Schedule The Resource Pro® CD-ROM gives you maximum flexibility for planning your instruction for any type of schedule. Resource Pro® contains Planning Express®, an advanced scheduling program, as well as the entire contents of the Teaching Resources and the Computer Test Bank.

CHAPTER PLANNING GUIDE

Program Resources	Assessment Strategies	Media and Technology
UR Chapter 19 Project Teacher Notes **UR** Chapter 19 Project Overview and Worksheets	**SE** Performance Assessment: Present Your Project, p. 635 **TE** Check Your Progress, pp. 599, 613, 621 **UR** Chapter 19 Project Scoring Rubric	Science Explorer Internet Site at www.phschool.com Student Edition on Audio CD, Chapter 19
UR 19-1 Lesson Plan **UR** 19-1 Section Summary **UR** 19-1 Review and Reinforce **UR** 19-1 Enrich	**SE** Section 1 Review, p. 599 **TE** Ongoing Assessment, pp. 595, 597 **TE** Performance Assessment, p. 599	Concept Videotape Library, Grade 6, Tape 4, "For the Love of Astronomy"
UR 19-2 Lesson Plan **UR** 19-2 Section Summary **UR** 19-2 Review and Reinforce **UR** 19-2 Enrich **UR** Chapter 19 Real-World Lab	**SE** Section 2 Review, p. 604 **TE** Ongoing Assessment, pp. 601, 603 **TE** Performance Assessment, p. 604	Concept Videotape Library, Grade 6, Tape 3, "Sunny Days"; Tape 4, "Wired to the Sun" Transparency 94, "Exploring the Sun" Lab Activity Videotapes, Grade 6 Tape 4
UR 19-3 Lesson Plan **UR** 19-3 Section Summary **UR** 19-3 Review and Reinforce **UR** 19-3 Enrich	**SE** Section 3 Review, p. 613 **TE** Ongoing Assessment, pp. 607, 609 **TE** Performance Assessment, p. 613	Transparency 77, "The Inner Planets"
UR 19-4 Lesson Plan **UR** 19-4 Section Summary **UR** 19-4 Review and Reinforce **UR** 19-4 Enrich **UR** Chapter 19 Skills Lab	**SE** Section 4 Review, p. 621 **TE** Ongoing Assessment, pp. 615, 617, 619 **TE** Performance Assessment, p. 621	Transparency 78, "The Outer Planets" Lab Activity Videotapes, Grade 6 Tape 4
UR 19-5 Lesson Plan **UR** 19-5 Section Summary **UR** 19-5 Review and Reinforce **UR** 19-5 Enrich	**SE** Section 5 Review, p. 627 **TE** Ongoing Assessment, p. 625 **TE** Performance Assessment, p. 627	
UR 19-6 Lesson Plan **UR** 19-6 Section Summary **UR** 19-6 Review and Reinforce **UR** 19-6 Enrich	**SE** Section 6 Review, p. 631 **TE** Ongoing Assessment, p. 629 **TE** Performance Assessment, p. 631	Concept Videotape Library, Grade 6, Tape 4, "Evolution of Cells"
RCA Provides strategies to improve science reading skills **GRSW** Provides worksheets to promote student comprehension of content	**SE** Chapter 19 Study Guide/Assessment, pp. 633–635 **PA** Chapter 19 Performance Assessment **CUT** Chapter 19 Test **CTB** Chapter 19 Test	Computer Test Bank, Chapter 19 Test

Key: **SE** Student Edition
CTB Computer Test Bank
ISAB Inquiry Skills Activity Book
GRSW Guided Reading and Study Workbook
TE Teacher's Edition
PTA Product Testing Activities by *Consumer Reports*
RCA Reading in the Content Area
PA Performance Assessment
UR Unit Resources
LM Laboratory Manual
IES Interdisciplinary Explorations Series
CUT Chapter and Unit Tests

Meeting the National Science Education Standards and AAAS Benchmarks

National Science Education Standards	Benchmarks for Science Literacy	Unifying Themes
Science as Inquiry (Content Standard A) ◆ **Develop descriptions, explanations, predictions, and models using evidence** Students design scale models of the solar system. *(Chapter Project; Section 4)* **Physical Science** (Content Standard B) ◆ **Transfer of energy** Energy from the sun is the source of energy in our solar system. *(Section 2)* **Earth and Space Science** (Content Standard D) ◆ **Structure of the Earth system** Earth's structure is the basis for understanding the structure of other planets. *(Section 3)* ◆ **Earth in the solar system** The heliocentric model of the solar system is the basis for our modern understanding. *(Section 1)* **Science in Personal and Social Perspectives** (Content Standard F) ◆ **Risks and benefits** Space exploration has many benefits but is very costly and risky. *(Science and Society)* **History and Nature of Science** (Content Standard G) ◆ **History of science** The struggle that occurred when society changed from a geocentric to a heliocentric model of the solar system is an example of the development of a scientific paradigm. *(Section 1)*	**1A The Scientific World View** Students learn about the observations and hypotheses that led to the shift from a geocentric to a heliocentric system of planets. *(Section 1)* Investigations into potential life on other planets are described. *(Section 6; Science and Society)* **2C Mathematical Inquiry** Applied mathematics helped scientists predict the existence of the planet Neptune. *(Sections 1, 4)* **4A The Universe** Each category of solar system object has distinct characteristics that reveal information about the nature of that object. *(Sections 1, 2, 3, 4, 5; Skills Lab; Real-World Lab)* **4B The Earth** The structure of Earth is used as the basis for making inferences about other planets. *(Section 3)* **4E Energy Transformation** The energy released by nuclear fusion in the sun's core is converted into light, heat, and other forms of energy at the sun's surface. *(Section 2; Real-World Lab)* **4G Forces of Nature** Gravity holds satellites in orbit around planets and the planets and other objects in orbit around the sun. *(Sections 1, 3, 4, 5)* **11B Models** Students construct scale models of the planets and sun. *(Chapter Project)*	◆ **Energy** Energy from reactions in the sun's core is transmitted as light and heat to all of the bodies in the solar system. *(Sections 2, 3, 4, 5; Skills Lab; Real-World Lab)* ◆ **Scale and Structure** Our understanding of the structure of the solar system depends on accurate observations. The sun is the largest body in the solar system. The outer planets, except for Pluto, are huge gas giants. The inner planets and Pluto are rocky and comparatively small. *(Sections 1, 2, 3, 4; Chapter Project)* ◆ **Unity and Diversity** Students compare the similarities of objects in the solar system and contrast their differences. The idea that conditions for life should be the same on all planets is considered, yet studies reveal that Earth is unique in the solar system because it supports life. *(Section 6)* ◆ **Stability** The planets are held in constant orbits by the force of the sun's gravity. *(Sections 1, 2; Skills Lab)*

Take It to the Net

Interactive text at www.phschool.com

Science Explorer comes alive with iText.

- **Complete student text** is accessible from any computer with Internet access or a CD-ROM drive.
- **Animations, simulations, and videos** enhance student understanding and retention of concepts.
- **Self-tests and online study tools** assess student understanding.

STAY CURRENT with 

Find out the latest research and information about The Solar System at: **www.phschool.com**

Go to **www.phschool.com** and click on the Science icon.Then click on Science Explorer: Life, Earth, and Physical Science under PH@school.

ACTIVITY	Time (minutes)	Materials *Quantities for one work group*	Skills
Section 1			
Discover, p. 594	10	**Nonconsumable** toy trucks, rocks	Predicting
Try This, p. 597	15	**Consumable** white paper, corrugated cardboard, 30-cm string **Nonconsumable** 2 pushpins, ruler, pencil	Predicting
Section 2			
Discover, p. 600	15	**Consumable** thin cardboard, masking tape **Nonconsumable** binoculars, ring stand, ruler, scissors, white paper	Observing
Try This, p. 602	10/day over 10 days	**Consumable** thin cardboard, masking tape, white paper **Nonconsumable** binoculars, ring stand, ruler, scissors	Interpreting Data
Science at Home, p. 604	home	No special materials are required.	Observing
Real-World Lab, p. 605	30	**Consumable** graph paper **Nonconsumable** pencil, ruler	Graphing, Interpreting Data
Section 3			
Discover, p. 606	10	**Nonconsumable** compass, ruler	Observing
Sharpen Your Skills, p. 609	15	**Consumable** graph paper **Nonconsumable** colored pencils	Graphing
Try This, p. 612	15	**Consumable** tape, paper **Nonconsumable** goggles	Inferring
Section 4			
Discover, p. 614	15	**Consumable** lined paper, butcher paper or poster board, string **Nonconsumable** quarter, ruler, compass, push pin	Classifying
Try This, p. 617	20	**Consumable** clear plastic sheet, tape, baking soda, peppercorn, glue (optional) **Nonconsumable** 8-cm plastic foam sphere, ruler, scissors, compass, 5 toothpicks	Making Models
Skills Lab, p. 622	45	**Consumable** string, 1.5 m **Nonconsumable** one-hole rubber stopper; plastic tube, 6 cm; stopwatch; weight or several washers; meterstick	Developing Hypotheses
Section 5			
Discover, p. 624	10	**Consumable** 3 10-cm lengths of string **Nonconsumable** modeling clay, pencil, small fan	Inferring
Science at Home, p. 627	home	**Nonconsumable** newspapers or almanacs	Observing
Section 6			
Discover, p. 628	15	**Consumable** yeast, warm water, sugar **Nonconsumable** bowl, thermometer, spoon, stopwatch or clock	Forming Operational Definitions
Science at Home, p. 631	home	No special materials are required.	Communicating

A list of all materials required for the Student Edition activities can be found on pages TVA34–TVA40. You can obtain information about ordering materials by calling 1-800-848-9500 or by accessing the Science Explorer Internet site at **www.phschool.com**.

This artist's conception shows the *Cassini* space probe arriving near Saturn's rings in 2004.

Section 1 Observing the Solar System
Discover How Do Mass and Speed Affect an Object's Motion?
Try This A Loopy Ellipse

Section 2 The Sun
Discover How Can You Safely Observe the Sun?
Try This Viewing Sunspots
Science at Home Solar Symbols
Real-World Lab Stormy Sunspots

Section 3 The Inner Planets
Discover How Does Mars Look From Earth?
Sharpen Your Skills Graphing
Try This Remote Control

592

CHAPTER 19 PROJECT

Model of the Solar System

Movies, books, and television shows have given most people a distorted understanding of the sizes of objects and distances between objects in the solar system. The Chapter Project will help students understand that the distances between the planets are very large relative to the sizes of the planets.

Purpose By creating scale models of the solar system, students will begin to understand the vastness of space, including the size of planets and the great distances between them. They will also discover difficulties in scaling the size of objects and distance between objects into the same scale measurements.

Skills Focus After completing the Chapter 19 project, students will be able to

- convert large numbers to the established scale;
- compare scaled distances and diameters to familiar distances and diameters;
- establish scale models to show the actual size of the solar system;
- discover why it can be difficult to build a scale model of the solar system's distance.

Suggested Shortcuts Allow students to do the mathematical calculations in groups. Since many distances in the solar system are given in astronomical units, an easy way to establish a scale is to let 1 AU = 1 m. Students can then brainstorm familiar objects that are comparable to the estimated planet sizes. If students have not had much experience with scaling, provide in-class time to assist students. You may decide to allow students to build the models in groups, or as a whole-class project.

Project Time Line This project requires about four weeks. Students will work on a different model each week, and the final week will be reserved for presentation preparation. Models should be completed sequentially, beginning with the planet sizes, then moving to the distance between the planets, and ending with the combination model. Students should complete the appropriate portion of the worksheets and get approval from you before they begin each phase of model building. The project should end with the presentations and a class discussion. Before beginning the project, see Chapter 19 Project Teacher Notes in Unit 6 Resources for more details on carrying out the project. Also, distribute the students' Chapter 19 Project Overview and Worksheets and Scoring Rubric in Unit 6 Resources.

Possible Materials For model building, students will need meter sticks or metric rulers and calculators. Since models of solar system distance usually involve large numbers, students may also need maps of their local community. Familiar objects such as tennis balls, beach balls, pieces of fruit (grapefruit, orange, etc.), marbles, dried beans, and ball bearings will make good planets, depending on the required diameters.

Other tools that may assist students in their model building are available from *The Astronomical Society of the Pacific,* 390 Ashton Avenue, San Francisco, CA 94112, USA.

CHAPTER 19 PROJECT

Model of the Solar System

If you could drive from Earth to the sun at 100 kilometers per hour, your trip would take 170 years. And most distances in the solar system are even greater! The *Cassini* space probe left Earth for Saturn in 1997 traveling much faster than highway speed, but will not arrive at Saturn's rings until 2004. Sizes in the solar system can be huge, too. Compared with some of the other planets in the solar system, Earth is very small. Saturn, for example, is about 10 times Earth's diameter.

In this chapter, you will get to know many of the objects in the solar system. To help you understand the huge distances and sizes, you will design three different scale models of the solar system.

Your Goal To design scale models of the solar system.

To complete this project, you will
- design a model to show the planets' distances from the sun
- design a model to show the planets' sizes relative to the sun
- test different scales to see if you can use the same scale for both size and distance in one model

Get Started Begin by previewing the tables with distances and diameters on pages 607 and 615. Brainstorm with a group of classmates how you will build your models. Prepare a data sheet to record your calculations of scaled-down distances and diameters.

Check Your Progress You will be working on this project as you study this chapter. To keep your project on track, look for Check Your Progress boxes at the following points.

Section 1 Review, page 599: Design a model to show distances.
Section 3 Review, page 613: Design a model to show diameters.
Section 4 Review, page 621: Design one scale model that shows both sizes and distances.

Present Your Project At the end of the chapter (page 635), you will present your design to the class.

The Outer Planets

Discover **How Large Are the Outer Planets?**
Try This **Model Saturn**
Skills Lab **Speeding Around the Sun**

Comets, Asteroids, and Meteors

Discover **Which Way Do Comet Tails Point?**
Science at Home **Watch a Meteor Shower**

Integrating Life Science

Is There Life Beyond Earth?

Discover **Is Yeast Alive or Not?**
Sharpen Your Skills **Communicating**
Science at Home **Message to E.T.**

A video entitled *The Powers of Ten* may help students do their calculations. Also available is a solar system chart that provides relative sizes, distances, orbits, and data about the planets and their place in the galaxy.

Launching the Project When introducing the project, bring in a scale model of an object familiar to all students (e.g., the Statue of Liberty). Ask: **How does the size of this model compare to the real object?** Discuss scaling. Take measurements of features of the model, and compare these to measurements of features on the actual object. If the model is proportional, the scaling should be the same for each measurement taken. Ask: **How big is Earth?** Discuss size. If you travel once around Earth, you would cover about 40,000 km. The United States is about 4,000 km across. It takes at least four or five days to make this journey by car, yet this is only 1/10 the distance around the Earth! Ask: **How could you compare size and distance in space with travel speeds on Earth?** Compare average travel speeds. *(Walking 3.6 km/hr, car 80 km/hr, jet 1,436 km/hr, light 300,000 km/sec)* Since the distance from Earth to the moon is about 386,000 km, it takes about 1.5 sec for light to travel this distance. Ask students how long it would take a jet to fly there.

Give students time to read about the project in their text and in the Chapter Project Overview in Unit 6 Resources. Pass out copies of the Project Worksheets in Unit 6 Resources.

Program Resources

- **Unit 6 Resources** Chapter 19 Project Teacher Notes; Chapter 19 Project Overview and Worksheets; Chapter 19 Project Scoring Rubric

Media and Technology

Student Edition on Audio CD
Chapter 19

You will find an Internet activity, chapter self-tests for students, and links to other chapter topics at this site.

Performance Assessment

The Chapter 19 Project Scoring Rubric in Unit 6 Resources will help you evaluate how well students complete the Chapter 19 Project.
Students will be assessed on
- how accurately they did their mathematical calculations;
- how well they selected model scales;
- how well they can discuss the concepts of size and scaling;
- the thoroughness and organization of their presentation.

By sharing the Chapter 19 Project Scoring Rubric with students when they start the project, they will learn what they are expected to do.

Section 1 Observing the Solar System

Objectives

After completing the lesson, students will be able to

- explain how the heliocentric and geocentric models of the solar system differ;
- explain how the observations and views of scientists such as Kepler and Copernicus contributed to the current understanding of the solar system;
- identify and explain the two factors that keep planets in their orbits.

Key Terms geocentric, heliocentric, ellipse, inertia

1 Engage/Explore

Activating Prior Knowledge

Show students a photograph of the night sky that shows stars and the moon. Ask them to identify the objects they see. Then ask: **Where was the sun when this picture was taken?** *(The sun could not be seen from the spot where the picture was taken because it was on the other side of Earth.)* Reinforce the idea that the objects in our solar system are moving.

Discover

Skills Focus predicting
Materials *toy truck, rocks*
Time 10 minutes
Tips A toy car, roller skate, or skateboard may be substituted for the truck. Remind students to push the truck gently at first. When they add rocks to the truck, students should be careful not to pile them so high that they fall out when the truck is pushed.
Expected Outcome Students should observe that it is harder to stop the truck when the truck is moving faster and when it has more mass.
Think It Over It would be easier to stop the truck if the partner pushed it more slowly. It would be harder to stop the truck if more mass was added.

Section 1 Observing the Solar System

Discover Activity

How Do Mass and Speed Affect an Object's Motion?

1. Have your partner push a toy truck across the table toward you. Stop the truck with your hands.
2. Repeat Step 1, but have your partner push the truck a little faster. Was it easier or harder to stop the truck than in Step 1?
3. Now add some rocks or other heavy objects to the truck and repeat Step 1. Your partner should push the truck at the same speed as in Step 1. How hard was it to stop the truck this time compared to Step 1?
4. Repeat Step 2 with the rocks still in the truck. How hard was it to stop the truck this time?

Think It Over
Predicting How hard would it be to stop the truck if your partner pushed it more slowly? If you added more mass to the truck?

Guide for Reading

- How do the heliocentric and geocentric descriptions of the solar system differ?
- What did Kepler discover about the orbits of the planets?
- What two factors keep the planets in their orbits?

Reading Tip As you read, make a list of the evidence that supports the heliocentric system.

Have you ever lain outdoors on a starry night, gazing up at the stars? As you watch, the stars seem to move across the sky. The sky seems to be rotating right over your head. In fact, from the Northern Hemisphere, the sky appears to rotate around a point near Polaris, the North Star, once every 24 hours.

Now think about what you see every day. During the day, the sun appears to move across the sky. From here on Earth, it seems as if Earth is stationary and that the sun, moon, and stars are all moving around Earth. But is the sky really moving above you? Centuries ago, before there were space shuttles or even telescopes, there was no easy way to find out.

Figure 1 This photo was made by exposing the camera film for several hours. Each star appears as part of a circle, and all the stars seem to revolve around a single point.

Reading Strategies

Reading Tip Students should list such evidence as Galileo's observation of the phases of Venus and the moons of Jupiter. After students have read the section, have them work in groups to compare their lists.

Study and Comprehension As students read the section, have them write brief summaries of the information under each heading. Remind students that summarizing involves stating briefly, in their own words, the main points and key details. In a class discussion, invite volunteers to give oral summaries of the information in the section.

Wandering Stars

When the ancient Greeks watched the stars move across the sky, they noticed that the patterns of most of the stars didn't change. Although the stars seemed to move, they stayed in the same position relative to one another. For example, the constellations kept the same shapes from night to night and from year to year.

As they observed the sky more carefully, the Greeks noticed something surprising. Five points of light seemed to wander among the stars. The Greeks called these objects *planets*, from the Greek word meaning "wandering star." The Greeks made very careful observations of the motions of the five planets they could see. You know these planets by the names the ancient Romans later gave them: Mercury, Venus, Mars, Jupiter, and Saturn.

Greek Ideas: Earth at the Center

When you look up at the sky, you can almost imagine that you are under a rotating dome with the stars pasted on it. The Greeks thought that they were inside a rotating dome they called the celestial sphere. Many Greek scientists, such as Aristotle, believed that the universe is perfect and finite and that Earth is stationary at its center. Since *geo* is the Greek word for Earth, an Earth-centered explanation is known as a **geocentric** (jee oh SEN trik) system. **In a geocentric system, Earth is at the center of the revolving planets.**

In A.D. 140, the Greek astronomer Ptolemy (TAHL uh mee) explained the motion of the planets in another way. Like the earlier Greeks, Ptolemy thought that Earth is at the center of the system of planets. Ptolemy also thought that the moon, Mercury, Venus, the sun, Mars, Jupiter, and Saturn revolve around Earth.

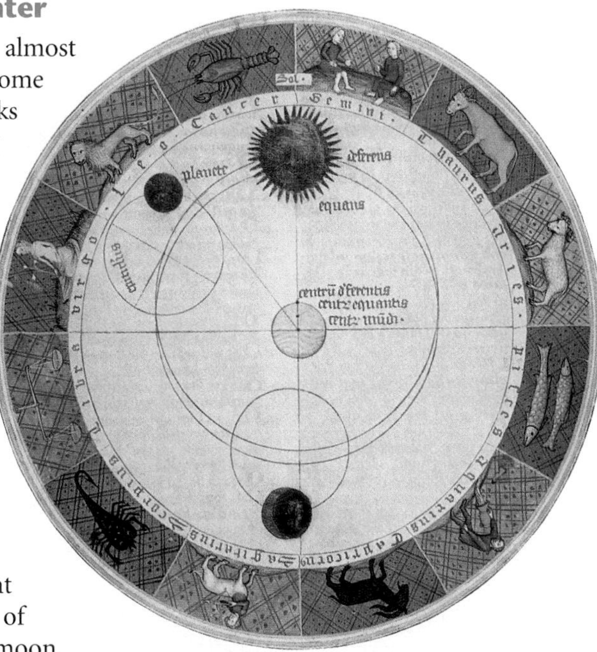

Figure 2 In the 1500s, an astronomy book published this illustration of Ptolemy's system. *Interpreting Diagrams Where is Earth located in this illustration?*

In Ptolemy's explanation, however, the planets move in little circles that move in bigger circles. Ptolemy thought that this explained why the planets seem to move at different speeds, and even backwards, among the stars. For the next 1,400 years, people believed that Ptolemy's ideas were correct.

☑ *Checkpoint* *What is a geocentric system?*

2 Facilitate

Wandering Stars

Building Inquiry Skills: Inferring

Guide students in evaluating what the ancient astronomers knew about stars. Ask: **Why did the Greeks only see five planets?** *(They did not have telescopes and could not see the other planets because they are too dim.)* **learning modality: verbal**

Greek Ideas: Earth at the Center

Cultural Diversity

Remind students that the Romans named the planets they knew after their gods. Tell them that other cultures gave objects in the sky names that were meaningful in those cultures. Ask students from other cultures to give examples of such names from their cultures. **learning modality: verbal**

Using the Visuals: Figure 1

Ask students to infer why exposing the film for several hours produced the circular effect shown in the figure. If they have difficulty, ask: **What is the single point around which the stars seem to revolve?** *(Polaris or the North Star)* Remind students that in the Northern Hemisphere, the stars seem to rotate around a point near the North Star. Leaving the camera shutter open as this rotation occurs produces the circular effect. **learning modality: visual**

Program Resources

- **Unit 6 Resources** 19-1 Lesson Plan; 19-1 Section Summary
- **Guided Reading and Study Workbook** Section 19-1
- **Interdisciplinary Exploration Series** "Mars the Next Frontier," pp. 22–23, 26–27

Answers to Self-Assessment

Caption Question

Figure 2 Earth is in the center.

☑ *Checkpoint*

A geocentric system is one in which Earth is at the center of a system of revolving planets.

Ongoing Assessment

Drawing Have students draw and label a diagram of a geocentric system. The diagram should include the sun, Earth, and at least one other planet.

Copernicus's Idea: Sun at the Center

In the early 1500s, the Polish astronomer Nicolaus Copernicus developed another explanation for the motions of the planets. Copernicus thought that the sun is at the center of the system of planets. His sun-centered system is called a **heliocentric** (hee lee oh SEN trik) system. *Helios* is Greek for "sun." **In a heliocentric system, Earth and the other planets revolve around the sun.** Copernicus's explanation included the six planets he knew about: Mercury, Venus, Earth, Mars, Jupiter, and Saturn.

Galileo's Observations

In the 1500s and 1600s, most people still believed Ptolemy's geocentric explanation. However, the Italian astronomer Galileo Galilei, who lived nearly 100 years after Copernicus, thought that the heliocentric explanation was correct.

Recall from Chapter 18 that Galileo was the first scientist to use a telescope to look at objects in the sky. With his telescope, Galileo made two discoveries that supported the heliocentric model. First, Galileo saw four moons revolving around Jupiter. Galileo's observations of Jupiter's moons showed that not everything in the sky revolves around Earth.

Figure 3 From this observatory, Tycho Brahe made accurate observations of the planets for nearly 20 years. His data became the basis for many important discoveries.

Galileo's observations of Venus also supported Copernicus's heliocentric system. Galileo discovered that Venus goes through phases similar to those of Earth's moon. Galileo reasoned that the phases of Venus could not be explained if Earth were at the center of the system of planets. So Ptolemy's geocentric system could not be correct.

Galileo's evidence gradually convinced others that Copernicus's explanation was correct. Today, people talk about the "solar system" rather than the "Earth system." This shows that people accept Copernicus's idea that the sun is at the center.

✓ ***Checkpoint** What two discoveries made by Galileo supported the heliocentric description of the solar system?*

Brahe and Kepler

Copernicus and Galileo had correctly identified the sun as the center of the system of planets. But Copernicus, like Ptolemy, assumed that the orbits of the planets are circles.

Copernicus's ideas were based on observations made by the ancient Greeks. In the late 1500s, Tycho Brahe (TEE koh BRAH uh), a Danish astronomer, made

Copernicus's Idea: Sun at the Center

Building Inquiry Skills: Comparing and Contrasting

ACTIVITY Have students diagram Copernicus's heliocentric model and then compare their diagram with the geocentric model in Figure 2. Ask: **How does Earth's motion differ in each system?** *(Geocentric—Earth is not moving; heliocentric—Earth rotates on its axis and revolves around the sun)* **How does the motion of planets differ in each system?** *(Geocentric—planets revolve around Earth; heliocentric—all planets revolve around the sun)* **learning modality: logical/mathematical**

Portfolio Students can save their diagrams in their portfolios.

Galileo's Observations

Including All Students

ACTIVITY Invite students who need additional challenges to research the phases of Venus in an astronomy textbook or other reference book. Students can draw diagrams to show how the sun, Earth, and Venus are aligned as Venus passes through its phases. Students can present their diagrams to the class. **learning modality: visual**

Building Inquiry Skills: Modeling

ACTIVITY Have students model the movements of the inner planets. Divide the class into groups of four. Have each group draw concentric circles of radii 3.5 m, 5.0 m, and 7.5 m. One student representing the sun will stand in the center. The other students will model the planets Venus, Earth, and Mars by walking around the circles at different speeds. The students must time their movement so that "Venus" on the inner circle takes three steps, in the same time as "Earth" on the second circle takes two steps and "Mars" on the outer circle takes one step. Make sure students observe their relative positions as they walk, especially how inner planets overtake outer planets. **learning modality: kinesthetic**

Background

History of Science Johannes Kepler believed the universe contained many profound mathematical patterns and relationships. One of his life-long endeavors was to identify a relationship between the mathematics of the movement of the planets around the sun and the mathematics of musical sound. Kepler compared the mathematics of many aspects of planetary motion to musical harmonies before asserting that he had discovered a clear relationship. In his book *Harmonice Mundi* (The Harmony of the World), Kepler assigned a range of sounds to each planet. Modern scientists do not accept Kepler's musical theories. However, his research may have led him to discover the relationship between the speed of a planet and its distance from the sun, a concept published in the same book.

much more accurate observations. Brahe carefully observed the positions of the planets for about 20 years.

In 1600, a German mathematician, Johannes Kepler, went to work analyzing Brahe's data. Kepler tried to figure out the shape of the planets' orbits. At first, he assumed that the orbits are circles. When Kepler tried to figure out the exact orbit of Mars, however, no circle fit the observations.

Kepler had discovered that the orbit of each planet is an ellipse. An **ellipse** is an elongated circle, or oval shape. Kepler found that if he assumed that Mars's orbit is an ellipse, his calculations fit Brahe's observations better.

Inertia and Gravity

Kepler had discovered the correct shape of the planets' orbits. But he could not explain why the planets stay in orbit. The work of the English scientist Isaac Newton provided the answer to that puzzle. **Newton concluded that two factors—inertia and gravity—combine to keep the planets in orbit.**

Galileo had discovered that a moving object will continue to move until some force acts to stop its motion. This tendency of a moving object to continue in a straight line or a stationary object to remain in place is the object's **inertia.** The more mass an object has, the more inertia it has. As you found if you did the Discover activity, an object with greater inertia is more difficult to start or stop.

Isaac Newton picked up where Galileo had left off. Late in his life, Newton told the story of how watching an apple fall from a tree in 1665 had made him think about motion. He hypothesized that the same force that pulls the apple to the ground also pulls the moon toward Earth. This force, called gravity, attracts all

Figure 4 Newton was a man of many achievements. Among them was the invention of this telescope.

A Loopy Ellipse

You can draw an ellipse.

1. Carefully stick two pushpins about 10 cm apart through a sheet of white paper on top of corrugated cardboard.

2. Tie the ends of a 30-cm piece of string together. Place the string around the pushpins.
3. Keeping the string tight, move a pencil around inside the string.
4. Now place the pushpins 5 cm apart. Repeat Step 3.

Predicting How does changing the distance between the pushpins affect the ellipse's shape? What shape would you draw if you used only one pushpin?

Brahe and Kepler

Building Inquiry Skills: Inferring

To help students understand elliptical orbits, diagram a planet and its orbit on the board. Challenge students to infer why scientists record a planet's average distance from the sun. Ask: **In an elliptical orbit, what happens to the distance between the planet and the sun?** *(It changes as the planet revolves.)* Have a volunteer point out where on the diagram the planet is closest and where it is farthest from the sun. Tell students that Earth is closest to the sun in the Northern Hemisphere winter. Ask: **What effect does the distance from the sun have on Earth's temperature?** *(The distance from the sun has little noticeable effect on Earth's temperature.)* **learning modality: visual**

TRY THIS

Skills Focus predicting
Materials *2 pushpins, white paper, corrugated cardboard, ruler, 30-cm string, pencil*
Time 15 minutes
Tips Provide students with pieces of cardboard the same size as a sheet of paper. Remind students to keep the string taut when drawing their lines.
Expected Outcome Students should predict that moving the pushpins closer together makes the ellipse more round. If they used only one pushpin, they would draw a circle.
Extend Challenge students to predict the shape of ellipses formed with pushpins 2.5 cm and 7.5 cm apart. Encourage them to test their predictions. **learning modality: kinesthetic**

Media and Technology

Concept Videotape Library
Grade 6, Tape 4 "For the Love of Astronomy"

Answers to Self-Assessment

Checkpoint

Jupiter's four moons revolve around the planet. Venus goes through phases similar to those of Earth's moon.

Ongoing Assessment

Writing Have students write a paragraph explaining in their own words the contributions made to the heliocentric model by Copernicus, Galileo, Kepler, and Newton.

Inertia and Gravity

Using the Visuals: Figure 5

As students examine the figure, have them trace the path the planet would take if the sun's gravity disappeared. *(The planet would continue to move in a straight path in the direction it was going when the gravity disappeared.)* **learning modality: visual**

More to Discover

Addressing Naive Conceptions

Explain to students that it is difficult to accurately represent the sizes and distances of objects in the solar system on a diagram such as Figure 6. If the sun and the planets were drawn to the same scale as the distances on the diagram, the sun would be a tiny dot about 0.10 mm in diameter and the planets would all be microscopic. On the other hand, if the distances were drawn to the same scale as the sizes of the planets, the diagram would have to be about 1.0 km wide! **learning modality: visual**

Real-Life Learning

In 1982, all of the planets were within 95° of each other as viewed from the sun. This alignment caused some sensationalist newspapers and books to predict earthquakes and global disasters. Assign students to groups of four. Have each group develop an explanation of why this kind of planetary alignment could never cause any noticeable effects on Earth. *(Gravity from the planets is far too weak.)* **cooperative learning**

Building Inquiry Skills: Graphing

To compare the distances between the planets and the sun, students can make a bar graph using the data in Figure 6. The x-axis should show the names of the planets and the y-axis the distance from the sun. Help students choose the intervals for the y-axis. They may want to have 1 cm equal 500 million km. **learning modality: logical/mathematical**

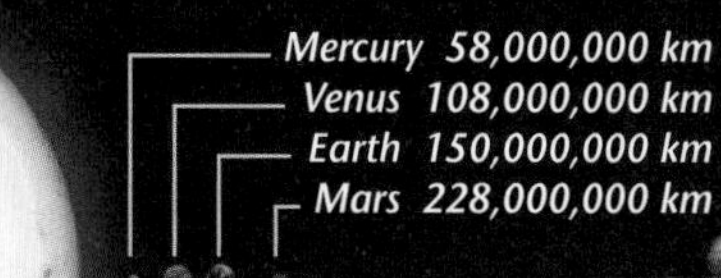

objects toward one another. The strength of gravity depends on the masses of the objects and the distance between them.

Newton figured out that Earth keeps pulling the moon toward it with gravity. At the same time, the moon keeps moving ahead because of its inertia. Earth curves away as the moon falls toward it, so the moon winds up in orbit around Earth.

In the same way, the planets are in orbit around the sun because the sun's gravity pulls on them while their inertia keeps them moving ahead. Therefore, the planets keep moving around the sun and end up in orbit.

Figure 5 If there were no force of gravity, inertia would make a planet travel in a straight line. But because gravity pulls the planet toward the sun, the planet actually travels in an elliptical orbit around the sun. *Interpreting Diagrams What would happen if a planet had no inertia?*

Background

Facts and Figures The planets of our solar system have been studied by spacecraft with one exception—Pluto. In 1991, employees of the Jet Propulsion Laboratory met with stamp collectors to view a new series of stamps showing planets and the spacecraft that had explored them. The stamp depicting Pluto said "Not Yet Explored." Challenged by this, JPL employees decided to develop a spacecraft to explore Pluto.

Because of this decision, NASA is now planning a robotic reconnaissance mission to Pluto and its moon Charon called the *Pluto-Kuiper Express.* The plan calls for two vehicles that will be launched around 2001 and fly past Pluto around 2010. If the mission to Pluto is successful, the spacecraft may continue beyond Pluto to the Kuiper Belt of minor planets, called *ice dwarfs.*

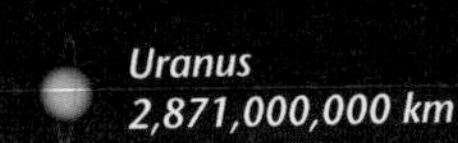

Figure 6 This illustration shows the average distances of the planets from the sun. The sizes of the planets and the sun are not to scale.

More to Discover

Since Newton's time, our knowledge about the solar system has increased dramatically. Newton knew of the same six planets the ancient Greeks had known—Mercury, Venus, Earth, Mars, Jupiter, and Saturn. Now astronomers know three more planets—Uranus, Neptune, and Pluto. Astronomers have also identified many other objects in the solar system, such as comets and asteroids, that you will learn about later in this chapter.

Galileo and later astronomers used telescopes on Earth to observe the solar system. Astronomers still use telescopes on Earth, but they have also made close-up observations of the planets from space probes sent far into the solar system. Our understanding of the solar system continues to change every day. Who knows what new discoveries will be made in your lifetime!

Section 1 Review

1. How is Copernicus's description of the system of planets different from Ptolemy's description?
2. How did Galileo's observations of Jupiter's moons help to show that the geocentric explanation is incorrect?
3. What shape are the orbits of the planets? How was the discovery of this orbit shape made?
4. What two factors act together to keep the planets in orbit around the sun?
5. **Thinking Critically Applying Concepts** People usually say that the sun rises in the east, moves across the sky, and sets in the west. Is this description literally correct? Explain.

CHAPTER PROJECT

Check Your Progress

Begin by making a table that shows the distances of the planets from the sun. To help visualize the solar system, you can reduce all the distances by the same amount: for example, divide all distances by 100,000 or 1,000,000. You can use the resulting smaller numbers to design a scale model of the solar system. Record your calculations on your data sheet. Now choose a different scale and repeat your calculations. Which scale makes it easier to see the relative distances between the planets and the sun?

Program Resources

- **Unit 6 Resources** 19-1 Review and Reinforce; 19-1 Enrich

Answers to Self-Assessment

Caption Question

Figure 5 The planet would be pulled into the sun.

3 Assess

Section 1 Review Answers

1. Ptolemy thought that Earth was in the center of the system of planets. The other planets, the moon, and the sun all revolve around Earth. Copernicus thought that the sun was in the middle of Earth's orbit, and that the other planets revolved around the sun in circular orbits.
2. Galileo's observations of moons revolving around Jupiter showed that not everything in the sky revolved around Earth.
3. The planets' orbits are elliptical. Kepler analyzed Brahe's observations about the motion of Mars and found that the data matched an elliptical orbit.
4. Gravity and inertia act together to keep the planets in orbit.
5. No. Earth is rotating from west to east. This causes the sun to appear to move across the sky in the opposite direction.

CHAPTER PROJECT

Check Your Progress

If students completed the Building Inquiry Skills activity on page 674, they can use that information here. They can also refer to the Addressing Naive Conceptions strategy on page 674. Suggest that students use lined paper or graph paper to keep their calculations neat and easy to follow. If students are having difficulty finding a good scale, suggest that they try 1: 10,000,000.

Performance Assessment

Organizing Information Have students create concept maps that illustrate the relationships among the following: Kepler, Ptolemy, Newton, Galileo, heliocentric, elliptical orbit geocentric, inertia, and gravity.

The Sun

Objectives

After completing the lesson, students will be able to

- describe how the sun produces energy;
- list and describe the layers of the sun's atmosphere;
- identify features of the sun's surface.

Key Terms nuclear fusion, core, photosphere, chromosphere, corona, solar wind, sunspot, prominence, solar flare

1 Engage/Explore

Activating Prior Knowledge

Invite students who have gotten sunburned to tell about their experiences. Encourage all students to imagine going outside on a clear, hot day and feeling the warmth of the sun. Then ask: **What do we receive from the sun?** *(Samples: Light, heat)*

DISCOVER ACTIVITY

Skills Focus observing
Materials *binoculars, ring stand, ruler, thin cardboard, scissors, masking tape, white paper*
Time 15 minutes
Tips If binoculars are not available, make a pinhole in a sheet of cardboard and project the sun's image through the hole onto the white paper. (If the pinhole is made very small, sometimes larger sunspots will be visible.) CAUTION: *Students must never look directly at the sun.* A small telescope can also be used to project the image. CAUTION: *The image of the sun focused to a point by a small telescope can cause burns and ignite paper.*
Think It Over Students should see a large bright circle. They may also see and draw sunspots.

The Sun

DISCOVER ACTIVITY

How Can You Safely Observe the Sun?

1. Clamp a pair of binoculars to a ring stand.
2. Cut a hole in a 20-cm by 28-cm sheet of thin cardboard so that it will fit over the binoculars, as shown in the photo. The cardboard should cover one lens, but allow light through the other lens. Tape the cardboard on securely. **CAUTION:** *Never look directly at the sun. You will hurt your eyes if you do.*
3. Use the binoculars to project an image of the sun onto a sheet of white paper. The cardboard will shade the paper. Change the focus and move the paper back and forth until you get a sharp image.

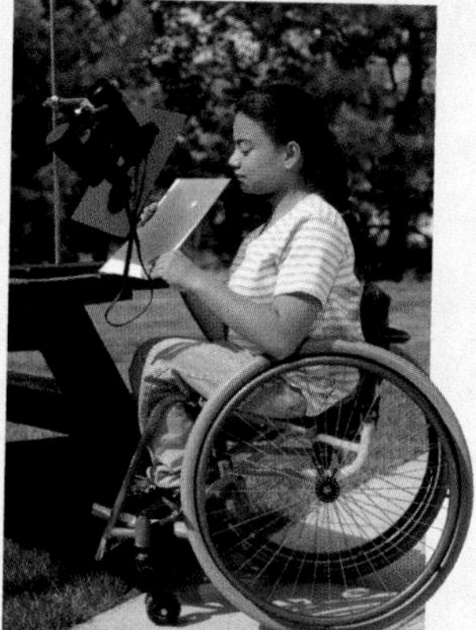

Think It Over

Observing Draw what you see on the paper. What do you see on the surface of the sun?

GUIDE FOR READING

- How does the sun get its energy?
- What are the layers of the sun's atmosphere?
- What are some features of the sun's surface?

Reading Tip As you read, write a sentence defining each boldfaced term in your own words.

The sun's gravity is by far the most powerful force in the solar system—strong enough to hold all of the planets and comets in orbit! The sun's gravity is so strong because the sun's mass is very large. In fact, 99.8 percent of the mass of the solar system is in the sun.

Like Earth, the sun has an interior and an atmosphere. Unlike Earth, however, the sun does not have a solid surface. The sun is a ball of glowing gas. About three fourths of the sun's mass is hydrogen, one fourth is helium, and very small amounts are other chemical elements.

The Sun's Interior

The interior of the sun is like a giant furnace. Like furnaces in houses, the sun produces energy. But the sun does not get its energy from burning fuels such as oil. **Instead, the sun's energy comes from nuclear fusion.** In the process of **nuclear fusion,** hydrogen atoms join together to form helium. Nuclear fusion occurs only under conditions of extremely high temperature and pressure. The temperature inside the sun's **core,** or center, reaches about 15 million degrees Celsius, high enough for nuclear fusion to occur.

READING STRATEGIES

Reading Tip Some sentences that students may write about boldfaced terms may include, "The core is the inner part of the sun." and "The photosphere is the layer of the sun that makes light." After students have written their sentences, have them read aloud their definitions to partners. Encourage partners to discuss their definitions.

Program Resources

- **Unit 6 Resources** 19-2 Lesson Plan; 19-2 Section Summary
- **Guided Reading and Study Workbook** Section 19-2
- **Laboratory Manual,** 19, "Measuring the Diameter of the Sun"

The total mass of the helium produced by nuclear fusion is slightly less than the total mass of the hydrogen that goes into it. The change in mass occurs because some of the matter is converted into energy, including light and heat. The light and heat gradually move from the core of the sun to its atmosphere and escape into space. Some of this light and heat reach Earth, becoming Earth's main source of energy.

There is enough hydrogen fuel in the core of the sun to last for a total of 10 billion years. The sun is now only about 5 billion years old, so you don't have to worry about the sun "burning out" any time soon!

☑ *Checkpoint* *Where in the sun does nuclear fusion occur?*

The Sun's Atmosphere

The sun's atmosphere has three layers: the photosphere, the chromosphere, and the corona. There are no boundaries between the layers of the sun.

The Photosphere The inner layer of the sun's atmosphere is called the **photosphere** (FOH tuh sfeer). The Greek word *photo* means "light," so *photosphere* means the sphere that makes light. When you look at an image or photograph of the sun, you are looking at the photosphere.

The Chromosphere During a total solar eclipse, the moon blocks light from the photosphere. The photosphere no longer provides the glare that keeps you from seeing the sun's faint, outer layers. At the beginning and end of a total eclipse, you can see a reddish glow just around the photosphere. This glow comes from the middle layer of the sun's atmosphere, the **chromosphere.** The Greek word *chromo* means "color," so the chromosphere is the "color sphere."

The Corona In the middle of a total solar eclipse, the moon also blocks light from the chromosphere. At these times an even fainter layer of the sun becomes visible, as you can see in Figure 7. This outer layer, which looks like a white halo around the sun, is called the **corona,** which means "crown" in Latin. From Earth's surface, the corona is only visible during eclipses or from special telescopes. But astronomers can use telescopes in space to observe the corona all the time and to study how it changes.

Figure 7 During a total solar eclipse, you can see light from the corona, the outer layer of the sun's atmosphere. ***Inferring*** *Why is it easiest to photograph the sun's outer layers during a solar eclipse?*

2 Facilitate

The Sun's Interior

Demonstration

Materials *2 large glass jars with lids, 2 plastic thermometers, black plastic, waterproof glue (hot glue works well)*
Time 45 minutes

Glue black plastic on one-half of the *inside* of the jar. Glue the plastic thermometer to the inside of the jar next to the black plastic so it can be read without opening the jar. Fill the jars with cold water, leaving 1.0 cm for expansion, and cap tightly. Take the class outside and place one jar in a shady spot and the other in direct sun propped up so that sunlight fully illuminates the inside of the jar. Read the temperature of each jar every five minutes for thirty minutes. Back in the classroom, have students graph the temperature versus time for each container. Ask: **What happened to the temperature of the jars?** *(Shady jar may have gone up or down slightly; sunny jar rose several degrees.)* **What caused the temperature to rise?** *(Energy from the sun)* **Where did this energy come from?** *(Nuclear fusion).* **learning modality: kinesthetic**

The Sun's Atmosphere

Including All Students

Show students color photos of the sun at various stages of an eclipse. Encourage students to point out the photosphere, corona, and chromosphere. **learning modality: visual**

Media and Technology

Concept Videotape Library
Grade 6, Tape 4 "Wired to the Sun"

Answers to Self-Assessment

Caption Question

Figure 7 During a solar eclipse, the sun's bright inner layers are blocked, making the outer layers easier to see.

☑ *Checkpoint*

Nuclear fusion occurs in the sun's core.

Ongoing Assessment

Drawing Have students diagram the sun's interior and atmosphere, then label where nuclear fusion occurs and where the greatest production of light occurs.

Features on the Sun

Including All Students

The terms used to describe the sun's features may be difficult or unfamiliar for students whose native language is not English. However, all of the terms are descriptive so students can use word skills to analyze the meaning. Have students separate the terms *sunspot* and *solar flare* into their parts. Allow students to look up the words and word parts in the dictionary. Encourage students to explain how the terms help describe the features of the sun. **limited English proficiency**

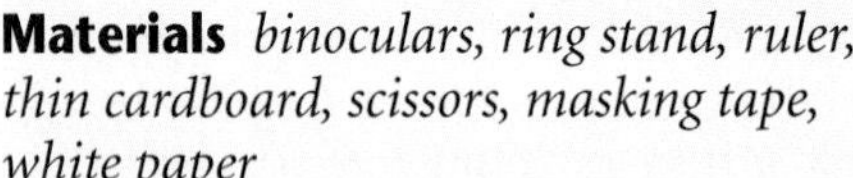

Skills Focus interpreting data

Materials *binoculars, ring stand, ruler, thin cardboard, scissors, masking tape, white paper*

Time 10 minutes per day over 10 days

Tips Warn students not to look directly at the sun because sunlight can injure their eyes. Students should identify the variables they must control to get the best data. Suggest students look for sunspots two or three times per day for ten days. Their data tables should include the number of sunspots recorded at each interval as well as the average number of sunspots per day. After the first five days, have students predict how the average number of sunspots will change over the next five days. When their observations are complete, students can draw conclusions about the accuracy of their predictions.

Extend Have students compile class results and evaluate the class average for the number of sunspots observed in a ten-day period. Invite students whose findings vary from those of other students to explain why. **learning modality: logical/mathematical**

Viewing Sunspots

You can observe changes in the number of sunspots.

1. Make a data table to record the average number of sunspots you see each day.
2. Decide on a time to look for sunspots each day.
3. View the sun in the way described in the Discover activity. **CAUTION:** *Never look directly at the sun. You will hurt your eyes if you do.*
4. Make and record your observations.

Interpreting Data How much did the average number of sunspots change from day to day?

The corona sends out a stream of electrically charged particles called **solar wind.** Normally Earth's atmosphere and magnetic field block these particles. However, near the North and South poles, the particles can enter Earth's atmosphere, where they hit gas molecules and cause them to glow. The result is rippling sheets of light in the sky called auroras.

☑ ***Checkpoint*** *During what event could you see the sun's corona?*

Features on the Sun

For hundreds of years, scientists have used telescopes to look at the sun. (To protect their eyes, they used a filter or projected the sun onto a white surface, as in the Discover activity.) The dark spots that they saw on the sun's surface became known as sunspots. The spots seemed to move across the sun's surface, which showed that the sun rotates on its axis, just as Earth does. **Features on or above the sun's surface include sunspots, prominences, and solar flares.**

Sunspots As you can see in Figure 8, sunspots look like small, dark areas on the sun's surface. But in fact, they can be as large as Earth. **Sunspots** are areas of gas on the sun that are cooler than the gases around them. Cooler gases don't give off as much light as hotter gases, which is why sunspots look darker than the rest of the photosphere.

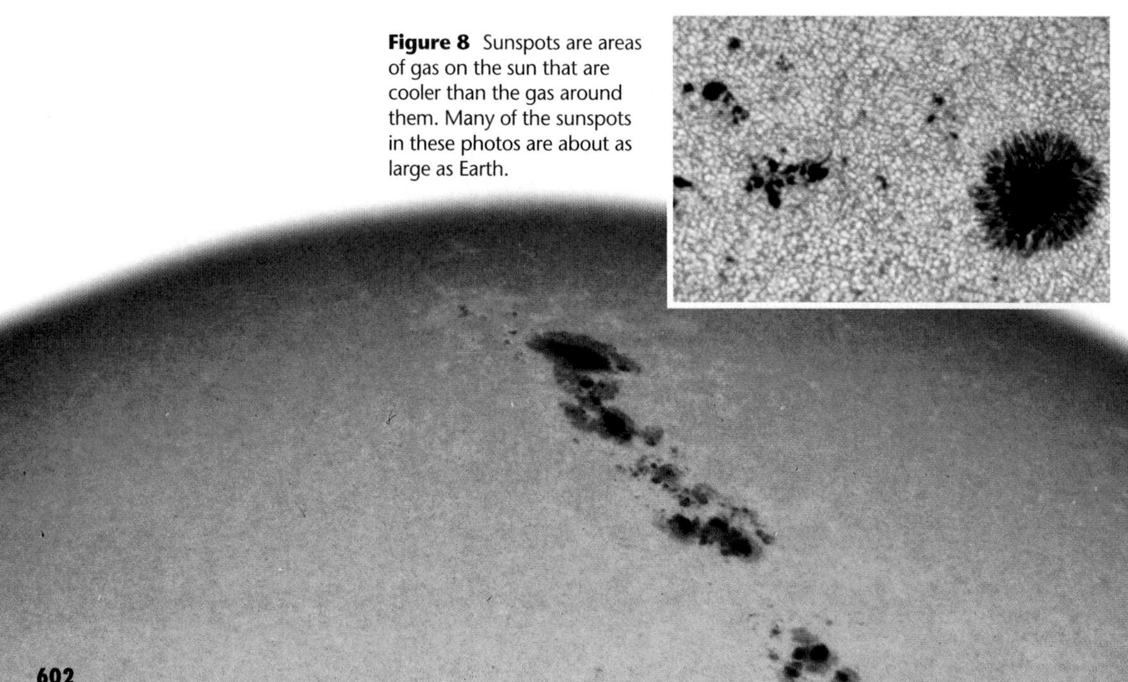

Figure 8 Sunspots are areas of gas on the sun that are cooler than the gas around them. Many of the sunspots in these photos are about as large as Earth.

602

Background

Facts and Figures Some scientists think that the sunspot cycle influences weather on Earth. Among the evidence for this is the so-called Little Ice Age, which took place from about 1550 until 1850. During this time, most parts of the world experienced cooler and harsher weather.

The Little Ice Age has been associated with a period of low sunspot activity between 1645 and 1715. This period is called the Maunder minimum after the English astronomer who described it. Sunspots were first detected about 1600, but there are few recorded sightings during the Maunder minimum. Sunspots sightings resumed after 1715.

There is evidence that such times of low sunspot activity occur about every 500 years. Perhaps another Little Ice Age will begin in 2050.

The number of sunspots on the sun varies over a period of 10 or 11 years. Some scientists have hypothesized that short-term changes in climate on Earth may be related to sunspot cycles. Satellites have recently collected data that show that the amount of energy the sun produces changes slightly from year to year. Some scientists think that these increases and decreases, which may be linked to the number of sunspots, may cause changes in Earth's temperature. Scientists need to make more observations in order to test this hypothesis.

EXPLORING the Sun

The diameter of the sun (not including the chromosphere and the corona) is 1.4 million kilometers.

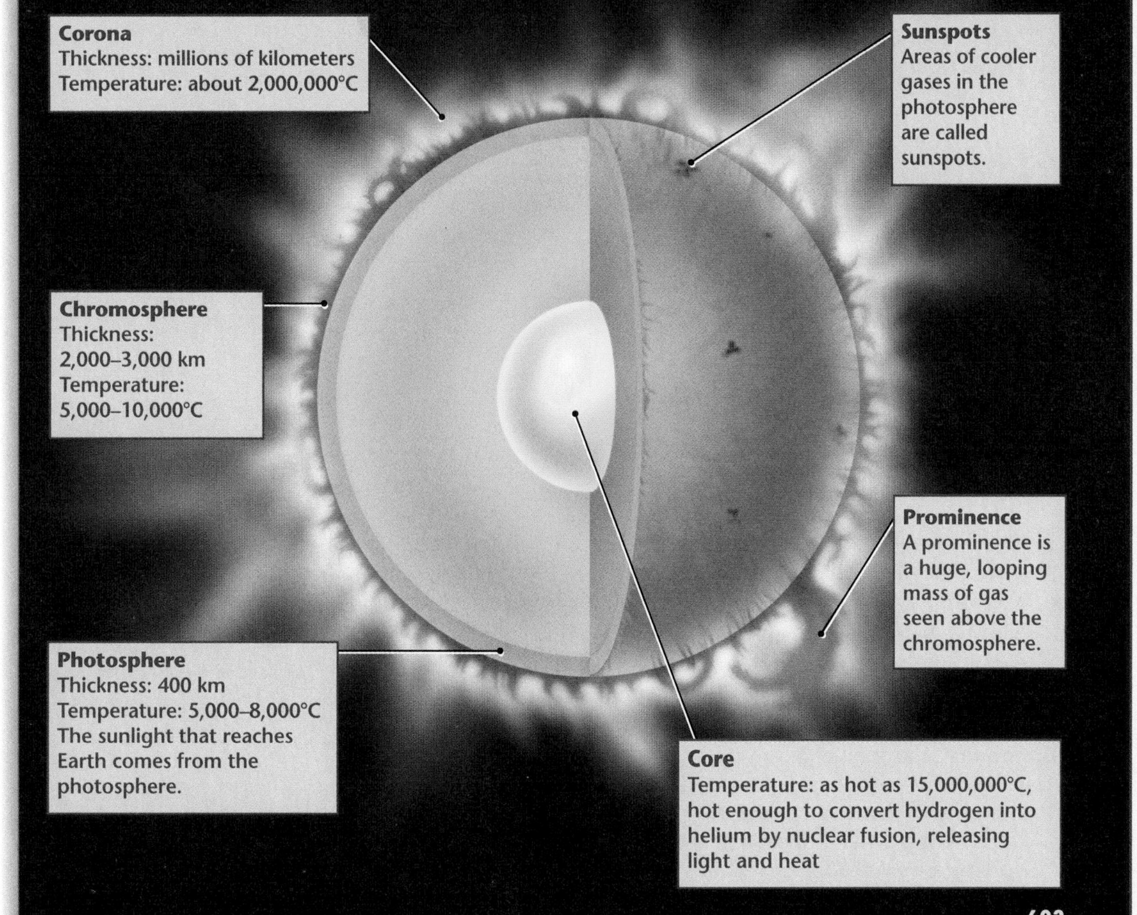

Corona
Thickness: millions of kilometers
Temperature: about 2,000,000°C

Sunspots
Areas of cooler gases in the photosphere are called sunspots.

Chromosphere
Thickness: 2,000–3,000 km
Temperature: 5,000–10,000°C

Prominence
A prominence is a huge, looping mass of gas seen above the chromosphere.

Photosphere
Thickness: 400 km
Temperature: 5,000–8,000°C
The sunlight that reaches Earth comes from the photosphere.

Core
Temperature: as hot as 15,000,000°C, hot enough to convert hydrogen into helium by nuclear fusion, releasing light and heat

603

EXPLORING the Sun

Have students look up the meanings of the word *corona* and the prefixes *chromo-* and *photo-*. Ask: **Why is the corona called a corona?** *(It surrounds the sun like a crown.)* **Why is the core called a core?** *(Because it's at the center)* **What is the source of light that reaches Earth from the sun?** *(the photosphere)* **What is the source of energy for the light and heat produced by the sun?** *(nuclear fusion)* Explain to students that the chromosphere lies just above the photosphere and has an intense red color when seen during an eclipse.

Extend Challenge students to explain why the surface of the sun is much cooler than the center. **learning modality: visual**

Media and Technology

Transparencies "Exploring the Sun," Transparency 76

Concept Videotape Library Grade 6, Tape 3 "Sunny Days"

Program Resources

◆ **Unit 6 Resources** 19-2 Review and Reinforce; 19-2 Enrich

Answers to Self-Assessment

Checkpoint

You can see the sun's corona during an eclipse.

Ongoing Assessment

Drawing Have students draw and label a diagram of the surface of the sun. Diagrams should include a sunspot, a flare, and a prominence. Have students include an explanation of what each solar feature is.

3 Assess

Section 2 Review Answers

1. Hydrogen fuel undergoes nuclear fusion and creates helium. Some of the energy from this process is released as light and heat.
2. photosphere, chromosphere, and corona
3. The solar wind is a stream of electrically charged particles sent out into space from the corona.
4. Sunspots are areas of gases on the sun that are cooler than the gases around them. Prominences are reddish loops of gas that link different parts of sunspot regions. Solar flares are explosions that occur when such loops suddenly connect.
5. Sunspots are made up of gases that are cooler than the gases around them. Because of this, they give off less light and thus appear darker.
6. The number of sunspots varies over a 10- to 11-year cycle.
7. A prominence is a loop of gas that links different parts of sunspot regions. A solar flare is an explosion that results when several prominences connect.

Science at Home

Suggest that students prepare a photo-essay or sketchbook collection of the items identified by their family. Some places to look for sun imagery include watches and clocks, artwork, product labels, and book illustrations.

Performance Assessment

Writing Have students create a travel brochure for an imaginary vacation trip to the sun. The brochure should include sites to visit, a map, and travel tips.

Students can save their brochures in their portfolios.

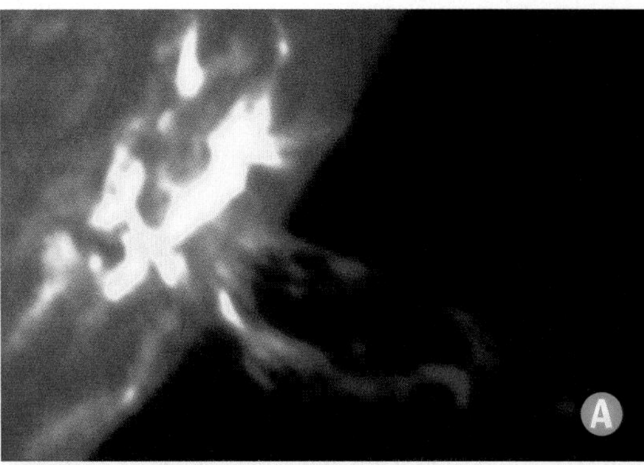

Figure 9 **A.** Prominences are huge loops of gas that connect different parts of sunspot regions. **B.** Solar flares on the sun release large amounts of energy. *Relating Cause and Effect How can solar flares affect communications on Earth?*

Prominences Sunspots usually occur in pairs or groups. Reddish loops of gas called **prominences** link different parts of sunspot regions. When a group of sunspots is near the edge of the sun as seen from Earth, these loops can stick out over the edge of the sun. If an eclipse hides the sun's photosphere, astronomers are able to see these loops. Prominences are about the same temperature as the sun's chromosphere, about 10,000 degrees Celsius.

Solar Flares Sometimes the loops in sunspot regions suddenly connect, releasing large amounts of energy. The energy heats gas on the sun to millions of degrees Celsius, causing the hydrogen gas to explode out into space. These explosions are known as **solar flares.**

Solar flares can greatly increase the solar wind from the corona, resulting in an increase in the number of particles reaching Earth's atmosphere. These solar wind particles can affect Earth's upper atmosphere, causing magnetic storms. Magnetic storms sometimes disrupt radio, telephone, and television signals. Magnetic storms can also cause electrical power problems for homes and businesses.

Section 2 Review

1. How is energy produced in the sun's core?
2. Name the layers of the sun's atmosphere.
3. What is the solar wind?
4. Describe three features found on or above the surface of the sun.
5. Why do sunspots look darker than the rest of the sun's photosphere?
6. How does the number of sunspots change over time?
7. **Thinking Critically Comparing and Contrasting** What is the difference between a prominence and a solar flare?

Science at Home

Solar Symbols As the source of heat and light, the sun is an important symbol in many cultures. With family members, look around your home and neighborhood for illustrations of the sun on signs, flags, clothing, and in artwork. Which parts of the sun's atmosphere do the illustrations show? Describe the layers of the sun's atmosphere to your family.

Background

History of Science In 1859, the English astronomer Richard C. Carrington became the first person to observe a solar flare. Carrington was studying a large sunspot when two brilliant ribbons of light crossed the sunspot. This flare only lasted about five minutes, but was followed by northern lights over much of Europe and as far south as Honolulu, as well as the failure of telegraph systems throughout the world.

Answers to Self-Assessment

Caption Question

Figure 9 Solar flares increase the solar wind in the corona, which can cause magnetic storms in Earth's upper atmosphere. These storms often disrupt radio, telephone, and television signals.

You and Your Environment

STORMY SUNSPOTS

Real-World Lab

Problem

How are magnetic storms on Earth related to sunspot activity?

Skills Focus

graphing, interpreting data

Materials

graph paper   pencil   straightedge

Procedure

1. Use the data in the table to make a line graph of sunspot activity between 1967 and 1997.
2. On the graph, label the *x*-axis "Year." Use a scale with 2-year intervals, from 1967 to 1997.
3. Label the *y*-axis "Sunspot Number." Use a scale of 0 through 160 in intervals of 10.
4. Graph a point for the Sunspot Number for each year.
5. Complete your graph by drawing lines to connect the points.

Sunspots

Year	Sunspot Number	Year	Sunspot Number
1967	93.8	1983	66.6
1969	105.0	1985	17.9
1971	66.6	1987	29.4
1973	38.0	1989	157.6
1975	15.5	1991	145.7
1977	27.5	1993	54.6
1979	155.4	1995	17.5
1981	140.4	1997	23.4

Analyze and Conclude

1. Based on your graph, which years had the highest Sunspot Numbers? The lowest Sunspot Numbers?
2. How often does the cycle of maximum and minimum activity repeat?
3. When was the most recent maximum sunspot activity? The most recent minimum sunspot activity?
4. Compare your sunspot graph with the magnetic storms graph. What relationship can you infer between periods of high sunspot activity and magnetic storms? Explain.
5. **Apply** During which years do you think electrical disturbances on Earth were most common?

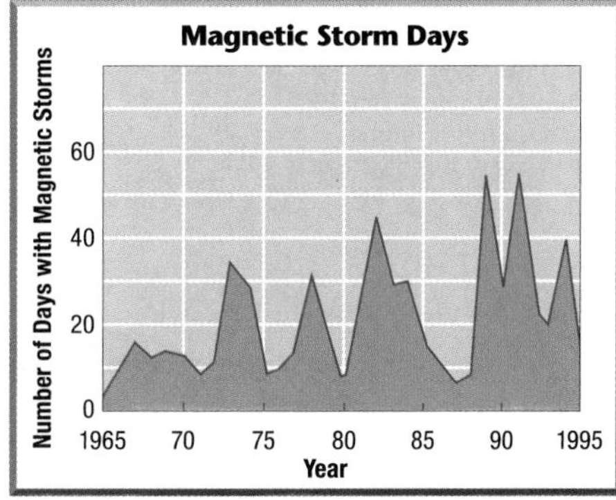

More to Explore

Using the pattern of sunspot activity you found, predict the number of peaks you would expect in the next 30 years. Around which years would you expect the peaks to occur?

Program Resources

◆ **Unit 6 Resources** Chapter 19 Real-World Lab

Media and Technology

 **Lab Activity Videotapes** Grade 6, Tape 4

5. Electrical disturbances on Earth were probably most common from 1967–1969, 1979–1981, and 1989–1991.

Extending the Inquiry

More to Explore Students add the time it takes to get a repeat to the year of the last maximum (1991) With a repeat of 10–11 years, you expect to get peaks around 2001–2002, 2012–2013 and 2023–2024.

Real-World Lab

You and Your Environment

Stormy Sunspots

Preparing for Inquiry

Key Concept Sunspot activity and magnetic storms on Earth can be related by analyzing sunspot activity over time.

Skills Objective Students will be able to
- ◆ make a graph of sunspot number versus year;
- ◆ compare a graph of sunspot activity to a graph of number of magnetic storms on Earth during the same time period.

Time 30 minutes

Advance Planning Distribute graph paper and straightedges to the students.

Guiding Inquiry

Introducing the Procedure

- ◆ "Sunspot number" is a technical term that represents both the number of sunspot groups and the number of individual sunspots.
- ◆ Tell students that a magnetic storm is defined as a brief disturbance in Earth's magnetic field.

Troubleshooting the Experiment

- ◆ Do not allow students to make a bar graph.

Expected Outcome

- ◆ Students will draw a graph that shows three peaks and three valleys in sunspot activity from 1967–1997.
- ◆ The sunspot activity valleys seem to coincide with valleys in the magnetic storm days graph.

Analyze and Conclude

1. Highest: 1967–1969, 1979–1981 and 1989–1991; Lowest: 1975–1977, 1985–1987 and 1995–1997
2. Every 10–12 years
3. Maximum: 1989; Minimum: 1995
4. The three sunspot activity valleys (1975, 1985, and 1995) occur at the same time as valleys in magnetic storm days. The three sunspot activity peaks (1970, 1980, and 1990) seem to precede by one or two years a magnetic storm peak (1973, 1982, and 1992).

SECTION 3 The Inner Planets

Objectives

After completing the lesson, students will be able to

- identify the main characteristics of the inner planets.

Key Terms terrestrial planet, retrograde motion, greenhouse effect

1 Engage/Explore

Activating Prior Knowledge

Show students a colored drawing of the solar system with the names of the planets covered. Ask: **Which planet is Earth?** *(The third planet from the sun)* Ask students to explain why they guessed that Earth was the third planet. *(Sample: The planet was colored blue, and Earth has water which makes it look blue from space.)* Then invite students to examine the map and point out other planets they think are most like Earth. *(Students should point out the inner planets.)*

DISCOVER

Skills Focus observing
Materials *compass, ruler*
Time 10 minutes
Tips Stress that students should make the small lines dark enough to be seen from a distance. To keep their drawings straight, suggest that they label them as *Original* and *Copied from a Distance.*
Think It Over The partner may see and draw patterns and lines that are not in the original drawing. The view from across the room is not an accurate representation of what the original drawing looked like.

SECTION 3 The Inner Planets

DISCOVER ACTIVITY

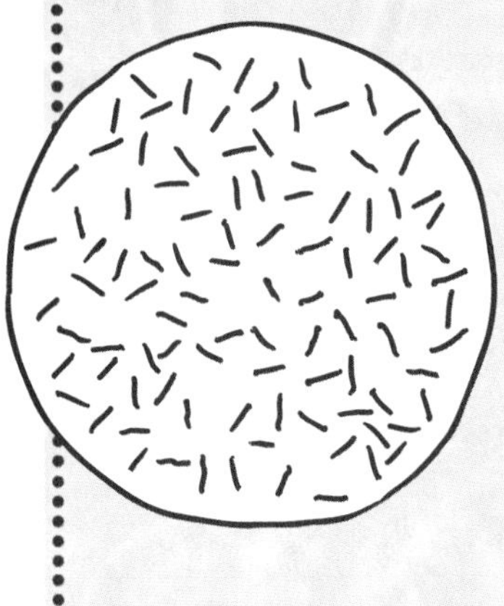

How Does Mars Look From Earth?

1. Work in pairs. On a sheet of paper, draw a circle 20 cm across to represent Mars. Draw about 100 small lines, each about 1 cm long, at random places inside the circle.
2. Have your partner look at your drawing of Mars from the other side of the room. Your partner should draw what he or she sees.
3. Compare your original drawing with what your partner drew. Then look at your own drawing from across the room.

Think It Over

Observing Did your partner draw any connecting lines that were not actually on your drawing? What can you conclude about the accuracy of descriptions of other planets as observed from Earth?

GUIDE FOR READING

- What are the main characteristics of the inner planets?

Reading Tip As you read about each planet, write down the similarities and differences between that planet and Earth.

Where could you find a planet whose surface is hot enough to melt lead? How about a planet whose atmosphere has almost entirely leaked away? And how about a planet with volcanoes higher than any on Earth? Finally, what about a planet with oceans of water brimming with fish and other life? These are descriptions of the four planets closest to the sun, known as the inner planets

Earth and the other three inner planets—Mercury, Venus, and Mars—are more similar to each other than they are to the five outer planets. **The four inner planets are small and have rocky surfaces.** These planets are often called the **terrestrial planets,** from the Latin word *terra,* which means "Earth." Figure 10 gives a summary of information about the inner planets.

Earth

Our planet's atmosphere extends more than 100 kilometers above Earth's surface. The oxygen you need to live makes up about 20 percent of the gases in Earth's atmosphere. Almost all the rest is nitrogen gas, with small amounts of argon and other gases. Earth's atmosphere also contains water vapor and clouds of water droplets. From space, astronauts can usually see past the clouds to Earth's surface.

Most of Earth, about 70 percent, is covered with water. Perhaps the planet should be named "Water" instead of "Earth"! No other planet in our solar system has oceans like Earth's.

READING STRATEGIES

Reading Tip Suggest that students use Venn diagrams to compare and contrast each inner planet and Earth. Demonstrate how to use a Venn diagram to compare and contrast two subjects. First, have volunteers read aloud the information about Earth and Mercury in the section. Then draw a Venn diagram on the chalkboard. As students name similarities between Mercury and Earth, such as small size and rocky surface, write these in the overlapping portion of the diagram. Then have students name differences, such as Mercury's lack of moon, and record these in the outer portions of the circles. Instruct students to complete additional Venn diagrams for the remaining planets.

Study and Comprehension Have students work in groups. Each member of the group can read the material on a planet, then teach the rest of the group about that planet.

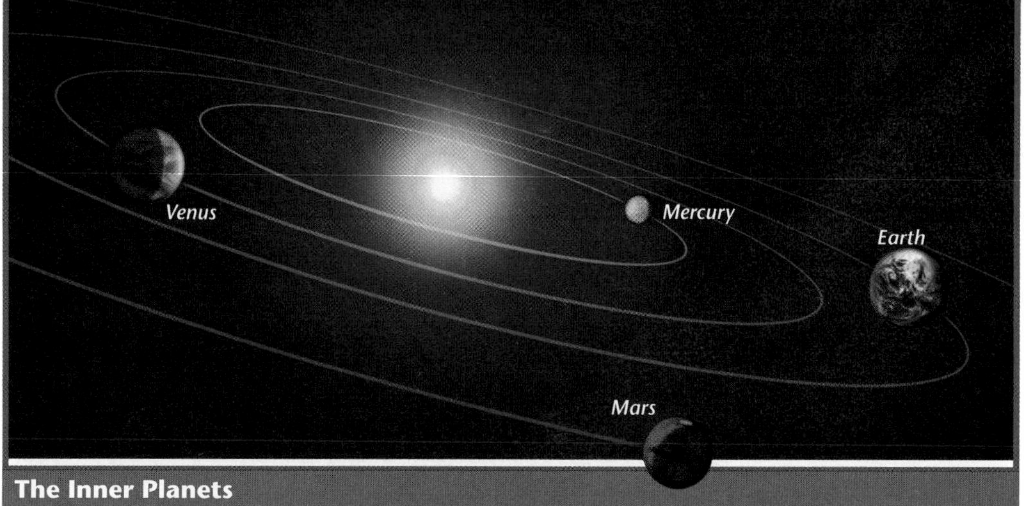

The Inner Planets

Planet	Diameter (kilometers)	Period of Rotation (Earth days)	Average Distance From the Sun (kilometers)	Period of Revolution (Earth years)	Number of Moons
Mercury	4,878	59	58,000,000	0.24	0
Venus	12,104	243	108,000,000	0.62	0
Earth	12,756	1	150,000,000	1	1
Mars	6,794	1.03	228,000,000	1.9	2

Figure 10 The inner planets take up only a small part of the solar system. The diameter of the entire solar system is more than 25 times the diameter of Mars's orbit.

INTEGRATING EARTH SCIENCE Earth has three main layers—the crust, the mantle, and the core. The crust includes the solid rocky surface. Under the crust is the mantle, a layer of hot molten rock. When volcanoes erupt, this hot material rises through the crust and flows out onto the surface. Earth has a dense inner core made up mainly of iron and nickel. The outer core is liquid, but the inner core is probably solid.

Scientists have been studying Earth for many years. They use what they know about Earth to make inferences about the other planets. For example, when astronomers find volcanoes on other planets, they infer that these planets have or once had hot material inside them. As we continue to learn more about our own planet, scientists will be able to apply that new knowledge to the study of the other planets.

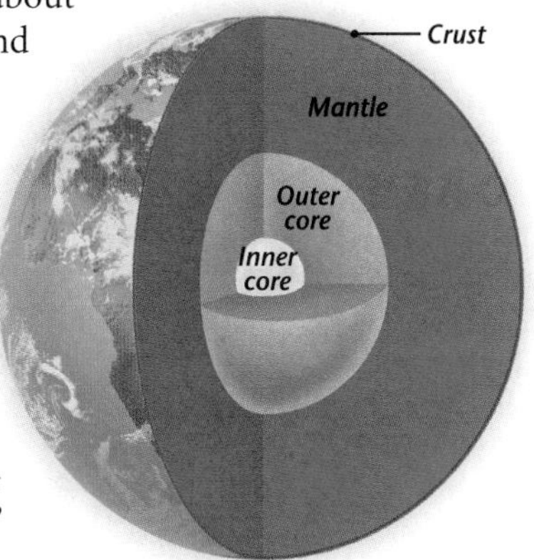

Figure 11 Earth has a solid, rocky surface. *Interpreting Diagrams What are Earth's three main layers?*

2 Facilitate

Earth

Building Inquiry Skills: Interpreting Data

To help students interpret the data in Figure 10, ask: **Which planets are most similar in size?** *(Venus and Earth)* Then ask: **How many times does Mercury revolve around the sun during one Earth year?** *(About 4)* Challenge students to make generalizations about a planet's average distance from the sun and its period of revolution. *(The farther from the sun, the longer it takes to complete one period of revolution.)* **learning modality: logical/mathematical**

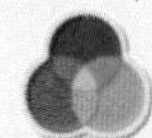

Integrating Earth Science

Materials *hard-boiled egg, blunt kitchen knife, paper towel*
Time 10 minutes
Tips Invite students to use hard-boiled eggs to model the layers of Earth. Have them place the eggs on paper towels, then use the knives to slice the shelled eggs crosswise. Ask students to identify what each part of the egg represents. *(Shell—crust; white—mantle; yolk—core)* Ask: **How is the model different from Earth?** *(Earth's core is liquid, but the egg yolk is solid.)* Students should take care when using kitchen knives. Make sure students do not eat the eggs. They should wash their hands after disposing of the eggs. **learning modality: kinesthetic**

Program Resources

- **Unit 6 Resources** 19-3 Lesson Plan; 19-3 Section Summary
- **Guided Reading and Study Workbook** Section 19-3

Answers to Self-Assessment

Caption Question
Figure 11 crust, mantle, and core

Ongoing Assessment

Drawing Have students draw a cross-section of Earth and its atmosphere and label the crust, mantle, outer core, inner core, and atmosphere.

Students can save their drawings in their portfolios.

Mercury

Building Inquiry Skills: Observing

ACTIVITY

Help students understand why scientists have difficulty making observations of Mercury. Pair students. Have one student hold a coin about 10 cm in front of a dim desk lamp. The head side of the coin should face away from the bulb. Challenge the other student to determine the date on the coin. Caution the student not to look directly at the light bulb. Ask: **What do you observe about the coin?** *(The brightness of the bulb makes it impossible to see the date.)* Have students explain why this is similar to the problems encountered by scientists who want to observe Mercury's surface features. *(The brightness of the sun makes it hard to see the features of Mercury's surface.)* **learning modality: kinesthetic**

Using the Visuals: Figure 12

Direct students to look at the picture of the moon on page 661. Point out that Mercury and the moon look very similar. Have students describe the features shared by the moon and Mercury. *(Heavily cratered surface, little atmosphere, no liquid water, little erosion)* Ask: **What difference do you see between the surface of the moon and that of Mercury?** *(Mercury's surface has no maria.)* **learning modality: verbal**

Figure 12 This photo of Mercury and the closeup view of some of its craters (inset) were taken by the *Mariner 10* space probe.

Mercury

The planet closest to the sun is Mercury. Mercury is not much larger than Earth's moon and has no moons of its own. Astronomers have been able to infer that the interior of Mercury is made up mainly of the dense metals iron and nickel.

Exploring Mercury Because Mercury is so close to the sun, people on Earth never get a good view of Mercury. Much of the knowledge that astronomers have about Mercury's surface came from a single probe, *Mariner 10.* It flew by three times in 1974 and 1975. *Mariner 10* photographed only half of Mercury's surface, so astronomers still don't know much about what the rest of Mercury is like.

Mariner 10's photographs show that, like the moon, Mercury has many flat plains and many craters on its surface. The craters on Mercury have been named for artists, writers, and musicians, including the composers Bach and Mozart.

Mercury's Atmosphere Mercury has an extremely thin atmosphere. Apparently the gases Mercury once had were heated so much that the gas particles moved very fast. Since they were moving so fast, the gas particles escaped from Mercury's weak gravity into space. However, astronomers have detected small amounts of sodium and other gases in Mercury's atmosphere.

Mercury is a planet of extremes. It is so close to the sun that during the day, the side facing the sun reaches temperatures of 430°C. Because Mercury has almost no atmosphere, at night all the heat escapes into space. The temperature drops to –170°C. Mercury thus has a greater range of temperatures than any other planet in the solar system.

☑ *Checkpoint* *Why is it difficult for astronomers to learn about Mercury?*

Background

Facts and Figures Until the 1960s, astronomers thought that Mercury's day was the same length as its year. In 1965, observations by Doppler radar showed that Mercury rotates three times in every two Mercury years. Mercury has a very eccentric orbit—sometimes 46 million km from the sun, at other times 70 million km.

Sunrise on Mercury would look strange to someone from Earth. At some places on the planet, the sun would appear to rise, increase in size, then stop, reverse, and stop again before rising again and decreasing in size.

Venus

Whenever you see a bright object in the west after sunset, it is probably Venus. When Venus shines brightly like that, it is known as the "evening star," though of course it really isn't a star. Stars shine with their own light, while Venus shines because it is reflecting light from the sun, just as the other planets and moons do. At other times, you see Venus rise before the sun in the morning. It is then known as the "morning star." At still other times, Venus is too close to the sun in the sky for you to see it from Earth.

Venus is so similar in size to Earth that it is sometimes called Earth's twin. Astronomers also think that the density and internal structure of Venus are similar to Earth's. However, in many other ways, Venus is very different from Earth.

Venus's Rotation Venus takes about 7.5 Earth months to revolve around the sun. It takes about 8 months for Venus to rotate on its axis. Venus rotates so slowly that its "day" is longer than its "year." Oddly, Venus rotates from east to west, the opposite direction from most other planets and moons. This type of rotation is called **retrograde rotation,** from the Latin words for "moving backward." One hypothesis proposed by astronomers to explain this unusual rotation is that Venus was struck by a very large object billions of years ago. Such a collision could have caused the direction of its rotation to change.

Graphing ACTIVITY

Using data in Figure 10 on page 607, make a line graph of the average distance from the sun and period of revolution of Mercury, Venus, Earth, and Mars. Describe how the two variables are related. If you wish, add data on Jupiter, Saturn, Uranus, Neptune, and Pluto from Figure 19 on page 614.

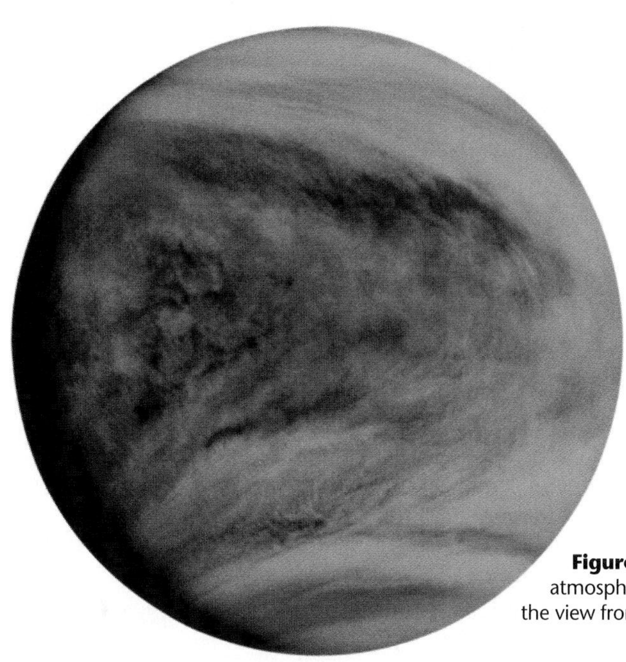

Figure 13 The thick atmosphere of Venus makes the view from space a cloudy one.

Venus

Demonstration

ACTIVITY

To help students visualize the unusual rotation of Venus, place one globe on a table to represent Earth. Spin the globe so that it turns from west to east. Ask: **How long does it take for Earth to spin once around its axis?** *(24 hours or 1 day)* Place another globe next to the first to represent Venus. Spin the globe very slowly so that it turns from east to west. Invite students to identify the differences between the rotations of Venus and Earth. *(Venus rotates from east to west, Earth from west to east. Venus is slower than Earth. On Venus, the sun "rises" in the west and "sets" in the east.)* **learning modality: visual**

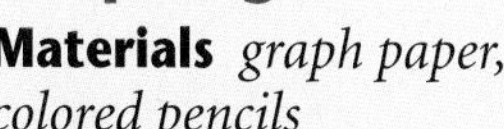

Graphing

ACTIVITY

Materials *graph paper, colored pencils*
Time 15 minutes
Tips Students should set up their graphs with the distances to the planets on the *x*-axis, and the period of revolution on the *y*-axis. Discuss the units. Suggest students use 1 cm = 10,000 km for units of distance and 1 cm = 0.01 year for time.
Expected Outcome Data should form a line with a positive slope. The inner and outer planets must be graphed separately because the same scale will not work for both.
Extend Ask students to predict the relationship between the diameter of a planet and its period of rotation, then create graphs to test their predictions.

Media and Technology

Transparencies "The Inner Planets," Transparency 77

Answers to Self-Assessment

☑ *Checkpoint*

Mercury is so close to the sun that it is difficult for astronomers on Earth to get a good view of it.

Ongoing Assessment

Writing Have students describe how sunrise on Venus differs from sunrise on Earth.

Including All Students

To help students who are still mastering English understand the origin of the term *greenhouse effect,* show them a picture of a greenhouse with plants growing inside. Explain that a greenhouse lets in sunlight and prevents convection from carrying heat away. The plants inside stay warm. Pair students who are still mastering English with native speakers, and have them each create flowcharts or sketches that compare the path of light and heat energy in a greenhouse with the path of light and heat energy on Venus. **Extend** Have students research possible environmental problems caused by changes in Earth's greenhouse effect. **limited English proficiency**

Music CONNECTION

Recordings of this work are widely available. ACTIVITY Check your school or public library for a copy. Holst was trying to musically describe the *astrological* and *mythological* characteristics of these seven planets. Encourage students to listen for *astronomical* connections. **learning modality: kinesthetic**

In Your Journal Students' responses will depend on the pieces they heard. They may suggest the use of specific instruments to give a feel or appearance of a planet. Students may describe the music with words such as *loud, soft, eerie, brash,* or *faraway.*

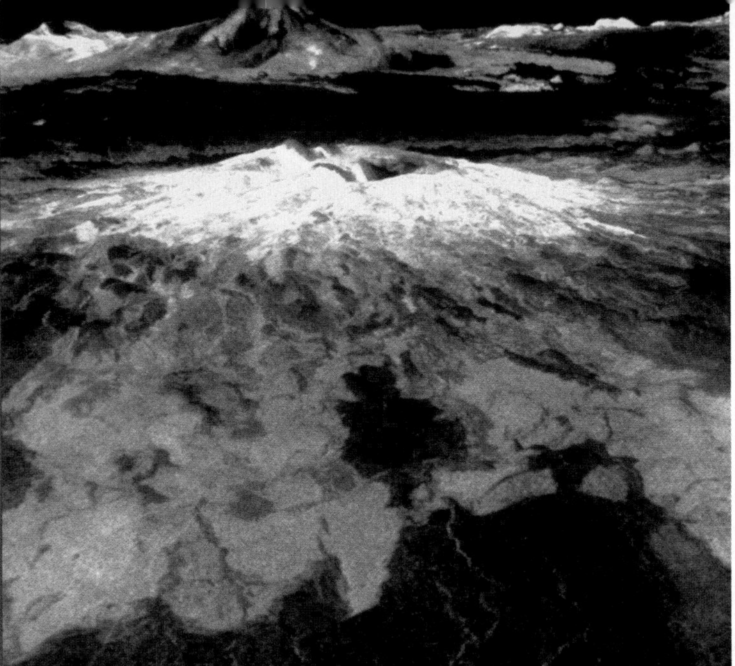

Figure 14 The *Magellan* spacecraft used radar to penetrate Venus's clouds. This three-dimensional image of a volcano on Venus was created by a computer using radar data. The height of the mountains is exaggerated to make them stand out.

Music CONNECTION

The English composer Gustav Holst, who lived from 1874 to 1934, composed a group of pieces for orchestra entitled *The Planets.* The seven pieces describe musically the planets Mars, Venus, Mercury, Jupiter, Saturn, Uranus, and Neptune.

In Your Journal

Listen to a recording of one of the pieces from *The Planets.* How did Holst use music to represent the planet? What words would you use to describe what you heard?

Venus's Atmosphere The atmosphere of Venus is so thick that every day is a cloudy one. Venus never has a sunny day. From Earth, astronomers see only a smooth cloud cover over Venus all the time.

If you could stand on the surface of Venus, you would quickly be crushed by the weight of its atmosphere. The pressure of Venus's atmosphere is 90 times greater than the pressure of Earth's atmosphere. You could not breathe on Venus because its atmosphere is mostly carbon dioxide. Also, its clouds are partly made of sulfuric acid.

Because Venus is closer to the sun than Earth, it gets more solar energy than Earth does. Ordinary light from the sun can penetrate Venus's atmosphere and hit its surface. The surface heats up and then gives off heat. Carbon dioxide traps this heat in the atmosphere. So Venus's surface becomes hotter and hotter, until it is about 460°C—hot enough to melt lead. This trapping of heat by the atmosphere is called the **greenhouse effect.**

Exploring Venus A total of 19 spacecraft have visited Venus, more than have visited any other planet. Some have even penetrated its clouds and landed on its surface. The first spacecraft to land and send back information, *Venera 7,* landed in 1970 but survived for only 23 minutes. Later spacecraft were more durable and sent back pictures and other data from Venus's surface.

Scientists have learned most of what they know about Venus's surface from data collected by the *Magellan* probe. The *Magellan*

Background

History of Science Because of Venus's extreme heat, high atmospheric pressure, and clouds of sulfuric acid, it would be almost impossible for astronauts to go there. To gather information about Venus, scientists have sent unmanned space probes. The Soviet Union was the first nation to attempt interplanetary exploration. In 1961, it launched the probe *Venera 1,* which passed within 99,000 km of Venus but did not transmit information. In 1966, the Soviets launched *Venera 3,* the first spacecraft to crash-land on another planet. In 1967, *Venera 4* parachuted a capsule of instruments to the planet's surface. *Venera 7* (1970) detected radioactive isotopes on Venus's surface. In 1975, *Venera 9* sent back the first close-up photographs of the surface of the planet.

probe reached Venus in 1990, carrying radar instruments. Radar works through clouds, so *Magellan* was able to map Venus's entire surface.

The *Magellan* views are so detailed that computers can be used to figure out what Venus would look like if you could fly just above its surface. Figure 14 shows one of these radar images. Venus is covered with rock, similar to many rocky areas on Earth. Venus has volcanoes with lava flows, many craters, and strange domes not found on other planets.

☑ ***Checkpoint*** *Why is the surface of Venus so hot?*

Mars

Mars is called the "red planet" because it has a slightly reddish tinge when you see it in the sky. The atmosphere of Mars is mostly carbon dioxide and has only 1 percent the pressure of Earth's atmosphere. You could walk around on Mars, but you would have to wear an airtight suit and carry your own air, like a scuba diver. Mars has clouds but they are very thin compared to the clouds on Earth.

Canals on Mars? In 1877, an Italian astronomer, Giovanni Schiaparelli (sky ah puh REL ee), announced that he had seen long, straight lines on Mars. He called them *canale,* or channels. In the 1890s and early 1900s, Percival Lowell, an American astronomer, convinced many people that these lines were canals that had been built by intelligent Martians to carry water. Astronomers now know that Lowell was mistaken. There are no canals on Mars.

Astronomers have found that some water remains on Mars in the form of ice at its north pole, as shown in Figure 15. During the winter, this polar ice cap is covered by a layer of frozen carbon dioxide. Mars' south pole has an ice cap made mostly of frozen carbon dioxide.

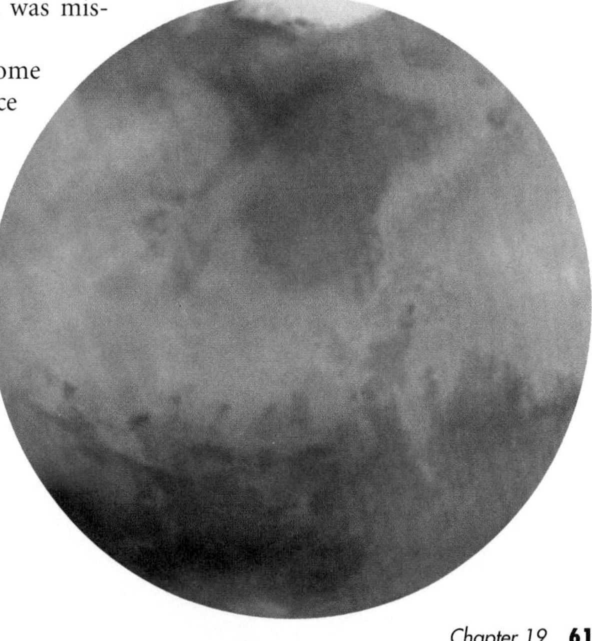

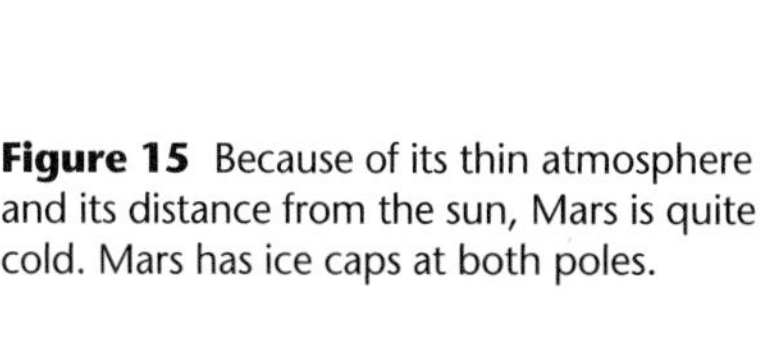

Figure 15 Because of its thin atmosphere and its distance from the sun, Mars is quite cold. Mars has ice caps at both poles.

Using the Visuals: Figure 14

Explain to students that radar images are formed when radio waves are bounced off a surface. Have students infer why scientists used radar to get an image of the volcano on Venus. *(They could not see the volcano because the thick atmosphere of Venus blocked the view.)* Explain that the radar-imaging technique exaggerates the heights of objects such as the volcano. Ask students: **Why might astronomers want to use an exaggerated scale when examining an image?** *(Astronomers increase the scale of an image so that they can examine details more clearly.)* Inform students that the colors in the figure are generated by the computer-imaging process. The actual volcano colors vary, and appear more like those of volcanoes on Earth. **learning modality: visual**

Mars

Addressing Naive Conceptions

Students' conceptions about the features and history of Mars may be based on science-fiction stories, television shows, and movies. As students complete their reading about Mars, have them prepare a Fact/Fiction sheet to distinguish scientific findings about Mars from science fiction. **learning modality: verbal**

Answers to Self-Assessment

☑ ***Checkpoint***

The surface of Venus is so hot because carbon dioxide traps heat inside the atmosphere. This is called the greenhouse effect.

Ongoing Assessment

Skills Check Instruct students to make a Venn diagram comparing the features of Venus's atmosphere with the features of Earth's atmosphere.

Skills Focus inferring ACTIVITY
Materials *tape, paper, goggles*
Time 15 minutes
Tips Perform this activity in a large open area. Make sure that there are no obstacles on which students might trip or hit their heads.
Answers Simple directions such as "Turn left" or "Take four steps forward" probably worked best. Students would have had to move slowly. This activity is similar to the way NASA engineers moved *Sojourner.* The rover could not move by itself but had to be given directions by remote control. The controller had to be careful not to have *Sojourner* run into anything, and the rover had to move very slowly.
Extend Have students infer difficulties NASA encountered when trying to get the rover to perform tasks on Mars. **learning modality: kinesthetic**

Building Inquiry Skills: Observing

Materials *sand, rectangular baking pans, large beaker, bucket for sand disposal* ACTIVITY
Time 15 minutes

Place large buckets in strategic locations around the room for sand disposal. Warn students to keep the sand out of the sinks. Have pairs of students build slopes with moist sand in one end of a rectangular metal baking pan. The sand should slope from just below the rim on one end to about the middle of the pan. Have students pour a slow, steady stream of water onto the top of the slope and observe what happens as the water runs down the slope. Have students continue pouring until there is about 1 cm of water in the pan. Ask: **How did the flowing water change the surface of the sand?** *(It formed channels.)* Ask students to infer why scientists believe water once flowed on Mars. *(Channels on Mars look similar to channels formed by flowing water on Earth.)* **learning modality: visual**

Remote Control

How hard is it to explore another planet by remote control? ACTIVITY

1. Tape a piece of paper over the front of a pair of goggles. Have your partner put them on.
2. Walk behind your partner and give him or her directions to move to another part of the room. **CAUTION:** *Do not give directions that would cause your partner to walk into a wall or corner, trip on an obstacle, or hit anything.*
3. Trade places and repeat Steps 1 and 2.

Inferring Which verbal directions worked best? How quickly could you move? How is this activity similar to the way NASA engineers moved *Sojourner* on Mars in 1997? How fast do you think the rover could move?

Seasons on Mars Because the axis of Mars is tilted, Mars has seasons just as Earth does. As the seasons change on the dusty surface of Mars, wind storms arise and blow the dust around. Since the dust is blown off some regions, these regions look darker. A hundred years ago, some people thought these regions looked darker because plants were growing there. Astronomers now realize that it is just that wind storms blow dust off the surface.

Exploring Mars The United States has sent many spacecraft to Mars. The first ones, in the 1960s, seemed to show that Mars is barren and covered with craters like the moon. Later spacecraft showed that regions of Mars have giant volcanoes. Astronomers see signs that hot material flowed down the volcanoes in the past, but they don't think the volcanoes are active now.

In 1976, two NASA spacecraft, *Viking 1* and *Viking 2,* landed on Mars. They sent back close-up pictures from Mars's surface. The pictures showed that the rocks look red because they are covered with a rusty dust. Other parts of the *Viking* spacecraft went into orbit around Mars, sending back detailed pictures.

In 1997, *Mars Pathfinder* landed on Mars. As Figure 16 shows, close-up photographs from *Mars Pathfinder* show no oceans or even puddles of water. Photographs taken from space do show evidence that water flowed on Mars millions of years ago.

Figure 16 The surface of Mars is rugged and rocky. The object at the bottom of the photo is the *Mars Pathfinder* lander. You can see the remote-control rover *Sojourner* in the middle of the photo.

Background

Facts and Figures In 1879, Giovanni Schiaparelli discovered another feature of Mars, a large crater he called *Nix Olympica.* Photographs from *Mariner 9* (1971–1972) showed that this crater was the caldera of possibly the largest volcano in the entire solar system, *Olympus Mons.* This volcano is one of several huge volcanoes on a plateau called *Tharsis.* Olympus Mons has ten times the volume of Mauna Kea in Hawaii, the largest volcano on Earth, and at 27 km, is three times as high as Mount Everest. The caldera of Olympus Mons is 85 km across, and the entire volcano covers a circular area 550 km across.

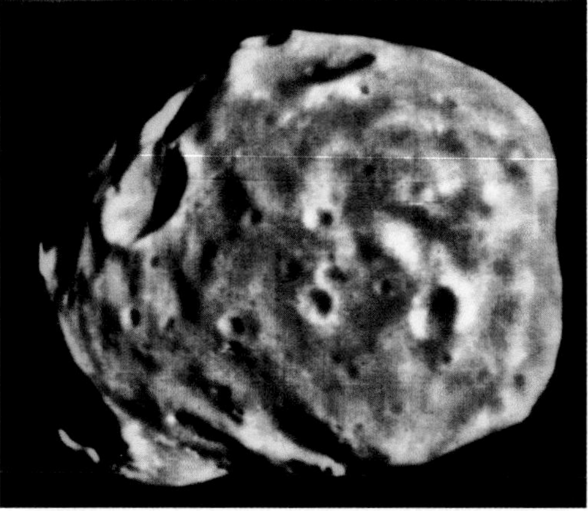

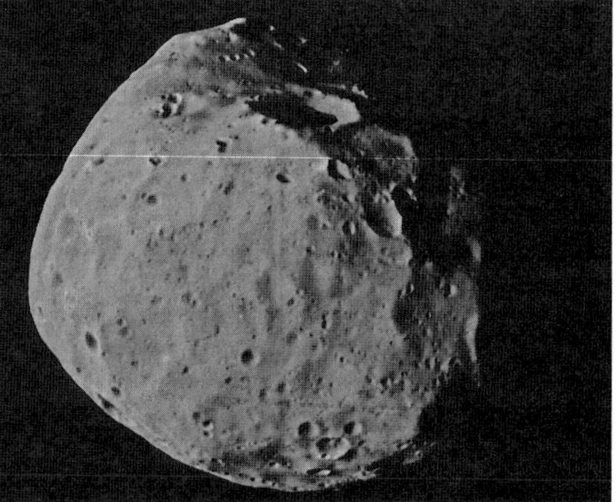

Figure 17 Phobos (left) and Deimos (right) are Mars's two small, crater-covered moons.

Mars Pathfinder carried a microwave-sized remote-control rover, called *Sojourner*, that investigated rocks on Mars. Also in 1997, another probe, *Mars Global Surveyor*, arrived in orbit around Mars, where it began mapping and photographing all of the planet's surface in detail.

Mars's Moons Mars has two very small moons. Phobos, the larger moon, is only 27 kilometers in diameter, about the distance a car can travel on the highway in 15 minutes. Deimos is even smaller, only 15 kilometers in diameter. Close-up views from space show that, like Earth's moon, Phobos and Deimos are covered with craters.

Section 3 Review

1. What features do all of the inner planets have in common?
2. What is Mercury's atmosphere like? Explain.
3. Why can astronomers see the surface of Mars clearly, but not the surface of Venus?
4. How have astronomers been able to study the surface of Venus?
5. What evidence do astronomers have that water once flowed on Mars?
6. **Thinking Critically Relating Cause and Effect** Venus is much farther from the sun than is Mercury. Yet temperatures on Venus are as high as those on the sunny side of Mercury. Explain why.

CHAPTER PROJECT

Check Your Progress

Now you will design a model that shows the relative diameters of the planets. Try several different scales to find one for which the smallest planet is clearly visible but the sun would still fit into your classroom. Convert the sun's and planets' diameters to scaled-down diameters and record your results on your data sheet. Compare your scaled-down diameters to objects you are familiar with, such as coins. Include your comparisons in your data sheet.

Program Resources

◆ **Unit 6 Resources** 19-3 Review and Reinforce; 19-3 Enrich

3 Assess

Section 3 Review Answers

1. They are all small and rocky.
2. Mercury has almost no atmosphere. The gases its atmosphere once had were heated so much by the sun that they escaped from Mercury's weak gravity into space.
3. The thin atmosphere of Mars is easy to see through; the very thick atmosphere of Venus is not.
4. Astronomers have been able to study the surface of Venus using unmanned spacecraft and by looking at radar images taken by the *Magellan* probe.
5. Astronomers have found that some water remains on Mars in the form of ice at its north pole, and patterns in photographs taken from *Mars Pathfinder* show evidence that water once flowed.
6. Venus's thick atmosphere traps heat due to the greenhouse effect.

CHAPTER PROJECT

Check Your Progress

If students have trouble finding a scale that works, suggest they try 1 cm = 10,000 km. At this scale, Mercury would be about the size of a pea, and the sun would be about the size of an easy chair.

Performance Assessment

Skills Check Have students create models of the four inner planets using art supplies and classroom items. Models should include some distinguishing characteristics of each planet.

Portfolio Students can save their models in their portfolios.

The Outer Planets

Objectives

After completing the lesson, students will be able to
- ◆ identify the main characteristics of the gas giant planets;
- ◆ compare Pluto with the other planets.

Key Term gas giant

1 Engage/Explore

Activating Prior Knowledge

Divide the class into groups of five. Give each student in a group an index card with the name of one outer planet written on it. Have students write three things they think they know about their planets. When they have finished, students can share their cards with the group. Collect the cards and use them to build a list of naive conceptions.

DISCOVER ACTIVITY

Skills Focus classifying
Materials *quarter, metric ruler, lined paper, butcher paper or poster board, compass, pushpin, and string*
Time 15 minutes
Tips A quarter has a diameter of 24 mm. Jupiter and Saturn will be too large to draw with a compass, so use a pin and string for them. CAUTION: *Compasses have sharp points and can cause injury. Warn students to be careful and watch for inappropriate behaviors.* For the best comparison, have students locate the center of each circle in the same place. Students will need large paper, such as poster boards or butcher paper, to fit the larger circles onto one sheet.
Expected Outcome Students' circles should have these diameters: Earth, 24 mm; Jupiter, 264 mm; Saturn, 226 mm; Uranus, 96 mm; Neptune, 94 mm; Pluto, 4 mm.
Think It Over Jupiter, Saturn, Uranus, Neptune, Earth, Pluto; Jupiter; Pluto

SECTION 4 The Outer Planets

DISCOVER ACTIVITY

How Large Are the Outer Planets?

Planet Diameters	
Planet	**Diameter**
Earth	1
Jupiter	11
Saturn	9.4
Uranus	4.0
Neptune	3.9
Pluto	0.17

The table shows the diameters of the outer planets compared to Earth. For example, Jupiter's diameter is 11 times Earth's diameter.

1. Measure the diameter of a quarter in millimeters. This represents Earth's diameter. Trace the quarter to represent Earth.
2. If Earth were the size of a quarter, calculate how large Jupiter would be. Now draw a circle to represent Jupiter.
3. Repeat Step 2 for each of the other outer planets.

Think It Over

Classifying List the planets in order from largest to smallest. What is the largest outer planet? Which outer planet is much smaller than Earth?

GUIDE FOR READING

- ◆ What are the main characteristics of the gas giant planets?
- ◆ How is Pluto different from the other outer planets?

Reading Tip Before you read, preview the photos and captions in this section. Then write down any questions you have. Look for answers as you read.

Most of what astronomers know about the outer planets has come from visits by NASA space probes. *Voyager 1* and *Voyager 2* reached Jupiter in 1979 and sent back close-up views of the planet. *Voyager 1* went on to visit Saturn in 1980. *Voyager 2* also visited Saturn, but then moved on to explore Uranus and Neptune. In 1995, the spacecraft *Galileo* reached Jupiter and dropped a probe into Jupiter's atmosphere.

Structure of the Gas Giants

Compared to Earth, some planets are huge. The largest planet, Jupiter, has a diameter that is 11 times Earth's diameter. Jupiter's mass is more than 300 times Earth's mass. If you could put Earth next to Jupiter, Earth would look like a tiny Chihuahua next to an enormous Great Dane. If Earth were the height of an average student, Jupiter would be as tall as a six-story building.

Jupiter and the other planets farthest from the sun, as seen in Figure 19, are called the outer planets. **The first four outer planets—Jupiter, Saturn, Uranus, and Neptune—are much larger than Earth, and do not have solid surfaces.** Because these four planets are all so large, they are also called the **gas giants.** The fifth outer planet, Pluto, is small and rocky like the terrestrial planets.

Figure 18 If the tiny Chihuahua were Earth's size, the Great Dane would be about half Jupiter's size.

READING STRATEGIES

Reading Tip Explain to students that previewing the photos and captions will help them understand what they are about to read. Write the questions below on the board. Suggest students answer the questions as they preview each image and its caption.
- ◆ How does the picture relate to the caption?
- ◆ How does the caption help me understand the picture?
- ◆ What do I already know about the information in the picture and caption?
- ◆ What else do I want to learn about the subject of this picture?

Compare/Contrast Table Have students make a compare/contrast table to show similarities and differences among the outer planets.

The Outer Planets

Planet	Diameter (kilometers)	Period of Rotation (Earth days)	Average Distance From the Sun (kilometers)	Period of Revolution (Earth years)	Number of Moons (as of 2003)
Jupiter	142,800	0.41	778,000,000	12	52
Saturn	120,540	0.43	1,427,000,000	29	30
Uranus	51,200	0.72	2,871,000,000	84	21
Neptune	49,500	0.67	4,497,000,000	165	11
Pluto	2,200	6.4	5,913,000,000	248	1

Figure 19 The outer planets are much farther apart than the inner planets. At this scale, the inner planets are so small and close to the sun that they cannot be shown. *Observing Which outer planet is closest to the sun?*

Atmospheres Because the gas giants have so much mass, they exert a much stronger gravitational force than the terrestrial planets. The strong gravity keeps the giant planets' gases from escaping, so they have deep atmospheres. The composition of their atmospheres is similar to the gases in the sun. They average about 75 percent hydrogen, 24 percent helium, and 1 percent other elements.

None of the giant planets has a well-defined surface. If you could parachute into Jupiter's atmosphere, you would sink into denser and denser gas. You would be crushed by the enormous pressure long before you got to the center, or core, of the planet.

Solid Cores Astronomers think that each of the giant planets has a partly solid core made of rock, ice, frozen carbon dioxide, and other compounds. Each of these cores may have several times as much mass as Earth. But they are buried so deep inside the planets that it has been hard to find out much about them.

☑ ***Checkpoint*** *Why do the gas giants have large atmospheres?*

2 Facilitate

Structure of the Gas Giants

Using the Visuals: Figure 19

Have students use their finger to trace the orbits of each planet in the figure. Ask: **Which planet has an orbit that crosses the orbit of another?** *(Pluto crosses the orbit of Neptune.)* Then draw students' attention to the data in the table. Allow them time to evaluate the distances of the planets from the sun. Ask: **Which planet is about twice as far from the sun as Jupiter?** *(Saturn)* **Which planet is about six times as far from the sun as Jupiter?** *(Neptune)* Astronomers using sophisticated new technology and software have recently identified a number of additional small moons in orbit around Jupiter, Saturn, and Uranus. In order to be officially recognized, additional observations are required to establish orbits for these moons. **learning modality: logical/mathematical**

Building Inquiry Skills: Applying Concepts

Invite students to imagine that they are sending a space probe to examine a gas giant. Encourage them to apply what they know about the planet's structure to describe what the probe would encounter as it approached the visible surface. *(There is no real solid surface, the atmosphere just gets thicker and thicker. Eventually, the combination of heat and pressure would probably cause the probe to fail.)* Ask: **Could the probe penetrate all the way to a solid surface? Explain.** *(Probably not. The solid core is buried deep inside the planet.)* **learning modality: verbal**

Program Resources

- **Unit 6 Resources** 19-4 Lesson Plan; 19-4 Section Summary
- **Guided Reading and Study Workbook** Section 19-4

Answers to Self-Assessment

Caption Question

Figure 19 Jupiter

☑ ***Checkpoint***

The gas giants have so much mass that they exert a strong gravitational force that keeps the planets' gases from escaping.

Ongoing Assessment

Writing Have students list features that characterize gas giants. *(Large size; far from the sun; partly solid frozen core; dense atmosphere made up mostly of hydrogen and helium)*

Jupiter

Building Inquiry Skills: Making Models

Materials *clear plastic 1-L bottle with lid, water, pepper, funnel or spoon*
Time 10 minutes
If students have completed *Weather and Climate,* point out the resemblance between the Great Red Spot and a hurricane on Earth. Allow students to model the motion of the Great Red Spot. Pair students. Have each pair fill a clear, plastic bottle half full with water. Using a funnel or a spoon, pour in a spoonful of pepper. Seal the bottle and swirl the water forcefully. Ask: **What happens to the pepper grains?** *(They spin in a large swirl.)* Have students compare the appearance of the spinning pepper to the photographs of the Great Red Spot. *(Both look like giant swirls.)* Challenge students to infer what forces are causing the Giant Red Spot to swirl. Ask: **What kind of data would you need to collect to test your inferences?** *(Sample: Differences in pressure in Jupiter's atmosphere cause the Giant Red Spot. Data that show the pressure of the atmosphere around the Giant Red Spot would be needed to test this inference.)*
learning modality: kinesthetic

Jupiter

Jupiter is the most massive planet. In fact, Jupiter is more than 300 times as massive as Earth.

Jupiter's Atmosphere Like all of the gas giant planets, Jupiter has a thick atmosphere made up mainly of hydrogen and helium. Jupiter's atmosphere contains many colorful bands and swirls of thick clouds. An especially interesting feature in Jupiter's atmosphere is its Great Red Spot, a giant area of swirling clouds many times bigger than Earth. The Great Red Spot, shown in Figure 20, appears to be an ongoing storm similar to a hurricane on Earth.

Jupiter's Moons Recall that the astronomer Galileo discovered four of Jupiter's moons. These moons are named Io (EYE oh), Europa, Ganymede, and Callisto. These four moons are Jupiter's largest. Three of them, Io, Ganymede, and Callisto, are larger than Earth's own moon. Since Galileo's time, astronomers have discovered and continue to discover additional moons revolving around Jupiter.

The *Voyager* and *Galileo* probes sent back images that showed detailed views of Jupiter's moons. Jupiter's moons are very different from one another, as you can see in Figure 21.

Figure 20 The larger photo of Jupiter was taken by the *Voyager 1* spacecraft. The small objects in front of Jupiter are two of Jupiter's moons, Io (left) and Europa (right). The Great Red Spot, shown in the inset, is a giant storm much larger in size than Earth.

Background

Facts and Figures

- Jupiter has a three-ring system that was discovered by *Voyager 1.* The main ring is about 7,000 km wide and contains the orbits of two small moons. The main ring merges into the halo, a broad ring of material about 20,000 km thick. Outside the main ring is a very broad, faint ring called the gossamer ring.
- In 2 B.C., Jupiter passed behind Venus as viewed from Earth. Since the planets all have slightly different orbital planes, this "occultation" of one planet by another is extremely rare. Astronomers use such events to gain additional information about our solar system.

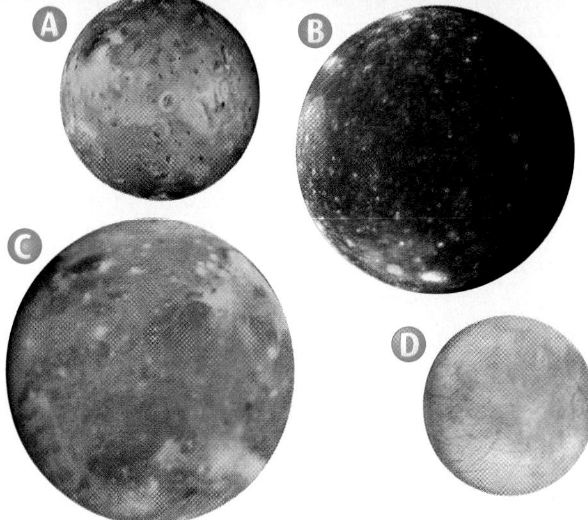

Figure 21 The astronomer Galileo discovered Jupiter's four largest moons. **A.** Io's surface is covered with large, active volcanoes. **B.** Callisto's surface is icy and covered with craters. **C.** Ganymede is the largest of Jupiter's moons. **D.** Europa's icy crust may have liquid water underneath. *Inferring Why was Galileo able to see only Jupiter's largest moons?*

Io is covered with volcanoes. Over a dozen huge volcanoes are erupting all the time, so Io's surface changes from year to year because of the flows of hot material. The sulfur in the flows gives a variety of colors to Io's surface. From space, Io looks like a giant pizza. Europa has an icy crust that may have liquid water underneath. You will learn more about Europa in Section 6.

Ganymede is the largest of Jupiter's moons and has about twice the mass of Earth's moon. Ganymede's surface is icy and partly covered with craters. Other parts of the surface show giant grooves in the ice. Callisto also has an icy surface. It is so heavily cratered that no part of its surface is free of craters.

☑ *Checkpoint What are Jupiter's four largest moons?*

Saturn

The second-largest planet in the solar system is Saturn. Saturn is slightly smaller than Jupiter, but including its beautiful rings it has a greater overall diameter. The *Voyager* probes showed that Saturn, like Jupiter, has a thick atmosphere made up mainly of hydrogen and helium. Saturn's atmosphere also contains clouds and storms, but they are less dramatic than those on Jupiter. Saturn is the only planet that is less dense than water.

Saturn's Rings When Galileo first looked at Saturn with a telescope, he could see that something was sticking out on the sides, but he didn't know what it was. A few decades later, another astronomer using a better telescope discovered that Saturn had rings around it. Astronomers later found that these rings are made of chunks of ice and rock, each traveling in its own orbit around Saturn.

TRY THIS

Model Saturn

ACTIVITY

Here's how you can build a scale model of Saturn.

1. Use a plastic foam sphere 8 cm in diameter to represent Saturn.
2. Use an overhead transparency to represent Saturn's rings. Cut a circle 18 cm in diameter out of the transparency. Cut a hole 9 cm in diameter out of the center of the circle.
3. Stick five toothpicks into Saturn, spaced equally around its equator. Put the transparency on the toothpicks and tape it to them. Sprinkle baking soda on the transparency.
4. Use a peppercorn to represent Titan. Place the peppercorn 72 cm away from Saturn on the same plane as the rings.

Making Models What do the particles of baking soda represent?

Saturn

TRY THIS

Skills Focus making models

Materials *8-cm plastic foam sphere, clear plastic sheet, ruler, scissors, compass, 5 toothpicks, tape, baking soda, peppercorn, glue (optional)*

Time 20 minutes

Tips You may want to cut circles from the center of the transparencies yourself so that students do not need to use sharp-nosed scissors.

Expected Outcome Students should understand that the particles of baking soda represent the chunks of ice and rock that make up Saturn's rings.

Extend Challenge students to use their model to demonstrate why the rings of Saturn are occasionally invisible from Earth. **learning modality: kinesthetic**

Media and Technology

Transparencies "The Outer Planets," Transparency 78

Answers to Self-Assessment

Caption Question

Figure 21 The other moons are too small and dim to have been visible through Galileo's telescope.

☑ *Checkpoint*

Io, Callisto, Ganymede, Europa

Ongoing Assessment

Oral Presentation Have students describe what they would see if they stood on the surfaces of Jupiter's four largest moons.

Using the Visuals: Figure 23

Have students write sentences describing the distinctive appearance of each of the moons shown in the figure. They should include any features that are visible, such as unusual color or large craters and note similarities to other objects in the solar system.

Students can save their sentences in their portfolios.

learning modality: visual

Building Inquiry Skills: Comparing and Contrasting

Students can make a table showing the similarities and differences between Saturn and Jupiter. The table should include size, density, appearance, composition, and any other features students wish to include. **learning modality: logical/mathematical**

Visual Arts Connection

The particles in Saturn's rings create an image of a solid surface when viewed from a distance. Artists who paint in the *pointillist* style use tiny dots to create a similar visual effect. One famous painting in this style has over 3,400,000 dots! Computer graphics images are built up in the same way, with hundreds of thousands of tiny colored dots forming the image. Obtain art reference books with examples of pointillist paintings to show to students. Challenge them to create pointillist-style drawings of one of the outer planets.

Portfolio Students can save their drawings in their portfolios.

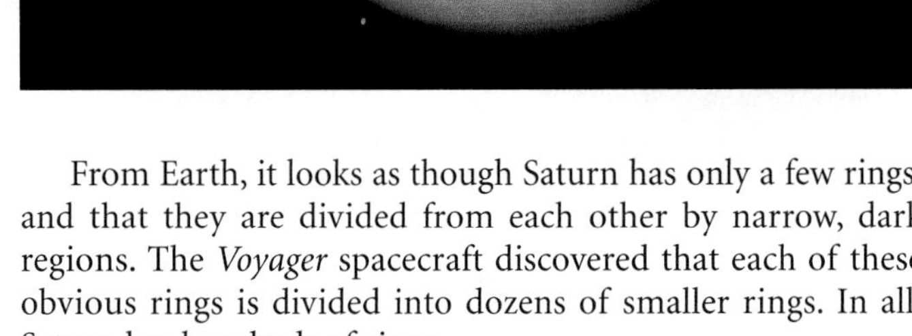

Figure 22 Saturn's rings are made up of ice chunks and rocks of many different sizes. The smaller photo shows that there are actually many small rings. The colors in this photo have been added by a computer. *Observing Why might it be hard to see Saturn's rings when their edges are facing Earth?*

From Earth, it looks as though Saturn has only a few rings, and that they are divided from each other by narrow, dark regions. The *Voyager* spacecraft discovered that each of these obvious rings is divided into dozens of smaller rings. In all, Saturn has hundreds of rings.

Saturn's rings are broad and thin, like a compact disc. Sometimes the rings are tipped so that observers see them at an angle. Occasionally, they are on edge, and then, because they are so thin, astronomers can't see them at all.

In the last few decades, rings have been discovered around the other three gas giants as well. But the rings around Jupiter, Uranus, and Neptune are not as spectacular as Saturn's.

Saturn's Moons Saturn's largest moon, Titan, is larger than Earth's own moon. Titan was discovered in 1665 but was known only as a point of light until the *Voyager*s went by. The probes showed that Titan has an atmosphere so thick that little light can get through it. Astronomers studying Hubble Space Telescope images can barely see Titan's surface.

Four other moons of Saturn are each over 1,000 kilometers in diameter. They are named Tethys (TEE this), Iapetus (eye AP uh tus), Dione, and Rhea. *Voyager* images show craters and canyons on these moons.

☑ *Checkpoint What are Saturn's rings made of?*

Figure 23 This image of Saturn and six of its moons combines photos taken by *Voyager 1* and *Voyager 2*.

Background

History of Science Like her brother William, Caroline Herschel (1750–1848) was born in Hanover in what is now Germany. William developed an interest in astronomy, even grinding mirrors for his own telescopes. At night, Caroline took notes on William's observations. During the day, she kept house, helped William grind and polish mirrors, and made the difficult computations connected with his observations.

Caroline also made her own observations. In 1786, she became the first woman to discover a comet. After William married in 1788, Caroline continued her studies, discovering seven more comets. William died in 1822, and Caroline returned to Hanover, where she completed the cataloguing of 2,500 nebulae and many star clusters. She died in 1848, two months short of her 98th birthday.

Uranus

Although the gas giant Uranus (YOOR uh nus) is about four times the diameter of Earth, it is still much smaller than Jupiter and Saturn. Uranus is twice as far from the sun as Saturn, so it is much colder. Uranus looks bluish because of traces of methane in its atmosphere.

Discovery of Uranus In 1781, Uranus became the first new planet discovered since ancient times. Astronomer William Herschel, in England, found an object in the sky that did not look like a star. At first he thought it might be a comet. But other astronomers soon calculated its orbit and realized that it was a planet beyond Saturn. The discovery made Herschel famous and started an era of solar system exploration.

Exploring Uranus In 1986, about 200 years after Herschel's discovery, *Voyager 2* arrived at Uranus and sent back our only close-up views of that giant planet. Images from *Voyager 2* show only a few clouds on Uranus's surface, but even these few allowed astronomers to calculate that Uranus rotates in about 17 hours.

Strangely, Uranus's axis is tilted at an angle of about 90° from the vertical, as shown in Figure 24. Viewed from Earth, Uranus is rotating from top to bottom instead of from side to side, the way most of the other planets do. Astronomers think that billions of years ago Uranus was hit by an object that knocked it on its side.

Uranus's Moons Photographs from *Voyager 2* showed that Uranus's five largest moons have icy, cratered surfaces. The craters show that the moons have been hit by rocks from space. Uranus's moons also have lava flows on their surfaces, suggesting that material has erupted from inside each moon. *Voyager 2* images revealed ten moons that had never been seen before. Since 1999, astronomers have discovered more moons orbiting Uranus.

Language Arts CONNECTION

The ancient Romans named the planets after the gods they worshiped. Mercury was the fast, winged messenger of the gods. Venus was the goddess of beauty and Mars was the god of war. Jupiter was the king of the Roman gods. Saturn was the Roman god of agriculture.

The planets discovered in the last 200 years have also been named after ancient gods. Uranus was the Greek god who was the husband of Gaea, Earth. Neptune was the Roman god of the sea. Pluto was the Roman god of the underworld.

In Your Journal

Look in a reference book to find out more about one of the gods for which a planet has been named. Make a poster showing that god and describing his or her character.

Figure 24 A. This composite image of *Voyager 2* photos includes Uranus and five of its moons. B. Unlike most other planets, Uranus rotates on its side.

Uranus

Using the Visuals: Figure 24

Some students may think that the axis of rotation of Uranus always points to the sun. Have students lay a pencil over the axis of rotation, then trace the orbit of Uranus by moving the pencil. The pencil should always point to the left edge of the paper.

Language Arts CONNECTION

ACTIVITY

Explain to students that the planets were supposed to share characteristics of the gods after which they were named. Provide reference books for students. Allow them to work in groups to find out more about the gods the planets were named for. They can try to think of a reason why each planet was given the name it has, both by the Romans and by modern astronomers. *(Sample: Mercury, the fastest moving planet, was named for the swiftest of the gods. Mars, with its distinctive reddish color, was named for the god of war.)*

Extend Have students rename the planets after famous characters from literature or popular culture. Ask them to explain their choices.

In Your Journal Students can consult mythology books and other reference books to read about ancient gods. If students wish to explore the names of bodies other than planets, allow them to research the names of moons of different planets. **learning modality: verbal**

Answers to Self-Assessment

Caption Question

Figure 22 The rings are so thin that when their edges face Earth they are nearly invisible.

Checkpoint

Ice chunks and rocks

Ongoing Assessment

Writing Have students create two fact sheets about Uranus. The first should include facts known about the planet before the *Voyager* images. The second should include facts learned since the *Voyager* images.

Neptune

Building Inquiry Skills: Relating Cause and Effect

ACTIVITY

Materials *small marble, large marble, medium-sized bowl, piece of spandex large enough to cover the bowl, large rubber band*
Time 10 minutes
Tips Invite students to predict how a large object's gravity could affect the orbit of a planet. To check their predictions, have students fasten a piece of spandex over the bowl and hold it in place with the large rubber band. The surface of the spandex should be smooth. Next roll the small marble across the surface several times and observe and record its motion. *(It rolls straight.)* Now place the large marble in the center so that the surface will be depressed in the center. Make sure it is still smooth. Have students roll the small marble in various paths across the spandex and observe its path. *(The small marble will be deflected by the curve in the surface of the fabric. The closer it comes to the large marble, the more it will be deflected.)* Ask students to compare the model to what happens in the space around a massive object like Neptune. *(The large marble models a mass like Neptune. The curve in the surface of the spandex models gravity. The small marble models other objects whose path is deflected by Neptune.)* **learning modality: kinesthetic**

Pluto and Charon

Building Inquiry Skills: Classifying

Pluto is unlike any other planet because it is much smaller than the gas giants and it is less dense than the inner planets. It is ten times larger than an asteroid, and only one other asteroid is known to have a satellite. So what is it? Challenge students to write a paragraph explaining why Pluto should be classified as a planet, an asteroid, or as some other object.

Students can save their paragraphs in their portfolios.

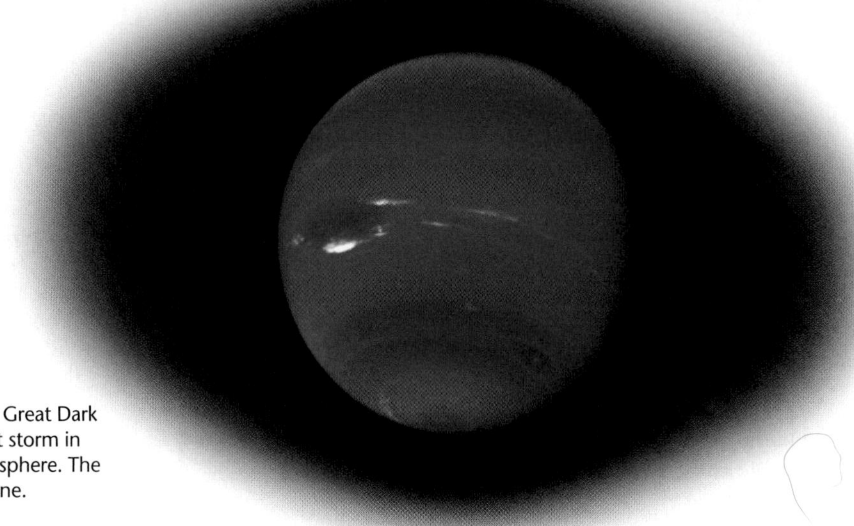

Figure 25 The Great Dark Spot was a giant storm in Neptune's atmosphere. The storm is now gone.

Figure 26 Neptune's largest moon, Triton, is covered with ridges and craters.

Neptune

Neptune is even farther from the sun than Uranus—in fact, it is 30 times Earth's distance from the sun. Unlike Uranus's nearly featureless blue atmosphere, Neptune's atmosphere contains visible clouds.

Discovery of Neptune The planet Neptune was discovered as a result of a mathematical prediction. Uranus was not quite following the orbit astronomers predicted for it. Astronomers hypothesized that there must be another, unseen planet whose gravity was affecting Uranus's orbit. By 1846, mathematicians in both England and France had calculated the orbit of this new planet. A few months later, an observer in Germany saw an unknown object in the sky. It was the new planet, now called Neptune.

Exploring Neptune In 1989 *Voyager 2* flew by Neptune, where it photographed a Great Dark Spot, as shown in Figure 25, about the size of Earth. Like the Great Red Spot on Jupiter, the Great Dark Spot probably was a giant storm. But the storm didn't last long. Images from the Hubble Space Telescope taken five years later showed that the Great Dark Spot was gone. Other, smaller spots and regions of clouds on Neptune seem to come and go.

Neptune's Moons Astronomers have discovered 11 moons revolving around Neptune. Neptune's largest moon is Triton. The *Voyager* photos show that the region near Triton's south pole is covered with a cap of ice, and that dark material erupts from underneath.

☑ ***Checkpoint*** *Before they could see Neptune, what evidence led scientists to conclude that it existed?*

Background

History of Science Clyde Tombaugh was only 24 when he discovered Pluto. As a boy he had been intrigued by the view of the heavens he saw through an uncle's telescope. After he finished high school, Tombaugh built his own telescope. When he sent sketches of his observations of Jupiter and Mars to the Lowell Observatory, they offered him a job—finding Pluto.

Astronomers had predicted the existence of Pluto based on calculations that indicated a distant planet was disturbing the orbits of Uranus and Neptune. They know now that Pluto's small mass could not have not have caused this disturbance, but they were looking for another planet, and Tombaugh found it!

Tombaugh received a scholarship to the University of Kansas, but he continued to work at the Lowell Observatory until 1946.

Pluto and Charon

Pluto and its single moon Charon are very different from the gas giants. **Pluto and Charon have solid surfaces and masses much less than that of Earth.** In fact, Pluto is less than two thirds the size of Earth's moon. Since Charon is more than half the size of Pluto, astronomers often consider them to be a double planet instead of a planet and a moon.

Pluto and Charon are so far from the sun that they revolve around the sun only once every 248 Earth years. Because Pluto and Charon are so small and far away, astronomers have been unable to learn much about them.

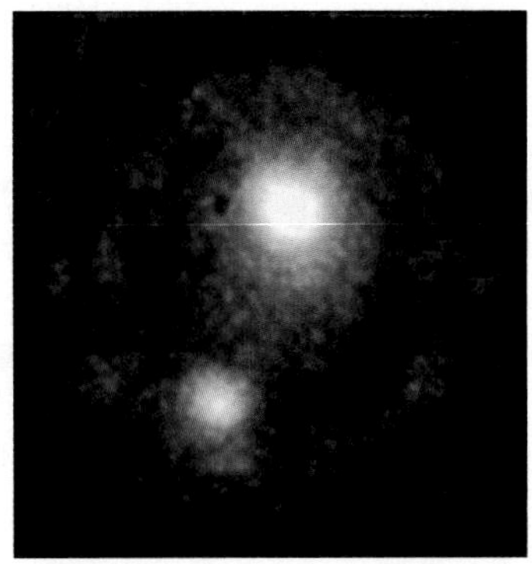

Figure 27 The space between Pluto and Charon couldn't be clearly seen from Earth until 1999, when Pluto and Charon were observed with new telescopes. This photo, taken with the Hubble Space Telescope, clearly shows them as two objects. *Inferring Why do astronomers often call Pluto and Charon a double planet?*

Discovery of Pluto and Charon The American astronomer Clyde Tombaugh discovered Pluto in 1930. He had been searching for a large object he thought might be affecting Neptune's orbit. Tombaugh spent 10 months looking at hundreds of thousands of images before he found Pluto. Charon was not discovered until 1978, by the astronomer James Christy. Christy was studying photographs of Pluto when he noticed that Pluto seemed to have a "bump." The bump turned out to be Charon.

Is Pluto Really a Planet? Pluto is so small that many astronomers do not think it should be called a planet at all. Pluto may be merely the largest of thousands of objects revolving around the sun out beyond Neptune. If astronomers had found these other objects before they found Pluto, they might not have called Pluto a planet.

Section 4 Review

1. How are the gas giants similar to each other? How are they different?
2. How is Pluto different from the gas giants?
3. What is the most prominent feature of Jupiter's surface? What causes this feature?
4. Why do astronomers think Uranus may have been hit by another object billions of years ago?
5. **Thinking Critically Predicting** Do you think astronomers have found all of the moons of the outer planets? Explain.

Check Your Progress

CHAPTER PROJECT

Once you have models that show size and distance separately, design another scale model of the solar system. This time, use the same scale for both size and distance. If your chalkboard is the sun, which planets would be in your classroom? Where would the other planets be with respect to your classroom, school grounds, and town?

Discuss with classmates any problems that would come up in building a model using the same scale for both size and distance. Revise your model as needed.

3 Assess

Section 4 Review Answers

1. They are all much larger than Earth, and do not have solid surfaces. They differ in size, number of moons, presence of rings, the tilt of their axes, and the presence of storms in their atmospheres.
2. Pluto is smaller and denser than the gas giants.
3. The Great Red Spot is Jupiter's most prominent feature. It is probably caused by a hurricane-like storm in the atmosphere.
4. Uranus's axis is tilted 90°. This could have been caused by a collision with another object.
5. No. Many of the moons were found only with the help of the *Voyager* photographs. Future probes will probably find other moons that *Voyager* may have missed.

Check Your Progress

CHAPTER PROJECT

By this time, students should have a model showing relative size and a model showing relative distance. The larger the model, the more successful it will be in accurately representing the sizes of the planets. It is difficult to find a suitable scale that will clearly show both sizes and distances between the planets . For example, if the distance to Pluto is made equal to 100 m, then the size of Pluto would be 0.03 mm! Jupiter would be the size of a BB. If the size of Pluto is made 1.00 mm, then the distance to Pluto would be 2.6 km!

Program Resources

- **Unit 6 Resources** 19-4 Review and Reinforce; 19-4 Enrich

Answers to Self-Assessment

Caption Question

Figure 27 Pluto and Charon are close in size and close together.

Checkpoint

Uranus was not following the orbit that scientists predicted. Scientists believed that the gravity of a large object, probably a planet, was affecting Uranus's orbit.

Performance Assessment

Drawing Have students draw diagrams of the outer planets that show their relative sizes, order, and at least one distinguishing characteristic of each planet.

Students can save their diagrams in their portfolios.

Skills Lab

Developing Hypotheses

Speeding Around the Sun

Preparing for Inquiry

Key Concept Since the pull of gravity is stronger, planets closer to the sun must move faster in order to maintain a stable orbit. Therefore, the length of time it takes a planet to go around the sun is related to the distance of the planet from the sun.

Skills Objectives Students will be able to:

- formulate hypotheses concerning the revolution of a planet around the sun related to its distance from the sun.
- test their hypotheses to determine if they are supported by the available data.
- determine whether their hypotheses should be accepted or rejected based on the results of their tests.

Time 45 minutes

Advance Planning Perform this activity on your own first to become familiar with any problems students may experience in keeping the stopper swinging at various distances from the plastic tube. Use the materials to assemble a sling and test it for safety. Make sure that there is enough open space for groups to work without hitting each other.

Alternative Methods If you are concerned about students hitting one another, carry out the physical aspects of the lab as a demonstration from which students can develop the skill of formulating a hypothesis. In place of the stopper, a tennis ball with rubber bands around it or any other soft object of suitable weight and density that can be safely tied to the end of the string can be used. In place of the plastic tube, a pen tube with smooth ends may be used.

Guiding Inquiry

Invitation Discuss the difference between a hypothesis and a scientific fact. A hypothesis is a possible explanation for a set of observations or answer to a question.

Skills Lab

Developing Hypotheses

SPEEDING AROUND THE SUN

In this lab, you will make and test a hypothesis about how a planet's distance from the sun is related to its period of revolution.

Problem

How does a planet's distance from the sun affect its period of revolution?

Materials

string, 1.5 m
plastic tube, 6 cm
meter stick
one-hole rubber stopper
stopwatch
weight or several washers

Procedure 

1. What do you think is the relationship between a planet's distance from the sun and its period of revolution? Write your hypothesis in the form of an "If . . . then . . ." statement.
2. To test your hypothesis, you need to make a model planet.
   a. Thread the string through the rubber stopper hole. Tie the end of the string to the main part of the string. Pull tightly to make sure that the knot will not become untied.
   b. Thread the other end of the string through the plastic tube and tie a weight to that end. Have your teacher check both knots.
   c. Hold the plastic tube in your hand above your head. Swing the stopper around above your head. Practice keeping the stopper moving at a constant speed. The circle represents the planet's orbit. **CAUTION:** *Stand away from other students. Make sure the swinging stopper will not hit students or objects. Do not let go of the string.*
3. Before you try different distances for your model planet, copy the data table into your notebook.

DATA TABLE

Distance (cm)	Period of Revolution (seconds)			
	Trial 1	Trial 2	Trial 3	Average
20				
40				
60				

4. Pull the string so the stopper is 20 cm away from the plastic tube. Swing the stopper just fast enough to keep the stopper moving.

622

Introducing the Procedure

- Have students think of the inward pull of the string as gravity.
- The activity should give students a "feel" for the effects of gravity and the increased speed as the orbit gets smaller.

Media and Technology

Lab Activity Videotapes
Grade 6, Tape 4

Troubleshooting the Experiment

- Students may have to practice keeping the stopper moving at a constant speed. They may try to keep the stopper moving with the same frequency. Tell them to keep the stopper moving just fast enough to keep it up.

Expected Outcome

- Students will see that it takes longer for a single revolution when the string is longer.
- Students may have to reformulate their hypotheses from Step 8.

5. Have your partner time how long it takes for the stopper to make 10 revolutions. Divide by 10 to find the period of revolution. Record this number as Trial 1.
6. Repeat Steps 4–5 two more times. Record your results as Trials 2 and 3. Add the results of the three trials together and divide by three to find the average period of revolution.
7. If you pull the stopper out to 40 cm, do you think the period of revolution will increase or decrease? To find out, pull the stopper out to 40 cm and repeat Steps 4–6.
8. Based on your results in Step 7, do you want to revise your hypothesis? Make any needed changes. Then pull the stopper out to 60 cm and repeat Steps 4–6.

Analyze and Conclude

1. Which object in your model represented the sun? Which represented the planet?
2. What force did the pull on the string represent?
3. When you pulled the stopper out to make the orbit larger, did the string then represent a stronger or weaker force of gravity? Why?
4. What happened to the period of revolution when you made the orbit larger in Steps 7 and 8?
5. Did your observations support your hypothesis? Summarize your conclusions based on your observations.
6. Which planets take less time to revolve around the sun—those closer to the sun or those farther away? Use the model to support your answer.
7. **Think About It** What information did you consider when you made your hypothesis? How did having some experimental data help you modify your hypothesis?

Design an Experiment

Write a hypothesis relating the mass of a planet to its period of revolution. Then, using a stopper with a different mass, modify the activity to test your hypothesis. Before you swing the stopper, have your teacher check your knots.

Program Resources

- **Unit 6 Resources** Chapter 19 Skills Lab

Sample Data Table

Distance (cm)	Trial 1 (sec)	Trial 2 (sec)	Trial 3 (sec)	Average (sec)
20	0.4	0.5	0.4	0.43
40	0.6	0.6	0.7	0.63
60	0.8	0.8	0.8	0.80

Safety

Any time there is a swinging stopper, make sure it is in an open space free to swing clear of all students and objects. Make sure that the object on the opposite end of the string from the stopper cannot be pulled through the pen tube. Check the strength of the string to make sure that it will not break. Tell students to wear eye protection throughout the lab. Review the safety guidelines in Appendix A.

- Some students may ask for more information regarding the planets themselves. Tell them that the circumference of the orbit increases as distance from the sun increases. In addition, as distance from the sun increases, the gravitational pull of the sun on a planet decreases. This means that the planet is traveling more slowly over a greater distance.

Analyze and Conclude

1. The plastic tube represented the sun. The rubber stopper represented the planet.
2. The pull on the string represented the force of gravity.
3. When the orbit was larger, the string represents a weaker force of gravity since the planet is farther away.
4. As the orbit became larger, the period of revolution became longer.
5. Sample: The period increased as predicted by the hypothesis. Observations supported the hypothesis.
6. Planets closer to the sun should take less time to revolve around the sun. When the string was short, the period of revolution was short.
7. Sample: String length determines orbit size, which determines the distance the stopper must travel in one orbit. We predict orbits of greater size will take longer to complete. The data supported the hypothesis.

Extending the Inquiry

Design an Experiment By adding additional rubber stoppers to the end of the string, the mass of the swinging object is increased. By repeating the swing of the increased mass in the same orbit, students will determine that planets have the same period at the same distance. They may also notice that the inward pull of the string has to be greater with more stoppers. The force of gravity between the sun and a planet is related to the mass of the planet. The inertia of a planet is also related to its mass. Thus, the effect of increasing the mass is to increase both the pull of the sun's gravity and the ability of the planet to withstand that pull through inertia. The resulting acceleration on the planet is the same, regardless of mass.

SECTION 5 Comets, Asteroids, and Meteors

Objectives

After completing the lesson, students will be able to
- ◆ identify the characteristics of comets and asteroids;
- ◆ describe the formation of meteoroids.

Key Terms comet, asteroid, asteroid belt, meteoroid, meteor, meteorite

1 Engage/Explore

Activating Prior Knowledge

Ask students if they have ever seen a shooting star. Invite them to describe what a shooting star looks like. Ask them to speculate about what it is. After the discussion, tell students that in this section, they will investigate the nature of comets, asteroids, and shooting stars, which are actually meteors.

DISCOVER ACTIVITY

Skills Focus inferring
Materials *modeling clay, pencil, 3 10-cm lengths of string, small fan*
Time 10 minutes
Tips You may wish to have more than one fan available and allow two or three students to test their models at the same time.
Expected Outcome The strings point away from the fan, behind the ball of clay.
Think It Over Moving the ball does not change the direction in which the strings point. A comet's tail always points away from the sun.

SECTION 5 Comets, Asteroids, and Meteors

DISCOVER ACTIVITY

Which Way Do Comet Tails Point?

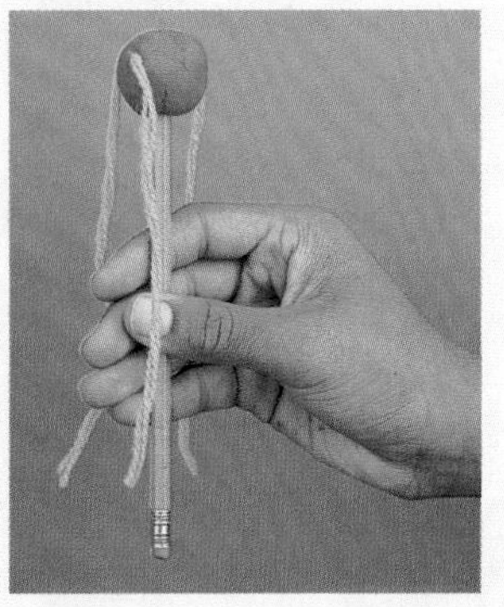

1. Form a small ball out of modeling clay to represent a comet.
2. Using a pencil point, push three 10-cm lengths of string into the ball. The strings represent the comet's tail. Stick the ball onto the pencil point, as shown in the photo.
3. Hold the ball about 1 m in front of a fan. The air from the fan represents the solar wind. Move the ball toward the fan, away from the fan, and from side to side. **CAUTION:** *Keep your fingers away from the fan blades.*

Think It Over

Inferring How does moving the ball affect the direction in which the strings point? What determines which way the tail of a comet points?

GUIDE FOR READING

- ◆ What are the characteristics of comets and asteroids?
- ◆ Where do meteoroids come from?

Reading Tip **As you read, make an outline of this section using the headings as the main topics.**

Imagine watching a cosmic collision! That's exactly what happened in July 1994. Eugene and Carolyn Shoemaker and David Levy discovered a new comet in 1993 that had previously broken into pieces near Jupiter. In 1994, the fragments returned and crashed into Jupiter. On Earth, astronomers were fascinated to see the huge explosions—some were as large as Earth!

As this story shows, the sun, planets, and moons aren't the only objects in the solar system. There are also millions of smaller objects, most of which are classified as comets and asteroids.

Comets

One of the most glorious things you can see in the night sky is a comet. A bright comet may be visible only for days or weeks or months, but is well worth seeing. In April 1997, for example, Comet Hale-Bopp and its bright dust tail were clearly visible even without a telescope.

You can think of a **comet** as a "dirty snowball" about the size of an Earth mountain. **Comets are chunks of ice and dust whose orbits are usually very long, narrow ellipses.** Because their orbits are so

◄ A dark ring on Jupiter caused by comet Shoemaker-Levy 9

READING STRATEGIES

Reading Tip Suggest to students that, as they outline, they leave space between the headings to fill in details. The completed outline can be used as a study guide.

I. Comets
  A. Structure
    1. nucleus
    2. coma
    3. tail
  B. Orbit (outline will continue)

Study and Comprehension Provide each student with three note cards, and have them write *comet, asteroid,* and *meteor* on the cards, one term per card. As students read the section, have them list the characteristics of the object on the opposite side of each card. Then have partners take turns using their sets of note cards as flashcards for testing each other's knowledge of comets, asteroids, and meteors.

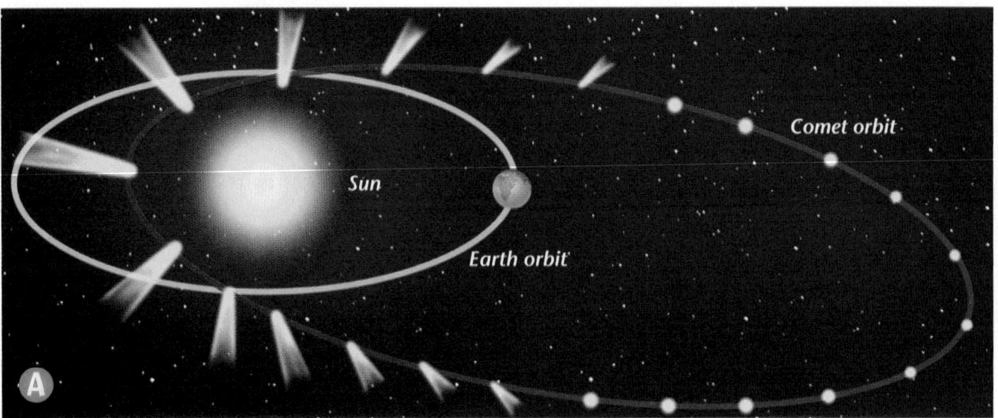

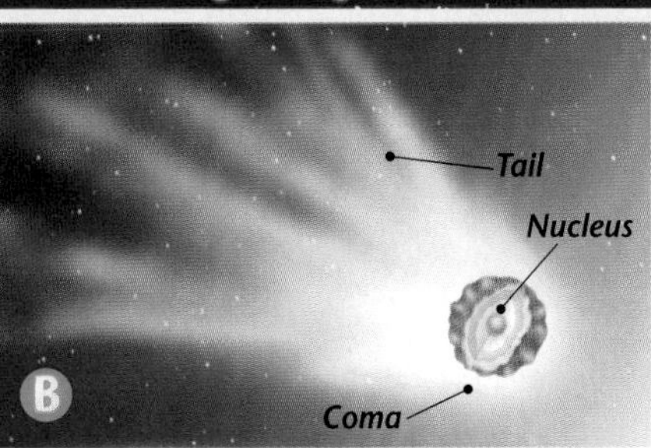

Figure 28 A. Most comets revolve around the sun in very long, narrow orbits. B. The main parts of a comet are the nucleus, the coma, and the tail. *Observing What shape is a comet's orbit?*

elliptical, few of them pass near Earth. They can usually then be seen only briefly. When a comet gets close enough to the sun, the energy in the sunlight turns the ice into gas, releasing dust. The gas and dust form an outer layer called the coma. Figure 28 shows the inner layer of the comet, which is then called the nucleus. The brightest part of a comet, the comet's head, is made up of the nucleus and coma.

Remember that the sun's corona produces a stream of particles called the solar wind. Solar wind pushes the gas from a comet away from the sun. Gas and dust form the comet's tail. The tail looks like hair; in fact, the name *comet* means "long-haired star" in Greek.

A comet's tail can be hundreds of millions of kilometers long and stretch across most of the sky. The material is stretched out very thinly, however, so there isn't much mass in a comet tail.

In 1705, Edmond Halley, an English astronomer, calculated the orbits of 24 comets that people had observed over hundreds of years. Halley realized that several of the comets seemed to have the same orbit and suggested that they were actually the same comet. Halley calculated that this comet appeared about every 76 years, and predicted that it would reappear in 1758. When this prediction came true, the comet was named Halley's Comet. In 1986, the last time Halley's Comet appeared in our sky, the European Space Agency's *Giotto* spacecraft flew within a few hundred kilometers of it.

☑ ***Checkpoint*** *How did Halley's Comet get its name?*

2 Facilitate

Comets

Using the Visuals: Figure 28

Ask students how the orbit of a comet is different from the orbit of a planet. *(The orbits of most comets are much longer and narrower.)* **learning modality: visual**

Building Inquiry Skills: Inferring

As students explore the structure of a comet, have them make inferences about observing comets from Earth. Ask: **Which part of the comet do we see? Why?** *(The coma and tail; they are the brightest parts of the comet.)* **Why would it be difficult to view the nucleus?** *(It is very small and obscured by the coma.)* **learning modality: verbal**

Building Inquiry Skills: Predicting

ACTIVITY

Ask students to predict whether they are likely to ever have the opportunity to see Halley's comet. *(Probably, for most students)* Encourage students to determine approximately how old they will be at that time. *(Most will be in their 70s.)* **learning modality: logical/mathematical**

Program Resources

- **Unit 6 Resources** 19-5 Lesson Plan; 19-5 Section Summary
- **Guided Reading and Study Workbook** Section 19-5

Answers to Self-Assessment

Caption Question

Figure 28 The shape of a comet's orbit is a long, narrow ellipse.

☑ ***Checkpoint***

Edmond Halley identified a comet, and calculated that it appeared every 76 years. He predicted the comet would reappear in 1758. When Halley's prediction came true, the comet was named after him.

Ongoing Assessment

Writing Have students explain how the coma and tail of a comet are formed.

Asteroids

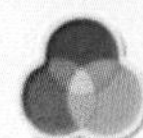

Integrating Earth Science

Have students locate the Yucatan peninsula on a world map. Ask: **Since a giant asteroid hit this area, why haven't scientists found the object that made the crater?** *(It probably exploded into dust on impact.)* Tell students that asteroids and other objects from space that land on Earth usually explode into dust or vapor. Ask: **What may have happened to the dust from the asteroid that hit the Yucatan?** *(Sample: It fell into the ocean, settled on the ocean floor, was buried by layers of sediment, and eventually turned back into rock.)* **learning modality: verbal**

Meteors

Building Inquiry Skills: Hypothesizing

ACTIVITY

Materials *plaster of Paris, water, disposable plastic trays, assortment of round objects with different sizes and masses, petroleum jelly*

Time 40 minutes

Since objects in the classroom don't explode on impact, it is only possible to model *some* of the aspects of crater formation. Assign students to groups. Have each group choose one variable to test, such as height, mass, or size of object, and develop a hypothesis relating crater size to the variable chosen. Coat the marbles with petroleum jelly. Prepare liquid plaster of Paris. Have students fill a clean polystyrene tray with the liquid. Wait a few minutes until the material begins to set, then quickly drop the marbles, controlling all except the manipulated variable. When the plaster of Paris sets completely, remove the marbles and examine the craters. Ask: **How did the variable you chose affect the size of the crater it made?** *(Answers will vary, but crater size should increase with height and mass.)* **learning modality: kinesthetic**

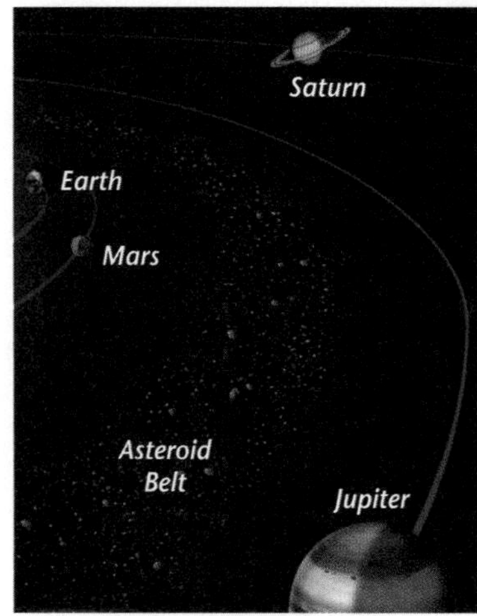

Figure 29 The asteroid belt (left) lies between Mars and Jupiter. Asteroids come in many sizes and shapes, as shown in this artist's depiction (center). NASA's *Galileo* mission photographed the asteroid Gaspra (right).

Asteroids

Between 1801 and 1807, astronomers discovered four small objects between the orbits of Mars and Jupiter. They named the objects Ceres, Pallas, Juno, and Vesta. Over the next 80 years, astronomers found 300 more. These objects, called **asteroids,** are too small and too numerous to be considered full-fledged planets. **Most asteroids revolve around the sun between the orbits of Mars and Jupiter.** This region of the solar system, shown in Figure 29, is known as the **asteroid belt.**

Astronomers have discovered more than 10,000 asteroids, and more are found every month. Ceres, Pallas, Juno, and Vesta are among the dozen that are over 250 kilometers across.

INTEGRATING EARTH SCIENCE Some asteroids come near the orbit of Earth. Someday, one of these near-Earth asteroids could hit Earth. When a large asteroid hit Earth 65 million years ago, it exploded, making a crater 200 kilometers in diameter near the Yucatán Peninsula of Mexico. The explosion almost certainly raised trillions of tons of dust into the atmosphere, blocking the light from the sun for months. Debris from the explosion probably started huge fires that destroyed much of Earth's forests and grass. Scientists hypothesize that as a result many species of organisms, including the dinosaurs, became extinct.

Meteors

Imagine being outside in the country on a clear night, looking up at the sky. Suddenly, you see a streak of light flashing across the sky. Within seconds, you see another streak. For an hour or so, you see a streak at least once a minute. You are watching a meteor shower. Meteor showers happen regularly, several times a year.

Background

History of Science Consider these facts about the first asteroid to be discovered, Ceres.

- Ceres was discovered twice, the first time by Giuseppe Piazzi, on January 1, 1801, in Palermo, Sicily. Piazzi named the asteroid *Ceres* after the Roman goddess of grain (who was also the patron saint of Sicily). Because Piazzi was ill, he only observed the asteroid for about one month, and it moved into the daytime sky. The German astronomer Franz von Zach rediscovered Ceres on January 1, 1802.
- Ceres is the largest known asteroid.
- When Piazzi named the asteroid he had discovered, he began the asteroid-naming convention astronomers still use today—asteroids are named *by* their discoverers, unlike comets, which are named *for* their discoverers.

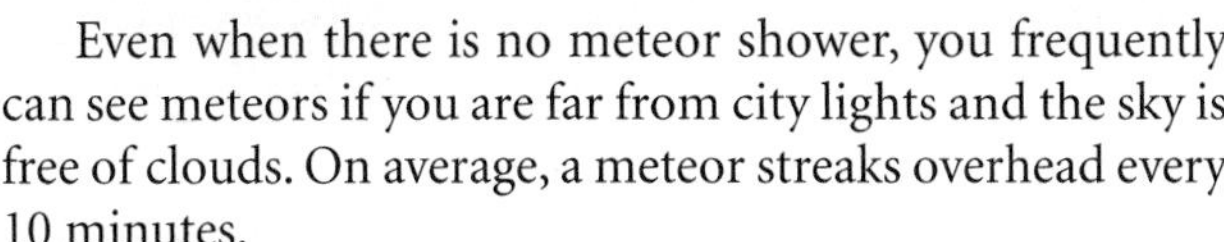

Figure 30 A. Meteor Crater in Arizona is the best-known meteorite crater on Earth. It was formed when a meteorite hit Earth about 40,000 years ago. B. Meteoroids make streaks of light, like the one above, as they burn up in the atmosphere.

Even when there is no meteor shower, you frequently can see meteors if you are far from city lights and the sky is free of clouds. On average, a meteor streaks overhead every 10 minutes.

A **meteoroid** is a chunk of rock or dust in space. **Meteoroids usually come from comets or asteroids.** Comets leave dust behind as they move through the solar system. When Earth passes through one of these dust clouds, bits of dust enter Earth's atmosphere.

When a meteoroid enters Earth's atmosphere, friction makes it burn up and produce the streak of light you see in the sky—a **meteor.** If the meteoroid is large, it may not burn up completely. Meteoroids that pass through the atmosphere and hit Earth's surface are called **meteorites.** The craters on the moon and on other objects in the solar system were caused by meteoroids.

Meteorites fall all over Earth. Most of them look just like stones, so nobody notices them. A few meteorites are made almost entirely of iron and nickel, and so are unusually heavy for their size. This makes them more likely to be identified as meteorites than as Earth rocks.

Section 5 Review

1. What is a comet made of?
2. Where are most asteroids found?
3. What are the main sources of meteoroids?
4. What is the difference between a meteor and a meteorite?
5. **Thinking Critically Predicting** Describe what might happen if an asteroid the size of the one that hit Earth 65 million years ago hit Earth today.

Science at Home

Watch a Meteor Shower Meteor showers occur regularly on specific dates. (The Perseids meteor shower, for example, occurs every August 12.) Look in the newspaper or almanac for information about the next meteor shower. With adult family members, go outside on that night and look for meteors. Explain to your family what causes the glow.

Program Resources

- **Unit 6 Resources** 19-5 Review and Reinforce; 19-5 Enrich

3 Assess

Section 5 Review Answers

1. Chunks of ice and dust
2. In the asteroid belt that lies between Jupiter and Mars
3. Most meteoroids come from comets or asteroids.
4. A meteor is a meteoroid that enters Earth's atmosphere and burns up. A meteorite is a meteoroid that passes through Earth's atmosphere and hits Earth's surface.
5. Effects would vary, depending on whether the object hit on land or water. In either case, the collision would raise huge clouds of dust, blocking light from the sun. Many species of living things could become extinct as a result of the blocked sunlight.

Science at Home

Since they will be outdoors after dark, caution students they should only view a meteor shower with an adult. Meteor showers are more easily seen outside cities, in areas where bright lights do not block the glow from the meteors. Students should explain that the glow is caused by friction caused by Earth's atmosphere heating the rock as it falls.

Performance Assessment

Oral Presentation Have students narrate the life story of an asteroid that orbits close to Earth and eventually hits the ground.

Is There Life Beyond Earth?

Objectives

After completing the lesson, students will be able to

- identify the conditions needed for living things on Earth;
- state why Mars and Europa are thought to be good places to look for signs of life.

Key Term extraterrestrial life

1 Engage/Explore

Activating Prior Knowledge

Show students a potted plant and a goldfish in a bowl. Invite students to suggest what is the same about these two. *(Both are alive.)* Ask: **How do we know these things are alive?** *(They grow, reproduce, excrete wastes.)* **What do these things both need to stay alive?** *(Water, space, energy)*

DISCOVER ACTIVITY

Skills Focus forming operational definitions

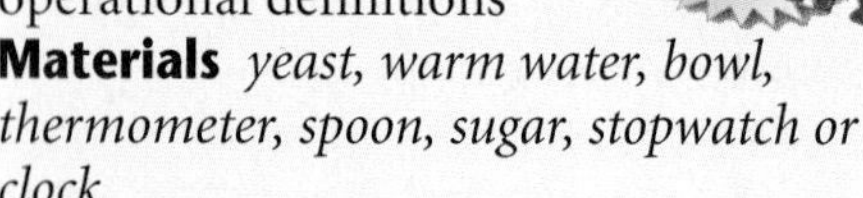

Materials *yeast, warm water, bowl, thermometer, spoon, sugar, stopwatch or clock*

Time 15 minutes

Tips You may wish to buy yeast in bulk rather than packets. A packet of yeast contains about one tablespoon. Provide a source of water at the correct temperature. Encourage students to record as many observations as they can.

Expected Outcome Before adding water, students will observe that the yeast is dry, brown, grainy, and not changing. After adding water, students should observe that the yeast is making bubbles and has a distinct odor.

Think It Over The observations that yeast is dry, brown, grainy, and immobile suggest that yeast is not alive. The observations that the yeast is bubbling, has a smell, and appears to be growing suggest that the yeast is alive. You can tell that something is alive if it eats, breathes, or grows.

Is There Life Beyond Earth?

DISCOVER ACTIVITY

Is Yeast Alive or Not?

1. Open a package of yeast and pour it into a bowl.
2. Look at the yeast carefully. Make a list of your observations.
3. Fill the bowl about halfway with warm water (about 20°C). Add a spoonful of sugar. Stir the mixture with the spoon. Wait five minutes.
4. Now look at the yeast again and make a list of your observations.

Think It Over

Forming Operational Definitions Which of your observations seem to suggest that yeast is not alive? Which observations suggest that yeast is alive? How can you tell if something is alive?

GUIDE FOR READING

- What conditions do living things need to exist on Earth?
- Why do scientists think Mars and Europa are good places to look for signs of life?

Reading Tip As you read, write down evidence to support this statement: Life may exist in other parts of the solar system.

Most of Antarctica is covered with snow and ice. You would not expect to see rocks lying on top of the whiteness. But surprisingly, in some places people have found rocks lying on the surface. When scientists examined the rocks, they found that the rocks are meteorites. A few of the meteorites came from Mars. Astronomers think that meteoroids hitting the surface of Mars must have blasted chunks of rock into space. The rocks eventually entered Earth's atmosphere and landed in Antarctica.

Recently a team of scientists announced that a meteorite from Mars found in Antarctica shows tiny shapes that look like fossils—the remains of ancient life preserved in rock. Many scientists doubt that the shapes really are fossils. But if they are, it would be a sign that life forms similar to bacteria once existed on Mars. Life other than that on Earth would be called **extraterrestrial life.**

Figure 31 Dr. Ursula Marvin (lying down) studies meteorites such as this one in Antarctica.

The "Goldilocks Conditions"

If you did the Discover activity, you saw that it can be hard to tell whether something is alive or not. But all living things on Earth have several characteristics in common. Living things are made up of one or more cells. Living things take in energy and use it to grow and develop. They reproduce, producing new living things of the same type. Living things also give off waste.

READING STRATEGIES

Reading Tip Before students read, explain that looking for evidence to support a statement is a good way to become involved with the ideas in a section. Students may list as evidence the presence of water or, possibly, fossils on Mars. After the activity, encourage students to discuss other evidence they have heard or read that supports theories of life in other parts of the solar system.

Program Resources

- **Unit 6 Resources** 19-6 Lesson Plan; 19-6 Section Summary
- **Guided Reading and Study Workbook** Section 19-6

A yeast cell, for example, is a living thing. Each yeast organism has one cell. Yeast cells take in sugar for energy. They reproduce and make new yeast cells. And yeast cells produce carbon dioxide as waste. A yeast cell, then, fulfills all the requirements for a living thing.

Nobody knows whether life exists anywhere other than Earth. Scientists often talk about the conditions needed by "life as we know it." **Earth has liquid water and a suitable temperature range and atmosphere for living things to survive.** Other planets do not have such favorable conditions, which scientists sometimes call the "Goldilocks conditions." That is, the temperature is not too hot and not too cold. It is just right. If Earth were hotter, water would always be a gas—water vapor. If Earth were colder, water would always be solid ice. On Earth, water exists as a liquid as well as a solid and a gas.

Are these the conditions necessary for life? Or are they just the conditions that Earth's living things happen to need? Scientists have only one example of life to study: life on Earth. Unless scientists find life somewhere else, there will be no way to answer these questions.

☑ *Checkpoint* *What are some characteristics of all living things?*

Sharpen your Skills

Communicating

ACTIVITY You are writing a letter to a friend who lives on another planet. Your friend has never been to Earth and has no idea what the planet is like. Explain in your letter why the conditions on Earth make it the ideal place for living things.

Life on Earth

In recent years, astounding discoveries have been made deep under the ocean. Sunlight never penetrates there. But deep-diving submarines have discovered giant tube worms and other animals that live at very high pressure in the dark. Single-celled forms of life have been discovered that are different from plants, animals, or bacteria. These newly discovered life forms get their energy not from sunlight, but from chemicals. Other scientists have found tiny life forms in caves and deep inside solid rocks. Still other scientists have found life surviving in hot springs that had been thought to be too hot to support life.

The range of conditions in which life can exist is much greater than scientists once thought. Perhaps life forms exist that do not even need the "Goldilocks conditions"!

Figure 32 These colonies of microorganisms were discovered deep in a cave in Mexico. *Inferring How does studying unusual organisms like these help scientists predict what extraterrestrial life might be like?*

Media and Technology

Concept Videotape Library
Grade 6, Tape 4 "Evolution of Cells"

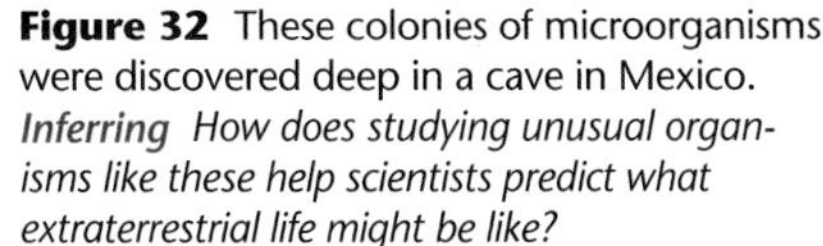

Answers to Self-Assessment

Caption Question

Figure 32 Scientists learn more about the wide range of conditions in which life on other planets might exist.

☑ *Checkpoint*

Living things are made up of one or more cells, take in energy and use it to grow and develop, reproduce, and give off waste.

2 Facilitate

The "Goldilocks Conditions"

Cultural Diversity

ACTIVITY When the *Voyager* spacecraft were launched, each had a time capsule that carried a message from Earth. The messages included languages, music, sounds, and images from many different cultures. As a class project, find out what messages were sent aboard the spacecraft. Then have students list the things that they would send to reflect their own culture. **learning modality: verbal**

Sharpen your Skills

Communicating

Time 15 minutes

Tips Have pairs of students critique each other's letters. Then have students write a final draft of their letters.

Expected Outcome Letters should include that Earth has liquid water and a suitable temperature range and atmosphere for living things.

Extend Challenge students to present the information in a chart listing the three Goldilocks Conditions and how Earth satisfies these conditions.

Life on Earth

Addressing Naive Conceptions

Some students may think that the search for extraterrestrial life is a search for only intelligent life forms. Ask: **Why would scientists be excited about discovering single-celled forms of life on other planets?** *(Single-celled life forms could suggest that multi-celled organisms may also exist on other planets.)* **learning modality: verbal**

Ongoing Assessment

Drawing Have students create a diagram showing characteristics of living things.

Life on Mars?

Building Inquiry Skills: Drawing Conclusions

Ask students: **What hypothesis were scientists testing when they sent the *Viking* spacecraft to Mars?** *(One hypothesis was that Mars may once have had life.)* Then ask: **What kinds of samples did the *Viking* examine?** *(Air and soil samples)* Next have students determine how these samples were useful to scientists. *(Scientists found no evidence of life on Mars.)* **learning modality: logical/mathematical**

Building Inquiry Skills: Making Judgments

ACTIVITY

Allow teams of students to debate the existence of life on Mars. Have each team prepare by making a list of all their arguments for one side of the debate. Then have pro and con teams present their arguments to each other and discuss the evidence on both sides. **cooperative learning**

Life on Europa?

Including All Students

ACTIVITY

Encourage students who need additional challenges to speculate on what kinds of life forms could exist beneath Europa's icy crust. Students should find out what living things survive under Earth's Arctic ice. Then have students suggest a possible test that could be done to find out whether similar kinds of life forms exist on Europa. **learning modality: logical/mathematical**

Language Arts Connection

Encourage students to read science-fiction short stories about life on other planets. Instruct them to try to distinguish fact from fiction. Encourage students to share stories with the class, and discuss the likelihood that they could ever take place. **learning modality: verbal**

Life on Mars?

Recall that Mars is the planet most similar to Earth. That makes Mars the most obvious place to look for living things similar to those on Earth.

The *Viking* Missions In 1970, a spacecraft found regions on the surface of Mars that look like stream beds with criss-crossing paths of water. These shapes, shown in Figure 33, were almost certainly formed by flowing water. **Since life as we know it requires water, scientists hypothesize that Mars may have once had the conditions needed for life to exist.**

Twin *Viking* spacecraft reached Mars in 1976. Each had one part that landed on Mars's surface and another part that stayed in orbit, taking pictures of most of the surface. Each of the *Viking* landers carried a compact biology laboratory meant to search for life forms.

The biology laboratories on the landers tested the Martian air and soil for signs of life. Each laboratory was designed to see if there were life forms that used oxygen and gave off carbon dioxide, as many living things on Earth do. A robot scoop brought some soil from Mars's surface into the lab and added water to see if the sample gave off oxygen. None of these tests showed any evidence of life.

☑ *Checkpoint* *What evidence shows that there may once have been running water on Mars?*

Meteorites From Mars Interest in life on Mars was increased by the report in 1996 about the meteorite from Mars that may contain fossils. The scientists' report started a huge debate. What were the tubelike things in the meteorite? Many scientists have suggested that the tiny shapes found in the meteorite do not prove that life forms once existed on Mars. Perhaps the shapes came from natural processes on Mars and are just lumps of hardened clay. Perhaps the shapes came from snow that got into cracks in the meteorite after it landed on Earth. Were the shapes

Figure 33 These patterns on the surface of Mars are probably evidence that liquid water once flowed on Mars. *Applying Concepts Why does this evidence make it more likely that there may once have been life on Mars?*

Background

Facts and Figures The tests performed by the scientific labs on the *Viking* landers gave no clear evidence of life on Mars. This conclusion, however, came after much debate, because the tests results were not negative. The tests were designed to detect life by exposing soil samples to controlled conditions, then detecting chemicals that would normally be produced by life processes. The tests not only detected these chemicals, but also detected them in much larger quantities than any life in the barren soil could possibly have produced. Obviously, something else was happening inside the test containers.

Scientists now hypothesize that the Martian soil contains chemicals similar to hydrogen peroxide that reacted with water and generated the positive test results. As a result, the *Viking* landers told us little about possible life on Mars.

too deep inside the rocks to be from Earth? Perhaps the shapes are too small to be the remains of life forms. They are only one-hundredth the size of any other known life forms.

The most effective way to answer these questions is to send more probes to Mars. Future Mars missions should be able to bring samples of rocks and soil back to Earth for detailed analysis. Scientists may not yet have evidence of life on Mars, but hope is growing that we can soon solve the mystery.

Life on Europa?

Many scientists think that Europa, one of Jupiter's moons, may have the conditions necessary for life to develop. Photos from *Voyager* and *Galileo* showed that Europa has a very smooth, icy crust with giant cracks in it.

Close-up views from *Galileo* show that Europa's ice has broken up and re-formed, resulting in twisted, house-sized blocks of ice. Similar patterns occur in the ice crust over Earth's Arctic Ocean. Could this mean that there is a liquid ocean under Europa's ice? The water in the ocean could possibly be kept liquid by heat coming from inside Europa. **If there is liquid water on Europa, there might also be life.**

How can scientists study conditions under Europa's ice sheet? Such studies are many years off. People will have to wait for the next generation of space probes to search for liquid water on Europa.

Figure 34 Europa is covered with a layer of ice similar to the ice covering Earth's Arctic Ocean. There may be liquid water under the ice.

Section 6 Review

1. What conditions does life on Earth need to survive?
2. Why do astronomers think there could be life on Europa?
3. How did the *Viking* missions search for life on Mars?
4. **Thinking Critically Applying Concepts** Do you think there could be life as we know it on Venus? Explain. (*Hint:* Review page 610.)

Science at Home

Message to E.T. Imagine that scientists have found intelligent extraterrestrial life. With family members, make up a message to send to the extraterrestrials. Remember that they will not understand English, so you should use only symbols and drawings in your message.

Program Resources

- **Unit 6 Resources** 19-6 Review and Reinforce; 19-6 Enrich
- **Interdisciplinary Exploration Series** "Mars the Next Frontier," pp. 8–11, 38–39

Answers to Self-Assessment

Caption Question

Figure 33 Since life as we know it requires water, evidence of liquid water flowing on Mars makes it more likely that there may once have been life there.

Checkpoint

Regions on the surface of Mars that look like stream beds with crisscrossing paths of water

3 Assess

Section 6 Review Answers

1. Liquid water, a suitable temperature range and atmosphere, and sunlight or other source of energy
2. Europa is covered by a layer of ice like Earth's Arctic Ocean, and there may be liquid water underneath the ice.
3. Both *Viking* landers had biology laboratories. Each laboratory examined the air and soil for signs of oxygen being used up and carbon dioxide being produced.
4. No, because life as we know it cannot exist at 460°C, the surface temperature of Venus.

Science at Home

Encourage students to consider what information about Earth and its inhabitants would be most important for extraterrestrials to know. Suggest that students ask each family member to contribute one piece of the message.

Portfolio Students can save their messages in their portfolios.

Performance Assessment

Writing Have students explain which of the planets and their moons in our solar system would be good places to search for signs of life and which would not.

Science and Society

Space Exploration—Is It Worth the Cost?

Purpose

To discuss the value of space exploration

Panel Discussion

Time 1 day to prepare; 1 hour for panel discussion

Have students discuss space exploration in groups of three or four. Allow them access to books, magazine articles, or the Internet to find information on the potential benefits of space exploration.

Once students have had time to discuss the issues in groups, bring them back together and lead a panel discussion on the pros and cons of space exploration. Have each group act as one panel member, representing one point of view and taking turns presenting points in the discussion.

Extend Ask students to come up with several questions concerning space exploration that they could ask their family or community members in order to gain other insights into the space program and its potential benefits. For example, students may not realize how inspiring Armstrong's trip to the moon was when it took place unless they talk to someone who was an adult in the 1960s.

You Decide

Have students complete the first two steps on page 708 before the panel discussion begins as a way to prepare themselves for taking part. After the discussion is concluded, students can complete Step 3 on page 708, using what they learned in the discussion to find solutions to the problem. Students may set priorities for Congress's budget in many different ways. Many will put feeding the poor or researching diseases near the top of the list and space exploration near the bottom.

Science and Society

Space Exploration—Is It Worth the Cost?

Imagine that your spacecraft has just landed on Mars after a two-month journey from Earth. You've spent years planning for this moment. Canyons, craters, and distant plains stretch out before you. You check your spacesuit and prepare to step out onto the rocky red surface of Mars.

Is such a trip likely? Would it be worthwhile? How much is space flight really worth to human society? Scientists and politicians have already started to debate such questions. Space exploration can help us learn more about the universe. But exploration is risky and expensive. Sending people into space costs billions of dollars and risks human lives. How can we balance the costs and benefits of space exploration?

The Issues

Should Humans Travel Into Space? Many Americans think that Neil Armstrong's walk on the moon in 1969 was one of the great moments in history. Also, learning how to keep people alive in space has led to improvements in everyday life. Safer equipment for firefighters, easier ways to package frozen food, and effective heart monitors have all come out of space program research.

What Are the Alternatives? Space exploration can involve a project to put a person on Mars. It also can involve a more limited use of scientific instruments near Earth, such as the Hubble Space Telescope. Instead of sending people, we could send space probes like *Mars Pathfinder* to other planets.

Is Human Space Exploration Worth the Cost? Scientists who favor human travel into space say that only people can collect certain kinds of information. And using simpler space vehicles that are cheaper to build can also save money. But no one knows if research in space really provides information quicker than research that can be done on Earth. Many critics of space research think that other needs are more important. One United States senator said, "Every time you put money into the space station, there is a dime that won't be available for our children's education or for medical research."

You Decide

1. **Identify the Problem** In your own words, list the costs and benefits of space exploration.
2. **Analyze the Options** Make a chart of three different approaches to space exploration: sending humans to another planet, doing only Earth-based research, and one other option. What are the benefits and drawbacks of each approach?
3. **Find a Solution** Imagine that you are a member of Congress who has to vote on a new budget. There is a fixed amount of money to spend, so you have to decide which needs are most important. Make a list of your top ten priorities. Explain your decisions.

Background

NASA has included a detailed justification of space exploration on their Web site. NASA argues that the basic knowledge about the universe gained through space exploration gives us a better understanding of Earth. Space exploration has allowed applications in satellite communication. Many technological breakthroughs have come as a result of the space program. The space program supports many jobs and is thus good for the economy. The exploration of space serves as an inspiration to people to explore the unknown and push back boundaries. Additional information is available at: **www.nasa.gov/** and **www.nss.org/**

CHAPTER 19 STUDY GUIDE

Observing the Solar System

Key Ideas

- Ptolemy thought that Earth is at the center of the system of planets.
- Copernicus thought that the sun is at the center of the planets. Galileo's observations supported Copernicus's theory.
- Kepler discovered that the orbits of the planets are ellipses.
- Newton concluded that two factors—inertia and gravity—combine to keep the planets in orbit.

Key Terms

geocentric
heliocentric
ellipse
inertia

The Sun

Key Ideas

- The sun's energy comes from nuclear fusion.
- The sun's atmosphere has three layers: the photosphere, the chromosphere, and the corona.
- Features on or above the sun's surface include sunspots, prominences, and solar flares.

Key Terms

nuclear fusion
core
photosphere
chromosphere
corona
solar wind
sunspot
prominence
solar flare

The Inner Planets

Key Idea

- The four inner planets—Mercury, Venus, Earth, and Mars—are small and have rocky surfaces. They are often called the terrestrial planets.

Key Terms

terrestrial planets
retrograde rotation
greenhouse effect

The Outer Planets

Key Ideas

- Four outer planets—Jupiter, Saturn, Uranus, and Neptune—are much larger than Earth.
- Pluto and Charon have solid surfaces and masses much less than that of Earth.

Key Term

gas giant

Comets, Asteroids, and Meteors

Key Ideas

- Comets are chunks of ice and dust that usually have long, elliptical orbits.
- Most asteroids revolve around the sun between the orbits of Mars and Jupiter.

Key Terms

comet
asteroid
asteroid belt
meteoroid
meteor
meteorite

Is There Life Beyond Earth?

INTEGRATING LIFE SCIENCE

Key Ideas

- Earth has liquid water and a suitable temperature range and atmosphere for living things to survive.
- Since life as we know it requires water, scientists hypothesize that Mars may have once had the conditions for life to exist.

Key Term

extraterrestrial life

Organizing Information

Compare/Contrast Table On a separate piece of paper, make a table comparing and contrasting the geocentric and heliocentric systems. Include information on the following: object at the center of the system; objects that move around the center; who first proposed the system; and who supported the system. (For more on compare/contrast tables, see the Skills Handbook.)

Organizing Information

Compare/Contrast Table

	Geocentric System	Heliocentric System
Object at center	Earth	sun
Objects that move around center	planets and sun	Earth and other planets
Proposed by	ancient Greek astronomers	Copernicus
Supporters	Ptolemy	Galileo and others

Media and Technology

Computer Test Bank Chapter 19 Test

Program Resources

- **Unit 6 Resources** Chapter 19 Project Scoring Rubric
- **Performance Assessment** Chapter 19
- **Chapter and Unit Tests** Chapter 19 Test; Unit 6 Test

CHAPTER 19 ASSESSMENT

Reviewing Content

Multiple Choice

1. d **2.** d **3.** c **4.** a **5.** c

True or False

6. ellipse **7.** true **8.** true **9.** Jupiter **10.** true

Checking Concepts

11. Galileo's observations of Venus' phases could not be explained by the geocentric system. His observations of the motions of Jupiter's moons showed that not everything in the sky revolves around Earth.
12. Newton concluded that gravity and inertia keep the planets in the orbits that Kepler found by looking at Brahe's observations.
13. It is usually impossible to see the sun's corona because its faint light is overwhelmed by the bright light of the photosphere and chromosphere.
14. Dark-looking areas of gas on the sun that are cooler than the gases around them
15. Mercury is so hot that the gases in the atmosphere escaped from Mercury's weak gravity.
16. One hypothesis is that Venus was struck by a large object billions of years ago and this collision caused Venus' direction of rotation to change.
17. The terrestrial planets are relatively small and rocky. The gas giants are much larger and lack a solid surface.
18. These astronomers think Pluto should not be a planet because it is so small. They think it may just be the largest of thousands of objects revolving around the sun beyond Neptune.
19. Solar wind pushes the gases in a comet's tail away from the sun.
20. No. Life on Earth can exist without sunlight, in caves, and in solid rock. Scientists could look for evidence of life in these places.
21. Students should include descriptions of the terrestrial planet and the gas giant that they visit. High marks should be given for accurate, clearly written descriptions.

CHAPTER 19 ASSESSMENT

Reviewing Content

Multiple Choice

Choose the letter of the answer that best completes each statement.

1. Copernicus thought that the solar system was
a. celestial.
b. elliptical.
c. geocentric.
d. heliocentric.

2. The part of the sun where nuclear fusion occurs is the
a. photosphere. **b.** chromosphere.
c. corona. **d.** core.

3. Planets with atmospheres composed mostly of carbon dioxide include
a. Earth and Mercury.
b. Venus and Mercury.
c. Venus and Mars.
d. Mercury and Mars.

4. The Great Red Spot is a huge storm on
a. Jupiter. **b.** Neptune.
c. Saturn. **d.** Pluto.

5. Most asteroids orbit the sun
a. between the sun and Mercury.
b. between Earth and Mars.
c. between Mars and Jupiter.
d. between Neptune and Pluto.

True or False

If the statement is true, write true. If it is false, change the underlined word or words to make the statement true.

6. The shape of the orbit of each planet is a circle.
7. Sunspots are regions of cooler gases on the sun.
8. The atmosphere of Venus has higher pressure than the atmosphere of Earth.
9. Aside from the sun, Saturn is the largest source of gravity in the solar system.
10. Conditions favorable to life as we know it are sometimes called the Goldilocks conditions.

Checking Concepts

11. How did Galileo's observations support the heliocentric system?
12. How did Newton's work on orbits add to the work Kepler had done?
13. Why is it usually impossible to see the sun's corona?
14. What are sunspots?
15. Why does Mercury have only a thin atmosphere?
16. How do astronomers explain that Venus rotates in the opposite direction from most planets and moons?
17. What are the major characteristics of the terrestrial planets? How do they differ from the gas giants?
18. Why do some astronomers think that Pluto should not be called a planet?
19. Why does a comet's tail always stream away from the sun?
20. Do living things have to live on the surface of a planet or moon? Where else on a planet or moon could scientists look for evidence of life?
21. Writing to Learn Imagine you are an astronaut on a mission to explore the solar system. Write a trip journal telling the story of your trip from Earth to another terrestrial planet and to a gas giant. Include a description of each planet.

Thinking Critically

22. Relating Cause and Effect How would Earth move if the sun (including its gravity) suddenly disappeared? Explain your answer.
23. Applying Concepts Explain why Venus is hotter than it would be without its atmosphere.
24. Comparing and Contrasting Compare and contrast meteoroids, meteors, and meteorites.
25. Making Generalizations Why would the discovery of liquid water on another planet be important?

Thinking Critically

22. Because of inertia, Earth would continue to move in a straight path in the direction it was going when the sun disappeared.
23. Venus's atmosphere creates a greenhouse effect that traps heat energy from the sun.
24. A meteoroid is a chunk of rock or dust in space. If a meteoroid enters Earth's atmosphere and burns up, a streak of light called a meteor is seen. If a meteoroid hits Earth's surface, it is called a meteorite.
25. Since water is essential to life on Earth, the presence of water on another planet increases the possibility that life may be found there.

Applying Skills

Use the diagram of an imaginary, newly discovered planetary system around Star X to answer Questions 26–28. The periods of revolution of planets A, B, and C are 75 Earth days, 200 Earth days, and 300 Earth days.

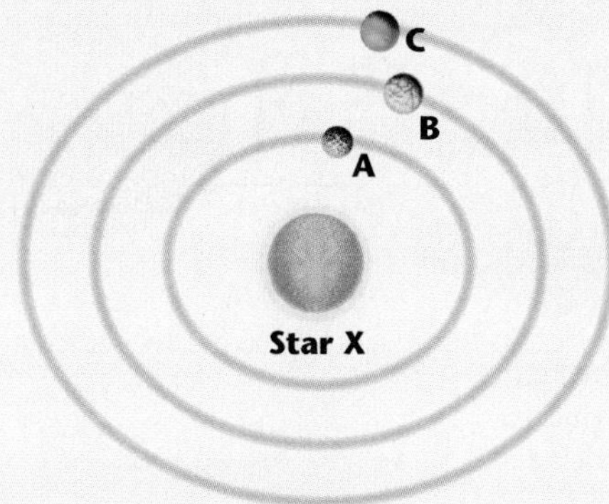

26. Interpreting Data Which planet in this new planetary system revolves around Star X in the shortest amount of time?

27. Making Models In 150 days, how far will each planet have revolved around Star X? Copy the diagram and sketch the positions of the three planets to find out. How far will each planet have revolved around Star X in 400 days? Sketch their positions.

28. Drawing Conclusions Can planet C ever be closer to planet A than to planet B? Study your drawings to figure this out.

Performance (CHAPTER PROJECT) Assessment

Present Your Project Now you are ready to present your solar system. Explain how you were able to work with large distances. Display your data tables showing how you did the calculations and how you checked them for accuracy. Compare the distances in your models to distances inside and outside your classroom.

Reflect and Record In your journal, explain what you would change in your model of the solar system. What would you do to improve the model? How effectively did you use computers or calculators to get the data?

Test Preparation

Use these questions to prepare for standardized tests.

Study the table. Then answer Questions 29–32.

Planet	Period of Rotation (Earth days)	Period of Revolution (Earth years)	Average Distance From the Sun (million kilometers)
Mars	1.03	1.9	228
Jupiter	0.41	12	778
Saturn	0.43	29	1,427
Uranus	0.72	84	2,871
Neptune	0.67	165	4,497

29. Which of these planet's orbits is farthest from Earth's orbit?
a. Mars **b.** Jupiter
c. Uranus **d.** Neptune

30. Which planet has a "day" that is most similar in length to a day on Earth?
a. Mars **b.** Jupiter
c. Uranus **d.** Neptune

31. Light takes about 8 minutes and 20 seconds to travel from the sun to the Earth, 150 million kilometers away. About how long does it take light to travel from the sun to Jupiter?
a. 10 minutes **b.** 25 minutes
c. 43 minutes **d.** 112 minutes

32. Which one of the following conclusions about planets is supported by the information in the table?
a. As distance from the sun increases, period of rotation increases.
b. As distance from the sun increases, period of revolution increases.
c. As distance from the sun increases, period of revolution decreases.
d. There is no relationship between distance from the sun and period of revolution.

Program Resources

- **Inquiry Skills Activity Book** Provides teaching and review of all inquiry skills

Applying Skills

26. Planet A which takes only 75 days
27. Planet A will have revolved around star X twice. Planet B will have completed three quarters of one revolution. Planet C will have completed only one half of one revolution. In 400 days, planet A will have completed five revolutions and be one third through a sixth; planet B will have completed two revolutions; and planet C will have completed one revolution and be one third through a second.
28. Yes. Planet A and C could be on one side of the star and B on the other. After 300 days, planet A and C are where they began, on the same side of star X, but planet B is on the opposite side of the star.

Performance Assessment

Present Your Project Students should explain that they scaled all distances by a constant amount to make them manageable. They could have checked their numbers by multiplying the scaled numbers by the reciprocal of their scaling factor to see if they obtained the correct planet sizes. Students should have a good understanding that the sun is very large, that planets vary considerably in size, and that space is mostly "empty space."
Reflect and Record Students might change the scale and present the model in a very large area in order to make the smallest planets visible. Students will reflect that it was not possible to find a scale that was good for comparing the sizes of the planets and the sun with one that was good for showing the distances between the planets and the sun. Since students are dealing with very large numbers with many zeros, they should have found calculators useful in avoiding arithmetic errors.

Test Preparation

29. d **30.** a **31.** c **32.** b

The Solar System

This interdisciplinary feature presents the central theme of exploring the solar system by connecting four different disciplines: science, social studies, mathematics, and language arts. The four explorations are designed to capture students' interest and help them see how the content they are studying in science relates to other school subjects and to real-world events. The unit is particularly suitable for team teaching.

1 Engage/Explore

Activating Prior Knowledge

Help students recall what they learned in Chapter 19, Section 3, The Inner Planets, by asking questions such as: **How many moons does Mars have?** *(two)* and **How does Mars compare in size to Earth?** *(Mars has a diameter a little more than half that of Earth.)*

Introducing the Unit

Discuss the fact that space exploration is a popular theme in entertainment. However, humans have explored very little of space so far. Ask: **Why is it so difficult for humans to explore space?** *(Accept all reasonable responses.)* Ask: **Where have humans been in the solar system outside of Earth?** *(In space stations orbiting around Earth and on the moon)*

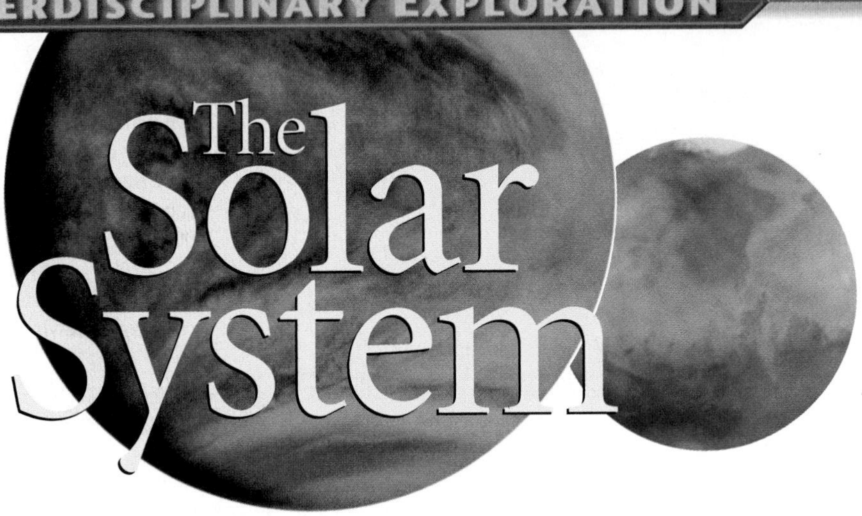

The Solar System

In the 1950s, the first artificial satellite was launched into orbit around Earth. Since that time, scientists and engineers have developed new technologies to send vehicles farther and farther from their launch pads on Earth.

Only the moon has been visited by humans. Other space missions have studied the solar system by sending vehicles to orbit or fly by planets, and sometimes to land on them. These missions have provided information that could not have been learned through observations through telescopes on Earth.

SURFACE OF MARS

A dog called Laika survived for a few hours in space aboard Sputnik 2.

SPUTNIK 2

YURI GAGARIN

Apollo 11 *lunar module approaches the surface of the moon.*

***APOLLO 11* MISSION**

1957 The Soviet Union launches the first artificial Earth satellite, *Sputnik 1*, into space. *Sputnik 2* follows a few weeks later.

1961 Russian Yuri Gagarin becomes the first person to orbit Earth, aboard *Vostok 1*.

1969 American astronauts Neil Armstrong and Edwin "Buzz" Aldrin, Jr. are the first people to step onto the moon, as part of the *Apollo 11* mission.

1972 The space probe *Pioneer 10* blasts off to study Jupiter and its moons.

1976 *Viking I* and *Viking II* space probes land on Mars and send back photos of the red planet's surface.

1950 1960 1970

Program Resources

- **Unit 6 Resources** Interdisciplinary Exploration
- **Interdisciplinary Explorations Series** "Mars the Next Frontier," pp. 1–43

Mission to Mars

In 1997, *Pathfinder* landed on Mars. It carried a rover, a six-wheeled vehicle about the size of a microwave oven. The rover, called *Sojourner*, was controlled from Earth. Engineers at the Jet Propulsion Laboratory in Pasadena, California guided the rover using remote controls. They maneuvered Sojourner around the rocky surface, stopping the rover at each rock, to allow the rover to collect data on the minerals in the rocks.

Science Activity

Study the timeline below. What event happened the same year as the Pathfinder mission? How many years were there between landings on Mars? How many years were there between missions to Jupiter? Suggest a reason for the long intervals between missions.

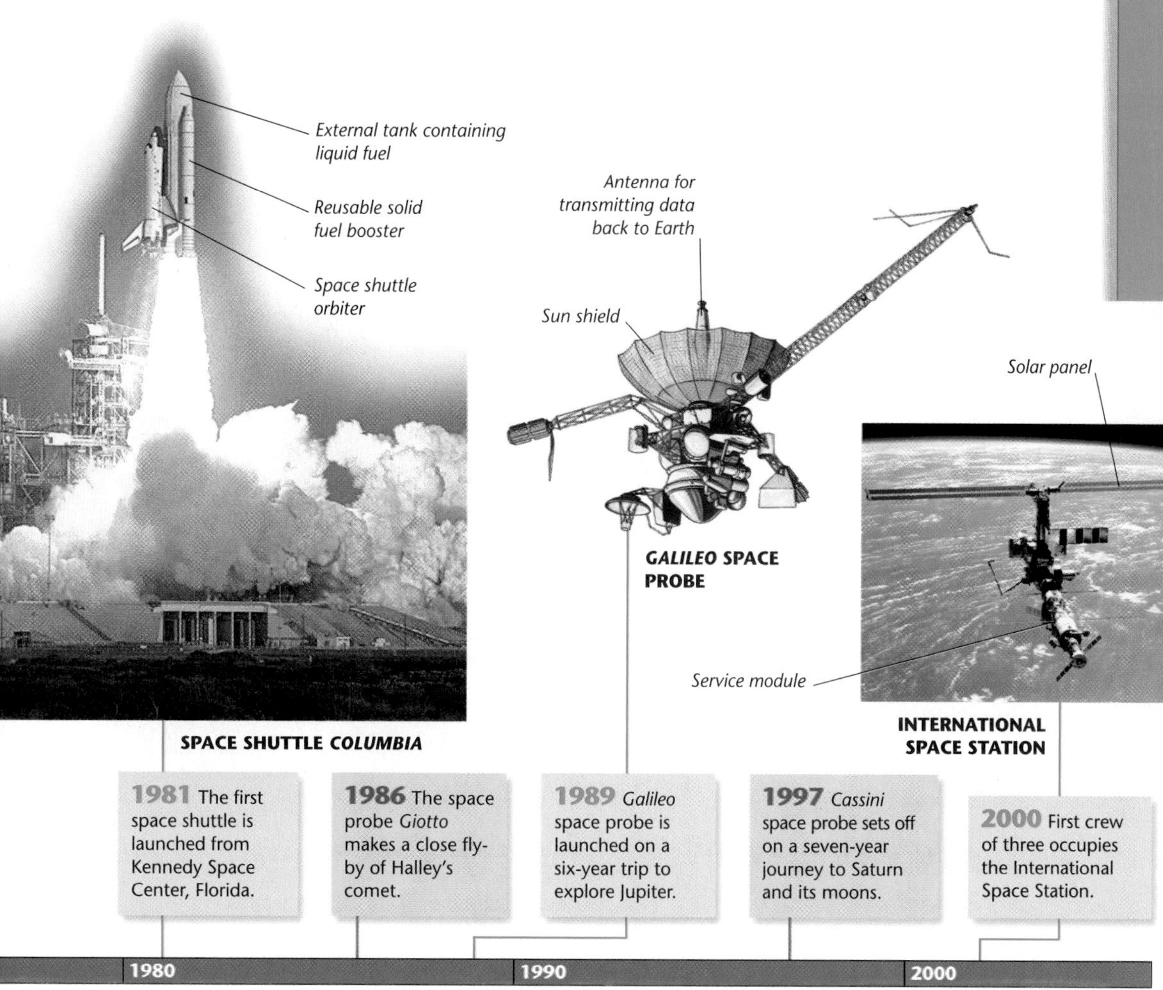

1981 The first space shuttle is launched from Kennedy Space Center, Florida.

1986 The space probe *Giotto* makes a close fly-by of Halley's comet.

1989 *Galileo* space probe is launched on a six-year trip to explore Jupiter.

1997 *Cassini* space probe sets off on a seven-year journey to Saturn and its moons.

2000 First crew of three occupies the International Space Station.

1980 1990 2000

Background

Facts and Figures If you've ever been in the rocky western deserts of the United States, the rugged Martian landscape of reddish rocks may look familiar. Mars has a "Grand Canyon," too, a series of huge canyons called Valles Marineris (named after the U.S. *Mariner* probe). These canyons are five times as deep as the Grand Canyon and more than 4,500 kilometers long, about the width of the continental United States.

Since there are no oceans, the total land area of Mars is about equal to the continents and islands on Earth. In the south, the rugged surface is pitted with craters. The northern hemisphere is sandy dunes or rolling plains covered with thin lava. Volcanoes have been important in forming Mars's landscape. One huge volcano, Olympus Mons, towers about 24 kilometers above the surface, three times as high as Mt. Everest.

2 Facilitate

- To extend this exploration, challenge students to find out more about space exploration. Students who have access to the Internet can look at NASA's Web site, **www.nasa.gov**, to find out what the rover *Sojourner* learned about conditions on Mars.

Science Activity

Divide students into groups of four. Have each group perform the activity. Urge students to use the amount of plant food marked on the container. Students who use more plant food than is recommended may damage their plants.

Assign a few minutes twice a week for the following three weeks for students to check that their plants have sufficient water and to record their progress.

Use this experiment to help students understand the scientific process. Scientists try to test every hypothesis rather than just assume it is true. Scientists can learn as much from hypotheses that are proved to be false as they can from hypotheses that are supported by scientific evidence.

Unit 6 Resources The following Interdisciplinary Exploration worksheets correlate with this page: Gravity on Mars; The Polar Caps of Mars; and History of Mars Exploration.

3 Assess

Activity Assessment

Help students read the timeline. They should be able to compare dates and answer the questions in the Science Activity.

Language Arts

2 Facilitate

- Have three volunteers each read one third of the essay aloud. Students may need help pronouncing "Sojourner." Have students use a dictionary to look up the meanings of words they are not familiar with, such as "reformer" or "eloquence."
- After students have read the essay, make two columns on the board titled "Person" and "Pathfinder." Have students review the essay and name ways in which Sojourner Truth and the *Sojourner* rover are similar.
- Challenge interested students to find out more about Sojourner Truth's life and make a bulletin board display for the class.

Language Arts Activity

Students can use reference books such as almanacs or the *New York Public Library Science Desk Reference* to find the names and achievements of some of the most famous scientists. Students can then research further those scientists they are most interested in. Urge students to include in their essays the ways in which the scientist is similar to the research station.

Unit 6 Resources The following Interdisciplinary Exploration worksheets correlate with this page: Ain't I A Woman?; Words From Mars Fiction; and Move to Mars!

3 Assess

Activity Assessment

Make sure students choose a person from science exploration or discovery, not a sports or entertainment figure. Make sure students' essays are persuasive. Look for students who clearly explained why the research station should be named after the person they chose.

Language Arts

Honor in a Name

Would you like to name a spacecraft? A 13-year-old student from Connecticut got that chance. Valerie Ambroise chose the name *Sojourner* for the small Pathfinder rover that explored the Martian surface in 1997. In a contest sponsored by NASA and The Planetary Society, Valerie wrote the winning essay for the best name. There were 3,500 student entries.

Valerie named *Sojourner* after Sojourner Truth, an African American reformer in the 1840s and 1850s. Here is Valerie Ambroise's essay.

Sojourner Truth (above), a powerful speaker against slavery, and Valerie Ambroise (right).

The name of the Pathfinder should be Sojourner Truth. I chose Sojourner because she was a heroine to Blacks, slaves, and women. She acted on her strong feelings about life and the way it should be. Her greatest companions were God and her beliefs. Her greatest achievements included the book of her life written through her by a friend, meeting President Lincoln, meeting President Grant, her speeches and tours, her work at hospitals for soldiers during the Civil War, and her intellect (considering that she was illiterate). She went on many journeys and told many truths. She spoke with such eloquence that she moved people with simple words and understandings.

It's only logical that the Pathfinder be named Sojourner Truth, because she is on a journey to find truths about Mars. The Pathfinder should be able to have strong personalities in order to go under harsh conditions like that on Mars. Truth, while on tours, went under many harsh conditions. Even before, she went under harsh conditions as a slave.

Like Sojourner, the Pathfinder should be able to survive with what she already has. She should not need any extra equipment for surviving. The Pathfinder could use its feet like wheels, for transportation. Sojourner used her feet to travel a lot.

To research Mars, first, Sojourner would find out all she could about it. She always tried to understand further about what she was fighting for. When she got her information; she would use this information in Mars to study it more and add it to hers. She would act quickly to get what she wanted or what she felt was needed. Her talents in her work would be the same on Mars. She would use her eloquent voice and powerful actions.

You must admit, Sojourner and the Pathfinder are important.

Language Arts Activity

You have the chance to name the first research station on Mars, honoring an important person in scientific exploration or discovery. Research your hero or heroine. Then write a persuasive essay explaining why the research station should be named after him or her.

Background

Facts and Figures The "Name the Rover" competition was announced in 1994. The rules were:

- the writer had to be born after January 1, 1976
- the essay had to be 300 words;
- the essay had to be fully researched;
- the rover could be named for any heroine from mythology, fiction, or history who was not living;
- the essay had to explain how the person's name was appropriate for the rover.

The essay organizers received 3,800 essays, of which 1,700 followed the rules. The essays came from all over the world. The second place essay proposed that the rover be named after Marie Curie. Curie's work in radioactivity related to the Mars mission because the rover used radioactivity to analyze rocks and soil.

Astronaut Shannon Lucid and a Russian cosmonaut examine food bins on *Mir* (left).

A cosmonaut, floating in space, repairs equipment on *Mir* (above).

Partners in Space

Many engineers and scientists are confident that humans will travel to Mars sometime in the next 25 years. Meanwhile, people have gotten a preview of a space voyage from astronauts and cosmonauts traveling on space shuttles, on *Mir*, Russia's former space station, and on the new International Space Station.

For years, the United States and the Soviet Union competed in a race to send missions into space. Beginning in 1997, Russia and the United States cooperated on *Mir*. Americans worked with cosmonauts to solve problems, make repairs, take spacewalks, and run the ship's computers. More recently, scientists from 16 countries have cooperated to construct and operate the International Space Station, which is being built in orbit.

What's it like for crew members from different backgrounds to live and work together in a cramped spacecraft? Besides having cultural and language differences, Russian and American crews have different training and different equipment. Even spacesuits are not the same.

Because *Mir* was an old station, space crews gained experience dealing with emergencies. On a long flight, such as one to Mars, those skills would be essential.

All this experience on *Mir* and the International Space Station should prove invaluable for a future expedition to Mars.

This is a 360-degree image taken from *Pathfinder.* On the rugged Martian landscape, sand and dust storms have carved rocks into fantastic shapes. Deep canyons and huge volcanoes also shape the surface.

Social Studies Activity

The first trips to Mars will probably take at least 6 to 8 months. Think about the difficulties you would have spending 7 months in a spacecraft about the size of a school bus. Set up rules and guidelines for your voyage. Plan for five astronauts from two different countries. Consider these issues:

- who will make decisions and give orders
- how you will communicate
- how you'll adjust for different living habits and backgrounds
- how you'll avoid getting bored
- how you'll resolve conflicts among crew members or with mission-control scientists on Earth.

2 Facilitate

- *Mir* is pronounced "mere" and means "peace."
- Mention that the International Space Station was begun in 1999 and that Mir re-entered Earth's atmosphere on a controlled trajectory and crashed into the Pacific Ocean in March 2001. Russia has more extensive experience than the United States with long stays in a space station. This experience will be useful both for the space station and for future trips to Mars.
- To extend this exploration, have students think about experiences they have had where people had to cooperate in cramped conditions. Ask students to brainstorm things they learned about how to get along with others under stressful conditions.

Social Studies Activity

Have students first work alone, then in groups. Have students share and discuss their ideas. As conflicts arise within student groups, use this as an opportunity to discuss ways the astronauts might have conflicts. Ask students to suggest strategies that people can use to make group decision-making easier. Ask: **What kinds of behavior help the group get along?**

Unit 6 Resources The following Interdisciplinary Exploration worksheets correlate with this page: Earth from Space; The Search for Life on Mars; and Map of Mars.

3 Assess

Activity Assessment

Evaluate the reasonableness of students' ideas. Watch for students who need concrete suggestions on how the astronauts can resolve conflicts. Watch for students who are unrealistic about the amount of stress that can occur when too many people are sharing too small a space.

Mathematics

2 Facilitate

- Review what causes days, years, and seasons. Ask: **Could a planet have a day shorter than an Earth day but have a year longer than an Earth year?** *(Yes, if the planet was spinning on its axis faster than Earth but revolving around the sun slower than Earth.)*
- To extend this exploration, encourage interested students to read books or magazine articles about what it is like to live in harsh climates. Eric Pinder's book, *Life at the Top,* describes living conditions at the Mount Washington weather observatory on top of Mount Washington, New Hampshire, which is known as the location of Earth's worst weather.

Math Activity

Point out that the values of the percents should correspond to the relative sizes of the segments. Remind students that the northern and southern hemispheres have seasons of different lengths, unlike on Earth.

Unit 6 Resources The following Interdisciplinary Exploration worksheets correlate with this page: A Year on Mars; Model the Mars Neighborhood; and Martian Seasons in Days.

3 Assess

Activity Assessment

Northern Hemisphere: Fall 21%, Spring 29%; Southern Hemisphere: Fall 29%, Spring 21%. Make sure the size of each segment is the right size for the percent.

Mathematics

Sols of Mars

Mars is the planet most like Earth. But its smaller size, greater distance from the sun, and different orbit cause some immense differences. A Martian day, called a sol, is only about 40 minutes longer than an Earth day. The Martian year, however, is much longer—669 sols.

Mars, like Earth, tilts on its axis, so it has seasons. Each Martian season lasts longer than an Earth season because the Martian year is longer. The shape of Mars's orbit makes the seasons unequal in length (see table below).

The climate in the southern hemisphere is more extreme than in the northern hemisphere. Winters in the south are longer and colder, while summers are shorter and warmer. Winter in the south, for instance, lasts 177 sols. In the northern hemisphere, winter lasts only 156 sols.

Seasonal changes affect Mars's north and south poles, which are covered with polar ice caps made of water and carbon dioxide. During winter in the southern hemisphere, the polar cap covers almost half the hemisphere. Here the ice cap is mainly frozen carbon dioxide—like dry ice. In spring, the ice cap partially melts, releasing carbon dioxide into the air. In a similar way, when spring comes in the northern hemisphere, the north polar cap melts. But in the north, the frozen core is made mainly of water ice.

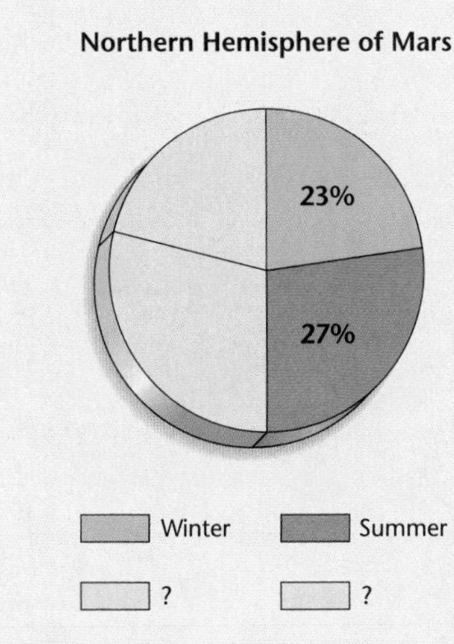

Martian Seasons in Sols (Martian Days)

	Northern Hemisphere	Southern Hemisphere
Winter	156	177
Spring	194	142
Summer	177	156
Fall	142	194

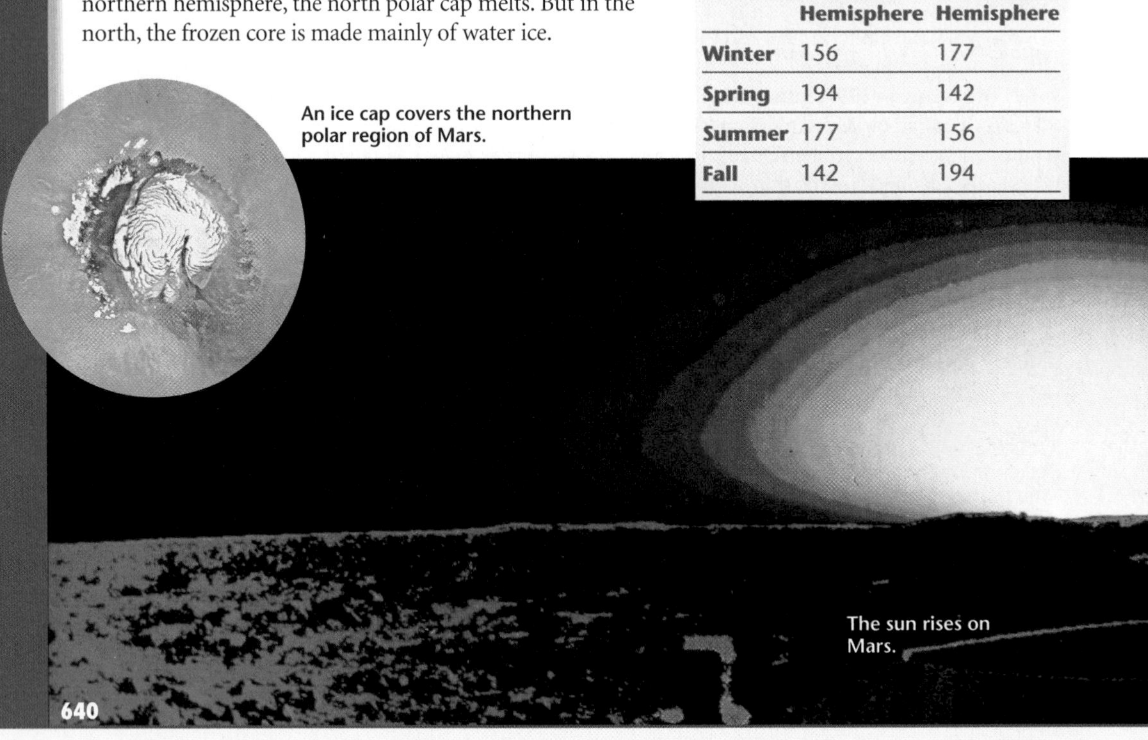

An ice cap covers the northern polar region of Mars.

The sun rises on Mars.

640

Background

Integrating Science and Technology Space scientists and engineers who have considered missions to Mars have taken two different approaches. One approach, in general, depends on transporting buildings, supplies, rocket fuel, and billions of dollars worth of other equipment to the planet—in short, taking along everything necessary to get along for two or three years. By contrast, the other approach depends on the pioneer settlers quickly making use of what is available on Mars. For example, an initial uncrewed flight would take just the equipment needed to use chemicals in the Martian atmosphere to make enough rocket fuel to return home.

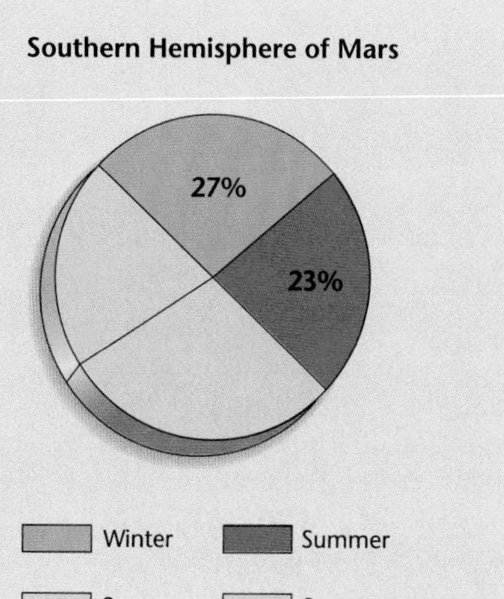

Math Activity

People working on Mars would probably go by Martian time. You know that there are 669 sols (Martian days) in a Martian year. Knowing the number of sols in a season, you can figure the percent of the year that's winter. For example, winter in the northern hemisphere is 156 sols ÷ 669 sols ≈ 0.233 ≈ 23%.

- Use the table on page 752 to figure out what percent of the Martian year in each hemisphere is winter, spring, summer, and fall. Round to the nearest hundredth.
- Make two circle graphs like those on pages 752 and 753. Label, color, and write the percent for each season in the northern and southern hemispheres.
- Choose a different color for each.

If you had a choice, which hemisphere would you choose to live in?

Tie It Together

Plan a Martian Station

At last, you will be going to Mars to set up the first human research station. For an expedition this long, good planning is essential. Review the major problems that Mars presents to humans, such as thin atmosphere, no oxygen, extreme temperatures, and so on. Remember that it's too expensive to send most supplies to Mars. Work in groups to make a plan for setting up Earth's research station. Include maps and drawings. As you make your plan, consider questions such as these:

- How will you supply oxygen? Water? Fuel?
- What site will you choose for your settlement? Consider the landscape and climate on Mars.
- What supplies will you bring with you?
- What will you use for building materials?
- What kinds of food will you get? How will you get food?

This painting shows how one artist imagined a human home on another planet.

Tie It Together

Time 1 week (1 day for planning, 2 days for research, 2 days for preparing maps, plans, and drawings)

Tips Have students work in groups of four or five. If possible, group students so that each group contains at least one student who knows how to research on the Internet or who can ask an adult for help.

- Most of the information that students' are searching for should be readily available from encyclopedias.
- Ask questions such as the following to prompt student thinking: **Will you construct domes like those in research stations in Antarctica? Could you make bricks out of frozen soil? How will you supply oxygen, water, food, and fuel? How can you grow food indoors in a laboratory or greenhouse? Can you use hydroponics or aquaculture? Keeping in mind what you have learned about the landscape and climate of Mars, what kind of site will you choose for a settlement? Do you want the protection of a valley or canyon? Do you want the smoother terrain and milder climate of the northern hemisphere?**

Extend Challenge students to find out what scientists have learned about building self-contained biospheres containing people.

Developing scientific thinking in students is important for a solid science education. To learn how to think scientifically, students need frequent opportunities to practice science process skills, critical thinking skills, as well as other skills that support scientific inquiry. The *Science Explorer* Skills Handbook introduces the following key science skills:

- Science Process Skills
- SI Measuring Skills
- Skills for Conducting a Scientific Investigation
- Critical Thinking Skills
- Information Organizing Skills
- Data Table and Graphing Skills

The Skills Handbook is designed as a reference for students to use whenever they need to review a science skill. You can use the activities provided in the Skills Handbook to teach or reinforce the skills.

Think Like a Scientist

Observing

ACTIVITY

Before students look at the photograph, remind them that an observation is only what they can see, hear, smell, taste, or feel. Ask: **Which senses will you use to make observations from this photograph?** *(Sight is the only sense that can be used to make observations from the photograph.)* **What are some observations you can make from the photograph?** *(Answers may vary. Sample answers: Water covers the road; two barriers block the road; trees line both sides of the road; telephone poles are on the left side of the road.)* List the observations on the chalkboard. If students make any inferences or predictions about the scene at this point, ask: **Can you be sure your statement is factual and accurate from just observing the photograph?** Help students understand how observations differ from inferences and predictions.

Inferring

ACTIVITY

Review students' observations from the photograph. Then ask: **What inferences can you make from your observations?** *(Students may say that the road is closed because of flooding waters caused by heavy rains.)* **What experience or knowledge helped you make this inference?** *(Students may have had experience with flash floods on roadways and they may have seen barriers placed across impassable roads.)* **Can anyone suggest another possible interpretation for these observations?** *(Answers may vary. Sample answer: The road may have been built in wetlands and over time has sunk lower than the water level)* **How can you find out whether an inference is correct?** *(by further investigation)*

Predicting

ACTIVITY

After students come to some consensus about the inference that the road was closed due to flooding, encourage them to make predictions about what will happen next. *(Students' predictions may vary. Sample answers: The water will rise higher with the next rain. Dry weather will cause the flood waters to recede and the road to reappear.)*

Skills Handbook

Think Like a Scientist

Although you may not know it, you think like a scientist every day. Whenever you ask a question and explore possible answers, you use many of the same skills that scientists do. Some of these skills are described on this page.

Observing

When you use one or more of your five senses to gather information about the world, you are **observing.** Hearing a dog bark, counting twelve green seeds, and smelling smoke are all observations. To increase the power of their senses, scientists sometimes use microscopes, telescopes, or other instruments that help them make more detailed observations.

An observation must be an accurate report of what your senses detect. It is important to keep careful records of your observations in science class by writing or drawing in a notebook. The information collected through observations is called evidence, or data.

Inferring

When you interpret an observation, you are **inferring,** or making an inference. For example, if you hear your dog barking, you may infer that someone is at your front door. To make this inference, you combine the evidence—the barking dog—and your experience or knowledge—you know that your dog barks when strangers approach—to reach a logical conclusion.

Notice that an inference is not a fact; it is only one of many possible explanations for an observation. For example, your dog may be barking because it wants to go for a walk. An inference may turn out to be incorrect even if it is based on accurate observations and logical reasoning. The only way to find out if an inference is correct is to investigate further.

Predicting

When you listen to the weather forecast, you hear many predictions about the next day's weather—what the temperature will be, whether it will rain, and how windy it will be. Weather forecasters use observations and knowledge of weather patterns to predict the weather. The skill of **predicting** involves making an inference about a future event based on current evidence or past experience.

Because a prediction is an inference, it may prove to be false. In science class, you can test some of your predictions by doing experiments. For example, suppose you predict that larger paper airplanes can fly farther than smaller airplanes. How could you test your prediction?

ACTIVITY Use the photograph to answer the questions below.

Observing Look closely at the photograph. List at least three observations.

Inferring Use your observations to make an inference about what has happened. What experience or knowledge did you use to make the inference?

Predicting Predict what will happen next. On what evidence or experience do you base your prediction?

Classifying

Could you imagine searching for a book in the library if the books were shelved in no particular order? Your trip to the library would be an all-day event! Luckily, librarians group together books on similar topics or by the same author. Grouping together items that are alike in some way is called **classifying.** You can classify items in many ways: by size, by shape, by use, and by other important characteristics.

Like librarians, scientists use the skill of classifying to organize information and objects. When things are sorted into groups, the relationships among them become easier to understand.

ACTIVITY Classify the objects in the photograph into two groups based on any characteristic you choose. Then use another characteristic to classify the objects into three groups.

Making Models

Have you ever drawn a picture to help someone understand what you were saying? Such a drawing is one type of model. A model is a picture, diagram, computer image, or other representation of a complex object or process. **Making models** helps people understand things that they cannot observe directly.

Scientists often use models to represent things that are either very large or very small, such as the planets in the solar system, or the parts of a cell. Such models are physical models—drawings or three-dimensional structures that look like the real thing. Other models are mental models—mathematical equations or words that describe how something works.

ACTIVITY This student is using a model to demonstrate what causes day and night on Earth. What do the flashlight and the tennis ball in the model represent?

Communicating

Whenever you talk on the phone, write a letter, or listen to your teacher at school, you are communicating. **Communicating** is the process of sharing ideas and information with other people. Communicating effectively requires many skills, including writing, reading, speaking, listening, and making models.

Scientists communicate to share results, information, and opinions. Scientists often communicate about their work in journals, over the telephone, in letters, and on the Internet. They also attend scientific meetings where they share their ideas with one another in person.

ACTIVITY On a sheet of paper, write out clear, detailed directions for tying your shoe. Then exchange directions with a partner. Follow your partner's directions exactly. How successful were you at tying your shoe? How could your partner have communicated more clearly?

On what did you base your prediction? *(Scientific predictions are based on knowledge and experience.)* Point out that in science, predictions can often be tested with experiments.

Classifying

ACTIVITY Encourage students to think of other common things that are classified. Then ask: **What things at home are classified?** *(Clothing might be classified by placing it in different dresser drawers; glasses, plates, and silverware are grouped in different parts of the kitchen; screws, nuts, bolts, washers, and nails might be separated into small containers.)* **What are some things that scientists classify?** *(Scientists classify many things they study, including organisms, geological features and processes, and kinds of machines.)* After students have classified the different rocks in the photograph, have them share their criteria for classifying them. *(Some characteristics students might use include shape, color, size, and texture.)*

Making Models

ACTIVITY Ask students: **What are some models you have used to study science?** *(Students may have used human anatomical models, solar system models, maps, stream tables.)* **How did these models help you?** *(Models can help you learn about things that are difficult to study, either because they are too big, too small, or complex.)* Be sure students understand that a model does not have to be three-dimensional. For example, a map in a textbook is a model. Ask: **What do the flashlight and tennis ball represent?** *(The flashlight represents the sun, and the ball represents Earth.)* **What quality of each item makes this a good model?** *(The flashlight gives off light, and the ball is round and can be rotated by the student.)*

Communicating

ACTIVITY Challenge students to identify the methods of communication they've used today. Then ask: **How is the way you communicate with a friend similar to and different from the way scientists communicate about their work to other scientists?** *(Both may communicate using various methods, but scientists must be very detailed and precise, whereas communication between friends may be less detailed and precise.)* Encourage students to communicate like a scientist as they carry out the activity. *(Students' directions should be detailed and precise enough for another person to successfully follow.)*

Making Measurements

Measuring in SI

Review SI units in class with students. Begin by providing metric rulers, graduated cylinders, balances, and Celsius thermometers. Use these tools to reinforce that the meter is the unit of length, the liter is the unit of volume, the gram is the unit of mass, and the degree Celsius is the unit for temperature. Ask: **If you want to measure the length and width of your classroom, which SI unit would you use?** *(meter)* **Which unit would you use to measure the amount of matter in your textbook?** *(gram)* **Which would you use to measure how much water a drinking glass holds?** *(liter)* **When would you use the Celsius scale?** *(To measure the temperature of something)* Then use the measuring equipment to review SI prefixes. For example, ask: **What are the smallest units on the metric ruler?** *(millimeters)* **How many millimeters are there in 1 cm?** *(10 mm)* **How many in 10 cm?** *(100 mm)* **How many centimeters are there in 1 m?** *(100 cm)* **What does 1,000 m equal?** *(1 km)*

Length ACTIVITY *(Students should state that the shell is 4.6 centimeters, or 46 millimeters, long.)* If students need more practice measuring length, have them use meter sticks and metric rulers to measure various objects in the classroom.

Liquid Volume ACTIVITY *(Students should state that the volume of water in the graduated cylinder is 62 milliliters.)* If students need more practice measuring liquid volume, have them use a graduated cylinder to measure different volumes of water.

Making Measurements

When scientists make observations, it is not sufficient to say that something is "big" or "heavy." Instead, scientists use instruments to measure just how big or heavy an object is. By measuring, scientists can express their observations more precisely and communicate more information about what they observe.

Measuring in SI

The standard system of measurement used by scientists around the world is known as the International System of Units, which is abbreviated as SI (in French, *Système International d'Unités*). SI units are easy to use because they are based on multiples of 10. Each unit is ten times larger than the next smallest unit and one tenth the size of the next largest unit. The table lists the prefixes used to name the most common SI units.

Common SI Prefixes

Prefix	Symbol	Meaning
kilo-	k	1,000
hecto-	h	100
deka-	da	10
deci-	d	0.1 (one tenth)
centi-	c	0.01 (one hundredth)
milli-	m	0.001 (one thousandth)

Length To measure length, or the distance between two points, the unit of measure is the **meter (m).** One meter is the approximate distance from the floor to a doorknob. Long distances, such as the distance between two cities, are measured in kilometers (km). Small lengths are measured in centimeters (cm) or millimeters (mm). Scientists use metric rulers and meter sticks to measure length.

Common Conversions

1 km = 1,000 m
1 m = 100 cm
1 m = 1,000 mm
1 cm = 10 mm

ACTIVITY

The larger lines on the metric ruler in the picture show centimeter divisions, while the smaller, unnumbered lines show millimeter divisions. How many centimeters long is the shell? How many millimeters long is it?

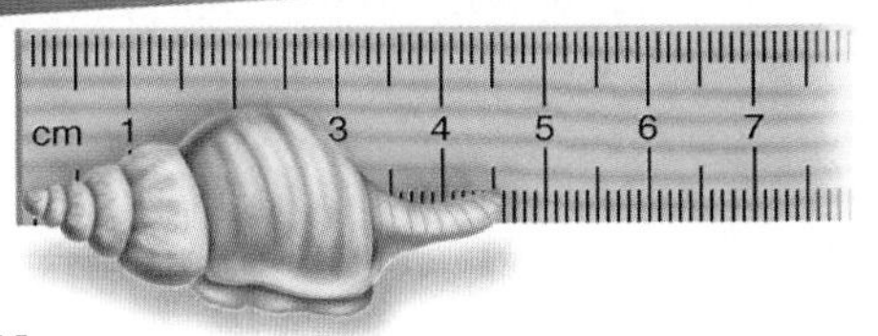

Liquid Volume To measure the volume of a liquid, or the amount of space it takes up, you will use a unit of measure known as the **liter (L).** One liter is the approximate volume of a medium-sized carton of milk. Smaller volumes are measured in milliliters (mL). Scientists use graduated cylinders to measure liquid volume.

Common Conversion

1 L = 1,000 mL

ACTIVITY

The graduated cylinder in the picture is marked in milliliter divisions. Notice that the water in the cylinder has a curved surface. This curved surface is called the *meniscus*. To measure the volume, you must read the level at the lowest point of the meniscus. What is the volume of water in this graduated cylinder?

SKILLS HANDBOOK

Mass To measure mass, or the amount of matter in an object, you will use a unit of measure known as the **gram (g).** One gram is approximately the mass of a paper clip. Larger masses are measured in kilograms (kg). Scientists use a balance to find the mass of an object.

Common Conversion

1 kg = 1,000 g

ACTIVITY

The mass of the apple in the picture is measured in kilograms. What is the mass of the apple? Suppose a recipe for applesauce called for one kilogram of apples. About how many apples would you need?

Temperature To measure the temperature of a substance, you will use the **Celsius scale.** Temperature is measured in degrees Celsius (°C) using a Celsius thermometer. Water freezes at 0°C and boils at 100°C.

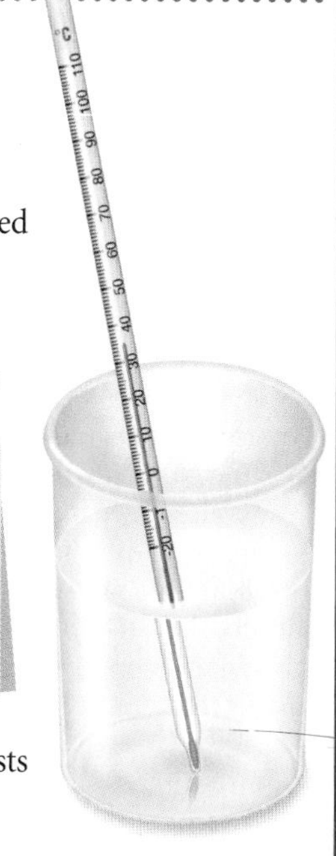

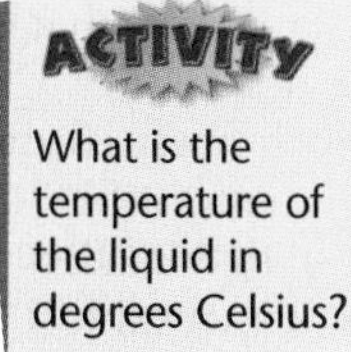

ACTIVITY

What is the temperature of the liquid in degrees Celsius?

Time The unit scientists use to measure time is the **second (s).**

Converting SI Units

To use the SI system, you must know how to convert between units. Converting from one unit to another involves the skill of **calculating,** or using mathematical operations. Converting between SI units is similar to converting between dollars and dimes because both systems are based on multiples of ten.

Suppose you want to convert a length of 80 centimeters to meters. Follow these steps to convert between units.

1. Begin by writing down the measurement you want to convert—in this example, 80 centimeters.
2. Write a conversion factor that represents the relationship between the two units you are converting. In this example, the relationship is *1 meter = 100 centimeters.* Write this conversion factor as a fraction, making sure to place the units you are converting from (centimeters, in this example) in the denominator.
3. Multiply the measurement you want to convert by the fraction. When you do this, the units in the first measurement will cancel out with the units in the denominator. Your answer will be in the units you are converting to (meters, in this example).

Example

80 centimeters = ___?___ meters

$$80 \text{ cen}\cancel{\text{timeters}} \times \frac{1 \text{ meter}}{100 \text{ cen}\cancel{\text{timeters}}} = \frac{80 \text{ meters}}{100}$$

$$= 0.8 \text{ meters}$$

Convert between the following units.

1. 600 millimeters = _?_ meters
2. 0.35 liters = _?_ milliliters
3. 1,050 grams = _?_ kilograms

Mass *(Students should state that the mass of the apple is 0.1 kilograms. They would need 10 apples to make 1 kilogram.)* If students need practice determining mass, have them use a balance to determine the mass of various common objects, such as coins, paper clips, and books.

Temperature *(Students should state that the temperature of the liquid is 35°C.)* If students need practice measuring temperature, have them use a Celsius thermometer to measure the temperature of various water samples.

Time Make sure students know how to convert from seconds to minutes or hours. *(Students should state that 60 seconds = 1 minute; 3,600 seconds = 1 hour.)*

Converting SI Units

Review the steps for converting SI units and work through the example with students. Then ask: **How many millimeters are in 80 centimeters?** *(Students should follow the steps to calculate that 80 centimeters is equal to 800 millimeters.)*

Have students do the conversion problems in the activity. *(**1.** 600 millimeters = 0.6 meters; **2.** 0.35 liters = 350 milliliters; **3.** 1,050 grams = 1.05 kilograms)* If students need more practice converting SI units, have students make up conversion problems and trade with a partner.

Conducting a Scientific Investigation

Posing Questions

Before students do the activity on the next page, walk them through the steps of a typical scientific investigation. Begin by asking: **Why is a scientific question important to a scientific investigation?** *(It is the reason for conducting a scientific investigation and how every investigation begins.)* **What is the scientific question in the activity at the bottom of the next page?** *(How is a plant's growth affected by the amount of water it receives?)*

Developing a Hypothesis

Emphasize that a hypothesis is a proposed explanation or suggested answer to a scientific question, but it is *not* just a guess. Ask: **On what information do scientists base their hypotheses?** *(Their observations and previous knowledge or experience)* Point out that a hypothesis does not always turn out to be correct. Ask: **In that case, do you think the scientist wasted his or her time? Explain your answer.** *(No, because the scientist probably learned from the investigation and may be able to develop another hypothesis that could be supported.)*

Designing an Experiment

Have a volunteer read the Experimental Procedure in the box on the facing page. Then call on students to identify the manipulated variable *(amount of salt added to water)*, the variables that are kept constant *(amount and starting temperature of water, placing containers in freezer)*, the responding variable *(time it takes water to freeze)*, and the control *(Container 3)*.

Ask: **How might the experiment be affected if Container 1 had only 100 mL of water?** *(It wouldn't be a fair comparison with the containers that have more water.)* **What if Container 3 was not included in the experiment?** *(You wouldn't have anything to compare the other two containers with to know if their freezing times were faster or slower than normal.)* Help students understand the importance of keeping all variables constant except the manipulated variable. Also be sure they understand the role of the control. Then ask: **What operational definition is used in this experiment?** *("Frozen" means the time at which a wooden stick can no longer move in a container.)*

Background

Facts and Figures The term *hypothesis* refers to a proposed explanation that can be tested. In science, many hypotheses are developed through logical thinking. But some hypotheses have been the results of imagination, creative leaps, chance events, even dreams. The key characteristic of a hypothesis is that it's a testable explanation.

Conducting a Scientific Investigation

In some ways, scientists are like detectives, piecing together clues to learn about a process or event. One way that scientists gather clues is by carrying out experiments. An experiment tests an idea in a careful, orderly manner. Although all experiments do not follow the same steps in the same order, many follow a pattern similar to the one described here.

Posing Questions

Experiments begin by asking a scientific question. A scientific question is one that can be answered by gathering evidence. For example, the question "Which freezes faster—fresh water or salt water?" is a scientific question because you can carry out an investigation and gather information to answer the question.

Developing a Hypothesis

The next step is to form a hypothesis. A **hypothesis** is a possible explanation for a set of observations or answer to a scientific question. In science, a hypothesis must be something that can be tested. A hypothesis can take the form of an *If . . . then . . .* statement. For example, a hypothesis might be *"If I add salt to fresh water, then the water will take longer to freeze."* A hypothesis worded this way serves as a rough outline of the experiment you should perform.

646

Designing an Experiment

Next you need to plan a way to test your hypothesis. Your plan should be written out as a step-by-step procedure and should describe the observations or measurements you will make.

Two important steps involved in designing an experiment are controlling variables and forming operational definitions.

Controlling Variables In a well-designed experiment, you need to keep all variables the same except for one. A **variable** is any factor that can change in an experiment. The factor that you change is called the **manipulated variable.** In this experiment, the manipulated variable is the amount of salt added to the water. Other factors, such as the amount of water or the starting temperature, are kept constant.

The factor that changes as a result of the manipulated variable is called the responding variable. The **responding variable** is what you measure or observe to obtain your results. In this experiment, the responding variable is how long the water takes to freeze.

An experiment in which all factors except one are kept constant is a **controlled experiment.** Most controlled experiments include a test called the control. In this experiment, Container 3 is the control. Because no salt is added to Container 3, you can compare the results from the other containers to it. Any difference in results must be due to the addition of salt alone.

Forming Operational Definitions
Another important aspect of a well-designed experiment is having clear operational definitions. An **operational definition** is a statement that describes how a particular variable is to be measured or how a term is to be defined. For example, in this experiment, how will you determine if the water has frozen? You might decide to insert a stick in each container at the start of the experiment. Your operational definition of "frozen" would be the time at which the stick can no longer move.

EXPERIMENTAL PROCEDURE

1. Fill 3 containers with 300 milliliters of cold tap water.
2. Add 10 grams of salt to Container 1; stir. Add 20 grams of salt to Container 2; stir. Add no salt to Container 3.
3. Place the 3 containers in a freezer.
4. Check the containers every 15 minutes. Record your observations.

Interpreting Data

The observations and measurements you make in an experiment are called data. At the end of an experiment, you need to analyze the data to look for any patterns or trends. Patterns often become clear if you organize your data in a data table or graph. Then think through what the data reveal. Do they support your hypothesis? Do they point out a flaw in your experiment? Do you need to collect more data?

Drawing Conclusions

A conclusion is a statement that sums up what you have learned from an experiment. When you draw a conclusion, you need to decide whether the data you collected support your hypothesis or not. You may need to repeat an experiment several times before you can draw any conclusions from it. Conclusions often lead you to pose new questions and plan new experiments to answer them.

ACTIVITY

How is a plant's growth affected by the amount of water it receives? Using the steps just described, plan a controlled experiment to investigate this problem.

SKILLS HANDBOOK

Interpreting Data

Emphasize the importance of collecting accurate and detailed data in a scientific investigation. Ask: **What if the students forgot to record the times that they made their observations in the experiment?** *(They wouldn't be able to completely analyze their data to draw valid conclusions.)* Then ask: **Why are data tables and graphs a good way to organize data?** *(They often make it easier to compare and analyze data.)* You may wish to have students review the Skills Handbook pages on Creating Data Tables and Graphs at this point.

Drawing Conclusions

Help students understand that a conclusion is not necessarily the end of a scientific investigation. A conclusion about one experiment may lead right into another experiment. Point out that in scientific investigations, a conclusion is a summary and explanation of the results of an experiment.

Tell students to suppose that for the Experimental Procedure described on this page, they obtained the following results: Container 1 froze in 45 minutes, Container 2 in 80 minutes, and Container 3 in 25 minutes. Ask: **What conclusions can you draw about this experiment?** *(Students might conclude that the more salt that is added to fresh water, the longer it takes the water to freeze. The hypothesis is supported, and the question of which freezes faster is answered—fresh water.)*

ACTIVITY

You may wish to have students work in pairs to plan the controlled experiment. *(Students should develop a hypothesis, such as "If a plant is given more water, then the plant will grow faster." They can test the hypothesis with two identical plants. One plant receives a small measured amount of water daily. The second plant receives a larger measured amount of water daily (the manipulated variable), but all other conditions are the same. Measure the growth of the plants daily (the responding variable).)* After students have designed the experiment, provide bean plants or other fast-growing plants and have students carry out the experiment so they can collect and interpret data and draw conclusions.

Thinking Critically

Comparing and Contrasting

Emphasize that the skill of comparing and contrasting often relies on good observation skills, as in this activity. *(Students' answers may vary. Sample answer: Similarities—both are dogs and have four legs, two eyes, two ears, brown and white fur, black noses, pink tongues; Differences—smooth coat vs. rough coat, more white fur vs. more brown fur, shorter vs. taller, long ears vs. short ears.)*

Applying Concepts

Point out to students that they apply concepts that they learn in school in their daily lives. For example, they learn to add, subtract, multiply, and divide in school. If they get a paper route or some other part-time job, they can apply those concepts. Challenge students to practice applying concepts by doing the activity. *(Many people have metal plumbing in their homes, therefore it is not safe to take a bath during a thunderstorm. Wires are also metal and can conduct electricity. Phones and other appliances that use electrical wires should be avoided. Metal lightning rods are used to conduct charge away from other objects.)*

Interpreting Illustrations

Again, point out the need for good observation skills. Ask: **What is the difference between "interpreting illustrations" and "looking at the pictures"?** *("Interpreting illustrations" requires thorough examination of the illustration, caption, and labels, while "looking at the pictures" implies less thorough examination.)* Encourage students to thoroughly examine the diagram as they do the activity. *(Students' paragraphs may vary, but should describe the formation of a meander, oxbow lake, and new river channel, including some reference to the roles of erosion and deposition.)*

Thinking Critically

Has a friend ever asked for your advice about a problem? If so, you may have helped your friend think through the problem in a logical way. Without knowing it, you used critical-thinking skills to help your friend. Critical thinking involves the use of reasoning and logic to solve problems or make decisions. Some critical-thinking skills are described below.

Comparing and Contrasting

When you examine two objects for similarities and differences, you are using the skill of **comparing and contrasting.** Comparing involves identifying similarities, or common characteristics. Contrasting involves identifying differences. Analyzing objects in this way can help you discover details that you might otherwise overlook.

Compare and contrast the two animals in the photo. First list all the similarities that you see. Then list all the differences.

Applying Concepts

When you use your knowledge about one situation to make sense of a similar situation, you are using the skill of **applying concepts.** Being able to transfer your knowledge from one situation to another shows that you truly understand a concept. You may use this skill in answering test questions that present different problems from the ones you've reviewed in class.

You have just learned that lightning can travel through metal and water. Use this knowledge to decide which objects in your home could act as conductors and therefore be dangerous during a thunderstorm.

Interpreting Illustrations

Diagrams, photographs, and maps are included in textbooks to help clarify what you read. These illustrations show processes, places, and ideas in a visual manner. The skill called **interpreting illustrations** can help you learn from these visual elements. To understand an illustration, take the time to study the illustration along with all the written information that accompanies it. Captions identify the key concepts shown in the illustration. Labels point out the important parts of a diagram or map, while keys identify the symbols used in a map.

▲ An oxbow lake begins to form as erosion and deposition create a meander, or bend, in a river.

Study the diagrams above. Then write a short paragraph explaining what you have learned.

Relating Cause and Effect

If one event causes another event to occur, the two events are said to have a cause-and-effect relationship. When you determine that such a relationship exists between two events, you use a skill called **relating cause and effect.** For example, if you notice an itchy, red bump on your skin, you might infer that a mosquito bit you. The mosquito bite is the cause, and the bump is the effect.

It is important to note that two events do not necessarily have a cause-and-effect relationship just because they occur together. Scientists carry out experiments or use past experience to determine whether a cause-and-effect relationship exists.

ACTIVITY

It is a hot day. You go to the freezer for ice and find only water in the trays. List some possible reasons for the missing ice. How would you determine which cause-and-effect relationship has left you without a cool drink?

Making Generalizations

When you draw a conclusion about an entire group based on information about only some of the group's members, you are using a skill called **making generalizations.** For a generalization to be valid, the sample you choose must be large enough and representative of the entire group. You might, for example, put this skill to work at a farm stand if you see a sign that says, "Sample some grapes before you buy." If you sample a few sweet grapes, you may conclude that all the grapes are sweet—and purchase a large bunch.

ACTIVITY

A team of scientists needs to determine whether the water in a large reservoir is safe to drink. How could they use the skill of making generalizations to help them? What should they do?

Making Judgments

When you evaluate something to decide whether it is good or bad, or right or wrong, you are using a skill called **making judgments.** For example, you make judgments when you decide to eat healthful foods or to pick up litter in a park. Before you make a judgment, you need to think through the pros and cons of a situation, and identify the values or standards that you hold.

ACTIVITY

Should children and teens be required to wear helmets when bicycling? Explain why you feel the way you do.

Problem Solving

When you use critical-thinking skills to resolve an issue or decide on a course of action, you are using a skill called **problem solving.** Some problems, such as how to convert a fraction into a decimal, are straightforward. Other problems, such as figuring out why your computer has stopped working, are complex. Some complex problems can be solved using the trial and error method—try out one solution first, and if that doesn't work, try another. Other useful problem-solving strategies include making models and brainstorming possible solutions with a partner.

Relating Cause and Effect

Emphasize that not all events that occur together have a cause-and-effect relationship. For example, tell students that you went to the grocery and your car stalled. Ask: **Is there a cause-and-effect relationship in this situation? Explain your answer.** *(No, because going to the grocery could not cause a car to stall. There must be another cause to make the car stall.)* Have students do the activity to practice relating cause and effect. *(Students should identify that the water remaining as liquid is the effect. Some possible causes include malfunction of the refrigerator, a loss of power to the home, or too many people using ice.)*

Making Generalizations

Point out the importance of having a large, representative sample before making a generalization. Ask: **If you went fishing at a lake and caught three catfish, could you make the generalization that all fish in the lake are catfish? Why or why not?** *(No, because there might be other kinds of fish you didn't catch because they didn't like the bait or they may be in other parts of the lake.)* **How could you make a generalization about the kinds of fish in the lake?** *(By having a larger sample)* Have students do the activity to practice making generalizations. *(The scientists should collect and test water samples from a number of different parts of the reservoir.)*

Making Judgments

Remind students that they make a judgment almost every time they make a decision. Ask: **What steps should you follow to make a judgment?** *(Gather information, list pros and cons, analyze values, make judgment)* Invite students to do the activity, and then to share and discuss the judgments they made. *(Students' judgments will vary, but should be supported by valid reasoning. Sample answer: Children and teens should be required to wear helmets when bicycling because helmets have been proven to save lives and reduce head injuries.)*

Problem Solving

ACTIVITY

Challenge student pairs to solve a problem about a soapbox derby. Explain that their younger brother is building a car to enter in the race. The brother wants to know how to make his soapbox car go faster. After student pairs have considered the problem, have them share their ideas about solutions with the class. *(Most will probably suggest using trial and error by making small changes to the car and testing the car after each change. Some students may suggest making and manipulating a model.)*

Organizing Information

Concept Maps

Challenge students to make a concept map with at least three levels of concepts to organize information about types of transportation. All students should start with the phrase *types of transportation* at the top of the concept map. After that point, their concept maps may vary. *(For example, some students might place* private transportation *and* public transportation *at the next level, while other students might have* human-powered *and* gas-powered. *Make sure students connect the concepts with linking words. Challenge students to include cross-linkages as well.)*

Compare/Contrast Tables

Have students make their own compare/contrast tables using two or more different sports or other activities, such as playing musical instruments. Emphasize that students should select characteristics that highlight the similarities and differences between the activities. *(Students' compare/contrast tables should include several appropriate characteristics and list information about each activity for every characteristic.)*

Organizing Information

As you read this textbook, how can you make sense of all the information it contains? Some useful tools to help you organize information are shown on this page. These tools are called *graphic organizers* because they give you a visual picture of a topic, showing at a glance how key concepts are related.

Concept Maps

Concept maps are useful tools for organizing information on broad topics. A concept map begins with a general concept and shows how it can be broken down into more specific concepts. In that way, relationships between concepts become easier to understand.

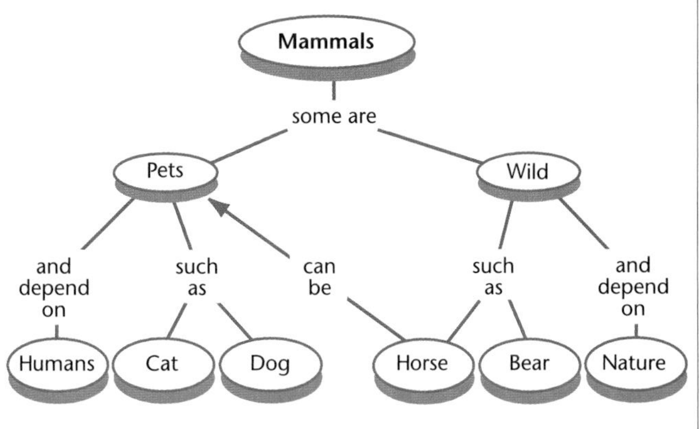

A concept map is constructed by placing concept words (usually nouns) in ovals and connecting them with linking words. Often, the most general concept word is placed at the top, and the words become more specific as you move downward. Often the linking words, which are written on a line connecting the two ovals, describe the relationship between the two concepts they connect. If you follow any string of concepts and linking words down the map, it should read like a sentence.

Some concept maps include linking words that connect a concept on one branch of the map to a concept on another branch. These linking words, called cross-linkages, show more complex interrelationships among concepts.

Compare/Contrast Tables

Compare/contrast tables are useful tools for sorting out the similarities and differences between two or more items. A table provides an organized framework in which to compare items based on specific characteristics that you identify.

Characteristic	Baseball	Basketball
Number of Players	9	5
Playing Field	Baseball diamond	Basketball court
Equipment	Bat, baseball, mitts	Basket, basketball

To create a compare/contrast table, list the items to be compared across the top of a table. Then list the characteristics that will form the basis of your comparison in the left-hand column. Complete the table by filling in information about each characteristic, first for one item and then for the other.

Venn Diagrams

Another way to show similarities and differences between items is with a Venn diagram. A Venn diagram consists of two or more circles that partially overlap. Each circle represents a particular concept or idea. Common characteristics, or similarities, are written within the area of overlap between the two circles. Unique characteristics, or differences, are written in the parts of the circles outside the area of overlap.

To create a Venn diagram, draw two overlapping circles. Label the circles with the names of the items being compared. Write the unique characteristics in each circle outside the area of overlap. Then write the shared characteristics within the area of overlap.

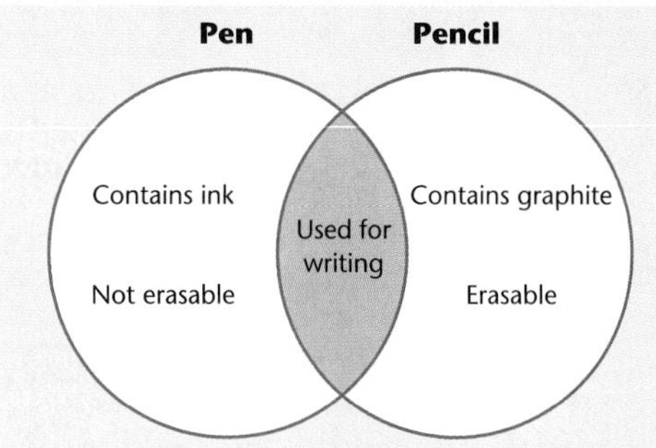

Flowcharts

A flowchart can help you understand the order in which certain events have occurred or should occur. Flowcharts are useful for outlining the stages in a process or the steps in a procedure.

To make a flowchart, write a brief description of each event in a box. Place the first event at the top of the page, followed by the second event, the third event, and so on. Then draw an arrow to connect each event to the one that occurs next.

Preparing Pasta

Boil water → Cook pasta → Drain water → Add sauce

Cycle Diagrams

A cycle diagram can be used to show a sequence of events that is continuous, or cyclical. A continuous sequence does not have an end because, when the final event is over, the first event begins again. Like a flowchart, a cycle diagram can help you understand the order of events.

To create a cycle diagram, write a brief description of each event in a box. Place one event at the top of the page in the center. Then, moving in a clockwise direction around an imaginary circle, write each event in its proper sequence. Draw arrows that connect each event to the one that occurs next, forming a continuous circle.

Steps in a Science Experiment

Pose a question → Develop a hypothesis → Design an experiment → Interpret data → Draw conclusions → Pose a question

SKILLS HANDBOOK

Venn Diagrams

ACTIVITY

Students can use the same information from their compare/contrast tables to create a Venn diagram. Make sure students understand that the overlapping area of the circles is used to list similarities and the parts of the circles outside the overlap area are used to show differences. If students want to list similarities and differences among three activities, show them how to add a third circle that overlaps each of the other two circles and has an area of overlap for all three circles. *(Students' Venn diagrams will vary. Make sure they have accurately listed similarities in the overlap area and differences in the parts of the circles that do not overlap.)*

Flowcharts

ACTIVITY

Encourage students to create a flowchart to show the things they did this morning as they got ready for school. Remind students that a flowchart should show the correct order in which events occurred or should occur. *(Students' flowcharts will vary somewhat. A typical flowchart might include: got up → ate breakfast → took a shower → brushed teeth → got dressed → gathered books and homework → put on jacket.)*

Cycle Diagrams

ACTIVITY

Review that a cycle diagram shows a sequence of events that is continuous. Then challenge students to create a cycle diagram that shows how the weather changes with the seasons where they live. *(Students' cycle diagrams may vary, though most will include four steps, one for each season.)*

Creating Data Tables and Graphs

Data Tables

Have students create a data table to show how much time they spend on different activities during one week. Suggest that students first list the main activities they do every week. Then they should determine the amount of time they spend on each activity each day. Remind students to give this data table a title. *(Students' data tables will vary. A sample data table is shown below.)*

Bar Graphs

Students can use the data from their data table above to make a bar graph showing how much time they spend on different activities during a week. The vertical axis should be divided into units of time, such as hours. Remind students to label both axes and give their graph a title. *(Students' bar graphs will vary. A sample bar graph is shown below.)*

Creating Data Tables and Graphs

How can you make sense of the data in a science experiment? The first step is to organize the data to help you understand them. Data tables and graphs are helpful tools for organizing data.

Data Tables

You have gathered your materials and set up your experiment. But before you start, you need to plan a way to record what happens during the experiment. By creating a data table, you can record your observations and measurements in an orderly way.

Suppose, for example, that a scientist conducted an experiment to find out how many Calories people of different body masses burn while doing various activities. The data table shows the results.

Notice in this data table that the manipulated variable (body mass) is the heading of one column. The responding variable (for Experiment 1, the number of Calories burned while bicycling) is the heading of the next column. Additional columns were added for related experiments.

CALORIES BURNED IN 30 MINUTES OF ACTIVITY

Body Mass	Experiment 1 Bicycling	Experiment 2 Playing Basketball	Experiment 3 Watching Television
30 kg	60 Calories	120 Calories	21 Calories
40 kg	77 Calories	164 Calories	27 Calories
50 kg	95 Calories	206 Calories	33 Calories
60 kg	114 Calories	248 Calories	38 Calories

Bar Graphs

To compare how many Calories a person burns doing various activities, you could create a bar graph. A bar graph is used to display data in a number of separate, or distinct, categories. In this example, bicycling, playing basketball, and watching television are three separate categories.

To create a bar graph, follow these steps.

1. On graph paper, draw a horizontal, or *x*-, axis and a vertical, or *y*-, axis.
2. Write the names of the categories to be graphed along the horizontal axis. Include an overall label for the axis as well.
3. Label the vertical axis with the name of the responding variable. Include units of measurement. Then create a scale along the axis by marking off equally spaced numbers that cover the range of the data collected.
4. For each category, draw a solid bar using the scale on the vertical axis to determine the appropriate height. For example, for bicycling, draw the bar as high as the 60 mark on the vertical axis. Make all the bars the same width and leave equal spaces between them.
5. Add a title that describes the graph.

Calories Burned by a 30-kilogram Person in Various Activities

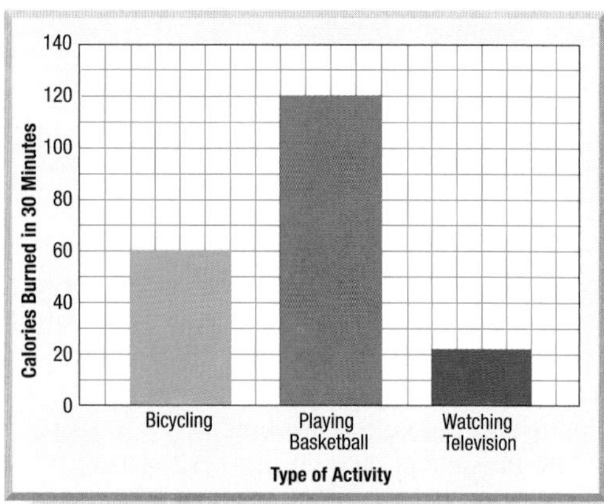

Time Spent on Different Activities in a Week (in hours)

	Going to Classes	Eating Meals	Playing Soccer	Watching Television
Monday	6	2	2	0.5
Tuesday	6	1.5	1.5	1.5
Wednesday	6	2	1	2
Thursday	6	2	2	1.5
Friday	6	2	2	0.5
Saturday	0	2.5	2.5	1
Sunday	0	3	1	2

Time Spent on Different Activities in a Week

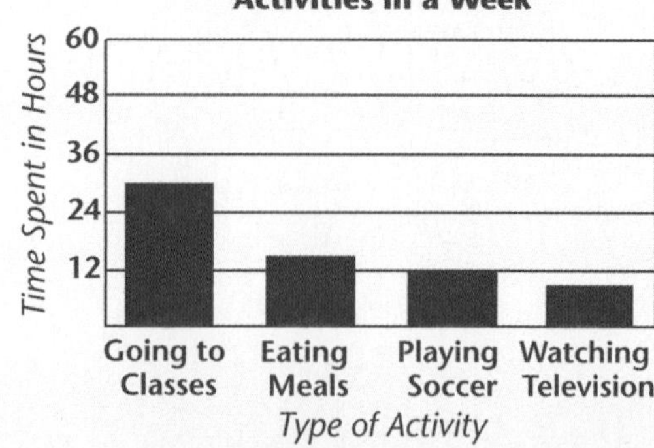

Line Graphs

To see whether a relationship exists between body mass and the number of Calories burned while bicycling, you could create a line graph. A line graph is used to display data that show how one variable (the responding variable) changes in response to another variable (the manipulated variable). You can use a line graph when your manipulated variable is *continuous,* that is, when there are other points between the ones that you tested. In this example, body mass is a continuous variable because there are other body masses between 30 and 40 kilograms (for example, 31 kilograms). Time is another example of a continuous variable.

Effect of Body Mass on Calories Burned While Bicycling

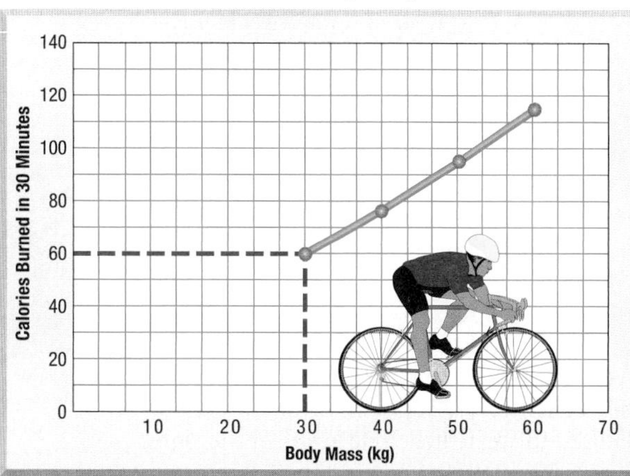

Line graphs are powerful tools because they allow you to estimate values for conditions that you did not test in the experiment. For example, you can use the line graph to estimate that a 35-kilogram person would burn 68 Calories while bicycling.

To create a line graph, follow these steps.

1. On graph paper, draw a horizontal, or *x*-, axis and a vertical, or *y*-, axis.
2. Label the horizontal axis with the name of the manipulated variable. Label the vertical axis with the name of the responding variable. Include units of measurement.
3. Create a scale on each axis by marking off equally spaced numbers that cover the range of the data collected.
4. Plot a point on the graph for each piece of data. In the line graph above, the dotted lines show how to plot the first data point (30 kilograms and 60 Calories). Draw an imaginary vertical line extending up from the horizontal axis at the 30-kilogram mark. Then draw an imaginary horizontal line extending across from the vertical axis at the 60-Calorie mark. Plot the point where the two lines intersect.
5. Connect the plotted points with a solid line. (In some cases, it may be more appropriate to draw a line that shows the general trend of the plotted points. In those cases, some of the points may fall above or below the line. Also, not all graphs are linear. It may be more appropriate to draw a curve to connect the points.)
6. Add a title that identifies the variables or relationship in the graph.

ACTIVITY

Create line graphs to display the data from Experiment 2 and Experiment 3 in the data table.

ACTIVITY

You read in the newspaper that a total of 4 centimeters of rain fell in your area in June, 2.5 centimeters fell in July, and 1.5 centimeters fell in August. What type of graph would you use to display these data? Use graph paper to create the graph.

S K I L L S H A N D B O O K

Line Graphs

Walk students through the steps involved in creating a line graph using the example illustrated on the page. For example, ask: **What is the label on the horizontal axis? On the vertical axis?** *(Body Mass (kg); Calories Burned in 30 Minutes)* **What scales are used on each axis?** *(3 squares per 10 kg on the x-axis and 2 squares per 20 calories on the y-axis)* **What does the second data point represent?** *(77 Calories burned for a body mass of 40 kg)* **What trend or pattern does the graph show?** *(The number of Calories burned in 30 minutes of cycling increases with body mass.)*

ACTIVITY Have students follow the steps to carry out the first activity. *(Students should make a different graph for each experiment with different y-axis scales to practice making scales appropriate for data. See sample graphs below.)*

ACTIVITY Have students carry out the second activity. *(Students should conclude that a bar graph would be best to display the data. A sample bar graph for these data is shown below.)*

Rainfall in June, July, and August

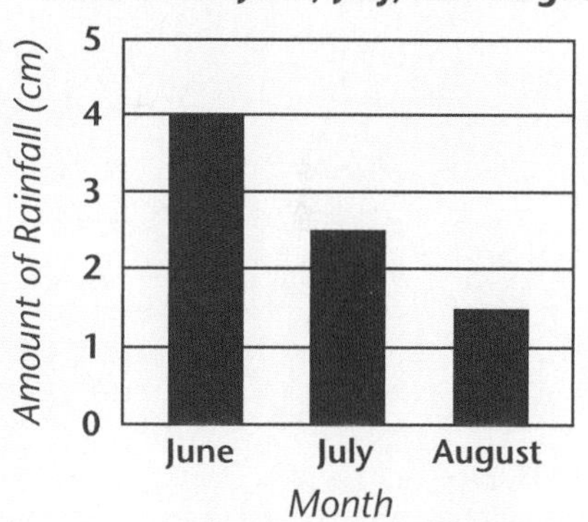

Effect of Body Mass on Calories Burned While Playing Basketball

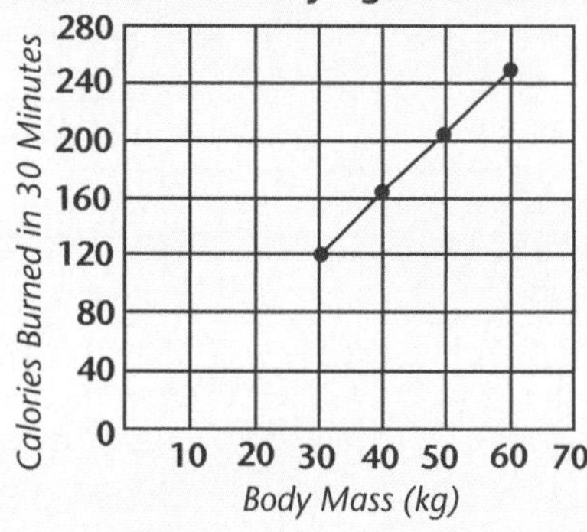

Effect of Body Mass on Calories Burned While Watching Television

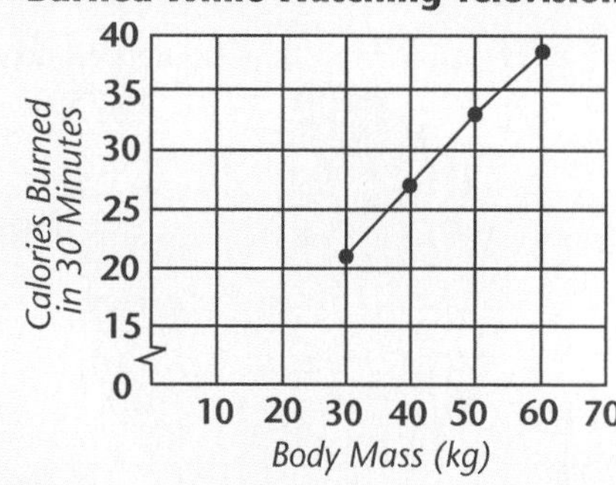

Circle Graphs

Emphasize that a circle graph has to include 100 percent of the categories for the topic being graphed. For example, ask: **Could the data in the bar graph titled "Calories Burned by a 30-kilogram Person in Various Activities" (on page 652) be shown in a circle graph? Why or why not?** *(No, because it does not include all the possible ways a 30-kilogram person can burn Calories.)* Then walk students through the steps for making a circle graph. Help students to use a compass and a protractor. Use the protractor to illustrate that a circle has 360 degrees. Make sure students understand the mathematical calculations involved in making a circle graph.

You might wish to have students work in pairs to complete the activity. **ACTIVITY** *(Students' circle graphs should look like the graph below.)*

Circle Graphs

Like bar graphs, circle graphs can be used to display data in a number of separate categories. Unlike bar graphs, however, circle graphs can only be used when you have data for *all* the categories that make up a given topic. A circle graph is sometimes called a pie chart because it resembles a pie cut into slices. The pie represents the entire topic, while the slices represent the individual categories. The size of a slice indicates what percentage of the whole a particular category makes up.

The data table below shows the results of a survey in which 24 teenagers were asked to identify their favorite sport. The data were then used to create the circle graph at the right.

Sports That Teens Prefer

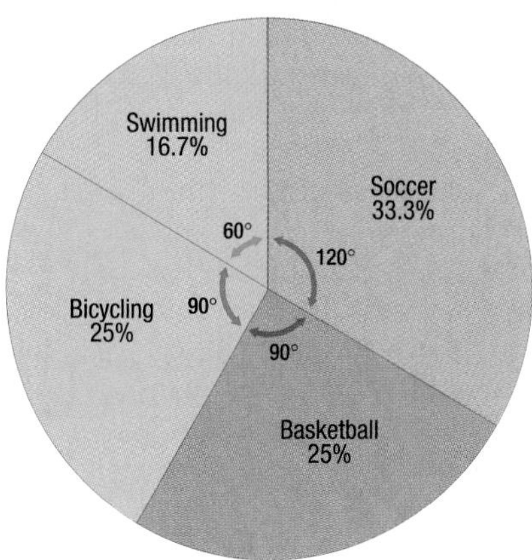

FAVORITE SPORTS

Sport	Number of Students
Soccer	8
Basketball	6
Bicycling	6
Swimming	4

To create a circle graph, follow these steps.

1. Use a compass to draw a circle. Mark the center of the circle with a point. Then draw a line from the center point to the top of the circle.
2. Determine the size of each "slice" by setting up a proportion where x equals the number of degrees in a slice. (NOTE: A circle contains 360 degrees.) For example, to find the number of degrees in the "soccer" slice, set up the following proportion:

$$\frac{\text{students who prefer soccer}}{\text{total number of students}} = \frac{x}{\text{total number of degrees in a circle}}$$

$$\frac{8}{24} = \frac{x}{360}$$

Cross-multiply and solve for x.

$$24x = 8 \times 360$$
$$x = 120$$

The "soccer" slice should contain 120 degrees.

3. Use a protractor to measure the angle of the first slice, using the line you drew to the top of the circle as the 0° line. Draw a line from the center of the circle to the edge for the angle you measured.
4. Continue around the circle by measuring the size of each slice with the protractor. Start measuring from the edge of the previous slice so the wedges do not overlap. When you are done, the entire circle should be filled in.
5. Determine the percentage of the whole circle that each slice represents. To do this, divide the number of degrees in a slice by the total number of degrees in a circle (360), and multiply by 100%. For the "soccer" slice, you can find the percentage as follows:

$$\frac{120}{360} \times 100\% = 33.3\%$$

6. Use a different color to shade in each slice. Label each slice with the name of the category and with the percentage of the whole it represents.
7. Add a title to the circle graph.

ACTIVITY In a group of 32 students, 24 are right-handed, 6 are left-handed and 2 use both hands equally. Create a circle graph to display these data.

654

Which Hand Students Use

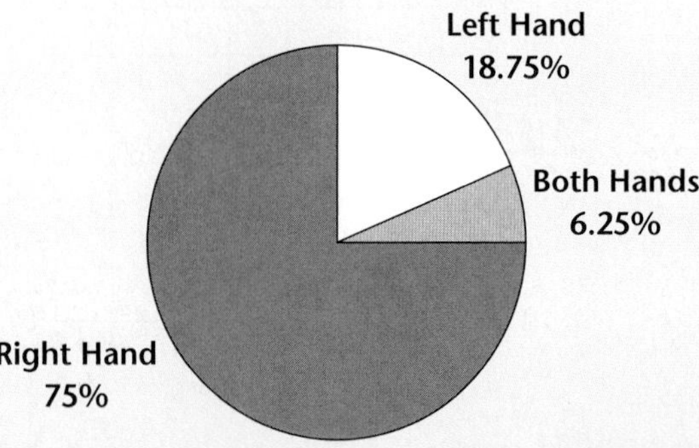

Laboratory Safety

Safety Symbols

These symbols alert you to possible dangers in the laboratory and remind you to work carefully.

Safety Goggles Always wear safety goggles to protect your eyes in any activity involving chemicals, flames or heating, or the possibility of broken glassware.

Lab Apron Wear a laboratory apron to protect your skin and clothing from damage.

Breakage You are working with materials that may be breakable, such as glass containers, glass tubing, thermometers, or funnels. Handle breakable materials with care. Do not touch broken glassware.

Heat-resistant Gloves Use an oven mitt or other hand protection when handling hot materials. Hot plates, hot glassware, or hot water can cause burns. Do not touch hot objects with your bare hands.

Heating Use a clamp or tongs to pick up hot glassware. Do not touch hot objects with your bare hands.

Sharp Object Pointed-tip scissors, scalpels, knives, needles, pins, or tacks are sharp. They can cut or puncture your skin. Always direct a sharp edge or point away from yourself and others. Use sharp instruments only as instructed.

Electric Shock Avoid the possibility of electric shock. Never use electrical equipment around water, or when the equipment is wet or your hands are wet. Be sure cords are untangled and cannot trip anyone. Disconnect the equipment when it is not in use.

Corrosive Chemical You are working with an acid or another corrosive chemical. Avoid getting it on your skin or clothing, or in your eyes. Do not inhale the vapors. Wash your hands when you are finished with the activity.

Poison Do not let any poisonous chemical come in contact with your skin, and do not inhale its vapors. Wash your hands when you are finished with the activity.

Physical Safety When an experiment involves physical activity, take precautions to avoid injuring yourself or others. Follow instructions from your teacher. Alert your teacher if there is any reason you should not participate in the activity.

Animal Safety Treat live animals with care to avoid harming the animals or yourself. Working with animal parts or preserved animals also may require caution. Wash your hands when you are finished with the activity.

Plant Safety Handle plants in the laboratory or during field work only as directed by your teacher. If you are allergic to certain plants, tell your teacher before doing an activity in which those plants are used. Avoid touching harmful plants such as poison ivy, poison oak, or poison sumac, or plants with thorns. Wash your hands when you are finished with the activity.

Flames You may be working with flames from a lab burner, candle, or matches. Tie back loose hair and clothing. Follow instructions from your teacher about lighting and extinguishing flames.

No Flames Flammable materials may be present. Make sure there are no flames, sparks, or other exposed heat sources present.

Fumes When poisonous or unpleasant vapors may be involved, work in a ventilated area. Avoid inhaling vapors directly. Only test an odor when directed to do so by your teacher, and use a wafting motion to direct the vapor toward your nose.

Disposal Chemicals and other laboratory materials used in the activity must be disposed of safely. Follow the instructions from your teacher.

Hand Washing Wash your hands thoroughly when finished with the activity. Use antibacterial soap and warm water. Lather both sides of your hands and between your fingers. Rinse well.

General Safety Awareness You may see this symbol when none of the symbols described earlier appears. In this case, follow the specific instructions provided. You may also see this symbol when you are asked to develop your own procedure in a lab. Have your teacher approve your plan before you go further.

Laboratory Safety

Laboratory safety is an essential element of a successful science class. It is important for you to emphasize laboratory safety to students. Students need to understand exactly what is safe and unsafe behavior, and what the rationale is behind each safety rule.

Review with students the Safety Symbols and Science Safety Rules listed on this and the next two pages. Then follow the safety guidelines below to ensure that your classroom will be a safe place for students to learn science.

- Post safety rules in the classroom and review them regularly with students.
- Familiarize yourself with the safety procedures for each activity before introducing it to your students.
- Review specific safety precautions with students before beginning every science activity.
- Always act as an exemplary role model by displaying safe behavior.
- Know how to use safety equipment, such as fire extinguishers and fire blankets, and always have it accessible.
- Have students practice leaving the classroom quickly and orderly to prepare them for emergencies.
- Explain to students how to use the intercom or other available means of communication to get help during an emergency.
- Never leave students unattended while they are engaged in science activities.
- Provide enough space for students to safely carry out science activities.
- Keep your classroom and all science materials in proper condition. Replace worn or broken items.
- Instruct students to report all accidents and injuries to you immediately.

Laboratory Safety

Additional tips are listed below for the Science Safety Rules discussed on these two pages. Please keep these tips in mind when you carry out science activities in your classroom.

General Precautions

- For open-ended activities like Chapter Projects, go over general safety guidelines with students. Have students submit their procedures or design plans in writing and check them for safety considerations.
- In an activity where students are directed to taste something, be sure to store the material in clean, *nonscience* containers. Distribute the material to students in *new* plastic or paper dispensables, which should be discarded after the tasting. Tasting or eating should never be done in a lab classroom.
- During physical activity, make sure students do not overexert themselves.
- Remind students to handle microscopes and telescopes with care to avoid breakage.

Heating and Fire Safety

- No flammable substances should be in use around hot plates, light bulbs, or open flames.
- Test tubes should be heated only in water baths.
- Students should be permitted to strike matches to light candles or burners *only* with strict supervision. When possible, you should light the flames, especially when working with sixth graders.
- Be sure to have proper ventilation when fumes are produced during a procedure.
- All electrical equipment used in the lab should have GFI switches.

Science Safety Rules

To prepare yourself to work safely in the laboratory, read over the following safety rules. Then read them a second time. Make sure you understand and follow each rule. Ask your teacher to explain any rules you do not understand.

Dress Code

1. To protect yourself from injuring your eyes, wear safety goggles whenever you work with chemicals, burners, glassware, or any substance that might get into your eyes. If you wear contact lenses, notify your teacher.
2. Wear a lab apron or coat whenever you work with corrosive chemicals or substances that can stain.
3. Tie back long hair to keep it away from any chemicals, flames, or equipment.
4. Remove or tie back any article of clothing or jewelry that can hang down and touch chemicals, flames, or equipment. Roll up or secure long sleeves.
5. Never wear open shoes or sandals.

General Precautions

6. Read all directions for an experiment several times before beginning the activity. Carefully follow all written and oral instructions. If you are in doubt about any part of the experiment, ask your teacher for assistance.
7. Never perform activities that are not assigned or authorized by your teacher. Obtain permission before "experimenting" on your own. Never handle any equipment unless you have specific permission.
8. Never perform lab activities without direct supervision.
9. Never eat or drink in the laboratory.
10. Keep work areas clean and tidy at all times. Bring only notebooks and lab manuals or written lab procedures to the work area. All other items, such as purses and backpacks, should be left in a designated area.
11. Do not engage in horseplay.

First Aid

12. Always report all accidents or injuries to your teacher, no matter how minor. Notify your teacher immediately about any fires.
13. Learn what to do in case of specific accidents, such as getting acid in your eyes or on your skin. (Rinse acids from your body with lots of water.)
14. Be aware of the location of the first-aid kit, but do not use it unless instructed by your teacher. In case of injury, your teacher should administer first aid. Your teacher may also send you to the school nurse or call a physician.
15. Know the location of emergency equipment, such as the fire extinguisher and fire blanket, and know how to use it.
16. Know the location of the nearest telephone and whom to contact in an emergency.

Heating and Fire Safety

17. Never use a heat source, such as a candle, burner, or hot plate, without wearing safety goggles.
18. Never heat anything unless instructed to do so. A chemical that is harmless when cool may be dangerous when heated.
19. Keep all combustible materials away from flames. Never use a flame or spark near a combustible chemical.
20. Never reach across a flame.
21. Before using a laboratory burner, make sure you know proper procedures for lighting and adjusting the burner, as demonstrated by your teacher. Do not touch the burner. It may be hot. And never leave a lighted burner unattended!
22. Chemicals can splash or boil out of a heated test tube. When heating a substance in a test tube, make sure that the mouth of the tube is not pointed at you or anyone else.
23. Never heat a liquid in a closed container. The expanding gases produced may blow the container apart.
24. Before picking up a container that has been heated, hold the back of your hand near it. If you can feel heat on the back of your hand, the container is too hot to handle. Use an oven mitt to pick up a container that has been heated.

Using Chemicals Safely

- When students use both chemicals and microscopes in one activity, microscopes should be in a separate part of the room from the chemicals so that when students remove their goggles to use the microscopes, their eyes are not at risk.

Using Glassware Safely

- Use plastic containers, graduated cylinders, and beakers whenever possible. If using glass, students should wear safety goggles.
- Use only nonmercury thermometers with anti-roll protectors.
- Check all glassware periodically for chips and scratches, which can cause cuts and breakage.

Using Chemicals Safely

25. Never mix chemicals "for the fun of it." You might produce a dangerous, possibly explosive substance.
26. Never put your face near the mouth of a container that holds chemicals. Many chemicals are poisonous. Never touch, taste, or smell a chemical unless you are instructed by your teacher to do so.
27. Use only those chemicals needed in the activity. Read and double-check labels on supply bottles before removing any chemicals. Take only as much as you need. Keep all containers closed when chemicals are not being used.
28. Dispose of all chemicals as instructed by your teacher. To avoid contamination, never return chemicals to their original containers. Never simply pour chemicals or other substances into the sink or trash containers.
29. Be extra careful when working with acids or bases. Pour all chemicals over the sink or a container, not over your work surface.
30. If you are instructed to test for odors, use a wafting motion to direct the odors to your nose. Do not inhale the fumes directly from the container.
31. When mixing an acid and water, always pour the water into the container first and then add the acid to the water. Never pour water into an acid.
32. Take extreme care not to spill any material in the laboratory. Wash chemical spills and splashes immediately with plenty of water. Immediately begin rinsing with water any acids that get on your skin or clothing, and notify your teacher of any acid spill at the same time.

Using Glassware Safely

33. Never force glass tubing or thermometers into a rubber stopper or rubber tubing. Have your teacher insert the glass tubing or thermometer if required for an activity.
34. If you are using a laboratory burner, use a wire screen to protect glassware from any flame. Never heat glassware that is not thoroughly dry on the outside.
35. Keep in mind that hot glassware looks cool. Never pick up glassware without first checking to see if it is hot. Use an oven mitt. See rule 24.
36. Never use broken or chipped glassware. If glassware breaks, notify your teacher and dispose of the glassware in the proper broken-glassware container. Never handle broken glass with your bare hands.
37. Never eat or drink from lab glassware.
38. Thoroughly clean glassware before putting it away.

Using Sharp Instruments

39. Handle scalpels or other sharp instruments with extreme care. Never cut material toward you; cut away from you.
40. Immediately notify your teacher if you cut your skin when working in the laboratory.

Animal and Plant Safety

41. Never perform experiments that cause pain, discomfort, or harm to animals. This rule applies at home as well as in the classroom.
42. Animals should be handled only if absolutely necessary. Your teacher will instruct you as to how to handle each animal species brought into the classroom.
43. If you know that you are allergic to certain plants, molds, or animals, tell your teacher before doing an activity in which these are used.
44. During field work, protect your skin by wearing long pants, long sleeves, socks, and closed shoes. Know how to recognize the poisonous plants and fungi in your area, as well as plants with thorns, and avoid contact with them. Never eat any part of a plant or fungus.
45. Wash your hands thoroughly after handling animals or a cage containing animals. Wash your hands when you are finished with any activity involving animal parts, plants, or soil.

End-of-Experiment Rules

46. After an experiment has been completed, turn off all burners or hot plates. If you used a gas burner, check that the gas-line valve to the burner is off. Unplug hot plates.
47. Turn off and unplug any other electrical equipment that you used.
48. Clean up your work area and return all equipment to its proper place.
49. Dispose of waste materials as instructed by your teacher.
50. Wash your hands after every experiment.

657

Using Sharp Instruments

- Always use blunt-tip safety scissors, except when pointed-tip scissors are required.

Animal and Plant Safety

- When working with live animals or plants, check ahead of time for students who may have allergies to the specimens.
- When growing bacteria cultures, use only disposable petri dishes. After streaking, the dishes should be sealed and not opened again by students. After the lab, students should return the unopened dishes to you. Students should wash their hands with antibacterial soap.
- Two methods are recommended for the safe disposal of bacteria cultures. *First method:* Autoclave the petri dishes and discard without opening. *Second method*: If no autoclave is available, carefully open the dishes (never have a student do this) and pour full-strength bleach into the dishes and let stand for a day. Then pour the bleach from the petri dishes down a drain and flush the drain with lots of water. Tape the petri dishes back together and place in a sealed plastic bag. Wrap the plastic bag with a brown paper bag or newspaper and tape securely. Throw the sealed package in the trash. Thoroughly disinfect the work area with bleach.
- To grow mold, use a new, sealable plastic bag that is two to three times larger than the material to be placed inside. Seal the bag and tape it shut. After the bag is sealed, students should not open it. To dispose of the bag and mold culture, make a small cut near an edge of the bag and cook in a microwave oven on high setting for at least 1 minute. Discard the bag according to local ordinance, usually in the trash.
- Students should wear disposable nitrile, latex, or food-handling gloves when handling live animals or nonliving specimens.

End-of-Experiment Rules

- Always have students use antibacterial soap for washing their hands.

Physical Map: United States

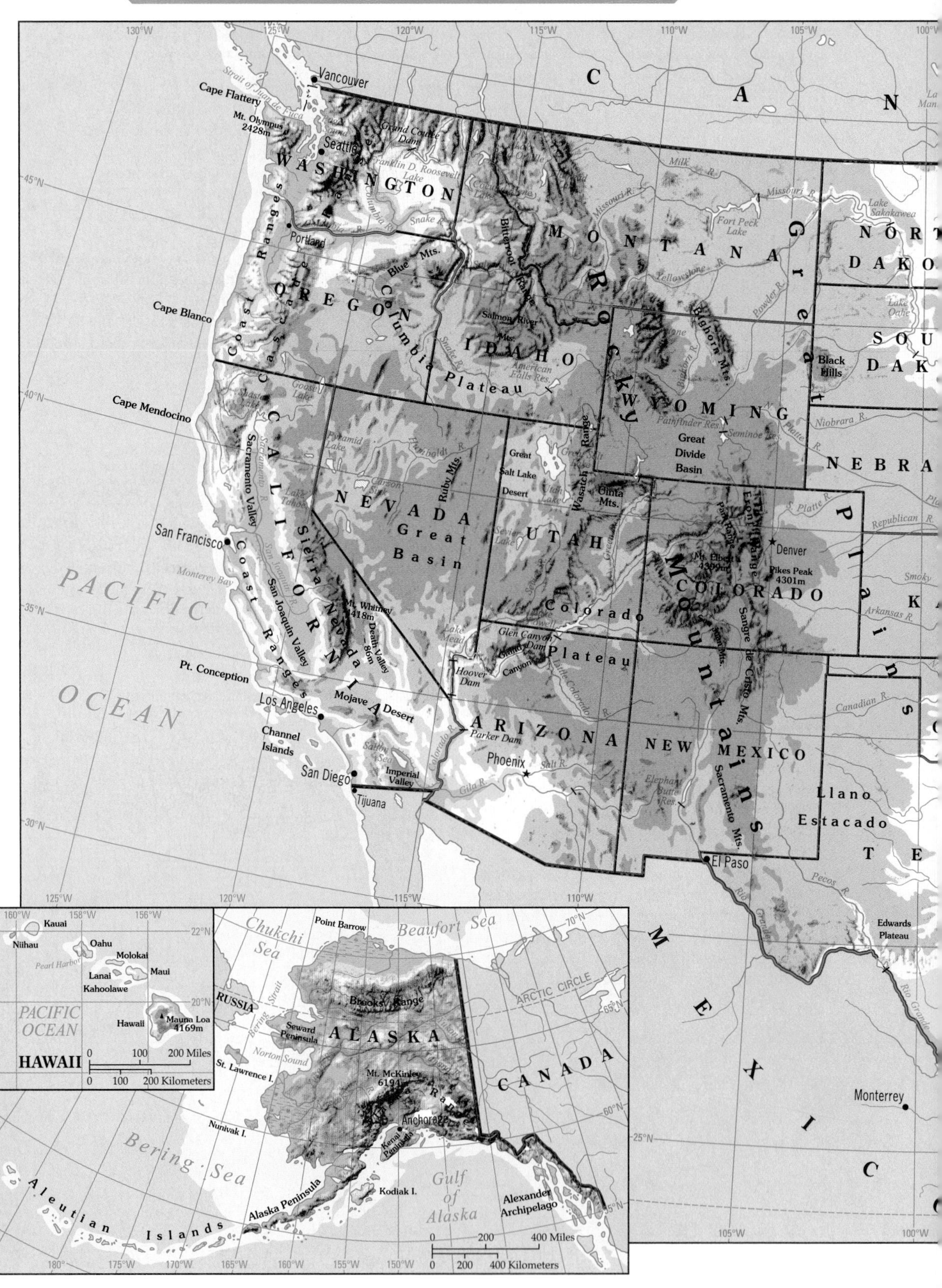

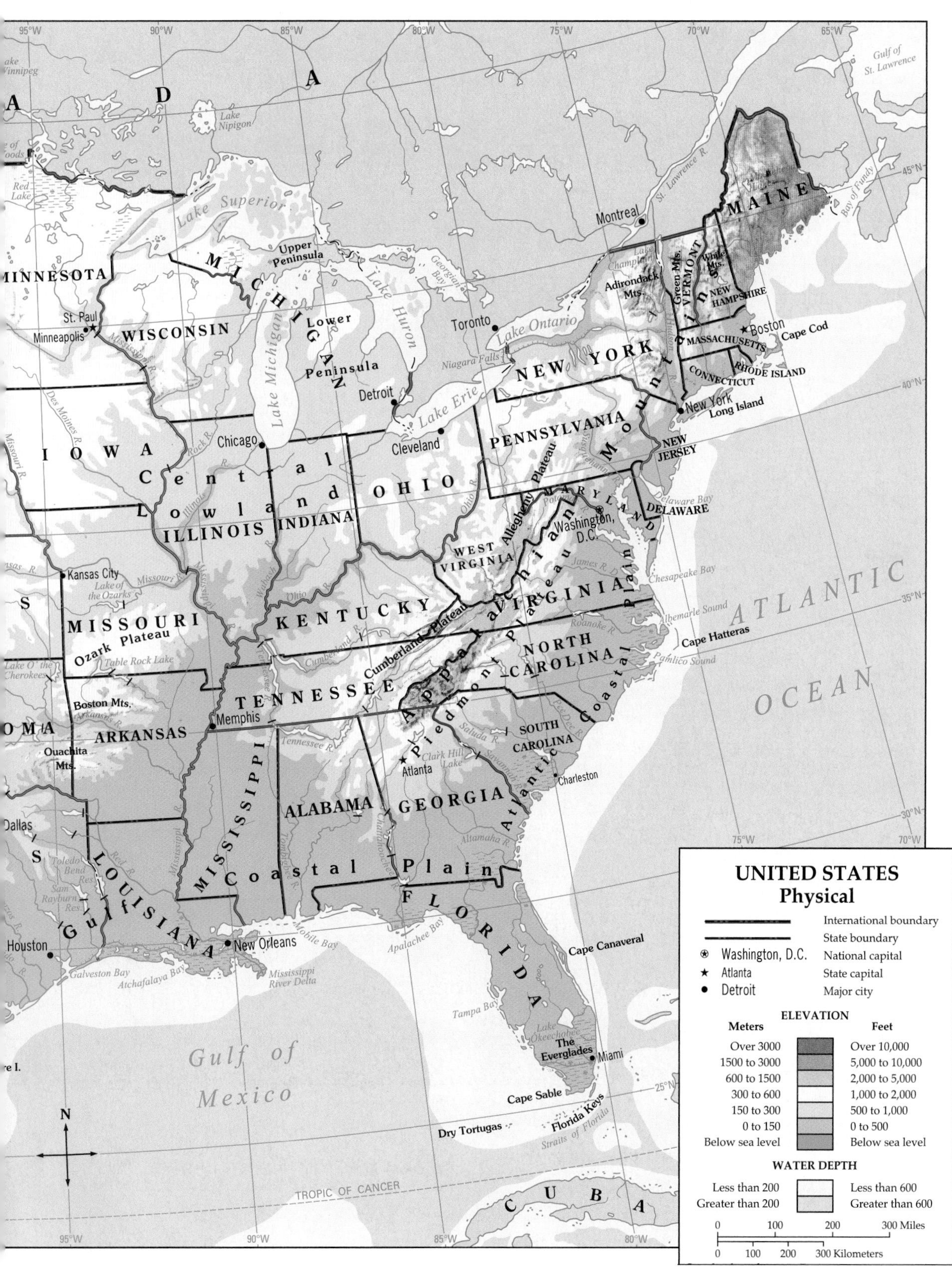
UNITED STATES
Physical
International boundary
State boundary
Washington, D.C. National capital
Atlanta State capital
Detroit Major city
ELEVATION
Meters
Feet
Over 3000
1500 to 3000
600 to 1500
300 to 600
150 to 300
0 to 150
Below sea level
Over 10,000
5,000 to 10,000
2,000 to 5,000
1,000 to 2,000
500 to 1,000
0 to 500
Below sea level
WATER DEPTH
Less than 200
Greater than 200
Less than 600
Greater than 600
0 100 200 300 Miles
0 100 200 300 Kilometers
95°W
90°W
85°W
80°W
75°W
70°W
65°W
45°N
40°N
35°N
30°N
25°N
N
TROPIC OF CANCER
ATLANTIC OCEAN
Gulf of Mexico
Gulf of St. Lawrence
Bay of Fundy
Lake Superior
Lake Michigan
Lake Huron
Lake Ontario
Lake Erie
Lake Nipigon
Georgian Bay
Lake Champlain
MAINE
VERMONT
NEW HAMPSHIRE
MASSACHUSETTS
RHODE ISLAND
CONNECTICUT
NEW YORK
NEW JERSEY
PENNSYLVANIA
DELAWARE
MARYLAND
WEST VIRGINIA
VIRGINIA
NORTH CAROLINA
SOUTH CAROLINA
GEORGIA
FLORIDA
ALABAMA
MISSISSIPPI
TENNESSEE
KENTUCKY
OHIO
INDIANA
ILLINOIS
MICHIGAN
WISCONSIN
MINNESOTA
IOWA
MISSOURI
ARKANSAS
LOUISIANA
CUBA
Montreal
Toronto
Boston
New York
Cleveland
Detroit
Chicago
St. Paul
Minneapolis
Kansas City
Memphis
Atlanta
Charleston
Washington, D.C.
New Orleans
Houston
Dallas
Miami
Upper Peninsula
Lower Peninsula
Adirondack Mts.
Green Mts.
White Mts.
Appalachian Mountains
Allegheny Plateau
Cumberland Plateau
Piedmont Plateau
Central Lowland
Ozark Plateau
Boston Mts.
Ouachita Mts.
Atlantic Coastal Plain
Gulf Coastal Plain
Cape Cod
Long Island
Cape Hatteras
Cape Canaveral
Cape Sable
Dry Tortugas
Florida Keys
Straits of Florida
The Everglades
Lake Okeechobee
Tampa Bay
Apalachee Bay
Mobile Bay
Mississippi River Delta
Galveston Bay
Atchafalaya Bay
Chesapeake Bay
Delaware Bay
Albemarle Sound
Pamlico Sound
Niagara Falls
Table Rock Lake
Lake of the Ozarks
Clark Hill Lake
Toledo Bend Res.
Sam Rayburn Res.

659

Periodic Table of the Elements

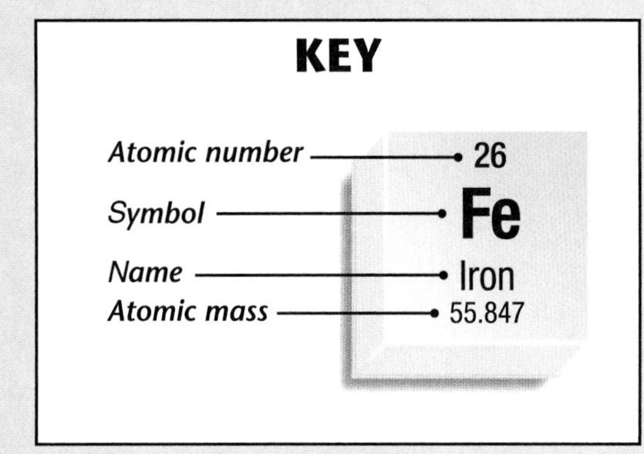

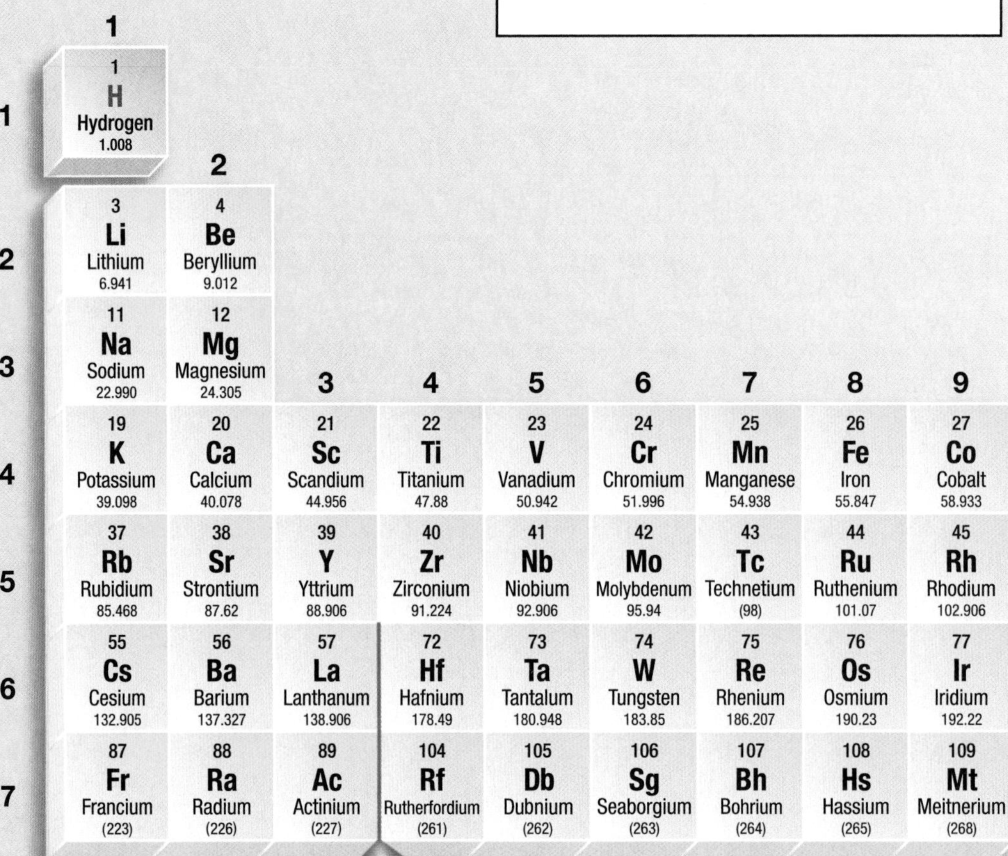

Period	1	2	3	4	5	6	7	8	9
1	1 H Hydrogen 1.008								
2	3 Li Lithium 6.941	4 Be Beryllium 9.012							
3	11 Na Sodium 22.990	12 Mg Magnesium 24.305							
4	19 K Potassium 39.098	20 Ca Calcium 40.078	21 Sc Scandium 44.956	22 Ti Titanium 47.88	23 V Vanadium 50.942	24 Cr Chromium 51.996	25 Mn Manganese 54.938	26 Fe Iron 55.847	27 Co Cobalt 58.933
5	37 Rb Rubidium 85.468	38 Sr Strontium 87.62	39 Y Yttrium 88.906	40 Zr Zirconium 91.224	41 Nb Niobium 92.906	42 Mo Molybdenum 95.94	43 Tc Technetium (98)	44 Ru Ruthenium 101.07	45 Rh Rhodium 102.906
6	55 Cs Cesium 132.905	56 Ba Barium 137.327	57 La Lanthanum 138.906	72 Hf Hafnium 178.49	73 Ta Tantalum 180.948	74 W Tungsten 183.85	75 Re Rhenium 186.207	76 Os Osmium 190.23	77 Ir Iridium 192.22
7	87 Fr Francium (223)	88 Ra Radium (226)	89 Ac Actinium (227)	104 Rf Rutherfordium (261)	105 Db Dubnium (262)	106 Sg Seaborgium (263)	107 Bh Bohrium (264)	108 Hs Hassium (265)	109 Mt Meitnerium (268)

Lanthanide Series	58 Ce Cerium 140.115	59 Pr Praseodymium 140.908	60 Nd Neodymium 144.24	61 Pm Promethium (145)	62 Sm Samarium 150.36
Actinide Series	90 Th Thorium 232.038	91 Pa Protactinium 231.036	92 U Uranium 238.029	93 Np Neptunium (237)	94 Pu Plutonium (244)

660

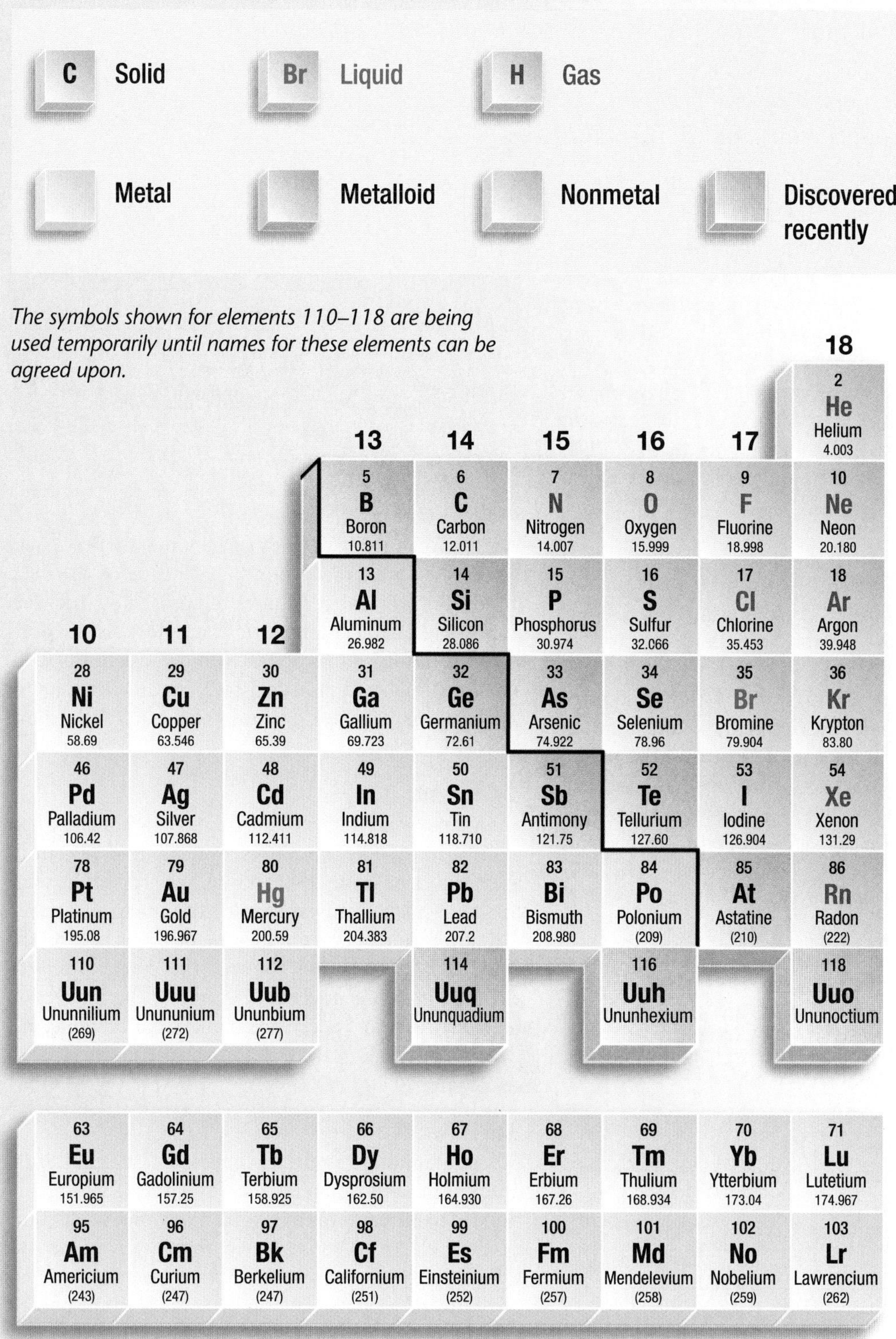

The symbols shown for elements 110–118 are being used temporarily until names for these elements can be agreed upon.

10	11	12	13	14	15	16	17	18
								2 **He** Helium 4.003
			5 **B** Boron 10.811	6 **C** Carbon 12.011	7 **N** Nitrogen 14.007	8 **O** Oxygen 15.999	9 **F** Fluorine 18.998	10 **Ne** Neon 20.180
			13 **Al** Aluminum 26.982	14 **Si** Silicon 28.086	15 **P** Phosphorus 30.974	16 **S** Sulfur 32.066	17 **Cl** Chlorine 35.453	18 **Ar** Argon 39.948
28 **Ni** Nickel 58.69	29 **Cu** Copper 63.546	30 **Zn** Zinc 65.39	31 **Ga** Gallium 69.723	32 **Ge** Germanium 72.61	33 **As** Arsenic 74.922	34 **Se** Selenium 78.96	35 **Br** Bromine 79.904	36 **Kr** Krypton 83.80
46 **Pd** Palladium 106.42	47 **Ag** Silver 107.868	48 **Cd** Cadmium 112.411	49 **In** Indium 114.818	50 **Sn** Tin 118.710	51 **Sb** Antimony 121.75	52 **Te** Tellurium 127.60	53 **I** Iodine 126.904	54 **Xe** Xenon 131.29
78 **Pt** Platinum 195.08	79 **Au** Gold 196.967	80 **Hg** Mercury 200.59	81 **Tl** Thallium 204.383	82 **Pb** Lead 207.2	83 **Bi** Bismuth 208.980	84 **Po** Polonium (209)	85 **At** Astatine (210)	86 **Rn** Radon (222)
110 **Uun** Ununnilium (269)	111 **Uuu** Unununium (272)	112 **Uub** Ununbium (277)		114 **Uuq** Ununquadium		116 **Uuh** Ununhexium		118 **Uuo** Ununoctium

63 **Eu** Europium 151.965	64 **Gd** Gadolinium 157.25	65 **Tb** Terbium 158.925	66 **Dy** Dysprosium 162.50	67 **Ho** Holmium 164.930	68 **Er** Erbium 167.26	69 **Tm** Thulium 168.934	70 **Yb** Ytterbium 173.04	71 **Lu** Lutetium 174.967
95 **Am** Americium (243)	96 **Cm** Curium (247)	97 **Bk** Berkelium (247)	98 **Cf** Californium (251)	99 **Es** Einsteinium (252)	100 **Fm** Fermium (257)	101 **Md** Mendelevium (258)	102 **No** Nobelium (259)	103 **Lr** Lawrencium (262)

Mass numbers in parentheses are those of the most stable or common isotope.

661

Appendix D

Chemical Formulas and Bonding

In your study of Earth Science, you will need to know some basic chemistry, including how to read a chemical formula and how atoms of different elements bond together chemically to form compounds. Earth Science topics for which a knowledge of chemistry is important include minerals, energy resources, the oceans, and the atmosphere.

Chemical Formulas

A chemical formula is a shorthand way to represent a compound. For example, H_2O is the formula for water. The letter symbols stand for the specific elements present in the compound—in this case, hydrogen and oxygen. The subscripts tell you the ratio of atoms of each element present in the compound. If there is no subscript, the number 1 is understood. The ratio of hydrogen atoms to oxygen atoms in water, then, is 2 to 1. The table to the right lists some common chemical formulas.

SOME COMMON CHEMICAL FORMULAS

Name	Formula	Name	Formula
water	H_2O	table salt	$NaCl$
carbon dioxide	CO_2	quartz	SiO_2
ozone	O_3	calcium carbonate	$CaCO_3$
methane	CH_4	pyrite	FeS_2

Atoms and Ions

You may recall that atoms contain negatively charged particles called electrons. Under certain conditions, atoms may gain or lose electrons and become electrically charged particles called ions.

The charge of an ion depends on the number of electrons gained or lost. For example, a sodium atom can lose one electron and become a positive sodium ion, written as Na^+. A chlorine atom, on the other hand, can gain an electron and become a negative chloride ion, written as Cl^-. (For many elements that form negative ions, the ending of the name changes to *–ide.*) The table below lists some common ions.

SOME COMMON IONS

Name	Symbol	Name	Symbol
sodium	Na^+	fluoride	F^-
magnesium	Mg^{2+}	oxide	O^{2-}
calcium	Ca^{2+}	sulfide	S^{2-}
aluminum	Al^{3+}	sulfate*	SO_4^{2-}
chloride	Cl^-	carbonate*	CO_3^{2-}

*Some ions consist of several atoms.

Ionic Bonds

When two atoms react with one another, they are held together by a chemical bond. One type of chemical bond, known as an ionic bond, forms between oppositely charged ions. For example, calcium ions (Ca^{2+}) can form ionic bonds with chloride ions (Cl^-). The ions react in a ratio of 1 to 2, that is, one calcium ion for every 2 chloride ions. The result is calcium chloride, or $CaCl_2$.

Covalent Bonds

A covalent bond forms when atoms share some of their electrons with other atoms. In covalent bonds, electrons are not lost or gained, so no ions are present. Instead, think of what happens when you close a snap on a jacket. A link is formed between one side of the jacket and the other as the two sides "share" the snap. Similarly, electrons may be shared between atoms. The connection between the atoms is a covalent bond. For example, in a water molecule, one oxygen atom shares electrons with two hydrogen atoms.

Metallic Bonds

Metallic bonding occurs in metals such as gold, iron, aluminum, and copper. In a solid metal, atoms are bonded to other atoms in several directions, while some of their electrons move freely among all the atoms. Often, the metal's atoms are described as being in a "sea of electrons." Metallic bonding gives metals some of their familiar properties, such as electrical conductivity.

662

Glossary

A

abrasion The grinding away of rock by other rock particles carried in water, ice, or wind. (pp. 93, 146)
abyssal plain A smooth, nearly flat region of the deep ocean floor. (p. 295)
acid rain Rain that is more acidic than normal, caused by the release of molecules of sulfur dioxide and nitrogen oxide into the air. (pp. 247, 338)
active solar system A method of capturing the sun's energy and distributing it using pumps and fans. (p. 509)
air mass A huge body of air that has similar temperature, pressure, and humidity throughout. (p. 396)
air pollution A change to the atmosphere that has harmful effects. (p. 336)
air pressure A force that is the result of the weight of a column of air pushing down on an area. (p. 346)
alluvial fan A wide, sloping deposit of sediment formed where a stream leaves a mountain range. (p. 137)
altitude Elevation above sea level. (p. 348)
anemometer An instrument used to measure wind speed. (p. 373)
aneroid barometer An instrument that measures changes in air pressure without using a liquid. Changes in the shape of an airtight metal box cause a needle on the barometer dial to move. (p. 347)
anticyclone A high-pressure center of dry air. (p. 402)
aquaculture The farming of saltwater and freshwater organisms. (pp. 313, 541)
aquifer An underground layer of rock or soil that holds water. (p. 212)
artesian well A well in which water rises because of pressure within the aquifer. (p. 213)
asteroid belt The region of the solar system between the orbits of Mars and Jupiter, where many asteroids are found. (p. 626)
asteroids Objects revolving around the sun that are too small and too numerous to be considered planets. (p. 626)
astronomy The study of the moon, stars, and other objects in space. (p. 561)
astronomer A scientist who studies the universe beyond Earth. (p. 11)
atmosphere The mixture of gases that surrounds Earth. The outermost of the four spheres into which scientists divide Earth. (p. 330)
atom The smallest unit of an element that retains the properties of that element. (p. 38)
aurora borealis A colorful, glowing display in the sky caused when particles from the sun strike oxygen and nitrogen atoms in the ionosphere; also called the Northern Lights. (p. 356)
autumnal equinox The day of the year that marks the beginning of fall in the Northern Hemisphere. (p. 567)
axis An imaginary line that passes through Earth's center and the North and South poles, about which Earth rotates. (p. 561)

B

barometer An instrument used to measure changes in air pressure. (p. 346)
beach Wave-washed sediment along a coast. (p. 157)
bedrock The solid layer of rock beneath the soil. (p. 101)
benthos Organisms that live on the bottom of the ocean or another body of water. (p. 299)
bioluminescence The production of light by living things. (p. 309)
biomass fuel Fuel made from things that once were alive. (p. 511)
biome A group of ecosystems with similar climates and living things. (p. 178)
boiling point The temperature at which a substance changes from a liquid to a gas. (p. 64)
brackish Water that is partly salty and partly fresh, characteristic of estuaries. (p. 302)

C

canopy A leafy roof formed by tall trees. (p. 179)
capillary action The combined force of attraction among water molecules and with the molecules of surrounding materials. (p. 52)
captive breeding The mating of endangered animals in zoos or preserves. (p. 550)
chemical bond The force that holds two atoms together. (p. 38)
chemical change A change in matter that produces new substances. (p. 25)
chemical equation A short, easy way to show a chemical reaction, using symbols instead of words. (p. 78)
chemical property A characteristic that is observed when a substance interacts with another substance. (p. 20)
chemical weathering The process that breaks down rock through chemical changes. (p. 95)
chemist Scientist who investigates the particles of matter and their interactions. (p. 10)
chlorofluorocarbons Chlorine compounds formerly used in air conditioners, refrigerators, and spray cans; also called CFCs. (pp. 341, 462)
chlorophyll A plant pigment that absorbs energy from sunlight for photosynthesis. (p. 484)
chloroplast Structure in plant cells that contains chlorophyll. (p. 484)

Glossary

chromosphere The middle layer of the sun's atmosphere. (p. 601)
cirrus Wispy, feathery clouds made mostly of ice crystals that form at high levels, above about 6 kilometers. (p. 384)
clear-cutting The process of cutting down all the trees in an area at once. (p. 538)
climate The average, year-after-year conditions of temperature, precipitation, winds, and clouds in an area. (pp. 448, 432)
coagulation The process by which particles in a liquid clump together; a step in the water treatment process. (p. 231)
coefficient A number placed in front of a chemical formula in an equation that indicates how many atoms or molecules of each reactant and product are involved in a reaction. (p. 82)
colloid A mixture with small undissolved particles that do not settle out. (p. 62)
combustion The burning of a fuel. (p. 489)
comet A ball of ice and dust whose orbit is usually a long, narrow ellipse. (p. 624)
compound A substance in which two or more elements are chemically joined in a set ratio. (p. 22)
concentration The amount of one substance in a certain volume of another substance. (p. 230)
condensation The process by which a gas, such as water vapor, changes to a liquid, such as water. (pp. 54, 383)
conduction The transfer of heat from one substance to another by direct contact of particles of matter. (p. 370)
coniferous trees Trees that produce their seeds in cones and have needle-shaped leaves. (p. 183)
conservation The process of using a resource wisely so it will not be used up. (p. 238)
conservation of mass The principle stating that matter is not created or destroyed during a chemial reaction. (p. 81)
conservation plowing Soil conservation method in which the dead stalks are left in the ground to hold the soil in place. (p. 113)
conservation viewpoint The belief that people should use natural resources as long as they do not destroy those resources. (p. 534)
continental (air mass) A dry air mass that forms over land. (p. 396)
continental climate The climate of the centers of continents, with cold winters and warm or hot summers. (p. 434)
continental glacier A glacier that covers much of a continent or large island. (p. 149)
continental shelf A gently sloping, shallow area of the ocean floor that extends outward from the edge of a continent. (p. 294)
continental slope An incline leading down from the edge of the continental shelf. (p. 294)
contour interval The difference in elevation from one contour line to the next. (p. 175)
contour line A line on a topographic map that connects points of equal elevation. (p. 175)
contour plowing Plowing fields along the curves of a slope to prevent soil loss. (p. 113)
control rod Cadmium rod used in a nuclear reactor to absorb neutrons from fission. (p. 516)
controlled experiment An experiment in which all factors except one are kept constant. (pp. 6, 647)
convection The transfer of heat by movements of a fluid. (p. 370)
core Earth's dense center, made up of the solid inner core and the molten outer core (p. 170); also, the central part of the sun, where nuclear fusion occurs. (p. 600)
Coriolis effect The way Earth's rotation makes winds in the Northern Hemisphere curve to the right and winds in the Southern Hemisphere curve to the left. (p. 377)
corona The outer layer of the sun's atmosphere. (p. 601)
crater A round pit on the moon's surface. (p. 585)
crest The highest point of a wave. (p. 262)
crop rotation The planting of different crops in a field each year. (p. 114)
crust The layer of rock that forms Earth's outer surface. (p. 171)
cumulus Clouds that form less than 2 kilometers above the ground and look like fluffy, rounded piles of cotton. (p. 384)
current A large stream of moving water that flows through the ocean. (p. 279)
cyclone A swirling center of low air pressure. (p. 401)

data The facts, figures, and other evidence gained through observation. (p. 7)
deciduous trees Trees that shed their leaves and grow new ones each year. (p. 182)
decomposer An organism that breaks down wastes and dead organisms. (p. 225)
decomposition A chemical reaction that breaks down a compound into simpler products.. (p. 84)
deflation Wind erosion that removes surface materials. (p. 159)
delta A landform made of sediment that is deposited where a river flows into an ocean or lake. (p. 137)

664

density The amount of mass in a given space; mass per unit volume. (p. 32)
deposition The process by which sediment settles out of the water or wind that is carrying it, and is deposited in a new location. (p. 127)
desalination The process of obtaining fresh water from salt water by removing the salt. (p. 240)
desert A region that receives less than 25 centimeters of rain a year. (pp. 180, 446)
desertification The advance of desertlike conditions into areas that previously were fertile. (p. 111)
development The construction of buildings, roads, dams, and other structures. (p. 110)
development viewpoint The belief that humans should be able to freely use and benefit from all of Earth's resources. (p. 534)
dew point The temperature at which condensation begins. (p. 383)
divide A ridge of land that separates one drainage basin or watershed from another. (pp. 135, 202)
drainage basin The land area from which a river and its tributaries collect their water. (p. 135)
drought A water shortage caused by long periods of low precipitation in a particular area. (pp. 237, 390)
Dust Bowl The area of the Great Plains where wind erosion caused soil loss during the 1930s. (p. 112)

E

efficiency The percentage of energy that is used by a device to perform work. (p. 522)
El Niño An abnormal climate event that occurs every 2 to 7 years in the Pacific Ocean, causing changes in winds, currents, and weather patterns that can lead to dramatic climate changes. (pp. 283, 422)
elastic potential energy The energy of stretching or compressed objects. (p. 471)
electrode A metal strip that gains or loses electrons during electrolysis. (p. 42)
electrolysis A process by which an electric current breaks chemical bonds. (p. 42)
electromagnetic wave A form of energy that can travel through space. (p. 362)
electron A tiny, negatively charged, high-energy particle that moves in the space around the nucleus of an atom. (p. 38)
element A substance composed of a single kind of atom, that cannot be broken down into other substances by chemical or physical means. (p. 21)
elevation Height above sea level. (p. 167)
ellipse An elongated circle, or oval shape; the shape of the planets' orbits. (p. 597)
emissions Solid particles and gases released into the air from a smokestack or motor vehicle. (p. 337)
endangered species A species in danger of becoming extinct in the near future. (p. 546)
endothermic reaction A reaction that absorbs energy in the form of heat. (p. 73)
energy The ability to do work or cause change. (pp. 19, 145)
energy conservation The practice of reducing energy use. (p. 521)
environmental scientist A scientist who studies the effects of human activities on Earth's land, air, water, and living things and also tries to solve problems relating to the use of resources. (p. 11)
equinox The two days of the year on which neither hemisphere is tilted toward or away from the sun. (p. 567)
erosion The process by which water, ice, wind, or gravity moves fragments of rock and soil. (pp. 127, 213)
estuary A coastal inlet or bay where fresh water mixes with salty ocean water. (p. 302)
eutrophication The process by which nutrients in a lake build up over time, causing an increase in the growth of algae. (p. 207)
evacuate To move away temporarily. (p. 410)
evaporation The process by which molecules at the surface of a liquid, such as water, absorb enough energy to change to a gaseous state, such as water vapor. (pp. 54, 194, 381)
exosphere The outer layer of the thermosphere, extending outward into space. (p. 356)
exothermic reaction A reaction that releases energy in the form of heat. (p. 73)
extinction The disappearance of all members of a species from Earth. (p. 546)
extraterrestrial life Life that arises outside of Earth. (p. 628)

fishery An area with a large population of valuable ocean organisms. (p. 540)
filtration The process of passing water through a series of screens that allow the water through, but not larger solid particles. (p. 231)
flash flood A sudden, violent flood that occurs within a few hours, or even minutes, of a heavy rainstorm. (p. 416)
flocs Sticky globs created by adding a chemical such as alum during water treatment. (p. 231)
flood plain A broad, flat valley through which a river flows. (p. 136)
food web The pattern of overlapping food chains in a habitat or ecosystem. (p. 299)

Glossary

force A push or a pull exerted on an object. (p. 468)
fossil fuel An energy-rich substance (such as coal, oil, or natural gas) formed from the remains of organisms. (p. 487)
freezing point The temperature at which a substance changes from a liquid to a solid. (p. 63)
frequency The number of waves that pass a specific point in a given amount of time. (p. 262)
friction The force that opposes the motion of one surface as it moves across another surface. (p. 147)
front The area where air masses meet and do not mix. (p. 399)
fuel A material that releases energy when it burns. (p. 487)
fuel rod Uranium rod that undergoes fission in a nuclear reactor. (p. 516)

gas giants The name given to the first four outer planets: Jupiter, Saturn, Uranus, and Neptune. (p. 614)
gasohol A mixture of gasoline and alcohol. (p. 511)
gene A structure in an organism's cells that carries its hereditary information. (p. 546)
geocentric A description of the solar system in which all of the planets revolve around Earth. (p. 595)
geologist A scientist who studies the forces that make and shape planet Earth. (p. 10)
geology The study of the solid Earth. (p. 171)
geosynchronous orbit The orbit of a satellite that revolves around Earth at the same rate that Earth rotates. (p. 581)
geothermal energy Heat energy in Earth's interior from water or steam that has been heated by magma. (p. 511)
glacier A huge mass of ice and snow that moves slowly over the land. (p. 149)
Global Positioning System A method of finding an exact location on Earth using satellites. (p. 177)
global warming A gradual increase in the temperature of Earth's atmosphere. (pp. 342, 460)
global winds Winds that blow steadily from specific directions over long distances. (p. 377)
grassland An area populated by grasses that gets 25 to 75 centimeters of rain each year. (p. 181)
gravitational potential energy Potential energy that an object has as a result of its position. (p. 471)
gravity The attractive force between two objects; its magnitude depends on their masses and the distance between them. (p. 578)
greenhouse effect The process by which heat is trapped in the atmosphere by water vapor, carbon dioxide, methane, and other gases that form a "blanket" around Earth. (pp. 342, 610)
greenhouse gases Gases in the atmosphere that trap heat. (p. 460)
groin A stone or concrete wall built out from a beach to reduce erosion. (p. 265)
groundwater Water that fills the cracks and pores in underground soil and rock layers. (pp. 140, 193)
gully A large channel in soil formed by erosion. (p. 133)

habitat The place where an organism lives and that provides the things it needs to survive. (p. 198)
habitat destruction The loss of a natural habitat. (p. 547)
habitat fragmentation The breaking of a habitat into smaller, isolated pieces. (p. 547)
hazardous waste A material that can be harmful if it is not properly disposed of. (p. 119)
heat The energy transferred from a hotter object to a cooler one. (p. 369)
heat transfer The movement of energy from a warmer object to a cooler object. (p. 367)
heliocentric A description of the solar system in which all of the planets revolve around the sun. (p. 596)
hibernation A low-energy state similar to sleep that some mammals enter in the winter. (p. 183)
holdfast A bundle of rootlike strands that attaches algae to the rocks. (p. 306)
humid subtropical A wet and warm climate area on the edge of the tropics. (p. 448)
humidity A measure of the amount of water vapor in the air. (p. 382)
humus Dark-colored organic material in soil. (p. 102)
hurricane A tropical storm that has winds of 119 kilometers per hour or higher; typically about 600 kilometers across. (p. 408)
hydroelectric power Electricity produced by the kinetic energy of water moving over a waterfall or dam. (pp. 252, 510)
hypothesis A possible explanation for a set of observations or an answer to a scientific question. (pp. 6, 642)

ice ages Cold time periods in Earth's history, during which glaciers covered large parts of the surface. (pp. 150, 456)
ice wedging Process that splits rock when water seeps into cracks, then freezes and expands. (p. 94)
impermeable Characteristic of materials through which water does not easily pass, such as clay and granite. (p. 211)
incineration The burning of solid waste. (p. 117)

666

inertia The tendency of a moving object to continue in a straight line or a stationary object to remain in place. (p. 597)
inference An interpretation based on observation and prior knowledge. (p. 5)
infrared radiation A form of energy with wavelengths that are longer than visible light. (p. 363)
insulation Building material that blocks heat transfer between the air inside and outside. (p. 523)
intertidal zone The area that stretches from the highest high-tide line on land out to the point on the continental shelf exposed by the lowest low tide. (p. 300)
International System of Units (SI) A system of measurement based on multiples of ten and on established measures of mass, length, and time. (p. 29)
ionosphere The lower part of the thermosphere, where electrically charged particles called ions are found. (p. 356)
irrigation The process of supplying water to areas of land to make them suitable for growing crops. (p. 196)
isobars Lines on a map joining places that have the same air pressure. (p. 422)
isotherms Lines on a map joining places that have the same temperature. (p. 422)

jet streams Bands of high-speed winds about 10 kilometers above Earth's surface. (p. 380)

karst topography A type of landscape in rainy regions where there is limestone near the surface, characterized by caverns, sinkholes, and valleys. (p. 141)
kettle A small depression that forms when a chunk of ice is left in glacial till. (p. 152)
keystone species A species that influences the survival of many others in an ecosystem. (p. 545)
kinetic energy The form of energy an object has because of its motion. (pp. 145, 252, 469)

land breeze The flow of air from land to a body of water. (p. 376)
landform A feature of topography formed by the processes that shape Earth's surface. (p. 167)
landform region A large area of land where the topography is similar. (p. 167)
land reclamation The process of restoring land to a more natural state. (p. 114)
latitude The distance north or south from the equator, measured in degrees. (pp. 378, 566)
leachate Water that has passed through buried wastes in a landfill. (p. 115)
leach field The ground area around a septic tank through which wastewater filters after leaving the tank. (p. 235)
leeward The downwind side of mountains. (p. 437)
levee A long ridge formed by deposits of sediments alongside a river channel. (p. 203)
lightning A sudden spark, or energy discharge, caused when electrical charges jump between parts of a cloud or between a cloud and the ground. (p. 404)
lithosphere A rigid layer made up of the uppermost part of the mantle and the crust. One of four spheres into which scientists divide Earth. (p. 170)
litter The loose layer of dead plant leaves and stems on the surface of the soil. (p. 104)
load The amount of sediment that a river or stream carries. (p. 146)
loam Rich, fertile soil that is made up of about equal parts of clay, sand, and silt. (p. 102)
local winds Winds that blow over short distances. (p. 374)
loess A wind-formed deposit made of fine particles of clay and silt. (p. 160)
longshore drift The movement of water and sediment along a beach caused by waves coming into shore at an angle. (pp. 157, 264)
lunar eclipse The blocking of sunlight to the moon that occurs when Earth is directly between the sun and moon. (p. 575)

manipulated variable The one factor that a scientist changes during an experiment; also called the independent variable. (pp. 7, 647)
mantle The layer of hot, solid material between Earth's crust and core. (p. 170)
maria Dark, flat regions on the moon's surface. (p. 585)
marine climate The climate of some coastal regions, with relatively warm winters and cool summers. (p. 434)
maritime (air mass) A humid air mass that forms over oceans. (p. 396)
mass A measure of how much matter is in an object. (p. 29)
mass movement Any one of several processes by which gravity moves sediment downhill. (p. 127)
matter Anything that has mass and occupies space. (p. 18)

Glossary

meander A looping curve formed in a river as it winds through its flood plain. (p. 136)
mechanical weathering The type of weathering in which rock is physically broken into smaller pieces. (p. 213)
meltdown A dangerous condition caused by overheating inside a nuclear reactor. (p. 517)
mercury barometer An instrument that measures changes in air pressure, consisting of a glass tube part filled with mercury, with its open end resting in a dish of mercury. Air pressure pushing on the mercury in the dish forces the mercury in the tube higher. (p. 346)
mesosphere The middle layer of Earth's atmosphere; the layer in which most meteoroids burn up. (p. 352)
meteor A streak of light in the sky produced by the burning of a meteoroid in Earth's atmosphere. (p. 627)
meteorite A meteoroid that has hit Earth's surface. (p. 627)
meteoroid A chunk of rock or dust in space. (p. 627)
meteorologists Scientists who study the causes of weather and try to predict it. (pp. 11, 420)
microclimate The climate characteristic of a small, specific area; it may be different from the climate of the surrounding area. (p. 437)
mid-ocean ridge The undersea mountain chain where new ocean floor is produced; a divergent plate boundary. (p. 295)
mixture Two or more substances that are mixed together but not chemically combined (p. 22)
monsoons Sea and land breezes over a large region that change direction with the seasons. (p. 376)
moraine A ridge formed by the till deposited at the edge of a glacier. (p. 151)
mountain A landform with high elevation and high relief. (p. 168)
mountain range A series of mountains that have the same general shape and structure. (p. 168)
municipal solid waste Waste produced in homes, businesses, and schools. (p. 115)

neap tide A tide with the least difference between low and high tide that occurs when the sun and moon pull at right angles to each other. (p. 269)
nekton Free-swimming animals that can move throughout the water column. (p. 299)
neritic zone The region of shallow water in the ocean that extends from the low-tide line out to the edge of the continental shelf. (p. 305)
neutron Small uncharged particle in the nucleus of an atom. (p. 38)
nodule A black, potato-shaped lump formed when metals build up around pieces of shell on the ocean floor. (p. 311)
nonpoint source A widely spread source of pollution, such as road runoff, that is difficult to link to a specific point of origin. (p. 243)
nonrenewable resource A natural resource that is not replaced as it is used. (p. 531)
nuclear fission The splitting of an atom's nucleus into smaller nuclei. (p. 515)
nuclear fusion The combining of two atomic nuclei into a single larger nucleus, as when two hydrogen atoms join together to form helium, releasing energy. (p. 518)
nucleus The central core of an atom that contains the protons and neutrons. (pp. 38, 515)

observation Using all five senses to gather information. (p. 5)
oceanographer A scientist who studies Earth's oceans. (p. 11)
occluded Cut off, as the warm air mass at an occluded front is cut off from the ground by cooler air beneath it. (p. 401)
open-ocean zone The area of the ocean beyond the edge of the continental shelf. (p. 305)
operational definition A statement that describes how a particular variable is to be measured or a term is to be defined. (p. 647)
orbit The path of an object as it revolves around another object in space. (p. 561)
oxbow lake The crescent-shaped, cutoff body of water that remains after a river carves a new channel. (p. 136)
ozone A form of oxygen that has three oxygen atoms in each molecule instead of the usual two; a toxic form of oxygen. (pp. 332, 337)
ozone layer The layer of the atmosphere that contains a higher concentration of ozone than the rest of the atmosphere. (pp. 340)

passive solar system A method of converting solar energy into heat without pumps or fans. (p. 509)
penumbra The part of a shadow surrounding the darkest part. (p. 574)
permafrost Permanently frozen soil found in the tundra climate region. (pp. 184, 450)
permeable Characteristic of materials such as sand and gravel that allow water to pass easily through them. (pp. 97, 211)
pesticide A chemical intended to kill insects and other organisms that damage crops. (p. 248)

668

petrochemical Compound made from oil. (p. 505)
petroleum Liquid fossil fuel; oil. (p. 504)
pH How acidic or basic a substance is, measured on a scale of 1 (very acidic) to 14 (very basic). (p. 229)
phase One of the different shapes of the moon as seen from Earth. (p. 571)
photochemical smog A brownish haze that is a mixture of ozone and other chemicals, formed when nitrogen oxides, hydrocarbons, and other pollutants react with one another in the presence of sunlight. (p. 337)
photosphere The inner layer of the sun's atmosphere. (p. 601)
photosynthesis The process by which plants use water, plus carbon dioxide and energy from the sun, to make food. (p. 483)
physical change A change that alters the form or appearance of a substance but does not make the material into another substance. (p. 24)
physical property A characteristic of a substance that can be observed without changing the substance into something else. (p. 20)
pigment Colored chemical compounds found in plants. (p. 484)
plankton Tiny algae and animals that float in water and are carried by waves and currents. (p. 299)
plateau A landform that has a more or less level surface and is elevated high above sea level. (p. 169)
plucking The process by which a glacier picks up rocks as it flows over the land. (p. 150)
poaching Illegal hunting of wildlife. (p. 548)
point source A specific source of pollution that can be identified, such as a pipe. (p. 245)
polar (air mass) A cold air mass that forms north of 50° north latitude or south of 50° south latitude and has high air pressure. (p. 396)
polar molecule A molecule that has electrically charged areas. (p. 51)
polar zones The areas near both poles, from about 66.5° to 90° north and 66.5° to 90° south latitudes. (p. 433)
pollution A change to the environment that has a negative effect on living things. (p. 531)
pores Tiny openings in and between particles of rock and soil that may contain air or water. (p. 211)
potential energy Energy that is stored and available to be used later. (pp. 145, 470)
power The rate at which work is done. (pp. 490)
precipitate A solid that forms from a solution during a chemical reaction. (p. 71)
precipitation Forms of water such as rain, snow, sleet, or hail that fall from clouds and reach Earth's surface. (pp. 387, 194)
pressure The amount of force pushing on a surface or area. (p. 345)
preservation viewpoint The belief that all parts of the environment are equally important, no matter how useful they are to humans. (p. 534)
product A substance formed as a result of a chemical reaction. (p. 80)
prominence A loop of gas that protrudes from the sun's surface, linking parts of sunspot regions. (p. 604)
proton Small, positively charged particle in the nucleus of an atom. (p. 38)
psychrometer An instrument used to measure relative humidity, consisting of a wet-bulb thermometer and a dry-bulb thermometer. (p. 382)

radiant energy Energy that travels in waves. (p. 473)
radiation The direct transfer of energy through empty space by electromagnetic waves. (p. 362)
rain forest A forest in the tropical wet climate zone that gets plenty of rain all year. (p. 443)
rain gauge An instrument used to measure the amount of precipitation, consisting of an open-ended can topped by a collecting funnel and having a collecting tube and measuring scale inside. (p. 389)
reactant A substance that enters into a chemical reaction. (p. 80)
reactor vessel The part of a nuclear reactor where nuclear fission occurs. (p. 516)
recharge New water that enters an aquifer from the surface. (p. 213)
recycling The process of reclaiming and reusing raw materials. (p. 117)
refinery A factory where crude oil is separated into fuels and other products. (p. 505)
relative humidity The percentage of water vapor in the air compared to the maximum amount the air can hold at that temperature. (p. 382)
relief The difference in elevation between the highest and lowest parts of an area. (p. 167)
renewable resource A resource that is naturally replaced in a relatively short time. (pp. 501, 531)
replacement A reaction in which one element replaces another in a compound, or in which two elements in different compounds trade places. (p. 86)
reserve A known deposit of fuels. (p. 503)
reservoir A natural or artificial lake that stores water for human use. (p. 206)
respiration The process by which glucose is broken down to release energy. (p. 486)

responding variable The factor that changes as a result of changes to the manipulated variable in an experiment; also called the dependent variable. (pp. 7, 647)
retrograde rotation The spinning motion of a planet from east to west, opposite to the direction of rotation of most planets and moons. (p. 609)
revolution The movement of an object around another object. (p. 561)
rill A tiny groove in soil made by flowing water. (p. 133)
rip current A rush of water that flows rapidly back to sea through a narrow opening. (p. 264)
river A large stream. (pp. 134, 264)
rock The material that forms Earth's hard surface. (p. 171)
rotation The spinning motion of a planet about its axis. (p. 561)
runoff Water that flows over the ground surface rather than soaking into the ground. (p. 133)

salinity The total amount of dissolved salts in a water sample. (p. 271)
sand dune A deposit of wind-blown sand. (p. 158)
sandbar A ridge of sand deposited by waves as they slow down near shore. (p. 264)
sanitary landfill A landfill that holds nonhazardous waste such as municipal solid waste and construction debris. (p. 116)
satellite Any object that revolves around another object in space. (p. 580)
saturated zone A layer of permeable rock or soil in which the cracks and pores are completely filled with water. (p. 168)
savanna A tropical grassland with scattered clumps of trees; found in the tropical wet-and-dry climate zone close to the equator. (pp. 181, 446)
scale Used to compare distance on a map or globe to distance on Earth's surface. (p. 174)
scattering Reflection of light in all directions. (p. 364)
science A way of learning about the natural world and the knowledge gained through that process. (p. 4)
scientific inquiry The diverse ways in which scientists explore problems and seek to answer questions about the natural world. (p. 4)
scientific theory A well-tested concept that explains a wide range of observations. (p. 8)
sea breeze The flow of air from an ocean or lake to the land. (p. 376)
sediment Small, solid particles of material from rocks or organisms which are moved by water or wind, resulting in erosion and deposition. (p. 127)
selective cutting The process of cutting down only some trees in an area. (p. 538)
septic tank An underground tank containing bacteria that treats wastewater as it passes through. (p. 235)
sewage Water containing human wastes. (p. 233)
sludge Deposits of fine solids that settle out from wastewater during the treatment process. (p. 234)
sod A thick mass of grass roots and soil. (p. 112)
soil The loose, weathered material on Earth's surface in which plants can grow. (p. 101)
soil conservation The management of soil to prevent its destruction. (p. 113)
soil horizon A layer of soil that differs in color and texture from the layers above or below it. (p. 103)
solar eclipse The blocking of sunlight to Earth that occurs when the moon is between the sun and Earth. (p. 574)
solar energy Energy from the sun. (p. 507)
solar flare An explosion of hydrogen gas from the sun's surface that occurs when loops in sunspot regions suddenly connect. (p. 604)
solar wind A stream of electrically charged particles produced by the sun's corona. (p. 602)
solstice The two days of the year on which the noon sun is directly overhead at either 23.5° South or 23.5° North. (p. 566)
solute The part of a solution present in a lesser amount and dissolved by the solvent. (p. 60)
solution A mixture in which one substance is dissolved in another. (p. 52)
solvent The part of a solution that is present in the largest amount and dissolves a solute. (p. 52)
sonar A system that determines the distance of an object under water by recording echoes of sound waves; gets its name from sound navigation and ranging. (p. 293)
specific heat The amount of thermal energy required to raise the temperature of one kilogram of a substance by 1°C. (p. 58)
spit A beach formed by longshore drift that projects like a finger out into the water. (p. 157)
spring A place where groundwater bubbles or flows out of cracks in the rocks. (p. 212)
spring tide A tide with the greatest difference between high and low tide that occurs when the sun and the moon are aligned in a line with Earth. (p. 268)
stalactite A calcite deposit that hangs from the roof of a cave. (p. 141)
stalagmite A cone-shaped calcite deposit that builds up from the floor of a cave. (p. 141)
states The three forms (solid, liquid, and gas) in which matter exists. (p. 24)
steppe A prairie or grassland found in the semiarid climate region. (p. 447)

storm A violent disturbance in the atmosphere. (p. 403)
storm surge A dome of water that sweeps across the coast where a hurricane lands. (p. 410)
stratosphere The second-lowest layer of Earth's atmosphere; the ozone layer is located in the upper stratosphere. (p. 352)
stratus Clouds that form in flat layers. (p. 384)
stream A channel through which water is continually flowing downhill. (p. 134)
subarctic A climate zone that lies north of the humid continental climate zone, with short, cool summers and long, bitterly cold winters. (p. 449)
submersible An underwater vehicle built of strong materials to resist pressure at depth. (p. 275)
subscript An underwater vehicle built of strong materials to resist pressure at depth. (p. 79)
subsoil The layer of soil beneath the topsoil that contains mostly clay and other minerals. (p. 103)
substance A single kind of matter that has distinct physical and chemical properties. (p. 19)
sunspots Dark, cooler regions on the surface of the sun. (pp. 457, 602)
surface tension The tightness across the surface of water caused by the polar water molecules pulling on each other. (p. 51)
suspension A mixture in which particles can be seen and easily separated by settling or filtration. (p. 59)
sustainable yield A regular amount of a renewable resource that can be harvested without reducing the future supply. (p. 538)
symbols On a map, pictures used by mapmakers to stand for features on Earth's surface. (p. 174)
synthesis A chemical reaction in which two or more simple substances combine to form a new, more complex substance. (p. 83)

taxol Chemcial in Pacific yew tree bark that has cancer-fighting properties. (p. 553)
telescope A device built to study distant objects by making them appear closer. (p. 585)
temperate zones The area between the tropical and polar zones, from about 23.5° to 66.5° north and 23.5° to 66.5° south latitudes. (p. 433)
temperature The average amount of energy of motion in the molecules of a substance. (p. 369)
temperature inversion Condition in which a layer of warm air traps polluted air close to Earth's surface. (p. 338)
terrestrial planets The name given to the four inner planets: Mercury, Venus, Earth, and Mars. (p. 606)
thermal energy The energy of motion in the molecules of a substance. (p. 369)
thermometer An instrument used to measure temperature, consisting of a thin, glass tube with a bulb on one end that contains a liquid (usually mercury or alcohol). (p. 369)
thermosphere The outermost layer of Earth's atmosphere. (p. 355)
threatened species A species that could become endangered in the near future. (p. 546)
tides The daily rise and fall of Earth's waters on shores. (pp. 267, 578)
till The sediments deposited directly by a glacier. (p. 151)
topographic map A map that shows the surface features of an area. (p. 173)
topography The shape of the land determined by elevation, relief, and landforms. (p. 166)
topsoil Mixture of humus, clay, and other minerals that forms the crumbly, topmost layer of soil. (p. 103)
tornado A rapidly whirling, funnel-shaped cloud that reaches down from a storm cloud to touch Earth's surface, usually leaving a destructive path. (p. 405)
transpiration The process by which plants release water vapor through their leaves. (p. 194)
trench A deep canyon in the ocean floor. (p. 296)
tributary A stream that flows into a larger stream. (pp. 134, 200)
tropical (air mass) A warm air mass that forms in the tropics and has low air pressure. (p. 396)
tropical zone The area near the equator, between about 23.5° north latitude and 23.5° south latitude. (p. 433)
troposphere The lowest layer of Earth's atmosphere, where weather occurs. (p. 351)
trough The lowest point of a wave. (p. 263)
tundra A polar climate region, found across northern Alaska, Canada, and Russia, with short, cool summers and bitterly cold winters. (pp. 184, 450)
turbulence A type of movement of water in which, rather than moving downstream, the water moves every which way. (p. 148)

ultraviolet radiation A form of energy with wavelengths that are shorter than visible light. (p. 363)
umbra The darkest part of a shadow. (p. 574)
understory A layer of shorter plants that grow in the shade of a forest canopy. (p. 179)
unsaturated zone A layer of rocks and soil above the water table in which the pores contain air as well as water. (p. 211)
upwelling An upward flow of cold water from the ocean depths. (p. 281)

valley glacier A long, narrow glacier that forms when snow and ice build up in a mountain valley. (p. 149)
variable Any factor that can change in an experiment. (pp. 7, 647)
vernal equinox The day of the year that marks the beginning of spring in the Northern Hemisphere. (p. 567)

W

water cycle The continuous process by which water moves from Earth's surface to the atmosphere and back, passing through the living and nonliving parts of the environment. (p. 194)
water pollution The addition of any substance that has a negative effect on water or the living things that depend on the water. (p. 243)
water quality The degree of purity of water, determined by measuring the substances in water, besides water molecules. (p. 228)
water table The top of the saturated zone, or depth to the groundwater in an aquifer. (p. 211)
water vapor The invisible, gaseous form of water. (pp. 192, 333)
watershed The land area that supplies water to a river system. (p. 201)
wave The movement of energy through a body of water. (p. 261)
wave height The vertical distance from the crest of a wave to the trough. (p. 263)
wavelength The horizontal distance between two wave crests. (p. 262)
weather The condition of Earth's atmosphere at a particular time and place. (p. 330)
weathering The chemical and physical processes that break down rock at Earth's surface. (p. 92)
weight A measure of the force of gravity on an object. (p. 29)
wetland An area of land that is covered with a shallow layer of water during some or all of the year. (p. 216)
wind The horizontal movement of air from an area of high pressure to an area of lower pressure. (p. 372)
wind-chill factor Increased cooling caused by the wind. (p. 373)
windward The side of mountains that faces the oncoming wind. (p. 437)
work The product of force and distance when a force is used to move an object. (p. 468)

672

Index

Index

674

675

Index

677

Index

678

679

Index

680

Index

682

683

Acknowledgments

Staff Credits

The people who made up the ***Life, Earth, and Physical Science*** team—representing design services, editorial, editorial services, electronic publishing technology, manufacturing & inventory planning, marketing, marketing services, market research, online services & multimedia development, production services, product planning, project office, and publishing processes are listed below.

Carolyn Belanger, Barbara Bertell, Peggy Bliss, Kristen Braghi, Roger Calado, Jonathan Cheney, Lisa Clark, Christine Cuccio, Patricia Cully, Patricia Dambry, Kathleen Dempsey, Judy Elgin, Jim Fellows, Barbara Foster, Bernard Gage, Julie Gecha, Joel Gendler, Adam Goldberg, Jessica Gould, Robert M. Graham, Dennis Higbee, Joanne Hudson, Anne Jones, Dorothy Kavanaugh, Toby Klang, Don Manning, Jeanne Maurand, Carolyn McGuire, Brent McKenzie, Natania Mlawer, Cindy Noftle, Julia Osborne, Caroline M. Power, Shelley Ryan, Robin Santel, Diane Walsh, Beth A. Winickoff, Helen Young

Illustrations

AccuWeather: 424, 425, 426
Peter Brooks: 29, 42, 223, 568, 576, 605, 622
Warren Cutler: 204-205, 218-219, 300-301
Kathleen Dempsey: 98, 108, 110, 142, 591 b
Julia Gecha: 426
Andrea Golden: 51, 52, 54, 199 bl, 212, 214 t, 422
JB Woolsey Associates: 7, 47, 94, 123, 133, 257, 321 b, 384, 417, 465 b, 486, 497, 502–503 b
John Edwards & Associates: 96, 171, 175 tl, 175 tr, 243, 246, 247, 251, 255, 262 tr, 263, 264, 267 tr, 269, 281, 305, 343, 350, 364, 376 t, 401, 409 bl, 460, 470, 477, 501, 511, 517, 565, 571, 572 overlay, 574 r, 575 l, 598 b, 598–599 t, 607 t, 615
GeoSystems Global Corporation: 179, 180, 182, 184
MapQuest.com, Inc.: 107, 111, 112, 135 t, 137, 150, 158, 167 t, 167 b, 504 t, 167 t, 167 b,
Martucci Studio: 102 b, 109, 521 b, 174, 193, 321 t, 331, 363, 423 b, 453, 531, 605
Matt Mayerchak: 45, 187, 255 br, 463, 456 t, 495, 589
Karen Minot: 543
Paul Mirocha: 309 t
Morgan Cain & Associates: 43, 61, 62, 75 l, 75 m, 75 r, 78, 82 tl, 82 tm, 82 tr, 102 t, 104–105 b, 126, 128, 135 b, 148, 159, 232, 239, 248, 252, 262 bl, 292 bl, 307 t, 338, 341, 342, 346 b, 347 tl, 348, 377 t, 377 b, 379, 387 b, 389, 393, 461, 505, 516, 561, 564, 568, 573, 579 b, 580 t, 581 t, 581 r, 603, 607 b, 609 r, 625 t, 625 m, 626 l
Ortelius Design: 6 bl, 30, 31, 196 tl, 196 bl, 196 br, 197 tl, 197 br, 197 bl, 202, 207, 242, 266 tl, 283, 291 inset, 297, 322, 322 inset, 324 all, 325 tl, 325 tr, 327 inset, 333 inset, 376 b, 402, 406 tl, 406 tr, 406 br, 407 t, 407 bl, 407 br
Judith Pinkham: 536
Matthew Pippin: 85, 103 bl, 103 bm, 103 br, 138–139, 152–153, 195, 211, 213, 223, 231, 234, 235, 253 t, 254, 346 t, 353, 385, 416 t, 488
Pond and Giles: 539
Rossi Illustration and Design: 208 t
John Sanderson: 398
Nancy Smith: 76, 492
U.S.G.S.: 176
Robert Warshaw: 34

Photography

Cover: S. Solum/PhotoLink

Introduction to Science
Page 4 t, John Sanford/Science Photo Library/Photo Researchers; **4 b,** The Granger Collection, NY; **5,** Robert E. Daemmrich/Tony Stone Images; **6,** Manfred Gottschalk/Tom Stack & Associates; **8,** Tsado/NCDC/NOAA/Tom Stack & Associates; **9,** Richard Haynes; **10,** Charles Cupton/The Stock Market; **11,** NASA; **12–13 t,** M.W.Franke/Peter Arnold; **12 l,** L. Gould/OSF/Animals Animals; **12 br,** M. W. Franke/Peter Arnold; **13 tr,** Peter Menzel/Stock Boston; **13 bl,** Frank Pederick/The Image Works; **13 br,** Bob Crandall/ Stock Boston; **14,** Tsado/NCDC/NOAA/Tom Stack & Associates.

Chapter 1
Pages 16–17, Cameron Davidson/TSI; **18,** both Russ Lappa; **19,** Thomas H. Ives/The Stock Market; **20,** PhotoDisc, Inc.; **21 l,** Stone/Cathlyn Melloan; **21 m,** Bernard Roussel/The Image Bank; **21 r,** Bob Firth/International Stock; **22 l,** Ken Lucas/Visuals Unlimited; **22 r,** Yoav Levy/Phototake; **24 t,** Michael P. Gadomski/Photo Researchers, Inc.; **24 b,** Stone/Lawrence Migdale; **25,** John M. Roberts/The Stock Market; **26,** Stone/Alan R. Moller; **27 t,** James Dwyer/Stock Boston; **27 b,** Tony Freeman/PhotoEdit; **28 t,** Richard Haynes; **28 b,** SuperStock; **29 l,** Russ Lappa; **29 r** Richard Haynes; **30, 31 t,** Corbis-Bettmann; **31 b,** The Granger Collection, NY; **32,** U.S. Fish and Wildlife Service/Greg Knadle; **35 both,** 1998, The Art Institute of Chicago; **36,** Rich Treptow/Visuals Unlimited; **37,** Chuck Feil/Uniphoto; **38,** SCI-VU-IBMRL/Visuals Unlimted; **39,** Ken Eward/Science Source/Photo Researchers, Inc.; **40 t,** Russ Lappa; **40 b,** Corbis-Bettmann; **41 t** Helga Lade/Peter Arnold, Inc.; **41 bl** E. R. Degginger/Animals Animals/Earth Scenes; **41 br,** Charles D. Winters/Photo Researchers, Inc.; **42,** Aron Haupt/David R. Fraizer Photo Library; **44,** Heine Schneebeli/Science Photo Library/Photo Researchers, Inc.; **47,** Corbis-Bettmann.

Chapter 2
Pages 48–49, Randy Linchs/Sharpshooters; **50,** Russ Lappa; **51 b,** Stephen Dalton/Photo Researchers; **52 inset,** Tom Bean/The Stock Market; **52 b,** Mark & Audry Gibson/The Stock Market; **54 l,** Steven C. Kaufman/Peter Arnold; **54 m,** Chris Sorensen/The Stock Market; **54 r,** Japack/Leo de Wys; **55 b,** Neal Mishler/Natural Selection; **57 b,** Russ Lappa; **58 t,** D. Adams/ Picture Perfect Images; **59,** Michael Newman/PhotoEdit; **60 t, m,** Russ Lappa; **60 b,** Leonard Lessin/Peter Arnold; **61,** Runk/Schoenberger/Grant Heilman Photography.

Chapter 3
Pages 68–69, Corbis; **70,** Steve Elmore/The Stock Market; **71,** Brian Sytnyk/Masterfile; **72 t,** Charles D. Winters/Photo Researchers; **72 ml,** Wood Sabold/International Stock; **72 mr,** Ken O'Donaghue; **72 bl,** Russ Lappa; **72 br,** Steven Needham/Envision; **73 t,** Michael Newman/Photo Edit; **73 b,** Reinstein, The Image Works; **74 l** Russ Lappa; **74 r,** J. Sulley/The Image Works; **75 both,** Richard Megna/Fundamental Photographs; **77,** Richard Haynes; **78, 80 all,** Russ Lappa; **81,** John D. Cummingham/Visuals Unlimited; **83 both,** E. R. Degginger; **84,** Donald Johnson/Tony Stone Images; **86 t,** Russ Lappa; **86 b,** Charles D. Winters/Photo Researchers.

Chapter 4
Pages 90–91, Mike Mazzaschi/Stock Boston; **92,** Russ Lappa; **93 l,** Ron Watts/Westlight; **93 r,** Jerry D. Greer; **94 l,** Breck P. Kent/Animals Animals/Earth Scenes; **94 r,** Susan Rayfield/Photo Researchers; **95 l,** John Sohlden/Visuals Unlimited; **95 tr,** Gerald & Buff Corsi/Visuals Unlimited; **95 br,** E. R. Degginger/Photo Researchers; **97 t,** Chromosohm/Sohm/Photo Researchers; **97 b,** Breck P. Kent/ Animals Animals/Earth Scenes; **99,** Richard Haynes; **100,** John G. Ross/Photo Researchers; **101 t,** Richard Haynes; **101 b,** Rod Planck/Tony Stone Images; **106,** J.M. Labat/Jacana/Photo Researchers; **108,** Richard T. Nowitz/Photo Researchers; **109,** Richard Haynes; **110 l,** Bertrand Rieger/Tony Stone Images; **110 m,** Chad Slattery/Tony Stone Images; **110 r,** Jacques Jangoux/Tony Stone Images; **111 t,** Corbis; **111 b,** Chris Sattleberger/Panos Pictures; **112,** AP/Wide World Photos; **113 tl,** Kevin Horan/Tony Stone Images; **113 tr,** Tom Bean 1994/DRK Photo; **113 bl,** Larry Lefever/Grant Heilman Photography; **113 br,** Martin Benjamin/The Image Works; **114 both,** Wally McNamee/Woodfin Camp & Associates; **115,** Russ Lappa; **117,** Hank Morgan/Science Source/Photo Researchers; **118,** Ray Pfortner/ Peter Arnold; **119 all,** Russ Lappa; **120,** Stephen Agricola/The Image Works.

Chapter 5
Pages 124–125, Jim Steinberg/Photo Researchers; **126,** Jim Steinberg/Photo Researchers; **127,** Paul Sequeira/Photo Researchers; **128 t,** Eric Vandeville/Liaison Agency; **128 b,** Thomas G. Rampton/Grant Heilman Photography; **129,** Steven Holt; **130, 131,** Richard Haynes; **132 t,** PhotoDisc, Inc.; **132–133b,** Walter Bibikow/The Viesti Collection; **133t,** Runk Schoenberger/Grant Heilman Photography; **134,** Inga Spence/Tom Stack & Associates; **135,** David Ball/The Stock Market; **136 l,** Glenn M. Oliver/Visuals Unlimited; **136 r,** Index Stock Imagery, Inc.; **137 t,** Gerald & Buff Corsi/Visuals Unlimited; **137 b,** NASA/SADO/ Tom Stack & Associates; **140,** Chuck O'Rear/Westlight; **141,** St. Petersburg Times/Liaison Agency; **142,** Russ Lappa; **143,** Richard Haynes; **144,** Doug McKay/Tony Stone Images; **145 t,** Richard Haynes; **145 b,** Eliot Cohen; **149 t,** Richard Haynes; **149 b,** Mark Kelley/ Stock Boston; **151,** Grant Heilman Photography; **154,** Craig Tuttle/The Stock Market; **156,** Randy Wells/Tony Stone Images; **157,** E. R.I.M./Tony Stone Images; **158 t,** Richard Haynes; **158 b,** Jess Stock/Tony Stone Images; **159,** Breck P. Kent; **160,** Connie Toops.

Chapter 6
Pages 164–165, Nick Vedros, Vedros & Assoc./TSI; **166,** The Granger Collection; **168 t,** Tom Bean; **186 b,** David Muench Photography; **170,** ESA/PLI/The Stock Market; **172,** Gardar Palsson/Mats Wibe Lund; **173 t,** Richard Haynes; **173 b,** Robert Rathe/Stock Boston; **175,** Paul Rezendes; **177,** Ken M. Johns/Photo Researchers; **178,** Russ Lappa; **179 t,** Renee Lynn/TSI; **179 m,** Frans Lanting/Minden Pictures; **179 b,** Mark Hones/Minden Pictures; **180 l,** Joe McDonald/DRK Photo; **180 inset,** Michael Fogden/DRK Photo; **181,** Art Wolfe/TSI; **182 l,** Carr Clifton/Minden Pictures; **182 inset, 183 r,** Stephen J. Krasemann/ DRK Photo; **183 inset,** Michael Quinton/MInden Pictures; **184, 185,** Michio Hoshino/Minden Pictures; **186,** Richard Haynes.

Chapter 7
Pages 190–191, Randy Linchs/Sharpshooters; **192 t,** Richard Haynes; **196 t,** O. Louis Mazzatenta/National Geographic Image Collection; **196 b,** Liba Taylor/Corbis; **197 t,**Tom Bean/Tony Stone Images; **197 b,** Gianni Dagli Orti/Corbis; **200 t,** Russ Lappa; **200 binoculars,** Superstock; **200 reflection,** Wernher Krutein/Liaison Agency; **203,** Les Stone/Sygma; **206 l,** David L. Brown/The Stock Market; **206 r,** John Shaw/Tom Stack & Associates; **207,** George Holton/Photo Researchers; **208 l,** Hulton Getty/Tony Stone Images; **208 r,** Superstock; **209,** Ralph A. Clevenger/ Westlight; **210 t,** Richard Haynes; **210 b,** Tim Olive/SharpShooters; **215,** Mark Thayer; **216,** Russ Lappa; **217 t,** Breck P. Kent/Animals Animals/Earth Scenes; **217 bl,** Greg Vaughn/Tom Stack & Associates; **217 br,** John Eastcott /Yva Momatiuk/ Animals Animals/Earth Scenes; **220,** Patrick M. Rose/Save the Manatee.

Chapter 8
Pages 224–225, Jeremy Horner/Corbis; **226,** Russ Lappa; **227,** Guy Marche/Tony Stone Images; **228,** Michael Newman/PhotoEdit; **233 t,** Ted Horowitz/The Stock Market; **233 b,** Deborah Davis/PhotoEdit; **236 t,** Russ Lappa; **236 b,** Laura Sikes/ Sygma; **237,** Calvin Larsen/Photo Researchers; **238,** Russ Lappa; **240 t,** Peter Skinner/Photo Researchers; **240 b, 241, 243 t,** Russ Lappa; **243 b,** Seth Resnick/ Stock Boston; **246,** Corbis-Bettmann; **247 t,** Mugshots/Stock Market; **247 b,** Wayne Eastep/Tony Stone Images; **249 t,** Carson Baldwin/Animals Animals/Earth Scenes; **249 b,** John Eastcott/Yva Momatiuk/Stock Boston; **250,** Peter Essick/ Aurora; **251 t,** Russ Lappa; **251 b,** I. Burgum/P. Boorman/Tony Stone Images; **253,** Robert K. Grubbs/Photo Network; **254,** George Gerster/Photo Researchers; **255,** Deborah David/PhotoEdit.

Chapter 9
Pages 258–259, Siegried Layda/Tony Stone Images; **260 t,** Richard Haynes; **260–261,** Aaron Chang/The Stock Market; **265,** (c)1996 The Art Institute of Chicago, Clarence Buckingham Collection; **266, 267,** Gene Ahrens/Bruce Coleman; **270,** Maher Attar/Sygma; **271 t,** Richard Haynes; **271 b,** Russ Lappa; **272,** Alon Reininger/The Stock Market; **273,** Corel Corp.; **275,** Russ Lappa; **277,** Mark Thayer; **278 t,** Richard Haynes; **278 b,** Russ Lappa; **280,** Raven/Explorer/Photo Researchers; **281,** Carol Roessler/Animals Animals/Earth Scenes; **284,** Ryan Ott/ AP Photo; **285,** Art Institute of Chicago.

Chapter 10
Pages 288–289, Fred Bavendam; **290 t,** Russ Lappa; **290 b,** The Granger Collection, NY; **291,** Courtesy, Peabody Essex Museum, Salem, MA; **292,** Norbert Wu/The Stock Market; **293 t,** SCRIPPS Oceanographic Institute; **293 b,** Scott Camanzine/Photo Researchers; **296 t,** Ted Streshinsky/Corbis; **296 b,** Russ Lappa; **298,** Richard Dunoff/The Stock Market; **299 t,** E. R. Degginger/Photo Researchers; **299 m,** Tim Heller/Mo Yung Productions; **299 bl,** F. Stuart Westmorland/Photo Researchers; **299 br,** Doug Perrine/Innerspace Visions; **302 l,** Maresa Pryor/ Animals Animals/Earth Scenes; **302 r,** Peter Weiman/Animals Animals/Earth Scenes; **303 t,** Lynda Richardson/Corbis; **303 b,** Andy Martinez/Photo Researchers; **304 t,** Richard Haynes; **304 b,** Jeff Foott/Tom Stack & Associates; **306 l,** Chuck Davis/Tony Stone Images; **306 r,** Randy Morse/Tom Stack & Associates; **307,** Mike Bacon/Tom Stack & Associates; **308,** Norbert Wu; **310,** D. Foster/WHOI/Visuals Unlimited; **311 t,** Richard Haynes; **311 b,** Nathan Benn/Stock Boston; **313,** Russ Lappa; **314,** Arnulf Husmo/Tony Stone Images; **315 l,** Bob Torrez/Tony Stone Images; **315 r,** Bill Nation/Sygma; **316 t,** Jake Evans/Tony Stone Images; **316 b,** Richard Haynes; **317,** Tim Hauf/Visuals Unlimited; **319,** Doug Perrine/Innerspace Visions.

Interdisciplinary Explorations—Chesapeake Bay
Page 323 t, Bettmann/Corbis; **323 m,** Nathan Benn/Corbis; **323 b,** Dave Bartruff/Corbis; **325,** Jim Romeo; **326,** Lowell Georgia/Corbis; **327,** Tim Rudviensky/Virginia Images.

Chapter 11
Pages 328–329, Jay Simon/Tony Stone Images; **330 t,** Russ Lappa; **330 b,** NASA/ Photo Researchers; **332 t,** Richard Haynes; **332 b,** Russ Lappa; **333,** George G. Dimijian/Photo Researchers; **334,** Eric Horan/Liaison Agency; **335,** Richard Haynes; **336 t,** Russ Lappa; **336 b,** NASA/Liaison International; **337,** Conor Caffrey/SPL/Photo Researchers; **340, 343,** Russ Lappa; **344,** Steve Casimiro/Liaison Agency; **345 t,** Russ Lappa; **345 b,** Eric A. Kessler; **347,** Ivan Bucher/Photo Researchers; **349, 351 t,** Russ Lappa; **351 b,** Steve Vidler/Superstock; **352,** Mark C. Burnett/Photo Researchers; **354 t,** The Granger Collection, NY; **354 b,** Corbis-Bettmann; **355 t,** The National Archives/Corbis; **355 b,** NASA; **356,** Jack Finch/Science Photo Library/Photo Researchers.

Chapter 12
Pages 360–361, William Johnson/Stock Boston; **362–363,** Photo Researchers; **367,** Richard Haynes; **368, 369, 372 t,** Russ Lappa; **372 b,** Victoria Hurst/Tom Stack & Associates; **373 l,** Gary Retherford/Photo Researchers; **373 r, 375,** Richard Haynes; **376,** Steve McCurry/Magnum Photos; **378,** Scala/Art Resource, NY; **380,** Ken McVey/Tony Stone Images; **381,** Russ Lappa; **382,** E.J. Tarbuck; **383,** Peter Arnold; **385 t,** Michael Gadomski/GADOM/Bruce Coleman; **385 tm,** Phil Degginger/ Bruce Coleman; **385 bm,** E. R. Degginger; **385 b,** John Shaw/Bruce Coleman; **386,** Wendy Shattil/Bob Rozinski/Tom Stack & Associates; **387,** Richard Haynes; **388 t,** AP/Wide World Photos; **388 inset,** Gerben Oppermans/Tony Stone Images; **388 b,** Nuridsany et Perennou/Photo Researchers; **390,** Bill Frantz/Tony Stone Images; **391,** Gerben Oppermans/Tony Stone Images.

Chapter 13
Pages 394–395, Pete Turner/Image Bank; **396 both,** Russ Lappa; **397,** Jim Corwin/Tony Stone Images; **403 t,** Russ Lappa; **403 b,** Dirck Halstead/Liaison Agency; **404,** Dan Sudia/Photo Researchers; **405,** Schuster/Superstock; **406 t, b,** The Granger Collection, NY; **407,** North Wind Picture Archives; **408,** Sheila Beougher/ Liaison Agency; **409,** NASA Goddard Laboratory for Atmospheres; **410,** Clore Collection, Tate Gallery, London/Art Resource, NY; **412,** NOAA; **414,** Tony Freeman/ PhotoEdit; **415 t,** Richard Haynes; **415 bl,** Keith Kent/Science Photo Library/Photo Researchers; **415 br,** Grant V. Faint/Image Bank; **418,** David J. Phillip/AP/Wide World Photos; **419 t,** Larry Lawfer; **419 b,** Corel Corp.; **420,** David Umberger/AP Photo; **421,** NOAA; **424, 425, 426,** AccuWeather, Inc.; **427,** Schuster/Superstock.

685

Chapter 14
Pages 430–431, David Muench Photography; **432 t,** Richard Haynes; **432 b,** Thomas D. Mangelsen/Peter Arnold; **434,** David Madison/Bruce Coleman; **436,** Duncan Wherrett/Tony Stone Images; **437,** Chris Cheadle/Tony Stone Images; **441,** Richard Haynes; **442 t,** Russ Lappa; **442 b,** Charlie Waite/Tony Stone Images; **443,** Geogory G. Dimigian/Photo Researchers; **446 t,** Thomas D. Mangelsen/Peter Arnold; **446 b,** Alex S. MacLean/Peter Arnold; **447,** Stephen Johnson/Tony Stone Images; **448 t,** Ann Duncan/Tom Stack & Associates; **448 b,** Margaret Gowan/Tony Stone Images; **449,** Corbis-Bettmann; **450 t,** Art Wolfe/Tony Stone Images; **450 b,** Thomas Kitchin/Tom Stack & Associates; **451,** Photodisc, Inc.; **452,** 1996 Ira Block; **453,** Tony Craddock/Science Photo Library/Photo Researchers; **453 inset,** George Godfrey/Animals Animals/Earth Scenes; **462,** NOAA; **463,** Tony Craddock/ Science Photo Library/Photo Researchers; **466,** Jane Love /NASA; **467 l,** NASA/ Photo Researchers; **467 r,** Jose L. Pelaez/The Stock Market; **468 both, 469,** NASA.

Chapter 15
Pages 466–467, Robin Smith/Getty Images; **468 t,** Richard Haynes; **468 b,** Stone/Charles Doswell III; **469,** Stone/Zigy Kaluzny; **471,** J. MacPherson/The Stock Market; **472 l,** John Shaw/Tom Stack & Associates; **472 m,** Paul Silverman/Fundamental Photographs; **472 r,** Daniel Cox/Allstock/PNI; **473 t,** William L. Wantland/Tom Stack & Associates; **473 b,** Howard Sochurek/The Stock Market; **474, 475, 476 t,** Richard Haynes; **476 b,** Ken Straiton/The Stock Market; **478 t,** Dr. Harold E. Edgerton/The Harold E. Edgerton 1992 Trust; **478 b,** Sipa Press; **479 l,** Richard Megna/Fundamental Photographs; **479 r,** Russ Lappa; **480,** "Waterfall" by M. C. Escher,©1998, Cordon Art-Baarn-Holland, All Rights Reserved; **481,** Courtesy of the Archives, California Institute of Technology; **482 t,** Russ Lappa; **482 b,** Ludek Pesek/Photo Researchers, Inc.; **483,** Runk/Schoenberger/Grant Heilman Photography; **484,** Carr Clifton/Minden Pictures; **485 r**, Stone/Cosmo Condina; **485 inset,** biophoto Associates/Photo Researchers, Inc.; **487,** Matthew Naythons/Stock Boston; **490,** Russ Lappa; **491,** Bill Bachmann/Photo Researchers, Inc.; **493,** Richard Haynes; **494,** The Granger Collection, NY; **495,** Stone/Zigy Kaluzny; **497,** Globus, Holway & Lobel/The Stock Market.

Chapter 16
Pages 498–499, Yamada Toshiro/Tony Stone Images; **500,** M. L. Sinibaldi/The Stock Market; **503 t,** Mike Abrahams/Tony Stone Images; **503 b,** Paul Harris/Tony Stone Images; **504,** Jbboykin Oil Prod./The Stock Market; **506,** UPI/Corbis-Bettmann; **507,** Chad Ehlers/International Stock; **508,** Nadia MacKenzie/Tony Stone Images; **510,** A & L Sinibaldi/Tony Stone Images; **512,** NASA; **513,** Richard Haynes; **514,** Herb Swanson; **515 t,** Russ Lappa; **515 b,** Photograph by Johan Hagemeyer, courtesy AIP Emilio Segre Visual Archives; **518,** Y. Arthus-Bertrand/Peter Arnold; **519,** U.S. Dept. of Energy/Science Photo Library/Photo Researchers; **521,** Richard Haynes; **522 l,** Mitch Kezar/Tony Stone Images; **522 r,** Leonard Lessin/Peter Arnold; **523,** Yves Marcoux/Tony Stone Images; **524,** Wolf/Monkmeyer; **525,** Nadia MacKenzie/Tony Stone Images; **528,** University of Wyoming Public Relations; **530 both,** Courtesy of Kelli Trujillo; **531,** University of Wyoming Public Relations.

Chapter 17
Pages 528–529, Rob Crandall/Stock Connections/PictureQuest; **530,** Frans Lanting/Minden Pictures; **531 l,** Inga Spence/Tom Stack & Associates; **531 r,** Charles D. Winters/Photo Researchers; **531 b,** Key Sanders/TSI; **532 t,** UPI/corbis-Bettmann; **532 b,** Corbis-Bettmann; **533 t,** UPI/Corbis-Bettmann; **533 bl,** Underwood & Underwood/Corbis-Bettmann; **533 br,** William Campbell/Peter Arnold; **534,** Jeff Gnass/The Stock Market; **536,** Russ Lappa; **537,** Martin Rogers/Stock Boston; **538,** Gary Braasch/TSI; **540,** Tom Stewart/The Stock Market; **541,** Greg Vaughn/Tom Stack & Associates; **542,** Russ Lappa; **543,** Richard Haynes; **544 tl,** Dave Watts/Tom Stack & Associates; **544 tm,** Frans Lanting/Minden Pictures; **544 tr,** George G. Dimijian/Photo Researchers; **544 b,** Fred Bavendam/Minden Pictures; **545 t,** Frans Lanting/Minden Pictures; **545 b,** Jim Zipp/Photo Researchers; **546,** D. Cavagnaro/DRK Photo; **547,** Randy Wells/TSI; **548 l,** John Shaw/Tom Stack & Associates; **548 m,** Dan Suzio/Photo Researchers; **548 tr,** Stephen J. Krasemann/DRK Photo; **548–549,** Phil A. Dotson/Photo Researchers; **549 tm,** Frans Lanting/Minden Pictures; **549 m,** David Liebman, **549 r,** Lynn M. Stone/DRK Photo; **550 l,** Roy Toft/Tom Stack & Associates; **550 r,** Frans Lanting/Minden Pictures; **551,** Tom McHugh/Photo Researchers; **552 t,** Richard Haynes; **552 b,** Greg Vaughn/Tom Stack & Associates; **553 l, r,** G. Payne/Liaison International; **554,** D. Cavagnaro/DRK Photo; **555,** Gary Braasch/TSI.

Chapter 18
Pages 558–559, NASA; **560 t,** Russ Lappa; **560 b,** Eric Lessing/Art Resource; **562,** Corel Corp.; **563 t,** Courtney Milne/Masterfile; **563 b,** Hazel Hankin/Stock Boston; **566,** Palmer/Kane/Tony Stone Images; **567,** Art Wolfe/Tony Stone Images; **569,** Richard Haynes; **570 t,** Richard Haynes; **570 b,** Larry Landolfi/Photo Researchers; **572 all,** John Bova/Photo Researchers; **574, 575 both,** Jay M. Pasachoff; **577,** Richard Haynes; **578 both,** Nancy Dudley/Stock Boston; **579,** Richard Haynes; **580, 581, 582,** NASA; **583 t,** Richard Haynes; **583 b,** NASA; **584 t,** John Bova/Photo Researchers; **584 the rest,** Courtesy of Alastair G.W. Cameron, Center for Astrophysics at Harvard University; **585 t,** NASA; **585 b,** Jay M. Pasachoff; **586,** N. Armstrong/ The Stock Market; **587,** Tony Stone Images; **588,** NASA.

Chapter 19
Pages 592–593, NASA; **594 t,** Russ Lappa; **594 b,** Anglo-Australian Observatory, photograph by David Malin; **595,** The Granger Collection, NY; **596,** The Granger Collection, NY; **597 t,** Richard Haynes; **597 b,** The Granger Collection, NY; **600,** Richard Haynes; **601,** Digital Vision; **602,** National Solar Observatory; **602 inset,** Space Telescope Science Institute; **604 t,** Space Telescope Science Institute; **604 b,** National Solar Observatory; **608,** NASA; **608 inset,** A.S.P./Science Source/Photo Researchers; **609, 610,** Digital Vision; **611,** NASA; **612,** Jet Propulsion Laboratory; **613 both,** NASA; **614,** Tony Stone Images; **616 both,** NASA; **617, 618 t,** Jet Propulsion Laboratory; **618 inset,** Digital Vision; **618 b, 619, 620 both, 621,** NASA; **622, 623, 624 t,** Richard Haynes; **624 b,** Space Telescope Science Institute; **626,** Jet Propulsion Laboratory; **627 l,** U.S. Geological Survey; **627 r,** Jerry Schad/ Photo Researchers; **628,** Ghislaine Grozaz; **629,** James Pisarowicz; **630,** U.S. Geological Survey; **631,** NASA; **632, 633,** Jet Propulsion Laboratory.

Interdisciplinary Exploration—The Solar System
636 m, Corbis; **636 tr,** NASA/Galaxy Picture Library; **636 mr,** KSC/NASA; **636 l,** Novosti/Science Photo Library; **637 m,** DK Picture Library; **636 l, 636 r,** NASA; **638 l,** Corbis-Bettmann; **638 r;** Valerie Ambroise; **639 b,** Jet Propulsion Laboratory; **639 tl, tr,** NASA; **640,** U.S. Geological Survey; **640 b,** NASA/Peter Arnold; **641,** Pat Rawlings/NASA.

Skills Handbook
Page 642, PhotoDisc, Inc.; **643 t,** Breck P. Kent; **643 m,** Richard Haynes; **643 b,** Russ Lappa; **646,** Richard Haynes; **648,** Ron Kimball; **649,** Renee Lynn/Photo Researchers.

Appendix
Pages 668–669, Bilderberg/The Stock Market